THE TRAVELER'S HANDBOOK

The insider's guide
to world travel

The editors

JONATHAN LORIE is the Editor of *Traveller* magazine and a Fellow of the Royal Geographical Society. He has travelled widely in Africa, Asia and Europe. Previously he worked in the international aid sector.

AMY SOHANPAUL has spent half her life in Kenya and the other half in the UK. Formerly in publishing, working for Penguin and Macmillan, she is now a journalist specialising in travel and food.

THE TRAVELER'S HANDBOOK

Eighth edition

Editor Jonathan Lorie
Assistant Editor Amy Sohanpaul

Guilford, Connecticut

This completely revised and enlarged edition first published in 2000.

Library of Congress Cataloging-in-Publication Data is available.

Every effort has been made to ensure that the facts in this Handbook are accurate. However, travelers should still obtain advice from consulates, airlines, etc, about current travel and visa requirements and conditions before traveling. The editors and publishers cannot accept responsibility for any loss, injury or inconvenience, however caused.

ISBN 0-7627-0727-5

Typography and typesetting by typo^G, London. Cover design by Wylie Design, London. Printed and bound by Legoprint SpA, Italy.

Copyediting by Natasha Hughes and Barbara Mellor. Proofreading by Galiena Hitchman. Indexing by Hilary Bird.

COVER PICTURES *Image Bank: Guido Alberto Rossi, John P Kelly, Grant V Faint; Telegraph Colour Library: PJ Wagner, Adastra; Photonica: Starrex; Basil Pau (picture of Michael Palin).*

Contents ❧

Part 2: Being there

Part 3: Logistics

Foreword

Expect the unexpected
by Michael Palin

THESE ARE EXCITING TIMES FOR TRAVELLERS. Never before in history has so much of the world been so accessible to so many people. Greater disposable income, less widespread political tension and the insatiable desire to move have overcome many people's reservations about setting out into the big wide world. The journeys I've made on television have been at times uncomfortable and chaotic, but they haven't put anybody off. Rather the opposite. The obscure, the unusual and the unexpected seem to appeal as never before.

Travel is a constantly frustrating business. It is like studying a catalogue of fine clothes or a good menu. It opens up a world of tantalising choices. The more I know about a place, the more I want to go there; and the more I go there, the more I want to know about it. I can never walk through a strange city or town without wishing I had taken this turning instead of that, or eaten at this restaurant instead of that, or climbed one hill, or explored one alleyway instead of another. It's the nature of the beast. It is also what makes travelling such a total, all-pervading, limitless pleasure.

And the joy of it all is that travel is not a finite process. You may say you want to see the world but you never will. No one can. The most common question I'm asked is: "Where is there left for you to go?" The short answer is the hundred or so countries that I still haven't seen. But travel is much more than country-spotting, much more than a series of ticks on a checklist. The real pleasure is that I could go back again and again to the places I have already visited and have a new experience each time.

My advice is to take as much advice, encouragement and information as you can, then go out and make your own adventure. Allow the world to surprise you, vex you, delight you and frustrate you. If you're not ready to expect the unexpected, you might as well not set out. 🙢

Introduction

The world in your hands
by Jonathan Lorie and Amy Sohanpaul

THERE'S STUFF IN THIS BOOK THAT YOU COULDN'T IMAGINE. Putting together the text, we have discovered countries where stone money is still the currency, where medieval Latin is the language, and where half the population are animists. We've learned how to mend a Land Rover engine with porridge, and what to say when accused of spying. We've been amazed by South Africa, which has 12 official languages, and confused by the Solomon Islands, which have 87 varieties of local pidgin: do all of them get printed on the road signs?

We remain perplexed by those countries with three different types of electricity supply. We fear the erratic railway and bus timetables of the world. And we applaud those nations which only work from 8 am to noon, Monday to Wednesday.

Constantly astonishing are the things that our author-travellers get up to. There's a doctor in love with the North Pole, and a colonel who invented white water rafting. There's a couple who took off on their motorbike in 1983 and have only just returned home. Wildest of all, there's a man whose job is to swim with sharks and shimmy with scorpions in pursuit of the ultimate wildlife film.

And then there are the clever games played by customs men the world over. In Jamaica you can't bring in honey, in Nigeria you can't import eggs. Afghanistan is choosy about carpets, while Armenia refuses loose pearls. Who thinks these things up? Booze and fags are an obsession, suggesting that travellers should carry a health warning. Top prize in this category goes to the UAE, whose duty-free allowance is a lung-busting 2,000 cigarettes – if you can carry that many.

Curiously, one or two African nations that are awash with diamond-smugglers and gun-runners are intricately fussy about how many millilitres of perfume you import. Others deploy strict driving regulations, when you're more likely to be stopped by an armed guerrilla than a traffic-cop. And there are places that are so awful – the ones with no roads at all, or typhoons all summer, or execrable cuisine – countries so deeply wretched that you wonder why they don't abolish visa regulations altogether and simply be grateful to receive any visitors at all.

But hey: that's the fun of a book like this. You can see in one view the sheer weirdness of all the places and peoples out there. And there is the wonder of it all, too: the great journeys by riverboat or greyhound bus, the glimpses of wildlife in the Serengeti or the South Atlantic, the exhilarations of sailing or cycling or climbing or galloping your way into the sunset.

You couldn't imagine or even invent this sort of stuff. It's too crazy and too marvellous. But it's all here, and it's all waiting for you to discover for yourself. Welcome to the world. ❧

Part 1: **First catch your dream** ❧

The travelling life

Departures and arrivals
by Eric Newby

WHATEVER ELSE WE REMEMBER OF OUR TRAVELS, we remember our departures and arrivals. Often they are the most enduring of all our memories of them. In 1963, together with Wanda, my wife, I embarked on the Ganges in an open boat to row from the foothills of the Himalayas to the Indian Ocean. Some 200 metres from our starting point, from which we had been seen off by an old man who dropped sacred sweets on us as provisions for the journey, and some 1,900 kilometres short of our destination in the Bay of Bengal, the boat grounded in some 40 centimetres of water which proved to be the uniform depth of the Ganges at this season at this point, and it took five-and-a-half days to cover the next 56 kilometres, mostly by pushing it.

Nothing in the course of the entire trip, which took three months to accomplish, left such an indelible imprint on our minds as the moment when we discovered that the Ganges was only 40 centimetres deep and that our boat drew 46 centimetres when loaded.

To depart is often more satisfying than to arrive unless you are the first on the scene. Nothing was more deflationary to Scott and his companions than to find that they were the second party to reach the South Pole. Would I have set off at all if I had known what the journey would be like or what I was going to find at my destination are questions I have often asked myself, reminded of the wartime poster which read 'Don't waste food! Why did you take it if you weren't going to eat it?' To which some wit added a codicil: 'I didn't know it was going to taste like this!'

For years explorers attempted to reach Timbuktu, the mysterious city on the edge of the Sahara that, ever since the twelfth century, had been the hub of the North African world, and in which salt had been traded for the seemingly inexhaustible gold of Guinea, a city in which, according to the Muslim traveller Leo Africanus, who visited it in 1526, there were plates and sceptres of solid gold 'some whereof weigh 1,300 pounds'.

The first-known European to reach Timbuktu and return in one piece was Réné Caillieé, a penniless young Frenchman who had been inspired to become an explorer by reading *Robinson Crusoe*. Too late to see it in its heyday – the trade in gold had more or less come to an end – he reached the fabled city after a terrifyingly dangerous journey on 20 April 1828. 'I looked around,' he wrote, 'and found the sight before me did not answer my expectations of Timbuktu. The city presented, at first view, nothing but a mass of ill-looking houses, built of earth. Nothing was to be seen in all directions, but immense plains of quicksand of a yellowish-white colour.'

No one really enjoys arriving anywhere by train. (Nor does anyone in their right mind enjoy departing or arriving by plane, with the possible exception of the pilot whose toy it is.) Will there be any porters? Will there be any trolleys for the luggage if there aren't? Will there be any taxis? Will they be fitted with meters? These and similar questions that even the most hardened travellers ask themselves as the train comes into the platform all help to contribute to the particular form of angst, the generally non-specific but nonetheless acute form of anxiety described by Cyril Connolly (disguised under the *nom de plume* Palinurus) in *The Unquiet Grave* as the *Angoisse des Gares*, the Agony of the Stations: 'Bad when we meet someone at the station, much worse when we are seeing them off; not present when departing oneself, but unbearable when arriving….'

The best arrivals are by sea, that is unless your engine has broken down and the Cliffs of Moher are a lee shore. The first sight of a great city from the sea is big medicine, powerful magic, unforgettable, however much of a let-down it may prove to be on closer acquaintance. New York seen from the Hudson in the early morning with the sun roaring up over the East River turning the tall buildings into gigantic Roman candles; Venice as your vessel runs in through the Porto di Lido into St Mark's Basin with the domes and campaniles liquefying and reconstituting themselves in the mirage; Istanbul as your ship comes up the Marmara and sweeps round Seraglio Point towards the Golden Horn and you see silhouetted against the evening sky the fantastic, improbable, incomparable skyline of Old Stamboul.

My passion for travel cools when I consider that it consists entirely of departures and arrivals.
– MARQUIS DE CUSTINE (1893)

It is not only the great cities that have this effect on the arriving traveller. This is how TE Lawrence described his first sight of Jidda, the then little port of Mecca, seen from the deck of a passenger ship in the Red Sea while he was on his way to meet the leaders of the Arab revolt in 1917: 'When at last we anchored in the outer harbour off the white town, between the blazing sky and its reflection in the mirage which swept and rolled over the wide lagoon, then the heat of Arabia came out like a drawn sword and struck us speechless…. There were only lights and shadows, the white and black gaps of streets in front, the pallid lustre of the haze shimmering upon the inner harbour; behind, the dazzle of league after league of featureless sand running up to an edge of low hills, faintly suggested in the far away mist and heat.'

It is these and similar vistas, whether wild or civilised, that make one want to shout 'How beautiful the world is!', that made an elderly lady of my acquaintance, when taken on an outing from her native village in the Po Valley which she had never previously left, cry on arriving on the watershed of the Apennines from which there was an extensive view, 'Com'è grande il mondo!'… 'How big the world is!'… and insist on being taken home. ❧

ERIC NEWBY is one of Britain's most distinguished travel writers.
He was made CBE in 1994. This extract is taken from 'Departures and Arrivals',
published by HarperCollins.

The independent traveller
by Dervla Murphy

QUESTION: WHEN IS A FREAK NOT A FREAK? Answer: When she feels normal. I was in my late forties before the realisation came, very, very slowly, starting as a ridiculous-seeming suspicion that gradually crystallised into an exasperated certainty. Many people think of me as a freak.

By middle age one should be well aware of one's public image, given a way of life that makes such an accessory unavoidable. But if what an individual does feels normal, and if people are decently reticent about analysing you to your face, it's quite understandable that for decades you see only your self-image, vastly as it may differ from the false public image meanwhile gaining credibility.

The freakish thing is, of course, not me, but the modern world – from which I, like millions of other normal folk, need to escape at intervals. Those of us born with the wandering instinct, and not caught in a job trap, can practise the most effective form of escapism: a move back in time, to one of the few regions where it is still possible to live simply, at our ancestors' pace. To describe this as returning to reality would be absurd; for us the modern world is reality. However, escapist travelling does allow a return to what we are genetically fitted to cope with, as we are not fitted to cope with the freakishly hectic, technological present.

Hence the notorious 'pressures', paralleling our marvellous conveniences. We have reduced physical effort to the minimum; everything is 'labour-saving' – transport, communications, entertainment, heating, cooking, cleaning, dressing, marketing, even writing (they tell me) if one uses a repulsive-sounding thing called a 'word processor'. Yet the effort of coming to terms with this effortless world is too much for many of us. So we get ulcers, have nervous breakdowns, take to uppers and/or downers, gamble on the stock exchange – or travel, seriously, for several months at a stretch.

Today's serious travellers are often frustrated explorers who would like to have been born at least 150 years earlier. Now there is nowhere left for individuals to explore, though there may be a few untouched corners (in Amazonia?) accessible only to expeditions. But the modern hi-tech expedition, with its two-way radios and helicopters on call for emergencies, naturally has no appeal for escapist travellers. Among themselves, these lament that their traditional, simple journeys have come to seem – by a cruel twist of the technological spiral – paradoxically artificial. A century ago, travellers who took off into the unknown had to be completely isolated from their own world for months or years on end. Now such isolation is a deliberately chosen luxury and, to that extent, phoney. Had I died of gangrene in the Himalayas or Simiens or Andes, that would have been my own fault (no two-way radio) rather than a sad misfortune.

So the escapist traveller is, in one sense, playing a game. But only in one sense, because the actual journey is for real in a way that the modern expedition, with its carefully prearranged links to home and safety, is not. Whatever happens, you can't chicken out: you are where you've chosen to be and must take the consequences.

Here some confusion arises about courage. There is a temperamental aspect to this issue: optimism versus pessimism – is a bottle half empty or half full? Why should your appendix burst or your bones break abroad rather than at home? Optimists don't believe in disasters until they happen. Therefore they are not fearful and have no occasion to display courage. Nothing puts my hackles up faster than being told I'm brave. This is nonsense – albeit significant nonsense. Where is our effortless civilisation at when physical exertion, enjoyed in remote places, is repeatedly mistaken for bravery?

Genuine travellers, far from being brave, are ultra cautious. That is an essential component of their survival mechanism and one of the dividing lines between them and foolhardy limelight seekers. Before they start they suss out all foreseeable hazards and either change their route, should these hazards seem excessive and the risk silly, or prepare themselves to cope with reasonable hazards. Thus what looks to outsiders like a daring journey is in fact a safe toddle – unless you have bad luck, which you could have at home. Six times I've broken my ribs; the last time was at home, falling off a ladder. The other times were in Afghanistan, Nepal, Ethiopia, Peru and Madagascar. You could say I have an unhappy karmic relationship with my ribs.

He travels the fastest who travels alone.
– RUDYARD KIPLING

Recently I was asked, "Why is independent travel seen as so much more of an intellectual challenge? And what does it take to cope with it?" That flummoxed me. I have been an escapist traveller for more than 40 years without it ever occurring to me that I was meeting an intellectual challenge. A stamina challenge, usually; an emotional challenge, sometimes; a spiritual challenge, occasionally. But an intellectual challenge? I don't see it. Unless by intellectual one means that slight exertion of the grey cells required to equip oneself more or less suitably for the country in view. Yet surely that is a matter of common sense, rather than intellect?

Granted, equipping oneself includes a certain amount of reading; but this, in a literate society, scarcely amounts to an intellectual challenge. I refer only to reading history, not to any sort of heavy sociological or political research – unless of course you happen to fancy that sort of thing, in which case it will obviously add an extra dimension to your journey. Otherwise, for the average traveller, enough of current politics will be revealed *en route*, should politics be important to the locals; and in those few happy regions where domestic politics don't matter, you can forget about them. But to travel through any country in ignorance of its history seems to me a waste of time. You can't then understand the why of anything or anyone. With this view some travellers violently disagree, arguing that all preliminary reading should be avoided, that each new country should be visited in a state of innocence and experienced purely subjectively. The mind on arrival should be a blank page, awaiting one's own vivid personal impressions, to be cherished ever after as authentic and unique. Why burden yourself in advance with loads of irrelevancies about the past and piles of other people's prejudiced interpretations of the present? On that last point I concur; travellers rarely read travel books – unless they have to review them.

Reverting to this odd concept of an intellectual challenge: is the adaptability required of travellers sometimes mistaken for an intellectual feat? That seems unlikely because we're back to temperament: some people slot in easily everywhere. If travellers saw the need to adapt as an intellectual challenge they probably wouldn't slot in anywhere, except perhaps on some pretentious radio show.

Maybe the overcoming of language barriers is seen as an intellectual challenge? Yet there could scarcely be anything less intellectual than urgently saying "P-sssss!" when you must get fast to the nearest earth closet – or at least out of the *tukul*, which has been locked up for the night. The basic needs of human beings – sleeping, eating, drinking, peeing – are so basic that they can easily be understood; all our bladders function in exactly the same way. The language barrier unnecessarily inhibits many who otherwise would seek out and relish remote regions. On the practical level, it is of no consequence. I can state this with total assurance, having travelled on four continents using only English and those courtesy phrases of Tibetan, Amharic, Quechua or whatever that you happen to pick up as you go along. Even on the emotional level, it is not as formidable as it may seem; the human features – especially the eyes – are wonderfully eloquent. In our own society, the extent to which we wordlessly communicate goes unnoticed. In Far Flungery, where nobody within 200 miles speaks a syllable of any European language, one becomes very aware of the range of moods and subtle feelings that may be conveyed visually rather than aurally. However, on the exchange-of-ideas level the barrier is, quite simply, insuperable. Therefore scholar-travellers – people like Freya Stark, Patrick Leigh Fermor, Colin Thubron – consider the learning of Arabic or Albanian or Russian or Mandarin to be as essential as buying a map. And there you have what seems to me (linguistically inept as I am) a bona fide intellectual challenge.

As a label, 'the independent traveller' puzzles me. It verges on tautology; travellers, being inherently independent, don't need the adjective to distinguish them from those unfortunate victims of the tourist industry who, because of sun-starvation on our islands, are happy to be herded annually towards a hot spot where tea and chips are guaranteed and there is no danger of meeting the natives.

I can, however, see that holiday-makers (the category in between travellers and tourists) may validly be divided into 'dependent' and 'independent'. The former, though liking to make their own plans, contentedly follow beaten tracks and book their guesthouses in advance. The latter are often travellers manqué for whom unpredictability gives savour to their journey: setting off at dawn with no idea of where one will be by dusk, or who with or what eating. Only a lack of time or money prevents them from reaching travellers' territory and usually time is their problem. Travelling can be done on quite a short shoestring, and often must be so done for the excellent reason that the traveller's theatre of operations offers few consumer goods.

Independent holiday-makers are in general much more tolerant and sociable than travellers, whose escapist compulsion causes them to feel their day has been ruined if they glimpse just one other solitary trekker in the far distance, and who break out in spots if they come upon even a vestigial trace of tourism. But that last nightmare contingency is unlikely; the paths of travellers rarely converge, unless one finds oneself within a few miles of somewhere like Machu Picchu and it seems 'stupid not to see it'. Incidentally, Machu Picchu provided me with my most grisly travel memory – an American helicopter landing amid the ruins and spewing forth a squeal of excited women whose paunchy menfolk were intent only on photographing them beside the mournful resident llamas. My timing was wrong; you have to get to Machu Picchu at dawn, as I did later.

The past decade or so has seen the emergence of another, hybrid category: youngsters who spend a year or more wandering around the world in a holiday-making spirit, occasionally taking temporary jobs. Some gain enormously from this experience, but many seem to cover too much ground too quickly, sampling everywhere and becoming familiar with nowhere. They have been from Alaska to Adelaide, Berlin to Bali, Calcutta to Cusco, Lhasa to London. They tend to wander in couples or small packs, swapping yarns about the benefits – or otherwise – of staying here, doing that, buying this. They make a considerable impact on wherever they happen to perch for a week or so, often bringing with them standards (sometimes too low) and expectations (sometimes too high) that unsettle their local contemporaries.

Of course one rejoices that the young are free to roam as never before, yet such rapid 'round-the-worlding' is, for many, more confusing than enlightening. It would be good if this fashion soon changed, if the young became more discriminating, allowing themselves time to travel seriously in a limited area that they had chosen because of its particular appeal to them, as individuals. ❧

DERVLA MURPHY has been an intrepid traveller and distinguished travel writer since the 1950s. She is particularly known for her travels by bicycle. Lately she has turned to more political subjects, for books on Laos and Rwanda.

The celebrity traveller
by Clive Anderson

Clive Anderson gives the inside track on the
ultimate celebrity travel – making TV travelogues

MAKING TELEVISION DOCUMENTARIES is a great way to travel. Since I have managed occasionally to creep out of the studio and onto the road (and rail and aeroplane), for the purposes of making television programmes, I have been despatched to Hong Kong, China, Mongolia, Hawaii, Cuba, Dominica, Goa, Calcutta, Kenya, Nigeria, Beirut and a variety of bits of the United States. Not to mention Montreal and Edinburgh to cover comedy festivals, and Bayeux to film a tapestry. Join the BBC, it turns out, and see the world.

Overall, I have enjoyed myself hugely – and I hope some of the programmes have turned out all right as well. But there are some disadvantages. Documentary-making is not one long holiday, nor even one long *Holiday Programme*, whatever viewers might suspect. Or indeed whatever I secretly hoped before I started. Sad to say, even though you might spend two weeks on location making a 40-minute film, there is precious little time to lounge around on the beach, or to spend 'researching' local night clubs. Rather disappointingly, even relatively straightforward films seem to take endless amounts of time to shoot. And films never seem that straightforward when you are on location trying to film them. Also, budgets being what they are, filming has to start virtually from the moment the presenter arrives and continue until the minute he leaves. Even rare days timetabled as days off turn all too regularly into days catching up.

There are, of course, plenty of meals and drinks to be had with the crew, but this is a vital part of bonding together as a group and should not be seen as a pure pleasure. And if you meet up with local people as well, this must be regarded as a vital process of learning about other cultures and not just partying for the hell of it.

Time to acclimatise never seems to be allowed at all. Take Hawaii. I landed late at night on the other side of the world. Had we crossed the international date line? I literally did not know what day of the week it was. But I soon discovered I had to be up at the crack of dawn the next morning to row in a Hawaiian canoe. Several gorgeous, sun-tanned twentysomething oarsmen teamed with me: pale of skin, lacking of sleep, slight of frame and spread of middle age. All to produce a few frames of *Hawaii 5-0* parody for the end credits. However, as the director pointed out, it could have been so much more if I had had the sense to fall in and start drowning on camera.

Then there is the travelling itself. As I know to my cost, the modern child requires a vast amount of baggage in order to get from A to B. Cuddly toys, backpacks and buggies, snack foods and nappies, plus an array of items constructed entirely from garish coloured plastic are *de rigeur*. This, however, is not a patch on a film crew. Even the most solitary-looking TV journey is made by a small army of voyagers: a cameraman, a soundman, a camera assistant, a director and/or a producer, and perhaps a researcher, translator or local fixer. With them come their equipment. Metal boxes full of film or video tape, metal boxes full of lights, reflectors, batteries, cameras, tripods, metal boxes full of tape recorders, tape and microphones. Metal boxes, for all I know, full of spare metal boxes.

All of these have to be dragged around airports, checked onto planes, and loaded into vans, boats and trains. On the first leg of the great railway journey across China, we were worried about getting our equipment stolen, so we locked it in a 'soft-class' sleeper, while we mere humans struggled onto 'hard-class' bunks at the cheaper end of the train. Who else would give up their seats, and their beds, to their luggage? On a later leg of the same journey, all the equipment travelled on to Beijing with just our Chinese-speaking translator for company, while the rest of us stayed the wrong side of the barrier at Jinan station getting arrested. On a later film, the whole lot flew to the wrong island because some idiot (me, since you ask) said the wrong thing at an airport check-in. Still, in these days of high security awareness, it is nice to know that 50 or so metal boxes can still fly unaccompanied on a small passenger plane without let or hindrance!

In Lagos, we managed to get arrested twice in two weeks. Firstly for filming for several days with the full knowledge of the Ministry of Information but without the express permission of the secret police, and secondly for filming a roadside food stall without the permission of the local police station. It is remarkable the effect that cameras have on insecure members of the security forces the world over.

Cameras do bring out the more adventurous side of some people, though. The most stressful part of my normal travelling life is attempting to hail a taxi in Oxford Street. But in my documentary existence I am forever leaping onto tiny aeroplanes, dodgy helicopters, over-laden Land Rovers, unstable fishing boats, unconventional ferries and unpredictable horses. Needless to say, each owner, pilot, guide or driver, inspired by the presence of a camera, races, shows off and generally pushes his or her vehicle to its limit. It is as though they want them and me to die on camera, or at any rate come close to it.

No matter where you go — there you are.
— EARL MACRAUCH

I know how they feel. I was fortunate enough to be given the chance to take over the controls of a small aeroplane flying over the sea between Cuba and Florida. You pull the joystick one way to go up, the other way to go down, left to go left, right to go right, in, out, in, out, shake it all about… I was ordered to stop by the director getting seasick and squeezed in the back. "For God's sake Clive," he said, "let the real pilot take over again and let's go back to base as soon as…." (Sound track then obscured by retching sound.)

Ah, illness. All travellers risk upset, infection and disease, but the TV presenter risks his particular bout of Delhi belly, sleeping sickness or raging fever being caught on camera for the delight of the watching millions. Indeed, when I turned to Michael Palin for advice on this point, he assured me that being ill on screen is vital to maintain viewers' interest. But when you feel your insides are about to become outsides, it is no fun being Our Man In A Pale Suit trying to conduct an interview in a steaming hot location miles away from your old friend Armitage Shanks.

This brings me to another danger. It is important that the film-maker does not wind up filming someone else's film crew. With Michael Palin circling round the world in every possible direction, with every holiday destination covered by the *Holiday Programme*, or *Wish You Were Here*, with every war zone attracting crews from all over the world, with every Amazon Indian tribe apparently attached to its own resident camera crew, with every part of the natural world negotiating a series with David Attenborough, with every exotic railway journey the subject of a TV travelogue, this becomes ever more difficult.

I was once filming on the beautiful but little-known island of Dominica in the Windward Islands. At exactly the same time, Tony Robinson was on the same island making another film for the BBC. Now what are the chances of that?

But it has to be said, documentary-making abroad is much less dangerous than

fighting a war, less demanding than relief work, better paid than vso, less exhausting than grape-picking, more fun than a sales conference, and less uncomfortable
than travelling on the Northern Line. In fact my only real complaint is that I am at
home writing this, rather than away on another trip. Maybe next year. ❧

*CLIVE ANDERSON has presented numerous travel documentaries on British
television, including the series 'Our Man In...'. As a chat show host, he has developed
a reputation for fearless and funny interviewing. He is perhaps best known for
presenting the comedy improvisation show 'Whose Line Is it Anyway?'*

How travel shaped my life
by Esther Freud

As a child growing up in rural Sussex, travelling by bus between East Grinstead and Tunbridge Wells, gazing out at the tiny, sleepy villages, the misty
green fields, the cricket pitch, I was always aware that there were other worlds out
there. Wilder, hotter, stranger worlds. Countries with mules and camels, horse-
drawn taxis, kaftans and hennaed hair. This knowledge had a huge effect on me.

I was four when I went off travelling with my mother and elder sister, and six
when we came back. For almost two years we wandered through Morocco. We
rented small rooms in Medina hotels, hitchhiked, bartered, attended festivals and
hammams, spoke Arabic and French. We ate the food they cooked in cauldrons in
the square of Marrakech, played with the beggar children, befriended the women
who sold drums. My sister went to a Moroccan school and learnt about the pillars
of Islam, the laws by which the people lived their lives. She also learnt the names
for all the animals and how to count to ten. My mother became interested in Su-
fism and started praying towards Mecca on a rug.

Sussex by comparison was quiet and still. I remember, age six or seven, sitting
in my classroom listening to the teacher ask if anyone had 'news'. 'News' was an opportunity for children with pressing things on their minds to reveal them then at
the beginning of the class, and hopefully remain quiet until break. "Yes," my hand
shot up, "I've got some news." And I darted to the front of the class and told them
how I'd once ridden in the saddlebag of a donkey, my sister on the other side, and
how terrified I was as the donkey clipped down the mountain path, how every second I was sure its hooves were going to slip. I wanted my school friends to see the
mountain, the procession of bright people scrambling down, and to know that at
the top, a camel decked in flowers had had its head chopped off.

"I think that's enough for today," the teacher quietened me with a restraining
hand, and reluctantly I went back to my desk.

For the next ten years I hardly left Sussex. The world outside became fixed in
my mind as impenetrable and very far away. I had no idea that people went on

package tours, arriving at their destinations within hours, or took weekend breaks that involved no life-threatening illness or delays. But the further away my own travels became the more determined I was not to forget them. My class at school received regular bulletins about orange groves and oases, the taste of cumin in *bissara* soup, and once when I had the floor all to myself I told them a long story about how my sister and I once saw a mirage. We were in the desert, riding on camels, half dead from thirst, when there in the distance we saw an island of palm trees and green grass. We trotted thankfully towards it only to find that it had disappeared. It's from this point that I can trace my future as a fiction writer. Of course I'd never ridden into the desert on a camel, never seen a mirage, although to this day I wish I had, instead I'd simply read about one in a Tintin book and exchanged the characters of Thompson and Thompson for my sister and myself. But by now I'd told my class so many unlikely stories it meant nothing to them to accept one more, and from then on I was free to elaborate and embroider, and the more I did it, the more natural it became.

But then something happened that stopped me in my tracks. A new boy arrived at our school and at 'news' he told us about Thailand. He'd seen a jellyfish, all wobbly and white, and he told us how it had floated up to him and brushed against his arm. The class shivered and gasped. "Did it sting you?" the teacher asked, and I thought I saw him hesitate before he launched into a detailed description of his rash. Thailand was fascinating and new, and no one wanted to listen to Moroccan adventures

Travel is more than the seeing of sights; it is a change that goes on, deep and permanent, in the ideas of living.
– MIRIAM BEARD

any more. My role had been usurped. Occasionally I did still tell the stories, but only to myself. I practiced them, honed them down, elaborated on them. If I was going to share them with anyone again I was going to make sure they were as good as they could get. And then slowly, slowly, my own life took over. I started living in the present, I made real friends, and Morocco faded into the past.

Years later, in my early twenties, I started going to a creative writing class, and after a series of assorted exercises we were set a task. Simply to write a longer piece. A five- or six-page piece about anything at all. What could I write about? I had no idea, and then as soon as I sat down, alone in a quiet room, my stories all came back to me. Of course I'd write about the camel festival and the cumin, the beggar girls, the drummer women in the square, and although when I closed my eyes I could remember, almost cinematically, my life as it was then, I realised I did have a head start. I'd practiced these stories before.

But sometimes, especially if my book was going well, I'd stop and gaze off into space. What if I could never write about anything else? What if I did think up another story, would I have to practice and embellish it for the next 20 years of my life? By now I'd fallen in love with the whole process of writing and I couldn't bear to think I'd ever have to do anything else. But as soon as I'd finished *Hideous Kinky*, (as my first novel became), I found there was a reservoir of stories waiting to be told. In fact Morocco had been so vivid and so colourful that it had almost submerged the importance of everything else.

I've since discovered that one of the most wonderful things about being a novelist is that, in your own mind at least, you can travel anywhere you want. I've just spent the last two years back in Sussex, conjuring up those mist-green fields, remembering the quiet of the country lanes where foxgloves and snapdragons grow tall. Once I set my mind to it, it was easy to find enough drama and suspense to fill a book, even on the Ashdown Forest golf course. Any number of things could happen in those leaded phone boxes, or even at the plank-board bus stops where as a teenager I'd been so overwhelmingly bored. Sitting in a London study with the sounds of the city never far away, I took great pleasure in sending my characters rustling through bracken, scooping up great armfuls of white hay or hacking down a gorse bush with an axe. But what I'll never know is how long it would have taken me to find my courage and become a writer if I hadn't had that first, pressingly urgent travellers' tale handed to me on a plate. ❧

*ESTHER FREUD is the author of 'Hideous Kinky' (which was made into a
feature film starring Kate Winslet), 'Peerless Flats', 'Gaglow' and 'The Wild'.
In 1993 she was chosen by 'Granta' as one of the Best of Young British Novelists.*

Coming home
by John Blashford-Snell

UNTIL RULA LENSKA JOINED US ON A QUEST IN NEPAL I had no idea that actors and expeditioners suffer from the same problem at the end of the show. Both tend to get 'post-project depression' (PPD) or 'after-expedition blues'.

When a play ends or the filming of a series finishes, Rula explained, the cast is suddenly split up, left to find new jobs or return home for a well-earned rest. The friendships and working relationships break up, the team disappears and a different lifestyle starts overnight. So it is with expeditioners and, I imagine, ocean voyagers.

Dr John Davies, one of Britain's leading exploration medics, once started a lecture at the Scientific Exploration Society with the statement: "Expeditions may endanger your health." He went on to point out that, for the novice, the experience can be an introduction to the negative aspects of one's personality that are easily suppressed in normal daily life. However, with appropriate counselling and support, this can be a journey of self-discovery leading to increased confidence and a more enlightened attitude to others.

Seasoned adventurers, like experienced actors, recognise post-expedition blues, the symptoms of which are similar to bereavement. This is triggered by the loss of one's new-found 'family' of expedition friends in a widely different culture and suddenly being cut off from the excitement on return home.

"I just can't face going back to nine to five in the Tax Office," groaned an Inland

Revenue Officer who had spent three months in the Gobi. A routine and mundane lifestyle aggravates the condition and, for many, it is cured only by involvement in another challenge. Returning explorers also face isolation from family and colleagues, who have no concept of their recent intense experience. They are often perplexed by the indifferent response to their stories and may end up silent and withdrawn. The envy and resentment of the uninitiated, who imagine that one has been on a jolly picnic or at best some self-inflicted masochism, is also common.

"Don't know what you've done to my mother," complained a son after his mum had returned from one of the Discovery Expeditions in South America. "She's awfully quiet." But meeting the lady in question at a reunion a few months later I found her in great spirits, reliving the experience with her old pals.

John Davies, with whom I have been on many trips, advises 'returnees', especially the older ones, to spend several days enquiring about the day-to-day problems that have occurred in their absence before slowly beginning to recount their experiences. So, on being met by my wife as I stepped off a comfortable British Airways flight from Delhi recently, I asked: "How are those new trees in the garden coming on?"

"Have you gone mad?" replied Judith, well used to a dozen tales of high adventure before we reached the car park. But perhaps I'm beyond hope!

However, there may be medical problems, as I discovered a year after a Sandhurst expedition in Ethiopia, when my right leg started shaking uncontrollably while I was lecturing. 'How strange,' I thought, trying not to notice the offending limb. Two weeks later, lying racked with a fever in hospital, it was found that I had malaria, by which time I also had blurred vision and had lost nine kilos in weight. But, once diagnosed, malaria is usually fairly easily cured, and the doctors knew I'd been to the tropics.

Once you have travelled, the voyage never ends, but is played out over and over again in the quietest chambers... the mind can never break off from the journey.
– Pat Conroy

Sadly not all ailments are so quickly dealt with, as I realised after 12 months of visits to the St Pancras Hospital for Tropical Diseases. Strange hot flushes, violent stabbing pains in my stomach, aches and itches in awkward places were making life extremely uncomfortable. "There's nothing wrong with you," boomed one of the world's leading specialists in tropical diseases after exhaustive tests proved negative. "You young fellows imagine you've caught everything under the sun if you spend six weeks in the jungle. When I was in Burma..." he droned on. My morale at was rock bottom and it took great courage to return to the hospital a few weeks later, after the symptoms had become almost unbearable.

As luck would have it, a charming and much more sympathetic Asian doctor was on duty and, in no time, he had me face-down on a trolley with a flexible viewing device inserted up my rear end and my shirt over my head. "Keep him still," he beseeched as two strapping Fijian nurses pinned me down. "Oh, my goodness," exclaimed the physician. "What a fine example. Excuse me, sir, but you have a splendid parasite. It is quite unusual to see one so well developed. Would you mind if we allowed a class of medical students to see it?" Before I could even protest, I was wheeled into a theatre full of students, many of them, I noted, looking between my legs, were extremely attractive young women. One by one they came forward, without even a titter, to peer intently up my bottom. At last I was taken away and the awful tube removed. "What now?" I asked.

"Oh – just swallow these pills and you'll be as right as rain," smiled the doctor.

So it is my advice that if you feel ill after an overseas visit, go straight to your GP and say where you have been. Mark you, they might diagnose jet lag, which can affect one more than most care to admit.

This handbook contains useful tips on surviving the onslaught and reducing its effects to the minimum, so I'll not dwell on it. Suffice to say that when I get home I keep going until nightfall, doing simple, uncomplicated things such as unpacking or weeding, then I take a very mild sleeping pill and totter off to bed. With luck I can usually sleep for six hours. The important thing is to avoid stressful situations and don't make any important decisions until after your body has readjusted. In my case this usually takes 24 hours. Indeed, even weeding may not be a good idea. Having stepped off a long flight from Mongolia, I pulled up all my wife's carefully planted ground cover instead of the weeds.

If I am still feeling low, I concentrate on writing my thank-you letters (if not done on the plane!) and amending my packing list while memory of all the things I forgot to take and all unnecessary items that went with me is still fresh. Then it's down to sorting out photos, slides, videos and writing reports and articles. Next come repairs to kit, getting cameras serviced and preparing lectures.

If you start to feel sorry for yourself, you are not really bringing the benefits of your experiences to your life at home. Indeed I expect you will find that you have changed but the world has not.

The whole point is to keep active and look forward to the next challenge, and, if you can't afford another trip, why not use your vigour and energy to help others in your area, sick children, old people or anyone who could use some voluntary assistance?

For the adventurous there is the opportunity of supporting organisations such as the Duke of Edinburgh's Award or Riding for the Disabled and there are dozens of environmental groups needing help.

The great cry is, if you want to avoid PPD, keep busy. 🐾

COLONEL JOHN BLASHFORD-SNELL is one of the world's foremost explorers. He is a founder of Operation Drake and Operation Raleigh, and President of the Scientific Exploration Society. He has led many expeditions, particularly in Africa and Latin America, and is currently engaged in the Kotamama project, to see whether ancient peoples might have sailed from the Andes to the Atlantic by river.

The world of travel

The global suburb
by John Simpson

O NCE WE HAD A PLANET. Now, at the start of the third Christian millennium, we're left with a suburb.

In our world, you can fly from any big city to any other in 24 hours or less. A few rogue places exist to which you can scarcely fly at all, but their number is going down all the time; as I write they include North Korea, Chechnya, Afghanistan and Somalia. Libya was taken off the list in 1999, and a dozen big international airlines immediately started flying to Tripoli again.

When, following the collapse of Communism, an American academic made himself famous by announcing the death of history, most of his colleagues disagreed. A decade later there are scarcely 20 countries which haven't adopted the politics and economics of liberal democracy. If it isn't quite dead yet, history, in the sense of a clash between different political concepts, does indeed seem to be withering on the vine.

Our world has been mapped with complete accuracy, and there can be scarcely any peoples or species left uncatalogued. In 1999 a surprisingly large new species of tree rat was discovered in Peru. The previous year two separate bands of unknown wandering tribesmen were discovered in Papua New Guinea. They possessed no spoken language, and conversed solely in signs. In the dense forest in the far west of Brazil I came across a man who had found the arrows of various different groups of Indians unknown to ethnography. Groups in the Congolese jungle or the Kalahari Desert have probably not made contact with the outside world. But that is just about all. There are more people alive now than in the whole of mankind's past, which creates problems for those who believe in reincarnation. Yet for the first time we all know one another.

Worse, the differences between us are disappearing as fast as the animal, bird and insect species we share our planet with. In the 1960s you could still work out where you were when you drove across the United States by the accents and the food; not any longer. In the 1970s French was still an important second language in countries as divergent as Iran, Yugoslavia and Romania; alas, for those of us who have laboured to improve it over the years, not any more. An inalienable sameness has settled over the globe. The spirit of place is evaporating fast.

We are losing our distinctiveness, our human biodiversity, with appalling speed. As Gertrude Stein wrote of Oakland, California, 'There's no *there* there.' We tend to think of the process as being American-inspired, but it is merely American-led; the United States has gone farther and faster down this particular road then the rest of us, that's all.

Europe is doing its utmost to catch up. The powerful sense of regional identity that used to exist throughout Europe has faded very quickly. The first time I stayed in Venice in the early 1970s I remarked to the old lady who was showing me to my room in the Pensione Seguso that there were a lot of tourists about.

"Ah well, you see, it's Easter in Venice," she told me.

It was as if this was something special to the city, which those of us who lived elsewhere wouldn't necessarily appreciate.

Not long afterwards I spent a weekend on the charming Ile St Louis in Paris, and needed to buy a bottle of ink to write some letters.

"I'm sorry, M'sieu," said the elderly lady in the general store on the corner, "we don't sell ink. I doubt if you'll get it anywhere on the island."

The Ile St Louis is about 50 metres equidistant from the Left and Right banks of the Seine. Nowadays it is full of twee shops selling crêpes and glove puppets and paintings by Bernard Buffet, and English buskers queue up on the bridge, waiting for their half-hour turn in front of the tourists. Then it was a separate place with its own clearly established sense of identity.

"It is," said General de Gaulle in the late 1950s, "impossible to hold together a country which has 265 specialities of cheese."

All but two or three of those specialities can still be found in France, though European Union regulations make it illegal to sell even Brie and Camembert if it is produced in the strictly traditional method. France, once the most idiosyncratic, regionally diverse and uncontrollable country in Europe, is settling into the same uniformity as the rest of us. There are Body Shops and Holiday Inns in large numbers there too, and more McDonald's in Paris than in London. Obesity, the defining disease of Western man and woman, distinctly hamburger- and Coke-related, is beginning to affect France as it has long affected Britain. As for America, airlines are beginning to introduce wider seats to accommodate the growth in American arse sizes, and lavatories are being manufactured two inches wider.

In other ways, too, the choices are lessening. Until about 1980 furniture shops in Wales sold what was known as 'the Welsh bed', wider and shorter than the types available in the rest of the United Kingdom. Officially, we are all the same size now. And we are all equal in the face of technology. There was a time when, travelling abroad, I could go for days without contacting my office. Now I am fortunate if more than a couple of hours pass without a call from London; even during the night, if they forget about time difference – the one major element of distinction between one place and another that no one has yet suggested ironing out.

When the local telecommunications system doesn't run to the use of mobile phones – and I have used one to call my office from the Khyber Pass, the Great Wall of China and the flat of a drugs baron in Medellin – then I can always take a satellite phone the size of a small briefcase with me. In the 1970s my foreign desk used to communicate with me by telex. The technology was untrustworthy and the language strange:

"All well w u? ga"

"Yeah, tho cash a prob ga"

"So what new, eh? ga."

("Ga" stood for "go ahead.")

By the late 1980s the office sent me faxes, though they were on a shiny paper which curled up, and the words faded fast. If you went into the hotel business centre, another '80s concept, and asked to use a desktop computer, you would never know which of a dozen or so types of software it might use. Now, from Damascus to Lahore to Xian, everyone uses Microsoft. Sometimes you have to work out how to get out of Chinese or Arabic characters and into Roman ones, but that's all. It probably won't be long before that little nuisance to the manufacturers is ironed out too, and everyone will speak and write a kind of English.

Convenience has driven out variety; and not merely in the hotel business centre. Which American mall doesn't have its JC Penney, its Radio Shack, its Häagen Dazs? Which British high street doesn't have its Marks and Spencer, its WH Smith, its Principles? And when you come across these shops abroad, your first response is not a pleasant flash of recognition but a dull sense that you haven't really reached anywhere different after all.

In the Yemeni capital, Sana'a, there are almost as many mobile phones per capita as there are in New York City. In Bokhara and Samarkand you can buy hamburgers and hot dogs on the street corner. In the remotest reaches of the Amazon the children who play in the dust wear T-shirts with the Nike or Coca-Cola logos. In Iran, I have seen posters advertising a Sylvester Stallone film on the walls of the holy city of Qom.

The feeling is growing, especially in the United States, that there is no need to travel abroad, since abroad is travelling to you. In Washington DC I have been driven by a taxi driver who had been the leader of an Afghan mujaheddin group, and in Paris by another who had been an Iranian air force general. In Denver I once found a taxi driven by a North Korean who spoke not a single recognisable word of English, and in New York City a taxi driver from, I think, Equatorial Guinea, who had no idea where or what Wall Street was.

The earth belongs to anyone who stops for a moment, gazes and goes on his way.
- COLETTE

In London there are colonies tens of thousands strong of Colombians, Thais and Ethiopians – people without the remotest colonial links to Britain. There are Japanese restaurants in Kinshasa, Beijing and Geneva, and Italian restaurants in Amman, Minsk and Pretoria. You find the best Thai food in the world in Australia, the best *balti* in northern England, and the best Persian *fesanjun* in Los Angeles. *Tandoori* has become the quintessential British dish, while curry has supplanted fish and chips as the most popular take-away food. Hamburgers are far more popular among the 13 to 18 age group in France than *steak-frites* or *magret de canard*.

"I recognised him because he was dressed like a foreigner," says a character in a pre-war Graham Greene novel, and as late as the 1970s you could still recognise Frenchmen by the cut of their jackets, Englishmen by their checks and brogues, Italians by the narrowness of their trousers, Americans by the shortness of theirs and the thickness of the welts on their shoes. Nowadays large parts of the entire world's population, from Kuwait to Sydney and from Galway to Dalian, buy the same kinds of clothes, often made in Indonesia or Guatemala.

Once, caught unexpectedly in St Petersburg, I had to kit myself out at short notice from head to toe from the local Hugo Boss shop (the original Hugo Boss, incidentally, prospered in the 1930s and '40s as a tailor to Himmler's ss, and still seems to favour black). I then found that half the members of my audience of Russian literati and local politicians were also wearing Hugo Boss clothes.

"Fundamentally," intones the complacent voice-overs on a television advertisement for an international hotel group which claims to be deeply sensitive to cultural differences, "we are all the same."

That's good for business, of course; biodiversity costs money, but sameness encourages economies of scale. Fortunately for the big corporations, everyone everywhere seems to want exactly the same thing: Sony Walkmans, Adidas trainers, Toyotas, Swatches, caps with the peaks worn at the back. (When I was on *The Spectator* we ran a cartoon which showed a teenager asking a salesman, "Have you got any of these with the peak at the front?").

There are only a handful of places left on earth where you can escape all this; as I write there is no McDonald's in Cuba, no Coca-Cola in Libya, and no television in Afghanistan. But in order to find real difference you have to travel well outside the political pale. If you want to get away from the English football results and *USA Today* and advertisements with Cindy Crawford or Sir Anthony Hopkins in them, you must take your courage in both hands and go to the few really difficult, independent, unpredictable places which are left.

Sooner or later even these last sandcastles of independence will be washed over. The Havana Libre Hotel will turn back into the Hilton, Tripoli will have Häagen-Dazs ice-cream parlours, Afghanistan will tune in to *Friends*, restaurants in Iraq will accept payment in Euros, and earnest tour guides will lead you in total safety across the dividing line between north and south Mogadishu to a Holiday Inn or a Sheraton. How wonderful, I can't wait. 🙦

JOHN SIMPSON is the BBC's World Affairs Editor and one of Britain's most distinguished broadcasters. The second volume of his autobiography, 'A Mad World My Masters', is published by Macmillan.

The ethical traveller
by David Bellamy

NOMADS TRAVEL IN ORDER TO MAKE A LIVING from harsh landscapes, conquerors and business people to search for power and resources, holiday-makers to escape the monotony of the workplace. Adventurers, backpackers and Grand-Tourers travel because they have to. Theirs is the quest for knowledge, a quest to be worldly-wise.

It is somewhat awe-inspiring to realise that many areas which were marked as *terra incognita* on the maps of my youth are now stop-overs on regular tour itineraries. So much so that the two-edged sword of tourism now hangs heavily over every aspect of the heritage of this world.

If it had not been for the spotlight which has been turned onto these special regions by Grand-Tourers, past and present, the threat, to coin a phrase, of 'Costa-Brava-isation' would not be there. Yet it is equally true to say that without those spotlights of interest and concern, much of their heritage could have been lost through apathy and ignorance.

Whatever regrets we weavers of travellers' tales may have, I believe the die is now cast. Tourism is the world's fastest growing industry and the only hope for much of our heritage, both natural and people-made, lies within the wise use of its tourist potential.

A row of toilets at Everest base camp, or the importation of food to service tourists in Bali, don't make for confidence in the sustainability of the industry, unless either the tourist industry grows up and shoulders all its responsibilities, or the expectation of all travellers sinks to the current norm of home entertainment: a diet of soaps and game shows.

Fortunately, there are some bright lights at the end of the tunnel. At one end are well-appointed and -run establishments like South Africa's Sun City. There, a fun oasis has been *Take only memories. Leave nothing but footprints. – CHIEF SEATTLE (1786–1866)* created out of what was degraded veldt. Many thousands of local jobs have been created and an adjacent area has been restocked with game both big and small. It packs the tourists in, corralling them where they can do little harm to local culture. The only really negative effect is the use of fossil fuel and too much water but, living up to its name, it could become solar-powered and water-wise. At the other end of the spectrum of caring holidays are groups like Earthwatch and Coral Cay Conservation, where customers pay to be trained and then work hard on scientific research. Furthermore, a recent study of caravan parks, not usually renowned for their eco-friendliness, revealed that some had already taken up the eco-challenge and were putting their houses into green order, caring not only for their customers but for the local community, wildlife and wider environment.

Unfortunately there is also much bad news, but that is where *you* all come in, for there is an immense amount of work to be done. Attitudes are changing, but is it fast enough with 1.3 billion Chinese about to be industrialised? If only ten per cent of them had the funds to travel, that would make an extra 130 million tourists. If all of them decided that they must visit the English Lakes in their travelling lifetime, that would mean an extra 2.6 million visitors a year in Cumbria. Could they be accommodated? The answer from the industry is "yes". But at what cost to Wordsworth's 'open air university'?

One thing the whole industry must do, and fast, is realise that its success depends on other people's resources, landscapes and lifestyles, so they must help pay for their upkeep. They must help create local jobs, pay for local infrastructure, give more than they get. If they don't, the resource will eventually collapse.

As you lap up the challenges of pushing back the bounds of your personally unknown lands, and discovering these pearls of heritage for yourselves, remember they are only there thanks to the natural living systems on which we all depend.

You are the ambassadors of everything that the concerned traveller should be. Set the golden example. Respect local customs and buy only local craft goods made from sustainable resources, and always put as much as you can into the local economy. Be careful where you put your tripod and your feet. Flowers have power, you know. Leave only ripples of good will – and if you see an operator disobeying national or local rules, refuse his services.Thank you for caring. ❧

Professor David Bellamy is one of the world's leading environmentalists.
He has championed the cause through television appearances, books, campaigns,
and his own charity, The Conservation Foundation.

Moral dilemmas of travel
by George Monbiot

IN 1999, THE OWNERS OF A TOURIST ATTRACTION in north-west Thailand appeared in court on charges of running a 'human zoo'. Twelve adults and twenty-one children of the Padaung tribe had been discovered by a British journalist and a Thai human rights campaigner in a compound near the Burmese border. They had been tricked into leaving a refugee camp, then displayed to tourists who came to see their famously elongated necks. They were forced to dance, sing and sell artefacts to the visitors, and those who tried to escape were beaten up. By the time the slaves were discovered, one woman had died, due, her husband said, to a 'broken heart'.

These were the lucky ones. Their human zoo was closed down when exposure forced the reluctant authorities to start an investigation. But in many parts of South-East Asia, slavery is either ignored or promoted by the state. As both tourists and Thai men demand HIV-free prostitutes in Bangkok, brokers and bawds scour the Thai hills for girls to trick or kidnap. Across the border in Burma, the entire tourist industry has been built on slave labour, as hundreds of thousands of men and women have been forced, on pain of death, to construct the roads, airstrips, hotels and golf courses demanded by an industry that neither sees nor cares. Thousands have died of beatings, malnutrition and exhaustion. Yet still the vampire tourists come, purchasing a pound of human flesh with every kyat they spend.

Of course, it's not the tourists who are imprisoning people, forcing them to work and beating or killing them if they refuse. Our ignorance is exploited, our perception of where we should and shouldn't tread is complicated by the knowledge that some tourism can do more good than harm. But we are the ones who buy these slaves: ours, as William Wilberforce first pointed out nearly two centuries ago, is therefore the primary responsibility. It is up to us to discover whether or not our money will ruin or enhance people's lives. Today, you don't have to be evil to be a slave-driver, only unthinking.

Tourism has often been presented as a force for global salvation, bringing people closer together and providing alternative livelihoods for the victims of exploitation. It has also, however, become one of the world's principal sources of oppression and destruction.

Clearances are a common component of national tourist industries. All over South-East Asia, farms, forests, villages, even suburbs, have been destroyed to make way for golf courses. Slums are razed for fear of offending visitors. In many parts of Africa, conservation is used to justify the creation of new parks and reserves for tourism. Their inhabitants are excluded from the lands they have possessed for centuries, and if they dare to re-enter them they do so (in Kenya) on pain of death.

Wherever it occurs, tourism is an extractive industry. It extracts the differences between our land and culture and those of the nations we visit, until they scarcely exist. Remote and romantic beaches become mundane resorts. Remote and remarkable people tailor their culture to suit those who pay for it, until, in the words of a Maasai man, "We have ceased to be what we are; we are becoming what we seem." The exotic, of course, is illusory: as we approach it, it disappears. Tourism will never be sated, therefore, even when it has penetrated the remotest parts of the world.

While organised tours may be most directly responsible for the muffling of diversity, it is the backpackers who blaze the trail others follow. An independent travellers' destination becomes a mainstream resort within a few years. Indeed as travel becomes easier and tourists more adventurous, the distinction between the two groups is breaking down: hundreds of tour companies organise journeys that mimic those of independent travellers. Independent travel itself has had an enormous impact on places such as Goa, the South African coast and several Thai resorts, which have become increasingly unwilling hosts of the European dance scene. Neither category – if they can still be categorised – is blameless.

He that travels far knows much.
– ENGLISH PROVERB

Whatever happens when you get there, travelling itself has begun to ruin the lives of millions of people. By 2016, for example, the number of passengers using London's airports is expected to double to 160 million, an average of nearly three flights per year for every man, woman and child in the United Kingdom. This, of course, means ever noisier skies. Sedative use increases by eight per cent (over the average) in areas affected by aircraft noise, while people living within ten kilometres of an airport consume 14 per cent more anti-asthma drugs. Around Los Angeles airport, mortality rates are five per cent higher than in quieter places: suicide accounts for much of the difference. One study shows that the reading ability of 12- to 14-year-olds whose schools lie under flight paths is impaired by 23 per cent, while children of all ages are more likely to develop anxiety disorders when routinely exposed to aircraft noise.

The impact on the environment is even graver. The transport specialist Dr Meyer Hillman has shown that every passenger on a return flight to Florida is single-handedly responsible for generating 1.8 tonnes of carbon dioxide. Climate scientists estimate that, if the worst effects of climate change are to be avoided, total emissions per person *per year* should be little more than half this amount.

Now several companies are vying to become the first to propel tourists into space. It is hard to think of a project better designed for maximum environmental destruction. If the industry takes off as some of its boosters would like us to believe, it will rapidly become the world's primary source of carbon dioxide emissions. In our quest to populate the barren interplanetary wastes, we threaten to lay waste to the only life-sustaining planet astronomers have been able to detect.

None of the ethical questions raised by tourism have easy answers. Tour organisers have justified their work to me on the grounds that it is a form of 'cultural exchange'. Yet what I have seen of their activities suggests that this is not how the transaction actually works. While the visitors get culture, the hosts – if they are lucky – get money. As identity is rooted in place, the tourists have little to offer.

Other people claim that tourism breaks down the barriers between our lives and those of the people we visit. Yet in most cases tourists remain firmly behind barriers, be they the windows of a coach, the walls of a hotel or the lens of a camera. In many parts of the world, tourism has served to compound misunderstanding and hostility, as local people's sensitivities are trampled.

Tourism, we are told, brings wealth to local people. My experience suggests that the opposite is more likely to be true: in most places, tourism makes a few people extremely rich while impoverishing the majority, who lose their land, their resources and their sense of self, gaining in return (if anything) a tiny amount of money.

Even the oldest maxim of all, that travel broadens the mind, is questionable. Tourists are the aristocracy of the New World Order. They are pampered and protected wherever they go; they are treated with deference and never corrected. Indeed, tour companies do their best to provide what the tourists expect, rather than educating the tourists to expect what the country can reasonably provide. For most tourists, the only surprises will be unpleasant ones, when the reality of the countries they visit pricks the bubble in which they travel. At this point the shock of discovery tends to compound fears rather than assuaging them, and thus many people return home more convinced than they were when they left that foreigners are dirty, deceitful and dangerous.

And yet it is also true that some people – those who manage to engage with the place they visit on its own terms – come back from their travels better than they were before, able to see both themselves and the rest of the world in a new light, able to grasp, perhaps for the first time, that theirs is not the only valid way to live. Visiting other countries can help us to understand the impacts that our lives exert on other people's.

Like almost everything else, travelling is much harder to do the right way than the wrong way. We must collectively reduce the number of flights we take, but as flights become cheaper and other forms of travel more expensive, this becomes increasingly difficult. Perhaps we should try to reverse the trends of the past few years, and either travel closer to home or take longer, less frequent breaks, which would enable us both to fly less and to engage more effectively with the people we visit. We should read as much as we can before we go and try to learn the rudiments of the local language, so that when we get there we can discover things for ourselves, rather than allowing intermediaries to tell us only what they want us to hear.

Travelling, like all other forms of consumption, is not a neutral activity. Everything we do affects other people, everything we own is taken from someone else. If you can't travel carefully, don't travel at all. ಶ

GEORGE MONBIOT *is a columnist for the 'Guardian' newspaper and author of 'Poisoned Arrows: an Investigative Journey through Indonesia', 'Amazon Watershed' and 'No Man's Land: an Investigative Journey through Kenya and Tanzania'.*

The world impact of tourism
by Sir Crispin Tickell

THE ONLY PROBLEM ABOUT TOURISM is the other tourists. We see yet another boatload in motorised canoes in the wide waters of the Amazon; yet more louts demanding lager and chips in Mediterranean villages; yet another tourist procession between endangered species in the Galapagos Islands; yet more feet along the ever-widening trails that expose the mountain rocks; yet another cruise liner pouring people like an ant army on to white Caribbean beaches or even whiter Antarctica; yet more Land Rover tracks across the African savannah. We love tourism and we hate it.

The problem is relatively new. As with the industrial revolution some 250 years ago, it was the British who started it. In the early days travel abroad was the preserve of the rich, who did it to enlarge their education and enjoy exotic pleasures. With the new wealth generated by business and industry, it moved rapidly down the social scale. While the Duke of Wellington was against railways because they gave the lower orders ideas above their station, Thomas Cook organised the first rail excursion from Leicester to Loughborough for a shilling. But it was only in the lifetime of present generations that tourism became the world's biggest industry, with all the impacts and consequences of industrial development: the generation of wealth and employment, the opening of minds to new horizons, the pleasures of new ways of life, the impact on the environment, consumption of natural resources, production of wastes and pollutants, and not least effects on the cultural attitudes of all in contact with it.

It is worth looking at some of the figures. Tourism accounts for over six per cent of world gross national product, and provides up to ten per cent of total employment. All this arises from the eight per cent of the world's population that travels. Most tourists come from just 20 countries. Last year there were well over five million tourists in the world, and this figure could double in the next 15 years. Some countries have become dependent on tourism for the good health of their economies: they range from Egypt, Spain, Jamaica and Kenya to the islands of the Caribbean and the Pacific. Some of the environment in such countries has been radically changed as a result.

There has been a substantial diversion of resources to tourist use. This is particularly important in countries short of water. Some figures produced by the United Nations Food and Agriculture Organisation illustrate the problem. Fifteen thousand cubic metres of water can irrigate one hectare of high-yielding modern rice; support 100 nomads and 450 cattle for three years; maintain 100 rural families for three years and 100 urban families for two years; or meet the needs of 100 guests in a tourist hotel for 55 days. The cost of meeting tourist needs, whether in terms of clearing land for golf courses, building major works of infrastructure, producing specialised foods, disposing of wastes and pollution and the rest, are immeasurably large. The cultural impact is also beyond measurement. I remember my shock when, as an academic at Oxford, I was the subject of tourist curiosity with flash-bulbs. For once I was at one with the Matabele guide or the Amazonian Indian (who reasonably charge for having their photographs taken). Like seeing television or hearing radio programmes from another world, tourists generate unrealisable expectations and consequent frustration in others.

Yet the right to travel has become an icon of liberty, especially for those under oppressive regimes. So it should be. But rights carry obligations, and if tourism is not to be like the Indian goddess Kali, the creator of wealth and at the same time the destroyer of what generated it, we need to see how tourism can be brought into balance, particularly in relation to its impact on the environment.

What can we do? I believe that the first requirement in this, as in so many other environmental matters, is to establish true costs, and make sure that they are met. It has been well said that markets are marvellous at fixing prices but incapable of recognising costs. Recently a brave attempt has been made to establish the true costs of the natural services – ranging from the fertility of the soil to its ability to absorb wastes within the natural ecosystem, of which humans are a tiny part – and, although the results were approximate, they are very interesting: the average works out at about $33 trillion a year, while the world's gross national product is around $30 trillion a year. A good example is the price of coal. In no country does it include the cost of the effects of burning it, whether on human health, on buildings or on the chemistry of the atmosphere. The same goes for transport.

It is not easy to establish environmental costs. The last Chancellor of the Exchequer justified a continuing increase in petrol prices on environmental grounds, and the new climate change levy will fall in the same category. As for tourism, there can be no question that tourists should, in one way or another, bear the cost of the effects of their actions.

A particular perversion is the lack of any tax on aviation fuel. It has become cheaper to convey people as well as materials by air than to use other means of transport, with effects throughout the economy. Air traffic contributes carbon to the atmosphere. It makes up 11 per cent of total transport fuel emissions, and some three per cent of the emissions that can be attributed to human activity. Sixty per cent of air travel is now tourist related.

Another perversion is that very little of the wealth generated by tourism goes to the people who live on the spot. This means that local communities increasingly resent tourism, and in sensitive environmental areas have little incentive to protect and conserve their surroundings. If local people are to identify themselves with the good health of their own environment, then they must see most of the return from it. Individual tourists could make a big difference by spending their foreign currency on goods and services bought directly from the local communities.

At present most fees charged for admission to National Parks or other areas of conservation are derisory. They scarcely cover the most elementary requirements of conservation. In a way, tourists rent other people's environments for brief periods, and should be ready to pay a fair price for them. This, in turn, requires stronger local control. Nothing is more important than control of numbers. This can be done relatively easily in such isolated places as the Galapagos Islands, Machu Picchu in Peru, or Bhutan in the Himalayas, but control elsewhere, notably in our own Lake District or the Scottish highlands, has been non-existent or ineffective. Many feel that the natural environment should come for free, without realising that nothing is for free, above all the impact on the natural world. The Earthwatch programme in Zimbabwe over the last few years is a good demonstration of what can be done. Yet the threat to the natural world continues to increase almost everywhere, and something like a fifth of the world's rich biological diversity could be lost in the next 20 years unless coordinated action is taken to conserve it.

I think that the tourist industry is already well aware of these problems. So far there are few signs that they are being taken as seriously as they deserve. So long as the philosophy is primarily commercial, with the usual stuff about competitive markets, economic growth and promotion of mass movements of people, things are not likely to change, whatever the gloss put on them. True environmental costing has to enter in at all points.

Just as the industrial revolution did much good but created multiple problems for the good health of our planet, so its product, tourism, risks doing likewise. Indeed it is already doing so, and things could get much worse before they get better. There is a simple principle we should always bear in mind: do not kill the goose that lays the golden eggs. ❧

SIR CRISPIN TICKELL, GCMG, KCVO, is one of the founders of the environmental movement. His seminal work was 'Climatic Change and World Affairs' (1977) and he has been Chairman of the Climate Institute of Washington, DC, and Director of the Green College Centre for Environmental Policy and Understanding Initiative, Oxford. A former British diplomat, he is Warden of Green College, Oxford, and Chancellor of the University of Kent at Canterbury.

Can tourism save the planet?
by Simon Beeching

Back in 1984 a 'new low price' for a Round-the-World airfare of £1,250 was announced by British Airways/Air New Zealand. Suddenly, jet travel had not only made foreign holidays affordable for mass tourism in the Mediterranean, but also opened up distant horizons for everyday travellers. Now, in the early twenty-first century, the price of a similar ticket has fallen to as low as £700, and a generation of students have grown up with the concept of taking a year out before university to see the world on just such a ticket.

As a result of such affordability of travel, both for leisure and business travel, the World Tourism Organisation forecasts a continuing explosive growth in international travel. Already there are 800 million international visits a year, and WTO predicts this will double again in the next two decades.

Such rapid growth has seen the travel industry grow from its initial 'luxury goods' status to become the biggest industry in the world, ahead even of oil. So with such massive economic considerations at stake, the industry is rapidly expanding its interests globally: airlines are forming global alliances and mergers, and large tour-operating concerns like Thomas Cook, Thomson and Airtours are becoming parts of multi-national conglomerates.

Naturally, such huge growth also precipitates huge infrastructure change. And whilst ever-larger aircraft may somewhat ease congestion at airports, and modern technology may continue to make aircraft quieter, the environmental lobby is inevitably stepping up its efforts to minimise the impact of tourism on historic monuments, on coastlines and on the biodiversity and cultural heritage of host countries – as well as the ozone layer.

When I worked for the large UK tour-operating group Thomson Travel in the late 1980s, a group of MBA students from France did a survey amongst the directors. Apparently I was the only one who was sceptical about their thesis that tourism could be made more 'environmentally friendly'. After all, at its core, the concept of chopping down forests for all the travel brochures (Thomson alone was printing over 30 million brochures a year in those days), and of fleets of aircraft flying millions of charter passengers to the Mediterranean and beyond, was hardly a propitious starting point; let alone the questionable aesthetics of many of the burgeoning tourist developments around the world's coastlines and beauty spots.

But during the 1990s my perspective on this was changed by a number of events and observations.

When I had first joined the travel industry in 1979, Spain was still a relatively poor, developing nation, just emerging from Franco's dictatorship. But by the 1990s it had joined the EU and was as thriving a first-world democracy as any of its northern European partners, with huge social and infrastructure advances for the whole population afforded out of the massive inflows of tourism income to its economy.

The concept of this 'levelling' of the economic playing field for poorer nations which can benefit from tourism (the Caribbean and Indian Ocean islands, such as Mauritius, are other good examples) is a powerful justification for the occasional tourist blackspot, given the economic and social empowerment that this redistribution of wealth can create for the local population over time. And, after all, who is to say that the high-rise red dots on the map representing Palma Nova/Magalluf, Pattaya or Ochio Rios have 'spoilt' Majorca, Thailand or Jamaica in their totality, any more than Blackpool or Bournemouth have 'ruined' Great Britain overall? The balance of the environmental and aesthetic downsides of such tourist playgrounds, versus the broader benefits that can result for local economies, is more evenly weighted as an argument than many a purist conservationist, who objects to tourism development simply on principle, might have us believe.

But even directly in terms of conservation, this flow of tourist income into poorer local communities can also transform their very ability to care for their local environment – an environment which might otherwise be threatened by the lack of basic economic welfare for the local human population, let alone for such relative 'luxuries' as heritage sites or wildlife preservation.

I was struck, for instance, by the transformation of local attitudes towards reef protection in Palawan in the Philippines, when I visited the remote area of El Nido for my honeymoon. Almost overnight, the locals had changed their main occupation from dynamite-fishing (which had disastrous consequences for one of the best reef areas of the world) into dive-guiding for tourists. They were thus transformed from destroyers of the reef into its very guardians, which is good news on a global scale.

This same poacher-turned-gamekeeper transformation due to tourism has also been seen to work in some parts of Africa, where locals have been educated to understand that protecting the wildlife and game – rather than hunting it into extinction – is good for promoting tourism, which in turn creates employment for their communities.

Now that the World Tourism Council has established that one in eight people globally is directly or indirectly employed by the tourism industry, such economic arguments are powerful motivators indeed – and they provide an inducement for local and national governments of tourism host-nations to become directly involved in preserving and protecting what might otherwise become lost to the world.

Another graphic example of this which I have seen in action is at the Cango caves in South Africa, the third largest cave complex in the world. These are now specifically being preserved as a tourist attraction, whereas previously – just like the caves in England's Cheddar Gorge – they were being completely despoiled by the very geologists who were exploring them.

So, far from being seen as inevitably a pariah in terms of conservation, there is in fact a strong argument to suggest that the tourism industry, as the world's largest employer, can and should harness its huge financial muscle directly in favour of conservation and the host economies, to promote local welfare and environmental good. And this argument becomes even more powerful when coupled with the fact that this must anyway be good for the travel industry itself: it will ensure a better balance for the future between the ongoing growth of the industry and the capacity of host nations and local environments to cope, and thus help to preserve the future of the travel industry too.

Evidence that such a harmonisation of interests and balancing-out of apparent opposites is already happening can be seen in a number of movements and initiatives now established or gathering momentum. The Tourism For Tomorrow awards (initiated by the UK's Federation of Tour Operators and sponsored annually by British Airways) now receives widespread international interest, both in terms of submission of entries and of media coverage for the winning tourism projects, which work in harmony with, or directly to protect, the local environment.

'Green Globe' certification is now recognised internationally as a symbol of environmental best practice for tourist developments, in particular for hotels. And the international charity Friends of Conservation, of which the Prince of Wales is patron in the UK, is receiving ever-increasing pledges of funding from British travel companies keen to support its funding of community-based conservation projects around the globe.

Governments and international politics are also playing their part. A recent United Nations initiative (UNEP) is attracting support from European tour operators to co-ordinate new sustainable tourism standards; and the British government's Department for International Development has announced funding for tourism projects which support sustainable environment programmes in poorer countries. The latter follows research which demonstrated that positive links could indeed be encouraged between tourism and poverty-reduction, and also environmental sustainability.

So the interests of conservation and tourism are becoming more in tune with one another as the travel industry matures, and the realisation dawns for shareholders of travel companies that the key 'asset' in their balance sheet which they must protect is the very environment in which they trade, and which their customers wish to enjoy. And in tandem with this, conservationists and scientists have awoken to the huge economic power of the tourism industry which can either work for the good or else cause despoliation and damage if not properly planned and environmentally audited.

Of course, the wheel may eventually turn full circle anyway, as the capacity of the planet eventually fails to be able to absorb further tourism growth, or if governments succeed in their intention to levy 'green taxes' on the travel industry (as they have for instance on petrol) in order to curb this very growth.

Or perhaps the explosive growth of international travel will be seen as only a twentieth-century phenomenon, curtailed in this new century by environmental constraints and by the fact that modern video-conferencing techniques may make business travel less necessary anyway. Furthermore, with the future possibility of our being surrounded by 3-D holograms of a place, with all the sights, smells and sounds recreated artificially, we may want to visit facsimiles of foreign places much nearer to home. Already, Americans can view the false Venetian canals and bridges of the Venetian Palace Hotel in Las Vegas. We may simply book virtual trips to far-flung places, without having to leave home at all.

Now that really would be good for the planet. 🙠

Simon Beeching is the Managing Director of Wexas International. He is also a trustee of the Friends of Conservation, Chairman of its Travel and Tourism Conservation Committee, and co-founder of the environmental consultancy Travelwatch. He is a Fellow of the Institute of Travel and Tourism and of the Royal Geographical Society.

Tomorrow's destinations
by Jonathan Lorie

WHERE'S HOT, WHERE'S HIP, WHERE'S 'HAPPENING'? The burning question for the independent traveller is how to find the next generation of destinations, the places that are 'special' but still unspoilt.

The reality, of course, is that there is almost nowhere left on the surface of this planet that is completely 'unspoilt'. Possibly on the steppes of outer Mongolia, but even there they're hooking up satellite television sets to oil-burning generators in an effort to enter the global culture. Even in the rainforests of central Africa, there are villagers clothed in T-shirts that read, bizarrely, 'Vote for Bill Clinton'. There is precious little escape from our modern world.

One solution, for those who can afford it, is to escape into the realm of luxury travel. There is a whole range of private islands, stucco hotels, grand trains and shiny yachts, in which the affluent traveller can recreate a version of how travel might once have been, in the days before cheap airfares filled the globe with package resorts.

Not so much a destination as a way of life, luxury travel is opening new frontiers all the time. Its big success right now is cruising. Three-quarters of a million British holiday-makers took a cruise in 1999, an increase of 11 per cent on the year before. The Passenger Shipping Association predicts that $10 billion will be spent on building cruise liners in the next five years worldwide, to launch 40 new ocean liners. The appeal behind all this is the fact that the scenery comes to you, as you lie on deck enjoying the comforts of five-star service.

Lolling on a sun deck quaffing champagne is nice work, if you can get it, but it's not the same as experiencing the reality – and the totality – of a country that is new to tourism. Such places do still exist. The ultimate example is probably Bhutan, a tiny kingdom high in the Himalayas, where only a trickle of travellers is permitted entry. Here you can find the most 'unspoilt' Buddhist culture on earth. Next door is tiny Mustang, another highly restricted kingdom, about which almost nothing is known.

Even less well-known areas exist in the inhospitable hinterlands of the world. In Borneo and Papua New Guinea, explorers do still encounter tribesmen who have not seen white skin before. The Amazon basin is opening up for tourism, especially wildlife and river safaris and including, I understand, a jungle nudist resort (which must offer plenty of skin for the locals). Even Australia has vast areas of outback that are uncharted territory: though there may be good reasons for this. Essentially, the rawest travel experiences will be found in those places that are the most unpleasant to visit – malarial swamps in the Congo, for example, or the wind-blasted islands off Cape Horn.

Slightly more feasible for the ordinary traveller are those countries which are just opening the door to foreigners. Vietnam was the classic example, five or six years ago, and still offers an authentic experience of the fragile beauty of Indochina. Then came Laos next door, where you couldn't even buy maps or phrasebooks when I visited it in 1995. Next will be Cambodia, if they ever stabilise the politics, because

I suggested that she take a trip round the world. "Oh I know," returned the lady, yawning with ennui, "but there's so many other places I want to see first."
– S J PERELMAN

it is home to the jungle-clad ruins of Angkor, one of the world's finest temple sites. Interestingly, the isolation of all three countries was a historical accident (caused by the Vietnam War) and it is such 'victims' of history which are proving the most rewarding to visit now.

Cuba is the outstanding example of this. Long embargoed by the United States, it is now emerging from Cold War quarantine and proving a massive hit with travellers. It offers hot music, fine beaches, picturesque towns and the frisson of history. Because it was isolated for so long from the modern world, its traditions and essential character have been preserved intact – for the time being at least.

The same is true of Libya, which has some of the finest and emptiest Classical sites in the Mediterranean. South Africa is benefiting from the same effect, and British tourism there is doubling annually as people flock to see wildlife and scenery which in the apartheid era they had heard about but not wished to visit. Its neighbour Namibia was hardly visited at all during the years of apartheid and independence struggle: now it offers spectacular safaris through rugged deserts and pristine game parks.

Could this be the future for Africa's other pariah states, if peace ever comes? It happened in post-war Mozambique, which was building a reputation among serious travellers before the unfortunate flooding of 1999. Could it happen in Angola or Sudan? Sierra Leone is an achingly beautiful country, but its return to travel brochures is some way off. Zimbabwe could go either way. In such places, the politics is everything.

Closer to home, the time-warp effect is visible in many post-Soviet countries. Romania and Hungary offer a glimpse of a picturesque older Europe as it existed before the Second World War. The Baltic republics bristle with fairytale castles and quaint towns in a classic northern European landscape of pine forests and lakes. Montenegro is a jewel of Ottoman imperial architecture. Georgia offers fine skiing and the cheapest champagne in the world.

Central Asia is the great beneficiary of the Soviet Union's collapse. Samarkand, Bokhara, Tashkent – these are names dripping with myth. Now you can fly direct from London. The Silk Route can be traced from start to finish, with or without an organised tour. No longer are you subject to endless red tape and incomprehensible official guides. Though you might find the disintegrating infrastructure something of a challenge.

And as Russia collapsed, so China relaxed. Foreigners have been able to travel through most of the celestial republic for a decade now. Some areas are closed off, others are just impenetrable, but in a country this big there's plenty to discover.

And with the current easing in world tensions (touch wood), other countries that were clients of the communist bloc have come onstream. Syria is little visited, but offers fabulous opportunities for those interested in crusader castles, Arabic culture and sweeping desert landscapes. Iran has dazzling Islamic architecture and impressively hospitable people. Mongolia, too, has opened up, though you have to be a good seat on horseback to really appreciate this steppeland. Nicaragua is now peaceful, beautiful and welcoming.

Moving on from the countries that came in from the cold, there are other places which ought to be simply ruined by tourism, but remain surprisingly unpopular. Bolivia is a case in point. A giant slumbering in the heart of Latin America, it spans the dramatic Andes, the mysterious *altiplano* and the luxuriant Amazon jungle – but no one goes there.

Madagascar is another obvious spot that's missed out. It's an island the size of Britain, but blessed with the sunshine and beaches of the Indian Ocean. The people are a beguiling mixture of African and Arabic, and its unique ecosystem ranges from rainforest to desert to mountains. And the place is almost empty of tourists.

Sri Lanka ought to be inundated with visitors. To be fair, it has suffered from a low-level civil war for decades now, but that doesn't impinge on most of this beautiful island. Imagine India without the madness, a lush and laid-back island where Buddhism sets a gentle tone and history has left resonant monuments. It's hard to resist.

Ecuador is slowly rising in popularity. Everyone yearns to visit the Galapagos Islands, where you can swim with sea lions and bask with giant tortoises. But few explore the mainland, a luscious country of jungles, beaches and Spanish colonial towns.

Botswana still doesn't receive many visitors, although the Okavango delta is one of the most magical places anywhere. Floating through the reeds in a dugout canoe surrounded by singing birds and flowering lilies, or walking the islands among giraffe and cheetah and zebra – there's nowhere on earth quite like it.

There are others: Belize (deep rainforest and Caribbean beaches), Pakistan (hill-tribe cultures and Moghul architecture), French Polynesia (Pacific paradise), Lakshadweep (exquisite islands), Chile (spectacular mountains).

Not all destinations are actual places, of course. There's a whole new category of holidays that are based around activities rather than places. Never mind painting holidays or wine-tasting tours. Eco-warriors are volunteering to conserve species from South African dolphins to Indian wolves. Charity fundraisers are rafting

Guatemala, trekking Nepal, cycling Jordan. Extreme sportspeople are colonising the globe, whether they're hang-gliding the Himalayas, snow-boarding the Rockies or dog-sledding the Arctic.

And the Arctic represents a real frontier that is opening for the mainstream traveller. Travel to the Arctic or Antarctic is necessarily by organised tour group, but the opportunities now exist to walk on the ice pack, indulge in polar transport and walk with the penguins. It takes several weeks to arrive via luxury cruiser, and you'd better be a good sailor for those wild seas, but you can now experience the most extreme environment on our planet.

Which only leaves one destination 'unspoilt': space, the final frontier for tourism, the place that Ronald Reagan called 'the face of God'. And guess what? Already you can buy a ticket. For £56,000 you can book onto the first sub-orbital flights in 2003. These will take you 62 miles above the earth's surface, from where you can see the curvature of our planet. You will experience total weightlessness and, I would imagine, a little vertigo.

Personally, I'll be staying on planet earth. Apart from the vertigo, I reckon there's enough down here to keep us busy for a good long while yet. I'll see you out there. 🍂

Jonathan Lorie is the Editor of 'The Traveller's Handbook'.

How travel has changed
by Ian Wilson

IT'S A HARD LIFE LIVING IN A SHRUNKEN WORLD that once brimmed with the chance to see new faces and places. Or so people keep telling me. Everywhere is supposed to be spoiled now. Spoiled for the locals and spoiled for the visitors. It's as if you might as well stay at home and just send your money instead.

Until recently I too felt this way, regretting that the places I used to enjoy had lost their charm. I have done a lot of travelling around the world since the 1970s, and it is true that, since then, the travel experience has changed hugely. Once, the world was your oyster; but now?

There were fads 20 years ago, much as there are fads now. The Seychelles had already come and gone, so to speak. Sri Lanka was just starting to happen, only to see its budding tourist industry hit by the civil war a couple of years later. Bali and Kenya, too, were taking off, but no one was thinking about Vietnam and Laos, and even Thailand and Malaysia were not on most travellers' visiting lists.

But the favourites of the old hippie trail of the 1960s and 1970s were still pulling in an ever-ageing tourist population of former hippies – in particular Kathmandu, Goa, Lake Toba in Sumatra and Jogjakarta in Java. Later there would be Koh Phangan in Thailand. But if the places to go were changing, so were the types who went there. In Bali, the hippies gave way to the surfies, who also took over the town of Jaco on the Pacific coast of Costa Rica.

Where you go depends a lot on your age and your income. Places that pulled in the impecunious with a good ration of cheap living and inspired the *$5 a Day* books in the pre-inflationary 1960s and 1970s included Morocco and Turkey, as well as Afghanistan and Iran, compulsory visits on the overland route to India and beyond in the days when the Magic Bus from London was part of the hippie vocabulary. After it was all over, the hippies all said the same thing: the experience was great, but like most rites of passage they wouldn't want to do it again.

The package holiday industry, which was really limited to Europe for most travellers in the 1970s, started to move further afield after that. The mass market ventured as far as Tunisia, then Florida, Barbados and St Lucia. Going east, there was coastal Turkey, then Israel. And for the really intrepid there was Kenya, the Maldives and the destinations pioneered by the hippies for the mainstream market that followed: Goa, Bali, Kathmandu and Thailand.

Where does that leave for the seasoned traveller to go and visit if he insists on sun and sea? The good news is that the world may have shrunk, and cities may have become polluted hellholes, but there is still plenty of unspoilt coastline out there. My own favourite, in some ways, is Nicaragua, with all that Costa Rica has to offer at half the price and with virtually no tourists at all.

Much of Africa has had a pretty bad press in recent years, but a lot of it is fabulous. In particular I like the coast of Ghana, while the southern part of Senegal, known as the Casamance, is a great place for a short winter break in the sun.

The Caribbean is hardly a new destination, but what most people don't realise is how interesting it is if you get away from the well-known spots. My favourites there include San Salvador, Cat Island and Mayaguana in the Bahamas. Then there are the Turks and Caicos Islands, especially Grand Turk. In the British Virgin Islands, I go

I have wandered all my life, and I have also travelled; the difference between the two being this, that we wander for distraction, but we travel for fulfilment.

– Hilaire Belloc

back from time to time to Anegada, a coralline island that is hardly visited. Carriacou, north of Grenada, is a weird and interesting place to spend a few days far from the crowds.

But it's the Indian Ocean I like most – places such as Sainte Marie, off the coast of Madagascar; or Rodrigues, to the east of Mauritius. The Pacific, by comparison, just doesn't compare with either the Indian Ocean or the Caribbean in the tropical islands' league tables. The sea can be great, but I have to admit I quickly get bored on most of the Pacific islands. The various cultures just don't grab me.

The point is that you can get away from it all just about anywhere. The secret, for me, is in following the coast away from the roads and any signs of habitation. You can do it almost anywhere in Europe, including England. I've walked the hundred or so miles of the Dorset coastal path, and even in summer it's possible to leave the crowds behind simply by walking a few miles.

Even when you're trying to get away from it all, the experience of flying has not got any easier in the last 20 years. Airports are still a nightmare in themselves; and if you're travelling from somewhere like London, it now takes twice as long to get to the airport from the centre of town as it did 20 years ago. Traffic congestion is the biggest cross the modern traveller has to bear. The second biggest is the growing crime problem all over the world and the sad fact that travellers have increasingly become targets for terrorism. Places such as Kenya, Egypt, Kashmir, Thailand, Zimbabwe, Colombia, Chechnya, Congo, Rwanda and South Africa all present real threats to foreign tourists, while Latin America, as a whole, is considered a danger zone by many thanks to a reputation for street and car crime. Particular cities, for instance, Rio de Janeiro, São Paulo, Bogotá, Caracas, Lima, Colon and Panama City, feature on my list of danger spots.

So don't go to the cities. Get out of them as fast as possible. The countryside is usually a far safer place, whether you're in South America or South Africa. You should rarely feel threatened in rural areas, assuming all reasonable precautions are taken. I am sure that there are plenty of exceptions, but on the whole the further you are from a city and other foreign visitors, the more hospitable and honest the local people tend to be. And travel with small children if you can. They act as great ice-breakers.

Where would I recommend for a really interesting experience? I've already suggested Nicaragua. How about Mauritania? Or the Azores in spring? Or, for spectacular scenery not too far from home, you could try the far north-west of Scotland. Or maybe you should just stay at home and send your money instead.

If you look hard enough, the world is still your oyster. ❧

IAN WILSON is the founder and Chairman of WEXAS International and one of the world's most-travelled travel agents.

The future of the travel industry
by Jeremy Skidmore

THE TRAVEL INDUSTRY HAS CHANGED RADICALLY SINCE THE 1970S, when two weeks at the English seaside were the norm and Mediterranean holidays were only just coming within reach of most families. Domestic holidays have survived, but these days most people holidaying in the UK are taking a short break of up to three nights and there has been a steady decline in the number of longer stays. Around 14 million UK residents took an overseas holiday in 1999 – around ten million in summer and four million in winter, and they spent, on average, £500 per head.

Spain is the clear favourite for the British, accounting for 42 per cent of all package holiday bookings. But while the Mediterranean has remained strong, UK holiday-makers now travel to all corners of the globe. The advent of charter flights to the United States, the Caribbean, the Far East and Australia in the 1980s opened new markets for UK holiday-makers, as did a fall in the price of cruises and all-inclusive holidays.

The travel industry today

Today the UK, and indeed the European, holiday markets are dominated by a few major players. During 1997 the UK government conducted a wide-ranging review of the package holiday market, which was dominated by Thomson, Airtours, Thomas Cook and First Choice.

At the time, the first three of those companies were all vertically integrated, which meant they owned tour operators, airlines and travel agents. But despite their dominance, the government found that they operated in a highly competitive market and offered consumers good value for money. This was the signal for the main players to expand further and a rapid programme of consolidation began.

Airtours bought up Panorama, direct-sell operator Direct Holidays, and more recently Jetset and Manos. Thomson acquired ski operator Crystal Holidays and a raft of small independent operators. The idea behind the acquisitions was to try to convince holiday-makers that they were not only good for mass market holidays, but that they could cater for any type of traveller.

The big companies also wanted to make sure you bought from their shops and began a policy of acquiring high street travel agencies. However, when Airtours stepped in to buy First Choice in early 1999, the planned purchase was a step too far for the European Commission, which decided to investigate. The EC concluded that, even though First Choice shareholders wanted the deal, it should not go through because Airtours would then hold a dominant position in the UK market and this would, potentially, be bad for consumers. Although at the time of going to press Airtours was fighting the decision in the court of appeal, it became clear to the major players that any further expansion in the UK market would be limited. If they wanted to get bigger, they had to expand on a European basis.

Thomas Cook is already 51 per cent-owned by German giant Preussag, and Airtours has various interests around the world, including a 36 per cent stake in FTi of Germany. In April 2000, German's other giant, C&N Touristic, made an offer for Thomson, the UK market leader, which has had a troubled time since its float in May 1998. The reason for the mass consolidation is simply to give the big companies greater buying power when it comes to negotiating hotel beds in resorts and buying aviation fuel. The profit margin on package holidays from the UK is only around four per cent, but economies of scale can help push that up considerably. These increased margins are unlikely to be passed on to the consumer in the form of cheaper holidays. UK holiday-makers already enjoy prices that are, on average, around 40 per cent cheaper than their German counterparts and high street discounts of 30 per cent are commonplace.

More likely is that the increased consolidation will lead to reduced competition among travel companies and give them the opportunity to charge what they would consider to be more realistic prices for the holidays they offer. Medium-sized tour operators will find it increasingly difficult to contract hotel beds when up against the buying power of the European giants.

Elsewhere, low-cost carriers such as EasyJet, Go, Ryanair and Buzz have exploited the market for cheap European fares. Operating out of cheap satellite airports such as Luton and Stansted, they have been able to offer flights to European cities at a fraction of the cost of such main scheduled airlines as British Airways.

Surprisingly, the cheaper airlines have appealed to business travellers on a budget as much as to holiday-makers. However, they have largely steered clear from operating on routes to Mediterranean resorts, where they would have to compete with the charter carriers, which offer flights as part of a keenly priced package.

The three big success stories of the mid- to late-1990s have been Florida, cruising and all-inclusive resorts. Florida, with its theme parks, guaranteed sunshine and great value for money, has appealed to families that want an alternative to the Costa del Sol. Unfortunately Florida did not capitalise on its popularity by promoting the whole state, and many families chose to holiday elsewhere after they had visited Walt Disney and Universal Studios.

Cruising and all-inclusive resorts, which have been most prevalent in the Caribbean, have proved to be an increasingly popular option for stressed-out workers who want to recharge their batteries. On both types of holidays all meals and activities are provided, leaving holiday-makers with little to worry about apart from topping up their suntans. But the holidays have not been without controversy. Many Caribbean islands have complained that cruise ships, which stop off for the day, add little to the local economy because tourists largely keep their money in their pockets, returning to the ships for meals and drinks. Similarly, all-inclusive resorts are self-contained and many guests never venture out of their safe complex.

Future directions

The biggest changes in the industry will be in distribution, or the sale of holidays. The major companies have stopped opening new travel agency branches and instead are pouring millions of pounds into new technology. So far less than one per cent of package holidays have been booked over the internet, but the big companies are banking on this changing. Not only will consumers become more used to booking in this way, but the costs to tour operators will fall because they will not have to pay travel agents' commissions if they can get holiday-makers to book direct on their own site.

Commodity bookings, such as flights and hotels, have already been sold over the internet to great effect, and EasyJet claims that it is taking over 30 per cent of its bookings via its website. So far only five per cent of British Airways' flights are booked over the internet, but the airline believes the figure could be as high as 50 per cent within five years.

In the future, the new technology will simply give customers greater choice. You will be able to call up the internet from your mobile phone and surf to find the best deals. You may choose to book holidays from an internet travel agency that is offering a range of different holidays or you could log directly on to a tour operator or airline site and book with the company itself. Alternatively, you will be able to see and speak to a travel agent on your phone who will carry out all the searching for you in return for a service charge or fee. A similar function will be available on television and people will be able to make bookings or call up an agent on the screen.

High street travel agencies won't disappear because there will always be people who want to talk face to face with an agent and enjoy the social experience of shopping. A peak-season Mediterranean holiday to a good standard hotel currently costs around a £1,000 per head, and for that sort of money many people want a chat with a friendly face they can trust. But, to survive, agents will have to offer a personal service and innovative ideas to capture the imagination of the public, and the new technology will undoubtedly weed out the worst retailers. Currently there are around 7,000 UK agents, and this is expected to drop to around 5,000 over the next five years.

A new development in towns is the holiday 'hypermarket' – huge warehouse-style agencies where people can practice driving on the other side of the road, and watch videos and relax in the comfort of a coffee bar. The idea was borrowed from America, where mall shopping is popular. Although it was slow to get off the ground in the UK, and bookings during the week are often poor, the hypermarkets have done good business at weekends.

The quality of holidays has improved beyond all recognition over the past 20 years and this trend will continue in the future. Programmes such as BBC's *Watchdog* have made people more aware of their rights, and it is no longer acceptable to offer holidays that do not fit the brochure description. However, the choice of holidays on the market is set to diminish as the big players continue to grow. Although the internet provides a relatively cheap form of distribution for anyone starting out as a tour operator, the real problem is gaining content, or hotel beds, in a resort. Most of the available properties in traditional hot-spots have already been snapped up by the big boys.

Futuristic travel

Talk of the future always sparks images of space travel, but in reality it would take a huge change in the cost of these trips for any family to even contemplate donning silver suits and travelling to another world. A Bristol-based company has offered trips on a space shuttle, but places are very limited and you won't get much change from £30,000 a head. Although the quality and types of holiday on the market and the way in which they can be bought are constantly changing, such old favourites as Spain, Greece, the Far East and Australia are set to remain popular for many years to come. ❧

JEREMY SKIDMORE is Editor of the trade newspaper 'Travel Weekly' and a regular contributor to newspaper and television on travel issues.

What kind of traveller are you?

The first-time traveller
by Jonathan Lorie

JUNE 27: LOMÉ BEACH, TOGO. My first night in Africa. Lying on a long beach, counting the shooting stars. Deep black sky. Sand between my toes as white as icing sugar, stars so close you could lick them. Coconut palms dancing in the sea breeze. Moonlight bright enough to write this.

Last night I was in a tapas bar in London, saying goodbye to friends. Sports cars whizzed past with their roofs rolled down, drivers in shades, jazz-funk blasting. I had a glass of wine and an ironed shirt, and people asked me what I'd miss in Africa. I said friends and books and clean sheets. Also toilets.

This morning I walked from the airport into Lomé. A capital city built from sheets of tin. The central market was a madhouse of stalls selling gaudy cottons, dead fish, bicycle tyres, voodoo skulls. Noise, people, heat, sunlight. Hands coming at me from the crowd, saying "Patron, patron." Boys frying bowls of rice and plantain on fires in the gutter. Old men in kaftans squatting outside the central bank, waving handfuls of filthy notes for exchange. Inside the bank a clerk took my English pounds, put them in his jacket pocket, produced an envelope of local currency at a generous exchange rate and said "Sans papiers."

Next door was a supermarché where white people were buying a little bit of home – ice buckets, saucissons, perfume, wine. It had air-conditioning. Outside there was a beggar on crutches with one leg stopped at the knee. Inside there were deep-frozen croissants.

Tonight the town's electricity failed but the street stalls were lit with candles and my taxi drove slowly between hundreds of soft flames in the hot velvet darkness.

THAT WAS A DIARY EXTRACT FROM MY FIRST VISIT TO AFRICA. And if you're contemplating your first big trip abroad – wherever it is – you might recognise some of these emotions. As a first-time traveller, perhaps the biggest hazard you'll encounter is your own state of mind. The trick is knowing how to handle yourself.

First there's the anticipation before you go, the sense of not quite knowing what you're getting into: the heady mix of fear and excitement. Don't be put off by this. Seasoned travellers will tell you that they still get this buzz – and still relish it – but like any addict, they have to go further and further to feel it. On the other hand, good pre-departure preparation can do wonders for your confidence – and for the trip itself.

So use this book (and perhaps a regional guidebook) to prepare yourself properly: there are lots of chapters here that would help you. And talk to people who've been there. Do some useful background reading to get your bearings, and pack carefully.

Then, when you arrive, there's the shock of being out there for the first time, in a strange place with different ways and values. You may have no way of understanding what's going on or being said. As many people say of India, it may challenge your entire view of the world. At the least, you won't know how to order a decent meal.

Again, don't despair. Many travellers find that the shock of the new is actually liberating: it allows them to leave behind the person they were at home, their inhibitions or preconceptions. Others never quite adjust. But if you don't want to be the kind of tourist who spends all day sheltering in the hotel compound or arguing with the locals, I suggest you try the adjustment option.

This may take a little time. It depends on how much difference you're adjusting to. For my first three weeks in India, I hated the place: the poverty, the dirt, the crowds. Travellers on short trips often get no further than this stage, because they don't have the time; it's important to allow yourself the right amount of time for the place you're visiting. India takes longer than most places, but slowly I began to enjoy things: a family who invited me home for rose-scented tea, pilgrims bathing in a river, even the hurly-burly of the trains.

The third and best emotion, if all goes well, is wonder. I don't need to tell you about that. You'll know it when it hits you and you wonder why you never did anything like this before.

So now we've sorted out your head, let's look at a few tips for handling the outside world.

Rules of the road

1. **TALK TO PEOPLE.** Whether it's fellow travellers or locals, the people you meet are one of the great pleasures of any trip. They're also the best source of inside information on what's really good to see or to avoid locally.

2. **DON'T PLAN TOO MUCH.** You'll find that local information or simple serendipity open opportunities which you could never anticipate – a side trip you hadn't planned, a festival you didn't know about, a place you want to savour for longer than expected. So be flexible: leave unscheduled gaps in your trip and try not to buy tickets you can't change.

3. **BE PATIENT:** especially in developing countries. Where the infrastructure is poor, getting things done can take ages. You stand more chance of achieving your goal by persisting very patiently and politely, than by demanding Western standards where they could not exist.

4. **NEVER LOSE YOUR TEMPER.** It goes down much worse than it might at home, and can escalate situations rather dramatically.

5. **TRUST YOUR INSTINCTS.** If a situation seems unnerving in any way, duck out of it. Always take your security precautions seriously. Learn to judge people and situations quickly and act accordingly. Equally, if something seems unexpectedly appealing, go for it.

6. **ENJOY.** Don't take everything too seriously. Allow yourself to appreciate the strangeness of foreign cultures, and exercise your sense of humour regularly.

And finally

Let me leave you with a portrait of another first-time traveller: my friend Marius. He's a game warden in South Africa, six foot six and built like a rhino. Out in the bush he's a bit of a daredevil, known to chase lions on foot and to fly his microlight above wild game. I drove with Marius right across the deserts of Namibia and none of our adventures scared him.

But Marius had never been outside southern Africa, until the day he visited London. I suggested we meet in Covent Garden, a trendy part of town. And there he was, an unmistakable figure among the glittering designer-shoppers and black-clad *cappuccino*-drinkers, dressed just as I had last seen him in the Transvaal: khaki shorts, dusty T-shirts, 'feltie' boots. On his belt he carried an enormous bush knife (until I said he'd better hide it, because in England it would be confiscated as an offensive weapon).

He stood on the kerb and we talked a long time, until I realised that he was rooted to the spot. "Pretty glad to see you, Jon," he said in his Afrikaans accent. "Man, I can take anything back home, but your traffic here scares me stiff."

And it was true. The cars down Long Acre had him running for cover. He'd rather walk round the block than cross the street. And the crowds of shoppers just baffled him. He stood there like a bull elephant sniffing the wind. How he managed the underground trains I cannot imagine.

Then I took him to see the Changing of the Guard outside Buckingham Palace, and he wept at the pageantry of it all. Later he explained that he'd never seen snow before, so I put him on a train for the Scottish Highlands – after buying him his first pair of jeans, just to keep him warm up there. And he still talks about that trip with fondness.

Which just goes to show that, however great our experience, we're all first-time travellers at heart. ❧

The woman traveller
by Isabella Tree

"THE ART OF TRAVELLING IS LEARNING TO BEHAVE LIKE A CHAMELEON." So said a woman friend of mine on her second year around the world and I don't believe a truer word was ever spoken. Blending into the background is not only a prerequisite to understanding and observing a different culture, it also keeps you out of trouble.

Indecent exposure

For women in particular, how you behave and especially how you dress can be construed as camouflage or an open invitation; it can make you one of the crowd or a moving target. This may be an unfair state of affairs but it's a fact of life and in someone else's country one is in no position to rail against it.

Call it ignorance or misdirected feminism, but many women make the mistake of travelling in a 'no compromise' frame of mind. They wear shorts and bra tops in Marrakech and Istanbul, G-strings in Goa and Phuket, and nothing at all in the Mediterranean. I know and you know that this does not mean they are 'loose women', but it does show a distinct lack of respect for local custom and the sensitivities of the men, and women, of the country.

Dress is the first line of defence and the most immediate symbol of respect. If you get that wrong you are starting your travels with a glaring disadvantage.

Of course codes of dress differ wildly from country to country. In southern Africa and part of the Indian subcontinent short sleeves and hemlines not far below the knee are fully respectable. In Iran and strict Muslim countries, the body must be totally covered, usually by a black *chador* which drapes you completely from head to foot. A woman not wearing a veil risks flogging or imprisonment, although as a foreigner you are likely to be let off with a caution and forced to cover up.

There are legally enforced dress codes at home as well, though they're so familiar we may take them for granted. But it serves to show that though conventions may differ, they are universal. In London, or Paris or New York, you would be a fool for walking the street topless, let alone racing across a cricket pitch, and not expecting to be arrested. In rainforest tribal communities from Sumatra to the Amazon, on the other hand, bare breasts are *de rigeur*.

A culture's standard of dress has a lot to do with what parts of the body are considered sensuous or provocative. In China the feet are still thought erotic, while in many countries direct eye contact can be as promiscuous as the offer of a spare key to your hotel room. In Papua New Guinea you can bare your breast to the world, but your thighs must be covered at all times. Not only that, but the space between your legs is so sexually suggestive that trousers can be as much of a turn-on as wearing nothing at all.

It pays to be prepared for the dress sense of your destination before you head off for a pre-holiday splurge in the high street, but clearly this is not always possible. As a general rule it can be said that tight and skimpy clothes are inappropriate for most countries outside Europe and the United States, and that generous, loose-fitting clothes are not only more comfortable to travel in, but less controversial.

If you don't want to wear dresses and skirts, you can't do better for propriety's sake, especially in tropical heat, than the kind of cool, cotton pyjamas worn by Chinese or Kashmiri women, or a Moroccan *jalaba*. However, in places like Burma, Thailand and Vietnam, particularly in the cities, this may be too casual. Asian women take a great deal of trouble with their appearance however poor their background, and while torn jeans and a tattered T-shirt may seem relaxed and inoffensive to the Westerner, it can seem dirty and disrespectful in Bangkok or Singapore.

If conventions are strict on the street they are doubly so in places of worship. I once met a French woman who had been stoned in Turkey – one of the most relaxed of the Muslim countries, for being dressed inappropriately in a mosque. In Greece you may be provided with frumpy, elasticated skirts to hide your trousers or miniskirt when entering an Orthodox Church. You may even be asked to cover your head. Never enter even a remote chapel on a beach in anything else than full daily dress. You may get away with it, but the distress you will cause a worshipper who stumbles on you wearing a bikini in the crypt is indefensible. In all these cases, a simple length of wrap-around cotton, like an Indian *lungi* or a sarong, or an African *kanga* or *kikoi*, is a handy extra to have.

The hands-off approach

Perhaps the most persistent and aggravating problem a woman has to deal with, particularly if she is travelling alone, is male harassment. Satellite TV and black market videos have a lot to answer for. In Third World countries Madonna and Sam Fox are seen as the archetypal western woman; while the steamier side of Swedish exports, now providing a boom business for the black market in Asia, gives the impression that American or European women have an indiscriminate and insatiable appetite for sex. Black western women fare even worse than blondes because they are considered 'exotic'.

The sad truth is that you can be dressed modestly and impeccably on a bus in Lima or Tangiers and still feel a hand on your bum. Ironically it is often in Catholic or Muslim countries, where impropriety is most despised, that local men feel they can take liberties with foreigners. Most self-defence experts advise: 'Never create a 1:1 confrontation'. "Get your hands off my bum, you filthy expletive," can exacerbate the situation or even incite a violent response. The best solution is to make a scene and enlist the support of other passengers. "Did you see what that man did to me?" creates a sense of moral outrage and people, when directly appealed to, will be more eager to leap to your defence. The same attitude that implies that Western women are 'loose', can work as an effective antidote to harassment when the groper, having been sprung, is hounded out of the bus and given a going-over by the other male passengers.

In general, the first rule of self-defence is awareness. Be alert, listen to the advice of locals and fellow travellers, develop a street sense and try not to be in the wrong place at the wrong time. Good judgement is every traveller's personal responsibility and the chances are, if you find yourself alone, late at night and being pursued up a dark alley, you could have avoided being there in the first place.

It is politically incorrect nowadays to suggest that women should ever play a 'passive' role, or – heaven forbid – that they could court disaster. But avoidance and weak-minded submissiveness are two completely different things, and the distinction is one that is crucial to survival, especially in foreign countries where the threat is an unknown quantity.

A woman is rarely a physical match for a man. And even if she is a black-belt in the martial arts, it would be unwise to launch into front kicks and elbow strikes if the man confronting her is just after money. Hand over the wallet and have done with it. Your pursuer may be armed, crazy or drunk and there is no need ever to find out if it can be avoided.

Most confrontational scenarios must be played by ear to a great extent, but there are a few universal rules. Don't turn a scary situation into a dangerous one if you can help it. Don't panic, don't show fear and don't allow the person accosting you to get the upper hand. Try to gain the psychological advantage by throwing him of his balance. In most cases a man who is attempting to intimidate a woman believes himself invulnerable and a strong show of resistance will unnerve him enough to make him back down. Never be persuaded to try and resolve the situation by moving to another place, like a car, a hotel room or someone else's house.

If you do find yourself in a dangerous, enclosed situation, try to anticipate the aggressor's next move and plan ahead for it. You may only get one chance to defend yourself – the earlier the better – and you won't want to miss it. As the innocent one in confrontation you have the advantage of surprise, but if you are forced to strike back physically, make sure it is a crippling blow that gives you a chance to escape. The last thing you want is to provoke a more serious physical attack. As one London-based martial arts master recommends: "There is only one thing better than a kick in the balls – and that's two kicks in the balls."

If you are worried about your ability to gauge dangerous situations and to defend yourself if they get out of hand, a few classes in the basic strategies of awareness and self-defence before you travel can boost your confidence immeasurably.

Warm receptions

Stay alert and these 'worse case scenarios' should never arise. I've travelled most of my life, some of it on my own, and though I'm certainly no Kate Adie, I've been caught up in anti-British demonstrations in Peru, tear-gassed in Czechoslovakia and Papua New Guinea, been ambushed by tribal warriors in Indonesia, and never had a hand laid on me in earnest.

Appreciation of the dangers should never stop you from sharing in the action, or making friends. One of the great advantages of being a woman is that men and women find you more approachable. Sometimes the offers of hospitality and kindness can be overwhelming. And any woman who has travelled with a child or a baby can regale you with stories of such warmth and tenderness that it melts the heart and restores all your faith in human nature. These are the moments one travels for and that stay with you for ever.

Contraception and feminine hygiene

Contraception is often difficult to come by abroad and should be acquired before you leave home. Time changes should be taken into consideration if you take a low dosage contraceptive pill. Stomach upsets and diarrhoea may also reduce or neutralise the effectiveness of oral contraception.

Condoms are not as freely available, especially to women, as they should be, and packets that you do find in clinics or chemists in areas off the beaten track may be past their sell-by-date and the rubber may break or corrode. Always take condoms with you, however remote the possibility of sex. AIDS and other sexually-transmitted diseases are, thanks to the ease and popularity of travel, a universal threat.

Safety tips for women travellers

1. Trust your instincts. If you have any doubts about getting into a car with someone or meeting them for a drink, don't do it. And don't feel bad about not turning up to a prearranged meeting if you've had second thoughts.

2. Dress to respect local customs, which in most cases is conservatively. It may seem archaic, but pick your principles or pick preservation. Long skirts instead of short, trousers not shorts, long sleeved not short. As a consolation prize, think of the comfort – and the protection against sun damage.

3. You may find it useful to wear a wedding ring, even if you're not married. Or carry photos of a scary-looking 'boyfriend'.

4. Walk confidently, and avoid direct eye contact with strangers. Wearing sunglasses should do the trick. Take a book or magazine into bars and restaurants with you to avoid eye contact with all those men staring at you. (Yes they do.)

5. Try and plan your arrivals into big towns before it gets dark. Plan any journey in terms of daylight hours.

6. Be aware of your surroundings (people, cars, doorways) so you know which way to head if you get into trouble. If you're being followed, walk into a tourist hotel or a shop and ask the staff for help.

7. Be careful about disclosing where you are staying. Lock your room when you are in it. Better still, take your own padlock (a common travellers' precaution). When staying in a hotel, check with reception staff before answering the door to visitors.

8. If groped on public transport, you may wish to draw attention to the fact – loudly.

9. Don't cut yourself off from the excitement of meeting new people. Befriend local women or families. You'll be surrounded by hospitality, so you can learn about their different culture – and they often have valuable advice about the area for the solo female traveller.

10. And just in case you do embark on a holiday romance, do carry your own supply of Western-manufactured condoms. (See also the chapter on *Sex Abroad*.)

Women should be aware that the physical stress of travel, jet-lag and time difference can upset the biological clock and throw even the most regular period out of kilter. Sanitary towels and tampons are also often difficult to buy abroad, especially in the Third World. A form of Tampax, with plastic or cardboard applicator, is perhaps the most hygienic and convenient to take with you, as on some occasions you may find it difficult to find clean water and soap to wash your hands. If you do prefer to take the more discreet-sized tampons without applicators, carry a sachet of disinfectant wipes to clean your hands which will guard against the transmission of germs.

Be sensitive about cultural attitudes to menstruation. In some places, especially tribal areas, men are really frightened of the powers a woman has when she is menstruating. Some cultures believe it is contaminating, and will not allow you to touch or even walk near their food. Of course, they need never know, but be careful how you dispose of sanitary towels and tampons in this situation.

In brief conclusion, don't be a loud tourist, keep an open mind, stay cool and be wise, and travelling, especially if you are a woman, will be a fulfilling and exciting adventure. ❧

ISABELLA TREE is a writer and journalist.

The family traveller
by Matthew Collins

WE RETURNED TO OUR CAMPGROUND OUTSIDE ORLANDO to find several gleaming, giant customised Harley Davidsons parked in the space next to ours. "Get off!" I bawled to my kids, who were clambering onto them, "or the owners will be really angry." The owners *were* angry. A group of greasy, dangerous-looking Hell's Angels approached, menace in their eyes.

"Why have you got tattoos?" asked Charlie, four.

"Be quiet," I muttered. "And get off those bikes now...."

"They're cool," said the ugliest one. "You wanna know why we got tattoos? 'Cos we're just a bunch o' dumb guys. You won't get tattoos when you're older, will you son?"

"Yes, I will," said Charlie. "I'm going to get a Postman Pat tattoo."

Oh the relief... Who would have thought that several hours later I would be discussing British and American children's TV with die-hard US bikers?

But that incident illustrates one benefit of travelling with kids: they are fantastic ice-breakers.

They also lend a fresh pair of eyes. A couple of days later we were at Seaworld, waiting for the *Shamu, The Killer Whale* show to start. Suddenly a 40-ton, aquatic mammal shot out of the massive swimming pool. "That's not a penguin, *is* it?" three-year-old Nicolai confirmed.

Moving on to Memphis we toured Elvis Presley's house. We spent four hours in Graceland, learning about the king. 'Maybe this trip is educational, after all,' I thought.

But two hours later, on Beale Street, downtown, we spotted a life-sized Presley poster. "So boys," I said. "Who is that man?"

"Is it John Major?" asked Charlie.

Our American journey (three months in a motorhome, two kids, no wife) was the most ambitious trip I've ever made. My wife, Khelga, was busy with work exams, so I proposed the idea of a drive across the States. I would fulfil a Kerouac dream. The boys and I would have a father-and-sons' adventure. She would have calm space in which to study.

Khelga took a while to buy the idea, but as soon as she was persuaded I remortgaged the house. For three months I had zero income, substantial expenses and 24 hours a day with two pre-school kids.

But that was a benefit. How many children and parents (especially dads) spend 24 hours a day together outside the annual summer holiday? The boys and I got to know each other extremely well and shared a unique experience.

"Wasn't it hard work?" people always ask. The answer is: no. At least, less hard than normal life in London. At home nearly everything has to be organised, outdoor activities are weather-dependent and the city often makes the kids feel claustrophobic.

Driving through the southern states in a motorhome in summer, stopping off at beautiful parks and campgrounds, they had space, sunshine and freedom.

"But how do you keep them entertained?" Americans asked constantly. "You don't even have an on-board VCR."

"We talk," I informed them. And we did, about anything – Elvis Presley, Bill Clinton, Fireman Sam, Mickey Mouse….

North America is one of the easiest countries to travel in with children, but the boys and I have ventured into other places too: Egypt, Israel, Iceland, Kenya, Europe, the Caribbean, Russia. We've driven, we've flown, we've taken trains and ferries, we've cycled, we've even hitchhiked together.

To progress from being a traveller to being a globetrotting parent is a fear-inducing, lifestyle-jolting, jump. But even the most jaded palate will find new sensations in a world suddenly filled with little people. There's no set formula for travelling with children and, as with any trip, there is always a risk. To help things go smoothly here are some tips I've acquired from my experiences, both good and bad.

When to start

"Do as much as possible while he's still being breastfed," friends advised when Charlie arrived. "You're much more self-sufficient and don't need so much junk." (I did need the wife though, which wasn't a problem).

The first trip was two weeks in Puerto Rico, followed by a winter stay in Canada. Charlie was two months old.

First disaster was the loss of our luggage when we flew to Montreal from San Juan. It had been plus 30°C when we took off. It was 30° below in Montreal. "Not to worry," I said cheerily, as we walked to our car in a blizzard, snow and ice strafing our arms and legs. My wife and I were dressed in shorts and T-shirts, Charlie was swathed in borrowed airline blankets.

Lesson one in travelling with children: always keep a spare supply of clothes as hand luggage. You never know when you might need them. And as for travelling while the baby's still breastfeeding – nothing can be taken for granted. The following week my wife's milk dried up.

As kids reach toddler stage they sleep less, and demand more attention and equipment. (It's only when you can chuck the buggy away that you finally begin to feel liberated.) Kids aren't really going to appreciate their travels until they begin to communicate. Of all the animals on safari in Kenya, two-year-old Nicolai loved the local sparrows best.

Preparation

Make sure that you've had all the required injections well in advance of your departure date.

Prepare lists of everything you need. As well as practical stuff, don't forget favourite teddies, toys or books. But don't go mad. Limit what you take – travellers accumulate stuff. And if you're going to North America, take very little (and buy over there – nearly everything is cheaper than it is in Europe). In hot and cold climates, remember that hats are extremely important.

As children get older, prepare them psychologically for travelling. If you're having an adventure (rather than a holiday) they should be aware that life will be different.

Flights

Flying with children isn't *always* a nightmare. Letting the kids go to bed late the night before is a high-risk strategy but it *can* work. My boys were so excited the night before one long-haul trip that they didn't settle until midnight. Such was their exhaustion, they fell asleep shortly after take-off and I spent most of the flight undisturbed. But you can't rely on that. You often have to think on your feet. One tip here: sick bags fascinate *all* children and, with some decoration, make good glove puppets, too.

Airlines vary in their attitude to kids. Virgin Atlantic are deservedly famous in that department. They give out lots of goodies and staff are very tolerant. But some charter airlines can be hell – even exhausted children can have problems sleeping in cattle truck conditions. If you're making a long-haul flight consider the advantages of scheduled over charter.

Manage expectations. If you're flying to South-East Asia and your children want to know if you've arrived just as you pass over Hounslow Heath, *be honest*.... Tell them they are going to be on the plane *a very long time*.

Flying dehydrates, so keep children watered.

Food

No matter how well airlines cater for children their idea of a child-friendly meal is usually revolting fast-food junk. Sugar and additives aren't the most child-calming ingredients for a flight. So don't feel obliged to order a kids' meal. As a precaution, pack your own in-flight snacks – with whatever healthy things your children like.

When it comes to food, I must confess to being totalitarian with my boys. So they're used to a varied diet and generally eat everything on their plate. This has been useful on our travels as they're happy trying out new things. Prepare children for a different diet by producing new dishes at home before travelling (and warn them that they won't be able to have burgers or chicken nuggets for every meal.) If your kids are fussy eaters, stock up on supplies they'll probably like – dried mince or noodles usually go down well. And use different tricks to lure them into trying new things: e.g. Superman eats *tom yum* when he's in Thailand; Mickey Mouse eats *pork fat* when he's in Costa Rica; Batman eats *turtle blubber* when he visits the San Blas Islands.

On the road

The most important requirement when travelling with children is flexibility. It's all very well making itineraries, but one tired toddler ruins everything. Never push kids. Go with the flow. If they seem tired, err on the side of caution.

Be prepared to do or see half the things you want to do or see. Be prepared for days of doing nothing – catching up on sleep (you *and* the kids); lounging by a pool, chilling out....

If you've crossed a time zone, give the children time to adapt. On the third day of our American trip I was woken at four in the morning by two naked boys cycling *inside* the motorhome.

Compromise. If you're a culture vulture don't expect your children always to share your interest. If you have to visit a museum, check whether it has a children's section. If it doesn't, take into account the kids' tolerance threshold and reward them for their patience with a treat – a visit to a waterpark, swimming pool or zoo, anything they're bound to enjoy.

Don't lose the children. But if you do (and you probably will) make sure they have some information – their own name, your name, where you're from. I had a frightening experience when Nicolai vanished on a campground outside Nashville. After 15 minutes he was delivered by a fellow camper. "Sir," said the man. "Are you Mr Collins?"

"Yes, I am," I said, hugely relieved.

"I thought you were," said the man. "Your son told me his dad was bald, not very tall and had huge, size-12 feet. So I guessed it had to be you...."

Illness

If you're away for more than a fortnight, it's likely your child will be ill. First tip: make sure you have good insurance. Second tip: choose the contents of your medical bag carefully – preferably in consultation with your family doctor (and keep it with you at all times). Third tip: (again) don't push your children. If they get overtired they're more likely to get ill.

Our worst experience was when Nicolai suffered febrile convulsions on a ferry from Santander to Plymouth. We had to watch helplessly while a nervous French doctor calculated the appropriate dose of sedative. Oh, the guilt... we'd travelled all the way from Seville that day.

Take the usual culinary precautions – peel fruit and veg, avoid buffet food (which has been left standing out), and avoid ice in drinks. Watch your child's fluid intake. Children dehydrate more quickly than adults. If they develop a fever or any illness involving diarrhoea or vomiting, get them to take water mixed with sugar and a little salt. The juice of an orange makes it palatable. Pack camomile tea. You can use it for everything from upset tummies (drink it) to heat rash (apply it).

If your child develops a temperature over 39°C, find a doctor, fast.

Final tip

Warn your child when he or she goes back to school that, just because he/she has spent the summer trekking up the Himalayas or sailing down the Amazon, he/she mustn't expect every other child in the class to have done the same. After my Charlie had recounted his tales of bear spotting, trout fishing and glacier crossing in Canada, his friend William informed the class he'd spent the summer in Clacton with his granny. But at least William was more interested in Charlie than a boy called Thomas, who hadn't been away at all. "Oh, be quiet," he said. "We're not interested in Charlie's boring travel stories." ❧

MATTHEW COLLINS was a reporter for the BBC's 'Travel Show' for ten years, before undertaking freelance book and television assignments. He has just published 'Across Canada With The Boys And A Granny'.

The older traveller
by Cathy Braithwaite

A ROUGH ORANGE DIRT TRACK IN THE SCORCHING MASAI MARA. In a small van, five travel journalists – the young and intrepid type – clutch their seats, knuckles white, jaws set, staring straight ahead, hating every minute of the bouncy, five-hour journey.

"These roads are just too bumpy, too uncomfortable. This is ridiculous – you can't possibly call this a holiday," complains one, just as another van carrying two elderly but beaming tourists bounces by.

Lesson one: journalists have tender bottoms and mature travellers can be a darn sight more adventurous. In fact, these days senior citizens think nothing of tackling the most demanding challenges, and relish new experiences at an age when they have the time and money. And this is the essence of the growing market for older travellers: time and money.

The retired can travel when and for as long as they choose. No jobs to groaningly return to; no children to force through school gates. You can break the journey up into manageable sections, pausing for periods of rest when necessary. This is good news for any travel operator or airline. Though it's hardly a problem to sell travel in the high season, it's a different story off-peak, which is when the buying power of older travellers really comes into its own.

The benefits of off-peak travel are many and varied: you can holiday when temperatures are kinder (avoiding the searing heat), when there are fewer crowds, lower prices and beaming smiles from travel industry staff delighted by your off-peak business. All you, the traveller, have to do is decide is where, how and when to go. There need not even by a 'why'. Your horizons are impressive, and while your age may prove a restriction with some operators and car hire companies (usually for travellers aged over 65), you will doubtless be spoilt for choice.

Whether you are a fit older person who can happily cope with a two-week camp-and-trek holiday in the Himalayas, or you feel a lack of stamina precludes a two-month tour of Australia's outback or a six-month journey around the world, if you recognise your limitations and are realistic about your expectations it is possible to make travel in retirement safe and exhilarating.

Destinations

Today even the most remote corners of the world are accessible, and it is tempting to embark on the most unusual and exciting journey you can find. First establish what you want from your holiday. Then weigh up your own ability to cope. Don't fool yourself: there is no shame in admitting that a whirlwind tour of six South American countries in 30 days would be too much for you. It is far worse to arrive at the start of what would be the experience of a lifetime, only to realise your holiday has turned into a test of endurance. The maxim 'different strokes for different folks' is never more apposite than in the context of older people and travel. What to one person is tame and unadventurous to another is the most daring project they've ever contemplated. But whether you are the type who would take out a mortgage to buy the latest walking boots or you follow the 'have timetable, will travel' school of travelling, building your own itinerary maximises your choice. You can choose how to travel, when and where to overnight and whether or not to spend a couple of days at a stopover, and you can make the whole experience as demanding or relaxed as you wish.

Preparation

While it is romantic and inspiring to think of intrepid 85-year-olds throwing more knickers than shirts into a bag and wandering wherever their fancy leads, life is so much easier if you take a few basic precautions.

Explore visa requirements and apply as much in advance as possible. Passport regulations can also differ. If you suffer from a medical condition, make sure the destination you visit easily meets your needs. Invest in insurance which will cover all eventualities including the cost of repatriation (not all insurance policies include this, so do check). You may need to shop around for a policy that will cover a traveller of advancing years, but they do exist.

See your doctor well before you embark on your trip. He or she will be able to advise and arrange vaccinations and will prescribe any regular medicinal needs during your time overseas. Doctors can normally only prescribe a limited quantity under the NHS, but your GP may be able to make an exception or advise you of what is available at your intended destination/s. The countries you visit may also impose restrictions on certain medicinal drugs. It is always a good idea to carry notification of any significant medical condition you suffer from.

Health

The older you are, the longer it takes to recover from an illness or broken bone. So

A reader writes...

I would strongly urge your older readers *not* to give up the enlivening and rejuvenating habit of travel. My travelling companion is in his early nineties, and by no means robust, but I guess if you have been adaptable, you stay that way.

On one of our four trips last year, we stopped over in Tromso for three days before the departure of our boat for Spitzbergen. There wasn't a room to be had. To compound the problem, my 91-year-old succumbed to an alarmingly bad head-cold plus bronchitis. But he insisted that the disappointment of cancelling the trip would be far more dangerous for his health than three nights on an airport bench followed by the temperatures of the Arctic.

In the end we were rescued by a kindly hotel porter. My friend retired to a camp-bed in an empty room, and by our first storm-tossed night *en route* to Spitzbergen he was on his way to recovery. It was one of our best trips ever – beautiful scenery and wildlife (polar bear and cub, walruses, whales, birds, seals…) and cosmopolitan company.

Here are my tips for elderly travellers:

1. Always carry a 'scissor seat' so you can sit down anywhere while waiting (airport check-ins, for instance). You can also use it instead of your usual walking-stick. The lightest one (2.5 lb) is the Quatro from Linden Leisure (telephone 01242 604545).
2. Don't be too proud to ask for a wheelchair at airports. Save your energy for more thrilling things than airport corridors – and get VIP treatment boarding the plane.
3. Always take a fairly laid-back younger friend with you.
4. Do keep rolling, fellow-wrinklies! *Mary Alexander, London*

it is common sense to preclude predicaments such as being stuck in a Nepalese hospital with a leg in plaster because you were convinced you could imitate that mountain goat – and failed. Assess your fitness before deciding where to travel.

Up-to-date information on health problems in any country you plan to visit is available from clinics across the UK. Contact British Airways Travel Clinics (01276 685040) for your nearest clinic, or try the Medical Advisory Service for Travellers Abroad (MASTA: 0113 238 7575, www.masta.org). It is also sensible to have a full medical check-up before you leave.

For a free copy of the Department of Health leaflet *The Traveller's Guide to Health* (ref. T6), see your doctor, travel agent, local post office or call 0800 555777. Remember, you will not enjoy your holiday if you are constantly tired. And if you feel tired, rest. Pushing yourself to the limit all day every day will only cause the excitement of being in a new place and witnessing a different culture to pall.

Services for older people

There are now a number of travel companies that provide holidays specifically for older travellers. Most offer packages, but there is an increasing demand for holidays which combine the advantages of package deals (easy travel arrangements and the support of large organisations should you need help) with independence once you reach your destination.

A number of specialist operators now cater for older travellers. Forty years ago, Saga pioneered holidays exclusively for the over-60s, long before anyone else realised the market potential. The company has since moved on a continent or two from UK seaside hotel holidays. It also includes travel insurance in the cost of all overseas travel and offers a free visa service. Numerous other companies such as Thomsons and Cosmos have followed the trend, offering package holidays tailored to the needs of older people, making it worth your while to shop around.

Practicalities

No matter how dauntless you are, nothing makes for a grouchier traveller than the lack of life's little comforts. So take small inflatable cushions to rest that weary head, and cartons of drink to quench that thirst when you are nowhere near civilisation. Use luggage with wheels or spread the load over a couple of soft-pack bags.

And if you are the type who would consider the ultimate travel experience ruined by a lack of milk, let alone tea, check that in the destination of your choice they also appreciate such basics. ❧

CATHY BRAITHWAITE has worked for the Saga Group,
which specialises in travel for the elderly.

The honeymoon traveller
by Lucy Hone

A HONEYMOON IS THAT ULTIMATE OF HOLIDAYS, one which we all hope to take at some stage in our lives. It will probably be the most expensive trip you've ever been on, so it should be your perfect holiday, one that provides you with memories to cherish for years to come. What a dreadful shame then that so many couples get it so horribly wrong. In my research for *The Good Honeymoon Guide*, I have come across scores of honeymoon couples with disappointing tales to tell: couples lured by discount deals to the Caribbean in August only to find themselves caught in a hurricane; couples promised wonderful ocean views but given a room overlooking an adjacent building site; and the surprise sailing honeymoon booked by a groom who didn't know that his spouse was prone to seasickness. Any seasoned traveller will tell you that the obstacles encountered while travelling are all part of the adventure, but for honeymooners such problems are nothing short of an intergalactic disaster.

The honeymoon traveller is unlike any other kind of traveller: the trip is billed as the holiday of a lifetime, and the pressure is on to enjoy every minute. As a result, couples regard their honeymoon in a totally different light than they would any 'normal' trip. Many couples have travelled extensively before their marriage, seeking out imaginative and far-flung destinations for in-depth exploration, but the moment the ring slips upon the finger all that changes: independent travellers who have, for years, lived and slept by their *Lonely Planet* bibles suddenly find themselves looking through brochures full of what they would normally refer to as 'boring beach holidays'. When it comes to booking a honeymoon, couples always seem to play it safe, which usually translates into them all trooping off to the same old trusted haunts. They flock in droves towards the reliable and idyllic islands of the Indian Ocean and the Caribbean: Mauritius, the Maldives, the Seychelles, St Lucia, Antigua and Barbados all appear regularly in the honeymoon Top Ten. If you are booking a honeymoon you'll know that this is largely because newlyweds want to be assured of that essential honeymoon ingredient: a romantic hotel with a bedroom to die for.

For many couples this is their first opportunity to stay in a luxurious hotel with all the trimmings, allowing them to revel in the glorious excesses of the hotel's room service, swim-up bars and jacuzzis. However, an all too common mistake is made by couples who dream of simply lazing around on the beach for two weeks on their honeymoon, and actually end up feeling bored and frustrated if there's nothing to do. Check with the hotel or travel agent and find out exactly what leisure facilities and cultural diversions are available should you get bored of the bedroom or the beach lounger!

Oh, the earth was made for lovers
– EMILY DICKINSON

Similarly, those planning an active honeymoon, with plenty of touring, sightseeing, and adventure activities, should take care to build in plenty of time for rest and relaxation: spend a few days lying on the beach or holed up in a mountain hideaway before you hit the trail. If you *do* decide on a really alternative destination, remember that you don't have to dash around and see every single highlight of that country in your two weeks. Many tour operators, particularly the specialist ones who are so enthusiastic about their countries, tend to push people into doing too much. Don't feel afraid to say no to some sightseeing and spend the day relaxing on your own instead.

Flights are also a big consideration when booking a honeymoon, as couples tend to be pretty exhausted after the wedding and may not necessarily feel like spending hours cooped up on an aeroplane. Don't think that romantic necessarily has to mean distant. It doesn't. Having said that, if you've absolutely set your heart on a country and a hotel that is thousands of miles away, why not take the plunge – there are always sleeping pills to fall back on.

Alternative honeymoon destinations

If you want to avoid the crowd, there are a comforting number of alternative destinations that offer culture, eco-tourism or adventure, as well as some really wonderful hotels where you can recharge your batteries and get into some serious honeymoon indulgence along the way. There's hardly a corner of the world now that doesn't boast some kind of superb hotel, making less-traditional honeymoon destinations such as Costa Rica, Indonesia, Morocco, Borneo, Chile, Tanzania, India, Thailand, Brazil and Egypt all realistic contenders for your dream trip.

Keep an open mind when selecting your destination. Many couples have looked aghast at the suggestion of India or Costa Rica, but have been readily convinced by the discovery that they would be staying in luxurious palace hotels if they chose India or exotic hand-crafted lodges set deep in the heart of the rainforest in Costa Rica.

The one golden rule of honeymoons is not to go somewhere that one of you has been to before – especially not with an ex, as there's nothing more tedious than being given a blow-by-blow account of a holiday they enjoyed, or even didn't enjoy, with someone else.

Who should book the honeymoon?

The first thing to do once you get engaged is to decide who is going to book the honeymoon. Although most couples now choose to plan this important holiday together, there are those who still believe in the tradition that it's a man's job. As one husband-to-be recently said to me: "Melissa is sorting out everything else, I just want to have something that I can say is totally and utterly all mine. She hasn't got a clue where we're going, but as soon as I saw it in a brochure I knew it was just perfect for the two of us, and I'm having such a great time planning it all in secret."

Surprise honeymoons are great. They are romantic, dreamy, exciting and thrilling, as long as you both feel that way. So before you take the ball off into your own court, do check that your other half is genuinely happy to go ahead with the plan. And check that they are still happy to hang in there until the departure lounge a week or two before the wedding, and once more a day or two before the big day. Bear in mind that many people also find it difficult to get excited about a holiday they cannot visualise.

If you are booking a surprise, the key is to really think about your other half and decide, honestly, what you think they would want. Don't book a trekking holiday in northern Thailand if all your fiancée wants to do is lie on the beach. If your opinions differ markedly on what constitutes the perfect holiday, the best trick is to plan a two-centre honeymoon with something for you both, say a few days on the beach at either end of the trip and a few days in the middle for your trekking, white-water rafting, canoeing, diving, temple tours, safari or whatever. Talk to her about the fundamentals – hot or cold – and the things that she wants to avoid – injections, spiders or a long flight.

Before you go

Some countries require proof of citizenship or visas, so make sure you check with your travel agent or the tourist commission that you've got everything you both need as soon as you book, as it can take weeks or even months to get through the bureaucracy.

If your plane tickets and your passport are under different names, take your wedding certificate along to the airport with you or, better still, arrange to send your passport off about three months prior to the trip to have it changed into your married name.

Consult your doctor about inoculations and anti-malaria pills: some countries require certificates of vaccinations and will not permit you to enter without them.

Lastly, whatever you decide, it's essential to get straight on with your booking as the best rooms, the best views and the best deals always go first. Also, don't forget to stock up on all necessary prescriptions (including contraceptives!) Try to leave these in their original bottles and keep a copy of the prescription to satisfy curious customs officials. ❧

LUCY HONE *is a freelance travel writer and author of 'The Good Honeymoon Guide'.*

The solitary traveller
by Nicholas Barnard

THE NOISE AND MOVEMENT OF AN ELDERLY LAND ROVER negotiating a footpath within dense bush was no foil to the impact of the tales of swamp life I was being subjected to. "Of course, you realise that the crocodiles are the least of your worries," the great white pot-bellied hunter paused, wrenched the wheel this way and that, before continuing with great deliberation, "no, the crocodiles will have what is left of you after the hippo have chewed up your dug-out." The 'Hip-po', previously a happy word of the nursery and cartoon, was instantly dismembered by his accent to create a clear onomatopoeic vision of a wobbly dug-out snapping in the jaws of the snarling monster. Turning to look at me in the bright moonlight, my congenial host shared with me a calabash-full of pertinent information. "As for the snakes for which this part of Africa is famous – don't worry, there may be a snake bite kit in the back, but if there is, what use will it be to you? Moments after most snake bites you will be completely paralysed and the polers will be standing around watching you die, for none speak or read a word of English."

By the time we reached our fishing camp near the Angolan border at dawn, I believed that I had come to terms with the prospect of travelling alone for at least eight days in such taciturn company; but dying alone in their presence was an untenable thought. To endure that journey down the Okavango to the Kalahari was an early and rigorous introduction to the art of travelling alone, to the condition of being able to survive alone.

Between the concept of travelling alone and the reality of the journey, there exists a gulf that will be bridged by painful as well as pleasing experience. From country to country and culture to culture, the act of travelling alone exposes the myths and expectations of a singular path. No manner of preparation and solitariness will disguise the fact that, by leaving a homeland, one becomes inescapably foreign and obtrusive. How the citizens of each culture will react to this small-time intrusion will make or break the experience of travelling alone. The solitary habit may help the desire to achieve inconspicuousness or it may increase the attention received: within one land one may know just how lonely a journey may be in the close company of others and, yet again, how intrusive a train compartment of strangers may prove. Dependent upon the age and sex of the would-be loner, the choice of destination certainly needs careful thought.

Travelling alone enjoys a different status within the varied regions of the world. Successful solitude may be found in the most unlikely destinations or modes of transport. Without exception, it is very difficult to travel alone outside Europe and North America. Consider how easy it is to take a railway or a bus journey across Europe in delicious isolation from the friendliness of the companions of the carriage. To ignore a possible foreigner is acceptable in those parts – in southern Asia it is unthinkable. If you want isolation from the land and its people when travelling the subcontinent, take the first class air-conditioned wagon or the Air India flight. There you will be forced to endure the foppish company of the politician, the government official or the corporation executive. I take the clamour of second-class reserved and share the ever-proffered tiffin with the broad-beamed smiles of the families in my compartment – and even answer all the questions I am able concerning the greatness of Manchester United, the Spice Girls and Tony Blair. Indeed, I have come to relish, to look forward to these casteless ceremonies of intimate hospitality so alien to my first desire to be alone – despite seeking to be that sentinel of isolation with my open and over-thumbed leaden volume of social history I never fail to pack, never finish and always discard at a faraway hotel for a more appreciative reader.

The obtrusiveness of being foreign has, seemingly, considerable demerits. Escaping to the Omayid mosque from the demographic froth of the most wonderful Damascene bazaar, I passed through a gate to behold for the first time that temple of temples to monotheism. Bewitched, I entered the cathedral-lofty prayer hall and sat near the tomb of John the Baptist (for reassurance, I suppose) and observed the interplay of women and children, men and boys, at prayer and at play. The all-pervading sense of tranquillity was an unparalleled experience and it was wise to have drunk so deeply, so rapidly, for my peace was to be cast aside by the introduction of a student of agriculture eager to exercise his World-Service English. It was not the interruption that was so galling, but the fact that he was so charming, so genial and good – characteristics that precluded any beastly dismissiveness on my part. As ever, so gentle a meeting converted solitude to a shared and unforgettable experience of being led with gusto to the hidden tombs, chapels and by-ways of ancient Damascus.

Being foreign and a woman alone in certain cultures is an unenviable circumstance. Certain countries are simply not enjoyable to visit for the single woman, whether for the mismatch of the religious, cultural or social mores with our own. Chittagong, like so many conurbations of Muslims the world over, is not a forum for the proselytising of worthy feminine liberal sentiments. The paucity of any kind of foreigners draws undesirable companionship, as mosquitoes to the ear. Boarding a bus, I was approached by an English girl and her train of admirers. After so long in the company of well-wrapped women I was as shocked and confused by the state of her lack of clothing as the gathered young Bangladeshis. The crowd was divided in sentiment – from the full-scale stoning party to lascivious indulgence – and I was delighted when the bus pulled out of the station. I had to ask about her dress, but I should have known that I was wasting my time. Fixing me with a stare that took my eyes permanently away from her partly dressed torso, she stated her view with a certain clarity: "Of course I realise what I should wear. These people simply will have to learn." I forfeited my 45p all-night bus ride and got off before the perimeter of the city.

The personal qualities needed for successful solitary travel are multifarious. Sitting at this desk to map out the requisite facets of character, I wrote:'foresight, diligence, flexibility and humour'. With a smile I scribbled over these worthy notions and thought of my most memorable expeditions. Many of my journeys were undertaken in a parlous mental condition for, from the experience of travel, I was seeking solutions. It is this balance of being able to allow the outside world to influence one's inward-beseeching world that makes a solitary expedition worthwhile. Take a reserve of worthy notions and a good health insurance policy, for there is nothing more miserable and frightening than to be ill or damaged while on the road alone.

What I appreciate about travelling alone are the extremes of experience so often encountered. The sense of solitude in a tropical land will be acutely felt in the early evening after eating – when the darkness falls like a shutter and the hours before sleep are many. A bright-beamed small torch is essential, for the lighting in inexpensive hotels is never unfailingly diabolical. The slim volumes of my favourite poets are dog-eared from browsing and memorising, and a capacious hip flask of fine whisky is always a soothing companion. By contrast, one may be transported without warning from a cycle of long evenings of quiet thoughtfulness to a night of wayward indulgence. The invasion of my private oceanside guest-house in Cochin by a group of exuberant and friendly New Zealanders resulted in days of parties that became nights with newfound companions, complete with the exhausting surfeit of conversation.

> *To awaken quite alone in a strange town is one of the pleasantest sensations in the world.*
>
> *– FREYA STARK*

Without companions the pace and direction of travel may vary to one's will. About to depart for the Amazon, I sat within a Quito hotel eating a silent breakfast, seeking not to overhear the siren conversations in English amid the guttural clutter of the local Spanish. From such precocious eavesdropping, I gleaned an introduction to a Galapagos ornithological enthusiast. His vision was an immediate inspiration: "You haff walked a jungle before?" He swung the questions with the directness of a large Swedish wood axe, "Well, you haff seen enough. Go to the Galapagos. If you like wildlife and, most important, the birds, then there is no decision!" So inspired, I ditched an elaborate and painstakingly calculated schedule of buses and aeroplanes and flew west to the Pacific. He was right, there is no decision.

If you had no notion of writing a journal, the action of travel in would-be solitude is the finest inspiration. Not only is there so much more time and space for the quiet dissemination and recording of days past, but the act of mute concentration over a pen and paper will deter all but the most callous interloper of personal privacy.

Whereas the lack of company may be a boon for privacy and quietude, the security of companionship is often sorely missed. That the urban centres of the world are hotbeds of energetic and endemic crime is obvious. The need for vigilance when alone is a source of debilitating fear for many, and so it is best to avoid taking a visible array of baggage that may create so much desire. I feel safest travelling light and take less and less each journey, looking to pack what is worthless to both parties or (as necessary with a camera, travellers' cheques and cash) securely covered by a reliable traveller's insurance policy.

No manner of personal privations, however, will dampen my enthusiasm for the act of travelling alone. The diverse memories I carry from such journeys are legion. From anguish to exhilaration, fulfilment to the most intense and destructive frustration that only alien bureaucracy will create, I may recall the extremes of experience with a shudder or a smile. It is ironic that what makes this practice of attempted solitude so consuming and addictive is the participation of others. Leaving home without a companion is an excellent beginning, for without a partner or friends one may be a susceptible witness to the openness of the human condition that is simple friendship. Of the greatest pleasures of travel, the new-found and often sweetly ephemeral companionship of others is my source of guiding inspiration and steadfast joy. ❧

NICHOLAS BARNARD specialises in writing on the tribal and folk arts.
His books include 'Living with Kilims', 'Living with Decorative Textiles',
'Living with Folk Art', 'Traditional Indian Textiles' and 'Indian Arts and Crafts'.

The escorted traveller
by Hilary Bradt

THEY USED TO BE CALLED PACKAGED TOURS, which conjured up an image of coach-loads of tourists thinking: 'If it's Tuesday this must be Belgium'. Rebranded as escorted journeys, these off-the-peg and tailor-made holidays cover almost every country on the planet, and certainly all those for which a tourist visa is obtainable. Not only are there hundreds of places to choose from, but dozens of ways to enjoy them, from museum tours to pottery workshops or, for the energetic, from kayaking to trekking or mountain biking. There is something for everyone, whatever their age, whatever their interests and whatever – let's be honest – their suitability for adventure travel.

The moment of truth comes at the airport check-in counter or departure lounge, where passengers cast covert glances at the luggage tags of their fellow travellers, with hearts lifting or sinking as they recognise those who are on the same tour. It is no exaggeration to say that a trip can be made or destroyed by the people on it and, on a fixed-departure trip, there is nothing you can do about it.

There is always the risk of encountering a nutter seeking a soul mate. And the more exotic the destination, the more likely it is to attract 'trophy hunters' who are more interested in bagging another country than they are in discovering the enjoyment it has to offer. It is not surprising, therefore, that more and more people are opting for the more expensive but less risky tailor-made tour, which is put together just for them, whether 'they' are a couple or a group of friends.

Although there are fewer risks inherent in a tailor-made trip there are still ways of ensuring that it goes smoothly. Couples will be fine – the problems arise when a group of friends and acquaintances get together for exotic travels. Bear in mind that people with whom you get on well at home may be disastrous travel companions and, since you are friends, you cannot simply ignore them. Remember, too, that many people who have only travelled in Europe and the Western world will be unprepared for the rigours of the developing countries. They may take it in their stride or they may spoil the enjoyment of the rest of the group with non-stop complaining. They will need someone to complain to, so one member of the group must take on the role of leader.

Apart from being willing to listen to grumbles, he/she should be an experienced traveller who will know what questions to ask the travel agent or tour operator before departure – such as, is there a danger of being combined with another group for certain tours? The risk here is that you could be put with a larger, non-English-speaking party. The leader should also consider the problems of smokers versus anti-smokers and decide on rules that suit both parties.

A compromise between a tailor-made tour and a fixed-departure trip is to get your own group together, decide on your preferred travel dates, and negotiate with a tour operator for a discount on one of their standard itineraries. With your agreement he can add some more clients to make up the numbers.

Whether tailor-made or fixed-departure, how do you choose the perfect holiday? First take a long hard look at… not the holiday brochures, but yourself. One of the paradoxes of travel in the developing world – and I am assuming that most readers of the *Traveller's Handbook* will be venturing to the more unusual destinations – is that the type of person who can afford the trip is often the type least suited to cope with a very different culture. In the West a strong sense of right and wrong, assertiveness and organisational skills are the personality traits that lead to success in business, and thus the income to finance exotic travel. But these 'A-type' personalities often find the developing world unbearably 'inefficient' and frustrating. By having control over their itinerary through a tailor-made tour, such people are more likely to get the most out of their trip with the minimum of frustration. A group tour, where they must 'go with the flow', may be the least successful option. Conversely, the happiest group travellers are often those who can adopt the attitude of one elderly woman, who announced to her tour leader: "I'm going to give up thinking; it doesn't work in Madagascar". It doesn't, and she had a great time!

If asked to pick out the two main reasons to choose an escorted tour over a tailor-made itinerary, I would say friendship and knowledge. When a group really jells the holiday will be remembered for all time, and reunions will take place each year because these new friends can't bear to let go after a fortnight of shared laughter and awe, when the lows become highs because of the feeling of camaraderie. Several of my close friends are people I met on group trips up to 20 years ago. Fixed-departure tours are an excellent choice for single people, who should be advised that the inevitable singles supplement is usually preferable to the risks of sharing with a stranger.

The knowledge part of the equation comes with the expert leaders provided by the best tour operators. A truly great leader is able to share his or her knowledge of the country in an enthralling way, so that no one is bored and no one feels diminished because their level of knowledge or interest is less than that of the others. Your leader should be an extrovert and a raconteur, as well as a smoother of ruffled feathers and a diplomat able to deal calmly with the trickiest situation. Such paragons are hard to find but they do exist. Personal recommendation is invaluable here.

After that long, hard look at yourself you need to take a long, hard look at your bank statement and promise yourself you'll spend as much as you can afford. If you are planning to go somewhere genuinely exotic, try not to be influenced by price or name. What matters is not saving the odd £100, but the itinerary and the leader, particularly in special-interest groups. Be wise to the false glamour of a posh name – once you arrive at your destination your holiday arrangements are likely to be in the hands of a ground operator who provides the same service to all their overseas partners, big and small.

Before you even start looking at brochures, buy a good guidebook and get a feeling for the country of your choice and the places you would most like to see. Then send for AITO's *Holiday Directory*. The Association of Independent Tour Operators has around 160 members, who are all extremely knowledgeable in their own specialised area. With the directory it is easy to see which tour operators cover the region or country you are interested in, and the activity that you find most appealing. Call 020 8744 3187 for a copy of the latest directory.

Magazines are the best source of information on tour operators offering special-interest trips. If you are looking for a riding holiday buy a horse magazine, if it's painting you are after look in an art magazine, and so on.

Travel shows such as the Daily Telegraph Adventure Travel Show and Destinations in London and the Independent Travellers' World in other parts of the UK give you the chance to meet and talk to tour operators as well as find inspiration. By the time you are ready to make a choice you will be well informed enough to pick out the tour operators who do not know the country they are selling (yes, it happens!). If place names are wrongly spelled or animal species incorrectly named you should be wary of travelling with that company. Much better to choose a specialist with a proven track record.

Don't hesitate to ask for the contact details of people who have been on the trip you are interested in. A successful tour operator will have no qualms about putting you in touch with former clients. If you enjoy your trip you can volunteer to be a referee for that company afterwards. It is also helpful to talk to the trip leader beforehand and to some of the other people who have signed up.

If you have an independent travel agent whom you trust and have worked with before, let them do the leg work – it will cost you no more. They will save you lots of time and can help sort out any serious problems that arise while you are away.

Here's a little story to close this section. Once upon a time in Bolivia a group of Americans assembled to enjoy a trek over the Andes and into the jungle. The first obstacle to holiday bliss was evident immediately: the party was made up of 11 women and one man. The next obstacle emerged a few hours later: the women were divided into two groups, one of which had signed up because they were ardent feminists and would only consider a trip that had a woman leader; the others were hoping to meet the man of their dreams. The one man was oblivious to both – he was a cocaine addict who was fully occupied by his quest for coca leaves. None of the 12 travellers was particularly interested in trekking.

The guide, Jean-Paul, was a Frenchman who looked like Rudolf Nureyev. He was a poet and a mountaineer, had romantically flared nostrils and a temper to match. One of his first comments was that he hated women and Americans.

Highlights, or rather lowlights, of the next six days included the news, on a village radio, of an attempted coup in La Paz ("Tanks and dead bodies all over the place," said Jean-Paul dramatically, but not entirely accurately), food-free days because the muleteers had sold our provisions to villagers along the way to make up for their lack of wages, part of the group becoming separated from the others and sleeping on the floor of a village school, and one of the feminists threatening to castrate Jean-Paul with her Swiss Army knife. The group divided into two factions, with one lot refusing to speak to, or sit with, the others. It rained incessantly.

The last night should have been spent in a luxury hotel recovering from the ardours of trekking. Instead it was spent with the group split between a pair of whorehouses. One had no bathroom of any kind and the most prudish of the women was reprimanded by the village policeman for squatting in the street, while the other had an outhouse that was occupied by a monkey chained to the lavatory seat.

Sometimes you need a truly dreadful trip to fully appreciate the good ones! ❧

HILARY BRADT is one of the pioneers of the modern guidebook, founding the Bradt travel guide series in 1974 and winning the 'Sunday Times' Small Publisher of the Year Award in 1997. She is also a tour leader and travel writer, specialising in South America and Madagascar.

The extreme sports traveller
by Steve Watkins

THE REALISATION, OVER THE LAST DECADE OR SO, that a refreshing holiday doesn't have to mean lounging on a beach with a good book has led to an explosion of operators offering extreme sports trips to satisfy almost anyone's desire for an invigorating adventure. While the vast majority of trips are based around activities where the perceived danger is far greater than the real danger, it is important to remember that there are some risks involved. It is worth putting extra effort into ascertaining the level of competency of any operator you intend using. Check their guides' qualifications and experience levels, ask about the safety equipment they use and how often it is maintained and replaced and inquire as to the guide/client ratio to ensure that you will receive a reasonable amount of personal tuition and contact. Once you are satisfied, hold onto your hat and prepare to be thrilled. Below are just some of the sports that can lift your adrenaline levels to new highs.

Canyoning

One of the new kids on the adventure sport block, canyoning has rapidly become one of the most popular of such activities in Europe, with its accessibility and high fun factor playing a significant part in its rise. It involves scrambling through rocky gorges, abseiling down waterfalls and leaping carefree into deep river pools while wearing a special, reinforced wetsuit and helmet to help protect against bumps and scrapes. If you like getting wet then canyoning could be your thing. A two-day introductory course would leave you confident of the simple ropework and scrambling skills needed, then it is just down to practice. Although it is possible to canyon independently, this should only be attempted by more experienced canyoners. It is far better and easier to link up with a local operator, who will have qualified guides who know the best areas and the possible problems associated with regional weather conditions. Canyons are constricted waterways and heavy rain can cause devastating flash floods. Canyoning was born in Europe and the Alps is still the Mecca, though there are usually operators in any suitable mountain area. In the UK, there are no real canyons, but gorge walking is a close parallel and takes place in Wales and Scotland.

Coasteering

This is the latest addition to the adventure sports' world and is suitable for anyone who is a reasonably strong swimmer and has a head (and heart) for leaping from rocks. It originated on the coastline of south-west Wales and the name was derived from the similar, inland, sport of canyoning. Clad in a wetsuit and buoyancy aid, topped off with a protective helmet, you get to scramble, swim and leap your way around spectacular and otherwise unreachable sections of rugged coastline. Being tumbled around in the ebb and flow of the tidal surge is an exhilarating experience, but nothing can match leaping from rocks into the ocean for adrenaline-rush value. Most courses are based around half-day excursions, with instruction on how to negotiate the obstacles safely. Although the coasteering word is spreading rapidly, it is still predominantly a UK-based activity, with west Wales remaining at the forefront. Courses are also available in north Wales, Scotland and Cornwall.

Hang-gliding

You may have dreamed of having wings and soaring high over the hills, but hang-gliding is as close as you can get at present. With a delta-shaped wing over you and your own prone position, your similarity to a bird lies in more than your ability to get airborne. If you correctly read and pick the thermal currents that rise from the Earth's surface, it is possible to stay in the air almost indefinitely. Beginners' courses start out on gentle slopes and tether the hang-glider to the ground to stop you from getting too high until you have mastered the feel of flying. Short-hop flights follow, and eventually you can take off alone and soar along a ridge. Taster courses are available if you just want to try it, as full pilot qualification training takes money and a reasonable amount of time. If you invest in your own hang-glider, then the costs are reduced. It is possible to fly anywhere you can find a hill and steady wind conditions, so the world becomes your potential playground.

Hydrospeeding

Think of white-water rafting and then personalise it with a one-person raft – that is the gist of hydrospeeding. There is no better way of getting up close to the frothing torrents of a river. The hydrospeed raft is like the front half of a small bobsleigh and allows you to protect your arms and head from impact while your finned legs dangle off the back to provide the power and steering. Extra-thick wetsuits are specially designed to protect any exposed parts of your body. The hydrospeeds are incredibly manoeuvrable and you can swoop through pounding rapids with ease. You need to be a competent swimmer and then a straightforward instruction session will teach you the basic skills for steering and reading the water flow. It has become very popular and courses are offered on most rivers where rafting takes place throughout Europe.

Ice climbing

Human interaction with the environment rarely comes in a more spectacular form than it does when you go ice climbing. The stark beauty of towering walls of ice, or even frozen waterfalls, contrasts sharply with the seemingly gravity-defying ascent of a person using only two axes and a pair of crampons, special pointed attachments to climbing boots. It is wonderful to feel the sprinkling shards of freezing ice shower your face each time you place an axe. Ice climbing is a highly skilled activity and involves the ropework aspects of rock climbing, so it is essential to get full and proper instruction. Although weekend courses are available, it is far better to dedicate a week to learning the fundamentals. Most course prices include the hire of all the specialist equipment needed, but you will have to supply your own suitable outdoor clothing. There are many places around the world where you can practice ice climbing, including the Rocky Mountains in Canada and the USA, the European Alps and Scotland. It is always advisable to check on weather conditions before booking as ice routes vary considerably throughout the winter months.

Paragliding

For those who find having their feet on the ground slightly mundane, paragliding is the ultimate way to fly. With only a thin seat between you and a plummet to Earth, you get to soar on thermal air ridges using a rectangular canopy that allows you to control both direction and speed. After a weekend starter course, you can be up and flying solo, though it is very advisable to take as much qualified instruction as possible to learn about the fine nuances that will eventually enable you to stay in the air longer and more safely. If you get hooked then it will be a relief to know that paragliding is one of the cheapest ways to get airborne, though it still doesn't cost peanuts. Some of the most inspiring places to paraglide are in the Alps, with Chamonix in France, the Jungfrau region of Switzerland and the mountains around Lake Constance being among the best. There are plenty of places to try your hand at flying in the UK, with the south coast area being a popular choice.

Rock climbing

Few activities require the level of concentration and ability necessary to subdue the body's natural reaction to danger as rock climbing does. Even when you are securely tied to a rope that will stop you from falling far, a tricky move has fear welling up inside you. By controlling those fears and directing that energy into your fingers and feet, it is possible to scale rock faces that, from the ground, seem to have no holds. It is essential to receive proper training in the techniques and ropework required, as the consequences can be dire if mistakes are made. A weekend course should be enough to get you started and then the world is your oyster. There are almost limitless places to climb, with some of the most renowned being in the USA, such as the huge granite walls at Yosemite, though Wadi Rum in Jordan and Arapiles, near Melbourne, may appeal too. Europe is awash with great rock routes, too, with the Alps and Spain being particularly good locations. Getting yourself fully kitted out can be expensive, but as you need at least two people to climb the costs can be split.

Scuba diving

Many people are unaware of the incredible world that exists beneath the sea, yet donning a mask and snorkel and glimpsing this other world for the first time is one of the most exciting and life-changing experiences around. While snorkelling is a great and easy way to see the bright colours of coral reefs and the plethora of rainbow-coloured fish that live on them, it is frustrating to have to surface for air continually. Scuba diving not only solves that problem, it adds a completely different dimension to the experience. To move around effortlessly for up to an hour or so, swimming among shoals of exotic fish and maybe even seeing dolphins, turtles, manta rays or sharks, is possibly the most refreshing and thrilling adventure sport you can do. It is essential to take a recognised instruction course, such as those offered by PADI, BSAC or NAUI, that shows you how to use the equipment, the standard methods of communicating underwater and how to handle emergencies. Most beginner courses can be completed in a total period of one week or so. Once you are qualified you are free to roam the world's oceans in search of the big blue.

Sea kayaking

Setting off on a voyage has always been one of the more romantic faces of adventure travel, and heading off for open oceans in a sea kayak is as challenging as voyaging becomes. The feeling of being really out there is almost tangible when waves roll through and you bob up and down, seeing the land appear and disappear behind each one. Thankfully for beginners, though, many sea kayaking trips are run in areas where the oceans are at their most placid and beautiful, and most rarely venture too far from a coastline. The paddling skills needed for kayaking can be learnt relatively quickly, a couple of days will give a grasp of the basics, but it does take time to learn enough about tides, weather, navigation and ocean currents to enable you to head off without a guide. If you think sea kayaking involves too much time spent on bland ocean, you may be surprised to hear that it is a great way to spot ocean wildlife, too. Turtles, dolphins, flying fish and even whales can be seen in some areas and the peaceful nature of paddling means the animals are less likely to be scared off. Baja California in south-western America is one of the prime areas for sea kayaking, but the more adventurous may fancy a trip to the glacial waters of Patagonia.

Ski touring/mountaineering

When winter bites, it puts paid to many adventurous opportunities, but at the same time creates others, such as ski touring and ski mountaineering, sports that may offer the most adventurous ways of getting out into wilderness areas during the coldest months. There can be few experiences more exhilarating than cresting a ridge on skis and taking in the panoramic view of a snow bowl filled with glacial ice and surrounded by craggy snow-capped peaks. Special hairy strips, known as 'skins', attach to the bottom of the skis and, together with bindings that allow your heels to lift, enable you to walk up very steep snow slopes. It is not vastly more exacting than mountain hiking, but you do need to be a competent off-piste skier to negotiate the testing terrain safely. Ski mountaineering simply involves ski touring and climbing to a summit, which may require climbing and ropework skills. While there are super opportunities to ski tour in the Alps, with the spectacular Vallée Blanche near Chamonix being one of the most accessible and do-able runs for newcomers, there are also great ski touring routes in Scotland, Scandinavia and the Rocky Mountains.

Skiing

Undoubtedly the most popular of adventure sports, downhill skiing is also one of the least physically demanding when practised in a good ski resort. Extensive lift systems carry you up the slopes, so all you have to do is enjoy the thrill of going back down again, although a bit of thigh burn usually accompanies long runs! The action is fast and exciting and there can be no better place to be than on a ski slope on a sunny day after a fresh fall of snow. For beginners, a week of morning sessions at ski school is usually enough to get you negotiating simple runs with ease and two weeks of skiing is ideal for further honing of your skills. However long you go for, though, it won't be enough. Skiing is addictive! With opposite seasons in the northern and southern hemispheres, it is theoretically possible to ski all year round, with the Rocky Mountains of North America, the European Alps and the New Zealand Alps offering some of the best locations. A popular offshoot from downhill skiing is heli-skiing, where a helicopter takes you to the top of untouched slopes of powder snow outside the resort area for the ultimate experience of wilderness skiing.

Skydiving

The thought of falling to Earth from a plane is a nightmare to some people and an exciting dream for others – the difference being that people in the latter group imagine doing it with a parachute on. If you want to have your entire body and mind overcome with a potent mixture of fear and excitement, then take yourself down to an airfield and find yourself a skydiving instructor. There are several variations available for beginners, with the simplest and cheapest being a static line jump. On this course, you are taught how to land properly, like the soldiers in those old Second World War movies. You're then launched from a plane at around 600 metres above the ground. The parachute is automatically opened on exit from the plane, so you just get to enjoy the descent. Tandem skydives involve you being lashed to the front of a skydive instructor and then launched together from a plane at around 3,500 metres. The instructor does all the work, so again you get the thrill without needing too many of the skills. If you want to fast track yourself to skydiving alone, then an accelerated freefall course can have you qualified in less than a week. Some of the best skydiving spots on the planet are in California and South Africa.

Snowboarding

With its rebellious image and street-style clothing, snowboarding is distinctly different from skiing and there has been a fair amount of tension between the two sports over the last decade or so. Things seem to have calmed now and the upstart sport of snowboarding is openly accepted at most ski resorts in the world. With only one piece of wood strapped to your feet to think about, it is easier to learn how to snowboard than it is to ski, but it requires many hours of practice to become really good. It is like surfing on snow and the techniques and body movements of the two sports are not dissimilar. There are snowboard instructors at all the major ski resorts of the world, and a day or two of learning the basics will have you whooshing down the slopes.

White-water rafting

Team spirit is the key factor in a successful rafting trip, and the exhilaration that comes with getting through a big rapid with a committed team effort puts other sports in the shade. Most rafts can seat up to six or eight people, and it is essential that everyone instantly obeys the commands of the river guide. "Forward hard", "back paddle" and "high side left" are all common commands that can make the difference between emerging safely from a rapid and the boat flipping over to send everyone swimming. There are no real courses where you can learn about rafting as it is one of the most straightforward of adventure sports. A half-hour briefing session will take you through all the commands and safety aspects and as long as you are a reasonable swimmer, you are free to go and get wet and wild. Most rafting rivers have grades between III and VI: the latter are the domain of experts who happen to have a screw loose and the former provide a fun and challenging ride for beginners. There are endless numbers of places to raft in the world, so if there are mountains in an area then there is usually rafting, too. ❧

STEVE WATKINS is a freelance photojournalist specialising in adventure travel, outdoor sports and cultural issues. He is a contributing author to the Adventure Travellers series from AA Publishing and is co-author of 'Action Guide Europe'. His travel photography has been exhibited at the Barbican Gallery, London.

The mountaineer
by Sir Christian Bonington

IT DOESN'T MATTER HOW BRILLIANT THE ADVENTURE, how talented the team – if a vital piece of equipment is missing, or the food or fuel has run out, not only could the expedition fail to achieve its objective, but lives could be put at risk. Sound logistical planning ensures that you have the right supplies to achieve the objective and survive, in relative comfort and with enjoyment. The principles are the same for any type or scale of expedition or journey, though the size of the party and the nature of the objective obviously must affect the complexity of the logistics. Since my own expertise is in mountaineering, I shall use the planning of a mountaineering expedition as my model, but the principles behind this could be transposed to almost any venture.

It is important to start by deciding exactly what the objective is to be – this might sound very obvious but it is amazing how many people become confused about precisely what they are trying to achieve and end up with a set of conflicting objectives, which in turn make it difficult, if not impossible, to prepare a workable plan. There could, for instance, be a conflict between trying to introduce a group of youngsters of different nationalities to the mountains and tackling a very difficult unclimbed peak.

Having clarified the aim, the next step is to formulate an outline plan of how to achieve it. In the case of a mountain objective the first consideration is the style of climbing proposed to tackle it. There are two approaches: alpine style – packing a rucksack at the bottom of the peak and then moving in a continuous push to the top, bivouacking or camping on the way; or siege style – establishing a series of camps up the mountain, linked by fixed rope on difficult ground. The latter inevitably demands a larger team, more gear and more complex logistics. These have to be worked out in detail, from the number of camps needed, the quality of rope to be fixed if the ground looks steep, the cooking gear needed for each tent, and then the amount of food and fuel necessary to feed the climbers and/or porters while they force the route and ferry loads.

It pays to start the calculations with a summit bid of, say, two people from a top camp of one assault tent, and then work back down the mountain. As a rule of thumb, estimate a camp every 500 metres which represents a reasonable distance for a load carry. Loads of around 15 kilos can be carried comfortably up to 7,000 metres, but the higher you get the lighter the load should be. It is also important to allow adequate rest periods, so that the team doesn't burn itself out. Using a spreadsheet on a computer makes the calculations easier and the various 'what if?' scenarios can then be played out.

Planning in this detail at an early stage automatically supplies information about the size of the team needed and the kind of skills required. This will help choose a team that is not only the right size but also the right composition. This may not appear to come under the heading of logistics but it most certainly does, for without the right people to carry out the tasks in hand, the best laid plans and logistics fall apart. From this point of view, in choosing a team it is essential to have a good balance between people who are capable of taking on organisational or management roles and those with skills to attain the objective – in the case of a climbing expedition, talented climbers, or for a scientific one, people with the right scientific qualifications and knowledge. It is also important that the team is compatible, that the brilliant expert – climber, canoeist or scientist – will work effectively for the team as a whole.

The foundations of the expedition are laid in this initial planning phase and are then built into the organisational stage in the home country when everything is being assembled. If vital items of food or equipment are left out, shipping arrangements mishandled or, perhaps most important of all, there is a shortfall in the amount of money to pay for the enterprise, it could be condemned to failure before even setting out. In this organisational phase it is important for the leader to delegate responsibility effectively (in the first instance ensuring that the right person has been given the right job), give briefs of what is required and the deadlines to be reached, and finally leave them to get on with it; but maintain a reporting-back system so that if there are any critical problems, the leader can take any necessary action. This role should be one of support rather than interference.

Sound budgeting and raising sufficient funds is obviously a key task in this preparatory phase. In getting sponsorship it is also very important to be realistic over what is promised, so that not only can the promises be fulfilled but, equally important, the commitments to a sponsor do not prejudice achieving the end objective or the way the expedition is conducted.

It pays to build some slack into the schedule to allow for delays and crises. In

1970 when I went to the south face of Annapurna, we sent all the expedition gear by sea, scheduled to arrive in Bombay a fortnight before we were due to reach Nepal by air. The ship carrying it broke down off Africa and was over a month late, giving us a major crisis at the very beginning of the expedition. We got round it with the help of an army expedition going to the north side of Annapurna. They allowed us to send some gear out with their air freight and loaned us some excellent army compo rations. This kept us going until the main gear caught up with us, but we experienced a lot of unnecessary worry and delay. Even today, when most expeditions use air freight for their baggage, gear can be lost, delayed in customs or sent to the wrong place. So it pays to allow plenty of time, particularly for clearing customs.

When packing, keep in mind at which stage of the trip the different items of food or gear will be used, and also how they are going to be carried to the base of operations. Put together all the items not needed until base camp. The gear and food for use on the approach march needs to be separate and accessible. It is best carried in lockable containers and it pays to get a set of padlocks with a uniform key so that any team member can get access to communal equipment.

It saves a lot of time and hassle if containers are kept to a weight that can be carried by local porters or pack animals, and are protected robustly to withstand rough treatment and exposure to the weather. It is best to distribute similar items in different loads, so that if a single box goes missing the total supply of a vital piece of equipment is not lost – all the oxygen masks, for example, or all the matches. The other vital task is to list everything and mark all the boxes clearly with some form of identification that gives no clue of the contents to the casual observer.

I think that maybe we do not climb a mountain because it is there. We climb it because we are here.

– JON CARROLL

Remember that certain items cannot be sent by air. It is irresponsible and dangerous to try to smuggle such items. Gas cylinders can be sent by cargo plane, but must be specially packed. The air freight agent can give advice on these matters.

Once at the roadhead, life becomes much simpler. At last everyone is together and, with luck, all the gear and food is there with you. It is just a matter of keeping the porters happy – not always easy – and keeping tabs on gear and loads. To make this easier, on some expeditions I have issued each porter with a numbered plastic disk to coincide with the number of their load, and then taken a Polaroid photo of him holding his disk and load.

An approach march can be a leisured delight or a nightmare, depending on the behaviour of the porters. Very often, problems with the porters are outside your control, since so much depends on the local situation, the attitude of the liaison officer and the conduct of the *naik* or overseer, who might have extracted a large commission from the porters in return for employment. It is very difficult to advise on any specific reaction other than to stay cool, to listen carefully and to bargain effectively.

And so to base camp. The objective – in my case, a mountain – is in sight and some might think that this is where the real challenge begins. However, the eventual success or failure will have been strongly influenced by everything that has been done in the preparatory phase and the approach. If the expedition has been planned in detail, all the essential gear that was packed in containers to go straight to base camp is now ready for use. Provided team members are fit and relaxed and happy, they certainly have a much better chance of success, or at least of having a good try at achieving the objective and enjoying themselves at the same time.

In the case of a mountain, particularly one that is unclimbed, the first priority, after making base camp comfortable, is to make a thorough recce, to check out if the actual terrain corresponds with what pictures and maps you have managed to get hold of, and to assess whether the plan of campaign needs changing or adjusting. A plan should always be flexible. It is possible to change and adapt it to circumstances, but it must be a well thought out plan in the first place. On the southwest face of Everest in 1975, we completed a detailed plan using a computer model in Britain, but made frequent changes during the actual expedition. However, without the original plan as a solid foundation, we could never have climbed the south-west face as quickly and smoothly as we did.

It is all too easy, when the weather is good, to believe it will last forever. Each fine day needs to be regarded as the last one you will get on the expedition. Equally, when the weather is bad, it is also easy to slip into lethargy. It is just as important to be poised to take advantage of a clearance.

We all want to achieve success, to reach our objective, but I believe it is important to remember that the journey is as important as the final objective. The way that journey is carried out not only determines the eventual outcome but, equally important, how you are going to feel about it in the future. If the logistics are right, if everyone works well together as a team, with each individual being prepared to sacrifice personal ambition for the good of the group as a whole, being aware of the needs of others and helping where necessary, then the venture has achieved complete success. Sound planning from the very beginning provides the foundations of that success. ❧

SIR CHRISTIAN BONINGTON, CBE, is one of the world's greatest mountaineers. He was the first to climb the south-west face of Everest in 1975. His most recent climbing book is 'Tibet's Secret Mountain'.

The equestrian traveller
by Robin Hanbury-Tenison

IF THE TERRAIN IS SUITABLE, THEN RIDING A HORSE is the ultimate method of travel. Of course, in extreme desert conditions, or in very mountainous country, camels, donkeys or mules may be more appropriate. The chapters on travelling by pack animal and camel, in Part 3, describe these methods clearly and give a great deal of excellent practical advice that is equally applicable to horses and which should be read by anyone planning a long-distance ride. This is especially the case if the decision is to take a pack animal or animals, since the care of these is as important as that of the animal you are riding yourself.

But for me the prime purpose of riding is the freedom that it can give to experience fully the sounds, smells and sights of the landscape through which I am passing; to divert on the spur of the moment so as to meet local people or look closer at interesting things; to break the tedium of constant travel by a short gallop or a longer canter in the open air, surely the closest man or woman can come to flying without wings.

One way to achieve this freedom is to have a back-up vehicle carrying food for both horses and riders, spare clothes, kit and all the paraphernalia of modern life, such as film, paperwork and presents. Often it may not be necessary to meet up with the support team more than once or twice a week, since it is perfectly possible to carry in saddle-bags enough equipment to survive for a few days without overloading your horse. In this way an individual, couple or group can live simply, camping in the open or in farm buildings. If a rendezvous is pre-arranged, the worries of where to stop for the night, whether there will be grazing for the horses and what sort of accommodation and meal awaits at the end of a long day in the saddle are removed.

Fussing about this can easily spoil the whole enjoyment of the travel itself, and it is well worth considering carefully in advance whether sacrificing the ultimate vagabondage of depending solely on equestrian transport for the serenity of mechanical support is worth it. It does, however, involve a certain amount of expense, although this may be less in the long run than being at the mercy of whatever transport is available locally in an emergency, and most significantly, as with ballooning, it depends on having someone who is prepared to do the driving and make the arrangements. The alternative is to use time instead of money and resolutely to escape from a fixed itinerary and desire to cover a pre-determined distance each day. This is quite hard to do, since we all tend today to think in terms of programmes and time seems to be an increasingly scarce commodity.

Where to go

After half a lifetime spent on other types of exploratory travel through tropical rainforests and deserts, I came to long-distance riding more by accident than design. My wife and I needed some new horses for rounding up sheep and cattle on our farm on Bodmin Moor in Cornwall, and we bought two young geldings in the Camargue, where the legendary white herds run free in the marshes. Riding them home across France we discovered that the footpaths are also bridle-paths and there is an excellent and well-marked network of *sentiers de grande randonnée*. Thanks to this, we were able to avoid most roads and instead ride across country. It was an idyllic and addictive experience during which we rode some 1,600 km in seven weeks. Leaving the horses to graze each night in grassy fields, for which we were never allowed to pay, we either camped beside them or stayed in remote country inns so far off the beaten track that the prices were as small as the meals were delicious. This was an unexpected bonus of riding: the need to arrange accommodation around a daily travelling distance of no more than 45 km or so – and that, in as straight a line as possible, took us to villages that did not appear on even quite detailed maps but where the culinary standards were as high as only the French will insist on everywhere.

Later, we were to ride 1,600 km along the Great Wall of China. There we had to buy and sell three different pairs of horses, and my suspicions were confirmed that horse dealers the world over tend to be rogues. We were luckier with our mounts on similar rides in New Zealand and Spain, but with horses nothing is certain and it is essential to be constantly on guard for the unexpected. However, this only serves to sharpen the senses and when something really wonderful happens, such as reaching a wide, sandy beach on the coast, riding the horses bareback out into huge breakers and teaching them to surf, then you know it has been worthwhile.

Practicalities

This piece is meant to be full of practical advice and information, but I am hesitant to give it where horses are concerned. People are divided into those who are 'horsey' and those who are not. The former know it all already and do not need my advice. The latter (and I include myself among them, in spite of having spent much of my life around horses) have to rely on common sense and observation. It is, on the whole, far better to fit in with local conditions than to try and impose one's ideas too rapidly. For example, we learned to appreciate the superb comfort of the Camargue saddles that we acquired for our ride across France and we took them with us on all our subsequent rides. But in both China and Spain, I found that mine did not suit the local horse I was riding and, to preserve its back, I had to change to a local model, which was much less comfortable for me but much better for the horse.

And it is the horses' backs that should be the most constant concern of all on long-distance rides. Once a saddle sore develops it is very difficult to get rid of and prevention is by far the best cure. To begin with, it is wise to use a horse whose back is already hardened to saddle use. Scrupulous grooming and regular inspection of all areas where saddle or saddle-bags touch the horse is essential. Washing helps, if water is available, and a sweaty back should be allowed to dry as often as possible, even if it does mean unsaddling during a fairly brief stop when one would rather be having a drink and a rest oneself. A clean, dry saddle-cloth is essential (felt, cotton or wool), so find out what the horse is used to.

There are many local cures for incipient sores. I have found surgical spirit good, though it will sting if the skin is at all sore or sensitive. Three tablespoons of salt to half a litre of water will help harden the skin if swabbed on in the evening, but complete rest is the best treatment. The same goes for girth galls, although these should be avoided if the girths are tightened level and a hand run downwards over the skin to smooth out any wrinkles. A sheepskin girth cover is a good idea too, as it prevents pinching. If it is absolutely essential to ride a horse with a saddle sore, the only way to prevent it getting worse is to put an old felt numnah under the saddle with a piece cut out so as to avoid pressure on the affected part.

It is also vital to keep checking the feet, ideally every time you rest and dismount. Stones lodge easily between the frog and the shoe and soon cause trouble if not removed. Small cuts and grazes can be spotted and treated with ointment or antiseptic spray at the same time and a hand passed quickly up and down each leg can give early warning of heat or other incipient problems. Once again the best general cure is usually to take the pressure off horse and rider by resting, if necessary for a day or two.

While putting on a new set of shoes is a skilled business that should not be attempted by the amateur, it is invaluable to have enough basic knowledge of shoeing to be able to remove a loose shoe or tighten it by replacing missing nails from a supply of new ones, which should always be carried in the saddle-bag. I have had to do this with a Swiss Army knife and a rock, but it is much better to carry a pair of fencing pliers since these are essential in an emergency if your horse should get caught up in wire.

Your own footwear is also important on a long ride, since it is often necessary to walk leading your horse almost as much as you ride. Riding boots that protect your calves from rubbing on the saddle are useful, especially at the start and if you are using an English or cavalry saddle, but you must be able to walk in them. With a Western type of saddle and once your legs have settled down, it is better to wear comfortable walking shoes or trainers. Leather chaps, which can be found at most country shows, are also invaluable. The protection they give to legs both against rubbing and from passing through bushes easily outweighs the heat and sweat they may generate in a hot climate.

Choosing your horse

As Christina Dodwell says in *A Traveller on Horseback*, a valuable horse is more likely to be stolen and what you need is 'a good travelling horse'. Tschiffely, on the most famous of all long distance rides, from Buenos Aires to Washington in the 1920s, had two Argentinian ponies, which were already 15 and 16 years old when he acquired them. He covered 16,000 km in two-and-a-half years, covering about 30 km a day on the days he rode, but making many long stops and side trips.

Tim Severin started out on his ride to Jerusalem on a huge Ardennes heavy horse, as used on the First Crusade. In spite of suffering from heat exhaustion, it reached Turkey before being replaced with a more suitable 13-hand local pony. The ideal horse for covering long distances in comfort is one possessing one of the various 'easy' inbred gaits, which lie between a walk and a trot. We were lucky enough to use 'amblers' in New Zealand. These had been bred to have a two-beat gait in which the legs on either side move together, giving an impression a bit like the wheels of a steam engine. Once we learned to relax into the unfamiliar rhythm and roll a little from side to side with the horse, we found it wonderfully comfortable and the miles passed effortlessly and fast. However, even then we seldom averaged more than seven kmph.

Unless you are setting out to break records or prove a point, the object of a long-distance ride should be the journey itself, not the high performance of your mount. The close relationship that develops between horse and rider is one of the bonuses of such a journey, and as long as your prime concern is your horse's welfare before your own you won't go far wrong.

On a horse it is uniquely possible to let an intelligent creature do most of the thinking and all of the work, leaving you free to enjoy and absorb your surroundings. Birds are not afraid to fly near and be observed; the sounds of the countryside are not drowned by the noise of a motor or the rasping of one's own breath; and if you are lucky enough to have a congenial companion, conversation can be carried on in a relaxed and pleasant way. Notes can even be taken *en route* without the need to stop or the danger of an accident, especially if you carry a small portable tape recorder. This helps greatly in taking down instant impressions for future inclusion in books and articles which are surely the chief justification of pure travel. Photographic equipment can be readily to hand in saddle-bags, and much more can be carried.

Above all, those you meet along the way, whether they be fellow travellers, farmers or remote tribes people, are inclined to like you and respond to your needs. ❧

ROBIN HANBURY-TENISON, OBE, is a distinguished explorer and energetic champion of indigenous peoples. He is the founder of Survival International (a charity defending tribal groups) and an author and broadcaster.

The sailor
by Sir Robin Knox-Johnston

SAILING BENEATH A FULL MOON ACROSS A CALM TROPICAL SEA towards some romantic destination is a wonderful dream, but to make it become a reality requires careful preparation, or the dream can turn into a nightmare.

The boat you choose should be a solid, robust cruiser. There is no point in buying a modern racing yacht as it will have been designed to be sailed by a large crew of specialists and will need weekly maintenance. The ideal boat for a good cruise should be simple, with a large carrying capacity, and easy to maintain. Bear in mind that it is not always easy to find good mechanics or materials abroad, and most repairs and maintenance will probably be done by the crew.

It is important to get to know the boat well before sailing so that you will know how she will respond in various sea states and weather conditions. Try changing her trim by moving weights fore and aft to see the response. Experiment with the sails to obtain the best balance. Remember that a well-balanced boat needs less rudder and will travel faster. Make a proper check-list for the stores and spares that will need to be carried. For example, there is no point in taking a spare engine, but the right fuel, oil and air filters, spare fan belts and perhaps a spare alternator, are advisable. Standardise things as much as possible. If the same size of rope can be used for a number of purposes, then a spare coil of that rope might well cover nearly all your renewal requirements.

Electronics

There is a huge array of modern equipment available and these 'goodies' can be tempting. It pays to keep the requirement to a minimum to reduce expense and complexity. Small boat radars are now quite cheap and can be used for navigation as well as keeping a lookout in fog. The Global Positioning System (GPS), with its worldwide coverage and position updates every few seconds, has proved a boon to the busy yachtsman, but anyone contemplating a long voyage should master astro navigation to fall back upon if the instrument fails or the batteries give up.

Radio communications are now everywhere and are important for the boat's safety. Short range, Very High Frequency (VHF) radio is in use worldwide for port operations and for communications between ships at sea. It is best to buy a good, multi-channel set and make sure that the aerial is at the top of the mast as the range is not much greater than the line of sight, so the higher the aerial, the better. For long-range communications, use Single Side Band in the medium- and high-frequency bands, but the shore stations that used to service these bands are fast disappearing.

The new Global Maritime Distress and Safety System (GMDSS) is already coming into force for commercial traffic for larger ships. By 2005 it will be universal. All vessels will be required to have digital selective calling on their VHF sets, and, if they are going beyond the range of shore VHF stations, MF, and beyond 450 km, HF as well. Satellite communications are also becoming common. The least expensive piece of equipment to handle it is Satcon-c which can handle telex and email. It is inexpensive, but brings instant distress, urgency, safety and general communications to the smallest yacht. All yachtsmen should take a GMDSS course to understand the new safety procedures.

There is a worldwide network of amateur radio operators or 'hams', which can provide a regular link for those who take the relevant licence.

Meteorology plays an important part in any voyage, and the rudiments of weather systems, and how they are going to affect the weather on the chosen route are essential knowledge for anyone making any voyage. Weather forecasts are broadcast by most nations, but it is possible to buy a weatherfax machine, which prints out the weather picture for a selected area and costs about the same as an SSB radio set. Alternatively, these weather faxes may be received with the normal SSB and displayed on a computer.

Charts are now computerised and, when interfaced with the GPS, will show the position of the yacht on the chart in use. There are some small anomalies due to the change in the data and you should, in any case, take the paper charts of the area you will be sailing through.

The crew

The choice of crew will ultimately decide the success or otherwise of the venture. Its members must be congenial, enthusiastic and good work-sharers. Nothing destroys morale on board a boat more quickly than one person who moans or shirks their share of shipboard duties. Ideally, the crew should have previous sailing experience so that they know what to expect, and it is well worthwhile going for a short shakedown sail with the intended crew to see if they can cope and get on well. Never take too many people, it cramps the living quarters and usually means there is not enough work to keep everyone busy. A small but busy crew usually creates a happy, purposeful team.

Beware of picking up crew who ask for passage somewhere at the last minute. For a start, you will not know their background and will only find out how good or bad they are once you get to sea, which is too late. In many countries, the skipper of the boat is responsible for the crew, and you can find that when you reach your destination, immigration will not allow the marine 'hitchhiker' ashore unless they have the onward fare or ticket out of the country. If you do take people on like this, make sure that they have money or a ticket, and I recommend that you take the money as security until they have landed. I once got caught out in Durban with a hitchhiker who told me I would have to give him the airfare back to the US. However, he 'accidentally' fell into the harbour, and when he put his pile of dollars out to dry, we took the amount required for his fare. Never hesitate to send crew home if they do not fit in with the rest of the team. The cost will seem small when measured against a miserable voyage.

Provisions

Always stock up for the longest possible time the voyage might take, plus ten per cent extra. The system that I use for calculating the food requirement is to work out a week's worth of daily menus for one person. I then multiply this figure by the number of weeks the voyage should take plus the extra, and multiply that figure by the number of crew on board.

Always take as much fresh food as you can. Root vegetables will last a couple of months, greens last about a week, Citrus fruit will last a month, if kept well aired and dry. Eggs, if sealed with wax or Vaseline, will last a couple of months. Meat and fish should not be trusted beyond a day or two unless smoked, depending on the temperature. Flour, rice and other dry stores will last a long time if kept in a dry, sealed container.

The rest of the provisions will have to be freeze dried or canned. Such foodstuffs are of good quality in Europe, the USA, South Africa, Australia and New Zealand, but not so reliable elsewhere. The USA does not produce canned stewing steak or minced steak, so if you are going to have to stock up there make sure you have plenty of ways of cooking corned beef, Spam or ham. Code all the cans with paint, then tear off the labels and cover the whole tin with varnish as protection against salt water corrosion and stow securely in a dry place.

When taking water on board, first check that it is fresh and pure. If in doubt, add chloride or lime to the water tanks in the recommended proportions. Very good fresh water can be obtained from rain showers. The most effective method is to top up the main boom, so that the sail 'bags' and the water will flow down to the boom and along the gooseneck, where it can be caught in a bucket. There are a number of desalination plants on the market. If the budget allows, they can be worthwhile in case the water tanks go foul and rain water is hard to come by.

Safety

The safety equipment should be up to the Offshore Racing Council's minimum standards. Ensure that the life raft has been serviced before sailing, and that everyone on board knows how to use their life-jackets and safety harnesses. A number of direction-finding and recovery systems have been developed recently for picking up anyone who falls overside, and this drill should be practised before the start of the voyage. A 406 Mhz EPIRB distress beacon is essential – make sure it is properly registered with its relevant authority. Take a search and rescue transponder (SART). These provide a short-range signal to radar sets and can be invaluable for rescuers looking for a life raft.

Paperwork and officialdom

Before setting out on a long voyage, make sure that someone at home, such as a member of the family or your solicitor, knows your crew list, their addresses and your intended programme – and keep them updated from each port. Make sure your bank knows what you are planning, and that there are enough funds in your account for emergencies. It is better to arrange to draw money at banks *en route* rather than carry large sums on board.

The boat should be registered. This is your proof of ownership and the boat's nationality, and it also means that your boat comes under the umbrella of certain international maritime agreements.

A certificate of competence as a yachtmaster is advisable. Some countries (Germany, for instance) are starting to insist on them. The crew must have their passports with them, plus any visas required for such countries as the USA, Australia and India. More countries are demanding visas these days, and you should check with the embassies or consulates of the countries you intend to visit for details. You should also check the health requirements and make sure that the crew have the various up-to-date inoculation or vaccination certificates. It is always advisable to have tetanus jabs before starting a voyage but most doctors' surgeries can provide list of recommended inoculations.

When you are at sea you know you must reach harbour, to restock and hope, rest in a warm caress. Then when you are in port, you can't wait to get back to the sea again. You need mother earth, but you love the sea.
– STEVEN CALLAHAN

Before setting out, obtain a clearance certificate from customs. You may not need it at your destination but it will be helpful if you run into difficult officials.

On arrival at your destination, always fly your national flag and hoist the flag of the country you have reached on the starboard rigging, on the yard if possible, and the quarantine flag (Q). If officials from the customs and immigration department do not visit the boat on arrival, only the skipper need go ashore to find them and report, taking the registration certificate, port clearance, crew passports and any other relevant papers.

Smuggling and piracy

Smuggling is a serious offence and the boat may be confiscated if smuggled items are found on board, even if the skipper knows nothing about the offending items.

There are certain areas where smuggling and piracy have become common and, of course, it is largely in the same areas that law enforcement is poor. The worst areas are the Western Caribbean, the north coast of South America, the Red Sea and the Far East, particularly near the Malacca Straits. There have also been a number of attacks on yachts off the Brazilian coast. The best protection is a crew of fairly tough-looking individuals, but a firearm is a good persuader. Never allow other boats to come alongside at sea unless you know the people on board and, if a suspicious boat approaches, let them see that you have a large crew and a gun. Call on VHF, or send an alert on the Satcom if you feel threatened. If the approaching vessel is official, they are probably listening to VHF channels. When in a strange port, it is a good rule never to allow anyone on board unless you know them or they have an official identity card.

If you do carry a firearm, make sure you obtain a licence for it. Murphy's law says that if you carry a rifle, you will never have to use it. ༄

SIR ROBIN KNOX-JOHNSTON, CBE, was the first man to sail around the world single-handedly and without stopping. He also set a global record for sailing around the world in a catamaran. He is the author of numerous books on sailing.

The cyclist
by Nicholas Crane

EVER SINCE JOHN FOSTER FRASER AND HIS BUDDIES Lun and Lowe pedalled round the world in the 1890s, the bicycle has been a popular choice of vehicle for the discerning traveller. The most efficient human-powered land vehicle, it is clean, green and healthy to boot.

The standard bicycle is also inexpensive, simple and reliable. Its basic form is similar the world over, with its fundamental parts available in Douala and downtown Manhattan alike. With the exception of remote settlements accessible only on foot, most of the world's population is acquainted with the bike. It can never be as symbolic of wealth as a motor vehicle, and neither is a bike-rider insulated from his or her surroundings by metal and glass. It's a humble vehicle. It is approachable and it is benign. Birdsong and scents are as much a constant companion as voices and faces.

Cycling is slow enough to keep you in touch with life; fast enough to bring daily changes. A fit rider ought to be able to manage an average of 80 to 100 kilometres a day. Pedalling puts you partway between pedestrians and motor cars: a bike can manage a daily distance four times that of a walker and a third that of a car.

Bikes can be carried in planes, trains, boats and cars, on bus roofs and in taxi boots. They can be parked in hotel bedrooms and left-luggage stores. They can be carried by hand and taken apart.

But isn't cycling hard work? Sometimes, but for every uphill stretch or headwind there's a descent or tailwind that's as fun as flying. What happens when it rains? You get wet or stop in a bar. How many punctures do you get? On my last ride (5,200 kilometres), two. How do you survive with so little luggage? It's leaving behind the clutter of everyday life that makes bike touring so fun.

Where to go

If you are doubtful about your stamina, choose somewhere docile such as East Anglia or northern France for your first trip. Beware of being tricked by the map: it's not always the places with the highest mountains that are the most tiring to ride. Scotland, where the roads often follow valley floors, is a lot easier than Devon, where the roads hurry up and down at ferocious angles. The Fens, Holland and the Ganges Delta may be as flat as pancakes, but it is this very flatness that allows the wind to blow unchecked – exhilarating if it's going your way, but not if it isn't....

You may already have a clear idea of where you would like to ride. Hilliness, prevailing winds, temperature, rainfall, whether the roads are surfaced or dirt: all these factors are worth quantifying before you leave. Then you must fit the route with places of interest and accommodation. There may be duller sections that you would like to skip; if so, you need to find out in advance whether you can have your bike transported on buses or trains.

You do not have to be an athlete to ride a bicycle, or even able to run up three flights of stairs without collapsing. It is a rhythmic, low-stress form of exercise. Riding to work or school, or regularly during evenings and weekends, will build a healthy foundation of fitness. If you have never toured before, try a day's ride from home (40 kilometres maximum), or a weekend ride.

Once you know how far you can comfortably ride in a day, you can plan your tour route. Always allow for a couple of 'easy' days to begin with: set yourself distances which you know you can finish comfortably, and this will allow you to adjust to the climate and the extra exercise. It will also let your bike and luggage 'settle in'.

Main roads are to be avoided. This means investing in some good maps. As a rule, a scale of 1:200,000 will show all minor roads. For safe cycling on rough tracks, you will need maps of 1:50,000 or 1:25,000. Stanfords (12-14 Long Acre, London WC2E 9LP, 020 7836 1321) is the best supplier of cycling-scale maps.

The type of accommodation you decide upon will affect the amount of luggage you carry – and the money you spend. Camping provides the greatest flexibility, but also requires the greatest weight of luggage. With (or without) a tent you can stay in all manner of places. Farmers will often let you use the corner of a field, and in some wilderness areas you can camp where you choose (leave nothing; take nothing). With two of you, you can share the weight of the tent, cooking gear and so on. If you are using youth hostels, bed-and-breakfasts or hotels, you can travel very lightly but your route is fixed by the available accommodation.

'Wild camping', where you simply unroll your sleeping bag beneath the stars on a patch of unused land, is free and allows you to carry a minimum of camping gear. Always be careful to check the ownership of the land, and bear in mind that you have no 'security' beyond your own ability to remain inconspicuous.

The best source of information on the geography of cycle travel is the CTC (Cyclists' Touring Club). To join, contact the CTC at Cotterell House, 69 Meadrow, Godalming, Surrey GU7 3HS, 01483-417217.

The bike and clothing

Unlike a motorised expedition vehicle, a bicycle need cost no more than a good camera or backpack. Neither need it be an exotic mix of the latest aluminium alloys and hi–tech tyres. John Foster Fraser covered 19,237 miles through seventeen countries on a heavy steel roadster fitted with leather bags. And while steel bike frames may be repaired by local blacksmiths if necessary, carbon-fibre, titanium or even aluminium alloys will be beyond their skills. Destinations are reached because of the urge to make the journey, not the colour of the bike frame.

Given a determination to arrive, virtually any type of bicycle will do. The writer Christa Gausden made her first journey – from the Mediterranean to the English Channel – on a single-speed shopping bike. My early tours across Europe were made on the heavy ten-speed I had used for riding to school. Spending time and money on your bike does however increase your comfort and the bike's reliability. So does reading *Richard's 21st Century Bicycle Book* (Macmillan), the updated classic that provides the answers to almost anything velocipedal.

For road riding the most comfortable machine is a lightweight multi-speed touring bike. Gear ratios in the UK and USA are measured, somewhat quaintly, in inches – the given figure representing the size of wheel that it would have been necessary to fit to a penny farthing to achieve the same effect. *Richard's 21st Century Bicycle Book* (among others) contains detailed gear ratio tables. For normal touring, the lowest gear should be around 30 to 35 inches; the highest, 80 to 90 inches. With these ratios, a fit rider ought to be able to pedal over the Pyrenees, while the top gear is high enough to make the most of tailwinds.

Good-quality wheels and tyres are important. If you can afford it, have some wheels built by a professional wheel-builder, asking him to use top-quality pre-stretched spokes and the best hubs and rims. For continental touring it is handiest if the rims are of the size to take the metric 700 C-tyres. Some rims will take a variety of tyre widths, allowing your one set of wheels to be shod either with fast, light, road tyres, or with heavier tyres for rough surfaces. Buy the best tyres you can afford. Quality tyres can be expected to run for 8,000 kilometres on a loaded bike ridden over mixed road surfaces.

'Drop' handlebars are more versatile than 'uprights', providing your hands with several different positions and distributing your weight between your arms and backside. Drops also permit for riding in the 'crouch' position – useful for fast riding or pedalling into headwinds. Drop handlebars come in different widths; ideally they should match the span of your shoulders. Flat, multi-position 'hybrid' bars are a recent alternative to drops. The saddle is very much a question of personal preference: try several before deciding. (Note that you should fit a wide 'mattress' saddle if you have upright handlebars, as most of your weight will be on your backside.) Solid leather saddles need treatment with leather oils then 'breaking in' – sometimes a long and painful process but one which results in a seat moulded to your own shape. Also very comfortable are the padded suede saddles which require no breaking in. Since they never change shape, be sure this sort of saddle is a perfect fit before you buy. Steer clear of plastic-topped saddles.

It is very important that your bike frame is the correct size for you. There are several different methods of computing this, but a rough rule of thumb is to subtract 25 centimetres from your inside leg measurement. You should be able to stand, both feet flat on the ground, with at least three centimetres between the top tube and your crotch. The frame angles should be between 71 and 73 degrees. The strongest and lightest bike frames are commonly made from Reynolds tubing. An option for those with fatter purses is to have a bike frame built to your own specifications and size. Many of the top frame-builders advertise in *Cycling Weekly* magazine and in *Cycle Touring and Campaigning*, the magazine of the Cyclists' Touring Club.

Generally speaking, the more you spend on your brakes and pedals, the stronger and smoother they will be. Pedals should be as wide as your feet (note that some Italian models are designed for slim continental feet rather than the flat-footed Britisher). Toe-clips and straps increase pedalling efficiency.

Luggage should be carried in panniers attached to a rigid, triangulated carrier that cannot sway. Normally, rear panniers should be sufficient. If you need more capacity, use a low-riding set of front pannier carriers (such as the Blackburn model) and/or a small handlebar bag. Lightweight items such as sleeping bags can be carried on top of the rear carrier if necessary. The golden rule is to keep weight as low down and as close to the centre of the bike as possible. Never carry anything on your back.

Clothing chosen carefully will keep you warm and dry in temperate climates, cool and comfortable in the heat. Choose items on the 'layer' principle: each piece of clothing should function on its own, or fit when worn with all the others. The top layers should be windproof, and in cold or wet lands, waterproof too. Goretex is ideal. Close-fitting clothes are more comfortable, don't flap as you ride, and can't get caught in the wheels and chainset. In bright conditions a peaked hat or beret makes life more comfortable, and cycling gloves (with padded palms) will cushion your hands from road vibration. Choose shoes with stiff soles (i.e. not tennis shoes or trainers) which will spread the pressure from the pedals and which are good for walking too. Specially designed touring shoes can be bought at the better bike shops.

The Touring Department of the CTC publishes technical information sheets on equipment for bike and rider.

Mountain bikes

If you are planning to venture off the beaten track, on rough roads and tracks, a mountain bike will provide strength and reliability. Mountain bikes evolved in

California from hybrid clunkers during the Seventies, first arriving in Britain *en masse* in 1982. Since then, they have become lighter, swifter and stronger. For tarmac riding, a mountain bike is still heavier, harder work and slower than a lightweight touring bike. The mountain bike's fatter tyres create greater rolling resistance, and the upright riding position offers greater wind resistance. The additional weight also requires more pedalling effort on hills. But on dirt roads and trails mountain bikes are in their element: easy to control, with excellent traction and superb resistance to vibration, knocks and crashes.

Mountain bikes generally come with 18 to 21 gears, with a bottom gear of around 25 inches (though in practice five or so of these gears are always unusable because of the sharp angle the chain is forced to make when it is running on the largest front chainring and smallest rear sprocket – and vice versa). Mountain bike brakes are generally more powerful than those on road bikes, and the heavy-duty ribbed tyres are virtually puncture-proof. Lighter tyres with smoother tread patterns and higher pressures can be fitted for road-riding. For sheer toughness a mountain bike is impossible to beat, but you pay for this toughness by pedalling more weight in a less efficient riding position. 'Hybrid' bikes, which fall somewhere between the pure mountain bike and conventional tourer, are extraordinarily versatile: well balanced and tough on road surfaces, fast and relatively light on roads.

Buying second-hand

Buying second-hand can save a lot of money – if you know what to look for. Touring bikes, 'hybrids' and mountain bikes are advertised regularly in the classified columns of the bi-monthly magazine of the CTC, the monthly cycling magazines, and in *Cycling Weekly*. Before you buy, check that the frame is straight, first by sight, and then by (carefully) riding no-hands. If the bike seems to veer repeatedly to one side, the frame or forks are bent. Spin the wheels and check they are true. Wobble all the rotating parts; if there is a lot of play the bearings may be worn. Above all, buy only from somebody you feel is honest.

On the road

The greatest hazard is other traffic. Always keep to your side of the road, watching and listening for approaching vehicles. In Asia and Africa, buses and trucks travel at breakneck speeds and expect all other vehicles to get out of their way. Look out too for carts and cows, sheep, people, pot-holes and ruts – all of which can appear without warning.

Dogs deserve a special mention. Being chased uphill by a mad dog is every cyclist's nightmare. I've always found the safest escape to be speed, and have yet to be bitten. If you are going to ride in countries known to have rabies, consider being vaccinated before departure. It goes without saying that you should check with your GP that you have the full quota of inoculations (including tetanus) suited for your touring area.

Security need not be a problem if you obey certain rules. Unless you are going to live with your bike day and night, you need a strong lock. Always lock your bike to an immovable object, with the lock passing round the frame and rear wheel. For added security, the front wheel can be removed and locked also. Before buying, check that the lock of your choice is big enough for the job. Note that quick-release hubs increase the chance of the wheels being stolen. Always lock your bike in a public place, and if you are in a café or bar keep it in sight. In most Third World countries it is quite acceptable to take bicycles into hotel bedrooms; elsewhere, the management can usually be persuaded to provide a safe lock-up. The CTC sells travel insurance and bicycle insurance policies.

Expedition cycling

Bikes have been ridden, carried and dragged in some ridiculous places: across the Darien Gap, through the Sahara and up Kilimanjaro. They have been pedalled round the world, many times. And they have been used as a sympathetic means of transport into remote, little-visited corners of the globe. The step up from holiday touring in Europe to prolonged rides to the back-of-beyond requires sensible planning. The choice of bicycle and equipment will have a considerable bearing on the style of the ride. If you want to be as inconspicuous as possible, the best machine will be a local black roadster. Such a bike will probably need constant attention, but pays

On a bicycle I am exposed to all local experiences as no other modern traveller can hope to be. Moving quietly along at gentle speeds allows me to see, hear, and smell the country, in a way that isn't possible encapsulated in a motorcar or a bus.
– BETTINA SELBY

off handsomely in its lack of Western pretension. I once pedalled across the African Rift Valley on a bike hired from a street market in Nairobi; the bike fell apart and had to be welded and then rebuilt, but the ride was one of the most enjoyable I've ever had.

For serious journeys defined by a set goal and a time limit, you need a well-prepared, mechanically perfect machine. If much of the riding is on dirt roads, a mountain bike may well be the best bet. If you can keep your weight down, a lightweight road-bike will handle any road surface too. On the *Journey to the Centre of the Earth* bike ride across Asia with my cousin Richard, our road bikes weighed ten kg each, and our total luggage came to eight kg each. We carried one set of clothes, waterproofs and a sleeping bag each, picking up food and water along the way. Our route included a crossing of the Himalayas, followed by a south-to-north traverse of the Tibetan Plateau and Gobi Desert. Objectivity obliges me to note that I've seldom come across other cyclists travelling this light, most voicing the opinion that they would rather carry their cooking stove, pans, food, tent and extra clothes.

Spares

Lightness gives you speed. One spare tyre, one spare inner tube and a few spokes are the basic spares. Rear tyres wear faster than front ones, so switch them round when they become partly worn. For rides of over 5,000 kilometres, in dry or gritty conditions, a replacement chain will be necessary too. In 'clean' conditions a good-quality, regularly lubricated chain will last twice that distance. The tool kit should include a puncture repair kit, appropriate Allen keys, chain-link remover, free-wheel block remover, small adjustable wrench and cone–spanners for the wheel-hubs. Oil, grease and heavy tools can be obtained from garages and truck drivers along the route.

Saving weight saves energy. Look critically at your equipment, and have some fun cutting off all unnecessary zips, buckles, straps and labels. Discard superfluous clothing and knick-knacks. Make sure there are no unnecessary pieces of metal on the bike (such as wheel guides on the brakes).

It is useful to know the absolute maximum distance you can ride in one day, should an emergency arise. For a fully fit person riding a loaded bike on tarmac, this could be as much as 2-300 kilometres, but it will vary from person to person. With a constant air-flow over the body and steady exertion, a cyclist loses body moisture rapidly, and in hot climates it is possible to become seriously dehydrated unless you drink sufficient liquid. You need a minimum of one litre carrying capacity on the bike; whether you double or treble this figure depends on how far from habitation you are straying. In monsoon Asia I've drunk up to thirteen litres a day.

You may have surmised (correctly) from all this that there are as many different ways of making an enjoyable bicycle journey as there are stars in the sky. I've yet to meet two cyclists who could agree on what equipment to carry. ❧

NICHOLAS CRANE is a celebrated long-distance walker and cyclist. He has walked the length of Europe and cycled in 29 countries. He has also worked for Afghan Aid in the Hindu Kush mountains and been president of the Globetrotters' Club. His books and television films are widely known.

The charity challenger
by Mick Kidd

OKAY, IT'S HANDS UP TIME. For me the initial motivation for doing a charity challenge was neither charity nor challenge but destination – in this case Cuba, a place I'd always meant to visit but never got round to. Like everyone else, I'd noticed the increasing number of adverts for charity challenges but disregarded them on the grounds that a) I'd never be able to raise the minimum sponsorship money and b) why go all that way to do them in mainly poor countries when you can cycle from say London to Brighton at considerably less administrative cost? Obviously trekking in Ladakh/Nepal/Peru beats bypassing Haywards Heath hands down *vis-à-vis* exotic allure. But what swung it for me was a friend in Devon who had done a charity cycle ride in Cuba and was knocked out by both the place and the experience.

So now that I've done one myself, what's my opinion? The trip I went on was for the National Deaf Children's Society. It was brilliantly organised, the cycling strenuous but never so arduous as to make it unenjoyable (I'd done plenty of preparatory training). We all bonded in a common cause and the charity made heaps of money even after deducting costs. There were 55 in our group (a mixture of teachers, journalists, doctors, nurses, freelance artists and students plus the inevitable website designer) and between us we raised £140,000. About half of everyone's minimum of £2,300 sponsorship went to cover costs, although most people surpassed the minimum target so it was in effect less than half. Ours was the last of seven rides in Cuba in the winter of 1999/2000, and there are other challenge rides/treks in China, Sri Lanka, Mexico, Jordan and Iceland.

But what does Cuba get out of it? Last year the charity donated £20,000 from its aggregate net income for local projects and equipment. A similar sum is expected to be donated this year. This may seem paltry, but is still a significant amount in local terms. Nevertheless, maybe a larger sum would offset using a beleaguered country (Cuba is still severely affected by the US trade embargo) as a venue. The trip was nine days in length, five days cycling at approximately 50 miles a day, two days flying there and back and a day at either end to acclimatise and unwind. The charity had delegated the nuts and bolts of the ride – flights, bikes, accommodation, food plus mechanical and medical support – to a tour company who invoiced the charity for their services. They weren't cheap but did an excellent job, taking part in the ride themselves (as did a couple of workers from the charity). They also provided an intelligent ongoing commentary on Cuban politics, economy and culture far removed from the patronising patter of the 'warmth of the people will remain with you long after your tans have faded' variety I've experienced elsewhere.

Our itinerary took us off the normal tourist routes and through agricultural landscapes (mainly sugar cane), villages and small towns where local residents, especially the children, often applauded us through. Whether this is because such sights are becoming familiar (apparently there was another charity ride going the other way not long after ours) I'm not sure. I like to think it was our being on bikes, albeit multi-gear hybrids, rather than in luxury coaches, that endeared us to Cubans for whom cycles are an integral part of getting around, as are horses and carts. One place we stayed in offered buggy rides, which in our ignorance we took to be for tourists but were in fact for residents, petrol being an expensive commodity thanks to the US embargo.

At the end of each day we'd arrive at our accommodation in state-run hotels or holiday chalets. This meant the money went back into the Cuban economy more directly than in the all-inclusive, hermetically sealed luxury hotel complexes in places like Varadero, which are funded and part-owned by international consortiums. We stayed in Varadero for two nights at the end of the ride, and I found it utterly soulless and devoid of Cubans except in ancillary roles.

Being in a large group tended to keep us separate from local life. Backpackers, for instance, can live and eat with families, whereas we were in hotels. And during the day we'd be toiling away on the bikes. Other than that, we did the usual tourist things in our free time – listening to the ubiquitous bands (music seemed to be on the wind), dancing to the salsa beats, hanging out in small bars drinking beers or *mojitos*, the rum cocktail beloved of Ernest Hemingway (at our own expense I hasten to add), or making visits to places mentioned in our guide books. My favourite was the Museum of the Revolution in Havana, with its extensive photographic record of the overthrow of Batista in 1959 and various memorabilia including Che Guevara's sock.

Tourism is a fairly recent development in Cuba – part of the adjustment following the collapse of the Soviet Union in 1991 . Tourism brings in much-needed revenue, but with it the dangers of a two-tier economy (those with and those without dollars) in a country dedicated to social equality. So our being there both helps and hinders. Still, *je ne regrette rien*. I've done my bit for charity and been somewhere I always wanted to go.

My friend down in Devon says the experience in part changed her life. I wouldn't go that far, but then I've always subscribed to the Roman poet Horace's take on travel. He wrote, 'they change their sky but not their soul who cross the sea', doubtless before setting off to do a chariot challenge in Asia Minor to raise funds for an Iron Age good cause. 🕭

MICK KIDD *is the acclaimed 'Guardian' cartoonist 'Biff' – and a recent convert to charity challenges.*

The serious walker
by Nicholas Crane

W E ARE ALL BIPEDS. WE ARE ALL EXPERTS AT WALKING. Legs require no skills to use or licence to operate. They're built in, cost us nothing to use and are greener than any other means of transport. Legs! Stick 'em in a couple of boots and they'll do thousands of miles without so much as a service. Marvellous things.

Legs have been a recent discovery for me. For years I've been travelling on bicycles, occasionally boats and, under pressure, some kind of motorised transport. Horses are fine, but are limited to particular types of terrain. Legs are versatile. You can vary your mode of transport on a whim. Rides in trains or hay-carts, buses and boats are all possible complements to a foot-journey.

At walking pace you become part of the infinitely complicated countryside. After a while, animals and birds tend not to take flight at your approach. Strangers stop to chat, flattered that you are exploring their neighbourhood at a civilised, respectful pace. On foot you pose no threat and appear to have nothing to hide.

My life as a leg-advocate began with a walk across Europe, following the mountain ranges of the continent from Cape Finisterre in Spain to the Black Sea. This 10,000-kilometre hike took me one and a half years, and was the greatest adventure of my life. I learned a lot from that walk and I hope that the notes below will be helpful to you. I must however ask you to remember that I am a newcomer to long-distance walking (my only other hikes have been a youth hostelling trip in the Peak District with my mother, a one-week hike in Wales, and another week in the Greek mountains) and so my 'tips' are based on a limited number of extremely vivid experiences rather than a lifetime's worth of muscled miles.

First, let us consider the principles.

Principles

When I began my trans-European walk I made the mistake of being so excited that I forgot to rest. I walked for eighteen days non-stop through the sierras of northern Spain. It did not occur to me to take a break until my right leg swelled up like a gourd and reduced me to an agonised hobble. After that I stopped every five to seven days for at least one day's rest. I learned that being conscious of incipient ailments will prevent them from becoming problems. Blisters, muscle strain and back-pain can be avoided by being continually aware of how your body is functioning.

The Romans, who were experts at thousand-mile marches, walked to a system of three days on, one day off, a routine which they found ideal for legions crossing continents. One other authority I'd like to mention is Christopher Whinney, who once walked from London to Rome and who subsequently set up the walking-holiday company Alternative Travel Group. After prolonged trial and error, Christopher found that, just like the Romans, his groups remained at their happiest and most cohesive if they took every fourth day as a rest day.

Ultimately, of course, you must find your own rhythm. There is no golden mean for everyone. If you walk one day and take two off, that's fine if it's bringing the best rewards from the journey. On several occasions on my European amble, I spent a week or so in one place, or made wide detours from my planned route, and on a couple of occasions walked *backwards* to visit places I'd missed the day before. There is no magic distance that should be covered each day; a fit walker with a medium-sized pack can cover say 20 or 30 kilometres in one day with no trouble. Sometimes I've walked over 50 kilometres in one day, but as a result have been wrecked the following day.

I'll just add that I'm not a believer in training. If you want to try a long-distance walk, just go. Take it easy and use the first days (or weeks) to get fit.

So much for the rhythm. Now, where to go? Because walking is the slowest form of travel, you do need to choose a route that brings variety on an almost hourly basis. Either you choose a landscape that is chock-a-block with physical diversity, or you learn to spot the interest in what to many would seem a dull landscape. An interest in flora and fauna, history, geomorphology, agricultural implements, mountain cultures… whatever (the list is endless) will turn a walk into a fascinating quest. Some landscapes hand the walker hourly interest on a plate. Rambling in mountains; following the courses of rivers; following coastlines: all are 'themes' which, through the natural lie of the land, will create a change of view with every hour. Also in this category is the long-distance footpath, way-marked and 'themed' to provide interest. The pilgrims' Camiño de Santiago, across northern Spain, falls into this category.

The one area of essential knowledge that is required before embarking upon a long walk in wilderness areas is navigation. This means being able to use a compass accurately and in gales and mists. It also means being able to read maps and to master 'dead-reckoning' – the ability to estimate how much time it will take to cover a certain compass-bearing. It is essential to know how to do this before walking in mountains.

There are some terrains, and I'm thinking of mountains in particular, which are potentially dangerous for inexperienced walkers. It is important not to be lulled into a sense of false security by a belief that superior equipment is a substitute for old-fashioned savvy. Had I not spent 25 years messing about trying to climb mountains in Scottish winter white-outs, I would not have survived my trans-European wander. To walk safely in mountains, it is essential to feel confident using a map and compass in zero visibility and gale force winds on precipitous ridges. This is unlikely ever to happen, all being well, but it is a possibility and you need to be ready to cope. This kind of knowledge can be built up over time, in the company of a more experienced companion, on, say, the hills of Wales, the Pennines, the Lake District or Scotland. The most testing ground I've ever found for navigation in mist was Dartmoor.

Saving weight has the dual benefit of making the walking less strenuous and reducing the clutter of everyday life to a minimum. I cut my comb in half, trim the edges of maps and keep my hair short, not because these minor weight reductions are noticeable individually, but because each reminds me daily not to overload my rucksack with unnecessary stores. Carrying a half-kilo of jam unopened from one town to the next is a waste of effort. And while a shortage of water is to be avoided at all costs (dehydration is lethal), it is worth remembering than one litre of liquid really does weigh one kilogram. It pays to think ahead. Ask locals where the next spring or tap can be found rather than loading up like a camel.

Practicalities

It is not worth getting obsessive about equipment, beyond the one rule of minimal weight and maximal safety. There are, however, a number of equipment items whose suitability to your needs will affect your enjoyment of the walk.

The single most important requirement is footwear. The first decision to make is between running/training shoes or boots. The former do not need wearing in, are far lighter than boots and have a 'softer' feel. Boots offer ankle support, a leather construction which breathes better than man-made fibres, a degree of waterproofness and grippy treads for steep or uneven surfaces. Again, it is down to personal preference. When my cousins Richard and Adrian made their foot-traverse of the Himalayas in 1982, they wore running shoes; when I made my European mountain hike ten years later, I wore boots. After much experimentation I settled on the British-designed 'Brasher Boot', which combines running-shoe technology with the construction of traditional leather boots. Brasher Boots are lightweight and comfortable.

Footwear, more than any other item of walking equipment, has the power to determine whether a hike is hellish or heavenly. A perfect fit is critical. My method for selecting the correct size (taught to me by Chris Brasher, the Olympic gold medallist runner and designer of the Brasher Boot) is to push my foot forward as far as possible in the unlaced boot or shoe. There should be space to fit a finger down the gap between the heel and the inside of the boot/shoe. Footwear which is slightly too tight is the most common cause of foot problems. No matter how good the footwear, extraneous factors such as wet weather or extreme heat can cause sores and blisters. On extended hikes, washing feet daily helps to prevent infection. Too-long toenails collide with the front of the boot or shoe during descents and, after a period of excruciating discomfort, will turn black then fall off. During my hike I lost a total of ten toenails, to no noticeable disadvantage. They seem fairly superfluous.

Foot problems can be largely circumvented by giving these put-upon appendages considered thought at least three times a day. At the end of a day's walk I wash my feet, even if doing so means using precious supplies of drinking water. With practice, it is possible to wash two feet in half a litre of water, tipped in a trickle from a mug. In winter, feet can be cleaned by running very fast on snow, but the subsequent pain as they thaw is dramatic. Washing feet in the evening means that they spend the night bacteria-free in the sleeping bag, thus encouraging the healing of any sores.

In the morning I inspect each toe and every point of wear on each foot. I always pierce blisters the moment they appear, using the tip of a sewing needle, sterilised in the flame of a cigarette lighter. Blisters are more likely to appear when the skin has been softened by waterlogged footwear or sweat. Morning is also the time to clip toenails which, left unattended, can wear holes in adjacent toes and abrade the ends of socks. At midday, I de-boot for lunch, giving my feet the chance to bask in ultra-violet light and my boots the opportunity to air. This pleasurable diversion has to be forsaken if lunch is being taken in a bar or restaurant.

Toe problems can be averted by using Scholl's Toe Separator. This is a small wedge of foam rubber which can be inserted into the gap between two quarrelling digits. For anyone prone to pronation (walking on the outside of your feet), a toe divider inserted between the two smallest toes on each foot will prevent the little toe being rolled under the ball of the foot and gradually eroded.

While I'm dealing with leg-matters, I'll briefly mention knees. After feet, these are the rambler's least reliable component. Aches (and damage) most frequently occur as a result of long descents or stumbles. I have no idea whether there is any physiological sense in this, but my own technique on long descents is to take exaggeratedly short steps, keeping my knees bent. Walking thus, the legs act like car shock-absorbers. The shorter strides also allow greater control and more precise placement of every footstep. It is easier to be thrown off balance while carrying a loaded rucksack, and knees are frequently the weak link which hit the ground first, or which suffer violent twisting. An accident can be caused by a minor misplacement of the foot: a boot skating on a tiny, unseen pebble, or glancing off a curl of turf, or a heel skidding on a coin-sized spot of ice.

Many walkers protect their knees by using a walking aid. There are three alternatives. A conventional walking stick is the least expensive and in most mountainous areas can be bought locally. They are usually heavy and cannot be adjusted for length. Far better is the lightweight, adjustable walking pole, such as the Hillmaster series sold by the Brasher Boot Company. These poles come with a variety of hand grips and can be adjusted to suit body weight and terrain. The carbon-fibre model weighs only 266 grams. When not in use, the sections retract, allowing the poles to be strapped to the side of the rucksack. Finally there is the combined umbrella/walking stick (see below).

After boots, the rucksack is the next most critical item of equipment. Like footwear, the rucksack should be carefully chosen to fit the wearer. A waist belt is essential, as is a chest strap. A properly-fitting rucksack divides the load between the shoulder straps and the waist-belt. Rucksacks of the same capacity can range widely in weight. In the Karrimor range, for example, the 35-litre capacity ultra-light 'Kimm 35' model weighs only 650 grams, while the high-specification 'Alpiniste 45+10' (45 litres) weighs 1,900 grams. After various experiments, I now find that it is worth carrying the extra grams to guarantee that a rucksack is comfortable. Rucksacks with non-adjustable backs are substantially lighter than the more sophisticated adjustable models. A zip compartment at the foot of the rucksack can be useful for stowing a tent, where it can be kept separate from the rest of the luggage; a sensible precaution since it will sometimes be wet.

Individual items of clothing should be chosen for their light weight, comfort and insulation properties. On my legs I usually wear poly-cotton trousers, which dry quickly and, with the 'poly' for extra strength, tend to last longer than all-cotton trousers. The most comfortable walking trousers I have ever worn were made from Ventile by Snowsled Clothing (01453 839090). Ventile is a very fine weave of cotton, which is both windproof and has an almost silk-like feel. Snowsled also make a superb range of Ventile smocks and jackets. My shirts are always 100 per cent cotton. With a rucksack semi-permanently glued to the shirt, natural fibres are easier on the skin. I favour shirts with two breast pockets for carrying my compass and money. If possible, the shirt should have double shoulders, to cope with the wear of the rucksack straps.

For summer walking I usually wear Marks and Spencer wool/nylon mix ankle socks, which are durable and which dry overnight after being washed. For extra insulation in the winter, the 'Thor-Lo' brand, with their differentially-padded panels, are comfortable and warm (and expensive). A foot-trick of which I am rather proud is my practice of carrying a spare set of 'footbeds' (the insoles which fit into the floor of the boot). When my boots get wet, I start the next day with the spare, dry pair of footbeds, thus thwarting the misery of early-morning rising damp.

I always carry an 'emergency layer' such as a second fleece jacket or a sleeping bag (which, wrapped around the torso beneath a waterproof jacket, works like a duvet). I have an 'emergency rule' which is that one set of thermal underwear is kept inside my sleeping bag, which is kept inside a plastic bag, inside the rucksack. Under no circumstances are the sleeping bag or underwear allowed to get wet. This means that in a crisis I always have a complete set of warm, dry insulation.

The item I feel most particular about is my hat, which should have a brim to keep the sun (the ultra-violet is intense at higher altitudes) from the eyes and the back of the neck. French berets are virtually indestructible but cast shade on only one part of the head at a time. More suitable is the Basque beret, with its greater diameter. Best of all is the lightweight travelling trilby, which can be rolled up like a cornet when not in use. On the head, its generous brim works well as a cranial parasol. The best trilby is made by Herbert Johnson of New Bond Street, London. It should be noted that the trilby does not perform well in high wind. I always carry supplementary headwear, in the form of a very lightweight thermal balaclava.

The sun blazes overhead and hours pass, while you trudge through the fiery inferno; scintillations of heat rise from the stones and still you crawl onwards, breathless and footsore, till eyes are dazed and senses reel.
– NORMAN DOUGLAS

And my waterproof jacket (whether Ventile or Goretex) has an integral hood. Reducing heat loss from the head is one of the most efficient methods of maintaining overall body temperature. The other item essential for head protection is a pair of sunglasses. In mountains some walkers prefer the glasses which have leather side-pieces fitted, which cut out lateral glare. Walking on snow with unprotected eyes can cause 'snow-blindness', both painful and damaging to the eyes.

The only item of equipment that I duplicate is my compass. Without one I am lost, literally and philosophically. I use liquid-filled, Swedish-made 'Silva' compasses. The Type 3 model tucks into my breast pocket, tied with cord to the buttonhole. The much smaller Type 23 model, which weighs only 15 grams and is supplied in a modified form for the pilots' survival packs in the seats of Tornado aircraft, is kept in reserve, in my rucksack.

Without maps, long-distance walking can be erratic. Every popular mountain area in Western Europe is mapped at a scale of 1:50,000 or, even better, 1:25,000. No other series is comparable for accuracy or clarity to the Ordnance Survey, however, so Britons heading overseas must prepare for a lesser quality of cartography. The best source for walking maps in Britain is Stanfords, 12-14 Long Acre, London WC2E 9LP. For hiking in Eastern Europe, the best source is Fretytag & Berndt, Kohlmarkt 9, Vienna 1010, Austria and the Bundesamt fur Eich-und Vermessungswesen at Krotenthallergasse 3, Vienna 1080, who sell the old maps of the Austro-Hungarian Empire. The sense of history imparted by these beautifully drawn maps compensates for the fact that most users will spend 90 per cent of the time completely lost. I relied on them for walking 3,000 kilometres through the Carpathians. They were invaluable.

There is an inverse relationship between the number of days you've been hiking, and the number of tent-pegs remaining to erect your nightly home. Pegs disappear in long grass, drop down rabbit holes, or get used as a tea-stirrer then left on a tree-stump. Peg loss can be reduced by reciting BBC-man Brian Hanrahan's famous Falklands quote ('I counted them all out; I counted them all back'), when inserting pegs in the evening and retrieving them next morning.

I've often noticed how that red-handled talisman, the Swiss Army knife, is more treasured than it is used. At the top of the Victorinox range of penknives is the 'Swiss Champ', whose 29 features (among them a hacksaw, a reamer and a ballpoint pen) would be useful for hikers who think that they might be called upon to construct a biplane using nothing but driftwood and the contents of their rucksack. I carry the smallest and lightest in the range, the two-bladed Pocket Pal. I use the larger blade for cutting food and the smaller blade for less hygienic roles such as emergency chiropody.

I would not go walking without an umbrella. Furled, it can be used for parrying dog-attacks or beating back briars. Driven spike first into the ground, it is handy for drying socks. Reversing the umbrella and holding the spike converts it into a harvesting tool for out-of-reach blackberries. In the open mode, it is both rain and snow shelter, a sun shade and – during exposed picnics – a handy wind-break. My favourite umbrella was obtained when I visited the 'Que Chova' ('What Rain!' in Galician) umbrella factory in Santiago de Compostela, one of the wettest places in Europe. The best mountaineering umbrellas are made by James Smith & Son (53 New Oxford Street, London): their hickory-shafted model is strong enough to serve as a walking stick, and unlike the metal-shafted models, does not act as a lightening conductor when strapped to a rucksack. A good mountaineering umbrella has 8 ribs, and it is fallacy to imagine that 10- and 16-rib umbrellas are tougher: the extra ribs create variable shrinkage in the umbrella's fabric, and thus encourage wear and tear.

After some experimentation, I have settled on the Parker 'Vector' fountain pen, which costs less than a round of beer and is available throughout Europe (on the Continent it is a favourite among French schoolchildren, an indication more of its durability than its writing quality). Such a pen is more suitable than a ballpoint, whose ink become treacly at low temperatures and leaks in the heat, while fancy fibre-tips are expensive and have to be thrown away once they have run dry – not a very green option. In sub-zero temperatures, the conventional ink in my fountain pen will thaw from frozen after a few minutes compression under an armpit. Ten spare Parker cartridges bunched in an elastic band lasted me about 1,000 kilometres of note-making and postcard writing. Uni-ball rollerball pens (by Mitsubishi Pencil Company) write well and are filled with waterproof ink.

Diet is not a facet of everyday life that many long-distance walkers are likely to be able to control to any great extent. You eat what you can find (I do not carry food from home, since part of the interest of travelling is in discovering the local food). But on extended walks, dietary deficiencies can lead to a lowering of the body's defences against bugs and a reduction of its capacity to heal wounds. During my 507-day hike across Europe I lived largely on bread and sardines, bread and pork fat, and bread and jam – the staples generally available in mountain villages. During the same period I ate 1,014 tablets of Vitamin B Complex, Vitamin C and zinc. I was never ill and wounds healed within 3 or 4 days, without the use of antiseptic.

I'll round off this fairly random checklist of my tips with a thought: the best way of finding out about long-distance walking is to start with a short walk and not to stop. ❧

The student traveller
by Nick Hanna, Greg Brookes and Susan Griffith

STUDENT TRAVELLERS CAN TAKE ADVANTAGE of a comprehensive range of special discounts – both at home and abroad – which enable them to go almost anywhere in the world on the cheap. To qualify for a range of discounts on train, plane and bus fares, on selected accommodation, admission to museums, etc., you need an International Student Identity Card (ISIC) which is recognised all over the world. The card is obtainable from local student travel offices for £6 or by post for £6.50 from ISIC Mail Order, PO Box 48, Horndean, Waterlooville, Hampshire, PO8 OFJ. The ISIC card is valid for 16 months from 1 September. All full-time students are eligible (though some flight carriers do not offer discounts to students over the age of 31); applications should include proof of student status, a passport photo, full name, date of birth, nationality, address and a cheque or postal order.

The ISIC card is issued by the Amsterdam-based International Student Travel Confederation (ISTC) which has a splendid website (www.istc.com) with links to all member organisations and discount information on goods and services available to students worldwide, from cafés in Armenia's capital to the national bus system of Egypt. These discounts and benefits are also listed in the *ISIC Student Travel Handbook* which comes free with membership. In addition, the handbook contains information on the ISIC emergency helpline for students who encounter medical or legal emergencies while travelling.

Several alternative travel discount schemes are not dependent upon student status but are available to young people under the age of 26. The Federation of International Youth Travel Organisations (FIYTO, Bredgade 25H, 1260 Copenhagen, Denmark, website www.fiyto.org) comprises 350 organisations and companies in 60 countries specialising in youth travel. A 'Go 25' membership card costs £6 and gives access to a range of concessions similar, although not identical, to those offered by ISIC; you can apply for one at any branch of STA Travel. Another similar card is the Euro Under-26 card administered by the European Youth Card Association (website www.euro26.org), available to Europeans under the age of 26. In the UK this card is administered by usit-Campus.

Accommodation

The international youth hostelling movement continues to thrive, despite keen competition from other hostel organisations and independent hostels. Hostelling International, to which the Youth Hostels Association (YHA) belongs, is still the first port of call for many travelling students and young people. Membership for people over 18 costs £12 a year and is available at any youth hostel or by contacting the YHA National Office (Trevelyan House, 8 St Stephen's Hill, St Albans, Hertfordshire AL1 2DY, tel 0870 870 8808 or 01727 855215, website www.yha.org.uk). Hostelling International has more than 4,500 hostels worldwide, listed and described in two books costing £8.50 each: Europe and the Mediterranean in one volume, Africa, America, Asia and Oceania in the other. Note that ISIC card holders aged 18–25 can claim a £1 discount on all hostel stays within Britain, bringing an average overnight stay down to less than £9.

An explosion of budget accommodation for students and young people has taken place around the world and many leads can be found on the internet. One such hostel network is the Hostels of Europe Group, based in Belgium (133-135 Langestraat, 8000 Bruges, tel +32 50 34 49 28, website www.hostelseurope.com). VIP Backpackers Resorts of Australia is especially strong in Australia and New Zealand but also offers an international network. You can get an up-to-date list of their hostels on the internet or on a pamphlet available from its head office in Australia (PO Box 600, Cannon Hill, Brisbane, Queensland 4170, tel +61-7-3395 6111, website www.backpackers. com.au). Another very useful website for worldwide hostel listings is www.hostels.com/hostels. The small, up-to-date *Independent Hostel Guide* is published every spring; it costs £4.95 from bookshops or from the Backpacker Press (2 Rockview Cottages, Matlock Bath, Derbyshire DE4 3PG, tel/fax 01629 580427). The bulk of the listings are in the United Kingdom and Ireland, but a growing number of European hostels is also included. With a little initiative, you may be able to negotiate use of student accommodation during vacation time. In West Germany, students can use university catering facilities (Mensas) which are decent, reasonably priced and open all year round. Most student and independent travel agencies can book budget accommodation or short backpackers' packages worldwide in hostels or 1-, 2- and 3-star hotels.

Travel discounts

Cheap rail travel is dependent chiefly upon age and is generally open to everyone under the age of 26. Inter-Rail is available on a zonal basis – from £129 for a 22-day 1-zone pass to £219 for a month-long all-zones pass covering all 28 countries on the network as well as offering discounts on Eurostar and cross-Channel travel. Inter-Rail passes are available from youth travel agencies and from Rail Europe (179 Piccadilly, London W1V 0BA, tel 08705 848848); alternatively they can be booked via the internet at a £5 discount (www.inter-rail.co.uk). For more flexible rail travel, Euro Domino is a go-as-you-please touring pass valid for three to eight days of travel during any one month. You simply buy a coupon for each country you wish to visit.

Europe's largest scheduled coach operator is Eurolines (4 Cardiff Road, Luton, Bedfordshire LU1 1PP, tel 0990 143219, www.eurolines.co.uk) which offer a ten per cent discount to passengers under 26. It pays to compare prices carefully between coach and rail because the differences are sometimes less than you might expect. Student travel agents such as usit-Campus (see below) sell European coach passes: 30 days of travel between 50 cities in 25 countries costs £195, for example, while the 60-day pass costs £227.

Within Britain, students with a Student Rail Card costing £18 are entitled to a third off all rail travel for one year (tel 0845 7484950). National Express markets a Young Person's Coach Card for £9 which gives holders a 20–30 per cent reduction on all standard fares; enquiries to the Coach Travel Centre (4 Vicarage Road,

Edgbaston, Birmingham, B15 3ES, tel 08705-808080, www.nationalexpress.co.uk).

Valuable discounts are also available for air travel. Student and youth discount flights are operated by the major student travel organisations under the umbrella of the Student Air Travel Association. Most of the flights are open to ISIC card holders under 30 (some have different age restrictions) together with their spouses and dependant children travelling on the same flight, and to young persons with a valid Euro Under-26 or Go 25 card.

Travel offices

Specialist youth and student travel agencies are an excellent source of information for just about every kind of discount. Staff are often themselves seasoned travellers and can be a mine of information on budget travel in foreign countries. But check out your High Street or local independent travel agent as well, in order to compare prices before making a final decision.

The two leading youth and budget travel specialists are STA Travel and usit-Campus Travel, both of which can organise flexible deals, domestic flights, over-land transport, accommodation and tours. Both publish brochures-cum-magazines which survey travel options for students: look out for STA's *The Guide* and usit-Campus's *Hit the Ground*. STA originally stood for Student Travel Australia, though it is now a major international travel agency with 250 branches worldwide; the UK head office is at Priory House, 6 Wrights Lane, London W8 6TA (tel 020 7361 6262 worldwide, 020 7361 6160 insurance and other travel services, website www.statravel. co.uk).Usit-Campus is Britain's largest student and youth travel specialist, with 47 branches in high streets, universities and YHA Adventure Shops. As well as worldwide airfares, they sell discounted rail and coach tickets, budget accommodation and insurance and many other packaged products. Their head office is at 52 Grosvenor Gardens, London SW1W OAG (website www.usitcampus. co.uk); the national call centre number is 0870 240 1010 (tel 0161 273 1721 in Manchester, 0131 668 3303 in Scotland or 0117 929 2494 in Bristol).

Council Travel, America's largest student travel agent, has branches across the States; to find the local address, ring 1-800-2council or visit the website at www.counciltravel.com.

Working abroad

Established organisations that run working abroad programmes are invaluable for guiding students and other young people through the problems of red tape, and for providing a soft landing for first-time travellers. BUNAC (16 Bowling Green Lane, London EC1R OBD, tel 020 7251 3472) is a student club which helps British students to work abroad. It offers a choice of programmes in the United States, Canada, Australia, New Zealand, South Africa, Ghana, Jamaica and Argentina, and in all cases assists participants in obtaining the appropriate short-term working visas. In some programmes participants have jobs arranged for them, for instance as counsellors or domestic staff at American children's summer camps; in others, individuals must find their own summer jobs once they arrive at their destination.

Usit-Council is affiliated to the Council on International Educational Exchange in New York and oversees work abroad programmes in the USA, Canada, Australia, Japan and China (52 Poland St, London W1V 4JQ, tel 020 7479 2000, website www. councilexchanges.org).

Many other youth exchange organisations and commercial agencies offer packages which help students to arrange work or volunteer positions abroad. Camp America (37a Queen's Gate, London SW7 5HR, tel 020 7581 7373, website www. campamerica.co.uk) and Camp Counselors USA (6 Richmond Hill, Richmond TW10 6QX, tel 020 8332 2952) are major recruitment organisations which arrange for thousands of young people to work in the US, mostly in summer camps. Other agencies specialise in placing young people (both women and men) in families as au pairs, as voluntary English teachers or in a range of other capacities.

The best way of finding out about these mediating agencies and companies is to visit the library of a student careers office. These have key reference books and other resources, such as the very useful series published by Vacation Work Publications, and titles such as *Working Holidays* from the Central Bureau for Education Visits and Exchanges.

Gap year students

An increasing number of school-leavers are deciding to take a gap year between school and higher education. A plethora of organisations both charitable and commercial offer a wide range of packaged possibilities to gap year students, from working on a kibbutz in Israel for eight weeks to teaching in Nepal or Ecuador for six or more months. Some placements are straightforward to arrange and require little more than phoning a UK partner agency, filling out some forms and paying a fee.

Pre-arranged placements are seldom self-financing, with some commercial organisations charging up-front fees of £3,000 plus for, say, a three-month placement in South America combining language instruction, a stint of voluntary work in a conservation or welfare project and an expedition. In a very few cases outside funding is available; for instance the European Union's European Voluntary Service (Connect Youth International, British Council, 10 Spring Gardens, London SW1A 2BN, tel 020 7389 4030, website www.britcoun.org/education/connectyouth/ evs.htm) has recently provided subsidised or even free training, flights and board and lodging for six-month voluntary attachments to social projects in Eastern and Central Europe.

An association of placement agencies called the Year Out Group was launched in 2000. It exists to promote the benefits of well-structured gap year programmes and publishes guidelines to help students and their parents choose a responsible and appropriate scheme. At present 22 member organisations belong to the Year Out Group (PO Box 29925, London SW6 6FQ, tel 07980 395789, website www. yearoutgroup. org). Students should apply as early as possible in their final year at school or college; early acceptance leaves more time for fund-raising which is usually an intrinsic part of the experience.

This is a small selection of the key organisations in the field of gap year placement abroad:

◼ GAP Activity Projects (GAP) Ltd, 44 Queen's Road, Reading, Berkshire RG1 4BB, tel 0118-959 4914, website www.gap.org.uk. With voluntary work placements in 33 countries, GAP offers a wide range of volunteering opportunities. These include assisting with the teaching of English as a foreign language, general assistance with sport, drama, etc. in schools, working with the disabled and disadvantaged, conservation work and outdoor education. Placements last from four to eleven months. Applicants pay a fee (currently £490), their own airfares, insurance and medical costs, and receive free accommodation, food and in most cases pocket money.

◼ Gap Challenge, Black Arrow House, 2 Chandos Road, London NW10 6NF, tel 020 8537 7980, website www.world-challenge.co. Part of World Challenge Expeditions, Gap Challenge provides gap year students and graduates aged 18-25 with three- and six-month voluntary work placements in a range of countries. Departures are in August/September and January/February for India, Nepal, Malaysia, Tanzania, Zanzibar, Malawi, South Africa, Ecuador, Belize, Costa Rica and Peru. Fees range from £1,600 to £2,500 exclusive of airfares and board and lodging.

◼ Project Trust, Hebridean Centre, Ballyhough, Isle of Coll, Argyll PA78 6TE, tel 01879 230444, website www.projecttrust.org.uk. An educational trust that places volunteers overseas each year in posts in Africa, South and Central America, Asia and the Middle East. Most of the work offered falls into the categories of English language teaching, conversation assistants and social service. Participants must raise funds to contribute towards the cost of their placement: £3,250 in 2000.

◼ Raleigh International, 27 Parsons Green Lane, London SW6 4HZ, tel 020 7371 8585, website www.raleigh.org.uk, is a UK-based charity which offers young people aged 17-25 the chance to undertake demanding environmental and community projects overseas. Recent destinations include Chile, Belize, Namibia, Ghana and Mongolia. The fundraising target is about £3,000.

◼ Students Partnership Worldwide, SPW, 17 Dean's Yard, London SW1P 3PB, tel 020 7222 0138, website www.spw.org, is a youth development charity which offers young people aged 18-25 the chance to work in rural communities in Nepal, India, Tanzania, Zimbabwe, Uganda, Tanzania, Namibia and South Africa (former homelands of Ciskei and Transkei). Participants must raise £2,200-£2,500.

A number of books on how to fill the gap year are available, including *Taking a Gap Year* from Vacation-Work Publications (£11.95), *Taking a Year Out* (Hodder & Stoughton) and *The Gap Year Guidebook* (Peridot Press).

Studying abroad

To study abroad you must first be sure you can cope adequately with the local language. Organisations such as the Central Bureau and possibly the British Council should be able to advise, as should the Cultural Attaché at the relevant embassy. If possible, ask someone who has just returned for details about local conditions.

The Socrates-Erasmus programme enables students to obtain financial assistance for 3-12 months' study in another European country. This is normally taken as part of a recognised degree course, e.g. third year university year abroad for language students. A Socrates-Erasmus grant will contribute towards the extra costs that arise from studying abroad, but it does not cover all the usual student living expenses. Anyone interested in taking part in the Erasmus programme should look for universities that participate in the Erasmus exchange. This information is contained in The UK Guide to Socrates-Erasmus available from ISCO Publications (12A Princess Way, Camberley, Surrey GU15 3SP).

Lingua offers the opportunity to go on an educational exchange to improve foreign language communication skills. Lingua Action C enables future language students to spend up to one year working as a language assistant in another EU country.

Ask your university, college, higher education department or local authority if they have any special trust funds for study abroad and student travel. Two handbooks on grants are the *Directory of Grant-Making Trusts* and the *Grants Register*. Both are expensive (£90 and £99 respectively) but should be in student and some local libraries. ✎

NICK HANNA is a freelance travel journalist and author of the 'Tropical Beach Handbook' and 'The Greenpeace Book of Coral Reefs'. GREG BROOKES has spent the last four decades alternating periods of full-time study and teaching in Europe and Africa. SUSAN GRIFFITH writes books for working travellers.

The safari traveller
by Amy Sohanpaul

YOU CAN TAKE A SAFARI ANYWHERE NOW, most holiday brochures to most countries offer them. After all, the Swahili word means 'journey', and not specifically 'journey in a jeep through African bush'. So strictly speaking, it can apply to tiger trekking in India, whale watching in the Atlantic, a trip down the Amazon or perhaps even round the supermarket....

And yet... for the purist, for the smitten, a safari is only a safari in Africa. It's a journey, yes, but one under vast skies through savannahs shimmering under the sun: savannahs softened by swirling dust, punctured by thorn trees, made surreal by upside-down baobab trees. It's stopping for still, silent afternoons that hide languorous, lethargic, simply-can't-be-bothered-to-move lions. It's the sharp, hot smell of Africa. It's the excited, rustling burst of noise from the bush as darkness falls, campfires roar reassuringly and a hundred million sparkling stars appear. Above all, it's a window to the world as it must have been at the beginning of time. At least – that's how it feels.

Catch it while you can. The winds of change blow swiftly in Africa. I spent 14 years in Kenya and even in that dot of time the decline in wildlife was astounding. Somehow, seeing it disappear in front of your eyes is more alarming than reading statistics about it. On one journey, driving on the main road from Nairobi to

Mombasa, we stopped and marvelled as a herd of elephants loomed out of the bush and crossed the road – not a common experience outside a game reserve, but not an infrequent one either, in those days. A few years later we drove for days around a nearby game park, and didn't see a single elephant. That's just one example. The park, Tsavo, was ravaged by drought and poaching at the time. The situation has improved; and now, like most parks in Africa where you can still see plenty of game, the animals survive mainly because of the tourist dollar.

The name of the game

Everyone has an animal they really really want to see more than any other. Elephants, lion, buffalo, leopards and rhinos are the classic 'Big Five' species. For some people, the gawky giraffe with its supermodel legs and eyelashes-to-die-for is top of the list, others find grunting warthogs curiously engaging, plenty want to witness the sleek speed of a cheetah.

It's best not to get too obsessed about ticking off a list, however. No matter what the brochures tell you, there are no guarantees that you will see everything on one trip. Animals have their own patterns and, while experienced guides can second-guess where they might be at any given time, this isn't fool-proof. And animals are no fools. In some reserves, cheetahs have wised up to the fact that most game drives take place in the early morning or late afternoon and have started to avoid going out at those times. For that reason, it's best to spend a few days in one reserve. Relax, soak

How can one convey the power of Serengeti? It is an immense, limitless lawn under a marquee of sky. The light is dazzling, the air delectable; kopjes rise out of the grass at far intervals, some wooded; the magic of the unraped prairie blends with the magic of the animals as they existed before man.
- CYRIL CONNOLLY

up the glory of the bush and of the more common creatures. If you're on constant standby for a 'big' beast, you might miss the drama of an ostrich mating dance; or the delightful 'zic-zic' sound of the delicate dik-dik; or fail to appreciate the graceful bounds and leaps which impalas insist on making out of sheer *joie de vivre*. The Big Five will probably stroll up – eventually. If you only have a week (a minimum of ten days is best, to allow for travel to the reserves), try to spend it at one place or, at most, split it between two. You can cram in more reserves if you try hard, but will probably see less. And you will be very sore from bumpy travel.

Safari etiquette

Game reserves seem so vast that it's easy to forget that they are home for numerous animals, which were there first but may not be for much longer if their habitat and habits are not protected. The rules of the wild are essential for your enjoyment, your safety and their survival:

■ Most parks have a list of rules that they give out as you enter. Stick to them. Most close at sundown – make sure you're out by then or in a game lodge or camp. If you miss this and can't leave for any reason as night falls, stay in your car until found – all night, if necessary.

■ Never leave your vehicle except at designated places. And never go for a walk without an experienced guide. Some parks have areas deemed 'safe' for walking – heavenly after being shaken and stirred on the road for hours. Many of these spots are chosen for their stunning views.

■ Don't leave your vehicle if it breaks down, not even to change a tyre. If you're not on an organised safari, wait for the park wardens to find you on their rounds.

■ Make sure that you/your driver stick to designated tracks. Off-road driving injures smaller game, particularly young animals concealed in bushes and grass. It also destroys the ecosystem: Amboseli in Kenya was reduced to a dustbowl by stampeding 4x4s. It's also illegal in many African game parks.

■ Don't under any circumstances follow a predator chasing dinner. The chances of a successful kill are greatly hampered if a lioness or cheetah is accompanied by a crashing jeep. And particular care is needed with cheetahs. However thrilling it is to watch them running at full speed, they get extremely agitated if followed, can turn much faster than the average four-wheel drive in the bush and have been known to crash into them.

■ Don't join the vultures circling the feast. It's better to watch animals with their kill from a distance. Some animals are so used to the presence of cars that they will carry on eating, if you don't get too close. Others find it very stressful and try and drag the kill away – don't follow them. Some will abandon their meal altogether and then have to summon up the massive energy needed to make another kill – they don't get take-aways.

■ Stick to the speed limit – *pole pole* (a favourite Swahili phrase meaning 'go slowly'). Your chances of spotting animals are greatly increased, and slowness gives you time to stop should an animal leap out onto the road.

■ Blend into the surroundings (as much as you can in a lumbering Land Rover). Leave bright coloured clothes at home. Be very silent in the presence of animals. Low murmurs of awe inspired by the beauty in front of you are fine. Loud cries of 'cute, amazing, wonderful, awesome, did you ever, oh my' – loud cries of any sort are just not on. They frighten the animals and ruin the spectacle. Persistent offenders are at risk from their fellow travellers, who may want to throttle them with the nearest camera strap.

■ However hot and dusty you are (and you will be, very) don't be tempted to take a dip with hippos, crocodiles or bilharzia. That means avoiding most rivers and lakes.

■ Don't interact with the animals in any way. This means not feeding them – people have lost fingers giving bananas to baboons. It also means not provoking them by revving the engine, making sudden movements or calling out to them. No big cat is going to obey calls of 'here kitty kitty' (this has been heard – honestly).

What kind of safari?

The possibilities are as varied as the wildlife.

Once, the only way to go on safari was to go with a mobile camp. Trucks with tents, cooking equipment and staff would follow. Thankfully this is still possible, in two versions: budget, where you pitch your own tent; or luxury, where someone

Safari survival list

Pack to be prepared – but only take essentials, particularly if you're flying between reserves – the allowance for light aircraft is minimal; and soft, 'squashable' bags are better than rigid suitcases. The basics are:

- Wide-brimmed hat or scarf for sun protection – and to keep the dust at bay.
- Long-sleeved shirts – preferably in cool but tough cotton, to protect against mosquitoes, tsetse files and sunburn.
- If you plan to walk through the bush, wear comfortable but sturdy boots and impenetrable trousers, and you should be safe from snakes and scratches.
- Clothes in neutral colours – it doesn't have to be khaki, but a sand/sludge spectrum is best.
- A fleece or jumper. Early morning and evening game drives can be cool, and temperatures plummet at night in the higher regions.
- A small torch or flashlight just in case you need to wander about at night.
- A good penknife.
- Insect repellent, mosquito coils (possibly a small portable mosquito net), anti-bacterial cream or wipes.
- Sunscreen, sunglasses
- Camera – with at least 300mm zoom, dust cover, waterproof cover and plenty of film.
- Binoculars.
- Water bottle.
- Swimming gear – plenty of lodges have swimming pools.

does it for you and feeds you with delicacies. Most people stay at permanent tented camps (which range from basic to blissful) or at game lodges (ditto).

After the accommodation decision has been made, you only need to decide if you want to safari by jeep (the usual method), on horseback, on foot or by bicycle (with experienced guides, obviously) – you can even take a houseboat safari on Lake Kariba in Zimbabwe or a canoe safari in the Okavango delta. Or you could stay in a private game reserve – the latest, most luxurious trend, and go on night-drives with spotlights to glimpse all that nocturnal activity. Then there's flying safaris – light aircraft drifting close to the game – very *Out of Africa* – or hot air balloon safaris. Take your pick.

There are hundreds of specialist safari operators to choose from, many online. If you want to leave it until you get in-country, speak to as many local operators as possible and make your choice. Be aware that some operators may swap vehicles between themselves depending on availability – make sure you know what kind you're getting – and that you will get a window seat. That usually means a maximum of four to six people, depending on the car. Another thing to bear in mind is that some parks and game-lodges don't allow children under the age of eight or 12,

Some things never change

(From the 1949 edition of the *South and Eastern African Yearbook and Guide*)

Please:

Don't molest or frighten the animals you see along the roads by chasing them with your motor car, or alarm them in other ways. You will make them afraid to stay near the road; and they will run off when they hear a motor car coming. Moreover, it is a most unsportsmanlike thing to do, seeing that it is very unfair towards others who might be following you by the same road. The animals are now confiding only because they have not yet learned to be afraid of cars.

Don't leave your car to take photos of animals near the roads; they will run away as soon as they see you get out of the car.

Don't bathe; there are often crocodiles in the smallest pools.

Don't become alarmed if lions stand and stare at your car. They mean no harm and in fact are looking at your car and not at you. The lion's nose tells him at once that a car is not good to eat and only smells of petrol.

Don't imagine because the lions are passive that they are therefore tame, and that you can go up and pat them. If you get out of your car in close proximity to lions you are courting trouble. Remember that a startled or frightened lion is just as dangerous as an angry one. A lioness with cubs, though she may take little notice of cars, is almost certain to attack a human being walking towards her cubs.

Don't forget that if you wound a lion or lioness you are making unnecessary trouble and creating a danger to yourself and other visitors. The animal, probably merely curious before, will become indignant and may attack you and others

Don't travel at a speed exceeding 25 mph. Remember the slower you travel the better your chances are of seeing game.

When passing through **Elephant Country** visitors are warned:

(a) To travel very slowly especially round corners, and not to pass any cow elephants with young ones, but to get away back as soon as possible, or if that is not possible to remain perfectly quiet till the elephants have gone.

(b) In the case of bull elephants which it is desired to photograph near the road, drive a little past the animal before stopping the car, and not to stop to take photographs, while he is still in front.

(c) Not to stop and photograph a herd of cows and calves, but to make haste to get away.

depending on the country: check this before you go. And don't go during the rainy season – most parks become quagmires.

You can organise a safari yourself, but by the time you've sorted out the right vehicle, equipped it, paid the park fees and found an authorised camping site, the cost will be the same as getting an expert to do it for you. In any case, breakdowns are common in the bush and it's better to have an experienced hand with you. Unless you're an experienced hand yourself, in which case you don't need to read this.

Where to go

SOUTH AFRICA: Despite a tendency for surfaced roads in some reserves, which somehow feel all wrong, South Africa takes its wildlife very seriously. It is home to Africa's oldest national park, the Kruger, which is larger than Wales and slightly wilder. A long stay is best in the Kruger: it is so vast that it's easy for the animals to hide. Still, the roads do lead to popular watering-holes so you will see the local animal population popping in for a pint if you time it right. Private game reserves line the unfenced western boundary of the Kruger – Sabi Sands, Timbavati, Manyeleti and Thornybush all offer high concentrations of game. In KwaZulu Natal, the Hluhluwe-Umfolozi game reserves are the best place on the continent to see black and white rhinos in numbers. Also worth a look is the Greater St Lucia Wetland Park, which houses the highest forested dunes in the world, swamps, sandforests, a palm belt, hippos, crocodiles and outstanding bird life.

BOTSWANA: With the exception of elephant, almost every other variety of game can be found in the Central Kalahari Game Reserve – the Kalahari is the desert with the highest species diversity in the world. An organised safari is best; there are no permanent camps and facilities are minimal. The Okavango delta is Botswana's 'don't miss' attraction. The northern end is permanently etched with deep channels, placid pools and papyrus; the south is interspersed with wooded islands; all of which are home to large numbers of small mammals and birds. Venice has gondolas, the Okavango has *mokoros* – canoes that are the best way to explore this lush region. Finish off with a visit to Chobe National Park, famous for elephants, or Moremi Game Reserve, encompassing almost every wildlife habitat – and animal.

NAMIBIA: It's got to be Etosha. The 'place of dry water' houses elephant, giraffe, cheetah, leopard, lion, and black rhino – all against a stunning backdrop of desert and dunes. And although the infrastructure is improving all the time, Etosha is far from crowded – which means that the animals are relaxed. This and the clear light make for superb photo opportunities.

ZIMBABWE: Gonarezhou National Park – packed with animals, well off the beaten track, beautiful, wild and real. Matobo – take a horse-ride through the rocky hills which shelter caves and rock-paintings as well as white and black rhino. Mana Pools National Park in the north is one of the few where visitors can walk – after arriving by canoe safari along the Zambezi. Hwange is the most accessible park, and has a healthy game population – this park is easy to visit on a self-drive holiday. Lake Kariba, as mentioned, offers idyllic houseboat safaris.

UGANDA: Bwindi Impenetrable Forest is the place to visit. There are only about 600 mountain gorillas left on the planet. Half of them live within Bwindi. Take a trek through the dense brush and swinging vines for the exhilarating experience of coming face to face with a silverback.

KENYA: The old favourite, the best known safari destination, and therefore more crowded than other countries. As a result, the concept of staying on private ranches or houses is a growing one here. On the other hand, Kenya's variety of parks is superb, from the suburban Nairobi National Park (easily accessible for a morning or afternoon) to the lofty heights of Mount Kenya National Park. The parks are so varied and spread out that it's best to combine just one or two – or stay for a couple of months. Try an overnight at the Ark hotel in the hilly, forested Aberdares and watch animals all night long from the balcony, or spot sable antelope in tiny Shimba Hills National Reserve (just 30 miles away from the delightful marine park at Wasini on the coast), or elephants covered in red dust in Tsavo. Every animal you see in Amboseli will be against the stunning backdrop of Mount Kilamanjaro.

Then there's the northern trio – Buffalo Springs, Samburu and Shaba – all Born Free territory. A hot air balloon trip over the Masai Mara at dawn, watching the world and the animals awake, is like flying over an earthly Eden – but better, because you stop for a champagne breakfast. The real 'don't miss' however, is the wildebeest migration between the Mara and the Serengeti in Tanzania.

TANZANIA: As above, try and catch the wildebeest migration. Dry, dusty, endless Serengeti Plain is home to over 3 million animals, so despite its size – over 5,000 miles – spotting large concentrations of prides or herds is easy. Ngorongoro Crater is a self-contained paradise concentrated and protected within one crater, with exceptional game viewing. The crater is one of the best places to view a lion or hyena hunt – try and get there early in the morning. It can get busy, however. Tanzania is starting to catch up with Kenya in tourist traffic, but one place where you can say "I want to be alone" and mean it is the Selous Game Reserve, the largest reserve in Africa. The main attraction is the space, and a speciality is walking safaris where you are likely to encounter no other humans but plenty of game – although the elephant population is no longer what it was – great herds, some 300,000 strong once roamed the reserve. You'll still see a few though. ❧

AMY SOHANPAUL is the Assistant Editor of 'The Traveller's Handbook'.

The clubbing traveller
by Chris Mooney

"OF COURSE, IT WAS BETTER IN 1990." It's the one thing that links the clubbing veteran and the seasoned traveller – an unshakeable conviction that everything was better at a vaguely defined point in the past. So if you are going around the world with the express purpose of visiting the legendary locations you've heard about, uncovering new and exciting music in its home country and meeting like-minded enthusiasts, it's something you're going to have to get used to.

It is, of course, total rubbish. Just as every traveller brings a fresh set of eyes to the world, so does the world of sweating, dancing and chatting constantly renew itself. Unfortunately, this perennial moan is the only thing that unites the concept of 'the clubbing traveller'. How, for example, do you reconcile these experiences…?

Bouncing in the perennially popular Banana Club in Cusco, Peru, to the background of head-drilling hardcore techno randomly mixed with local salsa. The floor has at least a metre of give in the centre, so even retiring wall-flowers standing meekly by the edge jig helplessly, catapulted into the air by the laws of physics.

Negotiating the sticky-floored Cocktails and Dreams in Australia's Surfer's Paradise, where every Tuesday punters claim one hour of free beer, and where ten bottles in that hour is not only common practice, but positively expected.

Laying on a straw mat on Hat Rin's white sand beach in Thailand, taking delivery of a cold melon juice and watching a flawless purple-bruise sunrise, while in the background a squealing voice declares: "harrrrrcore techno y'know, foo moon partaaaay" to the accompaniment of head-splitting firecrackers.

Negotiating the velvet rope outside New York's The Tunnel by peering over a bouncer's shoulder at a name on the guest list, only to find yourself at a party celebrating 'sadomasochistic art through the ages'.

No jaunt around the world is going to be the same. This guide can only give the merest hint of what is going on in every corner of the globe. The only advice you need, which is what every budding traveller wants to hear, is: get out there and define your own clubbing map of the world. But we all need a helping hand, so let's start with some familiar names…

The big three: Ibiza, Goa, Ko Phan Gan

Whatever your opinion of patchouli oil or The Grateful Dead, hippies do deserve our thanks for establishing three of Earth's grandest clubbing institutions.

Throughout the 1960s and 1970s, intrepid longhairs on their meandering trail round the world gradually tired of all that movement and stuck a stick in the ground. Ibiza and Goa in the 1960s, and Thailand's Ko Phan Gan in the early 1990s, became semi-permanent tie-died enclaves. All three offered the winning double of cheap accommodation and the opportunity to frolic naked, which may also explain their lasting appeal. These days, of course, all three are well stomped parts of any young and excitable traveller's itinerary, but don't let that put you off.

Ibiza needs no introduction – the white isle can now claim to be the clubbing capital of the world without causing too many raised pierced eyebrows. If you've even a passing interest in the repetitive beat, you'll be familiar with the names if the main clubs – Ku and Pacha in particular are absolutely stunning, and that goes for the decor, the music and the bar staff.

Stay out of San Antonio if you don't like beer and football, make sure you see at least one sunset from Café Del Mar and don't fall asleep on the beach. The main season runs from June to September – www.ibiza-info.com/night contains unbiased updates and sensible advice if you intend a visit.

Goa, the former Portuguese colony on the south-west coast of India, is the original hippy port that is now home to backpackers looking to see if all they've heard is true. By and large, it is – Calangute is the 'party beach', but if you're planning a long stay it can become oppressive after a while. A good plan is to stay in Baga, a bit further north – it has all the beauty of Calangute, but more opportunities to escape the crowds. Don't expect groundbreaking music – a psychedelic trance regime is strictly enforced – but the white beaches, sunsets and transcendental conversations are all beautiful. Man.

Hat Rin beach on Ko Phan Gan is home to the infamous 'full moon parties', held, well, every full moon. Until fairly recently you could only get here by bribing a willing local fisherman to take you from Ko Samui, but you can now catch a ferry straight from Surat Thani on Thailand's east coast. Hat Rin is surprisingly small, and it's worth exploring the island, which comes close to the conventional descriptions of paradise. Back on the main beach, time seems to obey different rules – many people have lost whole weeks falling into the papaya shake, seafood and sun lifestyle. It's also not to everybody's taste – the scathing parody in Alex Garland's *The Beach* is transparently based on Ko Phan Gan, complete with travelling one-upmanship and some seriously damaged psyches.

Warning: If you come across someone at any of these three destinations who has been there since "the very beginning" (a sliding date that will tend to vary with each storyteller), don't try and get much sense out of them. You won't.

Where else can I go?

One of the world's more timeless clubbing events is The Berlin Love Parade – the one time that the city completely throws off its somewhat drab reputation and takes to the streets in style. The two days of homespun techno, sequins and Teutonic mayhem make you wonder where on earth these people get to for the rest of the year. It tends to take place around May, but not much forward planning is needed – accommodation is cheap and plentiful.

Forward planning, however, is vital if you're going to the Rio Carnival. This needs no introduction, running from Sunday to 'Fat Tuesday', 40 days before Lent (usually February or March). You won't be alone in the crowds of tourists, but it's guaranteed to leave a smile tattooed to your mouth for the duration of the full four-day celebration. The usual caution applies when travelling in Rio – don't carry large amounts of money, keep to the main streets and don't stray too far from the town centre.

The Sydney Mardi Gras also takes place around March; it's a time when the city's gay and lesbian population celebrate as only Australians can. Last year's highlights included a float made entirely from beer cans, a mobile lesbian wedding centre and a 'tallest tranny' competition. End the evening in the clubs of Kings Cross and Pitt Street and you'll have enough tales to bore your friends for weeks. Not one for colonials with a stiff upper lip.

Ayia Napa in Cyprus is fast becoming a world convention for garage and R'n'B every summer, with top DJs promising residencies. The town itself shares Ibiza's beered-up temporary clientele, but the atmosphere rarely goes beyond frisky. Seeing Mickey Finn and the Ganja Kru gleefully playing their raucous drum'n'bass to a small crowd of bewildered Cypriots is just one lasting memory – although now there are likely to be Ibiza-style crowds to match the music.

If you're heading to Japan, Tokyo's Shibuyaku district is unparalleled for ice-cool posing, superb homegrown techno and hip-hop and a strict 'no-dancing' policy – look cool at all costs. The clothes and styling are obsessively dapper, and you're also likely to pick up some superb outfits to mail home. Just don't expect them to be fashionable for a few years.

But look at the itinerary of any big DJ for the full story of clubbing around the world. Carl Cox, for example, visited Cologne, Paris, Albufeira, New York, Belfast, Finland, Denmark and Australia in the space of two months in early 2000. Keep your eyes open, and you'll find an unexpected bonus wherever you turn.

And always remember a golden rule – follow the heavens. If you're in a beautiful part of the world and there's a full moon or eclipse, someone somewhere will be hosting a party worth being at.

Dos

Like the best restaurants and the best guesthouses, the best clubs are not always listed in handy guides like these. You'll need to get out there and talk to people (locals, fellow thrill-seekers, the melon-seller, anyone). A truly unique clubbing experience is one of the only joys left in travelling that can't be exhaustively researched and printed in a book – in a year it will be gone.

Visit local record shops, whether it's DownTown Records on New York's West 25th St – a vinyl junkie's dream – or a tin shack booming out *merengue* in Cancun. Buy a tape in each one and you'll have an amazing set of memories, not to mention reams of unlistenable-to tat that 'sounded good at the time'. Given the right surroundings, even Chinese opera can gain a certain charm. And as at home, search out any magazines, flyers and fanzines – the quickest route to where you want to be.

Young men should travel,
if but to amuse themselves.
– Lord Byron

The internet is now essential to the traveller – it's more up to date than the advice you picked up two months down the road, and chat rooms are often full of like-minded people only too willing to trade stories. www.clubplanet.com has reliable guides to the major cities around the world, and www.wwideweb.com/chat-pro.htm gives you access to the busiest chat rooms, where you'll more than likely find like-minded nightlife fans.

One tip that may surprise you: carry a reasonably smart, crease-free outfit in your backpack, including shoes that aren't trainers. Heavy and annoying, yes, but if you're intending to go out anywhere grander than the local pub in a major Western city, they won't let you in wearing Birkenstocks and a 'Free Tibet' T-shirt. Australia, France and the US are particularly strict. It's less of a problem in Goa.

ID with a photo is also a must for city nightclubs – even a UK driving licence often isn't enough if it doesn't have a picture. If you're younger than 21 you may have the occasional problem, but an international student card with a slightly 'optimistic' birth-date will get you past most doormen.

Don'ts

Be careful that you're not the kind of 'clubbing traveller' who is also the 'selfish hedonist'. Don't throw your rubbish everywhere – beautiful places became popular for a reason. Respect local customs at all times – there may be a big discrepancy between acceptable behaviour at home and the country you're in. You may offend religious sensibilities and local custom by assuming the world loves to dance to loud drum'n'bass in Lycra and bikinis. Anyone who has spent time in Thailand or India, among a tolerant and religious people, will have seen their occasional dismay at behaviour they cannot condone. Be aware of your surroundings.

And, most importantly, remember that nightclubs picked up a seedy reputation for a reason. Tales of clubs in Patpong in Bangkok being locked until everyone pays to get out are not urban myths. Use your head – which brings us onto the next subject.

Drugs

Whether you like them or not, and it's impossible to deny that many people do, drugs are part of many clubbing cultures. But before you join in, consider the following facts carefully.

You're often nowhere near the kind of medical help you may need, you're not in a controlled environment, and you're more likely to be experimenting with something you haven't tried before. Most importantly, drug laws are usually harsh and, contrary to travelling rumour, often enforced.

One full moon party I attended in Ko Phan Gan in 1992 was thrown into perspective after two young German men died trying to swim home after some magic mushroom omelettes. And there's no fun to be had in foreign prisons, deportation, confiscated passports or massive fines. For more advice, read the chapter on *In Trouble With The Law*.

Working as a DJ

Working in clubs abroad is not as hard as you may think, although the pay is likely to be restricted to board and expenses. Budding DJs will need their own records, something that obviously needs planning. You're unlikely to lug mountains of vinyl around on the off chance, but most people looking for work leave them in a left-luggage locker and chance their arm.

Often the right accent, the right record names to drop and a convincing sounding DJ history (even if it's three nights at The Wheeltappers and Shunters, Armley) will go far in a world that often slavishly follows Western Europe and the US when it comes to dance music trends. Happily, though, a lot of the world has yet to discourage enterprising and talented DJs, a complaint you hear more and more in the UK. So if you know you can mix and entertain a crowd – rather than just think you can – give it a go.

The up and coming scene

If you really want to join the club of 2010, who will confidently and dismissively claim that "it was better in 2000", then you should know that Eastern Europe is rapidly destroying its reputation for bad haircuts and worse music. A refreshing lack of cynicism and pragmatic creativity is throwing up some enterprising and forward-thinking clubs. A recent trip to Talinn in Estonia revealed hidey-holes such as Club Enter – an internet café by day and drum'n'bass sardine tin by night. DJs returning to the UK are also talking of small but growing club scenes in Prague, Moscow, Warsaw and Helsinki.

Canada is also emerging from America's shadow – particularly in Vancouver. The happy coincidence of a snowboarding community, beautiful scenery, and the same idealistic anti-corporate vibe that spawned such places as Goa are coming together to offer more fine venues to dance until sunrise.

Have a great time

And don't forget – if you're setting off on a trip around the world there's much, much more to travelling than music and dancing. Make the most of every place you visit, see the sights, meet the people and take time to relax. Nightlife is all very well, but the world looks better in daylight. Have a great time. 🐾

CHRIS MOONEY is a freelance journalist and copywriter based in London. He was named Radio 4 Young Critic of the Year in 1993, and is eagerly awaiting his next award.

The spiritual traveller
by Rupert Isaacson

IT WAS NEVER MY INTENTION TO BECOME A 'SPIRITUAL TRAVELLER'. Nor do I know if I really qualify for the title, having never stayed in an ashram or followed a guru. It all happened in spite of myself, through a series of accidents rather than any thought-out design. It began, I think, when I was 19, on my year off between school and university. I was visiting a cousin who was a born-again Christian and lived in Botswana. "So Rupert," he asked me on my first night in his hot, drought-ridden country, while huge moths and other insects I didn't recognise fluttered at the candles: "At what stage in your spiritual odyssey are you?"

I had no answer. I was a teenager, concerned with girls, adventure and, well, girls. It had never occurred to me that my life might be a spiritual journey. But despite my inability to respond, and my innate resistance to my cousin's rather rigid brand of spirituality, the question resonated. And three years later, while living on my wits as an illegal immigrant in Canada, it raised its head again. I had been surviving any old how, doing various kinds of labouring jobs, when it occurred to me that I might be able to make my living by my pen – or rather, begin the long, long process of establishing such a living. I was living in Montreal at the time. While there, a story much in the Canadian newspapers concerned the intention of a government-sponsored power company called Hydro Quebec to flood an area of land equivalent to the size of France in Northern Quebec. The water and hydro power would be sold to America. Problem was, the land belonged to the Cree Indians, and they didn't want the flooding. No one was reporting on the story back in the UK. I managed to get an on-spec commission for a British magazine and headed north to do my first reportage.

What I found was a people intimately connected with the land, and who were not afraid to apply the words God and spirit to everything around them. Trees, rocks, water, animals, people, even machines – everything was seen as a manifestation of divine spirit. The woods around the Crees' canvas settlements echoed to the clack of bones and antlers tied to the trees to honour and invoke animal spirits they had taken. Medicine bundles full of prayers were fastened with strips of caribou hide to the forks of silver birch trees. They believed that to take more from the forest than was needed was to abuse God, but that to take as much as was needed was to honour God. This deliberate, focused, intimate relationship with a God of all things seemed to give the Cree a palpable strength of resolve. They won their battle against Hydro Quebec, and safeguarded the land. And I came away questioning my own world view. The Crees' belief in the interconnectedness of things had a kind of instinctive logic to it that was hard to ignore.

A few months later, back in Britain, the chance came my way to update a guidebook to – as it happened – spiritual retreats. I spent several months tramping up and down the UK, staying in Benedictine monasteries, Buddhist centres, New Age/Pagan communities such as Findhorn in Scotland, and even colleges of the pan-religious Ba'Hai faith. During that time I learned that – interested though I was – I was not yet ready for the rigour of a specific, regular spiritual practice. Yet I could see that life without such a practice was only half a life – the people in all these places were just too damn fulfilled by their own spiritual practices to dismiss. And I could see that, whether I liked it or not, my life was – as my cousin had once told me – a journey towards finding my own spirituality. But I was hung up on the idea of virtue: how could I try to follow a spiritual path when I had a young man's libido and thirst for adventure to contend with? It seemed an insoluble quandary.

The following years – the mid to late 1990s – brought a succession of contracts to write guidebooks to South Africa, Zimbabwe, Botswana and Namibia. These projects revived an old interest in the wild Kalahari area, the vast dry grassland that lies at the centre of all four countries, and which my South African mother had told me stories of when I was a child growing up in grey, unexotic London. Many of those stories had been about the svelte, golden-skinned hunter-gatherers who inhabited that vast land of singing grasses – the people known as Bushmen. I began to get more curious about these people, whose culture (it was said) dated back at least 30,000 years. Yet it wasn't easy to make contact with them. After several attempts to overcome the obstacles of vast distance, the need for an expensive 4x4, language barriers and lack of local knowledge, I finally managed to meet and make a friend among the Ju'/Hoansi Bushmen of northern Namibia. One of the last clans to live almost entirely by hunting and gathering they – like the Cree – were resisting the appropriation of their land; in this case by aggressive, cattle-owning tribes such as the Herero, Batswana and Ovambo, who wanted the Bushman hunting grounds for grazing.

Perhaps inevitably, I became quickly drawn into reporting on the Bushmen's emerging political struggle. Two communities, the Xhomani of South Africa and the Nharo of Botswana, eventually became sufficiently comfortable with me to invite me to the trance, or healing, dances for which the Bushmen are famous. These dances last all night, a chorus of women weaving a sonic web of hand-clapping rhythm and shrilling song while the men dance a slow-stamping circle between them and the fire, led a by a healer. When the healer achieves his trance, the sight is spectacular; he shrieks, sobs with the pain of it. Blood and mucus pour from his mouth and nose. Quite miraculous healings take place – I have seen, for example, a woman cured of angry red swellings on her legs, and a child's whooping cough taken away in a single night of dancing. But almost more important than the individual healings is the effect these dances have on the communities themselves. Ancestral spirits are called in to flush out any tensions and conflicts that threaten the unity of the group. The importance of this cannot be over-empha-

A good traveller is one who does not know where he is going to, and a perfect traveller does not know where he came from.

– Lin Yutang

sised. As Dawid Kruiper, leader of the Xhomani Bushmen, once told me: "We are the jackals, the little ones who sit in the dunes and wait while the lions eat." A pacifist culture surrounded by warrior societies – both black and white – the Bushmen were certain that this continual renewal of spiritual strength through the trance dance had given them the strength to survive the continual assaults that it has been their lot, historically, to suffer.

They also showed me, sometimes very graphically, how leading a spiritual life does not necessarily require being a saint. All the Bushman healers I know drank (though not to achieve trance). Many of them cheated on their wives, fought sometimes, and said and did thoughtless things. And the same is true of healers I have met at home. Though not so extreme a character as the Bushman shamans, one Cornish healer I know is very much a red-blooded male. Yet his ability to heal – by channeling love, as he calls it – is extraordinary. He once healed me, long distance, of a blinding toothache (he was in Cornwall, I was in Idaho, trying to live-capture a mountain lion in a snowstorm as part of a wildlife study). Another time, when I fell from a horse in Colorado and got up coughing blood, I made a successful mental appeal to him – 9,500 kilometres away – to stop the bleeding. And these episodes pale beside what he has done for cancer patients. As he says: "God expects devotion, not perfection."

Recently, during this life of travelling to and fro between the Kalahari (where most of my work is), England (where my commissions come from) and America (where I now live), I have become more interested in the Eastern traditions. Most of this has come through my wife, whom I met in India. Neither of us were there for any spiritual purpose – she was collecting data for her psychology PhD among Indian high school students and I was in between Africa projects, writing another guidebook. But my wife, whose hippy-minded Californian parents introduced her early to the Hindu and Buddhist traditions, already had a daily meditation practice. The equanimity this brought her was evident from the start of our relationship. I felt inspired to follow. Though my practice is, as yet, much more erratic than hers, together we have been exploring yoga and the teachings of the Vietnamese Buddhist monk Thich Nhat Hanh, who preaches a philosophy of non-attachment to objects and ideas, and who was highly influential in the peace talks that brought an end to the Vietnam War. Coming soon is my first yoga retreat – which will take place on a remote ranch in northern Texas. And I am working up the courage to try, this summer, the discipline of my first meditation retreat, hopefully at Thich Nhat Hanh's Plum Village community in Southern France.

Which brings us back to where we began – travelling with a spiritual purpose. It is a cliché to say that life itself is a spiritual journey. But, like most clichés, it holds true. Although I never set out to travel as a means to a spiritual end, it happened anyway. Through the Cree and the Bushmen I learned the necessity of honouring God in all things and applying love to all situations – or at least as much as possible, given the limitations of ego and desire. Without the strength that their beliefs brought them, these two peoples might well have succumbed to the outside aggressors. And from the isolated spiritual communities of the West I have learned that a life lived in fear of the word God is a life devoid of any real meaning. Now, it seems, I am at last about to start travelling with more of a direct spiritual purpose in mind. But where this will lead, I have no idea. All one can do – in this as in all journeys – is begin. ❧

Rupert Isaacson's account of his time with the Bushmen, 'The Healing Land', is due to be published by 4th Estate. He hopes, one day, to be able to practise what he preaches.

The retreat traveller
by Stafford Whiteaker

'Going on retreat' is the alternative holiday that is winning new converts by the thousand every day across Europe and the United States. Here is the ultimate journey to that most mysterious place of all – your inner space. It is a way of recharging your energies and getting some peace and quiet in a hectic and demanding world. It is a chance to get away from it all, to think things through, and to reflect on your life and relationships. Travelling this way means shedding stress and rediscovering the inner person.

Who goes on retreat?

Going on retreat can be an exciting adventure for anyone. You meet people of all ages and from every kind of background – students, housewives, grandparents, business people, the rich, the famous and the unemployed. You do not have to be a Christian or Buddhist or indeed religious at all, or know anything about spiritual things, even if you stay in a monastery. People of all faiths and none go on a retreat. But a retreat is a spiritual adventure, and so the mind, body and spirit are all involved, with unity of the whole person as the goal. This process can be a lot of fun as well as a way to renew the inner person.

What is a retreat?

A retreat is simply a deliberate attempt to step outside your ordinary life and relationships and take some time to reflect, rest and be still. It is a concentrated time in which to experience yourself and think about your relations to others – and, if you are fortunate, to gain a sense of the eternal. It can give you a view of the world that surpasses the one from the highest mountain and is bigger than any ocean.

There is a wide and international choice of retreat places, from Christian, Buddhist and Hindu to Yoga and Alternative Spirituality centres. Alternative Spirituality is a collection of many ideas and practices aimed at personal growth, which may range from alternative healing practices, reincarnation, environmental concern, inner voice singing and telepathy to occultism and spiritism. Many of these ideas, techniques and approaches spring from well-established traditions of healing, self-help and self-discovery.

No matter where you go – traditional monastery or ashram, healing centre or workshop on shamanism – the result should be the same: self-discovery and a new view of life. A retreat may last from a day to many months, but for most people a long weekend or a week make the best lengths of stay.

Almost all places of retreat in Europe are Christian, Buddhist or Alternative Spirituality based and the use of a particular approach in the form of spiritual exercises is common. These incorporate various ancient and modern forms of meditation, contemplation, vocal and mental prayer, ways of looking at reality, and other techniques that clear up mental clutter, put your body in a relaxed state and serve to open up the inner person. Such activities are designed to make you fully aware of yourself and others in new and refreshing ways.

The ways in which humanity handles its spiritual dimension are innumerable, and dozens of approaches are available today. For Christians, the spirit is helped to become open to love and to the discovery of God's will. Buddhist practices develop a capacity for awareness and compassion, so that we may become more awakened to reality. Retreats based on Native American shamanistic practices may lead into the spirit world. Other spiritual traditions aim to bring consciousness of the unity of all creation and of the eternal.

These are enormous goals – but then, why not? Unlike the mind and body, your spirit goes forth with unlimited prospects. You were born fully equipped for this kind of travel.

Different kinds of retreat

Retreats divide into two major groups : private retreats to which you go alone, and group retreats, which often have a theme and cover a particular topic or approach to spirituality and inner healing. Many group retreats take the form of workshops lasting a week or a weekend. Some are specially designed to help you unwind. Others are highly structured around a particular system of spiritual exercises, such as those of Ignatius Loyola, or based on a well defined-form of meditation such as Vipassana.

The private retreat

Here you are strictly on your own. You decide what you will do and how you will approach your sanctuary time. You can opt for self-catering if you don't want the meals on offer. There will be time to walk, read and just rest. No radios or television or mobiles here – just your inner voices. All is simple, easy and peaceful.

The traditional retreat

Traditional weekend retreats are the most popular option, and if you are in a group are likely to run along the following lines. You arrive on Friday evening, find your room and meet the retreat leader and other guests. After supper there may be a short discussion about the programme. Then you might go for a walk in the garden or spend some time getting acquainted. Early to bed is the usual rule, but not necessarily early to rise. From the first night, you cease doing much talking except when gathered together for a group discussion. There may be prayer or meditation. If you are in a monastery there may be set times for spiritual practices such as sung prayers, which you can attend if you want to.

Theme and activity retreats

These offer a wide range of courses and study that combine body and spiritual awareness. The methods used spring from alternative healing practices, group psychology, or are based on rediscovering traditional religious forms of creating spiritual awareness. You enter an activity, such as painting or dance, through which you may gather your feelings, senses and intuition together into a greater awareness of yourself, of others and of life as part of the cosmic creation. There are a great number of ways to explore this form of retreat. Some are ancient arts and others very much of our own time. Yoga retreats employ body and breathing exercises to achieve greater physical and mental stillness as an aid to meditation and contemplation. Embroidery, calligraphy, and painting retreats focus on awakening personal creativity. Nature and prayer retreats help you to see things freshly, appreciating colour, shape and texture to heighten your awareness of creation at work all around you.

Healing and renewal retreats

Ancient and modern techniques are drawn upon to help achieve this goal in a healing retreat. These may range from discovering the child within you, to flotation sessions, nutritional therapy, holistic massage or aromatherapy. The established churches have regained their awareness of this almost lost aspect of their faith. Now inner healing and healing of the physical body through prayer and the laying on of hands have become prominent features of many Christian ministries.

Renewal retreats

A renewal retreat is usually Christian and is seeking to find a new awareness of the presence of Christ, a deeper experience of the Holy Spirit, and a clearer understanding for the committed Christian of his or her mission in the Church.

Taking the family or going just for the day

For those places that have suitable facilities, a whole family may experience going on retreat together – even the family dog may be welcomed in some places. These retreats need to be well-planned and worked out so that each member of the family from the youngest to the oldest has a real chance to benefit from the experience. Buddhist centres and monasteries often have a children's Dahampasala, which is a school study session held each Sunday. Some convents offer crêche facilities for mother-and-baby day retreats. Many places have camping facilities or a family annex.

Meditation retreats

These are for the study and practice of meditation from the beginner level to the advanced practitioner. It is a way of opening yourself to an inner level of wellbeing. There are many kinds of approaches to meditation from the various Buddhist traditions to those of the Christian and Hindu faiths as well as non-religious ones.

The experience of silence

The most ancient retreat of all is the one of contemplation and solitude. Here you live for a few days in that great school of silence in which the legendary hermits and saints of old sought God and made all else unimportant. Silence and stillness are very great challenges in this age of diversion and aggression. Even after a few hours of stillness, an inner consciousness arises and those bound up in busy lives are often surprised at the feelings which surface. This kind of retreat is best done in a monastery or convent where the atmosphere is very peaceful.

Going on retreat

Once you decide to go, select a place which strikes you as interesting and in an area you want to visit. Most places have a brochure or list of activities which includes charges. Write, giving the dates you would like to stay with an alternative, and making it clear whether you are a man or a woman, for some facilities are single gender. You need not declare your faith or lack of it or your age. Enclose a stamped, self-addressed envelope.

Going on retreat for people with disabilities

The number of retreat places offering facilities for independent people with disabilities is increasing all the time, but always double-check before booking so that you know exactly what is on offer.

How much does it cost?

Room and food are usually included in the price. Costs are modest in comparison with ordinary holiday hotel rates. In Spain, for example, you can expect to pay from 1,000 to 2,000 pesetas, and in France 300–400 francs per day for full board.

In Britain the range is £25 to £35 a day, and weekends cost between £55 and £250. Expect most courses and workshops to cost about the same as programmes of similar quality at colleges or craft centres.

Alternative Spirituality places, offering healing therapies and special counselling, usually charge a commercial rate for accommodation, treatments and courses. These range from £75 a day to over £350 for a weekend, plus individual treatment fees. Many Christian and Buddhist retreat houses refuse to put a price on their hospitality and ask only for a donation. If you are a student or unwaged, a special lower rate is often possible. Some places offer camping or caravan facilities or a room with a common kitchen for DIY eating.

Food

Vegetarians and special diets are often catered for in Britain and the United States, if you give advance notice. The food in other countries is apt to reflect the national diet and include meat. Self-catering facilities often exist in retreat guesthouses and this is one way around diet problems.

A bed for the night

The hospitality traditionally offered by monasteries and convents around the world is still available today. If you have little money, knock on the door and say so – you are likely to find a meal and a bed for the night. A bit of gardening or cleaning is usually welcomed as a way of repaying such hospitality, bearing in mind that many religious communities are either poor or have too few members to fulfil their practical needs. Many monasteries still have rooms only for guests of the same gender as members of their own community, though this is changing.

Further information

The Good Retreat Guide by Stafford Whiteaker (Rider £12.99) lists over 400 places in Britain, Ireland, France and Spain; *Sanctuaries* by J & M. Kelly (Bell Tower, NY) covers the USA. In France try the *Guide des Centres Bouddhistes en France* (Editions Noésis, Paris) and the *Guide des Monastères* by Maurice Colinon (Editions Pierre Horay). For India, *From Here to Nirvana* by Anne Cushman and Jerry Jones (Rider £12.99). A variety of guides to retreat centres is published annually in Italy. For other countries you will probably need to contact a religious organisation to find out what is on offer.

OTHER CONTACTS: Retreats Association, 256 Bermondsey Street, London SE1 3UJ (020 7357 7736); Friends of the Western Buddhist Order, 51 Roman Road, Bethnal Green, London E2 OHU (020 7981 1225).

STAFFORD WHITEAKER is author of 'The Good Retreat Guide'.

The travelling artist
by Mary-Anne Bartlett

TRAVEL INCREASES CREATIVITY. Making art has become my reason to travel. Over the course of the past eight years, I have found myself exchanging portraits with Siberian snow sculptors, painting murals in international airports, sketching curry-eating camels in India, drawing colourful market scenes across Europe and recording countless exhilarating sights in National Parks in Africa, most recently tracking black rhinoceros, sketchbook in hand....

Travel is inspiring. It requires us to think and act creatively. Nomadic artists can take their skill anywhere in the world and, with few materials, can enjoy brilliant cross-cultural communication and follow other interests, such as social development or wildlife conservation. Travel art is a healthy throwback to Victorian-style documentation, first-hand message-bearing in a medium packed with memory and personal information – and it allows its future viewers to travel in their imagination.

All artists should travel with a flexible mind on subject matter. However, if you are determined to catch a particular subject, then do your research and go to the right place for it. Nudist beaches are great if you want to do life drawing!

What kind of an artist are you?

There are three types of artists who travel: the 'painting traveller', the 'artist on holiday' and the 'travel artist'.

The painting traveller travels to see the world, but takes a sketch-book, pencil and paints as an alternative to diary and camera. Filling the pages is highly enjoyable and relaxing, can fill the empty hours spent waiting for buses, creates an essential time-out space apart from fellow travellers and makes for a fascinating record.

The artist on holiday usually has a sketching or painting habit, so has planned to allow room for this. Over the last 15 years there has been a proliferation in enticing art interest holidays and courses worldwide, from luxury to trek style, for all standards and all media, often also offering gallery and museum opportunities for culture vultures. *Painting Holiday Directory* editor, Anne Hedley, advises potential bookers to read publicity material carefully and ask the right questions about teaching, media, style, accommodation and comfort. Art magazines *Artists & Illustrators, The Artist* and *Leisure Painter* publish special holiday issues and have cornered the advertising market for art courses and holidays.

The travel artist is a professional who travels in order to collect images, either as sketches or as source material, for studio work back home, for exhibition and publication.

Expeditions occasionally take professional artists with them to document the trip. Invariably the artist is roped into doing some research work and needs to strike a balance between this and their own work. The Royal Geographical Society should be the first port of call when you're trying to find out about expeditions, though my first expedition was with a university.

Travel bursaries for artists do exist (for artists to develop their own work and take influence from other cultures and craft expertise), as do artist-in-residence schemes abroad (where you are developing your own work *in situ*) and international commissions (where you have a specific subject to document creatively). The *Artist's Newsletter* gives details of residencies and travel grant information in each issue. The national grants register in your local library and your regional arts board will also be valuable as sources of information.

Equally, if you are brave enough to go to an unknown country and show your work and say, "I'm an artist", then expect to have incredible adventures, encounter brilliant people and be shown rare sights. Research and relevant contacts are essential, being open to opportunities is more important still. If you are spending a long time in a country it is possible to set up an exhibition. The artist and expat communities will feed you with ideas and contacts, and give you the courage to visit the embassies, NGOs, government offices, businesses and individuals who might be able to help. Financial assistance is unlikely, but help in kind can be overwhelmingly generous. Key cultural contacts vary between countries, according to historical activity and the current directorship. I have found that the British Council, the French Cultural Institute, the British and American embassies, and various countries' government ministries for arts or culture, are all extremely helpful.

> *Moonlight is sculpture, sunlight is painting.*
> – NATHANIEL HAWTHORNE

Audiences

Whichever kind of travelling artist you are, you will be a performance artist. Whether it's Leicester Square or Machu Picchu, a crowd will appear to watch. Adults and children can keep up an excited chatter of comment and laughter as you build the image, blocking the view and challenging your concentration and patience to breaking point. I find that if you remain unruffled and concentrate on your subject, with a certain amount of polite and jovial view-clearing, people will allow you to continue with your work. If you're lucky there might be a chorus of "ooohs" and "aaahs"; drawing is often seen as magical and treated with respect and awe in countries where images are still scarce. I always hold up the finished item for the crowd to see, however dreadful I think it is. It's rare to get immediate audiences for visual art, so we should enjoy it!

Materials

The amount and type of equipment you need will depend on your medium and how quickly you go through materials. You will need to consider whether you want exhibition-quality materials. Don't rely on being able to find art materials in the country you're travelling to; you can always give away excess materials at the end of your stay to local artists.

I take pencils and watercolour equipment when travelling, with a mass of sketch-books and loose-leaf paper of all formats. I then take the odd diversion into local crafts if I feel the whim (most embarrassingly when an ebony tree was presented to me because I had said I enjoyed woodcarving).

As a rough guide, this is the list of materials that I took for a recent six-month painting trip in East Africa:

1. Full pan 24-colour watercolour box.
2. Travellers' full pan 12-colour watercolour box.
3. Watercolour brushes in a tube.
4. Ten sketch-books (avoid spiral-bound books).
5. Loose-leaf watercolour and drawing paper (in waterproof A1 portfolio).
6. Selection of pencils and graphite sticks.
7. White gum rubber.
8. Putty rubber.
9. Water bottle and mug.
10. Scalpel.
11. Lightweight board.
12. Bulldog clips.

I took two sets of watercolours, as I thought these would be difficult to replace. In addition, I find that binoculars, clothing with big pockets, a hat, a good daysack and A1-size plastic bags are vital equipment.

The creative dimension

I feel very strongly that creativity adds a further dimension to the riches of travel. The keen observation needed for taking down visual images gives a heightened awareness of a new environment. You take time to look at detail, recognise the differences, appreciate and gently imbibe the wonders, without judgement.

If you spend longer than a couple of days painting in a place you will soon be regarded as a regular, even as a fellow worker, and you find that you are accepted and welcomed by local people. This brings a great sense of belonging.

Your images (especially portraits) can work for you as passports in tourist-hostile places and you can win people's hearts if you depict subjects of local pride (be it the fish market, the bus stop or the village pump), providing you with an accurate social document.

Lastly, remember that the time you spend is encapsulated in the finished artwork, meaning that in months and years to come you can look at a painting and recall that concentrated timeframe in all its magical detail.

Contacts

The Arts Council of England, 14 Great Peter Street, London SW1P 3NQ (tel 020 7333 0100, fax 020 7973 6590, email enquiries@artscouncil.org.uk, website www.artscouncil.org.uk)

The British Council, 10 Spring Gardens, London SW1A 2BN (tel 020 7930 8466, fax 020 7389 6347, email general.enquiries@britcoun.org, website www.britcoun.org)

The Directory of Grantmaking Trusts (held in public libraries)

The Writers' and Artists' Handbook (published by A&C Black)

The Royal Geographical Society, Kensington Gore, London SW7 2AR (tel 020 7591 3000, fax 020 7591 3001).

The Painting Holiday Directory, PO Box 1 Ponteland, Newcastle upon Tyne NE19 2EB (tel/fax 01830 540215, website www.wavenet.co.uk/users/kirkland/phd)

Artists and Illustrators, Quarto Magazines Ltd, The Fitzpatrick Building, 188-194 York Way, London N7 9QR.

Leisure Painter, The Artists' Publishing Company Ltd, Caxton House, 63-65 High Street, Tenterden, Kent TN30 6BD.

Artists' Newsletter (and helpline), 1st Floor, Turner Building, 7-15 Pink Lane, Newcastle upon Tyne NE1 5DW (website www.anweb.co.uk)

Asekela Painting Holidays, 14 Model Cottages, Vapery Lane, Pirbright, Woking, Surrey GU24 0QB (tel 01483 480092).

Indian Romance, 46 Masbro Road, London W14 0LT (tel/fax 020 7603 9616).

Paint Away, Indus Tours and Travel Ltd, MWB Business Exchange, 2 Gayton Road, Harrow, Middlesex HA1 2XU (tel 020 8901 7320, fax 020 8901 7321). 🐚

MARY-ANNE BARTLETT is a travel artist and printmaker, specialising in East Africa. She has undertaken work on location for the Scientific Exploration Society and the British Council, among others.

The cultural traveller
by Kenneth Asch

THERE ARE OCCASIONS IN (A JOURNALIST'S) LIFE when, telling others where you've been or are about to go, you find yourself hearing the inevitable. "Goodness," my audience usually exclaims, a tinge of envy colouring their voice, "you must have seen the whole world."

"Far from it," is my instant response. The world is vast and the more I travel, the more I know there is yet to be seen. This is something that is especially true in the interior sense. How often has the joy of discovery been greatest when I have found myself at the most unheralded, least picturesque turning in the road, among the local inhabitants?

I had a favourite aunt, a *grande dame* wealthy enough to indulge every desire that a young nephew could only dream of. I sweated over times tables, she flew, she cruised into the sunset, she travelled. There was one particular journey she relished describing, a round-the-world expedition on a fabled ship. Her discoveries in the most exotic ports of call, it eventually became apparent, extended all the way to the ship's rail. She was as pleased as punch to recite in detail such journeys. And she always brought out the evidence, the trinkets paddled by the natives from shore to ship where they would be exchanged for coins chucked from the deck into the bobbing canoes.

I have no doubt that cruising in sight of foreign shores with an occasional tentative foray into the town beyond to break the spell is precisely the kind of holiday that, now and then, is the only kind that will do. If, however, you are the kind of traveller who takes a cue from a thoughtful guidebook, chances are that you are looking for something more substantial.

Which is where a much-abused word – *culture* – enters the scene. In fact, there are two words here, one with an upper-case 'C', the other its lower-case cousin. It's the latter version that's the more fascinating, as lower-case culture embraces just about every aspect of the destination you are giving so much of yourself to enjoy.

Can you imagine that there are people who disdain Holland because it is flat? Or ridicule Switzerland because it has, allegedly, created nothing more useful to civilisation than the cuckoo clock? (This was Orson Welles's error, Germany's Black Forest being the home of this cute invention.) If these people could see beyond such prosaic perspectives they would find enough to lure them back time and again. As a specialist in organising cultural travel explained, the secret of discovering and understanding a place is finding the most congenial avenue into it.

For example, I lived in New York for long periods, and suddenly finding myself having to write about it as a travel destination, was confronted with the obvious challenge. Too much to do in too cramped an area with far too few comfortable benches for sitting back and taking it all in. Central Manhattan alone is more than most people can cope with, so they concentrate on the popular, blockbuster sights. Customarily they emerge from the experience exhilarated by the city's legendary buzz, but the cost is virtual exhaustion. And ultimately how much of the essential Manhattan have they really seen?

The solution I discovered – New York via the Art Deco Route – has become a formula I began applying to other destinations. The idea, in Manhattan's case, was that by tracing the development of an architectural style around the borough, I first of all gave myself a necessary focus. I was immediately aware that many of Manhattan's other sights, especially the ones that had always seemed relatively inaccessible and less familiar, suddenly took on interesting new perspectives.

Because of its vast sweep of natural beauty, history and culture contained in such a tiny area, Israel similarly is among the most challenging places to visit, but hugely rewarding given a sensible route. My Art Deco experience suggested itself and I came up with a formula that has taken me and my photographer to every corner of the Holy Land. We call it "Israel, a musical focus". There aren't many nations where every imaginable kind of music is so successfully combined with its surroundings, making the whole experience greater than the sum of its parts.

I am particularly fortunate. My principal line of work, being music, has opened doors to unexpected and unfamiliar worlds from which otherwise I would largely be excluded. But if music journalism based on a working knowledge of some of the world's great stages is not a career that is open to everyone, it is still possible for the casual traveller to enjoy the interior worlds which exist beyond the experiences of, well, my wealthy aunt.

Fortunately there are excellent tour operators in the UK offering imaginative packages along these lines, often accompanied by expert guides. The exciting aspect of culture is that there is a wide variety of possible avenues by which a destination's character may be enjoyed. ATG (Alternative Travel Group) Oxford's trips are based on the premise that the best way to see a country is on foot. All aspects of the local and historical culture are absorbed into the itinerary: ancient trails linking medieval hill towns, wine, food, fresco-filled churches – and you reside in characteristic hotels that are often family run. ATG's own Romanesque monastery, Pieve a Castello in Tuscany, for example, offers residential week-long courses in painting, cookery and music, the latter tying in with the nearby Siena Music Festival. All escorted trips (you can book independently as well) are guided by trilingual graduates in order to assure that clients understand all aspects of the area visited. For more information, contact ATG Oxford, 69-71 Banbury Road, Oxford OX2 6PE (tel 01865 315664/fax 01865 315 697/8/9).

If you want to broaden your horizons beyond opera, Liaisons Abroad is your ticket. Maxine Caneva is the heart and soul of something rather unique, in that her company has privileged access to tickets for Siena's Palio, Venetian carnival balls, Six Nations rugby, Formula One racing, UEFA Cup football, Italian 'A league' and more. Drag hunting near Rome, personal shopping in the most famous fashion houses and dinners in private *palazzi* are just some of the subsidiary pleasures that add that memorable extra dimension, perhaps, to witnessing productions of Verdi's greatest operas at Verona's historic Arena,

As for churches, and pictures, I have stared at them till my brains are like a guide-book.
– LORD BYRON

or Puccini's at the Torre del Lago open-air festival. Liaisons Abroad has its own ticket allocations with most of Europe's leading opera houses and festivals, as well as for special events such as the Pavarotti International, which takes place in the great tenor's hometown Modena; Three Tenors' concerts and celebrity performances worldwide. The provision of tickets to those booking through mainstream package holiday operators is a unique feature of this service. Contact Maxine Caneva on tel 020 7376 4020, fax 020 7376 4442, email info@lisiaonsabroad.com, website www.liaisonsabroad.com

Voyages Jules Verne is among the travel industry's premier names. I like their description of an Andalucian experience that commences at the Palace of the Alhambra and culminates at Gibraltar. 'Take the attitude to life of its inhabitants or the local culture,' says its brochure, 'which owes more to its "*Gitano*" Flemish roots in the vigour of the Flamenco and its Moorish ancestry than it does to Spain proper. There is a vibrancy and a lust for living that is apparent in the music and the pursuits of its people – the horsemanship, the *Zapateado* dance, or the Flamenco guitar.' For more information, call Voyages Jules Verne on 020 7616 1000 or fax 020 7723 8629, email sales@vjv.co.uk, website www.vjv.co.uk

Of all the travel services I have researched, Martin Randall Travel is perhaps the most comprehensive, culturally speaking. One example from its brochure suffices. 'The festival in Aix-en-Provence is one of the most enjoyable and esteemed of Europe's summer music events. The utterly charming old capital of Provence, graced with a profusion of seventeenth- and eighteenth-century mansions, quiet squares, arcades and a lively café life, provides a superb setting for a feast of first-rate opera and concerts. As with all our music tours, there is a gentle programme of walks and excursions designed to show the best of the region's art and architecture without taxing the participants' energies at the expense of the music'. Contact Martin Randall Travel for more information (tel 020 8742 3355, fax 020 8742 7766, email info@martinrandall.co.uk).

If I were choosing to go in search of life under one of Europe's most powerful and controversial rulers, the Habsburg Emperor Charles v in 2000, the 500th anniversary year of his birth, the British Museum Traveller would be where I would register myself. Operating curator-led tours the world over, both for members and non-members, this world-famous institution claims to be among the pioneers, over the past ten years of its own existence, of culturally focused trips to unusual destinations such as Libya, Georgia, Armenia, Sudan, Madagascar, Saudi Arabia and along the Silk Route. Call the British Museum Traveller on 020 7323 8895, or fax on 020 7580 8677.

Cox & Kings is the longest-established travel company in the world – it was founded in 1758 to act as agents for the British Army in India. Two and a half centuries on and the company still specialises in cultural and natural history tours of the subcontinent. It maintains offices in every part of the country and provides personalised service, as much for those on the trail of the most-often visited destinations – the Taj Mahal and Jaipur being two distinguished examples – as it does for those travelling to the offbeat but equally enthralling places found in every corner of this vast region. In recent years the company has broadened its horizons by offering specialist cultural programmes in Latin America, the Middle East and southern Africa. In all instances Cox & Kings offers both brochure-designed tours for groups as well as individuals in addition to custom-made itineraries designed by expert travel consultants at the company's London HQ.

Contact Cox & Kings Cultural Tours on 020 7873 5000, or by fax on 020 7630 6038, email: Cox.Kings@coxandkings.co.uk, website: www.coxandkings.co.uk ✍

KEN ASCH is a freelance arts journalist and broadcaster. For 20 years he was a principal bass soloist for various opera companies and symphony orchestras, and has also stage-managed many musical and theatrical performances.

The wine-loving traveller
by Andrew Barr

IN ORDER TO TASTE GOOD WINE, YOU DO NOT NEED TO LEAVE HOME. You do not even need to leave your house. One telephone call, and the finest wines in the world can be delivered to your front door. Such a wide range of wines is imported into Britain and North America nowadays that it is possible to drink wine instead of travelling, as a means of experiencing another country's culture vicariously.

Nothing captures the smells and tastes of the place from which it comes better than a bottle of wine, made from grapes harvested in a single vineyard in the autumn of a single year.

The taste of the soil

Admittedly, most ordinary wines are made from a blend of grapes from different vineyards and are subjected to extensive processing, causing them to taste much like one another, but it is the purpose of fine wines to express the character of the raw material from which they have been made, to allow the flavours inherent in the grapes to express themselves. The buzz word in the wine world at the moment is '*terroir*', which literally means 'soil' but actually refers to the whole environment in which the grapes are grown. This should be expressed in the taste of the wine, through a '*goût du terroir*'. A Cabernet Sauvignon from California will never taste like a red Bordeaux (claret) nor a Chardonnay from Australia like a white burgundy, however hard the wine-makers may try to follow the same methods, because the warmer climates naturally express themselves in riper, fruitier flavours in the wines. In general, however, the characteristics of terroir are much less obvious than this; and are expressed through subtle differences that can only be appreciated by travelling to the place where the grapes have grown, by gaining one's own sense of the environment.

Out of the way

This environment may well be one that you would not otherwise experience, because most fine wines are produced in out-of-the-way places. Historically, in Europe, fertile farmland was too precious to waste on growing a crop intended for inebriation rather than nutrition, and vines were restricted to poor soils that could not support other forms of agriculture. Ironically, this accounts for the origin of fine wine. In poor soils, vines have to dig deep to find moisture and nutrients, and produce small crops of finely flavoured fruit. If they were to be grown on lush farmland, they would have it too easy, and produce large quantities of fat but tasteless grapes. The best vineyards are situated on the sides of hills and valleys, and sometimes half-way up mountains.

The same is true of countries in what wine connoisseurs still insist quaintly in describing as the New World – the Americas, Australasia and South Africa – but for a different reason. These countries are generally too warm for fine wines: grapes ripen too quickly, and develop coarse, 'cooked' flavours. The solution is to go up hills and mountains, where the climate is cooler, or (in the case of California) to seek out remote coastal valleys that are cooled by afternoon fogs.

As a result, vineyard scenery can be magnificent. Best of all is probably Rippon Vineyard on the South Island of New Zealand, on the shores of Lake Wanaka and overlooked by the Southern Alps. The price of their beauty is that the vineyards can be hard to find. If you contact the trade department of the relevant embassy in Britain or the United States, they should be able to put you in touch with the official representative body of the wine region you are intending to visit, which should be able to supply you with information and maps. Guides to a few vine-growing regions are also produced by Mitchell Beazley under the series titles, *Touring in Wine Country* and *Wine Atlas*, but be warned that Hugh Johnson's famous *World Atlas of Wine* is not detailed enough for this purpose.

When to go

The difficulty of finding some vineyards can be compounded if you visit them at the one time of year you can be sure the wine-maker will be able to receive you – the middle of winter. I spent several years travelling through fog, ice and snow in Burgundy in January because estates there are essentially one-man operations and I needed to see the person in charge. The underground cellars were slightly warmer than the air outside but I still kept on my overcoat. I also found it essential to wear thermal socks and boots with thick soles. If this does not appeal, then wine-makers also have some free time in the middle of summer – of which they often take advantage in order to go on holiday.

The period when wine-makers are busiest and are least able to see you is unfortunately also the best time to visit, during the harvest in the autumn. You can see the grapes being picked (still usually by hand) and the wine being made, and taste the previous year's vintage. Grapes are harvested in the northern hemisphere in September and October, and in the southern hemisphere in March and April. (It took me a long time to accept that natural events really do occur the other way round in the southern hemisphere. When Australian wine-makers first told me that their vineyards faced north, towards the sun, rather than south, as in the northern hemisphere, I was convinced they were pulling my leg.)

Catching your wine-maker

You will definitely miss out, however, if the wine-maker is unable to see you. Like dogs and cars, wines tend to reflect the character and self-image of the people responsible for them. It is very difficult to appreciate the style of a particular wine without meeting the man or woman who has made it. Contrary to what a wine-maker may claim ("the wine just makes itself"), personality does influence terroir.

In order to persuade a wine-maker to make the time to see you, it is helpful to obtain a recommendation, through a merchant who imports the wine into Britain or America, through the official representative body in the area, or through a local restaurant. The last of these is often a very good place to try a wine that you might not have encountered back home. The restaurateur will generally be flattered if you ask to try an interesting local wine, and, if you like it, will be especially keen to give you a recommendation that will ensure you are well received by the producer.

Communication

Once you have caught your wine-maker, he is likely to be friendly. People who grow grapes and make wine generally do so because they love it. If they happen to have inherited a vineyard but are not interested in wine, they will not bother to make wine themselves but will sell their grapes to someone else. Wine-makers are certainly not in the business to make money. It is often said that, in order to make a small fortune in the wine business, it is necessary to invest a large one.

Wine-makers are friendly but, in a business where the product continues to be consumed for decades after it was made, they have long memories. If, when being shown round an estate in France by an older wine-maker, he asks you whether you are German before taking you down to his cellar, please remember that the correct answer to this question is "No". In that case, he will warn you to avoid knocking your head on the stone lintel above the steps.

Because they make wines as an expression of their personality, wine-makers are generally keen to communicate. They are not necessarily comprehensible, however. Many of them use technical language or refer philosophically to the influence of *terroir*. There are also a number of ex-pot-heads in the wine business in California and Oregon who lost part of their brain to drugs a generation ago and may have some difficulty in expressing themselves in a manner that other people can readily understand. Nor do wine-makers tend to be linguists. Large commercial wineries in Europe will organise guided tours in English, but at small estates the wine-maker will almost certainly be able to speak only in his own language (and often with a heavy regional accent).

Commercial wineries

I would not generally recommend visiting large commercial wineries, where you will be forced to relinquish all hope of dialogue with a like-minded individual and abandon yourself to a well-organised publicity machine. Worst of all, you will probably be obliged to spend some time observing the workings of the company's bottling line, an experience that provides roughly the same degree of enjoyment as filling in one's annual tax return.

This said, it is well worth visiting one of the big Champagne companies in order to see the huge underground cellars where they mature their wines, and where they will demonstrate the elaborate process by which the bottles are gradually turned to bring the sediment to the cork. With the exception of the wine, however, Champagne is a pretty boring part of the world. There is Rheims cathedral, but otherwise its main virtue lies in its proximity to Paris.

Organised tours

The easy solution to the problems of travelling at the time of your choice, of arranging appointments with English-speaking wine-makers, and of avoiding the most commercial wineries, is to take an organised wine tour with a specialist company. These are package tours, it is true, but of a very civilised kind. In traditional wine regions they will enable you to see prestigious estates that would not otherwise receive you. For example, the American company France In Your Glass organises visits to top Bordeaux châteaux such as Margaux and d'Yquem and leading Burgundy estates, including those of Roumier and Dujac. The premier British wine tour company is Arblaster and Clarke. If you want to touch the cutting edge of the wine revolution, you might think of taking their tour to Chile and Argentina. There are also wine-and-walking tours, wine-and-cycling tours, wine-and-camping tours, wine-and-skiing tours, wine-and-cruise tours, wine-and-big-game tours, wine-and-classical-music tours, and so on *ad infinitum*.

Specialist wine tour operators

Accompanied Cape Tours, Hill House, Much Marcle, Ledbury, Hereford and Worcester HR8 2NX (tel 01531 660210).

Allez France, 27 West Street, Storrington, West Sussex RH20 4DZ (tel 01903 748100).

Arblaster and Clarke, Farnham Road, West Liss, Hants GU33 6JQ (tel 01730 893344, website www.arblasterandclarke.com).

Backroads, 9 Shaftesbury Street, Fordingbridge, Hants SP6 1JF (tel 01425 655022).

DER Travel Service, 18 Conduit Street, London W1R 9TD (tel 020 7290 1111).

Eurocamp, Hartford Manor, Greenbank Lane, Northwich, Cheshire CW8 1HW (tel 01606 787878).

France In Your Glass, 814 35th Avenue, Seattle, WA 98122, USA (tel 1-800-578-0903, website www.inyourglass.com).

Friendship Travel, Bullimores House, Church Lane, Cranleigh, Surrey GU6 8AR (tel 01483 273355).

Fugues en France, 11 square Jean Cocteau, 91250 St German les Courbell, France (tel 33 1 6075 8833).

HCP Wine Tours, The Old Signal Box, Railway Station, Rathmore Road, Torquay, Devon TQ2 6NU (tel 01803 299292).

KD River Cruises, 28 South Street, Epsom, Surrey KT18 7PF (tel 01372 742033).

Moswin Tours, 21 Church Street, Oadby, Leics LE2 5DB (tel 0116-271 4982).

Page and Moy, 136-40 London Road, Leicester, Leics LE2 1EN (tel 0870-010 6400).

Tanglewood Wine Tours, Tanglewood House, Mayfield Avenue, New Haw, Surrey KT15 3AG (tel 01932 348720).

Wessex Wine Tours, 1 King Edward Road, Saltash, Cornwall PL12 4EQ (tel 01752 846880).

The Parker Company, 319 Lynnway, Lynn, MA 01901, USA (tel 1-800-280-2811, website www.theparkercompany.com).

Winetrails, Greenways, Vann Lane, Ockley, Dorking, Surrey RH5 5NT (tel 01306 712111, website www.winetrails.co.uk).

Wink Lorch, 5 Drovers Way, Seer Green, Beaconsfield, Bucks HP9 2XF (tel 01494 677728).

Spit or swallow

Tasting with a wine-maker in his cellar may seem a bit daunting, but he knows that you are not a professional and will expect only that you show an interest in his wine. Using a pipette, he will draw a sample of his latest vintage from a tank or wooden barrel and empty it into glasses so that you and he can taste it together. You should look at the wine against the light (if any is available), swirl it in the glass and smell it before you sip. If you can, you should suck air over the wine while holding it in your mouth, which helps to bring out its flavour, but don't worry if you can't manage this at first.

The decision whether to spit or swallow is purely personal. Obviously, if you are driving, it is wiser to spit, and the wine-maker will not be offended if you insist on so doing, but he will be flattered if you swallow the wine and then explain that it was too good to spit out. Professionals always spit, but then they can taste hundreds of wines a day. In many European wineries, tasters spit on the floor, although it is best to aim in the general direction of a drain; in America, spitting on the floor is illegal and the wine-maker may insist that you use a spittoon or bucket.

If you cannot already suck or spit like a professional, you may well find it helpful to practise these skills in the bathroom or kitchen at home before attempting them in public.

Appropriate comments

The wine-maker will expect you to make some appropriate comments about his produce. You may well have a great deal to say but, if not, the key is to remember to offer an observation that appears to have been carefully considered rather than simply describing every sample he offers you as 'delicious'. References to balance, harmony and length on the palate are always appreciated. The latter applies to the length of time you can taste the wine after spitting or swallowing and is generally considered a sign of high quality.

If the wine is tasteless, I would suggest describing it as 'elegant' or 'delicate'; if bad, then there is always 'interesting'. Alternatively, take on the wine-maker at his own game and explain how, in your opinion, his product expresses true regional character in the form of a *goût du terroir*.

Bringing wine home

You should never tip a wine-maker for showing you his wares, and you are not obliged to buy them. Wines are always much cheaper bought direct from the grower, often costing only half as much as you would pay in a shop back home, but, remember, they always seem better on the spot. They are designed to suit the local weather and food – not just in Europe, but also in the New World, where the vibrantly fruity style of many wines perfectly suits currently fashionable 'fusion' or 'Pacific Rim' cuisine. Serve them with a plate of good old British stodge in damp, grey weather and they do not taste the same at all. ❧

ANDREW BARR is a wine writer and historian, and the author of 'Wine Snobbery', 'Pinot Noir' and 'Drink: a social history'. He no longer visits Burgundy in mid-winter.

The gourmet traveller
by Paul Wade

A S A CHILD I WAS LUCKY. MY FAMILY ROAMED EUROPE during the holidays, spending time in what were then exotic spots: Dubrovnik in the former Yugoslavia, Rapallo in Italy and Salzburg in Austria. My memories are of scorched, rocky shores, pavement cafés, hulking castles and... food. Post-war Britain was still strictly a 'meat-and-two-veg' country, with powdered eggs and stock cubes in every pantry. Like a jangling alarm clock, the Mediterranean flavours of fresh tomatoes and giant watermelons woke up my taste buds. Slurping spaghetti splashed with purple squid sauce and munching a properly prepared schnitzel ensured they would never go back to sleep.

Ever since this awakening, food has been an integral part of any trip, whether it's a day out in the nearby English countryside or weeks in the distant pueblos of Mexico. With my wife, who shares the same enthusiasm, I pore over guidebooks, searching for the elusive tip that might send us to a restaurant where we can eat what the locals regard as traditional dishes. Our aim is to add taste and smell to the other three senses, which are sharpened by being on holiday.

Guided tours

Sadly, many guidebooks concentrate on museums and mosques, shopping and beaches, with food little more than an afterthought. How often is the list of 'best places to eat' merely a roll-call of the poshest French restaurants in town – whether you happen to be in Chicago or the Caribbean, Munich or Manchester? These are lists for business executives, keen to impress clients with the size of their tips and their knowledge of over-priced wines. But how can you say you understand Catalonia if you have not attended a *cocotada* (an onion barbecue, washed down with the local black wine) in Valls? How can you boast that you 'know' the USA if you have not put on a bib and tucked into a lobster in Maine or made a pilgrimage to the birthplace of the hamburger or the pizza?

By eating what we rate as the best rice in the world (in Iran), the best grass-fed beef (in Argentina), the most delicious oysters (straight from the squeaky-clean waters off the coast of Tasmania), my wife and I have rounded off our experience of those countries. We also have had the bonus of meeting the people. Interest in good food overcomes any language or cultural barrier. The fastest way to get into conversation with locals is to ask about their specialities.

Word play

Before I forget, let's be clear about what I mean by that much over-used word: 'gourmet'. Too often, along with 'connoisseur' and '*bon viveur*', it screams snob. It also shouts 'expensive'. But in my dictionary a gourmet is 'a judge of good fare', and in my experience, real 'gourmet travellers' don't need a gold credit card. Sure, once in a while, it is fun to splurge, but it is just as educational to seek out local produce that is prepared with care, in which freshness is rated higher than fashion and flavour is more important than fancy frills. That is why our holiday highlights include just as many simple meals as complex creations. The mountain *taberna* in Spain where we enjoyed thick pork chops, drizzled with lemon juice and grilled quickly over vine roots, is in no guidebook that I know – and never will be. The old lady near Cortina d'Ampezzo in Italy who used to open up her house for dinner on two nights a week died several years ago, but we will always remember her holding a vast copper pan and whipping up the most sensual warm zabaglione we have ever eaten. The texture and flavour of a pink-fleshed giant trout, freshly hooked and hot-smoked on the shore of New Zealand's Lake Taupo is forever etched on our gastro-memory.

Star signs

The problem is how to find these honest-to-goodness local dishes. Let's start with France, a country where food is so important that great chefs commit suicide if they lose a Michelin star. The famous red guide, with its mind-boggling array of wingdings, may be the bible of gastronomy, but it lacks the Bible's poetry and description. Back in the 1970s, we added the more outspoken, idiosyncratic Gault Millau guide to our library. Founded by a couple of journalists who focused on new French cooking and dared to praise innovation, this big yellow guide has rarely let us down. Years later, when the trendy wave of nouvelle cuisine and its descendants threatened to eradicate France's traditional regional dishes, Gault Millau introduced its *Lauriers du Terroir* awards. This laurel wreath symbol signifies restaurants offering dishes that *gran'mère* would have been proud of, often with portions to match. These have helped us to find unusual sweet wines in the Loire Valley, black radishes in Albi and *mouclade* (mussels in cream) on the Ile de Ré. Michelin has taken up the challenge, introducing a grinning Michelin man to point out value-for-money restaurants where food rather than formality is the priority.

These renowned guides are reliable in France but less trusty beyond its borders. The Michelin guide for Britain is notorious for praising French chefs and French-style restaurants. This is no Anglophobia; other neighbours suffer from similar chauvinism. When we are asked to choose our gastronomic heaven, we usually sigh and dream of the Engadine Valley in Graubunden, in western Switzerland. Look up five of our memorable hotel–restaurants in the Michelin guide to Switzerland, however, and the symbols tell you that they are pleasant and quiet, have terraces, exceptional views and let in dogs. What they do not and cannot tell you is that this valley is a foodie enclave, with five of our favourite chefs working close to one another, conjuring up some of the best nosh in the universe.

Empire-building

A few years ago, we were in Montreal reporting on Christmas in this most Francophile of cities. Everyone we talked to recommended 'authentic' French restaurants. These turned out to be run by expatriate Frenchmen serving up food that was considered *haute cuisine* 30 years ago. It was a classic example of the emperor's new clothes. Yet, right in the city, talented young Québecois chefs were, and still are, following the French rules on techniques and use of strictly local ingredients, yet producing totally individual results that we rated ten on the foodies' Richter scale.

It is not fair to expect such a momentous meal every night. We are just as happy with simple, clean flavours and honest dishes. Even that, however, can be difficult to find. Take the Caribbean, where the demands of the American tourist have stifled local ambition in the kitchen and swamped supermarkets with foodstuffs processed in the USA. On some small islands, it is impossible to buy locally caught fish or locally raised fruit and vegetables. Food has been replaced by T-shirts and baskets in the market, and restaurants serve American hamburgers, Italian veal *piccata* and New Orleans blackened shrimp.

When we were on the relatively unspoiled island of St John in the US Virgin Islands, we searched in vain for true Caribbean cuisine. We even tried having lunch with the taxi drivers and road builders, but heavy stews and gristly pigs' trotters defeated us in the tropical heat. The best meals we had were cooked in a tiny restaurant by an American with a Thai mother. He knew how to wheedle chickens and vegetables from the islanders' own backyards and his use of spices contributed to the sense of place that is important when in another country.

The English disease

Although the 'think local' campaign has won the hearts and minds of many chefs, another food phenomenon has swept through other kitchens. This is the 'United Nations' attitude to cooking, where ingredients from anywhere in the world are combined, with results veering between triumph and disaster. It has taken hold, in the main, in countries where English is the common language. Perhaps that's because, for example, in the USA and Australia, much of the food used to echo Britain's: plain and hearty home cooking that rarely translated successfully on to the restaurant plate.

As in the UK, chefs in these countries are now so eclectic that critics try to wedge them into pigeonholes so that readers have some idea of what to expect: 'Floribbean' for Miami chefs who draw on Florida and the Caribbean for inspiration; 'Pacific Rim' for the mixing and matching of, say, Asian spices with Peruvian purple potatoes and low-cholesterol kangaroo meat. Perhaps these novelties will eventually become classics in their own right. Perhaps not.

In trendy cities such as New York and London, 'new' has come to mean 'good', whilst 'newest' is equated with 'best'. Restaurants open every week but the star chef who stood at the stove when the first diners came through the door may have moved on to another project after a few months, leaving a deputy to maintain his and the restaurant's reputation. What was tantalising yesterday may be tired today.

Tried and tested

Consistency: that is the problem. In countries such as France and Italy, where restaurants are often family enterprises going back decades, the secret of success is to do the same thing well, day after day, year after year. Not so long ago, deep in the countryside of southern France, we ate in the same restaurant that Elizabeth David had immortalised decades before. We ordered the same chicken dish (roasted, with mushrooms stuffed under the skin) that she had enjoyed. The owners saw no reason to change a winning formula, which appealed equally to guests old and new.

Cultural cringe

So how do you find a 'good place to eat'? The restaurants we like least are those that advertise most. We avoid anywhere that sells its charms in an airline magazine or on a card at the airport. To avoid ending up in a culinary ghetto with other foreigners, we rarely take advice at hotels unless the concierge seems particularly in tune with our tastes. Unfortunately, tourism is such a rampant industry that standardisation in hotels and restaurants is not only commonplace, but even embraced by local people as a sign of new-found sophistication.

What Australians refer to so vividly as 'the cultural cringe' is a major handicap when it comes to food. Why should anyone have to imitate European-style restaurants to gain gastronomic credibility? Italian restaurants in Africa, Greek restaurants in South America, pseudo-French bistros in Japan may offer an alternative for the inhabitants but are sheer torture for us.

Heard it on the grapevine

The way we dig out good restaurants is by talking to people in the trade. If we like the look of a bakery or delicatessen, a butcher or fishmonger, we go inside and chat. Wine and cheese makers are usually a good bet, since they supply the better restaurants. Once two agree on their favourite spot, off we go.

We not only keep our eyes and ears open, we keep our noses sniffing. We watch where locals head when offices close. We listen for the happy hum of contented eating. We track down the source of delicious smells.

Then, we order the daily special, even though we may have no idea what it is. When, in a suburb of Buenos Aires, the waiter announced that the dish of the day was *mondongo*, I chose it, only to discover that it was what I hate most: tripe. My sole consolation was that it was cheap and that I had expanded my vocabulary by one word. In Tasmania recently we came across a 'bush restaurant', part of a growing trend to utilise indigenous produce, as opposed to plants and vegetables introduced by the Europeans. Here, bunya nuts, native limes and rosella petals flavoured dishes ranging from crocodile and sweet potato spring rolls to wattle grubs. Although these may not be recipes to replicate at home, they certainly provide the raw ingredients for travellers' tales.

How often persons who have travelled around the world tell you so earnestly that they found a place in Venice where they served American ham and eggs.
– ALFRED CARL HOTTES

Of course, you don't have to go to such extremes of geography and gastronomy. Europe may seem old hat since we are all part of the EU, but familiarity need not breed contempt. After all, with barely a wave of a passport, we can order mouthwatering meals in 15 different countries, each with dozens of regional cuisines.

Travel only broadens the mind when you meet and talk to people. You don't get into discussions of pop music or politics while touring a castle or cathedral. You don't expect to argue about education or the environment while bronzing on a beach. Understanding another culture comes more easily with a glass in one hand and a fork in the other. Years ago, in a bar in Madrid, we ordered some tapas, including *pulpo*. The Spaniard next to us was incredulous: "Do you really want *pulpo*? Do you know what it is? Do you like it?" When we answered "Si" to each question, he grinned his approval and quipped, "You cannot be English if you like octopus." It was the beginning of a long and enjoyable evening. ❧

PAUL WADE is a freelance travel journalist, guidebook writer and broadcaster.

The vegetarian traveller
by Andrew Sanger

WHAT DOES A VEGETARIAN DO WHEN INVITED by a smiling, rough-and-ready truck-driver in Eastern Turkey to join his family for dinner in a small village at the end of a long, dusty track?

In many ways, limitations on what you eat, what you do and where you will go are anathema to the traveller. An open mind and a willingness to adapt make a much better approach. However, we all carry a few ethical ideas in our mental rucksack, and some of these principles are worth keeping. After all, we preserve our own moral standards when at home – even if the 'locals' don't agree with us – so it's reasonable to do the same when abroad.

For vegetarians, this isn't easy. It's not just the food, but attitudes. In most parts of the world, vegetarians are regarded as mere harmless foreign lunatics. Certain countries do have vegetarians of their own: they generally have either opted to give up meat for health reasons, or they are enjoined to do so on religious grounds. Some in Europe (mainly Holland and Germany) have a political commitment to avoiding meat because of the waste of resources that it entails. Few outside the Anglo-Saxon world have any sympathy with the notion (or have even come across it) that wantonly killing animals is actually wrong. Indeed, if they were to hear it, most would fiercely oppose the idea.

A problem arises when your morality is totally at odds with that of the people around you – especially when your views are seen as a Western luxury or as an absurd ethnocentricity.

Culture and circumstances impose a diet that is right for a given people. So it can sometimes be wise (if all you want is food and no arguments) to offer the most acceptable explanation for your own vegetarianism. Among friends this may not be necessary. In everyday encounters, however, you'll get the best out of people if you can either claim to be "on a diet", possibly under medical supervision, or dress

Websites for vegetarian travellers

www.focusguides.com/p172.htm#vegetarian – links for vegetarian travellers

www.vrg.org/travel/travelbb.htm – a bulletin board for vegetarian travellers

up personal ethics as part of some religious persuasion. Above all, don't try to persuade people that they, too, should give up meat.

On the road it's essential to be flexible. Even meat-eating travellers may be faced with food (sheep's eyes, for example) that they find hard to swallow. My approach is simply to avoid meat and fish as much as possible. Usually it is possible, and with no greater hardship than a rather monotonous diet at times.

In Greece, for example, a vegetarian must be happy with lots of delicious *horiatiki* salad, fresh bread and oily vegetables; or, in France, some marvellous four-course meals in which the main dish is always omelette; or, in a dozen other countries, meals consisting entirely of snacks or a succession of starters. Some countries are easier than others. In Italy, where pasta usually comes before the main course, it usually is the main course for vegetarians. Mercifully, Italy is one of those places where nobody bats an eyelid at such eccentricities, and pasta comes in a score of different forms with a dozen different meatless sauces. Meatless pizzas are everywhere, and many Italian cheeses, such as gorgonzola, are made commercially without animal rennet.

In north-west Europe, eating habits are decidedly meaty, or fishy (especially in Scandinavia). But there are so many vegetarians that almost all cities and a good number of provincial towns have eating places that cater to meat-free consumers. Holland and Germany, like Britain, have thousands of such establishments. You can hit cultural differences with your fellow vegetarians, though. For example, to a typical Anglo-Saxon lacto-vegetarian (i.e. milk products allowed) there can seem a streak of masochism in the monastic simplicity – the alcohol-free, raw food veganism – espoused by so many Scandinavian vegetarians.

Further east in Europe, there's a hefty meat culture – often just artless slabs accompanied by potatoes and cabbages, and followed by lard-rich sticky cakes. This is not invariably the case. The Czech Republic, or at least Prague, seems now to enjoy an abundance of cuisine of all kinds.

One of the best parts of the world for vegetarian travellers is the Middle East. Israel, above all, is a land of meat-free snacks and meals. All sorts of cultural reasons account for this. Many Jews are vegetarian, but in any case Jewish dietary laws prohibit the mixing of meat and milk within several hours of each other. This has led to a proliferation of 'dairy' restaurants in which nothing on the menu (not even the cheese) contains any meat products. Note, though, that dairy restaurants do serve fish.

Israelis particularly like salads, even for breakfast, eaten with yoghurt-like milk products. More salad at lunch time or in the evening is accompanied by fried, meat-free items such as *falafel* (like meatballs, but made of chickpeas), *blintzes* (filled, rolled pancakes), *latkes* (fried grated potato) and *borekas* (little savoury pastries with fillings). Some of these have been brought to the country from Eastern Europe, others are native Middle Eastern dishes, reflecting the differing origins of the refugees who make up Israel's population.

In neighbouring Arab countries (not the Maghreb, though), and in Turkey, several of the same delicious snacky dishes can be found. A traditional Arab *mezze* (a meal consisting of many small items served all at once) can be made of such dishes, although in the Islamic world it is hard indeed to get anyone to accept that you truly don't want any meat.

That's not particular to Islam. In much of fervently Christian South America, meat is the be-all and end-all of cookery. While I was in Brazil, a crisis involving farmers led to meat shortages that actually sparked off riots – even though nothing else was in short supply. There I managed happily, mainly on salads, fruit and bread. North America has followed a similar path, despite closer historic links with north-western Europe. True, there's a good magazine called *Vegetarian Times* (website www.vegetariantimes.com), and hundreds of 'veggie' eateries scattered about – in the big cities or around university campuses – but on the whole North America is still hooked on meat. Often the only alternative seems to be a cheese sandwich (with dubious American 'cheese'). One consolation: American vegetarians are not usually into austerity and self denial.

It's perhaps too reminiscent of holiday-makers who go abroad loaded with the familiar foods of home, but don't be unwilling to put some emergency rations in your luggage. I have staved off hunger on countless occasions – and in every continent – with a small bag of muesli mixed with milk powder. It can be turned into a nourishing, tasty and filling snack just by adding water. If there's milk, yoghurt or fruit juice on hand, so much the better.

The one country where vegetarianism is really normal and meat-eaters in the minority is India. Hindus are supposed to steer clear of all meat (including eggs), but yoghurt is eaten in abundance. Most Hindu eating places at the poorer end of the scale are completely vegetarian, as are the smarter (but entirely un-Western) Brahmin restaurants. Travellers tend to find themselves in a different class of establishment, quasi-European in a dignified, old-fashioned way, as if the days of Raj were not quite forgotten. Railway stations, for example, usually have a good dining room divided into meat and vegetarian sections. Many hotels do likewise. Muslim or Christian regions, say Kashmir or Goa, are less reliable. But similarly, beyond India, pockets of Hinduism provide resources throughout South-East Asia.

The places where vegetarianism is best known, and often quite well catered for, tend to be those countries formerly under British influence. Australia – which also benefits from Middle Eastern and Indian immigration – is an obvious example. And, though most major scheduled airlines have now come to grips with providing meatless tray meals, it's not for patriotic reasons that I often commend British Airways to vegetarian travellers. They are more aware of what vegetarians want and more serious about providing it than most of their competitors. When booking, you can opt for lacto-vegetarian, vegan or Oriental vegetarian in-flight meals. Other airlines capable of providing (rather than just promising to provide) a decent meatless meal include Air India, El Al and Swissair.

But to return to earth. I did accept the Turkish truck-driver's invitation. A goat was slaughtered and served, with no accompaniment but bread. I picked reluctantly at the meat, hoping no one would notice. While we men ate and the women peeked from the kitchen door, the severed head of the animal gazed at us horribly from the end of the table. Rough drinks were poured and we toasted mutual understanding. ❧

ANDREW SANGER *is the author of 'The Vegetarian Traveller',*
published by Grafton (available from www.focusguides.com).

The expeditionary
by Shane Winser

FOR MANY, INDEPENDENT TRAVEL IS A DAUNTING TASK, and the prospect of joining a group with a pre-determined objective is attractive. Others may feel that they wish to make a contribution to the communities or environment through which they travel. The options open to such individuals are enormous: from adventure holidays to community work and scientific fieldwork overseas. The better-known and well-established groups can be found in specialist directories or on the internet. It may be more difficult to find out about the credentials of smaller and/or newly emerging groups. Almost all will require some sort of financial contribution. Don't be afraid to ask questions, either about the organisation itself or what your payment covers. Try and get a feel for the organisation, and if you are not happy with its overall aims or the attitudes of the people who run it, don't sign up.

Whether you want to climb Everest, walk to the South Pole or visit a remote tropical island, there is now a tour company out there to help you achieve your dream. Naturally, you pay for someone else to organise your expedition, but the preparation time and responsibilities for you are correspondingly less. For example, the WEXAS members' Discoverers brochure has many such trips; others are advertised in outdoor-interest magazines and the national press. The useful directory *Adventure Holidays* (Vacation Work Publications, 9 Park End Street, Oxford OX1 1HJ, tel 01865 241978, website www.vacationwork.co.uk) lists holidays by the type of sport or activity. Magazines such as T*raveller, Wanderlust, Global Adventure* and *Geographical*, and the travel sections of the weekend newspapers, are useful for finding out more about the unusual and exotic.

There is an increasing trend to combine an adventurous journey with the challenge of raising funds for a charitable cause. The initial financial contribution required to join these charity fund-raising expeditions is often low, but the effort required to meet both challenges can be immense. Be prepared to train hard. Whatever the organisers tell you, you need to be fit and acclimatised to the conditions you are going to meet. And when it is all over and your friends' hard-earned cash is on the way to the charity, satisfy yourself that it is being well spent on a cause dear to your heart.

Adventure holidays and genuine expeditions differ in many ways. A scientific expedition will be expected to add to human knowledge, to 'discover' something new. Those joining such expeditions will usually be expected to give up considerable time to help with preparations, be whole-heartedly committed to the project's overall aim and objectives, and be capable of working as a skilled member of the team. And that is to say nothing of the efforts required to raise the necessary funds for the expedition.

In Britain, the Royal Geographical Society (with The Institute of British Geographers) at 1 Kensington Gore, London sw7 2ar (website www.rgs.org) is the principal organisation concerned with helping those carrying out scientific expeditions overseas. Through the work of its Expedition Advisory Centre (tel 020 7591 3030), the rgs-ibg provides information, advice and training to 500 or so groups each year – groups that carry out scientific and adventure- and youth-oriented projects abroad. For those who have a clear idea of what they want to do and have already formed a group of like-minded individuals, the centre has a number of useful services, including the annual seminar on planning a small expedition that takes place each November.

Many of the groups helped by the centre are based at schools and universities, as the principle of outdoor adventure and challenge is widely accepted as an important training ground both for young people and potential managers alike. As a result, a number of charitable and commercial organisations now offer expeditions to people of all ages. The Expedition Advisory Centre publishes a directory of these, entitled *Joining an Expedition.* The directory includes advice on choosing an appropriate project and ideas for raising funds to join projects. Many of the organisations listed in the directory can also be accessed via the Expedition Advisory Centre's website (www.rgs.org/eac). Individuals with special

We climbed and climbed, and we kept on climbing; we reached about 40 summits, but there was always another one just ahead.
– Mark Twain

skills to offer – doctors, nurses, mechanics and scientists – are invited to become listed in the register of personnel available for expeditions that is maintained by the centre and used by expedition organisers to recruit skilled volunteers and staff.

Amongst the well-established youth-focused exploration societies, there are:

■ Brathay Exploration Group (Brathay Hall, Ambleside, Cumbria la22 ohp, tel 015394 33942, website freespace.virgin.net/brathay.exploration) and The Dorset Expeditionary Society, (Budmouth Technology College, Chickerell Road, Weymouth, Dorset dt4 9sy, tel 01305 775599, website www.wdi.co.uk/des). Both send out several expeditions each year, both within the uk and abroad, and members tend to be between the ages of 16 and 21.

■ The British Schools' Exploring Society, (1 Kensington Gore, London sw7 2ar, tel 020 7591 3141, website www.bses.org.uk) organises six-week-long expeditions for 17- to 20-year-olds during the summer holidays and six-month-long expeditions for those in their 'gap' year between school and university. BSES Expeditions has always had a strong scientific component to its work and provides an excellent training for those hoping to go on and organise their own research expeditions.

■ Raleigh International (27 Parsons Green Lane, London sw6 4Hz, tel 020 7371 8585, website www.raleigh.org.uk) regularly recruits 17- to 25-year-olds to take part in demanding community projects and conservation programmes that last up to 12 weeks.

With increasing public concern for the environment, a number of other organisations offer a chance to get involved in conservation projects overseas on a fee-paying basis. Among them are:

■ The British Trust for Conservation Volunteers (36 St Mary's Street, Wallingford, Oxfordshire ox10 oEU, tel 01491 839766, website www.btcv.org), which has links with many similar organisations in Europe.

■ Greenforce (11-15 Betterton Street, Covent Garden, London wc2H 9BP, tel 020 7470 888, website www.greenforce.org) uses volunteer field assistants on ten-week research expeditions in Zambia and the Peruvian Amazon as well as on reef surveys in the South Pacific and South China Sea.

■ Trekforce Expeditions (34 Buckingham Palace Road, London sw1w 9sa, tel 020 7828 2275, website www.trekforce.org.uk) has been carrying out rainforest conservation work throughout the Indonesian archipelago since 1990, and is now working in Sabah, Malaysian Borneo and Belize.

■ Coral Cay Conservation Programme (154 Clapham Park Road, London sw4 7DE, tel 020 7498 6248, website www.coralcay.org) recruits qualified divers to help monitor the reefs in a marine reserve off the coast of Belize.

■ Earthwatch Europe (Belsyre Court, 57 Woodstock Road, Oxford ox2 6Hu, tel 01865 311600, website www.earthwatch.org) teams paying volunteers with scientists who need their help to study threatened habitats, save endangered species and document our changing environmental heritage. Volunteers do not need to have any special skills to join Earthwatch expeditions and anyone aged 16 to 75 may apply.

■ For budding archaeologists, Archaeology Abroad (31-34 Gordon Square, London wc1H opy, tel 020 7383 2572, website www.britarch.ac.uk/archabroad) helps directors of overseas excavations find suitable personnel through its bulletins.

■ For those taking a gap year, a new organisation, The Year Out Group, (po Box 29925, London sw6 6FQ, tel 07980 395789, website www.yearoutgroup.org) promotes the concept and benefits of a well-structured year for young people between school and university, or between university and work. It has drafted a series of questions to help young people decide which year-out experience might be best for them. GAP Activity Projects (tel 0118 959 4914, website www.gap.org.uk) and Gap Challenge (tel 020 8537 7980, website www.world-challenge.co.uk) are specialists in this field.

For many, the experience of meeting and working alongside people in the host country is one of the great attractions of travel:

■ Wind, Sand & Stars (2 Arkwright Road, Hampstead, London nw3 6AD, tel 020 7433 3684, website www.windsandstars.co.uk) specialises in journeys and expeditions to the desert and mountain areas of Sinai, travelling and working with members of the local Bedouin tribes.

■ Teaching and Projects Abroad (Gerrard House, Rustington, West Sussex BN16 1AW, tel 01903 859911, website www.teaching-abroad.co.uk) and I to I International (tel 0870 333 2332, website www.i-to-i.com) arrange work placements in a number of different disciplines.

■ Quest Overseas (tel 020 8673 3313, website www.questoverseas.com) and VentureCo Worldwide (Pleck House, Middletown, Moreton Morrell, Warks CV35 9AU, tel 01926 651071, website www.ventureco-worldwide.com) both offer a combination of language training, community projects and an adventurous expedition.

Those wishing to work or study abroad without necessarily joining an expedition should consult the Central Bureau (10 Spring Gardens, London SW1A 2BN, tel 0207389 4004, website www.britcoun.org/cbeve), whose publications are extremely useful. The Bureau, which also has offices in Edinburgh and Belfast, holds details of jobs, study opportunities, youth organisations and holidays in some 60 countries. Vacation Work Publications (9 Park End Street, Oxford OX1 1HJ, tel 01865 241978, website www.vactionwork.co.uk) publishes many guides and directories for those seeking permanent jobs or summer jobs abroad, unusual travel opportunities, voluntary work and working travel.

Often travel for its own sake seems insufficient for those who wish to provide practical help for locals in the country they are to visit. If you feel that you have both the time and the specialist skills needed to be a volunteer with one of the aid and development agencies, you should probably start by reading two very helpful directories: *Volunteer Work* (Central Bureau) and/or *The International Directory of Voluntary Work* (Vacation Work). Both books give an outline of the organisations which are willing and able to accept volunteer workers on overseas projects, as well as information about the skills and level of commitment required of the volunteer. At this stage you should be aware that the majority of host countries that welcome volunteers usually require skilled personnel such as nurses, teachers, agronomists and civil engineers. They may be unable to pay even your airfares (although many provide board and lodging) and you may be expected to help for at least one or two years. Remember that during that time you probably won't be travelling but will be based in a poor urban community or remote rural village.

If you feel that you are suitably qualified and have the emotional maturity to be a volunteer, you may like to discuss your hopes and ambitions to serve with someone who has already been on such an expedition.

If you wish to work for an international aid organisation, the World Service Enquiry (Bon Marché Centre, Suite 233, 241-251 Ferndale Road, London SW9 8BJ, website www.wse.org.uk) has been advising people wanting to work overseas in the developing world for more than 25 years. Its annual guide outlines a range of options and organisations and its monthly magazine, *Opportunities Abroad,* lists the latest aid, development and mission agencies' vacancies. Volunteer Work Information Service (Case Postale 90, 1268 Begnins Vaud, Switzerland, website: www.workingabroad.com) provides the *Complete Resource Guides to Voluntary Work*, a specialist publication listing voluntary work opportunities by continent and personalised service, which provides individual country information to enable volunteers to work or travel overseas.

Finding the right organisation to suit you can take time, so don't expect to leave next week. Four major agencies which send out volunteers from the UK as part of the British Government's overseas aid programme are International Cooperation for Development (ICD) (Unit 3, Canonbury Yard, 190A New North Road, London N1 7BJ), UNAIS (Suite 3A, Hunter House, Goodramgate, York YO1 2LS), Skillshare Africa (126 New Walk, Leicester LE1 7JA) and Voluntary Service Overseas (VSO) (317 Putney Bridge Road, London SW15 2PN). Over 400 volunteers go abroad each year through these organisations; all of them are over 21 years old and have relevant professional work experience.

Those with medical skills to offer might like to contact Health Projects Abroad (PO Box 24, Bakewell, Derbyshire DE45 1ZW, tel 01629 440051, website www. hpauk.org), which publishes a useful booklet, the HPA *Guide to Voluntary Nursing Overseas*, and recruits unskilled volunteers for health-related projects in Tanzania. The International Health Exchange (8-10 Dryden Street, London WC2E 9NA, tel 020 7836 5833, www.ihe.org.uk) publishes job vacancies, runs training courses and maintains a register of healthcare professionals wanting to work in developing countries. Merlin (Medical Emergency Relief International) (5-13 Trinity Street, London SE1 1DB, tel 020 7378 4888, www.merlin.org.uk) is a well-respected agency sending qualified medical and support staff to emergency zones worldwide.

So, whatever motivates you to go on your expedition of a lifetime, you can be sure there is someone out there to help you realise your dream. There is nothing like travelling with a purpose to help you to understand the world and all its complexities better.

SHANE WINSER runs the Expedition Advisory Centre at the Royal Geographical Society, and has helped to organise scientific expeditions to Sarawak, Pakistan, Kenya and Oman.

The polar traveller
by Sir Ranulph Fiennes

"After a memorably unpleasant night Mike and I followed an unnamed tributary that descended steeply into the crevasse-streaked maw of the Mill Glacier. The horizons which now opened to us in slow motion were awesome, a sprawling mass of rock and ice locked in suspended motion. This was the headwater of a moving ice-river. Constrictions caused by 15,000-foot-high mountains had formed, and were even now renewing savage whirlpools and mighty maelstroms of cascading pressure-ice. Huge open chasms leered from distant foothills and standing ice-waves reared up at the base of black truncated cliffs.

I found this canvas full of power and wonder and thanked God for this moment of being alive. Nothing else lived here nor ever had since the dinosaurs of Gondwanaland. No birds nor beasts nor the least bacteria survived. Only the deep roar of massive avalanche, the shriek and grind of splitting rock, the groan of shifting ice, and the music, soft or fierce, of the winds from a thousand valleys, moved to and fro across the eternal silence. " – SIR RANULPH FIENNES

THERE IS A DANISH WORD, *POLARHULLAR*, meaning 'a yearning for the polar regions' that grips the soul of a traveller so that nowhere else will ever again satisfy his appetite for the essence of 'over there and beyond'. A victim of *polarhullar* will forever be drawn back to the very extremities of Earth.

Antarctica is expensive and difficult to reach, which is why, blocked by the roughest seas in the world, nobody penetrated its fastness until, only 90 years ago, Scott, Amundsen and Shackleton struggled over the Ross Ice Shelf and on to the vast inland plateau; while the Arctic Ocean, peopled by Eskimos, who, for centuries, have survived along its coastlines, is infinitely more accessible to travellers. Sledgers who cross Greenland, the Canadian north and Svalbard often describe themselves as polar travellers, using the Arctic Circle as their yardstick. Thus there are a great many more veterans of the Arctic than of Antarctica.

Travel in the remote polar reaches of the Arctic Ocean itself and the high plateaux of Antarctica demands careful preparation and constant wariness due to unpredictable weather and local hazards, which can rapidly prove lethal. On the other hand, during the summer season, polar travel can be easy and almost temperate on windless days and away from problem areas. I have travelled to both poles without suffering unduly from the cold, yet I lost part of a toe from frostbite during a weekend army exercise in Norfolk. A need for wariness is not a uniquely polar prerogative.

A brief history of previous polar travellers in Antarctica would have to start in 650AD when, according to the legends of Polynesian Rarotonga, their chief Uite headed south in a war canoe until the ocean was covered with 'white powder and great white rocks rose into the sky'.

Soon after the discovery of America by Columbus and Cape Horn by Drake, Britain annexed Australia (1616). Then, in 1700, the astronomer Halley reached South Georgia, and by 1774 Captain Cook had sailed south of the Antarctic circle. He then circumnavigated Antarctica without ever sighting land. Nobody overwintered on the continent until the British–Norwegian Southern Cross expedition of 1900, which preceded the 'heroic age' of the pole racers, made famous by the deaths of all Scott's team soon after Amundsen reached the south pole in 1911. In 1914 Shackleton attempted to traverse Antarctica. He failed, but in 1958 the crossing was successfully achieved by the team led by Dr Vivian Fuchs and Sir Edmund Hillary.

A full resumé of Arctic travel that stretched over three centuries would fill many pages. Ships' captains from America and Britain vied with each other throughout the nineteenth century to find a 'north-west passage'. Entire expeditions disappeared in a mist of rumoured mutiny, murder and cannibalism.

The urge to be the first to the north pole ended early this century with mutually disputed claims by two Americans, Peary and Cook. Both were later accused of fudging their records and the first proven journey to the north pole was that of Ralph Plaisted, an American preacher, in 1968, a year before Britain's Wally Herbert completed the first surface crossing of the Arctic Ocean via the pole.

The achievement of linking up expeditions north and south into a circumpolar journey encircling the earth was proposed by Charles de Brosses, an eighteenth-century French geographer, and finally executed by the Transglobe Expedition (1979-1982). This expedition's ice group, myself and Charles Burton, travelled from Greenwich across Antarctica and the Arctic Ocean, then back to Greenwich. We became the first people to reach both poles by surface travel and to circumnavigate Earth on its polar axis.

In 1993, with Mike Stroud, I crossed the Antarctic continent on the longest unsupported polar journey in history. This took nearly 100 days but, a year later, various types of wind-powered kites and parawings emerged that enabled Antarctica to be crossed with far less effort in a mere 50 days. Now it is possible to traverse both Antarctica and the Arctic Ocean with no 'outside' support, by harnessing the wind with lightweight sails.

A sledger, using modern kites, can pick up and harness winds from over 180 degrees. Until 1994, the great journeys of Shackleton and his successors utilised crude sails, which could only run before a directly following wind. Should Mike and I have described our 1993 expedition, or Shackleton's, as 'unsupported' when we harnessed the wind, albeit in a minimal way? Should I, in 1996, have used a vastly improved modern kite gadget and still have called my journey 'unsupported'? It is a question of definition, for there is, after all, no polar version of the International Olympic Committee.

In 1993 Mike Stroud and I suffered considerable physical damage crossing the Antarctic continent by manhaul and minimal use of sails that could only use following winds. Our sledge loads, each in excess of 215 kg, required brute force to shift and 16 km a day was a fair average manhaul stint, costing a daily deficit of 8,000 calories and leading to slow starvation.

In 1996, again towing a load of nigh on 225 kg, I deployed a 4.5 kg kite and managed up to 190 km a day with minimal physical effort and correspondingly less calorific expenditure. My sledge load could be halved in terms of fuel and food. What had previously proved remarkably difficult was now comparatively simple.

Polar travel has been truly revolutionised by such wind devices. It is now possible to cross Antarctica in under two months. Of course the element of luck can still play tricks. Broken equipment, unusually bad weather, sudden illness and well-hidden crevasses can still prevent a successful outcome, but at least the reality of polar travel is now within the grasp of the many, not just the few.

My instructions for this section of the *Handbook* are to provide practical information, and this would be difficult without lists. These are the result of a dozen polar journeys in many regions and with differing purposes. I have spent more days and nights out on the Arctic pack and Antarctic plateau than anyone alive, but my kit lists and general tips are by no means infallible. They will not prevent you falling into the sea or an ice crack. You may still become hypothermic, snow blind or lost or eaten by a polar bear, but I hope they will at least help you get started as a polar traveller of reasonable competence.

First of all, read as much available literature by previous travellers in the area of your chosen trip. Study the annexes at the rear of expedition books. Lists of sponsors and manufacturers are often quoted and can save you time.

Then apply, perhaps through the Royal Geographical Society's expedition advisory office, for information on expeditions currently planning to go into your area of interest. It will help if you have a skill to offer (cook, communications, photographer, mechanic, etc.).

Go on other people's trips to Greenland, Svalbard, Iceland, Norway, anywhere with snow and ice, to gain experience before progressing to the deep south or north and to leading your own projects, eventually to and across the poles if that strikes your fancy.

Here are some guidelines. Feel free to ignore or alter them wherever you can garner more appropriate advice elsewhere.

Equipment

Clothing:

1. Fleece jacket with hood.
2. Ventile outer trousers with braces and long-length anorak (baggy).
3. Down duvet jacket with hood attached (for periods when not manhauling).
4. Wick-away underwear (long sleeves and legs).
5. Meraklon headcover.
6. Duofold balaclava with mouth hole.
7. Separate lip protector mouthpiece with elastic to hold in place.
8. Ski goggles and ski glacier glasses with nose-protecting felt pad glued in place.
9. 1 pair thick wool socks.
10. 1 pair thin Helly Hansen socks.
11. 1 pair vapour barrier socks.
12. 1 pair Dachstein mitts.
13. 1 pair Northern Outfitters heavy gauntlets.
14. 1 peaked cap, kepi-style and with under-neck strap
15. 1 pair thin working gloves.
16. 1 pair vapour barrier mitts (optional). Some folk swear by them.
17. Footwear, as advised by polar travellers of your acquaintance (or from their books!). There are too many alternatives to be specific here. Correctly fitting boots are of great importance.
18. For polar work when using snow machines, skis or dogs, shops specialising in the relevant sports gear will be able to advise you best.

NOTE: *The heavier the weight you tow when manhauling with no wind support, the more difficult the selection of clothing, as you will sweat, despite the cold, when working and various parts of your body, especially feet and crotch, will suffer if your clothing choice is not excellent.*

General items:

1. Geodesic dome tents are best (two- or three-man), but beware of the elastic holding the poles together. When cold it loses elasticity so, if you have room on a sledge, keep as many of the pole sections permanently taped together as possible. Black tents make the most of the sun's heat and can be seen nearly as well as fluorescent colours.

2. Sledge harness and traces (solid traces are best for crevassed areas). In the Arctic Ocean pack ice, your sledge should be 'amphibious'.

3. Skis, skins, ski sticks and relevant spares. (Make sure your ski bindings mate well with your boots.)

4. With your sleeping bag and tent, use stuff sacs that don't need too much effort to squeeze in. In 2000, the best custom-made down gear in the UK comes from Peter Hutchinson Designs in Stalybridge.

5. MSR (Mountain Safety Research) cooker. Coleman fuel is best in extreme cold. (Be sure to get a secure fitting fixed to the lid of the box you carry your cook gear in.) Clip the MSR fuel bottle into it firmly before priming. You need a firm base. Take a spare MSR and bag of spares, especially a pricker. (Ensure your MSR fuel bottle tops have winterised washers if you intend to use them in extreme temperatures.)

6. Brush to clear snow (hard bristles).

7. Insulated mug and spoon. Set of cooking pots and pot holder.

8. Zippo lighter and spare flints. Use Coleman fuel.

9. Spare lighter.

10. Silva (balanced) compass and spare compass.

11. Reliable watch and spare.

12. Optional: a light rucksack.

13. Optional: windsail kit and spares in bag (unless travelling 'unsupported').

14. 2 ice screws. 1 pair jumars with loops.

15. Ice axe (very small, light model).

16. 16 m length of para cord.

17. 30 m of thinnest relevant climbing rope.

18. Optional: foldaway snow shovel.

19. Karabiners.

20. Karrimat.

21. Sleeping bag with inner (and optional outer) vapour barriers.

22. Pee bottle (Nalgene or Rubbermaid).

23. PLB (Personal Locator Beacon) and spare lithium battery.

24. GPS (Global Positioning System) and spare lithium battery (Garmin model is recommended).

25. Optional: HF radio and ancillaries (or Global Satellite mobile phone).

26. Video and still camera kit. Polythene bags to avoid misting up.

27. Steel thermos.

28. Rations (high-calorie and low-weight). Be-well Nutrition is best for extreme polar work. Pack as for a 24-hour day per tent.

29. Personal bag. This may contain: small adjustable spanner, pin-nose pliers, dental floss, needles, thin cord, Superglue, wire, diary and pencil, Velcro, charts and maps, Swiss Army knife (all necessary) and spare underwear (optional).

Medical kit:

This should include all that polar travellers advise, and may well include:

▪ **PAIN:** Paracetamol for mild pain. For more severe pain and when inflammation is involved, use Ibuprofen. For severe pain, MST tablets or Buprenorphine or morphine (on prescription). Voltarol suppositories are a good additional painkiller. Be sure to study the instruction paper that comes with each of the above.

▪ **INFECTIONS/ANTIBIOTICS:** Augmentin for dental and chest infections. Ciproxin is excellent for severe spreading infections of skin or gut or anything non-responsive to Augmentin. Cicatrin powder for dressing superficial cuts and rashes. Chloromycetin for eye infections. Flucloxacillin is powerful. Good for painful frostbitten toe areas.

▪ **WOUNDS:** For deeper wounds, take threaded surgical needles. Take Lignocaine for self injection for local anaesthetic. Use Steristrips for smaller wounds. For open blisters, burns and frost injuries, Flamazine cream is effective. Take alcohol swabs to clean wounds. Tegaderm second-skin dressings are useful. Granuflex dressings are good for open blisters and frostbite areas. Canesten powder for crotch fungal infection.

▪ **SICKNESS:** Immodium is best for diarrhoea. If not effective, use Ciproxin. Buccastem is good for nausea (absorb in mouth, don't swallow).

▪ **SUNBLINDNESS:** Take Amethocaine drops.

▪ **TEETH:** Take oil of cloves. Also dental cement pack.

▪ **OTHER:** Jelonet dressings for burns/scalds. Rolls of sticky plaster and gauze dressings. Bonjela for mouth ulcers. Neutrogena for hand sores. Anusol for haemorrhoids.

Other considerations

Remember that insurance, fully comprehensive and including possible search and rescue costs, is often mandatory and always sensible.

In Antarctica the best air charter company, Adventure Network International, will give you all the necessary advice on every side of your expedition. In the Canadian Arctic, First Air is the best (based at Resolute Bay, NWT). Remember that your cargo will cost a great deal at both ends. (In Antarctica, count on US$70 per kg above your basic allowance to get you there from Chile.)

Final advice

Don't go to the Arctic or Antarctica to do difficult journeys with folk you don't know about. They should be reliable, easy-going and experienced. You can get to both poles by paying expert guides to help you there. Some are to be avoided. Others, such as Pen Hadow, are excellent. All are expensive. Pay more and an aircraft will take you all the way to either pole and allow you an hour or two there, before whisking you back to warmer climes.

Never leave litter nor harm life in any form while you are there. The Everest climbers have polluted their grail. Keep our poles clean.

Plan with great care and never rely on gizmos working, PLBS and GPSS for instance, or count on immediate rescue, since storms can keep search planes away for days, even weeks, so play safe.

If you aim to join the weirdos' section by bicycling across Ellesmereland or 'collecting' different poles (geomagnetic, magnospheric, lesser accessibility, etc.) then plan accordingly. For example, if you intend doing the south pole on a pogo-stick, don't forget lots of low-temperature grease and your haemorrhoid cream. Have fun and stay cool. ❧

SIR RANULPH FIENNES, BT, is one of today's greatest polar explorers.
He has been awarded the Founder's Medal of the Royal Geographical Society,
and the Polar Medal (with bar).

The motorbiker
by Ted Simon

IT SEEMS POINTLESS TO ARGUE THE MERITS OF MOTORCYCLES as against other kinds of vehicles. Everyone knows more or less what the motorbike can do, and attitudes to it generally are quite sharply defined. Most are against it – and so much the better for those of us who recognise its advantages. Who wants to be part of a herd? Let me just say that I am writing here for people who are thinking of travelling through the broad open spaces of Africa and Latin America, or across the great Asian landmass.

Here then are some points in favour of motorcycles for the few who care to consider them. In my view, the motorbike is the most versatile vehicle there is for moving through strange countries at a reasonable pace, for experiencing changing conditions and meeting people in remote places. It can cover immense distances and will take you where cars can hardly go. It is easily and cheaply freighted across lakes and oceans, and it can usually be trucked out of trouble without too much difficulty, while a car might anchor you to the spot for weeks.

Sit up and take notice

In return, the bike demands the highest levels of awareness from its rider. You need not be an expert, but you must be enthusiastic and keep all your wits about you. It is an unforgiving vehicle that does not suffer fools at all. As well as the more obvious hazards of potholes, maniacal truck drivers and stray animals, there are the less tangible perils such as dehydration, hypothermia and plain mental fatigue to recognise and avoid.

The bike, then, poses a real challenge to its rider – and accepting it may seem to be almost masochistic, but my argument is that by choosing to travel in a way that demands top physical and mental performance you equip yourself to benefit a thousand times more from what comes your way, enabling you quite soon to brush aside the discomforts that plague lazier travellers.

You absolutely must sit up and take notice to survive at all. The weather and temperature are critical factors; the moods and customs of the people affect you vitally; you are vulnerable and sensitive to everything around you; and you learn fast. You build up resistances faster, too, your instincts are sharper and truer, and you adjust more readily to changes in the climate, both physical and social. Here endeth the eulogy upon the bike.

One's company

I travelled alone almost all the way around the world, but most people prefer to travel in company. As a machine, the motorcycle is obviously at its best used by one person, and it is my opinion that you learn faster and get the maximum feedback on your own, but I know that for many such loneliness would be unthinkable. Even so, you need to be very clear about your reasons for choosing to travel in company. If it is only for security, my advice is to forget it. Groups of nervous travellers chattering together in some outlandish tongue spread waves of paranoia much faster than a single weary rider struggling to make contact in the local language. A motorcycle will attract attention in most places. The problem is to turn that interest to good account. In some countries (Brazil, for example) a motorcycle is a symbol of playboy wealth, and an invitation to thieves. In parts of Africa and the Andes, it is still an unfamiliar and disturbing object. Whether the attention it attracts works for the rider or against him depends on his own awareness of others and the positive energy he can generate towards his environment.

It is very important in poor countries not to flaunt wealth and superiority. All machinery has this effect anyway, but it can be much reduced by a suitable layer of dirt and a muted exhaust system. I avoided having too much glittering chrome and electric paintwork, and I regarded most modern leathers and motorcycle gear as a real handicap. I wore an open face helmet for four years, and when I stopped among people, I always took it off to make sure they saw me as a real person.

Don't...

Finally a few things I learned not to do. Don't ride without arms, knees and eyes covered, and watch out for bee swarms, unless you use a screen, which I did not. Don't carry a gun or any offensive weapon unless you want to invite violence. Do not allow yourself to be hustled into starting off anywhere until you're ready; something is bound to go wrong or get lost. Do not let helpful people entice you into following their cars at ridiculous speeds over dirt roads and potholes. They have no idea what bikes can do. Always set your own pace and get used to the pleasures of easy riding. Resist the habit of thinking that you must get to the next big city before nightfall. You miss everything that's good along the way and, in any case, the cities are the least interesting places. Don't expect things to go to plan, and don't worry when they don't. Perhaps the hardest truth to appreciate when starting a long journey is that the mishaps and unexpected problems always lead to the best discoveries and the most memorable experiences. And if things insist on going too smoothly, you can always try running out of petrol on purpose. ⚗️

TED SIMON has circled the globe on a Triumph 500cc motorcycle, a journey described in 'Jupiter's Travels'.

The hitch-hiker
by Simon Calder

WHY HITCH? HITCH-HIKING AS AN ART, OR SCIENCE, is almost as old as the motor car. Originally the concept was largely synonymous with hiking. You started walking, and if a car came along you put out your hand; mostly you ended up hiking the whole way. From this casually optimistic pursuit, hitching has evolved into a fast, comfortable form of travel in some parts of the world. Elsewhere it remains one big adventure.

Hitching has many virtues. It is the most environmentally sound form of motorised transport, since the hitcher occupies an otherwise empty space. Socially it can be rewarding, enabling you – indeed obliging you – to talk to people whom you would not normally meet. Financially it is highly advantageous: hitching allows you to travel from A to B for free or next to nothing, whether A is Aberdeen or Auckland, and B is Birmingham or Bucharest.

Yet standing for hours at a dismal road junction with the rain trickling morosely down your neck as heartless motorists stream past is guaranteed to make you question the wisdom of trying to thumb a ride. And placing yourself entirely in the hands of a complete stranger can be harrowing. Some travellers dislike the degree of dependence upon others that hitch-hiking engenders. Hitch-hiking can also be enormously lonely. Expect the elation of getting the ideal lift to be tempered with stretches of solitude and frustration and bear in mind that motorists rarely give lifts out of pure philanthropy. Your role may be to keep a truck driver awake with inane conversation, to provide a free English lesson or to act as a sounding board for a life history. But no two rides are ever the same. Techniques and conventions of hitch-hiking vary considerably around the world, most notably the divergence between fast, money-saving hitching in the West and the slower and more chaotic practices of lift-giving in less developed countries.

The West and the Developed World

In Europe, North America and Australasia, hitching can be an almost mechanically precise way of travelling. The main criteria are safety and speed. To enable a motorist to decide whether or not to pick you up, he or she must be able to see you and stop safely. The driver must evaluate whether he or she can help you, and if you would enhance the journey. Make yourself as attractive as possible by looking casual but clean. Hitching in a suit raises driver's suspicions (normal dress for an average hitcher being denim). Looking as though you've been on the road for a year without a wash is equally counter-productive. So freshen up, choose a suitable stretch of road, smile and extend your arm. The actual gesture is a source of possible strife. In most parts of Europe and North America, the raised thumb is understood to be an innocent gesture indicating that a lift is needed. Elsewhere it represents one of the greatest insults imaginable. A vague wave in the general direction of the traffic is safest.

Never accept a lift with anyone who is drunk, high or otherwise gives you cause for concern (e.g. by squealing to a halt in a cloud of burning rubber after crossing six lanes of traffic to pick you up). Turning down a ride is easier said than done, especially if you have been waiting for six hours on a French *autoroute* and night is falling, but try to resist the temptation to jump into a van full of dubious characters. If you find out too late that you've accepted a dodgy ride, feign sickness and ask to be let out. It sometimes works.

Some offers should be turned down simply because they are not going far enough. Hitching through Germany from the Dutch border to the Polish frontier can be done in a day, but is best achieved by discriminating in your choice of lifts. Refuse a ride that would take you only 20 km to the next town. By hopping from one *autobahn* service area to another, you can cover ground extremely quickly.

All kinds of gimmicks can help you get rides more easily. The most effective device is a destination sign. Road systems in developed countries are often so complex that a single road may lead in several different directions. The only commonly enforced law on hitching is the one forbidding hitching on motorways, freeways or *autopistas*. By using a sign you minimise the risk that the driver who stops will want to drop you at an all-motorway junction such as those on London's M25 or the Boulevard Peripherique in Paris. Make your destination request as modest or as bold as you wish – from London you could inscribe your sign 'Dover' or 'Dar Es Salaam', but always add 'Please'.

Hitch-hiking is a cumulative experience, a never-ending happening of unknown factors which contribute to a memory of what real travelling is all about – the feeling that at one time, somewhere, even if only for an instant, you felt like you had become part of the land through which you travelled.
– KEN WELSH

Sophisticated hitchers concentrate their attention on specific cars. The real expert can spot a Belgian number plate at 100 metres. He or she will refuse lifts in trucks (too slow), and home in on the single male driver, who is easily the most likely provider of a lift. So good is the hitching in Germany that if you vowed to accept only lifts in Mercedes, you would still get around. Neighbouring France, in contrast, is hell for hitchers, as is much of southern Europe and Scandinavia.

Hitch-hikers fare well in the newly liberated nations of eastern Europe, especially Poland. It has a Social Autostop Committee – effectively a ministry for hitch-hiking – which provides incentives for motorists to pick up hitchers.

Having taken Lou Reed and Jack Kerouac's advice, and hitch-hiked across the USA, I would hesitate to recommend the experience to anyone. While the chances of being picked up by an oddball or religious fanatic in Europe are tiny, in the States almost every lift-giving motorist is weird and not necessarily friendly. New Zealand could not be more different nor less threatening: if you need a place to stay, just start hitching around nightfall, and a friendly Kiwi will almost certainly offer you a ride and a room. In Australia, the hitcher is the object of greater abuse than anywhere else, with insults (and worse) hurled from car windows alarmingly often.

One exception to the hitching lore of the developed world is Japan. Western hitch-hikers are picked up, usually very quickly, by one of the extremely considerate local drivers. In the absence of any other information, he or she will assume that you want to go to the nearest railway station. But upon learning that your final destination is hundreds of kilometres away in, say, Kyoto, the driver may feel duty bound to take you all the way there.

Japan is one place where women can feel comfortable hitching alone. The conventional wisdom is that women should never hitch alone. Single women hitch-hikers are all too often victims of male violence. Nevertheless, women continue to hitch alone, and get around without problem; some maintain that safety is largely a question of attitude: if you are assertive and uncompromising, you survive.

If 'real' hitching does not appeal, ride-sharing agencies exist in many countries. The idea is simply that travellers share expenses, and often the driving, and pay a small fee to the agency that arranges the introduction. Be warned, however, that there is no guarantee that a driver you contact in advance will not turn out to be a psychopath or a drunk as you hurtle through the Rocky Mountains or central Australia.

The concept of hitching can be extended to boats and planes. Hitching on water can involve anything from a jaunt along a canal in Europe to a two-month voyage to deliver a yacht from the Canary Islands to Florida. And in countries where private flying is popular, rides on light aircraft have been successfully procured.

Less-developed countries

At the other extreme are the dusty highways of Nigeria or Nicaragua. In the Third World, the rules on hitching are suspended. Almost any vehicle is a possible lift-provider, and virtually every pedestrian is a potential hitch-hiker. Amid such good-natured anarchy, hitching is tremendous fun.

You have to accept any form of transport, from a horse and trap upwards. To make the most of opportunities, it helps to be adept at riding side-saddle on a tractor engine, or pillion on a moped for one.

Purists who regard paying for petrol as contrary to the ideals of hitch-hiking, and dismiss the idea of asking a driver for a ride as capitulation, can expect a miserable time in the Third World. Definitions of what constitutes a bus or a taxi, a truck or a private car, are blurred. Sometimes the only way to reach a place is by hitching, and local motorists may exploit their monopoly position accordingly.

El Salvador's transport system has been devastated. Everyone hitches, and you are expected to pay the equivalent of the fare on the (notional) bus. The same applies in large swathes of Latin America, Africa and south Asia. Unless you have insurmountable moral objections or a serious cash-flow crisis, you should always offer something for a ride. More often than you might expect, the ride will cost nothing more than a smile. In Indonesia, for example, the Western hitch-hiker is a curiosity, to be taken (temporarily) home and paraded in front of friends and relations as an exotic souvenir. You too can become an instant celebrity.

Cuba has massive transport problems, some of which are solved by an intriguing form of mass hitch-hiking. Little old ladies and large young louts join forces to persuade passing trucks to stop, or pile into a Lada saloon driven by a grumbling member of the bourgeoisie.

In such places hitching is at its simplest and most effective. Thumbing a ride enables you to see corners of the world that might otherwise remain hidden, and to meet people whom you would surely pass by. And, in the final analysis, there are worse ways to travel than being chauffeur-driven. ❧

SIMON CALDER is the Travel Editor of 'The Independent' and the author of several guidebooks, notably the 'Hitch-hiker's Manual (Britain and Europe)' and 'Panamericana'.

The happy camper: 1 Survival strategies
by Anthony Smith

THE FIRST REAL CAMPING I EVER DID was on a student expedition to Persia. There I learned the principle of inessential necessities. We were travelling by truck and could therefore pile on board everything we might possibly need. The truck could transport it all and we only had the problem of sorting through the excess whenever we needed something. Later we travelled by donkey and, miraculously, the number of necessities diminished as we realised the indisputable truth that donkeys carry less than trucks. Later still, after the donkey drivers had failed to coerce higher rates of pay from very empty student pockets, we continued on foot.

Travelling light

Amazingly, the number of necessities decreased yet again as a bunch of humans realised they could carry far less than donkeys and much, much less than trucks. The important lesson learned was that happiness, welfare and the ability to work did not lessen one iota as the wherewithal for camping decreased in quantity. It could even have been argued that these three blessings increased as less time was spent in making and breaking camp.

This lesson had to be learned several times over. Some time later I was about to travel from Cape Town to England by motorbike. As I wished to sleep out, provide my own meals and experience a road network that was largely corrugated dirt, I found no difficulty in compiling a considerable list of necessities. We must all have made these lists (of corkscrews, tin openers, self-heating soup) and they are great fun, with a momentum that is hard to resist. "Why not a spare tin opener?" "And more medicine and another inner tube?" "Isn't it wise to take more shirts and stave off prickly heat?" Fortunately the garage that sold me the bike put a stop to such idiotic thinking. I had just strapped on a sack containing the real essentials (passport, documents, maps, money and address book) when a passing mechanic told me that any more weight would break the machine's back. (It was a modest machine.) Thus it was that I proceeded up the length of Africa without a sleeping bag, tent, groundsheet, spare petrol, oil, tools, food or even water, and never had cause for regret concerning this lack of wealth. Indeed I blessed the freedom it gave me. I could arrive anywhere, remove my one essential sack and know that nothing, save the bike itself, could be stolen. To have possessions is to be in danger of losing them. Better by far to save the robbers their trouble and start with nothing.

Kippered hammock

A sound tip is to do what the locals do. If they sleep out with nothing more than a blanket, it is probable that you can do likewise. If they can get by with a handful of dates at sunset, it is quite likely that you too can dispense with half a hundredweight of dried egg, cocoa, vitamin tablets, corned beef, chocolate – and self-heating soup. To follow local practice and then try to improve on it can, however, be disastrous. Having learned the knack of sleeping in a Brazilian hammock as if it were a bed, I decided one thunderous night to bring modern technology to my aid. I covered myself with a space blanket to keep out the inevitable downpour.

Unfortunately, while I was asleep the wretched thing slipped round beneath me and I awoke to find my body afloat in the pool of water it had collected. Being the first man to drown in a hammock is a poor way of achieving immortality. I looked over at my Indian travelling companion. Instead of fooling around with sub-lethal blankets, he had built a fire longitudinally beneath his hammock. Doubtless kippered by the smoke but certainly dry, he slept the whole night through.

Planning and adventure

One trouble with our camping notions is that we are confused by a lingering memory of childhood expeditions. I camp with my children every year, and half the fun is not quite getting it right. As all adventure is said to be bad planning, so is a memorable camping holiday one in which the guys act as trip wires, the air mattress farts into nothingness and even the tent itself falls victim to the first wind above a breeze.

Adults are therefore imbued with an expectation that camping is a slightly comic caper, rich with potential mishap. Those who camp a lot, such as wildlife photographers, have got over this teething stage. They expect camping to be (almost) as smooth and straightforward a business as living in a house. They do their best to make cooking, eating, washing and sleeping no more time-consuming than it is back home. The joy of finding grass in the soup or ants in the pants wears off for them on about the second day. It is only the temporary camper, knowing he will be back in a hotel (thank God) within a week, who does not bother to set things up properly.

Surviving natural hazards

I like the camping set-up to be as modest as possible. I have noticed, though, that others disagree, welcoming every kind of extra. A night spent beneath the stars that finishes with the first bright shafts of dawn is hardly a punishment, but some seem to think it so, and concentrate on removing as much of the natural environment as possible.

I remember a valley in the Zagros mountains where I had to stay with some colleagues. I had thought a sleeping bag would be sufficient and placed mine in a dried-up stream which had piles of sand for additional comfort. Certain others of the party erected large tents with yet larger fly sheets (however improbable rain might have been at that time of year). They also started up a considerable generator which bathed the area in sound and light. As electricity was not a predominant feature of those wild regions, large numbers of moths and other insects, idling their way between the Persian Gulf and the Caspian Sea, were astonished at such a quantity of illumination and flew down to investigate. To counter their invasion, one camper set fire to several of those insect repellent coils and the whole campsite was shrouded in noxious gases. Over in the dried-up stream I and two fellow spirits were amazed at the camping travesty down the way. We were even more astonished when, after a peaceful night, we awoke to hear complaints that a strong wind had so flapped at the fly sheets that no one inside the tent had managed to get a wink of sleep.

The most civilised camping I have ever experienced was in the Himalayas. The season was spring and tents are then most necessary both at the lower altitudes (where it rains a lot) and at the higher ones (where it freezes quite considerably). Major refreshment is also necessary because walking in those mountains is exhausting work, being "always up", as the locals put it, "except when it's down." We slept inside sleeping bags on foam rubber within thick tents. We ate hot meals three times a day. We did very well – but we did not carry a thing. There were 36 porters for the six of us, the numbers falling as we ate into the provisions the men carried for us. I laboured up and down mighty valleys, longing for the next refreshment point and always delighted to see the ready-erected tents at each night's stopping place.

Personally, I was burdened with one camera, the smallest of notebooks and nothing more. The living conditions, as I have said, were excellent but what would they have become if I had been asked to carry everything I needed myself? It is at this point, when neither donkeys nor incredibly hardy mountain men are available, that the camper's true necessities are clarified. For myself, I am happy even to dispense with a toothbrush if I have to carry the thing all day long. ❧

The happy camper: 2 Camping rough
by Martin Rosser

IT'S NOT THE EXPENSE OF CAMPSITES THAT I OBJECT TO, but rather having to put up with the others that are crammed in around you. I camp to find peace and solitude, to commune with nature. How to do that in a canvas conurbation is beyond me. As for facilities, I can and do bathe in the woods and prefer it to slopping around in an overcrowded concrete shower block.

If you make the decision to camp freely, you have to decide whether to ask the landowner for permission or remain discreetly out of sight. Which you do will depend solely on the circumstances. I am aware that trespassing campers have an awesomely bad reputation, so I prefer just to get on with it quietly. Nine times out of ten I am not discovered and leave everything as it was except for a piece of flattened grass. I doubt if anyone is the wiser. If you are discovered, your best defence is the clean and tidy way you are camping, so that it can be readily seen that nothing has been, is being, or will be damaged. It helps if you can greet the person without guilt (I have only once received more than a general caution to take care and that once was well deserved – we had left a cooking fire unattended).

When you come to select a spot, remember to avoid all extremes. If the climate you are in is hot, seek shade; if the land is marshy, look for high, well-drained ground. Don't leave selecting your site till the last minute, stopping in late twilight and having to choose within a small area. From late afternoon on you should keep an eye open and be prepared to stop a little short of your planned destination – or backtrack a mile or so if need be. A bad night's sleep or wet and damaged gear are well worth avoiding.

The selection of a resting place that is not to be final involves experience: here I can do little more than outline the general dos and don'ts. After that, bitter experience starts to take over. I rarely camp with a tent, preferring a bivi-bag, which makes my choice of spot very versatile. Generally, I select a spot protected by trees or in a sheltered dip. The patch need not be bigger than eight by four feet for me and my gear. I have even slept on substantial slopes – the record being 45°. I avoid all low-lying wetlands (and even streams in summer) because flying bloodsuckers enrage me to the point of sleeplessness. In areas I know will be bad, I try to find ground high enough to have a stiff breeze. This is the surest way I know of deterring the Scottish midge or the Australian mosquito.

I was determined, if not to camp out, at least to have the means of camping out in my possession; for there is nothing more harassing to an easy mind than the necessity of reaching shelter by dusk.
– ROBERT LOUIS STEVENSON

For those who carry tents, the rules are slightly different. The ground you are after has to be as flat and rock-free as possible. Take a leaf out of the book of London taxi drivers, who know the exact dimensions of their cab. Just as they are able to slide their cab into the most unlikely looking gaps, you too should know where to and (more importantly) where not to pitch. Sleeping in a tent, you have less to worry about on the insects front, but you should be more wary of falling branches and the like. Tents are far easier to damage than bivouac sheets, and more expensive to repair or replace. If you can, face the tent doors eastwards. That way you don't have to get up, or even fully wake up, to watch the dawn break. For the rest, just apply common sense. Don't pitch a tent with its only door facing into a gale, and don't camp in a dry river bed when the rains are due, although it has to be said that dry river beds are very comfortable in the right season – flat floor and plenty of firewood to hand.

The reason I prefer bivouacking is that it forces you to take greater notice of the terrain that surrounds you. You become more adaptable in your camping and more ready to sleep anywhere. I have slept in derelict buildings and under bridges while experiencing the low life; up trees; in caves; and I once found a sea cliff with a horizontal crack running three feet high and over ten feet deep. Sleeping in there was an experience and a half as it was 60 feet above a rocky shore on which the waves crashed all night.

A friend went on to greater things and slept behind a waterfall (and once in the shovel of an ancient and abandoned mechanical digger). So if there is a moral to this tale of where to camp, it would be somewhere along these lines: use your common sense; break all the rules in the boy scout manual – but sensibly; be adventurous and try new ways. Even if you carry a tent you don't have to use it. ❧

The happy camper: 3 Fixing a tent
by Jack Jackson

IF YOU AREN'T WORRIED ABOUT WEIGHT, and you are not constantly on the move, you might as well make yourself as comfortable as possible, which can mean virtually building a tented village. Large groups will find it very useful to have a mess tent where the party can all congregate during bad weather and for meals.

On hard, sun-baked ground in hot countries, pegs normally supplied with tents are of little use, so have some good, thick, strong ones made for you from 60 mm iron (or use 15 cm nails). As wooden mallets will not drive pegs in, carry a normal claw hammer – you can also use the claw to pull the pegs out again. In loosely compacted snow, standard metal pegs do not have much holding power, so it is useful to make some with a larger surface area from 2.5 cm angle alloy. Even this does not solve all the problems because any warmth during the day will make the pegs warm up, melt the snow around them and pull them out, causing the tent to fall down. The answer is to use very big pegs or ice axes for the two main guys fore and aft. Then for all the other guys, dig a hole about 25 cm deep, put the peg in horizontally with the guy line around its centre and compress fresh snow down hard on the peg with your boots to fill the hole.

A special 'tent anchor' for snow and soft sand is now available from good suppliers; it is not any better in snow than the method described above, but is good in soft sand. Four of these would normally be all you would carry per tent.

If you sleep without a tent, you need a mosquito net in some areas. There are several types on the market, including ex-army nets that have the advantage of needing only one point of suspension: a camera tripod or ice axe will do for this if there is not a vehicle or tent nearby. However, commercial manufacturers have now produced lighter and more compact nets, and special impregnation kits are available which enhance their effectiveness.

Since tents take heavy wear, carry some strong thread and a sailmaker's needle for repairs, plus some spare groundsheet material and adhesive. Tents that are to be carried by porters, on donkeys or on a vehicle roof rack are best kept in a strong kit bag, or they will soon be torn. If it is not windy, a space blanket covering the reflecting side of the tent will help keep the tent cool during the day. ‌❧

The happy camper: 4 Choosing your campsite
by Melissa Shales

I F A LARGE GROUP OF YOU ARE TRAVELLING TOGETHER in the more civilised parts of the world, you won't have the option of just choosing a suitable area to camp, particularly if you want to explore the towns. In many countries and in national parks it is actually illegal to camp outside the official sites. These, however, are often a very good option, far cheaper and cleaner than inexpensive hotels. Some motels have campsites attached that allow you the option of using their restaurant facilities, swimming pools, etc. The Caravan Club of Great Britain (East Grinstead House, East Grinstead, West Sussex RH19 1UA, 01342 326944) is a useful source of information about good sites in Europe (for tented camping as well as caravanning) and also runs various small sites around the UK. Contact the club for details about their publication *Continental Sites Guide*.

If you have the option, aim for a smaller site first. At the height of the tourist season, larger ones tend to get crowded, to the point where guy ropes are overlapping and you can hear the conversation in the tent next door. Some have hard stands which, while conveniently clean, are exceptionally hard unless you are travelling with the full paraphernalia of air beds etc. They also become horribly sterile areas that destroy virtually the entire ethos of camping. Avoid them if possible.

Many of the better sites will have either barbecues or special sites for fires. You will rarely be allowed to have a fire wherever you choose. The caretaker will often be able to supply wood if you ask in the morning. Check the toilets and washing facilities before you book in. Unless the site is very small, when all you can expect is a primitive or chemical toilet and a stand-pipe, there should be showers and laundry facilities and a plentiful supply of hot water. In some countries, such as Zimbabwe, the sites will even have servants attached who will do your washing, sweep out the tent, run errands and build your fires for a small fee. As with hotels, there are listings, and even star ratings in many places. If you want to go to a site that is obviously a highly rated or the only one in the area, or if you are travelling in high season, try to book in advance. ❧

ANTHONY SMITH *is a co-founder of the British Balloon and Airship Club and a veteran of many expeditions – including a motorcycle ride down the length of Africa.* JACK JACKSON *is an expedition leader, mountaineer and diver.* MELISSA SHALES *is a previous Editor of 'Traveller' magazine and now writes guidebooks.* MARTIN ROSSER *is a freelance writer and traveller.*

The luxury traveller
by Amy Sohanpaul

THE WORD LUXURY HAS BEEN USED SO LAVISHLY – and so slavishly – by press officers and chocolate makers that we're in danger of forgetting what it really means. Not that the dictionary definition is perfect: 'something desirable for comfort or enjoyment, but not indispensable.' Not indispensable? It's essential for one's sanity. Happily, luxury doesn't always have a hefty price-tag. Stretching out in a sunny spot, finding time to stand and stare, having the papers delivered to the doorstep, a glass of wine in the bath: everyone has their own personalised version.

Luxury and travel
However, if you have a lot of time and a lot of money, or even just the latter, travel is one of those areas where you can find absolutes of luxury. A stratospheric price tag equals a whole exclusive world, far from the madding crowd. And if you're travelling first class, it starts at the airport – or if you're flying with Virgin it starts on your doorstep as they send a chauffeur to pick you up. At the airport you're whisked through the speediest check-in to a private lounge and ushered into first class and, on some planes, tucked into bed. British Airways beds come with velvet head cushions and real cashmere blankets. If you must eat or drink, simply summon staff just desperate to serve you *haute cuisine* at 20,000 feet. Is the world your oyster or is the oyster your world?

The sky's the limit
What could be better than flying by first class? Travelling by private jet? TCS Expeditions will sort it out for you. Passengers travel aboard specially modified Boeing

757s. These give you access to the smaller airports in remoter places: you can hop between one exotic destination and the next as easily as a grasshopper leaps between blades of grass. The staff-to-passenger ratio is high – including chefs and professional expedition leaders and academic guides. A few sample itineraries include *Around Africa by Private Jet* – Zanzibar, Namibia and Marrakech are just a few of the stops on this trip. Or spend 21 days rediscovering *History's Lost Cities* from Angkor to Uzbekistan. If that isn't good enough, they can custom-make your own private jet expeditions (www.tcs-expeditions.com). Many upmarket tour operators will organise exclusive private arrangements for you – fancy flying to the Caribbean at short notice and need a private jet, limousine transfers and a fully crewed and catered sailing ship? WEXAS and Abercrombie & Kent are just two companies who will organise it all while you pack your bikini. If you only want a jet and aren't going too far, then try Euro Executive Jet, who fly to over 1,500 European destinations (email enquiries@exec-jet.co.uk).

Of course, you don't have to fly. Cruising is even more laid back than a reclining seat in first class, and increasingly popular. But don't let that put you off. The independent Cruise Advisory Service (35 Blue Boar Row, Salisbury SP1 1DA, tel 01722 335505) should be your first port of call to sift the standard from the sublime. Their standards are so high that they have no hesitation in describing the newest, biggest ship on

> *The world is his who has money to go over it.*
> – RALPH WALDO EMERSON

P&O's books – the superliner *Aurora* – as 'standard bucket-and-spades four star', notwithstanding the ship's penthouse suites, butler service and 30-foot cascading waterfall. Even the QEII only qualifies for four stars, despite staff who endeavour to satisfy your every whim, fantastic suites with private balconies, and ever-changing views. You might choose to ignore the ratings, since this *grande dame* remains a favourite for the classic transatlantic crossing, and is justifiably loved for its World Cruise – three months of non-stop glamour and luxury.

In case you're wondering, the lines that do qualify as five star include Silversea Cruises, Crystal, Seabourn (part of Cunard), Radisson and Peter Dielmann. If you're still not convinced, then hire yourself a superyacht instead – complete with helicopter landing pads, mahogany bedrooms, jacuzzis on deck and cinemas inside (www.eliteyacht.com).

If you get sea-sick even in superliners, there's always the humble train. Such as the splendid Rovos *Rail Pride of Africa* trains – two restored steam trains that wind their way from Cape Town to Dar Es Salaam, or shorter routes, taking in overnight stays at selected game reserves. Still in South Africa, the *Blue Train* is another delight, and a spectacular way to travel between Pretoria and Cape Town. You can relax in *en-suite* compartments with crisp white bedding, telephones and televisions. Some even boast CD players, for playing blue savannah songs as Africa rolls past. After this hotel on wheels, try the *Palace on Wheels* – the only way to travel through Rajasthan. Passengers view forts and resplendent royal residences during stops and then retire to the air-conditioned elegance of their 'bed-chambers' or a pink gin in the bar as the train moves onto the next glorious location.

Or try the legendary *Orient-Express*; well, you don't have to try very hard. The food is splendid, the service even more so. This quality is a standard on all *Orient-Express* trains, which include the *Great South Pacific Express* between Cairns and Sydney, and the *Eastern & Oriental Express* between Bangkok and Singapore. On the *Venice-Simplon-Orient-Express* the brass gleams, the wood shines, the original carriages (rescued from dereliction and restored) are inlaid with marquetry. The view from the windows isn't too bad either, when you wake up in the Swiss Alps. And at the end of it all, there's Venice. Glorious even if staying in a sleeping bag, sublime when staying at the Hotel Cipriani, with its elegance, sumptuous simplicity and views of the lagoon. The Gritti Palace runs it a close second for style and comfort, and houses Harry's Bar, the best place in the world to drink a *bellini*.

That's Venice, which only leaves the rest of the globe to choose from. There simply isn't room to list all the most luxurious rooms and hotels within this chapter. Suffice to say that any member of Small Luxury Hotels of the World, of the reliable Relais & Chateaux group or of The Leading Hotels of the World is probably going to meet the mark. There are some hotel groups which you just know will provide the best of the best – Four Seasons' hotels, from New York to the Maldives, hit the perfect spot every time; while the Aman hotels aren't so much hotels as experiences – of sheer indulgence.

Take their Amanwana resort in Indonesia, for example. It's as rough and ready as an Aman hideaway gets – tents on a jungle-covered island. It's a long hop, skip and jump to this remote retreat and the final leg is on a motorcruiser, when the fun begins as the taste of champagne mingles with the delicious spray of the ocean. Winding paths of sand lead to each tent – which seems as appropriate as calling Windsor Castle a wee wigwam. They come complete with living room, writing desks and state of the art bathrooms with his and hers sinks. Staff outnumber guests by at least three to one.

People do get addicted to the Aman group. In the Amanwana bar I met a couple on honeymoon who had decided to spend it visiting various Aman resorts. They had planned on a year, which seemed fair. Or vastly unfair!

I want to be alone

Of course, even the most exclusive hotels can seem a little crowded at times, which is when only a villa will do. It's possible to have anything from a château to a re-worked cowshed at your disposal, with or without maid service. Some villas are part of hotels so you get full-on service and privacy. For instance, the two bedroom Royal Villa, is part of the beautiful Rajvilas resort in Jaipur, comes complete with grand dining-room, private garden and its own pool. Traditional, private villas are just as luscious. Villas of the World offer gems such as Casa Careyes in Mexico – five air-conditioned bedrooms, four bathrooms, a dramatic, thatched, open-air living area with a freeform swimming pool, plus a full-time staff of eight, including a chauffeur. Smaller companies come up with the goods too, and the better ones have personal knowledge of all the properties on their books. Tuscany Now is particularly good for anything from a one-bedroom cottage to a thousand-year-old castle in Italy.

The most scenic, most idyllic privacy belongs to island retreats. Mnemba Island off the coast of Zanzibar is a shoeless haven, serenity lapped by gentle waves. Some of the Maldive resorts are worth a retreat before the islands disappear altogether, due to rising water levels. The Four Seasons at Kuda Huraa (with wonderful water-villas built on stilts over the lagoon) and Soneva Fushi (notable for its splendid spa) are among the best resorts on these enchanted islands. Fiji is paradise for *Robinson Crusoe* fans: with over 330 islands to choose from, one or two going make the perfection grade. Vatulele Island Resort does, with just 17 villas fronting a fantasy white beach.

The ultimate has to be Turtle Island, with 14 two-room Fijian-style *bures* (thatched huts) and 14 private beaches. The bliss of a beach each is not to be taken lightly – a minimum of 6 nights is required. A maximum stay limit might be more appropriate.

Dream on

The most wonderful thing about luxury travel is that the possibilities are endless. The best of the best is out there and there are numerous companies who will be delighted to put it together for you, such as WEXAS. Fancy a personalised safari with your own guides, virtually your own game reserve, as well as exquisite three course dinners in the bush? A private pool to float in between game watching? No problem, speak to Abercrombie and Kent or any number of safari specialists. A personalised shopping tour in India? Western and Oriental, or Cox and Kings, are India experts. Not sure when to go or where to go, but money no object? See any of the above, or the small but knowledgeable Nomadic Thoughts, whose offices I visited on a bleak rainy day in London. Large gin and tonics were poured as map after map of the world was unfurled and route after route was planned and plotted.

Deciding where you're going to go, whether you choose an old jalopy or a private jet is the most fun. But perhaps the simple privilege of being able to travel is the greatest luxury of them all. ❧

The green traveller
by Matthew Brace

FIRST A DEFINITION. 'ECOTOURISM', a buzz word for the millennium, is a portmanteau word used to describe a wide range of approaches, from ultra-green forest lodges operating in complete harmony with their environment to hotels that trample acres of precious forest and then name their rooms after the rare birds that used to live there. A better term, and the one preferred by the pressure group Tourism Concern, is 'sustainable tourism'.

By its very nature, tourism is rarely wholly ecologically friendly. Even if you sailed on a home-made driftwood raft to a holiday island, dropped no litter, killed only time and left only footprints (to quote a wise if oft-used phrase), you would still inevitably have some impact on the environment.However, it is possible to explore this wonderful planet while at the same time dramatically reducing your impact on its ecosystems, and in some cases actively helping by contributing tourist money to conservation programmes. No self-respecting independent traveller with a passion for the environment should leave home without the will to seek out the most ecological way to travel.

What is needed is respect. Respect for a rainforest's beauty, respect for a tribal people's beliefs and customs, respect for nature. A little more respect, say, than is currently being displayed by a company offering what they call an 'eco-safari', in which tourists are given the opportunity to shoot pellets of washable luminous-pink paint at the noble elephants of Zimbabwe. And just in case the elephant takes offence, a hunter is on hand to shoot it with a real bullet.

So when you step out on your trip, take time to check that, along with the sun creams and guidebooks, you have also spared a thought for why the destination attracted you in the first place and what impact your visit will have.

Why should we care?

Increasing numbers of people are travelling to more and more distant destinations. One exotic spot that has gained huge popularity for its wildlife and beauty is the tiny Central American nation of Costa Rica. Its position – forming a bridge between North and South America – means it is blessed with some of the most diverse flora and fauna on Earth. But all is not well in the forests. In 1980, Costa Rica had just 3,000 international visitors. By 1992 that figure had jumped to 64,000. Tourism brought in US$700 million in 1996, which was 30 per cent of total exports and 8.5 per cent of GNP. 1998 heralded a $4 million government publicity campaign, and in 1999 Costa Rica welcomed over 800,000 visitors.The country is now at a crossroads in terms of tourism development. Biological reserves such as Monteverde face the problem of balancing the preservation of their sensitive eco-systems with the streams of tourists that come to marvel at them.

Rodrigo Carazo, former Costa Rican president, is very much aware of the problem but views the situation as a positive opportunity to reduce deforestation: "It is about selling one tree a million times through tourism, rather than once through timber logging." Throughout the 1980s, however, Costa Rica had one of the highest deforestation rates in the world, mainly as a result of the demand for land for cattle-ranching and timber production. Forests covered 72 per cent of Costa Rica in the late 1950s. Now the only remaining forest is within protected areas and represents just 14 per cent of the country.

The world's most popular tourist honeypots are also under intense threat. According to United Nations predictions, visitors to the Mediterranean could total 760 million by 2025, adding to a resident population of 150 million. This would put tremendous further strain on the local environment, vastly increasing the amount of sewage discharged into the sea and thus endangering the natural habitat of marine animals and plants.

Coral reefs are the most endangered of all the world's ecosystems (more so even than the rainforests), yet only recently have conservation projects begun in earnest. Among other measures, these aim to protect them against the tourist habit of breaking off coral (accidentally or intentionally) to provide ornaments for their mantelpieces back home.

Programmes for change

On paper...

Ecotourism has burgeoned to such an extent that an international agency has been set up to monitor its growth. The International Ecotourism Society (TIES) was established in Washington DC with the aim of influencing the direction of ecotourism worldwide, and balancing the needs of conservation with those of the multi-million pound/dollar travel industry. The year 2002 has been declared the United Nations International Year of Ecotourism. Non-governmental organisations (NGOS) such as Tourism Concern will be working to ensure that this does not end up as a meaningless marketing ploy. Instead, campaigning organisations will be focusing international attention on the impact our holidays have on local people and their environments.

And in action...

Major TIES projects have included visitor management schemes in the Galapagos Islands (a rapidly growing tourist destination with a fragile ecosystem); national park-user fees in Costa Rica; and guidelines and monitoring programmes for nature tour operators with sustainable planning and design recommendations. Most recently, they have embarked on a consumer education campaign highlighting the impact of travel and how to choose responsible tour operators.

Governments the world over have formulated national ecotourism projects, and many have even signed up, via the United Nations Commission on Sustainable Tourism, to international commitments to sustainable tourism. At the same time, local communities are also taking matters into their own hands, making a success of smaller projects that bring positive results for local residents. These are the communities who know only too well that 'sustainable tourism' is an empty concept if it does not include people as well as flora and fauna.

Environmental and ecological protection tends to work best when it takes into account the social and economic benefits for local people. Tourism Concern's *Community Tourism Guide* includes community-based projects and tours all over the world.

Some simple steps for sustainable travel

Do your homework. Choose your destination with care. Read up and and inform yourself about the current issues of environmental contention. Ecotourism is the flavour of the month for travel agents and tour operators. A number of them are far from green, however, and are merely using the phenomenon of green travel as a device to sell more holidays. Tourism Concern has some useful questions to ask your travel agent before you go:

■ Can you assure me that the hotels you use do not diminish the supply of water to local people for domestic, animal or agricultural use?

■ Is adequate provision made for the disposal of sewage and waste without damaging the local environment?

■ Can you assure me that the hotels are not built on sacred sites or burial grounds?

■ Is any of the hotels you use owned or managed by local residents?

■ Can you assure me that the tourism developments you are offering have not deprived people of their homes or livelihoods?

■ Are you working with Tourism Concern or any human rights organisations to work out how to deal with these issues?

They may not have the answers at their fingertips, but give them time to check. And Tourism Concern urges independent travellers to write and tell them what they say.

And when in paradise?

The renowned conservationist David Bellamy believes certain rules must be adhered to if tourism is to function in harmony with the environment:

■ Visitor numbers must be limited.

■ At least 50 per cent of all profits should go back to the local community.

■ Accommodation should be built on land that has already been altered.

■ Alternative sources of energy and renewable local resources must be used where possible.

■ Local travel should be by foot or boat, with the use of internal combustion engines kept to a minimum.

"If that sounds boring," adds the great professor, "then please stay away. If you demand more, many people and their resources will not stand a chance. I sincerely believe that this is both their and our last chance."

Take Bellamy at his word and add a few more sustainable travelling tips to your list. Use public transport whenever possible to save fuel. If public transport is not available, get together with other sustainable travellers you meet along the way and hire a minibus (it will save you money, too). Bicycle hire can be very cheap, and can offer you access to areas that you would not be able to reach by motor vehicle. Don't drop litter (not long ago piles of pink toilet paper were reported in the foothills of the Himalayas). And when walking through eco-sensitive areas such as national parks, keep to the trails. This will not merely help to preserve the beauty of these areas – it might also save you from a close encounter with a territorially defensive snake. ❧

Matthew Brace is a freelance travel journalist specialising in environmentally-aware tourism.

The gay traveller
by Tony Leonard

W HEN DID GAY TOURISM BEGIN? Was it in 1895, when the trial of Oscar Wilde sent society homosexuals scrambling *en masse* to the Continent to escape a similar fate? Or were the ancient Spartan warrior-lovers the first great gaggle of gays to hit foreign climes for one hell of a party? The Grand Tour of Europe must surely have held sensual as well as cultural delights for a 'sensitive' young man of the eighteenth century. And Morocco had its fair share of theatrical ex-pats long before Joe Orton so elegantly chronicled his little escapades in Marrakech.

San Francisco first became a Boystown (and consequently a Gay Mecca) after the Second World War, when discharged sailors discovered they could have far more fun sticking together than they would back with their folks in Nowheresville, Illinois. The package tour found the clones of the Seventies charting all the major trade routes that remain well trampled to this day. They pitched camp, founding colonies that would become the staple destination of gay tourism for three decades and counting.

In the US, affluent New York 'A-gays' have decamped each summer to Fire Island. There they have created an alternative homosexual high society where social status permeates the rituals and traditions that have become as unchanging as anything the British class system has created.

Europe's gay hot-spots have always been rather more egalitarian, based around hedonism rather than social standing. The sun, sex and sangria of Sitges provide an opportunity for men whose everyday lives are constrained by heterosexual conventions to let rip in an atmosphere of mutual abandon. As our heterosexual counterparts discovered the delights of Torremelinos and Majorca, so gay men have made their annual pilgrimages to Sitges, Mykonos, Gran Canaria, etc., to do much the same, revelling in the sort of atmosphere epitomised by the package tours of Club 18-30.

Gay travel companies have been among the most successful of gay businesses, building primarily on a portfolio of conventional package tours to friendly resorts in Europe and North America. The most important qualification for becoming a gay resort was the perceived liberalism of the locals. Pretty soon, an area builds up an infrastructure of gay bars, clubs and hotels and the colonisation is complete.

For the gay holiday-makers of the last few decades, there is safety in numbers. For most, a gay lifestyle was something they were only able to experience on occasion, be it once a week, once a month or even once a year. No surprise then, that they should wish to holiday almost exclusively among other gay men, away from the bigotry and petty prejudices of everyday life. And no surprise that they should make the most of a scene that they have little access to for 50 weeks in a year.

But Joe and Joel Average have started to become rather more adventurous of late. The last few years have seen a surge in confidence amongst the gay community, matched by a greater recognition and acceptance from the wider population. As we recognise the diversity of our community, more highly specialised gay travel operators have sprung up to cater for every conceivable destination and activity.

For the physically active traveller, there are adventure holidays aplenty, from canyoneering and mountain biking in the wilds of Utah to discovering Aboriginal culture in the Australian Outback, white-water rafting, scuba diving, whale watching, mountaineering, skiing, snowboarding, trekking through the Amazon – the sky's the limit. Or rather it isn't; there are hang-gliding and ballooning trips. And you can be sure that when the first travel agents start sending people into space, one of them will be a gay operator.

More sedentary pursuits include painting, cookery, art history and music. Self-development on a Greek island or group bonding on a Turkish yacht, or perhaps a spa getaway in Iceland: the choice seems limitless. All these holidays are marketed directly to gay men and lesbians, by gay or gay friendly companies. Straight friends may come along, but only in the company of a responsible homosexual.

The development of the gay travel market can be ascribed directly to the concept of the Pink Pound. This developed in the late Eighties, with the realisation that because of their lack of dependants gay people have a greater disposable income than their straight counterparts. This, combined with the fact that in gay couples both are likely to be in full-time work, has made the gay sector a dream consumer group for marketeers of all persuasions.

Research in the US has since suggested that gay men are four times more likely to hold a current passport than heterosexual men, and have a greater propensity for travel. In Britain, a survey of *Gay Times* readers found that 76 per cent take holidays abroad at least once a year and that 34 per cent travel at least twice a year.

How representative these figures are of the gay population as a whole is open to debate, but the response to such data has been phenomenal. Major international travel companies have suddenly become interested in courting this previously shunned group.

And this new found interest is not confined to companies. Cities, states and even countries are bending over backwards to attract and accommodate the gay visitor. Sydney's Mardi Gras brings millions of dollars into the city in tourist-generated revenue, a fact that the city is eager to exploit and expand on. Florida's Tourist Board had long targeted the gay visitor, as has Amsterdam. Hawaii, since its change in legislation, now promotes itself as the gay wedding capital. Politics are not entirely market-driven, however. A government-produced leaflet aimed at attracting gay visitors to Spain was withdrawn after a change of administration.

Gay travel trade shows now take place regularly in London and throughout the US, and workshops and seminars on selling to the gay consumer are legion. While specialised companies thrive, the traditional gay holiday firms have grown substantially, and are combing the globe to find new gay destinations. Prague has joined Amsterdam as an ideal location for a weekend break, while Mexico is being touted as the next big thing.

Exclusively gay resorts and developments are being created, where people can stay and never see a heterosexual during their entire visit. Man Friday is one such location, encompassing ten acres of exquisitely manicured lawns, gardens and

Pink pink sunshine

Bangkok: back in vogue, after losing some of the seedier elements. Attracts gay traffic as a stopover for Sydney.

Barcelona and Seville: Close enough to Sitges to combine as two-centre breaks: culture and clubs.

Cape Town: Gay-only safaris – excellent wildlife *and* excellent nightlife.

Most requested destinations at Ferrari Guides website: Amsterdam, Key West, London, Miami, Mykonos, New York, London, Paris, San Francisco and Sydney.

rainforest along Fiji's Coral Coast, where guests stay in 'traditional' thatched huts.

The Desert Tropics Inn in Las Vegas, a city not noted for its tolerance, is an all-male, clothing optional complex to which the management aims to add an all-gay casino in the near future. Even Disney got in on the act, with the Annual Gay Day at Walt's Magic Kingdom.

Of course, all this activity needs media outlets to cover it. The numerous gay travel guides on the market have now been joined by an American monthly magazine called *Our World*, a travel journal for lesbians and gays, focusing on a different part of the world in every issue.

The electronic media have become extremely important to all this. The internet has played a major role in the development of the more specialised companies, giving gay people the world over immediate access to the smallest operators.

This has made it particularly easy to find the gay holiday of your choice. IGTA, the International Gay Travel Association, is the network of the travel industry businesses and of professionals involved in the gay travel market. From a group of 25 when it formed in 1983, it has grown into an organisation with over 1,200 members, and is the ideal starting point in the search for the perfect holiday.

Another excellent site is www.ferrariguides.com, created by the publishers of the Ferrari Guides. Here you can look up holidays by destination, activity, operator or date of travel. If you can't find something that appeals here, perhaps you're better off staying at home.

The gay community has come a long way in the last few decades, and increasingly that journey is becoming measurable in air miles. Please note that this article concentrates exclusively on gay men, as the lesbian market is a rather different though equally vibrant area. It is too soon to tell whether the market can sustain such levels of exploitation, and consequently whether the intervention of the mainstream companies will continue. Current opinion is optimistic but corporate attention can be fickle, if companies don't make their quotas. In the meantime, the gay traveller can bask in all the attention, and rest assured in the knowledge that he faces a choice that – for the first time – is second to none. ❧

Tony Leonard is a freelance writer and a regular contributor to 'Gay Times'.

The disabled traveller: 1 A personal view
by Quentin Crewe

M Y DOCTOR, WHEN A PATIENT ASKS WHETHER IT IS WISE for him or her to travel, nearly always says, "Yes, it will do you good."

He takes the view that, unless it is obviously impossible or plainly dangerous, any patient who wants to go will be happier going. Only twice in his long career has he lost a patient. He still reckons that it was a good way for them to go and they might just as well have died if they had stayed at home. This is the principle I have always worked on. I live my life in a wheelchair, as I have muscular dystrophy, but I have been round the world many times. I have been blown up by a land mine in Mauritania, nearly drowned in Niger, robbed by bandits in Brazil, lost in the Saudi Arabian desert, embraced by a snake in Kenya, threatened by a bear in India, but I am still here, as John Major has been known to say.

Disability takes many forms. What is true for one person does not necessarily apply to the next, but my hope is that as many disabled people as possible will, as it were, have a go. They will have many agreeable surprises. For instance, who would guess that Bogotá is one of the best cities in the world for wheelchairs, almost every pavement carefully ramped? It is a pleasure to wander around, but I would carry a little mugging money with you.

Obviously, the easiest way to travel is by car, and I must admit that most of my major journeys have been by road, including 24,000 miles round South America in a Toyota Landcruiser, which involved 1,000 miles floating down the Amazon river for five days and nights on a barge, sleeping on the deck, under some lorries.

Air is my next preferred method of travel. This has improved immensely in the last few years. On the whole, I do not warn anyone of my situation when I buy a ticket, taking the view that disabled people should be able to do things on the spur of the moment, like everyone else. I just turn up at the airport and leave it to them. I have found that if one goes to a travel agent and alerts them, they create problems and ask for doctor's certificates to say one is fit to travel. I have seldom had trouble. Some years ago in Tunis, I was asked to sign an indemnity saying that if there were a crash and I impeded someone's escape, I would be liable. It seemed a reasonable chance to take.

Forgetting my own rules, not long ago in India I went myself into the airline office. They asked for a doctor's certificate. There was a doctor in the same street. For a few rupees, he wrote a certificate to my dictation.

Before landing, it is essential to check that the pilot has radioed ahead to ask for help to be ready at your destination. In more remote places, the airport may not have one of those narrow chairs for getting disabled people to their seats and up and down aircraft steps. On the other hand, in remote places, there are usually strong, helpful people ready and eager to carry you on and off the plane. If this could hurt you, it is worth checking beforehand. I have often been carried off upside down with all my change falling out of my pocket – to the delight of the helpers. If you are flying with your own chair, it is important to make sure they have put it in the hold. Taking off from Beirut once, I looked out of the window to see my chair sitting abandoned on the runway.

A major drawback to air travel is the impossibility of getting to the toilets. Fortunately, air travel is dehydrating and it is amazing what, with the help of a friend, can be achieved discreetly, by a man at least, under a rug – as I dare say members of the 'mile high club' would testify. Otherwise, a GP could give you advice about aids to incontinence.

Rail travel in Britain used to mean a chilly ride in the guard's van. These days, things have improved, but it is well to warn them ahead, especially when there is a question of taking a seat out to make room for your chair. ❧

The disabled traveller: 2 The facts
by Carey Ogilvie

S O ACCESSIBLE HAS THE WORLD BECOME IN THE LAST 20 YEARS or so that no one now blinks an eyelid if you click on to www.lastminute.com on the spur of the moment and dash off to Paris for the weekend. The ease with which we are able to travel the world grows annually. With more people travelling, the industry fights for our custom; airlines negotiate new routes and tantalise us with special offers on the internet; operators offer more and more irresistible deals; and guidebooks and information abound as never before: the world, in short, is our oyster. The same is not true for disabled travellers, however. Although numerous organisations and charities have consistently offered help and advice, it is only in the last five years or so that attitudes have begun to change within the tourist industry. As with most changes in any industry, this has been market-forced: according to the US National Organisation of Disability, 54 million Americans have some sort of disability. In the UK, meanwhile, even with the 1995 Disability Discrimination Act in force, there is still a long way to go before travel becomes plain sailing for the wheelchair-bound.

But success as a disabled traveller often depends on your attitude of mind, and great things are possible even though you may not always find that the system works for you. Nevertheless, there are a number of organisations that exist in order to help you.

Independent travel

On the whole, public transport wherever you may be is not designed with the disabled in mind, but improvements are taking place and in the UK are set to continue with the implementation of the transport regulations of the Disability Discrimination Act.

Airlines have greatly improved the facilities they offer, and most now have set procedures for assisting disabled passengers. But – unlike other forms of transport – there are no discounts available, and there is a strong feeling among disabled people that airlines do not actively encourage us to travel by air.

Generally, the best advice is to give the airline as much notice as possible and to obtain detailed advice from the airline regarding exactly what they can and will provide. If you are in a wheelchair, you are more than likely to remain in your wheelchair until just before boarding. Most airlines provide an on-board wheelchair, but it all depends on the aircraft, the airline and the airport. Tales of being hoisted up through the cargo holds are not unknown. *Everybody's Airline Directory* (www.everybody.co.uk) offers a listing of each airline's disabled policy, including whether they will carry guide dogs, whether the cabin staff are disability trained, whether disabled passengers must be accompanied or not, and so on. Most of the major leading airlines have some planes equipped with accessible toilets. Check with the airline concerned, but do not assume either that this will be the case or that they will not change the aircraft at the last moment.

Like your suitcase, your wheelchair runs the risk of being damaged by the time it is returned to you, but on the whole airlines do try to make an effort. A notable exception is Ryanair, which instead tries to make money: their policy is to charge passengers with disability a handling charge of £12.50 per assistance required, i.e. on boarding and disembarkation. A return fare therefore costs an extra £50, making Ryanair not quite the low-cost carrier it claims to be.

If you are travelling by ferry, the general rule again is to let the ferry company know your needs. Ask them if you can board your vehicle at the head of the queue, so that you can get out of it before another car is parked alongside it (making it almost impossible to open a door, let alone move a wheelchair). Discounts on ferry travel are available to members of the Disabled Drivers' Motor Club, Cosy Nook, Cottingham Way, Thrapston, Northamptonshire NN14 4PL, tel 01832 734724 or the Disabled Drivers' Association, Ashwellthrope Hall, Ashwellthrope, Norwich, NR16 1EX, tel 01508 489449. Even if you are not a member of one of these organisations, some ferry companies still offer discounts, so do enquire.

> Too often… I would hear men boast only of the miles covered that day, rarely of what they had seen.
> – LOUIS L'AMOUR

The main challenge of travelling by rail in the UK is not so much the rolling stock but the stations, many of which have footbridges and stairs. Each rail operator is required to offer a dedicated number that disabled passengers may ring to arrange assistance. The national rail travel helpline, on 0345 484950, will be able to give you individual numbers for the required rail service. All credit to Eurostar, who have really got their act together: all their facilities are fully accessible to people in wheelchairs, those with walking difficulties, the partially sighted and people with hearing difficulties. Blind people and wheelchair users with one travelling companion are entitled to a preferential fare, moreover. The equivalent of less than the regular Standard Class price, this includes seating in First Class accommodation, which features a special wheelchair area.

Useful books

■ *Smooth Ride Guides – Freewheeling Made Easy* (Smooth Ride Guides, Duck Street Barns, Furneux Pelham, Hertfordshire SG9 0LA, tel 01279 777966) are a series of comprehensive guides for travellers in wheelchairs. Two are currently in print: the *Smooth Ride Guide to the United Kingdom*, and the *Smooth Ride Guide to the United States Eastern Seaboard*. Guides to France, Spain and Italy are also planned.

■ Mobility International USA (PO Box 10767, Eugene, OR 97440, USA, tel 00 1 541 343 1284) publish a comprehensive two-volume guide entitled *A World Of Options* ($45). Its 600+ pages are packed with personal travel accounts and essential information on travelling, working or being a volunteer abroad. It also offers in-depth critiques of various airlines, car rental companies, hotels, cruise ships and adventure packages.

■ If you are worried about the challenge of travelling, Patrick Simpson's *Wheelchair Around the World*, telling the story of how he and his wife Anne fulfilled their lifelong dream to travel around the world, is inspirational. The Simpsons' advice could stand as a resourceful guide for all, and their story exudes an addictive spirit of adventure that will inspire many to follow in their tracks.

■ For the past 20 years, RADAR has published *Holidays in Britain and Ireland – A Guide for Disabled People*. The current edition includes detailed information on over 1,300 places to stay. It is available at £8 (including postage and packing) through their web site (www.radar.org.uk) or by post (12 City Forum, 250 City Road, London EC1V 8AF; 020-7250 3222). RADAR also produces three excellent *Holiday Facts* packs to guide you through every stage of a holiday.

Getting to most airports and railway stations – and above all getting across London – almost invariably requires a sense of humour and a great deal of patience. Although no longer banned from the London Underground, wheelchair users will find the London Underground system almost impossible (the Manchester Metrolink, by contrast, is fully accessible and has one wheelchair space in each carriage).

Two publications are available to help you across London. *Access to the Underground* is available from RADAR (the Royal Association for Disability and Rehabilitation, 12 City Forum, 250 City Road, London EC1V 8AF, tel 020 7250 3222), price £1. It provides a general description of each line, a guide to fixed stairs in stations with escalators, access details from station entrances to platforms and interchange information. The excellent guidebook *Access in London*, available in bookshops, includes chapters on travel in and around the capital.

And what about hotels? Unlike airlines, the hotel industry caters well for the disabled traveller. When choosing a hotel (especially abroad), check that the facilities that are important to you are accessible. They might have a room designed for the disabled, but then you may find five steps leading up to the restaurant. As always, explain your needs and wishes when you book. An excellent alternative to staying in a hotel is a home exchange. Accessible Home Exchange, run by the Swedish organisation Independent Living, has a web site (www.independentliving.org) offering a good choice of homes. Swapping homes with another person with similar needs in another part of the world is a low-cost and practical solution to accommodation problems.

Cruising is one of the easiest and most popular forms of travel for the disabled. The choice of cruise ships and destinations grows each year, as a wider choice of accessible ships becomes available. On the whole, the most recently built ships offer the most facilities for the disabled traveller. The *2000 Guide to Cruising* (Berlitz, £16.95) is a good place to start your research into different cruise lines and ships. As well as assessing all cruise ships and offering advice on selecting and booking a cruise, it also has an entire chapter dedicated to cruising for the disabled.

Organisations offering general help and advice on travelling with disabilities include not only RADAR but also Tripscope (Alexandra House, Albany Road, Brentford, Middlesex TW8 ONE, tel 0208580 7021) and the Holiday Care Service, 2nd Floor, Imperial Buildings, Victoria Way, Horley, Surrey RH6 7PZ, tel 01293 774535; www.holidaycare.org.uk). Holiday Care Service, a registered charity established in 1981, has been instrumental in changing attitudes within the industry. It now publishes UK regional guides to accommodation that is accessible for the wheelchair user, all of which can be booked through the organisation at discounted prices. The free service provided by Tripscope is perhaps the most informative of all: although they are not a travel agent and therefore cannot arrange bookings, their suggestions pave the way.

A number of travel agents (generally run by people with disabilities) specialise in travel for the disabled. Can be Done (tel 020 8907 2400, www.canbedone.co.uk) can arrange both group and individual travel for people with all types of physical limitation. Gloucester-based Travelability based is run by Richard Thompson and Paul Derbyshire, both of whom have spinal cord injuries. With nearly 20 years' experience in the travel trade, they can tailor an itinerary to suit virtually any needs (www.travelability.co.uk, The Ferns, Framilode, Gloucester GL2 7LH, tel 01452 740820).

Organised tours

Numerous companies organise tours for the disabled. Some are mixed ability tours while others are solely for the handicapped; some are charities and others work on a commercial basis. The opportunities, however, are endless.

One of the most inspiring charities is Across, who organise tours and pilgrimages for the severely disabled in their Jumblances. They started in 1972 with a transit van to Lourdes, and now offer a wide range of holidays in Europe and the Holy Land. Jumblances are fitted with adjustable tubular aluminum beds, sleeper and reclining seats, resuscitation equipment, oxygen, pressure mattresses and every other facility necessary for the comfort and safety of their passengers.

For those who want to go below the surface, the Scubatrust (tel 01797 361975) was launched in 1996 at the London International Dive Show, the brainchild of a group of diving enthusiasts and instructors who were determined to give people with physical disabilities an equal opportunity to experience the pleasures of snorkelling and diving.

AdventureQuest.com, based in Maine, usa, is an on-line agent specialising in adventure tours, with a section devoted to disabled adventures. Neverland Adventures (715 J Street Suite 201, San Diego, California 92101, tel 00 1 619 696 6068, www.neverland-adventures.com) is a company owned and staffed by people with disabilities, whose specialty is adventure trips to Australia and now New Zealand. Their Outback Experience includes a hot-air balloon trip at Ayers Rock.

Another sporting holiday on offer is skiing. As they say at the Uphill Ski Club, "Why shouldn't you have a wheelchair at the top of a mountain?" Founded over 25 years ago, the club is committed to providing winter sports activities for people with a wide range of disabilities, including cerebral palsy, spina bifida, epilepsy, learning difficulties, head injuries and sensory handicaps. For further information, contact them at 6a Emson Close, Saffron Walden, Essex cb10 1hl, tel 01799 525406, or through their Northern Office at Glenmore Lodge, Glenmore, By Aviemore, Invernesshire p22 1qu, tel 01479 861 272, or visit their web site at www.ccksb.freeserve.co.uk.

The most important thing for both the consumer and the travel industry to remember is that there is no such thing as a holiday that is unsuitable for people with disabilities, whatever their needs: everything depends on the degree of disability and the attitude of all concerned.

Happy freewheeling. 🐾

The late QUENTIN CREWE *was a highly respected author, traveller and restaurateur, who had been confined to a wheelchair since childhood.*
CAREY OGILVIE *was Assistant Editor of a previous edition of 'The Traveller's Handbook' and now works in the travel industry.*

Classic journeys

Overland through Africa
by Warren Burton

IT IS NO WONDER THAT THE VASTNESS OF AFRICA'S LANDMASS, unknown and untamed, should have presented the ultimate challenge to Europeans for centuries. Africa is a huge and incredibly diverse continent stretching from the Mediterranean to the southern oceans – the eastern 'horn' jutting into the Arabian Sea to the Atlantic coast of Senegal. Its size was fully realised only by seafaring explorers who began charting the coastlines during the seventeenth and eighteenth centuries. It contains the world's largest desert and its longest river, but this represents only a part of Africa's statistics. So much about it remains unknown, yet the Great Rift Valley contains evidence of the birthplace of mankind. Tales of the expeditions undertaken by Livingstone, Burton and Speke (amongst many others) still inspire many to take on Africa's challenge. There is never a dull moment in Africa – it is forever changing. Politically it is often in turmoil, but it is a big place and the regions/countries affected normally only represent a small proportion of the continent. But travellers should be informed and definitely open-minded – any day can throw up unpredictable events that have no equivalent in any other part of the world. A journey through even a part of Africa will probably represent the major travel experience of a lifetime.

Up-to-date medical advice should be sought before departure because of the ever-present health risks in Africa. Malaria is now on the increase, particularly in sub-Saharan and West Africa. And HIV has become a major hazard throughout Africa (see chapter on Sex Abroad).

Crossing the Sahara to Central Africa

Hardly a year goes by without some part of Africa being categorised as a 'no-go' region. The Sahara is no exception, and quite apart from its usual challenges – extremes of heat, lack of roads, closed frontiers – it is now the Sahara's own internal unrest that stands in the way of travellers. The established and rather traditional route followed over the past 25–30 years now carries much greater risks.

In the past (and it is to be hoped that these options will soon return), journeys either started from Morocco, crossing the Atlas Mountains into Algeria, or alternatively began by sailing from Italy and entering at Tunis. Either route takes you south on the 'Trans Sahara Highway' to the oasis towns of Ghardaia, El Golea, In Salah and finally Tamanrasset, at the foot of the mighty Hoggar Massif. More adventurous overlanders, with well-equipped 4x4 vehicles and ample supplies of fuel and water, opted for the dramatic and somewhat tortuous route east via the Tassili plateau and the extraordinary rock formations around Djanet. Discovered in the caves here are 3,000-year-old rock inscriptions, records of life in the Sahara before the expanding sands engulfed much of its vegetation. Desert tracks marked occasionally by oil drums then lead south to Tamanrasset and the ever-elusive 'Highway'. The Sahara has its own way of dealing with development – no sooner do the Algerian and Niger governments lay a few more kilometres of bitumen than along comes a typical desert 'flash flood', sometimes destroying years of work in just a few hours.

A less popular but more practical alternative, again requiring a suitable vehicle (carrying long-range fuel and water supplies), was to travel due south from Bechar to Reggane, before following the Tanzerouft route in Mali. Either way, the present political unrest and rise of Islamic fundamentalism in Algeria renders the country unsafe and these routes largely non-viable. Regrettably this has followed a long period of unrest in the south of the Sahara, on the frontier lands of Algeria, Niger and Mali. During the early- to mid-Nineties, unruly factions of Tuareg, seeking autonomy, set about attacking and robbing any vehicle entering the region, with isolated reports of shootings. Alternative routes had to be found. Crossing Libya into Chad is still really out of the question, so all attention was focused on a route through the former Spanish Sahara (now administered by Morocco) into Mauritania. However, while overlanders have obtained permits from the Moroccan authorities, the Mauritanian government has never really acknowledged this and permission to enter from Morocco is often refused – though this situation now seems to be improving and there is talk of 'legal' northbound crossings.

Still, with careful preparation it can be done – so you are strongly advised to investigate this route thoroughly first. While many travellers still attempt and succeed in crossing Africa without a 4x4, it is still the wisest means of travel, particularly as this alternative route certainly presents some tough days of soft sand in northern Mauritania. It is all the more necessary if you are considering exploring the remoter areas of Mali, Niger and Chad.

Carnet de Passage documents are required for your vehicle once you leave Morocco, and most (if not all) countries in Africa are now very well-informed as to the requirements of vehicle insurance, so you will need to secure minimum third party cover in all countries.

Visas are required to enter Mauritania, and you are advised to obtain these in Europe (Bonn, Paris or Madrid). It is reported that they are also obtainable in Rabat, Morocco – but this is possibly leaving it too late should they be refused. It is also best to obtain visas for Mali while in Europe, thus avoiding the risk of not being able to obtain them before leaving Mauritania. Most other visas can be obtained *en route* in neighbouring countries.

Your route through Morocco should certainly take in the imperial city of Fes, renowned for its huge walled Medina. Then crossing the High Atlas to Todra Gorge and the edge of the Grand Erg Occidentale, with its 'sea of sand dunes'. Marrakech still retains its mystic aura, and is your last 'semi-civilised' centre before heading south to the coastal sands of the Western Sahara. Following the Atlantic coast via Layounne you arrive in Dakhla, the formal exit point from Morocco. Here at least a day of tedious paperwork and form-filling will enable you to join a twice-weekly 'convoy' south to the frontier post at La Gouria. A short but tricky desert crossing brings you into Mauritania at Nouadhibou – a strange town, servicing the rail link and port essential to the export of the country's phosphate reserves.

Mauritania is an Islamic republic and thus prohibits the import of alcohol, so it is wise to consume or dispose of this prior to entry. Furthermore, overland travel has only recently arrived on Mauritania's doorstep – so it is as well to tread lightly and savour the rather timid reception you may receive, though generally local people are very friendly and helpful.

Entry formalities are slow, and you must obtain a '*Laissez Passe*' (permit) to travel south to Nouakchott. For the more adventurous, and with the assistance of a local guide and plenty of sand-matting, try the route due south. You then have to catch the low tide in order to drive the last 150 kilometres along the beach into Nouakchott. A bitumen road takes you east to Nema before joining some rough tracks south into Mali and on to Bamako.

Borders with Mauritania and Senegal are open, so a route encompassing most of West Africa can be considered – but check for the rainy season, when many routes are impassable.

If time permits, Mali presents a wealth of culture, history and tradition, much of which is found around Mopti and Djenne in the lands of the Songhai and even up to Timbucktu (weather permitting). A little to the east is the Bandiagara Escarpment, the home of the Dogon people, with their traditional lifestyle in evidence. South from here you cross into Burkina Faso (formerly Upper Volta), through Ouagadougou and on to Niger. Niamey, the capital, offers little of interest but does provide the opportunity to obtain several visas before heading off to Nigeria. The popular route now is to Kano in northern Nigeria, offering time out to service vehicles and restock for Central Africa and the Congo. Then head on into northern Cameroon and the spectacular route through the Kapsiki Mountains.

The alternative is to head south from Ougadougou to the Ivory Coast, Ghana, Togo, Benin and southern Nigeria. This route provides more varied insights into West Africa but will obviously add a considerable amount of time to your journey. From Nigeria you enter Cameroon by the southern route, visiting Douala and the capital Yaounde *en route* for the Central African Republic. While visas are readily available to enter Gabon and the Republic of Congo, any route further south appears doubtful. Angola has reverted to a state of unrest and civil war and former Zaïre, now the Democratic Republic of Congo, is still highly volatile.

Back on the traditional overland trail, you enter the Central African Republic via Bouar to reach Bangui, the sleepy but shifty colonial capital renowned for its French pâtisseries. Make the most of them: you won't find too many in the Congo.

Democratic Republic of Congo to East Africa

The route east through the Central Africa Republic to southern Sudan, Juba, and on south to Kenya, has effectively been out of bounds for many years now. The continuing conflict with the North shows no real signs of abating, causing much suffering to the Dinka and Nuer peoples who roam these lands.

So far, and for the foreseeable future, the only route open to East Africa is through the Democratic Republic of Congo (DRC) which, after struggling under President Mobutu for over 30 years now has a new and unstable regime led by Laurent Kabila. At the time of going to press, travel in the DRC is not recommended, but this situation is not necessarily long-term and this is still the best route through to East Africa. Corruption is rife, fuel and food shortages are common, and the 'roads' deteriorate by the year. Anyone considering this route is advised to go prepared, with a vehicle in sound condition (very little in the way of spares or assistance is available on the way). Reserve food and fuel supplies are a must.

There are presently two entry points into DRC from Central Africa, both involving a ferry crossing of the rivers that form the frontiers. Entering at Zongo (across the river from Bangui) will take you south-east via Gemena to Lisala and the Zaïre River. Here you may be able to board a barge or one of the river ferries travelling upstream to Kisangani (Stanleyville during the colonial days of the Belgian Congo). The overland route follows the north bank of the river via Bumba and Buta and then south to Kisangani.

Night silence in Africa holds the far sea-sound of urgent stars.

— LAURENS VAN DER POST

Either way progress is slow. The ferries and barges constantly run aground on shifting sand bars, whereas the road will inevitably be the worse for wear especially during and after the long rainy season (July to November).

The other alternative is to travel further east in the Central African Republic, viewing the awesome Kembe Falls *en route* to Bangassou. Having crossed the Mbomou river you join a 'secondary road' (more like a track) south to Bondo then to Buta; makeshift bridges on this route are very suspect and should always be checked.

Into eastern DRC via the Ituri Forests and the home of various pygmy peoples, you arrive at a point where the best option is to cross into Uganda; alternatively, you can travel further south through the Virunga National Park and enter Rwanda, but this is not recommended. Previously the route south from Komanda to the Virunga National Park and Rwanda was the popular one, but the state of civil war and the Rwandan refugee crisis have left this region in a state of constant disruption, and it is therefore best avoided. The Mountain Gorilla projects in DRC are temporarily suspended, so it is best to seek these out in Uganda or possibly Rwanda (entering from southern Uganda).

Leaving DRC and entering directly into Uganda, a route taking you through Murchison Falls National Park, you will be well rewarded. Here you are at the meeting points of the Victoria and Albert Niles, as they form the mighty White Nile at the start of its long slow journey to the Mediterranean. Uganda, once the 'Jewel of Africa', has endured a long road to recovery following the horrific periods of rule by Amin and Abote, which left this friendliest of countries in rack and ruin. Uganda's people offer you wonderful hospitality: definitely include it on your route.

From Kampala there are several choices of route. Either head directly into Kenya and through the rift valley and its lakes of Baringo, Naivasha and Nakuru to

Nairobi. Or take the southerly route round Lake Victoria directly into Tanzania and on to Mwanza. By doing this you can then visit the game-filled plains of the Serengeti, discover the Olduvai Gorge and climb to the rim of the Ngorongoro Crater. This natural haven for wildlife can be visited by driving down in a Land Rover, chartered locally at the park's wildlife headquarters.

From here you descend into Tanzania's rift valley, via Lake Manyara and the Masai tribelands to Arusha, at the foot of Mount Meru. It is well worth exploring the game reserves of Kenya, the Indian Ocean coast from Lamu to Malindi and the old Arab trading port of Mombasa. Then head south via the slopes of Kilimanjaro, Africa's highest peak. With the support of local guides and porters, you can make a non-technical climb to its snow-capped summit at 19,000 feet.

A completely different route to East Africa for the adventurous would be to go from Niger into Chad, crossing the southern Sahara to enter the Sudan at El Geneima, then head for Khartoum. But you need to choose your season and really research the route and local formalities beforehand – Chad does go through periodic political upheavals and it is not always easy to find reliable, up-to-date information for this region. Several overland companies as well as some independent travellers have taken this route during 1999 and 2000. Travel in northern Sudan is slow but generally straightforward, and you are required to check in with local authorities at every centre. From Khartoum you need to head directly south-east to Ethiopia via Wad Medani, over a very seasonal road. The more viable route via Kassala to Eritrea is out of the question at present, owing to the recent border conflict with Ethiopia. From Ethiopia this route takes you into northern Kenya: again check beforehand on the current situation, as there can often be bandit movements (of Somali origin) in this area. Always join the daily police escorts from Moyale to Marsabit and on to Isilio.

The Rift Valley to the Cape

It seems an age since the days of apartheid in South Africa when travel to neighbouring countries was very restricted. Now travel in the south has been transformed, with the whole of the Nairobi to Cape route becoming a relative highway. Gone are the days of questioning border controls, intent on stalling your progress south through Tanzania, Zambia and Botswana, knowing full well that your destination was ultimately South Africa. Now very few visas are even required to travel through this section and the only real challenge is deciding on your route and preferences. It is easy to stick to the popular main route, but by adopting a more adventurous approach you can still get off the beaten track.

The popular route is south via Dar es Salaam, taking time out to visit the exotic spice island of Zanzibar, where life is dramatically different from on the mainland. By joining the 'Tanzam Highway', you then enter the eastern fork of the Great Rift Valley, which leads you down into Malawi and the characteristic fishing villages dotted along the shores of its beautiful lake. After visiting Lilongwe, Malawi's peaceful capital, you enter Zambia. Your choice is then either to head south via Lake Kariba into Zimbabwe and Harare, or to head for Livingstone and the thundering Victoria Falls on the frontier of Zimbabwe and Zambia. Here activities include white-water rafting, bird's eye flights over the falls and – would you believe – bungy jumping off the bridge joining the frontiers.

There are many different routes from here to the Cape, but most now prefer to cross Botswana, including an excursion into the waterways of the Okavango Basin. The 'islands' of the delta are a haven for wildlife and birds. Carry on through the Caprivi Strip into Namibia, the unique Etosha Pans and the vast mountainous sand dunes that fall dramatically into the Atlantic. The rugged shoreline is littered with skeletons of the shipwrecks for which the coastline is notorious. Sea life havens can be visited as you travel south via Walvis Bay and Luderitz. The Fish River Canyon is a must before leaving Namibia to cross the Orange River into South Africa. Several days' drive brings you to the end of an incredible journey – and Cape Town, overlooked by its distinctive Table Mountain, is an ideal place to end.

An alternative and rewarding route from Harare takes you through the eastern highlands of Zimbabwe into Mozambique, following its wonderful Indian Ocean coastline to Maputo and then into South Africa. From here you can go south to Durban, the Drakensbergs, Lesotho and the garden route to the Cape.

The alternative Cairo to Nairobi route

Regrettably, with southern Sudan still a 'no go' zone, the route directly south from Egypt up the Nile to Khartoum, Kosti, Juba and into Kenya is still not possible. The little-used route from Wad Madeni to the gorges of the Blue Nile into Ethiopia and Lake Tana is seasonally passable, but the borders between Sudan and Ethiopia are periodically closed.

The most practical route from Khartoum used to be to travel via Kassala into Eritrea to Asmara, the capital, then south to Ethiopia, following the dramatic highlands route to Addis Ababa. But the last two years have seen these two neighbours in periodic conflict over their borders, which recently led to an all-out invasion and declared victory by Ethiopia. So the journey via Eritrea is really out of the question for some time. From Addis Ababa, perched on the 'wall' of the Great Rift Valley, there is a viable route south through the lakes and desert lands bordering on Kenya. This is harsh country that experiences extreme temperatures, but it is at least part of an overland route that was not generally possible for some twenty years between the mid-Seventies and mid-Nineties. ❧

WARREN BURTON is Operations Manager at Encounter Overland, having led expeditions for them worldwide.

Overland through South-East Asia
by Myfanwy Vickers and Rachel Flower

THE PRINCIPLE UNDERLYING OVERLAND TRAVEL is that it is as good to travel as to arrive. Most guidebooks will jump you from site to site, city to city, beautiful beach to ancient temple, and tell you little if anything about the stretches in between – which is a shame, as this is often where you will find the vital heart of a country.

For anyone with a sense of adventure, overland travel is best undertaken independently, using whatever local transport is available, self-propelled or otherwise. This way, not only do you have total freedom of movement, but your pace is adjusted to that of the life going on around you. If you travel by train, bus, jeep or any other local means, you still have the opportunity either to take a side road or to get out mid-way to do some exploring. If you don't feel like going off the beaten track completely, however, 'independent' travel can hover reassuringly close to the well-travelled tour routes. The down side of this is that you meet the same people on the same route in the same places, and the mystique of the exotic somehow eludes you.

Throughout South-East Asia, the choices of available transport are many and varied, and this is part of the fun. Not only are there buses and trains (which may bear little resemblance to their Western namesakes), but also trucks and jeeps, taxis and *tuk-tuks*, *bemos* and *becaks*, rickshaws and trishaws, pony and traps, coming in all shapes, sizes and speeds. For the weary traveller, a ride around town in a bicycle rickshaw – a sort of open-air armchair on wheels, decked out with bells and bunting – is a luxury hard to beat. You're also much closer to the action, namely the constant stream of tempting invitations at your ear ("Batik? Statues? Sarongs? My cousin's factory? I give you good price!"). What is more, it will probably only cost you about 30p an hour.

Nevertheless, travel on public transport can be less than fun. Simply buying a ticket can be a chaotic and frustrating experience, more akin to a perverse treasure hunt or mystery tour that you hadn't bargained for (and not speaking or reading the local language can be a huge disadvantage in such situations). In combination with the practice of some local drivers of refusing to set off before their vehicle is filled to three times its capacity, this conspires to prove a maddening and crushing experience for the average Anglo-Saxon traveller.

Once aboard, you have to contend not merely with your (numerous) fellow passengers, but also with their baskets and boxes, goats, birds (caged and uncaged) and occasionally even bats, babies and elbows, airlessness and cramp, perhaps the distorted wail of an amplifier in your ear, and a nagging feeling that you have paid over the odds for a conveyance that is heading in the wrong direction and provides nowhere for you to put your feet. Few experiences can be more alarming than being inside an Indonesian public bus as it bears down, avenger-like and with its holy shrine swaying in hectic fashion, on a group of yet more passengers waiting on a bend in the road – apparently intent on carrying them off into the next world (all too grim a reality on occasion).

In desperate straits such as these, try telling yourself that it is all part of the 'experience'. Assertiveness when necessary and an inexhaustible sense of humour are invaluable assets. And since your schedule is up to you, once you arrive at your destination you can give yourself time to recover from the rigours of getting there.

Most tourists in South-East Asia fly into Bangkok and head north to trek in Chiang Mai, then south to the beaches. For those who have been overlanding across India and Nepal, Thailand is a blessing, for travel is cheap, easy and relatively clean. When I cycled through the country, barely a day passed without a vehicle stopping to offer me a ride. Hitch-hikers should have no problem, and Thailand's public transport system is increasingly modern, efficient and relatively punctual.

The four trunk routes of the state rail system run to the north, north-east, east and south; long-distance trains have sleeping cars and/or air-conditioned coaches which are extremely comfortable. Slower than buses, they are also safer, and you have the added advantage of not being pinned to your seat.

Both state and private buses are cheap and uncomfortable, and the cheapest ones tend to be accident-prone; this is not unusual in Asia, and many travellers are not put off. The more expensive private buses are in some ways more civilised and safer, though you may find curtains sealing off the view while a video of 'Life in Rural Thailand' blares through the bus. Try not to be tempted by some of the ridiculously cheap bus fares on offer (for example £1 for Chiang Mai to Bangkok). If you can't resist, at least refuse all offers of food or drink: people have been known to wake from a peculiarly deep sleep to find all their belongings gone.

Reputable car rental companies such as Avis and Budget Rentacar operate out of Bangkok and Chiang Mai, and there is also the usual panoply of taxis, *tuk-tuks* and *bemos*. Travel by motorbike or bicycle is easy, and increasingly seems the only way to see parts of the country that lie off the beaten track. Mae Hong Son, long cut off by mountains, is being promoted as one of the last undeveloped areas for trekking – but when you learn that Thai Airways flies from Bangkok and twice daily from Chiang Mai, you begin to see why the in-between bits become almost essential. Head out to the north-east, a dry plateau known as 'Isaan', meaning 'vastness', before the hordes arrive.

Overland travel is interrupted by Myanmar (Burma), impenetrable at present through any of its five land borders: unless you decide to ford a river, you have no choice but to take to the air. Some border crossings between Thailand and Myanmar are open to day-trippers or for short excursions, however. The situation could change, so check on the latest developments with travel agents or websites.

Travellers to Myanmar should note that visiting this country is the subject of fierce controversy, particularly among human rights activists, and has been criticised by the imprisoned pro-democracy leader and Nobel Laureate Aung San Suu Kyi. You should brief yourself on the issues before deciding whether to visit.

Those who do decide to visit Myanmar can now get a visa for one month, which allows plenty of time to visit the main sights and more. There are some restrictions on places open to tourists, however, so check this before deciding your itinerary. Avoid using state-run tour agencies, as they feed the coffers of the repressive, military-run State Peace and Development Council (formerly the State Law and Order Restoration Council, SLORC).

Trains in Myanmar are cheap, and tourists may use most lines. Cheap buses run everywhere. Jeeps run at random, leaving when they are full. Hiring is expensive, and if you stray off limits you may waste time being stopped. Bicycle trishaws and pony traps can be hired for the day – but you may end up walking some of the way out of compassion. Ferries are an excellent way of getting around: the 12-hour trip down the Irawaddy from Mandalay to Pagan is certainly a journey worth making.

To make the most of your time and concentrate on Pagan, take the night train from Yangon to Mandalay. After exploring Mandalay, fly to Pagan (or take a ferry in season). In Pagan, don't miss Mount Popa. Next fly to Heho, then take a bus to Yaunghwe for a scenic boat tour of Lake Inle. Then take a bus to Thazi followed by the night train to Yangon, getting off two hours short of Yangon to explore Pegu in the early morning and catching a later train out.

The 13,000 islands making up the Indonesian archipelago seem to offer as many different variations on the theme of transport. Only Java and Sumatra, for example, have a railway (consult a specialist guidebook for details). Java and Bali are now well served with new roads, but getting off the beaten track in Indonesia means just that: the road may be hard to locate. Parts of the so-called Trans-Sumatran highway are like a battlefield, pitted with pot-holes and scattered with boulders. Wooden bridges built for buffalo carts now take heavy goods traffic. Lorries favour a technique involving grinding to a virtual halt at the bridge, throwing themselves into top gear, and then lurching across with engines roaring, as if taking the bridge by surprise might somehow forestall its collapse. Roads in the less developed south-eastern islands, Nusa Tenggara, are even bumpier and likely to have been flooded and washed away in the rainy season (November to March). Here, outlying areas are served by an irregular public transport system, and you are better off under your own steam. At present, the Moluccas are a no-go area.

In Kalimantan, dense jungle, a sparse population and a natural network of waterways make rivers the main arteries. If they are not navigable, travel is virtually impossible except by air. Take outboard motor boats, longboats, dug-outs, ferries and water taxis. In Irian Jaya, you will need a spirit of adventure and a sharp implement for cutting your way through tangled vegetation.

Overland travel in the Philippines may be difficult, but is not impossible. Travel in the deep south, where Muslim insurgency has seen a recent upsurge, may be inadvisable: check with the local authorities first. While the Philippines boast very cheap internal flights, these get heavily booked, so be prepared for a wait. Overland travel here is quite hard work: boats are a must, but bear in mind that only the luxury end of the market will be relaxing. Every type of tub and ferry is available; ask at the port if you get no joy in the office.

Be wary of travelling in bad weather: safety precautions are non-existent and people regularly drown in shipping accidents. Unique to the Philippines is the jeepney, an ex-US jeep festooned with flashing lights, garishly painted cut-out characters, bells and baubles. Shout and gesticulate when you want to get out.

Although most current guidebooks will tell you it is not possible to travel independently overland in Indo-China, it is. Unlike Malaysia and Singapore, where travel is simple and far from alien, these countries have only recently been opened up after long periods of devastation, and there are things you need to know.

Vietnam has an extensive network of decrepit, overcrowded and exhausting buses. Trains are more reliable, but can average as little as 15 kilometres an hour. Thanks to the war efforts of the Americans, the roads are not bad, and you can always hire a car with driver. Initially, foreigners had to ask for an inter-province pass and report every time they came to a new provincial centre. This is no longer the case, but with the recent troubles the system may be instigated again. Talk to other travellers to find out the latest regulations.

In Laos, investigate flights: the country is incredibly mountainous, has no railway, and the roads are abysmal even by Asian standards. Tortuous dirt roads will defeat you utterly between June and September (the rainy season). The major towns are linked by air, and rivers form some of the country's main thoroughfares.

Tourists are no longer forbidden to travel on buses in Cambodia – although huge areas are without roads anyway. Again, ferries provide a useful service, and the railway functions despite frequent delays. A limited number of flights is available on set routes, and others are added when there is sufficient demand.

Everything about transport in Indo-China reinforces my initial point: self-propelled means are the most effective. People are already walking and mountain-biking in Indo-China; I do urge you, with undisguised bias, to try it. Paradoxically, self-propulsion is often less tiring than mechanical modes of transport, and it has an uncanny way of making everything seem more wonderful. Perhaps you are simply grateful for small mercies when you finally arrive. But appreciating the little things, and the everyday, is what overland travel is all about. ৰ৯

MYFANWY VICKERS is a traveller, writer and radio producer.
RACHEL FLOWER is a travel journalist based in Chiang Mai, Thailand.

Overland through Asia
by Warren Burton

THE JOURNEY ACROSS ASIA must still be considered the most venerable of all overland routes. History provides us with sketchy accounts of the great overland journeys of Alexander, Hannibal and Marco Polo. Further afield, ancient stories of Ghengis Khan and more latterly of the explorers along the Silk Route still provide inspiration to travellers to explore the further reaches of Asia. Overland journeys to India and beyond are still practicable, despite international conflicts such as the 1991 Gulf War and continuing tribal warfare in Afghanistan. The Middle East continues to present some instability, yet there has always been a safe and viable alternative route to follow. Now that the revolution in Iran is some 20 years in the past, the country is no longer the bureaucratic and logistical nightmare that it was during those few years of turmoil. Visas are available to all, even holders of US passports, and even five-day Transit Visas can be extended to up to 14 days with relative ease within Iran. But in the wake of the Gulf War, and despite promises to the Kurdish people by the West, there is still unrest in south-east Turkey (Turkish Kurdistan). As the suppressed and isolated Kurds struggle once again for autonomy, the Turkish government's answer – as ever – is to send in the army. This is definitely a region to be avoided, but fortunately (for travellers) there are alternatives.

With the continuing effects of the break-up of former Yugoslavia, the most direct route to Istanbul via Zagreb (Belgrade following the E5) is still not recommended. A diversion through Hungary, Romania and Bulgaria can nevertheless bring you into Turkey (and Asia) without covering too many more kilometres. It also provides a glimpse of countries that have experienced considerable change since the break-up of the Eastern Bloc. Alternatively, you can travel via Italy, taking a ferry to Greece from Brindisi and continuing via Thessaloniki.

The crossing of Asia remains a bureaucratic challenge, however, so go prepared with the necessary vehicle documentation, and most importantly a *Carnet de Passage* and vehicle registration document, both correct in every detail as border officials can be very uncompromising. In addition you must have minimum third party insurance. Most international insurance companies will cover you with a 'Green Card' at least as far as Turkey and possibly Iran, but afterwards you will be purchasing locally as you go. Furthermore, virtually all nationalities now require a visa for all countries east of Turkey. These must be obtained before departure, as they cannot be issued on entry and are often not obtainable in neighbouring countries.

Istanbul and all routes east

Istanbul, where Europe meets Asia, is the perfect place to pause in order to finalise your plans and timings. The city is well serviced, and although it is not the Turkish capital most countries on your route have diplomatic representation here. It also makes an ideal meeting point for travellers heading east, and you may be fortunate to meet some who are returning westbound: recent experience is always the most reliable source of current information.

The most direct route to Iran and beyond is via Ankara (the capital), then up to the Anatolian Plateau through Sivas, Erzincan, Erzurum to Dogubayazit (last stop in Turkey). This region has been affected sporadically by Kurdish unrest, so check with the local authorities before leaving Ankara. Never travel at night and stay in towns rather than camping out.

The alternative route, longer and more rewarding by far, heads south from Istanbul via the Gallipoli Peninsula, crossing the Dardanelles to Canakkale. After that the choice is yours, but why not visit Troy, Bergama, Kusadasi (and Ephesus), then go east to Pamukkale before crossing the mountains to the south coast? You could spend a few days lazing around the beaches and coves of Olu Deniz, before following the dramatic coastal route from Fethiye via Kas to Antalya, Side and

Anamur. This route is not only scenically spectacular but also dotted with ancient Roman sites, Crusader castles and typically Turkish coastal villages.

Once you have travelled virtually the entire length of the south coast, you reach Adana, which lies at a crossroads: south to Syria and a diversion to the Middle East (see below) or north across the Taurus Mountains to Cappadocia (and the environs of Goreme) and on to rejoin the main E5 route at Sivas.

Diverting into the Middle East

If time and money permit, you should certainly consider visiting Syria, the Lebanon and Jordan. More recent conflicts and friction between neighbours restrict travel possibilities, but the situation is constantly changing. At time of going to press, the Israel/Palestine peace process could well change the entire area – even Syria and Israel are at last talking to each other over conference tables.

Visas are required for both Syria and Jordan and should be obtained before you leave Europe. You do not require any other special paperwork for your vehicle, but be patient with Syrian border procedures, which can be very autocratic and time-consuming. Lebanese visas may be obtained either in Damascus or on the border.

From Adana, head south to the coastal town of Iskenderun, cross into Syria at the Baba el Hawa border and carry on to Aleppo, which has both the largest medieval citadel in the world and the largest bazaar/*souk* in the Middle East. Further south you come to the waterwheels of Hama, then on to Homs and Damascus, Syria's bustling capital. A visit to Lebanon can be arranged from here. Cross the Jordanian border at Dar'a, then carry on to Amman, the capital. The city offers little of interest, but the ancient site of Jerash to the north is well worth a visit.

Jordan holds surprises for many travellers. Not only are the people extremely friendly and hospitable (65 per cent of the population being Palestinian), but the country is also geographically stunning and historically dramatic. A route via the Dead Sea takes you along the King's Highway from Madaba to Kerak and Petra, the hidden city of Nabateans. Several days here would not be wasted, before heading south to the Aqaba on the Red Sea.

You can complete a circuit by returning to Amman along the Desert Highway, with a highly recommended excursion *en route* to Wadi Rum (famous in the days of Lawrence of Arabia). Take a local Bedouin guide and you will travel through some of the most spectacular desert scenery to be seen in the Middle East.

From Amman it is possible to take an excursion to the 'West Bank' of the Jordan River, namely Israel, but you require a special permit (obtainable in Amman) and you are not permitted to take your own vehicle. Fortunately, border controls between Jordan and Israel do not stamp your passport. On returning from Jordan, however, you must ensure that you have no evidence of Israeli goods, souvenirs etc., or you will run into great difficulty when you attempt to re-enter Syria and afterwards Iran.

At the time of writing, there is still no recommended route into Iraq. Furthermore, travelling overland through Saudi Arabia is still prohibited, though (if you were considering shipping to the Gulf States or beyond) transit permits are occasionally issued for travel from Jordan to coastal parts.

On re-entering Syria from Jordan and returning to Damascus, consider heading north-east to the remote desert ruins of Palmyra – the Roman city built on an ancient Greek site dating back to 1000 BC. Your route could then take you to Lake Assad on the Euphrates, returning via Aleppo to re-enter Turkey. Owing to the present Kurdish unrest, the regions to the east and north-east of Gaziantep and Diyarbakir are best avoided, and certainly any route around Lake Van is usually considered out of bounds.

Iran to India

The only practical point of entry into Iran from Turkey is the border of Barzagan. Before entering, in order to conform with Islamic dress codes women must equip themselves with a *chadoor*, a long loose-fitting gown covering head and shoulders and concealing the outlines of the body. This must always be worn in public. Alcohol is strictly forbidden, so dispose of any supplies before the border. This apart, the border control is slow but usually very civil, and as long as everything is in order all should run smoothly.

The direct and most travelled route leads to Tabriz and Zanjan, then south to Esfahan via Hamadan, avoiding Tehran – unless of course you want to tackle some of the worst traffic jams in Asia. Esfahan is the cultural centre of Iran, and still houses some of the most valuable craft workshops and bazaars of the Middle East. The Shah Abbas Mosque is spectacular, with turquoise-blue ceramics covering its domes and minarets. In the summer months, a rewarding journey will take you north of Tehran and over the Albarz Mountains to the Caspian Sea, before heading south through the Kavir Desert and the Dasht-e-Lut to rejoin the route to Pakistan.

You could consider an alternative route from Iran into what is commonly known as Central Asia, though reports on the viability of taking your own vehicle on this journey are mixed. From the north-eastern Iranian city of Mashad, capital of Turkmenistan, the main route heads east to Bukhara and Samarkand in Uzbekistan. However, for several years the Iranians have apparently refused to offer visas allowing foreigners to leave or enter via this route. There are presently no overland operators running vehicles on this route.

Afghanistan is still considered a no-go area for any form of overland travel, as the Taliban regime in power is in conflict with regional resistance groups. In addition, the country is heavily landmined following the Russian involvement in the Eighties, rendering many areas unsafe.

Back at Esfahan, a day's drive south will bring you to Shiraz, the garden city renowned for its hospitality, and the nearby ruins of Persepolis. This 2,500-year-old city was built by the Persian king Darius the Great, only to be destroyed by Alexander the Great around 300 BC.

You now follow the old southern trade routes across Dasht-e-Lut, via Kerman and Zahedan. The way is punctuated with *caravanserai* and desert fortresses; one of these in particular, the mud brick city at Bam, is still virtually intact and is a must to visit. Crossing the Baluchistan desert is now the only viable route into Pakistan, but this is a highly sensitive region in which you need to proceed with caution, avoiding any night-driving and camping out. You should also avoid any form of disagreement or conflict, no matter who is at fault. The volatile Baluchi people are usually armed and often smugglers, so diplomacy is called for in order to avoid any problems.

The rather chaotic border post at Mijaveh/Taftan is usually straightforward and travellers are often welcome to sleep overnight at the Pakistan customs post.

The construction of the bitumen road through the desert to Quetta is now at last complete, but constantly drifting sand and seasonal flash floods often have an adverse effect on conditions.

Quetta is very much a frontier town: a colourful mountain oasis, bazaar and crossroads for traders and smugglers alike. While it has very little in the way of architectural interest, the people who throng the streets and markets – Afghanis, Baluchis and Pathans – provide lively colour and character.

Following ancient nomad routes into the Indus Valley, Pakistan's lifeline, the most direct route now takes you via Sukkur and Multan to Lahore. If time and resources permit, however, a route into Pakistan's northern frontier region is a must, especially during the summer months (June to September).

The frontier region of north-west Pakistan, bordering on Afghanistan, is tribal and access is restricted. If you intend to visit the north, follow the Indus Valley via Dera Ismail Khan to Khot and on to Peshawar. At Peshawar you have the choice of exploring the North-West Frontier (home to peoples with such firmly established indigenous cultures that time seems to have stood still here) or taking the Raj-built Grand Trunk Road down to Lahore. From Peshawar you can also explore the Khyber Pass and the Swat Valley. Further north, Chitral and the Kalash Valleys are inhabited by the Kafir people, possibly descended from Alexander the Great.

From Peshawar, this route crosses the Indus river, overlooked by the mighty Attock Fort, before continuing to to Rawalpindi and Islamabad, Pakistan's satellite capital. From Islamabad another excursion is possible, this time north to the Hunza Valley and the Karakorams. Although the land border is open over the Khunjerab Pass to China and Xinjiang Province, this crossing is possible only on local public transport (the Chinese authorities still make it very difficult to obtain permission to enter China with foreign-registered vehicles). Public transport provides an interesting alternative route, passing via Kashgar and Urumqi to follow the ancient Silk Route through the lands of Ghengis Khan and on to Beijing and Shanghai.

From Islamabad continue south again, into the heart of the Punjab to Lahore, with its Moghul Red Fort and Shalimar Gardens. A bustling thriving city, Lahore is an ideal centre in which to make any mechanical repairs before entering India.

From Lahore the Grand Trunk Road takes you the short distance to the Wagah/Attari Road border with India. Here strict times of opening and rampant bureaucracy welcome you to India. You will immediately see and feel the change.

India and beyond

This fascinating country of diverse cultures, terrains, languages and religions has a population in excess of 900 million people, making the largest democracy in the world. Though predominately Hindu, it nevertheless has the largest Muslim population of any country in the world. The history and sights of India offer the overland traveller unique itineraries, whether pursuing the direct route to Nepal or following the Grand Trunk Road to its destination at Calcutta.

The first stop in India, in the wealthy state of Punjab, is Amritsar, the centre of the Sikh religion. The holy shrine to the Sikh faith is the Golden Temple, which welcomes visitors and pilgrims alike. Now the route takes you on to Delhi – and from here the choice is yours.

In autumn, winter and early spring, the colourful desert state of Rajasthan makes a rewarding diversion; some head further south to Goa and its beaches, or further still to the hill stations of the south.

During the summer months, the Himalayan foothills offer some respite from the heat and the effects of the monsoon. Simla, the Kulu Valley and Manali are wonderful spots in which to relax, or try venturing further north into Ladakh.

Following the overland route, do not miss Agra and the Taj Mahal, the highlight of any journey to India. Head east to Varanasi on the Ganges, sacred to Muslims and one of the holiest places of the Hindu faith, with early morning cremations on the historic *ghats*. Nearby, at Sarnath, is the site of the Buddha's first sermon.

The traditional route of the past 30 years or so takes most overlanders to the Himalayan kingdom of Nepal and to Kathmandu. Once the cloistered capital of a relatively secluded kingdom, it is now a busy tourist centre offering climbing, trekking, and rafting expeditions. With its friendly people and its splendid scenery and climate, Nepal will always provide a welcome rest at the end of a long journey, or a refreshing pause to those venturing further.

There is no silence in the East.
– W. SOMERSET MAUGHAM

During the summer months, many of those who choose to continue cross the passes of the Himalaya on to the Tibetan plateau, slipping in through the back door of China. Entry is still generally restricted to organised tour groups with a minimum of five people, however, and again it is impossible to enter with foreign-registered vehicles without very special (and costly) permission. The alternative route via Bangladesh and Myanmar (Burma) is not yet possible, but times are changing: recent reports indicate the opening of some land borders between Myanmar and Thailand.

In the future there may yet be the possibility of a complete land route to Singapore, and (with a few sea crossings) on to Australia. London to Sydney: now that would be a classic overland journey. ❧

Around South America
by Chris Parrott

The 'Gringo trail' (not to be confused with the Inca trail) is what everyone calls the most frequently travelled route through and around South America. Gringo derives either from 'green go home' (in the days when the US Army used to wear green uniforms), or from *greigo*, the Spanish for Greek. Despite assurances in the guidebooks that the term is widely used in friendly reference to anyone with a pale complexion, this is definitely not a complimentary form of address. Just watch how a blond Argentine reacts to being called a gringo.

The trail begins in whichever gateway happens to be the cheapest to fly into from Europe or the USA. Let's start in the north, in Colombia. The coast here boasts beautiful golden beaches, clear water and crystal streams cascading down from the 5,800 m summits of the Sierra Nevada. To the south is the big industrial port of Barranquilla, followed by Cartagena, an impressively fortified town dating from 1533 which for nearly 300 years served as a conduit for gold and treasures looted by the Spanish from their colonies. Continuing further south through hot swampland, then inland up the attractive forested slopes of the Cordillera Occidental, the traveller emerges on to the high plateau where Bogotá is situated, at an altitude of 2,620 m. Here the magnificent Gold Museum has over 10,000 examples of pre-Colombian artefacts. An hour away are the salt mines of Zipaquira, in the bowels of which is an astonishing 23 metre-high cathedral carved by the miners.

South of Bogotá are the Tequendama Falls, the splendid valley of the Magdalena river and, high up in the Magdalena Gorge, the village of San Agustín. Here, hundreds of primitive stone statues representing gods of a little-known ancient Indian culture guard the entrances to tombs. The road then loops back over high moorland to Popayan, a fine city with monasteries and cloisters in the Spanish style. The tortured landscape near here resembles violently crumpled bedclothes; recent reports suggest that it is not safe to travel on public or private transport in this region, so check with local sources before you go. Now the road crosses into Ecuador. Just north of Quito, the Equator – La Mitad del Mundo – straddles the road a few hundred metres from the grand stone monument built to mark the meridian. Quito itself lies at an altitude of 2,700 m, ringed by peaks including the volcanoes of Pichincha. The city's fine colonial architecture boasts (according to the South American Handbook) no fewer than 86 churches, many of them gleaming with gold.

The Andes

Crossing the Andes, travellers pass from near-Arctic semi-tundra, through temperate forest and equatorial jungle and down to the hot total desert of the Peruvian coast, punctuated by oases of agricultural land where irrigation has distributed the melt-waters from the Andes over the littoral. Here, too, the ancient empires of the Chavin, Mochica, Nazca and Chimu people flourished. Ruined

Chan-Chan, near Trujillo, was the Chimu capital; nearby Sechin has a large square temple, 3,500 years old, decorated with carvings of victorious leaders and dismembered foes.

A popular detour from here turns inland at the fishing port of Chimbote to head for the Callejon de Huaylas. The route passes through the spectacular Canóon del Pato, where the road is literally drilled through the rock wall of the canyon, with 'windows' looking down to the roaring maelstrom of the Santa river below.

The Callejon de Huaylas valley runs along the foot of the Cordillera Blanca; here a 1970 earthquake buried the town of Yungay under an avalanche of mud. The towns of Caraz and Huaraz make good centres for walking and trekking in the Cordillera, and the road south across the mountains offers spectacular views of the snow-capped Cordillera Blanca.

The coast near Lima is picturesque and rich in fish and birdlife, owing to the effects of the Humboldt Current. Lima itself has both shanty towns (*barrios*) and affluent suburbs, parks and fine beaches. Well worth seeing are the National Museum of Anthropology and Archaeology and the Gold Museum at Monterrico on the outskirts of town.

South from Lima

From Lima there are two routes south. One branches into the mountains (the pass reaches 4,800 m), passing through the zinc-smelting town of La Oroya and on to Huancayo. The railway line along this route has recently been reopened – check departures at Des Ampararados station, behind the presidential palace in Lima. The road continues through Ayacucho and Abancay to Cusco. The alternative route follows the fast coast road through the desert, past the wine centre of Ica to Nazca, with its vast network of ancient and mysterious lines, and on to Arequipa. There are several short-cuts – from Pisco or Nazca, for example – or you can take the train in a great circle from Arequipa to Cuzco.

One thing is certain: any route across the Peruvian Andes is tortuous, time-consuming, and stunningly spectacular. Although the route from Lima to Cuzco looks relatively short on the map, for instance, it actually represents about 50 hours of continuous travelling overland. Cuzco, sitting in a sheltered hollow at 3,500 m, was the capital of the Inca Empire. Inca stonework forms the foundations of many of the later Spanish buildings, and the ancient city layout survives to this day.

Overlooking Cuzco's red roofs is the ruined fortress of Sacsahuaman. Within a couple of hours' drive are the Inca ruins of Pisac and Ollantaytambo. Accessible by train only, down the valley of the Urubamba (called the Vilcanota further upstream), is the 'Lost City of the Incas', Machu Picchu. The magnificent ruins, near ly 500 m above the river, were invaded and overgrown by the jungle until their discovery in 1911. Several legends add to the mystery of the lost city. According to one, the Incas fled after the sacking of Cusco to this city, whose existence was unknown to the Spanish invaders. According to other legends, the Incas themselves erased all mention of the city from their oral histories as retribution for some (now forever censored) local uprising long before Pizarro and his men set foot in Peru.

From Cuzco, the road crosses the watershed of the Andes to the dry and dusty Altiplano, a high, treeless plateau stretching across much of the Bolivian upland. Here lies Lake Titicaca, at 3,810 m the world's highest navigable lake, blazing a deep blue through the effects of strong ultra-violet rays. On its rocky islands the Uru-Aymara Indians continue their traditional lifestyle. Across the border in Bolivia are the ruins of the ancient temples of Tiahuanaco, with the famous carved Gate of the Sun. La Paz sits in a valley just below the rim of the Altiplano, the city centre lying at approximately 3,500 m.

La Paz and beyond

From La Paz, there are three possible routes, depending on the size of the circuit you intend to make:

1. Eastwards through the relatively low-lying city of Cochabamba to Santa Cruz, then on by rail to Corumba on the Brazilian border, from where you can head for Saõ Paulo or the Iguaçu Falls. The road from Santa Cruz to Corumba and all routes from Bolivia to Paraguay are suitable for four-wheel-drive vehicles only.

2. Southwards via Cochabamba to Sucre and the mining town of Potosi, and on to Villazón on the Argentine border and points south.

3. Southwards to Arica in northern Chile. The roads gradually peter out over the salt pans and quicksands that cover this region, which should only be traversed in the dry season (May to November) and then with very great care. The road passes through the very beautiful Lauca National Park before continuing (for the most part tar-sealed) through the Atacama desert and the farmlands and vineyards of central Chile, and on to the so-called 'Little Switzerland' of mountainous southern Chile.

The road south of Puerto Montt goes only as far as Coyhaique. The most usual point for crossing the border south of Santiago is near Osorno, which brings you to Bariloche, now a fashionable ski resort in Argentina. This route may not be passable in winter (June to October). The road from Santiago to Mendoza via Uspallata is kept open all year round; it uses the railway tunnel and does not pass the famous statue of Christ of the Andes. Travel south from Bariloche takes you over frequently unmade roads in the foothills of the Andes,

"You must not judge people by their country," a lady advised me. "In South America it is always wise to judge people by their altitude." – PAUL THEROUX

through the beautiful Argentine lake district to Viedma and El Calafate. Here the lakes are fed by melt-waters from the Patagonian ice cap, and their creeks are sometimes blocked by tongues of glacial ice. The scenery around Lago Argentino is some of the most spectacular to be found anywhere in the world. Roads here are passable at most times of year, though from June to October four-wheel drive vehicles are advisable.

Alternatively, you can combine the Pan-American highway with local ferries, travelling via the island of Chiloe and the Chonchi-to-Chaiten ferry. You can also travel east out of Puerto Montt, using the local balsa or ferries to cross the numerous rivers and fjords on the way to Chaiten. The road continues down to Cochrane, but ferry services stop from June to October. Bear in mind that heavy rains periodically cause landslides which put an end to all hope of travel.

The south

It is possible to reach South America's southernmost tip, Tierra del Fuego, by ferry from near Rio Gallegos, or from Punta Arenas across the border in Chile. From June to October it is often impossible to cross the mountains by road in order to reach the small town of Ushuaia on Tierra del Fuego's south coast, but there are regular flights throughout the year from nearby Gallegos and Rio Grande.

It is well worth making an excursion from Punta Arenas in Chile to Puerto Natales and the famous Torres del Paine National Park: a must for mountaineers, and an unforgettable experience for anyone who thinks that those etchings by early explorers always made mountains look improbably precipitous.

The fast and straight east coast road takes you north again through temperate scrubland, via Comodoro Rivadavia and Puerto Madryn, with its Welsh-speaking colony, to Bahia Blanca and Buenos Aires. This cosmopolitan city of nearly ten million inhabitants lies on the estuary of the Rio Plata, a few hours by ferry from Montevideo in Uruguay.

Most travellers tend to bypass the rolling cattle-grazed plains of Uruguay in favour of the roads northwards, either through Santa Fé and Resistencia to Asunción, or direct to Iguaçu via Posadas and the Misiones province. Ferries are now almost extinct, but new bridges (Ponte President Tancredo Neves between Argentina and Brazil, and the Friendship Bridge between Brazil and Paraguay) make the journey quicker, if less interesting. There are also three bridging points across the Parana River between Buenos Aires and Asunción: the first is at Zarate; the second is the tunnel from Santa Fé to Rosario; and the third is the bridge between Resistencia and Corrientes.

There is a good fast road from Asunción to Foz do Iguaçu, where a bridge straddles the frontier. Another bridge links Foz do Iguaçu (Pôrto Meira) in Brazil with Puerto Iguazu (or Iguassu) in Argentina, making it possible to visit these spectacular falls from both sides of the river.

The plantations of Brazil

The dense forest that once spread across Brazil from Iguaçu to Rio and beyond is gradually giving way to coffee and soya bean plantations. A particularly special stretch of forest road follows the Serra do Mar coastal range from Curitiba to São Paulo, its east- and west-bound carriageways frequently separated by several kilometres of jungle-clad mountain.

From São Paulo there are two routes: one through Santos and Angra dos Reis along a beautiful coast road; the other a fast motorway following the ridge of the mountains via the steel town of Volta Redonda. Rio is a focal point from which routes divide once more:

1. The north-east coast road through Salvador, Recife and Fortalaza to Belém at the mouth of the Amazon. Many travellers feel that this route, passing through the

regions first settled by the Portuguese and their slaves four centuries ago, is the real Brazil.

2. North-west via Belo Horizonte and the old mining towns of Minas Gerais province, such as Ouro Preto, Congonhas, Tiradentes and Mariana. This route leads to that oasis of modernity and the ultimate in planned cities, Brasilia.

From Brasilia, several routes lead up to the Amazon basin, the fastest and easiest heading direct to Belém via Anapolis. This road offers a short cut at Estreito, along the Transamazónica Highway to Altamira and Santarém.

Alternatively, you can follow the newer road west to Cuiabá and then take the Transamazónica north to Santarém. From both Belém and Santarém there are river steamers to Manaus, though car ferries are few and far between. A more practical route for travellers with their own vehicles heads west to Cuiabá and Pôrta Velho, then north along the new road via Humairá to Careiro on the south bank of the Amazon, opposite Manaus. From here there are three ferries daily to Manaus.

In the heady days when Brazil enjoyed the world monopoly on rubber production, Manaus built a splendid (and recently restored) opera house for the best mezzo-sopranos in the world, and the rubber barons lit their cigars with 1000 millreis notes. Most of that glitter has now faded, though edifices built from stone imported from Britain can still be seen.

From Manaus, river boats ply the Rio Negro and the Rio Branco, tributaries of the Amazon, providing a break from overlanding and a convenient, if primitive, way of visiting remote villages. North of Manaus, the authorities have 'subdued' unrest among the local Indians, and the route is now passable in safety.

Angel Falls

The road between Boa Vista and the gold mining town of El Dorado in Venezuela winds through spectacularly beautiful country, passing the sheer-sided 'lost world' of Mount Roraima at the point where Venezuela, Brazil and Guyana meet. Trips can be taken to the world's highest waterfall, Angel Falls (979 m), from El Dorado or from Puerto Ordaz (now part of the new city of Ciudad Guayana).

After crossing the Orinoco, you soon reach Caracas, having completed almost a full circle of the continent. If you still want to see more, you can take a route eastwards that is definitely not on the Gringo trail. Border disputes make it impossible to cross the frontier from Venezuela to Guyana.

From Boa Vista in Brazil, however, a road of sorts leads to the frontier and a fordable river into Lethem. In the dry season, it is possible to drive all the way to Georgetown, and on along the coast to the Corentyne river. Getting across the river and into Nieuw Nickerie in Surinam will cause problems for those with their own vehicles, though there is an infrequent ferry. It is in fact possible to drive all the way to Cayenne in French Guiana, though the road is little more than a sand track in places and a number of rivers have to be crossed by ferry.

Saint Laurent lies just over the river from Surinam, in French Guiana, and the remnants of both this penal colony and the better-known one on the Isles de Salut (including hard-to-reach Devil's Island) are beginning to prove something of a tourist attraction.

At Cayenne the road comes to an end, though it is possible to fly either direct to Belém at the mouth of the Amazon or to Saint Georges just across the river from the Brazilian river port of Oiapoque, from where a road runs all the way to Macapa. From here there are ferries to Belém, which puts you back on the route southwards to Rio, either along the north-eastern coast or south to Brasilia. In fact, you could just keep circling and recircling the continent in ever decreasing circles, clockwise and anti-clockwise. It's a very dizzying part of the world in every respect. ⁊❧

CHRIS PARROTT is a Director of Journey Latin America.
He has lived in France, Singapore, Spain and Brazil.

Inter-Railing through Europe
by Max Thorowgood and Rachel Hammond

VAST SOCIAL AND TECHNOLOGICAL CHANGES have given the twentieth-century traveller unprecedented access to the remotest regions on earth. Consequently, the classical marvels that enticed eighteenth-century dilettantes from the serenity of their country residences seem hidebound to the modern grand tourist. However, in their anxiety to taste the delights of the newly accessible, today's travellers too often fail to examine their more immediate cultural stimuli before thrusting themselves upon the unsuspecting objects of their wanderlust. In so doing they limit the benefit to themselves and their victims. An Inter-Rail or Eurail ticket is the cure to these ills and heir to the spirit of the grand tour.

In 1972 the Inter-Rail ticket burst upon the scene and Britain joined the Common Market. The former event was the more genuinely pan-European in scope. The object of the International Confederation of Railways (which included, even then, the less regressive East European countries) was to promote international rail travel. It devised a system whereby a single ticket afforded the bearer one month's unlimited rail travel on the participating networks. In so doing, it did much to foster European integration because the Inter-Rail ticket affords an unrivalled opportunity to discover European civilisation.

Inter-Rail permits the spirit of European integration and enlightenment to flourish not only because of its amazing scope, but because train travel is a wonderfully convivial means of transport, and no conveyance is so congenial as the compartments that still form the large part of European rolling stock. You can roam the train; enjoy the ride, or the people riding with you and their picnics; and when the general gaiety begins to pall, make a moderately uncomfortable bed from the compartment's sliding seats. With the exception of hitch-hiking, there is no cheaper way to travel in Europe – by the time you reach Nice, your card has all but paid for itself, and the plains of Italy spread out at your feet. The grand tourist may drink deeply of the spirit of the Renaissance, while the connoisseur of more ephemeral pulchritude can scan a good proportion of Europe's beaches and costas, rivieras and islands. Europe, from the Atlantic to the Carpathians, and from the land of the midnight sun to the fleshpots of Morocco, is your oyster.

Ticketing

The under-26 ticket system divides the participating networks into seven zones, as follows: zone a is the Republic of Ireland and Great Britain; zone b is Scandinavia; zone c, Germany, Switzerland, Austria and Denmark; zone d is the Czech and Slovak Republics, Poland, Hungary, Bulgaria, Romania, Croatia and Serbia; zone e, Benelux and France; zone f is the Iberian Peninsula and Morocco; and zone g is Italy, Greece, Turkey, Slovenia and what remains of Yugoslavia. A global ticket costs £279 at the time of going to press. Alternatively, up to three zones can be selected for reductions (one zone for 15 days costs £185; two zones for one month costs £224; three zones for one month costs £249). The beauty of the Inter-Rail ticket is in the amazing freedom of movement it offers, but that freedom is unduly restricted by the zonal system –the global ticket, therefore, is much the most desirable option. A ticket for those over 26 is now also available for the price of £275, but it does not include France, Italy, Belgium or Morocco.

Best routes

A cursory glance at the map supplied with the ticket reveals that Central Europe has the most comprehensive rail network. In Holland, Germany, Poland, the Czech Republic, Slovakia and Hungary it is quite easy to get to anywhere you are likely to want to go by train. The same is broadly true of Italy and France, though in Italy the non-supplement trains, of which there are a limited number, tend to be very busy. Switzerland has good coverage but many of the lines are privately owned and offer only a 50 per cent discount (Switzerland is expensive). Rail travel on the Iberian Peninsula leaves a lot to be desired, fast trains aside. This can only be recommended to serious Hispanophiles and to those whose destination is Morocco – don't be taken in by the timetable, do take a month.

Such is the facility of movement offered by the Inter-Rail ticket, and the myriad opportunities offered by Europe that the prospect of recommending a route is daunting. Divide Europe, as Charlemagne did, into three (vertically): East, Middle and West. You then have roughly four different route choices – two outside-ins and two inside-outs. Decide upon the furthest extent of your trip, then think in terms of convection currents and proceed accordingly.

If that is too schematic, I offer an example: Folkestone to Ostend, then Ostend to Munich, from where you get the Hellos Express. Travel through the fabulous scenery of Slovenia to Zagreb, Belgrade, Skopje and eventually Thessaloniki. From Thessaloniki you can get access to the coast and the islands of the north Aegean. If that does not appeal, proceed through Greece to Athens, where cheap accommodation is readily available. See the Parthenon, even if you don't like climbing hills, and try the street kebabs. Take a boat to an island, explore it and do the beach thing in Poseidon's enchanting waters (take *The Magus* by John Fowles as reading matter). Then get another boat to Izmir, check that out, and move on to Istanbul by train and boat for a peek at the Sultan's palace, from which you get the top-down view on the gateway to the Orient. Say your *salaams* to the Byzantine world and proceed along the Greek coast, via Thessaloniki again, to Belgrade. Get a train to Prague, suffer the hordes, and move swiftly on to Dresden, the Florence of the Elbe. If you have time, take it to sample the Saxenschweiz, the gorge through which the Elbe flows so adroitly. This is a short day trip from Dresden – Konigstein can safely be recommended as a sight of interest. Also, just outside Dresden is the Schloss Pilnitz, which is quite lovely. Time will be short now, but don't bottle up. Go to Berlin, sample the after-dark scene, then try Amsterdam for size to round things off. Finally, return via Hoek van Holland to Harwich.

If you want to go to Greece, there are four routes: by ferry from Brindisi in southern Italy, the ticket should get you a reduction; from Munich on the fancifully named *Hellos Express* through what used to be Yugoslavia, taking in Zagreb and Belgrade; from Venice by way of Sarajevo; and, avoiding the former Yugoslavia, by a circuitous route via Hungary, Romania, Bulgaria and Turkey, which would certainly be a challenge but good if you are committed to enjoying the journey. The routes through the former republic of Yugoslavia are open again, though their condition (which was never exactly the best) is doubtful. Croatian and Slovenian railways, it seems, are independent but the rest remain under the umbrella of Jugoslav Railways. Whichever way you cut it, getting to the Big Olive is liable to be a somewhat lengthy business on crowded trains, but it is a treat when you get there.

> I have seldom heard a train go by and not wished I was on it.
> – PAUL THEROUX

Because the Aegean islands are so vital to the Greek tourism industry they are exceedingly well served by ferries from Piraeus (and other ports), for which there are Inter-rail discounts. For your discount you will have to sleep on the deck, so avoid the bow and the waves. It will be cold, but the stars will be brilliant. From islands such as Samos you can get boats to Turkey. Visas are necessary and can be obtained for a relatively modest charge. The train from Izmir takes you to the Sea of Marmara, where you will need to take another ferry to Istanbul.

Some rules of the rails

■ The Inter-Rail ticket only covers ordinary trains, fast trains and couchettes are extra. The tariff varies considerably depending on the conductor, so you've got to haggle, but generally France and Italy are more expensive, Germany is cheaper, and in most other countries almost all trains are standard. It is not normally necessary to take fast trains, but couchettes are well worth it if you are interested in sleeping – and they are cheaper than hotels.

■ Although it is generally possible to buy food on trains, it is invariably of low quality and high price. It is worth packing a penknife and buying your supplies in town before boarding anything – European railway platforms are not a patch on their Eastern counterparts when it comes to provisioning yourself for a journey. A good supply of comestibles can work wonders in the cut and thrust of the search for a comfortable berth.

■ Don't worry about getting value for money from your ticket. Unless you are spectacularly unadventurous it cannot fail to pay. The new city every day approach much vaunted by the International Rail marketing men is ultimately sterile. Cultural overload is a danger. Vary the diet – inter-railing is not the preserve of the culture vulture.

■ I could advocate travelling light, but this is a peculiarly fruitless exercise since aptitude for it is genetic. However, the art becomes doubly important when it is necessary to walk along crowded narrow corridors in unstable trains while carrying your luggage. It is desirable, therefore, to keep the number of trips you have to take to a minimum. One trip down the corridor, fat rucksack on back, will be more than enough to make the bearer heartily unpopular.

■ The hottest tip of all is 'left luggage'. Money spent on left luggage is money well spent. Take a small pack for essentials and dump your bag at the station upon arrival. The cheapest hotels are normally near the station, but that does not mean they will be easy to locate or that they will have rooms, so a recce without luggage is strongly recommended. ✌

MAX THOROWGOOD is a veteran Inter-Rail traveller and, more recently, a barrister. RACHEL HAMMOND works in the travel industry.

Part 2: **Being there** ❧

Working travellers

Business travel
by Gillian Upton

THE JURY'S OUT AS TO WHETHER THE BUSINESS TRAVELLER is to be sympathised with or envied. On the one hand they roam the world for free, seeing places and experiencing vastly different cultures, travelling with a degree of comfort few other people enjoy. Once their business is finished, they are able to put their briefcases away and tack a local side-trip on to their excursion at prices mere mortals will never be offered.

On the other hand, they work long, anti-social hours and spend extended periods away from home and their families, often in alien cultures or high-risk destinations; they suffer from higher stress levels than their non-travelling colleagues, are connected to their offices virtually 24 hours a day, and pay higher airfares and hotel and car hire rates than leisure travellers because of their pressing need for flexibility.

Surveys that attempt to determine which of these snapshots is a more accurate representation of the life of the business traveller abound – but their results are inconsistent and so it is difficult to conclude whether the business traveller doth protest too much. Either way, business travellers are a growing and demanding group of executives. What turns them on and off is becoming clearer – and gender plays a big role in the results.

Female business travellers tend to worry about the cost of travel, while men are more concerned by check-in queues. Men choose their hotel by cost, but women choose them by location, which is a reflection of their greater concern over security. In a recent survey, twice as many women as men (52 per cent against 21 per cent) said that they were concerned about security issues in the UK, although men became more security-conscious when travelling overseas (up to 43 per cent).

Across the board, though, the biggest turn-offs are – not surprisingly – late flights, road congestion, the high airfares to many destinations, long check-in queues, the lack of sleep that business travel entails, and the risk of potential downgrades to economy class.

All these concerns give an accurate picture of the current sorry state of the business travel market. Corporate down-sizing and cost-cutting are the order of the day, and more business travellers are having to squeeze themselves into economy-class seats and budget hotels these days than ever before.

And airline punctuality is just getting worse. Sympathise with any traveller who flies regularly into airports such as Milan, Geneva or Munich, as these regularly top the lists of European airports most affected by delays. Generally, over a quarter of intra-Europe departures are delayed more than 15 minutes, according to figures released regularly by the Association of European Airlines (AEA).

Flight delays exacerbate what is already a stressful and tight business schedule. Reduced budgets and the availability of flights to business destinations at either end of a working day has forced many business travellers to forgo an overnight stay – and the inherent cost – and squeeze all their appointments into one long day. And because more business travellers are flying from airports such as Luton and Stansted, where the 'no-frills airlines' such as Buzz, Go and Ryanair are based (Ryanair, for example, claims that 40 per cent of its passengers are business travellers), the businessperson often has a longer than usual trip home once the flight finally lands.

Meanwhile, it's a travesty that the UK, home to so many low-cost carriers, stings business travellers. *The European Corporate Travel Index*, published by American Express, revealed that British companies pay 76 per cent more than the European average for business-class fares to New York. The cost of a business-class seat to New York has increased by 50 per cent since 1994.

The great advantage of a hotel is that it is a refuge from home life.
– GEORGE BERNARD SHAW

A UK-based company that takes, say, 200 flights to New York in business class each year, will pay an average of £275,000 more than an equivalent company based in Germany, and £217,000 more than a French company – even though the distances involved are shorter. A British business traveller can expect to pay 46 per cent more for a direct flight from the UK to New York (£3,234) than they would if travelling from Paris (£2,217), and 55 per cent more than a traveller from Frankfurt (£2,086).

Stretching budgets for long-haul travel has meant that companies now send their executives via hub airports. In the same American Express survey, it was pointed out that British companies can save almost 30 per cent by sending executives bound for Los Angeles via Paris, for example.

But it's not all doom and gloom for the business traveller. The good news in that survey came on short-haul flights, where flights of less than 750 miles are significantly cheaper from the UK than the European average. And business-class cabins have never been so comfortable. These days they're fitted with seats that incorporate personal video screens, laptop power points, telephones, head rests, lumbar support – all operated electronically by the touch of a button. Some, notably cabins on British Airways' long-haul flights, are now fitted with seats that recline fully to become a flat bed. This is the sort of comfort that travellers used to get only in first class.

While first-class cabins are half the size they used to be in the 1980s, there are still business travellers who are able to pay £5,000 or £6,000 for a first-class ticket across the Atlantic. These tend to be the chairmen of large companies, city institutions, bankers, insurers, consultants and lawyers, all of whom can charge the enormous fare back to a client.

For them the status of flying in first class, being first off the aircraft, enjoying *à la carte* service and the privacy of sitting with probably only half a dozen others, is in direct contrast to the experience of those travelling in the business-class cabin, where there are upwards of 50 other passengers. There is also the advantage of superior food and drink and the much higher staff-to-passenger ratio, which

Buying smart

Air:

■ Fly via an intermediate hub on long-haul routes (via Amsterdam or Paris to get to New York, for instance) and save up to £1,000.

■ The purchase of an air pass if you're flying to several points within a region will give you significant savings.

■ The only way to save money on short-haul flights is to downgrade to a 'no-frills' airline, or squeeze all your appointments into one day to avoid the cost of an overnight stay.

■ Consider buying consolidated airline tickets to save up to 70 per cent, but be aware of the restrictions attached to such fares. Participating airlines are generally of good reputation.

■ Back-to-back airline tickets can save hundreds of pounds on long-haul economy class airfares, as long as you spend a Saturday night at your destination.

Rail:

■ If your company spends over £500,000 a year on rail travel, you can negotiate volume discounts from the rail operators.

■ When travelling less than 500 km within Europe, forget flying and opt for rail travel, as the European train system is infinitely superior.

■ If you travel off-peak and, in many European countries, purchase an annual travel card, you will gain a discount of up to 50 per cent on the cost of your fares.

■ It pays to book in advance if journey dates and times are fixed, as you will benefit from heavily discounted ticket prices.

Hotels:

■ Don't accept the first rate a hotel offers – always ask for better deals.

■ Getting a rate from the hotel direct can be cheaper than ringing that hotel chain's central reservation number.

■ Consolidate and place your hotel bookings with fewer hotels, giving each of them a higher number of bed nights, to score a heavier discount.

■ Specialist hotel-booking agencies are worth looking at as an alternative to booking through a general travel agent/management company.

■ Think about booking a room on the executive floor. Yes, it costs about 20 per cent more, but the sum total of all the free benefits and services may make it worthwhile.

■ Stay just outside your destination, where hotel rates can be significantly lower.

■ Check out airline stopover packages; their hotel rates can be amazingly cheap.

■ Look out for cheaper rates at new hotels or hotels re-opening after refurbishment and trying to win your loyalty.

■ Don't stay in a hotel at all if your stay extends to weeks rather than days; opt instead for an apartment and save money.

translates to virtually one-on-one service. Compare one member of airline staff for every ten passengers in business class, to three crew members for every 14 passengers in first class. And bear in mind the fact that the first-class cabins are generally half full. It's the nearest you get to personal service in the air. And, once on the ground, the pampering doesn't stop, whether for first- or business-class travellers. Some airlines, such as Virgin Atlantic, treat them to chauffeur-driven cars to and from the airport.

Don't feel too sorry for the business traveller, though. Check-in options nowadays have increased enormously, so they can avoid the long queues at the counter. They can check in by fax or phone, from their car on the way to the airport, or at Victoria or Paddington train stations. And the comforts of business travel don't stop there. On arrival back in Britain, British Airways and Virgin, for example, have opened arrivals lounges that enable business travellers to shower, eat breakfast and go straight into the office after a 'red-eye' flight.

And when it comes to staying in hotels, downgrading to a three- or four-star property is not the depressing experience that it was some years ago. Budget accommodation has improved in leaps and bounds; the hotels are usually modern, well-maintained and up to the minute in terms of hi-tech gadgetry such as dataports, inn phones, decent-size desks and ergonomic seating in the rooms. Greater hotel choice has helped the process. At the end of 1999, there were 62 hotel chains, up from 30 just 15 years ago.

Business travellers are, naturally, fêted by the airlines and hotels. It is these customers that account for the highest profits, so they need to be looked after and recognised as such. It is for this reason that frequent flyer programmes and hotel loyalty schemes have proliferated. Business travellers can earn miles or points while travelling on business, then use them at their leisure. One of the most useful benefits of being a member of such a scheme is the access it gives to airline lounges, upgrades and priority wait-listing on over-booked flights. Finding the time to redeem thousands of air miles is often a problem, though, and billions of them go unused each year.

Technology, of course, is playing an increasing role in alleviating the hassles of travelling on business, with the internet increasingly pivotal in all developments. Business travellers can already surf the net to check the lowest prices for flights and accommodation, then book online. However, some corporations have grave doubts over productivity issues if their staff are booking for themselves. Why should their high-paying executive 'waste' time doing that when a travel agent, who is paid far less, could do it instead?

A survey of 70 UK travel managers and business travellers by Carlson Wagonlit Travel, in 2000, unearthed an almost Luddite attitude towards new technology. Over half of the business travellers questioned said that they had never logged on to the internet to make travel arrangements, with some questioning the speed of the web compared with traditional booking methods. Even the web enthusiasts favoured it for leisure rather than business travel. Meanwhile, corporate travel managers were unimpressed by direct booking tools. Almost 90 per cent said they do not book on the internet, and would only use it for arranging the simplest itineraries. They saw several obstacles: the difficulty in consolidating accounting practices, the tracking of travel policy compliance, executive productivity issues, their lack of experience and skills when it comes to booking complicated itineraries, and the concern that suppliers may not offer their best prices to the direct booker.

On the plus side, the thumbs up was given to electronic ticketing because of its speed, the removal of queuing at tickets desks and the fact that it generates less paperwork. The process of organising refunds on e-tickets is straightforward but time consuming and some companies are concerned that millions of pounds' worth of unused e-tickets are going uncollected.

Only 40 per cent of the travellers surveyed had used video-conferencing, and most of them said they thought it would be unlikely to reduce the need to travel. Corporate travel managers agreed, with 75 per cent claiming that it had no impact on the frequency of business travel – one even said that it probably generated more travel. One cannot underestimate in such cases the low status of video-conferencing. Business travellers appear to like bragging to their colleagues that they have to travel to head office for a meeting.

Other technological innovations may be more readily accepted. Already the humble mobile phone is turning into a pocket-sized computer terminal. New WAP ('wireless application protocol') mobile phone technology gives dial-up web access, which means that the phone becomes an airline ticket and a check-in and loyalty mechanism. *En route* to the airport, it will know the status and location of your flight and, once you have arrived, it will guide you to the right terminal and car park.

Even better will be the newer mobile phones that will be introduced by the end of 2000, giving instant access to the web, with charges only be levied on receipt of information. These advances in telephony also mean that the airline will know exactly when the last passenger will board the plane, which could easily translate into fewer delays.

When all's said and done, business travellers don't have a bad life after all. And it's going to get a lot better. ❧

GILLIAN UPTON is a freelance journalist specialising in business travel.

The expatriate traveller
by Doris Dow

NOWADAYS GOVERNMENTS, LARGE ORGANISATIONS and big companies all compete for the expertise and skills they require. More and more people leave their own country to live and work abroad. These expatriates go off with high hopes and expectations, but in spite of increased earning power, some are disappointed and frustrated and return home for good. Others adapt well to the challenge of a new life and continue in the expatriate scene for many years, sometimes even finding it difficult to repatriate.

Contracts

It is important that the terms of the contract are understood and signed by the employer and the employee; if the contract is in another language, a reliable translation should be obtained before signing on the dotted line. Contracts should set out the terms and conditions of employment, including the minimum length of contract; working hours and overtime; remuneration; allowances for or provision of accommodation, car, education, medical and dental cover; leave and terminal gratuities/bonuses; dismissal clauses and compassionate leave arrangements.

Many jobs abroad offer what seem to be on paper very large salaries, but the attitude of employers, their willingness to accept responsibility and to offer support when necessary are often worth more than money. There are several excellent websites dedicated to expat issues and these are worth a look if you need information or reassurance.

Try www.expatnetwork.co.uk, which has good links (Expat Network, International House, 500 Purley Way, Croydon, Surrey CRO 4NZ, tel 020 8760 5100). Other websites, www.expatexpert.com and www.escapeartist.com, are also good. *The Weekly Telegraph*'s website for Britons living abroad, www.globalnetwork.co.uk, has useful contacts and links as well as articles dealing with the psychological aspect of relocation.

Documentation

Before departure, visas, work permits, driving licences, health regulations and other documentation must be attended to. Getting the necessary visas from embassies can entail many visits and long waits, but the first lessons of an aspiring expatriate are quickly learned – the acquisition of tolerance, patience, perseverance and good humour. For those working for a large company or international organisation, the documentation is usually done for them.

Preparations for the move

Time spent doing some 'homework' on the country you are going to, its lifestyles, traditions and customs, is very worthwhile. Mental preparation is just as important as the practical plans – working and living in a country is quite a different experience from a holiday visit.

Try searching libraries and bookshops for travel books and up-to-date guides. Embassies should also be helpful on specific information on currency, import regulations, etc., as well as giving advice on what not to import. Other valuable sources of information include Corona Worldwide, c/o The Commonwealth Institute, Kensington High Street, London W8 6NQ (tel 020 7610 4407), its *Notes for Newcomers* series features over 100 countries (£5.00 and £7.50 per set, plus postage) and gives practical details on what to take, education, leisure activities and health, etc. Employment Conditions Abroad, Anchor House, 15 Britten Street, London SW3 3TY (tel 020 7351 5000) is another useful source of information.

Cultural confusion

Watch out for:

■ Attitudes towards women: Equal opportunities don't always apply, and many countries have different laws about what women are allowed to do. Strict dress codes may apply, driving may be forbidden. Whatever your personal beliefs, the only practical solution is 'to go with the flow'. Doing otherwise is at best discourteous, at worst breaking the law. In any case, it will probably be too hot to wage constant battles against the system.

■ Intoxication: Alcohol may be a social lubricant, and having a drink or two may be a nice way to pass the time, but this does not apply everywhere. Some countries may allow foreigners to indulge, others uphold a total ban. If faced with the latter, try and take comfort from the fact that 'the deleterious social, domestic and professional hazards of prolonged alcohol abuse are well-recognised problems for expatriates', to quote tropical medicine expert Dr Nick Beeching.

■ Bribery: Take advice from local businessmen and the business section of the embassy. Where a culture of bribery exists, it often permeates so many levels, that parting with some '*chai* money' may be the only way to proceed – however much it hurts, offends or infuriates.

■ Despite all this, cultural differences are also the reason that so many expatriates have a wonderful time, exchanging and sharing customs. Those who come away enthused are the ones who immersed themselves in the experience. In the words of an ex-expat: "When you go, unpack your bags and plant your trees. Even if you don't get to eat the fruit, someone else will. Wherever you live, live there fully."

Finance

Arrangements should be made to continue National Health Insurance contributions, as these are an extremely good investment. All financial aspects of the move should be studied and arranged before departure – tax clearance, financial regulations and exchange controls in your country of destination, investments, etc. There are firms and consultancies specialising in this field, such as Wilfred C Fry Ltd, Crescent House, Crescent Road, Worthing, West Sussex BN11 1RN (tel 01903 231545).

Despatch and arrival of effects

There are many international firms that specialise in overseas removals. For those who have to make their own arrangements, it is advisable to approach more than one firm for an estimate. When travelling by air, include as many basic essentials as possible in the accompanying luggage so that you are self-sufficient for the first few days (include a few paperbacks to get through lengthy waits and sleepless nights due to jet lag).

Always ensure that personal luggage is locked and insured. Many people find airfreight the quickest, easiest and safest way of consigning goods. Lists of all contents should be available for customs clearance, shipping agents, insurance, etc., and two copies of these lists should always be retained. Baggage allowances are usually generous and first entry into a country generally permits duty-free import of personal and household effects.

In many countries there is a ready sale for second-hand possessions at the end of a contract, often at advantageous prices, so it is worthwhile making full use of the allowance. There are only a few instances where what is imported must be taken away again in its entirety. Heavier items for sea freight should be crated and listed – translation into the appropriate language can often hasten customs clearance. Hiring a good local agent who knows the ropes can also be a good investment. Realistic insurance of all effects is essential.

Arrival at destination

If possible, arrange to be met at the airport, and/or have a contact telephone number. Make sure that hotel accommodation has been booked and keep all receipts for later reimbursement. Salary may be delayed so try to have some interim financial support to cover this eventuality. A long journey and the shock of new climatic conditions can be depressing until you are acclimatised, so use your common sense and allow yourself time to adjust. Be prepared for long delays at customs and immigration control – patience and good humour will pay dividends here. Don't judge the country by its officialdom! Do not exchange money except through official channels.

Housing

It is unlikely that permanent accommodation will be available immediately, necessitating a few days' or even week's stay in a hotel. Make use of this freedom to get acquainted with local sources of supply, etc. To many expatriates, disappointment can begin with housing and furniture, which often does not match up to expectations. Reserve judgement at the beginning, because what may seem a drawback can turn out to be an advantage. There is a big difference in standards between local and expatriate employers, and there is no firm basis for comparison. In oil-rich states, it may well be that expatriate housing is much humbler than that of the nationals. On the other hand, accommodation may be very luxurious and spacious. The less fortunate expatriate should refrain from envious comparisons and, with careful thought and inexpensive ingenuity, make the best of what comes along. Work camps/compounds and high-rise flats are all very real challenges to the good homemaker.

Medical care

Primary medical care is sometimes much better than one might expect, easily contacted and near at hand. Further care may be available but, if not, serious cases are flown out for emergency or specialist treatment. Large organisations often have their own hospitals, clinics and doctors. Government contracts usually provide free medical facilities. It is always wise to have a good dental check-up before departure from home. Anybody needing medication on a regular basis should take a good supply to last until an alternative source is established.

Education

Very young children are often well catered for by playgroups and nursery schools. For older children, there are international schools, company schools, and private or state schools. These vary considerably, but given a good school and parents who take advantage of all there is to offer in the locality, a child will make a good start. There is often a waiting list and information about schools should be obtained and an early approach made for enrolment well ahead of departure. For those going to outlying areas, it may be necessary to consider correspondence courses, such as those offered by World-Wide Education Service, Blagrave House, 17 Blagrave Street, Reading, Berkshire RG1 1QA (0118 958 9993).

Many contracts provide for boarding school in the UK and regular holiday visits to parents. As the older child might well lack stimulation and local schooling might be inappropriate, early consideration should be given to choosing a boarding school. It is a hard decision to take, but the partings at the end of the holidays are compensated for by the pleasure with which children look forward to travelling out to their parents at the end of term. In some expatriate communities, special events are laid on for the children, they feel special having a home overseas and the experience of travelling alone can make them more responsible, confident and resourceful. If required, Corona Worldwide may be able to provide an escort service from airport-to-school trains, etc. Children are often used as an excuse for wives to return home, but when it comes to children at boarding school, it can be more important for them to feel that they have a solid family base than to have Mum on the doorstep.

Marriage

The move should be talked over very carefully as it can have a profound effect on a marriage. For busy working parents and weary commuters, expatriate life can be an opportunity to spend more time together as a family, and if both partners are keen, the novelty of the strange environment can be a rewarding experience. I would advise against any married person taking up a single person's contract or splitting the partnership for long periods of time, as this places a great strain on communication. Starting again could help to rebuild a shaky marriage, but it could also split it apart if an unwilling person is ripped away from everything familiar. So think before you move.

Single men and women

Single (or unaccompanied) men often live in work camps that are isolated. They have frequent short leaves and money to spend. A special interest – sport or hobby – gives them a chance to form stable friendships and does away with propping up the bar for company in their spare time. Conversely, a single woman may find herself in more demand in a lively social whirl. But this needs to be handled with great care. She is often an object of great interest to the local population, who may find it difficult to understand that she has no husband, and she may receive many offers of various sorts. However, a single woman with a job, with a real and worthwhile challenge, may have an advantage over a married woman without a job, who can find herself with nothing to do all day but keep house.

Partners without jobs

The stress on both partners should not be underestimated, if only one has employment. Naturally, the unemployed person will wish to be supportive of their partner as he or she settles into a new job; but they too will need support and encouragement as they establish a new home, meet new people and adapt to a different lifestyle.

Many women give up careers or interesting part-time jobs to accompany their husbands overseas, and in a number of places, there is no opportunity for them to get a job. Work permits can often be obtained in the teaching or medical professions, but not always near to where the husband is posted. If your husband is working for a big company, it might be worth asking the company about jobs, or considering the possibilities of working on your own or doing voluntary work.

Careful planning and preparation for the use of leisure time (whether it is a result of having no outside employment, or enjoying greater freedom from household duties thanks to servants) is essential to counteract boredom and initial loneliness. There are many hobbies and interests to be resurrected or embarked upon. Join groups with local knowledge, such as those involved in archaeology, history, wildlife, photography, amateur dramatics, etc. Involvement in the local scene through clubs and organisations helps understanding and leads to more tolerant attitudes towards cultural differences. Learning the language or taking a correspondence course are just two possible alternatives for the unemployed partner determined to make the most of his or her stay in another country.

There may be a lack of facilities, and the posting may entail putting up with a number of uncongenial conditions, but there are so many other rewards to compensate. Expatriates are on the whole friendlier and less inhibited than they are in their home environment. In hot climates, the sun and outdoor pursuits can often make people seem more attractive and relaxed. Social life is also important because, with the exception of those living in big cities, you will frequently have to entertain yourselves. This often provides scope for great ingenuity and many find latent and surprising talents hitherto undeveloped.

In what is often a male-orientated society, it is important for a wife to cultivate her own interests, making sure of her independent identity, rather than identifying herself too much with her husband's job and position. And with servants, there is more time to experiment, as she is no longer saddled with the day-to-day chores involved in running the house.

Servants

The availability of domestic help brings with it an easier lifestyle and is recommended for hot and humid climates where your energy will be easily sapped. Many people are diffident about employing servants and don't know how to cope with them. With an initial trial period and the advice of someone who speaks the language and has had a servant for some time, it is possible for a good relationship to be formed. Settle for a few qualities or skills suitable for the family's needs and be tolerant about other shortcomings. Establish what is wanted and agree time off. A servant who is respected becomes part of the extended family.

Lifestyle

Wherever possible, try to respect local customs of behaviour and dress, and be prepared for what might appear odd or rude behaviour. Cultural differences can lead to all sorts of misunderstandings, so reserve judgement, take advice from happily established residents and concentrate first on personal relations. Forget efficiency and don't expect things to happen in a hurry. Polite conversation and courtesy are priorities – sincere interest, tolerance and a joke work wonders. Beware of criticising before you have attempted to understand a situation.

At all times, the laws of a country should be obeyed. Western women in particular may find some cultures inhibiting, especially in a Muslim country, and it is essential to prepare for this. One-day briefing courses for men and women, Living Overseas, are run by Corona Worldwide to counsel on adaptation to a new lifestyle and provide an opportunity to meet someone with current knowledge of their future country of residence. They also offer telephone briefings. Call to confirm costs as these vary depending on the country in question.

Security

Security can be a problem, but common-sense measures, security guards and alarm systems are used in greater or lesser degree according to local hazards. Wilful violence is rare. It is possible for the expatriate to get caught up in political reprisals, but this is fortunately very rare indeed. It is wise to register with the consular section of your embassy or high commission so they know where to find you in cases of emergency – don't wait until trouble arises as communications can become difficult under such circumstances.

Summary

The expatriate can suffer considerable privation through lack of consumer goods and a low standard of living, or can be handsomely rewarded with higher standards of housing and a hectic social life, as well as a worthwhile job. The challenge of helping a country to develop can be very stimulating and even addictive (whatever the conditions encountered), which is why so many expatriates return overseas again and again. Friendships made abroad are often more binding and congenial, through shared experiences, than those made at home, and valuable experience in a job often leads to promotion. The tolerance and understanding of other races and cultures learned through the expatriate experience of shorter or longer duration means that life will forever afterwards be enriched. ❧

DORIS DOW lived the expatriate life for 24 years in central Africa. She is a secretary and teacher and has become actively involved with the Women's Corona Society.

Work your way around the world
by Susan Griffith

SHORT OF EMIGRATING OR MARRYING A NATIVE, working abroad is the best way of experiencing a foreign culture from the inside. The plucky Briton who spends a few months on a Queensland cattle station will have a different tale to tell about Australia from the one who serves behind the bar in a Sydney pub. Yet both will experience the exhilaration of doing something completely unfamiliar in an alien setting.

Working abroad is one of the means by which it is possible to stay overseas for an extended period, to have a chance to get below the surface of a foreign culture, to meet foreign people on their own terms and to gain a better perspective on your own culture and habits. The kind of job you find will determine the stratum of society in which you will mix and therefore the content of the experience. The traveller who spends a few weeks picking olives for a Cretan farmer will get a very different insight into the life and times of modern Greece from the traveller who looks after the children of a wealthy Athenian shipping magnate. And both will probably have more culturally worthwhile experiences than the traveller who settles for working at a beach café frequented only by his or her partying compatriots.

Anyone with a taste for adventure and a modicum of nerve has the potential for exploring far-flung corners of the globe on very little money. In an ideal world, it would be possible to register with an international employment agency and wait to be assigned to a glamorous job as an underwater photography model in the Caribbean, history co-ordinator for a European tour company or ski tow operator in New Zealand. But jobs abroad, like jobs at home, must be ferreted out. The internet has had an enormous impact and those prepared to surf can make their way through the deluge of information to specific job listings overseas.

Exchange organisations and agencies

At the risk of oversimplifying the range of choices, the aspiring working traveller either fixes up a definite job before leaving home or takes a gamble on finding something on the spot. There is a lot to recommend prior planning, especially to people – students taking a gap year for instance – who have never travelled abroad and who feel some trepidation at the prospect.

A range of mediating organisations and agencies (whether public or private, charitable or commercial, student or general) exist and can offer advice and practical assistance to those who wish to fix up a job before leaving home. Some accept a tiny handful of individuals who satisfy stringent requirements, others accept almost anyone who can pay the required fee. For example, various agencies arrange for large numbers of young people to spend the summer working at children's summer camps in the US, as English teachers in Eastern Europe and as volunteers on Israeli *kibbutzim*.

Students occupy a privileged position since a number of schemes are open only to them. Student exchange organisations can help with the nitty-gritty of arranging work abroad (see factbox): for example BUNAC (British Universities North America Club) has a choice of programmes – not all confined to students – in the US, Canada, Jamaica, Australia, New Zealand, South Africa, Ghana and, most recently, Argentina. Council Exchanges offers working opportunities in the US, Japan, Korea, China and Australia, including some for people pursuing specific careers. Lesser-known organisations can arrange short-term jobs on Latvian or Polish summer camps, Norwegian or Swiss farms, French or Italian archaeological digs, in Maltese youth hostels and Nepalese villages.

It would be wrong, of course, to assume that the love (or shortage) of money is at the root of all decisions to work abroad. Paid work in developing nations is rarely available outside mainstream aid agencies, such as VSO, which require specific training and skills and (in most cases) a two-year commitment. Yet many world travellers arrange to live for next to nothing while doing something positive for a local community. For example, enterprising working travellers have participated in interesting projects that range from helping a local native settlement to build a community centre in Arctic Canada to working at Mother Teresa's charity in Calcutta. Almost without exception, volunteers must be self-funding. For anyone with a green conscience, numerous conservation organisations throughout the world welcome volunteers for short or long periods who want to plant trees, count endangered birds and carry out research on coral reefs; again, volunteers must be prepared to pay for the privilege of helping.

Seasonal work

Most itinerant job-seekers will have to depend on the two industries that survive on seasonal labour: tourism and agriculture. Campsite operators, hoteliers and catering managers from Cannes to Cape Town depend on a temporary workforce. Anyone with some home-town restaurant experience and possibly an acquaintance with a second language is well placed to fix up a job ahead of time by sending a mass of speculative letters to winter and summer tour operators or to the hotels and campsites listed in tourist guides.

Farmers throughout the developed world are unable to bring in their harvests without assistance from outside their local community and often reward their itinerant labour force well. Finding out where harvesting jobs can be found is a matter of asking around and being in the right place at the right time. The organic farming movement is a useful source of agricultural contacts. The national co-ordinating bodies go by the name of WWOOF (Willing Workers on Organic Farms), and the organisation now has affiliates in such places as Hungary and Togo as well as Europe, North America and the Antipodes. For a modest joining fee, WWOOF will send lists of organic growers offering free room and board in exchange for helping them to minimise the use of chemicals.

The other major fields of temporary overseas employment are English teaching (see separate essay) and au pairing. Even the Louise Woodward case could not undermine the popularity of au pairing among young Europeans keen to escape Basingstoke or Bremen for up to a year. Au pair agencies abound in the Home Coun-

Working

Archaeology Abroad, 31-34 Gordon Square, London WC1H 0PY, tel 020 7504 4750, fax 020 7383 2572, www.britarch.ac.uk/cba/archabroad. Publishes lists of 200 digs abroad that need volunteers.

British Universities North America Club (BUNAC), 16 Bowling Green Lane, London EC1R 0QH, tel 020 7251 3472, fax 020 7251 0215, www.bunac.org.

Camp America, 37a Queen's Gate, London SW7 5HR, tel 020 7581 7333, www.campamerica.co.uk.

Central Bureau for International Education and Training, 10 Spring Gardens, London SW1A 2BN, tel 020 7389 4004, fax 020 7389 4426, www.britcoun.org/cbeve. Also at 3 Bruntsfield Crescent, Edinburgh EH10 4HD (0131-447 8024) and 1 Chlorine Gardens, Belfast BT9 5DJ, tel 01232 664418.

Council Exchanges UK, 52 Poland St, London W1V 4JQ,tel 020 7478 2000, fax 020 7734 7322, www.councilexchanges.org. Part of Council on International Educational Exchange, 205 East 42nd St, New York, NY 10017, USA, tel 212 226-8624.

Eurocamp, Overseas Recruitment Department, tel 01606 787522.

International Agricultural Exchange Association (IAFA), Young Farmers' Club Centre, National Agricultural Centre, Stoneleigh Park, Kenilworth, Warwickshire CV8 2LG, tel 01203 696578, fax 696684, www.agriventure.com. Places agricultural trainees on farms abroad.

WWOOF (Willing Working on Organic Farms), PO Box 2675, Lewes, Sussex BN7 1RB, tel/fax 01273 476286, www.phdcc.com/wwoof.

Useful web addresses: www.iAgora.com; www.jobsabroad.com/listings; www.travelnotes.org/Travel/working.abroad.htm; www.summerjobs.com

Further Reading: Vacation Work Publications, 9 Park End Street, Oxford OX1 1HJ, tel 01865 241978, fax 01865 790885, www.vacationwork.co.uk, publishes a wide range of titles for the working traveller, including *Work Your Way Around the World* (new edition every other year), *Taking a Gap Year*, *The Au Pair & Nanny's Guide to Working Abroad* and a number of titles for specific careers, e.g. *Working in Ski Resorts*, *Working with Animals* and *Working with the Environment*.

---

ties and, increasingly, outside London. Their job is to match vaguely domesticated young women (and a handful of men) with families on the continent or the USA, normally for the maximum allowed fee of £47.50.

The more unusual and interesting the job, the more competition it will attract. For example, it is to be assumed that only a small percentage of applicants for advertised jobs actually get the chance to work as history co-ordinators for a European tour company, assistants at a museum bookshop in Paris or underwater photographic models in the Caribbean.

Advice will be freely given by expats and fellow travellers if sought. The casual-cum-seasonal job is always easier to secure on the spot. If looking for casual work on farms or trying to fix up a passage on a transatlantic yacht, for example, a visit to a village pub frequented by farmers, yachties or the local expatriate community is usually worth dozens of speculative applications from home.

Less-structured possibilities abound. Enterprising travellers have managed to earn money by doing a bizarre range of odd-jobs, from selling home-made peanut butter to American tourists or busking on the bagpipes, to doing Tarot readings on a Mediterranean ferry or becoming film extras in Cairo or Bombay.

Red tape

Every country in the world has immigration policies that are job-protection schemes for their own nationals. The European Union is meant to have done away with all that, though red tape snags persist for those who want to work for more than three months. Outside the 15 member nations, work authorisations become decidedly tricky, unless you participate in a government-sponsored scheme such as the Japan Exchange & Teaching (jet) programme or the Swiss Hotels Association's summer placement scheme for eu students, or unless you qualify for special schemes, such as the recently expanded New Zealand working holiday visa for *bona fide* travellers aged 18 to 30.

Apart from these specific programmes, the job-seeker from overseas must find an employer willing to apply to the immigration authorities on his or her behalf well in advance of the job's starting date, while they are still in their home country. This is easier for high-ranking nuclear physicists and pop stars than for mere mortals, though there are exceptions, especially in the field of English teaching. Bureaucratic difficulties do make participation in an organised exchange programme appealing, as the red tape is taken care of by the sponsoring organisation.

Planning in advance

Anyone contemplating a stint of serious travelling funded by jobs *en route* can take some practical steps in the months before departure to prepare for such a trip. In addition to the obvious ones, such as working overtime to save money and investigating visa regulations, you can enhance your employability by collecting together potentially useful documents (character or job references, copies of a short cv, first aid certificate, diplomas in sailing, cooking, computing) or even by doing a course (language, tefl). And don't forget to pack a smart outfit for interviews.

As in any job hunt, contacts are often the key to success. It is always worth broadcasting your intentions to third cousins, pen friends left over from when you were 12 and visiting Oriental professors in case they divulge the details of potentially useful contacts.

Some travellers have their future career prospects in view when they go abroad, for example to teach English as a foreign language, to work on an English-language newspaper or for a marketing company. This is easier for people with acknowledged qualifications who can seek information from the professional body or journals in their field of expertise. The internet is a particularly worthwhile tool in this case.

Whether you set off to work abroad with the help of a mediating organisation or with the intention of living by your wits, you are bound to experience the usual rewards of travelling, encountering interesting characters and lifestyles, collecting a wealth of anecdotes, increasing your self-reliance, feeling that you have achieved something. Setbacks are inevitable, but it is amazing how often a setback leads to a success once you are on the track.

True 'working holidays' are rare, though they do exist. For example, travellers have exchanged their labour for a free trip with an outback Australian camping tour operator or on a cruise to the midnight sun. But in most cases, the expression 'working holiday' is an oxymoron in the same way as 'cruel kindness'. Jobs are jobs wherever you do them. There is seldom scope for swanning around art galleries, cafés and clubs if you are picking grapes seven days a week or teaching English on a Saudi oil base. Sometimes the most distasteful jobs of all are the ones that allow you to save quickly to finance the next leg of your journey.

Those who have shed their unrealistic expectations are normally exhilarated by the novelty and challenge of working abroad. Any individual with guts and gusto, whether a student or a grandmother, has the potential for funding him or herself to various corners of the globe. Persistence, optimism and resilience are the only ingredients essential for such a venture. 🍂

SUSAN GRIFFITH writes articles and books for working travellers, including 'Work Your Way Around the World', 'Teaching English Abroad', 'Taking a Gap Year', 'The Au Pair & Nanny's Guide to Working Abroad'.

Diplomatic service
by Sir David Hannay

THE DIPLOMAT TRAVELS NOT JUST BECAUSE HE ENJOYS TRAVEL, although it is as well that he should do so since he is fated to spend much of his professional life on the road, but because it is an essential part of his job. He travels to and from his posts abroad, he travels around the countries to which he is posted and, even when he is based in London, he tends to be caught up in the constant round of international meetings of which the web of modern diplomacy is composed. It all sounds pretty glamorous but, like so many other forms of modern business travel, it can easily become exceedingly humdrum if you let it. Similar airports, with similar flight delays, similar hotel rooms in impersonal international chains, and similar meeting rooms are not the stuff of which romantic travel experiences are made. The modern diplomat who wants to enjoy and benefit from his travel is going to have to work at it, not just sit back and have it ordered up by the travel section in the Foreign Office or his embassy.

Diplomatic travel begins with the journey to your posting, which can be extremely banal if you are heading for a western European capital or merely crossing the Atlantic, or potentially a bit more interesting if you are going further afield. Of course it will still be a far cry from the journey described so delightfully by Lady Macartney in *An English Lady in Chinese Turkestan*, when she set off in the nineteenth century with her husband, the British Consul General in Kashgar: they travelled on the newly completed Russian railway system to Tashkent and then covered the final leg of their journey by riding hundreds of miles over the Pamirs to reach their destination.

One personal rule I did try to stick to was always to travel to your post overland. This made for some very interesting experiences, particularly driving out to Tehran in 1960 – which involved some circuitous avoidance of East European Communist countries, then out of bounds to mere travellers – and through Eastern Turkey and Western Iran where a hard-top road was a rarity.

My system finally broke down after 25 years, when I was sent first to Washington and then New York, but I did manage a kind of revenge by returning on retirement from the latter via a long land journey through China and Central Asia. The object of going by land to your post is not mere whimsy, it is to try and arrive for the first time with some idea of what the country and its people look like and live like, and it is something you are unlikely to achieve on the road between the airport and the embassy.

Once you are in your posting, the opportunities for travel are greater, but again they need to be carefully planned. It is all too easy to get trapped into the bureaucratic grind of modern diplomacy – a far greater pitfall than the fabled cocktail party circuit, now largely a thing of the past – producing paper for the slave-drivers at home and missing the opportunities to get to know the complexities and attractions of the country you are in, not just its government. Once again it is a good deal less easy than it used to be to take off for a few weeks or even months into the wild blue yonder, as Sir Fitzroy Maclean chronicled in *Eastern Approaches*, a record of his travels in the Soviet Union in the 1930s, or as Hugh Carless did when he accompanied Eric Newby on *A Short Walk in the Hindu Kush* in the 1950s. Nor are there many opportunities such as I had in Afghanistan between 1961 and 1963 when I was grandly titled the 'Oriental Secretary' and managed to persuade my ambassador that I was more use to him on the road than in the office. It seems odd to think that we used to camp in the Panjshir Valley or catch trout at Bamyan in the shadow of the 50-metre-high statues of Buddha, where now the various factions of Afghanistan's eternal civil war are slugging it out.

It is almost equally odd to think that, as a Persian language student, I was encouraged, i.e. paid, to travel around southern Iran, on the condition that I went by public transport, which meant bus if I was lucky and the back of a lorry if I was not. It brings home the reality of the fact that war and instability are as often rapidly closing off places to which the diplomat may travel, just as technological advances are opening them up. But political developments are not always obstacles, as is demonstrated by the scope now for travel in China where not so long ago it was hard to get permission to go outside Beijing.

It would be nice if the diplomat only had to plan his own travel, but it is not so. One of his more demanding and thankless tasks is to act on occasion as a cross between a travel agent and a courier. A spell as a private secretary comes the way of many, and that is when qualities such as improvisation and endurance are put to the test. It is not just a question of getting your boss to the right place at the right time, it is a matter of getting there in the right frame of mind, often a good deal less easy. I worked for four years for Christopher Soames when he was a European Commissioner, during which we travelled pretty widely. One of his main characteristics was not simply to insist on absolute punctuality, reasonable enough when catching aeroplanes or calling on Prime Ministers, but also to avoid ever arriving anywhere more than 30 seconds ahead of the appointed time. The second part of the equation caused his private secretaries a good deal of anxiety, particularly when travelling in Asia and Latin America, or trying to calculate in advance the density of traffic between the airport in, say, Paris or Rome and the Foreign ministry. His other principal characteristic as a traveller was to insist that, if he was to go sightseeing – and he was not averse to that – then there had to be a three-star restaurant handy in which to recuperate. Travel as a private secretary is not, on the whole, life-enhancing, though it can provide a good deal of amusement, particularly in retrospect.

The most daunting challenge for the diplomat as traveller is to make something of those one-day stands which involve rushing from airport to meeting room, endless tours of the table, which have nothing to do with travel, and then a rush back to the airport – which is now the general form of modern diplomatic life. It is not easy to do. The frequency of airline flights makes it hard to convince one's employers that one simply had to travel the night before. The tendency of all international meetings to conform to a Parkinsonian law, which ensures that they last slightly longer than the time available for them to complete their work, is another complication. Nevertheless the really determined diplomatic traveller, whether his tastes be cultural, artistic or merely gastronomic, can usually manage to squeeze in the odd visit to a cathedral, an exhibition or a restaurant if he is sufficiently ruthless. Just occasionally the country caters for the travelling propensities of their guests by arranging the meetings in surroundings of beauty and interest; more often, unfortunately, they calculate that you will get more work out of people if you prevent their surroundings from being too attractive. Certainly, of the many meetings of the European Council I attended while I was dealing with the European Union, a great deal more fell into the latter rather than the former category. It took a hardy spirit, when Mrs Thatcher was leading the British delegation, to slip away, say, to that fascinating modern museum in Stuttgart.

The idea of national characteristics has been much overdone.
– Stephen Leacock

But of course the diplomatic traveller is not limited to professional travel, important a part of his life though that may be. If he is really bitten by the bug and if he can persuade his long-suffering family to share his passion, a lifetime of diplomacy provides some ideal jumping-off points for wider travel. Brussels may not be exciting in itself, but it is a remarkably good base from which to travel the European continent. New York is quite exciting for a traveller, but so is the possibility of using it as a base for visiting the furthest corners of Latin America. There are few better ways to spend a tedious afternoon in one of those subterranean meeting rooms at the United Nations than in planning how to get from Machu Picchu across Lake Titicaca to Bolivia (the answer: take the train from Cusco to the lake and hydrofoil across it).

So do 35 years or so of diplomacy dull the taste for travel? In my own case apparently not. The list of places still to be visited and '*vaut le detour*', in Michelin's inimitable phrase, seems if anything to grow longer. A willingness to rough it has certainly diminished, but so, fortunately, has the need to do so. The real challenge is to resist successfully what one could call the homogenisation of travel, the tendency to sell travel as McDonald's sells hamburgers. The diplomatic travellers should be in the vanguard of consumer resistance to any such tendency. ❧

SIR DAVID HANNAY was a British diplomat for 36 years, latterly as Britain's Ambassador to the European Union and the United Nations. He has also served in Tehran, Kabul, Brussels, Washington and New York.

Teaching English abroad
by Susan Griffith

EVERY MORNING AND EVENING THE STREETS OF BOGOTÁ, Bratislava, Beijing and a thousand other cities are thronged with people rushing to their English lessons. The demand for instruction or just conversation practice with people who speak English as their mother tongue is enormous, and will continue to increase for the foreseeable future. The most recent impetus to learn English has come from the explosion in use of the internet, as the vast majority of its sites employ the English language. Even in countries where English has been kept at a distance (such as Italy), people are flocking to English classes so that they won't be left behind.

However the time for assuming that a charming manner and a neat haircut are enough to land you a job is over in all but a handful of places, such as Bangkok and Mexico City. Standards are creeping up, partly because of a dramatic increase in the number of people gaining a qualification in TEFL (Teaching English as a Foreign Language). The number of both public and private institutes in the UK, North America, Australia and New Zealand turning out certified TEFL teachers has greatly increased in the past five to seven years, creating a glut of teachers, especially in the major cities of Europe.

Having sounded that warning note, there are still areas of the world, from Ecuador to Slovenia, Lithuania to Vietnam, where the boom in English language learning seems to know no bounds. In cowboy schools and back-street agencies, being a native speaker and adopting a professional manner are sometimes sufficient qualifications to get a job. But for more stable teaching jobs in recognised language schools, you will have to sign a contract (minimum three months, usually nine) and have some kind of qualification, which ranges from a university degree to a certificate in education with a specialisation in ELT (English Language Teaching is now the preferred label).

TEFL training

The only way to outdo the competition and make the job hunt (not to mention the job itself) easier is to do a TEFL training course. If interested, contact the British Council (Bridgewater House, 58 Whitworth St, Manchester M1 6BB, tel 0161 957 7755, www.britishcouncil.org) for its TEFL information pack.

The two standard recognised qualifications that will improve your range of job options by an order of magnitude are the Cambridge/RSA certificate in English Language Teaching to Adults (CELTA) and the certificate in TESOL (Teaching English to Speakers of Other Languages) offered by Trinity College in London. A list of centres, both in the UK and abroad, is available from these two accrediting bodies: the University of Cambridge Local Examinations Syndicate (UCLES TEFL Unit, 1 Hills Road, Cambridge CB1 2EU, tel 01223 553997, www.edunet.com/ciltsrsa) and Trinity College London (89 Albert Embankment, London SE1 7TP, tel 020 7820 6100, www.trinitycollege.co.uk).

Certificate courses involve at least 100 hours of rigorous training with a practical emphasis. They are offered full time for four weeks or part time over several months, and the cost averages at between £800 and £900. Although there are no fixed prerequisites, apart from a suitable level of language awareness, not everyone who applies is accepted.

Short introductory courses in TEFL are also available, and these vary enormously in quality and price. Although they are mainly intended to act as preparatory programmes for more serious courses, many people who have completed a brief training course go on to teach. Many (but not all) training centres have good contacts with language schools worldwide and can assist with the job hunt.

Finding a job

Teaching jobs are either fixed up from home or sought out on location. Obviously it is less nerve-racking to have everything sorted out before departure, but this option is usually available only to the highly qualified or to paying volunteers. It also has the disadvantage that you don't know what you're letting yourself in for. One of the possible advantages of fixing up a job well in advance is that you then have a chance of obtaining the appropriate work permit.

English teaching is one area of employment in which governments are relatively generous, since locals are not being deprived of jobs. Yet few nations will process visas unless applications are lodged outside the country. Employers of TEFL teachers in many countries (for example Korea, Taiwan, Hungary, Turkey and Morocco) can usually sort out visas or at least set the wheels in motion before their employees' arrival.

To fix up a job in advance, make use of the internet – increasingly the preferred recruitment tool – and check adverts in the education section of the *Guardian* every Tuesday and in the weekly *Times Educational Supplement*, which is published on Fridays. The best time of year is between Easter and July. In a few cases, a carefully crafted CV and an enthusiastic personality are as important as ELT training and experience. Well-qualified ELT teachers will already be aware of possibilities at the prestigious end of the market, for example with major ELT providers such as the British Council and International House.

The major language school chains hire substantial numbers of teachers, many of whom will have graduated from in-house training courses. Commercial recruitment agencies maintain a database of teachers' CVs that they then try to match with suitable vacancies in their client schools. In order to be registered with such an agency it is normally essential to have at least the certificate plus some experience. ELT opportunities are available through voluntary organisations such as VSO and educational charities. There is also increasing scope for untrained but eager volunteers who are willing to pay an agency to place them in a language teaching situation abroad.

The alternative to pre-arranging a job is to present yourself in person to language school directors. Jobs in any field are difficult to get without an interview, and English teaching is no different. Language institutes cannot, under normal operating circumstances, hire someone sight unseen merely on the basis of a CV and photo. Moreover, when the need for a teacher arises, that vacancy must usually be filled immediately. Therefore it is often more effective to base yourself in your preferred destination, introduce yourself to the directors of language schools and relevant companies and be prepared to wait for a vacancy to arise.

It is still possible for people who are well spoken and well dressed and have a confident manner to charm their way into a classroom. A university degree often cuts more ice than a TEFL qualification, particularly in the Far East, where a degree is a prerequisite to getting a visa. If you are job hunting in a capital city, the British Council may be able to provide a list of language schools or advise (informally) on the availability of teaching jobs: much depends on the goodwill of the staff. To gather together a list of addresses where you can ask for work, consult the *Yellow Pages*, read the adverts in the English-language papers, visit centres where foreigners study the local-language or English-language bookshops to check the noticeboards and ask the staff for leads. Business schools and vocational training institutes often need teachers of commercial English.

Several factors will affect the length of time it will take to find an opening. Timing can be crucial; aim to conduct your job hunt in the month before term begins (usually late August/September or around Christmas; summers are usually hopeless). Of course, a knowledge of the vernacular language is an advantage (especially in the Spanish-speaking world), as is the ability to look convincing while carrying a briefcase. If you have no luck in the major cities, consider trying provincial cities less frequented by foreigners (Plzen rather than Prague, Eskisehir not Istanbul, Chongqing rather than Beijing).

An alternative to working for a language school is to set yourself up as a freelance private tutor. While undercutting the fees charged by the commercial institutes, you can still earn more than you would as a contract teacher. Normally you will have to be fairly well established in a place before you can attempt to support yourself by private teaching, preferably with some decent premises in which to give lessons (either private or group) and with an aggressive self-marketing strategy. You should bear in mind the disadvantages of working for yourself, such as frequent last-minute cancellations by clients, unpaid travelling time (if you teach in clients' homes or offices), no social security and an absence of professional support and teaching materials.

If you are less interested in making money than in integrating with a culture, exchanging English conversation for board and lodging may be an appealing possibility, which usually relies on having contacts or good luck.

The job itself

Native speaker teachers are nearly always employed to stimulate conversation rather than to teach grammar. Yet a basic knowledge of English grammar is a great asset, especially when more advanced pupils ask awkward questions.

At least some of the thousands of young people who blithely set off to market their tongue abroad should pause to picture in detail the range of likely scenarios they may encounter. The classroom might be an alcove in a Chinese teacher training college where there are no desks and insufficient light but 25 eager learners. It might be a 'conversation lounge' in a Japanese city, which has an atmosphere more akin to a dating agency than a classroom. You could be faced with a room full of exuberant Taiwanese seven-year-olds who expect you to sing songs and draw pictures rather than talk about verb tenses. Or you might find yourself standing in front of a class of bored and disaffected Greek teenagers, forced by their ambitious parents to attend lessons after school to improve their chances of passing crucial exams for university entrance. Your 'class' may consist of a lone Peruvian businessman who, despite knowing very little English, expects to be able to swing a big deal with an American company after a few lessons from you. How far does your 'native speakerhood' get you in these circumstances? Even a minimum of training and/or experience in teaching English is a tremendous advantage.

The wages paid to English teachers are usually reasonable, and in developing countries are quite often well in excess of the average local wage. In return you will be asked to teach some fairly unsociable hours, since most private English classes take place after working hours, and so schedules split between early morning and evening are commonplace.

Teaching of any kind is a demanding job and those who are doing it merely as a means of supporting their travelling habit may find it a disillusioning experience. At the same time, it offers opportunities for creativity, learning about other cultures and attitudes, making friends and, of course, travelling. ❧

Being a tour leader
by John Warburton-Lee

How many times have you been in some exotic part of the world and, caught up in the euphoria of the moment, looked at a guide leading a group on the sort of adventure that you enjoy and thought, 'I would love to do that job'? By comparison to their apparently carefree, action-packed, outdoor existence, your office job appears mundane, depressingly unadventurous and lacking any form of excitement. At that moment, the thought of waking up on the banks of the Zambesi or in a remote camp on the Annapurna circuit, and of spending your days battling your raft-full of excited clients down raging rapids or trekking in the shadow of the Himalayas appears far more romantic than the concept of leaving your home to fight with the commuter crush on the way to a desk full of flickering computer screens and ringing telephones. But before you fire off a letter of resignation to your managing director and shower an unsuspecting adventure tourism industry with your newly rewritten cv, it may be worth considering some of the practicalities.

To begin with, you should ask yourself what it is about foreign travel and adventure holidays that you enjoy so much. Apart from the more obvious pleasures, do you associate travelling with being free from all responsibilities, away from the pressures of deadlines and demanding clients? Is it about being able to take every day as it comes, moving on at whim, without a care in the world, not needing to answer to others? Is it about pushing yourself on challenges that take you towards your physical limits? Is travelling in the comforting knowledge that your secure job will ensure that your mortgage and all other bills are paid a subliminal part of your enjoyment? If any of these scenarios strike a chord, you have some hard truths to confront before putting the stamp on that resignation letter.

First of all, you may as well recognise that no one ever got rich from guiding. It is a lifestyle choice that has little, if anything, to do with paying mortgages or saving a nest egg for your retirement. Rates of pay are low, in many cases amounting to your keep plus a small amount of pocket money. Many companies get enough staff purely by giving them a free trip, and in some cases companies expect staff not only to work for them but also to pay a contribution towards their expenses for the privilege of doing so.

Secondly, working as a guide or tour leader requires an extremely high level of commitment. You are on call 24 hours per day and take on considerable responsibility for your the safety of your clients, as well as their wellbeing and enjoyment. In addition to any specialist technical skills, such as mountain leadership or kayaking experience, guides often need to be able to act as group motivator, administrator, cook, driver, mechanic, equipment repairer, camp manager, medic, social worker and agony aunt. Every problem, from the most serious to the most trivial, will find its way straight to your tent door.

One company with a regular requirement for tour leaders is Encounter Overland, which employs around 20 leaders at any one time. The leaders normally work alone, driving groups of up to 24 clients of mixed nationality on itineraries lasting between two and 32 weeks through Africa, Asia and South America. Leaders may be deployed for up to 18 months at a time. They are on the road for roughly nine months of a year, with most of the remainder of the time dedicated to the maintenance of their vehicles.

"It is taken as read that our staff need to be very good drivers with an aptitude for mechanics, but the over-riding requirement is excellent people skills", says Moira Welikanna, Encounter Overland's operations director. "We demand absolute honesty, guts, stamina and an unbelievably cheerful disposition. The leaders have to do much more than drive and maintain their vehicles. They must be able to manage all of the bureaucracy *en route*, handle the paperwork and formalities at border crossings and deal with any corruption. They must always be thinking ahead, picking up local route information and remaining alert for security threats. Within the group they need to be motivators with limitless stamina, be constantly aware of group dynamics and be ready to mediate if problems begin brewing between group members."

Welikanna reckons that she can normally spot the qualities that she is looking for in a leader within five minutes of meeting someone. "During a recruitment drive we probably take three out of every 100 who apply, but those who come to us independently tend to be more motivated and we may take on 30 per cent of those who do so."

Those that are taken on are put through a six-month training programme in the UK, which concentrates mainly on learning to drive, repair and maintain the company's vehicles (potential leaders must obtain their passenger carrying vehicle driving licence at their own expense). They also do some first aid training, learn how to recognise tropical diseases and spend three weeks in the London office to meet the staff and see the UK end of the business, dealing with clients, obtaining visas, organising airport runs and seeing how crises are handled. On completion of the training a leader/driver spends up to four months apprenticed to an experienced leader in the field in either Africa or Asia before leading their own trips.

Encounter Overland's leaders work for the company for an average of four years. "If new leaders are going to have problems," says Welikanna, "it will normally be difficulty in handling the groups or simply not having the stamina to cope with living in close proximity to 24 people for whom they are responsible, operating on an average of five hours sleep per night."

The emphasis on people skills for group leaders is reiterated by Mark Hannaford, managing director of Across the Divide, a company specialising in mounting treks and cycle rides in remote parts of the world. "Our staff need to have a high level of experience in outdoor education and skills, but the job is mainly about being able to fit into the team and work well with clients. The core values that we look for in our staff are maturity, loyalty, integrity, dependability, good communication skills with people of all ages and backgrounds and the ability to remain calm in a crisis and manage a situation effectively until other help arrives. We tend to have people who are well travelled and have a broad view of the world.

It is important that everyone is fit and able to carry heavy loads – and a good sense of humour is essential."

Across the Divide mounts expeditions of between 30 and 100 clients, and operates in the field for a week to ten days, deploying staff in teams under the guidance of an expedition leader. Group leaders are responsible for up to 20 clients on a daily basis, working together with a local guide. Expedition doctors provide routine and emergency care for up to 50 people, normally with the support of a nurse or paramedic. Doctors are required to have recent accident and emergency department experience and need to be able to operate in field conditions without the level of back-up to which those used to working in hospital will be accustomed.

Managing large groups in remote areas requires special skills and operating procedures. Across the Divide uses radios and satellite telephones to keep groups in close contact with each other and to facilitate overall control by the expedition leader.

"The ethos of the company is that of a small, close-knit family," says Hannaford. "We mainly recruit new staff through personal recommendations or through other members of staff, although occasionally we meet people whose personality and skills fit our way of doing things. We have a very small permanent staff and maintain a cadre of roughly 30 group leaders and doctors who take part in expeditions as required. In many ways our staff are the company. We have developed the company culture together, both on expeditions and through our twice-yearly staff training camps. The proof of the success of this formula has been evident when there have been serious incidents to manage and everyone has known exactly what their role is and how each other will react and the expedition leader has been able to work to each member of staff's particular strengths."

Each company in the adventure travel field has its own individual style of operating. Some guides enjoy the autonomy of working on their own, whilst others prefer the camaraderie and support of working in a close-knit team. It is extremely important to identify exactly how you will be expected to operate – only work in situations which you feel comfortable with. Dealing with exercise casualties on training courses is excellent practice, but it is a very different matter when you are leading a group on your own and you become faced with a real situation involving a traumatic injury and a group of novices who are frightened by what they have seen when help is a long way away.

Although many companies stress the importance of people skills, that does not in any way diminish the need for technical skills and qualifications. Companies looking for trekking, mountaineering, canoeing or diving guides, for example, will normally specify minimum standards of qualifications from the appropriate British authority such as the Mountain Leader Training Board or the British Sub Aqua Club. In addition, first aid qualifications or validated training will not only make you much more attractive to an employer but give you a great deal of confidence on the ground.

I am constantly amazed by the number of clients who come on arduous adventure trips to remote areas of the world with serious medical conditions that they fail to mention until they find themselves in difficulty. Diabetics, on the whole, are perfectly capable of maintaining their insulin levels, but it as well to know what to do just in case. Of more concern are those who turn out to have a history of epilepsy, heart conditions, psychiatric problems or, as in one recent instance, a difficult pregnancy. Expedition medicine can involve much more than treating blisters, strapping sore knees and issuing the odd sachet of Immodium, and all of this comes on top of the many other claims on a guide's time.

The life of a tour leader is often far from the glamorous, carefree existence that it may appear to be at first glance. Working in remote areas of Third World countries often means that the kinds of support systems that we take for granted at home, from garages and hospitals to something as elementary as restaurants where the food is safe to eat, are no longer there. Clients can be unreasonably demanding, utterly frustrating and have a habit of doing the worst possible thing at the most inconvenient moment. As a tour leader you must guide well within your own technical and physical capabilities so that you always have reserves of expertise, strength and stamina to give your clients when they need assistance. By definition, this means that the trips that you lead for commercial organisations may well be fulfilling in a leadership sense, but they are unlikely to satisfy any personal cravings for a physical challenge that will stretch you.

The rewards, however, justify all of the hassle. I never cease to get a thrill from working in areas of great natural beauty. There is a special satisfaction derived from enabling people to realise their dreams or aspirations, whether that involves showing them a part of the world they have never seen before or helping them to complete a physical challenge. For many clients an expedition is truly the experience of a lifetime, one that leaves them profoundly moved. At the end of a trek across the Namib Desert recently, one of my group, a young 18-stone cockney pipe-lagger, burst into tears.

People don't take trips –
trips take people.
– JOHN STEINBECK

"John," he sobbed, "you cannot begin to understand what this means to me. Where I come from in the East End of London, the Namib Desert is unimaginable. It might as well be on Mars – and I have walked the whole way across it." The fact that he had been the joker of the party throughout the trek made his reaction all the more poignant.

If you do decide to post that letter of resignation and look for a job as a tour leader, it is worth looking at the classified section of the various outdoor and adventure travel magazines for companies advertising for staff. The Expedition Advisory Centre at the Royal Geographical Society maintains a register of personnel available for expeditions, with cvs for each person, and also publishes a bulletin of expeditions looking for people with particular skills. Some commercial companies do access the register of personnel when looking for staff, but it is more likely to produce positions on private adventures or scientific expeditions.

Finally, it is beholden to all tour leaders to remember that they bear a responsibility not only to their clients and the organisations that they work for, but to the peoples and places that they visit. Part of doing so is to ensure that you are in a position, through a combination of experience and research, to pass on as much information about the country that you are visiting as you can to assist your clients' ability to enjoy and understand the environment that they are in. It is up to a tour leader to set a standard for group behaviour and attitudes. Groups sometimes need to be educated to respect local cultures, act in a way that is mindful of the sensitivities of the people whom they meet and at all times minimise their impact on the environment through good camp-craft and trail discipline. ❧

JOHN WARBURTON-LEE is a travel writer and expedition leader. He has led expeditions in Africa and Latin America, which were described in 'Roof of Africa' and 'Roof of the Americas', and is a council member of the Scientific Exploration Society.

Crewing boats
by Alison Muir Bennett

IMAGINE A VOYAGE LIKE THIS… sailing out of Cape Town with Table Mountain and the great continent of Africa behind you, it takes a few days to get away from the influence of coastal currents before picking up the ocean breeze that will take you to the lonely island of Saint Helena, caught in a time warp. As you voyage you will be accompanied by sea birds and schools of dolphins that come to investigate the boat, and maybe the sighting of a whale. Then you have the chance of heading for the laid-back Caribbean or sailing into the spectacular Bay of Guanabara, where Rio de Janeiro and a whole new continent and culture to is waiting to be explored.

If the demands, pleasures, and challenges of ocean voyaging are your dream, it's easy enough to make your dream come true.

If you are considering the possibilities of sailing on a private yacht as a crew member, the best way to proceed is by registering your name for a small fee with organisations such as the Cruising Association (tel 020 7537 2828, website www. cruising.org.uk) or Crewseekers (tel 01489 578319, website www.crewseekers.co. uk). They hold lists of members or contributors requiring crew. Consult the personal advertisements in yachting magazines such as *Yachting* or *Yachting World*. Check out your local yacht club – ask the secretary what the procedure is. If you place an advertisement of your own, it should include the following information: name, nationality, sex, age, crewing experience, skills, date available and proposed duration of trip, desired destination, financial arrangements (contributory basis/ proposed payment) and a place/address where you can be contacted. It helps if you date the advertisement and add a photo.

It is very important to meet the skipper and see their yacht, as you will need to make assessments about their ability and the vessel's seaworthiness. Does it have the necessary equipment on board for all weather conditions: sails, navigation lights, navigation sextant and satellite, communications, life-raft, emergency tracking system and dinghy? Is the galley properly set up, are the heads adequate, what are the sleeping arrangements? Are the vessel's documents and the skipper's sailing certificates in order?

In return, they will want to know about your skills. You will be expected to have basic sailing skills at least, but more important than being an expert sailor is a willingness to do anything that may be required. Desirable skills include cooking, computer literacy, an aptitude for diesel mechanics, diving, electronics expertise, an inventive engineering ability, languages, medical knowledge, musical talent, navigation, sewing, experience as a teacher or nanny, and radio/communications experience. You will need to be organised to carry out your duties; for instance, if you've signed on as a cook, do you have recipes and adequate equipment on board? Mechanics should brush up on marine engines, check that manuals and tools are on board. If that's going to be your responsibility, you may want to take overalls. For sewing, do you have sail-repairing needles, 'palms' and other material on board?

Your own gear must be kept to a minimum and packed in a foldaway synthetic holdall. Keep your clothes in plastic bags. Your equipment should include: foul-weather gear, scarf, life-vest, safety harness, deck shoes, gloves, peaked hat, sun screen, sea-sickness remedy, personal medication, sunglasses and spare prescription glasses or lenses.

Keeping in touch needs to be organised. Before you leave, make sure that there is one person at home with whom you can co-ordinate your activities – that way you don't have several people to advise of your schedule. Your nominee can also collect your correspondence and forward it on to you. Make sure people understand that timings will be extremely flexible to save them anxiety when you don't call from, say, Cape Town, on a predetermined date.

Make sure people only use your surname with initials on correspondence, then it won't be accidentally filed under your christian name at your *poste restante*. International telephone calls are often a major exercise in those areas with limited facilities and major time differences. Email has made life easier, so you could consider using a service such as info@nautimail.com, website www.nautimail.com.

Skippers will ask you to contribute to general running costs, including food, mooring and immigration fees. The rate varies according to the situation, but it is usually around US$20-25 a day. It is not usual to contribute financially to yacht maintenance, although your elbow grease will be required. Apart from the 'on-board' living costs you agree, you will have to have a return ticket/MCO or the equivalent amount in travellers' cheques. Be prepared to 'bond' these with the skipper as he will be responsible to immigration and port authorities for crew members' repatriation. Keep all your documents in sealed plastic bags: passport, inoculation certificates, letters of reference, skill certificates, cash, cheques, tickets and insurance documents.

If you are looking for a paid job as skipper, deckhand or cook you will need references from previous skippers and certificates of competence. Information about certificates for all levels of competence is available from the Royal Yachting Association (tel 02380 627400, website www.rya.org.uk). Wages are minimal as living is 'all found' on board. Work is usually seasonal with charter and flotilla holiday companies or yacht deliveries. There are training establishments for skills associated with marine leisure activities and agencies which specialise in marine placement. Try the Hamble School of Yachting & Professional Training (tel 02380 452668, email tuition@hamble.co.uk) or Leisure Management International (tel 01983 280641, email mail@lmitraining.com). Consult the small ads in the yachting magazines.

Having agreed on finances, duties, and intended destination, the last but most important factor of all is compatibility. In the end it does not matter whether the vessel is state of the art or just adequate or the weather is foul or fair, if you do not get on well together the voyage could be disastrous. This is the hardest thing to get right, since there is no real way of knowing before you are on the high seas. A weekend 'shake-down' cruise is recommended to give everyone the chance to assess each other and the situation, but you could still be in for some surprises if you are considering a long voyage – even if you are sailing with someone you already know well! Personality problems are greatly emphasised in the limited environment of a yacht at sea, the boat has a greater chance of surviving than the crew, and the skipper has the last word on everything, so you must be prepared to obey – like it or lump it!

There are pros and cons for leaving from your country of origin. Skippers usually have family and friends to sail with at the beginning of their voyage, so finding a place can be harder even if you are on home ground. It is when these friends have to return home that the skipper will need to find crew *en route*, and at certain seasonal bottlenecks itinerant crew can be much in demand. Some of the major ones include the Solent in May, Las Palmas and Saint Thomas in November, Grenada and Durban in December, Cape Town in January and Tahiti in April and September. So sometimes it is worth flying out to the area you wish to sail in and putting up a notice in the local yacht club, meeting place, *poste restante* or launderette. Groups of yachts travelling together often operate a 'net' on ham radio or VHF, where crew requirements can be announced. These opportunities for finding a crew position come easier with experience. If you are sailing from the UK, the beginning of May to the end of August is the optimum time; in the Mediterranean it is between the end of March and the end of September. The Caribbean season runs from the end of November until March, but if you are sailing from Europe you should be leaving to cross the Atlantic between the end of September and early November. The Pacific season is from April to September, so yachts should be transiting the Panama Canal during March. The season for the Indian Ocean, via the southerly islands, is July to October. The growing popularity of rallies provides added opportunities to crew for yachts that enter them, find out when the major ones take place from the Cruising Association, details as before or the World Cruising Club (tel 01983 296060, website www.worldcruising.com).

You should remember that sailing is an archaic form of transport. When you travel by yacht you are reliant on the elements to get you from A to B, not a timetable. You play a major role in achieving this, living by a 24-hour watch, sleeping, cooking, eating, cleaning, sail changing and taking the helm to fit in with that routine. Life at sea has to be learnt: the motion of the boat and sea conditions must be accommodated while you fulfil all your roles. Your normal routine: sleeping, washing, eating, all must to be adapted to life on board ship.

The golden rule is: one hand for you, one for the boat. Everything has to have its place, and must be returned there after use and be stowed away properly. Doors, hatches, portholes, cupboards and drawers all have safety latches that must be used or the vessel will become unsafe and unmanageable. You cannot have an untidy boat at sea. The practice of conserving (in as much as it is possible) fresh water (usually for drinking purposes only), fuel, battery power and light is extremely important. You must learn how to use all the pumps properly, from the galley to the bilges – and particularly the heads – if you don't you could sink the vessel.

Life at sea is completely different to life on land. You are always exposed to the elements: sun, wind, rain squalls, and you are absolutely reliant on yourself and your crew mates on the high seas. There will be great challenges and periods of calm, there will be both companionship and solitude, and, above all, there will be the freedom of the oceans and the excitement of landfall and new places to see. ❧

ALISON MUIR BENNETT sailed her own yacht and crewed for others for ten years before becoming a writer. She spent three years on a voyage from from the Far East to South Africa, and has also sailed the coast of Brazil.

The aid worker
by Lucy Markby

TRAVELLING ABROAD AS AN AID WORKER is increasingly popular, because it offers some in-depth experience of a country plus the challenges and satisfactions of helping some of the world's neediest people. But it's no longer a game for amateurs.

The myths

"So what do you do?" —"I work for a humanitarian relief organisation…. Actually I've just come back from Afghanistan."—"Oh."

This is usually followed by one of the following stock responses:

a) "How fascinating, did you have a nice time? You haven't got much of a tan, though."

b) "How wonderful. I do think you people are doing a brilliant job out there."

c) "Don't you think it's immoral to support communities of such extremists?"

d) "What a bunch of cowboys!"

There are many stereotyped images of aid workers, even within the sector itself. Mercenary, missionary or misfit? Or, in one of their latest manifestations – Land Cruising, Caterpillar boot-wearing, Marlboro-smoking, bullet-dodging, hairy-

Emergency relief

These agencies look for experienced staff who can travel at very short notice to areas of instability, where local capacity cannot meet the basic needs of shelter, safe water, food and medical care:

Merlin (Medical Emergency Relief International) www.merlin.org.uk

MSF (Médecins sans Frontières) www.msf.org

Concern Worldwide www.concern.org.uk

AAH (Action Against Hunger) www.aah-uk.org

British Red Cross www.redcross.org.uk

legged war hero – 'le macho'. As a French survey in 1995 revealed, there is a certain thrill associated with aid workers: the ideal French lover, apparently, would be a doctor working for Médicins sans Frontières and offering an irresistible combination of intelligence, confidence, professionalism, adventurous spirit and sex appeal – oh, and a little altruism as well.

The truths

The views of aid workers are as varied as the people who choose to do this kind of work. All but a few would agree, however, that it is an experience that challenges your perspectives on life, work and social ethics. In my experience as an aid worker, this kind of work allows you to meet the most remarkable people and develop the strongest of relationships with colleagues from many countries.

The work itself can involve a level of responsibility that would be beyond most people's dreams (or nightmares) at home. This is matched by an intense degree of emotional and physical energy, combined with an equal measure of frustration in the face of antiquated and bureaucratic procedures overseas, for instance, or the laborious paperwork required to clear customs and satisfy donor reporting requirements.

The working environment tends to involve hard work in hot, sticky, mosquito-ridden and remote locations with unreliable water and electricity supplies. But many new aid workers are surprised by the level of technology available to support them, including high-tech satellite communications equipment and well-maintained four-wheel drive vehicles. They may also receive considerable support from domestic staff, employed to maintain the cars, clean the house, cook and even do the laundry, so that aid workers are free to do aid work.

But many organisations avoid this type of conspicuous consumption and find some kind of middle ground. In my experience as a volunteer in Gaza, home was a shared three-bedroom villa surrounded by orange and lemon groves, and transport was a half-share in a dilapidated Renault 4, whose rattling shell gave year-round ventilation but limited protection from stone-throwing youths.

The diversity of staff living standards, as well as general terms and conditions, will depend largely on the resources of the agency you choose. Some overseas staff find themselves posted to a far-flung corner of a country by themselves, while others may be living with a team of twenty- to thirtysomethings and attending NGO (non-governmental organisation) parties in villas in the sun.

On a serious note, any prospective field worker should be aware that aid work is almost inherently a risky business. Staff are vulnerable to disease, to theft, and to being stopped at tense checkpoints by Kalashnikov-toting boys. At worst, aid workers have been a specific target for kidnap or violence. Not all aid work is carried out in conflict areas, but much is conflict-related. It is essential to consider such issues in decisions about where, when and which organisation to choose.

Security management while overseas takes many forms, from armed guards to simple strategies such as adopting appropriate dress codes. When I was in Gaza, a 35-minute drive from Gaza City to the nearby town of Rafah would require a few quick changes: first there was some nifty work with a headscarf to create the impression of a modest, respectful, culturally sensitive woman showing solidarity with the Palestinian refugees; then at the Israeli military checkpoints the scarf disappeared as I metamorphosed into a hair-tossing young Western thing.

Professional considerations

More and more professionals are taking time out from work, or making a deliberate move away from the mainstream. Their motivation may be a desire to do something in response to the world's disasters that they see unfolding in the news, to teach their professional skills to others who desperately need them, or to learn new professional skills and experience in a fresh geographical and cultural environment – or a combination of all three.

The development of the 'global village' means that companies are now looking for global managers. So if you are to hoping to transfer your skills to something more meaningful that satisfies an aspect of your social conscience, or to develop your skills in a truly international context, this may be the path for you.

Aid workers as amateur enthusiasts are a dying breed. Increasingly they are being replaced by highly competent professionals, who work to agreed sector-wide

Volunteer-sending agencies

Terms in the field are of varying length. You can usually expect your costs to be covered, possibly plus an in-country allowance comparable with a local wage.

International Service (two-year contracts) www.oneworld.org/is

International Co-operation for Development www.ciir.org

VSO (two-year placement, or secondment) www.vso.org.uk

Raleigh International www.raleigh.org.uk
(two- to three-week corporate sponsorship, or three-month self-funded placements)

Unipal (EFL teaching to Palestinians in Gaza, West Bank, Lebanon) 0208 299 1132

Health Projects Abroad (age 17–28 years) www.hpauk.org

BESO (age range 35 to post-retirement) www.beso.org

standards and are monitored by donors who demand high levels of accountability and cost-efficiency.

Experienced aid workers, particularly those in senior management positions, can expect to command competitive salaries and benefits packages. The levels of responsibility commensurate with these posts should not be underestimated, however. Operational budgets frequently run to millions of dollars, and are implemented by large numbers of staff.

In less senior posts, remuneration for aid workers varies enormously. The minimum you can expect is to have all expenses covered for the period of work, plus a monthly allowance to cover any ongoing costs you might have at home, such as your mortgage.

What kind of people become aid workers?

Most aid agencies do their best to avoid recruiting people who fall into the stereotypes mentioned at the beginning of this article. It should be noted that war-hungry adrenaline junkies are almost universally unwelcome in the field.

In reality, a broad range of skills and professional backgrounds is potentially in demand from developing countries. VSO, for example, requires experienced professionals from many sectors, including industry, business, media, education, agriculture and more. Even organisations that have a specialist focus, such as the British medical agency Merlin, will want not only medical staff but also all manner of other personnel able to provide the programme with vital support services, such as mechanics and accountants. What unites almost all aid workers is the capacity to be functionally and intellectually flexible, with a skills tool kit that includes some heavyweight common sense.

Other personal requirements include a certain sensitivity and concern for the welfare of other people. But this must be focused by keen pragmatism and a strong determination to make a professional rather than emotional contribution. Even in disaster relief, field workers have to remember that their aim is often to transfer knowledge appropriately into another community.

All this is neatly summed up in S. George's description (albeit satirical) of the ideal aid worker:

'First they must take graduate degrees in social anthropology, geography, eco-

Agencies working in both development & relief contexts

These look for skilled, qualified and experienced overseas staff.
Employment tends to be paid, with some opportunities to take partners.

Save the Children Fund www.savethechildren.org.uk

Oxfam www.oxfam.org.uk

World Vision www.worldvision.org.uk

Christian Aid www.christian-aid.org.uk

Tear Fund (The Evangelical Alliance Relief Fund) www.tearfund.org

Central registers & humanitarian websites: specific jobs

IHE (International Health Exchange) www.ihe.org.uk

RedR (Registered Engineers for Disaster Relief) www.redr.org

APSO www.apso.ie

WSE (guide to working in development at home and overseas) www.wse.org.uk

Reliefweb www.relief.int

AlertNet www.alertnet.org

Bond www.bond.org.uk

nomics, a dozen or so difficult and unrelated languages, medicine and business administration. Second, at a slightly more practical level, they must demonstrate competence in agronomy, hydrology, practical nursing, accounting, psychology, automotive mechanics and civil engineering. In addition, they must learn to give a credible imitation of saintliness and it would be well if they could learn sleight of hand as well, since they will often be called upon to perform feats of magic.'

This vision found echoes in an article in *People Management*, which likened the level and diversity of competencies required of field staff to that of the most senior executives in most companies.

And as if this were not enough, there are still more requirements. The prerequisite skills and experience must be complemented by an ability to live and work in close proximity with a very mixed team of people, often in a harsh or demanding physical environment.

A survey of aid workers in 1995 revealed that health professionals form the single largest functional/professional group sent overseas. Support staff, including managers, administrators and logisticians, made up the second largest functional group (28 per cent of the 3,000 appointments), followed by teachers and trainers (12 per cent). Other highly sought-after specialists are those who can offer skills in engineering, agriculture, construction, business development, social work and mine clearance. The survey indicates a general lack of opportunities for unskilled volunteers to work overseas. This is a trend that is set to continue, as many agencies are increasingly concerned with providing appropriate training for host country nationals, enabling them to take on the responsibilities that were once the domain of expatriate aid workers.

How to get into aid work

Make a few calls to big charities and you'll find the story is the same. You need at least two years' field experience before they will even take a look at your CV. But don't get disillusioned and don't be put off – you are not going for the easy life, after all.

There are some 116 international NGOs in Britain alone, so there is something out there for everyone. But it may take you a while to achieve the right match between what you are looking for, what the agencies are looking for, and what posi-

tions happen to be available at the time. NGOs are inundated with people genuinely wanting to help, but to get a look-in you need the right personal qualities as
well as the technical/professional skills and experience.

Whatever your profession or work history, all the agencies will want to see you
demonstrate some pretty sound skills and an ability to apply them in a relief or development context. Increasingly they like to see an aptitude for transferring your
knowledge to your overseas colleagues, both national and international.

There are times, of course, when you just happen be in the right place at the
right time, and that is likely to be in the field itself. Merlin, like many other respectable agencies, has a rigorous recruitment process but is not over-burdened
with bureaucracy: a chance meeting in the field with the right person might well
turn into a genuine work opportunity.

My strategy for entering the sector led me down the quick and well-trodden
path of training as a qualified teacher of English as a foreign language (EFL). On
condition that I passed the course, indeed, I was promised a job even before I had
started. A major plus of being an EFL teacher is that you can find work anywhere,
and the nature of the work takes you right into the heart of a community – giving
you a intriguing insights into people's culture, lifestyles, interests and preoccupa-
tions. This was how I came to be among the Palestinians in Gaza.

Before you make that first step towards meeting a new challenge, do give your
personal circumstances some serious thought. Consider, for example, the impact
that working overseas might have on your partner, your children, your friends and
family; what financial commitments you are obliged to maintain; what training
courses, work opportunities, births, deaths or marriages you may miss while you
are overseas.

And if you can't get in

■ Find out which skills are the most useful and realistically attainable.

■ Join a training course specific to the aid sector, such as those run by Merlin,
RedR and International Health Exchange.

■ Make applications to organisations with an educational or experiential element, such as Operation Raleigh or Health Projects Abroad. (Raleigh have now
started a secondment scheme, so you might consider persuading your present
employer to let you be their first 'guinea pig'.)

■ Volunteer some time in the UK-based office of an aid agency – but be sure that
both you and they know what you are volunteering for.

■ Finally, learn a language. French, Spanish and Portuguese-speakers are in
hottest demand. But bear in mind that a language alone is usually not enough.

The agencies

Aid agencies, like people, come in all shapes and sizes. There are fat cats, rebels
with a cause (as well as those without), cowboys and 'happy-clappies'. An agency
might be a community-backed band of two people with a truck and a map of Eastern Europe, or conversely it might be part of the United Nations family with an international task force and the bureaucracy to go with it.

The NGO jungle can at first glance be daunting, but once you cut through the thickets of marketing, the interior reflects a high degree of biodiversity. There is a huge variety of technical, professional and geographical specialisations, ages and sizes, levels of bureaucracy, and operational focus.

The most widely known UK sending agencies fall into two main categories: development work and emergency relief. The majority of agencies (88 per cent) focus primarily on long-term development objectives. During the Nineties, however, many agencies chose to diversify into emergency relief work, in response to demand on the ground. Only nine agencies of the 116 surveyed by IHE and People in Aid specialise in relief.

All agencies will have their own selection criteria, requirements, terms and conditions, which you need to consider when choosing which to approach. A summary of the main agencies and contacts can be found in the fact boxes above. It should be stressed, however, that this is only a tiny sample of the better-known agencies, selected from many others that are looking to recruit the right staff. ❧

Lucy Markby worked in the overseas aid sector for several years and is now a human resources specialist.

Travels with my camera
by Benedict Allen

IT IS AN EXCITING PROSPECT TO HAVE YOUR TRAVELS shown on television to a potentially huge and enthusiastic audience. Thanks to the advent of comparatively cheap and light broadcast-quality video cameras, as well as the proliferation of television channels, this is now a real possibility. However, it is still a highly specialised field, and one that is strewn with ghastly difficulties.

Getting your idea commissioned

Let's face it, you are not going to be granted a 'TV spectacular' about your forthcoming round-the-world gypsy caravan odyssey. Why not? Because it all comes down to cost. A standard-length (say 50-minute) travel programme would be budgeted at about £150,000 – this is for a three-week shoot. Surprisingly, the cost of a Video Diary (a format made without a film crew) isn't exactly chicken feed either – here the expense lies in the editing.

This means that your film proposal has to be a very bankable proposition in order to even be considered – you are expected to be notable in your field and to be undertaking a journey that is unique as well as fascinating. And, as if that weren't enough, unlike a writer or a photographer you must be able to communicate your own feelings, even when under pressure – the pressure of, say, working under the constant attention of four bored, moronic members of a film crew – and you must be authoritative, articulate and 'personable'. In short, climbing Everest – even climbing it solo, without oxygen, up the southwest face – nowadays simply isn't good enough.

Still not put off?

An independent production company would consider itself lucky if one in 25 of its programme proposals were to be commissioned by a TV channel – this ratio might be as high as one in ten for the first rank of 'independents'. The process is this: whether through independents or directly, your proposal is submitted on paper (one or two sides of A4, maximum) to a TV channel, and its merits assessed, along with hundreds of other, through *A border is always* the long (up to nine months) selection process. Your pro- *a temptation.* posal might find a slot in a magazine programme – it *– LARRY MCMURTRY* might become a five-minute item on *Blue Peter* by a teenager questing after hairy-footed gerbils in the Kalahari. Alternatively, it might end up as a full programme on one of the occasional 'strands' so beloved of TV programmers – examples include Channel 4's *Travels with My Camera* or the BBC's *Great River Journeys*.

Of these two options, the magazines are most likely to offer the commissions – they have more slots because they are always looking for 5- or 10-minute items and will probably accept Hi-8 video quality. Although the emergence of digital Hi-8 technology will bring down the cost of foreign filming and open other avenues, at present the only other option is to ask a channel for a whole TV series – and there's fat chance of getting one of those beauties unless you already have a proven track record on telly.

Although the BBC has its own production base, and so can be approached directly with an idea, most channels – including the other two major travel programme outlets, Channel Four in the UK and The Discovery Channel in the US – commission from independents. One way or another, unless you are an experienced operator, with a nose for a marketable storyline, the general rule is that you need a commission, or at least a definite expression of interest, before you set off. The obvious exceptions are regional news programmes, which might welcome a 'local explorer' item, especially if you have potential headline material – which, sadly, means that you'll need to be involved in some kind of disaster story yourself or become a witness to someone else's misery as they succumb to massacre, coup or mudslide.

Behind the camera

Before undertaking this tedious commissioning process, it is as well to consider whether dragging about camera equipment or – horror of horrors – a camera crew is quite your cup of tea in the first place. For many travellers, it suffices simply to have a visual record of the journey – on your return you might want to give a presentation to the worthy businessmen who supported your venture, or wish to use a film clip as an educational tool for the local primary school.

Similarly, footage brought back on a recce trip might raise sponsorship prior to you setting out in earnest, or act as valuable briefing material for the main body of the expedition team. For such purposes it's enough to pack into your rucksack a Hi-8 camcorder, tripod and a stash of batteries.

For those who are prepared to 'go the whole way', and try for that TV commission, there are obvious financial advantages. The income you are likely to accrue from the programme probably will not do more than cover the cost of a modest expedition, but television coverage can have a pleasing effect on those to whom you are indebted. This can mean commercial sponsors – though rules on product placement are now very strict – or even political ones.

A few years ago I applied to the Namibian government to walk up the Namib Desert, something a TV crew had never previously been permitted – not least because diamonds lie scattered in the sands. Armed with a commission, I was in a position to offer the Namibian government worldwide coverage of an exquisitely beautiful portion of the country, which I suggested would be a fillip to its tourist industry; but the master stroke turned out to be that I had also persuaded the BBC to offer free broadcast of the programme on Namibian television, which would allow Namibians to make the journey themselves by watching my rather painful progress across the sand dunes on TV.

So, for the first time, total access was granted by the government to this very special place, while chunks of the delicate desert were still protected from the impact of tourists. However, there was a proviso: I would be filming my progress alone, without a camera crew. And this is where the real problems with telly begin.

The dreadful film crew

There's no escaping the fact that travelling with a film crew is not travelling at all. In bringing a crew, you bring a part of your world with you, and that part happens to be a circus. However hard you try, travelling becomes an act. Forget the lone caver, inching forward through slime on his belly. As likely as not the cameraman, lighting man, soundman and director have got there first.

It's the same for every market scene and every mountain-top soliloquy. In Kenya and Uganda, filming a BBC *Great Railway Journey*, I found myself lumbered with a crew that was ten-strong, including the official government minder, two local 'fixers' and two minibus drivers, who served as roadies, ferrying everyone else around along with their kit.

And here we come to the main point: keeping this show on the road costs a fortune, so before you even leave home, an hour-by-hour itinerary has to be worked out – worked out according to the needs of a film crew, not a traveller. 'Chance encounters' are arranged, tribal dances ordered up. Effectively, the film-maker is re-assembling the components of a journey for the enjoyment of others. He or she is not actually making a real journey at all. There may be many justifications for this – for me, watching the film crew scrambling aboard a crowded Kampala train was in itself good for a comedy sequence. But if you say you are doing your trek along the Great Wall of China for your own sake, and it just happens to be filmed, then you are deceiving yourself. The answer is that, like the very best circus act, it's little more than a stunt.

Video – the one-man band

There is another option. Modern technology now enables expeditions to be filmed on video with the help of a small, or no, additional film crew. In addition to the possibilities offered by the somewhat cumbersome Beta video camera, the Hi-8 camcorder, now with digital technology, brings the small camera well up to broadcast standard. While glossy shots and a first-grade soundtrack are still best captured by a crew, these cameras and the tape they use are cheap and robust. For the first time ever, expeditions can now be recorded comprehensively as they unfold. Thus for my three-and-a-half-month Namib trek, I simply strapped solar panels either side of the hump of Nelson (my lead camel) and used them to recharge the batteries for my little Hitachi vm-80. I was totally self-sufficient with the aid of the Hi-8 and tripod, recording whatever befell me (and camel companions) as we plodded hopefully through the dunes.

In the Peruvian Amazon, a camcorder (Sony tr805) again enabled me to record a journey over an extended period. The use of video also helped me in recording the everyday life of my guides. Instead of feeling like a predatory outsider, as I'd always felt before when taking photographs of indigenous people, I was now able to involve them in the process, in this case getting the local Matses Indians to film themselves. The hundred or so hours of tape from the expedition proved to be an invaluable record of life in the jungle – there was footage of drug dealers, and even of an ocelot-type cat, which, rightly or wrongly, the Matses believe often exhibits aggressive behaviour to humans.

A further note of warning. Just when you are congratulating yourself on having survived the film crew, the tangles of the battery charger units, the frogmarch to jail, it's time to begin battling back home in the cutting room. Your producer knows what makes 'good tv' – and that usually means giving your precious journey a 'comic twist'. That said, tv at its best gives the traveller something unique – the chance to pass on to others direct experience of different worlds. This is far more than simple gratification. Travellers must nowadays be able to justify the act of imposing themselves on foreign turf. Sharing their journey with the millions back home who are not privileged to have made it themselves is one way of doing that. ໕

Benedict Allen is an explorer, author and broadcaster. His television series have documented arduous journeys across the Gobi desert, along Namibia's Skeleton Coast, and in search of the world's last remaining shamen.

Travel writing for beginners
by Jonathan Lorie

'Dear Editor, You probably won't bother to read this letter, but if you do I can assure you that my article is much better than the ones you have been printing recently. Please consider it for publication.'

'Dear Sir/Madam, This is the first of a constant stream of letters which you will receive from me over the next two months, keeping you up to date with every day of my round-the-world adventures.'

'Dear Tim, I know that your magazine does not publish articles on package tourism, but I am sure you will be interested in my autobiographical manuscript 'Memoirs of a Tour Rep'. I enclose the first 50 pages.'

I DIDN'T MAKE UP THOSE LETTERS. I COULDN'T. They are real examples which I have received from people who would like to become travel writers. And who wouldn't? But there are ways and ways, and the aim of this article is to help you get a lot further than the people above did.

As the editor of *Traveller* magazine, I receive proposals for articles from travel writers of all kinds – Fleet Street journalists, published authors, commercial publicists, compulsive travellers and enthusiastic beginners. And it's clear that there are just as many versions of what travel writing is: the factual report on a popular destination, the sensitive literary impression of a distant culture, the free 'plug', the backpacker's tale of glory, the raw talent that needs a little technical guidance. Which is where you come in. So let's start at the beginning. What kind of writer do you want to be – and why?

Let me be Devil's Advocate here and put the case against becoming a travel writer. Contrary to popular belief, it won't pay your way around the world. A handful of newspaper and magazine journalists make a regular living and take a lot of trips, but the rest don't. The rest are either travelling anyway, or do something else for a living. And even the successful journalists tend to get short trips that include a lot of factual research (best hotels, cheapest fares, etc.). If you want to spend time savouring a foreign culture, it will usually be at your own expense.

Also contrary to popular belief, the reading public is not waiting breathlessly to hear your – or anyone else's – personal views on the world and all that is in it. Readers want information that is useful or interesting in itself: they don't want deeply personal musings on experiences they are unlikely ever to share.

On the other hand, travel writing might just make you famous. In the wake of Bill Bryson's global success, the market for travel books seems to expand inexhaustibly. Since there's almost nowhere on the planet that's not been written about already, book-publishers are hungry for new angles on old journeys. Hence some current titles that are weird but popular – travelling round Ireland carrying a fridge, for example, or travelling round the globe touching only deserts. And remember that Bryson's bestsellers are actually based on places most of us can visit (Europe, Australia, America), but described in his own inimitable style.

Other would-be travel writers do it not for the fame or the money, sensibly enough. They do it because they genuinely love to write, or because they have been somewhere that fires them up. In my experience, these are the ones worth watching. A writer who combines talent and passion can go a long way, eventually.

So how do you get your writing published? If you're a total beginner, then the classic route is to slowly build up a reputation through journalistic articles (see below). Having a portfolio of articles in print can help even if you're aiming at book-publishing, because it gives you credibility and something solid to show publishers. It gets your name out there, and establishes your area of expertise.

If your ultimate goal is books rather than articles, you should know that many book-publishers rely largely on literary agents for new talent, so you might do best to approach the agents. There are lists of them in the *Writers' and Artists' Yearbook*, or you may have personal contacts who can help. The classic approach is to send in a one-page summary of your book idea, giving the overall theme and a breakdown of the chapters, plus a sample chapter in full – perhaps the opening chapter, so they can see whether you can grab the audience. You should anticipate quite a long haul as you do the round of the agents.

But before that, for most writers, comes the stage of trying to sell your work to newspaper or magazine editors. The rules here are fairly simple:

1. KNOW THE MARKET. Research who is publishing what, and make sure you send them what they want. There is absolutely no point in submitting articles which are unsuitable because of style, subject matter or length. No matter how good they are, they just won't get published. Equally, find out who takes unsolicited material, and don't waste your time on those who don't.

2. CHOOSE YOUR ANGLE. You can place the same story with several publications, if you find a different angle for each. The crucial trick is to find the angle that will make your material relevant to that particular publication. For example, a woman writer just back from a safari could find distinct angles for the women's, environmental and tourism sections of the press.

3. MAKE A CRISP PRESENTATION. Send in your ideas on one side of A4, keep them short and sharp, don't send too many. You might include back-up material, such as photos or clippings, or perhaps the whole article, but there should be a cover letter that allows a busy editor to assess your proposals quickly and easily.

4. DON'T WASTE THEIR TIME. Journalism is a high-pressure business and editors are often ridiculously busy. Don't expect to reach them in person by phone – but if you do, keep the conversation brief and to the point. Don't hassle them for decisions they haven't made yet. But do keep gently reminding them or their staff about your proposal: polite persistence does pay off.

5. BE RELIABLE. Always meet your deadlines, check your facts, write to length. If you fail on any of these, you're leaving the editor in a real pickle. And it won't be forgotten, either. On the other hand, you'd be surprised at how many journalistic careers are based on being reliable rather than being brilliant.

If you compare these rules of thumb with the letters quoted at the start of this article, you can see where they went wrong. The first letter – apart from its off-putting rudeness – doesn't convey the proposal at all (rule 3). The second letter doesn't suggest an angle (rule 2) and would have most editors scared of a deluge of material. The third letter does have a strong angle but, as the author says, it is unsuitable (rule 1). Interestingly, all three letters break rule 4 in their own delightful ways. Unfortunately, none of them got far enough to test rule 5.

Much better than these is a straightforward letter like this, which just arrived: *'Dear Mr Lorie, I have spent the last 25 years chasing and photographing the world's last remaining steam trains. This might interest your readers, perhaps in your 'Eyewitness' section. I enclose the article written to your length, 25 original photographs of trains in India, and a stamped addressed envelope for their return. This material has not been published in the UK before.'*

Doesn't it sound intriguing? Wouldn't you want to know more? The writer has got lots of things right here – for starters, the name of the editor. He's told us the angle, the location, and his own credentials for writing about this. It's clear that he's looked at the magazine and tailored his material to fit one of the sections. He's also made it easy for the busy editor, by enclosing the pictures and a reply envelope. Crucially, he's explained that this article would be a UK 'first': editors love to publish something before their rivals. And all of that is conveyed in 66 words.

Now we've got a grip on how not to sell a story, let's consider what not to submit to an editor. He or she won't want unedited chunks of your travel diaries, since they won't suit the publication's style. Nor postcard-style reminiscences of happy holidays, which are too personal to interest the general reader. Nor thinly disguised 'plugs' for hotels/tour agents/resorts/airlines or anyone else who's obviously done the author some favour or other. Nor, sadly, reminiscences of the travels of ten, 20 or even 30 years ago: no matter how much they mean to the author, they won't be topical enough for the editor.

What the editor does want to receive is material that suits his or her publication, is entertainingly written, and tells the reader something worth knowing. It must be up-to-date and accurate. It should be written in 'house style'. It could be topical. And it helps if the story can be easily illustrated with photographs. Getting of all that right will get you in print.

So, having passed the test and got your proposal or article accepted, what happens next? My best advice is to regard the publication of your article as a beginning rather than an end. Regard that magazine or newspaper as your prime target, on the assumption that if they liked your material once, they will do again. Try to work out why that particular article got published, and offer them the same 'formula' a second or third time. Try to build some contacts there: perhaps get known for some area of expertise on which they might call you. Crucially, start a contact book in which to note any useful names and addresses, and keep careful track of your submissions and conversations.

With this combination of professionalism and patience, you might find that first article in print is a door opening into your future. ❧

JONATHAN LORIE is Editor of 'The Traveller's Handbook' and 'Traveller' magazine.

Writing on the road
by Martin Roberts

'I was on the beach and it was hot' – No.
'The sun was shining on the beach where I was sitting and it was hot.' – Um, no.

I'LL NEVER FORGET THE FIRST TIME I tried to write an article on a place I'd been to. After four years of presenting reports for BBC Radio 4's travel show *Breakaway*, I'd decided it was time to put pen to paper and actually write about my travels. Now I was sitting at a word processor trying to encapsulate the essence of a particularly magical afternoon spent on the powder-fine sand of a Venezuelan beach, drinking cold beers and eating freshly cooked lobster plucked from the ocean moments earlier. The experience needed to be transcribed from image to word and I was failing dismally.

'The beach where I was sitting was a great place to be eating lobster.' Delete, delete, delete. *'Sand formed the table for my bottle of cold beer which I was drinking on a beautiful beach prior to eating lobster.'* Bin the thing and give up in despair.

I felt like a schoolboy struggling with his first essay. In desperation, I rang a friend who was editor of one of the *Country Life* stable of magazines.

"I just can't seem to get it," I confessed.

"Don't think about it too much," she advised. "Just write down the first thing that comes into your head. Improve it and change it later."

It was the single most useful piece of advice I have been given in my writing career. It's so much easier to edit than to originate. Get something down on paper, then turn it into quality literature afterwards.

I tried (unsuccessfully) for another hour before calling her back.

"I still can't get it right," I moaned.

"OK," she said, " describe the scene."

I described the scene.

"How about: *'The most energetic thing I had done that day was to decide if I wanted the seafood sauce with my freshly caught lobster. I pondered the thought as a droplet of condensation formed on my ice-cold beer bottle and dropped lazily into the crescent of powdery white sand that stretched before me',"* she suggested off the top of her head.

I was hooked.

Despite those initial feelings of inadequacy in the face of my inability to string a few words together in a creative way, travel writing has proved to be a fascinating, exciting and fulfilling avenue of journalism, and one which has literally taken me all over the world.

If you can figure out a style and way of writing which appeals to readers and editors alike, you'll have the opportunity to tap into one of the world's most desirable professions. Obviously it's not always as glamorous as it appears, and making it pay the mortgage is a whole different ball game, but the opportunities it presents are incredible. Suddenly every situation you find yourself in becomes a potential story. A humorous account of 24 hours spent in Gatwick airport can be just as entertaining as a report on a climb of Kilimanjaro. Believe me, I've written both.

Good travel writing is about capturing the imagination. The reader's mind is a blank canvas onto which you have the opportunity to paint the most vivid of pictures. Steven Spielberg and a budget of millions could not create the kind of intricate pictures you can with a few well-chosen words.

Consider the following:

'The fort stood above the harbour.'

'The fort growled down from above the harbour.'

A few extra words. A big change in atmosphere. However, such subtleties can be worked on when you return from your travels. In general, while you are there, you need to get as much background and local colour as you possibly can. As a journalist you have to adopt a different approach from that of a holidaymaker. In a few days, you have to capture the essence of a place.

A few hints and tips that I have found helpful

■ Research as much as possible beforehand. Guidebooks, the internet and published articles will all give a starting point for your exploration. A working knowledge of the local language will give you an added advantage and a chance to get under the country's skin.

■ Once at your destination, visit places that will provide you with the most to write about. Eating re-fried beans with the locals at a traditional café is going to inspire you more than lunch at McDonald's. An uncomfortable journey by overcrowded bus will give you far more story ideas than jumping into a taxi.

■ Gather enough information while you are on location. You don't have to visit exotic destinations to practise this. In fact it is much more of a challenge to write a compelling travel article on somewhere local and unglamorous. Bring Runcorn to life and Bali will be a doddle. Try and find what makes the place special, its unique selling points. Describe and expand on these. Make notes of everything you see and everything that happens to you.

■ Observe the finer details. Just as a wide-angle view of a crowded market scene will have much less impact than a close-up shot of a barrow of oranges, so a travel article that brings out the details will win out over one that skims over a scene. Compare, for instance, *'A crowd of people gathered in the square below me'* with *'I watched as a small girl, eyes wide with wonder, gripped her mother's hand tightly as she was led through the heaving crowd that had gathered in the square below me.'*

When you are looking at a scene, look for that finer detail. Remember it, write it down and use it to paint your picture. There are various tools that you can use to help you. Make photographs or videos. Dictate what you see into a tape recorder. Jot down key words and images. Make sketches. There are no hard and fast rules – find what works best for you. But whatever the method you choose, do make notes. Overall images you will remember, finer details you won't.

■ Start your articles with an anecdote, using it to draw the reader into your work and set the scene for your destination. Factual stuff at the beginning of an article is a real turn-off. Compare, '*At nearly 10,000 feet, Quito is one of the world's highest capitals. My hotel was centrally located and well appointed,*' with, '*I collapsed against the check-in desk of my hotel, sucking air into my lungs as if through a cocktail straw. I would normally have skipped up the short flight of steps from the road, but for the first few days after I arrived in the Ecuadorian capital, Quito, I felt like I had been puffing on 40 Marlboros a day for the past 20 years.*' Continue including your feelings and emotions in what you write, and be passionate.

■ Don't write as if you're compiling a diary. When it comes to travel reportage, the 'Today we started with a tour of the cathedral. It was a very grand building with a lot of stained glass and while we were there we saw an old woman praying at the front,' approach is about as riveting a read as the back of a cereal packet. Remember: details, images, passion.

As a test, re-arrange the following words in any order you like:

The; pencil; face; window; the; stained; sunlight; of; woman; glass; of; praying; on; old; and; ancient; skinned; streamed; a; the; beam; an; through; to; olive; quietly; in; knave.

If you started with '*The old woman skinned the olive with a pencil...*' maybe it's time to consider another career.

Travel writing gives you the opportunity to be creative and let your mind explore avenues of expression without being tied to the realities of, say, news reporting. Make the most of it.

■ The people you meet are a major source of colour. Chat with as many locals and fellow travellers as you can. Use a tape recorder for longer conversations, or make detailed notes as soon as you have finished. Fellow travellers are also an invaluable source of hot leads to the more interesting places to visit.

■ Find an unusual angle if you want to sell the story to an editor or book publisher. An article on the Taj Mahal alone probably won't get their juices going. But one on the journey there by clapped out Hindustani Ambassador (a Morris Oxford lookalike), bringing in the characters and experiences encountered *en route*, just might.

A detailed description of a trip to the top of the Eiffel Tower has been done before. The same experience seen through the eyes of an excited six-year-old you have observed may not have been. Read the travel sections of newspapers and magazines to see how other people do it. You'll soon get a feel for the difference between a good travel writer and a mediocre one.

■ One last piece of advice: talk from the heart. There are enough guidebooks out there to provide all the facts and figures, times and dates. It's up to you to paint pictures and fire the imagination. And you can do it. Book a ticket on the next train to Runcorn or Basingstoke and give it a try. ❧

MARTIN ROBERTS is chairman of the British Guild of Travel Writers.
He is Travel Editor of Woman magazine and a presenter on CNN International's travel show, 'Hotspots', and ITV's 'Wish You Were Here...?'

Taking travel photographs
by Steve Watkins

ON MANY OCCASIONS YOU WILL HEAR disappointed travellers complaining that their photographs just didn't capture the spirit of their trip. They resolve to take a better camera next time or maybe even leave the camera behind. Yet, with a little thought and by following a few guidelines, any camera can take reasonable pictures if their limitations are understood and the traveller develops an eye for interesting images.

Equipment: 'light is right'

Cameras

The performance gap between single lens reflex (SLR) and compact cameras has narrowed considerably in recent years. The benefits of the SLR are more important if you wish to sell your pictures afterwards. These include bigger, more accurate viewfinders for better composition, a wide selection of top-quality, interchangeable lenses and more control over the camera's operation, allowing changes to apertures and shutter speeds to create dynamic images. Most modern SLR cameras also offer an intelligent program, or point-and-shoot, mode that can automatically adjust the settings to suit the subject matter, whether it is landscape, portrait or action. They are not foolproof but can be useful when something sudden happens, such as your travel buddy falling out of a dugout canoe on the Amazon, and you want to snap it. The disadvantages of these cameras are that they are bulkier and heavier than compacts, cost more and require slightly more maintenance.

Today, compact cameras offer excellent zoom lens options, high-quality lenses and the most expensive ones even allow a reasonable amount of operation control. They are light, easy to tuck into a pocket or bumbag and unobtrusive in sensitive shooting situations. In short, unless you want to use your pictures for more than personal memories, compacts offer a very convenient way of getting images that capture the spirit of your trip.

Advanced Photo System (APS) format cameras are available in both compact and SLR specification. These provide very user-friendly features, such as a choice of three print sizes, including panoramic, for each shot rather than a whole roll, automatic film loading and the ability to change rolls mid-film and to reload the partly used one later. The latter feature allows the use of different film speeds with only one camera body. Being a smaller format than 35mm, it means that the cameras can be smaller and lighter. Good news for travellers.

Digital cameras are now a viable choice for travellers. Picture quality has improved significantly and prices have fallen dramatically. Image quality is very important and the more pixels you can afford the better. A reasonable compact digital camera that has the ability to take images of over two million pixels currently goes for around £500 and prices are sure to fall further. One million-plus-pixel cameras currently go for around half that price and can still be used to make reasonable-sized prints, similar to those you would normally get done. The other thing to check is how the images are stored. A removable memory card is the only option for travellers as you can then carry several cards; though bear in mind the extra cost of these, which can add up to a whole wad of money. Remember that the larger you want to print the image, the more space it takes up on the memory card. It is better to have some way of downloading the pictures you want to keep. If you don't, then digital cameras are still only suitable for short trips. The big advantage of digital cameras is that they almost all have preview screens, allowing you to dispose of any poor pictures immediately so as not to waste memory.

For those who choose SLR cameras, a frequent dilemma is whether to buy a totally mechanical, manual focus camera or a computerised, autofocus model. Some of the world's best travel photographers still use manual cameras, but, generally, it would be wiser for the inexperienced photographer to take an autofocus model. They still require a reasonable knowledge of photography, but should ensure that travellers produce a far greater percentage of good shots. Modern autofocus systems can accurately focus on subjects far quicker than even the most experienced shooter with a manual system. Using manual cameras as backup on particularly rough trips seems to be less important these days as computerised ones are proving themselves to be as reliable, if not more so. On my mountain biking and hiking trips, the cameras have rarely given any problems that couldn't be solved by simply using fresh batteries. Before the trip, ensure that your insurance policy covers your equipment properly. Small, single-item figures can often include cameras and lenses as one item. Also, if you sell pictures, then most travel policies deem you to be a professional and will not cover any losses.

Lenses

Unless you fancy carrying around a heavy bag filled with fixed, or prime, lenses, travellers should use zoom lenses (a standard feature on most compacts). My personal favourites are a 24-85mm and a 100-300mm, though a 28-80mm and a 70-210mm would cover most situations. Wide-angle lenses, those below 50mm, give a large area of view and are great for landscapes or in tight situations, such as markets. They suffer less from camera-shake at slow shutter speeds, but can give a distorted effect around the outside and in the centre of the image. A full-face portrait with a 28mm lens would make your subject's nose seem huge. Telephoto lenses, those above 50mm, are good for portrait shots and allow you to shoot from a respectable distance, with those above 100mm particularly useful for clandestine pictures. To shoot wildlife, a minimum of 300mm is needed for safari-type journeys, and most professional wildlife photographers would be using 600mm or above, but these lenses are enormous and heavy on the wallet. Teleconverters are small adaptors that magnify your biggest lens. Available in 1.4 and 2 times magnification, they are a cheap alternative to buying a big lens, but do not match the quality. They reduce the speed of the lens by one and two stops respectively, e.g. an f5.6 lens becomes f11 with a x2 converter. Telephotos can also be used creatively for flattening perspective in landscape shots. Buy the best lenses (generally those with smaller minimum f-stop numbers) you can afford, such as those made by the main manufacturers, Nikon, Minolta, Pentax and Canon, as they, rather than the camera body, make the difference. If you want to carry one lens then choose a 28-80mm, though both Sigma and Tamaron make compact, lightweight 28-200mm lenses that deserve consideration.

Flash guns

Natural light is the most appealing way of lighting a scene, but at times it is either impossible or produces shadow problems, so it's worth having a flash unit. Flash units built into the camera are okay for close work, up to about five metres, but do not light up the Grand Canyon! With an in-camera flash, make sure that it can be turned off, otherwise low-light photography of distant objects becomes impossible. With SLR cameras, it is definitely worth carrying an off-camera, more powerful flash. These can provide fill-in flash to eliminate facial shadows in portraits and are ideal for lighting indoors. Make sure that the flash covers the same area as your wide-angle lens or shots will darken around the edges. And try to buy one that at least allows a degree of manual control and that has a GN rating (an indication of power) greater than 20m. A very useful accessory is a flash diffuser. Bare flash light is harsh and unflattering and should be softened. The Sto Fen Omni Bounce (seen on most news photographers' flashes) is a small, ultra-lightweight plastic cover that fits over the head of off-camera flash guns. It is quick to attach and very light, but it does reduce the power of the light output by two stops. The LumiQuest Pro-Max folds flat for storage and attaches via velcro to the head. It gives very even light and only reduces power by one stop, but it is more fiddly to attach and rather large when opened. Remember that flashes normally only work between shutter speeds of 1/60th and 1/200th second, so ensure your camera's settings are right.

Film

Certainly prints are easier to show your friends when you get back, more forgiving with exposures that aren't quite right and they are relatively cheap. However, they are almost impossible to sell for publication. Using 100 or 200 ISO-rated film, such as the highly rated Fuji Superia or Kodak Gold, should suffice for most conditions and produce sharp images. For telephoto lenses, it may be worth taking some ISO 400 or 'pushing' ISO 200, by manually setting the ISO rating on the camera to 400 and then telling the processing lab when you get it developed. (Keep a note of the film used by numbering them all with labels). Faster film has less contrast and weaker colours than slower film. High street processing is cheap, but it is usually poor quality. Professional labs are more expensive but produce far better prints.

Transparency, or reversal, film produces sharper, more colour-saturated images and is essential for selling to magazines and libraries or giving lectures. Transparencies are not as convenient as prints for showing to friends but, projected onto a screen, they do have more impact. Exposures must be very accurate, particularly in variable light situations. Most professional photographers use slower films, such as Fuji Velvia, ISO 50, or Kodachrome 64, but these can make it hard to hold the camera steady in low light without a tripod. There are some excellent ISO

100 films available that produce very sharp images and rich colours. Fuji Provia 100 and Fuji Sensia 100 are virtually identical (they have the same emulsions but Sensia is released before it has reached its prime, Provia is batch dated and released at optimum quality). Kodak Elite 100s is another good choice. A recent addition to the professional stable of films that is ideal for travel photography is the Fuji MS 100-1000, which can be shot at any speed between the two and still produces remarkable result (well, at least up to 800). I have used it at ISO 400 for assignments and been hard pressed to spot the difference in grain and colour from a 100-speed film. It isn't cheap, though, but negates the need to carry lots of different types of film. Don't worry too much about storage problems with so-called professional films. I have never had a problem in extreme heat or cold with them, nor have I heard of any problems from other photographers. Non-professional films, such as Sensia, are supposed to be more stable, though. All films requiring E6 processing have shorter archival lives (six to ten years) than films using other processes, such as Kodachrome (25 years plus).

Black-and-white film can produce strong travel pictures, but it requires careful processing and printing. This is expensive if you don't have access to or the inclination to use a darkroom yourself. They can be sold to magazines and newspapers, but the market is rather limited. However, they are perfect for exhibitions and it is possible to use faster-speed films as the image quality is much higher than equivalent colour films. Kodak now produces a black-and-white film, simply called Black and White+400, that can be processed in C41 labs, the labs that are all over the high streets. It works very well indeed and makes it easier and cheaper to get the film processed.

Film care

Don't leave film in extremely hot or cold places. In below-freezing temperatures, E6 transparency film becomes brittle and is prone to tearing, so warm it up before use and manually rewind it rather than allowing the motordrive to do it. It is widely believed that x-ray machines at airports damage films. Generally, this is untrue at airports in developed countries, where low-dosage machines are 'film-safe'. However, in other countries, using older machines, you should insist on having your film checked by hand. Keep it handy in a clear plastic bag. x-rays should not be a problem for slower films up to ISO 400, but faster films, especially colour negative ones, should be hand checked at all airports as they are more sensitive. It is better to be safe than to find out after a trip that the film was fogged. Radiation dosages build up, so the more times the film is checked by machine the greater the likelihood of damage. Don't take leftover film on subsequent trips. Always take film in your hand luggage as checked luggage scanners are ten to 20 times more powerful. A soft cool-bag, such as those used for carrying cold drinks, is ideal for storing film while you are travelling around.

Filters

It is not always feasible to wait for great natural light during a journey, though it is preferable. Filters can be used to enhance an image, to mimic a lighting situation

Five tips for better pictures

People portraits:

1. A 70–100mm lens.
2. A big aperture (f4 or f5.6).
3. Focus on the eyes.
4. Fill-flash with high sun.
5. Shoot a dummy shot of rigid poses, then shoot again.

Landscapes:

1. A 24-35mm lens for general scenes or 200-300mm for compressed abstract.
2. A small aperture (f16 upwards).
3. Include people to give sense of scale.
4. Use a tripod for slow exposures.
5. Put horizon on a third rather than in the middle.

Wildlife:

1. A 300–600mm lens.
2. A big aperture for animal portraits (f5.6 or less).
3. Focus on eyes.
4. Use a bean-bag or tripod for low-light shots.
5. Use the highest possible shutter speed (1/350th second and above).

Architecture:

1. With wide angle lenses, don't point the camera up too much, lines converge.
2. With large buildings, shoot details/abstracts.
3. Include people to give sense of scale.
4. Check map for best time of day for sunlight.
5. Use small apertures (f11 or above).

Festivals:

1. Find a high vantage point for sense-of-place shots.
2. Use slow shutter speeds and fill flash to emphasise motion.
3. Use wide-angle lens and get in amongst the action.
4. Shoot around the main action, e.g. crowds, drunken revellers.
5. Take plenty of film and keep shooting.

that would naturally happen or to help the film to record more accurately what the eye can see. Basic filters for travel are the skylight (neutral colour, reduces haze and protects the lens from scratches) and the polariser (minimises haze, saturates colours, turns hazy skies blue and cuts reflections from water or glass). The polariser reduces the light entering the camera by two stops and is most effective when used at 90 degrees to the sun. Autofocus cameras require a circular polariser. Other filters worth considering are an orange warm-up filter (adds warmth to shots taken in brighter light and for flashed portraits) and graduated neutral-density/grey filters. The graduated filters are more important with transparency film as it can only record detail to around +/- two stops. The human eye can see detail in light varying up to 13 stops. The graduated filters help to balance out bright skies and dark foregrounds, without altering the colours. Use fancy colour filters if you wish, but they do little to impress potential markets and, in my view, look terrible. There are no filters available for compact cameras.

Light meters and grey cards

Although in-camera meters have reached a high level of sophistication, they all suffer from reading only reflected light. All meters are based around a standard reflectance of 18 per cent grey, so if you have photographed a snow scene and wondered why it comes out grey, this is the answer. If your main subject is brightly coloured in a dull scene, the camera will underexpose, if it is a darker colour in a bright scene, it will overexpose, as the meter does not take colour into account. To reduce this problem, it is necessary to measure the light falling onto the subject rather than the light being reflected off it. A hand-held light meter is the best method and prices and sizes are falling all the time. The Sekonic L308BII is tiny and reasonably priced. Another option is to buy a grey card, which can be placed near the subject and the in-camera meter used to read off it.

In hurried situations or if you don't have the above, then nature lends a hand. In the northern hemisphere, a reading from the sky, 90 degrees from the sun and roughly 45 degrees up from the land, is equivalent to 18 per cent grey, as is green grass in bright sunshine. Snow in sunshine is one-and-a-half to two stops brighter than the standard setting. The other method is to experiment with taking readings off the back of your hand in different light situations and then adjust the camera settings to match. Caucasian skin is normally one to one-and-a-half stops over 18 per cent grey. Beware of suntans changing this!

Tripods

Many of the most memorable moments on a trip are around sunrise and sunset, when the light is warmer and softer. It is much easier to capture these scenes with a tripod, as it is almost impossible to hand-hold the long exposures needed with slower film. A number of mini-tripods, weighing very little, are available. They can be rested on a rock, fence or table to get the necessary height, but are not suitable for use with big lenses.

Lightweight, full-size tripods are OK, but check that they are solid enough when the telescopic legs are extended. Stability can be increased by taking a nylon bag that you can fill with stones and hang from the centre column. Gitzo makes superb, lightweight tripods, but they are rather expensive. Try to use a shutter release cable when shooting on tripods as the slightest touch on the camera can cause shake, especially with telephoto lenses. On safari, bean-bags offer a versatile method of steadying yourself on car bonnets or windows, but beware of vibration if the engine is left running.

Without a tripod, it is possible to build supports from stones or to place the camera on a high surface and use the self-timer. Monopods can be of some use at fast-moving events, such as festivals, but they don't help in really low light.

Straps

SLR cameras can be quite heavy so a wide, well-padded shoulder strap significantly eases the burden. The best ones, such as those made by Op-Tech, contain neoprene, which acts as a shock absorber. A useful strap for travel and action photography is Op-Tech's stabiliser. Made of neoprene, it straps around your midriff and has a hole cut into it to slide the lens through. It stops the camera swinging around, deters thieves and keeps the camera to hand for quick photography.

Camera bags

Whether using a compact or a comprehensive SLR kit, it is essential to protect it from the elements and shocks encountered on your journey. There are padded bags of every size and description to choose from, so it's a case of trying a few. Good brands include CCS, Lowe, Billingham, Heritage and Tamrac. I have found the half-moon-shaped bumbags, such as the LowePro OrionAW, particularly good. The camera is easily accessible, with the lid opening away from the body, and the closed bag provides a platform for changing lenses. The OrionAW also features a foldaway waterproof cover for extra protection against rain, dust and sand. Karrimor makes good, handlebar-mounted camera bags for bicycles. Canvas bags, such as Billingham and Heritage, are naturally waterproof. For watersports or particularly rough trips, consider storing the gear in a solid, waterproof case, such as the excellent ones made by Pelican. They come in plastic or metal and provide the ultimate protection, but are more cumbersome to work from. Ortlieb makes good waterproof camera bags that are similar to ordinary camera bags and are a great option where you need to stay light and dry. Keep some packets of silica gel in the bag for absorbing moisture.

Cleaning

Only use special lens cloths and blower brushes to remove dust from lenses and inside the camera. Check the lenses frequently and the camera every time you change a film. A tiny piece of dust in the film gate can scratch a whole film. Never touch the sensitive shutter curtains or the mirror with your hands.

Useful accessories

A roll of duct tape is useful for all sorts of things, from sealing camera openings against fine dust to fixing broken tripod legs. A must for all camera bags. Small torches are perfect for checking camera settings in the dark and can even provide the necessary illumination for focusing in poor light. A Swiss Army knife, especially those that feature the jeweller screwdriver for tiny screws, will always be used at some stage. Cotton buds are perfect for cleaning the nooks and crannies of the camera body. A small, reporter's notebook is great for recording details of pictures or grabbing addresses of people you meet. Take plenty of spare batteries for cameras, light meters and torches. AA-size batteries are available in most countries, but you will not find special lithium batteries in many places. No matter how well you know your camera, take the manual. A compass can help you get to the right place for sunrise and sunset. Lastly, take a good supply of zip-loc plastic bags or lightweight dry bags (from kayak stores), for protecting cameras and film in wet conditions.

Techniques: 'little change, big difference'

Composition

Using some simple guidelines (not rules, because intuition and creativity are more powerful than rules ever can be) when composing images in the viewfinder can have a dramatic effect on how interesting the resulting picture is to the eye. Divide the frame into thirds both horizontally and vertically. Rather than placing the main subject in the middle of the frame, position it on one of the third intersections. Use visual lines, such as roads, rivers, fences or beaches, to draw the viewer's eye into the image by running them diagonally into the frame. Think of the image as having three levels, fore, middle and background. Try to have something interesting in each area, as it helps to create depth and gives perspective. Another dynamic shape to include is the triangle. It may consist of three points, two hands and a head or two nomads and a horse, for instance, or a triangular block of colour or light.

Angle of view

An instant way to capture a viewer's attention is to shoot from strange angles. Stand on a wall, shoot down from a hotel balcony, crouch, lie on your back or even tilt the camera 45 degrees. Whatever works with the subject. This approach can be particularly effective for capturing the dynamic nature of festivals.

Sense of place

National Geographic photographers are superb at adding a sense of place to their pictures. Rarely, if ever, will you find a full-face portrait or abstract image in their pages. Subjects are shot in their surroundings, either by using telephoto lenses to compress people into a landscape or, more often, through the creative use of wide angle lenses to include the person and the background. Not every shot needs to use this principle, but it does help people to build a better mental picture of your trip. Think like a movie director. Open with an establishing shot, a wide view of the general location, and work your way into more detailed pictures.

The moment

The difference between a good picture and a great picture is that fleeting moment when everything comes together to create a magical image. It can be a smile, a twist of the head, a momentary splash of sunlight breaking through the clouds, the festival drummers beating in unison. It is what many photographers spend their whole life chasing, so don't expect to capture it in every image. The odds of success can be shortened by observation, anticipation and relaxation. Great shots rarely happen when you are rushing to catch a bus. For me, one of the great benefits of travel photography is that it makes me slow down and observe. By acquainting yourself with the ebb and flow of a market scene, for example, you can begin to predict the most interesting moments for your pictures. The magical moment may never come, or you may press the button just as it disappears, but at least you will leave with a better feel for the lives of the people you encounter.

Exposure

With colour print film, exposures are not so critical as the film is able to record detail across a large variation of light in a scene. Transparency films are not so forgiving, requiring very accurate exposures to within half a stop. If you rely on the camera's in-built light meter, it is important, with both SLR and compact cameras, to know how that meter measures the light. Many cameras take a 'centre-weighted' reading, meaning that it reads the light from most parts of the viewfinder area, but it gives extra importance to the section in the middle. Compacts offer few ways of controlling this, but a good tip is to exclude any excessively bright or dark areas from the viewfinder when you partially depress the button and then recompose the picture to how you want it. Be careful to make sure that it focuses on something at the same distance as the subject.

Modern SLR cameras have sophisticated metering systems that are hard to fool, including matrix metering (light is read individually from up to 14 honeycomb segments and account is taken of which segment contains the subject), centre-weighted and spot metering (reading is taken only from a tiny circle in the centre of the viewfinder). Thoroughly learn how the camera's light meter works and think briefly before shooting. If a scene is fairly evenly lit then most meters should produce reasonable results. If there are excessive areas of light and shadow, stop and meter from your subject. An easy guideline is to always expose for your most important highlight.

Speeds

Shutter speed is the most important setting to get right for reasonable pictures. To freeze action, use faster shutter speeds – 1/250th or 1/500th should cover most travel situations. Faster speeds are needed for subjects moving across the lens than those moving towards it. For people shots, 1/125th should eliminate any slight movements. In low light it is necessary to set a speed that can be hand held without causing blur. A simple rule for any lens is that the slowest safe speed for hand-held shots is 1/focal length of the lens, for instance, a 28mm lens needs 1/30th second, a 100mm lens needs 1/125th or a 200mm needs 1/200th second. At slower speeds, pull your arms in tight to your body, press the camera against your forehead and exhale before pressing the button.

Apertures

The aperture (size of the hole in the lens) determines how much of the image is in focus (depth of field). Big holes (rather confusingly the lower aperture numbers on the camera, e.g. f4 or f5.6) give little depth of field. They are useful for portraits as they throw the background out of focus or to concentrate the viewer's eye on your subject. Small holes, f11 and upwards, make most things in the shot appear sharp, which is great for landscapes. If your camera has a depth of field button, press it to view the effects of any given aperture.

Approach: 'mental shots'

Photographs – who needs them?

The first question to ask yourself before a trip is how important photographs are to you. Good images require some effort, which can alter the nature of your trip. If travelling alone, this may not be such a big deal, but it can cause friction when you are with a non-photographic companion. Few people share a photographer's enthusiasm for standing around waiting for the sun to hit the right spot in your epic landscape image.

It is a question of compromise. Unless you are going to try to sell the images afterwards to pay for the trip, then it is best to just strike when you can and concentrate on enjoying the journey. If your main aim is photography, then it may be wise to travel alone and join up with other travellers when you want to socialise, or pick a partner with a similar or complementary interest, such as drawing or painting. You can then split up during the day and meet up again later with your pictures taken.

Planning

The best planners get the most luck. Research your destination – go to the bookshops, scan newspaper travel sections, surf the internet. Remember though, if you plan your trip down to the last detail, it will blinker you from the impromptu opportunities that always crop up on a journey. Plan, but stay open-minded. Most trips do not allow for extended stays in one place so a shortcut to improved local knowledge is to check out postcards or magazines of the area. Don't just copy them, though. Try to find a different vantage point. Buy a local map, take a compass and plan your shots around the best times of day for the sunlight.

Shots in your head

Some of the most memorable travel pictures were conceived long before the photographer's plane touched down in the location. A useful way to pass the flight time is to think visually about where you are going. What are the important aspects that can sum up a place? Is it the beach, palm trees and a local fisherman casting a net or an ice-encrusted climber camping on a tiny snow ledge with a background view of distant mountains? Get some picture ideas in your mind and then try to find them when you are there. Even if you don't get exactly that shot, the previsualisation will help to you to recognise strong images when they appear.

Patience

If photos are important then be prepared to spend the time trying to get them. The longer you are out on the streets or hiking in the country, the better chance you have of seeing something special. Few great travel photographs were taken sitting in a hotel room. Find an interesting scene and hang around, watching and waiting for someone to walk by or something to happen to make it into a good image. Using a modest degree of common sense, talk to as many people as you can. Many picture opportunities can arise from a chance conversation and may even get you a free meal with a family or see you whisked off to some local vantage point that isn't in the guidebook.

Head first

Imagine your overland group having to wade through a raging brown river in deep jungle. A good photograph would bring the memories flooding back when you return home. The secret to really showing how deep and dangerous the river was would be to capture your companions' fearful faces as they resist being swept away. It's no use being the last person to cross if you want to get the picture. If there is an adventure to be photographed, be the first to do it. You then know where the best grimaces are likely to take place!

Up early, out late

Travel photography is not for late risers or early drinkers. Some of the best light is from one hour before to two hours after sunrise, and from a couple of hours before sunset onwards. It certainly isn't easy to crawl out of a warm bed on the off-chance that you may get a great shot of the rising sun glinting through the icicles hanging from the roof of your mountain hut, but it has to be done if you want that special image. Likewise, after a long day of walking around markets, museums and galleries, it is very tempting to slope off for an early beer instead of walking up that hill to shoot the last rays clipping the town's impressive church tower. If you want the image, you have to be there... period.

Focus on the bad times

When things get tough, it is difficult to keep taking pictures, yet these events often form the defining moments of a trip. If you can have the presence of mind to get off a few quick shots when your partner is fighting blizzards on a mountain, slumped in despair after losing their passport or suffering from a vehement dose of Delhi belly, then you will treasure the shots for years to come.

Guidance control

In many destinations, local guides are either unavoidable or useful enough to employ for your visit. However, remember that they are probably stuck in a rut of where to go, what to see and even the pace at which you should see things. All of these factors can limit the photographic opportunities in a place that you may never visit again. Take control. You are employing them and customers' wishes should always come first.

If you want to go off their normal route to check out something that catches your eye, do so, but be as pleasant about it as you can. If you seriously delay them, then consider paying them more for their time, as you are reducing their chances of picking up other clients, but don't be hurried by their well-honed ability to look impatient.

Respect

To really have a chance of capturing the spirit of a place on film, you have to be accepted by the local people. Show respect for their customs, private space and intelligence and you've already gone a long way towards getting good pictures. If you fail to realise that they have different values and refuse their offers of hospitality, then do not be surprised if your images have a distant feel, too. Spend time with the people, take a genuine interest in their lives and, again using a modest amount of common sense, go with the flow when they want to take you to particular places. It is almost always worth it. Remember, though, that there is a fine dividing line between respect and reticence. Don't automatically assume that people don't want their picture taken. Not all places are receptive to outsiders. A good test is to learn how to say "hello" in their language and use it. Their reaction should tell you if they want you around. Another good icebreaker is to have a portable party trick. Juggling, playing an instrument, a magic trick or simply being able to pull silly faces can all help to put local people at ease.

Camera in, camera out

Whether to approach people with your camera out or hidden away is a personal dilemma. My favoured method is to have the camera showing at all times. By doing this, people know exactly who I am and that it is likely that I would like a photograph of them. Building a level of trust is essential and I think that suddenly pulling out a camera after a seemingly innocent conversation is too much of a shock, often resulting in the person refusing to pose for a picture. This is particularly relevant to brief meetings. If you have plenty of time, it can be worth getting to know the person well first and then introducing the camera. Try both approaches to see which works best for you.

To ask or not to ask

Photographing people from a distance, possibly without their knowledge, adds a documentary feel to an image, something that many publications desire. Recreating that feel after asking permission to take the picture can, at best, be difficult. Few people have the ability to pose naturally when faced with a camera. If I do take a clandestine picture and the person gets upset, then I go over to them, shake their hand and have a joke about it. Don't sneak off with your tail between your legs. If you do ask and are confronted with a poker-faced, hands-by-the-side pose, then shoot one frame, then, when they relax, shoot another couple. There are no hard rules, though. It is a case of trusting your own judgment, something that only improves with experience of success and failure.

To pay or not to pay

With increasing frequency, travellers are facing demands for payment for photographs. These can range from half-hearted appeals to your good nature to quite intimidating threats. For guidance, I normally refuse to pay for pictures. If the demand is made before I take the shot then, unless the image is so outstanding that I have to get it and there isn't a crowd, I put the camera away and walk off. This is most important with children, for it can only be damaging to their future to make them dependent on begging. If I ask the person to do something for the picture, then it is reasonable to expect to pay them something for their time. With market sellers, a good way of avoiding the link between photography and payment is to buy something from their stall, which, in developing countries, is often sold at an inflated price to visitors. Both parties get what they want and retain their dignity.

Fun or photos

Most, if not all, people are travellers first and photographers second. There is little point in going on a journey and not enjoying it because of the pressure of trying to capture the place on film. The importance of the experience will always win over the importance of a photograph. 🙠

STEVE WATKINS is a photojournalist specialising in adventure travel, and the Editor of the new 'Action Guide Europe'.

Selling travel photographs
by John Douglas

A TWO-MAN CANOE EXPEDITION UP THE AMAZON... a one-man trek through Afghanistan... a full-scale assault on Everest involving a party of 60... a once-in-a-lifetime overland trip through Africa.

> QUESTION: *What might these travellers have in common?*
> ANSWER: *They will all probably be short of money and they'll all be taking at least one camera.*

The object of this section is to draw attention to the fact that these two features are not unrelated. Too few expeditions or independent travellers – whether they be on the grand scale or simply a student venture – are aware that the camera can make a substantial contribution to much-needed funds. When it is pointed out that a single picture may realise hundreds of pounds, the hard-pressed traveller begins to see that he or she may be neglecting a very substantial source of revenue. While it is true that income from photography may not be received until some considerable time after arriving home, it can be used to pay off debts – or perhaps to finance the next excursion.

If photography is to pay, then advance planning is essential. Too often planning is no more than quick decisions regarding types of camera and the amount of film to be taken. Of course, these are essential questions and something might first be said about their relevance to potential markets. Unless sponsorship and technical assistance are received, a video camera is not worth taking as a possible money-spinner. The production of a worthwhile expedition film or travelogue is such an expensive, specialised and time-consuming matter that it is best forgotten. In order to satisfy television and other markets, a film must approach near-professional standards, with all that implies in editing, cutting, dubbing, titling and so on, to say nothing of filming techniques By all means take along a good camcorder, but don't think of it as a source of income.

Format and colour

With still photography, the position is quite different. It is worthwhile investing in a good range of equipment (or having it on loan). It will probably be advisable to take perhaps as many as three cameras: two 35mm SLRs and a large-format camera with an interchangeable back. If the latter is not available, then contrary to advice sometimes given, 35mm format is quite satisfactory for most markets (except some calendar, postcard and advertising outlets).

Digital photography has its attractions especially if an expedition is sending regular reports back home. However, there has, of course, to be access to a computer and, for any revenue-gaining use, the camera has to be able to produce images of a high and saleable resolution.

Most travellers hoping to sell their work will use colour reversal film though some might find a wider market if they can offer black-and-white images as well. A majority of markets for photography now pay the same fees for mono as for colour. The advantage of monochrome is the ability to 'improve' the image during processing. Colour prints are not welcomed by publishers.

It is advisable to keep to one type of film with which you are familiar. Different colour films may reproduce with contrasting colour quality and spoil the effect of an article illustrated with a sequence of colour pictures.

Outlets

Before leaving, the travel photographer should contact possible outlets for his work. Magazines generally pay quite well for illustrations, especially if accompanied by an article. You can approach UK markets such as *Traveller* magazine or the colour supplements of the Saturday and Sunday newspapers. Although they may not be able to give a firm "yes", their advice can be helpful. Specialist journals, assuming they are illustrated, may be approached if the trip is relevant, but it should be remembered that the smaller circulation of such journals yields a lower rate of payment. It can be worth advertising the journey in the hope of obtaining lucrative photographic commissions.

Overseas magazines, such as *National Geographic*, often pay exceptionally high rates, but the market is tight. Much nearer home, local and national newspapers may take some pictures while the traveller is still abroad. If the picture editor is approached, he may accept some digital images if they can be channelled through a UK agent or a friend at home. In the case of an expedition that is regionally based, local papers will usually be quite enthusiastic, but it is important to agree a reasonable fee beforehand, otherwise the payment may not cover the costs involved.

Local papers may also agree to take an illustrated story on the return home, but again it is important to ensure that adequate payment will be made for the pictures published. Don't expect a fortune from the local or regional press.

It is not the purpose of this article to discuss techniques of photography, but before he or she leaves home, the photographer working with an expedition is well advised to seek guidance from others who have worked in the area. There can be problems with climate, customs and the like, of which it is as well to be aware before starting out.

Finally, one potentially contentious point must be settled before the first picture is taken. This is the matter of copyright ownership and the income received from the sale of photographs. In law, copyright is vested in the photographer, unless the work has been commissioned.

Universal appeal

Once the trip has started, the travel photographer should look for two sorts of photograph. Firstly, of course, there will be those which illustrate their travels and the changing scene, both human and physical. But secondly, and so easily neglected, are those pictures that have a universal appeal, irrespective of their location. Such shots as sunsets, children at play, brilliant displays of flowers and so on always have a market. It is important, too, not to miss opportunities that are offered *en route* to the main location in which the travel photographer is to operate. Don't pack away your film while travelling to your destination. Have the camera ready on the journey.

Not unnaturally, the question "What sells?" will be asked. There is no simple answer, except to say that at some time or other almost any technically good photograph may have a market. (It is, however, assumed that the photographer is able to produce high-quality pictures: there is never a market for the out-of-focus, under-exposed disaster.) Such statements as: "The photograph that sells best is the one that no one else has," may not seem very helpful, yet this is the truth. It is no use building a collection that simply adds to an already saturated market. For example, a traveller passing through Agra will certainly visit the Taj Mahal – and photograph that splendid building. Yet the chances of selling such a photograph on the open market are dismal. It's all been done before, from every angle in every light and mood. Perhaps a picture of the monument illuminated by a thunderstorm might be unusual enough to find a buyer, but the best that can reasonably be hoped for is that the photographer will hit on a new angle or perhaps a human interest picture with the Taj as background. On the other hand, a picture of village craftsmen at work might sell well, as will anything around which a story can be woven. Landscapes have a limited market but, given exceptional conditions of light, then a good scenic picture might reap high rewards in the calendar or advertising markets. The golden rule is to know the markets well enough to foresee needs. Sometimes the least obvious subjects are suddenly in demand.

Severe and unusual weather conditions sell well: a sudden rainstorm in an arid region, storms at sea or droughts. It's a fact of life that pictures of disasters have a good market. In the knowledge that subjects seen from an unusual viewpoint attract picture desks and art editors, consider aerial photography. This may seem to be prohibitively expensive, but the more remote the area the more likely it is that light aircraft will be a regular form of transport. Hitch a lift or pay a bush pilot for a short flight. If the availability can be foreseen, get some advice on technique before you leave.

Record keeping and processing

One most important but easily overlooked point is the matter of record keeping. In the conditions experienced by many travellers, this will not be easy – yet it cannot be emphasised too strongly that meticulous care must be taken to ensure that every picture is fully documented. It is true that certain photographs may be identified at a later date (macro-photography of plants, for example) but no shot should be taken without some recording of at least its subject and location. It is usually best to number the films in advance and to have an identification tag on the camera that will indicate the film being exposed. A notebook can also be prepared before the traveller leaves.

With the advertising market in mind, it maybe helpful to make sure that good photographs are taken that include the traveller's equipment. Less obviously, there is a market for photographs of proprietary brands of food, magazines, newspapers, items of clothing and equipment and so on in exotic and unusual settings.

If the traveller is to be away for a long time, it can be important to get some of the exposed film back home. There are dangers in this procedure because of the uncertainty of postal services, but provided some care is taken – perhaps with arrangements made through embassies – then there are advantages. Apart from the obvious problem of keeping exposed film in sub-optimum conditions, some preparatory work can be carried out by the traveller's agent. Of course, if the film is sent home, it is essential that labelling and recording are foolproof.

Serious selling

Once the travel photographer has returned home, the serious business of selling begins. Topicality is a selling point, so there is no excuse for taking even a few days off, no matter how exhausted you may feel. Processing the film is clearly the first task, followed by cataloguing. No one is going to buy if the goods are badly presented, so it is worth making sure that a portfolio of high-quality mono enlargements and colour transparencies is prepared with a really professional appearance. Put together a stock-list of all your photos (what countries and subjects, colour and black and white, and how many you have in each area) and circulate it around all the magazines and papers you can think of. As long as it is kept up to date, you should be able to sell one-offs for some way into the future.

The first market to tackle might well be the local newspapers. Following up the advances made before you set out is very important, no matter how lukewarm the original response. It often looks more professional if there are both a writer and a photographer to produce a magazine article, but it should be made clear to editors that a separate fee is expected for text and illustrations. This is invariably better than a lump sum or space-payment.

A direct source of income from photography can be slide shows for which the audience is charged. These are relatively easy to organise but must be prepared with slides of maps and accompanying tape or live commentary. Incidentally, try to avoid a mix of vertical and horizontal frames. It gives an untidy appearance to the show – even when the screen actually accommodates the verticals. The bigger the screen the better. If these shows are to have a wide audience, it may be necessary to put the organisation in the hands of an agent.

A photographic exhibition can provide helpful publicity, but it will probably raise little or no income itself. Branch librarians are usually helpful in accommodating exhibitions and, if these showings precede some other event like a lecture or slide show, they can be indirect money-spinners. For an exhibition, great care should be taken in making the display as professional as possible. Again, the bigger the enlargements, the better. As far as photography is concerned, 'big is beautiful', and it is worth investing in a few really giant enlargements.

If the traveller has not been too far off the beaten track, then travel firms may take photographs with which to illustrate brochures and posters. However, as with the calendar and postcard market, it must be pointed out that this is a specialist field, requiring not only particular sorts of photographs but images of a very high technical quality. This also applies to photographs used for advertising, although suggestions made earlier regarding pictures of proprietary brands leaves this door slightly wider open than usual.

Whenever an original transparency or negative is sent to or left with a publisher or agent, a signature must be obtained for it, a value placed on it should it be lost or damaged (probably £500 per original) and a record kept of its location.

Using an agency

Lastly, when the catalogue is complete, the travel photographer will wish to put the whole of his saleable photograph collection on the market. Now a decision must be reached on the thorny issue of whether or not to use an agency or picture library. Of course, direct sales would mean an almost 100 per cent profit, while the library sales will probably net only 50 per cent of the reproduction rights fee. But, as so often happens, it is the enlargement of the market, the professional expertise and marketing facilities of the library that are attractive. It is worth making enquiries of a number of photo libraries (see the *Writers' and Artists' Year Book*) and finding a company that offers the sort of terms and assistance that satisfy the travel photographer's requirements. It may be preferable to deal with a company that does not expect to hold the collection but simply calls for pictures when needed. This allows much greater freedom to the copyright owner, as well as being a check on what is happening in the market. Some libraries offer additional services to associate photographers in the way of help with the placing of literary as well as photographic material, and in the organisation of lecture services.

It may even be better to contact a picture library before leaving. For a small consultancy fee, a good agency may be able to advise on the sort of pictures that sell well and on the level of reproduction fees that should be charged. There is nothing more annoying than selling rights for £50 and then finding that the market would have stood £100. Many amateurs sell their pictures for too low a fee and others assume that there is a set price, irrespective of the use to which the photographic material is put. In fact, the market for photographic reproduction is something of a jungle and it may be better to gain professional advice rather than get lost. The same applies to locating markets. It is almost impossible for the inexperienced amateur to identify likely markets for his work. There are thousands of possible outlets and a small fortune could be lost in trying to locate a buyer for a particular picture, no matter how high the quality.

An ambitious and skilled travel photographer should expect to make a significant profit from his photography, providing an effort is made along the lines indicated. In the case of a specialised and well-publicised trip, it is not unknown for the whole of the cost of mounting the venture to be recouped from the sale of pictures. There are some simple points to remember: don't treat the camera as a toy, don't give the job of photographer to a non-specialist, don't put all those transparencies and negatives in the back of a drawer when you get home. As a money-spinner, the camera may be the most important piece of equipment the traveller carries. ❧

JOHN DOUGLAS *is a Director of Geoslides Photo Library and the author of* 'Creative Techniques in Travel Photography'. *He has travelled solo on expeditions through Asia, Africa and the Arctic.*

Underwater photography
by Dave Saunders and Rick Price

ANYONE WHO HAS PUT ON A MASK AND SNORKEL and floated over a coral garden or sunken boat will have had a glimpse of the fascinating world beneath the surface of the ocean. But we are not built to exist for long underwater and nor are most cameras. It is an alien environment with new rules for the photographer.

The nice thing about underwater photography is that you can approach it at any level. It is possible to take satisfactory pictures with an ordinary land camera through the 'window' of a glass-bottomed boat, or even in rock pools using a polarising filter, bucket or watertight box with a glass base. If the sun is shining on the subject, the pictures will be bright and clear.

But be careful when you are near water, especially salt water. Ordinary land cameras are like cats – they just don't want to get involved with water, and one drop of salt water in the wrong place could ruin your camera. So if you want to take a camera underwater, you will need either a purpose-built underwater camera or a watertight housing.

Kodak and Fuji now make a disposable waterproof 35mm camera with a built-in flash which can be used to a depth of two metres for very simple photographs.

Canon produce the 35mm compact automatic Sureshot A1 with built-in flash which is waterproof to five metres, and Minolta make a fully automatic Vectis Weathermatic APS compact camera with built-in flash which is rated to ten metres depth. For deeper diving, Sea & Sea produce three models of 35mm underwater camera. The simplest is the MX5, a 'point and shoot' fully automatic camera rated to 36 metres. The MX10 is a basic 35mm automatic camera with built-in flash, but other lenses, which can be changed underwater, and a detachable flash are also available. The Motormarine 11 EX is a more sophisticated camera with TTL metering and a choice of dedicated flash accessories as well as a built-in flash. This too is a modular system, and lenses can be carried and changed underwater. Both these cameras are rated to 45 metres. Bonica also manufacture the Snapper, rated to 40 metres and another modular system that you can upgrade as your interest grows.

The great advantage of the modular system is that you can change from wide-angle to close-up lenses and vice versa underwater very quickly. Inevitably, when you have set up your camera at the surface with a particular subject in mind, something else will turn up on the dive which you cannot photograph with the lens on the camera. With camera systems that allow lenses to be changed underwater this is no longer a problem.

The Nikonos is probably the underwater camera most used by scuba divers. No larger than an ordinary 35mm camera, it is easy to operate and can give excellent results. Based on the French Calypso design, it is continually being improved. The Nikonos v has a fully automatic exposure system and a range of TTL automatic flash guns. There is no rangefinder for focusing, so you have to estimate focusing distances. As it is a non-reflex camera, with a direct vision viewfinder, you may have problems with parallax when close to your subject, but there is a compensation within the viewfinder to overcome this. An external sportsfinder frame can be fixed to the top of the camera to make viewing easier. The Nikonos v offers a choice of auto or manual exposure. An LCD display in the viewfinder tells you the shutter speed, warns of wrong exposure and provides a 'flash ready' signal.

The standard lens is the W-Nikkor 35mm, f2.5, and 15mm, 20mm, 28mm and 80mm lenses are also available. Special close-up lenses or extension tubes allow detailed shots of coral and tame fish.

Underwater housings

Rather than investing in a whole new camera system, an alternative approach is to use an underwater housing around your land camera. In shallow water of less than ten metres, flexible plastic housings provide a relatively cheap method of protecting your camera. Controls are operated through a rubber glove set into the case.

In deeper water the flexible design is unsuitable, as the housing collapses under increasing pressure. Ikelite housings can be made for most cameras. These are rigid and some models can safely be taken to a depth of 100 metres. They have controls which link into the focusing and aperture rings, as well as shutter release and film advance mechanisms.

Rubber 'o' ring seals produce a watertight chamber which keeps the camera dry. To avoid flooding, the rings must be cleaned and lightly greased with silicone each time a film is changed. A range of aluminium alloy housings is also readily available; the housings are strong and durable, but heavy and bulky. Plexiglass housings are lighter and cheaper, and are available for a wide range of cameras.

Most serious photographers will already have a camera and range of lenses, so a cheaper option may be to buy a ready-made housing which will tend to be more versatile. Most camera features such as autofocus and motordrive can be used underwater. A comprehensive range of housings is available off the shelf from many manufacturers, who can also produce individual housings for unusual cameras without any difficulty. Housings and lights are also readily available for many types and makes of video cameras, including the new generation of compact digital video cameras.

How light behaves

Light is refracted (or bent) more in water than in air. Underwater objects appear larger and nearer than they really are. Your eye perceives the same distortion as the lens, so with a reflex camera you simply focus through the lens and the subsequent picture will then be in focus. The subject may be 1.5 metres away, but will appear closer to the eye and to the lens. However, if you then look at the focusing ring, it will be set at about one metre.

Because of the way light refracts through water, the effective focal length of the lens is increased, making it more telephoto when a flat underwater porthole is used. So a 35mm lens underwater is approximately equivalent in effect to a 45mm lens on land. Likewise a 15mm lens is equivalent to a 20mm.

A dome-shaped porthole, on the other hand, enables light from all directions to pass through it at right angles. This eliminates the problem of refraction and the angle of view of the fitted lens is unchanged.

Lenses

Wide-angle lenses are generally more useful underwater. Visibility is seldom as good as above water, especially if there are numerous suspended particles. For a clear image it is important to move in close so as to reduce the amount of water between the camera and the subject. To include the whole of a diver in the frame when using a 35mm lens on a Nikonos, you need to be about two metres away. A wider lens, say 15mm, means you can move in much closer to the subject and thus minimise the amount of obstructing material between the camera and the subject.

Generally camera-to-subject distance should not exceed a quarter of the visibility. If the visibility is only 1.5 metres (as it often is in temperate seas or inland lakes), you should restrict yourself to subjects up to 0.3 metres from the lens.

Flash

With high-speed emulsions such as Ektachrome 400 (transparencies) and Kodacolor 400 (prints) it is often possible to get away without using flash, especially near the surface where it is brighter. When the sun is shining through the surface layers of water, you can obtain good results down to about two metres without flash. However, the deeper you go below the surface layers of water, the more the light is filtered out by the water. At ten metres below the surface, the red has been filtered out of the ambient light, and flash is needed to restore the absorbed colour.

In tropical waters, the guide number of the flash gun (which indicates its power) is usually reduced to about a third of the 'in air' number. It is much safer to bracket your exposures, as the expense of film is nothing compared to the trouble and expense of getting into the water.

Underwater flash guns are either custom-made or normal land units in a plastic housing. Custom-made guns generally have a good wide-angle performance, whereas units in housings generally have a narrow angle.

Instead of using a flash gun mounted close to the camera, place it at arm's length or even further away to give a better modelling light to the subject. Having two flash guns is even better, and will give much greater control over lighting. With the flash gun further from the camera, fewer particles between the camera and the subject will be illuminated. If the flash gun is near the camera, the particles will be illuminated and detract from the subject.

Aiming the flash can be tricky. Although your eye and the camera lens 'see' the subject as, say, two metres away, it is actually further. As the flash must strike the subject directly in order to light it, the unit must be aimed behind the apparent position of the subject. Some flash guns now have modelling lights so that you can see exactly where the flash is aiming.

Diving Problems

Test your equipment in a swimming pool before you take it into the sea. Plan the shots in advance. It is always better to have a good idea of what you want before you go into the water, so that you have the right lens on the camera to do the job.

Keeping yourself stable while trying to take a picture can be a problem. Underwater you should be slightly negatively buoyant, so that you can lie or kneel on the sea bed or hang suspended in the water without moving up and down. By breathing in you should make yourself rise slowly, and by breathing out you should sink. Wearing a stabiliser jacket will allow you to increase or decrease your buoyancy by letting air into or out of the jacket.

Sometimes you may need to grab a handy piece of coral to steady yourself. A wetsuit or thin Lycra one-piece suit will help protect you against stings and scratches. As you will be moving around slowly when taking pictures, you will feel the cold earlier than if you were swimming energetically, and you will appreciate the warmth the wetsuit gives you.

Near the sandy sea bed it is easy to churn up the water and disturb the sand, making the water cloudy. The secret is to keep as still as possible and use your fins gently. Restricting rapid movements also avoids scaring the more timid fish away. Taking a plastic bag of bread down with you usually guarantees plenty of potential subjects.

Good Subjects

Even with very simple equipment it is possible to record interesting effects simply by looking at what is naturally around you underwater. Rays of light burst through the water in a spectacular way, and are especially photogenic when they surround a silhouette. And you can get impressive effects by catching reflections on the surface when you look up at the sky through the water. Macro photography with an automatic camera and a frame placed over the subject is a good place to start, as it takes at least some variables out of the equation and makes success more likely.

The best pictures are usually simple and clear. Select a subject, such as an attractive piece of coral, then position yourself to show it off to best advantage without too many distractions in the picture.

Do not be deterred by a high initial failure rate: with a little thought and planning, achieving good results underwater is quite straightforward.

The following companies will be only too willing to talk to you or send you brochures, and their websites contain a wealth of information for both the beginner and the more advanced photographer:

Cameras Underwater: 01404 812277   Sea & Sea: 01803 663012
Ocean Optics: 020 7930 8408   Videoquip: 0116 2558818 🖉

RICK PRICE *is a wildlife and underwater cameraman.*
DAVE SAUNDERS *is a freelance journalist specialising in photographic issues.*

Culture shock

Culture shock
by Adrian Furnham

NEARLY EVERY TRAVELLER MUST HAVE EXPERIENCED culture shock at some time or other. Like jet lag, it is an aspect of travel that is both negative and difficult to define. But what precisely is it? When and why does it occur? And, more importantly, how can we prevent it – or at least cope with it?

Although the experience of culture shock has no doubt been around for centuries, it was only 25 years ago that an anthropologist called Oberg coined the term. Others have attempted to improve upon and extend the concept and have come up with alternative jargon, such as 'culture fatigue', 'role shock' and 'pervasive ambiguity'.

Strain

From the writings of travellers and interviews with tourists, foreign students, migrants and refugees, psychologists have attempted to specify the exact nature of this unpleasant experience. It seems that the syndrome has six facets. Firstly, there is strain caused by the effort of making necessary psychological adaptations – speaking another language, coping with the currency, driving on the other side of the road, etc. Secondly, there is often a sense of loss and a feeling of deprivation with regard to friends, possessions and status. If you are in a place where nobody knows, loves, respects and confides in you, you may feel anonymous and deprived of your status and role in society, as well as bereft of familiar and useful objects. Thirdly, there is often a feeling of rejection – your rejection of the natives and their rejection of you. Travellers stand out by virtue of their skin, clothes and language. Depending on the experience of the natives, they may be seen as unwanted intruders, an easy rip-off or friends.

A fourth symptom of culture shock is confusion. Travellers can become unsure about their roles, their values, their feelings and sometimes about who they are. When a people lives by a different moral and social code from your own, interaction for even a comparatively short period can be very confusing. Once one becomes more aware of cultural differences, typical reactions of surprise, anxiety, even disgust and indignation occur. The way foreigners treat their animals, eat food, worship their god or perform their *toilettes* often cause amazement and horror to naive travellers. Finally, culture shock often involves feelings of impotence, due to an inability to cope with the new environment.

Little England

Observers of sojourners and long-term travellers have noted that there are usually two extreme reactions to culture shock: those who act as if they 'never left home' and those who immediately 'go native'. The former chauvinists create 'little Englands' in foreign fields, refusing to compromise their diet or dress and, like the proverbial mad dogs, insisting on going out in the midday sun. The latter reject all aspects of their own culture and enthusiastically do in Rome as the Romans do.

Most travellers, however, experience less dramatic but equally uncomfortable reactions to culture shock. These may include excessive concern over drinking water, food, dishes and bedding; fits of anger over delays and other minor frustrations; excessive fear of being cheated, robbed or injured; great concern over minor pains and interruptions; and a longing to be back at the idealised home, "where you can get a good cup of tea and talk to sensible people."

But, as any seasoned traveller will know, often one begins to get used to, and even learns to like, the new culture. In fact writers have suggested that people go through a number of phases when living in a new culture. Oberg, in his original writings, listed five stages. First, the 'honeymoon', which is characterised by enchantment, fascination, enthusiasm and admiration for the new culture, as well as the formation of

I dislike feeling at home when I am abroad.

— GEORGE BERNARD SHAW

cordial (but superficial) relationships. In this stage, people are generally intrigued and euphoric. Many tourists never stay long enough to move out of the honeymoon period. The second phase heralds crisis and disintegration. It is now that the traveller feels loss, isolation, loneliness and inadequacy, and tends to become depressed and withdrawn. This happens most often after two to six months of living in the new culture.

The third phase is the most problematic and involves reintegration. At this point people tend to reject the host culture, becoming opinionated and negative, partly as a means of showing their self-assertion and growing self-esteem. The fourth stage of 'autonomy' finds the traveller assured, relaxed, warm and empathic because he or she is socially and linguistically capable of negotiating most new and different social situations in the culture.

And finally the 'independent' phase is achieved, characterised by trust, humour and the acceptance and enjoyment of social, psychological and cultural differences.

U-curve

For obvious reasons, this independent phase is called the 'u-curve' hypothesis. If you plot satisfaction and adaptation (x axis) over time (y axis), you see a high point at the beginning, followed by a steep decline, a period at the bottom, but then a steady climb back up. More interestingly, some researchers have shown evidence not of a u-curve but a w-curve, i.e. once travellers return to their home country, they often undergo a similar re-acculturation, again in the shape of a u. Hence a double-u- or w-curve.

Other research has shown similar intriguing findings. Imagine, for instance, that you are going to Morocco for the first time. You are asked to describe or rate both the average Briton and the average Moroccan in terms of their humour, wealth, trustworthiness, etc., both before you go and after you return. Frequently, it has been found that people change their opinions of their own countrymen and women more than that of the foreigners. In other words, travel makes you look much more critically at yourself and your culture than most people think. And this self-criticism may itself be rather unhelpful.

The trouble with these stage theories is that not everyone goes through the stages. Not everyone feels like Nancy Mitford did when she wrote: 'I loathe abroad, nothing would induce me to live there… and, as for foreigners, they are all the same and make me sick.' But I suspect that Robert Morley was not far from the truth when he remarked: "The British tourist is always happy abroad, so long as the natives are waiters."

Then there is also the shock of being visited. Anyone who lives in a popular tourist town soon becomes aware that it is not only the tourist but also the native who experiences culture shock. Of course, the amount and type of shock that tourists can impart to local people is an indication of a number of things, such as the relative proportion of tourists to natives, the duration of their stay, the comparative wealth and development of the two groups and the racial and ethnic prejudices of both.

Of course not everybody will experience culture shock. Older, better-educated, confident and skilful adults (particularly those who speak the language) tend to adapt best. Yet there is considerable evidence that sojourners, such as foreign students, voluntary workers, businessmen, diplomats and even military people, become so confused and depressed that they have to be sent home at great expense. That is why many organisations attempt to lessen culture shock by a number of training techniques. The Foreign Office, the British Council and many multinational companies do this for good reason, having learned from bitter experience.

Training

For a number of reasons, information and advice in the form of lectures and pamphlets, etc., is very popular but not always very useful. The 'facts' that are given are often too general to have any clear, specific application in particular circumstances. Facts emphasise the exotic and ignore the mundane (how to hail a taxi, for example). This technique also gives the impression that the culture can be easily understood; and even if facts are retained, they do not necessarily lead to accommodating behaviour.

A second technique is 'isomorphic training'. This is based on the theory that a major cause of cross-cultural communication problems comes from the fact that most people tend to offer different explanations for each other's behaviour. This technique introduces various episodes that end in embarrassment, misunderstanding or hostility between people from two different cultures. The trainee is then presented with four or five alternative explanations of what went wrong, all of which correspond to different attributions of the observed behaviour. Only one is correct from the perspective of the culture being learned. This is an interesting and useful technique, but depends for much of its success on the relevance of the various episodes chosen.

Perhaps the most successful method is 'skills training'. It has been pointed out that socially inadequate or inept individuals have not mastered the social conventions of their own society. Either they are unaware of the rules and processes of everyday behaviour or, if aware of the rules, they are unable or unwilling to abide by them. They are therefore like strangers in their own land. People newly arrived in an alien culture will be in a similar position and may benefit from simple skills training.

This involves analysing everyday encounters such as buying and selling, introductions and refusal of requests. You will also observe successful culture models engaging in these acts and will practice yourself, helped in the learning process by a video tape of your efforts. This may all sound very clinical, but can be great fun and very informative.

Practical advice

Many travellers, unless on business and with considerable company resources behind them, do not have the time or money to go on courses that prevent or minimise culture shock. They have to leap in at the deep end and hope that they can swim. But there are some simple things they can do that may well prevent the shock and improve communications.

Before departure it is important to learn as much as possible about the society you are visiting. Areas of great importance include:

LANGUAGE: Not only vocabulary but polite usage, when to use higher and lower forms, and particularly how to say "yes" and "no".

NON-VERBAL CUES: Gestures, body contact and eye gaze patterns differ significantly from one country to another and carry very important meanings. Cues of this sort for greeting, parting and eating are most important, and are relatively easily learnt.

SOCIAL RULES: Every society develops rules that regulate behaviour so that social goals can be attained and needs satisfied. Some of the most important rules concern gifts, buying and selling, eating and drinking, timekeeping and bribery and nepotism.

SOCIAL RELATIONSHIPS: Family relationships, classes and castes, and working relationships often differ from culture to culture. The different social roles of the two sexes is perhaps the most dramatic difference between societies, and travellers should pay special attention to this.

MOTIVATION: Being assertive, extrovert and achievement oriented may be desirable in America and Western Europe but this is not necessarily the case elsewhere. How to present oneself, maintain face, etc., is well worth knowing.

Once you have arrived, there are a few simple steps that you can take to help reduce perplexity and understand the natives:

CHOOSE LOCALS FOR FRIENDS: Avoid mixing only with your compatriots or other foreigners. Get to know the natives, who can introduce you to the subtleties and nuances of the culture.

PRACTICAL SOCIAL ACTIVITIES: Do not be put off more complex social encounters but ask for information on appropriate etiquette. People are frequently happy to help and teach genuinely interested and courteous foreigners.

AVOID 'GOOD/BAD' OR 'US/THEM' COMPARISONS: Try to establish how and why people perceive and explain the same act differently, have different expectations, etc. Social behaviour has resulted from different historical and economic conditions and may be looked at from various perspectives.

ATTEMPT MEDIATION: Rather than reject your or their cultural tradition, attempt to select, combine and synthesise the appropriate features of different social systems, whether it is in dress, food or behaviour.

When you return home, the benefits of foreign travel and the prevention of the w-curve may be helped by the following:

BECOME MORE SELF-OBSERVANT: Returning home makes one realise the comparative and normative nature of one's own behaviour, which was previously taken for granted. This in turn may alert one to behaviour that is culturally at odds (and, perhaps, why) – in itself helpful for all future travel.

HELPING THE FOREIGNER: There is no better teaching aid than personal experience. That is why many foreign language schools send their teachers abroad not only to improve their language but to experience the difficulties their students have. Remembering this, we should perhaps be in a better position to help the hapless traveller who comes to our country. Travel does broaden the mind (and frequently the behind), but requires some effort. Preparation, it is said, prevents a pretty poor performance, and travelling in different social environments is no exception. But this preparation may require social, as well as geographic, maps. ❧

ADRIAN FURNHAM is a lecturer in psychology at London University. He is the co-author of 'Culture Shock: Psychological Consequences of Geographic Movement'.

Keeping a sense of humour
by Mark McCrum

MUCH AS I LOVE TRAVELLING, I also find it intensely irritating. The American 'mom' next to you on the Eurostar sharing a crackling sack of candy with her fat-faced kid while her equally plump older sister, the child's *ant*, tells him that he's got a bit of French in him, in fact he's got a bit of German in him, in fact he's got a bit of everything in him, in fact he's *whad ya call a mutt*. This wasn't what you went to Paris for, was it?

So look at it another way. It's funny! And contemporary! And a darn sight more real than a train full of claret-sipping onion-sellers in berets would ever be! So stop trying to read your boring book and just enjoy. And when the ant asks the French guard how long it is before the train goes into the channel tunnel, and the French guard goes "Pff," turns his back and walks off – that's hilarious.

Keeping your sense of humour not only leavens the traveller's way, it brings relief from the inevitable frustrations of travel. At Malaga airport I was once on the verge of strangling the representative of a charter flight operator who had shame-lessly diverted our plane to service a football match in Dublin. Then, suddenly, watching a woman from Newcastle asking the glowering Spanish barman repeat-edly, and ever more loudly, for "a small cock", my anger melted into laughter. In the end, she got her Coke (with ice, in a glass, no less) and we got our flight. What's a few hours of your life compared to the profits of a dodgy bucket shop anyway?

For the serious, long-term traveller, being able to see the funny side of things can be a lifesaver, not just when it comes to external problems, but also when pit-ted against the internal bogeymen: the exhaustion, loneliness and depression that can ambush you in even the most gorgeous of places.

Towards the end of a seven-month trip around Australia I found myself driving for three days along the coast road from Adelaide to Melbourne. I'd started out cheerfully in the lovely Adelaide hills, felt exhilarated as I sped across the vast-skied, dazzling salt flats of the Coorong. But by the time I reached the wild-flow-ered hedgerows of Victoria and, finally, the spectacular rollercoaster they call the Great Ocean Road, I was drained and nervy. At seven pm I finally had to admit to myself that I wasn't going to make my jolly Saturday night rendezvous in the Two Dogs Bar, St Kilda. It was going to be another grim hotel room in another resort where I knew nobody. But even that wasn't available. Typically, I'd picked one of the busiest weekends of the year and there wasn't a bed to be had on the coast. Just as I was in danger of driving off the cliff in a stupor of tiredness, I finally saw a gleaming pink vacancies sign. The only free room the place had cost $140 a night, the lisping Greek receptionist told me, but it had a "luck-thurry double thpa". For some reason, that *thpa* did it. My self-pity alchemised into careless extravagance. I threw my budget to the Southern Ocean winds and lay alone in the huge, heart-shaped pool of bubbles laughing, profoundly grateful that a single word had delivered me from certain death.

> *"To what end was this world formed?" said Candide.*
> *"To infuriate us," replied Martin.*
> *– FRANÇOIS-MARIE VOLTAIRE*

Can humour actually protect you from physical danger? In Belfast I went ex-ploring with an English friend down the infamous Falls Road, through the bleak estates where pro-IRA slogans are scrawled on every dirty grey concrete wall to a pub known as The Fort, whose windows were entirely covered with thick steel mesh. We ordered pints of the black stuff and sat down, sharing a booth with a pair of white-haired gents who seemed genial enough, yarning away to each other as Irishmen do. But on hearing our English accents their mood changed. The older of the two leant forward to warn me that I should be very careful, an Englishman walking into a republican pub in an area like this. "Ten years ago, five years ago," he told me, "if you'd walked in here with that accent they'd have had you out the back." In the toilet, he elaborated fiercely, with a gun to my head, finding out exact-ly who I was. Maybe I was writing a book, but there were plenty of undercover Brits who'd come up with stories like that.

I was as open as I could be with him. I wasn't anti-republican, I said, if I could get to interview Gerry Adams I would. The other man laughed loudly. "Well, you've got the right feller here," he said. "This is Gerry Adams's brother-in-law." He was, too. The laughter broke the ice and half an hour later the brother-in-law paid us the compliment of telling us that the *craic* had been good. We wrote our names on a piece of paper and left feeling considerably safer.

There are numerous instances where a shared sense of the ridiculous can break down even the most vexed of cultural barriers. Visiting South African townships in the last days of apartheid, it was always laughter that bonded. "You know what that stands for," one township host told me, pointing thoughtfully to the label of his bottle of lager. "Let Africans Get Equal Rights." I was in another cramped dwelling with a few guys when there was a knock at the door and a pair of po-faced white American missionaries stood before us. Everyone was very polite to them, even when they asked, in deeply patronising tones, what we all "did". Geoffrey, whose house it was, went round with formal and elaborate career descriptions for each of our group in turn, ending, "and Mr McCrum tells us he is a writer. Indeed we were just saying how unusual it was for us to have a white person among us and now I'm beginning to feel like this is my lucky day." The missionaries nodded seriously, and suddenly I felt that the colour barrier was much less important than the humour barrier.

Being actively prepared to have the mickey taken out of you is in general a wise move. In Kalgoorlie, Western Australia, I stumbled one evening into a bar full of miners, yelling their heads off as they let off steam from their long day in the gold pits. Trying to buy a drink I was harangued by a huge bearded bloke with shaved head and elaborate tattoos who was intrigued by my unusual accent. "We've got a bloody Pom here!" he was soon bellowing, hand clamped on my arm, half turned in his seat towards the gallery of mates behind. Then to the bargirls, who were wearing – this being one of WA's famous "skimpy" bars – nothing more than bra and panties. "Mark's a Pom. The Pom wants to see your tits, Donna – I didn't say that, the Pom said it. Ha ha ha!" Not a situation I'd choose to be in again, but non-directional loud laughter did the trick and Rob ended up showing me the town.

While keeping your sense of humour, don't go thinking that it is the answer to everything. It's at the point where you're getting a joke that others aren't, that you have to be most careful. Especially if they're carrying a machine gun or have the capacity to lock you up. On those occasions the ability to keep a straight face is even more important. Even the twitch of a smirk could be your undoing. ❧

MARK MCCRUM has published three travel books – 'Happy Sad Land' (about South Africa), 'No Worries' (about Australia) and 'The Craic' (about Ireland). He has also had seven one-man shows of his landscape watercolours, in galleries from London to Botswana.

Breaking the barriers
by Jon Gardey

BARRIERS TO COMMUNICATION OFF THE BEATEN TRACK exist just because of who you are: a visitor from another civilisation. It is necessary to show the local people that underneath the surface impression of strange clothes and foreign manners exists a fellow human being.

The first step is to approach local inhabitants as if you are their guest. You are. It is their country, their village, their hut, their lifestyle. You are a welcome, or perhaps unwelcome, intruder into their familiar daily routine. Always be aware that they may see very few faces other than those of their family or the other families in the village. Their initial impression of you is likely to be one of unease and wariness. Be reassuring. Move slowly.

If possible, learn a few words of local greeting and repeat them to everyone you meet in the village. It is very important to keep smiling; carry an open face, even if you feel exactly the opposite. Hold your body in a relaxed, non-aggressive manner.

In your first encounter, try to avoid anything that might anger them or make them shy with their initial approaches to you. If they offer a hand, take it firmly, even if it is encrusted with what you might consider filth. Don't hold back or be distant, either in attitude or voice. On the other hand, coming on strong in an effort to get something from a local person will only build unnecessary barriers to communication.

Words and pictures

Begin with words. If you are asking for directions, repeat the name of the place several times, but do not point in the direction you think it is, or suggest possible directions by voice. Usually the local person, in an effort to please his visitor, will nod helpfully in the direction in which you are pointing, or agree with you that, yes, Namdrung is that way, "if you say so". It may be in the opposite direction.

Merely say "Namdrung" and throw up your hands in a gesture that indicates a total lack of knowledge. Most local people are delighted to help someone who is genuinely in need, and, after a conference with their friends, will come up with a solution to your problem. When they point, repeat the name of the place several times more (varying the pronunciation) to check if it is the same place you want to go. It is also a good idea to repeat this whole procedure with someone else in another part of the village (and frequently along the route) to check for consistency.

In most areas it is highly likely that none of the local people will speak any language you are familiar with. Communicating with them then becomes a problem in demonstration: you must show them what you want or perform your message.

If you are asking for information that is more difficult to express than simple directions, use your hands to build a picture of what you need. Pictures, in the air, on the sand, on a piece of paper, are sometimes your only means of communication and, frequently, the clearest. Use these symbols when you receive blank stares in answer to your questions. Use sound or objects that you have in your possession that are similar, or of which you would like more.

Giving and getting

Not all of your contact with local people will be about getting something from them. Don't forget that you have a unique opportunity to bring them something from your own culture – try to make it something that will enrich theirs. Show them what it looks like with the help of postcards and magazines. Let them experience its tools. If you have a camera, let the local people, especially the children, look through the viewfinder. Put on a telephoto lens so they can get a new look at their own countryside. If you have a Polaroid camera, photograph them and give them the print (a very popular offering, but be careful, you might end up being asked to photograph all the villagers). And, most important of all, become involved. Carry aspirin to cure headaches – real or imagined. If someone in the village seems to need help, say in lifting a log, offer a hand. Contribute yourself as an expression of your culture.

If you want to take photographs, be patient. Don't bring out your camera until you have established a sufficient rapport, and be as unobtrusive as possible. If anyone objects, stop. A bribe for a photograph or payment for information is justified only if the situation is unusual. A simple request for directions is no reason for a gift. If the local people do something out of the ordinary for you, reward them as you would a friend at home. The best gift you can give them is your friendship and openness. They are not performers doing an act, but ordinary people living out their lives in circumstances that seem strange to us.

> *If you reject the food, ignore the customs, fear the religion and avoid the people, you might better stay at home.*
> – JAMES A. MICHENER

I have found myself using gifts as a means of avoiding contact with remote people – especially children – as a way of pacifying them. I think it is better to enter and leave their lives with as much warmth as I can give, and now I leave the sweets at home. If you are camped near a village, invite some of the local people over to share your food, and try to have them sit among your party.

On some of the more travelled routes, such as Morocco or the main trekking trails of Nepal, the local children, being used to being given sweets by passing trekkers, will swarm around for more. I suggest that you smile (always) and refuse them. Show them pictures or your favourite juggling act, then give them something creative, such as pencils.

If a local event is in progress, stand back, try to get into a shadow, and watch from a distance. You will be seen and noticed, no matter what you do, but it helps to minimise your presence. If you want to get closer, edge forward slowly, observing the participants, especially the older people, for signs that you are not wanted. If they frown, retire. Respect their attempts to keep their culture and its customs as free as possible from outside influence.

Many people in remote places are still in an age before machines, and live their lives close to the earth in a comfortable routine. Where you and I come from is sophisticated, hard and alien to them. We must come into their lives as gently as possible, and when we go, leave no trace.

Officialdom

In less remote areas where the local people have had more experience of travellers, you must still observe the rule of patience, open-mindedness and respect for the lifestyle of others. But you will encounter people with more preconceived notions about foreigners – and most of those notions will be unfavourable.

In these circumstances – and indeed anywhere your safety or comfort may depend on your approach – avoid seeming to put any local person, especially a minor official, in the wrong. Appeal to his emotions, enlist his magnanimous aid, save his face at all costs. Your own calmness can calm others. If you are delayed or detained, try 'giving up', reading a book, smiling. Should you be accused of some minor misdemeanour, such as 'jumping' a control point, far better to admit your 'mistake' than to be accused of spying – though even this is fairly standard practice in the Third World and shouldn't flap you unduly.

Wherever you go in the Third World, tones and pitches of voice will vary; 'personal distance' between people conversing may be less than you are used to, attitudes and priorities will differ from your own. Accept people as they are and you can hope that, with time and a gentle approach, they will accept you also.

Language

When you have the opportunity of learning or using a smattering of the local language, try to make things easier for yourself by asking questions that limit answers to what you understand and prompt responses which will add helpfully and manageably to your vocabulary. Make it clear to your listeners that your command of the language is limited. Note down what you learn and try constantly to build on what you know.

Always familiarise yourself with the cultural limitations that may restrict topics of conversation or choice of conversation partner.

Keep your hands to yourself

Gestures can be a danger area. The British thumbs-up sign is an obscenity in some countries, such as Sardinia and parts of the Middle East, where it means roughly 'sit on this' or 'up yours'. In such places (and anywhere, if in doubt) hitch a ride by waving limply with a flattened hand.

The ring sign made with thumb and forefinger is also obscene in Turkey and other places. And in France it can mean 'zero', i.e. worthless – the exact opposite of the meaning 'OK' or 'excellent' for which the British and Americans use it.

By contrast, our own obscene insult gesture, the two-finger sign, is used interchangeably in Italy with the Churchillian V-sign. Which way round you hold your fingers makes no difference – it's still understood as a friendly gesture meaning 'victory' or 'peace'.

In Greece, as the anthropologist Desmond Morris tells us, there is another problem to do with the gesture called the *moutza*. In this, the hand is raised flat, 'palm towards the victim and pushed towards him as if about to thrust an invisible custard pie in his face'. To us it means simply to 'go back', but to a Greek it is a hideous insult. It dates from Byzantine times, when chained prisoners were paraded through the streets and abused by having handfuls of filth from the gutter picked up by onlookers and thrust into their faces. Though naturally the brutal practice has long since ceased, the meaning of *moutza* has not been forgotten. ཚ

Jon Gardey is a writer, traveller and film-maker.

Respecting Hinduism
by Justine Hardy

HE LOOKED AT ME WITH SLIGHTLY GLAZED EYES through the pulse of bodies on the banks of the Ganges.

"Hinduism is as big as your mind or as small as your mind," said the smiling *sadhu*, stroking a belly that was as swollen and smooth as a spacehopper. Well, that seemed to wrap it all up really, one of those great throwaway lines that the wandering holy men of India, the *sadhus*, know the foreigners want to hear and will cogitate over for hours in the shimmering heat of the subcontinent. But beneath the glaze-eyed guru gimmick was the nut of Hinduism.

It is a huge religion, the oldest in the world, with a confusion of thousands in the Hindu pantheon of gods. And even if you were to crack the caste of thousands, each one of them has a vehicle, an animal of some description, that flies or trundles them around the heavens on their otherworldly missions. It is this hugeness that is daunting, but Hinduism is an onion religion that is heavy with the ritual paraphernalia attached to it by the Indian nature and culture. As you peel away the layers you'll find the simple moral codes of human behaviour that are at the root of Hinduism. If you dig down through the extraordinary scriptures to one of the main works, the *Upanishads* (400-200 BC), you'll find a text that incorporates the central theme of the majority of the world's main religions: 'The Great God is One, and the learned call him by different names.'

Hinduism's thousands of gods lead to the big three – Brahma the creator, Vishnu the preserver and Shiva the destroyer (sometimes also seen as a creator) – three in one, and also to the physical representations of the unseen omnipotent God, Parabrahma.

When the glaze-eyed *sadhu* with the spacehopper belly said that it was "as big as your mind", he was referring to the ability of Hinduism to embrace so many forms of worship; every family has a favourite god or goddess to whom they turn for guidance, support and comfort. But from out of all the layers of belief comes one core creed: the acceptance of *Samsara, Moksha, Karma* and *Dharma; Samsara*, the cycle of rebirth through many lives on the way to attaining perfection; *Moksha*, spiritual salvation and release from the cycle of reincarnation; *Karma*, the law of cause and effect, whatever you do, good or bad, there will be a consequence and crimes and good deeds that are not recognised in the current life may be punished or rewarded in the next; and *Dharma*, the natural balance of the universe, the law of the caste system and the moral code that each person should follow.

For the visitor to India and Asia, whether travelling through Hindu societies or living in them, a basic understanding of the caste system is important. The control of the caste system has been profoundly challenged for centuries, most dramatically in 1947 when Jawaharlal Nehru became the first prime minister of independent India and called for secular government. Nehru's hope, to form a government free of religious undertone, was an idealistic cry for a newly independent nation that has always ebbed and flowed on the tides of religious passion. The caste system is deeply ingrained in the Indian psyche and, even though it no longer officially exists as a class structure, the four main castes still affect daily life at every level. It has become largely diluted in the cities but it remains the rule of thumb in most rural areas. To ignore it is to bypass a great chunk of India at its pulse.

There are two things about Hinduism that were historically set in stone: you were either born a Hindu with a caste or you were not, and you could not truly convert to Hinduism. This may well be one of the reasons that foreigners have found Hinduism so fascinating, because ultimately we could find out as much about it as we liked, we could read the *Mahabharata*, the *Bhagavad Gita*, the *Ramayana*, the *Vedas*, the *Upanishads* and the *Puranas*, we could go to *puja* prayer rituals, we could pray with Hindus, sing their mantras, accept the blessing of their priests, but we could not claim a caste and convert, in spite of the openness that the religion offered to non-Hindus. Aspects of that are changing as times change and, increasingly, people marry across religions. Within its own fluidity, Hinduism has become more relaxed about conversions beyond the caste system.

So from the big stuff of gods and systems to the smaller but equally important stuff. Hinduism is a living religion in that it is a part of the daily round and there are some things that need to be understood.

Some people think that the Indians are prudish, that they cover up and hide everything. By Western standards they do, but there is a very beautiful sensuality in that very covering. When I work in India with men fresh out of England, when they catch their first sight of sari-clad bathers in a river or beside a village tank, the material wrapped and clinging to their curves, their response has always been to be awed by the feminine beauty. Hindus find it difficult to deal with the Western idea of stripping down to as little as possible in a hot country. If you have ever lived through a hot season in India you become only too aware of the fact that loose, flowing, light cotton clothes are the coolest and most practical. You just get burnt and bitten in shorts and T-shirts.

I had one of my closest shaves with the early edges of middle age when I was taking a young American student out to a primary school project located in a Delhi slum. She was gorgeous, blonde and curvy, and she turned up wearing a sleeveless shirt that showed a fantastic display of cleavage and a flippy skirt. She challenged my disapproval with a tone of voice that made me feel 30 going on 90.

She had picked up the skirt in a local market without realising that it was actually a sari petticoat. She was unintentionally breaking every code of decent dressing in Hindu eyes. She was wearing underwear, for a start, and she was also displaying her upper arms and cleavage. All that is fine and acceptable in the nightclubs and bars of Delhi and Mumbai, but it is just not fair outside of these cities, particularly in rural areas. It is confusing for the people and unfortunately helps to reiterate the belief held by many rural and village Indians that all white women are basically asking for it.

When it comes to going into a temple or attending a family prayer puja, both men and women should cover their heads, arms and legs. No naked flesh is the easiest rule to follow. You will almost always be asked to take your shoes off before going into a temple by an official shoe-minder. It is worth checking that you are handing your precious shoes over to the official minder rather than a likely lad who is going to skip off down the road with his booty, leaving you hopping around on boiling roads where rats and broken glass loiter. The official minder should be tipped a few rupees for his labours.

Weddings have a dress code all of their own. My pet theory is that it is wise for foreigners is to stick to Western dress, but keep it simple and elegant, and again no exposed flesh. Hindu weddings are all about glitter and show and there is just no point in trying to match the efforts of the native population. I don't know why but it always make me a bit sad seeing Western girls struggling with saris at weddings or parties. Indian women were born to it and carry this exquisite garment with grace. Most Westerners just get it a bit wrong and would look much more elegant and have more fun if they stuck to their own clothes. I've lost count of the number of Western girls and women that I have seen in glitzy hotel loos tacking saris up with safety pins, and looking totally miserable about their failure to float within the folds of silk, while their sinuous Indian counterparts waft on by.

While on the female take, historically and culturally Hindus have great respect for women – one of their favourite deities is the gorgeous Lakshmi, goddess of wealth and prosperity and consort of Vishnu, the preserver in the big three. But if a woman does not carry herself within the cultural boundaries of Hindu sensibilities men will understandably regard it as OK to leer and provoke to their hearts' content. If you give them something to stare at, they will stare and go on staring.

Hindus do not eat beef. The cow is sacred to them, hence the vast numbers of cows, decorated with gaily painted horns, wandering around the streets, half-chewed plastic bag in mouth, looking not unlike fag-ash Lil on jaunty hat day. Many people are vegetarians, but just as many eat meat – mutton and chicken being the most popular.

The eating implement of India, and most of Asia, is the right hand. If you are eating with locals and joining in with your hands, too, don't use the left, it is reserved for the washing of the bum. To use it for eating is both offensive and embarrassing for your hosts or fellow eaters.

One further warning about partying with Hindus, or more generally Indians: theoretically most of them do not drink as it is against some aspect of their religion, but at flash weddings or parties the booze flows freely and for a long time.

And the drinking goes on until about midnight. Then, when most people are very blurred around the edges, a great dinner is produced. Everyone eats hugely and then rolls off home repeating the Indian late-night chorus of indigestion. If you get hungry early, eat before you go and nibble politely at the midnight binge.

Hinduism is a bright, brilliant culture and religion that, like its partying, can seem indigestible if taken on too quickly but, when absorbed slowly, is as deep and voluptuous as the Ganges – or your mind, as the man with the spacehopper belly said. ❧

JUSTINE HARDY is a globe-trotting journalist and the author of 'Scoop Wallah' and 'Goat, a Story of Kashmir and Notting Hill'.

Respecting Islam
by Peter Boxhall

LIKE ANY NATION WITH AN IMPORTANT HISTORY, the Arab people are proud of their past. Not only because of an empire which once stretched from the far reaches of China to the gates of France, or their many great philosophers, scientists, seafarers, soldiers and traders, but because they are one people, sharing a common language and culture and following the same religion, which has become an integral part of their lives and behaviour.

Language
Arabic is a difficult language for us to learn, but it is a beautiful, expressive one, which, in the early days of Islam, came to incorporate all the permissible culture, literature and poetry of Arab society. Small West African children sitting under cola trees write their Koranic lessons on wooden boards, infant Yemenis learn and chant in unison *suras* of the Holy Book, school competitions are held perennially in the Kingdom of Saudi Arabia and elsewhere to judge the students' memory and knowledge of their written religion.

So, as in any foreign environment, the traveller would do well to try and learn some Arabic. For without the greetings, the enquiries, the pleasantries of everyday conversation and the ability to purchase one's requirements, many of the benefits and pleasures of travel are foregone. Best, too, to learn classical (Koranic) Arabic, which is understood throughout the Arabic-speaking world (although the further away one is from the Arabian Peninsula in, for example, the Mahgreb countries of Morocco, Tunisia, and Algeria, the more difficult it is to comprehend the dialectal replies one receives).

Not long ago, before the advent of oil, when one travelled in the harsh environment of the Arabian Desert, the warlike, nomadic Bedu tribes would, if they saw you came in peace, greet you with *salaam alaikum* and afford you the hospitality of their tents. If 'bread and salt' were offered to you, you were 'on their face': inviolate, protected, a welcome guest for as long as you wished to stay. *Baiti baitak* (my house is your house) was the sentiment being expressed. This generous, hospitable principle still prevails throughout the Arab world.

Bureaucracy

Although they are subordinate to the overall sense of Arabness, each of the Arab kingdoms, emirates, sultanates and republics has its own national characteristics. In those far-off medieval days of the Arab Empire, there were no frontiers to cross, no need for passports, there was a common currency, a purer language. Today it is different. There is bureaucracy abroad in the Arab world – mostly, it can be said, a legacy of former colonial administrations. So be patient, tolerant and good humoured about passports, visas, immunisation, currency controls and customs. And remember that many of the Arab countries emerged only recently to their present independent status and it has taken us, in the West, some hundreds of years to evolve our systems of public administration and bureaucratic procedure.

One has to remember that, in general, the Arab does not have the same pressing (obsessional?) sense of urgency that we do. No discourtesy is meant. Does it really matter? Tomorrow is another day and the sun will rise again and set. Neither in his bureaucratic or even everyday dealings with you does the Arab take much notice of your status, official or induced.

When I was Personal Secretary to the Governor of Jeddah, important corporation chiefs and industrialists used to visit him in his *majlis*. They were received courteously and served the traditional *qahwa*. The Arab, however, is a great democrat and even these important people had, often to their annoyance, to wait their turn. Yet on one occasion, a comparatively poor *shaiba* came straight up to His Excellency, kissed him on the shoulder and extracting a scroll from the voluminous folds of his *thobe* (the uniform dress worn by all Saudis), proceeded to read its full, eulogistic length in a high-pitched quavering voice.

To the Arab, it is of little importance to know who or what you represent; he is more interested in who you are. If he likes you, you will soon be aware of it. The sense of touch is, to the Arabs, a means of communication. Westerners, who come from colder climates, should not therefore be too reticent, distant or aloof.

Watch and listen, for example, how the Yemenis greet each other: the long repetitious enquiries as to each other's state of health; the handshake, the finger that will sometimes curl towards the mouth to indicate they are merely on speaking terms, casual acquaintances, sometimes to the heart to indicate that they are intimate friends. The embrace, the kiss on both cheeks, which are mainly customary in the Near East and Mahgreb countries…. If you allow the Arab to take you as a friend in his way, he may even invite you to his house.

Social conventions

Baiti baitak is the greatest courtesy. Do not, however, be critical or admiring of the furniture in the house. If you admire the material things, your hospitable host may feel impelled to give you the object of your admiration. Conversely, remember that if your taste in furnishing does not correspond with that of your host, don't, whatever you do, exaggerate how much you admire the material goods!

If it is an old-style house, you must always take your shoes off, and may be expected to sit on the floor supported by cushions. Then all manner of unfamiliar, exotic dishes may be served. If it is painful to plunge your fingers into a steaming mound of rice, and difficult to eat what are locally considered to be the choice pieces of meat, forget your inhibitions and thin skin, eat everything you are offered with your right hand and at least appear to enjoy it. Remember, your host is probably offering the best, sometimes the last remaining provisions in his house.

Once, in the Jordan desert, I was entertained by an important tribal sheikh in his black goat-hair tent. An enormous platter, supported by four tribal retainers, was brought in and put in our midst. On the platter, surmounted by a mound of rice, was a whole baby camel, within that camel a sheep, within that sheep, pigeons. Bedu scarcely talk at all at a meal; it is too important, too infrequent an occasion. So we ate quickly, belching often from indigestion, with many an appreciative *Al hamdulillah*, for it is natural to do so. When replete, rose-water was brought round for us to wash our hands and we men moved out to the cooling evening sands to drink coffee, converse and listen to stories of tribal life, while the tribal ladies, who had cooked the meal, entered the tent from the rear with the children to complete the feast.

In some Arab countries, alcoholic drink is permitted. In others it is definitely not. From my two years' experience in Saudi Arabia and three in Libya, I know it is actually possible to obtain whisky, for example, but it is at a price – perhaps as much as £70 a bottle – which, for me at least, is too expensive an indulgence, even if it were not for the penalties for being caught.

Coffee and tea are the habitual refreshments: in Saudi Arabia, as was the custom in my municipal office, the small handle-less cups of *qushr* are poured from the straw-filled beak of a brass coffee pot. 'Arabian coffee' is also famous: almost half coffee powder, half sugar. One should only drink half or two-thirds, however, and if you are served a glass of cold water with it, remember that an Arab will normally drink the water first (to quench his thirst) then the coffee so that the taste of this valued beverage may continue to linger in the mouth.

In North Africa, tea is a more customary drink. Tea *nuss wa nuss* with milk in Sudan, for example; tea in small glasses with mint in the Mahgreb; even tea with nuts in Libya. Whoever was it said that the English are the world's greatest tea drinkers? Visiting the Sanussi tribe in Libya, I once had to drink 32 glasses of tea in the course of a morning. The tea-maker, as with the Arabian coffee-maker, is greatly respected for his art.

Dress

In most of the Arab world, normal European-type dress is appropriate, but it should be modest in appearance. Again if, as we should do, we take notice of Arab custom, which is based on sound common sense, we might do well to remember that in hot, dusty conditions, the Bedu put on clothes to protect themselves against the elements, not take them off, as we Westerners do.

The question of whether one should adopt the local dress in the particularly hot, arid countries of the Arab world is probably a matter of personal preference. The *thobe* is universally worn in Saudi Arabia, the *futah* in the Yemen and South Arabia. I personally used to wear the *futah*; in Saudi Arabia, however, the Governor suggested I should wear the *thobe*, but I felt inhibited from doing so as none of the other expatriates appeared to adopt it.

Religion

The final, and perhaps most important, piece of advice I can offer to the traveller is to repeat the need to respect Islam. The majority of Arabs are Muslim, and Islam represents their religion and their way of life, as well as their guidance for moral and social behaviour. In the same sense that Muslims are exhorted (in the *Koran*) to be compassionate towards the non-believer (and to widows, orphans and the sick), so too should we respect the 'Faithful'. Sometimes one may meet religious fanatics, openly hostile, but it is rare to do so and I can only recall, in my many years in Arab countries, one such occasion. Some schoolboys in south Algeria enquired why, if I spoke Arabic, I was not a Muslim, and, on hearing my answer, responded: "*Inta timshi fi'n nar*" (You will walk in the fires of Hell).

In some countries you can go into mosques when prayers are not in progress, in others entry is forbidden altogether. Always ask for permission to photograph mosques and (in the stricter countries) women, old men and children.

Respect, too, the various religious occasions and that all-important month-long fast of Ramadan. My Yemeni doctors and nurses all observed Ramadan, so one year I joined them, to see exactly what an ordeal it was for them. Thereafter, my admiration for them, and for others who keep the fast, was unbounded, and I certainly do not think we should exacerbate the situation in this difficult period by smoking, eating or drinking in public.

Ahlan wa sahlan: welcome! You will hear the expression often in the Arab world, and it will be sincerely meant. ❧

Lt Col Peter Boxhall is an explorer, writer and Arabist.

Respecting Buddhism
by Gill Cairns

"DALAI LAMA PIC-A CHUR? YOU HOW MUCH? How much you say?" Anyone who has travelled in Tibet will have heard this constant refrain from children, accompanied by a relentless tugging on your shirt sleeve. A photograph of Tibet's spiritual leader, who has lived in exile since 1959, is a highly prized item in this part of the world, followed closely by "School pens, miss?" Any photos of the Dalai Lama are scattered on the shrines in Buddhist temples, along with rice grains and *katha*, or white offering scarves. These are only part of the rich panoply of offerings made by the devotees who circumambulate the shrines, strings of *mala* beads in their hands, counting the mantras that they murmur intensely and repeatedly.

Buddhism has been entwined with the fabric of Tibetan culture since as long ago as the seventh century. Today there are still practising Buddhists, men and women, lay and monk, despite the desecration of their temples by the Chinese occupation in the Fifties and the Cultural Revolution in the Sixties and Seventies, and intensifying imposition of Chinese culture on the area. In the wake of the invasion of Lhasa in 1959, those who fled with the Dalai Lama into exile at Dharamsala have set up communities on the Indian side of the Himalayas, in parts of Nepal and beyond.

Buddhism has its origins in the teachings of Siddharthur Gautama, who was born some 2,500 years ago, the son of Suddhodana of the Sakya clan, in Lumbini on the border of Nepal and India. Having heard that there was life beyond the confines of his luxurious palace, he went forth to seek and eventually gain 'Enlightenment' and liberation from the cyclic existence of birth, death and rebirth. After his Enlightenment he became known as Buddha, meaning 'Awakened One', and the influence of his teachings spread from India to Sri Lanka, Myanmar (Burma), Thailand, Cambodia and east into Tibet, China and Japan. Within India, Buddhism was subsumed into Hinduism and then eroded by the Muslim Moguls. Since Independence, however, it has enjoyed a small but significant revival, with pockets of Buddhists notably around Bombay, in the south of the country, and in the north-eastern region near the border with Tibet. This includes Ladakh, now known as 'Little Tibet', Sikkim, and the area around Dharamsala, where the Dalai Lama and his government-in-exile are based.

Today there are several schools of Buddhism. The *Theravadins*, who maintain traditional rules regarding discipline for monks and practitioners, based on the original teachings of Buddha, are found in parts of southern India, Sri Lanka, Myanmar (Burma), Thailand and Cambodia. The *Mahayana*, who grew up in northern India and Nepal among the lay as well as the monastic population, emphasise not only the historical teachings of Buddha but also the Buddhas of the past and future and the altruistic ideal of seeking Enlightenment for the benefit of all beings (the Bodhisattva Ideal). In the eighth century, Mahayana Buddhism was introduced into Tibet, where it developed a distinct flavour of its own with the beginning of *Lamaism*, in which religious teachers of high spiritual development are revered as incarnations, or *tulkus*, of their predecessors. It is believed that the current Dalai Lama, the fourteenth in the lineage, is the embodiment of the compassionate aspect of Enlightenment. This is symbolised in religious paintings by the Bodhisattva Avalokoteshvara, whose most common form has eleven heads and a thousand arms. A further development from the Mahayana in Tibet was the *Vajrayana* or *Tantra*, an even more devout approach (not for the faint-hearted) which introduced the possibility of reaching Enlightenment in one lifetime.

Today, Buddhism flourishes in pockets of Asia. In some countries, such as Bhutan, it is the state religion; in others it is virtually outlawed. In some places tradition allows people to be a Buddhist monk for a week, while in others sincere practitioners may not be members of a monastic order. All this may seem a little confusing to the Western traveller. Perhaps it is enough to say that even if the people around you are not wearing Buddhist robes, you may still be travelling among Buddhists.

In Tibet, Ladakh, and the Himalayan regions, the outward expression of Buddhism is found not only in the richly decorated monasteries or *gompas* (places of meditation) that are often wedged in impossibly inaccessible mountain tops, but also in the character of the people, both lay and monastic. It is as if all the positive emotion generated by Buddhist practice has infused its people with a remarkable cheerfulness, humour and lightness. The rugged monochrome landscape is sprinkled with the intense colours characteristic of Buddhist devotion: brightly coloured prayer flags fluttering from the golden rooftops of temples; boulders painted with Buddhist deities; the famous mantra of Avaolkiteshvara '*Om Mani Padme Hum*'; and *chortens*, stone structures containing relics and built on a stack of geometrical shapes representing the five elements (earth, fire, water, air and ether).

Many of the *gompas*, are encircled by a pilgrim circuit, a narrow trail followed by devotees, who prostrate themselves repeatedly (raising their hands above their heads, and then flinging their bodies forward to the ground) until the circuit is complete. The practice of prostration is believed to engage the body, mind and powers of speech fully in the devotion of one's life to the Buddha and the ideal of Enlightenment.

On approaching a *gompa*, you may find built into the perimeter walls a row of prayer wheels; inside these brass and wooden barrels are scrolls inscribed with hundreds of mantras, and as they are turned (clockwise) the *Dharma* or Buddhist teachings and prayers are sent.

When you enter a *gompa*, remove your footwear and ensure that you are modestly dressed. Monks take vows of celibacy and it is deemed disrespectful to wear revealing clothing. At the entrance of larger temples, white offering scarves are on sale: these may be placed on the shrines, along with small amounts of change. The darkness of the interior of the *gompa* takes some adjusting to: a torch is therefore handy for close inspection of the walls, every inch of which is painted with scenes from the life of the Buddha or other Buddhist iconography, or hung with *Thangkas* (wall hangings depicting particular deities, mounted on silk). It is disrespectful to touch any of the Buddhist statues (*rupas*) or these paintings. Butter lamps are lit as prayers, and often you can approach a *konyer* (chaplain) and give him money to light one for you. Buddhists make their way round the shrine room in a clockwise direction, and to do otherwise is considered offensive. On leaving places of worship, Buddhists either back out or bow gently to the shrine before turning to leave; it is courteous to do the same.

You may be lucky enough to witness a *puja* (devotional worship), which involves the chanting of *sutras* or scriptures and mantras, orchestrated by the occasional ringing of bells, beating of drums, and the haunting call of strange horns fashioned from brilliantly white giant conch shells. Sit quietly at the back of the gathering while the ritual is carried out. Monks at *puja* ceremonies sit on the ground: take care not to step over them, or over texts or books. During the course of the ceremony offerings are made to the shrines of the Buddhas and Bodhisattvas, including incense, rice grains and yak butter lamps. At the end of the ceremony, a bowl of salty butter tea may be put in front of you. This is definitely an acquired taste, but it is disrespectful to show distaste; if you find it undrinkable, simply leave the bowl full without any fuss.

As a general rule, taking photographs in temples is regarded as an intrusion – the dark interior would require a flash and this interrupts the concentration of devotees. In some *gompas*, however, monks will allow photography, normally for a modest fee.

Taking pictures of the Dalai Lama into Tibet as gifts should be considered with caution. While they might be very much appreciated, there is no doubt that this is a politically sensitive issue. According to the Tibet Information Network, several tourists have recently experienced problems with the Chinese authorities. It is more prudent to show pictures of the Dalai Lama in your guidebook, rather than making presents of them.

One recent abhorrent development that has affronted Tibetan sensitivities is the increasing number of tourists who have shown a morbid fascination in witnessing the sky burial ritual. In a sky burial, the corpse is taken to a special site on a mountainside, where it is cut into pieces and left to be eaten by birds. Some tourists have not only photographed but also videoed this ritual, as a result of which Westerners have now been banned from such ceremonies in Lhasa. In other parts of Tibet you may still be invited, but you are strongly advised to turn down the offer as a mark of respect to the dead and their relatives.

Although Tibetan culture appears to be generally happy-go-lucky, this does not necessarily mean that anything goes. Politeness is an integral part of Tibetan culture, to the point where many Tibetans are loathe to refuse requests from travellers. If a woman in a short skirt asks the incumbent monk of a temple if she can go inside, for example, he may mutter that it is rather cold inside, indicating he feels uneasy about it, but would be unlikely to refuse her entry.

Finally, for those who want to learn more about Buddhism, there are a number of centres where travellers can not only learn about the religion and meditation, but also go on a meditation retreat. The Friends of the Western Buddhist Order in Kathmandu runs meditation courses and retreats, held in Pulchowk monastery in Patan (contact PO Box 5336 Thamel, Kathmandu, Nepal). The Mount Everest Centre for Buddhist Studies at the Kopan Monastery, GPO Box 817, Kathmandu, can also be of help. ❧

GILL CAIRNS is a freelance writer and an active Buddhist.

Healthy travel

Health planning
by Drs Nick Beeching and Sharon Welby

The most carefully planned holiday, business trip or expedition may be ruined by illness, much of which is preventable. It is logical to put as much effort into protecting your health while abroad as you have into planning your itinerary and obtaining the necessary equipment and travel papers.

Unfortunately, it is not in the best commercial interests of travel companies to emphasise the possible health hazards of destinations that are being sold to potential customers: most holiday brochures limit health warnings to the minimum legal requirements, and some travel agents are woefully ignorant of the dangers of travel to more exotic climates. We have recently treated a travel agent for life–threatening malaria caught on the Kenyan coast. He had not taken malaria prophylaxis, despite the long and widespread recognition of the dangers of malaria in this area.

Happily, travellers' health problems are usually more mundane. Fatigue from overwork before a business trip or much needed holiday, the stress of travel itself, exposure to new climates and over-indulgence in rich food, alcohol and tobacco, all contribute to increased vulnerability to illness. Short-lived episodes of diarrhoea affect up to 50 per cent of travellers, and up to one fifth of tourists on some Mediterranean package holidays will have mild respiratory problems such as head colds, 'flu-like illnesses or, rarely, more severe pneumonias such as Legionnaires' disease. Sunburn or heat exhaustion are common, and accidents associated with unfamiliar sports such as skiing are an obvious hazard. But the most common cause of death among expatriates is road traffic accidents – not exotic infections.

Pre-travel health check-list

Starting three months before you travel, consult your family doctor and specialist agencies, as necessary, to:
1. Obtain information about specific health problems at your destinations.
2. Consider current health, medical and dental fitness and current medications.
3. Obtain adequate health insurance (and form E111 if travelling to an EC country).
4. Check again that health insurance is adequate.
5. Plan and obtain necessary immunisations and malaria prophylaxis.
6. Plan and obtain other medications and first aid items and any documentation.
7. Consider need for first-aid training course.

Sources of information

The depth of preparation required before travel clearly depends on the general health of the individual and on his or her destination(s). In the last few years, accessible information on health for travellers has improved considerably. The sections in this chapter are intended to provide a brief outline of the steps to be considered.

Travellers to areas outside Europe, North America or Australasia are advised to invest in a copy of *Travellers' Health: How to Stay Healthy Abroad* (3rd edition, OUP) by Dr Richard Dawood – a guide which contains a wealth of information on all aspects of travel medicine. This is updated by regular features in *Traveller* magazine (published by WEXAS), and is particularly recommended for those planning to work abroad or embarking on prolonged overland trips or expeditions in remote areas.

British travellers should obtain the booklet *Health Advice for Travellers Anywhere in the World*, prepared by the Department of Health and the Central Office of Information (booklet T5). This contains details of the documentation required for entitlement to free medical care and can be obtained from post offices, GPS' surgeries and vaccination centres, or by telephoning the Health Literature Line (freephone 0800 555 777). The leaflet is also constantly updated, on pages 460-464 of CEEFAX and on the computerised data services PRESTEL and ISTEL to which most travel agents have access.

Some useful web-based sources of information include the Department of Health travel advice (www.doh.gov.uk/hat/index.htm), the Foreign Office (http://193.114.50.10/travel/countryadvice.asp), the American Centers for Disease Control – Travel Health (www.cdc.gov/travel/), the World Health Organization (www.who.org), and Shoreland's Travel Health Online (www. tripprep.com/index.html).

When travelling outside Europe, it is wise to obtain information about compulsory immunisation requirements from the appropriate embassy, consulate or high commission of each country that you plan to visit. However, do not expect their personnel to be able to give you general medical advice, and their information is not always as up to date as it should be. British travellers to exotic locations should also consult their District Public Health Department or one of the centres of specific expertise listed in the *Directory* for the latest information on immunisation requirements and malaria prophylaxis.

Those planning to work abroad should try and contact an employee of the company to ensure that adequate provision for medical and dental care is provided within their contract. If necessary, they should also consider taking out health insurance in addition to company policies.

Medical and dental health

If in any doubt about possible hazards of travel because of a pre-existing medical condition, consult your family doctor. People with heart or chest problems, recurrent blood clots in the legs or lungs, recent strokes, uncontrolled blood pressure, epilepsy, psychiatric disorders or chronic sinus or ear problems may be at risk when flying.

Late pregnancy is a contra-indication to flying, diabetics taking medication will need special advice, and the disabled will have specific requirements that may need to be notified to airline and airport authorities. People with chronic health problems or women who are obviously pregnant should ask their doctor to complete a standard airline form certifying their fitness for flying. This form should be obtained from the airline concerned.

Adequate supplies of all routinely-prescribed medications, including oral contraceptives, should also be obtained before departure. For short trips within Europe, these will be provided as NHS prescriptions. Those planning longer stays abroad should determine the availability of their medication overseas or take adequate supplies (you may need to pay for these on private prescription). It is also strongly recommended that you obtain a certificate from your doctor detailing the drugs prescribed, including the correct pharmacological name, as well as the trade name. This will be necessary to satisfy customs officials and you may need to obtain certified translations into appropriate languages. Some drugs readily obtainable in the UK are viewed with great suspicion elsewhere (codeine, for example, is considered a controlled drug in many countries, and tranquillisers such as diazepam can cause problems). Women working in Saudi Arabia should take adequate supplies of oral contraceptives and will need a certified Arabic translation of the certificate stating that the contraceptives have been prescribed for their personal use.

A journey is a person in itself; no two are alike.
– JOHN STEINBECK

Those with recurring medical problems should also obtain a letter from their family doctor detailing the condition(s) – the letter can then be shown to doctors abroad if emergency treatment becomes necessary. People with surgically implanted devices are also advised to carry a doctor's certificate to show security officials. Artificial hip replacements frequently set off metal detection security alarms at airports, as do in-dwelling intravenous (e.g. Portacath) central venous lines. People with cardiac pacemakers are unlikely to run into problems due to electrical interference from British or North American airport metal detectors, but should try to avoid going through them and arrange instead for a personal body check by security officials.

Individuals with specific chronic health problems such as epilepsy, diabetes or long-term steroid treatment, should obtain a 'Medic-alert' bracelet or similar, which is more easily located in a medical emergency than a card in your pocket.

Many countries insist on a negative HIV-antibody test before allowing foreigners to work. Some will not allow any known HIV-positive individual to enter the country (http://travel.state.gov/hivtestingreqs.html) despite advice from the World Health Organisation (WHO) that such regulations are ineffective as a means of controlling the spread of HIV infection. HIV-positive travellers should consult their medical specialist and local support groups about specific travel insurance problems and the advisability of travel.

Dental health is often taken for granted by British citizens who get a rude shock when faced with bills for dental work overseas. Those embarking on prolonged travel or work abroad, or planning to visit very cold areas, should have a full preventative dental check up before leaving.

Spare spectacles, contact lenses and contact lens solutions should also be obtained before travelling. If you are planning a vigorous holiday or expedition (e.g. skiing, hill-walking etc.) it might be a good idea to begin an appropriate fitness regime before you leave.

It is worth noting that expatriates taking up a contract abroad will often have to submit to a detailed medical examination as a condition of employment.

On your return

On returning from a long trip, most travellers will experience some euphoria and elation, as well as family reunions and the interested enquiries of friends. After this, as relaxation, and possibly jet lag set in, a period of apathy, exhaustion and weariness can follow. Recognise this and allow a few quiet days if it is feasible. There are usually many pressures at this stage, especially if equipment is to be unpacked and sorted, photographs processed, etc.

Another pressure for most people is the none too welcome thought of returning to the mundane chores involved in earning one's daily bread. If your travels have been challenging, then a couple of recovery days will probably make you work more efficiently thereafter and cope more expeditiously with the thousands of tasks which seem to need urgent attention.

After a time of excitement and adventure, some will go through a period of being restless and bored with the simple routine of home and work. They may not be aware of this temporary change in personality but their families certainly will be. Having pointed out this problem, we cannot suggest any way of overcoming it except perhaps to recommend that everyone concerned try to recognise it and be a little more tolerant than normal. This may not be a sensible time to take major decisions affecting career, family and business.

Some will be relieved to arrive in their hygienic homes after wandering in areas containing some of the world's nastiest diseases. Unfortunately, the risk of ill health is not altogether gone as you may still be incubating an illness acquired abroad – incubation for diseases such as hepatitis or malaria could take a few months or in the extreme case of rabies, a few years.

After your return, any medical symptoms or even just a feeling of debility or chronic ill health must not be ignored – medical help should be sought. Tell your physician where you have travelled (in detail), including brief stopovers. It may be that you are carrying some illness outside the spectrum normally considered. Sadly this has been known to cause mistaken diagnosis so that malaria, for example, has been labelled as influenza with occasionally fatal consequences.

Tropical worms and other parasites, enteric fevers, typhus, histoplasmosis (a fungal disease breathed in on guano, making cavers particularly vulnerable), tuberculosis, tropical virus diseases, amoebic dysentery and hepatitis may all need to be treated. For these illnesses to be successfully treated, many patients will need expert medical attention.

Routine tropical disease check ups are provided by some companies for their employees during or after postings abroad. They are not generally required by other travellers who have not been ill while abroad or after their return. People who feel that they might have acquired an exotic infection or who have received treatment for infection abroad, should ask their doctor about referral to a unit with an interest in tropical diseases. Most health regions have a suitable unit. All travellers who have had freshwater exposure in a bilharzia (schistosomiasis) area (see section on schistosomiasis) should be screened 3 months after the last freshwater contact or sooner if symptoms develop.

All unprotected sexual encounters while travelling carry high risks of infection with various sexually transmitted diseases in addition to HIV and hepatitis B. A post-travel check up is strongly advised, even if you have no symptoms. Your local hospital will advise about the nearest clinic – variously called genito-urinary medicine (GUM) clinics, sexually-transmitted disease (STD) clinics, sexual health clinics, VD clinics or 'special' clinics. Absolute anonymity is guaranteed, and no referral is needed from your general practitioner.

After leaving malarial areas, many will feel less motivated to continue their anti-malarial drugs. It is strongly recommended that these be taken for a minimum of 28 days after leaving the endemic area. Failure to do this has caused many travellers to develop malaria some weeks after they thought they were totally safe. This is more than a nuisance: it has occasionally been fatal.

Fortunately, the majority of travellers return home with nothing other than pleasant memories of an enjoyable interlude in their lives. ૐ

Dr Nick Beeching is Senior Lecturer in Infectious Diseases at the Liverpool School of Tropical Medicine. He has worked in India, Australia, New Zealand and the Middle East, and collaborates with medical colleagues in many parts of the tropics. Dr Sharon Welby is a Lecturer in Travel Medicine at the Liverpool School, where she runs the medical clinic.

The essential medical kit
by Drs Nick Beeching and Sharon Welby

INDIVIDUAL REQUIREMENTS VARY GREATLY and most travellers do not need to carry enormous bags of medical supplies. This section covers a few health items that the majority of travellers should consider. Those going to malarious areas without ready access to medical care should read the Medical Kit Checklist, in the *Directory*.

First-aid training is appropriate for travellers to remote areas and those going on prolonged expeditions which might include a medical officer. As the medical needs of expeditions vary so much, an expedition kit bag list has not been included here. Expedition leaders should consult their own organisation or one of the specialist agencies for advice.

PAINKILLERS: We always carry soluble aspirin (in foil-sealed packs) which is an excellent painkiller and reduces inflammation associated with sunburn (just be careful about the water you dissolve it in). Aspirin should not be given to children aged less than twelve, and take paracetamol syrup for young children. Both paracetamol and aspirin reduce fever associated with infections. Adults who cannot tolerate aspirin because of ulcer problems, gastritis or asthma should instead take paracetamol (not paracetamol/codeine preparations). To avoid potential embarrassment with customs officials, stronger painkillers should only be carried with evidence that they have been prescribed.

CUTS AND GRAZES: A small supply of waterproof dressings (e.g. Band-Aids) is useful and a tube of antiseptic cream such as Savlon – especially if travelling with children.

SUNBURN: British travellers frequently underestimate the dangers of sunburn and should take particular care that children do not get burnt. Protect exposed areas from the sun, remembering the back of the neck. Sunbathing exposure times should be gradually increased and use adequate sunblock creams (waterproof if swimming), particularly at high altitude where uv light exposure is higher. Sunburn should be treated with rest, plenty of non-alcoholic drinks and paracetamol or aspirin. Those who burn easily may wish to take a tube of hydrocortisone cream for excessively burnt areas.

MOTION SICKNESS: If liable to travel sickness, try to sleep through as much of the journey as possible and avoid reading. Avoid watching the horizon through the window and, if travelling by boat, remain on deck as much as possible.

Several types of medication give potential relief from motion sickness when taken before the start of a journey, and sufferers should experiment to find out which suits them best. Antihistamines (e.g. Phenergan) are popular, especially for children, but should not be taken with alcohol. Adults should not drive until all sedative effects of antihistamines have worn off. Other remedies include Kwells (hyoscine tablets), Dramamine (dimenhydrinate) and Stugeron (cinnarazine). Scopoderm patches, only available on prescription, release hyoscine through the skin for up to three days. Hyoscine taken by mouth or by skin patch causes a dry mouth and can cause sedation.

CONSTIPATION: The immobility of prolonged travel, body clock disruption, dehydration during heat acclimatisation and reluctance to use toilets of dubious cleanliness all contribute to constipation. Drink plenty of fluids and try to eat a high-fibre diet. Those who are already prone to constipation may wish to take additional laxatives or fibre substitutes (e.g. Fybogel).

DIARRHOEA: Although this is a common problem, it is usually self-limiting and most travellers do not need to carry anti-diarrhoea medication with them. Diarrhoea reduces absorption of the contraceptive pill and women may wish to carry supplies of alternative contraceptives in case of this.

FEMALE PROBLEMS: Women who suffer from recurrent cystitis or vaginal thrush should consult their doctor to obtain appropriate antibiotics to take with them. Tampons are often difficult to buy in many countries and should be bought before travelling. Periods are often irregular or may cease altogether during travel but this does not mean that you cannot become pregnant.

INSECT BITES: Insect bites are a nuisance in most parts of the world and also transmit a variety of infections, the most important of which is malaria. Personal insect repellents will be needed by most travellers and usually contain DEET (diethyltoluamide). Liquid formulations are the cheapest but are less convenient to carry. Lotions and cream are available and sprays are the easiest to apply but are bulky to carry. Sticks of repellent are easier to carry and last the longest. All these should be applied to the skin and to clothing adjacent to exposed areas of skin, but should not be applied around the eyes, nose and mouth (take care with children).

DEET dissolves plastics, including carrier bags etc., so beware. An alternative to DEET-containing repellents is Mosiguard Natural. Marketed by MASTA, this is made from a blend of eucalyptus oils and is as effective as repellents based on DEET. It is more suitable for people who are sensitive to DEET.

When abroad, try to reduce the amount of skin available to biting insects by wearing long sleeves, and long trousers or skirts. If a mosquito net is provided with your bed, use it. Permethrin-impregnated mosquito nets are effective and can be purchased before travel to malarious areas. 'Knock-down' insecticide sprays may be needed, and mosquito coils are easy to carry. Electric buzzers (that imitate male mosquito noises) are useless and candles and repellent strips (containing citronella) are not very effective. If bitten by insects, try to avoid scratching, which can introduce infection, particularly in the tropics. Eurax cream or calamine lotion can relieve local irritation, and antihistamine tablets may help those who have been bitten extensively.

Antihistamine creams should be used with caution, since they can cause local reactions, and we prefer to use weak hydrocortisone cream on bites that are very irritating. Hydrocortisone cream should only be used if the skin is not obviously broken or infected. Increasing pain, redness, swelling or obvious pus suggest infection, and medical attention should be sought.

HIV PREVENTION: Most HIV infections are acquired sexually (see *Sex Abroad*). All adults should consider taking a supply of condoms. Travellers to countries with limited medical facilities should consider taking a supply of sterile needles and syringes so that injections required abroad are not given with re-usable needles of doubtful sterility.

Personal supplies of syringes and needles can make customs officials very suspicious, and condoms are not acceptable in some countries – particularly the Middle East.

To avoid problems at the border, it is worth buying these items as part of a small HIV/AIDS prevention pack which is available from most of the medical equipment suppliers listed in the directory. Larger 'HIV prevention packs' which include blood product substitutes are rarely worth carrying. ✤

Common health problems
By Dr Nick Beeching

IT GOES WITHOUT SAYING that travellers should always seek qualified medical attention if any illness they are suffering from gets worse despite their own remedies, or, for that matter any of those mentioned in this book! Large hotels usually have access to doctors, typically a local family doctor or private clinic. In remote areas, the nearest qualified help will be a rural dispensary or pharmacist, but seek advice from local expatriate groups, your consulate or embassy for details of local doctors.

Mission hospitals usually offer excellent care and they often have English-speaking doctors. In large towns, university-affiliated hospitals should be used in preference to other hospitals. The International Association for Medical Assistance to Travellers produces useful lists of English-speaking doctors overseas (www.sentex.net/~iamat/ci. html).

If you feel that your medical condition is deteriorating despite (or because of) local medical attention, consider travelling home or to a city or country with more advanced medical expertise – sooner rather than later.

Medication

Medicines sold in tropical pharmacies may be sub-standard. Always check the expiry date and check that medications that should have been refrigerated are not being sold on open shelves. There is a growing market in counterfeit drugs and locally-prepared substitutes are often of low potency. Stick to brand names manufactured by large international companies, even if these cost more. Insist on buying bottles that have unbroken seals and, wherever possible, purchase tablets or capsules that are individually sealed in foil or plastic wrappers. It is difficult to adulterate or substitute the contents of such packaging.

It is usually wise to avoid medications that include several active pharmacological ingredients, most of which will be ineffective and will push up the cost. Medication that is not clearly labelled with the pharmacological name as well as the brand name of ingredients is suspect (e.g. Nivaquine contains chloroquine).

Fevers

Fever may herald a number of exotic infections, especially when accompanied by a rash. Fever in a malarious area should be investigated by blood tests, even if you are taking antimalarials. A raised temperature is more commonly due to virus infections such as influenza, or localised bacterial infections that have obvious localising features such as middle ear infections or sinusitis (local pain), urinary tract infections (pain or blood passing water), skin infections (obvious) or chest infections including pneumonia (cough, chest pain or shortness of breath).

If medical attention is not available, the best antibiotic for amateurs is cotrimoxazole (Bactrim or Septrin) which contains a sulphur drug together with trimethoprim. This covers all the above bacterial infections as well as typhoid fever. Travellers who are allergic to sulphur drugs could use trimethoprim alone or coamoxyclav (Augmentin) which is a combined oral penicillin preparation.

Local infections

ATHLETE'S FOOT: Can become very florid in the tropics so treat this problem before departure. The newer antifungal creams e.g. Canesten, are very effective and supersede antifungal dusting powders, but do not eliminate the need for sensible foot hygiene. In very moist conditions, e.g. in rain forests, on cave explorations or in small boats, lacerated feet can become a real and incapacitating problem. A silicon-based barrier cream in adequate supply is essential under these conditions.

BLISTERS: Burst with a sterile blade or needle (boiled for three minutes or hold in a flame until red hot). Remove dead skin. Cover the raw area with zinc oxide plaster and leave in place for several days to allow new skin to form.

EARS: Keep dry with a light plug of cotton wool but don't poke matches in. If there is discharge and pain, take an antibiotic.

EYES: If the eyes are pink and feel gritty, wear dark glasses and put in chloromycetin ointment or drops. Seek medical attention if relief is not rapid or if a foreign body is present in the eye.

FEET: Feet take a hammering so boots must fit and be comfortable. Climbing boots are rarely necessary on the approach march to a mountain; trainers are useful. At the first sign of rubbing put on a plaster.

SINUSITIS: Gives a headache (feels worse on stooping), 'toothache' in the upper jaw, and often a thick, snotty discharge from the nose. Inhale steam or sniff tea with a towel over your head to help drainage. Decongestant drops may clear the nose if it is mildly bunged up, but true sinusitis needs an antibiotic so seek advice.

SKIN INFECTIONS: In muddy or wet conditions, many travellers will get some skin sepsis or infections in small wounds. Without sensible hygiene these can be disabling, especially in jungle conditions. Cuts and grazes should be washed thoroughly with soap and water or an antiseptic solution. Large abrasions should be covered with a vaseline gauze, e.g. Jelonet or Sofratulle, then a dry gauze, and kept covered until a dry scab forms, after which they can be left exposed. Anchor dressings are useful for awkward places e.g. fingers or heels. If a cut is clean and gaping, bring the edges together with Steristrips in place of stitches.

TEETH: When it is difficult to brush your teeth, chew gum. If a filling comes out, a plug of cotton wool soaked in oil of cloves eases the pain; gutta-percha, softened in boiling water, is easily plastered into the hole as a temporary filling. Hot salt mouth-washes encourage pus to discharge from a dental abscess but an antibiotic will be needed.

THROAT: Cold dry air irritates the throat and makes it sore. Gargle with a couple of aspirins or table salt dissolved in warm water, or suck antiseptic lozenges.

Unconsciousness

The causes range from drowning to head injury, diabetes to epilepsy. Untrained laymen should merely attempt to place the victim in the coma position – lying on

their side (preferably the left side) with the head lower than the chest to allow se-
cretions, blood or vomit to drain away from the lungs. Hold the chin forward to
prevent the tongue falling back and obstructing the airway. Don't try any fancy
manoeuvres unless you are practised, as you may do more harm than good. *All unconscious patients, from any cause, but particularly after trauma, should be placed in
the coma position until they recover. This takes priority over any other first aid manoeuvre.*

In cases of fainting, lay the unconscious person down and raise the legs to return extra blood to the brain.

Injury

Nature is a wonderful healer if given adequate encouragement.

BURNS: Superficial burns are simply skin wounds. Leave open to the air to form
a dry crust under which healing goes on. If this is not possible, cover with Melolin
dressings. Burn creams offer no magic. Deep burns must be kept scrupulously
clean and treated urgently by a doctor. Give drinks freely to replace lost fluids.

SPRAINS: A sprained ankle ligament, usually on the outside of the joint, is a
common and likely injury. With broad Elastoplast 'stirrup strapping', walking may
still be possible. Put two or three long lengths from mid-calf on the non-injured
side, attach along the calf on the injured side. Follow this with circular strapping
from toes to mid-calf overlapping by half on each turn. First Aid treatment of
sprains and bruises is immobilisation (I), cold e.g. cold compresses (C), and elevation (E); remember 'ICE'. If painful movement and swelling persist, suspect a fracture.

FRACTURES: Immobilise the part by splinting to a rigid structure; the arm can
be strapped to the chest, both legs can be tied together. Temporary splints can be
made from a rolled newspaper, an ice-axe or a branch. Pain may be agonising and
is due to movement of broken bone ends on each other; full doses of strong pain
killers are needed.

The aim of splinting fractures is to reduce pain and bleeding at the fracture site
and thereby reduce shock. Comfort is the best criterion by which to judge the efficiency of a splint, but remember that to immobilise a fracture when the victim is
being carried, splints may need to be tighter than seems necessary for comfort
when at rest, particularly over rough ground.

Wounds at a fracture site or visible bones must be covered immediately with
sterile material or the cleanest material available, and if this happens, start antibiotic treatment at once. Pneumatic splints provide excellent support but may be inadequate when a victim with a broken leg has a difficult stretcher ride across
rough ground. They are of no value for fractured femurs (thigh bones). If you decide to take them, get the Athletic Long Splint which fits over a climbing boot
where the Standard Long Leg splint does not.

WOUNDS (DEEP WOUNDS): Firm pressure on a wound dressing will stop most
bleeding. If blood seeps through, put more dressings on top, secured with ab-
sorbent crêpe bandages and keep up the pressure. You should elevate the injured
part if possible.

On expeditions to remote spots, at least one member of the party should learn to put in simple sutures. This is not difficult – a friendly doctor or casualty sister can teach the essentials in ten minutes. People have practised on a piece of raw meat and on several occasions this has been put to good use. Pulling the wound edges together is all that is necessary, a neat cosmetic result is usually not important.

Swimming

SAFE SWIMMING: Try to swim in pairs: a friend nearby in the water is more likely to distinguish between waving and drowning.

WHEN TO SWIM: Drowning seems rather too obvious a risk to mention here but it is simultaneously the most common and the most serious risk of any water sport, and in many cases alcohol is involved. Don't swim drunk. Some authorities still maintain that swimming after meals runs a risk of stomach cramps, although this is now a minority view.

WHERE TO SWIM: Safe swimmers find local advice before taking to the water. Deserted beaches are often deserted for a reason, whether it be sharks, invisible jellyfish, or vicious rip tides. Beware of polluted water as it is almost impossible to avoid swallowing some. Never dive into water of unknown depth. Broken necks caused by careless diving are a far greater hazard to travellers than crocodiles.

FRESHWATER SWIMMING: Is not advisable when crocodiles or hippopotamuses are in the vicinity. Lakes, ponds, reservoirs, dams, slow streams and irrigation ditches may harbour bilharzia (schistosomiasis). This is a widespread infection in Africa, the Middle East and parts of the Far East and South America, and is a genuine hazard for swimmers.

STRONG CURRENTS: In the sea and rivers, watch out for tides and rips: even a current of one knot is usually enough to exhaust most swimmers quickly. Swimming directly against a strong current is especially exhausting, and, if possible, it is best to swim across the flow, and so gradually make your way to the shore.

SNORKELLING: Snorkelling is a great way to see the seabed, provided that a proper mask is used, enclosing the nose. Eye-goggles can cause bruising and eye damage from the pressure of water. A more serious risk is the practice of hyperventilating (taking several deep breaths) before diving, in the hope of extending a dive. This can kill. Normally, the lungs tell the body to surface for air when the carbon dioxide level is too high. Hyperventilation disrupts this mechanism, so the body can run out of oxygen before the lungs send out their danger signals. This can lead to underwater blackouts, and drowning.

SCUBA DIVING: Scuba divers should be sure that local instruction and equipment is adequate and should always swim with a partner. Do not fly within three hours of diving, or within 24 hours of any dive that requires a decompression stop on the way back to the surface. Travellers who anticipate scuba diving in their travels are strongly advised to have proper training before setting out. 🙰

Travel stress
by Hilary Bradt

THE SCENE IS FAMILIAR: A CROWDED BUS STATION in some Third World country; passengers push and shove excitedly; an angry and discordant voice rings out, 'But I've got a reserved seat! Look, it says number 18, but there's someone sitting there!' The foreigner may or may not win this battle, but ultimately he will lose the war between 'what should be' (his expectations) and 'what is' (their culture) – becoming yet another victim of stress.

It is ironic that this complaint, so fashionable among businessmen, should be such a problem for many travellers who believe they are escaping such pressures when they leave home. But, by travelling rough, they are immediately immersing themselves in a different culture and thus subjecting themselves to a new set of psychological stresses.

The physical deprivations that are inherent in budget travel are not usually a problem. Most travellers adjust well enough to having a shower every two months, eating beans and rice every day and sleeping in dirty, lumpy beds in company with the local wildlife. These are part of the certainties of this mode of travel. It is the uncertainties that wear people down: the buses that double-book their seats, usually leaving an hour late but occasionally slipping away early; the landslide that blocks the road to the coast on the one day of the month that a boat leaves for Paradise Island; the inevitable *mañana* response; the struggle with a foreign language and foreign attitudes.

Culture shock

It is this 'foreignness' that often comes as an unexpected shock. The people are different, their customs are different – and so are their basic values and moralities. Irritatingly, these differences are most frequently exhibited by those who amble down the Third World Corridors of Power that control the fate of travellers. But ordinary people are different, too, and believers in Universal Brotherhood often find this hard to accept – as do women travelling alone. Many travellers escape back to their own culture periodically by mixing with the upper classes of the countries in which they are travelling – people who were educated in Europe or America and are westernised in their outlook.

Come to think of it, maybe this is why hitch-hikers show so few signs of travel stress: they meet wealthier car owners and can often lapse into a childlike dependence on their hosts.

Fear and anxiety

At least hitch-hikers can alternate between blissful relaxation and sheer terror, as can other adventurous travellers. Fear, in small doses, never did anyone any harm. It seems to be a necessary ingredient of everyday life; consciously or unconsciously, most people seek out danger. If they don't rock climb or parachute jump, they drive too fast, refuse to give up smoking or resign from their safe jobs to travel the world. The stab of fear that travellers experience as they traverse a glacier, eye a gun-toting soldier or approach a 'difficult' border is followed by a feeling of exhilaration once the perceived danger has passed.

A rush of adrenaline is OK. The hazard is the prolonged state of tension or stress, to which the body reacts in a variety of ways: irritability, headaches, inability to sleep at night and a continuous feeling of anxiety. The budget traveller is particularly at risk because money shortages provoke so many additional anxieties to the cultural stresses mentioned earlier. The day-to-day worry of running out of money is an obvious one, but there is also the fear of being robbed (no money to replace stolen items) and of becoming ill.

Many travellers worry about their health anyway, but those who cannot afford a doctor, let alone a stay in hospital, can become quite obsessional. Yet these are the people who travel in a manner most likely to jeopardise their health. Since their plan is often 'to travel until the money runs out', those diseases with a long incubation period, such as hepatitis, will manifest themselves during the trip. Chronic illnesses, such as amoebic dysentery, undermine the health and well-being of many budget travellers, leaving them far more susceptible to psychological pressures. Even the open-endedness of their journey may cause anxiety.

Easing the situation

Now I've convinced you that half the world's travellers are heading for a nervous breakdown rather than the nearest beach, let's see what can be done to ease the situation (apart from bringing more money). There are tranquillisers. This is how most doctors treat the symptoms of stress since they assume that the problems causing the anxiety are an unavoidable part of everyday life. Travellers should not rule tranquillisers out (I've met people who consume Valium until they scarcely know who they are), but since they have chosen to be in their situation it should be possible to eliminate some of the causes of stress.

They can begin by asking themselves why they decided to travel in the first place. If the answer is that it was 'to get away from it all', journeying for long distances seems a bit pointless – better to hole up in a small village or island and begin the lotus-eating life. If the motive for travel is a keen interest in natural history, archaeology or people, then the problems inherent in getting to the destination are usually overridden in the excitement of arriving. However, those who find the lets and hindrances that stand between them and their goal too nerve-racking (and the more enthusiastic they are, the more frustrated they will become) should consider relaxing their budget in favour of spending more money on transportation, etc., even if it does mean a shorter trip.

I believe I have a sunny disposition, and am not naturally a grouch. It takes a lot of optimism, after all, to be a traveller.
– PAUL THEROUX

The average overlander, however, considers the journey to be the object and will probably find that time on the road will gradually eliminate his anxieties (like a young man I met in Ecuador: he was forever thinking about his money, but when

I met him again in Bolivia he was a changed man, relaxed and happy. 'Well,' he said, in answer to my question, 'You remember I was always worrying about running out of money? Now I have, so I have nothing to worry about!').

If a traveller can learn the language and appreciate the differences between the countries he visits and his own, he will come a long way towards understanding and finally accepting them. His tensions and frustrations will then finally disappear. But travellers should not expect too much of themselves. You are what you are, and a few months of travel are not going to undo the conditioning of your formative years. Know yourself, your strengths and weaknesses, and plan your trip accordingly. And if you don't know yourself at the start of a long journey, you will by the end. ❧

Hilary Bradt is one of the pioneers of the modern guidebook, founding the Bradt travel guide series in 1974 and winning the 'Sunday Times' Small Publisher of the Year Award in 1997. She is also a tour leader and travel writer, specialising in South America and Madagascar.

Eating and drinking
by Dr Nick Beeching

AIRLINE CATERING APART, ONE OF THE GREAT PLEASURES of travel is the opportunity to sample new foods. Unfortunately, the aphorism 'Travel broadens the mind and loosens the bowels' holds true for the majority of travellers.

A huge variety of micro-organisms cause diarrhoeal illness, with or without vomiting, and these are usually ingested with food or water. Food may carry other health hazards – unpasteurised milk and milk products transmit brucellosis in the Middle East and parts of Africa, and raw fish and crabs harbour a number of unpleasant worm and fluke infections. Even polar explorers face hazards – the liver of carnivores such as polar bears and huskies causes human illness due to Vitamin A poisoning.

Some basic rules

Although it is impossible to avoid infection entirely, the risk can be reduced by following some simple rules. The apparent prestige and expense of a hotel are no guide to the degree of hygiene employed in its kitchens, and the following guidelines apply equally to luxury travellers and those travelling rough.

Assurances from the local population (including long-term expatriates) that food is safe should not be taken too literally. They are likely to have developed immunity to organisms commonly present in their water supply. Sometimes it is impossible to refuse locally prepared food without causing severe offence, and invitations to village feasts will need to be dealt with diplomatically.

The major sources of external contamination of food are unclean water, dirty hands, and flies. Pay scrupulous attention to personal hygiene, and only eat food with your fingers (including breads or fruit) if you have thoroughly washed your hands. Avoid food handled by others who you suspect have not been so careful with their hands – and remember that in many countries toilet paper is not used.

Water

The mains water supply in many countries is contaminated with sewage, while streams, rivers, lakes and reservoirs are freely used as toilets and for personal bathing and washing clothes. The same water may be used for washing food (especially salads and fruit) and may also be frozen to make ice cubes for drinks. Water should always be boiled or treated before drinking or use in the preparation of uncooked food (detailed advice is given in the chapter on *Water Purification*).

Hot tea or coffee are usually safe, as are beer and wine. Bottled water and carbonated drinks or fruit juice are not always safe, although the risk of adulteration or contamination is reduced if you keep to internationally-recognised brands. Insist on seeing the bottle (or can) before it is opened, thus confirming that the seal is tight and the drink has not been tampered with.

If you have any doubts about the cleanliness of plates and cutlery, they can be rinsed in a sterile solution such as tea or coffee, or wiped with an injection swab. If this is not feasible, leave the bottom layer of food on the plate, especially if it is served on a bed of rice. If drinking utensils appear to be contaminated, it may be preferable to drink straight from the bottle.

Food

Food that has been freshly cooked is the safest, but must be served really hot. Beware of food that has been pre-cooked and kept warm for several hours, or desserts (especially those containing cream) that have been inadequately refrigerated after cooking. This includes many hotel buffets. Unpasteurised milk or cheese should be avoided, as should ice cream. Food that has been visited by flies is certain to have been contaminated by excrement and should not be eaten.

Salads and peeled fruit prepared by others may have been washed with contaminated water. In some parts of the tropics, salads may be highly contaminated by human excrement used as fertiliser. Salads and fruits are best avoided, unless you can soak them in water that you know is clean. Unpeeled fruit is safe, provided that you peel it yourself without contaminating the contents. 'Wash it, peel it, boil it or forget it' remains excellent advice.

Shellfish and prawns are particularly high-risk foods because they act as filters, concentrating illness (they often thrive near sewage outfalls). They should only be eaten if thoroughly cooked, and I recommend resisting the temptation altogether. Shellfish and prawns also concentrate biological toxins at certain times of the year, causing a different form of food poisoning. Raw fish, crustaceans and meat should always be avoided.

Hot spices and chillies do not sterilise foods, and chutneys and sauces that are left open on the table may have been visited by flies. Be cautious with chillies: they contain capsaicin which is highly irritable to the bowel lining. Beware of trying to impress your hosts by matching their consumption of hot foods.

Alcohol

The temptation to over-indulge starts on the aeroplane, but in-flight alcohol should be taken sparingly as it increases the dehydration associated with air travel and worsens jet lag. Intoxicated airline passengers are a menace to everybody, and drinking impairs your ability to drive on arrival.

In hot countries, beware of dehydrating yourself with large volumes of alcoholic drink. Alcohol promotes the production of urine and can actually make you more dehydrated.

Excessive alcohol consumption promotes diarrhoea, and prolonged abuse reduces the body's defences against infection. The deleterious social, domestic and professional hazards of prolonged alcohol abuse are well recognised problems for expatriates. ❧

Water purification
by Julian McIntosh

POLLUTED WATER CAN AT BEST LEAD TO DISCOMFORT and mild illness, at worst to death, so the travelling layman needs to know not only what methods and products are available for water purification, but also how to improvise a treatment system in an emergency.

Three points about advice on water treatment cause misunderstanding. Firstly, there is no need to kill or remove all the micro-organisms in water. Germs do not necessarily cause disease. Only those responsible for diseases transmitted by drinking water need be treated. And even some water-borne diseases are harmless when drunk. Legionnaires' disease, for example, is caught by breathing in droplets of water containing the bacteria, and not by drinking them.

Secondly, in theory, no normal treatment method will produce infinitely safe drinking water. There is always a chance, however small, that a germ might, by virtue of small size or resistance to chemicals or heat, survive and cause disease. But the more exacting your water treatment process, the smaller the risk – until such time as the risk is so tiny as to be discounted. The skill of the experts lies in assessing when water is, in practice, safe to drink. Unfortunately different experts set their standards at different levels.

Thirdly, beware the use of words like 'pure', 'disinfect' and 'protection', common claims in many manufacturers' carefully written prose. Read the descriptions critically and you will find that most are not offering absolutely safe water but only a relative improvement.

Suspended solids

If you put dirty water in a glass the suspended solids are the tiny particles that do not readily sink to the bottom. The resolution of the human eye is about one-hundredth of a millimetre, so a particle half that size (five microns) is totally invisible to the naked eye – and yet there can be over ten million such particles in a litre of water without any visible trace. Suspended solids are usually materials such as decaying vegetable matter or mud and clay. Normally mud and clay contamination is harmless, but extremely fine rock particles including mica or asbestos occasionally remain in glacier water or water running through some types of clay.

Microbiological contamination

EGGS, WORMS, FLUKES, ETC: These organisms, amongst others, lead to infections of roundworm (*Ascaris*), canine roundworm (*Toxocara canis*), guinea worm (*Dracunculus*) and bilharzia (schistosomiasis). They are relatively large, although still microscopic, and can be removed by even crude forms of filtration. The tiny black things that you sometimes see wriggling in still water are insect larvae, not germs, and are not harmful. Almost any form of pre-treatment will remove them.

PROTOZOA: In this group of small, single-celled animals, are the organisms that cause giardiasis (*Giardia lamblia*), an unpleasant form of chronic diarrhoea, and amoebic dysentery (*Entamoeba histolytica*). Both of these protozoa have a cyst stage in their life cycle, during which they are inert and resistant to some forms of chemical treatment. However, they quickly become active and develop when they encounter suitable conditions such as the human digestive tract. They are sufficiently large to be separable from the water by the careful use of some types of prefilter. This is not always true for a common water borne protozoan called *Cryptosporidium parvum* that causes diarrhoea in all parts of the world and which may be lethal in immunocompromised people, e.g. those with advanced AIDS. The cysts are small enough to pass through many filters and are relatively resistant to chlorine, and are best destroyed by boiling water.

BACTERIA: These very small, single-celled organisms are responsible for many illnesses from cholera, salmonella, typhoid and bacillary dysentery to the less serious forms of diarrhoea known to travellers as Montezuma's Revenge or Delhi Belly. A healthy person would need to drink thousands of a particular bacterium to catch the disease. Luckily, the harmful bacteria transmitted by drinking contaminated water are fairly 'soft' and succumb to chemical treatment – their minute size means only a very few filters can be relied upon to remove them all.

VIRUSES: These exceptionally small organisms live and multiply within host cells. Some viruses such as hepatitis A, and a variety of intestinal infections, are transmitted through drinking water. Even the finest filters are too coarse to retain viruses. The polio and hepatitis viruses are about 50 times smaller than the pore size in even the finest ceramic filter.

Selection of a water supply

Whatever method of water treatment you use, it is essential to start with the best possible supply of water. Learning to assess the potential suitability of a water supply is one of the traveller's most useful skills.

GOOD SOURCES: Ground water, e.g. wells, boreholes, springs; water away from or upstream of human habitation; fast-running water; water above a sand or rock bed; clear, colourless and odourless water. Fast running water is a hostile environment for the snails that support bilharzia.

BAD SOURCES: Water close to sources of industrial, human or animal contamination; stagnant water; water containing decaying vegetation; water with odour or scum on its surface; discoloured or muddy water. Wells and boreholes can be contaminated by debris or excreta falling in from the surface, so the top should be protected. A narrow wall will stop debris. A broad wall is less effective, as people will stand on it and dirt from their feet can fall in. Any wall is better than no wall at all.

Pre-treatment

If you are using water from a river, pool or lake, try to not to draw in extra dirt from the bottom or floating debris from the surface. If the source is surface water, such as a lake or river, and very poor, some benefit may even be gained by digging a hole adjacent to the source. As the water seeps through, a form of pre-filtration will take place, leaving behind at least the coarsest contamination.

Pouring the water through finely woven fabrics will also remove some of the larger contamination. If you have fine, clean sand available, perhaps taken from a stream or lake bed, an improvised sand filter can be made using a tin can or similar container with a hole in the bottom. Even a (clean) sock will do. Pour the water into the top, over the sand. Take care to disturb the surface of the sand as little as possible. Collect the water that has drained through the sand. The longer the filter is used, the better the quality of the water, so re-filter or discard the first water poured through. Discard the contaminated sand after use.

If you are able to store the water without disturbing it, you could also try sedimentation. Much of the dirt in water will settle out if left over a long enough period. Bilharzia flukes die after about 48 hours. The cleaner water can then be drawn off at the top. Very great care will be needed not to disturb the dirt at the bottom. Siphoning is the best method.

If the water you are using has an unpleasant taste or smell, an improvement can be achieved by using coarsely crushed wood charcoal wrapped in cloth. When the 'bag' of charcoal is placed in the water, or the water is run through the charcoal (like a sand filter), the organic chemicals responsible for practically all the unpleasant tastes and smells will be removed. Some colour improvement may also be noticed. The water will still not be safe to drink without further treatment, but you should notice some benefit.

Treatment of a water supply

Boiling

Boiling at 100°C kills all the harmful organisms found in water, except a very few such as slow viruses and spores which are not dangerous if drunk. However, as your altitude above sea level increases, the weight of the atmosphere above you decreases, the air pressure drops, as does the temperature at which water boils. A rule of thumb for calculating this is that water boils at 1°c less for every 300 metres of altitude. If you are on the summit of Kilimanjaro, at 5895 metres, water will boil at only 80°c. At temperatures below 100°c, most organisms can still be killed but it takes longer. At temperatures below 70°c, some of the harmful organisms can survive indefinitely and as the temperature continues to drop, so they will flourish.

There is one more important consideration. When water is boiling vigorously, there is a lot of turbulence and all the water is at the same temperature. While water is coming to the boil, even if bubbles are rising, there is not only a marked and important difference between the temperature of the water and the temperature at a full boil, but there can also be a substantial difference in temperature between water in different parts of the pan, with the result that harmful organisms may still be surviving. To make water safe for drinking, you should bring water to a full boil for at least two minutes. Boil water for one minute extra for every 300 metres above sea level. Do not cool water down with untreated water.

Filtration

The key to understanding the usefulness of a filter is ensuring that you know the size of the particles that the filter will reliably separate, and the dirt-load the filter can tolerate before it clogs up. If the pores in the filter are too large, harmful particles can pass through. If small enough to stop harmful particles, the pores can block up quickly, preventing any more water from being filtered.

To reduce this problem, manufacturers employ ingenious means to increase the filter area, and filter in at progressively smaller stages. But even in one apparently clean litre of water there can be a hundred thousand million particles the same size or larger than bacteria. And to stop a bacterium, the filter has to take out all the other particles as well. If the filter is small (of the drinking straw type for instance) or if the water is at all visibly dirty, the filter will block in next to no time.

There are three solutions: water can be filtered first through a coarse filter to remove most of the dirt, and then again through a fine filter to remove the harmful bacteria; a re-cleanable filter can be used; or finally, only apparently clean water could be used with the filter. The use of a coarser filter is called pre-filtration. Viruses are so small they cannot be filtered out of drinking water by normal means. However, because they are normally found with their host infected cells and these are large enough to be filtered, the finest filters are also able to reduce the risk of virus infection from drinking water.

A filter collects quite a lot of miscellaneous debris on its surface and, in order to prevent this providing a breeding ground for bacteria, the filter needs to be sterilised from time to time. Some are self-sterilising and need no action, but others should be boiled for 20 to 30 minutes at least once every two weeks.

Where filters are described as combining a chemical treatment, this is for self-sterilisation. The chemical is in such small concentrations and in contact with water passing through the filter for such a short period that its use in improving the quality of the filtered water is negligible.

PRE-FILTRATION: Pre-filters should remove particles larger than five to ten microns in size and be very simple to maintain. They will be more resistant to clogging since they take out only the larger particles. They will remove larger microbiological contamination including protozoal cysts, flukes and larger debris that might form a refuge for bacteria and viruses. Pre-filtration is normally adequate for washing. Further treatment is essential for safe drinking supplies.

FINE FILTRATION: To remove all harmful bacteria from water, a filter must remove all particles larger than 0.5 microns (some harmless bacteria are as small as 0.2 microns). Filters using a disposable cartridge are generally more compact and have high initial flow rates, but are more expensive to operate. Alternatively there are ceramic filters that use porous ceramic 'candles'. These have low flow rates and are fairly heavy. Some need special care in transport to ensure they do not get cracked or chipped thus enabling untreated water to get through. Ceramic filters can be cleaned easily and are very economic in use.

ACTIVATED CARBON/CHARCOAL FILTERS: These remove a wide range of chemicals from water, including chlorine and iodine, and can greatly improve the quality and palatability of water. But they do not kill or remove germs, and may even provide an ideal breeding ground unless self-sterilising. Some filters combine carbon and other elements to improve taste; this also removes harmful organisms.

Chemical treatment

Broadly speaking, there are three germicidal chemicals used for drinking-water treatment. For ease of use, efficiency and storage life, the active chemical is usually made up as a tablet suitable for a fixed volume of water, although the heavier the contamination, the larger the dose required. Germs can also be embedded in other matter and protected from the effects of a chemical, so where water is visibly dirty you must pre-filter first. Chlorine and iodine have no lasting germicidal effect so on no account should untreated water be added to water already treated.

SILVER: Completely harmless, taste-free and very long-lasting effect, protecting stored water for up to six months. The sterilisation process is quite slow and it is necessary to leave water for at least two hours before use. Silver compounds are not effective against cysts of *Amoeba* and *Giardia*, so use pre-filtration first if the water is of poor quality.

CHLORINE: Completely harmless, fast-acting and 100 per cent effective if used correctly. A minimum of ten minutes is required before water can be used. The cysts of *Amoeba* and *Giardia* are about ten times more resistant to chlorine than bacteria, but both are killed if treatment time and dose are adequate. If in doubt, we recommend that the period before use be extended to at least 20 and preferably 30 minutes. If heavy contamination is suspected, double the dosage. Alternatively, pre-filter. Some people find the taste of chlorine unpleasant particularly if larger doses are being used. The concentration of chlorine drops quickly over several hours and more so in warm temperatures so there is very little lasting effect. Excess chlorine may be removed using sodium thiosulphate or carbon filters.

IODINE: Fast acting and very effective, normally taking ten minutes before water is safe to use. It has a quicker action against cysts than chlorine. Double dosage and extended treatment times or pre-filtration are still very strongly recommended if heavy contamination is suspected. Iodine is more volatile than chlorine and the lasting effect is negligible. Excess iodine may be removed by sodium thiosulphate or a carbon filter.

NOTE: Iodine can have serious, lasting physiological side effects and should not be used over an extended period. Groups particularly at risk are those with thyroid problems and the unborn foetuses of pregnant women. Thyroid problems may only become apparent when the gland is faced with excess iodine, so in the unlikely event of the use of iodine compounds being unavoidable, ask your doctor to arrange for a thyroid test beforehand – or use a good carbon filter to remove excess iodine from the water.

Rules for treatment

ORDER OF TREATMENT: If chemical treatment and filtration are being combined, filter first. Filtration removes organic matter which would absorb the chemical and make it less effective. If of a carbon type, the filter will also absorb the chemical leaving none for residual treatment. In some cases, the filter may also be a source of contamination. If water is being stored prior to treatment then it is worthwhile treating chemically as soon as the water is collected and again after filtration. The first chemical dose prevents algae growing in the stored water.

STORAGE OF WATER: Use separate containers for treated and untreated water, mark them accordingly and don't mix them up. If you are unable to use separate containers take particular care to sterilise the area round the filler and cap before treated water is stored or at the time treatment takes place. In any case, containers for untreated water should be sterilised every two to three weeks. Treated water should never be contaminated with any untreated water. Treated water should never be stored in an open container. Treated water left uncovered and not used straight away should be regarded as suspect and re-treated. ❧

JULIAN MCINTOSH has lived in Africa and travelled extensively. His overland experiences prompted him to set up his own tropical equipment company.

Diarrhoeal illness
by Dr Nick Beeching

THE WORLD-WIDE DISTRIBUTION OF TRAVELLER'S DIARRHOEA is reflected in its many geographical synonyms – Delhi belly, the Aztec two-step, Turista, Malta dog, Rangoon runs, to name a few. Typically, the illness starts a few days after arrival at your destination and consists of diarrhoea without blood, nausea with some vomiting and perhaps a mild fever. The mainstay of treatment is adequate rehydration and rest, and the illness is usually self-limiting within a few days. Antibiotics to treat or prevent this common illness are not usually prescribed in anticipation of an infection. Exceptions to this rule are business travellers or others embarking on short trips (less than two to three weeks) for whom even a short period of illness would be disastrous, e.g. athletes attending international meetings.

The most important aspect of the treatment of diarrhoea is the replacement of fluids and salts that have been lost from the body. For most adults, non-carbonated, non-alcoholic drinks that do not contain large amounts of sugar are quite adequate. For adults with prolonged diarrhoea and for children, it is more important to use balanced weak salt solutions which contain a small amount of sugar that promotes absorption of the salts. These can be obtained in pre-packaged sachets of powder (e.g. Dioralyte, Rehidrat) that are convenient to carry and are dissolved in a fixed amount of sterile water. Dioralyte can also be bought in the UK as effervescent tablets, or as Dioralyte Relief sachets which contain pre-cooked rice powder. This has the advantage of returning the watery stools to normal more rapidly, as well as replacing the salts which have been lost in the diarrhoea. If pre-packaged mixtures are not available, a simple rehydration solution can be prepared by adding eight level teaspoonfuls of sugar or honey and half a teaspoon of salt to one litre of water (with flavouring to tempt small children).

In every book I ever read
Of travels on the Equator,
A plague, mysterious and dread,
Imperils the narrator.
- HILAIRE BELLOC

Nausea, which frequently accompanies diarrhoea, can usually be overcome by taking small amounts of fluid as often as possible. For small children it may be necessary to give spoonfuls of fluid every few minutes for prolonged periods. If you or your child have severe vomiting which prevents any fluids being taken, medical attention must be sought immediately.

Anti-diarrhoeal drugs are not usually recommended and should rarely be given to children. Kaopectate is safe for children aged over two years but not very effective (Kaolin and morphine should not be carried). For adults, codeine phosphate, loperamide (Imodium or Arret) or diphenoxylate (Lomotil) are sometimes useful. These drugs should never be given to children and should not be used for bloody or prolonged diarrhoea. They are best reserved for occasional use to prevent accidents while travelling – for example before a prolonged rural bus trip. Prolonged use of these medications may prevent your body from eliminating the diarrhoea – causing organisms and toxins which may lead to constipation.

Preparations containing clioquinol are still widely available outside the UK, where it was previously sold under the trade name Enterovioform. These preparations are useless and should not be taken (they have been linked with severe side effects in some parts of the world). Other than rehydration solutions or the medications discussed in this article, I do not recommend purchasing medicines for diarrhoea from pharmacies or chemists.

Prevention

Travellers who wish to prevent diarrhoea should consult their medical adviser about preventative medication (a controversial issue within the profession) before travel. Liquid bismuth preparations (not an antibiotic) are effective but huge volumes need to be carried in luggage (very messy if broken), and bismuth tablets are difficult to obtain in the UK. Various groups of antibiotics may be used, including tetracyclines (e.g. doxycycline), sulphur containing antibiotics (e.g. Steptrotriad or cotrimoxazole, Septrin or Bactrim) and quinolone agents (e.g. ciprofloxacin, norfloxacin).

Prophylactic antibiotics are not recommended for the majority of travellers because of the limited duration of effectiveness and the possibility of side effects, including, paradoxically, diarrhoea. Vaccines are currently being developed to help prevent traveller's diarrhoea. The most promising vaccine is currently undergoing field trials in travellers and is looking safe and effective. This may be a good option for the future.

Self-treatment

Self-treatment with antibiotics for established diarrhoeal illness is usually inappropriate unless qualified medical attention is impossible to obtain. Travellers to remote areas may wish to carry a course of antibiotics for this eventuality.

- ■ Bloody diarrhoea with abdominal pain and fever may be due to bacillary dysentery (shigella organisms) or a variety of other organisms such as campylobacter or salmonella. The most appropriate antibiotic would be a quinolone such as ciprofloxacin, or a sulphur drug such as cotrimoxazole.
- ■ Prolonged bloody diarrhoea with mucus (jelly), especially without much fever, may be due to amoebic dysentery which is treated with metronidazole (Flagyl) or tinidazole (Fasigyn).
- ■ Prolonged, explosive diarrhoea with pale creamy motions may be due to giardia, a common hazard for overlanders travelling through the Indian subcontinent. This responds to metronidazole or tinidazole. These two antibiotics should not be taken at the same time as alcohol because of severe reactions between them.

If you have to treat yourself, obtain qualified medical investigation and help at the earliest opportunity. This is essential if symptoms do not settle after medication. Diarrhoea may be caused by other, more severe illnesses, including typhoid and malaria, and these would need specific treatment

Travellers who anticipate the need for self-treatment should take Richard Dawood's book *Travellers Health: How to Stay Healthy Abroad* (OUP). ࿓

Health in the heat
by Dr Richard Dawood

TRAVEL BROADENS THE MIND AND BRINGS UNTOLD BENEFITS to the human spirit, but in doing so it often rains a multitude of physiological insults upon the human body. Dehydration is one of the most fundamental of these, but there have been some important recent developments in our understanding of its mechanisms and how to avoid it.

Dehydration

In a temperate climate, most people need a daily fluid intake of two litres of water to remain in balance. In a hot, humid climate, and with increased physical activity, ten litres a day (one seventh of body weight) and sometimes more may be needed.

It takes about three weeks for people who normally live in a temperate climate to acclimatise to a hot one: for most trips by British holiday-makers, there is therefore no chance of acclimatising fully. During acclimatisation, sweat glands develop the ability to produce more sweat, to respond more quickly and to lose less salt; stomach and intestines also adapt to become better able to absorb salt and water more efficiently. Without acclimatisation, newcomers to hot climates have difficulty conserving water and salt and are at a significant risk of developing heat-related illnesses. (Excessive physical exertion increases the risk; avoid this until acclimatisation is complete.)

Acclimatisation is usually much more difficult in hot and humid climates than hot and dry ones. In humid climates, sweat does not evaporate easily and temperature and humidity tend to remain high through the night. This is a continuous stress, whereas in dry climates they both tend to fall at night, allowing the sweating mechanism to rest.

Small, thin people tend to acclimatise most easily to the heat – because their body surface area is relatively higher in relation to their volume, giving a relatively greater area from which to sweat and lose heat. Unfit, overweight people acclimatise more slowly, and do badly in the heat. People with high blood pressure and heart disease may be at risk from complications.

To remain in balance under such conditions, the body needs a greatly increased intake of salt and water. The trouble is that thirst and taste give an extremely poor indication of exactly how much is required. Many people have a reduced appetite on first arrival in a warm climate, which may reduce salt intake even further.

Deficiency of salt, water, or both, is called heat exhaustion. Lethargy, fatigue and headache are typical features, eventually leading to coma and death. Many sufferers do not even feel thirsty, and may have no idea that they are suffering from this problem. They feel 'hung over'. In fact, most symptoms of a typical, bad hangover are the direct result of dehydration. They feel irritable, and simply want to be left alone.

Prevention is by far the best approach. Perhaps the best method is the British

Army's pre-salted water regime. Salt is added to all fluids —tea, coffee, soup, fruit juices, water. The required amount is one quarter of a level teaspoon (approximately one gram) per pint – which results in a solution that is just below the taste threshold. (Don't use salt tablets: they are poorly absorbed, irritate the stomach and may cause vomiting.) Plenty of pre-salted fluid should be the rule for anyone spending much time in the tropics.

The only reliable guide to how much you need to drink in a tropical climate is the colour of your urine. Always drink enough to ensure that it is consistently pale in colour, and don't just wait until you feel thirsty before drinking.

Heat exhaustion should not be confused with heatstroke (formerly called sunstroke). Although dehydration is almost always a factor, the main problem is a failure of the body's heat control mechanisms. Sweating diminishes and the body temperature rises, headache and delirium also occur. Prompt treatment is essential. Once the body temperature begins to rise, death may occur within four hours. The priority is to lower body temperature. Remove clothing, and cover the victim with a wet bed-sheet, while arranging transfer to hospital. There are well-documented cases of travellers who have been left in their hotel rooms to die, simply because their condition was mistaken for a drunken stupor.

Infectious diseases that cause a fever can sometimes be mistaken for heatstroke, again with potentially fatal results. Malaria and meningitis are especially important in this context, because in both cases deterioration is rapid if treatment is not given.

Prickly heat

Prickly heat is the most common heat-related skin disorder – a sweat rash occurring on the sweatier parts of the body and consisting of tiny blisters on sore, reddened, mildly inflamed skin. You can prevent it with frequent showers and by keeping the skin clean and dry. Treat with calamine lotion.

Brown without burning

The effects of the sun on skin include sunburn, thickening and – in the longer term – drying, loss of elasticity, wrinkling, loosening, discolouration, premature ageing and skin cancer. People with fair, blond or red hair are most at risk, even after they've turned grey. Acute sunburn is a miserable way to begin a holiday. It results in a blotchy uneven tan and is all the more miserable for children whose skin is easily damaged.

If you're not bothered about a tan, cover up and use a high-protection factor sunscreen. But if vanity gets the better of you, tan very slowly. The protection factor numbers on skin preparations provide a rough measure of how much longer you can stay out in the sun without burning. If your skin normally burns in strong sunlight after 20 minutes' exposure, for example, a sunscreen with a protection factor of four will allow you to stay out for four times as long (80 minutes). After that, you would have to cover up; you would have had your maximum dose of sunlight, and more factor four would not protect you. If you wanted to stay out in the sun for 160 minutes, you would burn if you used anything less than a protection factor of eight. Protection factor numbers refer mainly to UVB protection – protection against the rays that cause acute sunburn. Protection against UVA – the rays mainly responsible for ageing and skin cancer effects – is usually shown by means of a 'star rating' system. Clearly, using a sunscreen that only protected against UVB rays but allowed people to spend more time in the sun, might actually increase the possibility of long-term damage. Check that any product you use gives protection against both.

Apart from cosmetic acceptability and protection factor, there is, however, little else to choose between the different brands of sunscreen. Whichever brand you pick, you should re-apply it frequently, especially when swimming or sweating. Most of the leading manufacturers now produce waterproof sunscreens which are particularly useful for children.

Some parts of the body are especially vulnerable and need extra care – the face, particularly the nose and forehead, neck and ears; parts of the body that are normally covered; the tops of the collar bones, bald patches on the scalp; and feet. Avoid sunbathing in the hottest part of the day and be guided by the habits of those more accustomed to hot climates, who take a relaxing indoor siesta instead.

If you burn, calamine lotion will soothe affected areas and mild painkillers are often helpful. More extensive or severe burns should be treated with a mild antiseptic and kept clean and dry. Stay out of the sun or use a total block sunscreen until the skin has healed.

The eyes, too, can be affected by the sun. The conjunctiva and retina are sensitive to ultra-violet light and are easily damaged. Pain usually begins several hours after exposure, when the delicate cells of the conjunctiva swell and become painful and inflamed. In the long term, excessive exposure to the elements causes a pterygium – an unsightly yellow patch on the white of the eye that may need to be removed. Good quality sunglasses provide effective protection.

Skin cancer and the sun

In the last few years, the number of cases of skin cancer in the UK has risen. The number of people taking holidays abroad has also risen, so the Royal College of Physicians in London commissioned a special study to determine whether or not there was a link. The results of this work have important implications for travellers: it found that the risks of skin cancer and skin damage from strong sunlight relate not just to long-term exposure, but also to the number of episodes of acute sunburn.

Skin cancers grow slowly and tend to destroy the area of skin in their immediate vicinity. Since they usually occur on exposed areas – President Reagan's nose was one well-publicised site – they can inflict much cosmetic damage. Some types – melanomas especially – become able to spread through the body. The Royal College of Physicians advises examining every pigmented patch and mole on your skin as follows:

1. Does it itch, or sensation alter over it?
2. Is its diameter 1 cm or more?
3. Is it increasing in size?

4. Is its border irregular in shape?
5. Does the density of black or brown colour within it vary?
6. Is the patch inflamed?
7. Is there bleeding or crusting?

If the answer is 'yes' to three or more of these questions, seek medical advice. The treatment is simple if the cancer is detected at an early stage. 🐾

DR RICHARD DAWOOD is Medical Director of the Fleet Street Travel Clinic and the author of 'Traveller's Health: How to Stay Healthy Abroad'.

Altitude sickness
by Dr Richard Dawood

MY FIRST EXPOSURE TO THE EFFECT OF HIGH ALTITUDE was in Nepal several years ago. I was on a trek six days' journey from Kathmandu. It is a bizarre and unnerving feeling to discover that your exercise tolerance is suddenly no more than a few slow paces, that your pulse races with each step you take, and that you are obliged to stop to catch your breath every few feet, waiting for the palpitations to subside while local people of all ages – some carrying heavy loads – stop, stare, then overtake. I was a fit young medical student, but my body felt as though it belonged to the victim of some dreadful disease that I had just been studying – chronic bronchitis, perhaps emphysema or asbestosis. I developed a hammering headache, and became more and more breathless, even at rest.

I was lucky, although I didn't know it at the time; these are important warning signs of acute mountain sickness (AMS). I decided to come down. In fact, members of the medical profession have a poor track record when it comes to heeding their own symptoms, and an especially poor record at high altitude. In a report on seven deaths from mountain sickness on Himalayan treks, three of the seven who died were themselves doctors.

The tragic fact about deaths from mountain sickness is that they are preventable in every case. The purpose of this article is therefore threefold: to offer some practical information about AMS, its warning signs and prevention; to discuss the merits of the drugs that are sometimes suggested for its prevention; and to consider other approaches to emergency treatment.

Mountain sickness

The driving force for the absorption of oxygen through the lungs into the bloodstream is atmospheric pressure – the 'weight' of the column of air that extends for ten miles or so above our heads. As we ascend, atmospheric pressure is reduced. Complex mechanisms exist to compensate for the resulting lack of oxygen: these include an increase in breathing rate and depth, as well as changes in the blood and tissues that increase their efficiency in carrying and using oxygen. However, the increased breathing results in reduced levels of carbon dioxide, causing the body to become more alkaline and, in turn, causing numerous other physiological changes to occur, not all of which are clearly understood. The kidneys are able to compensate for changes in alkalinity and acidity, but the process of acclimatisation to high altitude can take several days – longer under conditions of low temperature and increased exercise.

AMS tends to occur within two days of exposure. It usually begins with loss of appetite, headache, nausea, vomiting and sleeplessness. This is the early, benign form. It may simply resolve, but may also progress to a more serious, so-called 'malignant' form. It should be regarded as an important warning.

Malignant AMS can be fatal, and it may begin with little or no warning. Pulmonary oedema develops – a build-up of fluid in the lung tissues – which further interferes with absorption of oxygen, leading to breathlessness that persists even at rest. There is also a cough, with white, pink or frothy sputum, and the lips may turn blue. A build-up of tissue may also occur in the brain – cerebral oede-

> *Did any man know of any good befalling him from going up a mountain?*
> *– ANTHONY TROLLOPE*

ma. This results in headache, drowsiness, impaired co-ordination, abnormal or drunken behaviour, confusion, impaired consciousness and coma. Progression to coma may occur quite rapidly.

Benign AMS can be handled initially by remaining at the same altitude until symptoms resolve. If they do not improve, the best treatment is prompt descent. Victims of malignant AMS need to be brought down immediately, and most sufferers need to be carried down. Experts on AMS advise that descent should not be delayed while aid is summoned, and should start even at night, if necessary.

Mountain sickness is most often a problem at altitudes over 2,600 to 3,000 metres, though in some people it may occur as low as 2,350 metres. This means that a hazard exists at many popular travel destinations. Crucial factors in determining susceptibility to AMS are speed of ascent, and the altitude at which you sleep. If possible, begin by avoiding sleeping above 3,000 metres for the first few nights. 'Climb high, Sleep low', is the rule to follow. Then increase your sleeping altitude by no more than 300 or so metres per day – even this may be too fast for some people to adapt to.

High on drugs

While the most important approach to treatment is descent, there is an increasing trend towards advising trekkers and climbers to consider carrying medication. There are two drugs for the treatment and prevention of AMS, acetazolamide (Diamox) and dexamethasone. A third drug, nifedipine, has shown promising results.

Acetazolamide is a diuretic drug that increases excretion of bicarbonate by the kidney, tending to counteract the increase in alkalinity referred to above. Some experts consider that it speeds acclimatisation, while others believe that it may mask early symptoms that are not a great nuisance in themselves, but that provide useful warning signs that severe AMS may be developing. There is no consensus. I have spoken to doctors who swear by acetazolamide, and to others who are greatly troubled by such side-effects as nausea, tiredness, poor sleep, and 'pins and needles' in the arms and legs. There are many cases on record of malignant AMS occurring despite the use of acetazolamide. It may, nonetheless, provide some worthwhile benefit.

Dexamethasone is a powerful 'steroid' drug that has many actions; the most beneficial of these, as far as high altitude is concerned, is a tendency to reduce oedema. It does not affect acclimatisation, but merely alleviates some of the symptoms. It is safe for most people when taken for only short periods, but serious side-effects do occur, especially in people with diabetes. It may be useful to carry this drug for emergency use in descent.

Portable recompression chambers

The best treatment for a victim of the effects of reduced oxygen pressure is, obviously, to increase the pressure. Bringing the victim down to a lower altitude is usually the fastest and simplest way of doing this. However, a new approach also has its appeal. This is the use of a simple, portable compression chamber. These look like oversized sleeping bags that can simply be inflated with a foot-pump. It has to be pumped continuously, to eliminate waste gases, and this can be tiring at altitude. Alternatively, a carbon dioxide extractor is available for it. A larger model capable of accommodating two people is also available.

Achievable compression is roughly equivalent to a 1,500-metre descent, depending on your altitude. This would certainly buy time in an emergency, though there is no substitute for real descent for people who are seriously ill. It has already been used with great success by expeditions to remote places where rescue is difficult. Its cost makes it suitable for groups and expeditions rather than routine treks.

In one case, however, one victim of AMS died while left unattended overnight in such a chamber. It is very important for people with AMS to be carefully monitored throughout the course of their illness and to be brought down if there is no rapid response to the increased pressure.

Conclusion

The best approach to AMS is prevention, and the most important measure is gradual ascent. Problems are particularly common with people on a tight time schedule, who fly in to high-altitude destinations and try to cram in the maximum amount of sights and activity into the shortest time possible. One simply cannot expect to be able to fly in to such places as La Paz, Cusco or Leh and carry on sightseeing without allowing ample time – perhaps several days – for rest and acclimatisation. Yet there are cases on record where unfit, elderly people have been booked on tours to Peru without any warning about the dangers of high altitude, and have died as a result. Mountain sickness is a preventable illness, and all travellers to high-altitude regions should make sure they are fully informed about it. ❧

Sex abroad
by Dr Richard Dawood

Have you talked to your doctor about sex, lately? Doctors who give pre-travel health advice are generally more inclined to launch into a discussion of the latest research into malaria, or even travellers' diarrhoea, than raise the issue of casual sex. After all, doesn't everybody already know about HIV? The truth is, however, that one important fact about HIV seems to have escaped most people's attention: HIV infection resulting from sex abroad has now overtaken every other tropical and infectious disease hazard to become the single most frequent cause of lethal infection in travellers.

The comparison between HIV and malaria is an interesting one. Malaria's place in the pantheon of travel-related disease, and in the thoughts and fears of departing travellers and their doctors, is secure. There are approximately 2,000 cases of malaria in British travellers every year, causing between ten and 15 deaths. We agonise over each fatal case that occurs in the near-certain knowledge that it could have been prevented, and we scrutinise every detail for lessons that can be learned for the future. Yet during 1999 there were 969 confirmed cases of HIV infection resulting from heterosexual sex abroad. These cases include migrants to the UK, not just travellers; but in view of the long delay before infection becomes apparent, they represent the tip of a much larger iceberg: the true rate of infection is probably twice this number. The HIV infection rate in travellers is currently 100 times higher than the fatality rate from malaria, and it is rising.

These figures mean that no fewer than 85 per cent of British HIV cases in heterosexuals are acquired abroad. So far, most of these overseas infections have originated in Africa, but other regions are catching up – especially Asia and the countries of the former USSR.

In developing countries worldwide, the rates of HIV infection are mounting, and the pattern of infection is also changing. HIV is increasingly a disease of the young: some 60 per cent of new infections are in people aged between 15 and 24. Young women are particularly at risk: in Uganda, for example, the rate of infection among women in the 13 to 19 age group is 20 times higher than it is in men, and a recent survey of pregnant teenage women in Zimbabwe found 30 per cent of them to be HIV positive. Among people of both sexes in the commercial sex industry, infection rates in many parts of the developing world approach 100 per cent.

Other sexually transmitted diseases, from gonorrhoea and syphilis to more exotic and unfamiliar diseases such as chancroid, may seem to pale into insignificance beside the risks of HIV, but they have not disappeared from the scene: STDs are now nearly as common as malaria, with more than 250 million new cases worldwide every year: each year, one in 20 adolescents worldwide contracts a sexually transmitted disease.

How have travellers responded to these growing risks? In a survey of 782 returning travellers at the Hospital for Tropical Diseases, in London, 18.6 per cent reported having sex with at least one new partner while away, almost half of them with more than one partner. Another, smaller survey, found that 12 out of 17 people who admitted to having sex with a new partner while abroad had carried condoms, but had failed to use them on account of getting very drunk. A recent Swiss study found that four per cent of Swiss visitors to Kenya had sex with local people, often without using condoms, while a survey of Swedish travellers found that 28 per cent had sex with a new partner while travelling in Europe. These figures appear to reflect remarkable levels of restraint by comparison with a British survey of visitors to Torquay, where, out of 1,000 people aged 16–29, 600 said that they had had sex with a new partner without a condom during their visit. (Another finding from the same study: holiday-makers who were engaged to be married but had left their partners at home were more likely to report a sexual encounter than other visitors.)

Sex with fellow travellers rather than local people is not necessarily an entirely safer option since surveys have shown that many people are prepared to lie in order to have sex. One survey of young, sexually active Californians showed that 47 per cent of the men and 60 per cent of the women claimed that they had been lied to for the purposes of sex; 34 per cent of the men and ten per cent of the women admitted that they themselves would also be prepared to lie. Twenty per cent of the men said that they would lie about having a negative HIV-antibody test, and nearly half of both men and women said that they would understate their number of previous partners. Of those who had been sexually involved with more than one person at a time, more than half said their partners did not know.

Fastidiousness is a wretched travelling companion.
— WILLIAM WORDSWORTH

In Thailand, where the sex tourist once reigned supreme, public attitudes are only now beginning to change. Largely through the efforts of former government minister Mechay Viravaidya (widely known in his country as Mr Condom), an energetic programme of public education and condom distribution is under way. In the Philippines, a British travel agent received a 16 year prison sentence for organising paedophile sex tours into the country as part of a new drive by President Fidel Ramos to curb sex tourism. Such initiatives are still relatively rare in the developing world, and will have to be carefully planned, vigorous and sustained before they will have any real impact upon the health of local people.

When Edwina Currie advised travellers to avoid temptation by taking along their partner, she at least managed to hit the headlines. Current British efforts to educate departing travellers consist of distributing soft-sell leaflets to GP waiting rooms and an occasional poster at Heathrow. Until we can find more effective ways to increase public awareness of the problem, and to persuade travellers to avoid or reduce their exposure, HIV infection will remain the most formidable disease hazard of modern international travel. ❧

The pregnant traveller
by Dr Richard Dawood

PARADOXICALLY, SOME OF THE HAZARDS OF TRAVEL during pregnancy have increased in recent years. This is partly due to the continuing spread of drug-resistant malaria, and also arises from the fact that countries with poor medical care have become increasingly accessible to the adventurous traveller.

Good antenatal care has brought about a dramatic reduction in the complications of pregnancy, and travel has become almost too easy – it is often taken for granted. Perhaps the first hazard that the pregnant woman faces is a psychological one; pregnancy is not the ideal time for adventurous travel, but there is a widespread belief that travel to any country should be possible and that the fact of pregnancy should not be allowed to get in the way.

The early weeks of pregnancy are an important time to be at one's home base. It is necessary to begin planning antenatal care, and to arrange routine blood tests and ultrasound scans. Morning sickness is common, and as a result many women have no particular interest in travel at this stage. Early pregnancy is also a time when miscarriage is relatively more common. Travel itself does not increase the risk of miscarriage, but the consequences in a country where medical facilities are poor could be serious. If bleeding is severe, blood transfusion may be necessary. In many poor countries the risk of AIDS from unscreened blood transfusions is high, and facilities for surgery (including supplies of sterile medical instruments) may be difficult to obtain. Poor medical treatment may have serious consequences for future pregnancies.

Towards the later stages of pregnancy, premature delivery becomes a possibility. It is not generally feasible to predict which pregnancies are at risk. Survival of a premature baby depends upon immediate access to sophisticated neonatal intensive care facilities, and the greater the prematurity the more important this becomes. Even when such facilities are available they may be extremely expensive, and the cost of neonatal intensive care may not be covered by travel insurance. Severely premature babies may not be able to travel for several weeks, adding further to the cost. Facilities for skilled medical care during delivery, surgical facilities and access to adequate blood transfusion facilities may again be a problem.

Aeroplanes do not make good delivery suites, and while air travel does not in itself induce labour, long flights should be avoided during late pregnancy; in any case, most airlines do not accept passengers beyond the 32nd week of pregnancy.

Chief hazards

Two direct hazards of travel deserve mention. The first is the fact that there is an increased tendency for blood to clot in the veins of the legs – deep vein thrombosis. This tendency is accentuated by dehydration and prolonged immobility, both of which are common during long air journeys. The preventive measures are simple: drink plenty of fluids, stand up and walk around the aircraft cabin at least every two hours during a flight. The same applies to travel by road: take a rest and stretch your legs at least every one to two hours on a long journey.

The second hazard has received much attention over the last two years and relates to exposure to radiation. It has long been known that exposure to cosmic radiation at normal flying altitudes (10,500m) is more than 100 times greater than at ground level. There has been increasing concern about the effect of low-dose radiation and calculations show that it is possible for frequent flyers to build up a significant radiation exposure. Solar flares – bursts of energy on the surface of the sun – account for periodic increases in such exposure, and occur in unpredictable patterns. The radiation exposure for a return trip between London and New York is roughly equivalent to the exposure from a single chest x-ray (0.1 milliSievert); a return flight between London and Los Angeles would clock up 0.16 mSv. Calculations on the extent of harm associated with radiation exposure are generally based on exposure to much larger doses – such as those that occurred at Hiroshima.

It is difficult to be sure how such results extrapolate to lower doses and it is conceivable that low doses may be relatively more harmful. It is also difficult to document the effects and to know whether subtle changes such as differences in intelligence or minor defects can be attributed to such exposure rather than nature. For this reason, it has been suggested that pregnant women should avoid unnecessary long-distance flights during the early, most vulnerable stages of pregnancy.

Vaccinations involving a live virus should be avoided during pregnancy: these include the oral polio vaccine, and the vaccines for measles, rubella and yellow fever. If a yellow fever vaccination certificate is necessary for travel, a medical certificate can circumvent the requirement. Protection against polio can be provided using a killed, injectable vaccine. Vaccines that commonly cause a fever, such as the one giving protection against diphtheria and the injectable typhoid vaccine, should be avoided during pregnancy and the BCG vaccine should not be given.

Drug-resistant malaria continues to spread, and the particular problem with malaria in pregnancy is that malaria attacks tend to be considerably more severe. Both mother and foetus may be at very high risk. There are now relatively few parts of the world where chloroquine and paludrine – the two safest drugs for use in pregnancy – provide reliable protection. Mefloquine (Lariam) is a newer antimalarial drug that is now widely used for travellers to resistant areas, but there are parts of the world – especially in the region of the 'Golden Triangle' of South-East Asia – where resistance to mefloquine is common. Mefloquine has not been in use long enough for a clear picture to have emerged regarding its safety for use in pregnancy; there is no objective evidence of a risk, but caution is still advisable, especially during early pregnancy.

In addition to medication, insect repellents and other anti–insect measures (mosquito netting, suitable clothing, insecticide sprays, etc.) should also be used assiduously to reduce the number of mosquito bites. However, there is a strong case to be made for avoiding all unnecessary travel to malarial areas during pregnancy – particularly to areas with drug-resistant malaria.

Other tropical or infectious diseases tend to affect pregnancy only indirectly, such as causing dehydration or a high fever, both of which put the foetus at risk.

Great care should be taken to avoid diseases such as dengue fever (by use of anti-insect measures) and to observe careful food and water hygiene measures.

If travel during pregnancy is considered essential, it is important to find out as much as possible about local medical care – names and addresses of doctors, hospitals and facilities for neonatal intensive care, should anything go wrong. It is also important to take particular care to insure adequate insurance cover for both mother and child.

Experts consider that the most suitable time for an overseas trip during pregnancy – provided that there have been no complications or other problems – is after the majority of the ante-natal tests have been completed and the main risks of miscarriage are over, but before the foetus becomes viable and would need neonatal intensive care facilities if born prematurely. This period lies between the 18th and 24th week of pregnancy, though my own view is that high-risk countries should definitely be avoided throughout the pregnancy. ❧

The diabetic traveller
by Geoff Gill and Robin Perlstein

H OLIDAYS AND TRAVEL SHOULD BE SOMETHING to look forward to, but it is important to plan ahead – even more so if you have diabetes and you want your journey (and blood sugars) to run smoothly.

Vaccinations

Some countries insist on certain immunisations for visitors, so it is wise to check in advance what (if any) vaccinations are required. There are no vaccinations contra–indicated because you have diabetes, but be aware that some may affect your control of your blood sugar levels in the hours or days that follow.

Identification and custom

It is sensible to wear some form of identification bracelet/necklace indicating that you are diabetic – especially if you are insulin-dependent. It is wise to carry a letter from your doctor stating you have diabetes and the treatment you use, or a British Diabetic Association photo identification card. This could be crucial if you are taken ill or if you have any problems going through customs. You are not required to declare insulin/medicines/syringes, as these are personal medical requirements.

Insurance

The cost and availability of medical services differs from country to country. Some countries have a reciprocal health care agreement with the UK, so emergency medical treatment is free or available at a reduced cost. All EEC countries have such reciprocal agreements with the UK, for which you need to present an E111 form at the point of treatment (available from post offices). In many countries, all consultations, treatment and medical supplies must be paid for. This can be very costly, and adequate medical insurance is vital. Insurance policies that will reimburse you if you need to be flown home in an emergency are advisable. Ensure also that holiday insurance packages do not exclude pre-existing conditions such as diabetes.

Illness

Being ill is unpleasant and can spoil a holiday, especially if you are unwell in a country where foods are different and hygiene standards dubious. Knowing what to do regarding your medication and food intake is essential, so discuss this with your diabetes nurse or specialist before you leave. Find out about anti-diarrhoea medication and motion sickness tablets as well as food hygiene. Having the name and address of the local diabetes association may also be useful if you are taken ill.

Medical supplies

It is very important to take enough medical supplies (insulin, syringes, etc.) so that you don't have to waste valuable time and money. Your GP can only write a prescription for three months' supply of some items, so if you are going away for longer you will need to consult a local doctor. Many of the insulins and/or oral hypoglycaemics available in the UK are available in other countries. The manufacturers of most products can also give you an idea of worldwide availability. Have both the generic name and the brand name of your medication to hand, as brand names often differ in other countries.

The most important thing is to take everything you need with you if possible. This is especially true if you are visiting more remote and adventurous countries, where medication that is apparently 'standard' in Europe may not be available. Even U40 and U80 insulin may still be used.

On the journey

Whether you are travelling by train or plane, boat or car, take food with you in case of delays or extensions to journey times. Include quick-acting carbohydrates, such as sugar and glucose tablets, as well as the longer-acting variety, such as biscuits, fruit, chocolate, sandwiches, etc. If you are prone to travel sickness you may also need to take motion sickness tablets before your journey.

If you are driving, remember to test your blood sugars before leaving, and eat regularly on the journey. If you take sulphonylureas or insulin, test your blood sugars every two hours over long journeys in order to avoid hypoglycaemia.

Long periods of sitting relatively motionless may cause your blood sugars to rise, but on balance it is preferable to have them running a little high rather than low, as hypos can be very dangerous at the wheel and embarrassing and inconvenient on buses and trains. Remember, though, that you may be quite active at the beginning and end of a trip, as you rush to get to the station or airport (and then to the platform or departure gate), cart heavy bags about or pack the car.

Don't bother to request a 'diabetic diet' when flying – it almost invariably comes too early or too late, and then turns out to be either unappetising or inappropriate or both. Take what comes and adapt as usual (your own extra carbohydrate supplies may prove useful here).

Packing for the trip

Pack insulin in your hand luggage, as flying altitudes can cause baggage in the hold to freeze, and checked luggage may be lost or delayed. It is wise to keep all essential items, such as your insulin and blood glucose meter, close at hand, or at least split between yourself and a travelling companion.

Crossing time zones

Timing your insulin injections when flying across time zones can present problems. As you fly westwards (e.g. UK to USA), the day lengthens and you may need an additional injection of short-acting insulin. Conversely, as you fly eastwards (e.g. UK to Far East), so the day contracts, and you may need to reduce your insulin doses to compensate for the shorter gap between injections. It is impossible to give advice to cover all eventualities, so before you leave discuss your trip with your diabetes nurse or specialist, armed with local times of arrival and departure and the duration of the flight. Although the whole process sounds complicated, it rarely causes serious problems. As mentioned above, as a general rule of thumb it is prudent to let yourself 'run a little high' in order to avoid the risk of hypoglycaemia.

Insulin storage

Though extremely high temperatures can cause a drop in insulin activity, this is a problem that is often exaggerated. Unless you are planning a prolonged stay in a very hot country, it will be sufficient to keep your insulin in a reasonably cool and shady place. For lengthy travels and in very hot climates, use an insulin-carrier with a frozen water container to act as a coolant. Make sure freezing facilities are available and keep vials out of contact with the frozen blocks. Alternatively, keep your insulin in a plastic sandwich box and keep it cool. Wide-necked vacuum flasks and polystyrene containers are other useful cheaper options.

Climate

Take sensible precautions in extremes of temperatures. In hot climates, use a good sunscreen and drink plenty of fluids; in cold climates, conversely, wear warm socks and comfortable sturdy shoes to protect your feet. Remember that some blood glucose test strips over-read in very warm conditions and under-read in colder climates. Hypoglycaemia can be more of a risk in hot climates, perhaps because insulin is absorbed more rapidly when the skin temperature is higher. Reduced and more erratic carbohydrate intake also play a part. It is important to be aware of this possibility, and to watch food intake and blood glucose levels closely.

Activity

Generally people are more active on holiday than they are at home, taking long walks, trying out new sports, etc. Others may do less, missing out on their usual

Holiday check-list

- Ensure you have had all the required vaccinations.
- Carry a diabetic ID card and doctor's letter.
- Adequate travel insurance (not excluding diabetes) is imperative. In Europe an E111 form may suffice.
- Consider strategies for dealing with becoming ill while away.
- Find out the name and number of the local diabetes association.
- Take sufficient supplies (approximately twice your normal amount for the same period) of insulin, syringes, oral hypoglycaemic agents (with generic and trade name), blood glucose meter and spare batteries, testing strips, lancets, needle clipper, any other medication, glucose gel, glucose tablets/sweets, Glucagon, tissues and longer-acting carbohydrate foods (biscuits/bread/fruit/chocolate).
- Make a note of useful foreign phrases.
- Take local currency (to purchase food/drinks on arrival).
- Take insulin storage containers for long trips or hot climates.
- Pack a good sunscreen and comfortable socks and shoes for walking.
- Remember your record book.

daily activities to lie on the beach and relax. Monitor and record your blood sugars regularly, as this will provide useful information for future travel.

Foot care

Some people with diabetes return from holidays in warm climates with foot ulcers. This usually affects older Type 2 (non-insulin dependent) diabetic people, often with peripheral neuropathy (numbness of the feet). Walking barefoot on hot flagstones or stony beaches can commonly cause the trauma that precipitates ulceration. This can ruin a holiday, so it is sensible to take care of your feet and avoid going barefoot.

Food

Remember that a holiday is a time to sample new and different foods. Many people are daunted by the prospect of selecting from strange menus and eating unaccustomed foods. Yet in most places food consists of the same basic ingredients: fruit, vegetables, meat or fish and usually plentiful amounts of starchy foods such as rice, potatoes, bread and pasta.

Most people drink more alcohol on holiday, but remember that if you are taking some tablets or insulin it can lower your blood sugars It is wise to drink only with food, and where possible to choose low-alcohol or alcohol-free alternatives. Drink plenty of water, bottled if you are doubtful about the purity of the local water supply.

For more information, contact the British Diabetic Association (10 Queen

Anne Street, London w1M 0BD, tel 020 7323 1531). The BDA produces general travel information as well as information specific to certain countries. ༃

DR GEOFF GILL *is Senior Lecturer in diabetes and endocrinology at the University of Liverpool and the Liverpool School of Tropical Medicine, and has written the definitive book on diabetes in the tropics.*
ROBIN PERLSTEIN *is a Registered Dietician who has worked at the British Diabetic Association, where she provided advice on a range of health issues.*

Battles with jet lag
by Dr Richard Dawood

THE HUMAN BODY HAS IN-BUILT RHYTHMS that organise body functions on roughly a 24-hour daily cycle. These rhythms can be influenced and adjusted to a large extent by environmental factors – the time on your wristwatch, whether it's light or dark, and changes in temperature. Rapid passage across time zones disrupts the natural rhythms, outstripping the ability of the body to readjust.

Few people who travel are unfamiliar with the resulting symptoms: general discomfort, fatigue, inability to sleep at the appropriate time, reduced concentration, impaired mental and physical performance, altered bowel habit and disrupted appetite and eating patterns – all are typical features of jet lag.

Adaptation

The body adapts to time changes at a rate of roughly one hour per day, so after a journey across eight time zones it may take up to eight days to adjust fully to the new local time. Many people tolerate westward travel slightly better than eastward journeys: westward travel results in a longer day which benefits those whose natural body rhythm is longer than a 24-hour cycle. Clearly a flight that does not cross time zones – north/south travel, for example – will not cause jet lag.

Further problems may also be experienced by those on medication that has to be carefully timed (people with insulin-dependent diabetes have to plan their insulin doses with care, for instance, and women on low-dose contraceptive pills may lose contraceptive protection if doses are missed or much delayed).
Children are often less affected by jet lag than adults, while the elderly may have great difficulty. Altogether, around 70 per cent of travellers are significantly disturbed by the symptoms. A wide variety of solutions has been proposed for those unfortunate enough to be badly affected.

Solutions

MELATONIN: Melatonin is a naturally occurring hormone that functions in the body as a powerful internal signal of the approach of night. Melatonin is secreted by the pineal gland in the brain, in a pattern that normally follows a strict daily cycle. Melatonin secretion is suppressed by the presence of bright light.

In a number of placebo-controlled studies, small evening doses of melatonin have been shown to have a significant effect on speeding up recovery from jet lag – by about 30 per cent. Unfortunately, conducting trials on a large scale is complicated. The fact that melatonin is cheap and difficult to protect with patents means that pharmaceutical companies have had little commercial incentive to explore its potential in full. They are however working on melatonin analogues – synthetic substances that might have similar properties, but that could be patented.

Melatonin is available in capsule form in the USA as a food supplement, and may be bought off the shelf in health food stores. It has not been approved by the FDA or by drug regulating bodies elsewhere, and the situation has become further confused by recent extravagant claims that melatonin is a cure for almost everything, from impotence to old age. Consequently, regulatory bodies are reluctant to make it readily available. A recent informal survey of travel medicine practitioners attending an international conference suggested that over half of them had taken melatonin themselves, and more than 80 per cent were satisfied with the resulting beneficial effects.

LIGHT EXPOSURE: Exposure to light suppresses melatonin secretion, and controlled exposure is known to alleviate jet lag. Various strategies have been proposed, some of which are difficult to understand and follow. At the simplest level, it is possible to use daylight simply as an environmental cure. More complex formulas claim to use precisely timed light and darkness to achieve dramatic jumps in 'clock setting'. Researchers at Harvard have attempted to patent various regimens of light exposure, a controversial move that will be interesting to follow.

THE JET LAG DIET: With its 'jet lag diet', Ehret and Scanlon's book *Overcoming Jet Lag* (1983) became an instant bestseller, trading heavily on the claim that this was the strategy used by Ronald Reagan during his presidency. In this diet, protein and carbohydrate intake is scheduled in an attempt to enhance the synthesis of certain neurotransmitters within the brain at appropriate times. The claim is that, taken at breakfast and lunchtime, protein-rich meals that are high in tyrosine increase catecholamine levels during the day, while evening meals high in carbohydrates promote tryptophan for serotonin (and therefore melatonin) synthesis at night. In travel medicine circles, the diet has achieved a reputation for being almost impossible to follow – and so almost impossible to disprove.

It remains true, none the less, that meal timing is an important *zeitgeber* – a significant factor in influencing the body clock in its adaptation to a new time zone. So if it is not your habit to eat heavy meals in the middle of the night, resist the temptation to accept in-flight meals at times that are inappropriate to the time at your intended destination.

SLEEPING MEDICATION: Carefully timed sleeping medication can help reduce the fatigue of the journey – an issue quite separate from that of jet lag. The important points are to choose a drug that is short-acting and leaves no hangover, and to avoid alcohol while taking it. It is important only to take sleeping medication during flights that are long enough to permit at least six hours' sleep.

Widespread use of the drug Halcion during the late Eighties, taken halfway across the Atlantic (often with alcohol), resulted in an epidemic of short-term travel amnesia, in which travellers were unable to remember anything about the first few hours following their arrival.

Sleeping medication can also reduce fatigue during adjustment to a new time zone: it can help you get some sleep when you need to rest at what – for your body – is still an inappropriate time, and it can also help you sleep through the night. Zopoclone is believed to cause the least sleep disturbance. When using any drug, always take the lowest dose in the recommended range.

Melatonin also has a soporific effect, which some specialists have argued is the only explanation for any influence it may have on jet lag.

EXPERIENCE: There is no doubt that, over time, frequent travellers develop their own strategy, almost without thinking about it. This is one reason why any formal evaluation of cures for jet lag is so difficult – unscrambling the influence of other factors is a major problem, and large numbers of travellers are necessary for scientific study.

Planning your own jet lag strategy

Whatever your approach to jet lag, here are some tips to bear in mind:

1. Flying westbound has the effect of lengthening your day. Avoid taking naps during the flight – this may prevent you from falling asleep later.
2. Avoid alcohol, tea and coffee during and after your flight: all interfere with sleep.
3. During eastbound overnight flights, such as the transatlantic 'red-eye', eat only a light meal before take-off and ask the cabin crew not to disturb you during the flight, so that you can get the maximum amount of sleep possible. Consider taking a mild sleeping tablet.
4. If you can afford the luxury of time, take daytime flights where possible. Although they do not necessarily help you adjust better to the time difference, they cause least fatigue and loss of sleep, allowing you to arrive in best shape.
5. Expose yourself to cues from your new time zone as soon as you can: reset your watch, eat meals and go to bed at appropriate times, and spend time outdoors.
6. As body temperature falls naturally during the night, a common symptom of jet lag is feeling cold during the day: try a hot bath.
7. Accept that there is bound to be some loss of performance when you first arrive in a new time zone, and plan your trip to avoid important business meetings for the first 24 hours after arrival; if you have to schedule a meeting on arrival, choose a time of day when you would normally – on home time – be at your most alert.

On arrival

On arrival at your destination, try to stay awake until night time without taking a nap. For the first night in the new time zone, a sleeping tablet is useful to help you to get to sleep at an unaccustomed time.

This type of occasional use of short-acting, mild sleeping tablets can be valuable and does no harm. Most doctors are willing to prescribe small quantities for this purpose. Possibly the most useful drug is zimovane, as it is short-acting and causes very little sleep disturbance.

Clearly, sleeping tablets should only be used on flights that are sufficiently long: it is pointless to take a tablet that will make you drowsy for eight hours when you are already two hours into a five-hour flight. Use the lowest dose that will work, and avoid alcohol. And remember that alcohol, sleeping tablets, fatigue and jet lag do not mix well with driving: too many people stagger off aircraft after a long journey and attempt to drive, when they are clearly not in a fit state to do so.

Whatever your approach, it is important to recognise that your performance is almost inevitably going to be reduced, so try to avoid important commitments and business arrangements for at least the first 24 hours after arrival. ❧

Fear of flying
by Sheila Critchley

M ORE PEOPLE FLY TODAY THAN EVER BEFORE, yet many experienced air travellers, as well as novices, suffer anguish and apprehension at the mere thought of flying. A survey by Boeing suggested that as many as one in seven people experiences anxiety when flying, with women outnumbering men two to one. Crew members know them as 'the white-knuckle brigade'.

A certain amount of concern is perhaps inevitable. The sheer size of modern jet aircraft, which appear awkward and unwieldy on the ground, makes one wonder how they will manage to get into the air – and stay there. Most of these fears are irrational and are perhaps based on the certain knowledge that as passengers, once we are in the aircraft we are powerless to control our fate (this being entirely dependent on the skill and training of the crew). These nervous travellers find little comfort in the numerous statistics demonstrating that modern air transport is many times safer than travelling by car or rail.

According to Lloyd's of London, it is 25 times safer to travel by air than by car. A spokesman for Lloyd's Aviation Underwriting stated that if you take into account all the world's airlines, some 600 to 1,000 people are killed every year on average. This figure compares to an annual toll on the roads of some 55,000 in the United States, 12,000 in France and 5,000 in the UK. One sardonic pilot used to announce on landing: 'You've now completed the safest part of your journey. Drive carefully'.

Anxiety

Most people's fear remains just that – anxiety that causes stress but remains on a manageable scale. For some, however, the anxiety can escalate into an unimaginable fear, known as aviophobia or fear of flying. Symptoms include feelings of panic, sweating, palpitations, depression, sleeplessness, weeping spells, and occasionally temporary paralysis. Phobias are deep-seated and often require therapy to search out the root cause. Psychologists studying aviophobia suggest that in serious cases there may be an overlap with claustrophobia (fear of confined spaces) and aerophobia (fear of heights).

Professional help can be obtained from specialists in behavioural psychotherapy. But unlike sufferers from other phobias, which may impair their ability to function in society, sufferers from aviophobia may simply adopt avoidance of air travel as a means of coping. Only those whose lifestyles necessitate a great deal of foreign travel are forced into finding a solution.

One source of many people's fear of flying is simply a lack of knowledge about how aircraft work and what sort of noises to expect. Visiting airports and observing planes taking off and landing can help overcome this problem. Reading about flying can also help (though air disaster fiction can hardly be recommended).

What to do...

Talking to people who fly regularly can be reassuring. Frequent air travellers are familiar with the sequence of noises indicating that everything is proceeding in normal fashion, including the dull 'thonk' when the landing gear retracts on take-off and the apparent deceleration of the engines at certain speeds. Most people are familiar with the sounds their cars make, listening almost subconsciously to the changed 'tones' that

I'm not afraid of flying – I'm just afraid of falling.
– RAY BRADBURY

indicate mechanical difficulties, and aircraft passengers who are unsure about flying often feel a certain disquiet when they cannot distinguish 'normal' from 'abnormal' sounds in an aircraft.

Air turbulence can also be upsetting. Most modern aircraft fly above areas of severe winds (such as during thunderstorms), and pilots receive constant reports of upcoming weather conditions. Air currents up to 20,000 feet may buffet aircraft, none the less, and the resulting 'cobblestoning' effect can be alarming even for experienced air travellers. Flight crews are aware of this problem and usually make an announcement to allay undue worries.

If you are afraid to fly, tell the stewardess when you board so that the crew can keep an eye on you. Hyperventilation is a common symptom of anxiety: the remedy is to breathe slowly and deeply into a paper bag. Remember that all aircraft crew are professionals who have undergone comprehensive training.

Emergencies

The chief responsibility of the cabin crew is not to dispense food and drink at regular intervals but rather to keep a constant watch on the safety of everyone on board. There is usually a minimum of one flight attendant for every 50 passengers. The briefings on emergency procedures that are given at the beginning of every flight are not routine matters: they can mean the difference between life and death and should be taken seriously. Each type of aeroplane has different positions for emergency exits and oxygen supplies, and different design and positions for life jackets. The air crews' demonstrations of emergency procedures are for the benefit

Recommended reading
Taking the Fear Out of Flying (David and Charles)
Stress-Free Flying (Mark Allen Publishing)
Flying? No Fear! (Summersdale)

of everyone on board and should be watched and listened to attentively. In an emergency situation, reactions in the first fifteen seconds are vital: there is no time to discover that you do not know where the emergency exits are. Learning about what to do in an emergency should reduce fear, not increase it.

Relaxation

One way of coping with fear of flying (at least in the short term) is to learn how to relax. In-flight alcohol (in sensible quantities), movies, reading material and taped music are all conducive to relaxation.

If these are not sufficient to distract you, some airlines conduct programmes for those they call 'fearful flyers'. These seminars consist of recorded tapes offering advice on relaxation techniques, statistical information on how safe flying really is, group discussions in which everyone is encouraged to discuss their fears, and simulated recordings of the sounds to be expected in flight.

Familiarisation is the key concept behind all of these behaviourist therapy programmes. Instruction in rhythmic deep breathing and sometimes even hypnosis can also help in learning to control the physical signs of anxiety. A graduate of one of these programmes confirmed its beneficial effects: "I enjoyed the course, especially sharing my misgivings with other people and discovering I wasn't alone with my fears. At the end of the course, we actually went up on a one-hour flight and I was able to apply all the techniques I had learned. In fact, I actually managed to enjoy the flight – something I would not have ever believed I could do."

A certain amount of anxiety about flying is to be expected. For most people, a long-distance flight is not something they do every day. On the other hand, there is always a first time for everyone – even for those who have chosen to make flying their career. The more you fly, the more likely you are to come to terms with your fears. Some anxiety is inevitable, but in the case of flying it is best to remember that the statistics are on your side. ❧

SHEILA CRITCHLEY is a freelance journalist specialising in in-flight magazines.

Staying alive

Avoidable hassles
by Tony Bush and Ian Wilson

A TRAVELLER'S BEST FRIEND IS EXPERIENCE, and it can take dozens of trips to build this the hard way. Fortunately, there are some tips that can be passed on to help the inexperienced traveller before they even step on a plane.

Travel planning

Most people have the good sense to work out their journey time to the airport and then add a little extra for unforeseen delays. But is that enough, should something major go wrong – if the car breaks down, for instance, or there are traffic tailbacks due to roadworks or an accident? Remember, too, to try and avoid travelling at peak periods such as Christmas, Easter and July and August, when families are taking their holidays. This applies particularly to weekends, especially Saturdays.

The traveller should find out in advance of flying whether he will be required to pay an airport tax on departure and, if so, how much. This is normally only a token sum, but it would be frustrating to have to change a £50 travellers' cheque in order to pay it. Departure taxes are almost always payable in local currency. Occasionally an equivalent sum in US dollars will be accepted. The ideal arrangement is to work out roughly how much transport to the airport will cost, add on the airport tax, if any, and then throw in a little extra for incidentals.

Taking taxis

Most travellers would agree that the task of dealing with taxi drivers could be elevated to a science. In some parts of the world, overcharging alone would be a blessing. What is really disconcerting is the driver who cannons through red lights or uses part of the pavement to overtake on the inside.

And what about the fare? Without a meter, the obvious foreigner will almost certainly be overcharged. But even the sight of a rank full of taxis with meters should not raise too much hope. Meters often 'break' just as you are getting in.

Two good tips for dealing with the drivers of unmetered taxis are:

1. Know a little of the local language – at least enough to be able so say "hello" "please take me to...", "how much?" and "thank you". This throws the driver a little. After all, the driver's aim is only to try and make an extra pound or two. He doesn't want to get involved in a major row at the risk of being reported to the authorities.

2. Try and have the correct amount ready to hand over. It prevents the driver pleading that he has not got sufficient change – a ruse that often succeeds, particularly when the passenger is in a hurry. It also avoids 'misunderstandings'.

A typical misunderstanding might go like this: the traveller hands over a note worth, say, 100 blanks for a trip that he believed was going to cost him 20 blanks.

However, the driver, with the note safely tucked into his pocket, tells him he was wrong, he misheard or was misinformed. In fact, the journey cost 30 blanks and 70 blanks is handed back as change. This leaves the passenger in an invidious position. He cannot snatch his note back, and is faced instead with the indignity of having to argue for a relatively small amount (very rarely would a driver attempt to cheat on too large a scale). In most cases, the traveller will shrug his shoulders, walk away and put his loss down to experience. And this is what the driver is relying on. That is the reason he is not greedy: he knows that even the most prosperous-looking passenger would baulk at too big a reduction in his change.

Tea oils the wheels

If you must spread around a little 'dash' to oil the palms that facilitate your progress, do so carefully, after checking how to do it properly with someone who knows the ropes. You may be able, for instance, to avoid a few days in a Mexican jail for a mythical driving offence. On the other hand, you could end up in jail for trying to bribe an officer of the law – and then you might have to hand out a great deal more to get out rather than rot for months awaiting trial. The $1 or $5 bill tucked in your passport is the safest approach if you do decide on bribery, as you can always claim that you keep your money there for safety. But it may only be an invitation to officials to search you again, and since all officials ask for identity papers, you could go through a lot of dollars this way. When you think a bribe is called for, there's no need for excessive discretion. Ask how much the 'fine' is, or whether there is 'any way' of obtaining faster service.

Even disasters – there are always disasters when you travel – can be turned into adventures.
– MARILYN FRENCH

Bribes, by the way, go under an entertaining assortment of different names. 'Dash' is the term in West Africa, except in Liberia, where the euphemistic expression is 'cool water'. 'Mattabiche', which means 'tip', 'corruption' or 'graft', oils the wheels in Zaire. In East Africa, the Swahili word for tea, 'chai', serves the same function. 'Baksheesh' is probably the best-known name for the phenomenon, and is widely used in the Middle East. It is a Persian word, found also in Turkish and Arabic, that originally meant a tip or gratuity, but took on the connotation of bribe when it was used to describe money paid by a new sultan to his troops. 'El soborno' is 'pay-off' in Spanish-speaking countries, except Mexico, where the word for 'bite' ('la mordida') is used. In India you have the 'back-hander'; in Japan 'wairo' or, when referring more generally to corruption, 'kuori kiri', which translates lyrically as 'black mist'. The French refer to the 'jug of wine' or 'pot de vin'. The Italians use the term 'little envelope' ('bustarella') and Germans have an honestly distasteful term for a distasteful thing: 'schmiergeld' which means 'lubricating money'. Even there, however, exporters gloss over the matter by simply using the abbreviation 'NA', 'nuzlich abgabe', which means 'useful contribution'.

Smiling strangers

Beware of the 'Smiling Stranger' when abroad. It is here that experience really counts, as it is often extremely difficult to separate the con man from a genuinely friendly person. A favourite ploy is for him to offer his services as a guide. If he asks for cash, don't say "I would like to help, but all my money is tied up in travellers' cheques." The Smiling Stranger has heard that one before and will offer to accompany you to your hotel and wait while a cheque is cashed.

The warning about confidence tricksters also applies to some extent to street traders: not the man who operates from a well set-up stand, but the one who wanders about with his arms full of bracelets or wooden carvings. He may give the souvenir hunter a good deal, but prices on the stands or in the shops should be checked first. Sometimes they will be cheaper in the latter, when, frankly, they should not even compare. After all, the wanderer does not have any overheads.

The ultimate avoidable hassle

Do not try smuggling anything through customs, especially drugs. Soft drugs may be common in the countries you visit, but think twice before buying. A local dealer may be a police informer. Prosecutions are becoming more common and penalties increasingly severe – from ten years' hard labour to mandatory death – and in some countries, sentences are hardly more lenient for mere possession.

Local courtesies

One of the biggest minefields for the unsuspecting traveller is local courtesies and customs, and most of us have our pet stories about how we have unwittingly infringed them.

It is worth knowing that you should not insult a Brazilian by talking to him in Spanish. The Brazilians are proud of the fact that they are the only nation in South America to speak Portuguese.

It's also important to understand that the Chinese, Japanese and Koreans believe in formalities before friendship, and that they adore business cards. Everyone should realise that they must not ask a Muslim for his Christian name. And it is of passing interest that Hungarians like to do a lot of hand-shaking.

It is easy to become neurotic about the importance of local customs. Respect is always crucial, but many people today, especially in the major towns, have access to modern global culture through their television screens and will be somewhat familiar with the ways of Western travellers. In any case, civility, politeness, warmth and straight dealing transcend most linguistic or cultural barriers.

The model visitor

If you wish to be respected, wear respectable clothes. If travelling on business, wear sober business clothes. Apart from when you're on the beach, in many countries women would be well advised to make sure their skirts are below the knees, their necklines demure and their arms, if not always their heads, are covered. Sometimes dark glasses are not a good idea – take them off, so your eyes can be seen.

In practice, none of this is much fun when the temperature is 45 degrees in the shade, the humidity is 100 per cent and your luggage weighs 35 kg. Nevertheless, try to keep your clothes clean. If not backpacking, use a suitcase instead of a rucksack and (if male) shave and get your hair cut as close to a crew-cut as possible without looking like an astronaut. A moustache is better than a beard, but avoid both if possible. Long hair, as long as it is suitably neat, is usually more acceptable for women.

There's no excuse for failing to research the countries you intend to visit. Talk to people who have lived in or visited them and find out what problems you are likely to encounter. If you go prepared and adopt a sympathetic, understanding frame of mind you should be able to manage without trouble.

You might also check the section on *Culture Shock* for further useful advice. ❧

IAN WILSON is the founder and Chairman of WEXAS International and one of the world's most-travelled travel agents. TONY BUSH is author of 'The Business Travel Planner' and was Editor of 'Export Times'.

Daylight robbery
by Christopher Portway and Melissa Shales

O BVIOUSLY ONE OF THE MOST IMPORTANT THINGS to keep in mind while travelling is the safety of your possessions. Do your best to minimise the chances of theft and you will run far less risk of being left destitute in a foreign country. Try to separate your funds, dividing them between your luggage and your person, so as to frustrate thieves and reduce losses. And before you leave home, make arrangements with a reliable person whom you can contact for help in an emergency.

American Express probably issue the most reliable and easily negotiable travellers' cheques, have the most refund points in the world and possibly hold the record for the speediest reimbursements. If you don't have plenty of plastic to keep you going for the two to three weeks it can take to get replacement cheques or new funds via the bank, take these.

Play for sympathy

If you come face to face with your robbers, use all the communication skills you have picked up on your travels. Try humour. At least try to elicit their sympathy, and always ask them to leave items which will be of no immediate value to them but are inconvenient for you to replace. They are usually after cash, and valuables that are easily converted into cash. Try to get the rest back, and risk asking for enough money for a taxi fare if you feel the situation is not too tense. Acting mad can help, as can asking for help or advice. On being approached in Kenya, one man claimed to be a priest and put on such a convincing act that the robbers ended by giving him a donation.

Many thefts will be carried out (without your noticing) from your hotel room – or by pickpockets in a crowded street. Never use a handbag without a zip, and keep your hand over the fastener at all times. Robbers can still slit the fabric or leather, but the odds are lengthened against their success. Never carry anything valuable in the back pocket of your trousers or the outside pocket of a jacket. Even the top inner pocket can easily be picked in a crowd. A money-belt is the most secure method of carrying valuables, although even this is not foolproof.

Never leave valuables in a hotel room, even out of sight. A good thief will know far more tricks than you and is probably likely to check under the mattress or behind the drawers of the dressing table before searching elsewhere. As long as the hotel is fairly respectable and is not likely to be in cahoots with local criminals, put valuables in the hotel safe and make sure you get a proper receipt.

While on the move, never let your luggage out of your sight. Wrap the straps of your bag round your leg while sitting down (a good reason for a longer shoulder strap) so you can feel it if not see it. Lock or padlock everything. This will not deter the most hardened types, but should lessen the chance of casual pilfering. A slightly tatty case is far less inviting than brand new leather Gucci luggage.

Violence

Violence is usually committed with a view to robbery. My advice in this unhappy eventuality is to offer no resistance. It is virtually certain that those who inflict their hostile attentions upon you know what they are doing and have taken into account any possible acts of self-defence on the part of their intended victim. It may hurt your pride, but this way you live to tell the tale – and after all, if you are insured, the material losses will be made good by your insurance company following the submission of a police report of the incident.

In many poorer countries, it is advisable not to wear or hold anything that is too obviously expensive, especially at night. You should be particularly wary in Africa and South America. The most robbery-with-violence-prone city I know is Bogotá, Colombia, where in certain streets you can be 99 per cent certain of being attacked. Having had most of my worldly goods lifted off me – but not violently – in neighbouring Ecuador, I made sure I lost nothing else by walking Bogotá's treacherous streets with a naked machete in my hand. This is probably a little drastic, however, and not generally advised. You could become a target for the macho element – and you could get arrested for carrying an offensive weapon.

A British exporter robbed three times – once at gunpoint – in as many days in Rio spent his remaining week there avoiding *favelas* (shanty towns on the outskirts of the city where many thieves live) and making sure that he was in a taxi after nightfall (when local drivers start to shoot the lights for fear of being mugged if they stop). Sometimes rolled-up newspapers are thrust through quarter-lights and drivers find themselves looking at the end of a revolver or the tip of a sheath-knife.

One of the worst cities in Africa for theft is Dar es Salaam, where locals tell of Harlem-style stripping – a practice that is spreading across the continent anywhere cars or parts are in short supply. Drivers return to where they parked to find that their car's wheels, and often anything else that can be removed down to the windscreen and doors, have been removed. An expert gang can pick a vehicle clean in under ten minutes.

In 1977, I walked right across Peru not knowing that the region was infested with cattle rustlers with a reputation for killing without mercy if they thought they'd been seen. Occasionally, ignorance can be bliss. Since then, of course, the situation in Peru has worsened, the bandits being joined by guerrillas to make the mountains decidedly unsafe.

In urban areas, the best advice is to stay in the city centre at night. If it is imperative to move away from the lights, go by taxi and try not to go alone. And don't forget to press down the door locks when you get in. There are some countries – Egypt is a prime example – where other people just jump in if the car has to stop for any reason. They are normally just an extra fare, but you can never be certain.

If by some mischance you do find yourself walking along a remote, unlit road at night, at least walk in the middle of it. This will lessen the chances of being surprised by someone concealed in the shadows. And when you have to move over for a passing car, use its headlights as your searchlight over the next ten or 20 metres.

Protecting yourself from attack by carrying a firearm is not recommended. Even in those countries that do permit it the necessary papers are difficult to come by, and in countries where the law is ticklish over the subject of mercenaries, a gun of any sort could brand you as one. One traveller was arrested in Zambia just for having a bullet on him. In any case, the idea that a pistol under the car seat or your belt offers protection is usually nonsense. In many countries a gun is a prize in itself to a violent thief, who will make every effort to procure one.

What to do next

Consider what action you can take if you find yourself penniless in a foreign land. Report thefts to the police and obtain the necessary form for insurance purposes. You may have to insist on this and even sit down and write it out for them to sign. Whatever it takes, you mustn't leave without it. It may be essential to you for onward travel.

Local custom may play a part in your success. In Lima, for instance, the police would only accept statements on paper with a special mark sold by one lady on the steps of an obscure church found with the help of a guide. They have a way of sharing in your misfortune – or sharing it out, at any rate.

If there is an embassy or consulate, report to them for help. In a remote spot you are more likely to get help from the latter. You may have to interrupt a few bridge parties, but insist on your right to be helped. In cases of proven hardship, they will pay your fare home by (in their opinion) the most expedient route, in exchange for your passport and the issue of travel papers. If your appearance suits, they may also let you phone your family or bank for funds.

Have the money sent either to the embassy via the Foreign Office or to the bank's local representative, with a letter or cable sent to you under separate cover. This will give you proof that the money has been sent when you turn up at the bank. I have met many starving people on the shiny steps of banks being denied money which is sitting there in the care of a lazy or corrupt clerk – or in the wrong file. Other countries do not always use our order of filing and letters could be filed under 'M' or 'J' for Mr John Smith. Have your communications addressed to your family name followed by initials (and titles if you feel the need).

An effective, proven way of moving on to a more sophisticated place or getting home, is to phone your contact at home and ask him to telex or fax air tickets for a flight out. They pay at home and the airline is much more efficient than the bank. This has the additional advantage of circumventing the Mickey Mouse currency regulations that various countries impose. Algeria is a perfect example. The country insists that air fares be paid in 'hard' currency, but the money transferred into the country is automatically changed into Algerian currency as it arrives. So you then have to apply to the central bank for permission to change it back (at a loss) in order to buy your air ticket. A telexed ticket can have you airborne in a couple of hours (I've done it).

Local generosity

In desperate situations, help can be obtained from people locally. These fall into two main groups. First come expatriates, who generally live unusually well and are often not too keen on the image that young travellers seriously trying to meet the local scene create, but once you have pierced the inevitable armour they have put up from experience, they are able to help.

They often have fax facilities at their disposal, business connections within or outside the country and friends amongst the local officialdom. Their help and experience is usually well worth having.

The come the missionaries. From experience I would suggest you try the Roman Catholics first, as the priests often come from fairly poor backgrounds themselves and have a certain empathy with empty pockets. Other denominations tend to live better but put up more resistance to helping. (I came across an American/Norwegian group in the Cameroons suffering from a crisis because the last plane had left no maple syrup). Swallow your principles or keep quiet and repay the hospitality when you can. They often need their faith in human nature boosted from time to time. You will receive kindness from other temples, mosques and chapels and can go there if you are starving. Again, do not abuse assistance and repay it when you can.

Real desperation may reduce you to selling blood and branded clothes, in which you have thoughtfully chosen to travel, in exchange for cheap local goods. But local religious communities are the best bet and usually turn up an intelligent person who can give advice.

In Third World countries, being poor and going without is no big deal – you may be in the same boat as some 90 per cent of the population. A camaraderie will exist, so you will probably be able to share what little is available. It would be wrong to abuse such hospitality, but do be very careful about hygiene, so as not to compound your problems with illness. ❧

CHRISTOPHER PORTWAY was a travel correspondent for DC Thomson magazines for 15 years, and has written 15 books, including several based on his wartime experiences. At the age of 70 he cycled from the Baltic to the Black Sea.
MELISSA SHALES is a freelance guidebook writer and previous Editor of 'The Traveller's Handbook'.

A safe hotel stay
by Samantha Lee, Sarah Thorowgood and Patricia Yates

ONE OF THE FIRST RECORDED HOTEL FIRES TOOK PLACE at Kerns Hotel in Lancing, Michigan, on 12 November 1934. Thirty-five people lost their lives. Just over a decade later, in 1946, 119 people perished in one of the worst hotel fires ever, again in the US but this time in Georgia.

On New Year's Eve 1986, 96 unfortunate souls met their maker as a result of a huge conflagration at the Hotel Dupont Plaza in Puerto Rico. After the disaster it was found that the building, on which no expense had been spared in the luxury department, had been totally unprepared for emergencies of any description. Safety precautions were so inadequate as to be almost non-existent. The hotel had no evacuation plan and provided no training for staff in emergency procedures. There was no smoke detection system to alert the occupants to danger, exits from the casino were woefully sparse, and the hotel boasted a number of unprotected vertical or horizontal openings.

And as was shown with stark and tragic clarity by the recent fire in an Australian hostel – a low-rise building in a country many would regard as safe – barred windows and a lack of safety measures can conspire even today to produce a terrible death toll.

Fire regulations in the UK are tight and generally strictly enforced (though youth hostels are technically private clubs so do not have to comply with hotel fire safety legislation), but travellers would do well to remember that not all countries are quite so well organised. In 1996, *Holiday Which?* found major problems when it inspected hotels in Turkey and Gran Canaria in Spain. In Turkey, seven out of 20 hotels inspected were rated as 'poor', meaning that in the event of a fire guests might not be able to escape. Problems identified included staircases that were not separated from bedroom corridors and that would therefore act as smoke funnels; long dead ends; and buildings with only a single staircase, which if blocked by fire would mean that guests were trapped. *Holiday Which?* experts also reported that in both countries staff received no training in fire safety procedures, and liaison with local fire brigades appeared to be infrequent and haphazard.

In Britain, the provisions of the 1977 Fire Precautions Act require that every hotel with space to sleep more than six people should possess a Safety Certificate indicating that the building is equipped with protected escape routes, fire doors, a fire alarm system and portable fire extinguishers. In addition, the former Trust House Forte chain made it a policy to install smoke detectors in all their hotels, both at home and abroad. As a further precaution, the night porter in each establishment checks the building from top to bottom every two hours between 11 pm and 7 am, inserting a key into a time clock at strategic points in order to provide a record of his or her route.

If a hotel or hotel chain is known to have poor safety standards, some big companies have a policy of boycotting them for their personnel. Wherever possible, stay in a hotel with sound fire safety regulations, but do remember that not all fires are caused by negligence: no one can anticipate with any certainty where arsonists or terrorist groups may strike. Ultimately, responsibility for your safety lies in your own hands – so be prepared.

After a long and gruelling journey, searching out the nearest hotel fire exits is probably not going to be your number one priority. But it should be. A few minutes 'casing the joint' before you order up that G&T or slip into that pre-prandial bath could mean the difference between life and death should the unthinkable occur.

If fire does break out, remember that it is the smoke, rather than the fire itself, that is the major killer. If the hotel has a large open-plan ground floor with wide unprotected stairways leading upwards, smoke will permeate the upper reaches of the building quickly and easily. If there are no alternative stairways or exits from the ground floor, and if dining rooms, bars and discos seem cramped or inadequate, you might want to lift your bags off the bed and find yourself another place to lay your weary head.

A traveller should always be furnished with some iron machine to shut his door on the inside… for it frequently happens that the doors of the lodging-rooms have neither locks nor bolts, and opportunity, according to the old proverb, makes the thief.
– Sir Thomas Nugent (1749)

If the hotel seems to have covered these points adequately, you might move on to a few responsible measures of your own. Preparation is the key. Virtually anyone caught unprepared in a life-threatening situation will panic. And with good reason in the case of fire, since trying to find the nearest fire exit when the smoke is already filtering under the door will waste precious moments that could mean the difference between life and death. Below are a few sensible precautions that will maximise your chances of survival.

On arrival

Check the ground floor layout and identify escape routes. Read the fire emergency instructions in your room and find the fire exit, making sure that it is free of obstruction (if it is not, notify the management and complain). Remember that fire doors are no use at all if they are wedged open. Walk the nearest escape route, counting the doors from your room to the exit (an *aide-mémoire* should the lighting fail or smoke obscure visibility). Note the location of fire alarm call points in the vicinity of your room, and familiarise yourself with the layout of your room and the way to the door (this is particularly important if you've arrived late after a large and liquid dinner). Find out what (if anything) lies outside and beneath the window and keep your valuables next to the bed for easy access. Don't smoke in bed, and never ignore a fire alarm.

In case of fire

Report the outbreak immediately, by phoning reception or breaking a fire alarm. Don't attempt any fire-fighting heroics unless you are an off-duty fireman. Close the door(s) and windows of the room where the fire is located (to restrict the

spread of flames and poisonous fumes) and use the nearest exit to leave the building. Don't use the lift. Don't open any closed doors without first feeling them for
heat (there may be a fire directly behind them). If your escape route is filled with
smoke keep low, getting down on your hands and knees, where air quality and visibility will probably be better. Stay close to the wall to avoid disorientation. On
leaving the hotel, report to your evacuation point so that people know you are safe
and won't risk their lives unnecessarily looking for you.

If you are cut off by fire, try to inform reception. Close the door of the room.
Run the bath to soak towels, bedding, curtains, carpets, etc., and use these to block
up any cracks. Fill the wastepaper bin with water in order to douse any outbreak of
fire inside the room, and go to the window to attract attention. If possible, open
the window if you need to vent smoke from the room. Don't break the glass, since
you may have to close the window to prevent smoke from below blowing in.

Jumping from even a second-floor window is not advisable (you might like to
specify in advance that you want a room on the first floor).

Security

Theft is rife in hotels all over the world, from bag-snatching and pick-pocketing in
the lobby to full-scale theft of thousands of pounds' worth of jewellery from hotel
rooms. Not surprisingly, hoteliers are reluctant to be drawn on the subject of security, and it appears that they rarely take the perpetrators to court.

Some hotel chains – Sheraton are a notable example – are by contrast highly
aware of the problem, and have adopted security policies involving installing
video surveillance throughout their hotels and training their staff accordingly.
Training highlights the importance of such measures as not disclosing names and
room numbers over the telephone, ensuring discretion at reception, and being
aware of security measures during the cleaning of occupied rooms (such as keeping the door closed or blocking it with a trolley).

The travel safety consultant Virginia Duncan recently advised readers of *Business Traveller* magazine to consider the following points when choosing a hotel:

- Do the room doors open on to a hallway or directly to the outside (the safer option)?
- What sort of keys system does the hotel use? The electronic card keys and metal
  keys with a magnetic strip now used in most Western business hotels provide
  greater security than traditional locks, as they can be changed after each visitor.
- What sort of locks do the doors have on the inside? Ideally the door should be
  self-locking, with a deadbolt, peephole and security chain or bar. Also check the
  door frames to make sure they sturdy.
- Is the front desk staffed on a 24-hour basis?
- Never leave your room key exposed in a public place, such as on a bar table.
- Never leave valuables of any description in your hotel room. Buy a good insurance policy and leave valuables in the hotel safe.
- Budget travellers may find there are no locks on the doors at all, in which case
  the best strategy is probably to take no valuables and carry the essentials with
  you at all times.

As with everything, prevention is better than cure. A constant awareness of the potential threat of theft will make the thief's job considerably more difficult without necessarily (once it has become a matter of habit) making your life any harder. ?▲

Patricia Yates is the Editor of 'Holiday Which?'. Samantha Lee is a freelance journalist. Sarah Thorowgood is an editor at Footprint Handbooks, and previously was Assistant Editor of 'The Traveller's Handbook'.

In trouble with the law
by Christina Georgiou

YOU GET ARRESTED ABROAD... THE NIGHTMARE BEGINS. You are locked up in a dirty cell awaiting questioning... the nightmare continues. Police officials are interrogating you in a language you don't understand... the nightmare worsens.

Getting arrested abroad, whether you are guilty or innocent, can be a terrifying experience. Local cultures can be very different, and what may be legal or culturally acceptable in the UK may be illegal in other countries and carry with it a harsh sentence. Most of all, the fear invoked by not understanding what is happening or knowing what the implications are of being locked up abroad could make this experience your worst nightmare.

Taking on board some of the advice and information outlined in this section could help you survive a potential nightmare.

Committing the crime

People can get arrested abroad for a multitude of reasons. Travellers, in particular, are vulnerable either wittingly or unwittingly to arrest, and offences can include expired visas, photographing military buildings and breaking local laws such as purchasing alcohol without a licence or drinking alcohol in a public place. The list of potential offences is vast. However, many travellers who get arrested and subsequently receive a prison sentence do so because of drugs. No matter how trivial or serious the drug offence, of which there are many, sentences are likely to be severe, and in some countries could even mean the death penalty.

Police officials will not normally care whether you claim to be innocent or not; just being in a room or vehicle where there is a stash of drugs or someone who is carrying drugs can land you in prison. Even if you did not know about the drugs, you could find yourself arrested and detained. Also, be aware of the consequences of transporting drugs across country borders, whether knowingly or unknowingly. Be wary of the person who befriends you and gives you a sob story about their sick uncle, who was unable to make it to their wedding. Coincidentally, your next stop just happens to be where the uncle lives – would it be too much to ask you to take a copy of the wedding video across the border with you? They don't want to post it in case it gets lost or damaged. Be warned, you could be carrying a cassette filled with heroin not videotape.

Don't be coerced into transporting drugs across borders in return for money; the financial gain may appear to be huge but you could be caught and left with nothing but 40 other cellmates sharing a room built for ten. In particular, young female travellers are targets for drug trafficking; they often fall victim, all too easily, for the charming, rich drug dealer who promises them the earth in return for transporting a package. However, the young woman is nothing more to the dealer than a decoy who is intended to be caught at the airport in order to allow a much bigger package to go through unnoticed.

Sentences for trafficking offences are among the harshest, especially in Asia, South America and the West Indies.

Upon arrest

On your arrest, despite the serious and frightening situation, try to keep as calm as possible. You will probably be feeling panic stricken and scared, this is natural, but try to keep your cool and avoid showing anger and aggressive behaviour towards the police; they are in a more powerful position than you and will want to maintain their power and not lose face in front of their colleagues. Do not resist arrest through violence and unless demanded on your arrest, keep hold of your passport.

There may be language differences: if so, communication will be extremely difficult. This in itself can cause problems due to misunderstandings. Ask for an interpreter or someone who is familiar with the language to be with you before you answer any police questions or sign a document that you do not fully understand.

Ask that the British consul be notified of your arrest. He or she will be able to offer you advice and support, and will contact your family for you.

Conditions of police cells and prisons will vary from country to country. Depending on which country you are in, you may be held in conditions that you find totally unacceptable – but this is the harsh reality and you must deal with it. Conditions in South America and South-East Asia are particularly grim; extreme overcrowding, poor sanitation and lack of nutritious food are commonplace.

Make sure family and friends back home know what has happened to you. You will probably be feeling lonely and scared and will need their support. Your family will also feel extremely anxious, but this is better than the worry and uncertainty they would feel if they had not heard from you at all. They may also be in a position to help you as they will have access to telephones, faxes and computers, etc., and will be able to find out what is going on, in a way that you will not be able to.

Help is at hand

As previously mentioned, insist that the British consul for that area be notified. This is your right. British consuls are there to protect the interests of Britons abroad; this includes helping Britons who have got into trouble. They can not get you out of prison, but will offer advice and support. The consul will visit you as soon as possible.

You should also contact Prisoners Abroad, details below. You can do this directly, or through the British consul or your family and friends. Prisoners Abroad is the only UK charity that provides practical support and campaigns for the welfare of Britons imprisoned abroad. It is a non-judgemental, humanitarian organisation with a team of caseworkers who have detailed knowledge of specific countries and will be able to provide you and your family with support and advice by explaining criminal justice systems, prisoners' rights and prison conditions; by contacting other agencies, including the Foreign and Commonwealth Office and foreign Ministries of Justice; and by providing families with advice on how to send money abroad and helping to arrange visits.

Unofficial help can come in the form of the friends you have been travelling with and locals, especially expatriates. Being locked up, far away from family and friends, can be extremely isolating; local people, especially those that you have a common language with, can keep you in touch with the outside world, bring you things you need such as extra food or clothing and get messages to consuls, family and friends.

Doing the time

After the initial arrest and questioning phase it is unlikely that you will get bail due to being a foreigner. This means that you will be held in prison on remand until the trial date. The length of time you will be held on remand varies, but it is not unheard of for this to last for two years and more.

Being held far away from home, probably isolated from others by language and culture, it will be important to try to keep your spirits up. Your consul should visit you regularly, keeping you in touch with the outside world, and Prisoners Abroad can provide a service to ensure that your specific needs are met. This includes providing advice about lawyers; translating documents, letters and court papers; supporting any application for parole, remission, pardon and appeal; negotiating with prison authorities; providing essentials such as medicine, food and clothing; linking prisoners with pen pals; sending out magazines and books, particularly to non-English-speaking countries with limited library materials.

False accusations

It has been known for travellers to find themselves falsely accused of committing a crime. If it is simply a case of mistaken identity, stay calm. Do not panic and aggressively protest your innocence, this may only aggravate your captors and fuel them into pinning something on you.

You could find yourself in the situation where police officials have set you up and are demanding a pay-off. Police and prison officials, particularly in Asia, are on a meagre wage and some supplement their income by demanding pay-offs from travellers. You will need to use your judgement to decide whether, if you have the funds, to give money to such officials. There is no guarantee that it will stop at one payment and that, afterwards, they will leave you alone. However, if you decide to do so, you could be making a number of expensive pay-offs to each police official involved.

If you get arrested

- Keep calm and do not argue with the police.
- Try to hold on to your passport.
- Make sure someone knows that you have been detained.
- Demand to see the British consul.
- Contact Prisoners Abroad.
- Ask for an interpreter.
- If you are going to trial, make sure you have a lawyer.

If you find yourself falsely accused, immediately inform the consul and tell them exactly what has happened.

Buying yourself out

Once you are being held in custody, there are some countries where you may be offered freedom in exchange for unofficial payments or bribes to certain officials. You or your family may be tempted to try this, but it is extremely dangerous and you may lose a lot of money with nothing to show for it – there is no guarantee that the officials will uphold their part of the bargain. You may also find yourself in the difficult position of being charged with bribery.

If you are actually being held on remand in prison it is important to know that bribery and corruption are rife in many prisons around the world and are a way of life. You may find that you have to pay for a space in a cell, your bedding, even food.

Holiday hotspots

In India, if you are caught with ten grams of cannabis, you face a mandatory sentence of ten years.

In Thailand, if you are caught in possession of less than 20 grams of heroin, you could receive a sentence of up to ten years and a fine. If you are caught trafficking any amount, no matter how small, of heroin you will automatically receive the death penalty. Possession of 30 grams of ecstasy can see you spending seven years in prison.

In Nepal, if you overstay your visa you will be fined $4,000 or receive a ten-year jail sentence.

In Japan, if you are caught in possession of 800 grams of hashish you could receive a four-year jail sentence.

In Spain, if are caught in possession of cannabis, the minimum sentence is three years. For possession of cocaine, you could be looking at anything between nine and 14 years. If you are arrested, it is highly unlikely that bail will be granted being a foreigner and this could mean spending anything up to a year on remand while the investigation takes place.

IN SOUTH AMERICA, conditions are extremely harsh and prisoners often have to buy basic items such as mattresses, beds and bedding as well as food and water. Foreigners are at a disadvantage as they do not have a local family network to supply them with these basic necessities.

IN FRANCE, possession of even a very small amount of drugs can result in a sentence of six months to one year. Foreigners are unlikely to be granted bail and you will be fined the street value of the drugs in your possession, which, even for small amounts, will be a substantial amount of money. Therefore, even if you serve your full sentence, you will not be released until the fine is settled.

Prevention is better than cure

Prevention is always better than a cure. There are a number of factors that travellers should take into consideration to ensure that they avoid getting into trouble abroad:

■ Check your passport and visa and make copies of them. Make sure you keep them safe, that the information contained in them is correct and that they are valid.

■ Make sure you have adequate insurance cover. Some insurance companies will pay legal costs; check that to make sure they provide this cover before you buy the policy.

■ Find out about and respect local laws and regulations.

■ Watch your luggage at all times at airports, as well as on trains and buses when crossing borders.

■ Be wary of taking lifts across borders; the one between France and Spain is particularly notorious as it is a well-known drug route into Europe from North Africa.

■ Do not agree to carry a suitcase or package for a friend or acquaintance, especially if you are offered large sums of money.

■ Do not get drunk and into fights.

■ Carry a list of British consular offices for the countries you plan to visit.

■ Let your family and friends back home know your movements and any changes you make to your route.

■ Make sure you prepare yourself and know the consequences of your actions; saying you didn't realise that something was illegal is no excuse. This advice may seem obvious, but it is surprising how many people say "If only…."

For more information

Contact Prisoners Abroad, 89-93 Fonthill Road, Finsbury Park, London N4 3JH, tel 020 7561 6820, fax 020 7561 6821, email info@prisonersabroad.org.uk. ❧

CHRISTINA GEORGIOU works for Prisoners Abroad.

Surviving a kidnap
by Daniel Start

IRIAN JAYA – INDONESIAN NEW GUINEA – is a vast tropical wilderness of glacier-capped mountains, pristine rain forest and lowland swamps, sparsely populated by tribal peoples living much as they have done for thousands of years. It might seem an unlikely place to be taken 'hostage' by 'terrorists', both words being so modern in their connotations, but this is what happened to our group of 12 biologists in January 1996. It goes to show that no corner of the world is so remote and untouched that it can be assumed immune from such threats.

Every country has some form of internal strife, some group that is fighting the state. Even if there is no history of kidnapping, there is no guarantee that one of these groups might not decide to take hostages as part of some crazy new strategy. However, if you are an independent traveller who stays on the beaten track and follows FCO or State Department advice closely, the chances of ending up in shackles are negligible. But those people whose work, study or inquisitive nature takes them to more unusual places must do extra research.

Our group spent two years in preparation. We knew about the existence of the OPM Papuan independence movement and knew that the Indonesian military had committed atrocities in Irian Jaya. The missionaries, mining companies, governments and many other organisations that we consulted suggested there was no risk. It seemed a sensible conclusion. The atrocities were too far in the past, the current trouble spots were too far away from us and the OPM had too few supporters. We were all wrong. Resentment among a people lingers and spreads. The OPM had wide support and although they could not read or write and had only bows and arrows they were still very dangerous. It is essential to understand the history of an area: don't ever underestimate the risks and don't always believe the experts' advice, however much you want to.

When we first arrived by light aircraft at our remote village in the mountains everything seemed peaceful and trouble-free. The village head men greeted us and smiled happily and for two months everything went very well. It is easy to be lulled into a false sense of security, and important to be aware that there may be other factions who see your arrival differently. In our case they numbered 200, were from the next valley and they ambushed us on 8 January 1996. We knew some of them already. Almost all of them were young men about our own age living normal Papuan lives. These are the type of people who make up most guerrilla outfits.

The ambush was a very frightening experience. The crowd had worked themselves into a frenzy and sported painted bodies, head-dresses and machetes. We thought we would be killed, but much of the aggression was theatre and no harm was done to us. When it started to rain the mood seemed to pass, they introduced themselves as OPM rebels and we all went inside and ate lunch together.

At first we were worried that they would abuse the women (men in large phallic penis gourds tend to look quite threatening) but none of the five women was seri-

Top ten countries for kidnapping

1. Colombia	6. Nigeria
2. Mexico	7. India
3. Former Soviet Union	8. Ecuador
4. Brazil	9. Venezuela
5. Philippines	10. South Africa

Source: Kidnap Monitor, Hiscox Group, 2000

ously molested. One of the hostages was pregnant, and was greatly respected because they believed pregnant women could cast powerful curses. We made it clear that each woman was married to at least one of the men. We were also very concerned for the Indonesians – the obvious enemies of the Papuans. Thankfully the OPM had accepted that we were all there with good intentions, so we were treated with respect; more like guests than prisoners.

In fact our group was seen as a gift from the Lord. White people are almost revered by the Papuans because of the work of the missionaries. In our case it was naïvely believed that we were so important and powerful that we could be traded for independence – a 'free country'. The unborn child of the pregnant hostage was even perceived as the new Messiah who would lead the Papuans to victory. These interpretations helped to seal our fate. Be aware that other cultures may see things in radically different ways from us. To minimise the effects of this, keep visits short. It takes time for rumour and superstition to spread and even longer for people to act on it.

The first night in the village seemed quite exciting, but it was so bizarre I found it difficult to take seriously. The next morning, however, our captors announced that they were taking us into the forest to hide us, and I suddenly became very frightened. We packed up everything; about half a tonne of the stuff. Much of the useless equipment made good presents for people – even cameras and Walkmans were valued for their shiny components. As we were marched into the jungle I remembered the old army adage that 'the longer you wait the harder it becomes to escape', and began to make many daredevil plans. Thankfully I didn't attempt any, but from then on I always kept a knife, compass, matches and iodine in my pocket – just in case.

At first we were sure it would all be over within days, but we quickly realised the situation was very serious. For a start, they declared that the baby – the new Messiah – had to be born on Papuan soil, and it wasn't due for another six months. Our main fear, though, was that the Indonesian military would come in and bomb the whole place and declare we had been murdered by the rebels. The OPM were as frightened of them as we were. Almost immediately we found we had common ground. The first priority was to get news of our kidnapping to the outside world, so that our embassies could prevent the military from wiping everyone out. As only one or two of the OPM men could read or write, we prepared all the letters for them. They were sent out by runner to the nearest town (about a week away), but finally our short band radio was found and used to negotiate with the missionaries. Thankfully in those first days we were able to communicate a lot of information about our situation. We also became very involved with the negotiations on the OPM's behalf and got quite carried away with our demands, thinking that we could organise both sides into compromising a little. It is tempting to imagine that your situation is a special case: always remember, however, that no respectable authority will openly make concessions to terrorists.

This alliance with our captors ensured they treated us well. Many were very nervous at first and hid this with a false bravado which was fairly easy to break through. I made a concerted effort to joke and laugh with the men, believing they would be less likely to kill me if they liked me. In fact we soon realised that all the OPM actively wanted to be our friends, because it gave them status. We used this to our advantage by giving presents only to those who treated us well or seemed to think we should be released. This created competition and jealousy among the OPM and gave us more power.

While we also wanted the OPM to like us, we had to be careful not to be too compliant. The odd refusal or confrontation made them think twice about asking us to do stupid things. As time went by we made a point of showing our frustration and unhappiness, so that they would not forget that they had taken innocent people prisoners.

Over the four months of our captivity, conditions in the mountainous jungle were harsh. We were moved 28 times; sometimes staying in villages but more often being hidden in remote forest. Although we were never tied up and were able to wander around reasonably freely, there was little chance of escape. Our captors knew we were almost totally dependent on them for food, shelter and direction.

Many of us suffered from malaria, dysentery, tropical ulcers and infections, but we had just enough basic medicines to treat ourselves. Thankfully we suffered no serious accidents and no run-ins with snakes or poisonous spiders. For me, boredom and hunger were the worst things, especially when

Don't panic.
– Douglas Adams

they were combined. You can only make conversation with your companions for so long. After that it is a matter of reliving old journeys, daydreaming, making plans or playing games – if you can find the material to make dice or a pack of cards. The OPM worked hard to find us what food they could (mainly sweet potatoes), but we soon learned to appreciate anything that moved: frogs, rats, bats, tree kangaroos, weevils. More than once we got food poisoning from meat that was too old.

Food was so limited and we were so hungry that initially this became the cause of all major arguments. After a while we realised that if we could rise above our animal instincts, giving a little extra rather than taking a little extra, the world became a much more pleasant place to be. Despite these conflicts, the entire group became very loyal to one another, like a family. But it was a lonely time. You can't expect to find a soul mate in everyone. In a way this was good because we learned to be strong, independent and self-supporting. This made us better able to take care of each other in a crisis. Images of family and home were very important in

How to survive a kidnapping

▓ Force yourself to be calm and compliant; there is little you can do by reacting violently.

▓ Do whatever your captors tell you to do without argument.

▓ Communicate with your captors to make them understand that you want to stay alive

▓ Take control of your mental and physical state. Develop a routine that will include mental and physical exercise.

▓ If you think you can escape, do so, but stop if under threat of death or being shot.

▓ If you are being rescued by armed troops or police, stay flat on the ground. Make it difficult for your captors to drag you away, but do not resist. The greatest risk of death is during a rescue attempt.

Source: Fielding's The World's Most Dangerous Places

battling with depression and despair. Some found solace in fantasy worlds, others in prayer or meditation. Certainly we all rekindled the remnants of any faith we had once had.

The OPM promised many times to release us, but not one promise was kept. There was so much conflicting news that it was tempting to attach too much significance to rumours of release. The disappointments were bitter and it took us several months to realise that the most painless way to get through was to let go of our hopes of release. Once I had resigned myself to being there forever I began to appreciate the present more, taking pleasure in the small things in life such as a beautiful sunrise or a moment of shared laughter. I also gained comfort and enjoyment from simple habits and routines, such as going to wash, collecting water or preparing food. The moment I stopped counting the hours the days seem to pass more quickly. Most important for me was understanding that this captivity wasn't wasted time, but an experience that would make me stronger and become an important part of who I was.

After about two months, the Red Cross made contact. From then on we were able to receive and write letters to our families about once a fortnight. There were also medicines, books and food, but soon the OPM came to enjoy the free presents so much that the Red Cross had to stop bringing in anything. This made the OPM angry but also focused their minds on the negotiations. Finally they agreed to hold a pig feast and release us on 8 May 1996, but at the last minute they refused. Perhaps they thought they should hold out for more. Maybe it was an act of angry defiance. Whatever, the next day we heard helicopters, gunfire and then a series of huge explosions (possibly blanks, but certainly powerful enough to blow down trees and start landslides).

This was the military operation we had dreaded. After an initial period of intense fear and panic we managed to think rationally. We had been told by the Red Cross that if things got nasty we should just lie down. But this was not an option, as we had to get away from the house in case the military bombed it or the hardline OPM came to get us. We heard about four helicopters circling, trying to find us, but the canopy was too thick. Then we heard a high-pitched whine which I now know was the sound of troopers being winched down into the forest. In hindsight, we should probably have split up and hidden in the forest close by until the military found the house. Instead, we made for a clearing from which we could signal but were intercepted by a group of OPM before we got there. We were taken into the mountains, and for five days the military tracked us with sniffer dogs, a heat-imaging camera mounted on a pilotless drone and trackers who followed our footprints (the Papuans do not wear shoes). On the sixth day, quite unexpectedly and very calmly, our captors attacked us and killed the two Indonesian men. The rest of us were able to get away. We ran down to a river, where we found a small military patrol camped on the bank. The OPM had seen the patrol, realised everything was over and killed the Indonesians to show that they would not be beaten.

We were flown out by helicopter and looked after incredibly well by the Indonesian government and British Embassy, but it was difficult to celebrate with the horror hanging over us. The press followed us everywhere and were such a problem that we decided to do an exclusive for one newspaper so that the others would leave us alone. Although we would have liked to address the political and human rights issues in a broadsheet interview, we were so confused and angry that we felt happier telling our story to a tabloid who would leave these things well alone. We chose the *Mail on Sunday*, which did one big feature, treated us exceptionally well, reported very accurately and paid us enough to provide some security in the coming months of readjustment.

For a few weeks I found I was very nervous and frightened of simple things such as going outside alone. It was exhausting speaking to friends on the telephone, so everybody wrote instead. We were offered counselling by the Foreign Office, but we needed to arrange it through our GPs and in the end it all seemed too much hassle and none of us bothered. I decided the best therapy was time with my family in Cornwall. Within three weeks I plucked up the courage to go and see friends in Cambridge, and I was amazed at how quickly I was back in the swing of going to pubs and parties. I felt very detached from my experiences in Irian Jaya, perhaps because they seemed so surreal. It might have been easy to pretend the whole thing never happened, but I could feel the experience had changed me and I was not happy having all these subconscious emotions inside me. I decided to write a book, not only for cathartic reasons but also because I felt it was a story that needed to be told.

Writing the book was a gruelling experience which felt a little like a penance, but those six months helped me to come to terms with my anger and guilt. Once the book was finished I found I had little idea of what I wanted to do. But perhaps that is no bad thing. Being taken hostage teaches you that you never know what's around the corner.... ❧

DANIEL START was kidnapped in Irian Jaya while on a conservation expedition in 1995. He was released after being held hostage for four months by the Free Papua Movement. He described these experiences in 'The Open Cage'.

Surviving a hijack
by Mike Thexton

HIJACKING COMES AND GOES AS A FASHION AMONG TERRORISTS. It is probably something that most travellers will think about at some time – to some it may be a vague anxiety; to others, part of a Rambo-style daydream. Anyone who worries about it a great deal is likely to be too nervous to be a regular traveller.

The most important thing is not to worry about it. The whole point of terrorism is to create a fear completely out of proportion to the risk – to get the maximum effect for the minimum effort. Don't give them that victory. Think about the huge number of trouble-free flights every day. It's very unlikely to happen to you.

However, it sometimes does. It happened to me on 5 September 1986, when four Palestinian terrorists stormed a Pan Am 747 on the ground at Karachi airport, Pakistan. All hijackings are likely to be different (the security forces try to bolt all the stable doors, so the successful terrorist will have to do something original) but there are some points which could be useful in any such situation. Armed men ran up the steps and took over the cabins as the last passengers were boarding. Accept that you will not react very fast in this situation, nor should you. Civilians are usually stunned by violence, or the threat of it, because it is so shocking. If you do have an opportunity to escape at this point, make sure that it is a clear and safe one – the terrorists are also very hyped-up, and are most likely to shoot you. It may be better to wait a while.

You will need to get control of yourself. If fear takes over, you will not be able to do anything useful if an opportunity presents itself. Everyone has to fight their own battle in their own head. I started by thinking that some people usually escape hijacks, and I saw no reason why I should not be included. I admit that I took comfort from the fact that there were Americans aboard. Since Ronald Reagan had ordered the bombing of Libya, they had to be more unpopular than the British – not much, but a bit.

Make yourself inconspicuous. It is generally fatal to be memorable: if the terrorists single someone out, it is usually to shoot them. Don't volunteer for anything, even if you think you might ingratiate yourself with them. Keep your head down. Don't catch their eyes. I was wearing a red duvet jacket, which was a bad start, but I knocked my Panama hat off my head with my raised hands, and sank into the seat as far as possible.

Do what they say, within reason. I would not co-operate to the extent of joining them (as happened in a famous Stockholm siege), but if they say, "Hands up, no moving", do it. We all sat in silence with our hands above our heads, looking into our laps.

There is a problem here. Two terrorists kept about 350 passengers completely quiet for the whole day. No one dared to look round. They could have gone away for a cup of tea and come back in half an hour, and we would still have been in our seats – no one would have looked round, for fear that a terrorist was standing right behind them. If you can, you want to get as much information as possible about the number of terrorists, weapons and position, but you are safer taking no risks.

The pilots escaped right at the beginning, so we were stuck on the ground – a great relief. We sat with our hands in the air for the first three hours of the siege. I was beginning to think it would really be all right when one of the flight attendants came around collecting passports. If you can avoid giving your papers in, do – they become a means of singling you out. Take any opportunity to dispose of anything which might be 'incriminating' in the mind of the terrorist. Of course, if you have a wholly 'terrorist-credible' nationality, it matters less, but I heard one of them venting his hatred for "all Westerners". He listed practically every nation, including the Spanish. I didn't think the Spanish had ever done anything to offend anyone. These people are indoctrinated.

The flight attendant knew that American passports were what the terrorists were after, so she dropped them all under the seats as she went. This was very brave and quite proper, but it promoted the British as second most unpopular nation. My passport was picked out, and I was summoned to the front of the plane. I didn't think that it would be possible to play hide-and-seek, so I went.

Controlling fear at this point is an entirely different exercise. I went from thinking, "Some people always get off," to "Someone always gets shot." Dealing with the expectation of imminent death must be very personal. I started with blind panic; I moved on to prayer, but felt very hypocritical ("Er, God, remember me? I haven't been good at keeping in touch, but could you …"); I made some promises to God in case he was listening, but only ones that I felt I could keep (and I did). What seemed to work best was to think of all my family and friends in turn, and to say goodbye to them. I thought about the mountaineering expedition I had just completed, and what a good time it had been. I settled in my mind any arguments I had with my friends so that the sun would not go down on my anger. I also determined that I was not going to die frightened – if they wanted to shoot me, I would stiffen my upper lip, shake them by the hand, and tell them to make a decent job of it. I doubt if I could have done it, but I felt better for the intention.

They kept me at the front of the plane for twelve hours or so, thinking about shooting me to emphasise some particular demand. I think it is important to retain your dignity – begging would not have helped, nor would offering bribes or assistance. You don't have anything they need. To them, you are simply a piece of breathing merchandise, to be traded or cashed in. If you can obtain their sympathy, or in some way turn yourself into a human being, try it – but don't speak unless spoken to, and don't irritate them. They may be trigger happy. I think that the sight of me praying, and my calm acceptance (after a while) of my situation may have impressed them. As the day went on, it became harder for them to shoot me.

I thought about telling them that I was Irish, and a fervent supporter of the IRA, but I doubt if it would have helped. If they know enough for it to benefit you, they will also probably know enough to see through it. They asked me if I was a soldier, and I guessed that it was important to say "No". I gave 'teacher' as a neutral occupation – after all, no one admits to being a chartered accountant. When asked later if I liked "Mogret Thotcher", I was able to give the required answer with conviction.

It would have been more difficult if they had asked me to say something I really disagreed with (perhaps in a statement to those outside) – but it might seem safest to go along with them, and it might be extremely dangerous to do anything else. However, you may need to keep your self-respect to avoid mental collapse, and you may need to keep their respect as well. I am glad I did not have this test.

You must not raise your expectations of release. Set long horizons. Disappointment could be crushing. This was easy for me, as I was convinced I was not getting out anyway. You should ignore any information given to you by the terrorists. Remember that the authorities are the 'good guys', and they will be trying hard to get you out, but they cannot give in – if they do, there will be another plane-load of passengers in your situation the following week, and the week after. Hostages are sometimes convinced by their captors that the authorities are being uncooperative, that it is all the authorities' fault: hold on to reality. They aren't, and it isn't.

Make yourself as comfortable as possible. It might be a long stay. Massage your joints, if you are allowed to. Stretch whatever you can. Clench your fingers and toes to keep the blood moving. Any movement will stop you seizing up, and will give you something to do. It can be very boring. Any exercise for the mind is also useful – you do not want to dwell on the nastier possibilities of the position. Remembering favourite pieces of writing, picturing peaceful scenes, daydreaming – all help.

Back in economy, the passengers enjoyed a slightly more relaxed atmosphere for a while. Afterwards I met two who spent the afternoon playing cards. Anything which passes the time is useful. It also helps to exchange names, addresses and messages for next-of-kin.

Take advantage of any opportunity you get to do anything that may make you more comfortable or safe – get a more inconspicuous seat, go to the toilet, eat or drink. You don't know whether you will get another chance for days. However, you should probably not take advantage of an opportunity to make yourself a hero. You will probably get killed, and will also cause the deaths of a number of others.

Movies are unrealistic. A large man with a Kalashnikov is very hard to take on with your bare hands; a man holding a grenade in his hand with the pin between his teeth cannot be overpowered, unless you want a posthumous medal for bravery. In case you are wondering, you can't put the pin back in once he's dropped the grenade. It will explode.

The most important piece of advice is to be ready to get out if the opportunity comes. Some experienced travellers think it's 'cool' to sleep through the safety announcements. It's more cool to know where the doors are, and to be sure how to open them. Think through the quickest way out, and have alternatives ready in case your exit is blocked. Think about how far down it is, and know about pulling the red handle if the chute does not come down. Remember that all this takes time, and that it will not be possible to get out of a door in the time that one of your captors has his back turned.

After twelve hours, they put me back with the rest of the passengers. The lights went out because the generator had broken down. I could feel the tension increasing, and crouched as low as possible in my seat. For a reason that has never been

Responding to events

During the first few minutes:
The take-over of an aircraft could be chaotic or it could be controlled. Either way, the first few minutes of a hijacking are crucial:

- Stay calm, and encourage others around you to do the same.
- Remember that the hijackers are extremely nervous, possibly scared and potentially trigger-happy.
- Comply with your captors' directions.
- If shooting occurs, keep your head down and drop to the floor.

During the hijacking:
The crew may be forced to fly the aircraft to another destination; the hijackers may enter into a negotiation which could last indefinitely; they could use passengers as bargaining tools or threaten lives. This will be the longest phase of the hijacking:

- Prepare yourself mentally and emotionally for a long ordeal.
- Try and remain inconspicuous.
- If addressed by the hijackers, respond in a regulated tone of voice. Be responsive but do not volunteer information.
- If you are told to keep your head down or maintain another body position, talk yourself into relaxing into position; you may need to stay that way for some time.
- Use your time to observe the terrorists – physical features, numbers, dress – anything that might be useful later. But do this discreetly.

During a rescue operation:
This could be similar to the take-over, with noise, chaos, possibly shooting:

- If you hear shots fired, immediately take a protective position – head down or drop to the floor.
- If instructed by a rescue force to move, do so quickly, putting your hands up or behind your head; but don't make any alarming movements.
- If fire or smoke appears, attempt to open emergency exits and use the chutes or wings. Once on the tarmac, follow the instructions of the rescue force: if no official person is there to help you, move away from the aircraft as quickly as possible.

Source: the Overseas Security Advisory Council, US Department of State.

established, they started shooting at random in the darkness, and throwing hand-grenades about. Some of the passengers decided that they had had enough, and opened the emergency doors. The man in the next seat told me to keep down, but I was not staying – the plane had been refuelled for an eight-hour flight. I pushed him in front of me towards one of the doors ... I was out on the wing, looking for a way down ... the chute had not come out automatically ... I'm afraid of heights, but I jumped off the back of the wing without much hesitation (about two storeys up but still the lowest point) and ran away. Many people were hurt jumping off the wings because they had taken their shoes off to make themselves comfortable. Be ready, and move quickly.

It was a bloody event, with more than twenty dead and over a hundred injured. I was very lucky to escape with a scratched elbow. But I was very unlucky to be hijacked in the first place – it won't happen to you. ❧

MIKE THEXTON is a chartered accountant whose life took an unexpected turn in 1986 when he was trapped on a hijacked aeroplane.

Surviving a skiing accident
by Arnie Wilson

SKIING INJURIES CAN AND DO HAPPEN when you least expect them, let alone when you are taking risks: there are documented cases of skiers breaking a leg as they climb down the aircraft steps before even setting foot in a ski resort. And some years, ago a producer working on a television commercial – in which the hero clutching a box of chocolates had to out-ski an avalanche – fell over and broke her leg while standing on a mountainside watching.

Not so long ago, I met a ski holiday rep who had damaged his cruciate ligament while skiing without even falling over – he hit a bump awkwardly and tore it. Konrad Bartelski, Britain's most successful world cup skier ever, once damaged his cruciate ligament during a race without even realising until he crossed the finishing line. Ligaments, cartilages and tendons are the things that get hurt these days. Thanks to modern equipment, including more and more sophisticated bindings, broken legs are much rarer than they used to be. But something's got to give, and if it's not your leg, it's likely to be your cruciate.

Although advanced skiers travel at speed and are vulnerable to spinal and head injuries, surprisingly it is the beginners who frequently prove to be most at risk. They tend to ski slowly, and more often than not it is the slow, sickening, twisting fall that causes the damage – not the high-speed fall that catapults the skier out of his bindings – unless of course the fall hurls the unfortunate victim against a rock. Which leads us to head injuries, and protective helmets. Are they really necessary? In Scandinavian resorts they are virtually compulsory for young children, and many people believe that adult skiers should also be required to wear them. Yet statistics show that remarkably few skiing accident cause head injuries. They also show that a frightening number of accidents on the slopes are drink-related.

Drink is freely available – and its consumption encouraged – in a host of mountain restaurants. Marco Grass, a member of the Saas Ski School in Klosters, Switzerland, warns: "Drinking when you are skiing is just as dangerous as when you are driving a car. You think you are in control but in reality your reactions are slow and ill-judged. Statistics relating to injuries in this major ski area of Klosters/Davos show that more and more are drink-related. And we have no reason to think this trend is only happening here."

In North America, reckless skiers can have their lift ticket confiscated and even be put under arrest. In practice – unless they actually injure another skier – they often get away with it. Having monitored American skiing in almost 100 resorts right across the continent, the closest I have come to seeing an errant skier being punished was in Snowshoe, Virginia, when a member of the ski patrol leapt onto a chair to catch the culprit but lost him on the mountain.

Colin Allum, whose Fogg (as in Phileas) Travel Insurance Services specialises in skiing insurance, observes: "Skiing is a high-risk sport. About one person in 50 who goes skiing is liable to receive some form of medical treatment during the course of a normal winter-sports holiday. This can range from a twisted ankle or bruised shoulder to the extreme cases of serious back or head injury, or – fortunately very rarely – to death."

If you happen to be first on the scene after an accident, it is important to cross two skis in the snow about ten metres up the slope from the injured skier. Don't try to move the victim, and if there is a leg injury, don't try to remove the boot, as it can act as a splint. Keep the injured person warm, and do not give him or her any alcohol. Knees are the most prone to injury, but almost no part of the human body is immune from one sort of skiing injury or another.

A fracture or damaged cruciate ligament are among the worst things than can happen to your legs: but it is not always the big injuries that cause the most pain and curtail skiing. Some skiers – myself included –endure endless agonies because of ill-fitting boots. Like many other skiers, I am the unfortunate owner of feet that are fundamentally the wrong shape for most boots (one expert boot-fitter in Aspen described them as 'brick-shaped').

I remember cracking, or at least bruising, a rib or two when I was learning to ski in Verbier, Switzerland, and a friend of mine is always damaging hers. You can't do much with cracked ribs except perhaps strap them up, but she always continues to ski regardless. As with many skiing injuries, it is often less painful to carry on skiing than to walk around or even lie down in bed. The same goes for shoulders.

In California, I fell heavily on my left shoulder twice in two days and the pain affected me for months. Skiing was not a problem (except the worry of falling on it again), but lying in bed could be agony. Usually an anti-inflammatory cream and resting it will do wonders in such cases. Wearing a sling can help.

Shoulders are always a problem. They have such a sophisticated collection of moving parts, any one of which may be damaged in an accident without the others being affected. You may find you can ski yourself silly without so much as a twinge, but looking at your watch almost kills you. Still – at least I haven't torn my dreaded cruciate ligament yet (though no doubt it is only a matter of time).

Says Allum: "The advent of quick-release bindings has dramatically reduced the number of fractures – but dramatically increased the number of ligament injuries. In the days when bindings simply did not release, it was almost inevitable that a leg would be broken. Nowadays, 50 per cent of what may be regarded as 'serious' injuries – those which in due course will require some operative treatment – are knee ligament injuries.

"Many accidents are caused by people skiing across the tops of protruding rocks which are seen too late. This type of accident tends to produce head injuries, because the skier is released from the bindings and propelled forward, rather on the lines of a swimmer at the start of the 100-metres Olympic swimming trials.

"Skis themselves can cause accidents if they are the wrong ski for the skier concerned. It is always important that skiers ski within their limitations, and ski a length of ski to which they are suited rather than one decided by bravado. It is much more sensible to have a happy and successful holiday skiing a 195 centimetre ski than to finish up in hospital skiing a 210."

So much for the skis. But what about the skier? "There are those of us who may readily admit to being beginners even after 20 years of skiing. And there are others who will only admit to being advanced after 20 minutes," says Allum.

One good way to try to prevent injury on the slopes is to get fit before you go. Enter the Cybex machine, used by better fitness clinics. It sounds like something out of *Dr Who*, but what it actually does is check the strength of your hamstrings, quads abductors and adductors, and then targets any of these for strengthening with a customised programme of weight-training and exercises.

Weather and altitude can also play their part in making a skier's life a pain. Some people get serious altitude sickness in America, where skiing in the Rockies can mean altitudes of 11,000 or 12,000 feet or more. At such heights it is not unusual to feel some effects, including headaches, nausea, breathlessness etc. These should wear off after two or three days (a good reason not to go skiing in the USA for just a week, as your holiday may well be half over before you're ready to face it), but if they persist you should see a doctor. Drinking plenty of water – much more than you think you need – helps to alleviate the problem. But serious altitude sickness can only be dealt with by getting the patient to a lower altitude as quickly as possible. Your doctor can prescribe tablets to lessen the impact of altitude.

As for weather: watch out for frostbite. I got my first taste of it in Colorado, skiing Breckenridge's peak 7. The trouble is, you don't know you've been affected unless someone tells you. My nose went white, but I had no idea. As a damage limitation exercise, it is important to cover any frostbitten extremity and keep it warm. Experts argue over whether it is better just to cover it or knead it slightly to restore the blood supply. Those against kneading claim it could damage the cells while they are frozen. The consensus is just keep it warm.

Strong sunlight can be a major problem too. Always wear good protective creams, even when it may seem that the sun is not coming out that day. As the saying goes, you may not be able to see the sun, but the sun can see you. Even a couple of hours' skiing in high altitude without protection, especially during the later months of March, April and May, can cause serious sunburn and even sunstroke because of the strong ultra-violet rays.

Much has been said and written of the dangers of skiing off-piste, and it is true that skiers leaving marked trails without a guide may cause avalanches or be caught up in them, or even fall into a crevasse. However, skiing in a resort on a

Prevention is better than cure

Gliding over crisp snow in sparkling air – probably the most fun you can have without sprouting a pair of wings and taking flight. However, skiing also equates to repeated muscle stress and exertion at high altitude – a combination that can result in injury. That risk is considerably lower if you're fit to begin with and know the basics about equipment and safety.

Before you go:

- Increase your aerobic fitness by running, cycling, going to an aerobics class or dancing for at least 20 minutes, three times a week. This is worth a few extra hours on piste.

- Strengthen those muscles. Skiing puts pressure on thighs, hamstrings, calves, hips and groins, so some advance exercise targetting these muscles should reduce the chance of jelly legs on the slopes. Many fitness clubs offer special ski-preparation classes before the season starts

On the slopes:

- Make sure your equipment works. Bindings must release properly during falls, boots should fit securely enough to protect the ankle from moving inside the boot, but not so tightly that you lose all sensation.

- Stretch – without bouncing – before and after skiing. Hold each stretch for thirty seconds. A hot tub at the end of the day always helps – or a massage.

- If you are a beginner: before hitting the slopes and playing desperate catch-up as your expert friends zoom off, you should take a few lessons from a qualified instructor to learn proper techniques.

- Whatever your level, stop and have a rest if you're tired. Many injuries occur when skiers are tired. Always ski within your own limitations, even if you're skiing in a group.

marked run is arguably just as dangerous. When you compare the numbers of people on piste with those who ski off them, the chances of a collision in a resort must surely be just as high as those of falling foul of nature outside a resort.

Almost ten per cent of skiers who end up in Davos hospital have been involved in collisions. And collisions nearly always cause injuries, and sometimes serious ones. I found this out in a very tragic way when my girlfriend Lucy Dicker was killed in La Grave, following our successful mission to ski every day in 1994. Even skiing off-piste with a guide is no guarantee that no harm will come to you. Or to the guide for that matter. There is a cynical saying that all the avalanche experts are dead. Tragically, there is some truth in it.

According to the rescue service SOS which operates in the Parsenn area of Davos – one of the most extensive ski areas in Europe, which also prides itself on its avalanche research centre – "Avalanches are a natural phenomenon and therefore no absolute safety from them can be guaranteed. We must emphasise that even after the most experienced judgement and safety measures have been taken, an avalanche can still break loose and run over an open and marked piste."

Always obey avalanche warning signs and stay out of high-risk areas unless a qualified high mountain guide is skiing with you. He or she will have specialist knowledge and will certainly not take you off-piste if there is a serious risk.

Just as experts argue over the best way of dealing with frostbite, so they have different views about how to try to survive an avalanche. There is no way of guaranteeing that you will not die. There are all sorts of avalanche patterns, from powder avalanches which drown you to slab avalanches which can break every bone in your body, or at least batter you senseless. You might start it yourself, or you might be engulfed in one started by another skier. Most likely it will start spontaneously and trap you in its path.

Avalanches can move frighteningly fast. You may have only a second or two to react. One possible reaction is to ski diagonally out of the avalanche's path. Another is to take your skis off and try to 'swim' on the surface of the snow. If you are sucked under the surface, try to keep a pocket of air in front of you by cupping your mouth and nose with your hand. When skiing off-piste wear an avalanche transceiver, never ski alone and if possible always take a guide.

Ueli Frei, President of the Mountain Guides Association in Grindelwald, who specialises in helicopter skiing and regularly rescues climbers stranded on the much-feared north face of the Eiger, remarks: "You have to respect the mountain. But for me there is more risk in crossing a busy street in London." But he admits that two of his most experienced colleagues have recently died in avalanches.

In general though, skiing statistics are encouraging. While the risk of minor injury – sprains, bruises, cuts – is high; major injuries – broken bones or torn ligaments – are much rarer, occurring once in every 200 days worth of skiing. For most recreational skiers, that is the equivalent of 20 years.

Incidentally, three per cent of injured skiers each year suffer from broken thumbs. But you can break a thumb even before you go skiing. Many people who practice on dry ski slopes sprain or break thumbs when they fall on the unforgiving plastic surface and sandwich a thumb between the slope and their body. But don't let that encourage you to give skiing the thumbs down. It's far too much fun. Just take it easy. And take care. ✌

ARNIE WILSON is the skiing correspondent of 'The Financial Times', and the author of 'Tears in the Snow', an account of spending a record-breaking 365 consecutive days on skis in 1994.

Surviving wild animals
by Nigel Marven

EVEN WITH A WETSUIT ON I WAS COLD. The waters south of Cape Town in South Africa are closer to Antarctica than they are to the tropics. The creature ahead of me was chilling, too: its girth was so huge I couldn't have circled its body with my arms. And its environment was alien to me. In the sea, I was comparatively clumsy, coping with the twin problems of staying afloat and breathing with a snorkel. Unless underwater technology changes radically, we'll always be half blind and deaf in the ocean – but that doesn't mean that what I could see wasn't magnificent. Sunlight splashed onto the shark's eye and the dead black hole transformed itself into a shining blue-black, coming alive in the process. On the side of the creature's head, five gill slats flared open. I imagined I could see the vortices of oxygen-stripped water spiralling away from the clefts, which looked like knife cuts in blotting paper. The five-metre-long animal seemed curious and circled slowly. Its great head was tapered to a point, which is why Australians call the most feared of all sharks the white pointer.

The image of its mouth is forever burned into my consciousness – it was smiling with a clownish grin. This rictus smile was fixed, so the teeth were always on show. The great white shark was thrilling, more like a jet fighter than a fish. If it wanted to it could have given me a devastating, perhaps lethal, bite. I wasn't in a cage and a wetsuit was my only protection (my companion André Hartman had a spear gun, but it didn't work). I didn't want this encounter to end, but after a while the great white became a little too curious and André gave it a sharp rap on the nose with his heavy camera housing and sent it on its way.

This sequence was the finale to a film I produced about the world's largest sharks. My purpose was to show that great whites are not malicious monsters with a taste for human flesh. But then they're not harmless herbivores either – there is no doubt they have the potential to eat us, and that's what makes them so exciting, one of the last predators of humanity.

I would never have dared do what I did if I hadn't spent ten days observing the behaviour of great whites – and nearly the same amount of time reading everything I could about them. I also had a companion who'd swum with great whites hundreds of times before. I'd seen that the great fish are careful about what they bite; white marks, as if a child had scribbled with chalk on their snouts, bore testament to injuries caused by the teeth or claws of fur seals, their main prey. Great whites are cautious before they bite – their eyes are vulnerable. I also knew that they aren't particularly fond of humans as food: we don't have enough blubber to be energy-rich, fur seals are power bars compared to us. Andre had also waited until the visibility was good. In dirty water the sharks couldn't see us clearly and we wouldn't be able to see them.

Most attacks by great whites (there have been 245 since 1846, and of these only 60 were fatal) have been cases of mistaken identity. The hungry shark has seen movement at the surface of the water and has launched a vertical lunge before discovering that it has bitten a human rather than a seal. The predator doesn't even bother delivering the *coup de grace* to our scrawny bodies, which is why many human victims survive shark attacks.

But even with all this knowledge and my direct experience, I still wouldn't recommend that other travellers swim freely with great whites. By all means, view them from a cage, but even then, without expert help and perfect conditions you could be taking a risk.

Most divers feel elated if they catch a glimpse of a shark. Tales of waters infested with them, just like those of deserts teeming with scorpions or rainforests writhing with venomous snakes, are usually just that, travellers' tales. As a wildlife filmmaker, it didn't take me long to find this out. It takes weeks, possibly months, of meticulous planning to ensure that you are in the right place at the right time to get the pictures used in documentaries. If we just turned up on the off chance, with a vague hope of seeing animals, hazardous or otherwise, it's unlikely that any wildlife film would ever be completed. But we do have more opportunities than most other travellers to meet potentially dangerous creatures – and, most importantly, to do so safely.

If you follow a couple of simple rules, shark watching shouldn't be any more hazardous than badger watching. I've dived with tiger sharks, hammerheads and reef sharks without any problems at all. Spear fishing when sharks are around is, of course, a no-no: the blood in the water and the death throes of the punctured fish excite sharks too much so they tend to come too close for comfort. Don't touch or approach sharks too closely, just watch and marvel. If a shark is going to attack, it usually displays warning signs, arching its back, raising its head and lowering its pectoral fins (the big wing-like ones at the front).

If a shark does look likely to attack (this really is a million to one chance), the worst thing you can do is panic and try to flee – the shark is far swifter in the water than you are, and may confuse your flailing behaviour with that of an ailing fish. Instead, stand your ground and remember that the eyes and heads of sharks are vulnerable. If one comes at you, be prepared to give it a punch or even gouge its eyes with your fingernails. If possible, seek a retreat on the reef or rock wall, making sure you keep your back against something solid.

As well as sharks, there are other potentially hazardous animals in the sea. Animals made of jelly, the sea gooseberries, salps, sea butterflies and jellyfish, are some of my favourites – then there's the glories of the plankton, some of which have brightly coloured tentacles or delicate air-filled floats. Others have rows of cilia that flash with iridescent colours when they catch the light. Sea butterflies live up to their name, flapping languidly through the water with transparent wings. Many of these animals, particularly jellyfish, have a battery of stinging cells for catching prey – but they can also lash unwary swimmers.

Most cause nothing worse than a mild prickling or tingling sensation, perhaps with some swelling and reddening of the skin, but stings from the infamous Portuguese man o' war can be excruciating, and those from the box jellyfish lethal. To avoid the former watch out for dead man o' wars washed up on the shore (this creature is usually quite big, with tentacles up to nine metres long that hang from a gas-filled flotation bladder that is tinted with blue, purple and pink). If a few of these are beached, the waters could be infested, so avoid swimming there. If you can't resist a dip, wear long pants and a long-sleeved shirt, as these will give protection from the stinging cells.

The box jellyfish is a different proposition. Travellers need to seek local advice about its presence or watch out for warning signs. It's prevalent in some regions of the Pacific and Indian oceans, particularly in the tropical waters of Australia. This jellyfish has been responsible for the deaths of 90 people to date, and about 70 of these fatalities were in Australian waters. This cube of jelly has four groups of trailing tentacles – blunder into these and they discharge into your skin, causing savage and excruciating pain. There's acute inflammation and a florid flare on the skin where the tentacles have made contact. Venom is absorbed into the bloodstream, attacking the victim's nervous system. I've seen the warning signs about stinger season in northern Australia, and I'd be petrified about swimming at that time without a stinger suit (a thin wetsuit) for protection. If anyone is unlucky enough to get stung, the injured region should be doused with vinegar for a minimum of 30 seconds (there are vinegar supplies on many of the beaches). This inhibits any of the other stinging cells from firing off; prompt medical attention must then be sought. If the victim loses consciousness, resuscitation techniques should be used. Unless the unfired stings have been deactivated with vinegar, no attempt should be made to rub or wipe off adhering tentacles.

There are other hazards that lie in wait for anyone getting to or from a swim. If you happen to be on a coral reef, beware of intricately patterned shells in the shape of a perfect cone. In 1935 in Queensland, Australia, a 27-year-old man handled such a cone shell. He felt an immediate mild stinging sensation in the palm of his hand, within ten minutes his lips felt numb, after four hours he was in a deep coma and dead an hour after that. Cone shells harpoon their prey, usually small fish, with poisonous darts; if we handle these molluscs with bare hands they can sting us, too.

Anywhere along the Australian coast, you may find miniature octopuses stranded in rock pools. When they get excited or annoyed circles of iridescent blue develop on their tentacles and bodies, but beware of picking them up, however much they may look like colourful toys. A bite from a blue-ringed octopus causes nausea, vomiting then paralysis. This can happen within minutes and a victim may soon experience difficulties with breathing. In such cases, first aid to maintain breathing is crucial until the patient can be got to an artificial ventilator.

Stingrays can be concealed on the muddy or sandy bottom of bays. At the base of their tails they have a venomous bony sting with short barbs along its length, which tear through flesh as it is withdrawn. If you've been told they're in the area, avoid stepping on them by shuffling your feet to disturb them as you're wading (the stings are long enough and tough enough to pierce plastic sandals). A stingray victim should put the affected area into a bath of hot water (as hot as they can bear) for 30 to 90 minutes, which denatures the proteins in the venom.

Stingrays are not restricted to salt water, either. I had to use the foot shuffling technique in the Llanos, a swampy region in Venezuela. I'd taken my shoes off for tactile sensitivity because I was feeling for anacondas with my toes. I certainly didn't want my snake hunt to be disrupted by a stingray sting.

I've always been a fan of snakes and whenever I get the chance I actively search them out. There are over 2,700 species, and only a small proportion of these are dangerous to us.

Given the chance, nearly all snakes will disappear into cover when they sense the vibrations from a human footfall. So stamp your feet when moving through snake country. Personally, I walk carefully and slowly so I can see them.

The big constrictors, species that suffocate their prey, rarely attack us; most fatalities are from people molesting them or accidents with captive snakes. Pythons or anacondas that hunt people are figments of the imaginations of Hollywood scriptwriters – our shoulders are just too broad for all but world-record-sized snakes (over eight metres) to work their jaws over to allow them to swallow us.

Venomous snakes can be hazardous to travellers. Boots and thick socks should be worn where they abound. I actively turn over rocks and logs looking for reptiles (I always gently replace them back in the position that I found them in when I'm doing this). I'm always careful not to put my hand underneath or into dark cracks and crevices. While most travellers won't be turning things over, the same rule applies when climbing or scrambling through snake country: don't plunge your hands into chinks in rocks or into hollow logs.

But I've had a close shave myself because of a failure to take common-sense precautions. Camping in Turkmenistan on the Iranian border I had to relieve myself at night. I didn't put on shoes or take a flashlight. When I shone one around the next night I found that there were rodent burrows with saw-scaled vipers laying outside in the sand, next to one of them there was a footprint I'd made the night before. That was a close shave. If I'd trodden on one of these snakes (they are highly venomous and can be irascible) in this remote region, far from medical help, I'd have put my life at great risk.

If I had been bitten, I would have put a compression bandage (this can be made from strips of towel or clothing) just above the puncture wound. This shouldn't block arterial flow and should be loose enough to get a finger between the constriction band and the affected area. The bandage will stop the venom spreading through the superficial veins and lymph vessels. I'd then try to keep calm and rest on the journey as I travelled towards the nearest medical care. In most parts of the world this is usually only a short distance away.

For most travellers the chances of being bitten by a snake are rare. Venom is a complex mix of organic chemicals, usually proteins, which are 'expensive' for the snake to make. Its main use is for immobilising prey and as a method of preliminary digestion. Venom is used in self-defence, but only as a last resort; that's why snakes have developed ingenious warning devices such as a cobra's hood, a rattlesnake's rattle or the bright warning colours of the coral snake. No snake will go after a human being (with one exception, a king cobra guarding its nest, but that would be a rare find indeed), so if you're lucky enough to come across one of these reptiles just stand back and watch. If you're patient, the snake will eventually move. I always marvel at the streamlined design and effortless flowing movement of a snake. If it's close enough or you have binoculars, you can make out its pattern and colour scheme – these can be dazzling. When the snake has disappeared into cover, as it will invariably do, just think for a while about a snake's elegant solution to life without limbs. Snakes will only bite us in self defence, so they should be treated with caution and admiration, not fear and hatred.

Furred predators rarely get as much of a bad press as snakes, sharks or creepy-crawlies, probably because, as mammals ourselves, we feel an affinity with them. Big cats are a potential danger in the tropics (there are some tigers in Siberia, but their numbers have declined so much it would be an honour to be attacked by one), as are bears in temperate or Arctic climates. While it's very unusual for people to be on their menus, there have been cases of rogue lions, tigers or bears that, because of injury or old age, are forced to treat us as food – but these individuals are so rare you've more chance of the plane that's taking you to your destination dropping out of the sky than you have of meeting one of them.

Usually big predators will run when a human approaches them on foot. Accidents tend to happen when they're surprised or when food brings them into close proximity with us. Most travellers will be escorted and/or in vehicles when viewing lions and tigers; but in North America and Russia bears can turn up in many areas – even outside protected parks. I spent two weeks in Alaska's Katmai National Park working on a film about brown bears. I'd never seen these magnificent creatures before, but on encountering them it soon became apparent that they were more interested in the succulent sedge grass and salmon than in us. We always remembered we were visitors to their home, so as we walked along their trails we talked and clapped so as not to surprise them – and, of course, they always had right of way. If they approached us, we'd talk to them calmly, "Hi, bear. Hullo, bear, we're still here," so that hey didn't forget we were there; but if they came to within ten metres or so of us, we slowly retreated.

Campers in bear country shouldn't put temptation in a bear's way. Food should be kept in sealed containers and away from the sleeping areas. Surprising as it may seem, recent research has shown that bears seem to be excited by the odours of menstruation or love-making; so, if possible, a trip should be planned to avoid these from happening when under canvas with bears prowling around outside. The same basic rules apply for polar bears. They can be seen around the town of Churchill in Manitoba, Canada, between July and November, and on the Norwegian island of Spitzbergen in spring.

It's clear that, in most habitats, animals aren't usually a threat to us – but there's just one case where they are – and this is somewhere I'd never venture. The habitat in question is the tropical freshwaters inhabited by saltwater crocodiles (northern Australia and some parts of South-East Asia) or Nile crocodiles (Africa). (If the river or pool was in Africa, hippos could mean a double whammy of danger. There's every chance they'd kill human swimmers, particularly when defending young.) Crocodiles aren't as fussy as sharks about what they attack: anything swimming in their territory is potential food. If I go for a dip in croc country I always check with the locals whether the water I'm entering is really clear of the animals. I don't want to experience becoming prey for an animal that can be up to ten times my size.

So, in conclusion, I think you can probably tell by now that I'd love it if the world were teeming with exciting and potentially dangerous animals, but this really isn't the case. While modern travellers can get anywhere and do anything with relative ease – we hike, camp or snorkel in areas that used to be exclusive territory for animals – when compared with the chances of being harmed by another human being, the danger posed by other creatures is negligible.

The Smithsonian Institute and US Navy have calculated that, right around the world, there are 50 shark attacks each year. During the same period, people in the United States suffer six million dog bites – our best friend causes ten deaths per year. However, there will be under 200 attacks by bears, sharks, crocodiles and alligators, with fewer than ten deaths. Snakes bite 3,000 people in Australia every year, but 90 per cent of these bites are from non-venomous species. Medical care and anti-venom treatment are so efficient nowadays that, even among the 300 or so people who are actually envenomated, deaths are extremely rare.

In most situations, all that's required to avoid a bite or attack is an awareness of the presence of animals that could be a threat. No creatures show malice aforethought, we just need to be careful and not blunder into a curtain of jellyfish tentacles or tread on a camouflaged viper. If we keep our eyes skinned and senses alert, an encounter with a predator can be one of the most thrilling and memorable experiences of our lives. ❧

NIGEL MARVEN has made numerous wildlife documentary films for BBC and ITV, most recently 'Giants', a round-the-world odyssey in search of the largest predators. He spends about five months each year seeking wild animals to film.

Survival at sea
by Sir Robin Knox-Johnston

A VERY SENSIBLE LIST OF SAFETY EQUIPMENT to be carried on board a boat was published by the Offshore Racing Council (ORC) in its *1994/5 Special Regulations Governing Offshore Racing*. The list is extensive, but because it is comprehensive, it is given opposite.

Medical

The health of the crew is the skipper's responsibility and he or she should see that the food is nourishing and sufficient, that the boat is kept clean and that the crew practise basic hygiene. A good medical kit must be carried.

There is an excellent book (published by HMSO for the British Merchant Navy) called *The Ship Captain's Medical Guide*. It is written for a ship that does not carry

Safety equipment

- Two fire extinguishers, easily accessible and kept in different places.
- Two manually operated bilge pumps.
- Two buckets, of strong construction, fitted with lanyards.
- Two anchors and cables (chain for cruising is sensible).
- Two flashlights: water resistant and capable of being used for signalling, with spare bulbs and batteries.
- Foghorn.
- Radar reflector.
- Set of international code flags and a code book.
- Set of emergency navigation lights.
- Storm trysail.
- Storm jib.
- Emergency tiller.
- Tool kit.
- Marine radio transmitter/receiver.
- Radio, capable of receiving weather forecasts.

- Life-jackets: sufficient for the whole crew.
- Buoyant heaving line at least 16m long.
- Life-buoys or rings.
- Set of distress signals.
- Twelve red parachute flares.
- Four red hand flares.
- Four white hand flares.
- Two orange smoke day signals.
- A hand-held VHF radio.
- A life-raft of a capacity to take the whole crew, which has: a valid annual test certificate, two separate buoyancy compartments, a canopy to cover the occupants, a sea anchor and drogue, bellows or pump to maintain pressure, a signalling light, three hand flares, a baler repair kit, two paddles, a knife, emergency water and rations, a first aid kit and manual.
- In addition, it is worth carrying a portable, waterproof VHF radio and an emergency distress transmitter (EPIRB).

a doctor and includes a recommended list of medical supplies. Most doctors will supply prescriptions for antibiotics when the purpose has been explained. Two other books to recommend are *The International Medical for Ships*, published by the World Health Organisation, and *First Aid at Sea*, by Douglas Justins and Colin Berry (Adlard Coles Nautical, London).

Safety on deck

Prevention is always better than cure. Everyone on board should know their way about the deck, and know what everything is for. A good way of training is to take the boat out night sailing so that the crew get to know instinctively where everything is and what to avoid. Train the crew to squat whenever the boat lurches – it lowers the centre of gravity and makes toppling overside less likely.

In rough weather, make sure that all the crew wear their life-jackets and safety harnesses when on deck, and that they clip their harness to a strong point. A good attitude on board is that crew should wear their lifejackets at night, when told to and when they want to. If the crew have to go out from the cockpit, they should clip the harness to a wire jackstay that runs all the way from right forward to the cockpit for this purpose.

Man overboard

If someone falls overside, immediately throw a life-buoy into the water and summon the whole crew on deck. The aim is to get back and pick them up as quickly as possible, so post a look-out to keep an eye on the casualty, and the rest of the crew should assist with turning the boat around. It is worthwhile putting the boat straight in the wind, as this stops you close to the casualty, then start the engine and motor back. On one occasion in the Southern Ocean, we lost a man overside, and we ran on more than a mile before we could get the spinnaker down.

I love the sea as one loves any capricious being who makes one suffer.
– CAROLUS DURAN

Because of the large swell, the only way we could locate him when we turned round was by heading for the sea birds that were circling him. We got him back, after about 20 minutes, by which time he was unable to assist himself because of the cold.

In the upper latitudes, there is a real danger of hypothermia, so it is vital to warm the person as quickly as possible. Strip off their wet clothing and towel them dry, then put them in a warm sleeping bag. The heat is retained better if the sleeping bag can be put into a large plastic bag. If the person is very cold, it may be necessary for someone else to strip and climb into the bag with the casualty and warm them with their own body.

If the casualty is conscious, feed them hot soup or tea. Remember that it can be a nerve-shattering experience and that they may need time to get over the shock. Do not give them alcohol.

Abandoning the boat

When, as a last resort, it becomes necessary to leave the boat, set off the EPIRB, and, if possible, send out a digital selective distress call on the appropriate frequency or by satellite communications. Inflate the life-raft and pull it alongside. Put one or two of the crew on board, and, if there is time, pass over as much food, water and clothing as possible, plus the EPIRB and SART. If the boat's dinghy is available, tie it to the life-raft, as it will give extra space and also help create a larger target for rescuers. Only leave the boat if there is absolutely no alternative. Life-rafts are small and not particularly robust, and it is always preferable to keep the boat afloat if humanly possible.

The usual reason for abandoning a boat is that it has been holed. One method of improving its survivability is to fit it with water-tight bulkheads so that its volume is roughly divided into three. The Marine and Coastguard Agency insists on water-tight sub-division on yachts that take paying crew, which means that if the boat is holed the chances are that it will lose only a proportion of its buoyancy and there will still be dry, safe shelter for the crew. From the comparative safety of one of the 'safe' parts of the boat, a plan can probably be made to fix the leak.

When it is necessary to abandon the boat, having got as much food and useful equipment aboard the life-raft as possible, cut the painter and get clear. Then take stock of what you have, and post a look-out.

Ration supplies from the start. The best way to do this is to avoid food for the first day, as the stomach shrinks and the body's demand for food falls. Ration water to about a quarter of a litre a day and issue it in sips. On no account should sea water be drunk, but it can be used for washing and cooling in hot weather. Humans can last for amazingly long periods without food, but they do need water. Any rain should be trapped and saved. The canopy of the life-raft can be used for this purpose, as could the dinghy, if it has been taken along. Do not eat raw fish unless there is a plentiful water supply, as they are very rich in protein and ruin the liver unless the surplus can be washed out of the system. As a general rule, one volume of protein will require two volumes of water. Where water is plentiful, fish should be hunted. Most pelagic fish are edible, and quite often they will swim around a boat or dinghy out of curiosity. Inedible fish are found close to land or on reefs.

Keep movement to a minimum to conserve energy and, in cold weather, hold on to urine as long as possible to retain its heat. In hot, sunny weather, try to keep everyone in the shade. Find some mental stimulus in order to maintain morale, and remember that the crew will be looking to the skipper to set an example, so remain positive. Humans have survived for well over three months on a life-raft, but only because they had a strong will to live and were able to improvise. My book, *Seamanship* (Hodder and Stoughton), may prove useful further reading. ❧

Sir Robin Knox-Johnston, cbe, was the first man to sail around the world single-handedly and without stopping. He also set a global record for sailing around the world in a catamaran. He is the author of numerous books on sailing.

Survival in the desert
by Jack Jackson

THE MOST IMPORTANT THING ABOUT DESERT SURVIVAL is to avoid the need for it in the first place! Be aware your vehicle's capabilities and do not overload it, and know how to maintain and repair it. Carry adequate spares and tools. Be fit yourselves and get sufficient sleep. Start your journey with 25 per cent more fuel and water than you calculated would be needed to cover extra problems, such as bad terrain, leaking containers and extra time spent over repairs or sitting out a bad sandstorm.

Know accurately where your next supplies of fuel and water are. Carry plastic sheets to make desert stills and take space blankets with you. Pack more than one compass and know how to navigate properly. When using magnetic compasses, keep them well away from vehicles and cameras. Do not rely exclusively on electronic Global Positioning Systems (GPS) or the batteries that power them, and do not leave the piste unless you really do know what you are doing. Travel only during the local winter months. Know how correct your odometer is in relation to the wheels and tyres fitted to the vehicle. Make notes of distances, compass bearings and obvious landmarks as you go along so that you can retrace your route easily if you have to.

Observe correct check-in and out procedures with local authorities. If possible, travel in a convoy with other vehicles. When lost, do not continue. Stop, think and, if necessary, retrace your route.

Backup plans

If you are travelling in a large party, you should arrange a search and rescue plan before you start out. This would include the use and recognition of radio beacons or flares for aircraft search. Many countries do not allow you to use radio communications, but if you can use them, carry modern portable satellite communications systems.

Should the worst happen, remember that, for most people, an air search is highly unlikely and high-flying commercial passenger aircraft passing overhead are unlikely to notice you, whatever you do. A search, if it does come, will be along the piste or markers. Most often this will consist of other vehicles travelling through the area, whose drivers have been asked by the local authorities to look out for you because you have failed to check in at a pre-appointed time and place.

Local drivers will not understand or appreciate coloured flares, so your best signal for local outside help is fire. If you hear a vehicle at night, cardboard boxes or wood are quickly and easily lit, but during the day you need lots of thick black smoke. The best fuel for this is a tyre. Bury most of a tyre in the sand to control the speed at which it burns (keep it well away from and downwind of the vehicles and fuel) and start the exposed part burning with a rag soaked in either petrol or diesel fuel. As the exposed part of the tyre burns away, you can uncover more from the sand to keep it going, or cover all of it with sand if you wish to put out the fire. You should always avoid inhaling the sulphurous fumes. While the battery still carries a charge, headlights switched on and off at night can also be used to draw attention to your plight.

Should you be lucky enough to see low-flying aircraft overhead, it's worth remembering that the international ground/air code for a request to be picked up by such a plane is to stand up with your arms held aloft in an obvious 'v' shape.

A need to survive

Once you are in a 'need-to-survive' situation, the important things are morale and water. Concentrate on getting your vehicles moving again. This will keep you occupied and help to keep up morale. To minimise water loss, avoid manual work during the day and, instead, work at night or in the early morning. Build shade and stay under it as much as possible, keeping well covered with loose cotton clothing. 'Space blankets', with the reflective side facing out, make the coolest shade. Keep warm and out of the wind at night. In really hot climates, replacing lost potassium with Slow κ can make a big difference to your general alertness.

Unless you are well off the piste with no chance of a search, you should stay with your vehicle. If someone must walk out, pick one or two of the strongest and most determined people to go. They must carry with them a compass and a GPS receiver, if available; a torch; salt; anti-diarrhoea medicine; loose, all-enveloping clothes; tough footwear; good sunglasses and as much water as they can sensibly carry. In soft sand, a jerrycan of water can easily be hauled along on a rope tied to the waist. On mixed ground, tie the jerrycan to a sand ladder, one end of which is padded and tied to the waist.

Those who walk out should follow the desert nomad pattern of walking in the evening until about 11pm, sleeping until 4 am, walking again until 10 am, then digging a shallow hollow in the sand and lying in it under a space blanket, reflective side out, until the sun has lost its heat. If it's a full moon they can walk all night. In this way, fit men would make 60–70 km on ten litres of water – less in soft sand.

Water

In a 'sit-it-out-and-survive' situation, with all manual labour kept to a minimum, food is unimportant and dehydration staves off hunger, but water is vital. The average consumption of water in a hot, dry climate should be eight litres per person per day. This can be lowered to four litres a day in a real emergency. Diarrhoea increases dehydration, so should be controlled by medicine where necessary. Salt intake should be kept up – in the worst scenario, licking your bare arms will replace some lost salt.

Water supply should be improved by making as many desert stills as possible.

The desert of Danakil is a part of the world that the Creator must have fashioned when he was in a bad mood.
– LADISLAS FARAGO

To make one, dig a hole about one-third of a metre deep and one metre in circumference, place a clean saucepan or billycan in the centre of the hole, and cover it with a two-metre-square plastic sheet weighted down at the edges with stones, jerrycans or tools. Put a stone or another heavy object in the centre to weigh it down directly over the billy. Overnight, water vapour from the sand will evaporate and then condense on the underside of the plastic sheet. In the morning, running a finger down from the edge of the sheet to the centre will cause the condensation to run down and drip into the pan. All urine should be conserved and put into shallow containers around the central billycan. The water so collected should be boiled or sterilised before drinking.

If you have antifreeze in your radiator, don't try to drink it as it is highly poisonous. Even if you have not put antifreeze in the radiator yourselves, there is still likely to be some left in it from previous use or from the factory at the time that the vehicle was first manufactured. Radiator water should be put into the desert still in the same way as the urine and the resulting condensate should be boiled or sterilised before drinking. Water from bad or brackish wells can be made drinkable in the same way. Note, however, that solar stills can take a lot of energy to create and will yield little water in return. Until the situation is really desperate, they are probably not worth considering as a viable means of collecting water.

The minimum amount of water per day required to maintain the body's water balance at rest in the shade is as follows: if the mean daily temperature is 35°C, you will need 5.3 litres per 24 hours. If it is 30°C, then 2.4 litres; if 25°C you need 1.2 litres; and at temperatures of 20°C and below, one litre will suffice. It must be stressed that this is the bare minimum necessary for survival. If such an intake is prolonged, there will be a gradual kidney malfunction and possibly urinary tract infection, with women more at risk than men.

The will to live is essential. Once you give up, you will be finished. If you find people in such a situation and do not have a doctor to handle them, feed them water to which rehydration salts have been added, a teaspoonful at a time, every few minutes for a couple of hours. If you do not have sachets of rehydration salts, you can make your own by adding one level teaspoon of salt and two tablespoons of sugar per litre of water. If the person is unconscious, the dissolved rehydration salts can be administered anally. It is essential to try to stabilise someone in this way before trying to take them on a long, tough drive to hospital. ❧

JACK JACKSON is an expedition leader, mountaineer and diver. He is the author of 'The Four Wheel Drive Book' and co-author of 'The Asian Highway'.

Survival in the jungle
by Robin Hanbury-Tenison

THE KEY TO SURVIVAL IN THE TROPICS IS COMFORT. If your boots fit, your clothes don't itch, your wounds don't fester, you have enough to eat and you have the comforting presence of a local who is at home in the environment, then you are not likely to go far wrong.

Of course, jungle warfare is something else. The British, Americans and, for all I know, several other armies, have produced detailed manuals on how to survive under the most arduous conditions imaginable and with the minimum of resources. But most of us are extremely unlikely ever to find ourselves in such a situation. Even if you are unlucky enough to be caught in a guerrilla war or survive an air crash in the jungle, I believe that the following advice will be as useful as trying to remember sophisticated techniques that probably require equipment you do not have to hand anyway.

A positive will to survive is essential. The knowledge that others have travelled long distances and lived for days and even months without help or special knowledge gives confidence, while a calm appraisal of the circumstances can make them seem far less intimidating. The jungle need not be an uncomfortable place, although unfamiliarity may make it seem so. Morale is as important as ever, and comfort, both physical and mental, a vital ingredient.

Clothing and footwear

To start with, it is usually warm, but when you are wet, especially at night, you can become very cold very quickly. It is therefore important to be prepared and always try to keep a sleeping bag and a change of clothes dry. Excellent strong, lightweight plastic bags are now available in which these items should always be packed with the top folded over and tied. These can then be placed inside your rucksack or bag so that if dropped in a river or soaked by a sudden tropical downpour – and the effect is much the same – they, at least, will be dry. I usually have three such bags, one with dry clothes, one with camera equipment, notebooks, etc., and one with food. Wet clothes should be worn. This is unpleasant for the first ten minutes in the morning, but they will soon be soaking wet with sweat and dripping in any case, and wearing them means you need carry only one change for the evening and sleeping in. It is well worth taking the time to rinse them out whenever you are in sunshine by a river so that you can dry them on hot rocks in half an hour or so. They can also be hung over the fire at night, which makes them more pleasant to put on in the morning, but also tends to make them stink of wood smoke.

In this glittering equatorial slum huge trees jostle one another for room to live. The soil bursts with irrepressible vegetations... laced and bound and interwoven with interminable tangles of vines and trailers. Birds are as bright as butterflies, butterflies as big as birds.
– WINSTON CHURCHILL (1908)

Always wear loose clothes in the tropics. They may not be very becoming but constant wetting and drying will tend to shrink them and rubbing makes itches and scratches far worse. Cotton is excellent but should be of good quality so that the clothes do not rot and tear too easily. There are now many excellent specialist manufacturers of tropical clothing. Some are expensive, but it is worth investing in good quality for comfort and durability. One of the best suppliers is Nomad Camping at 3 Turnpike Lane, London N8 (tel 020 8889 7014).

For footwear, baseball boots or plimsolls are usually adequate, but for long distances good leather boots will protect your feet much better from bruising and blisters. In leech country, a shapeless cotton stocking worn between sock and shoe tied with a drawstring below the knee, outside long trousers, gives virtually complete protection. As far as I know, no one manufactures these yet, so they have to be made up specially, but they are well worth it.

Upsets and dangers

Hygiene is important in the tropics. Small cuts can turn nasty very quickly and sometimes will not heal for a long time. The best protection is to make an effort to wash all over at least once a day if possible, at the same time looking out for any sore places, cleaning and treating them at once. On the other hand, where food and drink are concerned, it is usually not practical or polite to attempt to maintain perfectionist standards. Almost no traveller in the tropics can avoid receiving hospitality and few would wish to do so. It is often best therefore to accept that a mild stomach upset is likely – and be prepared. There is an excellent medical section in this book with the best up-to-date advice on prevention and cure of all the illnesses to which travellers in the tropics are likely to be exposed and they should read it carefully. However, constant use of prophylactics and antibiotics can produce side-effects. Many of us now use homeopathic remedies, including malaria pills, while carrying conventional cures as well. Try Ainsworths of 36 New Cavendish Street, London W1M 7LH (tel 020 7935 5330, fax 020 7486 4313, email enquiries@ ainsworths.com, internet www.ainsworths.com), which has a good travel kit.

In real life-and-death conditions, there are only two essentials for survival, a knife or machete and a compass (provided you are not injured, when, if possible, the best thing to do is to crawl to water and wait for help). Other important items I would put in order of priority as follows:

1. A map.
2. A waterproof cover, cape or large bag.
3. Means to make fire: lifeboat matches, lighter with spare flints, gas or petrol.
4. A billycan.
5. Tea or coffee, sugar and dried milk.

There are few tropical terrains that cannot be crossed with these, given time and determination. Man can survive a long time without food, so try to keep your food supplies simple, basic and light. Water is less of a problem in the jungle, except in limestone mountains, but a metal or lightweight plastic water container should be carried and filled whenever possible. Rivers, streams and even puddles are unlikely to be dangerously contaminated, while rattans and lianas often contain water, as do some other plants whose leaves may form catchments, such as pitcher plants. It is easy to drink from these, though best to filter the liquid through cloth and avoid the 'gunge' at the bottom.

Hunting and trapping are unlikely to be worth the effort to the inexperienced, although it is surprising how much can be found in streams and caught with hands. Prawns, turtles, frogs and even fish can be captured with patience and almost all are edible – and even tasty if you're hungry enough. Fruits, even those that are ripe and being eaten by other animals, are less safe, while some edible-looking plants and fungi can be very poisonous and should be avoided. Don't try for the honey of wild bees unless you know what you are doing as stings can be dangerous and those of hornets even fatal.

As regards shelter, there is a clear distinction between South America and the rest of the tropical world. In the South American interior, almost everyone uses a hammock. Excellent waterproof hammocks are supplied to the Brazilian and US armies and are obtainable commercially. Otherwise, a waterproof sheet may be stretched across a line tied between the same two trees from which the hammock is slung. Elsewhere, however, hammocks are rarely used and will tend to be a nuisance under normal conditions. Lightweight canvas stretchers through which poles may be inserted before being tied apart on a raised platform make excellent beds and, once again, a waterproof sheet provides shelter. Plenty of nylon cord is always useful.

Fight it or like it

The jungle can be a frightening place at first. Loud noises, quantities of unfamiliar creepy-crawlies, flying biting things and the sometimes oppressive heat can all conspire to get you down. But it can also be a very pleasant place if you decide to like it rather than fight it – and it is very seldom dangerous. Snakebite, for example is extremely rare. During the 15 months of the Royal Geographical Society's Mulu expedition, in Borneo, no one was bitten, although we saw and avoided or caught and photographed many snakes and even ate some! Most things, such as thorns, ants and sandflies, are more irritating than painful (taking care to treat rather than scratch usually prevents trouble).

Above all, the jungle is a fascinating place – the richest environment on earth. The best help for morale is to be interested in what is going on around you and the best guide is usually a local resident who is as at home there as most of us are in cities. Fortunately, in most parts of the world where jungles survive, there are still such people. By accepting their advice, recognising their expertise and asking them to travel with you, you may help to reinforce their self-respect in the face of often overwhelming forces that try to make them adopt a so-called 'modern' way of life. At the same time, you will appreciate the jungle far more yourself – and have a far better chance of surviving in it. 🦂

Surviving the cold: 1 Take it seriously
by Dr Mike Stroud

'THE WIND WAS BLOWING BRISKLY AS I STEPPED OUT OF THE TENT, but the sun was shining and it didn't feel too bad. When I had been out earlier, briefly, answering nature's call, the air had been still, and despite it being −40°c it had seemed quite warm in the sunshine. I had decided to wear only a cotton windproof over underwear and fleece salopettes. It was amazing how little one needed to keep warm as long as you kept on working hard.

Ran and I took down the tent and packed up our sledges. The south pole was only 30 km away and, with luck, we would reach it within two days. It helped to have it so close. We had been going 12 hours a day for more than two months, and the effort had taken a terrible toll. It had been both mental and physical hell. It was not long after we set off that I realised my mistake. As well as only putting on a single jacket, I was wearing only thin contact gloves inside outer mitts and, after an hour, with the wind rising even more, my hands were suffering badly and not warming up despite moving. They became so bad that Ran had to help me put on the extra mittens from my sledge, my fingers were too useless to get them on. When we set off again, I was getting generally chilled. After the long stop fighting with the gloves, I found that I could barely pull the sledge with my cold muscles. I was in trouble, and I realised I would have to stop and put my fleece jacket on as well, but to do this meant removing my outer jacket completely and once again my fingers were useless and I was unable to do up the zips. Ran was there to help again, but I had entered a vicious circle. My thinking was beginning to fade, and although I kept walking for another half-hour or so, I was never with-it. It is only through Ran's description that I know what happened next.

I had apparently begun to move very slowly and to wander from side to side. When Ran asked if I was OK, I had been unintelligible, and he had realised immediately that I must be hypothermic. He then tried to get me to help with the tent, but I just stood around doing nothing. So he put it up alone and pushed me inside. Eventually he got me in my sleeping bag and forced me to take some hot drinks. After an hour or so I recovered, but it had been another close call. Obviously we were getting vulnerable and we discussed pulling out at the pole....'

The above is an excerpt from my book, *Shadows on the Wasteland*, about my crossing of Antarctica with Sir Ranulph Fiennes. Under the circumstances, it was perhaps not surprising that I became hypothermic, for cold easily creates casualties and can even kill. Yet, with the correct preparation, man can operate successfully even in the harshest of climates. The secret is to match the body's heat production – chiefly dictated by activity – with its heat losses – chiefly governed by clothing and shelter. You should aim to neither overheat nor cool down. Both can have unwelcome consequences.

An inactive adult produces about a light bulb's-worth of heat (100 watts), which is not really much to keep the whole body warm in the face of the cold, wind and rain. It is, therefore, generally wise to keep moving for the most of the time in cold conditions, until you have either reached or created proper shelter. However, many reasons, such as getting lost or injured, may force you to halt or lie up under adverse circumstances, and you are then going to need to reduce your heat losses to less than the 100 watts that you will be producing. This may be an impossibility if ill equipped or conditions are really harsh. If you can't reduce heat losses enough, your body will cool and you will start to shiver. This can increase your resting heat production to as much as 500 watts, but even this may be inadequate and the shivering itself is uncomfortable and tiring for the muscles. If cooling still continues, you will become hypothermic and can be in great danger. It is definitely best to carry enough protection to deal with getting stuck out in the worst possible conditions you may meet.

When you are active, things are quite different. Working hard leads the body to produce as much as a good room heater – 2,000 watts or even more. It is therefore more common to get too hot rather than too cold, even in the worst conditions. Initially, getting too hot may not be important, but it does lead to sweating, which can ruin the insulation of your clothing by wetting it from the inside and later, when you have decreased your activity or the conditions have worsened, this wet clothing will have lost its ability to protect you properly. Sweating may also lead to dehydration, which in turn will make you vulnerable to fatigue, and it is with the onset of tiredness and the ensuing slow-down in activity that heat production will start to fall and you will cool rapidly to become at risk from the 'exhaustion/hypothermia' syndrome. Even the most experienced of people have become victims under such circumstances.

In order to match heat losses to heat production, clothing must have the flexibility to be both cool and warm. It must also be able to provide windproofing and waterproofing. Such flexibility can only be achieved by the use of layers, which must be easy to put on and take off and comfortable to wear together. In all but the very coldest regions – where rain or melting snow won't occur – I would favour the use of modern synthetics in the insulation layers as they tend not to degrade very much when wetted by sweat or the environment, and they also dry spectacularly quickly. If affordable, waterproofs/windproofs should be moisture vapour permeable (MVP) since these will limit the accumulation of sweat and condensation in inner garments and will allow the evaporation of some sweat, which will help to keep you cool if overheating. However, it needs to be remembered that even MVP garments are only partially vapour permeable (especially in the cold, when water vapour will condense or even freeze on the inner surface of the garment and will then be trapped by its waterproof qualities), and so it is always better to remove the waterproof if it is not actually raining and activity is making you too hot.

Additional flexibility when trying to maintain a comfortable body temperature can be granted by changing your head covering. In the cold, when wearing good clothing, as much as 90 per cent of your heat losses can come from your head, so by putting on or taking off a warm hat or balaclava and by adjusting a windproof hood, you can make enormous changes to your heat losses much more easily than by adjusting other garments. It is often said that if you get cold hands you should put on a hat.

Eating is also an important factor in keeping warm. Even at rest a meal will rev up your metabolism and make that 100-watt bulb glow brighter, while during exercise it will considerably increase your heat output for any given level of activity. More importantly, food also helps to sustain the supply of fuels to the muscles, and this will allow you to continue working, or for that matter shivering, for longer. In addition, it will make it much less likely that you will develop a low blood sugar – a factor now thought to be important in the onset of some cases of exposure/exhaustion. Almost any food will help, but it is probably best for it to contain a fair amount of carbohydrate. Grain-based snack bars are as good as anything, but snacks based on chocolate are also excellent, even if there is a greater fat content.

When hypothermia does begin to occur in an individual, a number of changes are seen that make the diagnosis pretty easy as long as the possibility is carefully considered. Unfortunately, the person suffering from the cold is often unable to consider things properly, since he or she may not realise what is happening and often, after feeling cold, shivery and miserable initially, they may feel quite happy and even warm. It therefore goes without saying that a problem may only become evident when things have already become quite bad, and that if a victim is alone or everybody in a party becomes hypothermic simultaneously, things are very serious. The signs to watch out for are quite similar to those seen when a person becomes increasingly drunk. At first the victim may slur speech and begin to be unnaturally happy with the situation. This normally corresponds to a core temperature of around 35°C, compared to the normal 37°C, although the actual temperature varies from individual to individual and some people feel quite unwell at 36°C. Then, as cooling continues, the victim may begin to stumble or stagger and may go on to become aggressive or confused. This often correlates with a core temperature of around 33°–34°C. Eventually, at a core temperature of around 32°C, they will collapse and become unconscious, and they can go on cooling to stop breathing at around 27°C. However, their heart may not stop until core temperature is as low as 22°C, and so it is vital to remember that, however bad things seem, attempting rewarming and resuscitation may still work.

When someone first starts getting cold, act quickly by increasing clothing insulation, increasing activity or by seeking shelter. However, if choosing to shelter, remember that it may entail lying up in bad conditions and the loss of activity will cut heat production right down. This may have devastating results, and so the decision to go on or to seek emergency protection requires great judgement. Generally, I would recommend that if the victim is only just beginning to cool, push on if proper warm conditions are likely to be reached reasonably quickly. Hot drinks and food are also of great value, but will only be helpful while the victim is conscious and cooperative. Once again, however, remember that sitting around preparing them may have adverse effects.

If the victim is worse and is actually showing signs of staggering or confusion, the situation is becoming dangerous. Obviously additional clothing, hot drinks or seeking a course out of the wind remain of paramount importance, but the question of carrying on becomes more difficult since now it is probably better to stop if reasonable shelter is available. When going out in cold environments, you should always plan to carry some sort of windproof and waterproof bivouac protection – noting that, although tempting weight-wise, lightweight silvered survival blankets have been shown to be no more effective than a plastic sheet and definitely worse than a plastic or more rugged waterproof bag. You may, of course, be planning on camping anyway, in which case you need only ensure that your tent is adequate and that you have practised pitching it when the wind is up. It is no good finding out that it cannot be done with your model when you need it in emergency. Ideally, you should also be carrying a sleeping bag, even if you had no plans to get trapped outside, for there is no doubt that putting a victim in a good bag, and if necessary getting in it with them, is the best course of action if you are forced to stop.

Obviously, shelter can be sought as well as carried. In an emergency, it is a nice warm building that is best, but this is not normally an option. The priority then becomes getting out of the wind and wet, and any natural feature that you can get under or into the lee of is of great value. Also remember that effective shelter may often be found close in on the windward side of an object, particularly if it has a vertical side that will generate back pressure and a 'dead spot' immediately in front of it. Much to many people's surprise, the shelter there may even be better than to leeward since swirling vortices of snow do not come curling round and drifting over you. In conditions with decent snow cover, compacted snow or ice can be used to create a whole range of possible shelters, ranging from simple snowholes to multiple-roomed camps, but really you need to have been taught how to make them and be carrying a suitable snow shovel. Reading about building such shelters cannot replace experience, and before going out in really severe conditions one should have practised in safe conditions. Ideally, you should have attended a proper course on winter survival such as those run by the British Mountaineering Council in Scotland or North Wales.

If a victim has cooled so much that they are unconscious, they need medical attention urgently. However, while this is sought or awaited, every measure mentioned above should be made to protect them from further cooling. As a general rule, never give up trying to protect and warm them, even if they appear to be dead. People have been successfully resuscitated many hours after they have apparently stopped breathing, and you cannot rely upon being able to feel a pulse or hear their heart. It is said that hypothermia victims are 'not dead until they are warm and dead' and so, generally speaking, it is impossible to be sure while you are still out in the field.

I would reiterate that, with the correct preparation, you can operate safely and relatively comfortably in terrible conditions, but doing so is an art. That art needs to be learned and it is a mixture of education, preparation and forethought. Remember that hypothermia could happen to you or one or your party even in a temperate climate and indeed, it is more likely to happen in milder, wetter conditions than in the truly cold regions of the Earth.

I will finish with another extract that illustrates just how easy it is to be caught out, and how simple it is to remedy the situation.

'As he approached, I wondered what was wrong. He was moving slowly and seemed to be fiddling with his clothing, trying to undo the zip on the front of his sodden jacket. He was smiling and certainly looked happier than he had done 15 minutes back but I noticed that he stumbled a couple of times despite it being pretty flat. He drew up beside me where I stood with my back to the gale.

"Jusht a moment," he said, and then after quite a pause, "I've jusht got to get thish jacket off."

His voice was slurred and I looked at him more closely. Although he smiled, there was a strange, wild expression on his face and his eyes were slightly glazed. He wasn't shivering any more but his skin was as white as marble and I noticed that he had taken his gloves off and they were nowhere to be seen. He was also swaying as he began to almost rip at his clothing, frustrated by his fruitless attempts to pull down the zip with cold fingers.

"Are you OK?" I asked, but I got no reply, only an inane black grin as he continued with his attempts to undress. The truth began to dawn on me.

"Come on," I said, grasping him by the arm and pulling him towards the edge of the ridge. "We'll go down here and drop out of the wind."

The effect was quite spectacular. As we entered the lee of the Cwm, the noise and buffeting that we had endured all day ceased and the world became an almost silent place. It seemed so much warmer that as I hurried downward, I began to sweat, but for my companion, who I almost dragged along beside me, the move into shelter brought a different experience. Although he, too, began to warm, it only brought him back towards the normal and, with it, he began to shiver and feel miserably cold.

I could scarcely believe what I had just witnessed. It was only September on Snowdon, yet my father had been to the edge of disaster….'

Remember, always treat the cold with respect and never underestimate what even the UK weather can produce. ❧

DR MIKE STROUD set a polar record with Sir Ranulph Fiennes by completing the longest unsupported journey in the Antarctic. He specialises in the effect of physical extremes on the body and is based at the Army Personnel Research Establishment at Farnborough.

Surviving the cold: 2 Some guidelines
by Dr Richard Dawood

COLONEL JIM ADAM, THE MILITARY PHYSIOLOGIST who was, until recently, responsible for maintaining 'combat-effectiveness' of British troops under all conditions, advises observing the following steps in the event of hypothermia:

1. Stop all activity.
2. Protect those at risk by rigging a makeshift shelter from the wind, rain and snow; lay the victim on the ground, on a ground sheet or space blanket.
3. Remove wet clothing, and insulate the victim in a sleeping bag.
4. Rewarm the victim with hot drinks, then hot food or high-energy snacks; unconscious victims should be rewarmed by a companion's body warmth.
5. Observe the victim for the cessation of breathing or pulse, and start mouth-to-mouth resuscitation or cardiac massage if necessary.
6. Send for help.
7. Insist on treating the victim as a stretcher case.

Acute hypothermia

This is a medical emergency, and is almost always the result of falling into water colder than 5°C. The victim shivers violently, inhales water, panics, may have respiratory or cardiac arrest, and is dead from drowning in about five to 15 minutes. Survival is more likely if the victim is wearing a life-jacket that keeps the face out of the water and is able to keep perfectly still. Careful first aid is essential. Following rescue from the water, do not allow the victim to move or make any physical

Some guidelines

■ Don't drink. Alcohol causes peripheral vasoldilation – it increases blood flow through the skin – which can dramatically increase heat loss in extreme temperatures.

■ Don't smoke. Nicotine can cause vasoconstriction – reduction in blood flow to hands, fingers and toes – increasing the likelihood of frostbite.

■ Carry high-energy carbohydrate snacks, such as glucose sweets or Mars bars.

■ Carry extra layers of clothing.

■ Carry chemical hand-warming sachets to put inside gloves and shoes.

■ If you are on an expedition, or are looking after a large group, carry a special low-reading thermometer to measure body temperature: normal clinical thermometers are not adequate for detecting hypothermia. You may also be well advised to carry instruments for measuring high wind speed and estimating wind chill.

■ Anything that reduces activity, such as being stranded on a chair lift or being injured, can result in a rapid fall in body temperature; if this happens to you, try to maintain some muscular activity to generate warmth.

■ Children are at special risk. In particular, they need extra head protection (mechanical as well as against heat loss). Frost nip and frostbite can affect later growth.

■ In cold conditions it is easy to underestimate the need to protect skin and eyes against excessive sunlight. Take extra care.

effort. Keep the victim horizontal or slightly head-down, protect against further heat loss and arrange transportation immediately to a hospital so that rapid re-warming may begin. The most effective way of rewarming is a bath – at 42°C or as hot as the bare elbow can tolerate. Until normal body temperature is restored, the victim is at high risk from sudden death, partly because rewarming may actually trigger an initial further drop in body temperature; many victims of accidents at sea die after they have been removed from the water – sometimes even in hospital.

Frostbite

Localised injuries from the cold can affect limbs with exposed skin even when core body temperature is entirely normal. This happens when insulation is not adequate or on account of other factors, such as a restricted blood supply due to clothing that is too tight. Injuries of this kind range from frostbite following freezing of the tissues of the nose, checks, chin, ears, fingers and feet, to more common problems such as frost nips and chapping of the skin, especially of the lips, nose and hands, and often compounded by sunburn.

The best way to deal with frostbite is to take careful steps to prevent it. Ensure, particularly, that gloves, socks and footwear are suitable for the conditions and the task in hand, and do not choose extreme conditions to wear any of these items for the first time. Carry a face mask to protect yourself from high wind and driving snow and carry chemical hand-warmers that can be used when needed.

Impending frostbite is usually signalled by intense pain in the part at risk, this should not be ignored and prompt rewarming is necessary. For example, hands and fingers should be slipped under the clothes and warmed in the opposite armpit. If the pain is ignored it eventually disappears, the part then becomes numb, white and hard to touch – it is frozen.

Established frostbite is a serious problem that may need lengthy hospital treatment. Once thawing has taken place, tissue is liable to much more extensive damage from even slight chilling. During evacuation, keep the affected part clean and dry and give painkillers and antibiotics (if available) to prevent infection. Never rub frostbite with snow or anything else, because the tissues are extremely fragile and will suffer more damage.

The executive target
by Roy Carter

ALL OVER THE WORLD, IN SUCH DIVERSE AREAS as Central America or the Middle East, the level of politically motivated violence increases almost daily. The victim's nationality – or supposed nationality – is often the sole reason for him or her being attacked. Gone forever are the days when kidnap and murder threatened only the wealthy and influential. Instead, political and religious fanatics often regard ordinary citizens as legitimate targets, and this view will become more prevalent as prominent people take ever more effective steps to protect themselves. The average traveller is much more vulnerable, but still worthy of publicity – which is generally the motive behind all terrorist action.

No one travelling to certain parts of the world can sensibly afford to ignore the danger. If the risk exists everywhere, it naturally increases dramatically in known trouble spots. Nor is it wise to rely on the law of averages for protection. Terrorism and crime thrive on complacency, and a fatalistic attitude can actually create danger. Awareness is vital, and it is surprisingly easy for any intelligent person to do the sort of homework that can pay life-saving dividends.

The first step is to understand something of the anatomy of political crime. Terrorist violence is rarely, if ever, carried out as randomly as it sometimes appears. Particularly in the case of kidnapping, the victim will first be observed – often for a period of days – for evidence of vulnerability. Translating an awareness of the threat into a few simple precautions means offering a difficult target to people who want an easy one. Invariably they will look elsewhere. It is impossible to say how many lives have been saved in this way, because the threat, by its very nature, is covert, but the number is undoubtedly high. The majority of terrorist abductions are facilitated by the victim developing a regular pattern of behaviour, or being ignorant of the dangers in a strange country. No experienced traveller would forego vital inoculations or fail to enquire about the drinking water. Testing the political climate should be regarded as a natural extension of the same safeguards. After all, the object is the same, and the price of failure at least as high.

Of course, the most straightforward response to ominous events is simply to cancel or postpone the visit. In extremes this option should not be disregarded, but there will be occasions, especially for the business traveller, when such a drastic answer is difficult or impossible. An intelligent interest in the press and television news is a fundamental requirement in making the final decision. Sensible analysis of media reports will answer many questions about known trouble spots and help predict others. If nothing else, it will highlight areas for further study. Equally important, but easily overlooked, sound research can help put less-serious situations into perspective. Unnecessary worry based on sensationalism or rumour can be a problem in itself.

Official attitude

It is crucial to get a balanced idea of the official attitude in the country to be visited. The host government's status and its relationship with the visitor's country are always critical factors. A basically hostile or unstable government will always increase the danger to individual travellers, either directly, or by such indirect means as ineffective policing. Examples of the former risk have been seen very clearly in the imprisonment of British citizens in Montenegro and Sierra Leone. Finding the truth will usually involve delving beneath the headlines. In Britain, an approach to the Foreign Office can produce surprisingly frank answers. Next, and more obviously, an analysis of recent terrorist activity should aim to answer three essential questions: when and where it happens, what form it takes and, most importantly, whom is it directed against? The first two answers will help establish precautionary measures. The third may indicate the degree of risk by revealing common factors. A series of identical abductions from motor vehicles in a particular part of the city, involving the same nationalities or professions, for example, should be augury enough for even the most sceptical observer.

Local feeling

It is also as well to know as much as possible about feelings among the local populace, which are by no means guaranteed to be the same as those of the government. National identity, and even religion, are often viewed quite differently 'on the street', although the bias is just as likely to be favourable as not. One need not even step outside the UK to demonstrate the validity of this advice, as an Englishman on the streets of west Belfast could quickly discover. And in a country with a large Western expatriate community, for instance, any Caucasian will generally be regarded as belonging to the predominant foreign nationality. Depending on the local situation, this type of mistaken identity can be dangerous or advantageous. At least one case, the 1985 abduction of three British visitors to Beirut by anti-American Muslim extremists, resulted from a mistake in the victims' nationality.

These attacks, and others involving French and US citizens, took place outside the victims' homes, highlighting perfectly standard terrorist methods. Known reference points such as home or places of work are always by far the most dangerous. The much-publicised kidnap and subsequent murder of former Italian premier Aldo Moro by the so-called Red Brigade was a notable example of this fact.

Soft targets

Such vital, but frequently forgotten, cases demonstrate more than a need for extra care at home and in the office. They show equally the terrorists' need for soft targets and their reluctance to proceed beyond basic research to find them. Terrorist resources and abilities are limited and to regard terrorists as being omnipotent is both mistaken and dangerous. Sensible precautions, such as varying times of arrival and departure, parking in different places – facing in different directions – watching for and reporting suspicious activity before leaving home, and entering and leaving by different doors, sound almost too simple, but they really do work. Only the most specific kind of motivation would justify continued surveillance of a clearly unpredictable and cautious target.

Company image

In addition to such general precautions, the business traveller will usually need to examine more particular issues. He will need to know how his company is perceived by various local factions. Previous threats or attacks on company employees should be studied with great care, as should incidents involving similar organisations. Where applicable, the local knowledge of expatriate colleagues will be useful, but watch for bias or over-familiarity. In the absence of any actual events, examine the company's standing in the community, especially where a conflict of interest exists between government and opposition groups. Never forget that a company will often be judged solely on the basis of its clients and associates. Always consider the status of the people you intend to visit. In these days of trade sanctions and mutually antagonistic markets, the chances are high that any association will offend someone.

Practical action

But analysis is only a partial answer. The results must be translated into coherent action. In extreme cases, the business traveller might need special training in such areas as defensive driving, emergency communication and surveillance recognition. Many of the larger companies will provide special briefings, but their failure to do so should never be taken as a sign that no danger exists. It could equally indicate a lack of awareness or a misguided decision not to cause alarm. There is nothing at all wrong with alarm if it is justified. It may even be a necessity.

Regardless of whether special training is given or not, all travellers to high-risk areas should follow certain basic rules as a matter of course. Keep friends and colleagues informed of your whereabouts and stay in company as much as possible. Use inconspicuous means of transport, but avoid public transport in favour of taxis. If in doubt, wait for the second cab in the rank. Never take a taxi if the driver is not alone. Dress down and leave expensive accessories at home. Don't book hotels in the company's name. In all, practise being nondescript in public.

In a hazardous location

- Kidnappers need prior warning, tip-offs or knowledge of routine schedules to do their dirty work. Vary your schedule, change walking routes, and don't be shy about changing hotel rooms or assigned cabs.

- Avoid restaurants frequented by expats and tourists. Don't make reservations in your own name. Don't sit outside.

- Get used to sitting near emergency exits, memorise escape routes so you can follow them in the dark, lock your doors and be wary at all times.

- Do not discuss your plans, accommodations, finances or politics with strangers.

- Do not show your name, country or hotel ID on luggage or clothing. When a clerk asks for your room number, write it down for him rather than say it aloud.

- Watch your drinks being poured.

Source: Fielding's 'The World's Most Dangerous Places'

Try not to think of these rules as an inconvenience but as a natural consequence of your stay in a strange country, like remembering to use a foreign language. Relaxing one rule might be tempting but it could be the mistake that negates all the rest. Better to extend precautions than limit them. For example, travelling regularly by the same route can undo all the good work on the home front. The kidnap and murder of German industrialist Hans-Martin Schleyer was carried out because his attackers were able to predict confidently both his route and timing. The murder in India of British diplomat Percy Norris by Middle Eastern terrorists likewise occurred along his regular route to work. Mr Norris was shot to death in the back seat of his chauffeur-driven car when it halted at traffic lights.

On the move

Make a habit of changing places in the car if you have a driver or use a taxi now and then instead. The chances of being attacked on the move are extremely remote. It follows that road junctions, traffic signals, etc., are always more dangerous than, say, stretches of dual carriageway. A prospective attacker will study his victim's route carefully and identify vulnerable spots. If he can do so, so can you. Be aware of these danger areas and stay on the alert when negotiating them. If driving yourself, keep the car in gear and ready for a quick getaway at temporary halts. Keep sufficient space between yourself and any leading vehicles to avoid being boxed in. Routinely lock all doors and keep the windows wound up.

Last of all, remember that you stand more chance of being an accident casualty than a victim of terrorism. Far from being dangerous, a little knowledge can stack the odds even higher in your favour. You'll probably never know if it passes the acid test – but you'll be in no doubt at all if it doesn't. ❧

ROY CARTER writes on corporate security and risk management and was a senior consultant for an international group of security companies.

Surviving a civil war
by Anne Sharpley

D ON'T TAKE IT TOO PERSONALLY WHEN THE SHOOTING STARTS. They are almost certainly not shooting at you – and if they are, it is even safer since the level of marksmanship is so low (at least in all street shooting I have been caught up in) that you are almost invulnerable. Hollywood never comes to your aid at such moments. You would have thought that the rigorous early training we all get at the movies in both armed and unarmed fighting would have got into our reflexes. But it is all so much more muddled when it happens. Far from knowing when and where to duck, I could never make out where the fighting was coming from or which side of the wall or handy car to duck behind.

As for hand-to-hand fighting, far from the balletic, clearly defined choreography of cinematic bouts, it is generally a messy, confused affair in which everyone gets puffed, or sick, or falls over in a shambles of misunderstood intentions. Nor is there that crack on the jaw to let you know who is being hit when. So it is even poor in terms of spectator interest.

As a reporter, it is usually my job to be there and see what is happening. This means I cannot follow my own best advice, which is to get out.

Sticking around is the easy bit. It is the next stage of events, which sets in during and after the street blocks, cordons, summary arrests and general paralysis as order is imposed on a troubled area, that presents the visitor with new problems.

Communications with the outside world cease, public utilities go wrong and airports close. This is the guaranteed scenario. So forget the bullet-proof vest you wish you had thought of and get on with the practicalities. The first and best rule is worth observing before you leave home – never pack more than you can run with. Always include a smaller, lighter bag such as an airline bag, because if things get really nasty you need something handy with a shoulder strap to pick up and clear out with in a hurry.

Essentials

If you are in a situation in which something is likely to happen, it is worth keeping this bag packed with essentials. Do not run about with suitcases – you can't do it for long.

Always bring in your duty-free allowances if you know things are likely to get tough. Even if you are a non-smoking, teetotaller who hates scent, cigarettes, alcohol and perfume are the stuff of which bribes and rewards for favours are made. And as banks close or the money exchange goes berserk, they may end up as your only bargaining resource. And remember that drink is a useful stimulant, as well as a solace. If I have to stay up all night, I do it on regular small nips of whisky.

The next bit of advice will seem absurd at first, but you will regret having laughed at it if you ever get into one of those long-standing, semi-siege situations that sometimes happen when you are stuck in a hotel that either cannot or will not

In a warzone

■ Avoid politics, do not challenge the beliefs of your host, be firm but not belligerent about getting what you need. Talking politics with soldiers is like reading Playboy with a priest. It kills time, but is probably not a rewarding pastime.

■ Travel only with permission from the controlling authorities. In many cases you will need multiple permission from officers, politicians and the regional commander.

■ Remember that a letter of safe passage from a freedom group presented at an army checkpoint could be your death warrant. Understand and learn the zones of control and protocol for changing sides during active hostilities.

■ Remember that it is very unusual for non-combatants to be wandering around areas of conflict. If you are travelling, make sure you have the name of a person that you wish to see, an end destination to mention, and a convincing reason for passing through.

■ Understand where the frontlines are, the general rules of engagement, meet journalists and photographers (usually to be found at hotel bars) to understand the local threats.

■ Carry a lot of money hidden in various places. Be ready to leave or evacuate at any time: this means travelling very light. Choose a place to sleep that would be survivable in case of a rocket or shell attack.

■ Carry critical information on a laminated card – your blood type, country, phone number, local contact, allergies.

■ Do not engage in intrigue or meetings that are not in public view. In many places, they still shoot spies. Do accept any invitations for dinner, tea or social activities: getting to know your hosts is important. Don't gossip or lie.

■ Carry a first aid kit with syringes, antibiotics, intravenous needles, anaesthetics and pain killers, as well as the usual medication.

■ Dress and act conservatively. Be quietly engaging and affable, and listen a lot. Your actions will indicate your intentions, as the locals weigh up their interest in helping you. It may take them some time to check you out before offering assistance.

Source: Fielding's 'The World's Most Dangerous Places'

provide for you. Take one of those little aluminium pans with a solid fuel burner, so small it will slip into your pocket. You can boil water at the rate of quarter of a pint to one solid fuel stick, which is about the size of a cigarette. The whole thing is available from camping shops relatively cheaply. If you take a few tea bags or a small jar of instant coffee, this will not only help if you are a caffeine addict but also help to win friends and allies in an hour of need. Serve it up in a tooth mug, but don't forget to put a (metal) spoon in before you pour in the boiling water, or you'll crack the glass.

As the water supply will either shut down completely or turn a threatening colour, it is just as well to have a means of making water sterile. And at the very least it provides a shave. If things look ugly, it is a good idea to fill the bath. You can keep filling it if supplies continue, but you cannot get water at all if they really stop. Not only do you then have a means of keeping the toilet in a less revolting state, but you can also wash yourself and stave off thirst (boil or sterilise the water first, of course). I always like to carry a small box of biscuits, although this is nothing more than a psychological trick to reinforce feelings of self-sufficiency.

If things get really hectic, nobody in a hotel wants to know about you but they get rather interested in your property. It is a great time for getting everything stolen. I came back from Prague in 1968 with scarcely a thing left. What is yours suddenly becomes theirs. So remember that overnight bag and carry it with you everywhere.

Whether you should try to look less conspicuously foreign is a moot point. War correspondents usually get themselves kitted out in a sort of quasi-military get-up, and where there are women soldiers, as in Israel, I have too. If nothing else, it meant I could fill my taxi with girl soldiers and let them get me past the road blocks with their papers. But when I found myself in action before I had time to change, I was told afterwards by a captured sniper that it was my pretty pink blouse that had saved me. He'd had me in his sights and liked the colour, so he couldn't bring himself to shoot me.

You are much more likely to be holed up in your hotel, however. If things are exploding under fire, it is as well to get any movable glass down on the floor, draw curtains and blinds against window glass and drape mirrors you can't take down with blankets and towels. Glass is the biggest danger you face. Locate the fire escape, and if it's remote get yourself somewhere else to stay either in the same hotel or elsewhere.

Identity in a crisis

It is always worth trying to pretend you are from a country they are not having a row with, although local knowledge of nationalities is always limited, so don't try Finnish or Papuan. This is for occasional use when they are running around looking for someone to duff up. Hit the right nationality and you are so popular they won't put you down. Crowds are very emotional and the least thing sends them one way or the other.

Women are still quite often treated chivalrously in the Middle East. In some countries, I found that to get through road blocks I could simply say I was an 'English Miss', without having to hand over my passport with the damning word 'journalist' in it. What echoes it evoked, why they were so responsive, I never quite found out; but I liked to think that I had some modest affinity with those amazingly bossy English women, from Hester Stanhope onwards, who have travelled undaunted in the Middle East. Certainly I found that Muslim sentries were unable to challenge me. I always walked straight through, looking determined.

Another useful tip for visiting women in tricky situations in Muslim countries is to apply to visit the chief wife of whoever is in power. There is always a go-between who will arrange it for a sum, escort you there and help generally. As women in harems are bored out of their minds, they are usually delighted to see another woman from the outside world. If they like you, and you must make sure they do (that's where the duty-free scent or your best blouse or scarf come in), they will do a great deal to help. They always have more power than is generally believed.

Keep calling

While ordinary communications often stop altogether, it is a good idea to tell your family or company to keep on telephoning you from the outside. So often I have found it impossible to get calls out, while incoming calls made it.

You can always try the journalist's old trick of getting out to the airport, picking a friendly face about to board whatever aircraft is leaving and giving them a message to take.

One belief I have always held, which may not necessarily be true but has always worked for me, is that befriending a taxi driver can be extremely useful. They are a much-maligned lot. What you do is to practice your basic physiognomy – a derided skill, but it's all you've got – and pick a driver you think you can trust. Then use him all the time, paying him over the odds of course. Take an interest in him and his family, and you will find a friend.

A taxi driver not only knows where everything is and what is going on, but can also act as interpreter and spare hand. Explain what you are trying to do and they soon enter into the spirit of things. One taxi driver in Cyprus virtually did my job for me. Not only was he fearless, he was also accurate.

The late ANNE SHARPLEY won awards as Woman Journalist of the Year and Descriptive Writer of the Year.

Espionage and interrogation
by Christopher Portway

B EING SOMETHING OF AN INQUISITIVE JOURNALIST with a penchant for visiting those countries which normal people don't, I have, over the years, developed a new hobby. Some of us collect stamps, cigarette cards or matchboxes. I collect interrogations. And the preliminary to interrogation is, of course, arrest and detention, which makes me, perhaps, a suitable person to dwell for a few moments on some of the activities that can land the innocent traveller in prison, as well as the best way of handling matters arising thereof.

In some countries, there are no set rules governing what is and is not a crime. Different regimes have different ways of playing the game, and it's not just cut-and-dried crimes such as robbing a bank or even dealing on the black market that can put you behind bars. Perhaps a brief resumé of some of my own experiences will give you the idea and suggest means of extracting yourself from the clutches of a warped authority.

That nasty word 'espionage' has become a stock accusation, beloved by perverted authority worldwide. Spying covers a multitude of sins and is a most conveniently vague charge to lay against anyone who sees more than is good for him (or her). It is often in dictatorial countries that you have to be most careful, but some other states have picked up on the idea, too. Spying, of a sort, can also be directed against you. In my time, I have been followed by the minions of the secret police forces in Prague and Vladivostok for hours on end. Personally, I quite enjoyed the experience and led them a merry dance through a series of department stores in a vain effort to shake them off. If nothing else, I gave them blisters.

During World War ii, to go back a bit, I escaped from a pow camp in Poland through the unwitting courtesy of the German State Railway. The journey came to an abrupt end at Gestapo hq in Krakow. In post-war years, the then Orient Express carried me, visa-less, into the Stalin-controlled former Czechoslovakia. That journey put me inside as a compulsory guest of the stb, the former Czech secret police. I have met minor inconveniences of a similar nature in countries such as Russia, Albania and Yugoslavia, as well as several Middle Eastern nations, but it was only in the 1970s that I bumped into real trouble again – in Idi Amin's Uganda. Interrogations à la James Bond....

The venues of all my interrogations have been depressingly similar. In Kampala, for instance, it consisted of a bare, concrete-walled office containing a cheap desk, a hard-backed chair or two, a filing cabinet, a telephone and an askew photograph of Idi Amin. This consistently describes Krakow, Prague and Kishinev, except that in Nazi days nobody would have dreamt of an askew Fuhrer. Prague boasted an anglepoise lamp, but then communist methods of extracting information always did border on the cinematic.

Methods of arrest or apprehension obviously vary with the circumstances. For the record, in World War ii, I was handed over to the Gestapo by a bunch of Bavarian squaddies who could find no excuse for my lobbing a brick through the window of a bakery after curfew. In Czechoslovakia I was caught crossing a railway bridge in a frontier zone and, with five guns aligned to one's navel, heroics are hard to come by. In the Soviet Union it was simply a case of my being caught with my trousers down in a 'soft-class' toilet while in possession of an out-of-date visa valid only for a place where I was not. And in Uganda there was no reason at all, beyond an edict from Idi that stipulated a policy of "Let's be beastly to the British".

But in Uganda, the line of questioning was different. It wasn't so much why had I come, but why had I come for so brief a period? The other sticking point was the presence of the young Ugandan law student arrested with me. Being in close confinement in a railway carriage for 24 hours, we had become travelling companions, which, coupled with my suspiciously brief stay, spelled 'dirty work at the crossroads' to the Ugandan authorities.

Upon rummaging about in our wallets and pockets, they found bits of paper on which we had scribbled our exchanged addresses. It had been the student's idea and a pretty harmless one but, abruptly, I was made aware how small inconsistencies can be blown up into a balloon of deepest suspicion. All along I maintained I hardly knew the guy. (Which reminds me that the Gestapo, too, had an irksome habit of looking for a scapegoat among the local populace.) Then we came to the next hurdle. "How is it your passport indicates you are a company director but this card shows you are a journalist?" To explain that I was once a company director and had retained the title in my passport in preference to the sometimes provocative 'journalist' would only have complicated matters. So I offered the white lie that I was still a company director and only a journalist in my spare time.

In another of Kampala's Police HQ interrogation rooms, all my proffered answers had to be repeated at dictation speed. It was partly a ruse, of course, to see if the second set matched the first – and I was going to be damn sure it did.

And, you know, there comes a moment when you actually begin to believe that you are a spy or whatever it is they are trying to suggest. It creeps up in some harmless answer to a question. In Kampala I felt the symptoms and resolved to keep my answers simple – and remember them for the second time round.

For instance: "What school did you attend?" I named the one I was at the longest. There was no need to mention the other two.

My regimental association membership card came up for scrutiny. "What rank were you?" I was asked. —"Corporal," I replied, giving the lowest rank I had held. Pride alone prevented me from saying "Private". —"Which army?" came the further enquiry. I had to admit that it was British.

Every now and again, I would put in a bleat about having a train to catch – more as a cornerstone of normality than a hope of catching it. And finally, in most interrogations, there does come a point when there is a lull in proceedings during which you can mount a counter-attack. The "Why-the-hell-am-I-here? What-crime-am-I-supposed-to-have-committed?" sort of thing, which at least raises your morale if not the roof.

Of course, in Nazi Germany such outbursts helped little, because in a declared wartime one's rights are minimal, and the Gestapo had such disgusting methods of upholding theirs. But in the grey world of undeclared wars, the borderline of bloody-mindedness is less well defined. At Kishinev, the KGB had the impertinence to charge me a fiver a day for my incarceration in a filthy room in a frontier unit's barracks. I voiced my indignation loud and clear and eventually won a refund.

In Czechoslovakia, my outburst had a different effect. The interrogator was so bewildered that he raised his eyes to the ceiling long enough for me to pinch one of his pencils. And in the cell that became my home for months, a pencil was a real treasure.

I should add that, in general, the one demand you have a right to make is to be put in touch with your own embassy or consulate. I once wasn't – and it caused an international incident.

I suppose one lesson I ought to have learnt from all this is to take no incriminating evidence, such as press cards, association membership cards, other travellers' addresses and the like. But a few red herrings do so add to the entertainment. ❧

CHRISTOPHER PORTWAY has been a freelance travel writer for over 20 years.

Countries in conflict
by Andrew Duncan

With the end of the Cold War and the break-up of the Soviet Union it might be thought that the world would be a safer place. Unfortunately this is not so, and there are now more places which are unsafe to visit than ever before. It is true that the number of wars between states has significantly fallen; but sadly the instances of civil war, or situations which fall short of full-scale civil war but where violence or terrorism can erupt without warning, have dramatically increased. Now the bloodshed is caused by AK-47 rifles, machetes and, of course, land mines.

All such situations are included in the global review that follows. This report also takes into account the advice offered by the British Foreign and Commonwealth Office and the United States' State Department; their advice does not always coincide, and often the threat to Americans is seen as greater than that to British travellers.

The end of the Cold War means that the possibility of a Third World War starting in Europe between the forces of the communist world and those of the Western Alliance (NATO), which would probably have escalated into all-out nuclear war, has now disappeared. However, in the developing world, the cessation of superpower hostilities has had a mixed effect. The superpowers, who invariably took sides in any minor Third World conflict or civil war so as to embarrass each other and vie for influence, also made sure that such conflicts did not get out of hand, preventing a direct confrontation between them. So now that the US no longer wishes to be a world policeman, and Russia is unable to be one even in its own sphere of influence, the result is that conflicts are less influenced by outside powers and so are more vicious and bloody than before. And there are more of them.

In short, my dear Sir, we must take the world, and the things in it, as they are; it is a dirty world, but, like France, has a vast number of good things in it.
– PHILIP THICKNESSE (1789)

For a time, the United Nations, finding it easier now to get Security Resolutions passed where once they would have been vetoed by either the US or the USSR, embarked on a record number of peace-keeping missions, some of which were spectacularly unsuccessful. More recently, the threat of Russian and Chinese vetoes in the Security Council has returned, and this has led to the unilateral use of force without UN authority, as in the bombing of Serbia over Kosovo.

Another result of the end of the cold war and the collapse of communism has been the rise in nationalism and religious extremism that re-ignited many long-standing disputes, which communism had kept firmly under control.

Countries do not become automatically safe just because a cease-fire has been arranged, nor even when this is converted into a peace settlement. For many years after fighting stops, the land will still be littered with unexploded bombs and other munitions. Far worse, vast areas are usually highly dangerous to enter because of the hundreds of anti-personnel mines left by the contestants, more often than not without any warning signs. (A number of de-mining groups believe that the UN's estimates are grossly exaggerated – not that this is any comfort to those still being maimed.) There is also often a residue of armed men who can find no other way of life than that of violent crime.

In countries recovering from conflict, fragile political settlements may lead to the rise of terrorism. Terrorist attacks are often aimed at achieving publicity and, as terrorists choose soft targets, these often include tourists and the facilities frequented by them. In such countries, too, poverty often leads to crime: there are a number of countries where the crime rate makes them unsafe for holiday-makers – though potentially less dangerous for business travellers, who are unlikely to leave the centre of major towns.

Europe

Europe is now less dangerous than it was, say, two or three years ago. The terrorist war in Northern Ireland (and to a lesser extent in the UK) appears to be over, though there is the appearance of a rise in the activities of dissident terrorist factions. It was also thought that, in Spain, the Basque separatists ETA had ended their terrorist campaign, but sadly ETA announced that it was resuming its use of violence in its fight for independence; its attacks have now spread over the border into south-west France. Terrorist outbreaks elsewhere in Europe, by dissident groups such as Algerian Islamists or Turkish Kurds seeking international publicity (a bomb in a foreign capital is worth two at home) are much reduced. These are now low-risk dangers and should not deter travellers so long as local advice is heeded.

The Balkans present a more complex picture. In Bosnia-Herzegovina and Croatia, the fighting has been stopped but ancient hatreds remain. In Bosnia, freedom of movement is meant to be available everywhere, but there are many checkpoints and the Serbian entity (Republika Srpska) is virtually independent. Many landmines still have to be lifted. In Kosovo, tragic events have brought peace and temporary freedom to most of that province, but it is still a dangerous place, particularly in the north and around Mitrovica, a city that is spilt between Albanians and Serbs. (The borders west and south of the city are the scene of Albanian efforts to provoke Serbian action in the predominantly Albanian-populated areas just across the border in Serbia.) There is still a danger from mines and unexploded ammunition and bombs (particularly US cluster bombs, of which a percentage usually fail to explode). The future of the region is uncertain and the next area to see fighting could be Montenegro, which is distancing itself from Belgrade; violence here could drag NATO forces into the conflict as well as neighbouring states. Albania is still a relatively lawless state and the level of poverty there is an incitement to crime. Travel in Serbia and Montenegro is not recommended.

In the Russian Caucasus and in the former Soviet Republics of the Transcaucasus, an uneasy peace exists. The Russians have assaulted Chechnya for a second time, with greater success, but guerrilla warfare is likely to continue for some time – and not just in the mountains, but wherever the Chechens can exact revenge on the Russians. Fortunately, the war has not spilt over into neighbouring republics;

nor have any of the other Caucasian Republics followed the Chechen example of breaking away from the Russian Federation. To the south of the Caucasian Mountains, the civil wars in Georgia and over the Armenian enclave of Nagorno Karabakh in Azerbaijan have abated, but the causes of war are not yet resolved and violence could recur at any time.

In Turkey, the Kurdish uprising in the east and south-east of the country continues, but at a lower intensity than before. There is still a very large military presence and clashes still occur.

North Africa

There is still no solution to the long-standing problem of the Western Sahara, which was annexed by Morocco, and has been the scene of many years' fighting between the Moroccan Army and Polisario guerrillas based in Algeria. No progress has been made on holding a un-monitored referendum on the region's future. Though there is little violence at present, travel to the Western Sahara is still not recommended. The Algerian-Moroccan border is closed.

In Algeria, the vicious struggle between the military government and the Islamic Salvation Front (fis) appears to be over, although some hardliners are still holding out and are being hunted by the army.

The un ban on air travel to Libya has been lifted since the handover of two Libyans suspected of causing the Lockerbie air disaster. Organised tourist groups are now being allowed to visit the country.

Western and Central Africa

This is still the most conflict-torn region in the world. The Angolan civil war seemed to be over, but the un has withdrawn its mission after fighting broke out again. In Liberia, the level of violence has decreased substantially, but full peace eludes the several parties to the conflict there, and it remains a dangerous place. In Sierra Leone, five years of civil war appeared to come to an end when the government and the rebels of the Revolutionary United Front reached agreement. However, the implementation of the peace accord is not progressing well and violence has broken out again in various parts of the country. A un peace-keeping force has been deployed, and the mainly Nigerian-backed West African peace-keeping force that also caused much violence has been withdrawn.

Burundi and Rwanda are beginning to settle down, after periods of genocide and enormous refugee flows, but it remains very unwise to visit these countries. Rwanda's civil war was continued among the many thousands of refugees who fled to the Democratic Republic of Congo (formerly Zaire). These refugees included many perpetrators of the genocide, and their activities so affected Zaire's Tutsi population that they began their own revolution against President Mobuto's corrupt regime – and overthrew it. However, a counter-revolution then started against the replacement President, Laurence Kabila; six neighbouring states have become embroiled, sending in troops to support one side or the other in the new civil war. It has been feared that the war would spread to those countries, but so far it has not, though their troops still fight in the drc. Over the Congo River, the

Republic of Congo (Brazzaville) is also experiencing civil war, as rival factions fight and as guerrillas from the DRC cause trouble.

Civil unrest and army mutinies make it unsafe to travel to the Central African Republic, which experienced two army revolts in 1996 and one in January 1997. The latter was put down by French troops who have now withdrawn, and a UN peace-keeping force has been deployed. Côte d'Ivoire, Guinea Bissau (the border area with Senegal), Mali (the Kayes region and the borders with Niger and Mauritania), parts of Nigeria (particularly Kaduna Province), the border with Mali in Niger, and the Casamance region of Senegal are all dangerous to visit.

East Africa and the Horn of Africa

In southern Sudan, civil war continues and spreads as, for the first time, the mainly Christian Sudan People's Liberation Army receives active backing from Muslim opposition groups.

Ethiopia and Eritrea have been at war since May 1998 over a border dispute at Badame that has spread to other border areas. Now a severe drought has brought famine back to the region. This is affecting Ethiopia, Eritrea and Somalia, which still remains ungoverned and at the mercy of feuding warlords. Northern Somalia (formerly British Somaliland) is more stable, but seafarers are warned of piracy along the Somali coast. In the Comoros Islands, Anjouan has declared its independence and should not be visited.

In Uganda, the border areas with the DRC and Sudan are unsafe as the civil wars there spill over; also the Ruwenzori region is unsafe because of rebels of the Allied Democratic Front.

Southern Africa

This appears to be one area in the world where there are currently no civil wars. The main worry for travellers must be the high rate of violent crime in South Africa. The civil war in Mozambique ended in 1992, but the country suffers from uncleared landmines and high levels of armed robbery, and now it has been devastated by tropical floods. Namibia's Caprivi and Kavango regions are unsafe to visit, because the Lozi population is rebelling against the Ovambo led government that rules them, and also because the Angolan civil war has spilled over the border.

The situation in Zimbabwe is still volatile at time of going to press. During and after the parliamentary elections in 2000, President Mugabe encouraged the seizure of white-owned farms, with squatters terrorising farmers and their labour force. Political demonstrations have been attacked by both Mugabe supporters and the police. How events will unfold is difficult to predict. Travel is, in any case, virtually impossible, owing to a shortage of fuel caused by the economic crisis, which in turn was sparked by the costs of Zimbabwe's large-scale military support for President Kabila in the Congolese civil war.

Middle East

A great deal of optimism was evinced at the return of a Labour government in Israel, led by Ehud Barak. It was hoped that good progress would be made in both the Syrian and Palestinian peace processes. Barak launched a number of initiatives, but has found making real progress as difficult as his predecessors did. Nevertheless, Israel is a safe a place to visit. Travel to the West Bank and Gaza Strip can be another matter and should not be attempted without local, up-to-date advice. At the moment there is a resurgence of violence in Israel and all reports should be checked at the time of travel.

Parts of Lebanon are still unsafe for travellers, though this may change following the withdrawal of the Israeli Army from the south, and the disintegration of its allies in the South Lebanese Army. The Beka'a Valley in the east of the country is used by Hizbollah for its base-camps and training schools and tends to be the target of Israeli retaliatory air raids. There have been clashes in the northern Dannet hills. Only visit the Beka'a, Tyre and Sidon in organised groups.

The Yemen is still considered a dangerous place for travellers as there is the likelihood of kidnapping by tribesmen, who favour capturing foreigners, and many areas are not under government control. Few are likely to want to holiday in Iraq, and it would certainly be unwise to travel in the Kurdish-populated far north, where the Turkish army and air force mount raids against Turkish Kurd rebels close to the border. Britain's Foreign Office does not warn against travel in Iran, although the US State Department does; Iran is improving its relations with its neighbours in the Gulf and lifting many of the restrictions imposed on its own population.

Central Asia and the Indian subcontinent

In early 1995 a new force appeared in the Afghanistan civil war. Known as Taliban, it was originally a movement composed primarily of Islamic students studying at *madrassas* in northern Pakistan and in southern, Pashtun-populated, Afghanistan. Taliban now controls the country, bar the far north-east, where a mainly Tajik opposition still holds out. Landmines, refugees, food shortages and Islamic intolerance combine to make Afghanistan a no-go area.

In Tajikistan there is talk of peace, but this has not yet materialised. It is estimated that more than 30,000 have died as a result of civil war since 1992, despite the presence of 25,000 Russian troops. The government is weak, with many rebel leaders doing as they please. United Nations staff and other aid workers have been the target of kidnappers.

Nepal is experiencing terrorist threats for the first time, but foreign visitors are not being targeted. The remote western end of the country is the most dangerous area, currently experiencing a Maoist insurgency.

In India, the state of Jammu and Kashmir is still the scene of frequent clashes between the government and Muslim terrorists, who the Indians claim are supported by Pakistan. Exchanges of artillery fire occur regularly across the 'line of control' (the *de facto* frontier), but there has not been a major incursion into Indian Kashmir since that at Kargil in mid-1999. North-eastern India is a disturbed region and the situation should be checked before visiting Arunachal Pradesh, Assam, Manipur, Mizoram, Nagaland and Sikkim, where separatist movements have been active in the recent past.

In Pakistan, the security situation in Karachi is much improved, where only a short time ago there were serious outbreaks of communal violence caused by Urdu-speaking Muslims who had migrated there from India after the 1947 partition. Elsewhere in Pakistan, the areas bordering Afghanistan, India, Iran and the Kashmir 'line of control' should be avoided.

The Sri Lankan civil war is in its seventeenth year with no apparent reduction in the intensity of fighting between government troops and Tamil Tiger separatists. The north and east of the country are a potential battlefield, and terrorist attacks take place from time to time elsewhere, mainly in Colombo.

South-East Asia

In Myanmar (Burma), the State Peace and Development Council (formerly the State Law and Order Restoration Council) is widely condemned for its human rights record. This military junta enforces its control with torture, execution, forced labour and relocation of ethnic minority groups. There are areas of dissident activity and military operations along the eastern border with China and along the southern border with Laos and Thailand, where non-Burmese tribespeople live.

There have been several cases of banditry on some main roads in Laos recently.

Indonesia is facing a number of separatist movements against whom the government, and particularly the army, have reacted with undue force. East Timor, a former Portuguese colony that Indonesia invaded over 20 years ago, has finally gained independence, which can only encourage separatists elsewhere. There are still a large number of East Timorese refugees, including aggressive, pro-Indonesian militiamen in West Timor. Aceh in the west, the Moluccas (Ambon), and Irian Jaya in the east, have all witnessed violence. There have also been inter-ethnic clashes in West Kalimantan. Tourists had to flee Lombok in 1999, but nearby Bali is considered safe.

The Strait of Malacca, the Java Sea, the Makassar Strait and the Celebes Sea are vulnerable to piracy, with over 60 attacks there reported in 1999.

Islamic insurgency continues in the Philippines. North and South Luzon, western Mindanao and the islands to its south-west, are all affected. In March this year, the Moro Islamic Liberation Army carried out daily attacks for nearly a month and the government has now mounted a strong military campaign. As a result, nearly 100,000 people have fled from their homes in Mindanao.

Central and South America

Once the most violent region of the world, South and Central America have become much safer to visit in recent years. But there are exceptions. Colombia is the scene of fighting between government forces, terrorists of both the FARC and the ELN, and the private armies of drug cartels; the terrorists and the drug barons also fight each other. The fear is that the activities of the drug traffickers and the terrorists will spill over into neighbouring Panama, Ecuador and Venezuela, which have already been used as safe havens and training grounds by the FARC.

Some parts of the interior of Peru still suffer from the terrorist activities of the

Sendero Luminoso ('Shining Path') guerrillas, but generally the situation is much improved. Ecuador has very recently witnessed and is recovering from a successful and bloodless coup. Civil disturbance broke out in Bolivia in April 2000; the Zapatista rebellion continues in the Chiapas region of Mexico.

In the Caribbean, Haiti still witnesses large-scale violent crime. The Caribbean is the second-worst area in the world for piracy.

The outlook

Travelling in any of the countries mentioned above obviously carries risks. The risks are not worth taking in those countries which the Foreign and Commonwealth Office advises against visiting.

In many of the countries described, the main centres are relatively, if not entirely, safe to visit. Here, as in many countries not mentioned, the problem is usually violent crime rather than war. It all depends on where you go and when, and this can only be decided just before you travel. 'Discretion is the better part of valour' is just as true for travelling as it is for war. So take and follow advice.

The most up-to-date advice for travellers – and situations can change rapidly – is provided by the Foreign and Commonwealth Office, which maintains a Travel Advice Unit (tel 020 7238 4503/4); its website is www.fco.gov.uk/travel. Good advice is also available on BBC 2 Ceefax, page 470. The subjects covered include not just the risks of war but of crime, health, floods and volcanic eruptions. The US State Department website is www.state.gov. ✍

COLONEL ANDREW DUNCAN is a defence analyst and commentator.
Previously he worked at the International Institute for Strategic Studies.

Part 3: **Logistics** ❧

When to go

Whatever the weather
by Jill Crawshaw

"YOU SHOULD HAVE BEEN HERE LAST WEEK/MONTH/YEAR!" is the knee-jerk reaction I've come to expect – and dread – in every season of the year, somewhere around the globe. When I spent a large chunk of January turning rusty on the Costa del Sol, it was "freak weather"; when I had to flee south of Marrakech in December as torrential floods had wiped out several roads, part of the railway line and hundreds of mud brick houses, they claimed it was unbelievable.

Then there were the winter wash-outs in Tahiti, or the time I spent during an Australian summer being cling-filmed in dust by the willy-willies – the violent tropical storms that can hit the north coast. Sure, Down Under is the place to escape our winter, but only in some places Down Under. Even Melbourne's climate can change as much as four times in the course of one day, and Sydney is regularly dowsed, while summer monsoons can bring down rainfall in buckets on the hot and steamy Barrier Reef holiday playgrounds.

In order to be a really slick traveller, one who knows to avoid Mal in June, Mali in August and Mah in December, you would need to carry around the weather charts in the *Directory*; but there are a few rules that have helped me decide whether to pack my swimsuit and beach mat or brolly and thermals.

For a start, any temperature above about 27°C in humid Turkish-bath zones or 30°C in dry climes precludes vigorous exploration and activity for most, while anything below 17°C means lots of walkabouts and sightseeing but no beach.

The sad sight of winter holiday-makers huddled over Trivial Pursuits in all too many rainswept and deserted Mediterranean resorts has taught me to distrust the Med's winter weather. Sizzling or drizzling, it's always a gamble; and there's a particular cloud that arrives in southern Europe around the third week in October (a month later in Cyprus, Lebanon, North Africa and other southern Mediterranean resorts) that sends a message warning beach-dwellers that their time is up.

Cold, hard statistics reveal that Gibraltar or Haifa have nearly twice as much rainfall as London in January, which in turn is drier than the Algarve, Monaco and even Cyprus and Malta, not to mention Istanbul in February.

Even in that so-called winter sun Mecca, Tenerife (on the same latitude as Delhi and parts of Florida), a daily cloud arrives at 2 pm at the lush northern resort of Puerto Cruz, while on the other side of the island the sun shines evenly all day on the bare slopes and concrete jungle of Playa de las Americas – which is why the north is lush and the south barren. Eilat, Israel's winter offering, can also be grey and grizzling in January, though at least you can get away from the weather by exploring the resort's technicolour wonders below sea level.

But if it's winter sunshine you're after, you'll have to head at least as far south as

Luxor, while the cheapest guaranteed hot stuff can be found in Gambia, followed by high probabilities in Goa and the Kenyan coast. Alas, the Caribbean is at its most pricey and exclusive during our winter.

Wherever you are travelling in desert conditions, you'll find surprisingly large diurnal variations with cool, even cold, snaps at night and at dawn. But on and around the equator you'll need to overdose on anti-perspirant as it is nearly always hot and humid. There are so few seasonal variations there that you find yourself dreaming wistfully of spring flowers in the Lake District, the autumn wine harvest in Provence or fall in New England. And just to remind you of the vagaries of weather, *The Times* carried a picture of New England under deep snow at the beginning of April this year.

From trial and error in the tropics, I've at least learned that December to February are the most tolerable months in which to tackle Bangkok, but that in the same months it is so steamy and wet in Singapore you won't ever get your smalls dry unless you have a hotel room with air conditioning.

Weather in the Far East, generally, can present tricky problems, even within the same or neighbouring countries. Backpackers who have boned up on their weather charts will know that the May rains signal the end of the tourist season in Phuket and that they must migrate to Koh Samui, moving on from there to Bali for their fun in July, August and September. Malaysia, and even relatively small islands such as Sri Lanka, have considerable climatic variations – bi-annual heavy rainfalls often happen at night, but winds can make the sea rough and dangerous for bathing during the day. And remember that in both of these countries – and others – where you can move from steamy lowlands to cool highlands in a few hours, you need to pack sweaters for evenings alongside your sun hat for midday.

A good traveller has no fixed plans and is not intent on arriving.
– Lao Tzu

The rains, both long and short, fall somewhere in Africa throughout the year: from December to February in Zimbabwe and southern Africa, March to May in Kenya and Tanzania; May to August in Cape Town. From November to February, just when holiday-makers are being lured to the Seychelles and Mauritius by the eternal sunshine on the glossy brochure covers, these Indian Ocean playgrounds are getting their biggest annual soaking – whereas they are both ideal escapes during our summer months, when the Med resorts have become blowsy with tourists.

East Africa's safari season runs during the dry months from December to April, when the grasses are low for better game spotting, and the animals will seek out and congregate around water-holes rather than dispersing through the bush. But even here, alas, the rains don't always watch the calendar, and timing can often be a matter of luck. It took me several false starts before I caught the beginning of the migration in Serengeti – but the brief moments before dawn waiting for the sun to rise over the flat endless plains, surrounded by the shadowy silhouettes of millions of wildebeest on their starting blocks, are heart-stopping memories that will last a lifetime.

Even if you get your timing wrong, there are other compensations: some countries are almost reborn with changes of weather, none more so than Africa. Unexpected early rains in Botswana once turned my dry and dusty campsite into a Garden of Eden overnight as we awoke to a *Jungle Book* fantasy of monkeys chattering in the trees, impala playing in the bush and dragonflies and butterflies dazzling us with their pirouettes.

I witnessed as one of the driest places on earth, the Namib Desert, was almost transformed into an Irish meadow by rain after several years of drought, so heaven knows what the unique species that have adapted to this burning environment must have made of it. The desert onyx has developed a brain irrigated by a special network of veins that enables it to withstand fiery temperatures, while the dune beetle does handstands each morning to let droplets of Atlantic fog roll down into its mouth. More soberly, in such communities, you learn to realise that the weather is a matter of death or life.

Moving across from Africa to the Atlantic, anyone who believes that America's weather is a breeze may be in for some shocks. The wettest place I've been is Hawaii, where I was stuck for days waiting for a helicopter trip to photograph the volcanoes, of which I got no glimpse. The hottest I've felt was in the humid concrete canyons of New York, though body temperatures plummeted to sub-Arctic levels in the icy air conditioning of the Big Apple's restaurants, hotels and even cabs.

It was Mark Twain who said "The coldest winter I ever spent was summer in San Francisco." British holiday-makers should take note of this, before flocking in droves to visit Florida when it's almost guaranteed to be humid and wet, the Everglades' mosquitoes are at their most bloodthirsty, and there's a real likelihood of hurricanes as well.

After 20 years of travelling from Alaska to Zanzibar, writing hundreds of travel articles and answering thousands of questions on radio and television phone-ins, I've learned to identify the hardy perennials: "How much?", "What are the beaches like?", "Is it safe and can you drink the water in…?"

I express my opinion on a few general rules, pull out some statistics and weather charts, and then get myself off the hook with warnings that little complications such as the *meltemi*, the *mistral* or the *sirocco* winds can make a mockery of the most reliable Mediterranean temperature statistics; that you can get a deep suntan north of the Arctic Circle, or catch pneumonia in the desert – in other words, that the world's weather can be astonishingly unpredictable.

What would we have to talk about if it wasn't? ❧

JILL CRAWSHAW is a travel journalist and broadcaster.
She has won the Travel Writer of the Year award three times
and is a regular columnist for 'The Times'.

A guide to seasonal travel
by Paul Pratt and Melissa Shales

CHOOSING WHEN TO VISIT A COUNTRY CAN AFFECT more than your suntan. In many places, climate is a key factor in the overall levels of hygiene and disease, as well as the prevalence of those annoying little insects....

Africa

EAST AFRICA: Although much of this area is on or near the equator, little of it has an equatorial climate. The lowlands of Djibouti in the extreme east have a very low, uncertain rainfall, creating near-desert conditions plagued by severe droughts. Further down the coast, the high lowland temperatures are moderated by constant sea breezes. The temperatures inland are brought down by high-altitude plateaux and mountain ranges to about the level found in Britain at the height of summer. Temperatures are reasonably stable all year round, although the Kenyan highlands have a cooler, cloudy 'winter' from June to September. There are rainy seasons in most areas in April and May and, in some areas, for a couple of months between July and November, depending on the latitude.

NORTH AFRICA: The climate here varies widely from the warm and pleasant greenery of a Mediterranean climate in the coastal regions to the arid heat of the deep Sahara. Rains on the coast usually fall between September and May and are heavy but not prolonged. It can get cool enough for snow to settle in the mountainous areas, but temperatures will not usually fall below freezing, even in winter. In summer, temperatures are high (up to around 40°C) but bearable.

The Sahara, on the other hand, is extreme, with maximum summer temperatures of around 50°C and minimum winter temperatures of around 3°C. The temperature can fall extremely rapidly, with freezing nights following blisteringly hot days. What little, if any, rain there is can fall at any time of the year. The desert is also prone to strong winds and dust storms.

SOUTHERN AFRICA: The whole area from Angola, Zambia and Malawi southwards tends to be fairly pleasant and healthy, although there are major variations from the Mediterranean climate of Cape Province, with its mild winters and warm, sunny summers, to the semi-desert sprawl of the Kalahari and the relatively wet areas of Swaziland, inland Mozambique and the Zimbabwe highlands to the east. In the more northerly areas, there is a definite summer rainy season, from December to March, when the temperatures are highest. On the south coast, there is usually some rain all year round. The west coast, with little rain, has cloud and fog due to the cold Benguela current, which also helps keep down the temperature. The best times of the year to visit are April, May and September, when the weather is fine but not too hot or humid.

WEST AFRICA: At no time is the climate in West Africa likely to be comfortable, although some areas and times of the year are worse than others. The coastal areas are extremely wet and humid, with a total of 2,500 mm of rain falling in two rainy seasons (May and June and then again in October). In the north there is considerably less rain, with only one wet period between June and September. However, the humidity is still high, only lessened by the arrival of the *harmattan*, a hot, dry and dusty north-easterly wind which blows from the Sahara. Temperatures remain high and relatively even throughout the year.

The Americas

CANADA AND USA: Almost half of Canada and most of Alaska in the north lies beyond the Arctic Circle and suffers from the desperately harsh weather associated with this latitude. The ground is tundra and rarely melts more than a couple of feet deep, and even though summer temperatures are often surprisingly high, the season is short-lived. Snow and frost are possible at any time, while the northern areas have permanent snow cover. The coast is ice-bound most of the year.

The whole centre of the continent is prone to severe and very changeable weather, as the low-lying land of the Great Plains and the Canadian Prairies offers no resistance to sweeping winds that tear across the continent both from the Gulf and the Arctic. The east is fairly wet but the west has very little rain, resulting in desert and semi-desert country in the south.

Winter temperatures in the north can go as low as −40°C and can be very low even in the south, with strong winds and blizzards. In the north, winter is long-lived. Summers are sunny and often scorchingly hot.

In general, the coastal areas of North America are far kinder than the centre of the continent. The Pacific coast is blocked by the Rockies from the sweeping winds, and in the Vancouver area the climate is similar to that of the UK. Sea breezes keep it cool further south.

Seasons change fairly gradually on the east coast, but the northerly areas still suffer from the extremes of temperature that give New York its fabled humid heat-waves in summer and frigid winter temperatures. New York, in spite of being far further north, is often much hotter than San Francisco. The Newfoundland area has heavy fog and icebergs for shipping to contend with. Florida and the Gulf States to the south have a tropical climate, with warm weather all year round, and winter sun and summer thunderstorms. This is the area most likely to be affected by hurricanes and tornadoes, although cyclones are possible anywhere.

CENTRAL AMERICA: The best time to visit this area is during the dry season (winter) from November to April. However, the mountains and the plains facing the Caribbean have heavy rainfall throughout the year, which is usually at its worst from September to February. The mountains and plains facing the Pacific have negligible rainfall from December to April.

Central and northern Mexico tend to have a longer dry season, and the wet season is seldom troublesome to the traveller as it usually rains only between 4pm and 5pm. The temperature is affected by the altitude. The unpleasant combination of excessive heat and humidity at the height of the wet season should be avoided, if possible, at the lower altitudes.

SOUTH AMERICA: The climatic conditions of the South American continent are determined to a great extent by the trade winds, which, if they originate in high pressure areas, are not necessarily carriers of moisture. With a few regional exceptions, rain in South America is confined to the summer months, both north and south of the Equator. The exceptions are: southern Brazil and the eastern coast of Argentina and Uruguay, the southern Chilean coastal winter rainfall region, the coastal area of northeast Brazil.

The highest rainfall in South America is in the Amazon basin, the coast lands of Guyana and Surinam, the coastlines of Colombia, Ecuador and southwest Chile. Altitude determines temperature, especially in the Andean countries near to the equator: hot – up to 1,000 m; temperate – 1,000 to 2,000 m; cold – above 2000 m.

ARGENTINA: The winter months, June to October, are the best time for visiting Argentina. Buenos Aires can be oppressively hot and humid from mid-December to the end of February. Climate ranges from the sub-tropical north to sub-antarctic in Tierra del Fuego.

BRAZIL: The dry season runs from May to October, apart from in the Amazon basin and the Recife area, which have a tropical rainy season from April to July.

BOLIVIA: Heavy rainfall on the high western plateau from May to November. Rains in all seasons to the eastern part of the country.

CHILE: Just over the border from Bolivia, one of the driest deserts in the world faces the Pacific coast.

ECUADOR: Dry seasons from June to October. The coast is very hot and wet, especially during the December to May period. The mountain roads can be very dangerous during the wet season owing to landslides.

PARAGUAY: The best time for a visit is from May to October when it is relatively dry. The heaviest rainfall is from December to March, at which time it is most likely to be oppressively hot and humid.

PERU: During the colder months, June to November, little rainfall but damp on the coast, high humidity and fog. From December to May, travel through the mountains can be hazardous owing to heavy rain, which may result in landslides, causing road blockage and long delays.

Asia

CHINA: Climate is very diverse across this vast land mass. Summer in most areas is very hot and humid, while winters are generally extremely cold. The far north has dry winters, with temperatures below zero, and hot summers. The north-west gets very hot but not humid in summer, and winters are bitter. The central region, including the Shanghai and Yangtze rivers, has almost continuous rainfall, hot humid summers, and cold winters. The south is subtropical, with wet humid summers from April to September, and typhoons on the south-east coast between July and September. Overall, the best time to visit is the spring, starting in the south and working north or west as summer approaches; or the autumn, starting in the north and working southwards.

INDIA: The climate of south India is similar to that of South-East Asia: warm and humid. The southwest monsoon brings the rainy season to most parts of India, starting in the southwest and spreading north and east from mid-May through June. Assam has an extremely heavy rainfall during monsoon seasons.

Generally speaking, the period from November to April is the best time to visit. From April until the start of the southwest monsoon, the northern Indian plains are extremely hot, though the northern hill stations provide a pleasant alternative until the start of the monsoon rains. These places usually have a severe winter.

JAPAN: Japan lies in the northern temperate zone. Spring and autumn are the best times for a visit. With the exception of Hokkaido, the large cities are extremely hot in summer. Hokkaido is very cold in winter. Seasonal vacation periods, especially school holidays, should be avoided if one is going to enjoy visiting temples, palaces and the like in relative comfort.

KOREA: Located in the northern temperate zone, with spring and autumn the best times for touring. The deep blue skies of late September/October and early November, along with the warm sunny days and cool evenings, are among Korea's most beautiful natural assets. Though it tends to be rather windy, spring is also a very pleasant time for a Korean visit. There is a short but pronounced wet season starting towards the end of June and lasting into early August. Over 50 per cent of the year's rain falls during this period and it is usually very hot and humid.

MALAYSIA: There are no marked wet or dry seasons in Malaysia. October to January is the wettest period on the east coast, October/November on the west coast. Sabah has an equable tropical climate, October and April/May are usually the best times for a visit. Sarawak is seldom uncomfortably hot but is apt to be extremely wet. Typhoons are almost unknown in East Malaysia.

NEPAL: March is pleasant, as this is when all the rhododendrons are in bloom. The monsoon rains begin in April.

THAILAND: Hot, tropical climate with high humidity. Best time for touring is from November to February. March to May is extremely hot and the wet season arrives with the southwest monsoon during June and lasts until October.

SINGAPORE: Like Malaysia, Singapore has no pronounced wet or dry season. The even, constant heat is mitigated by sea breezes. The frequent rain showers have a negligible cooling effect.

PHILIPPINES: The Philippines have a similar climate to Thailand. The best time to travel in the islands is during the dry season, November to March. March to May is usually dry and extremely hot. The southwest monsoon brings the rain from May to November. The islands north of Samar through Luzon are prone to be affected by typhoons during the period July to September. The Visayas Islands, Mindanao and Palawan, are affected to a lesser degree by the southwest monsoon and it is still possible to travel comfortably during the wet season south of Samar Island – long sunny periods are usually interspersed with heavy rain showers.

SRI LANKA: The southwest monsoon brings rain from May to August in Colombo and in the southwest generally, while the northeast monsoon determines the rainy season from November to February in the northeast. The most popular time for a visit is during the northern hemisphere's winter.

Australasia

AUSTRALIA: For such a vast land mass, there are few variations in the weather here. A crescent-shaped rain belt follows the coast to provide a habitable stretch around the enormous semi-desert Outback. The Snowy Mountains in the east do, as their name suggests, have significant snowfalls, although even here it does not lie long. The east is the wettest part of the country, owing to trade winds that blow off the Pacific. The rainfall pattern varies throughout the country: the north and north-east have definite summer rains between November and April, the south and west have winter rains, while in the east and southeast the rains fall year-round. Tropical cyclones with high winds and torrential rain occur fairly frequently in the northeast and northwest. Tasmania, further south and more mountainous than the mainland, has a temperate climate similar to Britain's.

New Zealand: Although at a different latitude, the great expanse of water around New Zealand gives it a maritime climate similar to Britain's. The far north has a sub-tropical climate with mild winters and warm, humid summers. There are year-round snow fields in the south, and snow falls on most areas in winter. Although the weather is changeable, there is a surprising amount of sunshine, making this country ideal for most outdoor activities. The best time to visit is from December to March, at the height of summer.

Papua New Guinea: The climate here is a fairly standard tropical one: hot and wet all year, although the time and amount of the rains are greatly influenced by the high mountains that run the length of the country. The rains are heavy, but not continuous. While the coast tends to be humid, the highlands are pleasant.

Europe

Only in the far north and those areas a long way from the sea does the climate in Europe get to be extreme. In northern Scandinavia and some of the inland eastern countries such as Bulgaria, there are long, bitterly cold winters with heavy snow and, at times, arctic temperatures. In western Europe the snow tends to settle only for a few days at a time. In Britain, the Benelux countries and Germany, winter is characterised chiefly by continuous cloud cover, with rain or sleet. In the Alps, heavy snow showers tend to alternate with brilliant sunshine, offering ideal conditions for winter sports. There are four distinct seasons, and while good weather cannot be guaranteed during any of them, all are worth seeing. Summer is generally short, and the temperature varies widely from one year to the next, climbing at times to match that of the Mediterranean.

For sun worshippers, the Mediterranean is probably the ideal location, hot for much of the year but rarely too hot or humid to be unbearable. Rain falls in short, sharp bursts, unlike the continuous drizzle to be found further north. Winter is mild and snow rare.

Middle East

A large proportion of this area is desert: flat, low-lying land with virtually no rain and some of the hottest temperatures on earth. Humidity is high along the coast and travellers should beware of heat exhaustion and even heat stroke. What little rain there is falls between November and March. To the north, in Iran and Iraq, the desert gives way to the great steppes, which are prone to extremes of heat and cold, with rain in winter and spring.

Melting snow from the surrounding mountains causes spectacular floods from March to May. The climate is considerably more pleasant in the Mediterranean areas, with long, hot, sunny summers and mild, wet winters. The coast is humid, but even this is tempered by steady sea breezes. The only really unpleasant aspect of the climate here is the hot, dry and dusty desert wind which blows at the beginning and end of summer. ಈ

Paul Pratt claims to have made the longest continuous journey in motorcycle history - a distance of nearly 165,000 km through 48 countries. His book of the trip is called 'World Understanding on Two Wheels'. Melissa Shales is a previous Editor of 'The Traveller's Handbook'.

Festivals of the world
by Jeremy Atiyah

Can't wait for Christmas? Why not go abroad for your festivals instead? There is always something going on somewhere. Visiting festivals is not only a way of crashing other people's parties, it is also a way to see local people at their best and take great photos. If you don't lose your camera in the mêlée, that is.

Humans have been cluttering the calendar with special dates since the dawn of history. Some of these have never stopped, other new ones started up yesterday. Some are a fantastic spectacle; others offer nothing to see. If you are going halfway round the world to see one, make sure you have got the dates right.

Not that you need to go far. Every country in the world, perhaps every city, contains its own festivals, and Britain is no exception. Annual examples here include the explosive Guy Fawke's Night on 5 November, as well as curiosities such as the 300-year-old Shrovetide football match in Ashbourne, Derbyshire, in February.

Worldwide however, the origins of the oldest festivals revolve round agricultural rites, marking seasonal changes like the beginning of spring or the coming of the rains. Such festivals tend to follow the lunar calendar (lunar cycles were easier to count), which means that tourists have to check their calendars carefully. Given common agricultural origins, it is no coincidence that the end of winter is marked almost simultaneously in Europe and China by two of the world's largest festivals.

Carnival, which takes place on the days leading up to Ash Wednesday, 40 days before Easter, is a mad party throughout the Catholic world. Fat Tuesday or Mardi Gras is the climactic finale of these celebrations. In Europe, Mardi Gras is celebrated in all Catholic countries, but perhaps most famously in Venice, where harlequins and incognito strangers in chalk-white masks stalk the streets. Fantastically ostentatious fancy-dress balls are also held in Vienna at this time, while in the German city of Cologne, women run around cutting off men's ties.

Mardi Gras in the Americas is even more outrageous. In New Orleans bizarrely dressed paraders march to the accompaniment of an insane amount of bead-flinging, flambeaux-carrying, chanting and boozing. But even this is nothing compared to what goes down in Rio de Janeiro, probably the single most famous street party in the world, where the emphasis is heavily on transvestism, erotic costumes, scantily clad dancers and alcohol. Finally Sydney's Gay and Lesbian Mardi Gras parade (which actually falls a couple of weeks into Lent) is the latest spin-off from the Carnival scene.

By contrast to which, the end-of-winter festival at the other end of the Eurasian landmass – Chinese New Year – is altogether low key. Instead of street parties, this is a time for families to come together, the main consequence of which is closed restaurants and horribly crowded train stations. From the traveller's point of view, it is a time to avoid China. You will see more by hanging around for the lion-dance festivities in London's Chinatown.

Other festivals with ancient roots are to be found all over Asia. No Ruz, the Iranian new year marking the spring equinox, provides travellers with a fascinating glimpse into the ancient heart of Iran; apart from feasting, one age-old custom is for everyone to join in leaping over street bonfires. The symbolism of this comes straight from the pre-Islamic fire-worshipping cult of Zoroastrianism.

Hindu and Buddhist communities, in countries such as India, Nepal, Thailand and the Indonesian island of Bali, retain traces of ancient cults in virtually every town and village, to the extent that travellers need hardly consult their calendars to be sure of running into colourful festivities.

India is the country with the oldest recorded surviving festivals. In the north particularly, the beginning of spring is marked by a major festival, Holi, the Festival of Colour, during which people bombard each other with water and paint. In Bombay, the holiday Ganesh Chaturthi is dedicated to the Hindu god Ganesh, (late August/early September: check dates), and sees huge processions carrying images of the god to immerse in the sea. The whole country in fact

Travel is fatal to prejudice, bigotry, and narrow-mindedness... .Broad, wholesome, charitable views of men and things cannot be acquired by vegetating in one little corner of the earth all one's lifetime.
– MARK TWAIN

gets through a lot of rampant celebrations at the end of the monsoons, ostensibly commemorating events from the great Hindu epic, the Ramayana.

In contrast to these ancient ceremonies, the holidays associated with the world's monotheistic religions represent attempts to modernise ancient festivals, to tie them into an up-to-date framework. It is not, for example, coincidental that Christmas falls at the time of the winter equinox, and Easter at the spring equinox. This probably reflects ancient Mediterranean beliefs in a god who is born at the coming of the winter rains, only to die again at the beginning of the summer heat.

Interesting though the myths may be, for the traveller Christmas is rarely more than a family affair outside Bethlehem and the Vatican in Rome, where huge crowds congregate to hear the Pope lead mass. Easter is a better time to travel: southern Spain, above all, celebrates Semana Santa (Holy Week) in flamboyant style, especially in the Andalucian city of Seville, where colossal processions of hooded, masked figures take place with figures of the Virgin Mary and Jesus being carted around in tow. Greek Easter, which follows some weeks later, is likewise an excellent time to be in Greece. Islamic festivals are widely observed in the religious sense, but are not exactly occasions for tourist gawping. Eid El Fitr (the breaking of the fast after the holy month of Ramadan) and Eid El Adha are big family occasions, though if you happen to be in an Islamic country at this time you may be invited to banquets involving the slaughter of goats.

The biggest Shiite festival is Ashura, commemorating the martyrdom of the Shiite hero Hussein, killed in the battle of Kerbala in 680 AD. This is an occasion for mourning and grief rather than celebration, with young men each competing to flagellate themselves more bloodily than the next. This can be seen in Iran and parts of Iraq and Lebanon, though tourists may not feel very welcome.

Jewish holidays are notable for their extreme frequency, and again, where travellers are concerned, these might not be the best times to actually visit Israel. Several of the holidays, notably Yom Kippur and Sukkoth, involve varying degrees of abstinence and self purification. Purim, on the other hand, (February/March-check dates) is an occasion for outright revelry – and it's the only chance you'll have to get drunk with orthodox Jews.

Moving away from ancient myths and religions, it is perhaps refreshing at the dawn of the twenty-first century to realise that festivals are not exclusively rooted in the remote past. In truth, most of us spend more time celebrating secular festivals than religious ones.

National holidays can be exciting occasions anywhere. Independence Day, the USA's birthday bash on 4 July is a great time to be around, with fireworks, music and large crowds gathering in towns and cities. France's Bastille Day, just ten days later on 14 July, is another patriotic extravaganza.

The secular holiday that comes nearer than any other to being a truly world holiday is 1 January. Huge crowds at places as diverse as the Vatican, Times Square, Trafalgar Square, the Brandenburg Gate and Sydney Harbour (to name but a few) spiritually unite for heavy drinking and singing of *Auld Lang Syne*, Robert Burn's song, which was composed to mark Scotland's own Hogmanay.

But the modern world's real contribution to the festival lies in the great sporting events of the twenty-first century: the football World Cup and, above all, the Olympic Games, two four-yearly events for which virtually the entire world comes to a standstill. Being able to attend either event in person is the equivalent – perhaps – of what a religious pilgrimage would have been in another age. Political occasions – the American elections spring to mind – can also make pretty good jamborees. If you are able to travel, it really can be Christmas every day. ❧

*JEREMY ATIYAH is Travel Editor of 'The Independent on Sunday'
and co-author of the 'Rough Guide to China'.*

Researching your trip

Planning with the internet
by Natasha Hughes

L ANDING AT BOMBAY AIRPORT RECENTLY, I found myself in the grip of culture shock. It wasn't the usual Westerner's problem with India – seeing entire families sleeping out on the pavements, not knowing how to respond to hollow-cheeked children begging with outstretched palms or how to escape from trades-men who clutch at your clothes as they try to drag you into their shops for "just a little look, nice antiques, Kashmiri shawls" or whatever else they happen to be sell-ing. No, my problem was that the last time I had been in India, some dozen years or so before, I had travelled round a country where the only cars on the road were antiquated-looking Ambassadors, and telephonic communications were, to say the least, limited and uncertain. This time I found myself in a country where – in the cities at least – every other car was a European or Japanese import, and a sig-nificant proportion of the population carried a mobile phone.

The change that made the biggest impact on me, however, was the fact that the advertising hoardings on each street corner no longer exclusively proclaimed the merits of agricultural equipment, the latest Bollywood extravaganza and Thums Up cola. Instead, most of them seemed to be touting the virtues of the computer age, and almost every company that advertised its wares seemed to be promoting its website as well. It was then that I realised what a profound impact the internet was having on the world and that, soon, no corner of the planet would be unaf-fected by its coming, no life left untouched by the digital revolution.

Here in the West, we have been swept up in the 'dot.com' revolution. It is only recently that the first wave of overhyped internet companies have had to face up to a realistic revision of their market value, bursting the bubble of investor enthusi-asm for a technology that is little understood and frequently overvalued. But there can be little doubt that the internet is changing our world – and it is here to stay.

Many home computers are limited in their memory and the speed of their modems, all of which affect the rate at which web pages can be downloaded, but within a very few short years all this will change, and the net will open up a world of possibilities, allowing virtual travel to take place in the comfort of our living rooms. But at the moment, when it comes to its relevance to travellers, cyber-sci-ence is in its infancy.

Currently, the biggest drive is towards e-commerce functions, and there are many sites around that allow you to book your flights and hotels speedily and effi-ciently, without having to spend an age on the telephone listening to a recorded voice telling you, without a trace of irony, that your call is valued and will be at-tended to as soon as an operator becomes available. So, if all you're after is a no-frills flight or a package deal, the computer world is your oyster, and there are plenty of sites, from the infamous www.lastminute.com to www.go-fly.com, that will be able to meet your needs with slick efficiency. If, however, you find yourself at the planning stages of a major trip, the internet offers a more limited, albeit constantly growing, set of resources.

First of all, if you need inspiration about exactly where you should be going on your trip, there are a growing number of online 'magazines' that, like the newspapers, publish articles about a range of destinations. Some even carry 'video diaries' of travellers' trips, allowing you to experience the journey in a way that no piece of prose, however embellished by still pictures, can. Try www.uksmart.co.uk or www.breathe.com for features on the most happening holiday locations of the moment. The added advantage of such sites is that, as well as carrying the basic story, embedded within the feature you'll find hypertext links to pages that will give you extra information that can help you to plan your journey. A short piece about the Sydney Olympics, for instance, may carry links to a list of the top ten hotels in the city, a guide to the best restaurants in town, the lowdown on the local beaches and suggestions for day trips, as well as information about flight prices, weather conditions and the latest exchange rates.

If you have a location in mind, but would like to research it in greater depth, www.roughguides.com, the website of the publishers of the *Rough Guide* series, carries all the information contained within its vast range of guidebooks. A recent check showed that the site carried details of more than 10,000 destinations on its database – and the figure keeps climbing. That other major publisher of guidebooks, Lonely Planet, also has a site: www.lonelyplanet.com. While its resources are not as extensive as those of the *Rough Guides*, it does carry a wealth of information, posted by travellers to all kinds of destinations, as well as a noticeboard that can help you find a travelling partner. Finally, *Time Out*, London's grooviest weekly city guide, publishes extensive information about 25 of the world's most happening cities, from Paris to Shanghai, at www.timeout.co.uk.

For some admittedly more biased advice, log on to www.towd.com. This site will put you in touch with the tourism offices of almost any country you could possibly want to visit. Don't expect to find a wealth of information on the site but, with any luck, you could be the recipient of a whole pile of brochures within weeks, possibly even days, of your initial contact.

For some fairly up-to-date information about risky destinations, www.fco.gov.uk or travel.state.gov/travel_warnings.html are UK and US government-sponsored web pages that can give you the gen on a country's political and criminal situations. Of necessity, though, the information carried on these sites tends to be cautious, so it's worth seeking a second opinion before cancelling your adventure on the basis of advice there. If you are seriously concerned, there are professional advisory services on the net, which, for a fee, will give you all the latest information. One of the best of these is www.krollassociates.com.

On a lighter note, the weather can make or break a trip. You can make sure the sun will be shining – but not too hard – by visiting one of the following sites: www.worldclimate.com, weather.yahoo.com or www.cnn.com/WEATHER/.

You can get a feel for how far your travel funds will take you by logging on to www.quote.yahoo.com/m3?u, which will give you up-to-date exchange rates for over 160 currencies. And make sure you never run out of the readies by planning an itinerary of cashpoint machines at www.visa.com/pd/atm/ or www.mastercard/com/atm/.

When it comes to finding somewhere to stay, www.hoteldiscount.com offers discounted rates on a large range of hotels, and if you're travelling on a budget, www.hostels.com is the site to visit for details of backpacker accommodation worldwide. If you're planning a long stay in one place, you might want to check out www.homexchange.com, which can arrange for you to swap addresses with strangers right around the world.

If you're interested in witnessing any kind of festival, from open-air rock concerts in the US to snake-boat racing in Kerala, www.whatsonwhen.com is the site with all the details of what's happening around the world. All you need to do is plug in the date of your projected visit and the details of the country you're visiting, and the search engine will tell you all about any exciting goings-on that happen to coincide with your trip. Alternately, if you want to go to a particular festival, but aren't sure when it's actually taking place, this site can help you to pick the right dates for your journey.

See one promontory, one mountain, one sea, one river, and see all.
– SOCRATES

Always fancied going on safari, but never quite made it? Log on to www.africam.com for an insight into life on the open plains. This site's strength lies in the fact that it carries constantly updated video images that vary from season to season so, depending on the time of year, you might catch glimpses of leopards on the prowl or migrating wildebeest on the hoof.

Finally, as any WEXAS member will know, the company's site, www.wexas.com, is chock-full of travel information, from the kinds of basic details you'll need to plan a successful trip, to insightful accounts of journeys posted by other travellers. The site also carries facsimile copies of recent issues of *Traveller*, WEXAS' glossy and thought-provoking magazine, which you can download from your computer and print off to read at your leisure. If you're not a Wexas member, check out www.travelleronline.com for a taste of what's available on the site.

Of course, by the time this book has been printed there will be many hundreds of new and fascinating websites out there to help you plan your trip, whether you're heading for a couple of weeks in the Algarve or an expedition to the hinterlands of the Amazonian basin. All I can suggest is that you keep your eyes peeled for news of such sites – and that, at the moment, the best place to find them is via the good old-fashioned medium of print: newspapers and magazines, especially ones that feature travel articles or guides to the web, are still great sources of information about the latest, most informative websites in cyberspace. ❧

NATASHA HUGHES is a freelance feature writer specialising in travel and food topics. She is also a regular contributor to 'Traveller' magazine.

A guide to guidebooks
by Tim Ellerby and Roland Butler

A GUIDEBOOK IS ONE OF THE MOST USEFUL ITEMS you can pack, and selecting a good one can make all the difference to a trip. Whether it is scholarly coverage of the religious history of the local monasteries, a means of finding a quick alternative to the dive of a hotel you were recommended before you left home, or detailed information about trekking routes on some of the world's highest mountains, you may well be glad of a guidebook's services on the road.

Since this chapter was last updated, the travel guidebook market has mushroomed. One of the main results of this expansion has been the increasing number of specialist or niche guides. There are now guidebooks for almost every type of holiday everywhere.

The main publishers and the main guides

Detailed here are the main guidebook publishers and their key general titles for the independent traveller. All the guides detailed here abound with practical information: where to stay, where to eat, what to see, how to get around and so on. All will include background information and some coverage of history and culture. However, this is where the similarities end. Each publisher has a different emphasis and each guide series a different sequence of information and style.

Lonely Planet is undoubtedly one of the most well-known publishers. It began in 1973, when Tony and Maureen Wheeler published their guide to *South-East Asia on the Cheap* (based on their own experiences of travelling across South-East Asia). Lonely Planet's reputation has been made by its general guides to the countries and cities of the world and its continental guides. These all offer massive amounts of detail, clear layout and uncompromising reviews. Lonely Planet is one of the biggest guidebook publishers and is moving towards become one of the most diverse. As well as its core titles, it produces walking guides and phrasebooks and, in recent years, has added restaurant guides, food guides, diving guides, map guides, healthy travel guides, picture books, condensed guides, first-time travel guides and an acclaimed series of travel writing titles to its list. For more details of some of these, please read on.

The first *Rough Guide*, to Greece, was written in 1982 by a group of English university graduates. They saw the need for guides that, as well as giving you practical information and candid opinions about the main sights, also offered considered cultural and political coverage. The Rough Guides have kept to this basic idea and refined it over the years to make their books easier to use on the ground. They now have a superb range of guides for over 100 destinations – whole countries and cities – each with maps, colour photographs and excellent coverage of off-the-beaten-track sites. They have recently introduced a series of *Mini Rough Guides* as well as a series of guidebooks for first-time travellers. Rough Guides are intended to be as easy and enjoyable to read as straightforward books.

Bradt Publishing is famous for its coverage of off-the-beaten-track destinations, and currently produces the only guide to Spitzbergen, as well as having been among the first to produce guides for Cuba, Zanzibar and Madagascar. Its guides take a more personal and less formulaic approach, and the company prides itself 'on providing a greater and often more considered insight into the history and people of a country' than other publishers in the field. As well as its general guides, it also produces a range of specialist guides: rail guides. walking guides, wildlife guides and a even a guide to eccentricity!

The reputation of Footprint Handbooks is largely built upon the encyclopaedic detail of its guides to Central and South America. No town or village is left out, no matter how obscure a place it might be. Indeed, many independent travellers to these two areas will take no other guidebook with them. Footprint also produce very good guides for a whole host of other destinations, and pride themselves on using writers who are authorities on their areas. They have recently restyled their books as sturdy paperbacks, which now include a colourful photographic introductory section. An interesting feature of the Footprint Handbooks is that the *Continent Handbooks* are published annually.

Moon Handbooks is an American publisher. Its strongest point is coverage of the US, where it has a guidebook for each state, as well as publishing guides to destinations in South-East Asia, particularly Indonesia and Bali. Its *Hong Kong Guide* comes highly recommended and its *Tibet Pilgrimage Guide* is easily the largest single guidebook Stanfords stocks on Tibet. These guides are packed with detailed and reliable research on all practical aspects of independent travel, and are enhanced by line maps, drawings and comprehensive, descriptive introductions.

Fodor's is another one of the giants of guidebook publishing. Its reputation is based on the accuracy and reliability of its *Gold Guides*. Younger travellers often regard these comprehensive general guides as stuffy. But *To lie about a far country is easy. — AMHARIC PROVERB* do not dismiss them; it is often said that travel may be less of an adventure with Fodor's, but it is also less likely to go wrong. Many *Gold Guides* are updated annually and maintain a good balance between their description of sights and their presentation of practical information on transport, money, accommodation and restaurants. The post-2000 guidebooks include excellent introductory sections and, usually, a fold-out road map. Fodor's is also responsible for a superb series of gay guides, a budget travel guide range, pocket guides, luxury photographic guides for the United States and the Karen Brown series of accommodation and travel guides.

Frommer's is another large American guidebook publisher. The stalwarts of its range are the *Frommer's Complete Guides*, a range of comprehensive guides for travellers on all budgets. The *$ Per Day* series, a range of country and city guides that emphasise value for money, are based around a specific daily budget. It produces many other guides, including shopping guides, National Park guides, pocket guides and guides for people travelling with children. These guides are often criticised for their American orientation, and the fact that most of the more specialist titles are concerned only with US destinations would seem to confirm this.

Cadogan Guides' books are elegantly written and emphasise personal opinion. As a result, they usually feature lively and literate texts. The accommodation and restaurant listings are minimal by some standards, but you can rest assured that the author of the book has stayed in all the places he or she recommends. The coverage of history and culture is very good and is firmly woven into the main text. Of particular note is the *Giant Caribbean Guide*.

APA publishes *Insight Guides*. These are highly visual and informative guides that use photographs and magazine-style articles to explain a destination and the everyday lives of the people who live there. The books are divided into three parts, with an extensive introductory section, followed by regional chapters and a list of practical information at the back. *Insight Pocket Guides* and *Insight Compact Guides* are two spin-off series, both providing more practical detail and both arranged around a series of itineraries, some of which are quite innovative, such as cycle touring around Kathmandu.

On a budget

While all of the books mentioned so far cater for independent travellers who are seeking value for money, there are a number of guidebook series designed specifically for travellers on a very small budget.

Let's Go Guides are considered by many to be the kings of budget travel. They are written and researched annually by teams of students from Harvard University and have a formidable reputation amongst backpackers. There are many tales of travellers tearing out sections of the enormous *Let's Go Europe* once used, and passing the much-needed extracts on to other travellers. Let's Go often bundles popular destinations together, i.e. Spain and Portugal, India and Nepal, so you save money and packing space by only having to buy one book.

Vacation Work is perhaps the most interesting publisher as it takes the view that instead of scrimping and saving before you go, you can actually earn money as you travel. Its *Live and Work* guides are packed with advice and ideas on how to get temporary and permanent jobs in the country of your choice. It also publishes a series of *Travellers' Survival Kits*, which are aimed at budget travellers, and are an ideal accompaniment to the *Live and Work* books or as guides on their own.

As well as these, there are a number of budget guides from smaller publishers. These are often very good, although you may have to go to a specialist travel bookshop to obtain them. Some current examples would be Canadian Budget Zone, which produces an excellent guide to Central America, and Get Lost, a DIY publisher of two guides, one for Amsterdam and one for San Francisco.

Trekking guides

General guides will often include information on the popular walking areas of a country and advice on where to find out more. But a specific walking guide will provide you with maps and far more detailed directions and route options. Even if you are not planning on doing much walking, the amount of extra detail a specific walking guide provides makes it worth carrying in addition to your general guide.

Two publishers already mentioned, Lonely Planet and Bradt Publications, produce some very fine specialised guides. Lonely Planet's excellent trekking guides to Spain, Italy, Australia, the Karakorams, Greece, Alaska and the Himalayas are just some of its current titles. Extensive sections on travelling in the country or region and specific advice for the trekker are followed by chapters detailing a wide variety of treks in a given area, there are day-to-day descriptions of each trek and special trekking maps of the area. Some of the first Bradt Guides were hiking guides and Hilary Bradt, the company's founder, has written many of the South American guidebooks. Other areas that Bradt is strong on include guides to the more obscure trekking destinations of South America, Eastern Europe and Africa. Each have sketched maps, accompanied by specific advice and route descriptions.

Cicerone, a long-established company, highly respected among walkers, has one of the most impressive ranges of trekking guides, covering almost every walking region in Europe as well as common trekking destinations across the world.

Trail Blazer is one of the most exciting specialist companies. It produces an excellent range of trekking guides that provide new perspectives on some well-known trekking areas in Europe, India and Nepal, and also publishes the first comprehensive guide to the Inca trail. All its books include detailed maps and plenty of background information.

Cultural and historical guides

Not everyone travels with a rucksack and not everyone travels independently. If you want more information about the history and culture of a place and less about such basics as where to stay and how to get about, then there are many guide series that will provide you with just this balance of information.

The superb guides published by Odyssey cover a range of both the popular and less-popular destinations. It is one of the few companies to produce anything for Georgia and Uzbekistan, although this is sure to change. Its main strength is the quality of the photographs and the writing: all contributions come from authors with extensive local experience and extracts of work by local writers and celebrated travel writers are always included.

Everyman Guides and *Eyewitness Guides*, have a distinctive format of almost entirely of their own – a very modern look, where text mixes delightfully with drawings, diagrams and photographs. Everyman offers exceptionally rewarding and intelligent coverage of history and culture, with sections on art and wildlife, too. As well as cutaway diagrams, the books often use a range of special devices, such as lavish fold-outs, to explain and illustrate. In addition to the main series, Everyman also produces a *City Guide* series that uses similar production values but concentrates on the practical side of a stay: where to eat, shop and sleep. *Eyewitness Guides* are famous for presentation, using cut-away diagrams and 3-D street elevation maps to explain the area and the sights.

Pallas Guides and *Companion Guides* are highly respected and scholarly series that offer unparalleled detail and intelligent comment on the art, architecture, history and culture of a place. *Pallas Guides* are few in number but giants of quality, with excellent writing style and content. Generally considered more readable than the *Blue Guides*, and with impressive colour and black-and-white photography, they are an ideal accompaniment to your travels and also contain many practical details, suggested walking tours and itineraries. *Companion Guides*, like the *Blue Guides*, are a well-respected, established series that contain lots of historical and cultural information, practical advice and maps. They are written in the style of a travel narrative, making them easy and enjoyable to read.

Blue Guides are justly renowned for their comprehensive treatment of the architecture and the arts. Although they used to be seen as being rather dry and impractical, many of the titles in the range have been revised and rewritten. As a result, many *Blue Guides* provide a lively and intelligent commentary and are far more functional then their reputation once suggested.

Touring guides

Touring Guides are aimed mainly at the driver and are based around two formats: the easy-reference format and itineraries, which detail the sights, a selection of places to eat and places to stay along a prescribed route.

The Automobile Association (AA) publishes some classic touring guides: *AA Explorer Guides, AA Essential Guides* as well as the *Baedeker Guides. AA Explorer Guides* and *AA Essential Guides* are usually arranged around a tour of the main sights, usually by car but sometimes on foot. *Baedeker Guides*, still regarded by many as the last word on the main sights of an area, are presented as colourful photographic gazettes of the main attractions. A distinctive feature of all these guidebooks is the inclusion of a folded road map.

Famous enough to be identified simply by colour, the *Michelin Red Guides* and *Michelin Green Guides* are an excellent choice of touring companion. The Red Guides are an incomparable source of reference for the affluent hotel and restaurant connoisseur, and feature location maps, information on facilities and prices and, of course, the famous symbols of recommendation. They are updated annually and, once you master their language, they are hugely informative. More substantial touring information can be found in the series of *Michelin Green Guides*. These contain introductions to the history and art of an area, followed by a detailed alphabetical survey of places of interest. Clear and easy to use, they provide near-comprehensive coverage of the sights, with many maps, photographs and detailed descriptions. Both the *Red* and *Green Guides* can be cross-referenced to each other and to a range of excellent Michelin maps.

Fodor's also publishes the *Mobil Travel Guides*, which are similar in layout to the *Michelin Green Guides*, but cover the main regions of North America. The guides are updated annually, and feature road maps and city plans, followed by selections of above-average hotels and restaurants and suggestions of things to do and see in each town in the region.

Literary guides

Literary guides act as an optional extra if you don't mind carrying the extra weight. They can give a wonderfully illuminating insight into a place. Equally they can prepare you for your plunge in culture shock before the trip, or remind you vividly of your happy memories after the event. The best are the *In Print* series, from John Murray. These cover Greece, India, Egypt, Rome and Florence, among other places, with a delightful compendium of extracts from writers great and unknown. Other series to look out for are *Travellers' Tales*, which collect many travellers' accounts of a destination, and *Odyssey Guides*, mentioned above.

City guides

If you are going to be spending most of your time in one city or are just going for a short break, you should consider a city guide. Even if you are planning to explore the surrounding countryside, many of the popular excursions will be covered.

Time Out Guides are laid out in a similar way to the magazine listings, giving them the feeling of a directory. The reviews are detailed enough to let you make an informed choice and the candid comments rarely fall short of the mark.

Access Guides are large, clearly laid-out guides that tackle a city area by area. A map of the area is followed by colour-coded listings (red for restaurants, blue for hotels, etc) making them exceptionally easy to use on the ground.

AA City Packs are slim, pocket-sized guides that offer a quick summary of all the main sights and activities. Maps and colour photographs are included and the guide comes complete with a fold-out street map in a plastic wallet, which is, incidentally, particularly useful for holding bus tickets and museum passes.

All the main publishers also produce city guides along the same format as their country guides. Of particular note are those from Lonely Planet and Rough Guide. Lonely Planet's titles cover cities and offer clear and comprehensive listings, accompanied by colour photographs and extensive mapping sections. Rough Guide is well established as a publisher of city guides, each of which feature excellent sections on history and detailed listings.

Women's travel

Rough Guide publishes *More Women Travel*, which covers over 60 countries and offers advice for female travellers in the form of first-hand accounts written by women. These accounts are supported by practical advice and some addresses. It is worth noting that most of the main guidebooks now have sections covering specific advice that women may require when travelling around a country.

Travelling with children

There is quite an extensive range of guides for anyone wishing to travel to us destinations, including Disneyland and Disneyworld, with children, most notably those by Frommer's, although many of the other companies also publish such guides. For anyone wishing to travel outside of the us mainland, there are few guidebooks aimed specifically at people travelling with children, although most of the major guidebook series, such as the *AA City Packs*, include advice on child-friendly sights and activities.

Gay guides

Nearly all the main guidebook series include some advice for gay travellers as well as, to a greater or lesser extent, listings. However, a specific gay travel guide will almost certainly be more up to date and include information about the gay scene and the gay friendliness of many non-gay establishments that you may want to stay in, eat in or visit, as well as the main tourist attractions.

The *Spartacus Guides* are the obvious ones to mention. There is a worldwide guide in the series, as well as some for specific countries such as Britain and Spain. These guides are generally regarded as being comprehensive, and feature lists of the bars, clubs, cruising areas, hotels, cafés and restaurants, all accompanied by good maps and background information about the gay scene. *Scene Gay Guides* is another series that covers such destinations as Berlin, Thailand and New York. Each *Scene Gay Guide* has an introduction to the gay scene, a section on dos and don'ts and listings of the bars and clubs.

Fodor's produces a neat series of *Gay Guides*. Apart from the US one, each guide is pocket-sized and contains details of the gay and non-gay sights of an area as well as an assessment of the gay friendliness of a place.

If you are travelling to San Francisco, one publication with a title to savour is *Betty and Pansy's Severe Queer Review of San Francisco*. Also, it is worth noting that a lot of the main travel guides, the *Time Out* and *Rough Guides* in particular, have very strong sections for gay travellers.

And finally

This survey is, inevitably, incomplete due to the fact that new guidebooks are being published all the time. So, if possible, visit a specialist travel bookseller before you go or even before you start to make plans and you will find inspiration, choice, and possibly some expert advice from someone who has already done exactly what you want to do. ❧

TIM ELLERBY and ROLAND BUTLER work at Stanfords,
the world's largest map and travel bookshop.

Choosing maps
by Tim Ellerby and Roland Butler

IN ALL THE HUSTLE AND BUSTLE OF PLANNING FOREIGN TRAVEL, it is easy to forget that a good map can be just as useful as a guidebook. Under some circumstances, one may even help to get you out of serious trouble. Maps are also an extremely concentrated source of information, one that can be inexpensive and light to carry. However, perhaps the most important point to make about maps is that, with a little application, they can take you far beyond your guidebook or even local knowledge in pursuit of the unknown and undiscovered.

Having said that, one reason that people often do not buy maps is that they are unsure of how to select and use them. I hope that the following comments will help those who have no previous knowledge to feel confident enough to select the right map and make good use of it. Finally, the serious international traveller should recognise the value of mapping as an aid to advanced planning and that, where possible, maps should be bought in advance because local sources can be both surprisingly difficult to locate and unreliable.

The components of a map

The purpose of a map is to provide information about the area covered so that the user can either locate any feature shown or visualise what it would be like to be there, allowing journeys to be planned or imagined. This information is captured in two ways: through the use of a quoted scale and by employing standard symbols to represent commonly occurring features.

The scale of the map is an indication of how much detail the map contains. Large-scale maps have the most detail while smaller-scale maps contain less detail but usually show a wider area, giving a more general picture of the land. The biggest source of confusion with scale arises because the maps referred to as small scale have the highest numbers, i.e. 1:7,500,000. To find out which scale is right for you, please read the section on choice of scale.

The symbols on the map also need a little explaining as they are, in effect, the cartographer's shorthand. This shorthand can be 'decoded' by the use of the map key, which tabulates all the feature codes and tells you what each one represents. It is also important to realise that while the location of any feature is accurately portrayed, the ideogram used to represent it is purely diagrammatic and not to scale. As an example, roads on motoring maps appear to be far wider than they really are for the sake of maximum clarity and to allow junctions and other features to be usefully displayed.

One other consideration regarding both the scale of the map and the symbols used is that there is inevitably a degree of selection when it comes to the information portrayed, otherwise the map would become completely cluttered and consequently unreadable. In practice, this means that some features will be omitted from the map, something to consider when selecting one. The decision about what is shown on any given map or series of maps is determined by the cartographer and publisher, and is often as much a matter of the tradition and style of that particular company as it is of general convention.

Choice of scale

If we now move on to some specific map scales, we can quickly build up an idea of the sorts of map to use for a given purpose. Most national surveys were originally based on the scale of 1:50,000, and the British ordnance survey was no exception. At this scale it is obvious that a series of maps is needed to cover an area the size of Britain, and so a grid is used to relate map sheets of equal size to the areas that they cover and to each other. Such grids can be referred to at the map shop or are sometimes available to take away so that you can work on your requirement at home. The 1:50,000 scale is ideal for cycling and slow, detailed motoring within a limited area. It can also be used by walkers, although it is not really ideal. At this scale you will see all the towns, villages and hamlets in a given area, together with all the roads, tracks, lanes and rights of way. Other features will depend on the style and type of mapping. For walking purposes, a map scale of 1:25,000 is ideal, as it allows you to see all the landmarks and features of the area in more detail, right down to field boundaries in some cases. When we move into the urban environment, where the number and density of features is very high, scales of 1:10,000, 1:15,000 and 1:20,000 are frequently used and these allow you to see individual street names and specific building locations. At the other end of the spectrum, map scales of 1:100,000 and 1:250,000 or even 1:500,000 are regularly used for long-distance motoring and regional touring, where the emphasis is on relating one major feature or area to another.

Having established the uses of scale and the importance of symbols on a given map, it is helpful to look at the types of map that are generally available so that other criteria for selection can be established.

Types of map

For the purposes of the traveller, most maps will be either topographic or thematic, or possibly a combination of the two. Topographic maps show the general nature of the country: physical features, type of terrain, location of watercourses, forests, marshes, foreshore features and all roads, railways and other lines of communication, as well as any other significant features, be they man-made or natural. In general, this type of mapping will have contours (lines connecting points of equal elevation) to indicate the physical relief and, as such, tends to be an ordnance survey type of map.

Thematic maps can be very different. The most common types a traveller will encounter are tourist and trekking maps. Tourist maps tend to suppress and simplify a lot of the geographical features and show only main roads or established walks and the main points of interest to tourists, such as viewing points, guesthouses and picnic spots, museums or beaches, at the expense of comprehensive road layouts, minor villages and physical relief. Trekking maps show the route of a trek overlaid on a landscape that has been simplified to show only the recognisable features for the trekker, such as ridges, rivers, rocks and settlements. As trekking routes are often well established, such maps are usually enough to stop you getting lost. However, if you are venturing off the beaten 'trek', you would be advised to take a more detailed survey map with you, if you can get one.

Having decided on the best scale and the kind of features you want the map to show, you are now ready to compare your criteria with what is available.

Choosing a map

While there is no doubt that many maps are sold each year purely on the basis of their appearance, there are a number of other points that should be given priority.

First and foremost, a map is a graphic representation of information, so it is important to establish how accurate that information might be. This can be established in a number of ways, but it is fair to say that the publication date is one of the most useful indicators because, assuming that an area continues to develop, the older the map the more current information will be missing. Again, as an indicator, this rule need not be taken to extremes as some elements of the map, such as relief, only change very slowly and so, if your primary purpose is walking, such consideration might not be so critical. In urban and semi-urban areas, rates of change to road networks and buildings can be extremely fast, so here you need to be much more critical. Needless to say, most map producers are sensitive to such relative rates of change and will revise their urban mapping much more frequently than their rural and wilderness coverage.

It is also a great mistake to assume that levels of mapping and rates of updating are equal the world over. This is not the case, and so you may have to accept the best available, which could date back some 40 years in some cases. Likewise with scale: by no means all areas of the world are mapped at 1:50,000, so you may be forced to accept a smaller scale than you would otherwise choose. The important underlying factor is to find a source for your map purchase that offers reliable advice and can explain all the current options.

Unfortunately it is not possible to detail all the main map producers throughout the world and give an appraisal of their relative merits, but we can provide a general overview by area, and highlight the sorts of problems you may encounter in trying to obtain maps.

Worldwide

There are some topographic map series that cover the whole world. Air navigation charts are available at scales of either 1:1,000,000 or 1:500,000. Although this does not immediately sound impressive, in some cases – and places – these are the best maps available and should be borne in mind if all else fails. If you require more detail and have more patience, Russian military survey maps can be obtained, usually at a scale of 1:200,000, but sometimes at 1:100,000, or even 1:50,000; urban areas are usually mapped at 1:10,000. They are all in Russian, and supply can be patchy, so they usually have to be ordered, but as with the air navigation charts, if normal commercial maps are unavailable these may be your only option.

Europe

For general travel and route planning, it is hard to beat the maps produced by Michelin, Geocenter, Freytag & Berndt, Kummerley & Frey, Cartographia and Collins. These publishers also produce good street mapping of the major towns and cities, for less important towns please refer to the country text. For want of a better way of listing the more detailed maps I shall start in the west and work along the Mediterranean coast to Turkey and then start northwards.

In Portugal, the main source of large-scale mapping is the Instituto Geografico e Cadastral, which produce maps at 1:50,000 and 1:100,000; some military maps are also available at 1:25,000. Detailed road and tourist mapping for the Algarve is available from a range of different publishers.

For the popular walking areas of mainland Spain, such as the Picos de Europa and the Sierra Nevada, excellent commercial maps are available from Editorial Alpina and also Miguel Adrados. Contoured walking maps for some of the Canary and Balearic islands are available from Freytag & Berndt. Tourist maps for the popular coastal regions are easy to get hold of. IGN Spain publishes a provincial series of maps at 1:200,000. These offer a good combination of topographic and road detail and are popular with cyclists looking to combine maximum detail with a small number of maps. If you are travelling to Barcelona or the Catalan end of the Pyrenees, Survey of Catalunya produces a superb series of 1:50,000 maps for the whole province. For all other areas of Spain, military maps at 1:50,000, 1:100,000 and sometimes 1:25,000 are available. Town plans are available from Distimapas Telstar.

France is extremely well provided for by its national survey, IGN France, which produces maps at 1:25,000, 1:100,000 and 1:250,000 (but no longer 1:50,000), plus many special sheets. Of particular interest to mountain walkers are the IGN France Top 25 series, the Didier et Richard series and Edition Randonnées Pyrenées. Town plans are available from Blay Foldex, Serie Bleau and IGN France.

Italy presents problems for the map user as its national survey is in a rather sorry state and, while supply is possible, many sheets remain unpublished. Consequently you will have to rely on the commercially produced maps. All the popular walking and tourist areas are well covered by such publishers as IGC, Tabacco, Edizioni Multigraphic or Kompass. But when it comes to off-the-beaten-track destinations, detailed map coverage is poor.

Nothing in Africa is adjacent to anywhere.
— JAMES CAMERON

TCI (Touring Club Italiano), the Italian equivalent of the AA, and the Instituto Geografico De Agostini both publish excellent road maps of the whole country at 1:200,000. These may be the best large-scale maps available. Town plans are available from TCI and FMB.

Freytag & Berndt publishes the best detailed maps of the Dalmatian coast and Croatia at a scale of 1:100,000. Coverage for the rest of the Balkans is understandably very bad, with the best maps available being Russian survey maps (see above). A map of Kosovo, however, is available at 1:250,000.

Greece used to be a dreadful country for which to find large-scale maps. Now a company called Road Editions produces many maps of the popular walking regions and the islands. The series varies in quality, but usually the maps offer good contour information, trekking and ski routes and up-to-date road detail. Good tourist maps of the islands are also produced by Toubi. And Harms Verlag produces 1:100,000 contoured maps of Crete.

Finding maps for Turkey can be difficult. The largest-scale mapping that is easily available, as a consistent series, comes from Ryborsch, at a scale of 1:500,000. The popular coastal areas, however, are covered by a selection of maps from Turkish and non-Turkish publishers. For more detailed mapping of the inland and non-tourist areas, Russian survey maps have to be used (see above).

The best maps of Switzerland come from the Swiss national survey, and are generally considered to be exemplary in terms of the accuracy and clarity of their mapping. Produced at the scales of 1:100,000, 1:50,000 and 1:25,000, the maps are a joy to use. Special editions are available with ski routes and walking trails. A good series of street maps is published by Orell Fussli.

Austria's national survey is a reliable source of mapping, but excellent coverage of walking and skiing areas is also given by Kompass, Freytag & Berndt and Alpenvereinskarte. Germany is more complicated as each state has its own mapping department. These usually produce good maps and the Baden-Wurttemberg survey of the Black Forest is particularly popular. German publisher ADAC probably supplies the most detailed street plans and has the most comprehensive list of titles.

The Benelux countries are well covered by their national surveys at 1:25,000 and 1:50,000, and there are also some very detailed road atlases available. Good cycling maps for the Netherlands are produced by Dutch publisher ANWB at 1:50,000. It also produces an excellent series of road maps at 1:100,000.

Moving east, the popular areas of the Czech and Slovak Republics are well mapped by local companies and the resulting maps are easily available from the specialist map store. Poland is also well mapped by both its national survey and various commercial publishers.

In the far north, the Scandinavian countries all have their own national surveys, which produce high-quality topographical mapping at the standard scale of 1:50,000. As well as the standard maps, many popular areas are covered by special sheets or sets that offer excellent value for money.

North America

Survey mapping is available for the United States and Alaska, however it is not of the highest quality. Perhaps this is understandable, considering the vast area covered. Scales range from 1:25,000 up to 1:500,000, and a number of special sheets are also produced for the more popular areas. Help is at hand, however, if you are travelling to any of the National park areas in the form of the excellent NGS/Trails Illustrated maps. Printed on waterproof, tear-resistant paper and based on USGS mapping, they are aimed specifically at the backpacker and explorer. Walkers in California should look out for the Tom Harrison series of maps, as these provide excellent detail. Detailed topographic atlases are available for each of the American states, courtesy of Delorme. Good regional and state road mapping is available from companies such as Rand McNally and Berndston & Berndston.

Canada has the Canadian National Survey. This is the main source of detailed information, and is readily available at scales of 1:250,000 and 1:50,000. Special sheets with tourist information are produced for some of the National Parks. General motoring coverage and town plans are available from Allmaps and Mapart.

Central America, Mexico and the Caribbean

Survey information for this group of countries is hard to obtain, but the patient purchaser should be able to obtain mapping for the majority of popular destinations. Good general maps come from ITMB. Mapping for Belize at 1:50,000 is available from the Ordnance Survey International (formerly the Directorate of Overseas Survey). In Mexico, local cartographer Guia Roji produced good road maps of the individual states, and some survey maps can be ordered. Of the remaining countries, survey mapping is available for Costa Rica and Panama, but not so readily elsewhere. There are many high-quality general maps, however. The

Caribbean islands are well provided for by IGN France, which produces some excellent detailed maps that are scaled for walking and general use.

South America

Topographic maps for many South American countries can be ordered from their respective survey organisations, although you should be wary – many of these will be very out of date. You should also remember to plan in advance, as ordering can take months. A variety of commercial maps covering most of South America's popular trekking destinations, such as the Inca trail, the mountains of Peru and Bolivia and Aconcagua in Argentina, are produced by such organisations as the South American Explorers Club. Street mapping of major cities is available from a variety of local sources and is usually available by order from specialist shops.

Africa

The African continent presents many problems to the traveller wishing to buy maps, and it is useful to know something of the colonial history of the countries you are visiting when you set out to locate survey information. In general, some ex-British colonies will still have mapping available from the Ordnance Survey International (formerly the Directorate of Overseas Survey). Ex-French colonies are covered by IGN France, and sometimes this can be the only mapping available, although often at no more detailed a scale then 1:1,000,000. Some African countries have their own surveys, and these include Algeria, Ghana, Gambia, Madagascar, Malawi and Namibia, but supply is generally very poor and you should be prepared for a long wait. South Africa has an excellent survey department, which produces maps of high quality. Many national parks, such as the Drakensberg National park, are mapped by commercial publishers to a very high standard. The rest of Africa is more of a problem, and availability will vary with the current political climate. In the end, you may have to rely on either general road maps, air navigation charts or the Russian military survey.

Middle East

In most Middle Eastern countries, survey mapping is restricted. At present, Israel is the only country selling maps to the general public. An excellent series of general maps that covers much of the Middle East is produced by GeoProjects. If more detail is required, you will have to rely on air navigation charts or the Russian military survey.

Indian subcontinent

Despite an immense amount of travel interest in India and its neighbours, there is very little in the way of detailed mapping available to the general public. As a result, a number of publishers have produced very good maps for the walking and trekking areas of northern India, Pakistan and Nepal. Nepal is very well covered, with a survey of its own that covers most of the popular areas and Nelles (Schneider) produces a wonderful series of contoured maps covering east and central Nepal. Two other companies, Mandala and the Himalayan Map House, also produce trekking maps for Nepal. Some specific sheets are available for Everest and its national park, notably from the National Geographic Society. Outside of Nepal, Leomann produces a series of sketched trekking maps that cover virtually all the accessible parts of the Indian Himalaya and the Karakoram. A good series of locally produced regional, state and city maps for India are available from TT Maps. Nelles produces an excellent regional relief mapping of the whole of India and Pakistan. Finally, a reprint of the AMS/U502 series at 1:250,000 is available only from Stanfords Map and Travel Bookshop, and these, combined with air navigation charts, should more than adequately fill in any gaps.

China, Japan and Korea and South-East Asia

Excellent survey mapping is available for Japan, but the text is in Japanese and it can be time-consuming and expensive to obtain. The only survey maps of China or Korea that are available are Russian survey maps and they are available at various scales. Nelles produces some good maps of the different regions of China and individual province and city maps are available, but often only with Chinese or Korean text. A series of basic topographic maps for Tibet is available.

The vast area of South-East Asia, Indonesia, Malaysia, Papua New Guinea, the Philippines and the Pacific Islands again poses many problems to the traveller who wishes to purchase accurate, detailed mapping, but there are a few notable exceptions. Survey mapping in Thailand, the Philippines and Papua New Guinea is generally available, although, again, you may have to wait some time for delivery and coverage may not yet be complete. Nelles and a company called Periplus produce good general maps, which often provide detailed insets of popular areas.

Australia and New Zealand

Excellent survey mapping is available for Australia and New Zealand and there is a good selection of commercial mapping, too. The only problem with Australia is identifying the maps you require from the vast grids that cover the country. Australian publisher UBD produces good state and regional maps and a range of town atlases is produced by UBD and Gregory's. New Zealand survey maps are published under the brand name Infomap and these range from walking scale up to route-planning scale maps of the whole country.

In conclusion

As a final plea. please remember that no shop, however large, could possibly hold stock of all maps that are currently available; so if you are venturing off into the unknown and you need to rely on maps, please make sure that you order them well in advance. Some foreign survey departments can take between six months to two years to respond, so give your retailer as much notice as possible – otherwise you may be disappointed. ❧

Choosing an airline
by Philip Ray, Annie Redmile and David Warne

AIRLINES SPEND HUGE AMOUNTS ON ADVERTISING to tell us about their exotic in-flight cuisine, their glamorous stewardesses and their swish new aircraft. But surveys conducted regularly among frequent travellers – particularly among those who have to fly on business – tell us that all these 'service' factors are not terribly important when it comes to choosing an airline.

What does count, however, is a particular airline's punctuality record. When Lufthansa did some market research a few years ago, it discovered that punctuality was the most important criterion demanded by business travellers, being mentioned by 98 per cent of the respondents. Close behind were favourable departure times, mentioned by 97 per cent, while separate check-in was demanded by only 78 per cent and a good choice of newspapers by no more than 44 per cent.

Another survey among readers of the Swedish business journal *Svensk Export* produced similar results. Asked to put a priority on the service features that they regarded as most crucial when choosing an airline, 92 per cent cited departure times and 87 per cent regarded punctuality as being 'very important'. It seems, therefore, that a lot of airline advertising probably does no more than reinforce a choice that the consumer has already made.

Going direct

Most people prefer a flight that involves few, if any, changes where possible. This can restrict choice of airline as these services are often offered only by carriers such as British Airways and other national airlines or the US majors.

But the scene is changing and with a choice, for example, of three mainstream London airports alone – Heathrow, Gatwick and Stansted – and London City and London Luton added for good measure, choice is greater than it has ever been. Added to that the increasing number of direct services from airports such as Manchester and Birmingham and the traveller is getting a much better deal.

One of the best ways of researching your choice is through the OAG Official Airline Guide (or AOAG in the US and some other parts of the world), or the BAA Airport timetable. One possible trap today for unwary travellers is the proliferation of 'code-sharing' deals between airlines. The same flight number does not necessarily mean the same aircraft or even the same airline any more and so it pays to check carefully.

Choice of airports

London's two largest airports, Heathrow and Gatwick, have direct flights to such a range of busy destinations that there is generally no need to fly to a continental airport and change flights there. Passengers living away from the South-East may be lucky enough to have access to one of the growing number of direct services from their local airport – particularly Manchester and Birmingham, which have expanded their international services considerably. If this is not the case then the alternatives include taking a flight to an airport in mainland Europe – and KLM has done much to encourage this approach, over Schiphol – or to London.

Airline standards

There are hundred of airlines to choose from, but some adopt lower safety standards and maintenance procedures than the major international carriers. Some domestic airlines in South America, for instance, have pretty poor safety records. There has been growing concern in the aviation industry that the explosion of growth in China's airline industry has affected standards, and the proliferation of airlines that now operate in the former Soviet Union causes question marks to be placed over a number of carriers where formerly there was only Aeroflot to cause concern. A number of these airlines compete on price, but it can be advisable to pay more and enjoy better comfort and a greater degree of reliability.

The standards of on-board service offered by carriers from the Far East are probably the highest in the world (service is not a dirty word in Asia) but, to generalise, it is probably true to say that the most efficient in terms of punctuality and operational integrity are those of Europe and North America. British Airways, for instance, has received a lot of criticism over the years, but it is generally regarded as a world leader in setting high operational and technical standards. Now that its punctuality and service have been vastly improved, it is a force to be reckoned with. Other highly regarded airlines include Virgin Atlantic, Swissair, SAS, Lufthansa, KLM, Japan Air Lines and Emirates.

Many passengers may be worried about terrorist attacks or hijackings after the events of recent years, although the chances of being involved in an accident of this kind are statistically remote. The most sensible advice is to make a mental note of any airlines or airports that appear to be particularly vulnerable and avoid them. Airlines serving the Middle East are not necessarily bad risks. Israel's national airline, El Al, probably has the most rigorous security standards of any carrier and it was thanks to its own security staff at Heathrow that a catastrophic mid-air bomb explosion was avoided in 1986.

Some Third World airlines that excel in in-flight service may not be so good on the ground. When travelling in Third World countries, never attempt to make your reservation by phone but visit the airline's office and get the staff to validate your ticket in front of you. Always check and double check your reservation – some airlines in out-of-the-way parts of the world do not have computerised reservation systems and mistakes are frequently made.

No-frills airlines

The network of charter flights both inside and outside Europe is wider than many people imagine. On international routes within Europe, charters account for more than half the market in terms of passenger kilometres. Most charter flights within Europe carry passengers going on conventional package tours, but more and more flights are taking passengers on a 'seat only' basis. The mid-1990s saw the spread of the no-frills airline from America to Europe. Carriers such as UK-based EasyJet and Ireland's Ryanair followed the example of Southwest Airlines in the us, offering very low, point-to-point fares with minimal cabin service. Typically, these airlines do not offer in-flight meals, other than nibbles, and charge for drinks. They do not always sell tickets through travel agents. If you buy their cheapest deals and miss the flight, or are forced to cancel it, you may have to pay all over again or fork out a hefty penalty. EasyJet offers its lowest fares on a first-come, first-served basis with prices rising in preordained increments as seats at the cheaper rates sell out. Though it is not invariably so, these airlines often fly from airports other than the main hubs of major carriers.

Charters

There is a wide choice of charter flights across the North Atlantic year round, mostly to Florida and Canada but also to lesser destinations. Recent years have seen a proliferation of fly drive deals, often advertised on Teletext, with basic prices well under £100 for travellers prepared to book at the last minute. But take care. These very low prices often more than double once you have added obligatory insurance and collision damage waiver for the rental car.

Extras and specials

For many scheduled flights it's possible to request certain special meals, such as kosher or vegetarian, and to put in seat requests – for example, window, aisle, smoking or non-smoking, etc. If travelling on a long-haul flight, it's a good idea to advise the airline of your contact phone number so that you can be informed on the day of your departure if there is a major delay.

VIP treatment can take the form of better handling on the ground. An airline representative will smooth you through all the hassles of check-in and will escort you to the airline's own vip lounge. The cabin crew will be informed of your presence and will make every effort to ensure that your flight is a comfortable and enjoyable one. Airlines normally grant vip treatment to senior government officials and commercially important customers. Some airlines will allow you to use their vip lounges if you have paid the first class or full economy class fare.

Other airlines insist that you must be a member of their executive or frequent traveller clubs before they grant you admittance, while some carriers merely charge an annual membership fee that allows you to use their executive lounge whether or not you're actually flying with them. But don't expect vip treatment if you're travelling at a discount rate.

Alternative flights

It is also possible to travel as a courier for a much reduced fare. The courier 're-sponsibility' tends only to be for one half of the journey, so it is an inexpensive way to get to your destination with just a little work to do on the way. ࿎

PHILIP RAY is a freelance travel journalist, previously Deputy Editor of the trade newspaper 'Travel News'. DAVID WARNE works in the travel industry.
ANNIE REDMILE has been a journalist specialising in aviation for over 20 years.

Flight discounts and deals
by Philip Ray, Annie Redmile and David Warne

THE HIGH LEVEL OF AIRFARES IS ALWAYS FAIR GAME as a topic of conversation when frequent travellers get together. It is an even more popular topic for politicians, who appear to believe, probably erroneously, that cheap fares are a good vote-catcher. Some fares are certainly high, but it is still possible to fly to most parts of the world for considerably less than the full standard fare, given the assistance of a professional travel agent.

The key word when it comes to the difference between high fares and low fares is 'flexibility'. If you are prepared to be flexible as to the day or time of year when you want to travel and let the airline slot you onto a flight that it knows is likely to have empty seats, you can nearly always find a cheap fare. But this may well mean you have to buy your ticket either several weeks in advance or at the very last minute. Frequently your stay at the destination must include at least one Saturday night – a frequently criticised requirement that is imposed by airlines to minimise the risk of business travellers trading down from the normal full fare to the cheap rate (on the theory that few business people want to spend a Saturday night away from home). And with most cheap fares, once you have booked your flight, you can usually switch to an alternative service only on payment of a fairly hefty cancellation or amendment penalty.

The other side of the flexibility coin is that if you want complete freedom to change or cancel your flight without penalty, you have to pay for the privilege, which means, in practice, the expensive full fare.

Economics

The economics of the wide gap that exists between the highest fare and the lowest is not quite so crazy as might appear at first sight. If business travellers want the flexibility to change or cancel their reservations at short notice, seats will often be empty because the airline has been unable to resell them, and the cost of flying that seat still has to be paid for. The price of a fully flexible ticket also has to take account of the 'no show' factor – those passengers who have a confirmed reservation but do not turn up at the airport and fail to notify the airline that they want to cancel their flight. So there is an implicit bargain between the airline and the passenger when it comes to a cheap fare. The airline offers a discount in return for a commitment from the passenger (underpinned by a financial penalty) that he or she will actually use that seat.

Flexibility

Many business travellers can probably be more flexible about their air travel schedules and can still save quite a lot of money, provided they don't mind travelling at the back of the aircraft with the masses. For example, if you are planning to attend a conference, the date of which is known a long time in advance, you can frequently buy an APEX fare at anything up to half the cost of the full fare. But always bear in mind those heavy financial penalties if you suddenly decide to cancel or change your flight.

Business travellers will also find that it is often worth looking around for a package trip, such as those offered by specialist tour operators to tie in with a trade fair. Some travel agencies and tour operators also offer attractive packages to business destinations that provide not only the airfare but also hotel accommodation for a total price that is often less than the normal business class fare. Needless to say, this type of package does not offer the flexibility of the full-fare ticket and you will probably not be able to change your flight if your business schedule overruns.

If you are planning an extensive tour within a region such as North America, the Far East or Australia, it is well worth investigating the many airpasses available, for instance those issued by US and Canadian domestic airlines, which offer multi-coupon or unlimited travel over their networks for a given period (although there are usually some restrictions on routing). For travel to the USA, there are also some remarkably good-value deals on fly-drive trips, with car hire being charged at only nominal rates in many cases.

Some of the best deals for business travellers are to be found in the round-the-world fares offered by a number of airlines, which can enable you to plan a complicated itinerary at a knockdown rate.

Frequent flyer programmes

In the competitive world of aviation, where the frequent traveller is king – or queen – 'loyalty programmes', as the 'frequent flyer' programmes are classified, have become the norm. Passengers collect points or benefits each time they fly with a particular carrier and they redeem them for a free ticket for a partner or for some other benefit. There was a time that fear of the various tax authorities' view on such schemes prevented most airlines outside the US from offering frequent flyer programmes. If they were to offer a scheme it was heavily disguised and travellers had to have a US address. Competition has forced a more open approach and nearly all airlines have their own scheme today or link in to that of another carrier, and the hotel chains are also now following suit.

There are specialist magazines – such as *Executive Travel* or *Business Traveller* magazine in the UK – aimed at frequent travellers that list all the latest offers on airfares, deals and frequent flyer programmes.

Bucket shops

The best-known source of discounted air tickets is the so-called 'bucket shop', a phrase that was first coined at a travel industry conference in the early 1970s to denote an outlet specialising in the sale of air tickets at an 'illegal' discount. Such is the power of the media that the term – which was derived from shady activities in the nineteenth-century US stock market – is now universally understood. The term consolidator is now more frequently used within the industry and has gained legitimacy as a result of lighter regulatory control.

Back in the early 1970s, the world of bucket shops was a pretty sleazy one, based on back rooms in Chinese supermarkets or in flyblown first-floor offices in Soho. One or two of the early entrepreneurs actually ended up in prison and some of the cheap tickets that found their way into the market place had, in fact, been stolen. One bucket shop, which traded as a 'reunion club', ended up owing more than £620,000 to thousands of people who had been saving up to visit relatives abroad, not to mention another £614,000 that was owed to airlines. The owner of this club was eventually jailed for trading with intent to defraud. He knew that the 'club' could not meet its liabilities and yet he continued to trade for almost a year.

Failures still do occur occasionally, but the aura of back-street sleaze has virtually disappeared. Outlets are being opened in the high streets of provincial cities by respected companies with long experience of the travel business, and most of the household names in retail travel are now able to supply discounted tickets. At one time the Association of British Travel Agents (ABTA) officially banned its members from offering 'illegally' discounted airfares, but dropped this rule when the restrictive practices legislation began to bite on the travel business. Nowadays many bucket shops are members of ABTA, and all discounted scheduled airfares are now covered by the Civil Aviation Authority's consumer-protection machinery. This makes it less likely that the consumer will be left out of pocket if a bucket shop goes bust as repayment will be due from a bond.

The CAA recently tightened its protection rules further, requiring all consolidators to be covered by bonds unless they hand over tickets to their clients on the spot, immediately after receiving payment. The agent must print details of bonding and an Air Travel Organiser's Licence (ATOL) number on its documents. Consumers can check the validity of the ATOL by calling the CAA.

It is worth taking a closer look at the discounting phenomenon and at what makes it 'illegal', if indeed it is. It is an economic fact of life that, on average, the world's scheduled airlines fill only two-thirds of their seats, so there is a very powerful inducement to fill the remaining one-third by any means possible. Assuming that overheads have been covered by the two-thirds paying 'normal' fares (although this is not necessarily a valid assumption), anything earned from one extra passenger means a bigger profit or a smaller loss – provided that the airline can earn some valuable hard currency.

The 'illegality' of discounting stems from the internationally agreed convention that governments can approve airlines using their airspace, and most countries have provision in their legislation that makes the sale of tickets illegal at other than the officially approved rates. In the UK, the legal position is not quite so clear cut. British airlines are regulated by the CAA and there is specific legislation that lays down heavy penalties against discounting. Foreign airlines are separately controlled by the Department of Transport and, depending on whether there is a specific provision on tariffs in their permits, they may or not be liable to be brought before the courts for discounting.

There is a third class of airline – the so-called 'offline carrier' – which does not actually operate services into the UK but maintains sales offices here. These airlines can, quite legally, do whatever they want in terms of discounting, because there is no law that can catch them.

All this is somewhat academic because no British government has ever tried to enforce the law, which suggests that perhaps it is time for it to be repealed. The CAA, too, has rarely refused to sanction a new low fare filed by an airline (although it could intervene if it felt the fare was 'predatory' – in other words, designed to put a competitor out of business). However, the authority has frequently refused applications by airlines to increase their full-price fares.

The passenger's viewpoint

The risk of losing money at a bucket shop has been reduced drastically by tighter consumer protection rules. Even the danger than an agency could go under, leaving you scrambling for an alternative deal, should not be exaggerated.

Only a tiny proportion of bucket shop clients suffer financial loss in any year, and there are plenty of satisfied customers who have managed to make substantial savings on their trip. Perhaps word-of-mouth recommendation from a friend is a good way to find a reliable outlet for a discount fare and in recent years the strengthening of consumer protection legislation means that any outlet displaying the ABTA and ATOL symbols is a pretty safe bet.

It is a good sign if a bucket shop has been established for some time in good premises with a street-level office. If possible, you should make a personal visit to assess the knowledge of the staff rather than just relying on a telephone call. Ask as many questions as possible and find out any likely snags such as a protracted stopover *en route* in an unattractive part of the world; and make sure you know which airline you're flying with.

It is a good indication of a bucket shop's reliability if it holds an Access or Visa appointment, because the card firms check the financial integrity of their appointed outlets thoroughly. Use of a credit card also gives you added security because, under the Consumer Credit Act, the card company becomes liable for provision of the service you have bought in the event of the retailer's failure. It is also a good sign if the office is a member of the Association of British Travel Agents (look for an ABTA sticker) or licensed by IATA (the International Air Transport Association) because you are then protected by the association's financial safeguards. ✌

Learning a language
by Natasha Hughes

I MAGINE FOR A MOMENT THAT YOU ARE AN ASTRONAUT. You've crash-landed on an alien planet and, within seconds, are surrounded by little green creatures no higher than your knee who burble away at you in an incomprehensible series of clicks and chirps. You'd probably feel confused, isolated and at a loss to tell whether the situation you were in was threatening and hostile – or whether what was being communicated was the Martian equivalent of "Come inside and have a cup of hot tea after your long journey."

Now imagine that you've just stepped off a boat and onto the shores of an island in South-East Asia. A gang of taxi drivers jostle for your custom and leaflets for hotels that range from fleapit to beachside luxury are thrust in your face. It's hard not to feel confused.

The two situations are not dissimilar, the only difference being that when you encounter humans, whatever the gap in verbal communication, body language goes a long way towards creating a mutual understanding of mood – wherever you are in the world, you'll have a good idea as to whether the person talking to you is about to invite you in for a meal or level a shotgun at you.

Language is a hallmark of humanity, such a constant, such a given, that we feel disoriented when we are put into situations where we are unable to communicate.

English speakers are fortunate in that – thanks in part to the pervasiveness of pop music and Hollywood films – the great majority of people around the world speak at least a few words of their language. And that's not even taking into account those countries where English is either the first or the second language, of which there is a long list.

Having said that, there are many countries where English will do you little or no good unless you happen to be conversing with a member of an educated elite.

No man should travel until he has learned the language of the country he visits. Otherwise he voluntarily makes himself a great baby – so helpless and so ridiculous.
– RALPH WALDO EMERSON

Few people in many Latin American countries, for instance, have more than a few words, if any, of English, and trying to get around without a basic Spanish vocabulary – enough to order a meal, book a train ticket or ask for a hotel room – can make the going nearly impossible. I once spent six weeks in Peru with a friend who was under the impression that Italian was close enough to Spanish to enable him to get by. By the end of the first week in the country, he had been reduced to near-despair by his inability to communicate the simplest of needs.

Even those countries where English is widely spoken can prove tricky to negotiate without a few words of the native tongue. Travelling round Israel many years ago, I ended up in Ashkelon when I was meant to be heading for Eilat, simply because I couldn't ask my fellow passengers which direction the bus was following.

Many people criticise the British for their apparent inability – or unwillingness – to make the effort to learn even the merest smattering of a new tongue. Europeans, in particular, tend to be vocal in their criticism of the English traveller who believes that by speaking a little bit slower and a little bit louder he will make his audience understand whatever it is he happens to be talking about. Many Europeans, particularly northern Europeans, take the trouble to learn to speak excellent English – so why should it be so hard, they feel, for the English to take the trouble to pick up a few words of the language of whatever country they happen to be visiting? And they could have a point.

Even those early faltering steps in a new tongue – learning how to say please and thank you, for example – go a long way towards creating an atmosphere of trust: people are usually delighted that you have made the effort. Go a bit further and learn how to ask the price of things in a shop or marketplace, book a hotel room or enquire into the state of someone's health, and a whole new world will start to open. And forget that very British concept of being embarrassed about using the wrong words, the imperfection of your grammar or your awkward accent. Most people you encounter will be more than happy to make allowances for your mistakes.

So if you're planning a trip, what's the best way of getting to grips with the language? The most elementary way, of course, is to buy a phrasebook. These are now carefully researched and marketed, and there is very little chance that you will come across one that contains outdated, clunky and irrelevant sentences. The best way to find one to suit you is to go into a bookshop and browse through as many versions in your chosen language as possible. Try and get an idea of the range of situations covered to make sure your kind of travel experience has been catered for. If you don't even want to go that far, most guidebooks have a section dealing with useful words and sentences.

There are some severe limitations to this approach, however. To begin with, although these books are usually sorted into questions and their related (potential) answers, the chances of someone responding by the book, so to speak, to your carefully phrased question are pretty slim. Just think of the number of ways you might answer a tourist who asked you for directions to a particular museum or restaurant, for instance, and you'll get some idea of why things can get very confusing very fast. And local accents and idiom can muddy the waters even further.

Perhaps less limited are the 'teach yourself' type of book, which gives you step-by-step lessons in a language, from the basics ("My name is…", "How much is…") to the expression of more complex ideas. These will usually give you a fuller appreciation of a language than a phrasebook would, especially as you can gain some insight into its grammatical framework, helping you to construct sentences which you have never actually been taught. However, you may still run into problems with the spoken language once you arrive at your destination. Cassette tapes can be helpful in giving you a taste of how a language is actually spoken, but will not help you explore it in any greater depth than a book would.

> *The treachery of the phrasebook is that you cannot begin to follow the answer to the question you've pronounced so beautifully – and, worse still, your auditor now assumes you're fluent in Swahili.*
> *– Pico Iyer*

The best approach – if you have the time – is to take some lessons before you leave home. If you are based in London, both *Floodlight* and *On Course* publish details of courses in languages that range from Arabic to Urdu, at various levels ranging from beginner to colloquial. Buy one of these guides well in advance of the start of term, as some courses book up quickly, and check the listings to find your nearest centre – chances are you'll find one near work or home. Classes are usually held in groups of anywhere from five people to 20, and all should give you at least an elementary facility in your chosen language. If you have a helpful teacher, he or she should be able to advise you on useful phrases for situations that you expect to encounter on your travels and will be able to recommend additional reading matter that may prove useful once you've mastered the basics.

If you need to learn an Oriental or African language, the School of Oriental and African Studies (SOAS) at the University of London teaches everything from basic Yoruba to Chinese poetry and runs both full- and part-time courses. SOAS is based near Russell Square (tel 020 7898 4888, fax 020 7898 4889, email languages @soas.ac.uk, website www.soas.ac.uk/languagecentre).

Other centres focus on one particular language, but run courses that vary in their intensity, duration and the degree of expertise required from you. The Institut Français in South Kensington (tel 020 7581 2701, fax 020 7581 2910, email michel.richard@ambafrance.org.uk, website www.institut.ambafrance.org.uk) is renowned for the quality of its tuition, and covers everything from French at work to an appreciation of french literature. The Istituto Italiano di Cultura (tel 020 7823 1887, fax 020 7823 2887, email italian.languageservices@gateway.net, website www.italcultur.org.uk) and the Instituto Cervantes (tel 020 7245 0621, email cenlon@cervantes.es, website www.cervantes.es), both of which are based in Belgravia, cover Italian and Spanish (respectively) in equal depth. Japanese is taught at the Institute of International Education in London, which is situated in the heart of Regent's Park (tel 020 7487 7678, fax 020 7487 7679, email humanet @dircon.co.uk); and Russian courses to suit all levels of experience are conducted by The Russian Language Experience (tel 020 7608 3794, fax 020 7608 3792, email Russian_Language@compuserve.com). Most of these organisations run one-on-one sessions, which might suit your needs better than group lessons.

Another way of finding a good tutor is to go to the language department of your nearest university and place an ad on the college noticeboard. The chances are that you'll end up in touch with a number of very fluent students who would be only too happy to pick up some extra money in exchange for a few private lessons. Alternatively, someone at the language department itself may be able to recommend a professional tutor.

Finally, if you have the time, the most thorough way to immerse yourself in a new language is to sign up for a residential course based in the country itself. Lessons are usually conducted during the morning, leaving you free to explore your surroundings and practice your lessons in a real-life situation in the afternoon. Accommodation ranges from very basic beds in student halls to thoroughly luxurious *palazzi*; alternatively you might like to stay with a local family, a crash-course experience that forces you to be brave and plunge right in and try out your new-found language skills.

Whichever method you choose for learning your new language, the amount of effort you put in will pay rich dividends in allowing you to enjoy travel experiences that would once have left you feeling like you'd just arrived on a spaceship from an alien planet. ❧

Support systems

The email revolution
by Chris Martin

I<small>T'S HARD TO EXAGGERATE THE EFFECT</small> that modern communications have had on today's traveller. The internet, faxes and mobile phones have laid a tight net across the world that penetrates even the remotest areas. Of these technologies, perhaps email has been the most significant. Email has certainly changed the traveller's daily routine; for some a visit to the cyber café has now become as important as changing money or finding a place to stay for the night. The ready availability and relative cost effectiveness of email has meant that the traveller is no longer alone on the road; despatches and updates can be sent back to loved ones, friends and even the workplace. Email is fast, efficient and refreshingly unconstricted by the time differences that plague long-distance telephone calls.

Furthermore, email allows solo travellers to alleviate some of the loneliness that comes from staying in a strange environment, as well as to make arrangements to meet those travelling from near or far to join them.

Some might argue that this kind of contact goes against the very nature of immersing yourself in a new culture, however, the practicality of the matter is that more often than not you will be fighting for computer time with the locals themselves. Cyber cafés in large Indian cities have become a hub for those trying to find wives in a painfully strict and repressive society. In Singapore unwitting travellers have found themselves embroiled in the teenage dating scene, receiving offers of ice cream and kisses from giggling girls. I myself found a blossoming email scene in Beijing, as students took advantage of the new political freedom to make contact with their Western counterparts.

Indeed, the social scene surrounding cyber cafés goes beyond locals. You're unlikely to be the only traveller in town wanting to check in with home, so it's not unusual to find a fellow traveller at the terminal next to you. You'll quickly find that the cyber café can be as much about fun as it is about keeping in touch.

Finding a cyber café and getting set up

Cyber cafés are now common right across the world; certainly most big cities will have them. Usually they consist of a room with five or six terminals inside; often drinks and refreshments will be on sale to those surfing inside. Costs vary, but you will normally be charged an hourly rate to use one of their PCs. I use the word PC wisely. A version of Windows is used on around 90 per cent of the world's computers, so if you're used to a Mac you may be as well to take a crash course in Windows before you leave. Be aware, too, that you will have problems using a Macintosh floppy disc with most PCs, so if you are carrying work, a journal or internet bookmarks with you, be sure to use IBM formatted discs.

The standard of the equipment you'll get to use will vary, but don't expect it to be too primitive. The ongoing mission of the Western world to get the rest of the globe 'wired' and the charitable activities of the big computer companies mean that often the poorer the country you are visiting the better the quality of its equipment. Most set-ups will offer web browsing and some form of email package. While they'll certainly have some word processing software (such as Microsoft Word), graphics packages are expensive, so don't count on them being available.

Finding your local cyber café is easy. A guidebook will give you some idea of their location. You can also research locations online at the *Internet Café Guide* (www.netcafeguide.com) or *The Internet Cafés Guide* (www.netcafes.com). Neither of these sites is comprehensive (new cyber cafés are opening every day), but they do give a general global coverage and offer easy searching by county and city as well as some idea of current costs. If you really can't find an internet café anywhere, it is always worth trying the area's top-end hotels. Better hotels will have a business centre with a web connection, though expect hire time to be pricey.

There are two ways to handle your email on the move. Firstly, you can reconfigure a rented machine's own email client so that it connects to your isp (internet service provider) at home. To do this you will need to have to hand the name of your isp's pop3 server for received mail and its smtp server to send mail from your account. You'll also need your user name and password to access its service. If you are finding these terms a little bit bewildering you will certainly be better off with the second option: using a web-based email system. Don't worry about losing mail from your regular account as you can arrange for your isp to forward your mail automatically to your new web-based mailbox.

Web-based email is the traveller's choice. An invariably free service, it allows you to dial into your mailbox via a standard web browser through any web-ready terminal anywhere in the world. You can set up an account for yourself online in a matter of minutes simply by filling in an online form on your email provider's website. You'll also return to this website to send and receive email, logging in with a personal user name and password. Make no mistake, web-based email is phenomenally popular. One of the biggest, Hotmail (www.hotmail.com), attracted over 40 million users in just three years. Other popular choices are attached to search engines such as Lycos (www.lycos.com), Excite (www.excite.com) and Yahoo (www.yahoo.com). Publisher Lonely Planet also offers free email, as well as voice messaging and budget international calls, through its Ekno (www.ekno.lonelyplanet.com/) website.

A few words of warning

Check with the café staff before you start you session about the dos and don'ts of their establishment, particularly if you intend to start reconfiguring their machine or downloading files from the internet. No matter how proficient you may be with a pc, the café owners will, understandably, not want their pcs damaged by viruses or heavily reconfigured to suit your specific needs.

Be aware that while your café of choice may be bang up to date with the communication revolution, the country it's in may not be. The speed and time at which you can effectively connect to the internet is at the mercy of the local telephone system. Some remote cafés depend on shaky satellite uplinks, while a friend of mine in Moscow claimed that avid surfers soon learnt which cafés were in physically proximity to a functional telephone exchange.

Finally, web-based email servers regularly clear out dormant users, so if you neglect your Hotmail account don't be surprised to find that it has disappeared after six months. For a comprehensive guide to operating email of all kinds, visit Everything Email at www.everythingemail.com.

Other ways of staying in touch online

VIA YOUR OWN LAPTOP: Apart from the problem of carrying a heavy and eminently stealable laptop computer around with you, those wishing to connect to the internet may have difficulties using local telephone lines. A line tester is required to differentiate between digital and analogue lines, furthermore telephone plugs, like electric plugs, differ from country to country, so you'll need to research your destination or carry a selection of multi-purpose jacks. At a push, a modem can be hard wired to a telephone connection, but some expertise is required. You can reamore about mobile telephony at *The World Wide Phone Guide* site at www.kropla.com/phones.htm.

IRC CHANNELS: IRC is an open channel that is located on a server, via which you can talk to people in real time. You can search for channels that may be of interest to you using a web search engine. Each channel, however, tends to be a tight community and of little use to the general visitor. You will also need some additional software to connect to these channels. For more information, visit www.mirc.co.uk/ircintro.html.

ICQ: ICQ is a real-time communication service similar to IRC. It has the great advantage, however, of allowing you to track and contact friends or acquaintances who may be currently online via a system of registration numbers and directories. For more information on ICQ, visit www.icq.com/products/whatisicq.html.

BULLETIN BOARDS AND NEWSGROUPS: These are open-access areas on the internet, usually grouped by subject, onto which messages can be posted and replied to in 'discussions'. There are many web-based bulletin boards, and most decent web browsers, such as Netscape (www. netscape.com) or Internet Explorer (www. microsoft.com), can read newsgroups. You'll need to do some research to find one relevant to your needs, but they can be an invaluable resource for up-to-date, on-the-ground accounts. For more information, visit *Travel Services Forum* at www.travel-services.com/bbs/index.htm.

The future

Technology is constantly moving, and it seems to be focusing on making personal communication smaller and more globally available. The new generation of palmtop computers will provide an adequate email service and can be used to carry maps and city guides. Meanwhile we're welcoming the arrival of WAP mobile phones, which look set to take advantage of low-level satellites to offer excellent global communications and even to exploit the GPS tracking system.

All of the above leaves the traveller with a quandary. While it's nice to keep in touch, it's up to each individual to decide how far they wish to go. Personally, I'd hate to find myself at the top of a mountain trying to ignore the ringing of a mobile phone. ❧

CHRIS MARTIN is Editor of the online literary magazine 'Bookends' and writes about he internet for the 'Sunday Times' and 'The Bookseller'.

Organising your finances
by Harry Stevens and Melissa Shales

WE BELONG TO THAT GENERATION WHOSE FIRST REAL EXPERIENCE of foreign travel was conducted under the auspices of Her Majesty's Government, when European towns were teeming with black marketeers trying to prove to every young serviceman that 200 British cigarettes were really worth 200 or even 300 Deutschmarks. Travellers' cheques and banks hardly existed and credit cards, like ballpoint pens, had not yet been invented. Our trust in ready cash as the essential ingredient for trouble-free travelling is no doubt due to this early conditioning.

Cash is, of course, intrinsically less safe to carry than travellers' cheques, especially when these are fully refundable when lost (this is not always the case, particularly if a 'finder' has cashed them in before the loss has been reported).

Nowadays, we carry all three: travellers' cheques, credit cards and cash. However, our book of travellers' cheques is a slim one, which we hold in reserve in case we do run out of cash – and for use in countries with restricted currencies (which basically means you can't obtain their cash outside their borders – Tanzania and Cuba are examples).

Credit cards can be a very useful way of getting hold of money, especially if you are on an extended trip and don't feel like carrying several months' worth of cash with you at all times. Try not to use them to get hold of cash, however, as most card providers charge higher rates of interest for cash withdrawals than they do for direct payment for goods and services. And remember that, if you *are* travelling for more than a month, it's vital to set up some kind of direct debit system back home to make sure that your credit card bill is paid off.

A new service which combines the advantages of credit cards and travellers' cheques is the Visa Travel Money card. This is a 'smart' card which can be 'loaded' with a finite amount of money and used to withdraw that amount in local currency at Visa cash machines abroad. When all the money has been withdrawn, you throw away the card. For security you have a PIN number, making this a safe and convenient system. Currently it is only offered by some banks in the UK (RBS, Alliance and Leicester, Bank of Scotland).

When it comes to both credit cards and travellers' cheques, it is worth taking photocopies of all you might need to recoup your losses should the worst happen. In the case of credit cards, this means photocopying the front so that the serial number is clearly visible; with travellers' cheques, this will be the list of serial numbers and the receipt from the bank or bureau de change where you purchased them. Also make a note of the emergency-line phone numbers all financial organisations provide. These tend to operate on a 24-hour basis and it is an intense relief, if your wallet does get stolen, to be able to cancel the old card and get another one issued and on its way to you with a simple ten-minute phone call.

Small change

There are a number of cogent reasons for equipping yourself with the currency of the country you are about to visit before you get there:

1. Even on the plane you may find you can make agreeable savings by paying in some currency other than sterling.

2. Immediately on arrival it may be difficult to change your money and you may be doubtful as to whether you are being offered a good rate of exchange.

3. The immediate problem of tipping a porter, making a phone call and paying for a taxi or airport bus must be solved long before reaching your hotel. And when you do eventually get there, this does not necessarily get rid of your problem as not all hotels exchange travellers' cheques for cash (and, even if they do so, the facility is not necessarily offered at any time of day or night) and if they do, the vexed question of the rate of exchange arises once more.

Many countries do not allow unrestricted import or export of their currency – and in a number of countries for 'unrestricted' read 'nil' – so one has to exchange travellers' cheques or hard cash on arrival (there is usually a small exchange rate advantage in favour of the cheques). In addition, if you plan to visit several countries, it is usually best not to keep bank notes of a currency no longer required on that journey (although we do hold on to small change and some low-denomination notes if there is a likelihood of another visit).

Remember that every exchange results in a loss, but the sums involved are usually not large. It is certainly not worth spending a morning traipsing from one bank and *bureau de change* to another in the hope that you will find a rate that is significantly better than the first one you tried. Check out, at most, two or three banks, and then make a decision on that basis. You'll find that any difference in the exchange tariffs is usually minimal – and is often balanced by the rates of commission charged by each organisation.

Finally, remember to keep a record of all financial transactions, particularly in sensitive countries, as you may well be asked to account for every note before you are allowed to leave.

Nest eggs

If you are planning to be away for a long time, and possibly travel through many countries, there is one other way to ensure that you don't have to carry too much with you and risk losing it all in some remote village. Before you leave home, set up a number of accounts along the way through banks affiliated to your own and arrange for money to be wired over to you at regular intervals. Ask the foreign section of your bank to advise you on the best way of doing this.

While this is a simple-sounding operation, as with most aspects of travel, the reality is infinitely more complex, each transaction taking weeks longer than claimed and your money being misplaced *en route* or misfiled on arrival. The bureaucracy alone could make the whole exercise too difficult to be worthwhile, never mind the fact that you are having to place an immense amount of trust in bank staff who may be corrupt. It is probably not worthwhile unless you are planning to spend some considerable time in any one country. Whatever you decide to do, don't rely on having money waiting for you – keep an emergency fund for survival while you are trying to wring your money out of the bank.

Even if you haven't set up accounts along the way, ask your bank for a list of affiliated banks in the countries you will be visiting. In an emergency, you can ask for money to be wired out from home to any bank, but if you can choose one that is already in contact with yours, it should make life considerably easier. Always ask for a separate letter, telex or fax confirming that the money has been sent and specify that it should be sent to SWIFT (express).

Be careful not to wire more money than you will need into countries with tight export restrictions. No one will mind the sterling coming in, but they may well object to it leaving again, and if you are not careful you could find yourself with a nest egg gathering dust in a country you are never likely to visit again. ❧

HARRY STEVENS is a businessman running his own engineering and electronics company, which takes him abroad frequently.

Applying for sponsorship
by Myfanwy Vickers

T HE QUEST FOR SPONSORSHIP FOR YOUR TRIP is not a bad test of the qualities that will stand you in good stead as a happy and successful traveller: grit, tenacity, enthusiasm and unflagging energy. It is also the aspect of travel most reminiscent of the job you thought you were getting away from: raising money is hard work. It generates bureaucracy and administration, photocopying and phone calls – all of which absorb your carefully saved funds.

But it can also be rewarding in more ways than the purely financial; indeed, the contact you will have with people during the preparations for your trip can be every bit as heart-warming as that which you will experience once you are launched in far-flung places. But if you are to persuade people to give you funds, you are embarking on a campaign as well as an expedition. Securing sponsorship is not the end of the matter either, as you will have to carry through the follow-up, contacting donors and sponsors once again in order to keep your side of the bargain, deliver the goods and say thank you. Be realistic and bear this in mind before you start. It is not easy; what is easy is getting caught up in the next stage of your own life once you're back home, having enjoyed all the backing. Don't promise more than you can deliver. You burn your boats for next time, and make it doubly difficult for everybody else who is seeking the same thing.

You can seek sponsorship from business and industry, the media, grant-giving organisations, clubs and local groups, friends and the public. The vast majority of it will come from business and industry (in kind rather than cash) and in return for publicity. Some firms will offer their services, e.g. free printing, and many will offer you goods at reduced or cost price.

Remember how many appeals land on the desk of the people you are targeting (Kodak receive 300 a week): they will be quick to dismiss a shoddy, ill-considered, greedy or otherwise unseductive approach. Capture their attention and command their interest from the word go. Make the package professional. Invent your own logo, and don't use those of other organisations without their permission – for all your good intentions, you could end up with a court case. Each letter should be typed, addressed personally, and tailored to the individual or his or her company (phone to get the right name if necessary). Don't send duplicated round-robins: canvassing indiscriminately is rarely worth the paper it is Xeroxed on.

Where appropriate, an eminent patron can give an expedition authority and gravitas. A copy of a patron's supportive letter will lend credibility to the venture, and tempt people to put their faith where others have already shown confidence.

Provide a clear outline of what you plan to do and why, and enclose a route map and a breakdown of costs. Indicate how much of the budget you are covering out of your own pocket, and stipulate what you would like, rather than issuing a general plea for anything and everything.

You should also provide a concise profile of the team members, with any relevant experience or achievements to date. Show in your letter that you have already done considerable planning, research and preparation (which you have, of course), and that your departure is not wholly dependent on backing; sponsors are much more willing to help those with evidently serious intent who are already helping themselves. Once you have done all this, feel pleased with yourself if you get a ten per cent response rate.

Think local when appealing to businesses, companies, equipment stockists and so on. Smaller businesses receive fewer requests and they may like to be involved. Often you will simply find greater goodwill and a more personal approach than in a rule-bound conglomerate or multinational. Can you find a connection between the business and its interests, your trip and the destination? The greater the logic you can give to any potential generosity, the better the response is likely to be.

The main – if not the only – thing that most people can offer sponsors in return is publicity, and securing this is not always easy. Be realistic about what you are offering, clear that you know just what the company is asking for, and certain you are able to provide the goods. Are you offering to sport a shirt with the sponsor's logo on it, and if so, is anyone going to see it except the lost ape men of Sumatra? If it is photographs you are providing, give evidence of your ability with a camera: very few people take really good shots that can be used in a national campaign. They do not happen by themselves, either – you will have to set them up, and the best ones always present themselves when you are at your most exhausted. Can you get media coverage? Only pre-paid commissions will impress firms who know how unlikely you are to make headline news otherwise. So try to sell articles to papers and magazines before you leave, finding out which angles in particular interest the editor. Any contract with film or television companies will assure you immediate and abundant offers of sponsorship, as there is no more powerful publicity for any product. Is there a promising audio angle? If so you could sell to radio.

If publicity *en route* is to be part of the deal, start setting up contacts in the country concerned: ask the embassy for advice, arm yourself with the names of the appropriate people in the media, and find ways of overcoming people's innate reluctance to give some sponsor a plug at their expense. Obviously, if you can give evidence of successful marketing in the past, and ways in which other companies have benefited from your efforts, you are at an advantage.

Having said all this, many companies and suppliers have a margin for those who will not in their opinion achieve much publicity, but whom they like, quite simply, as individuals. Some also invest in what they call 'good citizenship', a concept applied almost without exception to field projects or research-based expeditions through which a commercial company can be seen to be putting something back into the host country – while at the same time raising its profile in the minds of potential new recruits. The "we're going to Tibet and we want to do some science so as to help raise funds" approach tends not to wash, and a sponsor such as Shell or the Royal Geographical Society will look for a demonstrable degree of competence in, and commitment to, the field in question.

Most grant-giving organisations provide money only for specific 'scientific' or investigative projects, but it is worth sifting discriminatingly through libraries and specialist directories and targeting the few that you think likely. It may seem unpromising, but the money has to go to someone.

Finally, you can raise money by arranging your own special events – anything from a sponsored parachute jump to selling cakes at the local jumble sale. If your project has a charitable goal, give talks to schools, colleges, clubs, etc. This can be time-consuming, however, with lots of unsuspected hidden costs for results that will probably be disproportionately small.

It is naturally easier to persuade people to give money away if you are helping someone or something else in your turn. Consequently many travellers decide to raise money for charity: you personally are never going to make much out of this, and – let's face it – nor should you. A proportion of the money raised, say ten per cent, may go to defray your costs, but any more than this is likely to lose you sympathy. You must contact the charity concerned for their authority before you start; a letter from them will show that you are *bona fide*. And open a special bank account in the name of the cause, so as to keep careful track of the money.

Contacts are not essential in this game, but anybody can unearth them and even create them. Do not be timid about approaching people, however elevated they may seem, for their potential interest and support. More often than not you will be pleasantly surprised at the response and the extent to which people will put themselves out on behalf of a project they take to. Liaise with organisations that are happy to advise, such as the extremely helpful enthusiasts at the Royal Geographical Society.

Beware, however, of the danger of having the 'freebie' tag attached to your efforts. Although pleasure is as valid a reason for travel as any other, people can understandably be quick to resent the idea that they should help finance what they see as 'jolly' on your behalf. Bring your tact and conviction to bear if you come up against this attitude, but don't bang your head against a brick wall: if the reaction is resentful, try elsewhere.

Perhaps the best advice is quite simply to start early. Plan ahead. It may seem improbable, but some firms like as much as a year's notice, so that the project can be incorporated into their plans for the following financial year's budget. Everything takes much longer than you think, and many appeals fall on deaf ears because the departure date is just too imminent.

Sponsorship is one of the few surviving gentlemen's contracts. When you get back, stick to your word. Do not be disappointed if, after all this, they don't make full use of the material – but give them every opportunity to do so. Most companies say that they never hear from travellers again. A thank you, a copy of a published article – all will be appreciated, and will stand you in good stead next time.

Throughout the whole thing, be organised and efficient, and keep a record of all correspondence. Don't take rejections personally; cling to those who show interest like a limpet. Be lively and polite. They don't *have* to give you anything. But don't bury your individuality in business-like formalities: ultimately, it is you rather than a journey that you are selling. Apply your own flair, and enjoy it. ❧

MYFANWY VICKERS is a traveller, writer and radio producer.

Travel insurance
by Ian Irvine

INSURANCE PLAYS AN IMPORTANT PART in planning a trip abroad, but is frequently overlooked until the last minute. A 'rush job' can have serious consequences when you find yourself needing to be airlifted out of the Indonesian jungle with a broken leg, only to discover that your insurance doesn't cover air transportation and you will have to foot the £20,000 bill yourself. It is, therefore, essential that you obtain the correct insurance to suit the particular travel and activities to be undertaken. The vast range of choice can be daunting – different types of travel insurance are sold from numerous sources, including banks, building societies, the Post Office, airlines, credit card companies and even supermarkets, but if you are unsure of exactly what cover you need, you are best advised to seek free professional advice from an insurance broker. Make sure you read the policy, particularly the small print, and understand it before committing yourself.

In 1996, a major travel insurance scheme underwritten at Lloyd's of London produced statistics showing that almost 40 per cent of claims paid related to medical expenses, 30 per cent to baggage losses and 25 per cent to cancellation claims, with the most expensive claim costing £240,000 for medical expenses.

As long as the nature of travel is understood by the insurers, an inclusive policy will meet your requirements and cover the following principal risks.

Medical expenses

This is probably the most important form of insurance, as the consequences of a medical problem may be severe – one can replace, or do without lost belongings, but one cannot replace one's health or body. Advances in medical treatment and the general availability of medical attention have increased costs considerably, and so an absolute minimum cover of £1 million is necessary and these days most policies give higher cover.

Repatriation costs are an essential part of medical insurance and under no circumstances should be limited in the policy. They can be high if a person is in a remote area and any form of complicated or specialist medical treatment is necessary. Air ambulances are regularly used to bring seriously ill travellers to the UK from Europe at costs of several thousands of pounds. When these are required for destinations further afield, prices inevitably escalate rapidly. For example, an accident in Nepal might mean a short helicopter flight to a light aircraft landing strip, followed by a light aircraft flight to an international airport, where a fully equipped medical jet could be waiting to bring the casualty back home. For severe illness or a serious accident, a medical team would need to accompany the injured person, and the costs could be as high as £60,000.

Also, any travel insurance policy must include a 24-hour emergency service so that a sick or injured person, or a hospital or embassy acting on their behalf, can summon immediate assistance. Essential air evacuation anywhere in the world should be covered, but this will not include 'search and rescue' expenses if someone is missing, even if there is concern for their health. Additional insurance for this can be arranged at an extra premium, dependent on location, duration and type of travel.

Private medical insurance in the UK is increasingly popular and often applies on a worldwide basis. However, it is important to note that such insurance often only insures the cost of direct medical treatment, and that repatriation cover is not automatic. Generally, the cover is more restricted than that of a travel policy.

Personal accident

This insurance pays a lump sum benefit if a traveller is unfortunate enough to have an accident that results in death, permanent disablement or the loss of an eye or limb. Some travellers may already have life assurance that applies on a worldwide basis and, in the event of death, would also pay a lump sum. For that reason, the death benefit under travel insurance is normally limited to £10,000. However, benefits for permanent disablement in a travel insurance policy may be as high as £40,000 or £50,000 and, if necessary, can be increased.

Cancellation or curtailment

When a journey has to be cancelled or curtailed unavoidably, the cost of a deposit or payments made in advance for travel can be recovered through your insurance policy, but it is important to check that provision has been made for this. The sum insured must be adequate to cover a traveller's total costs and an amount of £3,000 is usually provided, although, again, this can be increased if necessary. It is important to remember that travel costs may include car hire, accommodation, excursions and tours as well as airfares or other transportation. Cancellation of travel immediately prior to departure could mean losing everything paid for unless the correct cover is in force.

Personal liability

If a traveller injures someone, or damages their property, they could be liable to pay compensation. Personal liability cover deals with such claims and should provide at least £1 million protection. Do note that this insurance *does not cover* claims arising from the use of cars or motorcycles, which must be insured separately.

Delayed departure or arrival

Delays are increasingly common and travellers, particularly on economy tickets, are often left to fend for themselves. If delays last 12 hours or more due to strike, industrial action, bad weather or the breakdown of the aircraft, insurers will pay compensation to assist with the cost of incidental expenses. This should be no less than £25 for the first complete 12-hour period, with subsequent enhancements for longer delays. If the delay affected travel at the point of departure to the extent that the trip had to be cancelled, compensation of up to £1,000 should be payable.

Personal effects and money

The majority of travellers take as little clothing as possible when travelling and, with the increased use of credit cards and travellers' cheques, cash is usually kept to a minimum. In addition, many travellers have household policies that automatically insure their personal effects on a worldwide basis. However, when taking out cover for your personal effects, it is important to make sure that their value does not exceed the provision in the policy, which should be for a minimum of £1,200. Money should be insured for at least £250.

All travel policies limit cover for valuables (defined as jewellery, gold and silver articles, watches, photographic equipment, binoculars, telescopes, personal radios, TV, hi-fi equipment, computer and electronic equipment) and impose conditions regarding security. Valuables are in use throughout the year and so are normally insured under a household policy, which is why travel insurers usually limit cover for valuables to, say, £250 for any one article and £350 for all articles. If valuables are worth more than this they will not be covered under the travel policy.

Security for valuables is important and most insurers insist that they either be kept in hotel safes, locked bedrooms or wardrobes, or carried on the traveller's person. With this in mind, policies should be read very carefully – valuables will *not* be insured if they are not secured in a way specified by the policy. Money insurance usually covers airline tickets as well. A fairly typical limit for tickets would be £1,500, but it is important to be aware that tickets are insured for their cost price and not their replacement value. If a ticket is lost, the travel agent should be contacted, or the travel insurance claims adjuster – very often they can arrange for tickets to be reissued, thus avoiding more expensive replacements.

Vehicle insurance outside Europe

Vehicle insurance in the UK is simple to arrange and can easily be extended to include Europe with a Green Card. Outside Europe, particularly in Third World countries, vehicle insurance is difficult to arrange and there is no such thing as a comprehensive policy. Insurance needs to be divided in two: third party cover to protect against claims from others and accidental damage, and fire and theft cover, to protect the traveller's own vehicle. Third party cover can normally only be purchased at the borders of countries; some insist on insurance, others are indifferent. This insurance cannot be arranged in the UK. The traveller's own vehicle can be insured for accidental damage, fire and theft risks on a worldwide basis, but specialist advice would be need to be taken from an insurance broker.

A word of warning: vehicle insurance in North America differs from state to state, but generally speaking has very low third party limits. Compared with UK limits, they are inadequate and, unless increased, would expose the traveller to unnecessary risk. The limits can be increased by purchasing top-up liability insurance when hiring a vehicle.

Carnet indemnity insurance

If you intend travelling by vehicle outside Europe, you should, technically speaking, pay import duty on your vehicle every time you enter a country. This is obviously impractical and the problem can be resolved by obtaining a *carnet de passage* before leaving the UK. This is a multi-page document that is stamped when entering a country and stamped again when leaving the country to show that the vehicle has both been imported and exported, and as such no duty is payable.

Carnet indemnity insurance is arranged in conjunction with *carnet de passage* documents issued by the Automobile Association and this avoids having to provide a bank guarantee and tying up funds. The AA will require a financial guarantee equivalent to the highest duty of the various countries through which travel is intended. This can be as high as three times the value of the vehicle in the UK.

Insurance premiums are normally calculated at five per cent of the indemnity figure, but if the indemnity is in excess of £25,000 a sliding scale comes into operation. The AA requires a service charge of about £75 to provide the *carnet de passage* and a refundable deposit of £500. Strict instructions for the use of the *carnet* are issued and it is important that these are complied with, in particular, getting the *carnet* document stamped when entering and leaving any particular country.

It is important to be aware that the insurance guarantee against a *carnet* only provides immediate funding if duty becomes payable. It does not absolve the responsibility of paying the duty at a later date. To avoid paying duty at all, a double indemnity can be arranged on a separate basis. All insurances for *carnets* issued by the AA can be arranged by Campbell Irvine Limited of 48 Earls Court Road, Kensington, London W8 6EJ, tel 020 7937 6981.

Life assurance

These policies normally grant cover on a worldwide basis and would therefore apply while travelling. If, however, you are contemplating a particularly unusual or hazardous form of travel, it would be sensible to check with your life assurance company to make sure that no limitations apply.

Claims procedure

Claims that necessitate immediate attention can be dealt with by emergency claims facilities, something made available these days by all insurance companies. This is particularly relevant for medical claims, especially those involving repatriation. However, it is important to remember that contact must be made to get the best use of emergency facilities. Routine claims can normally be dealt with at leisure or on return to the UK. Any documentation relevant to a claim needs to be kept secure, so if it has to be posted it is important to take copies.

If property is lost, claims loss adjusters normally require some evidence of value. Original purchase receipts may not be available, so it will normally suffice to state when and where lost property was purchased, and how much was paid for it.

All insurance policies carry excesses, which are normally deducted from the settlement figure of a claim. Travel insurance claims are usually subject to an excess that should not exceed £50, but vehicle insurance excesses tend to be higher and an amount of £250 would not be unusual. Excesses are always clearly shown on policy documents and if there are any doubts about this, the position needs to be checked before travelling rather than leaving it until a claim is made. 🐾

IAN IRVINE is a registered insurance broker specialising in adventure travel.

Protecting your trip
by David Richardson and Edwina Townsend

THE TRAVEL INDUSTRY HAS AN ENVIABLE RECORD in protecting customers' money, but when the system breaks down there are inevitably heartbreak stories in the media and the image of the travel industry suffers. This was common 20 years ago, before financial safeguards were put in place, but it can still happen today. The vast majority of travellers either continue their arrangements or get their money back if their travel organiser goes bust, but this is of little comfort if you are one of the unlucky ones.

Package holidays

The package holiday customer enjoys the highest level of financial protection, and it is well worth choosing a package rather than making your own arrangements if you are in the least worried about losing your money. And don't forget, a package holiday doesn't have to mean a chartered flight followed by a week on the beach in Benidorm. Tour operators are increasingly targeting the independent traveller, and many people who go trekking in the Himalayas or scuba-diving on the Great Barrier Reef are also on a package.

When Air Europe collapsed in 1991, travellers who had simply booked their own scheduled flight almost certainly lost their money. But those booked on the same flight as part of a package holiday were fully protected through arrangements made by tour operators, who have been regulated and licensed since the early 1970s. New regulations implemented in 1993 as a result of European Community (now European Union) legislation have widened the gap still further between the cosseted package customer and the independent traveller.

The situation with package holidays by air is straightforward, and the same is true for charter flight passengers buying a seat-only deal rather than a package. All tour operators must have an Air Travel Organiser's Licence (ATOL) issued by the Civil Aviation Authority (CAA), and to get one they must satisfy the CAA that they are financially secure, providing a bond that will be used to reimburse or repatriate customers if they collapse. If the bond proves insufficient, the CAA draws on the Air Travel Trust Fund, financed by a levy on package holidays since the 1970s.

The ATOL system is virtually fail-safe as regards package holidays by air departing from the UK, and now has been extended to cover packages using scheduled as well as charter flights. This includes most discounted scheduled air seats sold as 'seat-onlys' or as part of tailor-made itineraries for independent travellers. Some companies advertise themselves as 'agents for ATOL holders', and it is worth checking this out with the CAA. In such cases, the ATOL holder must take responsibility for travellers if the agent fails.

The situation regarding package holidays by surface transport is much more complex. Until recently, tour operators using coach or rail transport, cruises or ferries were not obliged to offer financial protection. Many opted to do so through various trade associations, but this was purely voluntary. But in January 1993, the British government adopted the EC directive on package travel, which introduced a wide range of consumer protection measures including the requirement for all package organisers to protect money. This was no great innovation in the UK, because of the ATOL system and the large number of tour operators providing bonds through trade associations. In some other EU countries, however, public protection lagged far behind the UK. But what might have seemed a good idea to the Eurocrats and MEPs gathered together in Brussels can in practice cause UK travellers a lot of confusion and give them a false sense of security.

The regulations affect all package travel arrangements sold in the UK, not just for travel to EU countries (including within the UK) but world-wide. It is generally believed that the EU's concern was to protect the traditional package holiday customer, but in fact the legislation goes much further. Many areas are poorly defined and the British government has not made things any clearer.

First of all, what is a package? According to the regulations, it is a combination of any two of three elements – transport; accommodation; and/or other tourist services making up a significant element of a package. The latter is open to interpretation, but could include theatre tickets, riding lessons, or golf, for example. Even a country hotel in England that includes a fishing licence in its weekend rates could be deemed to be selling a package, with the consequent requirement to protect any money paid in advance.

This goes far beyond the idea of a traditional holiday package. When the regulations were debated in Parliament, the British government admitted to having no idea how many package organisers there might be in the UK. Its 'educated guess' was between 10,000 and 20,000, when the total number of tour operators belonging to trade associations is less than 1,000. Many of the organisers are coach operators, who are considered to be package travel organisers even if all they do is a onenight trip to Blackpool. Others include social clubs, societies and even individuals, such as the local vicar leading an annual pilgrimage to the Holy Land. 'Occasional' organisers of package travel are exempt from the regulations, but the meaning of 'occasional' remains to be defined if and when a case comes to court.

Also unresolved at the time of writing is the role of the travel agent in putting together packages. If you ask a travel agent to put together a flight and hotel, it could well be that he or she will have to provide protection as a package organiser, even if the arrangements are not sold at an inclusive price. But business travel packages may not be affected, as most business travellers are on credit and do not pay until their return.

Not surprisingly, the regulations are causing grief not only in the travel industry but also among many other organisations and individuals who had no idea that they could be considered package travel organisers. But what is causing even more heartache among established tour operators is that there is no effective way of policing the regulations. A gaping consumer protection loophole is still there.

Organisers of packages using air travel must have an ATOL – that much is straightforward. But there is not a parallel licensing authority for surface travel operators. These are required to provide evidence to travellers that their money is protected in one of three ways: they can provide a bond, possibly to a trade association which has reserve funds in place; they can insure against the risk of financial failure; or they can place customers' money in a trust account and not touch it until travel has been completed.

Travellers taking a package by surface transport should look for some evidence that their money is protected – but the only policing authority is local trading standards officers, who by their own admission lack the resources and expertise to do the job properly. It is now a criminal offence to operate packages without protecting customers' money, but although the maximum fine is £5,000 the first case to come to court resulted in a fine of only £250. The unlucky traveller caught up in a collapse could try to sue the directors – but if the company has gone bust, the kitty will probably be empty.

Trade associations

The weakness of the new legislation means that trade associations continue to play a strong part in protecting travellers' money – especially the Association of British Travel Agents (ABTA), the only one with a strong public profile. Surveys show that members of the public identify strongly with ABTA because their money is safe, and this remains true despite its changing role.

Your money is still 100 per cent safe if you book with an ABTA tour operator, as ABTA has never reneged on its promise to repay customers who have booked a package holiday with a failed member. This is because ABTA requires all its 600 tour operators to be bonded, either with the CAA through ATOL, or through ABTA itself in the case of surface travel operators. In both cases, back-up funds are in place if bonds prove insufficient.

ABTA will not accept insurance against possible failure, or trust funds, as a substitute for bonding – as allowed by the government for non-ABTA members. It points out that insurance against failure is of no help to travellers stranded abroad after a collapse, while trust accounts are open to abuse.

ABTA is going through major changes, but its consumer promise remains intact. Before the new regulations it acted as a quasi-licensing authority, and tour operators had to join up if they wanted to sell through ABTA's 7,000 travel agents. But it is no longer a closed shop, and tour operators and agents can leave ABTA if they wish. When dealing with a non-ABTA company, the onus is on the traveller to ensure his or her money is safe –if in doubt, contact your local authority trading standards officers for advice.

ABTA will also protect your money if a member travel agent goes bust, whatever kind of travel arrangement you have bought. If you already have your tickets then normally you will be able to continue; if not, ABTA will reimburse you. This applies to independent travel as well as to packages, but only when the agent (rather than the travel provider) is the one who goes bust.

Other trade associations also bond their members to protect public money, although it is CAA member organisations such as AITO (the Association of Independent Tour Operators) who license all air packages. Other members include the Bus and Coach Council's Bonded Coach Holidays scheme, the Passenger Shipping Association (Cruises) and the Federation of Tour Operators, formerly known as Tour Operators Study Group. But remember, protection applies only to packages, not to simple ferry crossings or express coach tickets, for example.

The independent traveller

If you book independently rather than buying a package (depending on the definition of a package, which may one day become clear), your money is theoretically much more at risk. But in reality there are few occasions when a failure will leave you out of pocket. The main area of risk is scheduled airlines, bringing us back to the Air Europe collapse of 1991. Despite the outcry that followed, neither the

British government nor the EU in Brussels has yet made any moves to protect scheduled airline passengers' money, much to the outrage of tour operators and travel agents, who were bonded to the hilt. Another British airline, Dan Air, came within a whisker of going bust in 1992 before British Airways picked up the pieces.

The risks are definitely increasing as airlines all over the world go private, free of government control but also of government support. Several US airlines are technically bankrupt, but continue to operate under US bankruptcy laws. New private airlines are starting all the time, while new state airlines in the former Soviet Union look particularly unstable. The British government has failed to act on a CAA proposal for a levy, partly because it would involve only British airlines' passengers, and British Airways objected. As little as £1 added to ticket costs for even a short period would soon build up a substantial protection fund, but there seems no likelihood of this happening in the short term.

But the risk of a scheduled airline collapsing is small enough for most travellers to accept, and the same is true for ferries and scheduled coach companies, who will often help out passengers if a rival collapses. Car rental companies pose a slightly greater risk, while the position of a private railway company that collapses holding customers' money is unknown – a point to consider in the wake of the privatisation of British Rail. And although hotels go into liquidation all the time, they nearly always stay open in order to keep some money coming in.

There sale of discounted scheduled air tickets was a grey area for a long time, but the CAA has now cracked down, requiring agents offering them to be covered by ATOLS unless they hand over tickets on the spot, immediately on receipt of payment. More recently, it has acted to make agents accept responsibility when an airline goes bust.

It gives them three options. They can offer insurance against the possibility of a scheduled airline failure – either free or by charging a premium on top of the fare. They may sign a formal guarantee that they will accept responsibility for customers if an airline goes under, re-booking them on alternative flights. Or they can opt to do neither. But if they do opt out, they must warn customers in all their paperwork and promotional material – and in suitably large print – that they part with money at their own risk. Independent travel arrangements are further safeguarded if you book through an ATOL-bonded agent.

Another way of safeguarding your money is to pay by credit card. This is increasingly popular, and is much more convenient when booking direct with travel suppliers in foreign countries, who may not even be subject to package travel regulations. Credit card companies are to some extent required by the Consumer Credit Act to ensure that the service paid for is provided. But like all legislation this is open to interpretation. The waters are further muddied by the fact that there are now about 40 organisations in the UK issuing credit cards, and their attitude towards refunds varies. If in doubt ask your bank, building society or whatever, especially when an expensive travel purchase is at stake.

Some banks see this as an opportunity to boost card usage: since 1992, for instance, Barclays which has guaranteed to protect anyone buying a flight or holiday in the UK with Barclaycard, for transactions of over £100 with a ceiling of £30,000.

However, Barclays accepts no legal liability, and looks to the travel industry to take primary responsibility. Credit card companies tell customers to seek refunds from the CAA or ABTA in the first instance, but for non-packaged arrangements there are no bonds in place.

There are probably enough scenarios in this chapter to make even the most resolute traveller wonder if his or her money is safe, but in general the travel industry's record is good. If you pay in advance for a carpet, a cooker or almost any other consumer goods and the company goes bust, there is no equivalent to the CAA or ABTA to turn to. But the travel industry is, after all, selling dreams. A ruined holiday is more serious than not getting the carpet you wanted, and the sooner all travel arrangements are fully protected, the better. ❧

DAVID RICHARDSON is a freelance journalist specialising in the travel industry.

Understanding visas
by Ralph Whitmarsh and Duncan Mills

THE SUBJECT OF VISAS IS EVER-CHANGING. Not only are the rules and regulations frequently revised, but the way embassies and high commissions impart information to the public and process visa applications is also constantly being altered – and frequently not to the benefit of the traveller.

Today there is a steady drift of people trying to leave their country and rebuild their lives elsewhere, safe from war, famine or persecution. This puts an increasing strain on the immigration policies of various governments, and the regulations dictating whether you may enter any given country visa-free are constantly under review. While the situation for UK passport holders is reasonably static, members of other nationalities resident in the UK may be subject to different sets of rules.

The ever-increasing desire to travel and the spontaneity with which travel can be organised has had little impact on the authorities responsible for issuing passports and visas. Some countries have closed their provincial consulates in the UK, thus putting additional strain on their hard pressed London-based staff and guaranteeing long queues, especially at peak travel times. Spain, by contrast, insists that you apply to the consulate closest to your place of residence. It all adds up to the fact that while you can virtually arrange a round-the-world itinerary in a matter of minutes, if your documents are not in order you cannot travel. So some thought has to be given to the matter of your passport and the possible need to obtain visas for the countries you wish to visit.

Efficiency and bureaucracy

The cost to a government of maintaining an embassy or high commission overseas is enormous, and most if not all are conscious of the need to reduce costs or raise extra revenue. Some have introduced premium-rate telephone lines for public enquiries; others have installed automated switchboards, which is fine if you know the extension number you want. You may have to listen to a long message before reaching the information you want, and sometimes your question may not be answered at all. But these methods enable the embassy or high commission to reduce its staff (or with luck redeploy them to issuing visas) and raise revenue from premium-rate telephone lines.

You need to do your research regarding visas early in your travel planning process, for – according to where you are going, your reasons for visiting a country and your nationality – the issuing time can vary from a matter of hours to weeks. It is important to understand the role of the embassy or high commission and its staff. The decision as to whether or not a visa is granted lies in their hands, and any consular official has the authority to reject an application if he or she thinks fit. If a rejection takes place, it may only require an extra supporting document such as a bank statement to resolve the matter. Beware though: the US and India endorse the passport when an application is rejected, whereupon a fresh application needs to be submitted, the paperwork for which has to persuade the embassy to reverse its previous decision.

Understanding

When you set foot in an embassy you are entering the territory of another country; frustrated though you may be after hours of queuing, it is worth remembering to be polite and tolerant with the consular official who deals with you, and who is after all only carrying out the checks and procedures imposed by his government. It may help to remind yourself that British and US embassies abroad can be equally daunting to other nationals. Opening hours are limited in order to enable staff to issue visas once the public have left the premises, but this obviously poses problems for people living a long way out of London. Postal applications are

If you look like your passport photo, then in all probability you need the journey.
– EARL WILSON

treated as non-urgent, and your envelope may remain in the mail bag for some weeks before it is opened and dealt with by the embassy or high commission. It is unrealistic to expect them to spend time searching for your application among hundreds of others.

It also pays to inform yourself of public holidays, as these authorities close not only on UK public holidays but also on their own. This obviously disrupts the issuing process and causes a logjam on reopening. During the Muslim holy month of Ramadan, embassies of Islamic countries change their hours of business, before closing altogether at the end of it. Be aware also of dates for the Chinese New Year and other important religious festivals.

Your passport

Before you leave Britain you require a ten-year passport. The MRP (machine readable passport) is available in two versions, one costing £28 and the other with additional pages costing £38 at the time of writing (applications made in person or through an agency will be charged an additional £12). Many countries require a minimum of six months' validity remaining on the passport when you either enter or leave their territory, so first of all check your passport's date of expiry. Make sure the passport has a blank page for each visa required, and sufficient space for entry and exit stamps. Some embassies will only issue a visa on a right-hand page.

Ensure your passport is signed. Again many authorities, the Indian High Commission among them, will not grant a visa on an unsigned passport. Some embassies will grant visas with a validity exceeding that of the passport, but others restrict the visa validity to coincide with the passport expiry date.

Take great care of your passport not only when you are travelling but also between journeys. Keep it secure, as a UK or US passport can command many hundreds of pounds on the black market.

Visa requirements

There are many factors to consider here. Business or tourism? How many entries and for how long? The US has over 20 different categories of visas reflecting different reasons for travel – but only one application form. Saudi Arabia has four different forms covering various reasons for travel. Non-UK-passport holders may find their application referred, with a delay of about four weeks, if they are not permanently resident in the UK.

Most visas are valid from the date of issue, frequently for three months. Some, such as those for Russia, are valid from the date you enter the country: in this case the entry and exit dates are clearly stated on the visa and you cannot enter Russia before or leave after the given date. You therefore need to plan when to apply for a visa in order to avoid a situation where it expires before you even arrive in the country. Other countries issue visas which may be valid for twelve months and allow multiple entries with no restrictions.

You will also need to make financial provision for buying visas. The majority cost under £25, and some are free, but others cost considerably more, particularly for business travellers. The price may also vary according to your nationality, as the costs are agreed between governments. To these costs must be added those incurred in actually getting the paperwork to the embassy: are you going to employ the services of an agent who specialises in visa procurement, or resign yourself to spending a lot of time making trips to embassies and waiting in queues?

Some countries, for example Cambodia, Laos, Mali and Mauritania, have no representation in London. Their nearest embassy is in Paris, which can only add to the cost and complicate the logistics of acquiring a visa.

Many nationals have for some years been able to travel to the US for a maximum of 90 days without a visa, providing they meet the criteria set down on the 'waiver' form. If you have incurred a conviction, however, you must declare this and apply for a visa. The Australian Working Holiday visa for those under 26 years of age is valid for 12 months and is an attractive proposition, allowing a period of holiday to be combined with work in order to finance additional travel.

Beware of an Israeli stamp in your passport should you wish to visit the Arab countries in the Gulf area. Instead, ask the Israeli entry and exit controls to stamp a loose-leaf document. A South African stamp in your passport, by contrast, no longer presents the problem that it used to.

Ready to go?

Before you leave, check your visa for accuracy and ensure it covers you for your plans. Mistakes are frequently made owing to pressure of work in Embassies, and even computer-issued visas are only as accurate as those who input the data. If you are taking family members who are on your passport – husband or wife or children under 16 – ensure that the visa covers them as well, or that a separate one has been issued. Some visa application forms, such as those for India, Australia and Egypt, include space for all those included on the one passport; other countries require one completed form per person. Remember that children who have reached 16 years of age require their own passport.

Visa trends

In recent years we have witnessed the break-up of the USSR; the Iron Curtain has come down; Czechoslovakia has become two separate countries, and Yugoslavia has fragmented. In South America, Argentina and Brazil do not require a visa from UK nationals, but tourists to Venezuela will require a tourist card obtainable from the airline on which they arrive in the country (check this when booking your seat).

Although the CIS (formerly USSR) has become more accessible, the documents required for a visa have changed little: you need either an invitation from the company you are visiting, if travelling on business, or confirmation of your accommodation, if travelling as a tourist. Poland, Hungary, Bulgaria and the Czech and Slovak Republics no longer require a visa from UK passport holders, but Romania does. Those requiring a German visa must show the embassy proof of medical insurance cover: if you are a UK resident and registered under the National Health Service, an E111 from the Post Office is sufficient.

The requirements for entering France and Spain on a non-UK passport are complicated, although visas are issued free of charge if the applicant is married to an EC passport holder, on production of the partner's passport and the marriage certificate (not a photocopy). Australian passport holders no longer require visas for France and Spain, but they do need visas for Portugal.

India is an ever-popular destination and the High Commission offers a tourist visa valid for a six-month stay, starting from the issue date of the visa. The cost of the visa is £19.00, though non-UK residents will be charged £10.00 extra and their visas will take up to ten days to be issued (do not in any case apply by post as you will probably not receive your passport back in time). Taiwan has relaxed visa requirements for periods of up to 14 days, depending on nationality. Still in the Far East, UK nationals can stay in Thailand as tourists for 30 days, providing they are in possession of air tickets with confirmed bookings in and out of the country. A two-month stay is allowed in Indonesia visa-free, provided entry and exit are made through designated air and sea ports. Residing with friends and relatives during the visit is not allowed, and not all nationals are permitted this 60-day stay visa-free. China requires a visa for all visitors, as do Vietnam and Myanmar (Burma), which are now being visited in greater numbers.

Finally, even if you have got all your visas, immigration officials have the power to deny you entry to their country if they so wish, and they are not obliged to state their reasons. The US is perhaps the most formidable in this respect, so it is always sensible to have an onward or return ticket with you, together with proof of sufficient funds to support yourself and additional evidence that you have good reason to return to your country of residence from the US. 🕿

RALPH WHITMARSH is Head of the Passport and Visa Section at Thomas Cook in London. DUNCAN MILLS works for The Visa Service, a commercial visa agency.

Official permits and restricted areas
by Jack Jackson

TRAVEL IN THE THIRD WORLD USED TO BE EASY FOR WESTERNERS, with few restrictions and little in the way of police checks, paperwork or permissions, to hold travellers back. Europe, in those days, offered more barriers to travellers, with frequent customs and police enquiries.

Nowadays the position is reversed. In most Third World countries, the hindrances to free travel grow yearly, both in number and variety. Ambiguous taxes are demanded at borders and airports. The legality of these may be questionable, but the man behind the desk is all-powerful, so travellers do not have any choice. Many countries whose monetary systems are unstable and which therefore have flourishing black markets now require travellers to complete a currency declaration on entry, detailing all monies, jewellery, cameras, tape recorders, etc. This is checked on departure against bank receipts for any money changed. Some countries are very thorough in their searches of departing travellers, and border officials are often corrupt.

When it comes to groups, border officials naturally try to cut down on the massive form-filling process by completing just one form for the group leader. This can make life very difficult later if one person in a group wishes to change money at a bank or wishes to leave the group but does not have their own individual form and cannot immediately produce the group form or the leader to vouch for him or her. Individual forms should always be obtained, where possible.

Vaccinations

Make sure that you have all the necessary vaccinations and that they are still up to date. Some Third World border officials relish the opportunity to inject women if they can, and will also inject the men in the party to make it look legal; it is more than likely that the needle will have been used many times and is not sterile. Sometimes you have to get a certificate of exemption for the cholera vaccine, even though it has not been a legal requirement for many years in most countries. Avoid the need for any injection in the Third World that is not given by a Western-style doctor.

Deliberate delays

Some countries purposely delay the issue of permits in capital cities so that the travellers will spend more money there. As most travellers are limited for time, a straightforward tourist tax would be more acceptable.

Registration

In many places, the law requires that you register with the police within 24 hours of arrival. Often a fee is charged for this. Usually, if you are staying at a hotel, the registration is done for you by the hotel and the costs are included in your room charges; but if you are in a very small hotel, camping or staying with friends you will either have to do it yourself or pay someone to do it for you. As this often entails fighting through a queue of several hundred local people at the immigration office, with the possibility that you have chosen the wrong queue anyway, baksheesh to a hotel employee to do it for you is a good investment.

Most of these countries also require that you register with the police in each town in which you stop. In some cases, in the south of Sudan, for example, you have to report to the police in every town or village through which you pass. In smaller places the registration is usually much easier.

Permission from the central government may be necessary to travel outside major cities. Usually, to get this permission you go to the ministry of the interior, but if a tourist office exists, it is wise to check there first. Any expedition or trekking party will have to do this anyway. This system is not always just 'red tape'. If there is local strife it may be for travellers' safety.

Restricted areas

Many countries have restricted or forbidden areas. For example, much of Africa and Asia has large areas of desert or semi-desert. Restrictions on travel in these areas are formulated by governments for travellers' safety and take account of such obvious things as ensuring that travellers have good, strong vehicles carrying plenty of water and fuel and are spending the nights in safe places.

Unfortunately, officials in these out-of-the-way places tend to be the 'bad boys' of their profession. Forced to live in inhospitable places, they are usually very bored and often turn to drink and drugs. When a party of Westerners suddenly turns up, they see this as a chance to show their power, get their own back for the old colonial injustices, hold travellers up for a day or more, charge them baksheesh, or turn on a tape recorder and insist on a dance with each of the girls and suggest they go to bed with them. If there is a hotel locally, they may hold travellers there overnight so as to extract a percentage from the hotel-keeper.

Unfortunately, your permit from central government means nothing in such places. These people are a law unto themselves. Some have been known to insist on visas from nationals of a country who do not require one. This often requires you to go back to the nearest capital city, where incredulous officials may, or may not, be able to sort things out.

The police in very remote areas often arrange that you cannot get fuel to move on without their permission and to get that you have to spend a lot of money with the local tourist organisation and hotel, as well as fork out baksheesh to the police themselves. Local officials also have a habit of taking your government permit from you and then 'losing' it. This makes life difficult both there and with local officials in other areas later on. It is best to carry many photocopies of the original government permission (photocopying machines are always available in capital cities) and never hand over the original. Let officials see the original, if necessary, but always give them a photocopy instead.

If you are travelling as a group, most officials and most hotels will want a group list from you. Carry enough copies of a group list made up of names, passport numbers, dates of issue of passports, dates of expiry of passports, dates of issue of visas, dates of expiry of visas, numbers of visas and occupations.

Fortunately, new passports no longer quote occupations; but where these are asked for, never mention the following: photographer, journalist, writer or member of the armed forces, unless you are travelling in such a capacity officially.

Photography permits

Some countries, for instance Sudan, Mali and Cameroon, require that you obtain a photography permit. These are usually only available in the capital, so overland travellers will have problems until they can get to the capital and obtain one. As with currency declarations, officials obviously like to save work by giving one permit for a group, but it is best to get one per person. I have known several instances where big-headed students have made citizen's arrests of travellers taking photographs, who then had to spend a couple of hours at the police station waiting for their group leader with the photo permit to be located.

Possession of a photo permit does not necessarily mean that you can take photographs. It is usually best to enquire with the local police first. In some areas where photography is forbidden, local guides may goad you on to take photographs. Beware of this situation, they are then likely to blackmail you for money or other gifts by threatening to inform the police.

In theory, you should be able to find out about documents and permit requirements from the consulate in your country of origin, but for Third World countries this can never be relied on, as local officials make their own rules. Information from source books such as this one and from up-to-date travellers is best.

Visas

In an effort to control illegal immigrants, Western countries now often require visas from nationals of countries that did not require them a few years ago. In a tit-for-tat response, these countries now require visas from the nationals of Western countries and often charge extortionate prices to issue them in the West. These charges often cause the numbers of tourist visitors to collapse, so after a while the prices are lowered. Where such visas can be obtained at local airports, borders or consulates in neighbouring countries, they may be cheaper.

Before issuing visas, most countries will require at least two clear pages left in your passport and the passport to be valid for at least six months after your date of entry into the country concerned. Some countries will also require proof that you have suitable funds available and a return or onward air ticket. Some even require onward air tickets for overland travellers. You may also require a letter of introduction from your own government or a sponsor if travelling on business.

If you are travelling overland or on an extended continuous journey, visas for later destinations may become out of date before you reach your goal. So enquire whether or not you can get such visas while *en route*.

A few of the Gulf countries require a certificate of 'no objection'. Some Third World countries may hold your passport for six weeks or more while searching their archives for any previous records on applicants before issuing a visa. If you have to travel somewhere else during this period, UK citizens can obtain a temporary second passport. Never carry both passports on the same journey.

Visas for some countries, such as the ex-French or Belgian colonies, may not be obtainable in the UK: it is cheaper to have visa services get these for you than to go to Paris or Brussels yourself.

Many countries still refuse to issue visas to anyone whose passport contains Israeli stamps. If you visit this country, ask the immigration officials not to stamp your passport. If your passport does contain Israeli stamps, get a new passport as soon as possible.

If for some reason you have to obtain a new passport while you are away and your current passport contains an active visa, this will have to be retained and either the current passport extended or the older passport attached to the new one. If you have the right of residence in the UK, make sure that this is clearly stated in any replacement passport.

Business passports, with their larger number of pages, can cause problems in the Third World. If you have had many visas for the same country, local immigration officers may start questioning you as to why you keep coming back.

For the Third World, the standard EC-size passport is preferable and more convenient to carry under clothing for safety.

Do as much organisation as you can before you leave home. Carry plenty of passport-size photographs and be prepared for delays, harassment, palms held out and large doses of the unexpected.

Warning

Be especially careful of crossing borders with anyone that you do not know well because, if that person has a previous record or is carrying banned substances, you could also be arrested. Likewise, never take another person's belongings across a border. ❧

Passing through customs
by officers of the British Customs and Excise department

CONTRARY TO POPULAR BELIEF, CUSTOMS OFFICERS do accept that most travellers are ordinary citizens going about their legitimate business and are not smugglers. So why is it that most travellers claim to feel nervous whenever they approach Customs, and actually feel guilty when negotiating a Green Channel?

It may be uncertainty about the extent of allowances and precisely what is and is not permissible. It may also be apprehension about the possibility of being singled out for checking – having bags emptied and even being personally searched. The modern Customs service recognises these pressures and considerable effort is made to make checks highly selective and well targeted at areas of highest risk so that the vast majority of travellers are not inconvenienced.

Today, Customs face a dramatically changing scenario, as trade barriers are dismantled, fiscal and physical frontiers are removed, journey times are reduced and ever-increasing traffic flows demand fast and efficient customs clearance.

A balance must be struck between the often conflicting demands of the free movement of travellers while at the same time protecting society. But from what? Serious threats are posed by the considerable number of prohibited and restricted items that may be either unwittingly carried by the uninformed traveller, or smuggled by and on behalf of the unscrupulous. Customs, consulates and ministries can give advice, often in the form of leaflets, about what can and cannot be imported. Examples which may be encountered by travellers include the following:

PLANT AND ANIMAL HEALTH RISKS: Commercial importations are carefully controlled to prevent the spread of pests and disease, but thoughtless importation could quickly introduce an epidemic. Rabies is the most publicised threat but there are many more, including bugs and grubs which could devastate crops in a new environment. A health certificate, licence and/or quarantine is necessary for many plants and animals, and all live birds.

ENDANGERED SPECIES: Few people bring home a wild animal from their travels. But many buy articles made from them (a skin handbag and shoes, an ivory ornament) without knowing that the species is in danger of extinction. Even trade in tourist souvenirs can threaten the most endangered species. In many countries it is illegal to cut or pick wild plants and flowers for the same reasons. They may be freely available and on sale in the country you are visiting but if you do not get a permit before you import them they are likely to be seized.

OBSCENE AND INDECENT MATERIAL: Changing social and cultural attitudes make this a sensitive area so check first and you will not be embarrassed.

FIREARMS, WEAPONS, EXPLOSIVES, GAS CANISTERS: Travellers face stringent security checks before the start of their journey in an effort to separate them from even the most legitimate of these such as the sporting gun or the fisherman's knife. But on arrival at the destination their importation is likely to require a licence, and may be prohibited. Check first, or be sure to tell Customs on arrival.

Drugs: Personally-prescribed drugs and medicaments are best carried in labelled containers and, if for regular use, carry a letter from your doctor. Illicit drugs are a major and increasing concern for all Customs services and are often the principal reason for checks on travellers. Whilst the possession of very small quantities may be permissible in a few countries, their carriage across frontiers is invariably prohibited. Penalties are severe, and often carry a risk of imprisonment.

Countries with long land frontiers may choose to exercise some controls inland but travellers through ports and airports provide a concentrated flow which enables an efficient screening and checking by Customs. Particularly in the prevention of drug trafficking, the search at the frontier enables Customs to identify and seize large commercial shipments, before they are distributed inland for sale in small, usable quantities. In addition, Customs and police will often cooperate to monitor the delivery of a consignment to its inland destination in order to identify principals in smuggling organisations.

Many people think that drugs are found from tip-offs, and that routine checks are not necessary. That is not so. Valuable intelligence does come from co-operation between Customs and police services around the world. But detections made in the day-to-day work of ports and airports depend on the Customs Officer's initiative and experience in assessing risks and choosing the right passenger. The overall Customs effort against drug trafficking is a mix of intelligence, information, judgement and intuition. Officers are carefully trained to observe, select, question and examine. 'Profiles' are built up from instances where patterns have emerged, but they are but one tool in a large bag, and need to be constantly updated and refined as methods and types of courier change. Checks may need to be done to test out Customs' perception of risk, and that is where the innocent traveller may come under examination. Co-operation will help allay suspicion of the innocent, and full searches – including a body search – are only undertaken under strict supervision and where there are strong grounds for suspecting an offence.

Checking travellers

An officer who stops a passenger needs information before making a decision (whether or not a full examination is needed) and so questions must be asked. The officer is looking for tell-tale signs that something is not right. The smuggler cannot be completely honest about themselves and must tell lies to stand any chance of success. It is that deceit that a Customs officer is trying to see through. Travel documents, identification documents, questions about the purpose of the journey – all give a picture which the officer can test for credibility against what he sees and hears and, ultimately, feels. He may not get it right every time, but intelligent, intuitive assessments do result in the discovery of people attempting to smuggle.

The traveller who objects to the way he or she is dealt with at Customs should complain to a Senior Customs official at the time of the incident. In that way most complaints can be dealt with to everyone's satisfaction, and while events are fresh in everyone's mind. By all means follow up with a letter if you feel you have not got satisfaction. But a written complaint made for the first time several days after an incident is more difficult to investigate.

In addition to their role in protecting society, the Customs service has a duty to collect import taxes (which can still be substantial on luxury goods, despite moves to harmonise more tax rates and remove barriers to trade). The expensive watch, silk carpet, video camera or item of jewellery can still result in a hefty tax bill on arrival home. Goods in excess of allowances must be declared to Customs, or you risk having them confiscated, and criminal proceedings taken for smuggling. Many offences of this nature are settled between Customs and the traveller by the payment of a fine and few cases go to court. However, if you also have to buy your confiscated goods back, the overall penalty can amount to a large sum. In addition, the amount of time and effort spent by Customs dealing with such irregularities increases the opportunity for the drugs courier to get through undetected.

The business traveller can usually be relied on to know what personal allowances can be carried into each country, but a misunderstanding can occur when business goods are carried. Lap-top computers, replacement parts for equipment, parts for repair and sample prototypes can all find their way into a business traveller's baggage. Sometimes he will act only as a 'courier' for another part of his company. Such items are invariably liable to some form of control as frontiers are crossed and a declaration to Customs on each occasion is the safest way – unless you have personally checked with a reliable authority and you are confident you know what you are doing.

As a general rule, do not carry packages for anyone if you are unsure what they contain. Whether it is personal or business, your freedom or even your life could be at stake if something goes wrong.

On 1 January 1993, the Single European Act heralded the free movement of goods and people within the European Community (EC). For visitors, controls on goods and the collection of taxes generally take place at the first point of entry into the Community, and subsequent travel involves only checks for prohibited and restricted goods. Travellers within the Community do not have to pay any tax or duty in the UK on goods bought in other EU countries for their own use. 'Own use' includes gifts but remember that you may be breaking the law if you sell goods that you have bought; and that if you are caught selling the goods they will be taken off you and you could get up to seven years imprisonment. Any vehicle you use to transport the goods could also be confiscated.

The EU sets out guidelines for the amount of alcohol and tobacco a person can bring into the UK from an EU country. These are intended as indicative levels for 'own use' consumption. If you bring in more than this, you must be able to satisfy customs officers if you are asked that the goods are for your own use. If you can't the goods may be taken off you. For your information the indicative levels are:

SMOKING
- Cigarettes: 800
- Cigarillos: 400
- Cigars: 200
- Smoking tobacco: 1 kilogram

ALCOHOL
- Spirits: 10 litres
- Fortified wine (such as port or sherry): 20 litres
- Wine: 90 litres (of which no more than 60 litres sparkling).

Since the advent of the single market, Customs' controls on EC passengers at airports and ferry ports have been improved to provide a faster and more efficient service which targets the high-risk traveller, but permits the majority to move unimpeded through customs.

Make sure you are properly informed when you travel. A confident traveller will project his or her innocence and help Customs to concentrate on their own priorities, for all our good. ❧

The black market
by Jack Jackson

IT USED TO BE COMMON FOR DEALERS on black markets in Third World countries to offer money at three or more times the official rate. Nowadays, however, most such countries have black market rates of only ten to 20 per cent higher than the normal rate. Buyers should always weigh up the risk before dealing, remembering that in black market operations the traveller, just as easily as the dealer, can end up in prison. In countries recently ravaged by war or *coup d'état*, black markets usually continue to thrive at good rates.

Dollarmania

Black markets usually operate best in ports; where money can be easily smuggled out and goods back in and where, with the help of baksheesh to customs officers, nobody in government pay needs to know, or admit to knowing. However, a quasi black market is operated by expatriate technicians working in oil fields or international aid or construction programmes. Paid part of their salary in local currency, usually more than they need to live on, they are keen to get rid of some of it in exchange for US dollars, at a good rate to the buyer.

In much of Islamic Africa and the poorer Middle Eastern countries, you will also find Egyptian, Sudanese, Syrian or Palestinian teachers, employed in smaller villages, who are very keen to convert their local salary into US dollars.

Another method of dealing, common in countries where businessmen do not feel safe and cannot get their money out legally, is for businessmen or hotel owners to 'lend' you funds locally, which you repay in hard currency into a relative's bank account in the West. Those who travel regularly often arrange this in advance before departure; but local businessmen will take a risk on unfamiliar travellers, if they are reasonably dressed and staying in recognised smaller hotels, because their own local currency is worthless to them.

Even in large top-quality hotels, cashiers will often take payment in hard currency at near-black market rates, if the customer pays them outside of the manager's normal working hours.

Travellers should particularly avoid street dealings, as they are more likely to be short-changed, given bad notes, caught in a police 'sting' operation or robbed.

On-the-spot black market deals nowadays are always for cash and mostly for US dollars. A few countries with strong links and trade with the UK or Germany will trade in pounds sterling or deutschmarks, but other currencies, even strong ones such as the Swiss franc or Dutch guilder, will find few black market buyers. Deutschmarks go down well in Turkey, pounds sterling in Pakistan, India, Malaysia and Nepal, but elsewhere the US dollar is the prime requirement.

Normally, larger denomination notes fetch a higher rate, as they are easier to smuggle out. Avoid the older $100 bills that do not have 'In God We Trust' written on them: even though they may not be forgeries, most dealers will not touch them. Also avoid English £50 notes, which may be unknown to smaller dealers. It is worth carrying a number of $1 bills to pay off small bills and give as tips. Even for normal legal transactions, many countries now insist on clean, unmarked notes, i.e. those without any writing on them that is not part of the original printing.

There is no longer any problem in taking money out of the UK, so it is best to buy US dollars or US dollar travellers' cheques before you leave. Many countries are not happy about accepting American Express travellers' cheques and most will not accept those from smaller, less-known Australian or New Zealand banks.

Declaration forms

Many countries with black market problems insist on a declaration of all money and valuables on entry and check this against bank receipts on exit. Remember, you may be searched on entry and exit, and any excess funds will be confiscated.

If you want to take in some undeclared money to use on the black market, you should understand the risks. Obviously, you must change a reasonable amount of money legally at a bank and keep receipts so that you will be able to explain what you have lived on during your stay. You will also need these receipts if you are trying to change local currency back into hard currency when you leave. It is usually inadvisable to try to do so, however, since most countries make it very difficult for you, despite the literature claiming that you can.

Local officials, who probably don't read the literature, like to remove your excess local money and keep it for themselves. The bank clerk who tells you he cannot change your money back is often in on the act. He informs the custom officials how much money you have and they, acting on his tip-off, search you as you leave.

On the plus side, allowing officials to remove a reasonable amount of money from you at the point of departure often minimises further red tape.

Currency declaration forms are taken very seriously in some countries and you must have an explanation for any discrepancy. Make sure that the amount written agrees with the amount in figures. If any money that has been entered on your form is stolen, get a letter giving details from the police, or you may have trouble when you wish to leave the country.

Some countries get around some of the black market by making you pay for hotels in hard currency, at the official rate.

In such hotels you can usually get away with paying for meals with black market cash, so long as you pay for it at the time. If you sign a restaurant bill to be paid for later, then you will be charged in hard currency. Corrupt hotel staff may refuse to accept cash payment in the restaurant, in which case you will be better off taking your custom to restaurants outside the hotel.

International airline tickets will always be charged for in hard currency, plus a premium ordered by IATA, to cover currency fluctuations. Hence, such tickets are much cheaper if bought in Europe. Internal air tickets can usually be bought with black money, but you may have to pay a local ticketing agent to do it in his name.

Beware of black market currency quotations by normally acceptable press outlets, such as the broadsheet Sunday papers, *Newsweek* and the BBC. These may be quoting from local sources, who have to be careful what they say publicly.

Street trading

Black market dealers are usually found in the places where budget travellers are most likely to be, for example, smaller hotels, bars and shops selling tourist items; in very small towns try the pharmacy.

In the main streets of a city or port, street traders will chase you and, assuming that you do not know the correct rate, will start with a very low one. It is usually worth bargaining to see how high a rate you can get, then approach safer places, such as small hotels, to check the real rate. Street trading is very risky: you should never show that you have a lot of money. There is a high chance that you will be short-changed, given notes that are no longer legal tender, have money stolen from the bundle by sleight of hand, see all your money grabbed and run off with, or meet one of those dealers who has a crooked, profit-sharing partnership with the police. So, in general, show only the amount of money you want to exchange and keep all other money out of sight, beneath your clothes.

Refuse any approaches to buy your passport or travellers' cheques. This kind of trading has become so common that many embassies delay issuing fresh passports to travellers who, may or may not, have genuinely lost their own. Getting travellers' cheques replaced in the Third World can take months, as can funds wired to banks or American Express offices. Never rely on receiving hard currency transferred in this way, you are likely to be forced to accept local currency.

Black market rates fluctuate with both inflation and availability. Rates will increase dramatically in the Islamic world, when the time for the annual pilgrimage to Mecca (the *hajj*) approaches, and decrease rapidly when the pilgrims return, or when a lot of upmarket travellers are in town, or a cruise ship or fleet ship is in port. Dealing out of season usually commands a better rate.

Central London banks often carry an excess of Third World currency and one of their branches may be happy to off-load a weak currency at a good rate. It is always worth checking whether this is so before you buy; but remember that the bank notes may no longer be legal currency.

Wherever you are, always check that you have not been short-changed. Bank cashiers try this on regularly, in the Third World. Many people end up changing on the black market, just because it can take up to two hours to change money legally in some countries. Currently, the black markets of the Balkans, the eastern

European states and the Commonwealth of Independent States are strong. Many of these nations are technically bankrupt, have rampant inflation, pay their employees with unredeemable money and are changing their currencies. And you must be careful not to be given out-of-date banknotes. In Uzbekistan, when I legally changed US$4 for local currency, I was given a wad of newly printed 'Monopoly money' ten cm thick.

The best way to travel in countries such as these, or those with high rates of inflation, is to carry a large number of small-denomination US dollar bills, change a little at a time as you go along and, where possible, pay for everything in US dollars, so that you do not collect worthless change. UK banks do not like holding US$1 bills, so give them plenty of warning when ordering currency and stipulate clean, unmarked notes.

Beggars

Begging is probably the world's second-oldest profession. In the Muslim and Hindu world, giving a percentage of one's income to the poor is considered to be a legal form of paying tax. However, with the increase of mass up-market tourism, begging is becoming an increasingly popular way of making a living, not only among the obviously poor people of the Third World, but also among Western hippies and some better-dressed, professional confidence tricksters, who claim to be refugees. This form of begging is now common on the London Underground.

In some countries beggars are very persistent, knowing full well that wearing you down produces results. Mere persistence may not be too hard for you to repel, but worst of all are the young children, often blind or with deformed limbs, who are guaranteed to arouse your pity.

What you may not realise, however, is that the child may have been intentionally deformed or blinded by its parents or 'master' in order to make a successful beggar. The child is almost certainly encouraged by his family or ringleader to beg and may be the chief source of their income, since the child beggar can perhaps earn more in a day than his father working in the fields or factory. Remember that a child who is out begging is necessarily missing school.

An adult with no education or experience, other than begging, tends to be less successful than a child beggar. What are his options? Crime, if he is fit, destitution if crippled. Begging is obviously easier than work, but to give money is to contribute to a vicious circle. By withholding money, you may indeed be helping to eradicate these appalling practices. ❧

Phone home
by Stephen McLelland and Natasha Hughes

There has never been a better time for the traveller to go almost anywhere and still be in touch by means of telecommunications – but be careful, because convenience can come at a price. However, with a little thought and some background knowledge, it is possible to keep costs low – and still get what you want.

The first step is to consider what your needs actually are: for instance, are you travelling for business or pleasure? Where are you going? What degree of mobility do you require? Do you just need telephonic communication or do you need both voice and data services, including internet access? Is your use of telecommunications going to be frequent or occasional? Making a decision about the best option for you depends on an adequate assessment of all of these criteria. Moreover, products and services are not necessarily identical in every country and getting a single 'international' solution, usable anywhere, will probably be impossible or extremely difficult.

Voice communications

We tend to forget how amazing it is that you can now make a phone call to anywhere in the world. International direct dial (IDD), enabling effective person-to-person calling, is now available in almost all countries. A minority still require some form of operator connection, but bear in mind that such conditions exist mainly in war zones.

IDD is theoretically available from almost any public payphone, residential phone, mobile phone or hotel phone in the world. However, it's worth bearing in mind that it can be an expensive option, and may not always be available. In a number of countries, such as Japan, for example, international operators are separate from the local ones and require booked, pre-assigned or special access arrangements. Likewise, international payphones in Japan are distinguished from national ones.

Wherever you happen to be, watch out for hotels and other sites that simply bar international access altogether to avoid being caught with large unpaid bills. Outside in the street, using a payphone means you have to work out how to pay. Unless you are flush with foreign currency, the only option is likely to be the use of a card phone (see below).

You should also recognise that many hotels probably make as much profit from telephone calls as they do from renting rooms. Call charges from hotels are likely to be extremely high. Some have begun to reduce tariffs recently, due to the pressure of unfavourable media attention, and the more responsible hotels notify you of the charging structure in advance, but you should always check and, if possible, arrange for people to call you instead. Note that hotels often make high charges for faxes, too, and many charge for inbound faxes.

PTT bureaux exist around the world, especially in countries where telephonic access has, traditionally, been poor. They provide a walk-in service for IDD, fax, and telex services at stipulated IDD rates, on a cash or sometimes credit card basis. Tourist information offices should always know where they are located.

One of your best bets is to use some sort of card phone, of which there are several different types. Prepaid card phones are exactly what their name suggests: these are payphones for which you must buy a card in advance of calling from a store or hotel. Once you've bought the card, you put it in a slot, dial the number and the total value of the call is deducted from the cash value of the card. Such cards are convenient and have the big advantage that you know exactly what you can spend in advance; but, generally speaking, cards must be bought in the country of use and are not transferable.

Credit card phones are simple variations on the basic payphone, which accept credit cards as an alternative or substitute for pre-paid cards or coins. Be careful, credit card phones may well be convenient but rack up very high charges very quickly, beginning with a high standing connection charge. Unless you are desperate, they are best avoided, particularly in airports.

Avoid collect calling (reverse charging) services like the plague – use them only where there is absolutely no alternative: they are all incredibly expensive. So-called 'home direct' (sometimes called 'country direct') options that are available from payphones around the world are also a form of reverse charging, differing only in the fact that you usually set up the call via an operator in your home country rather than locally.

Practically every major operator in the world now issues some form of calling card. These credit card-sized items basically give you a pre-assigned identity (account) number and personal identification number (PIN). In use, you call the particular operator who has assigned you the card from your location, give the identification numbers and the destination number you want, and the operator picks up your call and re-routes it to the destination. With most systems, the final bill appears in a statement from the operator or is transferred directly onto your credit card bill, so make sure you have a method of payment in place if you are travelling. The big advantage of the calling card is that it should be significantly cheaper than calling from hotel rooms, although there are wide variations in actual pricing. Because of the latter, it pays to be careful or to check charges in advance with the operator. Note also that hotels have realised that their own charging is being short-circuited by this method and occasionally engage in such tactics as charging for freephone access from rooms (many calling cards have a freephone or low-rate access for the first leg of the call into the operator), or barring the use of such numbers altogether.

Another advantage of calling cards is that they can also give you access to all the clever services that networks now offer. Most have call redirection facilities, for example, to enable automatic transfer from one number to another, conference calling for multiple users, translation and help lines.

Callback services are, potentially, the cheapest of all, with savings of between 30 to 80 per cent possible on many expensive IDD routes. They have become available as a result of the wide disparities in international calling charges. Basically, a callback service offers the opportunity for a subscriber to route his or her call through a country that can provide cheaper international access (usually this is the USA), regardless of where the call actually originated. For example, if you want to call France from India, you first notify a callback provider (perhaps in the USA) and immediately hang up. The callback service (which invariably has a pre-arranged subscription with you) then calls you back in India (hence the name), but in doing so gives you a dialling tone that enables onward dialling to the final destination (in this case, France). The call is cheaper because of the much lower rates offered by the US to India and the US to France than India direct to France.

Callback services have mushroomed in popularity due to the value they offer. Official authorities, however, are not so sure of their virtues, given that the local exchanges are clearly losing substantial amounts of revenue on this basis. Some have even resorted to means – both legal and illegal – to block callback providers or bar access to them, particularly in Argentina, Uruguay and various West African countries. China is also said to take a dim view of the service. The tactics to which such countries resort work for a time, causing everyone inconvenience, but sooner or later the callback provider has circumvented the restrictions and the process starts again.

To be sure, callback services vary in sophistication, so check the facilities on offer. You may have to designate a particular phone you will use, for example. Some providers save you the expense of calling them by automatically detecting the signalling coming from your phone system and working out the number from which you are calling before calling back. Your call is not technically connected and so you will not be charged. Cheap fax services may also be available. The major callback providers generally advertise in the main English-language newspapers around the world (at least the sort that are likely to be read by travellers). A few unscrupulous ones exist, but generally the field has a good reputation. Check the degree of your advance financial commitment – you may be asked to put down a deposit debited from your credit card, for example.

Mobile communications are on a massive roll worldwide as investors and operators see it as being a big commercial money-spinner. The cellular phone, unlike other radio systems, acts in exactly the same way as a conventional fixed phone. In terms of making or receiving calls, the systems are therefore effectively interchangeable. However, in practically every country in the world, cellular services are invariably more expensive than fixed services over the same distance (the only exception I have found is Israel, where it is possible to make cheaper long-distance calls by mobile phone than by fixed-line phones).

Now for the bad news. There is no such thing as a world standard in mobile communications, so it is not necessarily possible to take a phone from one country to another and expect it to work, a facility the industry calls 'roaming'. The nearest thing to a world standard in digital cellular is GSM (Global System for Mobile) technology, now available in more than 90 countries and used by nearly 200 operators. It is overwhelmingly dominant in Europe, the Middle East, South East Asia, South Africa and Australasia. It is therefore possible for a European to travel to Australia or a Singaporean to travel to the Middle East and, without further fuss,

WEXAS membership offer

Free trial travel club membership

WEXAS IS THE TRAVEL CLUB FOR INDEPENDENT TRAVELLERS. Our 35,000 members enjoy the unbeatable combination of low prices, travel ideas and information, and outstanding service.

As a reader of *The Traveller's Handbook* you can take out a month's free trial membership and then become a fully paid-up member for less than a pound a week.

Take a look at the benefits you'll receive and see how you'll save your subscription many times over.

- Discount rates on airfares, hotels and car hire worldwide

- Annual travel insurance from just £59 per year (2000 rates)

- FREE subscription to *Traveller*, the highly acclaimed travel magazine

- Expert service from experienced travel consultants, and access to our members-only phone numbers

- Privileged access to VIP airport lounges

- Currency and travellers' cheques available by post, commission-free

- Special rates for airport parking

- Discounts at British Airways travel clinics

- £50,000 free flight accident insurance with every flight booking

- BagTag lost-luggage retrieval service

- Free international assistance 24 hours a day

- Discounts on local tours and sightseeing worldwide

- Additional benefits for business travellers

- Access to WEXASonline (members-only website)

- Customised round-the-world itineraries

- Quarterly *Update* newsletter on special offers and discounts

---

COMPLETE THIS FORM AND POST IT TODAY FOR FULL DETAILS OF WEXAS MEMBERSHIP AND THE FREE TRIAL OFFER.

You can post this form to us at WEXAS International, FREEPOST (no stamp required), London, SW3 1BR, UK.

Alternatively you can fax it to us on 020 7589 8418, or email mship@wexas.com for details.

Name (Mr/Mrs/Miss/Ms)

Address

Postcode

Telephone

Email   T252

Priority Membership Enquiry

Membership Services Department

WEXAS International

FREEPOST

London

SW3 1BR

switch on his or her mobile phone and find it working immediately – if coverage exists in his or her location. In all these cases, the network 'knows' where the phone is when it is switched on, and manages the call routing and billing back on the subscriber's home bill. The snag is that another set of standards exists for the Americas and a third for Japan. (China, awkwardly, is a mix of standards but has established a large number of GSM networks; Russia also has several in major areas but is likewise a hotch-potch.)

However, many of the more sophisticated mobile phones now on the market have a dual-band, or even a triple-band, facility. This means that, as long as you have set up a roaming agreement with your network, your phone will work around the world. If you do want to set up this facility, leave ample time before you set off on your travels to make sure the system is in place – a couple of weeks should do it; although, theoretically, it is possible for a network to implement a roaming facility on your account within 24 hours.

A final note on roaming: expect big bills. Roaming implies that the calls you make are international calls and, as such, are charged at international rates. Even calls that appear 'local' to you in the country in which you are travelling are still treated by the network as 'international'.

An alternative to roaming, of course, would be to sign up and subscribe to the local cellular network, although this is not really worth doing unless you are spending a significant period of time in that particular country, as the contract may prove an expensive commitment. Finally, airport bureaux often offer cellular phones on a short-term basis for travellers: these will be cheaper on an overall basis than making roaming calls, but they do incur high daily charges.

Another drawback of mobile networks is a lack of coverage in the most remote areas, particularly deserts and mountains where the population is too sparse to support a mobile system economically (although you may be surprised exactly how much coverage is available). Generally, the policy of network deployment in any country is to give major cities and commercial centres the priority; thereafter, deployment is to secondary centres on a planned or phased basis.

If you thought satellite technology was really only for sophisticated expeditions, you are in for a surprise. Over the next few years a number of systems will be activated that will girdle the globe. The idea is to give coverage practically anywhere on the planet using hand-held phones that will look like and directly compete with digital cellular technology. Costs should be comparable with those of cellular systems. These could represent the biggest breakthrough of all for the independent traveller.

Data communications

The explosion of the internet has made communications by email a highly effective tool, giving you enormous facilities at very low cost. There are many email systems now in use around the world; strictly speaking, these are separate networks, but they can all 'talk' to each other and to the internet itself. Each system differs in fine detail, but all perform the same basic functions in allowing computer-to-computer communications.

It is perhaps easiest to think of such systems as being directly analogous to the postal system. Every registered email possesses an 'electronic mailbox' with a unique electronic address in which messages may be stored or received or from which messages may be sent. The advantages of email are that it is nearly instantaneous and probably cheaper on a per-message basis than ordinary post. Email is suitable for messages of almost any length, although cost varies with message size and the number of messages sent. In many cases, different types of data can be transferred over the network, including both text files produced by word processing and spreadsheet information.

At its most basic, you can gain access to your emails by routing them through a web-based Internet Service Provider (ISP), such as Hotmail, UK Smart or Talk 21. Before you set off on your travels, choose one of these providers, register an email address and notify your friends, family and colleagues of your contact details. From this point on, you can log on to a computer anywhere in the world, download your ISP page and access your email. Of course, in some countries, this is easier said than done. But many cities now have internet cafés where travellers can use the computers provided for precisely this purpose. Internet facilities are also frequently available at airports, and are a convenient way of killing time while you wait for your plane. In both these cases, you will be charged for the time you spend online. Many hotels and resorts will also provide you with access to a computer – for a price – so that you can check your emails.

If you want more regular access to your emails, you will need to travel with a basic computing kit, consisting of:

- a data terminal device (a desktop, laptop or notebook-sized computer);
- communications software (usually part of your basic computing package), so the message may be written and formatted in a form suitable for sending, and browser software (again, part of the standard package), for internet access;
- a modem (often built into the computer), which converts the stream of computer data into a form suitable for transmission;
- appropriate email registration for the country/service you are using;
- access to a public telephone connection through a socket or phone;
- a printer, should you want to print your emails;
- cables to connect all the above (and power supplies/adaptors for the country).

The main problem with email is that, due to differences in technical characteristics, it remains generally difficult to connect a device such as a modem, specified for one country, to the PSTN or hotel room socket in another. The differences can be minor but infuriating: there are nearly 40 different types of phone sockets around the world, and even where they are physically similar, they may be wired differently. The modem dialling system may not work or may connect incorrectly because of national technical and numbering differences. There are ways around this, but you could be unlucky and find systems or hotels that are unforgiving.

That said, I have used the same laptop, modem and plug combination in hotel rooms in the UK, USA, Canada, Finland, Singapore, Taiwan and Hong Kong; with a payphone (equipped with a data socket) in Japan; and even while flying over California (with an aircraft seat phone, again equipped with a data socket). In many cases, the plug/socket combination you will require is termed RJ-11 (widespread in the USA). For hotel rooms equipped with this (and there will often be an RJ-11 data port in the side of the phone handset), there should not be too many problems.

However, there are other problems to bear in mind. There is always a risk that hotel switchboards, more properly called 'private automatic branch exchanges' (PABXs), may be incompatible with your modem and may even damage it. The most 'difficult' travelling areas are in mainland Europe, and there may also be problems in parts of the developing world.

TeleAdapt (tel +44 20 8421 4444 or website www.teleadapt.com) is a specialist in this area, and will probably have all the information, connectors and other hardware that you will ever need. If you continue to have real problems, you may be forced to buy a modem and suitable jack in the country. Another option would be to use what is known as an 'acoustic coupler', a modem device that fits over a conventional phone handset but requires no plug and socket connection at all, but these tend to permit low connection speeds, reducing your options.

A final option – one that may prove increasingly attractive in the future – is to forget about hotel room phones, jacks and sockets altogether, and use a mobile (cellular) phone for your connection. Should you do so, you will need a special modem unit. Remember, however, that sending data over a cellular network has the same limitations as does voice communication, in that you will need a dual- or triple-band phone and a roaming agreement. A recent innovation in the world of the mobile telephone is the WAP phone, which enables direct access to the internet and email facilities straight from the handset. Although this technology is still, relatively speaking, in its infancy, it is predicted to grow exponentially and will probably become standard within the next few years, combining voice and data communications in one pocket-sized package. Watch this space. 🙢

STEPHEN MCCLELLAND was Editor of 'Telecommunications Magazine'.
NATASHA HUGHES is a freelance feature writer.

Freighting your kit by air, sea or road
by Paul Melly

FEW PEOPLE BOTHER TO THINK ABOUT BAGGAGE. Until, that is, they become that annoying person at the front of the airport check-in queue, searching for a credit card to pay the extortionate bill for bringing home an extra suitcase on the same plane.

The alternative – shipping separately – is often disregarded, or looked upon as the sort of thing that people did in the days when Britain had an empire. Shipping luggage seems to conjure up images of capacious Victorian trunks or battered tea chests creaking home from the Far East in the hold of a mail steamer. But it is actually worth investigating. With just a little planning, you can save a fair sum of money for relatively little delay by sending your surplus bags as freight.

The alternative is to pay the full whack for excess baggage while making a handsome contribution to airline profits. This is such a good earner that it is given a separate entry in the multi-million dollar revenue graph of one Middle Eastern carrier's annual report.

Costly limits

The reason excess baggage charges are so high is the strict limit on how much weight an airliner can carry. There is a premium on the limited reserve space. So if you significantly exceed your individual quota as a passenger and want to take that extra bag on the same flight, you must pay dearly for the privilege. Of course, it then comes up on the luggage carousel with everything else at the end of your journey, which is convenient. But it is also very much more expensive than sending it unaccompanied by air, sea, road or rail. Advance planning can ensure that your baggage will be waiting for you on arrival.

For those caught unawares, one UK operator, the London Baggage Company (Gatwick London Air Terminal, Victoria Place, London SW1W 9SJ, tel 020 7828 2400) is conveniently located by Victoria Station, the London check-in terminal for several airlines flying out of Gatwick.

Your local *Yellow Pages* will give details of all the various specialist companies under 'Freight Forwarding and Shipping and Forwarding Agents', while the British International Freight Association (Redfern House, Browells Lane, Feltham, Middlesex TW13 7EP, tel 020 8844 2266) publishes the *Year Book*, listing all BIFA members with their freight specialities.

Of course freight services are not only useful for those who have too much travel baggage. If you are going to work abroad, take an extended holiday, or embark on a specialist expedition or even a long business trip, you may well have equipment or samples to take. And if you have just finished or are about to start a course of academic or vocational study, there could be a hefty pile of books for which your normal baggage allowance is totally inadequate.

The more you send...

Although one, two, three or even half a dozen cases may seem a lot to you, for a specialist freight forwarder, airline or shipping company it is peanuts. Generally in the cargo business, the more you send (by weight above a basic minimum), the cheaper the price. Naturally, you can send less than the minimum weight, but you still have to pay that standard bottom rate as most freight companies are in business to cater for the needs of industry, not individuals.

When industry does not come up with the traffic, however, they can be glad to get whatever private business is around. The depressed oil market in 1986, for example, led to an economic slowdown in the Gulf and a consequent slump in export cargo to the region, but airline freight bookings out of Bahrain, Abu Dhabi and Dubai were bolstered by expatriate workers sending home their goods and chattels after their contracts expired and were not renewed.

Specialist outfits do nevertheless exist to cater for private individuals, using their bulk buying power to obtain cheap rates which are then passed on to their customers. They can also help with technical problems, such as how to pack, what you cannot send, insurance and so on.

Sending by sea

Sea freight is little used these days except for shipments between Europe and Australia or New Zealand, where the great distances involved make it a lot cheaper than air. The time difference between air and sea freight is from seven weeks by sea as opposed to seven to ten days by air. Air takes longer than one might expect because of red tape, the time needed for goods to clear customs and the wait until the freight company has a bulk shipment going out.

The London Baggage Company reports that nearly all its sea freight bookings are for Australasia, with most of the remainder bound for New York or California. On these routes, there is enough business for freighting firms to arrange regular shipments of personal cargo, but when it comes to developing countries the traffic is more limited so the price is higher. In such cases it is often just as cheap – and more secure – to use the air. Sea freight is charged by volume rather than weight, and is therefore particularly suitable for books or heavy household items. The goods can be held in the UK and then shipped out to coincide with your expected date of arrival in, say, Melbourne or Auckland.

If you want to send stuff straight away, you should remember it will wait an average of seven days before actually leaving: freight forwarders book a whole container and send it only when there is enough cargo to fill it. Shipping on some routes is regarded as high risk, so insurance premiums increase – thus further reducing any price differential with air freight.

Road and rail

Within Europe, rail is a useful option, especially for Italy. While there is only limited and relatively expensive air freight capacity from London to Milan and Rome, a rail shipment to Naples from the UK may take just six to eight days. Rail has the added advantage that most stations are in city centres, so you can avoid the tiresome trek out to an airport cargo centre to collect your bags. Of course, it may well be cheaper to travel by train yourself and pay porters at each end to help you carry the cases, than to spend hundreds of pounds having items sent separately while you fly. There is normally no official limit on what baggage you are allowed to take free with you on a train.

Trucking is also an option for continental travellers. There is a huge range of haulage services and some carriers do take baggage. But prices are often comparable to air freight and journey times are probably a day or two slower. European air freight is a highly competitive business and can actually be cheaper than trucking if you measure size and weight carefully. There are direct routes to most destinations and delivery can normally be guaranteed the next day.

However, the short distances involved mean that rail and road operators can often compete on timing: although most flights last only a couple of hours (or less) many more hours can be used up waiting for a consolidation – bulk air shipment – or for customs clearance on arrival.

Express services, operated by the airlines themselves or specialist companies, are growing rapidly, but are expensive and only worthwhile for items of high monetary or commercial value, such as scientific equipment, computer disks, spare parts or industrial samples. Normally these will offer a guarantee of transit time.

Whatever your method of shipment, there are some practical problems to be wary of. For example, Spanish and Portuguese customs can be finicky if items are sent by truck, and you may find yourself paying duty on some goods on which you were originally told there would be no charge.

Into remoter regions

More surprising is the ease with which you can send stuff to quite remote, longhaul destinations. The key question is: how far is your final delivery point from the nearest international airport? Normally you, or someone representing you, will need to collect the bags at the place where they clear customs, and it is often impossible to arrange local onward shipment, at least under the umbrella of the baggage service in your home country. Delivery can sometimes be arranged within the city catchment area of the airport, but this rarely extends for more than 20 or 30 kilometres. If you are based in Europe, it is also often difficult to get detailed information about onward transport services in the developing world — whether by air, train, truck or even mule.

One option is to go to a specialist freight forwarder who has detailed knowledge of a particular region of the world and is competent to arrange for local distribution. However, as a personal customer providing a relatively small amount of business, you may not be able to obtain an attractive price, and it could prove cheaper in the end to collect the bags from the airport yourself. There do not have to be direct flights from London, as long as your cargo can be routed to arrive in a country at the right city and pass customs there.

You can take the bags into a country yourself across the land border but you may face more complications taking five suitcases alone through a small rural frontier post than if they arrive at the main airport under the aegis of an established freight company. Customs regulations are complex, and it is vital to that the status of research equipment or commercial samples is checked with customs on arrival by the freight group's local agent.

There is no firm rule as to which places are most difficult to reach, but perhaps the complications are greatest when you want to ship to a remote corner of a large country in the developing world. In these circumstances, you may well find the only reliable option is to collect the bags from the capital city yourself. Shipping to small island destinations, such as Fiji or the Maldives, can be fairly routine, but there are also good services to some places with particularly tough reputations.

Pricing

Prices in general include two elements: a standard service charge which covers documentation, handling and administration by the shipping agent, and a freight charge per kilo which varies according to the airline, destination and particular bulk shipment deal the agent has been able to negotiate. Storage can be arranged, as can collection within the company's catchment area – sometimes free of charge. Outside this radius you will probably have to use a domestic rail or road parcel service rather than asking the agent to arrange a special collection, although a few larger companies do have regional offices.

Dos and don'ts

There are a number of important practical tips to bear in mind. A highly individual distinguishing mark on a case or carton will make it easier for you to pick out when you go to collect it from a busy warehouse or office. It is also important to mark it with your address and telephone number in the destination country, so that the receiving agent can let you know when it has arrived.

If you must send really fragile items, pack them in the middle of the case and tell the freighting office. Many have full packaging facilities and will certainly let you know if they think a bag should be more securely wrapped: for some destinations they cover boxes with adhesive banding tape so that anyone can see if it has been tampered with. Do not overload a case and do watch out for flimsy wheels or handles that can easily be broken off. The agent's packers can provide proper crates if necessary. Proper packing is vital – especially if you plan to ship the luggage by road. In many countries the wet season turns cart tracks into swamps. Expeditions or development aid teams will often have to ship into remote areas with poor roads.

If you are moving abroad, do try and differentiate between household items and personal effects such as clothing or toiletries. The latter are covered by a quite strict legal definition for official purposes. You may find it best to send heavy household items separately by sea.

If you have something awkwardly shaped to send, such as a bicycle, remember that the agent will almost certainly be more experienced in packing such items safely than you are. They will also know what the airline rules are: some carriers will not accept goods unless they are 'properly' packed, which sometimes means banding with sticky tape.

Insurance is essential. You may find you are covered by your own travel or company policy, but agents can also provide cover specially designed for unaccompanied personal freight. Without insurance you are protected only against provable failure on the part of the freighting company with which you booked the shipment, and only in accordance with the limits of their terms and conditions.

As with normal airline baggage, there are certain items you cannot put in the hold of a plane. This extraordinarily eclectic list features a wide range of items including: matches, camping gas cylinders, magnetised material, most aerosols, poisonous weed killer, car batteries, flammable liquids, glue or paint stripper.

Shipments by sea or land are also governed by strict restrictions on dangerous goods, which must be packed specially. 🐌

PAUL MELLY is a freelance journalist specialising in foreign news, business and travel.

Guide or porter?
by Richard Snailham

THERE IS SOMETHING TIMELESS ABOUT THE PROBLEMS of travel with guides and porters. Stories in Henry Morton Stanley's late-Victorian bestsellers find their echoes today, and it was instructive to learn that a recent Cambridge University Expedition to Sangay in Ecuador had the same problems that I had had on an ill-fated expedition to Sangay ten years before: the local Indians had either refused to take their mules to the agreed objective or simply defected.

Nevertheless, a local guide is often useful, sometimes indispensable. Small boys hover outside the souk in Marrakech and we once spurned them only to become comprehensively lost in the myriad covered alleyways. Rather less useful is the young boy who tags along on the streets of a Third World city with which you might be quite well acquainted. He will get into a conversation with you and then offer to show you the principal sights. Before your tour is finished you may find you are sponsoring him through school.

Sometimes a guide is obligatory, as at a French château – and generally provides good value. Where they are not, a judgement has to be made. In wild, sparsely populated, ill-mapped country, I would say that a guide was essential, especially where you do not speak the prevailing language and the local people do not speak yours. In Samburu country recently, with a map that was far too large in scale, I needed our camel handlers to steer us to the objective.

How to get the best

Fix your price. If a journey is involved and you require any form of transport for any great length of time, it is best to find out the cost in advance – if only to minimise the shock of the often inordinate sum asked. Guides have no meters and rarely are they governed by any regulations. The price agreed at the outset, especially if there are other guides in the offing (and thus a choice), is often substantially less than that demanded at the end. Even in Nairobi I recently fell into the trap of failing to establish the price before taking a taxi to the outer suburbs (and was still mightily stung, even after an unedifying argument at the journey's end). Before you clinch the deal, bargaining is generally possible and is often expected.

Pick the right man. Your selection of the right guide is very important. Unfortunately this often involves a snap judgement based on appearances. Women often seem to have better intuitive judgement than men, I find, and a few quick questions on the spot before departure are valuable in ensuring you have a good man. For how things can go wrong, read Geoffrey Moorhouse's *The Fearful Void*. Some unscrupulous guides lead their charges into remote regions and then refuse to conduct them back without a big bonus. Never entirely trust a guide's navigational ability. He will not usually admit to being lost, but can often become so. Try to keep a check on distance covered, note all prominent landmarks and take their bearings from identifiable points on your route and the time that you took them.

Avoid questions like "Is it far?" or "Will we get there tonight?" Guides often have more inclination to please their employers than to tell the sometimes painful truth, and the answers to these two questions will invariably be "no" and "yes".

Problems with porters

The days of mammoth expeditions, undertaken with armies of porters, are probably over. I was once manager and paymaster of a constantly changing team of about 130 porters in Nepal, but smaller, faster-moving assaults are now the order of the day and they normally require less manpower. The problems are otherwise the same, however, and most have been hinted at above.

Here are a few further suggestions:

- Be totally familiar with the local currency and its exchange rate before you embark on any negotiation.
- Try and secure the services of a local 'minder' to help firm up the local *bundobust* (a useful Hindi word, meaning 'logistical arrangements'). On a recent camel safari I took a young NCO from the Kenya General Service Unit who was excellent in his dealings with porters and headmen. Policemen, soldiers, students have all served me well in this role.
- Remember that guides and porters have to have food and shelter. Who is providing this, you or they? You may have to offer advance payment and provide for their journeys home.
- This goes for their animals, too. Camels often have to carry their own forage across deserts and yaks carry theirs up the last stages of the climb to the Everest base camp. Remember that they always travel home faster than they travel out.
- A head porter or *sirdar* is often a good idea if you have a large number in your party. He will be worth his extra pay.
- Only pay a portion of the agreed fee at the outset. Keep the balance in your money belt until you get there.
- Guides should, of course, lead but porters should take up position in the middle of your party. This prevents 'disappearances' and enables you to react if a porter becomes ill or tired.

The brighter side

Finally, if in doubt, take a guide or porter rather than try to struggle on without them. They add colour to the whole enterprise, are generally honest and good hearted and could well end up firm friends. It is worth while taking a few presents with you as a mark of gratitude. Some of your own kit will be much appreciated. Otherwise, penknives, folding scissors and cigarettes go down well. British commemorative coins, postcards of the Queen, empty screw-top tobacco tins – even my old shirts – have proved acceptable gifts. ❧

RICHARD SNAILHAM is a veteran expeditionary and a co-founder of the Scientific Exploration Society. He has been on many expeditions to the Middle East, Africa, Asia and South America, most recently to write the book of the Kotamama expedition, which aims to trace ancient river routes from the Andes to the Atlantic.

What to take

Specialist clothing
by Clive Tully

THE WHOLE POINT OF TRAVEL CLOTHING is that it is not 'run of the mill'. When choosing what to pack for a big trip, therefore, comfort, robustness and ease of care should be the prime considerations. The way it all fits into your luggage should be a high priority, too, since there is no point in packing garments that are heavy or bulky.

Ease of care is also important. Naturally, the simplest way to travel lighter is to take fewer items of clothing, which means that what is taken should be as washable in a hotel hand basin as it is in a mountain stream. In most cases, synthetic fibres not only wash more easily, they dry more quickly, too. Personally, I have been a fan of the lightweight travel clothing (pioneered by Rohan) since it became available 20 years ago. It has the benefits of being both light and durable, and while cheap alternatives tend not to have reinforcing bar tacks stitched into the ends of the zippers or securing the belt loops and zipped security pockets (impossible to pick), I still recommend this style. You might not care to try it, but yes, a pair of Rohan's best-selling Bags trousers really does fit into a Coke can!

Local sensibilities

There are plenty of reasons why one should not want to draw undue attention to oneself while travelling. Inappropriate dress can cause unwanted attention when it is often preferable to blend in with the scenery – crossing borders, checking into hotels, even minding your own business waiting at railway stations. Yet often, when it comes down to it, being thin, tall and pale, I know I am going to stick out anyway. My advice is not to go over the top. Nobody expects me to wear a kilt when I go to Scotland (except perhaps for Burns Night), so dressing up in any kind of ethnic kit is likely to leave me looking pretty ridiculous.

Some years ago, DPM (disruptive pattern material) clothing was all the rage in outdoors circles, with everything from clothing to rucksacks sporting camouflage patterns in commando styles. And since the Gulf War, we've also seen a fashion in desert camouflage combat trousers. Great for a night out in Manchester, perhaps, but pretty stupid in Africa. I've even heard reports of DPM-clad backpackers in the Pyrenees being shot at by the local bandits.

Of course you may have to consider the way you are dressed in certain situations to avoid offending local sensibilities, or in order not to make yourself a target for muggers. There are times when common sense should also prevail. This generally means not exposing too much bare skin when it really is inappropriate (besides, see Sun protection, below), which will generally apply to women much more than men. Having said that, western style is prevalent all over the world, and there are few big towns and cities where you will not see the likes of Coca-Cola T-shirts and baseball caps. Out in the provinces, the situation may well be different. The best advice is simply to be guided by what you see around you.

The practical side of clothing

If we work on a system of layered clothing, you will find you can cater for just about every kind of climate from temperate to downright cold, with only a few adjustments needed for hotter or more humid conditions.

Base layers

What you wear next to the skin is of paramount importance. How comfortable you feel, and how efficiently the layers worn on top work all comes down to wearing the right base layer. In short, the kiss of death is anything made of 100 per cent cotton. The problem with cotton is that it absorbs moisture and it takes forever to dry out. More preferable is the 'wicking effect', where moisture passes through the base-layer fabric so the skin stays as dry as possible, rather like a high-tech nappy. This effect is important in cold conditions, where you have layers on top, because keeping the moisture moving away from you will prevent the chills when you stop moving. And it is particularly important if your outer shell is a breathable waterproof because if cotton is worn next to the skin, you might just as well wear a bin liner rather than a £200 or £300 Gore-Tex jacket.

I like wearing a safari suit for shooting tigers in.
– VIVIENNE WESTWOOD

In warmer conditions, where the base layer may be all you are wearing on top, it helps keep you cool by wicking the moisture to the surface of the garment where it can evaporate most readily and therefore cool one down. Helly Hansen started the ball rolling years ago with polypropylene base layers, but technology has moved on considerably since then. Polyprop tends to get smelly very quickly, while the latest polyester fabrics, epitomised by Polartec's BiPolar, have anti-microbial treatments that will keep them working and smelling sweet, even under the most arduous laundry-free conditions.

Mid layers

The traditional garment here is the woolly sweater, and devotees say that not only does wool absorb moisture, but it even generates a certain amount of heat when it does so. But once again, if you are wearing a high-tech breathable waterproof on top, it is not allowed it to do its job by encouraging moisture to hang about inside your little microclimate. The modern alternative is fleece, made from knitted polyester, napped and sheared in a wide variety of different velour finishes, depending on the performance and look required by the manufacturer. As with the polyester used in base layers, it absorbs a mere one per cent of its own weight in water, and the sophisticated techniques used in its construction ensure excellent insulation for the weight of the fabric. Fleece comes in different weights, and the most widely available weight – the best for a broad range of temperatures – is the 200 g/sqm fabric typified by Polartec 200. The heavier weights are better for very cold conditions or inactivity in less extreme temperatures, while the lighter ones are useful for warding off the chills of a summer evening, or as an extra 'thermal' layer.

On its own, fleece is not windproof. In many situations with high activity – cross-country skiing, for example – a certain amount of air permeability can be an advantage. If windproofing is needed then you can either wear your waterproof on top, or a lightweight windproof layer made from poly/cotton or synthetic microfibre. Windproof fleeces made with a laminate sandwiched by two thin layers of fleece fabric are available, and while they do an excellent job, it is unfortunately at the expense of flexibility in an overall layered clothing system.

The legs

Cotton canvas jeans have been around for over 100 years, but while they are robust, they have little else to offer. Unless you buy the stretch variety, jeans are unyielding and take forever to dry when washed. In my opinion, they make appalling travel clothing. Get them wet in cold, windy conditions and they become downright dangerous. Water conducts heat away from the body 26 times as efficiently as air, so cotton trousers that absorb gallons of the stuff are not good news for the legs unless you are a fan of hypothermia.

Polyester/cotton or polyester microfibre fabrics fare much better in unexpected extremes of climate because they dry off much quicker. Besides, most travel trousers made from these kinds of fabric look smarter, too. For trekking and mountain walking, the best performer without a doubt is Polartec Powerstretch fleece, but given that a pair of leggings made from Powerstretch will be 'form-fitting', do bear in mind any social considerations when wearing them away from the mountains.

Waterproofs

The buzzword these days is 'breathability'. Most will have heard of Gore-Tex, the best-known microporous laminate, but there are also microporous polyurethane coatings, and there are, in addition, coatings and laminates that are hydrophilic – Sympatex, for example, the biggest-selling breathable waterproof laminate in Europe. They work by different mechanisms, but the effect is the same. Moisture vapour on the inside gets transmitted through the membrane or coating to the outside. They work best when there is the greatest difference in both temperature and humidity between the microclimate inside your clothing, and the air outside. In other words, cold and dry conditions will see the best performance.

While there are differences in performance between fabrics, and even different versions of the same fabric, what is probably more useful is to concentrate on the design of the jacket. If the most robust waterproof is needed, you should aim for one of the laminated fabrics in a three-layer configuration. They are good performers, but not necessarily the best for looks if you are seeking something a little more general purpose. Here the two-layer laminate with a separate lining comes into its own, in fact all but budget jackets made from polyurethane-coated nylon or polyester will come with a drop lining as well. The advantage is that they feel softer and look smarter and more sophisticated.

The main zip needs protection to stop water getting through. This should be a double storm flap – either Velcro or press stud fastened – with the inner flap slightly oversized to form a gutter so that any drips managing to infiltrate that far can run down to the bottom hem.

A good hood is essential. A walking jacket may have a fixed hood, but more are now coming with rollaway hoods that stow in the collar – simply because people want the jackets to be multifunctional. The drawcord adjuster should bring the hood snug around your face without too much fabric bunching up, and it should allow you to turn your head from side to side without your face suddenly disappearing inside the hood. Something that started out as a feature on mountaineering jackets but is becoming widely available on general models is the volume adjuster. Usually an elasticated drawcord or webbing strap and buckle at the back of the hood, it allows you to take up excess volume in the hood, giving a better fit.

Also useful is a decent peak or visor to keep drips from running down your face. Visors made for typical hillwalking or mountaineering will tend to come with some form of stiffening – either a thin plastic strip or malleable wire. In recent years, however, the trend has been towards soft visors, which make stowing the hood in the collar easier, but it is at the expense of functionality when it really counts. In high winds, a floppy peak will simply collapse over your eyes. Old-fashioned designs do give a rather closed-in feel – the more up-to-date ones have cutaways at the side of the face so no peripheral vision is lost – important when you are picking your way across uncertain terrain.

If you really want to batten down the hatches in bad weather, look for elasticated drawcords at both waist and bottom hem as well as the hood, while cuffs need to have a good range of adjustment to allow for sealing around gloves.

Pockets are really down to one's own preference and needs. Certainly if you are navigating yourself through wild terrain, a map pocket in the proper place can save you some grief. Decent map pockets will be situated at chest height with the zipped opening beneath the main zip storm flaps, but outside the main zip itself, affording access to your map without opening up the main body of the jacket.

Insulated clothing

If you are heading for really cold climes, or maybe you just need something warm to wear around camp if the temperature plunges to freezing or below, you might consider an insulated jacket, something filled either with polyester wadding or down. As with sleeping bags, the two forms of insulation have their pluses and minuses. Duck or goose down provides the best insulation for the weight – it is also more compressible, and it regains its loft better after compression. The big minus is that it loses its insulation value if it gets damp. Even an insulated jacket with a breathable waterproof shell can suffer from a build-up of moisture that will affect its performance. The first line of attack is to make sure it doesn't get wet. You can also impregnate the whole garment with a waterproofing agent, which will enable the down to loft even in damp conditions.

Synthetic waddings tend to be cheaper than natural fillings and, in general, are bulkier and have a shorter lifespan, though with the huge advances being made in the technology over the last few years, this is not always the case. Their big winning point is the fact that damp does not affect their performance.

Intelligent clothing?

It is now possible to make garments from fabrics incorporating phase change technology, promising superior temperature regulation. The idea is that if, say, you were exerting yourself while wearing a jacket made of the material, it would prevent you from overheating by changing phase and absorbing the excess heat. Then, once you stopped moving and began to cool down, the phase change material would revert to its former state, releasing heat in the process. The technology itself is brilliant – the drawback is that in order to get it working really well, you would end up with garments that were prohibitively expensive. The garments that are currently on the market have such a small percentage of phase change material in their construction that the benefits are negligible.

Head and hands

The head radiates more heat per square centimetre of skin than any other part of the body (up to 70 per cent of the total heat loss from the body). The moment you start feeling cold it is advisable to put a hat on. A woolly hat is fine, although if you find wool next to the skin a bit irritating, there is a huge range of styles made from polyester fleece.For maintaining any dexterity, in order to operate a camera, for example, you are better off using thin liner gloves with heavier gloves or mittens on top.

Sun protection

The rate of increase in new cases of skin cancer is alarming, and the age of onset is getting lower. We now know there is no such thing as a healthy tan, but also that we can improve our protection against the sun by wearing the right kind of clothes. Most people are unaware that while parts of the body covered by light clothing do not get tanned or burned in strong sunshine, the skin is still being damaged. UVA rays cause tanning and burning but UVB rays go deeper, causing more long-term damage, and they can penetrate many types of light clothing. The average cotton T-shirt has a SPF (sun protection factor) of between six and nine. That drops to less than half if the T-shirt is wet.

We tend to regard lighter colours as more suitable in bright conditions because they reflect better. In fact the opposite is true. Darker colours absorb more UV and therefore provide better skin protection. The best fabrics for sun protection can still be lightweight, but are close-weave. Some travel clothing companies – Rohan and Craghoppers in particular – now quote SPF ratings for their products.

As with base layers, synthetic or synthetic/natural fabrics are best. First of all, synthetic fibres can be made finer than cotton, and are therefore capable of being closer woven. Secondly, their quick-drying ability means enhanced cooling in conditions where you are likely to be sweating. A hat makes good sense, too. The head and neck are prime targets, with one-third of all skin cancers occurring on the nose. A mesh-topped baseball hat or open-weave straw hat might feel good, but they do not offer sufficient protection. A hat with a ten cm all-round brim is much more effective.

Footwear

What one wears on the feet can make or break any trip. So whether your preferred footwear is trainers, loafers, deck shoes, brogues, walking boots, sandals or wellies, you can do yourself a big favour by making sure they fit properly, and not leaving it until just before you head off into the blue yonder to buy a new pair.

Boots

Walking boots used to be heavy, unbending lumps of leather that were designed to inflict major injuries on feet until they had stomped at least 100 miles in them. Nowadays, while boots may need a little period of 'acclimatisation', they are designed to fit and to be comfortable, straight out of the box. For non-demanding walking and trekking, lightweight boots, such as the mega-selling Brasher Boot, will be just the job, and they don't look too bad for wandering around markets.

The main choice is between all-leather and fabric/leather boots, and within those distinctions there are models built to cater for very wide levels of usage, from general ambling on undemanding terrain to four-season mountaineering. Much of it comes down to the stiffness of the sole unit, but even a boot designed for foot-path walking – with a reasonable amount of flex in the sole – should still not be able to twist too much. If it does, it will offer little support on rougher terrain, and the feet are likely to tire more quickly.

The key to ensuring a decent fit lies in making sure you have the socks you intend to wear with you when you are shopping for boots. Remember that you should leave space in front of your toes to allow for feet expansion, and the easiest way to do that is to slide your foot forward as far as it will go in the unlaced boot. You should then be able to slip your index finger into the space between the heel and the back of the boot. If you can move the finger about, the next size down is needed, if it is very tight – then the next size up. Any outdoors shop worth its salt will have the means to measure feet accurately.

Insoles

Since it is likely you will spend lots of time on your feet, it can be worth investing in a pair of specialised insoles to provide superior support. Those that are provided as standard in many walking boots and trainers are generally made from soft closed-cell foam. They help cushion the feet and prevent blisters, but aren't as supportive as they could be. Probably the best insoles you can get for boots, shoes or trainers are those made by the American company Superfeet. By providing better support for the feet, they prevent the elongation that occurs when you put weight on them, which in turn prevents a wide range of long-term problems.

Sandals

When the first sandals that took over from flip-flops came into being (mainly for rafting in the US), they were fairly basic – nothing more than a sole with Velcro-fastened nylon webbing straps. Now sports sandals are extremely sophisticated, employing all the technologies used in high-tech footwear to provide comfort and support. The soles are generally supportive, many with good gripping outsoles, with shaped footbeds to add to the feeling of support and comfort. The straps may be made from nylon webbing, leather or synthetic leather, and most will have soft padding or linings on the underside.

There are versions made for use where immersion in water is likely, but equally there are versions that are suitable for hard walking. Indeed, there are many hikers in the States who prefer to use sandals in hot conditions, even when backpacking heavy loads. Since it is likely that you will be wearing sandals in hot, sunny conditions, do be mindful of the fact that the skin on your feet is very sensitive, so either use sunblock or wear a pair of socks.

Happy feet

Decent socks are as much a key to foot comfort as the shoe or boot itself. Look for socks without bulky protruding seams over the toe or round the heel, and check that the elastication at the top is not too tight. For walking and general travelling, loopstitch socks provide greater cushioning underneath the heel and ball of the foot, and you do not have to burden feet with the extra insulation of a full loopstitch sock – socks with the loop pile just in the strategic areas are now available.

Remember that the layer principle gives the greatest means to mix 'n' match, both in terms of performance and looks. The good backpacker keeps his load light by using items of clothing and equipment, which, where possible, serve more than one purpose. So as one begins to select clothing to put into that rucksack, travel bag or suitcase, think versatility and don't take more than you really need. ❧

CLIVE TULLY is an expert and writer on outdoor clothing and equipment.
His work regularly appears in walking magazines and national newspapers.

Choosing your rucksack (and other luggage)
by Hilary Bradt

THE ORIGINAL MEANING OF 'LUGGAGE' is 'what has to be lugged about'. Lightweight materials and wheels have made lugging obsolete for sensible travellers these days, but a bewildering choice of containers for all your portable possessions is available.

What you buy in the way of luggage and what you put in it obviously depends on how and where you are travelling. If your journey is in one conveyance and you are staying put when you arrive, you can be as eccentric as the Durrell family, who travelled to Corfu with: 'two trunks of books and a briefcase containing his clothes' (Lawrence), and: 'four books on natural history, a butterfly net, a dog and a jam jar full of caterpillars, all in imminent danger of turning into chrysalids' (Gerald, who described this vast logistical exercise in *My Family and Other Animals*). If, however, you will be constantly on the move and will rarely spend more than one night in any place, your luggage must be easy to pack, transport and carry.

What to take

There are two important considerations to bear in mind when choosing luggage. First, weight is less of a problem than bulk. Travel light if you can, but if you can't, travel small. Second, bring whatever you need to keep you happy. If you can travel, like Laurie Lee, with a tent, a change of clothes, a blanket and a violin or, like some modern travellers, with only a day pack, you will indeed be free. It's perhaps significant that these supremely lightweight travellers usual go solo; you stop noticing your own pong after a few months. Most people, however, are dependent on their customary possessions and must pack accordingly.

Suitcase or backpack?

Your choice of luggage is of the utmost importance and will probably involve making a purchase. Making do with Granny's old suitcase or Uncle John's scouting rucksack may spoil your trip.

Anyone who's had to stand in a crowded Third World bus or the London Underground wearing a backpack will know what an antisocial item of luggage this is. You take up three times more room than normal and every time you turn round you knock someone over. It is no wonder backpackers have a bad name. The trouble is that most modern backpacks are designed for hill-walking rather than travelling. The ergonomic design is superb for distributing weight evenly on your shoulders and hips and the fabric keeps out the rain. Fine for hikers, but if you are a backpacker – in the sense of using public transport and being willing to walk a couple of miles to the bus station – you would do better to go for a combination bag and backpack. Basically, this is a sturdy bag with padded shoulder straps that can be hidden in a special zip compartment when approaching a sensitive border (where backpackers may be given a hard time) or when travelling by plane. Eagle Creek is a good manufacturer of such bags and Rohan now makes luggage as well as clothing. Look out also for a rucksack-cum-bag from Regatta that is designed to allow air to circulate between the pack and your back – ideal for the tropics.

If you are joining an organised group or do not expect to carry your own luggage, you will find a duffel bag the most practical solution. Or two duffel bags since you have two hands. These soft zipped bags are strong and light and can fit into awkward spaces that preclude rigid suitcases. They fit snugly into the bottom of a canoe or the back of a bus and are easily carried by porters or pack animals. When selecting a duffel bag, choose one made from a strong material with a stout zip that can be padlocked to the side or otherwise secured against thieves. If you are looking for a more sophisticated piece of soft luggage, check out the Kiva 'Big Mouth' bag, which, as the name implies, has an especially large opening.

Suppose you are a regular air traveller, what will be the best type of luggage for you? Probably the conventional suitcase and, in that case, you will be well advised – as with most travel purchases – to get the best you can afford, unless you want to replace your 'bargain' luggage after virtually every flight. Cheap materials do not stand up to the airline handling, which usually involves throwing luggage 20 feet onto a hard surface, then allowing it to stand on the tarmac in the rain. For sheer toughness, the traditional hard cases do best. Choose ones made from a strong material such as nylon. These can go up to 1,000 denier. Leather looks smart but is quite heavy. As with all items of luggage, check the zip, which should be strong, and the stitching, which should be even and secure with no gaps or loose threads. Airport carousels can leave black smears on light-coloured items –

He who would travel happily must travel lightly.

– ANTOINE DE SAINTE-EXUPERY

darker colours stand up to this treatment more happily but are harder to spot among a medley or similar cases. Tie a distinctive ribbon or tag onto the handle for identification.

Few people these days would buy a suitcase that doesn't have wheels. These increase your independence (and save your back). Some wheeled suitcases are far easier to control than others, so check potential purchases out properly in the shop before handing over your money. The classic wheeled suitcase may soon be a thing of the past: the latest design from Kiva uses rollerblades.

Before checking in a backpack or suitcase at the airport, take time to remove all unnecessary appendages (straps, hangers, clips, etc.) and make sure your name and address is both on the label attached to the outside and inside the case as well.

Luggage experts and even those in the airline business often recommend sticking to a carry-on bag if possible. It ensures a speedy exit from the airport and avoids possible damage or loss. In any case, use a carry-on bag for your valuables and anything you can't do without for a few days. To fit under an aeroplane seat, a carry-on bag must measure no more than 45 x 35 x 15 cm.

As well as a carry-on bag, you are allowed the following free items: a handbag (women only – as this is in addition to the carry-on luggage, better take as big a handbag as possible to make the most of your luck), an overcoat, an umbrella or walking stick, a small camera, a pair of binoculars, infant's food for the flight, a carrying basket, an invalid's fully collapsible wheelchair, a pair of crutches, reading material in reasonable quantities and any duty free goods you have acquired since checking in.

Some thought should be given to accessory bags. Everyone ends up with more luggage than they started with, because of presents, local crafts, maps, etc., collected on the way, and a light, foldable nylon bag is very useful. I'm devoted to plastic bags myself and always carry a good supply to separate dirty clothes from clean ones, as well as for those extras.

Security

Choose your luggage with security in mind. Your possessions are at risk in two ways: your bag may be opened and some items removed, or the whole bag may be stolen. Most travellers have been robbed at some time or other, the most frequent occurrence being that small items simply disappear from their luggage. Make sure that your luggage can be locked. With duffel bags, this is no problem – a small padlock will secure the zip to the ring at the base of the handle. Adapt the bag yourself if necessary. Combination locks are more effective than standard padlocks as they are harder to pick. It is harder to lock a backpack, so use your ingenuity. One effective method is to make a strong pack cover with metal rings round the edges, through which can be passed a cable lock to secure the cover round the pack. Luggage may also be slashed, but this treatment is usually reserved for handbags. Apart from buying reinforced steel cases there is little you can do about it. A strong leather strap around a suitcase may help to keep your luggage safe and will be a life saver should the clasps break.

During my travels, I've been robbed of five small bags. I finally learned never to carry something that is easy to run off with unless it is firmly secured to my person. If you keep your most valuable possessions in the centre of a locked, heavy pack or bag they are pretty safe. If you can barely carry your luggage, a thief will have the same problem.

Weight allowances for air travel

On international flights, the IATA tourist and economy class allowance is normally 20 kg, for first class it is 30 kg. For transatlantic flights and some others (e.g. USA to South America), however, you can take far more luggage since the only restriction is to two pieces of luggage no larger than 170 cm. Before you fly, always ask the airline about luggage allowances and ask if the same applies to the home journey. For instance, if you fly Ecuatoriana from Miami to Quito, you will fly down on the two piece system, but will be restricted to 20 kg for your return – a nasty shock for the present-laden tourist.

Packing

Before I go on a long trip I put a large cardboard box into my bedroom and throw in stuff I may need on the trip as I come across it. That, plus a list that is added to as I remember things, makes the build-up to departure relatively unstressful.

Bear in mind that the variable air pressure inside the luggage hold will cause leakage. Shampoos, lotions and other fluids should be in screw-topped tubes or containers. Give the top an extra turn before you pack it. Potentially leaky things such as fountain pens should be carried in your hand luggage. Remember that your Swiss army knife may be classified as an offensive weapon and confiscated.

When packing, put irregular-shaped and heavy items such as shoes at the bottom, remembering where 'bottom' will be when the case is being carried. Clothes crease less if rolled up, or folded round a magazine. Let no space go to waste – fill up shoes with soft or small items such as underwear or jewellery. Top the lot with something large, such as a dressing gown or shawl. Some travellers like to keep their toilet items in different groups, which makes sense when you consider that you do not wash your hair with the same frequency as you wash your face or go out in strong sun. Medicines should be kept in an easily recognised plastic bag. Keep aspirins, etc., in your sponge bag so they can easily be found.

Do not over-pack: if you have to force the lid of your suitcase, you may bend the frame or break the hinges, not to mention what you do to the contents. Better to have plenty of space for those extra purchases. Pad the gaps out with bubble wrap. Then, when everything goes wrong on your holiday, you can relieve the tension by popping the bubbles one by one! ❧

HILARY BRADT is one of the pioneers of the modern guidebook, founding the Bradt travel guide series in 1974 and winning the 'Sunday Times' Small Publisher of the Year Award in 1997. She is also a tour leader and travel writer, specialising in South America and Madagascar.

Lightweight equipment
by Martin Rosser, Natasha Hughes and Paul Goodyer

THE ART OF TRAVELLING LIGHT is to make sure you have nothing superfluous to your trip, while at the same time ensuring that what you carry will enable you to do what you want and live wherever you choose.

So careful thought about the countries and terrain you will be visiting, the mode of transport you are using and the type of activities you will be involved in will greatly help to reduce bulk. For example, if you are heading off on a trip to the Far East you will probably not need a tent as there are few places to camp, in fact accommodation is so cheap that the intrepid traveller will only need to take a mosquito net and hammock.

With the technical advances of recent years, as a rule of thumb you can safely assume that the more lightweight and compact the equipment is (all performance factors being equal), the more expensive it will be. For example, a good sleeping mat will cost approximately £20, while a modern self-inflating mat that combines both air and foam comes in at under a quarter of the size and is more comfortable, but will set you back around £60.

Adaptability and versatility are the key to travelling light. Use one item to fulfil many functions – for example, a poncho can be used as a rain garment to cover you and your pack, a ground sheet, a bivvi shelter or a sleeping bag cover.

When I first came to lightweight backpacking, I knew very little and did not bother to ask for advice. I learned from bitter experience and, interspersed with episodes of extreme misery, very exciting it was, too.

The main drawback to equipping oneself adequately is expense. Costs soon mounted to prohibitive proportions before I had what I wanted. The lesson? If you are beginning, a little advice is worth a lot. When you become more practised, that is the time for bitter experience to take over.

In this article, I intend only to cover the main purchases you will make, missing out food, clothing, and any technical sporting equipment. This leaves (in descending order of probable cost) tent or shelter, sleeping gear, rucksack, boots and cooking and eating gear.

If you are going backpacking, there are a number of objectives you should have in mind. Weight is usually at the top of the list: you want everything to be as light as possible. Performance: you want your equipment to be good enough for everything you are going to put it through. Expense: you have to be able to afford it. These three criteria form the eternal triangle of backpacking.

As we go on, you will see compromises arising, but one aspect of weight can be covered now. Most lightweight gear comes marked with a weight, but manufacturers being manufacturers, these are not always as accurate as they might be. Furthermore, some sleeping bags come marked with the weight of the filling only. It is easy to become confused or misled. The easiest answer is to shop for your kit armed with a spring balance (anything that measures up to eight kilos is sufficient, as long as it can be read to the nearest gram or two). If you want to know where to get a balance, ask a fisherman.

Tents and shelters

At one time, the ridge pole was the only tent you could get, short of buying a marquee. Then some bright spark designed an A-pole ridge so that the pole did not come straight down the doorway. Today both these designs are still around, and the ridge pole (in the form of the Vango Force Ten) is still preferred by many as a heavy-duty tent that can take a lot of punishment.

However, with the advent of flexible poles that could be shoved through sleeves, new designs became possible and these had their own advantages. Such models give you plenty of headroom, something as important as ground space if you intend to live in your tent during bad weather. There are disadvantages, of course. These tents are both more expensive and more fragile. To get a structurally strong flexible-pole tent, you have to go upmarket and seek out geodesic designs – and that costs a lot of money.

After the innovation that came with flexible poles, Gore-Tex was next to make its mark on the tent scene when it was used in the construction of single-skin tents. Water-tight with built-in breathability, the fabric gives you a condensation-free tent that weighs even less than regular flexible-pole types. These tents also tend to employ flexible poles, so the space inside is good. However, Gore-Tex is a very expensive material, so as the weight goes down, the prices go up.

Single-skin tents soon became available in one-man versions with only the barest skeleton of a frame. Because the material breathes, it does not matter if there is no circulation of air around it. With a hoop at the front, these tents resemble a tunnel that you have to crawl into feet first. Then the hoop was removed and the Gore-Tex 'bivi-bag' was born – a waterproof and fully breathable covering for your sleeping bag. These are probably the ultimate luxury in bivouacking, but the cost is again high. However, weighing in at next to nothing, these bags are well worth considering (although it is a bit like sleeping in a coffin).

Last, but not least, comes the humble bivouac sheet or, to use the army parlance, the 'basha sheet'. This two-by-three-metre piece of PU nylon has tags around the outside that allow it to be pegged down. It is the most versatile, lightweight, in-expensive and durable of all shelters so far discussed. It is limited only by the inge-nuity and expertise of the user – and therein lies its fault: you need to know how to use it. But if you do not have any money, or if you can put the occasional soaking down to experience, give it a go. (The alternative for the backpacker travelling in warmer climates would be a waterproof poncho that can be used as a basha in combination with a mosquito net and hammock.)

So which tent do you choose? Narrow the field by asking yourself these ques-tions: how many people do you want it to sleep? How high up are you going to camp? (The higher you camp, the harsher the conditions, so the sturdier the tent you need.) Is headroom important to you? (Perhaps you want a flexible hoop de-sign.) Do you want it to last a long time? (If so you will have to go for a more stur-dy, heavy-duty model.) It has to be said that even if you designed the tent yourself, compromises would have to be made, so be prepared to make them when buying. However, with care and proper scrutiny of the maker's specifications, you should get something suitable.

Whatever you end up with, try to get a tent with mosquito netting on every en-trance, even the vents. Rare indeed are the countries with no flying biters. The tent you end up with will probably have a super-thin groundsheet to save weight, so you might want to get some 2mm foam to use as an underlay. It will keep you sur-prisingly warm and will cut down on wear and tear. However, this will add to the weight and bulk of your tent system. Bear this in mind before you reject the heav-ier tent with the stronger groundsheet.

Sleeping gear

The difficulty in choosing sleeping gear for the traveller is more extreme than it is for the expedition member as an expedition is usually based in one area, allowing you to equip yourself for that particular environment. The traveller, on the other hand, will more often than not encounter a variety of conditions. For example, a trip to India might include lazing on tropical beaches, travelling on crowded trains and hiking through the high and cold Himalayas. The solution comes with 'layer-ing'. Go for the lowest common denominator for a sleeping bag, then make sure you have a good, thin base-layer top (many on the market now have high wicking properties and are stylish enough to wear as a T-shirt in warm weather), a down waistcoat or fleece jacket – when these are all combined you should have ample sleeping gear. If you end up travelling in more extreme conditions it is always pos-sible to buy cheap local bedding to add on to your kit and dispose of it after the need has passed.

Another lightweight luxury to take with you is a pillowcase into which you can stuff fleece or cloth for added padding – or with which you can cover suspect pil-lows in cheap accommodation.

Without a shadow of a doubt, the best you can sleep in is a down bag. It pro-motes fine dreams, is aesthetically pleasing, is lighter for any given warmth rating than any other fill and packs away smaller than any other bag, lofting up after-wards to cosset you at night. Nothing else comes close to down unless, of course, you are allergic to feathers. Yet down has a terrible Achilles heel. If it gets wet, it is next to useless and becomes very unpleasant. Furthermore, wet it a few times and it starts to feel extremely sorry for itself, losing efficiency rapidly. It is also worth bearing in mind that a down bag can be difficult to clean while away and can become fetid on extended expeditions, so constant airing and the addition of a sleeping bag liner becomes vital.

If your bag is likely to get wet, steer clear of down. The alternative is a man-made fibre bag. These come in many guises, but the underlying principle is the same. A long, man-made fibre is hollow and thus traps air. As with down, it is the trapped air that keeps you warm. Call it Holofill, Superloft, Microsoft or whatever, the consensus of opinion is that the difference in performance is marginal. The fibres probably differ to get around patents rather than to improve performance.

The advantages of artificial fibres are clear. The bags are cheaper than down, they are warmer underneath you (because they are harder to compress), they keep you warmer when wet and they are easier to keep clean. Disadvantages? They are somewhat heavier and bulkier than down (although this is becoming less of an issue as these fabrics improve), and will not last you anywhere near as long.

The compromise is clear. If you can stay out of the wet and can afford to pay more, invest in down, which lasts longer and therefore costs the same in the long run. If you camp a lot in areas where you are likely to get wet, buy a man-made fibre bag and stick to stroking the down bags in the shops lovingly.

Another alternative is the Buffalo Bag, which is made from fibre pile covered in Pertex. These bags are unique and have their own special advantages, though the disadvantages can be stated easily: they are very heavy and bulky. Buffalo Bags are based on the layer system, making it handy to add layers for cold weather and subtract them for hot. They are tough and washable. Thanks to the Pertex covering, they do not get wet easily, and if they do so, the pile wicks away moisture and the Pertex cover dries it out rapidly. The same Pertex covering makes the bag very windproof The bag is good for those who bivouac and can be used to effect with a good down inner bag. Handle, or better still, borrow one to try before you buy.

Another alternative for the 'lightweight tropical traveller' is the tropical quilt. This offers the best pack size and economy in tandem with a range of functions. It can be formed into a lightweight sleeping bag, wrapped around you on buses and trains and can be washed and dried in 20 minutes. It can also be doubled with a waterproof poncho to create a basic sleeping unit.

Try the bag on in the shop, however foolish you feel, and leave your clothes on while you do so. This minimises embarrassment, and one day you might be cold enough out in the wilds to sleep fully clothed. Pull the hood of the bag tight around your face to cover your head. If you cannot do this, the bag cannot be used in cold weather. A large part of the body's heat loss is from the head. Shove your feet into the bottom of the bag and wriggle. If the bag constricts you, it is too small. Any point where you press against the bag will turn into a miserable cold spot at night. If you are a restless sleeper, make sure the bag is wide enough around the middle to contain all your squirming. If you feel like a pea rattling in an empty pod, the bag is too large and you will waste heat warming up empty space.

General points to look for in a bag include a box- or elephant-type foot, a draw-cord at the shoulder as well as the headband the option of a right- or left-handed zip so that, in an emergency, you can share your warmth with an extra-special friend. Zips should all be well baffled to prevent loss of heat. If the sack you choose is of man-made fibre, check to see if it comes with a compression-stuff sack. If it does not and you want one, this will add a few pounds to the final price.

I have deliberately ignored baffle constructions as the subject is complicated and best covered with examples to hand. Seek advice on-site. Similarly with the season rating of the bag: a 'season' system is simple but should only be used as a rough guide. One season (summer) for very casual use in warm weather, two seasons (summer and spring) is a little better, three seasons should be good for winter use and five seasons for use in severe conditions. However, simple systems such as this leave room for manufacturers to fudge their claims. One man's three seasons is another man's four, it really depends on how much you feel the cold.

Query the general reputation of the bag you fancy with as many experts as you can find. I find that the 'lowest temperatures' quoted for the bags are next to useless: they are inevitably rated for still air, and who camps in that? As well as ignoring the massive effect of wind chill, they can also ignore the fact that some people maintain a higher body temperature at night than others.

Last but not least with sleeping gear, you would be well advised to put something under your sleeping bag; namely a 'kip mat'. The most widely used is the closed-cell foam type, which is bulky but lightweight and durable. Ignore all advice that tells you that they are all made of the same stuff and that, when it comes to the expensive ones, you simply pay for the name – it is patently untrue. A simple test is to inflict severe damage on various types – such damage as scoring, tearing, and compressing flat. Choose one that withstands these injuries best – it will probably be the one that feels warmest when pressed between the palms. It will probably cost more, but in my experience the cheap ones are simply not worth it. A modern alternative is the self-inflating mat. This is a quarter of the pack size of a traditional mat and uses a combination of air and foam. Its drawbacks are that it is three times more expensive than a conventional mat and that great care must be taken to avoid punctures. A puncture repair kit is, therefore, an essential extra.

I always take a pen-knife. It's invaluable for everything – taking thorns out of elephant's feet, hacking through the jungle, opening a can of beans, repairing things. I'd never travel without it.
– JOHN BLASHFORD-SNELL

Rucksacks

The first choice that needs to be made is between the conventional top-loading rucksack with side pockets (still probably the best for expeditions) and the newer-style 'travelsack'. The travelsack is a hybrid of a rucksack and a suitcase in that it has a zip that runs all the way around, allowing you to expose everything inside, a concealing flap to hide away the back harness and straps when they are not needed, a grab handle and shoulder strap for ease of carrying and, more often than not, they will come equipped with a detachable daysack. Travelsacks are extremely practical, but are inherently more expensive than traditional rucksacks because of the extra features.

It is very important to try on packs before buying one. There is a fantastic array of back systems and, as our backs are all different, the only way of finding out which one works best for you is to try a variety on.

For lightweight backpacking, choose the smallest pack you think you can get away with and check with the retailer that you can exchange it for a larger version if you really cannot get everything you want into it. Starting with the smallest is the best way to restrict yourself as there is always a tendency to fill space.

When it comes to rucksacks, two things are important from the outset: size and a capacity for being waterproof. Almost any size of sack you might want is available and (whatever the manufacturer may say to the contrary) none of them are fully waterproof. The capacity of a sack is measured in litres. A small day pack weighs in at about 25 litres. General, all-round sacks come in all sizes from that capacity upwards, culminating in one sized at 75 litres. One of these will allow you to manage anything, even mountaineering (at a push), but you pay a price for the facility. Having 75 litres to play with gives you a terrible urge to fill up all the space, even for summer camping in the lowlands.

Restricting yourself to packing what you need rather than what you have room for takes discipline. Because of this, some people prefer a 65- or even a 50-litre sack. Moving upwards from 75 litres, there is almost no end to the packs available, but the higher you go the more specialised the use: for expedition travel overseas, perhaps, or for humping all you need up to a base camp from which you intend making sorties with smaller loads.

When you look at the vast array of rucksacks on the market, you will find that fashion dictates two things. First is the anatomical, internal frame system. External frames are considered fuddy-duddy now, though the internal frame is not the all-round answer to carrying loads. The second (and far less valid) fashion is for adjustable harnesses. Try, if you can (and it gets harder every season), to avoid these. There are more fiddly bits that can go wrong, usually at an awkward moment (mine gave way halfway up the ascent to a glacier); and as your back should not be due to change shape significantly for the next 30 years, you may as well save yourself some bother. It is better to settle for a sack that is fixed at one size and just happens to fit you.

Something that has always been a very important asset to a rucksack is a hip belt. When walking, the hip belt transfers roughly 60 per cent of the pack weight to your legs, leaving only 40 per cent for your more delicate shoulders and back. Therefore any rucksack you buy should have a wide, sturdy, and very well padded hip belt. That thick padding should also appear at the shoulder straps. Thin bands will cut off the circulation, giving you the sensation of having two useless and heavy ropes dangling from your shoulders instead of arms.

After you've accounted for these important criteria, the rest more or less comes down to personal preference. If you are organised in the way you pack, a one-section rucksack is simpler and more effective. It is an advantage if your pockets can be detached, but having them fixed saves a bit of weight. Some harnesses leave more room for air to circulate between you and the sack. If you hate getting hot and sweaty as you walk, try for one of these.

When you buy your pack, enquire about the repair service. Well-established manufacturers such as Karrimor and Berghaus give excellent service, often without charging. Some will even give a lifetime's guarantee, though I can never work out if this applies to the life of the sack or the life of its owner.

Boots

Leather, suede and fabric are the materials most commonly used to make boots. Leather and suede are more breathable, durable and adequately waterproof – if well taken care of and treated often with a water-repellent substance.

Fabric boots, however, lend themselves better to the backpacker in that they are lightweight and have a more stylish, 'trainer' look and feel as far as general use is concerned (not every day is spent trekking). More often than not, they have a breathable and waterproof membrane. The waterproof function is excellent and needs little maintenance, while the breathable part tends not to work too well in hot, humid conditions. 'Breathable', in this context, seems to mean 'in comparison to wearing plastic bags on your feet'.

The modern answer is the cross-hiking boot. These provide a cross between the weight and comfort of a trainer with the sole and ankle support of a walking boot. The emphasis is on breathability and quick drying and, in conjunction with this, there is now a new generation of waterproof socks. This means that, when the need arises, boot and sock can be worn together and although the boot will get wet, your foot won't.

As with rucksacks, it is imperative to try on boots, and all feet are different. What suits one person may be wrong for the next. If you need to make several purchases within the shop, deal with the boots first so that you can keep them on in the shop for as long as possible while sorting out the other products. This will give you the chance to live with them, albeit for a short while, before making your final decision. Once you take your boots home, walk up and down some stairs while wearing them at least a dozen times before committing yourself to wearing them outside as, once you have done so, you will not be able to exchange them.

Leather is still the best for serious trekking. Spotting a good leather boot is fairly simple. As far as possible, it should be made from one bit of leather. The stitching is double, sometimes triple. The ankle is well padded to give comfortable support. The inside of the boot is lined with soft leather, and there are no rough seams around the heel. Feet tend to blister in disapproval of poor design.

Check the weight of several different pairs. It costs you energy to clump around with a heavy weight on each foot, and you may well decide that the terrain you usually walk on is not demanding enough to require such solidity.

If you intend to use your boots with crampons, however, you will need a fairly rigid sole. If you intend to go front pointing you will need a boot with a steel shank in the sole. For the common walker, though, these should be avoided as such boots become very heavy and uncomfortable to walk in over any great distance.

Traditionally, two pairs of socks are worn with boots, and some celebrated old-timers even wear more, choosing oversized boots to compensate. However, modern thinking says that boots are not as uncomfortable as they used to be and one pair of loop stitch socks is quite enough. So unless you suffer terribly from cold feet, prepare to try on your boots with just one pair of thick socks. With the boots laced up, rap the heel on the floor and check to see if you can wiggle your toes freely. If you can, the boots are not too tight for you, the blood will still circulate and you should be free from the horrors of gangrene and cold toes.

Cooking and eating

For this pleasant pastime you will need a stove, something to cook in, something to eat out of, something to eat with and (very importantly) something to carry water in.

A water container should hold between one and two litres and can be of any shape or design that takes your fancy. The solid plastic army types are the most robust. The thin aluminium ones are lighter but more fragile. Modern bladder-type bottles are excellent and take up no space in your luggage when not in use. They come in various sizes, up to 4 litres. The best of all of these is the us Army two-litre bladder with insulated cover, belt clips and shoulder strap. One rule applies for all water bottles, though. Put anything other than water in them and they will be tainted for life.

The essential part of the 'something to eat with' is a general-purpose blade. This will cut up anything you want to eat into manageable portions as well as whittle sticks and slice your tongue open if you lick it once too often. Beyond this, you only need a spoon. Anything more is redundant. Save the weight by cutting down on the number of utensils you take rather than by using flimsy 'camping' ones that bend the first time you use them.

For those who are into time and motion, what you eat out of is also what you cook in. Those who find this idea displeasing will know best what they want. However, when you look for a cooking/eating billy, make sure of two things. Firstly, it should have a good handle (preferably one that will not get too hot to hold while cooking is in progress). Secondly, it must have a close-fitting lid. This, too, must have a handle, allowing it to be lifted on or off or be used as a frying pan by those terrible people who can suffer fried eggs and bacon for breakfast.

There are many styles of billy available to choose from. I use a one-litre 'paint tin' type because I like the shape and enjoy hanging it over wood fires. Others choose the rectangular army-type mess tins. These fit nicely into the side pocket of a rucksack and can be filled with snack foods and brew kit.

Now let us look at the more complex subject of stoves. The choice here is between solid, liquid or gas fuels. Solid fuel comes in blocks that resemble white cough candy. A packet fits neatly into the metal tray that you burn them in. The whole affair is little bigger than a pack of playing cards. The system is foolproof since you merely set a match to the blocks and add more for extra heat, or take away for less heat. The fuel is resistant to water, though you may have trouble lighting it if it is damp. Its main drawback is that it does not produce an intense heat and so it is slow to use. It also produces noxious fumes and so should not be used in an enclosed space.

Moving on to liquid-fuel stoves, your choice increases considerably. Most simple of all is the meths burner. Here you have a container into which you pour meths and then set fire to it. The more sophisticated (and expensive) sets have a windshield built round the container, and which also neatly holds the billy. Again the design is foolproof. Its advantages include a clean-burning flame and quite a range of burners, from basic and inexpensive to high-tech and costly. However, the fuel is relatively expensive and may be difficult to get hold of if you are off the beaten track. Furthermore, the rate of burn cannot be controlled. The choice is simply on or off.

Still in the liquid fuel range, there are the pressurised burners that run on either paraffin or petrol. The burner for paraffin is the well known Primus stove. Though it is a relatively complicated device, compared with other stoves, it can be readily mastered. Once burning, the flame is intense and efficient and can be adjusted to give various rates of heat. As a fuel, paraffin is cheap and almost universally available. The disadvantages of pressurised paraffin are that a small amount of a second fuel must be carried to prime the stove, which will also need some maintenance. However, Primus stoves are known in most parts of the world, so spare parts should not be too much of a problem.

An alternative to pressurised paraffin is pressurised petrol. Again, this type of stove is quite complicated and needs occasional maintenance. Furthermore, it usually demands to be fed unleaded petrol, so buying fuel could present problems. Like paraffin, however, it burns hot and fast, heating quickly and efficiently. Petrol and paraffin also produce noxious fumes and both should be used in a well-ventilated space.

Gas stoves are simple to use. They are relatively cheap to buy but are expensive to run. They burn cleanly and the flame can be controlled, but when pressure runs low the flame stays stubbornly and annoyingly feeble. You can usually find somewhere to buy replacement canisters, but in out-of-the-way places the cost will be high. The little Camping Gaz canisters that are ubiquitous around Europe are difficult to find in the Third World and you are not allowed to take them on planes. Unlike paraffin, gas is not an everyday fuel in most places. Using gas stoves in low temperatures is inadvisable as their performance drops dramatically.

As with most areas of equipment, there is now a stove to beat all stoves. This is the multi-fuel stove. It can run on any type of liquid fuel you care to feed it, including (apparently) vodka, should you be so inclined. It comes with an attachment that screws directly into a regular metal fuel bottle, and so the burner itself has no fuel reservoir, making it much lighter and smaller than conventional stoves. The fuel runs through a hose to the burner and will be subject to frequent blocking if using poor-quality fuel, so constant maintenance is needed. Should you be interested in buying one, be prepared to spend a lot.

Once again, compromise is often the solution. You will generally find that a pressurised paraffin stove is the tried and trusted one used on most formal expeditions, and is the general favourite of many. I find solid fuel a handy last resort to have available when you are travelling light and having difficulty lighting wood fires. Gas fuel is simple to use in all but extreme conditions. You pays your money and you takes your choice.

Last thoughts

With so much wonderful equipment around, it is easy to get carried away and want to buy the best of everything: a large rucksack to carry a five-season down bag with a Gore-Tex bivi-bag, a 'superstove' and a geodesic dome tent. Thankfully, most people's pockets refuse to support such notions.

In reality, if you think carefully about the use to which your equipment will be put, you will often find that the 'best' is not suitable for you and that you are just as well off with something cheaper. Then, when your style of travelling or camping does demand the best, the expense becomes worthwhile and supportable. So do not end up being parboiled in a five-season sleeping bag that only ever gets uses in summer. The money could be better spent elsewhere. ❧

MARTIN ROSSER is a freelance writer and self-professed vagabond.
His writing and travelling have taken him to Africa, Australia and Europe.
PAUL GOODYER is the founder and Managing Director of Nomad
Travellers Store and Medical Centre.

The ultimate kit list
by Jack Jackson

IF YOU HAVE A ROOMY VEHICLE, ARE NOT WORRIED ABOUT WEIGHT and are not constantly on the move, you might as well plan to make yourselves as comfortable as possible. Do not stint on things that seem frivolous before you leave but can make an enormous difference to morale. This is particularly true if camping.

Fragile items and paperwork, which must be kept away from dust and water, are best kept in cases with watertight silicone gasket seals. These come in many sizes, with foam inserts that you can customise to fit fragile equipment. These cases are so effective that even if you have descended a thousand feet down an escarpment, you have to release the purge button before you can open them.

Cases containing clothes can be sealed with strips of foam. Good strong cases are now available in polypropylene, but are usually styled in awkward rounded-off shapes. Fibre suitcases are available in squared-off shapes that pack more efficiently, but they loose their shape if they get wet. Using cleats to lash the baggage down will keep things in place and cut down on annoying rattles.

If you plan to sleep outdoors without a tent you will need a mosquito net in many areas. There are several types on the market, but they are not usually big enough to tuck in properly all the way round the mattress, thus ensuring that no gaps have been left. The best types are designed like a tent, with supporting poles and a sewn-in groundsheet. Ex-military mosquito nets have the extra advantage of needing only one point of suspension; a camera tripod or ice axe will do for this if there is not a vehicle or tent nearby.

Malaria is an increasingly serious problem, so it is worth getting a net that is already impregnated with insecticide. On a long journey, carry a can of the correct insecticide to re-impregnate the net every so often.

If you do sleep without a tent, make a note of where the sun should rise and position yourself to be in the shade at dawn, or the sun could wake you up earlier than you would like.

A full-length roof rack covered in plywood not only makes a good sleeping platform but acts as a double skin, keeping the vehicle cooler in sunny conditions.

Mattresses

You should not sleep directly on the ground in cold places, so use some form of insulation. Air-beds are very comfortable and are preferred by some to foam, but they do have disadvantages: they are generally too heavy to carry unless you have a vehicle and inflating them is hard work. Thorns and sunlight both work against them and you will certainly spend a lot of time patching holes.

If you decide to use one, be sure it is made of rubber and not plastic, and only pump it up until it is half-full. If you inflate it any harder you will roll around and probably fall off. Perspiration condenses against the surface of air mattresses, and on cold nights you will wake up in a puddle of cold water unless you have put a blanket or woollen jumper between yourself and the mattress.

Camp beds tend to be narrow, collapse frequently, tear holes in the groundsheet and soon break up altogether. Even worse, cold air circulates underneath the bed because your body weight compresses the bedding. Only several layers of blankets under you will give you the insulation you need.

Open-cell foam mattresses are comfortable but often too thin, so it is best to have two thicknesses, or else to put a closed-cell foam mattress, such as a Karrimat, on the ground and an open-cell foam mattress on top of it. Open-cell mattresses wear quickly, but if you make washable cotton covers that fully enclose them, they will last for several years. Foam mattresses, being bulky, are best wrapped in strong, waterproof covers during transport. One advantage of foam mattresses is that the perspiration that collects in them evaporates very quickly when they are aired, making them easy to keep fresh and dry. Remember to give the foam an airing every second day.

The most popular mattresses these days are self-inflating ones. As with air-beds, a blanket or sweater between your sleeping bag and the mattress will help to keep you warmer in really cold climates.

Closed-cell foam mats, such as the Karrimat, also come in a 3 mm thickness, which is suitable for putting under a groundsheet for protection against sharp stones or ice, where otherwise the tent groundsheet could stick to the ice and be torn when trying to get it free.

On a long overland trip, you can combat changing conditions with a combination of two sleeping bags. First get a medium-quality, nylon-covered, down sleeping bag and, if you are tall, make sure it is long enough for you. This bag will be the one you use most often for medium-cold nights. Secondly, get a cheap all-synthetic bag, i.e. one filled with artificial fibre. These cheap, easily washable bags are best for use alone on warmer nights and outside the down bag for very cold nights. Make sure the synthetic bag is big enough to go outside the down bag, without compressing the down bag when it is fully lofted up.

In polar and high mountain areas, the golden rule when travelling is never to be parted from your own sleeping bag, in case a blizzard or accident breaks up the party. This would hold true when travelling anywhere that is cold.

Furniture and utensils

If folding chairs or stools are covered with cotton, the fabric rots quickly in intense sunlight; take nylon- or Terylene-covered chairs instead. Full-size ammunition boxes are good for protecting kitchenware and make good seats, too.

When buying utensils, go for dull-grey aluminium billies. The shiny type tend to crack and split with repeated knocks and vibration. Billies, pots and pans, plates, mugs, cutlery, etc., should be firmly packed inside boxes, with cloth or thin foam separating metal utensils and cutlery or they will rub against each other and become covered in a mass of metal filings. A pressure cooker will guarantee sterile food and can double as a large billy so, if you have room, it is a good investment.

Kettles with lids are preferable to whistling kettles, which are difficult to fill from cans or streams. For melting snow and ice, it is best to use billies. Aluminium billies are best bought at Army and Navy auctions or surplus stores. If you are flying to the Third World, good alternatives will be readily available in local markets.

A wide range of non-breakable cups and plates are available, but you will find that soft plastic mugs leave a bad after-taste, so it is better to pay a little more and get melamine. Stick to large mugs with firm, wide bases that will not tip over easily. Insulated mugs soon become smelly and unhygienic because dirt and water get between the two layers and cannot be cleaned out.

Many people like metal mugs, but if you like your drinks hot you may find the handle too hot to touch or burn your lips on the metal. Melamine mugs soon get stained with tea or coffee, but there are cleaners available. Alternatively, Steradent tablets are a perfectly adequate and cheaper substitute. Heavyweight stainless steel cutlery is much more durable than aluminium, something to remember when planning a long expedition.

Ex-military plastic jerrycans are best for carrying water as they are light-proof. This means algae will not grow inside – as it does with normal plastic containers.

Stoves and gas

The 2.7 kg cartridge or the 4.5 kg gas cylinder are the best sizes to carry. Gas is the easiest and cleanest fuel to use for cooking.

Liquid petroleum gas is usually called Calor Gas or butane in the UK and by various oil company names worldwide, such as Shellgas or Essogas. Though available worldwide, there are different fittings on the cylinders in different countries and these are not interchangeable. Where you use a pressure-reduction valve on a low-pressure appliance, there will always be a rubber tube connection. Make sure that you carry some spare lengths of the correct size of rubber tubing.

Gas cylinders are heavy and refilling can be difficult. Refillable Camping Gaz cylinders, as supplied in Europe, are intended to be factory refilled, but in some countries, Algeria, Morocco and Yemen, for example, they are available with an overfill release valve, so that you can fill them yourself from a larger domestic butane gas supply.

In Asia, enterprising campsite managers and gas suppliers have discovered ways of filling gas cylinders from their supply. You should stand well clear while they do this as the process involves pushing down the ball valve with a nail or stone, then over-filling from a supply of gas kept under higher pressure. This operation can cause flare-up problems when the cylinder is first used with standard cooking equipment, so if you use such a source of supply it is advisable to release some of the pressure by opening the valve for a couple of minutes (well away from any flame) before connecting up.

Lighting any stove is always a problem in cold climates or at altitude. Local matches never work, unless you strike three together, so take a good supply of the household size. The best solution seems to be a butane cigarette lighter, kept in your trouser pocket where it will be warm. Remember to carry plenty of refills.

There are many good camping gas stoves available, but when cooking for large groups outside, I prefer to use the large cast-iron gas rings used by builders to melt bitumen. These are wide and heavy, remain stable when very large billies are used and do not blow out in the wind. In cold areas, try to get propane gas instead of butane.

If gas supplies are a problem, there are good twin-burner stoves that use unleaded petrol or kerosene. There are single-burner, multi-fuel stoves, that will also operate on diesel fuel.

Space blankets

Space blankets are, on the evidence, not much better than a polythene sheet or bag. Body perspiration tends to condense inside them, making the sleeping bag wet so that the person inside gets cold. In hot or desert areas, however, used in reverse to reflect the sun, they are very good at keeping a tent or vehicle cool during the heat of the day. If necessary, a plastic sheet or space blanket can be spread over a ring of boulders to make an effective bath; they are also ideal for making desert stills.

Buying

When buying equipment, be especially wary of any shop that calls itself an expedition supplier but does not stock the better brands of equipment. All the top-class equipment suppliers will give trade discounts to genuine expeditions or group buyers, such as clubs or educational establishments, and some, such as Field and Trek and Cotswold Camping, have special contract departments for this service.

Check-list

For a party of four with no worries about travelling light:

1. Good compass, maps and guidebooks, plus a Global Positioning System (GPS) receiver if travelling off-road.
2. Selection of plastic bags for packing, waste disposal, etc.
3. Clingfilm and aluminium foil for food and cooking.
4. Large bowl for washing up and washing.
5. Four 20 litre water cans – strong ex-military type (polypropylene).
6. Fire extinguisher.
7. Large supply of paper towels, toilet paper, scouring pads, dishcloths and tea towels.
8. Large supply of good matches in waterproof box and/or disposable lighters.
9. Washing-up liquid for dishes (also good for cleaning mechanics' greasy hands).
10. Frying pan.
11. Pressure cooker.
12. Selection of strong saucepans or billies.
13. Kettle with lid (not whistling type, which is difficult to fill from cans or streams).
14. Tin opener – good heavyweight or wall type.
15. Stainless steel cutlery.
16. Plastic screw-top jars for sugar, salt, washing powder, etc (Nalgene are the best).
17. Large, sharp bread knife.
18. Two small, sharp vegetable knives.
19. Kitchen scissors.
20. Large serving spoon and soup ladle.
21. Plates and/or bowls for eating.
22. Wide-base mugs that do not tip over easily.
23. Good twin burner for your gas supply, otherwise petrol or kerosene twin-burner cooker – multi fuel single-burner stoves are available that will work with diesel fuel.
24. Good sleeping bags or sleeping bag combinations for the climate expected, plus mattresses of your choice.
25. Mosquito nets.
26. Combined mosquito and insect repellent spray.
27. Battery-powered fluorescent light.
28. Four lightweight folding chairs.
29. Short-handled hand axe, for wood fires.
30. Thin nylon line to use as clothes line, plus clothes pegs.
31. Washing powder for clothes.
32. Two separate six-metre lengths of plastic tubing, one to fill water tank or water cans. the other for fuel cans.
33. Two tubes of universal glue/sealant.

34. Chamois leather.
35. Sponges.
36. Six heavy rubber 'tie downs'.
37. Water purification filters plus tablets or iodine as back-up.
38. Phrasebooks/dictionaries.
39. Two torches plus spare batteries.
40. Ordinary scissors.
41. Small plastic dustpan and brush.
42. Soap, shampoo, toothpaste, towels.
43. Medical first aid kit, plus multivitamins and rehydration salts.
44. Elastic bands, sewing kit and safety pins.
45. Cassette player and selection of cassettes (it is not advisable to use CD players in rough conditions).
46. Selection of reading material, including books on local flora and fauna plus AA multilingual vehicle parts guide.
47. Hidden strongbox and money belt.
48. Passports, visas, travellers' cheques, cash, vaccination certificates, car papers, insurance papers, UK and international driving licences, permission to drive letter (if you do not own the vehicle), photocopies of travel and medical insurance policies and six (per person) spare passport photographs.

Many other things can be taken along, but most of these are personal belongings. They include: dental floss; waterproof watch; tissues (good for many other reasons besides blowing your nose); clothing, including a tie (for men) for formal occasions (store it rolled up in a jar with a lid) or a dress (for women on that same occasion), jackets, waterproofs, gloves, swimming costume, sweaters, parkas with hoods; moisturising cream; toothbrush; comb; Swiss Army knife; Leatherman-type tool or SpydeRench; camera; film; photographic accessories; anti-malaria tablets and salt tablets, where required; sun barrier cream; sunglasses; medicines; spare prescription spectacles if worn; insurance papers; airmail writing paper; envelopes and pens.

If you carry a portable computer, make sure that it is protected by a padded, waterproof case, can be charged from the vehicle battery and is regularly backed up to removable media to cover failure of the hard disc or computer theft. If you can afford, it there are also portable satellite telephones that will work anywhere in the world you can get to in a wheeled vehicle. ✒

Food on the move
by Ingrid Cranfield

L IVING A REGULAR LIFE, IN ONE PLACE MOST OF THE TIME, people get to know what foods they like and dislike, and they base a balanced diet on this rather than on textbook nutrition. The problem is, how do you ensure you will have good food on the move? When travelling, you are faced with new foods and can easily lose track of how you are eating, simply because your rule-of-thumb menu-planning breaks down. This can lead to fatigue, a lack of energy and even poor health.

Eating nutritiously

Essentially there are two ways of coping. You can either pick up local food as you travel, or you can take with you all your needs for the duration. Eating local food may give you a feeling of being closer to a country's way of life, but could also make you severely ill. Taking your own supplies is safe and very necessary if you are going into the wilds, but how do you stop your palate becoming jaded with endless supplies of dried food?

It is sensible to be able to recognise the constitution of all foods and to know what is necessary to keep you well fed. A balanced diet breaks down into six main areas: sugars, carbohydrates, fats, proteins, minerals/vitamins/salts and water all are necessary, some in greater quantities than others.

SUGARS: Technically called simple sugars, these are the simplest form of energy-stored-as-food. Because they are simple, the body finds them easy to absorb into the bloodstream – hence the term blood sugar. From here sugars are either turned directly to energy, or are stored as glycogen. The brain is very partial to using sugars for energy and if it is forced to run on other forms of food energy it complains by making you feel tired, headachy, and a bit wobbly-kneed.

Though it is important to have some sugars in your diet, try not to depend on them. Weight for weight they give you fewer calories than other foods. Also, if you take in lots of sugars at once, the body will react by over-producing insulin because your blood sugar is too high, so that in the end your blood sugar is taken down to a lower level than before. If you desperately need instant energy, try to take sugars with other food types to prevent this happening. While travelling, it is simple enough to recognise foods with lots of sugars – they are sweet. In less developed areas, sugar is still something of a luxury, so there will be less temptation.

CARBOHYDRATES: Carbohydrates are complex structures of simple sugars. Plants store energy as carbohydrate while animals store food energy as fat or glycogen. Carbohydrates have to be broken down into simple sugars by the body before they can be used as energy, so it takes longer to benefit from them after eating. Weight for weight, however, you will get three or four times more calories from carbohydrates than from sugars. Carbohydrates are stodgy, starchy and very filling: breads in the West, mealies in Africa, rice in the East. Most food energy comes from carbohydrates, so find the local equivalent and base a diet around it.

FATS: Next to carbohydrates, most of our energy comes from fats. Our bodies store energy as fat, because it is the most efficient way to do so. Weight for weight, fats give you nearly three times the energy of carbohydrates, so they are an extremely efficient way of carrying food energy.

Fats, of course, are fatty, oily, creamy and sometimes congeal. Foods high in fat include butter, dairy foods, etc., although there are other high fat foods that are less well known, such as egg yolk or nut kernels. Fats are necessary now and again because one reclusive vitamin is generated from a fat and, more obviously, because without these concentrated doses of energy it would take a lot longer to eat all the food you need, as with cows or elephants.

PROTEINS: One of the most misunderstood types of food in the West is protein. Traditionally thought of as something essential, and the more the better, the truth is that for adults very little is needed each day, and bodies in the West work very hard to convert unnecessary protein into urea so that it can be flushed away.

Protein is used to build and repair bodies, so children need plenty of it, as do adults recovering from injury. Otherwise, the amount of protein needed each day is small – maybe a small egg's worth. Other than that, protein cannot be readily used for energy, and the body does not bother converting it unless it is heading for a state of starvation. Those people on a red meat diet are using very little of the protein it contains, relying on the fat content which can be up to 45 per cent. When you are wondering where protein appears in your food, bear in mind that protein is for growth, so young mammals have protein-packed milk, unhatched chicks have their own supply in the meat of an egg, and to help trees off to a good start there is a healthy package of protein in nuts.

MINERALS, VITAMINS AND SALTS: All of these are essential for all-round health and fitness. Most of them cannot be stored by the body and so they should be taken regularly, preferably daily. Ten days' shortage of Vitamin C, for instance, and you feel run-down, tired and lethargic – perhaps without knowing why.

In the normal diet, most of your minerals and vitamins come from fresh fruit and vegetables. If you feel that you may not get enough fresh food, take a course of multivitamin tablets with you for the duration of your travels. They do not weigh very much and can save you lots of trouble.

If you are getting your vitamins and minerals from fresh foods, remember that they are usually tucked away just under the skin, or in the skin itself. Polished and refined foodstuffs have lost a lot, if not all, of their vitamins, minerals and fibre.

As regards salts, there is little cause for concern. It is easier to take too much than too little, and if you do err on the low side your body tells you by craving salty foods. Do not take salt tablets, you could upset your stomach lining.

How much to eat?

Nutritionists have a term for the amount of food energy needed to keep a body ticking over – the basal metabolic rate. Take a man and put him in a room at ideal temperature, humidity, etc., and make sure he does no work at all except stay alive, and he will use about 600 kCal in a day. This is his basal metabolic rate.

Those of us who do not lie stock still in a room all day need energy over and above that basic amount, to work and to keep warm. For living and working in average conditions, our daily energy requirement rises to about 2500 kCal. If you are going to be physically active (backpacking, say) in a temperate climate, your energy use will go up to around 3500 kCal per day. If we do the same hard work in an extremely cold climate, our energy rate could go up to 5000 kCal. To require more than this, we would need to do an immense amount of work or have an incredibly fast metabolism. Sadly for women, they do not burn up nearly as much energy doing the same work as men.

A little experience will tell you whether you need a little more or a little less than the average. With this knowledge, you are ready to plan just how much food you need to take for the number of days you are travelling. When you come to work out amounts of various foodstuffs that make up your calorie intake for the day, books for slimmers or the health conscious are invaluable. They list not only calories, but often protein and other nutritional breakdown. Nutritional information is also given on the packet of most foodstuffs.

Eating safely

Before handling food of any kind, always wash your hands in water that has been chlorinated or otherwise purified. This is especially important in developing countries when you may have been in contact with unhygienic materials.

Eating in developed countries is not entirely hazard-free. You should remember that Delhi Belly is no respecter of language and is just as likely to strike in Spain as in India. The rules for avoiding tummy trouble are: stick to foods that are simple and hygienically prepared, and as close as possible to those you know and love – at least until your digestive system slowly adapts to change.

Always look for food that is as fresh as possible. If you can watch livestock being killed and cooked or any other food being prepared before you eat it, so much the better. Do not be deceived by plush surroundings and glib assurances. Often the large restaurant with its questionable standard of hygiene and practice of cooking food ahead of time is a less safe bet than the wayside vendor from whom you can take food cooked on an open fire, without giving flies or another person the chance to contaminate it.

Buying foodstuffs: the rules

■ Rice and other grains and pulses will probably have preservatives added to them. These will need to be removed by thorough washing as they are indigestible.
■ In developing countries, canned, powdered and dried foods are usually safe to eat, provided they are made up with purified water. Staples such as flour and cooking oils are nearly always safe.
■ Meat, poultry, fish and shellfish should look and smell fresh and be thoroughly cooked, though not over-cooked, as soon as possible after purchasing. They should be eaten while still hot or kept continuously refrigerated after preparation. Protect freshly bought meat from flies and insects with a muslin cover. Eggs are safe enough if reasonably fresh and thoroughly cooked.
■ It is wise to avoid steak tartare and other forms of raw meat in the tropics, as

there is a risk of tapeworm. Meat that is just 'on the turn' can sometimes be saved by washing it in strong salty water. If this removes the glistening appearance and sickly sweet smell, the meat is probably safe to eat.

■ Cold or half-warmed foods may have been left standing and are therefore a risk. Boil such meats and poultry for at least ten minutes to destroy bacteria before serving. Remember that hot spices and chillies do not sterilise meat.

■ Milk may harbour disease-producing organisms (tuberculosis, brucellosis). The 'pasteurised' label in underdeveloped countries should not be depended upon. For safety, if not ideal taste, boil the milk before drinking. (Canned or powdered milk may generally be used without boiling for drinking or in cooking.)

■ Butter and margarine are safe unless obviously rancid. Margarine's keeping qualities are better than those of butter. Cheeses, especially hard and semi-hard varieties, are normally quite safe; soft cheeses are not so reliable.

■ Vegetables for cooking are safe if boiled for a short time. Do check, though, that on fruit or vegetables the skin or peel is intact. Wash them thoroughly and peel them yourself if you plan to eat them raw.

■ Moist or cream pastries should not be eaten unless they have been continuously refrigerated. Dry baked goods, such as bread and cakes, are usually safe even without refrigeration.

■ Ice-cream is especially to be avoided in all developing countries.

■ Fruit juice is safe if pressed in front of you.

In restaurants, the same rules apply for which foods are safe to eat. Restaurants buy their food from shops, just as you would.

Off the beaten track

There is no right menu for a camping trip, because we all have slightly different tastes in food and there is an almost endless number of menu possibilities. So, what should you pack? Here are a few points you will want to consider when choosing the right foods: weight, bulk, cost per kg.

Obviously, water-weighted, tinned foods are out. So are most perishables – especially if you are going to be lugging your pantry on your back. You will want only lightweight, long-lasting, compact food. Some of the lightest, of course, are the freeze-drieds. You can buy complete freeze-dried meals that are very easily prepared: just add boiling water and wait five minutes. They have their drawbacks, however. First, they are very expensive. Second, even if you like these pre-packaged offerings, and many people do not, you can get tired of them very quickly.

A much more exciting and economical method is to buy dehydrated foods at the supermarket and combine them to create your own imaginative dinners. Dried beans, cereals, instant potato, meat bars, crackers, dry soup mixes, cocoa, pudding, gingerbread and instant cheesecake mixes are just a few of the possibilities. But do not forget to pack a few spices to make your creations possible.

Most people tend to work up a big appetite outdoors: about 0.9 kg to 1.2 kg of food per person per day is average. How much of which foods will make up that weight is up to you. You can guess pretty accurately about how much macaroni or cheese or how many pudding mixes you are likely to need.

Last, but not least, what do you like? If you do not care for instant butterscotch pudding or freeze-dried stew at home, you will probably like it even less after two days on the trail. And if you have never tried something before, don't take the chance. Do your experimenting first. Do not shock your digestive system with a lot of strange or different new foods. Stick as closely as possible to what you are used to in order to avoid stomach upsets and indigestion. And make sure you pack a wide enough variety of foods to ensure you will not be subjected to five oatmeal breakfasts in a row or be locked into an inflexible plan.

After purchasing your food, the next step is to re-package it. Except for freeze dried meals or other specially-sealed foods, it is a good idea to store supplies and spices in small freezer bags. Just pour in your pudding powder, salt or gingerbread mix, drop an identifying label in, to take all the guesswork (and fun) out of it, and tie a loose knot. Taking plastic into the wilderness may offend one's sensibilities but it works well. Out in the wilds, you learn just how handy these lightweight, flexible, recyclable, moisture-proof bags really are.

Although cooking over an open fire is great fun, many areas do not allow and cannot support campfires, so don't head off without a stove. When choosing a stove, remember that the further off the beaten track you go, the more important size, weight and reliability become. Aside from a stove, you will also need a collapsible water container, means of water purification, and a heavy bag in which to store your soot-bottomed pans. You will need individual eating utensils: spoon, cup and bowl will do. Also take a few recipes with you, or learn them before you leave. You can even have such luxuries as freshly baked bread, if you are prepared to make the effort. Here are some tips about camp cooking, learned the hard way.

1. Cook on a low heat to avoid scorching.
2. Taste before salting (the bouillon cubes and powdered bases often added to camp casseroles are very salty: don't overdo it by adding more).
3. Add rice, pasta, etc., to boiling water to avoid sticky or slimy textures and add a knob of butter or margarine to stop the pan from boiling over.
4. Add freeze-dried or dehydrated foods early on to allow time for rehydration.
5. Add powdered milk, eggs, cheese and thickeners to recipes last when heating.
6. When melting snow for water, do not let the bottom of the pan go dry or it will scorch (keep packing the snow down to the bottom).
7. Add extra water at high altitudes when boiling (water evaporates more rapidly as you gain altitude) and allow longer cooking times – 20 minutes at 1000 m, for example, as against ten minutes at sea level.

CLEANING UP: soap residue can make you sick. Most seasoned campers, after one experience with 'soap sickness of the stomach', recommend using only a scouring pad and water. Boiling water can be used to sterilise and, if you have ignored the above advice, is good for removing the remains of your glued-on pasta or cheese dinners. Soak and then scrub.

Use these recyclable plastic bags to store leftovers and to carry away any litter. Leave the wilderness kitchen clean – and ready for your next culinary delight. ❧

INGRID CRANFIELD is a freelance writer and broadcaster.

A place to stay

Hotels for business travellers
by Carey Ogilvie and Sue Walsh

THE COST OF ACCOMMODATION AND FOOD undoubtedly eats up the biggest chunk of the business traveller's budget. Even in these post-recession times, it should be a high-priority area for most companies that send their executives abroad with any frequency. Seasoned business travellers often complain about the high prices of scheduled air fares yet, paradoxically, these same people are quite willing to pay the full rack rate in a five-star hotel when, more often that not, they could have got a much better deal for comparatively little effort.

This article by no means guarantees unbeatable prices at five-star hotels, but it will point you in the right direction and even get you additional benefits.

If you turn up at a hotel without prebooking, you will more than likely be offered a room on the rack rate. However, if you work for a large corporation, and your company regularly sends employees to that hotel or hotel chain, it is more than likely that a corporate rate will have been negotiated. Some hotels will offer corporate rates to any *bona fide* business traveller, although in most cases you will have to book a number of rooms to qualify.

Travel agents, clubs and associations are able to offer corporate rates, which they will have negotiated on behalf of their clients. These rates offer savings of between ten and 15 per cent off the published rates. The level of discount will depend on the volume of room nights the agent or company gives the hotel or hotel chain. Some hotel companies will offer agents who book a high number of clients with them a preferred corporate rate, which could represent a saving of up to 30 per cent on the rack rate. Guests staying on a preferred rate often receive added benefits as well as savings. For example, some hotels will give complimentary upgrades, subject to availability at check in. For these reasons, smaller corporate business, individual business travellers and businessmen who travel to a wide variety of destinations could consider joining WEXAS' travel club or IAPA (the International Airline Passenger Association). These companies negotiate discounts of between ten and 80 per cent worldwide. Such savings are greater than individual travellers or small- to medium-sized firms could ever hope to achieve. For example, at the time of going to press, WEXAS quotes a rate of 22,500 Spanish pesetas at the four-star Melia Madrid, compared to the published rate of 31,300 Spanish pesetas; 1400 French francs at the four-star deluxe Concorde St Lazare in Paris, compared to a rack rate of 1950 French francs; and 1080 Hong Kong dollars at the five-star Great Eagle in Hong Kong, as opposed to a published rate of 1950 Hong Kong dollars.

It is worth remembering that often the best deals of all can be obtained on your behalf by the firm you are visiting. In the Gulf or Far East, for example, local banks and trading houses often have financial stakes in the cities' better hotels. So it is a good idea to ask them to book your room as their influence may secure you a more competitive rate in a better room.

With budget in mind, off season rates are another option for the business traveller, whose travel is not limited to the school holidays. Many three-, fou and five-star hotel chains offer seasonal rates during quieter times of year, with savings of up to 50 per cent. Some hotels will offer a flat discount, and in other cases the rate will be made to look more attractive by value-added benefits that may include breakfast, free use of the health club and a late check out. Such schemes include the Great Affordable programme offered by Leading Hotels of the World.

Some hotel companies have year-round packages for individual business travellers, which they sell alongside their package and corporate rates. Initially these may look more expensive, but the additional benefits they offer mean they quickly pay for themselves. For example, if you book a non-discounted room rate at one of the city Shangri-la hotels in the Far East you automatically receive free return airport limousine transfers, free laundry and dry cleaning, complimentary breakfast, free local telephone and fax calls, IDD calls and faxes at cost and a late check-out. For the resort properties, you receive complimentary breakfast, free daily buffet dinner or an equivalent credit on room service or at any of the resort's dining facilities, free non-motorised water sports, free laundry, late check-out and IDD calls and fax at cost. Inter-Continental's Global Business Options provides a choice of upgrade to a club room or suite, full breakfast or double air miles.

> *It's the business of hotels to be one step behind the times – hotels, like colonies, keeping up a way of life that is already outmoded.*
> – ALAN BENNETT

As with airlines, some hotels offer APEX bookings (advance purchase rates). Guests must be prepared to book up to 30 days in advance in return for savings of up to 30 per cent. Marriott, Starwood, Hilton and Forte all offer APEX rates. Beware though, APEX bookings sometimes require full prepayment and have very steep penalties if you amend or cancel your booking.

All major chains have internet sites that provide valuable information on their properties. However, it can be very time consuming to check and compare offers made by the individual chains. Once again, that is where your travel agent or club can do a search for you to check the best possible rate at *all* the major chains.

Which hotel?

Location is a particularly important factor for the business traveller because, invariably, he or she will need to be near a city's business or financial centre. City hotels also tend to pamper the business traveller because more businessmen and women stay in their hotels than budget-conscious tourists. However, with the current buoyant market, major cities are running much higher occupancy levels and are therefore not as generous as they were some years ago.

It goes without saying that airport hotels are, on the whole, places to be avoided. They can be worthwhile, however, if you need a room for a day on a stopover, so you can have a wash and a rest, or if you need somewhere for business meetings. They are geared to short stays and odd arrival and check out times and will be far more likely to accommodate you than the most interesting city centre hotels. As a general hotel principle, small is beautiful. In anything under 50 rooms, more attention to detail and character are to be expected.

After location, the main factor in choosing a particular business hotel will be the facilities it offers. Many companies are prepared to pay for executives to stay in hotels with a wide range of facilities and benefits as it is felt that the advantages of less stress and a more comfortable hotel stay will result in a more successful and, ultimately, more profitable business trip.

Another factor that has come into play is the business executive's choice of hotel loyalty awards. Frequent flyer schemes were launched in the States by the major US airlines in the early 1980s and the hotel industry followed suit. Today virtually every major hotel group has its own reward programme for frequent guests and the majority of hotel loyalty programmes have travel industry partners. For example Hyatt Hotel's loyalty programme is called Gold Passport and is linked to Aeromexico, Qantas, American Airlines, Cathay Pacific, British Airways, Continental Airlines, Lufthansa and Singapore Airlines, to name a few, as well as Alamo Rent-a-car and Avis car rental companies. These loyalty clubs are a huge success, giving the member rewards and the hotels a database of guest information.

Most hotel chains do not charge for joining their frequent guest programme, basing the level of your membership (and subsequently the level of benefits) on the number of stays per calendar year. The Starwood Preferred Guest Programme covering Westin, Sheraton Hotels, Four Points Sheraton, St Regis, the Luxury Collection and the W Hotel brands is free; as is the Bass Priority Club Worldwide, which covers Inter-Continental and Crowne Plaza Hotels and resorts, Holiday Inn Express hotels, Holiday Inn Garden Court hotels and Staybridge Suites.

Rates are not normally affected by the hotel loyalty cards, however members of the frequent stayer schemes often receive priority booking, free upgrades subject to availability and early or late check outs, all of which enhance the business traveller's stay and, in turn, can save money. In addition, points can be collected and redeemed for travel packages, specially selected merchandise, room upgrades, free weekend stays and even free flights.

Airline frequent flyer schemes also attract travel partners in the shape of hotel chains. Executives who predominantly use one airline will tend to use associated hotel chains to boost their air miles.

What's in a room?

Long gone are the days where the only amenities a business traveller would find in his or her room were a telephone and a teasmaid. Today hotels try and offer not just the home away from home but the office away from the office.

Even with the laptop explosion, many hotels still provide a business centre – but these are being replaced by business accessories within the room itself. Modem points are almost statutory in all room categories, but hotels are offering additional benefits for the frequent business traveller in upgrading standard rooms to contain larger desk space, personal fax machines, multiple telephone lines, personalised voice mail and even personalised business cards for use while in-house.

Starwood offers 'smart rooms', which are specifically designed as a luxury bedroom and a fully functioning office. Marriott has 'the room that works', a scheme which includes bright direct lighting, an adjustable ergonomic chair, voicemail and multiple data ports.

Executive floors

Most business hotels offer an executive or club floor for business travellers. This is usually on the top floor of the hotel and is designed to offer privacy and a premium service. Benefits normally include superior accommodation and additions such as express check in, late check out, use of an executive or club lounge, which normally offers breakfast and evening cocktails on a complimentary basis, plus complimentary use of small meeting rooms. Other advantages may include a meet and greet service at the airport, complimentary use of health facilities, express laundry and dry cleaning service.

Despite the rush of the average business trip and the range of priorities of the individual business traveller, this group of travellers is in a very good position to get the most out of the hotels they use while away. More and more, hotels are gearing themselves towards their needs and making every effort to solicit and keep their valuable custom. The key is, of course, information, which is where the travel agent comes in, but equally the business traveller who wishes to have value for money must be aware of the increasing amenities available and expect more. ❧

SUE WALSH and CAREY OGILVIE work in the travel industry.

On a limited budget
by Pat Yale

AFTER TRANSPORT, ACCOMMODATION is likely to burn the biggest hole in budget travellers' pockets. Luckily this is one area where economies can still be made. The cheapest accommodation is of course completely free. Sadly, there's not much of it. In a few parts of the world it is fine to sleep on beaches. However, not only are the rules subject to unexpected change and the whim of the local police, but beach bums are deprived of necessities such as washrooms, making this an unsatisfactory way to pass more than the odd emergency night. Those with a tent may find local farmers prepared to let them use their fields and facilities, but such *ad hoc* arrangements tend to depend on negotiating skills.

Some Indian and African Sikh temples also offer free accommodation. Don't expect luxury – one large bed may serve for any number of visitors. Nevertheless staying in a temple can be a magical experience, offering the chance to find out about the religion at the same time. Visitors must abide by prohibitions on smoking or drinking on the premises, but will often be included when the post-service sweetmeats are being handed out. The communal meal or *langar* at Sikh temples is open to all. While there is rarely an official fee, most temples appreciate a donation and may keep a visitors' book indicating what is expected.

Networking can also produce free accommodation. Members of the Globetrotters Club (The Friends Meeting House, 52 St Martins Lane, London WC2; www. globetrotters.co.uk; no telephone number) can sometimes stay with fellow members in other countries. Home-owners can also swap their homes with others (see *Home exchanges* article).

Travellers who hitch or use public transport may find themselves invited to stay with people they meet on the way. This can be the perfect way to find out about a place, but in developing countries may mean staying in houses without running water or toilets, and where conventions, particularly concerning women, may be very different from those at home. The tradition of hospitality to strangers, especially in Muslim countries, is still strong and may mean someone going without to provide for the guest.

It pays to be aware of local customs: in some countries anything a guest admires must be given to them; in others refusing food can cause offence. Clearly women must be especially careful about accepting offers of hospitality, particularly in Islamic countries where such offers will often come from men. If you decide that you would like to take up offers of hospitality, you should squeeze suitable thank-you presents into your backpack – pictures of London, British coins, malaria pills and biros often do the trick.

Organised camping is the next best option, particularly in Europe and North America where there are lots of well-equipped sites. The main snag, unless you have a vehicle, is carrying the tent and cooking equipment. However, many companies now sell lightweight tents.

Campsites are frequently in the middle of nowhere: in developing countries you may find that by the time you have added the cost of getting to and from them to the site fee, it is cheaper to stay in a budget hotel or in a hostel. Staying in hostels can minimise accommodation costs while also ensuring you meet other travellers. There are more than 5,000 International Youth Hostel Federation hostels and most are open to members of all ages, with priority going to younger members at busy times. Although you can usually take out temporary membership on the spot, it is often cheaper to join before leaving home.

Although hostels vary in character, many have cut back on previously rigid regulations, staying open all day and removing the nightly curfew. The standard of accommodation has improved too, with central heating, cooking facilities and relative privacy. In developing countries, some serve as long-stay accommodation for the homeless. In Europe expect noisy school parties. Incidentally, despite their name, YMCA/YWCA hostels are not usually any more restrictive than other hostels.

If you want to stay in cheaper hotels you must normally rely on guidebooks and recommendations; travel agents and tourist offices rarely keep details of budget accommodation. If you haven't got a guidebook, the best hunting ground is likely to be near bus and railway stations (for a good night's sleep make sure you get a room at the back of the building).

In Europe the *pension* equivalents of British bed and breakfasts generally omit the breakfast. As with the more expensive hotels, some *pensions* are subject to tourist board inspection, ensuring reasonable standards. Travel agents usually charge for booking hotels, however cheap. Instead, get the address from a telephone book in the library reference section. If possible write in the relevant language, and enclose a Post Office international reply paid coupon. If you prefer to phone but would find this difficult, British Telecom's translation service can work out cheaper than paying an agent to make your booking – call the international operator on 155 for details. To cut down communication costs, use central reservation offices for cheaper hotel chains such as Travelodge.

Finding budget accommodation in the United States can be difficult, and package deals often offer excellent value. The US Tourism Administration has details of companies that can make bed and breakfast bookings. Groups of three or four people can reduce costs by sharing twin rooms, which often have two double beds. Avoid extra costs by carefully observing the latest check-out times, and never make phone calls from your room.

In developing countries, rooms costing a mere couple of pounds a night may be furnished with a bed and chair only. Where dormitories are more popular than individual rooms, some will not accept women travellers. Even when they do, the same rooms double as children's nurseries, guaranteeing sleepless nights. Before accepting a very cheap room, check that the fan works, that the door locks properly, that the window will close and is fitted with mosquito-protection where appropriate, that there are no peep-holes in partition walls, that the walls reach right to the ceiling and that there are no tell-tale signs of bed bugs, ants or other insects. Then check the state of the toilets and the water supply (in Islamic countries the *hammams* or public baths make private baths and showers less important).

For my part I try to take things as they come, with cheerfulness, and when I cannot get a dinner to suit my taste, I endeavour to get a taste to suit my dinner.
– WASHINGTON IRVING

Try and pair up with someone else before booking in, in order to avoid being charged a single supplement. Train travellers can evade accommodation costs if they are prepared to sleep sitting up in frequently crowded conditions. Within Europe you'll get a better night's sleep at a reasonable price by opting for a *couchette*, a sort of fold-down shelf-bed which comes much cheaper than a true sleeping berth. Bear in mind that not everyone can sleep through a train's stopping and starting and that ticket collectors often time their visits for the early hours. Outside Europe, some sleeping cars offer an experience not to be missed. Nairobi to Mombasa sleepers, for example, have fold-down sinks and dining cars of near-Orient Express splendour. Their route also ensures that you wake up with the Tsavo National Park drifting past your bedroom window.

Taking a camper van or caravan with you obviously eliminates accommodation costs. However, few budget travellers can afford the initial outlay, the extra ferry fares and the high cost of petrol. Nevertheless, package deals to the US including a camper van offer excellent value for money.

A cautionary note on false economy. In some parts of the world, hotel prices are ludicrously low in comparison with the UK. In Udaipur (India) it is possible to stay in the usual pound-a-night pit; however, you could also stay in the fairytale Lake Palace Hotel, once a maharajah's palace, for a fraction of what anything remotely similar would cost at home. Likewise in Yangon (Rangoon) you can find a cheap room or upgrade to the fading colonial Strand. Now that Raffles in Singapore has been resurrected in a new guise with London-style prices, it's worth snapping up the real bargains that still remain to be had. ✒

PAT YALE is the author of 'The Budget Travel Handbook' and lectures in tourism issues. She has travelled extensively through Europe, Africa, Asia and Central America, frequently alone and always on a shoestring.

Youth hostelling
by Emma Crump, Liz Lloyd and Amy Sohanpaul

THE TERM 'YOUTH HOSTEL' IS RAPIDLY BECOMING A MISNOMER. For one thing, most hostels are open to all people of all ages in virtually every country where they are located. And, fortunately for the budget traveller, many have started to offer more than the old concept of just a bed for the night (if you returned before the evening curfew).

If you're planning a trip on a limited amount of money, it's worth enquiring about membership and hostels before you set out. As the largest, and perceived by many as the most reliable budget accommodation in the world, the International Youth Hostel Federation tends to be a safe first port of call. Membership (£12.50 for adults; £25 for families and £6.25 for under-18s, for residents of England and Wales) brings a wide range of discounts, a guide to youth hostels and regular member magazines, along with an introduction to a worldwide network of 4,500 hostels in 60 countries in Europe, Asia, Africa, the Americas and the Pacific. You can join in your home country or take out international membership on arrival at most hostels. Alternatively, you can often stay at hostels without being a member, but may have to pay a bit more. In general, prices are low enough to enable the budget traveller to spend precious funds on exploring the country.

Standards vary widely – you'll get the best reviews by speaking to fellow travellers and asking around. Youth hostels belonging to the International Youth Hostel Federation (look for the distinctive blue-and-white sign) are safe bets as they are required to sign up to rigorous standards of cleanliness and security. The ethical traveller may be reassured to know that these hostels also have to meet 'care for the environment' guidelines.

Hostel accommodation has come a long way since the days of huge dormitories and unfriendly opening times. It isn't unusual to find small comfortable bedrooms with *en-suite* or adjacent facilities; and many hostels have single, double and family rooms which are popular and need to be booked well in advance. Depending on the hostel's location, you could benefit from a full catering service or self-catering kitchens geared to the needs of the traveller. Many hostels have bars and serve drinks with meals or welcome adults who wish to 'bring their own'.

The other big improvement in recent years has been the disappearance of 'lockouts' during the day and of curfews in the evening. In the main, opening times now vary to suit the visitor, with many city centre hostels staying open right around the clock. Other services available at popular tourist destinations include foreign exchange, travel deals, email facilities, activity breaks and guided walks along national trails.

While all hostels try to meet uniform standards, this doesn't mean that they are as bland as some cheap hotel chains. Hostels are certainly much much cheaper, they provide more social contact with other travellers, and each youth hostel is a unique experience. You won't wake up in Toulouse thinking you're in Toronto; but neither will you be so anxious about holding onto your money belt that you can't get your documents out in peace. Hostels are secure and friendly, offering a real sense of place. The old notion of asking each hosteller to undertake a chore before departure has largely disappeared, but a helping hand is still welcome, particularly in smaller rural hostels which are often run by volunteers. This spirit of camaraderie is part of the hostelling ethos and creates a feeling of belonging and ownership amongst members, which can be useful if you're suffering from travel stress or an unexpected bout of homesickness.

Hostels of the world

Youth hostelling started in Germany in 1907 and there are now over 600 hostels there. These are often larger than average and of a high standard. They are very popular with school groups. Priority is given to the under-27s; in Bavaria there is a maximum age of 26 imposed by local legislation, for those who are not group leaders or accompanying their children.

France has 200 youth hostels, ranging from the Alps to the Mediterranean and from Brittany to Paris. For instance, you can stay right in the heart of the medieval city of Carcassonne or in the popular ski area of Chamonix Mont Blanc, for only

Hostellers' websites

There are a number of websites which will help you further. Try the International Youth Hostel Federation website www.iyhf.org or www.hostels.com . Both provide information on hostels around the world and answers to frequently asked questions. Many Youth Hostel Associations have their own sites where accommodation can be booked online or additional information sought. For England and Wales, visit www.yha.org.uk, while information about Youth Hostels in Scotland can be found at www.syha.org.uk; Northern Ireland on www.hini.org.uk, and the Republic of Ireland on www.irelandyha.org. A full list of American hostels is available on www.hiayh.org.

72 French francs. In Italy there are 70 hostels in cities ranging from Venice to Rome as well as in the countryside – where some are even 'green hostels' in areas of particular environmental interest.

In Malaysia, it's possible to sample the bright lights of Kuala Lumpur or Penang, or the simplicity and peace of Melaka Beach very cheaply indeed, by checking into one of the country's five hostels.

New Zealand's 55 youth hostels are well placed in city centres, national parks and prime scenic areas. They are particularly well equipped – try the hot pool at Rotorua. Australia's youth hostels span the country. They range from big, well-serviced hostels on the tourist trails, to tiny places offering the chance to experience the 'outback', where you collect the key from a neighbour.

Hostels in Brazil have on average only 50 beds and are very cosy. Most stay open 24 hours a day, leaving you free to *samba* until the small hours. In Costa Rica, hostels follow ecological conservation regulations based on sustainable development. Each hostel has something different, from Spanish courses to white-water rafting.

South Africa's emerging tourist industry is well served by youth hostels. The Baz Bus, aimed at backpackers, picks up and drops off travellers at hostels along the way. One of the highlights is Sondzela Backpackers, located right inside the lovely Mlilwane Wildlife Sanctuary in the Ezulwini Valley: here you can see wildlife on foot, from a bicycle or on horseback.

There are 140 youth hostels in America, covering major cities and popular national parks and rural attractions. Extensive hostel chains can be found in California, Florida, Colorado, Alaska, the Pacific north-west and the north-eastern States. In Canada, you might not believe you're in a youth hostel as you walk into the elegant Canadian Alpine Centre/Lake Louise Youth Hostel, with its internationally renowned restaurant and every amenity for the ski-board enthusiast. Likewise at Banff Youth Hostel, a mile up the hill from Banff town at scenic Tunnel Mountain. Both have interactive information and email kiosks and bring skiing within the reach of the budget traveller. ❧

EMMA CRUMP and LIZ LLOYD work for the Youth Hostelling Association.

Taking a timeshare
by Kim Winter, Michael Furnell and Diana Hanks

THE MAJORITY OF PEOPLE BELIEVE THAT TIMESHARING is something new which has only developed over the last fifteen years or so, but in fact it is not really a new concept: as far back as the eighteenth century, villagers were timesharing water in Cyprus where there was no piped supply.

Property timesharing is believed to have started in the 1960s, when certain French developers of ski apartments experienced difficulties in selling their leisure accommodation outright, and decided instead to offer for sale the ownership of weekly or fortnightly segments at the same time each year for ever.

The idea spread to other parts of Europe, including Spain. On the Costa Blanca, a British company that was building apartments in Calpe offered co-ownership of two-bedroomed flats in the main shopping street near the sea. Prices were as little as £250 per week's usage in the summer in perpetuity. Winter periods were even cheaper, at £180 for a month, and easy terms were available on the payment of a £50 deposit, with the balance payable at £4.50 per month over three years.

The Americans soon recognised this form of holiday home ownership, and in the early stages converted condominiums, motels and hotels – non-viable in their original form – into time-share units. Often these had rather basic facilities, and it is only in recent years that developers in Florida and elsewhere have realised that top-quality homes with luxury facilities are the key to successful multi-ownership.

It was not until 1976 that timesharing was launched in Britain. The first site was in a beautiful loch-side location in the Highlands of Scotland. This was a luxury development with excellent sporting facilities and prices were set from about £5,000 per week.

How it works

The aim of timesharing is to provide luxury accommodation in return for a once-only capital sum is paid at current prices. Future holidays are secure without the need to pay hotel bills or holiday rents – though buyers still need to pay an annual sum to cover maintenance expenses and local taxes, as well as buying flights and food. Timeshares are sold by a variety of methods, and prices vary according to season and the quality of accommodation. In 1998, about 1.2 million European families owned timeshares. In 1996, there were over 1,410 European resorts (4,500 world-wide), over 3.5 million owners world-wide and at least 108 resorts in the UK itself. When a freehold is purchased, as in Scotland, the period of time that you buy is yours to use forever, and you may let, sell, assign or leave the property to your heirs. In England and Wales, the law permits ownership only for a maximum of 80 years, but in many parts of the world ownership in perpetuity is possible.

An alternative is membership of a club which grants the right to a club member to use specified accommodation in a specified property for either specified weeks in the timeshare calendar or for 'floating time' in the high/medium/low season time band (selecting your weeks annually for a stated number of years is an alternative scheme). Under this arrangement, the assets of the property (i.e. buildings, lands and facilities) are conveyed (or leased) to custodian trustees (often a bank or other institution), which holds the property for the benefit of the club members. The rights of all owners collectively are regulated by the club constitution. This legal structure works well both in the UK and, with modifications, overseas.

A third alternative is to buy 'points' in a timeshare club, which allows considerable flexibility for taking two short breaks of less than a week's duration, for example, rather than owning a specified week or weeks in a specified timeshare resort.

The formation of a public limited company, with the issue of ordinary shares varying in price according to the season and apartment size, is another form of holiday ownership, although not strictly a timeshare arrangement. Each share provides one week's occupancy for a set period, usually 20 or 25 years. The properties are sold on the open market and the proceeds divided among shareholders.

One company uses capital contributed by participants to purchase land and build holiday homes in various parts of Europe. Each member is entitled to holiday points, to be used for a vacation of a week or more in a chosen development at any time of year.

Another provides for the sums paid by participants to be converted into a single-premium insurance policy. Part of that premium is invested in fixed-interest securities and another portion is used to acquire properties (over 400 in about 20 locations). 'Bondholders' pay a user charge to cover the maintenance cost of the property for each week's holiday taken, on a 'points per week' basis depending on the accommodation's size, location and season chosen. Investors are permitted to cash their bonds (the price of which is quoted daily in the financial press) at any time after two years. A capital sum is repaid on the death of the bondholder, the amount being determined by the age at which the holder took out the insurance policy. Such bond schemes are subject to legal regulations which do not apply to timeshare arrangements.

Over the past few years, various schemes have sprung up that are not covered by timeshare legislation. These include 'trial packs', which act like a conventional timeshare but for a period of only 35 months; holiday clubs, where buyers pay for holidays up to ten years in advance and apply to the promoter for the accommodation they are interested in (usually timeshare resorts); and holiday or travel packs, where buyers join a club, paying around £3,000 for access to low-cost travel and accommodation (again, usually in timeshare resorts). Check out these offers very carefully: some promoters have been found to have no links with the resorts they are offering, so it may be very difficult for them to book you the accommodation you want, and if the promoter goes bust a few months after you have paid your money up-front, your chances of receiving a refund are pretty slim.

Golden rules

The rules to remember when buying a timeshare home are:

■ Do some research. Read up about the timeshare concept and the resorts available in Europe. Compare resorts to find the most suitable.

■ Buy from a well-established developer or selling agent who has a reputation for fair dealing and offering really successful schemes. Second-hand timeshares bought from a reputable resale agency are usually considerably cheaper than those bought from a developer.

■ The location of the property is vital, so be sure to select a well-situated development with adequate facilities and a quality atmosphere. Be sure that it appeals to the whole family, so that you are all able to enjoy regular visits. If you are likely to want to resell or exchange in the future, the location will prove even more important to your choice.

■ Remember that the UK Timeshare Act 1992 and the Timeshare Regulations of 29 April 1997 provide for a 14-day cooling-off period for those who are in the UK when they sign a purchase agreement (the actual location of the timeshare resort is irrelevant). The regulations also ban the company concerned from taking any deposit from you within those 14 days. However, the EU Directive on timeshare, which came into force in the member states on 29 April 1997, provides for a minimum ten-day cooling-off period rather than 14 days, and some member states allow deposits to be taken by third parties (for example a trustee/escrow account). Check what cooling-off period is allowed before signing any contract.

■ Get the contract checked, preferably before you sign it. A solicitor can check the wording of agreements relatively easily, but it will be a considerably greater task – and thus more expensive – to consider the occupation rights granted, the nature of the developer's title, details of any mortgages or encumbrances on the timeshare property, the granting of correct local planning permission, the legal structure of the scheme in the context of that country's property laws, the effects of jurisdiction, the safeguards for monies paid for an unbuilt or incomplete property and the arrangements at the termination of the period of lease. Your solicitor should also scrutinise the documentation and perform independent checks regarding payments held in trust pending the issue of title documents, club membership certificates and a licence to use. Is the trustee reputable?

■ If all the amenities promised by sales staff are not already in existence, obtain a written commitment from the vendors that they will be completed, and by when.

■ Check carefully the annual maintenance costs and be sure you know what they cover. Part of the yearly charges should be accumulated in a sinking fund by the management company to cover replacements, new furnishings and regular major redecorations. Be careful of extra levies to cover refurbishments.

■ Ascertain the rights of owners if the builder or management company gets into financial difficulties, and ascertain if it is possible for the owners to appoint a new management company if they are not satisfied with the service of the original one. Show the constitution and management agreement to a specialist lawyer to determine that the title is safeguarded and occupation rights protected. Talk to other owners to find out their views on the relationship between the owners and the management company.

■ If you wish to have the flexibility to swap world-wide, the timeshare resort should be affiliated to an exchange organisation, such as Resort Condominiums International (RCI) or Interval International. Check any claim to affiliation.

Investment

Timesharing is not a conventional money-making investment in property, although some owners who purchased time in the earliest schemes have enjoyed substantial capital appreciation over the past ten years. Essentially, you are investing in leisure and pleasure, but you cannot expect inflation-proof holidays. What you are buying is vacation accommodation at current prices. Expenditure on travel, food and entertainment is likely to rise in future years according to the rise of inflation.Owners who sell their timeshare a few years after buying are likely to get back considerably less than they paid for it. The number of owners wanting to sell their timeshare significantly exceeds the number of people wanting to buy; so if you only want to hold a timeshare for a few years it would be worth comparing the cost of alternatives.

Exchange facilities

It became clear a while ago that after a few years many timeshare owners may want a change of scene for annual holidays; as a result, organisations grew up to arrange exchange facilities for timesharing owners. There are exciting possibilities for owners wanting to swap their seaside apartment in, say, England's West Country, for a contemporary-style bungalow in Florida or an Andalucian pueblo in Spain. Today there are two major exchange organisations operating in the UK: RCI and Interval International.

There is normally an annual membership fee payable by each family wishing to join the exchange system. The developer usually pays this for each family for the first two or three years as a purchase inducement. An additional fee is due when an exchange is successfully organised.

Further information

Organisation for Timeshare Europe, 15/19 Great Titchfield Street, London W1P 7FB, tel 020 7291 0901. This is the European trade association for timeshare, representing the interests of developers, exchange organisations, resale companies, marketing organisations and finance companies. It has a code of ethics for members and offers an advisory and conciliation service to people dealing with its members.

Timeshare Consumers Association, Hodsock, Worksop, Nottinghamshire S81 0TF, tel 01909 591100, email info@timeshare.org.uk, website www.timeshare.org. uk. Produces useful fact sheets offering advice on various aspects of timeshare.

The Department of Trade and Industry publishes *The Timeshare Guide*, available free from its Consumer Publications order line on 0870 1502500 (quote reference URN 97/643). The text is available at www.dti.gov.uk/access/timeshare. ❧

KIM WINTER is Managing Editor of 'Holiday Which?' magazine.
MICHAEL FURNELL is the author of 'Living and Retiring Abroad'.
DIANA HANKS is has worked for the Timeshare Council.

Home exchanges
by Heather Anderson and Amy Sohanpaul

LOOKING FOR AN ALTERNATIVE HOLIDAY? Had enough of package tours that herd you into tower-block hotels with rooms the size of your wardrobe at home? If you are looking for a more comfortable base for your holiday which allows you to see a country and its culture in a more natural setting, then a home exchange could be the right holiday for you. Imagine what it would be like to have a

Home exchange companies

HomeLink International
Tel 01344-842642, website www.homelink.org.uk. Publishes five directories a year. Membership £95 for all five directories (around 12,500 listings). Fee includes internet listing for the full membership year.

Intervac
Tel 01225 892208, website www.intervac.co.uk. Publishes five directories a year. Membership £92 for one directory (around 5,500 listings) plus £27 each for the other four (around 1,000 listings in each. Fee includes internet listing for the 3-4 months (until the next directory is published). If you buy the next directory, your on-line listing period is extended.

Home Base Holidays
Tel 020 8886 8752, website www.homebase-hols.com. Publishes three directories. Membership £70 for all three (around 2,000 listings). Fee includes internet listing. Shares listings with Green Theme (below).

Green Theme.
Tel 01208 873123, website www.gti-home-exchange.com. Publishes three directories. Membership £55 for all three (around 2,000 listings). Fee includes internet listing. Shares listings with Home Base Holidays (above).

five-star holiday anywhere in the world, with all home comforts, and nothing to pay except travelling expenses? Around 50,000 people do just that by swapping their homes for a holiday.

Home exchange holidays started more than 40 years ago, and there are now a number of companies which help make it all possible. The oldest and largest, HomeLink International, has over 12,500 members in 50 countries. Others include Intervac, Home Base and Green Theme with between 2,000 and 9,000 members each. The procedure is relatively simple. Each member is listed in a directory with a detailed description and a photograph of the home, and contact details. Members give preferred holiday destinations and dates, although many are fairly flexible about both. It is then up to individuals to contact other members with whom they wish to exchange. Membership fees range from around £60 for the smaller companies to £95 for the largest.

The appeal of the home exchange concept is based on the mutual trust and bond of friendship that is built up between members as they correspond and get to know each other in the weeks before their exchange holiday. Ideally a swap should be with a like-minded family or group of a similar size, so both will feel at home, and will look after the property well. Devotees claim that once you have experienced a holiday in the luxury of someone else's home, it is very hard going back to those cut-price hotels and self-catering apartments with their minimalist furnishing and mini fridge.

Others have had more sobering experiences, finding themselves in unsuitable accommodation or returning to find their home looking decidedly scruffy. It depends on how you organise your exchange. Anyone wishing to exchange properties can advertise in a suitable publication, and there are numerous companies around. Whichever method is used, make sure that every eventuality has been covered and agreed in writing. If using a company, it does pay to pick carefully. Those that 'vet' clients thoroughly are obviously safer to exchange through. If you are unsure about anything, check and check again with the company. *Bona fide* organisations will take time to answer all your queries. In general you're safer with a long-established company that has built up a reputation.

The internet has had a big impact on the way home exchange companies operate, and made swapping disasters less likely as some companies, including HomeLink, will give you access to their on-line listings database (minus members' personal details), so that you can see what's on offer before you join. This will help you to determine whether the type and number of homes available and the range of destinations appeals to you. HomeLink also provides a facility for members to amend their on-line listing whenever they want, and they provide hot lists of last minute exchange offers.

The key point when looking for a suitable organisation is the number of members you can contact or who can contact you, as this factor will largely dictate how successful you will be in finding an exchange for the dates you want and in your choice of country. When HomeLink member Elsie Butler listed her average three-bedroom house, she was surprised by the response. The directories are published in December and by March she had received over 60 offers – letters, faxes, emails from all over the world. Elsie and her family took the offer of spending Christmas in Sydney followed by two weeks in France during the summer.

Once you have taken the plunge and got your listing into a directory, you will be provided with comprehensive advice on how to set up an exchange.

Seven easy steps to a successful exchange

1. Describe your home honestly in your listing and in all correspondence.
2. Leave your home clean. Standards of cleanliness vary, so make sure that floors are cleaned and rooms dusted, refrigerator emptied, oven grease-free, and with special attention to bathrooms and kitchen. No need to repaint the house! Leave space on shelves and in wardrobes and drawers so that your guests can empty their suitcases.
3. Compile a 'Guide to Your Home and Surroundings' which should include local tourist information and household notices about the use of electrical appliances, pet and plant care, etc. Phone numbers of a recommended doctor, dentist, babysitter, good restaurants, and helpful friends are always welcome too.
4. Use your Exchange Agreement form to avoid misunderstandings. If necessary, clarify who pays what in terms of telephone, gas and/or electric bills, and staple foods such as flour, sugar, oil, etc.
5. If arrangements are such that you cannot meet, arrange for a family member, neighbour or friend to call in and welcome your exchange partners when they arrive.

6. It has become a tradition amongst exchangers to leave a small gift of welcome: a bottle of wine or champagne, a local speciality. Always a pleasant surprise.

7. Close the door, turn the key, and go off on your holiday knowing that your home is in the good hands of another member just like you.

So is home exchanging the right type of holiday for you?

Yes:

- ☐ If you find hotels or self-catering too impersonal or restricting.
- ☐ If you're outgoing and enjoy experiencing other lifestyles.
- ☐ If you're a good organiser.

No:

- ☐ If you can't be flexible about dates and destination.
- ☐ If if you haven't got neighbours willing to be friendly to your guests.
- ☐ If if you would be too embarrassed even to let a cleaner into your home. ೕ

Heather Anderson is Managing Director of Homelink International.

Ways to go

By train
by Keith Strickland

'I HAVE SELDOM HEARD A TRAIN GO BY AND NOT WISHED I WAS ON IT,' wrote Paul Theroux at the start of *The Great Railway Bazaar*, his account of a train journey from London to Tokyo. Commuters on the London Underground or the New York Subway might not share this sentiment, but for those of us with a more relaxed attitude to time, there's nothing quite like the anticipation of boarding a train, settling into a window seat, and letting the pleasure of travel take over. For trains are more than just a means of getting from A to B.

At one extreme, they give the traveller an insight into the everyday life of the countries they serve. To see and experience India away from the main tourist attractions, there is no better way than to take the train. Railway stations themselves are a microcosm of Indian life. The homeless and beggars may spend their whole time cooking, drinking, washing, and sleeping on platforms. Then there are the tradesmen – *chai wallahs*, booksellers, stallholders – and, of course, the crowds.

At the other end of the spectrum, South Africa's *Blue Train* from Cape Town to Johannesburg has gold-tinted windows, *haute cuisine* and *en-suite* accommodation, and is generally reckoned to be the world's most luxurious train.

You can take a train for a one-off trip, or you can spend your whole holiday on one. Sometimes there is no alternative form of transport – unless you are a mountain climber, the only way of ascending the Jungfrau in Switzerland is by rail.

Planning the journey

Wherever you want to go, planning is essential. In some parts of the world, trains run much less frequently than in the UK. There's a line in Patagonia whose regular train plies only once a week. Miss it and you have to wait seven days for the next.

The most comprehensive guides are Thomas Cook's *European Timetable* and *Overseas Timetable*. Both include shipping services as well as railways; both concentrate on major routes. For minor lines, one must consult local timetables. The best known is Newman's *Indian Bradshaw*, which contains every passenger train on the 35,000 miles of India's rail network. Sometimes there is no way of getting advance information. In parts of South America, the timetable consists of nothing more sophisticated than a handwritten poster or a blackboard at the local station.

Tickets

1. No railway administration likes ticketless travellers. You might just get away without paying in places such as India, especially if you enjoy riding on the carriage roof, but in many countries fines are stiff for passengers without valid tickets. The same goes for riding first class with a second-class ticket.

2. Train travel can be incredibly cheap, particularly in developing countries. If you want relative comfort and space, use first-class accommodation (if it's available) – you won't have to raise a mortgage.

3. There is now a proliferation of discounted tickets. Age, time and day of the week, advance purchase, duration of journey – all may have a bearing on the price you pay. Rover tickets offering unlimited travel within a country or geographical area are real value for money. Finding out about the best buys is, however, not always easy. High-street travel agents are not the best informed when it comes to rail travel. Try to find one who specialises in railways, such as Ffestiniog Travel. As a general rule, it pays to book as much of your overseas journey as you are able to in the UK before you set out. This will save you money, as well as possible hassle later on. A lot of patience is sometimes required if you try to book locally. The sale of tickets is not always the relatively speedy process it is in the UK.

Luggage

Travel light. It's amazing, when looking at pictures of Victorian travellers, to see the massive trunks they took with them. What did they pack?

The station porter may be a rare species in Britain but flourishes elsewhere – at a price. Even so, a mass of luggage is an encumbrance on a train. Pack essentials only. Choose according to the length of the journey and the climate of the country.

A word about security. Petty theft is a fact of life almost everywhere. Unattended luggage is easy game. Remember that in many developing countries the value of a camera may equate to several months' average wage. Keep money and other valuables on you. If you have to leave baggage, make sure it is locked and try to chain it to some immovable object such as the luggage rack. Above all, make sure you have adequate insurance.

Food

On long train journeys, find out in advance if food and drink are likely to be available. On-board catering should be indicated in the timetable, though standards and prices vary enormously. South African dining cars offer superb food and wine at modest prices. France is disappointing – food on the high-speed TGV is no better than average aircraft-style meals. Catering on the *Trans-Siberian Express* is, by most people's accounts, hardly bearable.

Don't overlook the possibilities of station restaurants, though Western stomachs should be wary of platform vendors, especially in Asia. Their wares look colourful but can have devastating effects. Similarly, treat local drinks with caution. Peru has its own version of Coke – green Inca Cola – as nauseating to look at as to drink. *Chai* (sweet, milky tea) is the safest drink at an Indian railway station and the cry of the *chai wallah* is a distinctive feature of train journeys.

Health

The first item in my personal medical kit is a bottle of eye drops – essential for countries where trains are still pulled by steam engines. Sooner, rather than later, the inevitable smuts will be acquired.

Other than this, there are no special health hazards associated with trains, assuming you won't be riding on the roof or hanging onto the sides. But a long journey is not the best way to pass the time if you are unlucky enough to be ill, and on-board 'bathroom' facilities are pretty primitive in many places. So it's important to take the health precautions necessary for the country you are visiting.

Sleeping

There's no experience quite like sleeping on a train. Again, if you intend to do this, plan ahead. Find out from the timetable whether sleeping facilities are available, and if so, what they are. There may be a sleeping compartment with fresh sheets, its own loo, and an attendant. Couchettes are popular in some countries – beware, the sexes are not always segregated.

In India and Pakistan, sleeping accommodation means a bed-roll spread out on an ordinary compartment seat, if you're lucky; and it's worth remembering that the more important stations on the subcontinent have retiring rooms where a bed can be rented for the night.

Whatever the facilities, a supplementary fee and advance reservation are almost always essential, though greasing the palm of the conductor often works wonders in places where such dealings are a way of life.

How to travel

First or second class? Express or slow train? By day or by night? The answers depend on the money and time at your disposal, and on the aims of your journey. Do you want to be cosseted from the outside world and pampered with luxury? Do you prefer to mix with local people? It's entirely up to you. The choice is enormous. Remember one golden rule: the more comfort you want, the more you will have to pay; and the greater will be the likelihood of having to make reservations in advance. Conversely, second-class travel is cheaper, usually does not need to be booked ahead, but will inevitably be more crowded.

Incidentally, some countries have more than two classes. India has a plethora, though you won't necessarily find them all on the same train.

Suggested routes

Starting at the top of the market, the *Blue Train* has already been mentioned. In the same league is the *Orient Express*. Can there be a more romantic way to arrive in Venice than by this train of restored elegant carriages? So successful has this up-market concept been that sister trains now operate in Malaysia/Thailand and in Australia. Other trains designed specifically for the tourist trade include India's *Palace on Wheels* and Spain's *Andalucian Express*. Though the daily train that took passengers from Montreal to Vancouver and vice versa ceased running a few years ago, it is still possible for tourists to cross the Rockies by luxury train.

Canada aside, the long-distance train does survive in everyday use in many parts of the world. The *Trans-Siberian* (or *Rossiya* to use its local name) runs daily from Moscow eastwards to the Pacific coast. One can still cross the USA by rail, though not as one continuous journey. Trains travel vast distances in India, and in

China where a new 'first-class' train links Beijing and Hong Kong. The *Indian Pacific* traverses the complete width of Australia from Sydney to Perth, whilst the *Trans-Alpine* crosses the mountains of New Zealand's South Island.

There are not many railway-less countries, and the possibilities for train travel are limitless. Don't just stick to the well-known routes. Branch out and see what you discover. The most memorable journey is often the least expected. Tucked away in a remote mountainous part of Peru are the towns of Huancayo and Huancavelica. The train takes all day to go from one to the other, stops everywhere and is full of people going to market with their produce and livestock. There are tunnels, steep gradients and river gorges and, all the while, the Andes form a stunning backdrop. A humble line; an extraordinary and exhilarating experience.

Better known and in almost equally breathtaking scenery is the narrow-gauge railway linking the hill station of Darjeeling to the plains 1,800 m below. In just over 80 km, the diminutive engines of the Darjeeling Himalayan Railway climb by way of zigzags and spiral loops into the foothills with stunning views – on a clear day – of Kangchenjunga, at 8,500 m the world's third-highest mountain. Parts of the track are often washed away in the annual monsoons, and it's a wonder the line has survived, especially as the journey by road can be done in half the time it takes by rail. But if the trains are running, it's a journey not to be missed. Such is the unique character of the line that it has just been declared a World Heritage Site by UNESCO.

> *Most people have that fantasy of catching the train that whistles in the night.*
> – WILLIE NELSON

Special interests

To many, railways are a hobby; some would say an addiction. Every aspect of railway history and operation has been studied in great detail, but it is the steam locomotive that commands the most devotion. Steam has an atmosphere all of its own. One can see it, hear it, smell it, feel it and taste it. Steam buffs travel the world to experience its thrill.

China is the enthusiast's Mecca. With cheap labour and plentiful coal supplies, China was still building steam engines in the late 1980s, and there are hundreds at work on the country's railways. In contrast is Cuba, where ancient engines are brought out of retirement for the annual *zafra* (sugar harvest) to pull cane from the fields to the mills. In this steam paradise, it's possible to combine a beach holiday with the joys of watching trains.

Elsewhere, the number of countries where steam is in everyday use is dwindling. Poland and the eastern part of Germany are the only European ones. Further afield, steam lingers – just – in Zimbabwe, Indonesia, Burma and Argentina. Sadly India, long regarded as a bastion of steam, has finished with steam on all but a couple of branch lines. There is a compensating increase in museum and preserved railways, but to the purist these are a poor substitute for the real thing.

Specialist travel operators for the serious enthusiast include Steam & Safaris, Travel Bureau Railtours, and Dorridge Travel Service. Many tours include general-interest elements to cater for non-railway partners.

Train specialists

Thomas Cook Publishing
PO Box 227
Peterborough
PE3 6PU

Tel 01733 503571
Fax 01733 503596
Website www.thomascook.co.uk

Dorridge Travel Service
7 Station Approach
Dorridge
Solihull
West Midlands
B93 8JA

Tel 01564 776252
Tel 01564 770117

Ffestiniog Travel
Harbour Station
Porthmadog
Gwynedd
LL49 9NF

Tel 01766 512340
Fax 01766 514715
Website www.festtravel.co.uk

Steam & Safaris
Winhill House
Edale Road
Hope
S33 6ZF

Tel 01433 620805
Fax 01433 620827

Travel Bureau Railtours
High Street
Wombourne
West Midlands
WV5 9DN

Tel 01902 324343

Bradt Publications
41 Nortoft Road
Chalfont St Peter
Bucks SL9 0LA

Tel 01494 873478

Darjeeling Himalayan Railway Society
Membership Secretary
80 Ridge Road
London N8 9NR

Weighed down with cameras and all the accoutrements of photography, steam buffs are instantly distinguished from their fellow travellers. Do not despise them! Their motives for the journey may not be the same as yours, but they're the experts to turn to when the unexpected occurs.

Remember that trains run late the world over – sometimes very late. Occasionally they are cancelled. Connections are missed. Landslides block the line. In these circumstances, your timetable may not be much help. It's a fair bet the enthusiasts will know the solution to the problem – you hope.

Reading material

Trains are places for meeting people. You will rarely be on your own. It's only in England that strangers never converse. Nevertheless, make sure you put a good book in your luggage. Every journey has a dull moment.

Books about railways are legion. Thomas Cook has a series of handbooks for 'rail touring'; and Bradt has books on rail travel in specific countries such as India and Russia. Paul Theroux's *The Great Railway Bazaar* remains the most readable account of one person's journey. Start and you won't be able to put it down.

To appreciate the atmosphere generated by the steam locomotive, browse the transport section of any large bookshop. For a sample, your contributor immodestly suggests his own books *Steam Railways Around the World* and *Steam Through Five Continents*.

Above all, buy a timetable. It is a mine of information. My Pakistan Railways timetable tells me the cost of a bed in the retiring room at Karachi. Breakfast consists of 'choice of two eggs, two toasts with butter and jam, pot of tea'. If I want to take a rickshaw with me as part of my luggage, it will be deemed to weigh 150 kg and charged accordingly. On another page comes the solemn warning: 'Passengers are requested in their own interest not to light or allow any other passenger to light any oil stove or any other type of fire in the passenger carriages as this practice is not only fraught with dangerous consequences but is a penal offence under the Railways Act.' Fascinating! This timetable could keep me occupied for hours.

Finally, turn the pages of the timetable and look at the names of the trains. Whose imagination fails to be stirred by the *Frontier Mail, Himalayan Queen* or *Shalimar Express*?

Trains are not some sort of time capsule. They seem natural – almost a part of the landscape. They certainly reflect the characteristics and atmosphere of the countries and communities through which they run in a way air travel, cruise ships or air-conditioned road coaches can never do. Flanders and Swann put it rather differently in one of their songs: 'If God had meant us to fly, He would never have given us railways.' ❧

Keith Strickland has travelled the world for 25 years to indulge his passion for trains. He has photographed trains in 40 countries and published three books on the subject.

By bus
by Irma Kurtz

E VERY COUNTRY BOILS DOWN TO ONE-THIRD LANDSCAPE and two-thirds people. Let a traveller cover a nation from coast to coast. Let him visit every monument and admire all its natural beauties. Let him live off the fat of its land, take a million photos and send home ecstatic postcards. Unless the traveller meets locals, and learns to know them on their own turf, he will remain two-thirds short of even the foggiest notion of where on earth he has been. For any free spirit possessed of real curiosity and a degree of fortitude travelling by good old proletarian bus is an unceasing revelation: a way not just to see the country – a way to befriend it. And nowhere is this wonderful intimacy more likely to occur than in the United States of America, where the general populace is innocent of shyness or awe and the average length of a bus journey easily accommodates uninhibited confidences.

During happy months spent criss-crossing America on Greyhound Buses I met students and strippers, gamblers on their uppers, Quakers, Amish and similarly thrifty sectarians, and scores of ordinary Americans who for one reason or another – decrepitude or youth, poverty, criminality, illness or genuine concern for the planet – do not use a car. As the magnificent countryside unrolled outside the windows, loquacious strangers exchanged opinions and personal history. Occasionally overcome by a longing for silence and solitude, I learned that if I faked a hacking cough or – explain it if you can! – was seen to be writing in a notebook, new boarders gave me a wide berth. American buses are democratically filled, first-come, first-serve, and it is worth arriving early at the terminal to secure a window-seat. Sometimes, when there was no pregnant or disabled passenger with priority, I was bold enough to snare the front seat. The views through the windscreen of a Greyhound Bus – dawn waking the flatlands of Kansas, great cities gathering themselves slowly out of America' s rural heartland – are the most engulfing and dramatic on the open road. However, because of the front seat's proximity to the driver, whose authority on a long-haul bus is as absolute as a captain's at sea, its occupant is subtly raised and separated from his fellows. The position therefore tends to attract exhibitionists and snobs doing their best to show they wouldn't be there, except for the fact that their cars are in for servicing.

"There will be no smoking on this bus," said our driver on the road to Winnemucca, Nevada. "That includes them magic cigarettes. Anybody smokes them on my bus gonna find hisself magically turned into a hitch-hiker."

And the smug blonde in the front seat turned to smirk and nod at us lesser types.

Nice ordinary Americans choose the middle rows; by tacit agreement preferring to sit next to their own sex and race. Yea verily, as, since the first bus was launched, bad boys go straight to the back.

"Whenever there's trouble," said our driver into St. Louis, "I know it will come from them last five rows."

Often I chose my next stop – Dinosaur, Bald Knob, Sault Sainte Marie – simply because I liked the sound of it. My book of blank tickets, bought in advance from Greyhound's English agent, did not hold me to any itinerary. But 99 out of 100 of my fellow passengers were purposefully *en route*, some to visit family, others to job hunt, and a few to flee trouble or find a new place to make trouble, never to start it on the bus. Though we were boarded in South Texas by armed police searching for 'illegals', and by Louisiana troopers looking (fruitlessly) for a fugitive wife who had fatally ventilated her husband with a carving knife, there was no violence on board. On the contrary, whatever the boys in the back get up to – drinking bourbon camouflaged in Coke tins and cutting some quiet deals – the Greyhound Bus must be one of the safest places in the USA. Terminals, however, though heavily policed, define the wrong side of the tracks in any town, and the surrounding areas can be threatening. Fortunately, there are taxi ranks outside every station; not once was I steered wrong by a taxi driver when I asked about a clean, cheap place to stay.

The long-distance bus traveller will probably spend at least one night out of every two or three on board. Sleeping on board entails a weird descent through skin after skin of consciousness until the constant Greyhound rock and rumble finally delivers you, its passenger, into dreams. Except on Thanksgiving and holiday weekends, when all Americans go home, the neighbouring seat is likely to be free at night, and with the help of an invaluable inflatable pillow, it could be worse. Sometimes I'd wake momentarily to see the passing ghost of a small town; once I opened my eyes on a flotilla of fairyland lights that turned out to be an oil refinery outside Corpus Christi.

"But I'm not much over five feet tall, I can't imagine how you manage," I said to a six-footer on what he figured would be a four-, maybe five-day journey to Seattle from the depths of Florida.

"No problem, ma'am," he said. "I just close my eyes and curl up like a snake."

Eating, like boozing and smoking, is forbidden on American buses. Frequent rest stops allow passengers to avail themselves of a more commodious lavatory than the one on board, which is used only in emergencies. ("What do you do about the loo?" is the question most frequently put to old bus hands by bus virgins). While smokers light up, the others rush to satisfy an apparently national addiction to junk food. Too many of the stops are anonymous greasy-spoon burger chains. Once in a while, however, especially in the wild reaches of northern America, where the breadth of a smaller nation lies between cities, the regular stop is somewhere the driver is greeted by name and his 'usual' is already in the oven. For half an hour or so, passengers join authentic Americana in mom-and-pop places like, say, Del's Café. In the backroom of Del's, a bunch of local women setting up a jumble sale had stopped to try on hats and were howling with laughter.

"Won't you join us?" one of them in a fedora called when she saw me in the doorway. And, for an instant, I was truly tempted to stop and end my days as a matron of Melrose, Minnesota, population 2,235.

America is a road country, and in the modern era of one-man-one-car, the road uniting all its states can be a lonely, congested, irascible, scary place to be. But not on a big bus. On a Greyhound out of Fargo, I listened as two men behind me swapped recipes for venison sausage. A woman across the aisle had just told us a story about the ghost of a bear said to haunt a forest on Minnesota's Upper Peninsula. My neighbour, an 80-year-old local, bound for her son's home a few hundred miles down the road, began describing the old days, when all her neighbours were homesick immigrants from Russia who thought they had found a replica of the Steppes in the North Dakota landscape.

"Good-looking boys, those Russians," she said, with a big wink. "I speak pretty good Russian to this day."

From the close, safe warmth of the bus, I smiled out at the endless telephone poles etching a dusky sky: my neighbour called them "our local tree". Taking the bus is more than travelling in space: it is nearly travelling in time, too. Taking the Greyhound Bus is as close as any westerly romantic can ever again come to crossing America by stagecoach. ❧

IRMA KURTZ is the agony aunt of 'Cosmopolitan' magazine.
She is the author of several books, including 'The Great American Bus Ride'.

By cruise liner
by Tony Peisley

CRUISING HAS BEEN THE FASTEST-GROWING HOLIDAY CHOICE for travellers from Britain and North America for the past decade. Annual passengers have doubled from 4.5 million in 1990 to more than nine million in 1999, and there is no sign of this growth slowing down. New cruise ships have never been built at a faster rate. Between 1995 and 2000, nearly 50 new ships were delivered and already on the order books are another 63 for the 2000-2005 period. These 63 ships represent an investment by the cruise industry of nearly $22 billion (about £14 billion).

This is an unprecedented expansion, not just because of the number of ships but also because of their size. Most of the last 50, and the next 60-plus, will be more than 70,000-ton (a measurement of size rather than weight or displacement, by the way) and with the capacity to carry more than 2,000 passengers. A dozen will even top 100,000-ton, a size only reached for the first time in 1996 with the arrival of the 101,000-ton *Carnival Destiny*.

At the end of 1999, one line – Royal Caribbean – took delivery of *Voyager of the Seas,* the latest in a series of 1990s ships to earn the tag of the world's largest passenger ship. Only this time, she took the title by some distance. At 137,000-ton, she is three times the size *Titanic* was and twice the size of QE2. She also carries just short of 4,000 passengers and more than 1,000 crew – more people on a ship than at any time in cruising history – and among her huge range of entertainment facilities are an ice rink and a rock-climbing wall on the funnel. The ship immediately proved so popular that four sister vessels were ordered for delivery before 2004.

An even larger ship, provisionally named *Queen Mary 2*, is being built to cross the North Atlantic alongside QE2 – she will also make occasional cruises. Also owned by Cunard, she will be about 150,000-ton, although she will carry fewer passengers than the Royal Caribbean ships.

Cunard itself is now owned, along with several other lines, by the US-based Carnival Corporation, which is the largest cruise company in the world. Another US-based company, Royal Caribbean International, is number two, with the UK's P&O number three. Between them, they are building 36 of the 62 new ships currently on order and, overall, the number of cruise holidays on the market will increase by 50 per cent once they have all been delivered. By then, the number of worldwide cruise passengers should have increased to somewhere between 11 and 12 million.

Nearly six million of the nine million current cruise passengers come from North America, and the majority of them cruise in the Caribbean. The UK is the second largest cruise market, with nearly 750,000 passengers having taken ocean cruises in 1999. But the fastest-growing cruise market is Asia, where a local line, Star Cruises, has come from nowhere to a position where it is challenging P&O for the position of third-largest cruise company. Although it has recently (early 2000) bought the US-based Norwegian Cruise Line and Orient Lines brands, Star's eponymous brand has developed exclusively in Asia. Its ships cruise out of

Malaysia, Singapore, Thailand, Hong Kong, Japan and Vietnam, with some carrying Asian passengers only and others a mix of Asians, Australasians, Britons, Europeans and Americans.

Asia is also one of the destinations that features more often and more extensively in cruise line itineraries than it did a few years back. Singapore, Thailand, Hong Kong and Malaysia remain the most frequently visited countries, while first China and, more recently, Vietnam have also been opened up to cruise tourism.

Late in 1998, the South Korean shipping conglomerate Hyundai finally began operating cruises from South to North Korea. This followed tortuous political negotiations between the governments of two parts of a nation divided since the 1950s. There have been operational hiccups since then, but the cruises continue in 2000. Passengers remain exclusively South Korean, but Hyundai plans to begin selling the cruises to foreign tourists in the near future.

The huge growth in the number of cruise ships has meant that lines are constantly searching for new destinations. In the Indian Ocean, cruises are being packaged with safari holidays in East and South Africa. There are more cruises around Australia, with side tours to the Great Barrier Reef, and this trend will accelerate after the Sydney Olympics. Cruise ships were chartered in numbers to operate as hotel ships for the duration of the Games. There has been an even bigger increase in the number of ships heading for New Zealand, with its huge variety of scenic attractions, many of which are most easily accessible by sea.

> *Four hoarse blasts of a ship's whistle still raise the hair on my neck and set my feet to tapping.*
> – JOHN STEINBECK

The next 'in' places for cruisers will probably be South America and the Middle East. Until recently, South American cruises were limited to a few trips up the Amazon and Orinoco, voyages timed to coincide with the Rio Carnival, and, every other year or so, a long voyage right round Cape Horn. But, in the last couple of years, cruise lines have begun to offer full seasons of cruises round the Horn between Argentina and Chile and, from 2001, there will be regular weekly cruises from Santos in Brazil.

Cruises from the Middle East are still relatively rare, but this is also set to change. The authorities in Dubai have given the go ahead for a new, purpose-built cruise terminal as part of a drive to attract more ships. It is linking with other members of the United Arab Emirates and countries in the region to try and reduce red tape, particularly in the granting of group tourist visas, and to bring down the cost for ships calling at local ports. Even Iran has begun to appear on cruise itineraries, and Saudi Arabia could be next as the country gradually embraces the non-religious tourism it has eschewed in the past.

The size of many of the ships currently under construction does restrict where they can cruise. Some are even too large to transit the Panama and Suez Canals; and the number of passengers they carry is another barrier, as certain places simply do not have the infrastructure to cope with 2,000–4,000 passengers at a time.

There are, in any case, restrictions on the number of passengers allowed to land on the islands of Antarctica, so this keeps the mega-ships away. The largest to visit is Orient Lines' *Marco Polo*, which limits its numbers to about 500 passengers when it cruises in the region. But most of the ships that cruise there, to the Arctic and through the Northwest Passage are much smaller. They are called expedition ships, although a better term for the experience they offer is 'soft adventure' as they usually have a fair amount of home comforts on board, even if they lack the lavish entertainment facilities of the bigger ships. The most basic are the converted Soviet ice-breakers operated by Quark Expeditions, but the vessels operated by Hapag-Lloyd, Society Expeditions, Special Expeditions, Abercrombie & Kent, and Marine Expeditions offer high-quality small-ship cruise experiences. Some of the ships are of genuine five-star standard, and they all have specialist lecturers on board as well as nippy Zodiac boats to transport their passengers even closer to nature and its marine wildlife.

Slightly less adventurous but even more cerebral are the cruises of Swan Hellenic, which, after building up a reputation for high-quality cruises despite the poor quality of the ships it chartered, finally built a new ship to match its reputation. The *Minerva* now operates year-round around the world instead of only during summer, but the policy of hiring top lecturers in fields that include history, archaeology, botany, and architecture to accompany every cruise continues.

Ships that have their own history are also increasingly popular. Star Clippers made waves with its first two ships, both authentic recreations of turn-of-the-century clipper sailing ships. On these, passengers can help out with the rigging and even stand watches if they want to, while the captains regularly give sailing lessons.

In 2000, the same company added a third ship, the largest sailing vessel in the world and a recreation of a famous German sail ship. This will have more luxurious cabins and suites than its other ships. Some will even have butler service and their own private balconies. In fact, cabins with their own balconies is the other major trend of twenty-first-century cruising. At first only the five-star-plus cruise lines, such as Silversea, offered these but now some of the larger vessels among the less expensive ships have many cabins with this much sought-after extra.

Another important development has been the addition of alternative dining options on board the larger ships. This means there is no longer any need to eat at set times and at set tables – one of the previous downsides of cruising for some people. On this new breed of ship, there are bistros, pizzerias, grills and speciality Italian, Chinese, Japanese and Tex-Mex restaurants.

While ocean cruising grabs all the headlines, there has also been a steady growth of interest in river cruising and a major expansion in the choice of possible destinations. Although they are often spoken of in the same breath, ocean and river cruising offer quite different experiences.

Apart from their obvious appeal to those who are worried about seasickness, river cruises also offer a lot more time ashore than most ocean cruises. There are usually several stops a day, particularly on rivers such as the Rhine, which competes with the Nile to be the most popular river cruise destination of all. However, in recent years, popular new river cruise programmes have been established in many other countries, notably in Russia (the Volga – between St Petersburg and Moscow), Italy (the Po) and Portugal (the Douro).

The British and the Germans are the biggest fans of river cruising, with about 100,000 passengers apiece annually and the Danube and the Rhône among their other favourite destinations, but Americans also enjoy the experience and there have been a succession of new riverboats on the Mississippi and other US rivers. These are usually replicas of the original steamwheelers that plied these routes a century and more ago.

Cruising tips

■ If you enjoy dressing up, do take a smart suit or DJ or an evening/cocktail dress, for even the least formal ships have a couple of evenings where there is an (optional) formal evening.

■ Do remember to leave enough at the end of your cruise for tips. Some ships do include tips in the cruise price and others have a no-tipping policy, but on the others, allow about £5 a day per passenger.

■ Do book shore excursions as the cruise goes along. If you book loads at the start or even before you go, you might find yourself with no time to relax. Most ports, particularly in the Caribbean, can be seen just as well independently.

■ Don't worry about seasickness. Cruise ships mainly avoid the bad weather and iffy sea conditions; in any case, there are lots of preventative remedies nowadays. Ask your own doctor or the one on board.

■ Don't overdo the sunbathing, particularly on the first day. The sun is stronger at sea than it is on land and, in tandem with the cooling effect of ocean breezes, this can fool you into spending more time outdoors than you would otherwise. You can burn quickly at sea if you are not careful – and, if you do, it could ruin your whole cruise. ❧

TONY PEISLEY is a freelance journalist specialising in the cruise industry. He is a regular contributor for the television programme 'Wish You Were Here'.

By river boat
by John and Julie Batchelor

WHEREVER YOU WANT TO GO IN THE WORLD, the chances are that you can get there by river. Indeed, the more remote your destination, the more likely it will be that the only way of getting there, without taking to the air, will be by river. This is particularly true of tropical regions where, throughout the history of exploration, rivers have been the key that has opened the door to the interior. It is still the case that, for those who really want to penetrate deep into a country, to learn about a place and its peoples through direct contact, the best way to do so is by water. River travel splits neatly into three categories: public transport, private hire and your own transport.

Wherever there is a large navigable river, whether it be in Africa, South America, Asia or even Europe, you will find some form of river transport. This can range from a luxury floating hotel on the Nile to a dugout canoe in the forests of Africa and South America. And between these extremes, all over the world there can be found the basic work-a-day ferries that ply between villages and towns carrying every conceivable type of commodity and quite often an unbelievably large number of people.

Let's start by examining travel on an everyday ferry. First you must buy your ticket. The usual method is to turn up at the waterfront, find out which boat is going in your direction and then locate the agent's office. With luck, this will be a simple matter, but on occasion even finding out where to purchase your ticket can be an endless problem. Don't be put off. Just turn up at your boat, go on board and find someone, preferably someone in authority, to take your money. You'll have no difficulty doing this, so long as you do not embarrass people by asking for receipts.

Board the boat as early as possible

It is probable that it will be extremely crowded, so if you are a deck passenger you will need to stake out your corner of the deck and defend it against all comers. Make sure of your sleeping arrangements immediately. In South America this will mean getting your hammock in place, in Africa and the Far East making sure you have enough space to spread out your sleeping mat. Take care about your positioning. If you are on a trip lasting a number of days do not place yourself near the one and only toilet on board. By the end of the journey the location of this facility will be obvious to anyone with a sense of smell. Keep away from the air outlet from the engine room unless you have a particular liking for being asphyxiated by diesel fumes. If rain is expected, make sure you are under cover. On most boats a tarpaulin shelter is rigged up over the central area. Try to get a spot near the middle as those at the edges tend to get wet. Even if rain is unlikely it is still a good idea to find shade from the sun. For those unused to it, sitting in the tropical sun all day can be unpleasant and dangerous.

Go equipped

There may be some facilities for food and drink on board, but in practice this will probably only mean warm beer and unidentified local specialities which you might prefer not to have to live on. Assume there will be nothing.

Take everything you need for the whole journey, plus enough for a couple of extra days just in case. On the Zaire River, for instance, it is quite common for boats to get stuck on sandbanks for days on end. And don't forget the insects. The lights of the boat are sure to attract an interesting collection of wildlife during the tropical night, so take a mosquito net.

Occasionally, for those with money, there may be cabins, but don't expect too much of these. If there is supposed to be water, it will be only intermittent at best, and there certainly won't be a plug. The facilities will be very basic and you are almost certain to have the company of hordes of cockroaches who will take particular delight in sampling your food and exploring your belongings. Occupying a cabin on a multi-class boat also marks you out as 'rich' and thus subject to attention from the less desirable of your fellow passengers. Lock your cabin door and do not leave your window open at night. In order to do this you will also have to go equipped with a length of chain and padlock. On most boats the advantages of a cabin are minimal.

Longer journeys, especially on African rivers, tend to be one long party. Huge quantities of beer are drunk and very loud music plays through the night. It is quite likely that you will be looked on as a guest and expected to take an active part in the festivities. It's a good way of making friends, but don't expect a restful time.

Given these few common-sense precautions, you will have a rewarding trip. By the time you have reached your destination you will have many new friends and will have learned a few essential words of the local language, all of which make your stay more pleasant and your journey easier.

Private hire

In order to progress further up the river from the section navigable by larger boats, you will have to look around for transport to hire. This may be a small motor boat, but is more likely to be a dugout canoe with an outboard motor. When negotiating for this sort of transport, local knowledge is everything: who's trustworthy and who owns a reliable boat or canoe. With luck, your new-found friends from the first stage of your journey will advise you and take care of the negotiations over price. This is by far the best option. Failing that, it is a question of your own judgement. What you are looking for is a well-equipped boat and a teetotal crew. In all probability such an ideal combination doesn't exist – at least we have never found it. So we are back to common sense.

Look at the boat before coming to any agreement. If possible try to have a test run just to make sure the motor works. Try to establish that the boatman knows the area you want to go to. If he already smells of drink at ten in the morning, he may not be the most reliable man around. This last point could be important. If you are returning the same way, you will need to arrange for your boatman to pick you up again at a particular time and place. The chances of this happening if he is likely to disappear on an extended drunken binge once he has your money are remote in the extreme. Take your time over the return arrangements. Make sure that everyone knows and understands the place, the day and the time that they are required to meet you. Don't forget that not everyone can read or tell the time. If you have friends in the place, get them to check that the boatman leaves when planned. Agree on the price to be paid before you go and do not pay anything until you arrive at the destination. If the part of the deal is that you provide the fuel, buy it yourself and hand it over only when everyone and everything is ready for departure. Establish clearly what the food and drink arrangements are as you may be expected to feed the crew.

Going up that river was like travelling back to the earliest beginnings of the world, when vegetation rioted on the earth and the big trees were kings. An empty stream, a great silence, an impenetrable forest.
– JOSEPH CONRAD

Once you are on your way, it is a question again of common sense. Take ready-prepared food. Protect yourself from the sun and your equipment from rain and spray. If you are travelling by dugout canoe, it will be a long uncomfortable trip with little opportunity for stretching your legs. Make sure you have something to sit on, preferably something soft, but don't forget that the bottom of the canoe will soon be full of water.

Once you have arrived at your destination, make sure that you are in the right place before letting the boat go. If the boatman is coming back for you, go over all the arrangements one more time. Do not pay in advance for the return if you can possibly avoid it. If the boatman has the money, there is little incentive for him to keep his side of the bargain. If absolutely necessary, give just enough to cover the cost of the fuel.

Own transport

After exhausting the possibilities of public transport and hire, you must make your own way to the remote headwaters of your river. You may have brought your own equipment, which will probably be an inflatable with outboard motor or a canoe. If you have got this far, we can assume that you know all about the requirements of your own equipment. Both inflatables and rigid kayaks are bulky items to transport over thousands of miles, so you might consider a collapsible canoe, which you can assemble once you have reached this part of the trip. We have not used them ourselves but have heard very good reports of them in use under very rigorous conditions.

Your chances of finding fuel for the outboard motor on the isolated headwaters of almost any river in the world are negligible. Take all you need with you. Your chances of finding food and hospitality will depend on the part of the world you are exploring. In South America, you are unlikely to find any villages and the only people you may meet are nomadic Indians who could be hostile. You will have to be totally self-sufficient. In Africa the situation is quite different. Virtually anywhere that you can reach with your boat will have a village or fishing encampment of some description. The villagers will show you hospitality and in all probability you will be able to buy fresh vegetables, fruit and fish from the people. Take basic supplies and enough for emergencies but expect to be able to supplement this with local produce.

Another alternative could be to buy a local canoe, although this option is fraught with dangers. without knowing anything about mechanics, buying a second-hand canoe is as tricky as buying a second-hand car. You can easily be fobbed off with a dud. We know of a number of people who have paddled off proudly in their new canoe only to sink steadily below the surface as water seeped in through cracks and patches. This is usually a fairly slow process so that by the time you realise your error you are too far away from the village to do anything about it. A word or two about dugout canoes: these are simply hollowed-out tree trunks and come in all sizes. The stability of the canoe depends on the expertise of the man who made it. They are usually heavy, difficult to propel in a straight line, prone to capsize, uncomfortable and extremely hard work. The larger ones can weigh over a ton, which makes it almost impossible for a small group to take one out of the water for repairs. Paddling dugouts is best left to the experts. Only if you are desperate – and going downstream – should you entertain the idea.

Travel etiquette

When travelling in remote areas anywhere in the world, it should always be remembered that you are the guest. You are the one who must adjust to local circumstances and take great pains not to offend the customs and traditions of the people you are visiting. To refuse hospitality will almost always cause offence. Remember that you are the odd one out and that it is natural for your hosts to be inquisitive and fascinated by everything you do. However tired or irritable you may be, you have chosen to put yourself in this position and it is your job to accept close examination with good grace. Before travelling, take the trouble to research the area you intend to visit and its people. Try to have some idea of what is expected of you before you go to a village. If you are offered food and accommodation, accept it. Do not be squeamish about eating what is offered. After all, the local people have survived on whatever it is, so it is unlikely to do you much damage.

No two trips are ever the same, thank goodness! The advice we have tried to give is nothing more than common sense. If you apply this to whatever you are doing, you will not go far wrong. Just remember that what may be impossible today can be achieved tomorrow… or the next day. Don't be in a hurry. There is so much to be enjoyed. Take your time… and good luck! ❧

*JOHN AND JULIE BATCHELOR have travelled widely in Africa
and have co-written several books, including 'The Congo'.*

By cargo ship
by Hugo Verlomme

WHY, IN THIS AGE OF JET-PLANE COMMUTING, would one travel by freighter? Surely it must be a boring, wet, lonely, and above all terribly slow way to go?

In fact this is exactly why travel by cargo ship is such a pleasure. If you want to go on holiday then a cruise liner, which is a floating luxury hotel that rarely 'goes' anywhere, is for you. If you want to really travel the seas then freighters are the genuine experience. Etymologically, to travel means 'to follow a path', and not simply 'to arrive'. Robert Louis Stevenson understood the nature of leisurely travel when he wrote: 'To travel hopefully is a better thing than to arrive.'

I have indeed noticed that some of my most vivid memories have been related to unexpected events that have happened on my travels. It could be the tail of a typhoon in the China Sea, whales in the St Lawrence river or, most important of all, encounters with people – officers, crew or fellow travellers of different nationalities – of whom some have become friends.

Being on the move for days and days on the rolling hills of the ocean has been described as 'the royal way'. As we walk, drive, fly or travel overland, we tend to forget that 71 per cent of our blue planet is composed of oceans. Why limit our travelling to 29 per cent of the globe?

"But isn't the sea always the same?" is a question I have been asked many times. Anyone who hasn't seen the changing colours of the oceans – the British Channel's ochres, the Atlantic's ultramarine, the Mediterranean's lapis lazuli, the Caribbean's turquoise or the deep Pacific's indigo – might be forgiven for thinking so. The sea is an incredible, changing prospect full of surprises for those who keep their eyes open: islands, storms, calms, squalls, dolphins and whales, fish and birds, icebergs and atolls. Freighters are privileged platforms from which to observe seas and skies, human activity and marine life.

Not so long ago, liners were the standard way to reach any destination 'overseas'. These were glorious times when microcosms of society crossed the oceans, mixing together families and loners, travellers and businessmen, migrants and adventurers. Today's liners are exclusively dedicated to the holiday cruising industry, which is booming. I remember with nostalgia enchanting Atlantic crossings aboard a Polish liner, one of the last 'Transatlantics', the *Stefan Batory*, who made her last crossing in 1988.

Nowadays, freighters are the only way remaining to travel by sea. Many people believe that embarking on a cargo ship means sleeping in a small cheap cabin, and maybe giving a hand on deck or in the kitchen to pay the fare. The good old times when famous writers such as Joseph Conrad, Blaise Cendrars, Malcolm Lowry or Jack Kerouac travelled (and worked) on freighters are gone forever. The romantic old beaten tramp patched with rust, as in Alvaro Mutis' novels, has been replaced with armadas of modern container ships, some of them so wide they can no longer navigate the Panama Canal.

Tramps, ro-ros, reefers...

To grasp the array of possibilities in today's merchant navy, just try to guess the percentage of world trade that is transported by ship. The answer is no less than 98 per cent, leaving a meagre two per cent for trucks, trains and planes.

The sheer amount of cargo that can be piled aboard a ship is such that maritime routes remain the major axes of the world economy. Among the 40,000 or more freighters plying the seas, only a few carry passengers, and even then the available space rarely accommodates more than 12 people. Sometimes there might be only one passenger on board.

Many different kinds of freighters welcome passengers, from luxurious vessels to their more modest, weathered counterparts. Containers have radically changed the picture. These boxes can hold anything from objects large and small to liquids, perishable goods or dangerous chemicals, and because they are standard the world over they can be loaded with machinery direct from trucks or trains. The process is so fast that container ships often do not even spend a whole day in their ports of call, to the great disappointment of passengers wishing to go ashore.

For longer stops choose bulk carriers, which take longer to load and remain in harbour for several days. I once received a postcard from a friend who was delighted because his ship – a Polish bulk carrier on her way to Chile – was delayed for days in the Belgian harbour of Antwerp, as heavy rain prevented the loading of sacks of grain that had to stay dry. My friend took the opportunity to visit the city and its surroundings, using the ship as a floating hotel moored in the harbour.

Container ships, bulk carriers, good old ocean tramps (which take no definite route and may change their port of call mid-route if there is a better cargo to pick up somewhere else), ro-ros (from 'roll on/roll off') loaded with cars – each ship is a different experience. Real fans of cargo-ship travel are particularly fond of tramps, because of the unpredictability and hence added adventure of the route.

If you board one of the refrigerated container ships that carry fruit between the Caribbean and Europe, you will find yourself on the most luxurious of all freighters. Painted white, these so-called 'reefers' are the modern equivalent of 'banana boats': fast, top-of-the-range vessels. A steward will take care of you, and in your cabin you will find your own fridge, coffee machine and vcr, while meals and services are of a high standard. If you embark on a cargo-liner, such as the ship that sails from Great Britain to South Africa via the Canary Islands and St Helena, you will find a warm atmosphere and a happy but all-too-rare marriage between a freighter and a liner, carrying over a hundred passengers as well as cargo and even mail (the island of St Helena has no airport).

On board

Modern technology, computers and satellite communication systems have greatly reduced crews and incidentally allowed space for spare cabins. The number of officers does not exceed four on small ships, with the rest of the crew (usually from poorer countries, especially the Philippine Islands) carrying out work on deck, in the engine room, and general maintenance.

Cabins offered to passengers are usually officers' cabins, which means spacious accommodation (much more than on cruise liners), wide portholes, private bathroom and shower and the best location on the ship's higher decks. Meals are taken in the same room and on the same schedules as officers. Food varies greatly according to the standard of the ship, its nationality and the cook's country of origin. Travelling on a Chinese cargo-liner between Singapore and Hong Kong, I was introduced to jellyfish soup for breakfast. Later, boarding a French

'Holy sunrises and holy sunsets in the Pacific with everybody on board quietly working or reading in their bunks, the booze all gone. Calm days, which I'd open at dawn…
at the rail of the ship, and below me there they were, the smiling porpoises leaping and curlicueing in the wet air.'
– JACK KEROUAC

banana boat from Guadeloupe, I was served meals by a *maître d'hôtel* who proposed wine bottled by the shipping company itself. Most of the time, however, passengers are served Western food, unless they want to try spicy, exotic food prepared by a Kenyan or Filipino cook.

It should be remembered that freighters are first of all places of work, and that passengers should not infringe on the ship's life. I was told by a German captain of an indelicate passenger who almost triggered a mutiny by telling the crew that their wages were much too low.

On board freighters, passengers are expected to be self-sufficient as far as entertainment is concerned. Before you leave on an ocean voyage, make sure you take your own 'food for thought'. Time and quietness are among the principal luxuries on board. This is the perfect time to do things you have always wanted to do but never had the leisure for. Books are ideal companions. Some travellers take advantage of lengthy voyages to finally get to grips with the complete works of Proust or Dostoevsky. Others take along drawing or painting materials or music recordings. Some artists, painters, writers and poets travel by cargo ship in order to practise their art without any intrusion from the outside world.

Those who travel by sea range from the retired (in many cases) to young adventurers wishing to savour every mile of their journey. Facilities are shared with officers. It is not rare to find a swimming pool (filled with ocean water), sauna, small gymnasium, table tennis table, bar or video lounge aboard freighters. Since VCRs have become very common on merchant ships, video cassettes are popular among sailors and make good gifts.

So how much does all this cost? First, try to resist the temptation to compare sea-fares with air-fares, as you spend days and weeks aboard these comfortable sailing hotels, with room, board and facilities included, in addition to getting to faraway and exotic destinations. The average fare is around US$120 per day, which – when you consider what you get for your money – is moderate. Naturally prices vary from one ship to another, as well as according to the time of year.

Cargo travelling revival

Back in 1992, I wrote a guide to travelling by cargo ship as so many people were asking me how to go about it. While doing research for this guide – the first of its kind – I encountered scepticism (from merchant navy professionals among others): "You'll find hardly any freighters accepting passengers; not enough to fill a book. Those times are over," I was told many times. But the opposite proved to be true. *Travel by Cargo Ship* has since been published in French, English, German and Italian. It is now possible to sail to most major harbours throughout the world. Travel agencies specialising in freighters are growing and flourishing on all continents, and every day more and more people are discovering the joys of ocean crossings. There are fans who travel at least once a year by freighter, for the sheer pleasure of being on a ship, no matter where it is bound. The trend is clearly established. In Paris, a 'Cargo Club' meets on the first Wednesday of every month in a small bookshop on the Ile Saint-Louis, every time attracting more old salts returning from distant oceans, and dreamers eager to hear stories and gather tips before their departure.

But do not travel by freighter if you have a problem with not departing or arriving on schedule: at sea as in harbour, all kinds of delays can occur, caused by everything from weather to red-tape; some consider this sprinkling of the unexpected an added charm. Sometimes, even the port of call is changed at the last moment (particularly on tramp ships).

Distance and duration

Distances in Nautical Miles		Duration of Voyage

Distances in Nautical Miles

From Felixstowe to:

New York	3200
Sydney (via Suez)	11590
Hong Kong	9715
Rio de Janeiro	5200
Cape Town	6150

From Los Angeles to:

London	7677
Sydney	6511
Singapore	7867
Cape Town (via Panama Canal)	9421
Le Havre	7557

Duration of Voyage

Approximate journey times at an average speed of 15 knots (equivalent to 15 nautical miles per hour)

500 miles – 1 day 9hrs

1000 miles – 2 days 19 hrs

2000 miles – 5 days 3 hrs

3000 miles – 8 days 8 hrs

5000 miles – 13 days 21 hrs

10000 miles – 27 days 18 hrs

1 Nautical mile = 1.852km = 1.15 miles

Shipping companies themselves are also subject to change: ships change hands, names and flags, and new routes are opened while others are closed. If you are looking for a particular itinerary and are told that no ship is going there, my advice is not to take no for an answer. Faxes and telephones can work miracles. Remember too that public demand does shape the future.

Travelling by cargo ship is here to stay, and we can hope to see more and more space for passengers, not only on freighters, big and small, but also on liners and even scientific ships fully equipped with labs, drilling equipment and helicopters, designed to accommodate (wealthy) passengers wishing to sail in southern Antarctic seas.

If you have never tried sea travel, you could do a trial run of a few days with several ports of call, perhaps in the Baltic Sea or the Mediterranean. If you are seeking the ultimate freighter experience, you could embark on a round-the-world voyage through the Pacific islands, lasting almost three months. And who knows, perhaps the future will see silent, wind-propelled cargo-liners sailing the seas, carrying freight and a happy bunch of passengers? ଛ

HUGO VERLOMME is the author of 'Travel by Cargo Ship' and has written several other books, fiction and non-fiction, on nautical themes.

By pack animal
by Roger Chapman

THE DONKEY IS THE MOST DESIRABLE BEAST OF BURDEN for the novice and remains the favourite of the more experienced camper – if only because the donkey carries all the traveller's equipment, leaving him free to enjoy the countryside unburdened. Although small and gentle, the donkey is strong and dependable; no pack animal excels him for sure-footedness or matches his character. He makes the ideal companion for children old enough to travel into the mountains or hills, and for the adult who prefers to travel at a pace slow enough to appreciate the scenery, wildlife and wilderness that no vehicle can reach.

The rock climber, hunter, fisherman, scientist or artist who has too much gear to carry into the mountains may prefer to take the larger and faster mule, but if they are sensible, they will practice first on the smaller and more patient donkey. The principles of pack animal management are the same, but the mule is stronger, more likely to kick or bite if provoked, and requires firmer handling than the donkey. The advantage of a mule is obvious. Whereas a donkey can only carry about 50 kg, the mule, if expertly packed, can carry a payload of 100 kg. Although both are good for 24 km a day on reasonable trails, the donkeys will have to be led on foot; whereas mules, which can travel at a good speed, require everyone to be mounted, unless their handlers are fast hikers.

Planning

To determine the number of donkeys needed before a trip, the approximate pack load must be calculated. The stock requirement for a ten-day trip can be calculated by dividing the number of people by two, but taking the higher whole number if the split does not work evenly. Thus, a family of five would take three donkeys. It is difficult to control more than ten donkeys on the trail, so don't use them with a party of 20 or more unless certain individuals are prepared to carry large packs to reduce the number of animals. Mules are usually led by a single hiker or are tied in groups of not more than five animals led by a man on horseback. This is the 'string' of mules often mentioned in Westerns; each lead rope passes through the left-hand breech ring of the preceding animal's harness and is then tied around the animal's neck with a bowline. One or more horses are usually sent out with the pack mules because mules respect and stick close to these 'chaperones'.

Whichever method you decide to use, don't prepare a detailed itinerary before your journey; wait and see how you get on during the first few days, when you should attempt no more than 12–16 km a day. Later you will be able to average 20–24 km, but you should not count on doing more than 24 km a day although it is possible, with early starts and a lighter load, if you really have to.

Campers who use pack animals seldom restrict themselves to the equipment list of a backpacker. There is no need to do so, but before preparing elaborate menus and extensive wardrobes, you would do well to consider the price of hiring a pack animal. The more elaborate and heavy your equipment, the more donkeys or mules there are to hire, load, unload, groom and find pasture for. In selecting your personal equipment you have more freedom – a 'Karrimat', or a larger tent instead of the small 'Basha' – but it should not exceed 12 kg and should be packed into several of those small cylindrical soft bags or a seaman's kit-bag. You can take your sleeping bag as a separate bundle and take a small knapsack for those personal items such as spare sweaters, camera, first aid kit and snacks required during the day. But there are some special items you will require if you are not hiring an efficient guide and handler: repair kit for broken pack saddles and extra straps for mending harnesses. An essential item is a 45 kg spring scale for balancing the sacks or panniers before you load them on the pack animals in the morning. Remember, too, that each donkey/mule will be hired out with a halter, lead rope, tow 'sacks', a pack cover, and a nine-metre pack rope. In addition, there will be pickets and shackle straps, curry combs, frog picks, canvas buckets, tools and possibly ointment or powders to heal saddle sores.

Animal handling

The art of handling pack animals is not a difficult one, but unfortunately you cannot learn it entirely from a book. With surprisingly little experience in this field, the novice soon becomes an expert packer, confident that he can handle any situation that may arise on the trail and, above all, that he has learnt the uncertain science of getting the pack animal to do what he wants it to do. The donkey is more responsive than the mule and is quick to return friendship, especially if he knows he is being well packed, well fed and well rested. The mule tends to be more truculent, angry and resentful until he knows who is in charge. Therefore, an attitude of firmness and consideration towards the animal is paramount.

Perhaps the easiest way to learn the techniques of handling pack animals is to look at a typical day and consider the problems as they arise.

Collecting in the morning: Pack animals can either be let loose, hobbled or picketed during the night. The latter is preferable as even a mule that has its front legs hobbled can wander for miles during the night searching for suitable grass. If the animal is picketed, unloosen the strap around the fetlock that is attached to the picket rope and lead him back to the campsite by the halter. If the animals are loose, you may have to allow a good half hour or so to catch them. Collect the gentle ones first, returning later for the recalcitrant animals. Approach each animal cautiously, talking to him and offering a palmful of oats before grabbing the halter.

Tying up and grooming: Even the gentlest pack animal will need to be tied up to a tree or post before packing. The rope should be tied with a clove hitch at about waist height. Keep the rope short, otherwise the animal will walk round and round the tree as you follow with the saddle. It also prevents him from stepping on or tripping over the rope. It is advisable to keep the animals well apart, but not too far from your pile of packed sacks or panniers.

Often, donkeys in particular, will have a roll during the night, so they require a good work-over with the brush or curry comb to remove dust or caked mud. Most animals enjoy this, but you mustn't forget that one end can bite and the other end can give a mighty kick. Personally, I spend some time stroking the animal around the head and ears, talking to him before I attempt to groom him. Ears are very good indicators of mood. If the ears are upright he is alert and apprehensive, so a few words and strokes will give him confidence; soon the ears will relax and lie back. If the ears turn and stretch right back along his neck, then there is a good chance you are in for trouble. The first time he nips, thump him in the ribs and swear at him. He will soon learn that you do not appreciate this kind of gesture.

Your main reason for grooming is to remove caked dirt, which may cause sores once the animal is loaded. Remove this dirt with a brush and clean rag and, if there is an open wound, apply an antiseptic ointment or sprinkle on boric acid powder, which will help dry it up. Finally, check each hoof quickly to see that no stone or twig has lodged in the soft pad. Lean against the animal, then warn him by tapping the leg all the way down the flank, past the knee to the fetlock before lifting the hoof; otherwise you will never succeed. If there is a stone lodged between the shoe and the hoof, prise it out with a frog pick.

Saddling and loading

Animals are used to being loaded from the left or near side. First you fold the saddle blanket, place it far forward then slide it back into position along the animal's back so that the hair lies smooth. Check that it hangs evenly on both sides, sufficient to protect the flanks from the loaded sacks. Stand behind the mule or donkey – but not too close – and check it before you proceed further. Pick up the pack saddle (two moulded pieces of wood jointed by two cross-trees) and place it on the saddle blanket so it fits in the hollows behind the withers. Tie up the breast strap and rear strap before tying the girth tight. Two people will be required to load the equipment in the soft canvas sacks onto the saddle pack, but it is essential to weigh the sacks before you place them on the cross-trees; they should be within two kg of each other. If the saddle is straight, but one sack is lower than the other, correct the length of the ear loops.

On the trail

Morning is the best time to travel, so you must hit the trail early, preferably before 7 am. At a steady two km an hour, you will be able to cover the majority of the day's journey by the time the sun is at its hottest. This will allow you to spend a good three hours' rest at midday before setting off once more for a final couple of hours ride and the search for a camp-site. Avoid late camps, so start looking by 4 pm.

During the first few days you may have some trouble getting your donkeys or mules to move close together and at a steady pace. One man should walk behind each animal if they are being led and if there are any hold ups, he can apply a few swipes of a willow switch to the hindquarters. It is a waste of time to shout at the animals or threaten them constantly, as it only makes them distrustful and skittish. The notorious stubbornness of the mule or donkey is usually the result of bad handling in the past. Sometimes it is a result of fear or fatigue, but occasionally it is sheer cussedness or an attempt to see how much he can get away with. The only occasion when I could not get a mule moving was travelling across some snow patches in the mountains of Kashmir. Eventually, after losing my temper and lashing him with a switch, I persuaded him to move slowly across the icy surface, where he disappeared into a snow hole. It took us three hours to unload him, pull him out and calm him down before we could re-pack. I learned a good lesson from my lack of awareness of the innate intelligence of the mule.

Understanding

There is no problem with unpacking, which can be done quickly and efficiently. Just remember to place all the equipment neatly together so it is not mixed up. Keep individual saddles, sacks and harnesses close enough together to cover with the waterproof cover in case of rain. Once unloaded, the donkeys can be groomed, watered and led off to the pasture area where they are to be picketed for the night.

Not long ago, I took my wife and two young daughters on a 195 km journey across the Cevennes mountains in south-east France. We followed Robert Louis Stevenson's routes, which he described in his charming little book *Travels With a Donkey*. We took three donkeys – two as pack animals and one for the children to take turns in riding – on a trail which had not changed much over the past hundred years. It made an ideal holiday, and we returned tanned, fitter, enchanted by the French countryside and aware that it was the character of our brave little donkeys that had made our enjoyment complete.

The speed with which the children mastered the technique of pack animal management was encouraging because it allowed us to complete our task with enough time to explore the wilder parts of the mountains and enjoy the countryside at the leisurely pace of our four-footed companions. We also took a hundred flies from one side of the Cevennes to the other, but that is another story. ❧

ROGER CHAPMAN, MBE, has been involved in many expeditions —down the Blue Nile and Zaire rivers, to Central and South America, to East Greenland with the British Schools Exploration Society, and to Papua New Guinea with Operation Drake.

By camel
by René Dee

In this mechanised and industrial epoch, the camel does not seem to be an obvious choice of travelling companion when sophisticated cross-country vehicles exist for the toughest of terrains. Add to this the stockpile of derisory and mocking myths, truths and sayings about the camel and one is forced to ask the question: why use camels at all? Purely as a means of getting from A to B when time is the most important factor, the camel should not even be considered. As a means of transport for scientific groups who wish to carry out useful research in the field, the camel is limiting. It can be awkward and risky transporting delicate equipment and specimens. However, for the individual, small group and expedition wishing to see the desert as it should be seen, the camel is an unrivalled means of transport.

Go safely in the desert

From my own personal point of view, the primary reason must be that, unlike any motorised vehicle, camels allow you to integrate completely with the desert and the people within it – something it is impossible to do at 80 kmph enclosed in a 'tin can'. A vehicle in the desert can be like a prison cell, and the constant noise of the engine tends to blur all sense of the solitude, vastness and deafening quiet that is so intrinsic to the experience.

Travel by camel allows the entire pace of life to slow down from a racy 80 kmph to a steady 6.5 kmph, enabling you to unwind, take in and visually appreciate the overall magnificence and individual details of your surroundings. Secondly, camels do, of course, have the ability to reach certain areas that are inaccessible to vehicles, especially through rocky and narrow mountain passes, although camels are not always happy on this terrain and extreme care has to be taken to ensure they do not slip or twist a leg. They are as sensitive as they appear insensitive.

Thirdly, in practical terms, they cause far fewer problems where maintenance, breakdown and repairs are concerned. No bulky spares or expensive mechanical equipment are needed for repairs. Camels do not need a great deal of fuel and can exist adequately (given that they are not excessively burdened) for five to ten days without water. Camels go on and on and on and on until they die; and then one has the option of eating them, altogether far better tasting than a Michelin tyre.

Lastly, camels must be far more cost effective if you compare them directly with vehicles, although this depends on whether your intended expedition/journey already includes a motorised section. If you fly direct to your departure point, or as near as possible to it, you will incur none of the heavy costs related to transporting a vehicle, not to mention the cost of buying it. If the camel trek is to be an integral portion of a motorised journey, then the cost saving will not apply as, of course, hire fees for camels and guides will be additional.

In many ways, combining these two forms of travel is ideal and a very good way of highlighting my primary point in favour of transport by camel. If you do decide on this combination, make sure you schedule the camel journey for the very end of your expedition and that the return leg by vehicle is either minimal or purely functional for I can guarantee that after a period of ten days or more travelling slowly and gently through the desert by camel, your vehicle will take on the characteristics of a rocket ship and all sense of freedom, enquiry and interest will be dulled to the extreme. An overwhelming sense of disillusion and disinterest will prevail. Previously exciting sights, desert towns and Arab civilisation, will pall after such intense involvement with the desert, its people and its lifestyle.

First steps

For the individual or group organiser wanting to get off the beaten track by camel, the first problem is to find them and to gather every bit of information possible about who owns the camels. Are they for hire, for how much, what equipment/

stores/provisions are included (if any) and, lastly, what are the guides/owners capable of and are they willing to accompany you? It is not much good arriving at Tamanrasset, Timbouctou or Tindoug without knowing some, if not all, of the answers to these questions. Good pre-departure research is vital, but the problem is that 90 per cent of the information won't be found from any tourist office, embassy, library or travel agent. Particularly if you're considering a major journey exclusively by camel, you'll probably have to undertake a preliminary fact-finding recce to your proposed departure point to establish contacts among camel owners and guides. It may well be that camels and/or reliable guides do not exist in the area where you wish to carry out your expedition.

I would suggest, therefore, that you start first with a reliable source of information, such as the Royal Geographical Society, which has expedition reports and advice that can be used as a primary source of reference, including names and addresses to write to for up-to-date information about the area that interests you. Up-to-date information is, without doubt, the key to it all. Very often this can be gleaned from the commercial overland companies whose drivers are passing through your area of interest regularly and who may even have had personal experience of the journey you intend to make.

In all the best Red Indian stories, the guide is the all-knowing, all-seeing person in whom total faith is put. However, as various people have discovered to their cost, this is not always such a good idea. Many so-called guides know very little of the desert and its ways. How then to find someone who really does know the route/area, has a sense of desert lore and who preferably owns his best camel? I can only reiterate that the best way to do this is through personal recommendation.

Having found him, put your faith in him, let him choose your camels and make sure that your relationship remains as amicable as possible. You will be living together for many days in conditions that are familiar to him but alien to you, and you need his support. Arrogance does not fit into desert travel, especially from a *nasrani*. Mutual respect and a good rapport are essential.

Pack up your troubles

Once you've managed to establish all this and you're actually out there, what are the dos, don'ts and logistics of travel by camel? Most individuals and expeditions (scientifically orientated or not) will want, I imagine, to incorporate a camel trek within an existing vehicle-led expedition, so I am really talking only of short-range treks of around ten to 15 days' duration, and with a range of up to 400 km. If this is so, you will need relatively little equipment and stores, and it is essential that this is kept to a minimum. Remember that the more equipment you take, the more camels you will need, which will require more guides, which means more cost, more pasture and water, longer delays in loading, unloading, cooking and setting up camp and a longer wait in the morning while the camels are being rounded up after a night of pasturing.

Be prepared also for a very swift deterioration of equipment. In a vehicle you can at least keep possessions clean and safe to a degree, but packing kit onto a camel denies any form of protection, especially since it is not unknown for camels to stumble and fall or to roll you over suddenly and ignominiously if something is not to their liking, such as a slipped load or uncomfortable saddle. My advice is to pack all your belongings in a seaman's kit-bag that can be roped onto the camel's side easily, is pliable, hard-wearing and, because it is soft and not angular, doesn't threaten to rub a hole in the camel's side or backbone. (I have seen a badly placed baggage saddle wear a hole the size of a man's fist into an animal's back.)

If rectangular aluminium boxes containing cameras or other delicate equipment are being carried, make sure that they are well roped on the top of the camel and that there is sufficient padding underneath so as not to cause friction. Moreover, you'll always have to take your shoes off while riding because over a period of hours, let alone days, you could wear out the protective hair on the camel's neck and eventually cause open sores.

Water should be carried around in goat-skin *guerbas* and 20-litre round metal *bidons* which can, again, be roped up easily and hung either side of the baggage camel under protective covers. Take plenty of rope for tying on equipment, saddles etc., and keep one length of 15 metres intact for using at wells where there may be no facilities for hauling up water. Don't take any sophisticated tents either; they will probably be ruined within days and anyway are just not necessary.

I have always used a piece of cotton cloth approximately six metres square, which, with two poles for support front and rear and with sand or boulders at the sides and corner, makes a very good overnight shelter for half a dozen people. Night in the desert can be extremely cold, particularly in the winter, but the makeshift 'tent' has a more important role during the day when it provides shelter for the essential two-hour lunch stop and rest.

The day's schedule

Your daily itinerary and schedule should be geared to the practical implications of travelling by camel. That is to say that each night's stop will, where possible, be in an area where pasture is to be found for the camels to graze. Although one can take along grain and dried dates for camels to eat, normal grazing is also vital. The camels are unloaded and hobbled (two front legs are tied closely together), but you will find they can wander as much as three or four kilometres overnight and there is only one way to fetch them: on foot. Binoculars are extremely useful as spotting camels over such a distance can be a nightmare. They may be hidden behind dunes and not come into view for some time.

Other useful equipment includes goggles for protection in sandstorms, prescription sunglasses and, of course, sun cream. Above all, take comfortable and hard-wearing footwear, for it is almost certain that you will walk at least half the way once you have become fully acclimatised. I would suggest that you take Spanish felt boots or something similar, which are cheap, very light, give ankle support over uneven terrain and are durable and very comfortable.

The one disadvantage of boots by day is that your feet will get very hot, but it's a far better choice than battered, blistered and lacerated feet when one has to keep up with the camel's steady 6.5 kmph. Nomads wear sandals, but if you take a close look at a nomad's foot you will see that it is not dissimilar to the sandal itself, i.e. as hard and tough as leather. Yours resembles a baby's bottom by comparison, so it is essential that you get some heavy walking practice in beforehand with the boots/shoes/sandals you intend to wear. If your journey is likely to be a long one, then you could possibly try sandals, as there will be time for the inevitable wearing-in process with blisters, as well as stubbed toes and feet spiked by the lethal acacia thorn.

For clothing, I personally wear a local, free-flowing robe such as the *gandoura*, local pantaloons and *cheche*, a three-metre length of cotton cloth, which can be tied round the head and/or face and neck for protection against the sun. You can also use it as a rope, fly whisk and face protector in sandstorms. In the bitterly cold nights and early mornings of winter desert travel, go to bed with it wrapped around your neck, face and head to keep warm.

If local clothing embarrasses and inhibits you, stick to loose cotton shirts and trousers. Forget your tight jeans and bring loose-fitting cotton underwear. Anything nylon and tight fitting next to the skin will result in chafing and sores. Do, however, also take some warm clothing and blankets, including socks and jumpers. As soon as the sun sets in the desert, the temperature drops dramatically. Catching cold in the desert is unbearable. Colds are extremely common and spread like wildfire. Take a good down sleeping bag and a groundsheet.

Your sleeping bag and blankets can also serve as padding for certain types of camel saddle. In the Western Sahara you will find the Mauritanian butterfly variety, which envelops you on four sides. You're liable to slide back and forth uncomfortably and get blisters unless you pad the saddle. The Tuareg saddle is commonly used in the Algerian Sahara. This is a more traditional saddle, with a fierce-looking forward pommel that threatens man's very manhood should you be thrown forward against it. In Saudi Arabia, female camels are ridden, and seating positions are taken up behind the dromedary's single hump rather than on or forward of it.

Culture shock

Never travel alone in the desert, without even a guide. The ideal group size would be seven group members, one group leader, three guides, 11 riding camels and three baggage camels. The individual traveller should take at least one guide with him and three or four camels.

Be prepared for a mind-blowing sequence of mental experiences, especially if you are not accustomed to the alien environment, company and pace, which can lead to introspection, uncertainty and even paranoia. Travel by camel with nomad guides is the reversal of our normal lifestyle. Therefore it is as important to be mentally prepared for this culture shock as it is to be physically prepared. Make no mistake, travel by camel is hard, physically uncompromising and mentally torturing at times. But a *meharee* satisfactorily accomplished will alter your concept of life and its overall values, and the desert's hold over you will never loosen. ❧

RENÉ DEE has travelled overland to India and Nepal and led a series of trips to Morocco, specialising in treks by camel and mule.

Driving the world

Hiring a car
by Paul Melly and Edwina Townsend

FIRST HIRE YOUR CAR.... Yes, there are a lot of countries where it is a big advantage to have your own transport, especially if you must keep to a tight work schedule or have bulky luggage. Yes, it is relatively easy to book anything from a Fiesta to a limousine for a fair number of the world's destinations, including some that are surprisingly off-beat. Yes, it can be very expensive – and almost certainly will be if you neglect your pre-departure homework. One journalist acquaintance (who thought he knew what travelling was about) managed to burn up over £100 on car hire for a day and a half in Brittany, by the time he'd paid all the extras.

The key rule is: don't just read the small print; work out what it actually adds up to. For example, a mileage charge really can rack up the cost, especially if you have not calculated in advance quite how far you will be travelling. And it's no use nursing a lifelong grievance against the big car hire companies after the event. By and large they do fairly well in providing a comprehensive and reliable service in a wide range of countries, if at a price.

Travelling cheaply

If you want a better deal, expect to work for it and be prepared to tramp the back streets looking for a local outfit that is halfway trustworthy – but remember that you only get what you pay for. It costs Hertz, Avis, Europcar, Budget, Alamo and the rest a hefty investment to provide that easy-to-book, uniform service across national frontiers and linguistic boundaries. Centralised, computer-based reservation networks don't come free.

If you really want to keep costs down, perhaps public transport is worth a fresh thought. Shared long-distance taxis or minibuses are surprisingly fast and cheap in many parts of the Third World, and may give you an easier time at the police, army or customs road checks that spring up every few kilometres in some countries. If it's not you who is driving, then it's not you – foreign and unfamiliar with local situations – who is called upon to judge whether it is correct paperwork or a small bribe that is required. Quite apart from the ethical dilemma, there is the practical one: having to pay unavoidable back-handers is bad enough, but offering them when they are not expected is worse and can get you into far more trouble.

It would be a pity to allow such worries to discourage anyone from doing the adventurous thing, however, and hiring a car can give you the freedom to go where you want, stopping in small villages or at scenic viewpoints when it suits you.

The big car hire firms offer comprehensive coverage over much of the developed world, along with quite a number of tourist and/or business destinations in other regions. But they certainly do not have outlets everywhere and there are many places where you will have to rely on local advice in order to find a reliable rental outfit. Advance reservation may well prove impossible. In this case, if your time is tight, ask friendly officials in the country's embassy in your home country for suggestions. Most will have a telephone directory for their capital city at least, even if it is a little out of date. For a few pounds, you can then ring to try to book in advance, or just to check availability (easier, of course, if the country is on direct dialling). This could well be a more effective strategy than asking a small high street travel agent used to selling Mediterranean package tours to attempt and arrange something for you. Try also contacting any agencies specialising in the particular region of the world that you intend to visit.

For most places, it is still definitely worth considering the big hire companies. In recent years they have developed a good range of lower-price options to complement the plusher services designed for those with fat expense accounts. And even if you are abroad for work, with a little planning you can very often make use of the special packages designed for tourists. Not only are these cheaper, but they also have the advantage of simplicity, being tailored to the needs of leisure visitors who are either not used to or do not want to be bothered with organising everything for themselves.

If you are going on holiday, meanwhile, there is something to be learned from those who have to travel for work. Clearly, big firms have buying power in the car hire market, but they also pick up a lot of experience. Here are some useful tips suggested by the travel manager of one multi-national company: read the small print; get your own insurance; avoid mileage payments and large cars; and watch out for the chance to save money on pre-booked deals.

Price in particular takes some calculation, because of the extras that are hard to evaluate exactly. Car hire is sometimes offered per mile or per kilometre, but it is best to go for an unlimited mileage deal, even if the base price is slightly higher. While you cannot be sure how much petrol you will use or how much you will pay for it, at least the local currency cost of hiring the car for, say, six days is fixed.

Legalities

Car hire forms always include references to CDW (Collision Damage Waiver) and PAI (Personal Accident Insurance), which come in addition to the cost of renting the vehicle. The customer may legally be held responsible for a share of loss or damage to the hire vehicle, regardless of who is at fault. But if you accept the CDW clause and pay the daily charge for it, the rental company waives this liability to the financial level advised. This varies from country to country, and in the US from state to state, and is dependent on the customer respecting the conditions of the hire agreement. When you rent a car you must clearly be insured against damaging both it and, more importantly, any other people or vehicles. Accepting the CDW option can prove an expensive form of protection, however, so explore other possibilities. Your own car insurance may provide cover, for instance, or by paying a supplement you may be able to build it into your general travel insurance policy.

If you are contemplating hiring a car in the USA, it is particularly important to remember that the CDW charge included in the prepayment provides only the bare minimum amount of cover required by the laws of the state in question. You will more than likely be asked to top up this cover, but check first what it will cost you and what you are paying for.

With PAI, similarly, you will find that most travel insurance policies sold in the UK include medical expenses and hospital costs. So before you decide to pay the car hire company for PAI as an additional extra check your travel insurance policy, as you may be putting yourself to unnecessary expense.

Always check whether the hire agreement allows you to drive where you want. This may seem irrelevant to anyone intending to restrict themselves to a European city, say, but if you are visiting a country where you plan to go off the beaten track and drive on unmade roads it is vital. The car hire company's conditions may insist you stick to metalled roads, thus severely limiting your freedom. Or if they do allow driving off-road, you may find they charge an additional supplement.

Driving conditions

Drivers used to British roads should be aware that in many countries even major highways are dirt or gravel roads and can become almost impassable at rainy times of year. Important trading routes are even worse, as huge trucks lurch through the mud, cutting deep wheel ruts which then fill with water.

While good maps are clearly indispensable, they do not always indicate what roads are made of and are unlikely to give you the up-to-date or seasonal information you really need before setting out. In the dry season, such routes may be dusty but otherwise much easier to use. In areas where the vegetation is stunted, the absence of tarmac can make it quite hard to follow the road.

Nor do these warnings go for tropical countries only: the famed Alaska Hi-way, from Dawson Creek in Canada through to Fairbanks, is surfaced with gravel for much of its length. When it rains, many minor roads in Canada turn into muddy bogs, with cars sinking up to their axles in black gumbo. The worst time of year can be the spring thaw – just when European visitors might be expecting conditions to get easier.

If you are likely to drive through mountains, including the relatively domesticated Alps and Pyrenees, make sure your car comes equipped with snow tyres or chains and that you know how to fit them. The Alps may be crossed by motorways and tunnels, but winter blizzards can still cause major problems. The local police make spot checks – and impose on-the-spot fines – on roads where chains or snow tyres are obligatory (normally indicated by a sign as you enter the relevant stretch). This advice is particularly pertinent to business travellers in winter who decide on the spur of the moment to hire a car and pop into the mountains for a day's skiing. Tyres that feel OK in downtown Turin won't feel so great on the nineteenth hairpin bend up to the ski resort, with no room to turn round.

It also pays to check for road construction projects, especially in developing countries, where a sudden influx of foreign aid can prompt building work on a huge scale virtually overnight. The inevitable mess and inconvenience involved has to be weighed against the advantages of a new hard-top road where there was only a mud-track before, which incidentally opens up fresh areas for relatively easy exploration with a hired saloon car. Conversely, there is always the possibility of stumbling on gaps in otherwise fairly good networks.

The basic rule is: before you do something unusual, tell the car hire outlet where you picked up the vehicle and signed it out. Should you have an accident or breakdown, telephone the hire firm before paying for expensive repairs. Otherwise you may not be reimbursed. They may want to make their own arrangements.

What car?

Deciding what size of car to hire is relatively simple. The main companies use fairly standard makes with which you will be familiar at home. On balance, you are more likely to get Japanese makes in Asia, French in West Africa and, not surprisingly, American in the US. But when working out costs, don't forget that larger vehicles are also thirstier. If you book in advance, the rental deal may stipulate that if the car of your choice is not available the agency will provide one in a higher category for no extra charge. In other words, if you reserve a small car and then turn up to find it isn't there, you may end up with one that uses more petrol – which could be an expensive (if comfortable) penalty if you are embarking on a long trip.

Do not forget the cost of petrol when you return the vehicle. Under the terms of most agreements the car is provided with a tankful of petrol and should be returned with a full tank. Check that it is full before you take it out and make the final fill-up yourself. That way you will probably pay less than the charges made by the hire company, as they usually add a refuelling charge to the cost of the petrol.

When to book?

Booking a car in advance is usually worth considering, not only for peace of mind it brings but also because you may be able to take advantage of one of the many inclusive deals offered by the major car hire companies. You can choose either to pay before leaving home in exchange for a pre-paid voucher, or to book at a guaranteed rate in local currency, or do it over the internet and pay by credit card. These rates may include not only unlimited mileage, CDW and PAI, but also airport fees, an additional driver, a full tank of petrol and local taxes. This leaves you with just the petrol to pay for and any optional extras you may agree to take locally. These inclusive rates often apply only to rentals of a minimum of a three days.

Mandatory extra charges to be paid locally are becoming increasingly frequent. In a growing number of countries, for instance, the local authority charges either a fixed fee or a percentage of the rental for vehicles rented at airports. This is passed on to the hirer by the car hire companies. Some US States, notably Florida, now levy a mandatory tax of approximately $2 per day in addition to the standard charges. Rentals in Vancouver, meanwhile, are charged an airport improvement fee. In other words, beware of the extras.

To rent or not to rent?

If you are not sure whether to rent or not, why not take a pre-paid voucher with you for any number of days? Once you are on the spot, you can then assess the possible alternative forms of transport. If returned to the outlet where they were bought, unused pre-paid vouchers will normally be refunded in full: check before you buy. Partially used vouchers are often not refundable.

Even if you have a pre-paid voucher, car hire companies always require a deposit at the beginning of any rental. In most cases an imprint of your credit or charge card will suffice; if you do not have a credit card, cash or travellers' cheques may be acceptable. Some companies may refuse to hire vehicles to drivers under 25 years of age.

When you arrive at your destination, it is always worth asking for tips about reliable local car hire firms (hotel porters are usually a good source of information). Once at the hire company's offices, check if they have any local special offers before revealing that you have a pre-paid voucher. Providing that you can fund the cost of the voucher until you return home, and that you can afford to pay again locally, this could be another way of making extra savings.

The big hire groups claim to offer the same level of service in franchise companies as in their own offices. While you will invariably be provided with the best available, remember that in some countries new vehicles are scarcer than hen's teeth, and road conditions and driving standards leave much to be desired.

If you are staying somewhere for a lengthy period or regularly visit the same destination, you can cut costs and red tape by leasing. This option – normally provided for conventional business car fleets – may prove cheaper than car hire if you, or a group of people, regularly need a car in one place. The deal can also include repairs and servicing.

Safety

The bottom line when you hire a car is safety. Does the vehicle work and can you trust it? Unless you are a natural or professional mechanic, or at least a good amateur, there isn't much chance of really assessing whether a car is roadworthy. But a few simple checks are at least a pointer as to how well it is maintained. Try the steering and test out the brakes in the hire shop forecourt, and of course listen for any faults in the first mile or two. Have a look at the tyre treads to see if they are still fairly deep and test the lights. If you are in tropical country check the air-conditioning (if any), and in very cold climes, such as Canada between October and April, make sure the vehicle is winterised: when the snows start, conditions in city centres are not indicative of those you may encounter in the surrounding countryside or even the suburbs. Make sure that any faults such as bumps or scratches are detailed on the hire form before you take the car out. Otherwise you could find yourself held liable when you return.

Red tape

Tell the hire firm if you plan to cross national or state borders, just to make sure the insurance cover extends across the frontier. And remember that while many discount rental deals allow you to drop the car off anywhere in the country where you collected it, there is usually a surcharge for leaving it at a company offices in a different country.

Getting the right paperwork is vital. Take photocopies of all hire agreements, insurance etc., as well as basics such as an International Driving Permit for non-EU countries. When it comes to officialdom, patience and politeness are probably more important than anything else. ঽ

*PAUL MELLY is a freelance journalist specialising in foreign news, business and travel.
EDWINA TOWNSEND works in the travel industry.*

Driving off-road
by Jack Jackson

OFF-ROAD DRIVING CHALLENGES THE TRAVELLER in a completely new way, and driving techniques vary with the ability and weight of the vehicle, as well as with the driver. Some vehicles have greater capabilities than many drivers can handle and there may often be more than one way of solving a particular problem.

Before you start

Before driving off-road, look under your vehicle and note the position of its lowest points: exhaust pipes, towing plates, springs, axles, differentials, transfer box and gearbox. These may be lower than expected, on some vehicles they are not in line, and the differentials are usually off-centre. Remember their clearance and position when traversing obstacles. Position the number plates and lights above bumper level, to avoid damage from the terrain. Ensure there are strong towing eyes.

Rules of the road

Alert but restrained driving is essential. A light foot, and low gears in four-wheel drive, will usually get vehicles through difficult situations. Sometimes sheer speed may be better, but if you lose control at speed, you could suffer damage or injury. Careful driving saves time, money and effort. Careless driving breaks chassis, springs, half-shafts and clutches. And remember: never hook your thumbs around the steering wheel. A sudden twist of the wheel, when a front wheel hits a stone or rut, can easily break them.

Always travel at a sensible speed, watching for problems ahead. If you are on a track where it is possible that another vehicle may come the other way, have a passenger keep a lookout further ahead, while you concentrate on negotiating difficulties. Travel only at speeds that allow you to stop easily within the limit of clear vision. Travel slowly to the brows of humps or sharp bends; there may be large boulders, holes, or steep drops beyond them. Make use of the rhythm of the suspension, touch the brakes lightly as you approach the crest of a hump and release them as you pass over it; this stops the vehicle from flying.

When you come to a sharp dip, ditch, or rut, cross it at an angle, so that only one wheel at a time drops into it. Steer the wheels towards and over the terrain's high points to maintain maximum ground clearance. Always change to a lower gear before you reach problems, to remain in control. With permanent four-wheel drive systems, remember to engage lock before entering difficult situations.

Apart from soft sand and snow, most situations where four-wheel drive is needed also require low-range for better traction, torque and control. They will normally also require you to stop and inspect the route on foot first, so you can engage low-range before starting off again.

On soft sand it is useful to be able to engage low-range on the move. On some vehicles, this requires practice at double-declutching. For most situations, first gear low-range is too low and you might spin the wheels; use second or third gear, except over large rocks.

Watch the ground

Keep an eye on previous vehicle tracks, they will indicate trouble spots that you might be able to avoid.

If you cannot see the route or obstacles clearly from the driving seat, get a passenger to stand in a safe place where he or she can see the problem clearly and direct you. Arrange a clear system of hand signals with the person beforehand, since vocal directions can be drowned by engine noise. Only delegate one person to do this: more than one becomes confusing.

On slopes

Do not drive on the outside edge of tracks with a steep drop, they may be undermined by water and collapse under the weight.

Do not tackle steep hills diagonally, if you lose traction and slip sideways, you may turn over. Only cross slopes if it is absolutely necessary. If you must do so, take the least possible angle and make any turns quickly.

Before descending any steep incline, check that the vehicle is still in gear in both the main gearbox and the transfer box. When descending steep, loose or muddy inclines, there is a high chance of skidding. Use second gear, low-range engine-braking in four-wheel drive with any centre differential locked in. With automatic transmission, use first gear plus left-foot braking, and use the accelerator to keep the wheels moving. Depress the accelerator gently, when correcting a skid.

If you lose traction going uphill, swing the steering wheel from side to side – you may get a fresh bite and make the top. If you fail going up a steep hill, change quickly into reverse, make sure you are in four-wheel drive with the centre differential locked if you have one and use the engine as a brake to back down the same way you came up. Do not try to turn round or go down on the brakes.

Be prepared to stop quickly on the top of a steep hill, the way down the other side may be at a different angle.

Surface effects

All braking on loose surfaces or corrugations should be cadence braking, i.e. several short pumps, unless you have ABS brakes. In really loose situations, turn ABS systems off.

If you have been in four-wheel drive on a hard surface, when you change back into two-wheel drive (or, for permanent four-wheel drive systems, you unlock the centre differential lock) you might find this change and the steering difficult, due to wind-up between the axles. This scrubs tyres and damages the drive train. If you are lightly loaded, free it by driving backwards while swinging the steering wheel from side to side. If you are heavily loaded, free it by jacking up one front wheel clear of the ground; keep clear of the wheel, which may spin violently.

On loose surfaces, don't change gear going up or downhill, you'll lose traction.

Overcoming obstacles

If you cannot avoid a rock, drive over it square on with a tyre, which is more resilient and more easily repaired than your chassis. To traverse large boulders, use first gear low-range and crawl over, using the engine for both drive and braking. Avoid slipping the clutch or touching the brakes.

You may have to build up a route, putting stones or sand ladders across drainage ditches, or weak bridges, chipping away high corners, or levering aside large boulders. If you have to rebuild a track or fill in a hole completely, do so from above, rolling boulders down instead of wasting energy lifting them from below. Where possible, bind them together by mixing with tree branches or bushes.

Pistes and dirt tracks

Except on soft sand, use two-wheel drive: this gives more positive steering and avoids transmission wind-up. Tyres should be at correct pressures.

Watch out for stones thrown up by other vehicles, never overtake when you cannot see through the dust of the vehicle ahead, and use the horn to warn vehicles you are about to overtake. Culverts do not always extend to the full width of dirt roads, watch out for these when overtaking.

Avoid driving at night: potholes, culverts, broken-down trucks, bullock carts and people are difficult to see; many trucks drive at speed without lights and then blind you with full beam when spotting you. Many countries have unlit chains and logs across roads at night, as checkpoints.

Bull dust

Bull dust hangs in the air, obscuring vision. When travelling downwind you have to stop often to let it clear. If you cannot see to overtake, drop back and wait until the piste changes direction so that the wind blows the dust to one side, providing clear vision.

Corrugations

Corrugations give an effect similar to sitting on a pneumatic drill to both vehicles and their occupants. Corrugations also find weaknesses in the suspension and electrical cable insulation: coil springs dislodge, leaf springs break, shock absorbers fail and electrical shorts cause vehicle fires; a battery isolator is essential.

Avoid travelling beside the corrugations: other vehicles will have tried that before and given up – hence the corrugations. Take it steady and be patient.

Except on sand, long-wheelbase vehicles should not use four-wheel drive on corrugations. The rear axle supports most of the load and has the strongest differential; in four-wheel drive, snatch loads could damage the front differential or half-shafts.

Light vehicles may 'smooth out' the bumps by achieving enough speed to skim over the tops. Going fast over corrugations increases tyre temperatures, causing punctures. Softly sprung vehicles can go faster more smoothly, but often blow tyres and turn over. With minimal area of tyre in contact with the ground at any time, braking should be light cadence, and any turns of the steering wheel should be gentle. Short-wheelbase vehicles often become unstable on corrugations.

Radial tyres give a more comfortable ride. But do not lower the tyre pressures: there are usually sharp stones, and soft tyres run hotter.

Ruts and gullies

Where possible, you should straddle ruts with your wheels on either side. Larger ridges or ditches should be crossed at an angle in four-wheel drive. Ditches can be bridged or ramps built up to ridges with supported sand ladders. Ditches can be filled in with logs or stones; clear them again afterwards to avoid local flooding.

There will be points where the lowest parts under your vehicle may ground. Where these occur, try to remove the problem, or fill in the ruts with stones or brushwood: continually grounding differentials causes drain plugs that are not recessed to come undone and drop out.

Ruts negate steering. Even in four-wheel drive, turning the steering wheel has little effect on the vehicle's direction of travel. Check regularly out of the driver's window to ensure that the front wheels point straight ahead: otherwise, if they find some traction or the side of the rut is broken away, the vehicle may suddenly veer off the track.

If you are stuck in a rut on firm ground, try rocking out by quickly shifting from first to reverse gear. Do not try this on sand or mud, you will sink in deeper. If this fails, jack up the offending wheel and fill in the rut with stones or logs. A high-lift jack makes this easier and can, with care, also be used to shunt the vehicle sideways out of the rut.

Deserts and sand

Deserts are not all impassable sand dunes. Even large dunes are passable, and most deserts have larger areas of stone than of sand.

Most deserts freeze overnight in winter, making the surface crust firmer. Even if not frozen, there will be dew in the surface crust, making it firmest around dawn. This is the time to tackle dunes and the softest sections. Avoid travelling in the late afternoon, when low sun makes it difficult to spot sudden changes in dune strata (many accidents occur as vehicles fly off the end of steep drops).

Watch out for any changes in surface colour. If the surface you are driving on is firm and the surface colour remains the same, then the going is likely to be the same. If the colour changes, you should be prepared for possible softer sand. Moving sand dunes and dry riverbeds produce the most difficult soft sand.

Do not travel in other vehicles' tracks: the crust has already been broken and your vehicle's chassis will be that much lower and therefore nearer to sticking, to start with. Keeping your eye on other people's tracks will warn you of soft sections, but do not follow them for navigation, they may be 50 years old.

Never use aggressive-tread tyres on sand. Only a small percentage of desert sand is really soft; use tyres at normal pressures so that you can travel at comfortable speeds on the firm sections and make full use of speed where you have room on soft sections. Only lower tyre pressures where necessary.

In general, flat sand with pebbles or grass on its surface, or obvious windblown corrugations, will support a vehicle. If in doubt, get out and walk the section first. Stamp your feet, if you get a firm footprint then it should support your vehicle; but if you get a vague oval, then it is too soft.

If the soft section is short, you can make a track with sand ladders. Long sections require low tyre pressures and low-range four-wheel drive. Bedford trucks will not handle soft sand without the assistance of perforated plates and lots of human pushing power.

The key to soft sand is flotation and steady momentum; any abrupt changes in speed or direction can break through the firmer surface crust, putting the wheels into the softer sand below. Use as high a gear as is possible to avoid wheelspin. Speed up as you approach a soft section and try to maintain an even speed and a straight line across it. If you find yourself sticking, press down gently on the accelerator. If you have to change down, do so smoothly.

I travel not to go anywhere, but to go. I travel for travel's sake. The great affair is to move.
– ROBERT LOUIS STEVENSON

Dry river beds can be very soft and difficult to get out of. Drift sand will always be soft. If you wish to stop voluntarily on soft sand, find a place on top of a rise, preferably pointing downhill and roll to a stop without using the brakes and breaking the crust.

Most vehicles have too much weight on the rear wheels when loaded. These wheels often break through and dig in, leaving the front wheels spinning uselessly on the surface. A couple of passengers sitting on the bonnet can help for short bad sections; but you must not overload the front continuously or you will damage the front axle.

On firm sand, two-wheel drive (or with modern Land Rovers, the centre differential locked-out) gives more positive steering, avoids transmission wind-up and allows higher speeds.

Sand dunes require high-flotation sand tyres. You need speed to get up a dune, but you must be able to stop on top, as there may be a steep drop on the other side. Dunes are best climbed where the angle is least, so known routes, in opposing directions, are often some distance apart to make use of the easiest angles.

When descending steep dunes, use second gear low-range and drive straight down, applying some accelerator to control any slipping and retain steering control. If the vehicle noses in, use third gear low-range with your left foot on the brake and enough accelerator to keep the wheels moving.

The bottom of the well between dunes and the leeward faces of dunes have the softest sand.

If you have to sit out a sandstorm, turn the rear of the vehicle to face the wind and cover all windows, to prevent them becoming etched by sand.

Getting unstuck in sand

Once you are stuck in sand, do not spin the wheels or try to rock out: you will sink deeper and may damage the transmission. First off-load the passengers and, with them pushing, try to reverse out in low-range. The torque on the propeller shafts tends to tilt the front and rear axles in opposite directions relative to the chassis. So, if you have not dug in too deep, when you engage reverse, you tend to tilt the axles in the opposite direction to the direction involved when you got stuck, thus getting traction on the wheels that lost it before. If you stopped soon enough in the first instance, then this technique will get you out. If it does not, then the only answer is to start digging and use sand ladders.

It is tempting to do only half of the digging required, but this usually fails and you finish up working twice as hard in the end. Self-recovery with a winch does not work well either. Sand deserts do not abound with trees, and burying the spare wheel or several stakes deep enough to winch you out is just as hard as digging out the vehicle. Another vehicle on firm ground with a winch or tow rope can help, but you must dig out the stuck vehicle first.

Reconnoitre the area and decide whether the vehicle must come out forwards or backwards. Dig the sand clear of all points that are touching it. Long-handled shovels are required to get under the differentials: folding tools are useless. Dig the wheels clear and then dig a sloping ramp from all wheels to the surface, in the intended direction of travel.

Lay down sand ladders in the ramps – rear wheels only, if things are not bad, all four wheels if things are bad. Push the ends of the ladders under the wheels as far as possible, so that they do not shoot out. A high-lift jack helps here. Mark their position in the sand with upright shovels, because they often disappear when used and can be hard to find later. Then, with only the driver in the vehicle, and all passengers pushing, the vehicle should come out using low-range four-wheel drive.

Very fit passengers can dig up the sand ladders quickly and keep placing them under the wheels of the moving vehicle. Sometimes, if a ladder is not properly under a rear wheel when a vehicle first mounts it, it can tip up and damage a body panel or exhaust pipe; so an agile person has to keep a foot on the free end to keep it down. (Remember to move very quickly once the ladder settles, or you'll get run over.) Some sand ladder designs are articulated in the centre, or sectional and tied together, to correct this problem.

Do not tie the ladders to the rear of the vehicle, in the hope of towing them: they may cause you to bog down again. With a large convoy, a ramp of several ladders can be laid down on bad sections.

Driving the vehicle out backwards is usually the shortest way to reach firm ground, but you will still have to get across or around the bad section. Once out, the driver should not stop until he reaches firm ground. The passengers may then have a long, hot walk, carrying sand ladders and shovels, so they should also carry bottles of drinking water.

Vehicles of one tonne or under need only carry sand ladders that are just long enough to fit comfortably between the wheelbase. A single vehicle should carry four ladders; but vehicles in convoy require only two each, as they can help each other. Heavier vehicles require perforated steel or aluminium alloy plate.

Sand ladders and perforated plates bend in use. You can flatten them out again by laying them on hard ground, with the ends on the ground and the bend in the air, and driving over them.

Beaches

Where a beach is the only route, wait for low tide. Beaches are usually firm enough for vehicles between the high tide mark and a line four metres from the sea. In the sea itself there is likely to be an undertow. Beware of the incoming tide, which is often faster than you envisaged and can cut off your exit. Where there are large puddles or streaming water on a sea beach, beware of quicksand.

Salt flats

These behave like quicksand. You sink quickly and if you cannot be towed out quickly, it can be permanent! In areas known for salt flats (*sebkhas* or *chotts*), stick to the track, and convoy with other four-wheel drive vehicles. If you hit a salt flat, try to drive back to firm ground in a wide arc. Do not stop or try to reverse out.

Mud

Mud problems are found not only off-road but on main pistes after rain. Many routes immediately south of the Sahara and in South-East Asia become almost impassably muddy for months during their wet seasons.

If mud is heavy with clay, even ultra-aggressive tread tyres clog up. The answer is normal tyres fitted with heavy-duty snow chains.

Winches are useful among trees, but unless you are operating regularly in these conditions the extra weight and cost of these plus ground anchors are rarely worth it. More important is to adapt your vehicle to accept a high-lift jack without it slipping. Fit small sections of angle iron or tube longitudinally to front bumpers and rear chassis, or longer pieces transversely, with suitable notches cut out, to stop jacks slipping. Adaptors are available for fitting high-lift jacks to late-model Land Rover jacking sockets and Toyota Land Cruiser bumpers.

Choose the firmest ground, avoid boulders and tree roots. If necessary engineer a route, dig channels to drain away water, and dig away high points that could be awkward to climb or may cause the vehicle to lean or slip sideways. If the track slopes sideways over a drop, level it out. If the area freezes overnight, or the water is fed by glacier meltwater, then the route will be easier at dawn.

The key to getting through mud is momentum in four-wheel drive, using as high a gear as possible: but there may be unseen problems beneath it. If there are existing tracks or ruts that are not deep enough to ground your transmission, then use them. Otherwise, slog through, avoiding sudden changes in speed or direction.

If you get 'high centred', either jack up one side of the vehicle and build up the ground under the wheels, or shunt the vehicle to one side using a high-lift jack. If you have lost traction, but the vehicle chassis is not grounded, then locked-up drum brakes on wheels that have them, 'heeling and toeing' or left-foot braking if you have automatic transmission, are alternatives, to stop wheels spinning and divert traction to wheels that have grip.

When seriously stuck, digging out is heavy work and leaves the vehicle with a rise to climb. Jack up the vehicle and fill in under the wheels with stones, logs, brushwood and even spare wheels.

Perforated plate, placed upside down (i.e. rough side up), will give more grip to the wheels; but sand ladders become slippery.

Trying to tow out a stuck vehicle, if the towing vehicle is also on mud, usually fails. If the stuck vehicle is of similar size to the rescue vehicle, 'snatch-tow' (Kinetic Energy Rope Recovery using the correct KERR ropes) is the most effective solution; but you must thoroughly understand the technique and its dangers.

When you return to paved road, clear as much mud as possible off the wheels and propeller shafts, because the extra weight will put them out of balance and cause damage. Drive steadily for ten minutes to clear the treads, or you could skid.

Crossing water

If a turbocharger is fitted, allow it to cool before entering water.

The latest vehicles may have catalytic converters; in rough terrain these break up and cold water destroys hot catalysts. For Third World use, remove the unit to avoid an expensive replacement on returning home. If you cannot do this, or will be wading back home, fit a raised exhaust outlet. Any serious wading in cold water can damage catalysts.

Coat petrol engine ignition components with silicone sealant, including any breather holes in the bottom of the distributor; clear these breather holes as soon as possible after the crossing. Silicone sealant is preferable to grease, which melts in hot climates and runs onto electrical contacts.

On Land Rover vehicles, fit the clutch bell housing wading plug and, where supplied, the camshaft drive belt housing wading plug. These plug the holes that drain any leaking oil to prevent it getting onto the camshaft timing belt or clutch-driven plate. They should be removed after wading – not necessarily immediately, but within a few days. For regular wading, leave these plugs fitted; but remove them weekly, allow any oil to drain out, and then replace them.

Late-model vehicles should have remote axle breather tubes, venting above the engine; check their condition regularly. Older vehicles may have Poppet valves; check that these are clean and in working order. Hot axles fitted with poppet valves, if stuck in water for any length of time, will produce a vacuum on cooling and suck water in through oil seals. Poppet valve systems are easily converted to remote breather tubes.

Inspect the water on foot first. In warm climates, avoid wading in bare feet: in slow-flowing water there may be Schistosomiasis (bilharzia). In Africa, going about in bare feet is asking for worm and tick infections. Waders are more sensible than Wellington boots, as there may be unseen deeper sections. Use a shovel or staff to prod for depth, boulders or soft sections.

Choose a sensible angle of drive into the water and out on the other side. You may flood your engine if the angle in is too steep, and may not be able to get up the other side if the angle is too difficult.

If the riverbed is soft, lower the tyre pressures. Fast-flowing rivers will be faster and deeper, with more difficult entry and exit, where they narrow. If possible choose a wider section. Moving or stagnant water with an unbroken surface may be deep and is more likely to have a silt bottom, which vehicles could sink into. Moving water with a rippling or broken surface usually denotes a stony bottom, will be shallower and clear of silt; this is easier to cross. If there are dry patches, you can break up your crossing into stages. Rivers fed by glaciers or melting snow will be at their slowest and lowest level at dawn.

If the water will reach above bumper level, fix a waterproof sheet across the front of the vehicle to help create an efficient bow wave. If a waterproof sheet is not available, consider crossing the water in reverse.

If the water will come above the fan, remove the fan belt to cut down the spray onto ignition components. This is important with nylon or aluminium fan blades, which may flex and damage the radiator core, and essential if you decide to wade in reverse or have to back out. Only remove a fan belt for short periods, since the water pump no longer operates.

If the water will come above the floor, raise any articles that could be damaged by it. Have the rear door open and all baggage lashed down. The vehicle may float slightly, therefore losing traction.

Vehicles in convoy should cross one at a time. On deep crossings, the rear of a vehicle and its chassis take in water, which pours out on climbing the far bank, making this slippery and more difficult for following vehicles. Later vehicles should try alternative exits or allow time for the exit to drain and dry out.

Cross difficult water in second gear, low-range four-wheel drive, with any centre differential locked in, and avoid changing gear while in the water. Keep engine speed high enough for the exhaust pressure to stop the back pressure of the water from stalling the engine. It is worth adjusting the engine tick-over speed to a faster setting. Forward speed should be high enough to create a small bow wave. The trough created behind this bow wave keeps the engine bay and side doors in shallower water, lessening any spray over the engine. A fast walking pace is about right; if spray comes over the bonnet you are going too fast. In very deep water you will require first gear, to push the wave of water ahead of the vehicle.

If you stall in the water, remove the sparking plugs or injectors and try driving out in bottom gear low-range on the starter motor. This works for short distances.

If the bow wave cannot be maintained and there is a chance of the water being deep enough to reach the air intake, switch off before the engine stops. This is essential with a diesel. Water does not compress, so catastrophic damage can occur.

If fast-moving water is above bumper height, keep the vehicle at 45° to the direction of flow. The full force of water at 90° to the body will force the vehicle downstream and negate steering.

On easy crossings, keep the brakes dry by keeping your left foot lightly on the brake pedal. Once out of the water, dry out the brakes by driving for a few minutes this way. Disc brakes are self-cleaning, but drum brakes fill up with water and sediment; clean these regularly and don't forget the transmission brake.

If a petrol engine stalls or misfires, spraying WD-40 over all ignition components may get it firing again; if not, dry them all out thoroughly.

Flash floods in riverbeds

Although you may be in a river bed under a cloudless sky, heavy rain elsewhere can cause a flash flood that envelopes you. Most flash floods are seasonal, but freaks can occur at any time. Always be prepared and never camp overnight in a riverbed.

Where a riverbed has to be used in the rainy season, while driving upstream, watch out for possible flood-water. When driving downstream, have a passenger monitor the route behind you, while your own attention is on the terrain ahead.

Make mental notes of any places where you can quickly get up the bank out of danger. If you encounter flood-water coming down, get up the nearest bank. If this is not possible, drive quickly downstream to the first available escape route.

Third World ferries

Third World ferries should be embarked and disembarked in four-wheel drive with any centre differential locked in. This ensures that you do not push the ferry away from the bank, leaving your vehicle in the water.

Weak bridges

Inspect local bridges before using them. If there are signs that local vehicles cross the river instead of the bridge, then that is the safest way to go. If in doubt and the bridge cannot be avoided, unload the vehicle and cross slowly in four-wheel drive, with only the driver in the vehicle.

Snow and ice

Snow is deceptive because it does not always conform with the terrain it covers. In addition, areas subject to wind or shade may have black ice.

Off-road driving in snow will be easier at night, or in the early morning, when the snow is firmest and the mud below it frozen. As with sand, high-flotation tyres are an advantage on really deep snow. If they are fitted with snow chains, they should be at the correct pressures, not at low pressure, or the chains will damage them.

Snow chains should be located either on all four wheels, or on just the rear wheels. Having chains on just the front wheels will cause a spin if you touch the brakes going downhill. With vehicles that have large axle articulation, some designs of snow chains could sever the brake hoses, so check with your vehicle manufacturer before buying snow chains.

If the vehicle is empty, put some weight over the rear axle.

In very cold conditions, if you have a diesel engine, dilute the diesel fuel with one part of petrol to 15 parts of diesel, to stop it freezing up (use 1:10 for Arctic temperatures). This is illegal in the UK and could damage modern high-speed diesel engines, but is often necessary in the Third World.

On roads or tracks, keep to the middle to avoid sliding into ditches or culverts at the side. Drive slowly in four-wheel drive, in as high a gear as is possible, and avoid any sudden changes in speed or direction. Use the engine for braking.

If you drive into a drift, you will have to dig your vehicle out; it is easier to drive out backwards.

If you skid or spin, do not touch the brakes; depress the clutch, then, with all four wheels rolling free, you will regain control.

Convoy driving

Vehicles in convoy should be well spread out, so that each has room to manoeuvre, does not travel in another vehicle's dust, and has room to stop on firm ground should one or more vehicles get stuck. Adopt the system where any vehicle which gets stuck, or requires help, has its headlights switched onto mainbeam. This is particularly important in desert situations. All drivers should keep an eye out for headlights in their mirrors, as these can usually be seen when the vehicle cannot.

The last vehicle should have a good mechanic and a good spare wheel and tyre, to cover breakdowns.

Keep to the allotted convoy order to avoid confusion and unnecessary searches. The convoy leader should stop at regular intervals, to check that all is well with the other vehicles. 🙖

Overland by truck, van or 4x4
by Jack Jackson

TRAVELLING OVERLAND IN YOUR OWN VEHICLE gives you the independence and freedom to go where you like, in a way that no other form of travel can ever hope to match. It also provides you with a familiar bolt-hole that can take you away from the milling crowds and the alienation one tends to feel in a different culture. The vehicle may seem expensive to start with, and can involve you in mountains of bureaucratic paperwork, but considering the cost of transport and accommodation, it becomes a realistic way to travel, particularly when you can escape the bedbugs and dirt that often accompany cheaper accommodation.

Which vehicle?

The choice of vehicle will be a compromise between what can be afforded, what can best handle the terrain to be encountered, and whether spares, fuel, food and water have to be carried or are readily available en route.

Short-wheelbase Land Rovers or Toyota Land Cruisers, Range Rovers and Land

Rover Discoverys are ideal in the Ténéré sand sea, but it is impossible to sleep full-length in one of these without the tailgate being open and all the fuel, stores and water removed. Moreover, they are heavy on fuel. After a while, one may long for the convenience and comfort of a Volkswagen Kombi or another, similar-sized panel van!

For a protracted transcontinental or round-the-world journey, you need to consider what sacrifices have to be made to balance the benefits of the more cramped vehicles, including the length of time you expect to be on the road and the degree of home comforts you will want along the way.

Where tracks are narrow, overhung and subject to landslides, as in outlying mountainous regions such as the Karakoram, the only usable vehicles are the smallest, lightweight four-wheel drives, for instance, the soft-topped short-wheelbase Land Rovers or Land Cruisers and the smaller Jeeps. These vehicles also give the best performance when traversing soft sand and steep dunes, but their small payload and fuel-carrying capacity restrict them to short journeys.

Keep moving.

– HUNTER S. THOMSON

If you do not plan to encounter soft sand, mud or snow and your payload consists mainly of people, who, when necessary, can get out and push, you really only need a two-wheel drive vehicle, provided that it has enough strength and ground clearance.

Avoid large American-style conversions. They have lots of room and such home comforts as showers, toilets, microwave ovens and storage space; but their large size, heavy fuel consumption, high weight, low ground clearance, poor traction and terrible approach and departure angles make them unsuitable for any journey off the asphalt road. They also often have engines with electronic control systems, which are not repairable if they go wrong in the Third World.

If cost presents no problem and all spares are to be carried, the ideal vehicle would be an all-wheel drive with a payload of one tonne, evenly distributed between all wheels. Look for a short wheelbase, forward control, high ground clearance, large wheels and tyres, good power-to-weight ratio and reasonable fuel consumption. The vehicles best fitting this specification are the Mercedes Unimog, the Pinzgauer and the Land Rover Military 101 'one tonne'. These are specialist vehicles designed for best cross-country performance and are often soft topped to keep the centre of gravity low. However, the costs involved in buying, running and shipping such vehicles would deter all but the very wealthy.

Considering price, availability of spares and working life, the most commonly used vehicles are the long-wheelbase Land Rovers, the smaller Mercedes Unimogs and the Bedford M-type trucks. The VW Kombi and the smaller Mercedes panel vans are the most popular two-wheel drive vehicles. These are big enough to live in and carry food, water, spares, cooking stoves, beds, clothes, extra fuel and sand ladders. They also remain economical to run, small enough to negotiate narrow bush tracks and light enough to make digging out less frequent and easier.

These vehicles will carry two people in comfort, more if camping or using other accommodation overnight.

A high-roofed vehicle is convenient to stand up in and provides extra storage, but is more expensive on ferries. It also offers increased wind resistance, thus pushing up fuel consumption and making the engine work harder and run hotter. This shortens engine life and increases the risk of mechanical failure.

Trucks

Where heavier payloads are envisaged, such as in Africa, where you will often have to carry large quantities of fuel, the most popular four-wheel drive vehicles are the Bedford m-type trucks and Mercedes Unimogs. Bedford trucks are cheap, simple and, in some ways, crude. They have good cross-country performance when handled sensibly and slowly, but are too heavy in soft sand. They go wrong and bits fall off, but repairs can usually be improvised, and used spares are readily available.

Bedford m-type trucks are best bought ex-uk military, as are their spare parts.

Ex-nato Mercedes Unimogs are near to perfect for heavy overland or expedition work. Their cross-country performance is exceptional, and their portal axles give them extra ground clearance, though this also makes them easier to turn over. It is almost impossible to get them stuck in sand, though they will stick in mud. They usually have relatively small petrol engines, so you need to use the gearbox well, but fuel consumption is good. The standard six-speed, one-range gearbox can be converted to a four-speed, two-range gearbox, which is useful in sand. Four-wheel drive can be engaged at any speed without declutching. Differential locks are standard. The chassis is arranged to give good weight distribution over all four wheels at almost any angle, but this causes a bad ride on corrugations.

Mechanically, the Unimog is over-complicated. It doesn't go wrong often, but when it does it is difficult to work on and often requires special tools. Later models have the clutch set to one side of the transmission, instead of in line with it, making it much easier to change. Unimogs are best bought from nato forces in Germany. Spares must be carried with you. Diesel Unimogs are usually ex-agricultural or building contractor, and are therefore less well maintained than military vehicles and may have rust problems.

Land Rovers

Despite some weaknesses, Land Rovers are the most durable four-wheel drive small vehicles on the market. Their spartan comforts are also their main attributes! Most of their recent challengers are too softly sprung and have too many car-type comforts to be reliable in difficult cross-country terrain. Spare parts are readily available worldwide and they are easy to work on with most parts bolted on. The older Series iii leaf-sprung models, are more durable than the newer 'Defender' models, and leaf springs are easier to get repaired in the Third World. The aluminium alloy body does not rust, so bent body panels can be hammered back into rough shape and then forgotten. You don't have to be Hercules to change a wheel.

The short-wheelbase Land Rover is usually avoided because of its small load-carrying capacity; but in off-road use, particularly on sand dunes, it has a distinct advantage over the long-wheelbase models. Hard-top models are best for protection against thieves and safer when rolled, unless you have had a roll cage fitted.

When considering long-wheelbase models, it is best to avoid the six-cylinder petrol engine models. All cost more to buy, give more than the normal amount of trouble, are harder to find spares for and recoup less on resale.

The six-cylinder petrol engine uses more fuel and more engine oil than the four-cylinder petrol engine and the carburettor does not like dust or dirty fuel, which means that it often requires stripping and cleaning twice a day in very dusty areas. The electrical fuel pump gives trouble. The forward control turns over easily and, as with the Series IIa Land Rovers, rear half-shafts break if the driver is at all heavy footed.

The four-cylinder models are underpowered, but the increased power of the six cylinder does not compensate for its disadvantages.

The 109" v8 Land Rover has permanent four-wheel drive, with a lockable central differential. It is an excellent vehicle, but very costly on fuel.

The Land Rover 90 and 110, now renamed 'Defender', are designed for speed, economy and comfort on the newer, improved roads in Africa and Asia. Built on a strengthened Range Rover-type chassis and suspension, with permanent four-wheel drive and centre differential lock, stronger gearbox, disc brakes on the front and better doors all round, the vehicle is a vast improvement on earlier models. It is ideal for lightweight safari or personnel carrier use, but for heavy expeditions the coil springs should be upgraded or fitted with airbag-type helper springs.

In European Union countries, outside of the UK, 12-seat Land Rovers should be fitted with a tachometer and come under bus regulations.

Range Rovers and Land Rover Discoverys are not spacious enough for long journeys, nor do they have the load-carrying capacity.

Any hard-top or station wagon Land Rover is suitable for a long trip. If you buy a new Land Rover in a wet climate, run it for a few months before setting off on a trip. This allows the wet weather to get at the many nuts and bolts that keep the body together. If these bolts corrode a bit, it will save you a lot of time later. If you take a brand-new Land Rover into a hot climate, you will regularly have to tighten loose nuts and bolts, particularly those around the roof and windscreen.

Early Land Rover diesel engines were not renowned for their reliability. The newer five-bearing crankshaft diesel engines are better, but still underpowered. Land Rover Ltd still refuses to believe that the Third World requires a large, trouble-free diesel engine, and it is sometimes sensible to fit another engine, such as the Isuzu 3.9 litre or the Perkins 4,154.

With the new TDI turbo diesel engines, Land Rover appears to have fixed the problems of its earlier turbo diesel, and owners rave about their good fuel economy. The GRP camshaft timing belt is now 50 per cent wider, but still causes problems in hot, dusty climates, though, to be fair to Land Rover, many modern vehicles have engines fitted with this type of belt and suffer the same problems.

The latest Defenders and Discoverys have five-cylinder diesel engines with a chain drive to the camshaft, so they not only give more power but eliminate the problems of unreliable cam-belts. They are also available with electronic traction control, among other electronic gizmos, although this system is not suitable for Third World use as it is not user-repairable if it goes wrong.

Stretched 127/130 versions of Land Rovers are available, including crew cab versions, but they are underpowered when fitted with four-cylinder diesel engines. Modern Land Rovers do not have double-skinned roofs, so a loaded or covered roof rack is useful to keep the vehicle cooler in sunny climates.

Other 4x4s

The Land Rover Defender's superb axle articulation and lightweight body gives it a distinct advantage in mud, snow and soft sand. If these conditions are not likely to be encountered, then the leaf-sprung Toyota Land Cruisers are comfortable and reliable, though heavier on fuel. Many Toyota models have large overhanging front bumpers, rear steps and running boards, which negate off-road performance. Coil-sprung Toyota Land Cruisers are less reliable, and the latest models with independent front suspension are best avoided. Nissan Patrols lack off-road agility and, as with American four-wheel drives, their large engines are heavy on fuel.

Despite its Paris/Dakar successes, the Mitsubishi Shogun (called Montero in the USA and Pajero elsewhere) has not proved reliable in continuous Third World use. The Isuzu Trooper is not well designed for true off-road work. Suzukis are just too small. Spares for Japanese vehicles can be a problem to get hold of in some parts of the world.

As with Range Rovers, Mercedes Geländewagons have poor load-carrying capacity and their high costs limit their appeal. Several of the latest four-wheel drive vehicles are of monocoque construction, which leaves them without a strong chassis; together with the Suzuki Vitara, Toyota RAV4 and the new Land Rover Freelander, they are not suitable for overland or expedition use.

Four-wheel drive versions are available of most popular pick-up trucks. Those most common in Africa are based on the Peugeot 504 and the Toyota Hilux. The Synchro version of the Volkswagen Kombi has an advanced fluid-coupling four-wheel drive system but poor ground clearance.

Two-wheel drives

The Volkswagen Kombi is in use in almost every country outside the Soviet bloc and China. Anyone who has travelled overland through Africa, Asia, the Americas or around Australia will notice that the VW Kombi is still a popular independent traveller's overland vehicle. Its ability to survive misuse (up to a point) and carry heavy loads over rough terrain economically, while providing the privacy of a mobile home, are some of the factors that make it so popular.

The Kombi has a one-tonne payload and far more living space than a long-wheelbase Land Rover or Land Cruiser. It lacks the four-wheel drive capability, but partly makes up for this with robust independent suspension, good ground clearance and engine weight over the driven wheels. With experience and astute driving, a Kombi can be taken to places that will amaze some four-wheel drive vehicle buffs. The notorious 25 km 'sea of sand' between In Guezzam and Assamaka in the Sahara has ensnared many a poorly driven 4x4, while a Kombi has stormed through unscathed! With the use of lengths of chicken wire fencing, as sand ladders, plus some helpful pushing, a Kombi can get through quite soft sand.

The second most popular two-wheel drive vehicle for overlanders is the smaller diesel-engined Mercedes panel van, which is very reliable. All the stronger rear-wheel drive panel vans are suitable for overland use and most are available with a four-wheel drive conversion. Avoid vehicles that have only front-wheel drive; when loaded at the rear, they often lose traction, even on wet grass in a campsite.

Petrol versus diesel

Weight for weight, petrol engines have more power than diesel engines, but they have several disadvantages when it comes to hard usage in Third World areas. In hot countries there is a considerable risk of fire and the constant problem of vapour lock, which is at its worst on steep climbs, or on long climbs at altitude. Dust, which often contains iron, gets into and shorts out the distributor. High-tension leads break down, and if much river crossing has to be done, water in the electrics causes more trouble. A further problem is that high-octane fuel is not usually available and low-octane fuel will soon damage a sophisticated engine. However, petrol engines are more easily repaired by less experienced mechanics.

Avoid engines with electronic engine management systems. These are not normally repairable if faulty and a flat battery can cause problems with some of these.

Diesel fuel is messy, smelly and attacks many forms of rubber, but it does not have the fire risk of petrol and, outside Europe, is usually one-third of the price of petrol. It also tends to be more available, as it is used by trucks and tractors.

Diesel engines are heavier and more expensive to buy, but are generally more reliable and require less maintenance. An advantage is that extra torque is available at low engine revolutions. This allows a higher gear in the rough, which improves fuel consumption. This means that less weight of fuel needs to be carried for a section without fuel supplies – improving fuel consumption still further. There is also no electrical ignition to malfunction where there is a lot of dust or water. Against this is the fact that diesel engines are noisier and lack the acceleration of petrol engines, which can be tiring on a long journey.

A second filter in the fuel line is essential to protect the injection pump from bad fuel, and a water sedimentor is useful, but it needs to be well protected from stones and knocks.

Some Japanese diesel vehicles have 24-volt electrical systems.

Tyres

Long-distance travellers have to cover several different types of terrain, which makes it difficult to choose just one set of tyres for the whole route. Unless you expect to spend most of your time in mud or snow, avoid the aggressive-tread, so-called cross-country or all-terrain tyres. These have large, open-cleated treads that are excellent in mud or snow, but on sand they tear away the firmer surface crust, putting the vehicle into the softer sand underneath. Open treads tear up quickly on mixed ground with sharp stones and rocks.

If you expect to spend a lot of time in soft sand, you will require high-flotation tyres with little tread pattern. These compress the sand, causing the least disturbance to the firmer surface crust. Today's standard for such work is the Michelin xs, which has just enough tread pattern to be usable on dry roads but can slide about on wet roads or ice. The xs is a soft, flexible radial tyre, ideal for low-pressure use but easily cut up on sharp stones.

As most travellers cover mixed ground, they require a general truck-type tyre. These have a closed tread, with enough tyre width and lugs on the outside of the tread to be good mixed-country tyres, although obviously not as good in mud or soft sand. Such tyres, when fitted with snow chains, are better than any all-terrain tyre for snow or mud use and, if of radial construction, can be run soft to improve their flotation on sand. The best tyres in this category are the Michelin xzy series.

Radial or cross-ply, tubed or tubeless

Radial tyres are more flexible and have less heat build-up when run soft than cross-ply tyres. They have less rolling resistance, thus improving fuel consumption. For heavy expedition work, Michelin steel-braced radials last longer. You must use the correct inner tubes with radial tyres, preferably the ones produced by the same manufacturer. Radial and cross-ply tyres should never be mixed.

Radial tyres 'set' in use, so when changed around to even out tyre wear they should, preferably, be kept on the same side of the vehicle. A further advantage of radials is that they are easier to remove from the wheel rim with tyre levers when you get a puncture away from help.

Most radial tyres have soft side walls that are easily torn on sharp stones, so if you have to drive over such stones try to use the centre of the tyre, where the tread is thickest. For soft sand use, radial tyres can be run at 40 per cent pressure at speeds below 25 km per hour and 75 per cent pressure for mixed terrain below 50 km per hour. Remember to reinflate to full pressure when you return to firm ground. Tubeless tyres are totally impractical for off-road work, so always use tubed tyres and carry several spare inner tubes.

A vehicle travelling alone in difficult terrain should carry at least one extra spare tyre, as well as the one on the spare wheel. Several vehicles travelling together can get by with only the tyres on the spare wheels, so long as they all have the same size and type of tyres for full interchangeability.

Wide tyres

There is a tendency for 'posers' to fit wide tyres. Such tyres are useful in soft sand and deep snow, but in other situations they negate performance. Worse still, on asphalt roads, hard-top pistes or ice they lower the weight per unit area (and hence the grip) of the tyre on the road, leading to slipping and skidding.

Wheels and tyres that are larger than the vehicle manufacturers recommend can damage wheel bearings and cause problems with steering and braking

Never mix tyres of different sizes on four-wheel drive vehicles.

Roof racks

These need to be strong to be of any use. Many of those on the market are flimsy and will soon break up on badly corrugated pistes. Weight for weight, tubular section is stronger than box section, and it should be heavily galvanised.

To extend a roof rack in order to put jerrycans of water or fuel over or even beyond the windscreen is lunacy. The long-wheelbase Land Rover, for instance, is designed so that most of the weight is carried over the rear wheels. The maximum extra weight allowed for the front axle is the spare wheel and a winch. It does not take much more than this to break the front springs or distort the axle. Forward visibility is restricted when going downhill with extended roof racks. Full-length roof racks can be fitted safely, but must be carefully loaded; remember that Land Rover recommends a total roof weight of not more than 90 kg. A good full-length roof rack will weigh almost that on its own.

Expect damage to the bodywork and reinforce likely points of stress, in particular the corners of the windscreen. Good roof rack designs will have their supports positioned in line with the vehicle's main body supports, and will have fittings along the back of the vehicle to prevent the roof racks from juddering forward on corrugations. Without these fittings, holes will be worn in the roof.

Modern Land Rovers have aluminium roof channels, so roof racks fitted to these vehicles require additional supports to the bulkhead at the front and the lower body at the rear.

Nylon or Terylene rope is best for tying down baggage. Hemp rope deteriorates quickly in the sun and holds grit, which is hard on your hands. Rubber roof rack straps are useful, but those sold in Europe soon crack up in the sun. You can use circular strips cut from old inner tubes and add metal hooks to make your own straps. These will stand up to the constant sunlight without breaking. Ratchet straps should not be over-tightened.

In deserts, if one doesn't have a motor caravan, sleeping on the roof rack can be a pleasant way of avoiding spiders and scorpions. Fitting a full-length roof rack with plywood makes it more comfortable, as well as keeping the vehicle cool in the sun. Special folding tents for roof racks are available, at a price.

Conversions

An elevating roof or fibreglass 'pop-top' motor caravan conversion has advantages over a fixed roof van. It is lower on the move, can sleep extra people up top, provide extra headroom while camped and insulates well in tropical heat. Some of the better-designed fibreglass pop-tops do not collect condensation, even when you cook inside them. Some of the disadvantages are that they can be easier to break into, they look more conspicuous and more inviting to thieves than a plain top and they have to be retracted before a driver, disturbed in the night, can depart in a hurry.

In some vans, the hole cut in the roof to fit the pop-top weakens the structure of the vehicle. Driving on very bad tracks can cause cracks and structural failures in the body and chassis; failures that would not normally occur if the vehicle spent its life in Europe. Vans should have roof-mounted support plates added along the elevating roof to give torsional support.

A demountable caravan fitted to four-wheel drive pick-up trucks such as the Land Rover, Land Cruiser or Toyota Hi-Lux could provide a lot more room and comfort, but demountables are not generally robust enough to stand up to the off-road conditions of an overland journey. They also add considerably to the height and width of the vehicle and are more expensive than a proper conversion. Moreover, you cannot walk through from the cab to the living compartment.

Furnishing and fittings

Camper conversions should have fittings made of marine plywood rather than hardboard; it is stronger, more durable and not prone to disintegration when hot or wet. If your vehicle is finally destined for the US, it must satisfy US Department of Transport and state regulations for the basic vehicle and the conversion. The same applies to motor caravans destined permanently for Australia, where equally strict Australian design rules apply to both the vehicle and the conversion.

Most water filtration systems, Katadyn, for instance, are portable and many wall-mounted models can be fitted to a vehicle. On many motor caravans, the water tank and even gas cylinders are mounted beneath the floor, where they are most vulnerable off-road.

Front-opening vents or window quarterlights in the front doors are appreciated in warm climates, as are a pair of fans built in for extra ventilation. However, window quarterlights are attractive to thieves. Fresh air is essential when sleeping inside a vehicle in tropical climates and a roof vent is not enough to create an adequate draught. Equip open windows with mosquito netting and strong wire mesh.

On a long transcontinental journey, one will normally have to do without a refrigerator. (It is often preferable to use the space and weight for more fundamental items such as jerrycans or spare parts.) However, if you are carrying large quantities of film or medicines, you might want to consider using a lightweight dry-operating, thermoelectric 'Peltier-effect' refrigerator from Koolatron Industries, but fit an alternator and spare battery with a larger capacity and a split-charge system.

Stone-guards for lights are very useful, but you need a design that allows you to clean the mud off the lights without removing them (water hoses do not usually exist off the beaten track) and they should not be fitted with self-tapping screws. Such designs are difficult to find.

Air horns should be located away from mud, e.g. on the roof or within the bodywork, where they can be operated by a floor-mounted switch. An isolator may be located on the dashboard to prevent accidental operation of the horn.

For sunny countries, paint chrome windscreen wipers, wing mirrors and any wing steps matt black to stop dangerous reflections from the sun, and have fresh windscreen wiper rubber blades at the ready for when you return to wet climates.

A good, powerful spotlight fitted on the rear of the roof rack will be invaluable when reversing and will also provide enough light for pitching tents. Normal reversing lights will be of no use. Bull bars, also known as nudge bars, are usually more trouble than they are worth, may invalidate your insurance and damage the body or chassis if struck with any force. The EU wishes to ban them.

Paperwork

As well as the obvious requirement for passports, visas and personal insurance, you will require: vehicle insurance for the whole journey, the vehicle registration document, a letter of permission to drive the vehicle if you are not the owner, each of the two types of international driving licences (these vary in the languages of translation) and a *carnet de passage* for the vehicle. Have photocopies of all of these documents and spare passport-sized photographs. Some countries will insist that you also buy local insurance, but this will only give you the bare minimum of third party cover.

The *carnet de passage* acts as a passport for the vehicle and is intended to stop you selling it; it will be your largest single expense and is obtainable through the AA or RAC by depositing a bond or taking out insurance. A few countries will note the vehicle in your passport instead of requiring a carnet de passage.

All-important paperwork is best kept in a strongbox that is fixed directly to the vehicle chassis.

Finally, whatever type of vehicle you take and however you equip it, you should aim to be as self-sufficient as possible. You should have food to last for weeks, not days, as well as the tools, spare parts and personal ability to maintain your vehicle and keep it going. Without these, and in spite of the occasional genuinely kind person, you will be conned and exploited to the extent that the journey will become a major ordeal. With adequate care and preparation, however, your overland journey will be an experience of a lifetime. ✒

Running repairs
by Jack Jackson

BEFORE YOU DEPART ON AN OVERLAND JOURNEY, use your vehicle for several months, to run in any new parts properly. This will enable you to find any weaknesses and become acquainted with its handling and maintenance.

Give it a thorough overhaul before leaving. If you fit any extras, make sure that they are as strong as the original vehicle. For precise navigation, you should know how accurate your odometer is, for the tyres fitted: larger tyres, e.g. sand tyres, will have a longer rolling circumference. Fit a battery isolation switch: it could save your vehicle in a fire and is an excellent anti-theft device. (New models of these will allow enough power through, to run any necessary clocks and memory systems, when disconnected.)

Loading
Overloading is the largest single cause of broken-down vehicles and the easiest to avoid. Calculate your payload against the manufacturer's recommendation for the vehicle. Water is 1 kg per litre, fuel roughly 0.8 kg per litre, plus the weight of the container. Concentrate on the essentials and cut back on the luxuries. It could make all the difference between success and failure.

By using several identical vehicles travelling in convoy, you can minimise the weight of spares and tyres to be carried. The idea of using one large vehicle to carry fuel etc., accompanying several smaller, more agile vehicles, does not work out well in practice. The larger vehicle will often be heavily bogged down and the smaller vehicles will have difficulty towing it out, often damaging their drive train in the process. Also, the vast difference in general journey speed and the extra spares needed cause many problems, unless you are to have a static base camp.

For rough terrain, trailers are not advisable. They get stuck in sand, slip into ditches and overturn on bad tracks. Powered trailers have been known to overturn the prime vehicle. On corrugated tracks, trailer contents soon become so battered as to be unrecognisable. Trailers are impossible to manhandle in sand or mud, and make life difficult if you have to turn around in an awkward situation. They also reduce the efficiency of the front wheels' driving and put strain on the rear axle.

If you must take a trailer, make sure that it has the same wheels and tyres as the towing vehicle, that the hitch is the strong NATO type, and that the wiring loom is fixed above the chassis, where it will be protected.

Regular checks

Once in the field, check the chassis, springs, spring shackles and bushes, steering, bodywork, exhaust and tyres, every evening when you stop for the day. Every morning, when it is cool, check engine oil, battery electrolyte, tyre pressures and cooling water, and fill the fuel tank. Check transmission oils and hydraulic fluids at least every third day. In dusty areas, keep breather vents clear, on the axles, gearbox, and the fuel tank filler cap. Keep an eye on electrical cables for worn insulation, which could lead to a fire.

Make sure that you carry and use the correct oils and fluids in all systems. Deionising water crystals are easier to carry than distilled water, for batteries. Remember to lubricate door hinges, door locks, padlocks etc., and remember that in many deserts you need anti-freeze in the engine for night temperatures.

Brush all parts clear of sand or dust before working on them. When working under a vehicle, have a groundsheet to lie on and keep things clean, wear goggles to protect your eyes. A small vice fitted to a strong part of the vehicle will aid repairs. In scrub or insect country you'll need to brush down the radiator mesh regularly.

Punctures

Punctures are the most common problem in off-road travel. Rear wheel punctures often destroy the inner tube, so several spare inner tubes should be carried. Wherever possible, I prefer to repair punctures with a known good tube and get the punctured tube vulcanised properly, when I next visit a larger town. However, you should always carry a repair kit, in case you use all your inner tubes. Hot patch repair kits do not work well enough on the truck type inner tubes that are used in four-wheel drive vehicle tyres.

Michelin radial tyres have the advantage that their beads almost fall off the wheel rim when flat. If you cannot break a bead, try driving over it or using a jack and the weight of the vehicle. If the wheel has the rim on one side wider than the other, remove the tyre over the narrowest side, starting with both beads in the well of the wheel. Narrow tyre levers are more efficient than wide ones. Sweep out sand and grit, file off any sharp burrs on the wheel and put everything back together on a groundsheet, to stop any sand or grit getting in to cause further punctures.

When refitting the tyre, use liquid soap and water or bead lubricant and a Schrader valve tool to hold the inner tube valve in place. Start and finish refitting the tyre, by the valve. Pump the tyre up enough to refit the bead on the rim, then let it down again to release any twists in the inner tube. Then pump the tyre up again to rear tyre pressure. If the wheel has to be fitted on the front later, it is easy to let out some air.

Foot pumps have a short life in sand and are hard work. If your vehicle does not already have a compressor, then use a sparking plug socket fitting pump if you have a petrol engine, or a 12 volt electric compressor which can be used with either petrol or diesel engines. Keep all pumps clear of sand. When using electric compressors, keep the engine running at charging speed.

Damaged steel-braced radial tyres often have a sharp end of wire internally, causing further punctures. These should be cut down as short as is possible and the tyre then gaitered, using thicker truck inner tubes. The edges of the gaiter should be bevelled and the tyre must be at full pressure to stop the gaiter moving about. On paved roads, gaitered tyres behave like a buckled wheel, so they are dangerous. Most truck tyres (including Michelin xzy) can be re-cut when worn and these re-cuts are useful in areas of sharp stones or acacia thorns, where tyres damage easily. (These re-cuts are not legal on light vehicles in the uk.)

Wheel braces get overworked in off-road use, so also have a good socket or ring spanner available, to fit the wheel nuts. With a hot wheel after a puncture, you may need an extension tube on the wheel brace, to undo the wheel nuts; but do not retighten them this way or you will cause damage.

In soft sand, use a strong one-foot-square metal or wooden plate under the jack, when jacking up the vehicle. Two jacks, preferably including a high-lift jack, are often necessary in off-road conditions.

If your vehicle spare wheel is stored under the chassis, it can be difficult to get out, when you have a puncture off-road. Store it inside the vehicle or on the roof.

Fuel problems

Bad fuel is common; extra fuel filters are useful, and essential for diesel engines. The main problems are water and sediment. When things get bad, it is quicker long-term to drain the fuel tank, decant the fuel and clean it out. Always keep the wire mesh filter in the fuel filler in place. Do not let the fuel tank level fall too low, as this will produce water and sediment in the fuel lines. With a diesel engine, you may then have to bleed the system. If fuelling up from 40-gallon drums, give them time to settle and leave the bottom inch, which will often be water and grit.

If you have petrol in jerry cans in a hot, dry climate, always earth them to discharge any static electricity before opening, and earth the vehicle before touching jerry cans to the fuel filler pipe. Fuel starvation is often caused by dust blocking the breather hole in the fuel tank filler cap.

Electric fuel pumps are unreliable; carry a complete spare. For mechanical fuel pumps, carry a reconditioning kit. In hot countries or in low gear at altitude, mechanical fuel pumps on petrol engines often get hot and cause vapour lock. Wrap the pump in bandages and pour water onto it to cool it. If this is a constant problem, fit a plastic pipe from the windscreen washer system to the bandaged fuel pump and squirt it regularly.

Low-pressure fuel pipes can be repaired using epoxy resin adhesives, bound by self-vulcanising rubber tape. High-pressure injector pipes must be brazed or completely replaced. Carry spares of these and spare injectors.

Diesel engine problems are usually fuel or water, you should know how to bleed the system correctly. If this fails to correct the problem, check all fuel pipes and joints, fuel pump and filter seals, for leaks. Hairline cracks in the high-pressure injector pipes are hardest to find. Fuel tank leaks repair best with glass reinforced plastic kits.

Electrical problems

These are a constant problem with petrol engines. Carry a spare distributor cap, rotor arm, sparking plugs, points, condenser and coil; all tend to break up or short out in hot countries. Replace modern high-tension leads with the older copper-wire type and carry spares. Keep a constant check on sparking plugs and contact breaker points. If you are losing power, first check the gap and wear on the points. Spray all ignition components with silicone sealant to keep out dust and water.

Keep battery connections tight, clean and greased. Replace battery slip-on connections with clamp-on types. Keep battery plates covered with electrolyte, top up only with distilled water or deionised water. Batteries are best checked with a battery hydrometer. There are special instruments for checking the modern sealed-for-life batteries.

Alternators and batteries should be disconnected before performing any electrical arc welding on the vehicle. Never run the engine with the alternator or battery disconnected. Alternators are not as reliable as they should be. If the diodes are separate, carry spares; if not, carry a complete spare alternator. On some vehicles, the red charging warning light on the dashboard is part of the circuit, so carry spare bulbs for all lights. Make sure you carry spare fuses and fan belts.

Regularly check that batteries are well clamped down and that electrical wires are not frayed or passing over sharp edges. The risk of electrical fire due to shorting is very high on rough tracks.

Overturned vehicles

Given the nature of the terrain they cover, overturned vehicles are not unusual on expeditions. Normally it happens at such a slow speed that no one is injured, nor even windows broken. If this happens, your first action should be to make sure the engine has stopped and the battery is disconnected. Check for human injury, then completely unload the vehicle.

Once unloaded, vehicles can usually be righted easily using manpower, though a second vehicle or winch can make things easier, in the right conditions. Once the vehicle is righted, check for damage, sort out all oil levels and spilt battery acid, and any oil that may be in the intercooler (if fitted). Then turn the engine over several times with the sparking plugs or injectors removed, to clear the bores of oil above the pistons.

Caution: Stand well clear of the side of the engine that houses the sparking plug sockets or injector ports, and of any point in line with injector high pressure pipe outlets. Fluids will eject from these at pressure high enough to penetrate your skin or blind you. Replace the sparking plugs or injectors and run the engine as normal.

Short-wheelbase vehicles have a habit of breaking away or spinning on bends and corrugations, often turning over. So drive these vehicles with extra care.

Drowned vehicles

Make sure that the occupants are safe, rescue them first, then recover the vehicle to safe ground, where it will not obstruct other traffic. Empty the vehicle and allow it and all electrical components to drain and dry out. Check for water and silt in drum brakes, all oils and fluids, the air filter and the air inlet system, clear and clean as necessary. Water is heavier than oil, it sinks to the lowest point and can be drained at the drain plugs. If oil looks milky, it will have been emulsified by moving parts: wait several hours, drain off any free water and replace with new oils as soon as is possible.

Drowned engines

Note the 'caution' in 'Overturned vehicles' above.

With diesel engines, change the fuel filter and clean the sedimentor if fitted. Remove the sparking plugs or injectors and turn the engine over in short bursts with the starter motor. Continue until there is no sign of water in the cylinders. If there is sediment, strip the engine down. Refit all components and run the engine till warm; check for problems, especially for shorting out of electrical components – these could cause a fire. Stop the engine and recheck fuel filters for water, and drain or clean as necessary.

When you reach civilisation, have the vehicle hosed out with fresh water and replace all oils and fluids with new ones. With diesel engines, fully service the injector pump and injectors. If the vehicle drowned in sea water, have the complete wiring loom replaced and all electrical connections cleaned, or you will be plagued by minor electrical problems for evermore.

Extreme cold

Arctic temperatures are a very specialist situation. Vehicles are stored overnight in heated hangars. When in the field, engines are either left running or else have an electric engine heater, which is plugged into a mains power supply. Oils are either specialist or diluted to the maker's recommendations.

Petrol is the preferred fuel for lighter vehicles but, for heavier uses, diesel vehicles have heaters built into the fuel system and the fuel is diluted with petrol. All fuel is scrupulously inspected for water before being used. Batteries must be in tip-top condition, as they lose efficiency when cold.

General tips and improvisations

■ Steering locks are best removed; if not, leave the key in them permanently in dusty areas. A spare set of keys should be hidden safely, somewhere under the body or chassis.

■ When replacing wheel hub bearing oil seals, also replace the metal mating piece.

■ Wire hose clips are best replaced with flat metal Jubilee type clips. Carry spare hoses, although these can be repaired in an emergency with self-vulcanising rubber tape. Heater hoses can be sealed off with a sparking plug.

■ Bad radiator leaks can be sealed with epoxy resin or glass reinforced plastic. For small leaks, add some Radweld, porridge, or raw egg, to the radiator water.

■ Always use a torque wrench on aluminium cylinder heads or other aluminium components.

■ In sand, always work on a groundsheet and don't put parts down in the sand. In sandstorms, make a protected working area around the vehicle, using groundsheets. If possible, park the vehicle rear on to the wind and cover all windows to prevent them being etched by the sand.

■ If you get wheel shimmy on returning to paved roads, first check for mud, buckled wheels, gaitered tyres and loose wheel bearings. If it is none of these, check the swivel pins, which can usually be dampened by removing shims.

■ Carry any spare parts containing rubber well away from heat, including the sun's heat on the bodywork.

■ If you cannot get into gear, first check for stones caught up in the linkage.

■ If you use jerry cans, carry spare rubber seals. Always carry water in light-proof polypropylene cans, to stop the growth of algae. (Available ex-military in the UK.)

■ Lengths of strong chain with long bolts, plus wood or tyre levers, can be used as splints on broken chassis parts, axles or leaf springs. If you do not have a differential lock and need one in an emergency, you can lock the spinning wheel if it has a drum brake, by tightening up the brake adjuster cam, but only use this system for a few metres at a time.

■ For emergency fuel tanks, use a jerry can on the roof, with a hose connected to the fuel lift pump. Drive slowly and never let the can get lower than half full.

■ If one vehicle in convoy has a defunct charging system, swap that vehicle's battery every 100 kilometres.

■ For repair work at night, or camp illumination, small fluorescent lights have the least drain on the battery.

■ If the engine is overheating, it will cool down quickest going downhill in gear, using the running engine as a brake. If you stop with a hot engine, then unless it is showing signs of seizure, keep the engine ticking over fast; this will cool it down quicker and more evenly than if you stop it. If you switch off an overheating engine, you are likely to get a warped cylinder head.

■ Make sure that there are no pin holes in the rubber connecting hose, between the air filter and the engine inlet manifold.

■ If you have a partially seized six-cylinder engine, remove the piston and connecting rod involved, disconnect the sparking plug and high tension lead (or the injector if diesel). Close the valves by removing the push rods, or rocker arms if overhead cam. If diesel, feed the fuel from the disconnected fuel injector pipe to a safe place away from the heat of the engine, and drive slowly. If you have a hole in the block, seal it with any sheet metal plus glass reinforced plastic and self-tapping screws to keep out dust or sand.

■ In an emergency, you can run a diesel engine on kerosene (paraffin) or domestic heating oil, by adding one part of engine oil to 100 parts of the fuel, to lubricate the injector pump. In hot climates, diesel engine crankcase oils are good for use in petrol engines; but petrol engine crankcase oils should not be used for diesel engines.

■ Bent track rods should be hammered back as straight as possible, to minimise tyre scrubbing and the possibility of a roll.

■ With four-wheel drive vehicles, if you break a rear half-shaft, you can continue in two-wheel drive, by removing both rear half-shafts and putting the vehicle into four-wheel drive. If the front or rear differential is broken, remove both of the half-shafts on that axle and the propeller shaft concerned and engage four-wheel drive. If a permanent four-wheel drive jams in the centre differential lock position, remove the front propeller shaft and drive on slowly.

■ Temporary drain or filler plugs can be whittled from wood and sealed in with epoxy resin.

■ Silicone RTV compound can be used for most gaskets, other than cylinder head gaskets. Silicone RTV compound or PTFE tape is useful when putting together leaking fuel line connections.

■ Paper gaskets can be reused if smeared with grease.

■ If you develop a hydraulic brake fluid leak and do not have enough spare fluid, travel on slowly, using the engine as a brake. If the leak is really bad, you can disconnect a metal pipe upstream of the leak, bend it over and hammer the end flat, or fit an old pipe to which this has already been done. Rubber hoses can be clamped, using a round bar to minimise damage. If you have a dual system, then the brakes will still work as normal, but if not, you will have uneven braking on only three wheels. If you lose your clutch, you can still change gear, by adjusting the engine speed, as with double-declutching. It is best to start the engine with the gearbox already in second gear.

■ Four-wheel drive vehicles are high off the ground and it is often easier to work on the engine if you put the spare wheel on the ground and stand on it. If your bonnet can be hinged right back, tie it back so that the wind does not drop it onto your head.

■ Steering relays that do not have a filler hole can be topped up by removing two opposite top cover bolts and filling through one of the holes until oil comes out of the other.

■ If you burst an oil gauge pressure pipe, remove the 'T' piece, remove the electric pressure sender from it, and screw this back into the block. You will then still have the electric low pressure warning light. ❧

The art of motorcycle maintenance
by Chris Scott

SETTING OFF BY MOTORBIKE IS A BOLD BUT EASY DECISION TO MAKE. However, be under no illusions as to the monumental preparation required and the sacrifices needed for two-wheeled life on the road. Chief amongst these is a bike's limited ability to carry little more than essentials. Documentation for bikes is identical to that needed for cars, and one should always carry copies. The cost of a *carnet de passage* is one good reason not to take an expensive bike, the fact that a long journey will annihilate its resale value is another. Inexpensive bikes, well prepared, are the best way to go.

Before you go

Taking the UK as a departure point, two of the most popular itineraries are trips across Africa to Cape Town or across Europe and western Asia to India and beyond. Both routes are frequently undertaken by bikers. Africa, with its unavoidable desert and jungle is the harder of the two, a challenge of arduous terrain and tedious border crossings.

Before undertaking these big trips, you should consider taking an exploratory run, to Morocco, for example, to see how your bike will perform. Much can be learned on a test run, above all from the shock of finding out how your bike actually handles when fully loaded on dirt roads. Allow at least a year for preparation before starting your trip – and for finding your funding. A good place to start researching routes on the internet is www.adventure-motorcycling.com, which features over 100 trip reports from all around the world. Trans-Africa will cost about £4,000, plus the cost of your bike; India and back about £5,000 and round the world around £10,000, depending on your route and resistance to temptations.

When it comes to getting your bike to your starting point, remember that while shipping is cheap, it is also slow and unnecessarily complicated; air freight is much more efficient and reliable. Leave some money at home with a reliable friend, or a credit card number with a friendly bike shop, that way vital items can be quickly despatched with just one call.

Choosing a bike

A four-stroke, single-cylinder trail bike of around 600 cc is best for Africa. For the main overland route to India any road bike will do and, in this case, a big, comfortable, shaft-driven tourer makes a lot of sense. Road bikes will limit your ability to explore off the highway and are exhausting when you have to detour off-road, but they are a better option for passengers. Whatever bike you choose, consider these factors along with the total weight once loaded:

1. Lightness
2. Economy
3. Comfort

4. Mechanical simplicity
5. Agility
6. Reliability
7. Robustness

Once the most popular bike was Yamaha's xt600 Ténéré; pre-1989 models are best, being simpler, lighter and more economical to run, but these are now hard to find. BMWs are also famously popular, but stick to the old Boxer-engined models of between 800 and 1,000cc or the f650 Funduro. Suzuki drs (especially the new 400) and the bigger Honda xls are also good, particularly the xl650r, but avoid xrs, Yamaha tts and other enduro-type bikes, which are not built for the rigours of long-distance touring. KTM's 640 cc Adventure is, in some ways, an ideal bike – it has a huge tank and a bias towards off-roading, but at the cost of an uncomfortably narrow seat. Women or short-legged men might find lower-seated 350/400s easier to manage.

Bike modifications and tyres

If you're buying a bike, go for one with a big tank (i.e. at least 20 litres): this will solve a lot of logistical problems. Jerrycans are awkward to carry, but may be essential for a desert crossing. Water-cooled engines offer unnecessary complication, but oil coolers can be a useful addition in hot climates. Other tips are to get hold of a bigger footplate for your sidestand to support the bike on soft ground and to fit Barkbuster handlebar lever protectors and security bolts (rim locks) on wheel rims. Use only top-quality O-ring chains (did or Regina) with wheel sprockets (the manufacturers' originals are often the best). You are inviting trouble if you use cheap transmission and rolling components. DID, Excel or Akront rims, laced with heavy-duty spokes, are a good precaution for rough roads and heavy loads. Paper element in-line fuel filters are another wise modification, and if you don't trust foreign motor oil, change it every 3,000 km or so. Replace cosmetic, plastic sump guards with proper alloy bash plates. Carry a tool for every fitting on your bike, plus duct tape, wire and glue. Modern bikes (especially the ones recommended) are incredibly reliable, and so spares are up to you, but at least carry heavy-duty inner tubes, control levers and anything else that is likely to wear out or break before you can replace it.

Tyre choice is always a quandary. To cross Africa, run down to the Sahara on any old tyre and then fit Michelin Deserts, extremely tough desert racing knobblies that will last well beyond the mudbath of Zaire with barely a puncture. Less expensive, though not quite as tough, are Pirelli mt21s, an excellent road/dirt compromise. In sand or mud, knobbly tyres make the difference between constant slithering and prangs or sure-footed fun. If you're heading across Asia or round the world on roads, pick the longest-wearing rubber you can buy. Tubeless radial tyres are relatively new to overlanding, but last a long time and can be easily repaired on the wheel with plugs and glue, plus a pump or carbon dioxide cartridges. Even then, you must be completely at ease with tyre removal and repairs, the most common cause of breakdown – unless you choose to buy an Enfield Bullet in India. If this is the case, go for the 350 cc model and expect to meet many roadside mechanics. One overlander described her Bullet as being "always sick but never terminal".

Luggage and clothing

Overloading is the single most common mistake, but something to be avoided if your bike is to be manageable off the road. Every biking overlander ends up giving stuff away or sending it home. Although German bikers love their huge aluminium boxes, the only advantage of this system is security and neatness. Soft throw-over panniers in either tough woven nylon, ex-army canvas bags or rucksacks, or simply home-made leather bags are lighter, cheaper, crashable, repairable and not prone to fracture or inflict painful injury. They will not be water-, dust- or theft-proof, but if you keep your baggage nice and dirty no one will want to go near it. Small tank bags are also very handy for valuables, but Krauser- or Givi-type boxes will eventually break on your average Afro-Asian road. Bear in mind that widely loaded bikes use more fuel and, in all cases, pack heavy weights low and towards the centre of the bike. Bulky, light items such as sleeping bags can be carried high, even over the headlight, but tools are best stored in an old ammo box or pouch attached to the bash plate. Carry fuel in steel jerrycans, which also make useful bike props and stools and are resellable anywhere. Above all, think light: non-bike stuff can be replenished or replaced on the way.

Your choice of clothing is limited only by its usefulness and durability. You will only wear one jacket, so make sure it can protect you from the rain, wind, stones and crashes. Natural fibres are light and comfy, leather can be heavy and hot and takes ages to dry. Top-quality touring jackets, such as those produced by Hein Gericke, are expensive, but are also light, robust and functional. The merits of breathable fabrics such as Gore-Tex are dubious on a bike, but lots of big, secure pockets are very useful; use your jacket like a wallet or safe and never lose sight of it.

Helmet choice is personal, but remember that an open-faced one makes you appear more human to strangers. Always wear goggles or use a visor. Stout footwear will protect your vulnerable legs; proper motocross boots are best for off-road trips, otherwise ex-army boots will last.

Life on the road

Pull over from the roadside and camp out of sight of passing vehicles. Never ride at night or miss a chance to fill up with fuel and water. Be aware of you and your bike's limitations when driving off-road, especially in the early days when you have yet to learn the benefits of less baggage. Even if you are a loner, you will find yourself delighted to team up with other overlanders when faced with remote or dangerous sections of your trip, such as when crossing the Sahara or Baluchistan. The longer you travel, the lighter and more refined your equipment will become.

Resist the temptation to ride and ride and ride. Whatever your stated goal, it's the people you will meet on the road that will provide the longest memories, both good and, sometimes, if they are in uniform, bad.

Traditionally capricious, border guards are generally easy on bikers, recognising that two-wheel overlanding is no picnic. Nevertheless, approach a border as if you were going to be there for days. Bribes are usually small and clearly prompted, unless you are in trouble. If there is one common piece of advice most overlanding motorbikers come back with it is this: plan well but trust your ingenuity. Everything works out all right in the end. 🐾

CHRIS SCOTT has biked in the Sahara and West Africa several times, describing his trips in 'Desert Travels'. He also contributes to Rough Guides and has recently produced two overlanding guidebooks: 'The Adventure Motorbiking Handbook' and 'Sahara Overland'.

Buying and selling a car abroad
by Jack Barker and Paul Melly

WHO WANTS TO GET RID OF A CAR IN JAKARTA? Well, if you've just spent 17 weeks driving all the way from London, there's a fair chance that a plane, with a flight time of 17 hours, will seem much the most attractive way to travel back home. Either way, if you do sell a car or camper van, make sure that anybody who could be affected knows what you've done. Whether you think you still own the vehicle is merely the first stage. The important thing is to be certain that the authorities, both where you bought the vehicle and where you sell it, understand the position. What you have to tell them partly depends on where you bought the vehicle and what its status is.

Buying

Traditionally, the favoured market-place for those planning long overland trips, especially Australians and New Zealanders, used to be a car park on the South Bank of the Thames in London. That this has fallen foul of parking regulations is no great loss: many of those sold at the end of a European tour – or two – have already done a huge mileage and, although there may be nothing obviously wrong with the vehicles, vital parts can be almost worn out, landing you with hefty repair bills soon after the purchase. A better option is to look in the UK's trade papers (*Loot* in London, *Exchange and Mart* nationally, with any number of regional alternatives) and find an older model that is much less used. Auctions are another possibility if you know your way around an engine.

If you're planning on travelling in Europe, it is preferable to buy a left-hand drive car. Many vehicles are registered on the continent, with some of the cheapest coming from the Netherlands. Provided the car is not kept in the UK for more than 12 months at a stretch (unlikely if you are buying it specially for a trip), you will not incur the costs of UK registration. Buying on the continent will only suit seasoned travellers: the language barrier makes it hard to follow up advertisements and the costs of accommodation while you seek out the perfect vehicle will quickly erode any savings. Arranging insurance and registration while of no fixed abode can also be problematic: you can't get documents posted to a car park.

Outside Europe, regulations surrounding the purchase of vehicles vary. Many travellers wish to buy Enfield motorcycles in India, but to buy new you have to be a resident, so most people use a local to help, fraudulently, with the paperwork. In the best case it takes weeks for the paperwork to come through and, in any event, bending the law while abroad is fraught with risk. In many countries a cash-rich tourist is a magnet for people with shady vehicles to offload: it's the perfect opportunity to get rid of a stolen car with dodgy paperwork. Buying second hand from other travellers is often an easier option: check the noticeboards at travellers' hostels and don't hesitate to check the regulations with the police.

Obviously, tyres, brakes and suspension should be checked wherever you buy. But, if a long trip is planned through countries where spares will be hard to get, it is worthwhile investing in a professional mechanical check of the vehicle. In the UK the AA, among other organisations, offer this service. After all, even if the seller does provide some kind of guarantee, you're going to have difficulty enforcing it in Kurdistan or Mizoram.

Insurance

Before leaving, it is also essential, if you can, to get full details of the vehicle registration rules for any country you could be passing through. Although these are often available from tourist offices or embassies, the AA and RAC have collated most of the information you will need and provide advice for their members. Insurance cover providing for, at the very least, local vehicle recovery is also a good idea. As most countries charge duty on the importation of cars, those who drive in are also expected to take their vehicles out, even if it is involved in an accident or fire. In Italy, for example, it is illegal to dump a car, and computerised records mean you can always be tracked down.

The road was new to me, as roads always are, going back.
– SARAH ORNE JEWETT

Breakdown insurance can be expensive, but it probably won't be as expensive as the fine or recovery fee you may end up having to pay a foreign government's embassy for leaving them to clear away what was left of your camper van.

The AA and RAC have co-operation deals with their European counterparts, but once you've crossed the Bosphorous, Mediterranean or South Atlantic, you will probably have to turn to a company that offers near-worldwide cover, such as Europ Assistance (Perrymount Road, Haywards Heath, West Sussex, RH16 1DN, tel 01444 444631). When you come to sell at the other end, immediately contact the insurers to cancel the balance of breakdown insurance time remaining, for which you should get a rebate.

Before leaving the UK, you should take two photocopies of all your motoring documents, including those that prove insurance registration, ownership, road tax and, if applicable, MOT; together with your passport. You should take the originals with you, keep one copy in a locked compartment in the vehicle and deposit one copy in your bank or a PO box at home, where it can be checked out if necessary.

This should help you to prove ownership if the police in any country or the insurance authorities require it.

The papers will also be useful when it comes to selling the car – as they show that you own it and are therefore entitled to sell.

Selling

The complications surrounding selling a vehicle depend on where you sell it. If you have a *carnet de passage* you will need to get the *carnet* discharged by the local customs office, proving that the local taxes have been paid. Otherwise you will forfeit your bond. The easiest way to sell a car with a *carnet* in the developing world is to allow the *carnet* to be stamped out of one country and then enter the next without getting stamped in or having its details entered into your passport or your tourist card. Usually there's a form that can be 'bought' (in Africa a *laissez-passer* or *passavant*) that will permit this. This won't work at all borders, but once it does, your *carnet* will be in order and you'll be free to sell the car and fly home (if no other taxes are to be paid, fast). With or without a *carnet*, it is a good idea to make sure that the transaction is recorded in the presence of a witness who can be easily contacted later if necessary. Motoring journalist Brian Charig recalls the case of the American student who found a garage willing to buy his camper van in India. In this instance the customer asked the manager of the hotel where the student had just paid his bill with an American Express Card (which is traceable) to witness the deal formally. They wanted to be protected in case something went wrong.

Written proof of sale is a safeguard against someone else committing a motoring offence, or even using the car for a serious crime, after you have sold it. You can demonstrate to the local police that it was nothing to do with you. To tell the police when you sell the car is, in any case, the correct thing to do.

When you sell your car you hope to keep, or spend, all the money you have been paid for it, so it is vital to make sure the contract of sale stipulates that the local buyer will meet the cost of all taxes, import duties or other official fees involved. When a foreigner sells a vehicle to a local, that normally constitutes an import, so be certain that the price you agree is net of all customs dues, sales tax, etc. And before you leave home, check (anonymously) with the embassy of the country where you plan to sell as to how the deal will be viewed by officials. If they record the fact that you bring in a car on your passport or entry document then you're probably not in a good place to sell the vehicle: the people checking you out at the airport customs or passport control may well want to know what you have done with it.

There are one or two legal ways to beat import duties, which can be as much as 400 per cent of the value of the vehicle. If you have owned the car for at least a year, plan to own it for another two, and if it is the first you have imported into that country you can normally take it in duty free. If the buyer is remaining in the country, they could leave it in your name for the required two years. Only do this, however, if you know the buyer well enough, either personally or by repute, to ensure that they are trustworthy. Or you can legally sell it in the zone between two borders, although this would mean the buyer would have to have access to free passage of a fairly large sum of money across the borders. Usually such sharp practice sails too close to illegality to be recommended. The sale between borders scam more often means the buyer plans to dump you in no man's land with no re-entry visa and drive past bribed customs officials, leaving you high and dry – a common trick on Mauritania's borders. Selling to another traveller, diplomat or foreign resident who is, for whatever reason, not bound by local laws is usually safer and more straightforward.

Using the money

A further factor that could influence your choice of where to sell is the local currency status and regulations. Many developing nations have a currency that is not internationally exchangeable, and such regulations are often backed by controls on what you can take out, in both local money and foreign exchange. This means that even if you manage to get paid in a hard currency, a last-minute tip-off to the border guards can result, at best, in your hard-won cash being confiscated. At worst, you'll be locked up as well.

Ideally, choose a country with an internationally convertible currency, such as the Singapore dollar, or perhaps the CFA (African franc, underwritten by the Bank of France). That way, if you do take out the payment for the car, you will be able to change it into money you can spend at home.

If you cannot plan to land up in a hard currency nation, find out what the local exchange control rules are. Many countries are so short of hard currency they must restrict its use to buying essential imports, and these are unlikely to include fifth-hand cars from foreign tourists. Even some countries that do have a convertible currency restrict what funds can be taken abroad.

The simplest answer might be to check before you leave what you can buy with the local money – food, souvenirs, hotel accommodation or air tickets – and spend your takings on the spot. But most cars, in the developing world, are worth an awful lot of handicrafts. 🐾

JACK BARKER is a freelance travel journalist and guidebook writer.

Shipping a vehicle
by Tania Brown and Keith Kimber

WE'RE ASSUMING HERE THAT SHIPPING by the cheapest means is your goal. After all, if you have enough money, shipping a vehicle can mean nothing more than driving it to an agent and telling him where you want it to go.

First you need to find out who sails to your destination. If you have internet access, this is an excellent place to start. But remember, as we enter the internet age it is heretical to say this but, speaking from experience, not everything is on the internet. So it's a good idea to look through the *Yellow Pages* and contact shipping agents as well.

Other handy sources of information are the newspapers that serve the ports. They appear under a variety of names, such as *Shipping Times* or *Shipping Schedules*, and some less-obvious names, such as *The Bulletin* in Panama. Most are published weekly. If you can't find one of these useful publications, then shipping agents are usually happy to give away last week's copy.

These publications contain a gold-mine of information. Listed are the pier and berth numbers for all ships in port, telling you exactly where each ship is located. Also listed are the departure dates for each ship, their final destinations and arrival dates, the shipping line, its local agent and types of cargo carried. The same information is given for ships at sea that are scheduled to arrive. There's also usually a directory of agents' telephone numbers and addresses. In some countries all this information appears as a weekly supplement to a regular newspaper.

If you want really cheap shipping then you can try accompanying your vehicle as a working passenger. Whenever we did this, our vehicle was taken for free. Regular shipping lines are now quite reluctant to take working passengers but the newspaper will list unscheduled 'tramp' ships using the port – mission boats, training ships, all kinds of 'oddball' one-off vessels – that might take you on board. These ships don't always have agents at the ports, so you may have to contact the captain direct. Where port security is minimal and/or corrupt you can try to enter the docks and speak to the captain personally. Any visual material, such as photos and maps of your journey, are invaluable as an introduction. One good photo can jump the language and cultural barriers and get him interested enough to talk to you. If port security is strict, there is another way. When a ship docks, it is immediately connected to a telephone line. Each berth has a different telephone number. In Sydney, for example, the numbers for each berth are listed in the telephone directory. Consult your shipping journal for the ship's berth, look up the number for that berth in the phone book and you can speak directly to the ship. If the numbers aren't in the phone book, ask at the shipping and port manager's office.

If the captain will not allow you to work your passage then it's not a bad idea at this point to make him a realistic offer of payment. It might still work out cheaper than going through normal channels.

One final, very important point: before going to sea with anyone make sure you feel comfortable about the captain and crew. There are no witnesses and no one to help you once you leave port. Women travelling alone should be especially careful.

If you're on the kind of expedition that can generate publicity for a shipping company, you may be able to offer this in exchange for free shipping for your vehicle. We've sometimes received offers from regular shipping lines to take our vehicle unaccompanied to various parts of the world. For this, approach the operations manager or general manager of the shipping line or its agent. As well as generating your own publicity for the company, you could also offer to send them any number of photographs they can use in their own advertising: pictures showing the company logo on your vehicle as you tackle the next desert or jungle. A nice way of saying "thank you" is to give a talk and slide show for the staff.

If you are going to pay to ship your vehicle, things become more straightforward. Contact the agents that list sailings to your destination and compare freight costs. Shipping freight costs are always based on volume unlike airfreight costs, which are always based on weight. The basic freight rate usually has three surcharges added to it that you need to look out for. They are bunker surcharge, currency adjustment factor and wharfage charges. Bunker surcharge takes account of fluctuating fuel costs, currency adjustment factor takes account of fluctuating exchange rates and wharfage charges are the costs of using the dock. Make sure these are included in any quotes you receive. Sometimes the bunker surcharge and currency adjustment factors can be negative values, and represent a discount.

Countries with weak economies may insist you pay your freight in US dollars. It's advisable to carry enough US dollars (rather than pounds) for this purpose

Packing your vehicle

Your next concern is how the vehicle will travel. Try to avoid crating it if you can. Crating is either expensive or involves a lot of backbreaking work if you build it yourself. Even in countries where labour is cheap, timber can be costly. It's also inconvenient – you can't drive your vehicle to the ship when it's in a crate. However, having said that, we recently had a crate built for us in Vancouver, Canada. The crate was very cheap and, because timber is so plentiful in Canada, it was fabulously made. The carpenter even used hardwoods in it – hardwoods that were worth a small fortune in our destination, Japan.

Uncrated, the vehicle can go break-bulk, roll-on/roll-off or containerised. Containerised is best. The vehicle is protected from theft and the elements, can't be damaged during loading or unloading and you can leave all your luggage inside. Roll-on/roll-off services are very convenient. The vehicle is driven onto the ship and stored below deck – just like a regular car ferry. But these only operate on certain routes and your luggage shouldn't be left in the vehicle. Break-bulk means it is carried as it is, either in the ship's hold or on deck surrounded by all the other break-bulk cargo.

If you must crate your vehicle, visit an import agent to try and obtain a ready-made crate the right size.

Paperwork

A forwarding agent can do all the paperwork for you, but if money is a consideration you can save quite a bit by doing it yourself. The bureaucracy can often be very confusing, especially in less developed countries, so one way of getting the job done quickly is to team up with a 'hustler' who works for a forwarding agent. These young lads spend all day pushing paperwork through the system. They know where to find port trust offices, the wharf storekeeper's office, main customs building, port customs building, etc. These are buildings and offices that can often be spaced far and wide across the city. They know how to persuade customs officers to inspect the vehicle and wharf officers to certify documents. Better still, they know what kinds of 'tips' are expected down the line. We've always found them friendly, helpful types, with great sympathy towards anyone on the same side of the counter as themselves, pitted against the officials. They've never objected to our tagging along to push our own paperwork through the system. In return, we buy them cold drinks and a good meal each day we're together, and give them a few dollars to thank them for their help at the end.

Be well prepared if you do your own paperwork. Take a dozen sheets of carbon paper, a handful of paperclips (there will be a lot of copies), a good ballpoint pen, some large envelopes and a pocketful of small-denomination notes in the local currency. Commit your passport number, engine and chassis number, vehicle weight and local address to memory so you can double check details as the officials type them out (this is also good practice for any overland traveller when crossing land borders). Remember, if a single digit is incorrect in the serial numbers you will not be entitled to your own vehicle at your destination because it will technically be a different vehicle – and we've been in many countries where a technicality like that is what the local customs officers pray for. People have lost their vehicles this way. We also carry a rubber stamp kit to make up our own rubber stamps. It saves hours filling out forms – especially if you are doing a number of vehicles. It's normal practice in less developed countries to have to buy all the forms you need – either at the port or a stationer's in town.

Preparation

Clean the vehicle thoroughly before shipping (especially under the mudguards where dirt collects) to try to avoid the cost of it being quarantined or fumigated on arrival. In Australia it will probably be quarantined, no matter how clean it is.

From experience, we know not to rely on the crew to tie our vehicle properly. If you are travelling on the ship with your vehicle, here are some things to look out for: four-wheeled vehicles should ideally be lashed on deck with chains and bottle screws, not rope, which can fray and stretch. If only rope is available, a length of flexible hose, cut along one side to enable it to be 'clipped' over the rope, makes good anti-chafing gear. Motorcycles should be off the centre-stand, wheels chocked front and back and the bike tied to a post or railing using wooden spacers. Look ahead and be prepared to take your own rope. We ended up using the guy ropes from our tent and every webbing strap we owned on an Indian ship to tie our motorcycle securely.

Try not to leave a vehicle unaccompanied at the dock. This applies to some airports. Paperwork can be done two days before sailing, then the vehicle is inspected, cleared by customs and loaded the day it sails. In some countries you might want to try and supervise loading. While loading our motorcycle onto a Russian ship recently, we didn't bother to supervise too closely and they ended up breaking the luggage rack. If you can, use rope slings rather than a net. A four-wheeled vehicle should be lifted using pairs of boards or poles chained together under the wheels. If the crew is not set up to load four-wheeled vehicles one solution is to drive the vehicle into an empty container so that it can be lifted on board. To lift a motorcycle, sling a rope through the back wheel and under the steering head.

If your vehicle must be left on the dockside and loaded in your absence, don't leave any luggage with it.

In some countries it can be quite important to stay in the country until you've seen the vehicle leave.

Again, depending on the country, it's a good idea to meet the ship on arrival and confirm your cargo will be unloaded. When we arrived in Malaysia, they told us our bike was scheduled to continue to Singapore. We had a tough time convincing them they were wrong.

Once unloaded, the vehicle will be held in customs until you complete the paperwork to release it. It really ought to go inside a locked shed and it's worth paying to ensure this happens. The port usually charges for storage once the vehicle is unloaded. Sometimes the first few days are free.

Be philosophical about minor damage. Put any dents down to adventure!

Air freight

In recent years, airfreight rates have become quite competitive and are worth looking into for anything that will fit into an aeroplane – such as motorcycles. Sometimes airfreight is the only way of getting somewhere – inland, for example.

In a passenger aircraft, the motorcycle usually lies on its side in the cargo hold. A set of crash bars will support it without damage. It must fly completely dry: no fuel, engine oil, brake fluid, coolant, battery acid or air in the tyres. People worry their battery will be ruined by draining the acid. We've drained ours many times and once left it dry for more than two weeks without any ill effects. It didn't even lose any charge! But don't use it before refilling with acid. Don't plug the breather hole or the whole thing can explode. A wad of cotton wool over the hole will soak up any acid drops and allow it to breathe. Freight charges are based on weight.

Special notes

We have met people who have been obliged to spend a lot of money on anti-pollution devices for their vehicles on arrival in California to comply with state laws. This doesn't apply to everyone, but if in doubt, ship to one of the other 49 states. Amazingly, Florida has no vehicle-inspection or anti-pollution requirements.

On entering Panama, you have to specify the place from where the vehicle will be shipped. If undecided, you might specify 'Colon'. When you've organised your shipping, visit the customs head office at Ancon to make any changes.

Finally, shipping/air freighting really isn't all that bad. Things often go smoother and quicker than you think and there are frequently people who will help you out. If you encounter just a quarter of the potential problems mentioned here you've had an unusually bad time. 🐾

TANIA BROWN and KEITH KIMBER set off by motorbike to see the world in 1983. They returned 16 years and six continents later.

Up in the air

Aviation safety
by David Learmount

IT IS EASY TO SAY THAT FLYING IS SAFE; BUT SAFE COMPARED WITH WHAT? Fear of flying is only partly rational, which makes it difficult to persuade the afflicted with the unfeeling logic of statistics. Even when nervous fliers are provided with a comparison that brings the truth of flight safety into easy perspective, the ultimate hurdle is man's fear of falling from heights. The latter has never been reduced – let alone eliminated – by pointing out that people don't often fall to their death.

Those frightened of flying will hardly have been reassured by a grim procession of disasters in the 1990s, among them the TWA jumbo explosion off Long Island, New York. Worse still, the fundamental cause of this catastrophe may never be known. The likelihood of solving similar mysteries in future looks sure to be increased by the recent decision of the US safety authorities to demand that all airliners carry sophisticated flight data recorders, the 'black box'.

Despite recent events, flight safety should be put in statistical perspective. During 1999 the world's air travellers made just over 1.5 billion individual journeys on scheduled airlines. It was an average year for flight safety, compared with the last ten years: there were 48 fatal accidents to civil airliners of all kinds, including the domestic short-hop propeller-powered type and cargo flights. The world total of airline deaths was low at 730; the average number of fatalities each year is just under 1,200.

Given the world average, a traveller would have to take 1.5 million flights before facing his or her statistical end. If that means very little to you, read on to put it into perspective. If it sounds horrifyingly dangerous, read on to discover how you can improve your chances enormously by knowing how to be selective about airline safety.

In the average fatal accident, more than half the people on board survive. It has also been shown that frequent air travellers have a better chance of surviving accidents than occasional travellers: this is assumed to be because they know the aeroplane better, panic less, and so can get out faster. Since you will want to be one of those who survives any accident that your flight has, take the emergency procedures briefing seriously. This is not paranoid, it's pure sense. Look at where all the exits are relative to you and imagine finding your way to them in the dark. Count the seat rows to them. Read the emergency cards carefully, study the brace position, have your seat belt firmly (really firmly) fastened at take-off and landing, and slacken it in flight but always have it fastened. Look with particular care at the diagram showing how to open the exit doors, and imagine opening them yourself in the dark. Having done all this, sit back and enjoy your flight.

Airlines specialise in delivering travellers over long distances fast and safely.

Risk does not increase with distance on an airline flight, whereas it increases almost directly in proportion to the distance travelled in a car. According to statistics there is no country in the world where the average car driver could expect to survive 1.5 million journeys if each trip was 1,000 km, which is the safety level offered to airline passengers.

Multiple car journeys of 1,000 km may sound irrelevant, but the statistics could mean something to the traveller who is considering driving from, say, London to the Côte d'Azur by car: if the purpose is to enjoy the countryside and the local cuisine *en route*, then drive; if it is to avoid flying for perceived safety reasons, your mathematics are flawed; if you are driving because of an irrational fear of flying, then enjoy the route and good luck – in relative terms you will need it.

The world airline safety average, however, is a very rough guide indeed because of enormous regional variations. Actual safety depends heavily on what nationality the airline is, whether the flight is domestic or international, where the flight is taking place, whether the aircraft is jet- or propeller-powered, and what the prevailing weather is like at take-off and landing.

The world's most statistically safe flight would be with an Australian airline, on an international flight to an American destination in summer (American summer), using a jet aircraft. More about regional variations later. Conversely, the least safe would be a domestic flight in a country with a 'Third-World' economy (specific details later) in a propeller-driven aeroplane (particularly if the propeller is driven by a piston engine rather than a turbine), in bad weather.

Air travellers at the planning stage sometimes ask whether there is an airline safety league table. Surely, they say, the safe airlines will publicise their achievement, proudly laying claim to their place in the league? In fact, even the safest carriers do not dare to. Airline fatal accidents are so statistically rare that even a single fatal disaster could make the top-of-the-league carrier disappear from the top 50 – and what might that do to the clientele's loyalty? Beside which, the airlines know that high places in league tables do not eliminate the basic fear of flying anyway. All a league table would do is to imply that air travel is dangerous. Do travellers require a league table of railway operators? Of coach companies? Of taxi drivers? How would a league table be drawn up? Should it take into account accidents since flying began?… since jets took over?… during the last ten or 20 years? Should the accidents taken into account be those in which someone died, or in which everyone on board died, or include also those incidents in which people were injured? And where does the league table put a brand-new airline? It is unproven, inexperienced, but has not had an accident yet, it could be at the top of the league.

> *There are only two emotions in a plane: boredom and terror.*
> – ORSON WELLES

These difficulties of definition are among the reasons why airlines themselves steer clear of selling safety. But above all, selling safety clearly implies that there is something to worry about in the first place.

Probably the best indicator of the safety of any form of travel – if it were possible to get the information – is the size of the operator's insurance premium. If someone has offered you a lift in a car and you want to know how safe a driver he is, ask how much he pays for his motor insurance. The higher it is, the more likely you are to die. Airlines are the same. It is the plain truth that Third World airlines and carriers from developing economies generally pay the highest premiums. The Third World airline market does not, it is true, have the same bargaining power with the insurance underwriters that, for example, the US airlines have. But in the end, it is simply accident rates which determine the rate of the premiums. In the USA, airlines will face annual premiums less than 0.5 per cent of the value of their aeroplanes, whereas some carriers from Africa and South America will pay more than three per cent.

Airlines can be crudely graded for air safety by the continent in which they are based: North American airlines, as a whole, are the most consistently safe; the Middle East has had an excellent record for a long time now; western European airlines offer a high level of safety; Asia, the Indian subcontinent and South-East Asia has a mixture of adequate and bad, with patches of good; Central America is poor, but South America is making an apparently successful attempt to recover from a bad record in the 1980s and earlier; and finally African airlines score lowest for safety, with a few exceptionally good airlines among the bad records.

The disparity is enormous: an African airline is more than ten times as likely to have an accident involving fatalities than a North American, Middle Eastern or Western European one. As for where the accident is most likely to happen, the continents are ranged in a similar order, but the disparity widens still further, with Africa topping the league by far. Finally the majority of accidents happen to domestic airlines – international carriers have a better record on average.

As for the exceptional nations, Australia is the safest, along with the USA, then come the Western Europe and the Middle Eastern nations, and competing for bottom marks are Nigeria, Taiwan, Indonesia and Korea.

The safest airline in the world is Australia's Qantas, which has not harmed a soul since the days of wood-and-fabric biplanes in 1937, when it was known by its original name, Queensland and Northern Territories Air Services. But just to show how misleading – even unfair – an airline league table could be, Qantas, with its half-century perfect record, would not be at the top of a ten-year table chart because it is a relatively small airline. Bigger US or European carriers that had a clear record during the last ten years (even though they might have had a fatal accident in the preceding decade) would be higher in the league table than Qantas because they would have operated more accident-free flights in the period under review.

In December 1990, the US magazine *Newsday* carried out an airline safety survey of 140 carriers between 1969 and 1990 using some unusual premises in its calculations. Nevertheless the results again confirmed the well-established truth that the airlines of the world's richer nations tend to have the best records.

Newsday's method was to take not just fatal events against number of flights, but the on-board survival rate in the accidents. This made Swissair safest in the list of those airlines which, during the 22-year period, had at least one fatal accident. With a single crash in 2,036,000 flights and a 91 per cent survival rate in that event, *Newsday* gave the odds of dying on Swissair at one in 22,623,000. It is statistically extremely shaky to forecast Swissair passengers' (or any other airline passengers') safety in that detail on the basis of a single event in 22 years. It is more accurate to say that Swissair is a very safe airline. Of course in 1998 Swissair suffered a terrible accident when one of its aircraft crashed into the sea off Nova Scotia, which would have shaken the *Newsday* statistics, but it remains a safe airline.

In that same period, to take a random list, the following international airlines had not had any fatal accidents: Qantas, Ansett (Australia), Aer Lingus, Austrian Airlines, Air Madagascar, Air UK, Braathens (Norway), Cathay Pacific, Finnair, Malaysian Airlines, Sabena (Belgium) and Singapore International.

The biggest safety improvement in aviation's history came with the introduction of jets and turbo-prop engines because the turbines that form the core of both engine types are far more reliable than piston engines. So safety climbed steadily during the late 1950s and in the 1960s as piston-power gradually left the scene. Strangely, there was another upward hike from the 1970s to the 1980s, the reason for which was less clear. But during the last ten years of the millennium, flight safety, having reached a high level, is improving only slowly. To a large extent it is the law of diminishing returns.

The industry itself is becoming more concerned with 'human factors'. 'Pilot error' has always played a part in some two-thirds of all serious accidents, so now that aircraft technology has become progressively more refined and less likely to fail with disastrous results, the experts are looking for ways of making pilots safer. Aviation psychologists are studying pilot behaviour on the flight deck, communication between pilots, and the way they handle today's computerised cockpits.

There is some concern that aircrews are beginning to feel superfluous in machines that do all their tactical thinking and flying for them. The pilots' attitude to the task has to be totally different from what it once was: formerly the job was to fly the aeroplane, now it is to manage the flight in a progressively more complex and crowded environment. The British Civil Aviation Authority leads the world in the 'human factors' field, demanding of pilots that they take an examination in task-related behavioural psychology as a part of their commercial pilot's licence-qualifying procedure. The intention is that they become more aware of the kinds of human mistakes their environment can lead them to make.

> *The stride of passengers off an airplane is always jauntier than the stride on.*
> — TOM CLANCY

Obviously, there is a search for the reasons why airlines from economically poorer, less sophisticated nations have the worst safety records. There is good evidence that they are more likely to cut corners on maintenance and safety regulations than airlines from richer nations – often because government supervision of standards is less stringent. But the accidents themselves are, as in the richer nations, more often caused by pilot error than by technical failure.

Given the higher Third World accident rates, the implication is that training is less good, or that the pilots' attitude towards their job is different, or both. In the end, psychologists have concluded it is largely a cultural matter.

What is it about the Australian culture that makes its airlines so safe? First, discipline is accepted as the basis of cockpit behaviour. Also authority, while respected by Australians, is not put on a pedestal by them – meaning in this context that if the captain makes a mistake the co-pilot will challenge him. There have been many serious accidents in airline history that could have been prevented if the pilot had challenged the captain's actions. For example, the Japanese are a disciplined race and meticulous in their attention to technical detail; but culturally it is difficult for a subordinate to challenge authority and this cost Japan Air Lines a fatal accident in 1982. Recently in the Asia-Pacific countries the realisation has been taking hold that this culture may have a valid place in society, but not on the flight deck, and training programmes now reflect the need of the co-pilot to be a part of a team rather than just a subordinate. Since 1985 JAL has had a first-class safety record.

When considering 'below-average' airlines as a mode of transport in their home countries, the alternative surface transport should be approached critically, too. In a country where a cash-strapped economy and a *laissez-faire* culture lets an airline's standards drop, perhaps the same is true of the infrastructure that is supposed to preserve national road and rail safety. It may be true that the national air transport system, while it does not compare well with American or European airline safety standards, is still a relatively safe form of transport in absolute terms.

Finally, airline and airport security has become very much a part of air travel worldwide. In some parts of the world, security is token, but that is often because the perceived risk is low. Lockerbie jolted the airline world into a realisation that the subject of airborne terrorism was a serious one, and airlines and countries that are at risk usually have an adequate security system.

Hijacking is relatively rare now, but it tends to go in cycles. It will come back again. This danger is shown in the case of the December 1999 hijacking of an Indian Airlines aircraft for political reasons. It ended up in Afghanistan where the various national authorities gave in to the terrorist hijackers, releasing them with some of the imprisoned colleagues for the sake of whose freedom they had carried out the hijack in the first place. This kind of capitulation in the face of terror is understandable but flies in the face of all the world's accumulated wisdom on the ways of handling hijack. Sure enough, within a month, some Afghans hijacked one of their own national airline's aircraft to Britain. Capitulation was not forthcoming in the UK and the hijackers have been brought to justice, but the importance of international standards for the handling of hijacking has been suitably underlined.

Meanwhile most hijackings today are not of the terrorist type. Usually they are carried out by unbalanced individuals, or people looking for escape or political asylum. They almost invariably fail. The only workable advice to passengers afraid of the terrorist hijack threat is to decide which airlines are the targets of active terrorist groups, and then to travel with airlines which are not. However, the passengers who take that choice should bear in mind that if they cause the threatened airline's business visibly to suffer they have handed the terrorist a partial victory, encouraging further terrorism. ❧

DAVID LEARMOUNT has worked at 'Flight International' magazine for 20 years and is a specialist in aviation safety.

Reading an airline ticket
by Philip Ray, Alex McWhirter and David Warne

AN AIRLINE TICKET IS REALLY A LEGAL CONTRACT which specifies and restricts the services that passengers may expect and when they may expect them. On each ticket, the duties and liabilities of both passenger and airline are clearly stated – whether it is a scheduled or a charter flight – and each passenger must be in possession of a ticket for the journey to be undertaken. The Warsaw Convention limits the liability of most airlines in cases of injury or death involving passengers, and also of baggage loss or damage. This agreement is usually explained on the inside cover of the ticket or on a summary inserted in loose-leaf form.

The format of tickets issued by IATA-appointed travel agents in the UK and a number of other countries has been changed to conform with the requirements of the so-called Bank Settlement Plan (BSP). Instead of having to keep a stock of tickets for each airline with which they deal, agents now have one common stock of 'neutral' tickets, but a special plate is slotted into the ticket validator at the time of issue to indicate which airline is issuing the ticket. The whole BSP operation is essentially aimed at simplifying accounting procedures for both travel agents and airlines. Tickets issued direct by airlines still carry the normal identification.

Flight coupons contain a fare construction box which, on a multi-sector itinerary, indicates how the fare is to be apportioned among the different carriers. Cities are denoted by their three-letter codes, e.g. LHR is London Heathrow, ROM is Rome, CPH is Copenhagen, LAX is Los Angeles and so on. The fare construction may be shown in NUCS (Neutral Units of Conversion), a universal 'currency' in which fares are frequently expressed. The amount in NUCS is converted into the currency of the country of issue, which is shown in the fare box in the left-hand corner. The British pound sterling is shown as GBP so as to distinguish it from other sterling currencies. Where local taxes are to be paid these are also shown, and the final amount to be paid is shown in the total box.

At the bottom of the right-hand side is the 'Form of Payment' box. If you pay for the ticket by cash, this will either be left blank or the word 'cash' will be written in. If you pay by cheque, the word 'cheque' or abbreviation 'chq' will be used. If you pay with a credit card, the letters 'CC' will be entered, followed by the name of the issuing company, the card number and its expiry date. If you have an account with the travel agent the clerk will write 'Non ref', which means that no refund can be obtained except through the issuing office.

In the 'Baggage' section of the ticket, only the 'Allow' column is completed by the agent. This shows your free baggage allowance. The number of pieces, checked and unchecked weights are completed when the passenger checks in. 'PC' indicates that the piece concept is in operation, as it is on flights to and from North America. There are validity boxes immediately above the cities on your itinerary. These 'not valid before' and 'not valid after' entries relate to promotional fares with minimum/maximum stay requirements, and the relevant dates will be shown here. If you have a full-fare ticket where there is no minimum-stay requirement and the maximum is one year, these boxes are frequently left blank.

Immediately to the right of the itinerary is a column headed 'Fare/Class basis'. The letters most commonly inserted here are 'F' for First Class, 'C' for Business Class or 'Y' for Economy Class. The 'Y' may be followed by other letters to describe the fare, especially if it is a promotional type. For example, 'YH' would mean a high season fare, 'YZ' a youth fare, 'YLAP' a low season Apex, 'YE' an Excursion, etc.

Under the 'Carrier' box is the space for the carrier code, e.g. LH for Lufthansa or BA for British Airways. However, the airline industry has now run out of combinations of two-letter codes, so numbers have been added in conjunction with letters (e.g. Y2 is SA Alliance Air) and three-letter codes may be introduced in the future. Next follows the flight number and class of travel on that particular flight. Most international flight numbers consist of three figures, but for UK domestic flights four figures are frequently used. The date is written as, for example, 04 JUN for 4 June, while the time is shown according to the 24-hour clock, e.g. 14.30 hrs and not 2.30 pm (though the 12-hour clock is still used for domestic travel within the USA).

The 'Status' box will contain the letters 'OK' if the flight has been confirmed, 'RQ' if requested but not yet confirmed, and 'WL' if it has been wait-listed. If you have not decided when you want to travel, the word 'OPEN' will be written across the flight number, date, time and status boxes. Infants, who travel for a ten per cent fare on international journeys, are not entitled to a seat or baggage allowance, so the reservations entry will be marked 'No seat' and the allowance marked 'nil'.

Your ticket is valid for travel only when date-stamped with a travel agency or airline validator, complete with the clerk's signature or initials. ❧

ALEX MCWHIRTER was the Travel Editor of 'Business Traveller' magazine.

Making claims against an airline
by Alex McWhirter, Annie Redmile and Rajinder Ghatahorde

YOU HAVE ONLY TO READ THE CORRESPONDENCE COLUMNS in the specialist business travel magazines each month to see what a fashionable occupation it is to complain about airline services. Some people seem to enjoy writing letters of complaint so much that they make a profession of it. They complain at the slightest hiccup and write long letters detailing every flaw, claiming huge sums in compensation and threatening legal action if it is not forthcoming by return.

But the fact is that no matter how much their inefficiency costs you in time, trouble, missed meetings, lost deals and overnight hotel bills, the airlines, in many cases, are not obliged to pay you anything. They are covered for most eventualities by their conditions of carriage, which are printed on the inside cover of the ticket. However, this is not to say that, in an increasingly competitive environment, the more enlightened airlines do not take their customers' attitudes seriously. Some airline chief executives take a personal interest in passenger complaints and have frequent 'purges', when they insist on seeing every letter of complaint that comes in on a particular day.

If you have a complaint against an airline that you cannot resolve satisfactorily, it is worth contacting the Air Transport Users' Council (AUC), CAA House, 45-59 Kingsway, London WC2B 6TE (tel 020 7240 6061, fax 020 7240 7071). The council is funded and appointed by the Civil Aviation Authority, but operates completely independently and, indeed, has frequently been known to criticise some of the authority's decisions. It has only a small secretariat and is not really geared up to handle a large volume of complaints, but it has had some success in securing *ex gratia* payments for passengers who have been inconvenienced in some way.

All the same, the council likes to receive passenger complaints because it is a useful way of bringing to light some serious problems, which can lead in turn to high-level pressure being brought to bear on the airline or airlines involved. Some of the subjects dealt with by the council in 1990 included European and domestic airfares, passenger safety, the pressure on airport and airspace capacity, overbooking and baggage problems.

Procedure

Here are some tips which may make complaining to an airline more effective:

■ The first person to write to is the customer relations manager at the airline. You can write to the chairman if it makes you feel better, but it makes little difference – unless that happens to be the day that the chairman decides to have his purge. If you've made your booking through a travel agency, send the agency a copy of the letter and, if it does a fair amount of business with that carrier (especially if it is a foreign airline), it is a good idea to ask the agency to take up the complaint for you.

■ Keep your letter brief, simple, calm and to the point. Remember also to give the date, flight number, location and route where the incident took place. All this may seem obvious, but it's amazing how many people omit these details.

■ Keep all ticket stubs, baggage claims and anything else you may have from the flight involved. You may have to produce them if the airline requires substantiation of your complaint.

■ If you have no success after all this, write to the Air Transport Users' Council. Send the council copies of all the correspondence you've had with the airline and let it take the matter from there.

Lost luggage

Most frequent travellers will, at some time, have experienced that sinking feeling when the carousel stops going round and there is still no sign of their baggage. The first thing to do if your luggage does not appear is to check with an airline official in the baggage claim area. It could be that your baggage is of a non-standard shape – a heavy rucksack, for example – which cannot be handled easily on the conveyor belt. If this is the case, it will be brought to the claim area by hand. But if your baggage really has not arrived on the same flight as you, you will have to complete a property irregularity report (PIR), which will give a description of the baggage, a list of its contents and the address to which it should be forwarded. Ask for a copy for yourself as you will need this – together with the baggage receipt – if you later want to claim compensation from the airline or from your travel insurance.

It is sometimes worth hanging around at the airport for an hour or two because there is always the chance that your baggage may arrive on the next flight. This sometimes happens if you have had to make a tight flight connection – you just squeak on to the flight but your baggage doesn't quite make it – although the current strict security requirements mean that normally a passenger and his or her baggage must travel on the same flight. But if there is only one flight a day there is no point in waiting and the airline will forward the baggage to you at its expense. In this case, ask the airline for an allowance to enable you to buy the basic necessities for an overnight stay – nightwear, toiletries and underwear, for example.

If your baggage never arrives at all, you should make a claim against the airline within 21 days. The airlines' liability for lost luggage is limited by international agreement and the level of compensation is based on the weight of your baggage, which explains why it is filled in on your ticket by the check-in clerk. The maximum rate of compensation at present is US$20 per kilo for checked baggage and US$400 per passenger for unchecked baggage, unless a higher value is declared in advance and additional charges are paid.

The same procedure applies to baggage that you find to be damaged when you claim it. The damage should be reported immediately to an airline official and, again, you will have to fill in a PIR form, which you should follow up with a formal claim against the airline.

Overbooking

Losing one's baggage may be the ultimate nightmare in air travel, but the phenomenon of 'bumping' must run it a close second. Bumping occurs when you arrive at the airport with a confirmed ticket, only to be told that there is no seat for you because the flight is overbooked. Most airlines overbook their flights deliberately because they know that there will always be a few passengers who make a booking and then don't turn up ('no shows' in airline jargon). On some busy routes, such as Brussels to London on a Friday evening, some business travellers book themselves on four or five different flights, so that there is a horrendous no-show problem and the airlines can, perhaps, be forgiven for overbooking.

The use of computers has enabled airlines to work out their overbooking factors quite scientifically, but just occasionally things don't quite work out and a few confirmed passengers have to be bumped.

If you are unlucky enough to be bumped, or 'denied boarding', to adopt the airline jargon, you will probably be entitled to compensation. A few years ago the Association of European Airlines (AEA) adopted a voluntary compensation scheme based on a 50 per cent refund of the one-way fare on the sector involved, but early in 1991 the European Community agreed new rules, which put compensation on a statutory basis. The rules lay down that passengers with a confirmed reservation who are bumped at an EC airport should receive 150 ECU (about £200) for a short-haul flight or 300 ECU (about £400) for a flight of more than 3,500 km. These amounts are halved if the passenger can get on an alternative flight within two or four hours respectively. In addition, passengers have the right to full reimbursement of their ticket for any part of their journey not undertaken, and can claim legitimate expenses.

In 1997 the EU was reviewing these rules. Consumer groups had complained that compensation should cover the whole journey – and not just the sector on which the overbooking occurs. They note that a passenger flying to the Far East via Amsterdam, who is bumped off the first leg of the journey, might be held up for only an hour or so getting out of Schiphol. But the missed connection could result in a much longer delay in getting to Asia.

Compensation for delays

Whatever the conditions of carriage may say, airlines generally take a sympathetic view if flight delays cause passengers to miss connections, particularly if the delay results in having to obtain overnight hotel accommodation. Our own experience is that most of the better-known scheduled carriers will pull out all the stops to ensure that passengers are quickly rebooked on alternative flights and they will normally pick up the tab for hotel accommodation and the cost of sending messages to advise friends or contacts of the revised arrival time.

The position is not so clear cut when it comes to charter airlines because the extent of their generosity usually depends on whatever arrangement they have with the charterer. But a number of British tour operators have devised delay protection plans that are usually included as part of the normal holiday insurance. Thomson Holidays, for instance, will normally provide meals or overnight accommodation in the event of long flight delays, and if the outbound flight is delayed for more than 12 hours, passengers have the right to cancel their holiday and receive a full refund. If they decide to continue their holiday they receive compensation up to a maximum of £60, in addition to any meals or accommodation which may have been provided. Compensation is also paid on a similar scale if the return flight is delayed.

Injury or death

Airline liability for death or injury to passengers was originally laid down by the Warsaw Convention, which was signed in 1929. The basic principal was that the infant airline industry could have been crippled if it had been forced by the courts to pay massive amounts of compensation to passengers or their relatives for death or injury in the event of an accident. The trade-off was that the airlines undertook to pay compensation up to a set ceiling irrespective of whether negligence on their part was proved. The limit was set at 250,000 French gold francs, an obsolete currency, which is nevertheless still used to this day as the official unit of compensation, and converted into local currencies. ❧

RAJINDER GHATAHORDE works in the travel industry.

Flying yourself by microlight
by Christina Dodwell

TO TRAVEL LONG DISTANCE BY MICROLIGHT AIRCRAFT is sometimes harder to organise logistically than to carry out. It took me nearly three months to sort out the route and obtain the necessary permits for my four-month microlight flight through West Africa.

The most obvious essential is to fit the journey to the prevailing winds; travel is hard enough without wasting fuel in headwinds. My best advice about winds came from the locust control unit, whose London office has extensive reference wind charts. The Met Office in Bracknell was also helpful.

The second controlling factor of the route was the terrain, which had to offer plenty of open landing areas; we had no back-up ignition system. Our fuel tank size was increased to 49 litres, and we used an average of 12 litres per hour in flight. We were fortunate that Mobil sponsored us and agreed to stash sealed jerrycans for us at intervals along our route. The alternative of using a support vehicle would mean following roads.

When route and timing are known you should apply for flight clearances. This is done by letter, fax or telex to the CAA or relevant authority of each country *en route*, and in due course they should each give you a clearance number. While travelling you must put that number on all flight plans. If the country is a military state or dictatorship, you also need a military clearance number. Although I had received mine for Nigeria, I was arrested on arrival because the number was not on government-headed paper. It took 24 hours to sort out.

Nowadays one can use a clearance agent to arrange all these details. A recommended one is Overflight International (tel 01624 842311). For those who wish to organise their own clearances, there is excellent free advice and access to addresses from AIS (part of NATS – National Air Traffic Services Ltd). The telephone number to call for advice or to arrange a visit so that the pilot can access the documents they hold is 020 8745 3470 (Barry Davidson) or 020 8745 3440 (Doug Ferguson). Visits can be arranged at any time, but weekdays during normal office hours is most convenient as, at these times, there are staff available to assist with finding one's way through the maze of documents. They prefer a couple of days' notice of a visit but, if pushed, this can be arranged at short notice.

Pilots can request copies of bulletins to be faxed or posted on AIS' 24-hour number (tel 020 8745 3464), but the staff on that number are not in a position to provide much detailed information. Bulletins are split into four basic types: en route, aerodrome, navigation warnings, and 'low-level navigation warnings'. These categories are something of a misnomer as AIS covers all sorts of activity at all sorts of levels, including gliding, kites, parascending, parachuting, pyrotechnics, lasers, etc. – in fact, most things, apart from firing and military exercises. AIS is now only able to assist with overseas clearances where a diplomatic clearance is required, although it can provide information on addresses, telephone and fax numbers.

If pilots wish to use AIS's services for a flight outside Europe, it is best to start the planning well before the departure date (six to nine months) as there are considerable delays along the way when it comes to dealing with foreign government departments.

I would recommend that microlight pilots carry ELT (electronic locator transmitter) and navigate with GPS (global positioning system). GPS didn't exist in West Africa in my days, but I am assured there is now world coverage. We did have an ELT disaster signal but an inquisitive person pulled out its pin the day before the journey began, leaving it exhausted.

When flying in ultra-inhospitable regions (as I found out mid-Sahara), one is obliged by law to have or hire a support vehicle, and the aircraft must carry fuel and water for a minimum of about five days.

In parts of Europe, the regulations against microlights have recently tightened and they are banned from certain major airports. It would be simpler to enter such a country by road with the microlight in tow and assemble it there. This requires only a courtesy call to let the authorities know that you are a visitor asking to fly in their airspace, plus a copy of your flight plan. For all advice on procedures, contact AIS (above) and also the very helpful Department of Transport, whose international aviation section (tel 020 7890 5803) is run by Huw Hopkins.

If a microlight does not have the fuel capacity to reach an international airport in one hop, you can get permission to stop and re-fuel, and to check in with any immigration and customs post, but remember to report to the local police chief.

The type of fuel at roadside petrol stations was very low octane and in remote places was contaminated by transportation in unclean containers. In the mountains of Cameroon, petrol was being sold in old Coke bottles.

As to the practical side, it wasn't until we began our journey in Cameroon that we learnt that our compass was calibrated to northern latitudes and unusable in the tropics. The only tropical compasses for sale were brass maritime heavies. Even the most basic things have a way of growing complicated. Luggage, camping gear, tools of lightweight aluminium and spare parts were loaded into panniers strapped outside the cockpit, plus spare wheel and spare propeller, while water cans and oil were stowed under the seats and sleeping bags were securely tied to the trike's mast.

If things fall off, they usually get sucked into the propeller. I remember Mik Coyne saying when they threw cereal packets out of a microlight for promotional photography, the packets were drawn into the propeller and chipped it badly. Our propeller had chunks torn out of it on several occasions, usually by sticks and stones whirled up on landing and take-off. But we glued the chunks back into place, or refilled the gap with wood carved to shape. I also had to stitch patches on the wing when it was torn by thorns. Others have trouble from thorns in tyres, for which Richard Meredith Hardy recommended putting strips of carpet between tyre and tube.

My microlight was a standard Pegasus XL, which has an all-up weight capacity of 390 kg, inclusive of trike, wing, two people and everything. When we overloaded by 30 kg we had a total engine failure at 15 metres while taking off, and we fell to the ground like a stone. But nothing broke. At normal full weight there were no adverse effects, except for heavier fuel consumption (up to 19 litres an hour in take-off) and a longer take-off and landing run. Perhaps it made us more stable in the air, though on occasions when we were tossed about the stress was appalling and I was surprised that nothing snapped. It was a sturdy machine.

In fact the dangers were few but, naturally, we had a lot of narrow escapes, particularly when landing on roads with unforeseen traffic. Our worst was a steeply banked road where we landed after dark with no lights, only to find a truck with no lights driving towards us. Sandstorms were not much of a problem, you can usually jump over them. They grow bigger as they approach, but you can judge their size. Our standard type was just over one kilometre wide and 600 metres tall. Flight rules say that when storms blow up you must land and secure your aircraft, but often it would have been too dangerous to land and there was nothing to tie the wing to, so we stayed airborne. One time a storm grew so big we couldn't find its top and at 1,200 metres we were being pushed backwards by the strength of the wind. Wind speed increases with height, it was futile to go higher and we decided to try flying low down in the storm; it wasn't fun.

Thermal pillars used to start bouncing off the desert by 11 am. By midday they were uncomfortable. The only practical times for flight were a few hours morning and evening. If you arrive at an airport after sunset, approximately 6 pm, you will be charged for landing lights, which tend to be expensive.

When taking off near towns or villages with no airstrip there is a danger of causing harm to people. In their delight, the crowds go crazy and, not wanting you to leave, they dash forward to try and grab your moving wing-tips, or rush behind the propeller where a whirled-up stone can kill. Sometimes it is worth asking the local police or headman to hold crowds behind the aircraft. Don't allow people to form a corridor during take-off because they will run into your path.

The horrors were equalled by moments of pure joy; I loved the aerial perspective and being able to see how things fit together. We could pick out the shape of tombs and ancient fortresses that would be invisible from the ground, and we were free to land anywhere looked interesting. Some weirdly eroded rocks turned out to house caves with wall inscriptions and some bone fragments led to the discovery of a dinosaur skeleton. It all combines to make a memorable way to travel. ❧

CHRISTINA DODWELL is an inveterate traveller, horsewoman, writer, and microlight pilot. She has written a number of books, most recently 'Beyond Siberia'.

Part 4: **Countries of the world** ❧

AFGHANISTAN

STATE OF THE NATION

SAFETY Highly volatile. Few foreigners even work here. Women must observe strict *sharia* Islamic law and never travel alone.

LIFE EXPECTANCY 45.

PEOPLE AND PLACE

CAPITAL Kabul.

LANGUAGE Officially Pashtu and Persian. Also Dari, Turkmen, Uzbek, Persian.

PEOPLES Pashtu, Tajik, Hazara, Uzbek.

RELIGION Muslim (mainly Sunni).

SIZE (KM) 652,225.

POPULATION 17,000,000.

POP DENSITY/KM 26.

FOOD Indian-style, spicy, poor ingredients.

TRAVEL PLANNING

WHEN TO GO High altitudes and landlocked terrain create a cold continental climate, with wide temperature swings between seasons and day/night. Fierce summers (June-August), freezing winters (December-February).

MEDICAL CARE Very limited and primitive. Up-front cash payments required, insurance essential.

CURRENCY Afghani (= 100 puls).

FINANCE Credit cards not accepted. Traveller's cheques OK.

AIRPORTS Kabul (sometimes closed).

INTERNAL TRAVEL Risky. Few roads remain and most require 4x4 vehicles. Otherwise donkey is safest, helicopter quickest. Some internal air services from Kabul, depending on political/military conditions.

BUSINESS HOURS Sat-Wed 0800-1200, Thurs 0800-1330, Friday sabbath.

GMT +4.5.

VOLTAGE GUIDE 220 volts AC, 50 Hz.

RED TAPE

VISAS (AUS/CANADA/UK/US) Required.

REPS IN UK/US UK: 31 Prince's Gate, London SW7 1QQ, tel 020 7589 8891. US: 19th Floor, 369 Lexington Avenue, New York, NY 10017, tel 212 972 2277.

CUSTOMS REGULATIONS Duty free allowance: A reasonable amount of tobacco products, unlimited amounts of perfume. Prohibited: Alcohol. Licences required for furs, carpets and antiques.

DRIVING REQUIREMENTS International Driving Permit.

KEEPING IN TOUCH

BBC WORLD SERVICE MHz 15.58, 11.76, 9.410, 6.094.

ENGLISH-LANGUAGE NEWSPAPERS *The Kabul Times.*

EMERGENCIES

RED CROSS/CRESCENT SOCIETIES PO Box 3066, Shar-e-Now, Kabul, tel 873 682 32357.

UK/US REPS UK: Closed. US: Closed. (The embassies in Islamabad may be able to provide some consular assistance).

Global weather guide p 818, Rainy seasons worldwide p 829, Vaccinations required p 832, Recommended reading p 848, Dependent territories p 812.

ALBANIA

STATE OF THE NATION

SAFETY Low level civil conflict and general lawlessness make this a very unsafe destination.

LIFE EXPECTANCY M 69.9, F 75.9.

PEOPLE AND PLACE

CAPITAL Tirana.

LANGUAGE Albanian, Greek in the South. Some Italian and English.

PEOPLES Albanian, Greek.

RELIGION Islam, Catholicism, Eastern Orthodox Christianity.

SIZE (KM) 28,748.

POPULATION 3,400,000.

POP DENSITY/KM 13.

FOOD Turkish influenced kofte and kebabs, several private restaurants.

TRAVEL PLANNING

WHEN TO GO April-June, mid-September to mid-October are warm and dry and the best time to visit. Cool and wet from October to May.

MEDICAL CARE Medical treatment to be paid for, except infectious diseases, medical insurance recommended.

CURRENCY Lek (Lk) = 100 qindarka.

FINANCE MasterCard and Eurocard acccepted by banks and many hotels. Travellers' cheques less so.

AIRPORTS Tirana Rinas (TIA), 29km from the capital. Entry tax payable on arrival.

INTERNAL TRAVEL Limited rail network, roads in variable condition used by pedestrians, cyclists, herds of cattle, wagons, tractors and an increasing number of cars.

BUSINESS HOURS 7.30-15.30 Mon -Fri.

GMT +1 (+2 from last Sunday in March to Saturday before last Sunday in October).

VOLTAGE GUIDE 220 volts AC, 50 Hz.

RED TAPE

VISAS (AUS/CANADA/UK/US) Not required up to 3 months for tourists.

REPS IN UK/US UK: 4th Floor, 38 Grosvenor Gardens, London SW1W 0EB, tel 020 7730 5709. US: 2100 S Street, Washington, DC 20008, tel 202 223 4942 Email albaniaemb@aol.com

CUSTOMS REGULATIONS Duty free allowance: 250 cigarettes/50 cigars/250 g tobacco, 1 ltr spirits, 2 ltrs wine, 1ltr *eau de toilette*, 50 g of perfume. Prohibited: Firearms, ammunition, narcotics. Export permits required for precious metals, antiques, national costumes, books or artworks which form part of the national heritage.

DRIVING REQUIREMENTS International Driving Permit or national driving licence.

KEEPING IN TOUCH

BBC WORLD SERVICE MHz 15.49, 12.09, 9.410, 6.195.

ENGLISH-LANGUAGE NEWSPAPERS *Balkan News.*

EMERGENCIES

RED CROSS/CRESCENT SOCIETIES CP 1511, Tirana, tel/fax 42 25855.

UK/US UK: Rruga Skenderbeu 12, Tirana, Albania, tel 42 34975-5. US: Rruga Elbasanit 103, Tirana, Albania, tel 42 47285-9.

Global weather guide p 818, Rainy seasons worldwide p 829, Vaccinations required p 832, Recommended reading p 848, Dependent territories p 812.

ALGERIA

STATE OF THE NATION

SAFETY Very high risk area. In the last three years there have been many attacks on Westerners and thousands of political murders.

LIFE EXPECTANCY M 67.5, F 70.3.

PEOPLE AND PLACE

CAPITAL Algiers (El Djezair).

LANGUAGE Arabic and French.

PEOPLES Arabic, Berber, French.

RELIGION Sunni Muslim (99%).

SIZE (KM) 2,381,741.

POPULATION 27,900,000.

POP DENSITY/KM 13.

FOOD Local cooking includes roast meat and cous-cous with vegetable sauces. French influenced dishes in hotels in Algiers and coastal resorts.

TRAVEL PLANNING

WHEN TO GO High summer temperatures and sandstorms. Relatively low rainfall . Desert temperatures drop dramatically at night. Coastal resorts cooled by sea breezes. Best times north of the Sahara September to May, south October to April.

MEDICAL CARE Basic in rural areas, medical insurance strongly recommended.

CURRENCY Dinar (AD) = 100 centimes.

FINANCE Limited acceptance of credit cards and only more expensive hotels and government-run craft shops accept travellers' cheques.

AIRPORTS Algiers Houri Boumediene (ALG), 20 km from Algiers.

INTERNAL TRAVEL Internal air flights most practical for travel to the south. Slow rail services but reasonable road surfaces. Vehicles travelling in the desert must be well equipped as breakdown facilities are virtually non-existent. Car hire can be arranged at the airport, in most towns and at many hotels.

BUSINESS HOURS 0800-1200, 1300-1600, Saturday-Wednesday.

GMT +1.

VOLTAGE GUIDE 220 volts AC, 50 Hz.

RED TAPE

VISAS (AUS/CANADA/UK/US) Required (no Israeli stamps in passsports).

REPS IN UK/US/CANADA: UK: 6 Hyde Park Gate, London SW7 5EW, tel 020 7589 6885, fax 020 7589 7725 US: 2118 Kalorama Road, NW, Washington, DC 20008, tel 202 265 2800, fax 202 667 2174. Canada: 435 Daly Avenue, Ottawa, Ontario K1N 6H3, tel 613 789 8505, fax 613 789 1406

CUSTOMS REGULATIONS Duty free allowance: 200 cigarettes or 50 cigars or 250 g of tobacco; 1 bottle of spirits or 2 bottles of wine; 500 ml of eau de cologne or 150 ml of perfume (must be over 17 yrs). Prohibited: Gold, firearms and drugs.

DRIVING REQUIREMENTS International Driving Permit.

KEEPING IN TOUCH

BBC WORLD SERVICE MHz 17.71, 15.40, 12.10, 6.005.

ENGLISH-LANGUAGE NEWSPAPERS The daily *Horizons* has an English section.

EMERGENCIES

RED CROSS/CRESCENT SOCIETIES 15 bis, Boulevard Mohammed V, Alger 16000, tel/fax 213 2 725 407.

UK/US/CANADIAN REPS UK: Residence Cassiopee, Batiment B, 7 Chemin des Glycines, 6000 Alger-Gare, Algiers, tel 2 230 068, fax 2 230 751. US: 4 chemin Cheikh Bachir El-Ibrahimi, Algiers, tel 2 691 255, fax 2 693 979. Canada: 18 Mustapha Khalef Street, Ben Akmoum, Algiers, tel 2 914 951, fax 2 914 973

Global weather guide p 818, Rainy seasons worldwide p 829, Vaccinations required p 832, Recommended reading p 848, Dependent territories p 812.

ANDORRA

STATE OF THE NATION

SAFETY Safe.

LIFE EXPECTANCY M 74, F 81.

PEOPLE AND PLACE

CAPITAL Andorra La Vella.

LANGUAGE Officially Catalan, but French and Spanish also used.

PEOPLES Spanish, Catalan, French, Portugese.

RELIGION Roman Catholic (94%).

SIZE (KM) 467.8.

POPULATION 65, 227.

POP DENSITY/KM 139.

FOOD Catalan, with plenty of pork and ham dishes. Restaurants quite expensive.

TRAVEL PLANNING

WHEN TO GO Summer (May-September). Temperate climate with warm summers and cold winters.

MEDICAL CARE Good. Covered by mutual agreements with the UK.

CURRENCY Mainly Spanish pesetas. French francs.

FINANCE Major credit cards accepted.

AIRPORTS Nearest international is Barcelona (BCN) in Spain - 225 km.

INTERNAL TRAVEL One major east-west route. Buses and minibuses between villages.

BUSINESS HOURS Vary considerably - lunch is after 13.30 and can extend through the afternoon.

GMT +1 (+2 in Summer)

VOLTAGE GUIDE 240AC, 50Hz.

RED TAPE

VISAS (AUS/CANADA/UK/US) No requirements for entry into Andorra but the relevant regulations for Spain or France should be followed, depending on which country is transited to reach Andorra.

REPS IN UK/US/CANADA UK: Andorra Tourist Delegation, 63 Westover Road, London SW18 2RF, tel 020 8874 4806. US: Permanent Mission of the Principality of Andorra to the United Nations, 2 United Plaza, 25th Floor, New York, NY 10017, tel 212 750 8064, fax 212 750 6630.

CUSTOMS REGULATIONS Duty free allowance: Duty-free zone - check Spanish/French regulations as they mantain customs controls at the borders. Prohibited: Narcotics, firearms, ammunition, explosives, fireworks, flick knives, pornography, horror comics, radio transmittors, certain foodstuffs, plants, flowers, animals, items made from endangered species. No works of art can be exported without permission.

DRIVING REQUIREMENTS National Driving Licence accepted.

KEEPING IN TOUCH

BBC WORLD SERVICE MHz 12.09, 9.410, 6.195.

EMERGENCIES

RED CROSS/CRESCENT SOCIETIES Prat de la Creu 22, Andorra la Vella, tel 825 225,, fax 828 630, email creuroja@creuroja.ad.

UK/US/CANADIAN REPS UK: Prat de la Creu 22, Bloc D, Alt.2, PO Box 1041, Andorra la Vella, Andorra, tel/fax 867 731. US, Canada: The American and Canadian consulates in Barcelona deal with enquiries regarding Andorra.

Global weather guide p 818, Rainy seasons worldwide p 829, Vaccinations required p 832, Recommended reading p 848, Dependent territories p 812.

ANGOLA

STATE OF THE NATION

SAFETY Low-level conflict zone, many landmines, travel not recommended.

LIFE EXPECTANCY M 44.9, F 48.1.

PEOPLE AND PLACE

CAPITAL Luanda.

LANGUAGE Officially Portugese and Bantu Languages

PEOPLES Portugese, Umbundu, Kimbundu, Kikongo.

RELIGION Mainly Roman Catholic. Other Christian minorities. Local Animist beliefs are held by a significant minority.

SIZE (KM) 1,246,700.

POPULATION 12,000,000.

POP DENSITY/KM 10.

FOOD Severe food and drink shortages at present. Book well ahead at the few hotels and restaurants.

TRAVEL PLANNING

WHEN TO GO May to October, when it is dry and there is a slight decrease in temperature. The rest of the year is hot and wet.

MEDICAL CARE Free but generally inadequate, medical insurance recommended for evacuation.

CURRENCY Kwanza (Kzr) = 100 lwei.

FINANCE Credit cards are not generally accepted and travellers' cheques are uncommon. US Dollars widely accepted.

AIRPORTS Luanda (LAD), 4 km from the city.

INTERNAL TRAVEL Strictly controlled and most of the country is only accessible by air. Rail services are erratic and much of the road infrastructure has been destroyed. Local buses run in Luanda.

BUSINESS HOURS 0830-1230, 1400-1800, Monday to Friday. Some offices open 0830-1230 Saturday.

GMT +1.

VOLTAGE GUIDE 220 AC, 60 Hz.

RED TAPE

VISAS (AUS/CANADA/UK/US) Required.

REPS IN UK/US/CANADA UK: 98 Park Lane, London W1Y 3TA, tel 020 7495 1752, fax 020 7495 135. US: 1615 M Street, Suite 900, NW,Washington, DC 20036, tel 202 785 1156, fax 202 785 1258, email: angola@angola.org. Canada: 75 Albert Stree, Suite 900, Ottawa, Ontario K1P 5E7, tel 613 234 1152, fax 613 234 1179, email: info@angolan.org

CUSTOMS REGULATIONS Duty free allowance: A reasonable amount of tobacco products, 3 bottles of alcoholic beverages (each of different contents) and a reasonable quantity of perfume in opened bottles. Prohibited: Firearms and ammunition.

DRIVING REQUIREMENTS International Driving Permit.

KEEPING IN TOUCH

BBC WORLD SERVICE MHz 15.40, 11.94, 6.190, 3.255.

EMERGENCIES

RED CROSS/CRESCENT SOCIETIES Caixa Postal 927, Luanda tel 2 336543, fax 2 391 970.

UK/US/CANADIAN REPS UK: PO Box 1244, 4 Rua Diogo Cao, Luanda, tel 2 334 582/3, fax 2 333 331, email britemb.ang@ebonet.net US: Rua Major Konhugulo 132-136, Luanda, tel 2 396 727, fax 390 515. Canada: 113 Rei Katyavala Street, Luanda, tel 2 348 371, fax 2 349 494.

Global weather guide p 818, Rainy seasons worldwide p 829, Vaccinations required p 832, Recommended reading p 848, Dependent territories p 812.

ANTIGUA & BARBUDA

STATE OF THE NATION

SAFETY Safe.

LIFE EXPECTANCY 74.

PEOPLE AND PLACE

CAPITAL St John's.

LANGUAGE English.

PEOPLES Most of African descent, some Europeans and South Asians.

RELIGION Mainly Anglican and Protestant.

SIZE (KM) Antigua: 280, Barbuda 161.

POPULATION 66,000.

POP DENSITY/KM 150.

FOOD Superb seafood, extensive choice in hotels including local curries and roast suckling pig. Local drinks include coconut milk and rum punches.

TRAVEL PLANNING

WHEN TO GO Tropical, warm and relatively dry throughout the year. Some rainfall from September-December.

MEDICAL CARE One private and one public hospital, insurance recommended.

CURRENCY Eastern Caribbean dollar (EC$) = 100 cents

FINANCE Major credit cards, travellers cheques.

AIRPORTS VC Bird International (ANU), 8 km from St John's

INTERNAL TRAVEL Light aircraft and boats between islands, good all weather roads and car hire easy to organise on arrival. Local buses are infrequent.

BUSINESS HOURS 0800-12.00, 1300-1630, Monday to Friday.

GMT - 4.

VOLTAGE GUIDE 220/110 AC, 60Hz.

RED TAPE

VISAS (AUS/CANADA/UK/US) None.

REPS IN UK/US/CANADA: UK: 15 Thayer Street, London W1M 5LD, tel 020 7486 7073, fax 020 7486 9970. US: 3216 New Mexico Avenue, NW, Washington DC 20016, tel 202 362 5122, fax 202 362 5225. Canada: 130 Alvert Street, Suite 700, Ottawa, Ontario K1P 5G4

CUSTOMS REGULATIONS Duty free allowance: 200 cigarettes or 50 cigars or 250 g of tobacco, 1 ltr wine or spirits, 170 g of perfume. Prohibited: Weapons and narcotics.

DRIVING REQUIREMENTS Local Driver's Permit.

KEEPING IN TOUCH

BBC WORLD SERVICE MHz 17.84, 15.22, 6.195, 5.975.

ENGLISH-LANGUAGE NEWSPAPERS All in English - the main paper is the *Daily Observer*.

EMERGENCIES

RED CROSS/CRESCENT SOCIETIES PO Box 727, St John's, tel 462 0800, fax 460 9599

UK/US/CANADIAN REPS UK: Price Waterhouse Center, 11 Old Parham Road, St John's tel 462 0008/9, fax4622806, email: britishc@candw.ag US, Canada: The respective embassies in Bridgetown (see Barbados) deal with enquiries

Global weather guide p 818, Rainy seasons worldwide p 829, Vaccinations required p 832, Recommended reading p 848, Dependent territories p 812.

ARGENTINA

STATE OF THE NATION

SAFETY Beware petty crime (pickpockets, theft).

LIFE EXPECTANCY M 69.6, F 76.8.

PEOPLE AND PLACE

CAPITAL Buenos Aires

LANGUAGE Officially Spanish, English widely spoken.

PEOPLES Mainly European. Remainder Mestizo, Indian.

RELIGION Roman Catholic (90%).

SIZE (KM) 2,780,400.

POPULATION 36,100,000.

POP DENSITY/KM 13.

FOOD Beef of very high quality. Grill rooms abound. Local food is largely a mixture of Basque, Spanish and Italian, including *empanadas* and pork and maize stew.

TRAVEL PLANNING

WHEN TO GO Subtropical in the north, with rain throughout the year, the far south is sub-arctic. The central mainland is tempearate - visit throughout the year.

MEDICAL CARE Good. No health agreements with UK so insurance recommended.

CURRENCY peso (P) = 100 centavos.

FINANCE US dollars and major credit cards generally accepted. Often difficult to exchange travellers' cheques in small towns.

AIRPORTS Ezeiza Ministro Pistarini (EZE), 42km from Buenos Aires.

INTERNAL TRAVEL Air travel most efficient way to get around but the services are very busy and often subject to delay. Long-haul train services have been disrupted since recent privatisation. Buses are considered to be a more reliable form of long distance transport. Trunk roads fine, rural roads become impassable after rain.

BUSINESS HOURS 0900-1900 Mon-Fri.

GMT -3.

VOLTAGE GUIDE 220 AC, 50 Hz.

RED TAPE

VISAS (AUS/CANADA/UK/US) None, required although business travellers should check with the Argentinian consulate.

REPS IN UK/US/CANADA UK: 27 Three Kings Yard, London W1Y 1FL, tel 020 7318 1340, fax 020 7318 1349, email fclond@ mrecic.gov.ar US: 1600 New Hampshire Avenue, NW, Washington, DC 20009, tel 202 939 6400-3, fax 202 332 3171 Canada: Suite 910, Royal Bank Center, 90 Sparks Street, Ottawa, Ontario K1P 5B4, tel 613 236 2351/4, fax 613 235 2659.

CUSTOMS REGULATIONS Duty free allowance: 400 cigarettes and 50 cigars, 2 ltrs of alcohol, 5 kg of foodstuffs, goods to the value of US$300 (travellers over 18 only) . Prohibited: Animals or birds from Africa or Asia (except Japan) without prior authorisation, parrots, fresh foodstuffs. Explosives, inflammable items, narcotics and pornographic material. All gold must be declared.

DRIVING REQUIREMENTS International Driving Permit - must be stamped by the Automóvile Club Argentina.

KEEPING IN TOUCH

BBC WORLD SERVICE MHz 17.84, 15.19, 12.09, 6.195.

ENGLISH-LANGUAGE NEWSPAPERS *The Buenos Aires Herald*.

EMERGENCIES

RED CROSS/CRESCENT SOCIETIES Hipólito Yrigoyen 2068, 1089 Buenos Aires, tel 11 49 51 11 391, fax 11 49 52 77 15.

UK/US/CANADIAN REPS UK: Dr Luis Agote 2412/52, 1425 Buenos Aires, tel 11 48 03 70 70, fax 11 48 03 17 31, email ukembarg@starnet.net.ar. US: Avenida Colombia 4300, 1425 Buenos Aires, tel 11 47 77 45 33/4, fax 11 45 11 49 97. Canada: Tagle 2828, 1425 Buenos Aires, tel 11 48 05 30 32, fax 11 48 06 12 09.

Global weather guide p 818, Rainy seasons worldwide p 829, Vaccinations required p 832, Recommended reading p 848, Dependent territories p 812.

ARMENIA

STATE OF THE NATION

SAFETY Political and religious unrest, take great care and register with relevant embassy on arrival.

LIFE EXPECTANCY M 67.2, F 73.6.

PEOPLE AND PLACE

CAPITAL Yerevan.

LANGUAGE Armenian and Russian.

PEOPLES Armenian. Small Azeri and Russian minorities.

RELIGION The world's oldest Christian nation. The Armenian Apostolic Church remains predominant. Catholic, Protestant and Russian Orthodox communities.

SIZE (KM) 29,800.

POPULATION 3,600,000.

POP DENSITY/KM 121.

FOOD Typically *hors d'oeuvres* of peppers, stuffed vine leaves and vegetables followed by lamb served as kebabs with flat bread or prepared as soup. Armenian brandy has a good reputation.

TRAVEL PLANNING

WHEN TO GO June to September, when it is hot and dry (temperatures fall sharply at night). Winters are extremely cold with heavy snow.

MEDICAL CARE Arrangements for urgent medical treatment exist for those with proof of UK citizenship, but standards are low and insurance is recommended.

CURRENCY Armenian dram (AMD) = 100 luma.

FINANCE Credit cards and travellers cheques generally accepted in shops and hotels. US dollars are also widely accepted.

AIRPORTS Zvartnots (EVN) 10 km from Yerevan.

INTERNAL TRAVEL May be disrupted by fuel shortages. Poor road surfaces, some internal air travel.

BUSINESS HOURS n/a.

GMT +4.

VOLTAGE GUIDE 220 AC, 50 Hz.

RED TAPE

VISAS (AUS/CANADA/UK/US) Required.

REPS IN UK/US UK: 25A Cheniston Gardens, London W8 6TG, tel 020 7938 5435, fax 020 7938 2595. US: 2225 R Street, NW, Washington, DC20008, tel 202 319 2983, fax 202 319 2982.

CUSTOMS REGULATIONS Duty free allowance: 400 cigarettes or 100 cigars or 500 g of tobacco products; 2 ltrs of alcoholic beverages, a reasonable quantity of perfume for personal use, other goods up to the amount of US$5000, for personal use only (for travellers over 18). Prohibited: Weapons, ammunition, narcotics, pornography, loose pearls, anything owned by a third party that is to be carried in for that third party. These items are also prohibited for export, as are works of art and antiquities without permits, saiga horns, punctuate and red deer antlers and punctuate deer skins.

DRIVING REQUIREMENTS n/a.

KEEPING IN TOUCH

BBC WORLD SERVICE MHz 15.57, 9.410, 6.195, 3.955.

ENGLISH-LANGUAGE NEWSPAPERS *Yerevan News* (weekly).

EMERGENCIES

RED CROSS/CRESCENT SOCIETIES 21 Paronian Street, 375015 Yerevan, tel 538 964, fax 151 129.

UK/US/CANADIAN REPS UK: 28 Charents Street, Yerevan 375025, tel 2 151 842, fax 2 151 807, email britemb@ arminco.com. US: 18 Marshall Baghramian Avenue, Yerevan 375019, tel 2 151 551, fax 2 151 550. Canada: The Canadian Embassy in the Russian Federation deals with enquiries relating to Armenia.

Global weather guide p 818, Rainy seasons worldwide p 829, Vaccinations required p 832, Recommended reading p 848, Dependent territories p 812.

AUSTRALIA

STATE OF THE NATION

SAFETY Safe (except for virulent poisonous wildlife).

LIFE EXPECTANCY M 75.5, F 81.1.

PEOPLE AND PLACE

CAPITAL Canberra.

LANGUAGE English.

PEOPLES European 95%, Aboriginal, Asian and other peoples.

RELIGION Roman Catholic 26%, Protestant 24% and smaller minorities of all other major religions.

SIZE (KM) 7,682,300.

POPULATION 18,500,000.

POP DENSITY/KM 2.3.

FOOD Numerous speciality dishes and high quality local produce and seafood. Several ethnic cuisines available, Asian cookery has contributed to the lauded Pacific Rim style of cuisine.

TRAVEL PLANNING

WHEN TO GO Throughout the year.

MEDICAL CARE Free treatment for UK citizens in emergencies only, insurance recommended.

CURRENCY Australian dollar = 100 cents.

FINANCE Major credit cards and travellers cheques in major currencies accepted, although use may be restricted in Outback areas and in small towns.

AIRPORTS Sydney (SYD), Adelaide (ADL), Melbourne (MEL), Perth (PER), Brisbane (BNE), Darwin (DRW), Hobart (HBA), Cairns (CNS), Townsville (TSV).

INTERNAL TRAVEL Air travel is fastest due to vast distances. Well served by rail, although only one service goes from coast to coast (*The Indian Pacific*). Driving off major roads in the Outback is difficult from Nov to Feb because of summer rain. Car hire available at all major airports and hotels to those over 21.

BUSINESS HOURS 0900-1700 Mon-Fri.

GMT North-east/south-east +10, central +9.5, West + 8.

VOLTAGE GUIDE 220/240 AC, 50 Hz.

RED TAPE

VISAS (AUS/CANADA/UK/US) Required.

REPS IN UK/US/CANADA UK: Australia House, The Strand, London WC2B 4LA, tel 020 7379 4334, fax 020 7240 5333 US: 1601 Massachusetts Avenue, NW, Washington, DC20036, tel 202 7973000, fax 202 797 6318. Canada: 7th Floor, Suite 710, 50 O'Connor Street, Ottawa, Ontario K1P 6L2, tel 613 236 0841, fax 613 236 4376, email ahc1.otwa@sympatico.ca.

CUSTOMS REGULATIONS Duty free allowance: 250 cigarettes or 250g of tobacco or cigars, 1.125 ltrs of any alcoholic liquor, articles for personal hygiene, not including perfume, other goods to a value of A$400 (for travellers over 18). Prohibited: non-prescribed drugs, weapons, firearms, wildlife, domestic animals, foodstuffs.

DRIVING REQUIREMENTS International or National driving permits translated into English. International Drving Permit only valid with a valid national licence.

KEEPING IN TOUCH

BBC WORLD SERVICE MHz 15.36, 11.77, 9.740, 5.975.

ENGLISH-LANGUAGE NEWSPAPERS All in English: main paper is *The Australian*.

EMERGENCIES

RED CROSS/CRESCENT SOCIETIES PO Box 196, Carlton, South Vic 3053, tel 61 3 934 51800, fax 61 3 934 82513.

UK/US/CANADIAN REPS UK: Level 10, SAP House, Canberra Centre, Canberra, ACT 2600, tel 2 62 57 24 38, fax 2 62 57 58 57. US: Moonah Place, Canberra, ACT 2600, tel 2 62 14 56 00, fax 2 62 14 59 70. Canada: Commonwealth Avenue, Yarralumla, Canberra, ACT 2600, tel 2 62 70 40 00, fax 2 62 73 32 85, email cnbra@dfait-maeci.gc.ca.

Global weather guide p 818, Rainy seasons worldwide p 829, Vaccinations required p 832, Recommended reading p 848, Dependent territories p 812.

AUSTRIA

STATE OF THE NATION

SAFETY Safe.

LIFE EXPECTANCY M 73.7, F 80.2.

PEOPLE AND PLACE

CAPITAL Vienna.

LANGUAGE German.

PEOPLES German (93%), Croat, Slovene, Hungarian minorities.

RELIGION Roman Catholic (78%), non-religious (9%), Muslim, Jewish and Protestant minorities

SIZE (KM) 83,858.

POPULATION 8,200,000.

POP DENSITY/KM 99.

FOOD Viennese cuisine is strongly influenced by southeast European cooking. Mostly meat dishes, such as *Wiener Schnitzel*, with potatoes or dumplings. Over 57 varieties of *torte*, often consumed with coffee at a *Kaffehaus*.

TRAVEL PLANNING

WHEN TO GO Anytime. Warm, pleasant summers, sunny winters with high snow levels, ideal for winter sports.

MEDICAL CARE Free treatment for UK citizens in emergency with nominal fee, a refund may be available for treatment in private hospitals.

CURRENCY Austrian schilling (ASch) = 100 groschen.

FINANCE Major credit cards, Eurocheque cards, travellers cheques widely accepted.

AIRPORTS Vienna (VIE), Innsbruck (INN), Salzburg (SZG), Klagenfurt (KLU).

INTERNAL TRAVEL Efficient rail service, excellent road network.

BUSINESS HOURS 0800-1230, 1330-1730 Monday-Friday.

GMT +1.

VOLTAGE GUIDE 220 AC, 50 Hz.

RED TAPE

VISAS (AUS/CANADA/UK/US) Not required for stays of up to 3 months.

REPS IN UK/US/CANADA UK: 18 Belgrave Mews West, London SW1X 8HU, tel 020 7235 371, fax 020 7344 0292, email embassy@austria.org.uk. US: 3524 International Court, NW, Washington, DC 20008, tel 202 895 6700, fax 202 895 6750, email austroinfo@aol.com. Canada: 445 Wilbrod Street, Ottawa, Ontario K1N 6M7, tel 613 789 1444, fax 613 789 3431, email austemb@comnet.ca.

CUSTOMS REGULATIONS Duty free allowance: For non EU-members over 17: 200 cigarettes or 100 cigarillos or 50 cigars or 250 g tobacco, 2 ltrs of wine or fortified wine or spirits upto 22%, 1 ltr of spirits, 1 bottle of eau de cologne (up to 250 ml), 60 ml of perfume, other goods of up to ASch2400. No limits on tobacco and alcohol imported for personal use by EU members.

DRIVING REQUIREMENTS National driving licences issued by EU countries accepted, car registration papers issued in the UK are valid. A Green Card is compulsory.

KEEPING IN TOUCH

BBC WORLD SERVICE MHz 15.57, 12.10, 9.410, 6.195.

ENGLISH-LANGUAGE NEWSPAPERS National press in German but English-language papers are widely available.

EMERGENCIES

RED CROSS/CRESCENT SOCIETIES Postfach 39, 1041 Wien, tel/fax 1 589 000, email: oerk@redcross.or.at.

UK/US/CANADIAN REPS UK: Jauresgasse 10, 1030 Vienna, tel 1 7161 35151, fax 1 7161 35900. US: 4th Floor, Gartenbaupromenade 2, Vienna, tel 1 31339, fax 1 513 4351. Canada: Laurenzerberg 2, 1010 Vienna, Austria, tel 1 531 380, fax 1 5313 83321.

Global weather guide p 818, Rainy seasons worldwide p 829, Vaccinations required p 832, Recommended reading p 848, Dependent territories p 812.

AZERBAIJAN

STATE OF THE NATION

SAFETY A ceasefire has lasted since 1994, but western areas are volatile.

LIFE EXPECTANCY M 65.5, F 74.1.

PEOPLE AND PLACE

CAPITAL Baku.

LANGUAGE Azerbaijani.

PEOPLES Mostly Azeri. Very small Russian, Armenian and Jewish minorities.

RELIGION Predominantly Shia Muslim.

SIZE (KM) 86,600.

POPULATION 7,700,000.

POP DENSITY/KM 89.

FOOD Combination of Turkish and central Asian dishes, kebabs, rich soups, spinach, chickpeas, rice and yoghurt. Sturgeon still available - at a price.

TRAVEL PLANNING

WHEN TO GO Generally very warm. Low temperatures can occur in the mountains and valleys. Most rainfall in the west. June-September best for travel.

MEDICAL CARE Limited but free emergency treatment for a limited period only, insurance recommended.

CURRENCY Manat (AM).

FINANCE Generally a cash-only economy with US dollars, pounds sterling and deutschmark preferred currencies. Credit cards accepted in major hotels and all banks in Baku.

AIRPORTS Bina, 30 km from Baku.

INTERNAL TRAVEL Restricted - many regions near the border require special permission. Many roads in poor condition. Car hire available from Avis in Baku. Most visitors use taxis or private cars. 4x4 vehicles recommended for travel in the mountains.

BUSINESS HOURS n/a.

GMT +4.

VOLTAGE GUIDE 220 AC, 50 Hz.

RED TAPE

VISAS (AUS/CANADA/UK/US) Required.
REPS IN UK/US UK: 4 Kensington Court, London W8 5DL, tel 020 7938 5482, fax 020 7937 1783. US: 927 15th Street, Suite 700, NW, Washington DC 20005, tel 202 842 0001, fax 202 842 0004, email: azerbaijan@ tidawave.net.

CUSTOMS REGULATIONS Duty free allowance: 1000 cigarettes or 1000 g of tobacco products, 1.5 ltr spirits, 2 ltrs wine, reasonable quantity of perfumefor personal use, goods up to a value of US$10,000. Prohibited: Weapons, ammunition, narcotics, live animals (subject to permit), fruit, vegetables, anti-Azerbaijani photographs or printed material. Prohibited exports: weapons, ammunition, works of art and antiques without permission from the Ministry of Culture, and furs.

DRIVING REQUIREMENTS n/a.

KEEPING IN TOUCH

BBC WORLD SERVICE MHz 17.64, 15.57, 9.410, 6.195.

ENGLISH-LANGUAGE NEWSPAPERS None. The main daily paper is *Azerbaijan*.

EMERGENCIES

RED CROSS/CRESCENT SOCIETIES Prospekt Azerbaijan 19, Baku, tel 12 931 912, fax 12 931 578, email: azrc@ ifrc.azerin.com.

UK/US/CANADIAN REPS UK: 2 Izmir Street, 370065 Baku, tel 12 975 190, fax 12 922 739, email: office@britemb.baku.az. US: Avenue Azadlyg 83, 370007 Baku, tel 12 980 3356, fax 12 938 755. Canada: The Canadian Embassy in Ankara (Turkey) deals with enquiries relating to Azerbaijan.

Global weather guide p 818, Rainy seasons worldwide p 829, Vaccinations required p 832, Recommended reading p 848, Dependent territories p 812.

BAHAMAS

STATE OF THE NATION

SAFETY Safe.

LIFE EXPECTANCY M 70.5, F 77.1.

PEOPLE AND PLACE

CAPITAL Nassau.

LANGUAGE English.

PEOPLES Of African descendent, white minority.

RELIGION Christian denominations, mainly Baptist, Anglican, Roman Catholic.

SIZE (KM) 13,939.

POPULATION 293,000.

POP DENSITY/KM 29.

FOOD Seafood specialities include grouper, conch, baked crab, red snapper in anchovy sauce. Local drinks are based on rum.

TRAVEL PLANNING

WHEN TO GO Mid-December to mid-April slightly cooler than other Caribbean island groups due to the proximity of North American cold-air systems.

MEDICAL CARE Four hospitals where medical costs are high, insurance recommended.

CURRENCY Bahamian dollar = 100 cents.

FINANCE Major credit cards widely accepted. The US dollar is accepted as legal tender.

AIRPORTS Nassau International (NAS), 16 km from city, Freeport International (FPO), 5 km from the city.

INTERNAL TRAVEL Charter flights between islands. A mail boat serves the Out Islands. Car hire easy, but buses, bicycles and taxis readily available.

BUSINESS HOURS 0900-1700 Mon-Fri.

GMT -5 (-4 in summer).

VOLTAGE GUIDE 120AC, 60Hz.

RED TAPE

VISAS (AUS/CANADA/UK/US) None.

REPS IN UK/US/CANADA UK: 10 Chesterfield Street, London W1X 8AH, tel 020 7408 4488, fax 020 7499 9937, email bahamas.hicom.lon@cableinet.co.uk US: 2220 Massachussetts Avenue, NW, Washington, DC 20008, tel 202 319 2660, fax 202 319 2660, fax 202 319 2668, email bahemb@aol.com Canada: Clairca Centre, Suite 1313, 50 O'Connor Street, Ottawa, Ontario K1P 6L2, tel 613 232 1724, fax 613 232 0097, email ottawa-mission@bahighco.com

CUSTOMS REGULATIONS Duty free allowance: 200 cigarettes or 50 cigars or 454 g of tobacco, 1.136 ltrs of spirits and 1.136 ltrs of wine, goods up to the value of B$100. Prohibited: Weapons and drugs.

DRIVING REQUIREMENTS A national driving licence is valid for up to three months.

KEEPING IN TOUCH

BBC WORLD SERVICE MHz 17.72, 15.22, 6.195, 5.975.

ENGLISH-LANGUAGE NEWSPAPERS The Tribune, Nassau Guardian, Freeport News. International papers also available.

EMERGENCIES

RED CROSS/CRESCENT SOCIETIES PO Box N-8331, Nassau, tel 323 7370, fax 323 7404, email redcross@bahamas.net.bs

UK/US/CANADIAN REPS UK: Ansbacher House, 3rd Floor, East Street, Nassau, tel 325 7471, fax 323 387, email: celia.davies@nassau.mail.fco.gov.uk US: Mosmar Building, Queen Street, Nassau, tel 322 118, fax 328 7838, email: usemb@batelnet.bs Canada: Shirley Street Plaza, Nassau, tel 393 2123, fax 393 1305.

Global weather guide p 818, Rainy seasons worldwide p 829, Vaccinations required p 832, Recommended reading p 848, Dependent territories p 812.

BAHRAIN

STATE OF THE NATION

SAFETY Safe.

LIFE EXPECTANCY M 71.1, F 75.3.

PEOPLE AND PLACE

CAPITAL Manama.

LANGUAGE Arabic and English.

PEOPLES Bahraini. Also other Arab, Iranian, Indian and Pakistani.

RELIGION Islam.

SIZE (KM) 707.

POPULATION 594,000.

POP DENSITY/KM 874.

FOOD Spicy, strongly flavoured Arabic food. Several restaurants serve international cuisine. *Arak* (aniseed-flavoured grape spirit) and beer often drunk - while the sale of alcohol is not encouraged it is available to non-Muslims at clubs, good hotels and restaurants.

TRAVEL PLANNING

WHEN TO GO Spring and late autumn are the most pleasant months to visit. Jun - Oct hot and humid, Dec-Mar quite cool.

MEDICAL CARE Good and free emergency medical treatment.

CURRENCY Dinar (BD)=1000fils.

FINANCE Major credit cards accepted in hotels, large stores and restaurants. Smaller shops prefer cash.

AIRPORTS Bahrain International (BAH), 6.5 km from Manama.

INTERNAL TRAVEL Excellent road system, car hire easy at the airport. Over 300 internal flights a week. Travel between the smaller islands by dhow or motorboat.

BUSINESS HOURS 0800-1300, 1500-18/1900 Sat-Wed, 0800-1300 Thu. Some offices work 0800-1600 Mon-Thu with an hour's break for lunch.

GMT +3.

VOLTAGE GUIDE 230AC, 50Hz (Awali, 120AC, 60Hz)

RED TAPE

VISAS (AUS/CANADA/UK/US) Required.

REPS IN UK/US/CANADA UK: 98 Gloucester Road, London SW7 4AU, tel 020 7370 5132/3, fax 020 7370 7773, email information@bahrainembassy.org.uk US: 3502 International Drive, NW, Washington, DC20008, tel, 202 342 0741/2, fax 202 362 2192. Canada: 1869 René Lévesque Boulevard West, Montréal, Québec H3H 1R4, tel 514 931 7444, fax 514 931 5988.

CUSTOMS REGULATIONS Duty free allowance: 200 cigarettes and 50 cigars and 250 g of tobacco, 1ltr of alcoholic beverages and 6 bottles of beer (non-Muslim passengers only), 8 oz of perfume, and gifts up to the value of BD250. Prohibited: Firearms, ammunition, drugs, jewellery. All items originating in Israel may only be imported under licence.

DRIVING REQUIREMENTS International Driving Permit. Must be endorsed by the Traffic and Licensing Directorate.

KEEPING IN TOUCH

BBC WORLD SERVICE MHz 15.58, 11.76, 9.750, 9.410.

ENGLISH-LANGUAGE NEWSPAPERS *Gulf Daily News, Bahrain Tribune*.

EMERGENCIES

RED CROSS/CRESCENT SOCIETIES PO Box 882, Manama, tel 293 171, fax 291 797, email: hilal@baletco.com.bh

UK/US/CANADIAN REPS UK: Government Avenue, PO Box 114, Manama, tel 534 404, fax 533 307, email: britemb@batelco.com.bh US: PO Box 26431, Manama, tel 273 300, fax 272 594, email usismana@batelco.com.bh. Canada: The Canadian High Commission in Riyadh (Saudi Arabia) deals with enquiries relating to Bahrain.

Global weather guide p 818, Rainy seasons worldwide p 829, Vaccinations required p 832, Recommended reading p 848, Dependent territories p 812.

BANGLADESH

STATE OF THE NATION

SAFETY Safe if you're sensible. Observe Islamic customs carefully.

LIFE EXPECTANCY M 58.1, F 58.2.

PEOPLE AND PLACE

CAPITAL Dhaka.

LANGUAGE Bengali and English.

PEOPLES Bengali (98%0.

RELIGION Islam (Sunni), Hinduism.

SIZE (KM) 147,570.

POPULATION 124,000,000.

POP DENSITY/KM 61.2.

FOOD Limited availability of Western food, although served in some hotels and restaurants. Local specialities based on chicken, lamb and seafood, served with rice. Alcohol expensive and availability is limited due to strict Muslim customs.

TRAVEL PLANNING

WHEN TO GO Avoid the monsoon season from Apr -Oct when temperatures are highest. The best time to go is during the cool season, between Nov-Mar.

MEDICAL CARE Limited and basic, insurance strongly recommended.

CURRENCY Bangladeshi taka (Tk) =100 poisha.

FINANCE Limited acceptance of major credit cards. Hotel bills must be paid in a major convertible currency or with travellers cheques.

AIRPORTS Dhaka International (DAC), 20 km from the city.

INTERNAL TRAVEL Slow but efficient rail system, limited by geography but river ferries provide links. Road travel can also be slow, as frequent ferry services a necessity.

BUSINESS HOURS 0900-1700.

GMT +6.

VOLTAGE GUIDE 220/240AC, 50Hz.

RED TAPE

VISAS (AUS/CANADA/UK/US) Required.

REPS IN UK/US/CANADA UK: 28 Queen's Gate, London SW7 5JA, tel 020 7584 0081, fax 020 7225 2130, email bdesh.lon@dial.pipex.com. US: Suite 300, 2201 Wisconsin Avenue, NW, Washington, DC 20007, tel 202 342 8372/6, fax 202 333 4971, email banglaemb@aol.com Canada: 275 Bank Street, Suite 302, Ottawa, Ontario K2P 2L6, tel 613 236 0138/9, fax 613 567 3213, email bdootcanda@iosphere.net

CUSTOMS REGULATIONS Duty free allowance: 200 cigarettes or 50 cigars or 225 g of tobacco, 1 bottle of alcoholic beverages (non-Muslims only), a reasonable amount of perfume, gifts up to the value of Tk500. Prohibited: Firearms and some animals.

DRIVING REQUIREMENTS International Driving Permit.

KEEPING IN TOUCH

BBC WORLD SERVICE MHz 17.79, 15.31, 11.10, 9.740.

ENGLISH-LANGUAGE NEWSPAPERS The *Bangladesh Observer*, *Daily Star*, the *Daily New Nation*, the *Independent*.

EMERGENCIES

RED CROSS/CRESCENT SOCIETIES GPO Box 579, Dhaka, tel 2 933 0188, fax 2 831 908, email bdrcs@bdonline.com

UK/US/CANADIAN REPS UK: United Nations Road, Baridhara, Dhaka 1212, tel 2 882 705-9, fax 2 883 437, email banglaemb@aol.com US: Diplomatic Enclave, Madani Avenue, Baridhara Model Town, Dhaka 1212, tel 2 884 700, fax 2 883 648. Canada: House CWN 16/A, Road 48, Gulshan Model Town, Dhaka 1212, tel 2 988 7091, fax 2 883 043.

Global weather guide p 818, Rainy seasons worldwide p 829, Vaccinations required p 832, Recommended reading p 848, Dependent territories p 812.

BARBADOS

STATE OF THE NATION

SAFETY Muggings increasing: do not carry valuables.

LIFE EXPECTANCY M 73.7, F 78.7.

PEOPLE AND PLACE

CAPITAL Bridgetown.

LANGUAGE English.

PEOPLES African descendants, small groups of South Asians and Europeans.

RELIGION Christian, with an Anglican majority, Roman Catholic minority. Small Jewish, Hindu and Muslim communties.

SIZE (KM) 430.

POPULATION 263 000.

POP DENSITY/KM 61.2.

FOOD Restaurants offer international cuisine. Bajan specialities include superb seafood , including flying fish, lobster and sea urchins. Rum based cocktails.

TRAVEL PLANNING

WHEN TO GO During the dry season from December-June, although even the 'wet' season sees an average of 8hrs of sunshine per day.

MEDICAL CARE UK citizens entitled to free hospital treatment but medicines for anyone other than children and the elderly must be paid for.

CURRENCY Barbados dollar (Bd$) = 100cents.

FINANCE Major credit cards and travellers' cheques widely accepted.

AIRPORTS Barbados (BGI), 11km from Bridgetown.

INTERNAL TRAVEL Good road network. Petrol is comparitively cheap, and cars may be hired by the hour, day or week.

BUSINESS HOURS 0800-1600 Mon-Friday.

GMT -4 (-5 in summer).

VOLTAGE GUIDE 110 AC, 50 Hz.

RED TAPE

VISAS (AUS/CANADA/UK/US) None.

REPS IN UK/US/CANADA UK: 1 Great Russell Street, London WC1B 3JY, 020 7631 4957, fax 020 7323 6872, email barcomuk@dial.pipex.com. US: 2144 Wyoming Avenue, NW, Washington, DC 20008, tel 202 939 9200, fax 202 332 7467, email barbados@oas.org. Canada: 130 Albert Street, Suite 302, Ottawa, Ontario K1P 5G4, tel 613 236 9517/8, fax 613 230 4362, email barhcott@travel-net.com.

CUSTOMS REGULATIONS Duty free allowance: 200 cigarettes or 250 g tobacco, 750 ml of spirits and 750 ml of wine, 50 g of perfume, gifts up to a value of Bd$100 (for persons over 18). Prohibited: Foreign rum, fresh fruit and articles made from camouflage material.

DRIVING REQUIREMENTS Barbados Driving Permit required. Also a valid national or International Driving Permit.

KEEPING IN TOUCH

BBC WORLD SERVICE MHz 17.72, 15.22, 6.195, 5.975.

ENGLISH-LANGUAGE NEWSPAPERS The Nation, The Barbados Advocate.

EMERGENCIES

RED CROSS/CRESCENT SOCIETIES Red Cross House, Jemmots Lane, Bridgetown, tel/fax 426 2052, email bdosredcross@ caribsurf.com.

UK/US/CANADIAN REPS UK: PO Box 676, Lower Collymore Rock, St Michael, tel 436 6694, fax 430 7860, email britishhc@ sandbeach.net. US: Alico Building, Cheap-side, Bridgetown, tel 431 0225, fax 431 0179, email clo@state.gov. Canada: Bishop's Court Hill, Collymore Rock, St Michael, Bridgetown, tel 429 3550, fax 437 7436.

Global weather guide p 818, Rainy seasons worldwide p 829, Vaccinations required p 832, Recommended reading p 848, Dependent territories p 812.

BELARUS

STATE OF THE NATION

SAFETY Seek local advice.

LIFE EXPECTANCY M 62.2, F 73.9.

PEOPLE AND PLACE

CAPITAL Minsk.

LANGUAGE Belarusian.

PEOPLES Belarusian, Russian, Polish and Ukrainian.

RELIGION Russian Orthodox. Roman Catholic, Protestant, Muslim and Jewish minorities.

SIZE (KM) 207,595.

POPULATION 10,300,000.

POP DENSITY/KM 50.

FOOD Regional cooking often based on potatoes with mushrooms and berries as favourite side dishes. Belarusian *borshch* and *filet à la Minsk* are recommended. A good selection of international and Russian cuisine available.

TRAVEL PLANNING

WHEN TO GO Anytime: temperate continental climate.

MEDICAL CARE Free hospital treatment for UK citizens but medicines may be unobtainable, insurance recommended.

CURRENCY Belarusian rouble (BYR).

FINANCE Major credit cards accepted in the larger hotels, shops and restaurants, travellers' cheques are preferable to cash.

AIRPORTS Minsk, 43 km from the city.

INTERNAL TRAVEL 5488 km of rail track in use. Most roads are hard-surfaced.

BUSINESS HOURS 0900-1800, Mon-Friday.

GMT +2/3.

VOLTAGE GUIDE 220AC, 50Hz.

RED TAPE

VISAS (AUS/CANADA/UK/US) Required.

REPS IN UK/US/CANADA UK: 6 Kensington Court, London W8 5DL, tel 020 7937 3288, 020 7361 0005. US: 708 Third Avenue, 21st Floor, New York NY 10017, tel 212 682 5392, fax 212 682 5491, email cgrb@ ix.net.com. Canada: 130 Albert Street, Suite 600, Ottawa, Ontario, K1P 5G4, tel 613 233 9994, fax 613 233 8500, email: belamb@ igs.net.

CUSTOMS REGULATIONS Duty free allowance: 1000 cigarettes, 100 g of tobacco products, 2 ltrs of alcoholic beverages, a reasonable quantity of perfume for personal use, other goods to the value of US$ 2000. Prohibited: Weapons, ammunition, narcotics, photographs and printed matter directed against Belarus, and fruit and vegetables. Prohibited for export: Weapons, ammunition, precious metals, works of art and antiques without permission from the Ministry of Culture, and furs.

DRIVING REQUIREMENTS International Driving Permit

KEEPING IN TOUCH

BBC WORLD SERVICE MHz 15.58, 13.23, 9.410, 6.195.

ENGLISH-LANGUAGE NEWSPAPERS None.

EMERGENCIES

RED CROSS/CRESCENT SOCIETIES 35 Karl Marx Street, 220030 Minsk, tel 172 272 620, fax 172 271 417, email redcross@ un.minsk.by/brc@home.by.

UK/US/CANADIAN REPS UK: 37 Karl Marx Street, 220030 Minsk, tel 172 105 920/1, fax 172 292 306, email pia@ bcpost.belpak.minsk.by. US: Starovilenskaya 46, 220002, Minsk, tel 172 347 761, fax 172 347 853. Canada: The Canadian Embassy in Moscow deals with enquiries relating to Belarus.

Global weather guide p 818, Rainy seasons worldwide p 829, Vaccinations required p 832, Recommended reading p 848, Dependent territories p 812.

BELGIUM

STATE OF THE NATION

SAFETY Safe apart violent carjackings, which are very common.

LIFE EXPECTANCY M 73.8, F 80.6.

PEOPLE AND PLACE

CAPITAL Brussels.

LANGUAGE Flemish and French.

PEOPLES Fleming and Walloon. Italian and Moroccan minorities.

RELIGION Roman Catholic (88%), Protestant, Muslim and Jewish minorities.

SIZE (KM) 30, 528 km

POPULATION 10, 200, 000.

POP DENSITY/KM 331.

FOOD Generally of high quality, style similar to French. Several regional specialities, often rich in butter, cream, wine or beer. Sauces with everything, including *frites* with mayonnaise. Renowned for chocolate - and the local beers.

TRAVEL PLANNING

WHEN TO GO Warm from May-September, snow likely during winter months.

MEDICAL CARE UK citizens with E111 certificate entitled to a 75% refund on medical costs.

CURRENCY Belgian franc (BFr).

FINANCE Major cards, Eurocheques and travellers' cheques widely accepted.

AIRPORTS Brussels Zaventum (BRU) 13 km from the city. Antwerp (ANR) 3 km from the city. Ostend (OST) 5 km from the city. Liege (LGG) 8 km.

INTERNAL TRAVEL Good road and rail networks.

BUSINESS HOURS 0830-1730 Mon-Friday.

GMT +1/2.

VOLTAGE GUIDE 220 AC, 50 Hz.

RED TAPE

VISAS (AUS/CANADA/UK/US) None.

REPS IN UK/US/CANADA UK: 103-105 Eaton Square, London SW1W 9AB, tel 020 7470 3700, fax 020 7259 6213, email info@belgium-embassy.co.uk. US: ITT Building, 1330 Avenue of the Americas, 26th Floor, 54th Street, New York, NY 10019-5422, tel 212 5865110, fax 212 582 9657, email NewYork@diplobel.org. Canada: 4th Floor, 80 Elgin Street, Ottawa, Ontario K1P 1B7, tel 613 236 7267, fax 613 236 7882, email ottawa@diplobel.org/canada.

CUSTOMS REGULATIONS Duty free allowance: 200 cigarettes or 100 cigarillos or 50 cigars or 250 g of tobacco, 2 ltrs of wine, 1 ltr of spirits or 2 ltrs of sparkling or fortified wine, 50 g of perfume and 250 ml of *eau de toilette*, other goods up to BFr 7300, 500 g of coffee, 40 g of tea (for travellers over 17 from non-EU countries) No limits on tobacco and alcohol imported for personal use by EU members. Prohibited: Unpreserved meat products. Other unpreserved foodstuffs must be declared.

DRIVING REQUIREMENTS A national driving licence is acceptable.

KEEPING IN TOUCH

BBC WORLD SERVICE MHz 12.10, 9.410, 6.195, 0.648.

ENGLISH-LANGUAGE NEWSPAPERS None, although international papers available.

EMERGENCIES

RED CROSS/CRESCENT SOCIETIES Ch. de Vleurgat 98, 1050 Brussels, tel 2 645 4411, fax 2 646 0439, email: info@redcross-fr.be.

UK/US/CANADIAN REPS UK: 85 rue d'Arlon, B-1040, Brussels, tel 2 287 6211, fax 2 287 6360. US: 25-27 boulevard du Régent, B-1000 Brussels, tel 2 508 2111, fax 2 511 2725, email jaf@usinfo.be. Canada: 2 avenue de Tervuren, B-1040 Brussels, tel 2 741 0611, fax 2 741 0613.

Global weather guide p 818, Rainy seasons worldwide p 829, Vaccinations required p 832, Recommended reading p 848, Dependent territories p 812.

BELIZE

STATE OF THE NATION

SAFETY Muggings and thefts occur, but not as bad as some parts of Latin America.

LIFE EXPECTANCY M 73.4, F 76.1.

PEOPLE AND PLACE

CAPITAL Belmopan.

LANGUAGE English.

PEOPLES Mestizo, Creole, Maya groups, immigrants from Mexico, Guatemala, Asia.

RELIGION Roman Catholic. Smaller groups of Anglicans, Methodists, Mennonites.

SIZE (KM) 22,965.

POPULATION 200,000.

POP DENSITY/KM 9.

FOOD Generally cheap Latin-American and Creole influenced food. Some international-style and Chinese restaurants. Coconut rum with pineapple juice and the local beer - *Belikin* - popular drinks.

TRAVEL PLANNING

WHEN TO GO Subtropical, with prevailing winds from the Caribbean sea. Dry and hot from January-April, with rainy season from June-September.

MEDICAL CARE Cash payments will generally be demanded for all treatment, insurance strongly recommended.

CURRENCY Belize dollar (Bz$).

FINANCE Credit cards and travellers' cheques accepted.

AIRPORTS Philip S W Goldson International (BZE), 16 km from Belize City.

INTERNAL TRAVEL Local air services between main towns, also linked by all-weather roads.

BUSINESS HOURS 0800-1200, 1300-1700 Mon-Thurs, 0800-1200, 1300-1630 Friday.

GMT -6.

VOLTAGE GUIDE 110 AC, 60 Hz.

RED TAPE

VISAS (AUS/CANADA/UK/US) Required.

REPS IN UK/US/CANADA UK: 22 Harcourt House, 19 Cavendish Square, London W1M 9AD, tel 020 7499 9728, fax 020 7491 4139. US: 2535 Massachusetts Avenue, NW, Washington, DC 20008, tel 202 332 9636, fax 202 332 6888. Also deals with enquiries from Canada.

CUSTOMS REGULATIONS Duty free allowance: 200 cigarettes or 50 cigars or 225 g of tobacco, 568 ml of alcoholic beverages, 1 bottle of perfume for personal use. Prohibited: Pre-Columbian articles, marine products, unprocessed coral or turtle shells may not be exported from Belize.

DRIVING REQUIREMENTS A national driving licence is acceptable.

KEEPING IN TOUCH

BBC WORLD SERVICE MHz 17.84, 15.22, 6.195, 5.975.

ENGLISH-LANGUAGE NEWSPAPERS *The Belize Times, Government Gazette, The People's Pulse, Amandala.*

EMERGENCIES

RED CROSS/CRESCENT SOCIETIES PO Box 413, Belize City, tel 2 73319, fax 2 30998 email bzercshq@btl.net.

UK/US/CANADIAN REPS UK: PO Box 91, Embassy Square, Belmopan, tel 8 22146/7, fax 8 22761, email brithi.com@btlnet. US: 29 Gabourel Lane, Belize City, tel 2 77161, fax 2 30802, email embbelize@state.gov. Canada: 83 North Front Street, Belize City, tel 2 33722, fax 2 30060.

Global weather guide p 818, Rainy seasons worldwide p 829, Vaccinations required p 832, Recommended reading p 848, Dependent territories p 812.

BENIN

STATE OF THE NATION

SAFETY Armed robbery and muggings increasing. Roads poorly lit at night.

LIFE EXPECTANCY M 51.7, F 55.2.

PEOPLE AND PLACE

CAPITAL Porto Novo.

LANGUAGE French and indigenous tribal languages.

PEOPLES Fon, Bariba, Yoruba, Fulani.

RELIGION Indigenous and Animist (70%), Christianity and Islam.

SIZE (KM) 112,622.

POPULATION 5,900,000.

POP DENSITY/KM 53.

FOOD Restaurants in Cotonou serve French and African specialities, particularly seafood. No restaurants of note in Porto Novo.

TRAVEL PLANNING

WHEN TO GO The south has an equatorial climate, hot and dry from January-April and during August, and rainy seasons from May-July and September-December. More extreme temperatures in the north, hot and dry from November-June, cool and very wet from July-October.

MEDICAL CARE Very limited and cash payments expected, insurance strongly recommended.

CURRENCY Commnauté financiare aficaine franc (CFA) = 100 centimes.

FINANCE Major credit cards and travellers' cheques accepted on a limited basis.

AIRPORTS Catonou Cadjehoun (COO), 5 km from the city.

INTERNAL TRAVEL Roads in reasonably good condition but often impassable during the rainy season. A number of local car firms are available in Cotonou for hire. Trains connect main towns.

BUSINESS HOURS 0800-1230, 1500-1830 Mon-Fri.

GMT +1.

VOLTAGE GUIDE 220AC, 50Hz.

RED TAPE

VISAS (AUS/CANADA/UK/US) Required.

REPS IN UK/US/CANADA UK: Dolphin House, 16 The Broadway, Stanmore, Middlesex, HA7 4DW, tel 020 8954 8800, fax 020 8954 8844. US: 2737 Cathedral Avenue, NW, Washington, DC 20008, tel 202 232 6656, fax 202 265 1996. Canada: 58 Glebe Avenue, Ottawa, Ontario, K1S 2C3, tel 613 233 4429, fax 613 233 8952, email ambaben2@ on.aira.com.

CUSTOMS REGULATIONS Duty free allowance: 200 cigarettes or 25 cigars or 250 g of tobacco, 1 bottle of wine and 1 bottle of spirits, 500 ml of *eau de toilette* and 250 ml of perfume (for travellers over 15).

DRIVING REQUIREMENTS International Driving Permit.

KEEPING IN TOUCH

BBC WORLD SERVICE MHz 17.83, 15.40, 7.160, 6.005.

ENGLISH-LANGUAGE NEWSPAPERS None - all papers exclusively in French.

EMERGENCIES

RED CROSS/CRESCENT SOCIETIES BP No 1, Porto Novo, tel 212 886, fax 214 927.

UK/US/CANADIAN REPS UK: The British High Commission in Lagos (Nigeria) deals with enquiries relating to Benin. US: BP 2012, rue Caporal Anani, Cotonou, tel 301 792, fax 301 439. Canada: The Canadian Embassy in Accra (Ghana) deals with enquiries relating to Benin.

Global weather guide p 818, Rainy seasons worldwide p 829, Vaccinations required p 832, Recommended reading p 848, Dependent territories p 812.

BHUTAN

STATE OF THE NATION

SAFETY Safe.

LIFE EXPECTANCY M 59.5, F 62.

PEOPLE AND PLACE

CAPITAL Thimpu.

LANGUAGE Dzongkha.

PEOPLES Drukpa, Nepalese.

RELIGION Buddhist, Hindu

SIZE (KM) 46, 500.

POPULATION 1, 900, 000.

POP DENSITY/KM 40.

FOOD Restaurants scarce. Vegetarian based cuisine. Chillies, yaks cheese frequently used, rice ubiquitous. Bhutanese tea (*souza*) most popular drink.

TRAVEL PLANNING

WHEN TO GO October-November, April-mid-June are best, when rainfall is at a minimum. Nights can be very cold. Monsoon occurs June-August.

MEDICAL CARE Basic, insurance strongly recommended.

CURRENCY Ngultrum (NU) = 100 chetrum (Ch).

FINANCE American Express and Diners Club have very limited acceptability. Travellers cheques accepted in banks and hotels.

AIRPORTS Paro (PBH) - journey into Thimpu takes about 90 mins by bus or taxi.

INTERNAL TRAVEL No internal rail services, good internal road network.

BUSINESS HOURS 0900-1700, Mon-Friday.

GMT +6.

VOLTAGE GUIDE 220 AC, 50 Hz.

RED TAPE

VISAS (AUS/CANADA/UK/US) Required.

REPS IN UK/US/CANADA UK: n/a. US: 27th Floor, 2 United Nations Plaza, 44th Street, New York NY 10017, tel 212 826 1919, fax 212 826 2998. Canada: n/a.

CUSTOMS REGULATIONS Duty free allowance: 200 cigarettes or 50 cigars or 250 g of tobacco, 1 ltr of spirits, 250 of *eau de toilette*. Prohibited: Firearms, narcotics, plants, gold and silver bullion and obsolete currency. The export of religious objects, manuscripts, images and anthropological materials. Note: Cameras, videos, mobile phones and all other electronic equipment must be registered with the authorities on arrival and will be checked by customs on departure.

DRIVING REQUIREMENTS International Driving Permit

KEEPING IN TOUCH

BBC WORLD SERVICE MHz 17.79, 15.31, 11.75, 5.965.

ENGLISH-LANGUAGE NEWSPAPERS Very few papers. *Kuensel*, a government news bulletin, published weekly in English.

EMERGENCIES

RED CROSS/CRESCENT SOCIETIES n/a.

UK/US/CANADIAN REPS UK: n/a. US: n/a. Canada: n/a.

POSSIBLY USEFUL CONTACTS Tourism Authority of Bhutan, PO Box 126, Thimpu, Bhutan, tel 2 323 251, fax 1 323 695, email tab@druknet.net.bt. Bhutan Tourist Corporation Ltd (BTLC), PO Box 159 Thimpu, Bhutan, tel 2 322 045, fax 2 322 392, email btcl@druknet.net.bt. United Nations Development Programme: United Nations Building, Dremton lam, GPO Box 162, Thimpu, tel 2 322 424, fax 2 323 006, email fo.btn@undp.org.

Global weather guide p 818,   Rainy seasons worldwide p 829,   Vaccinations required p 832,   Recommended reading p 848,   Dependent territories p 812.

BOLIVIA

STATE OF THE NATION

SAFETY One of the safest Latin American countries, but take care in any cocaine-growing areas.

LIFE EXPECTANCY M 59.8, F 63.2.

PEOPLE AND PLACE

CAPITAL La Paz.

LANGUAGE Spanish.

PEOPLES Aymara and Quecha Indians.

RELIGION Roman Catholic.

SIZE (KM) 1,098,581.

POPULATION 8,000,000.

POP DENSITY/KM 7.

FOOD National dishes often based on meat, for instance *lechon al homo* (young roast pig). *Empanada saltena* is a pastry filled with diced meat, chicken, chives, raisins, diced potatoes, pepper and hot sauce). Bolivian beer (especially *paceña*) is reputed to be the best on the continent.

TRAVEL PLANNING

WHEN TO GO Temperate climate, but wide differences in temperature between day and night. Wettest between November-March. La Paz can be uncomfortable for some visitors because of the very high altitude.

MEDICAL CARE Basic in public hospitals, insurance strongly recommended.

CURRENCY Boliviano (Bs) = 100 centavos.

FINANCE US dollar travellers' cheques best form of currency at the moment. Very limited acceptance of credit cards.

AIRPORTS La Paz (LPB) 14 km from centre. Santa Cruz (VVI), 16 km from centre.

INTERNAL TRAVEL Air travel is the best mode of transport because of the topography and tropical regions. Separate rail networks in the eastern and western parts of the country. Work in progress to improve the condition of major highways. Car hire is possible in La Paz.

BUSINESS HOURS 0830-1200, 1430-1830 Monday-Friday, 0900-12300 Saturday.

GMT -4.

VOLTAGE GUIDE 110/220 AC in La Paz. 220 AC, 50 Hz in the rest of the country.

RED TAPE

VISAS (AUS/CANADA/UK/US) Not required for tourists.

REPS IN UK/US/CANADA UK: 106 Eaton Square, London SW1W 9AD,tel 020 7235 4248, fax 020 7235 1286. US: 3014 Massachusetts Avenue, NW, Washington, DC 20008-3603, tel 202 483 4410, fax 202 328 3712, email bolembus@erols.com. Canada: 11231 Jasper Avenue, Edmonton, Alberta T5K 0L5, tel 403 488 1525, fax 403 488 0350.

CUSTOMS REGULATIONS Duty free allowance: 100 cigarettes and 25 cigars and 200 g of tobacco and 100 cigarillos, 1 opened bottle of alcohol, a reasonable amount of perfume.

DRIVING REQUIREMENTS International Driving Permit required.

KEEPING IN TOUCH

BBC WORLD SERVICE MHz 17.84, 15.22, 6.195, 5.970.

ENGLISH-LANGUAGE NEWSPAPERS *The Bolivian Times* (weekly).

EMERGENCIES

RED CROSS/CRESCENT SOCIETIES Casilla No 741, La Paz, tel 2 202 930, fax 2 359 102.

UK/US/CANADIAN REPS UK: Avenida Arce 2732, Casilla 694, La Paz, tel 2 433 424, fax 2 431 073, email ppa@mail.rds.org.bo. US: Avenida Acre 2780, Casilla 425, La Paz, tel 2 430 251, fax 2 433 900. Canada: Avenida 20 de Octuber 2475, Plaza Avaroa, Sopocachi, La Paz, tel 2 432 838, fax 2 430 250, email cida-lapaz@mail.megalink.com.

Global weather guide p 818, Rainy seasons worldwide p 829, Vaccinations required p 832, Recommended reading p 848, Dependent territories p 812.

BOSNIA & HERZEGOVINA

STATE OF THE NATION

SAFETY Extremely dangerous. Many landmines and considerable tension remain. Roadblocks in many areas.

LIFE EXPECTANCY n/a.

PEOPLE AND PLACE

CAPITAL Sarajevo.

LANGUAGE Serb-Croat and Croat-Serb.

PEOPLES Before the war, 44% ethnic Bosnian, 31% Serb, 17% Croat, other minorities.

RELIGION Muslim 40%, Serbian Orthodox 31%, Roman Catholic 15%, small Protestant population.

SIZE (KM) 51,129.

POPULATION 4,510,000.

POP DENSITY/KM 88.2.

FOOD Turkish influenced cuisine, including *bosanski lonac* (meat and vegetable stew), Turkish delight, *Halva*.

TRAVEL PLANNING

WHEN TO GO Moderate continental conditions, hot summers and very cold winters.

MEDICAL CARE Very limited, insurance with repatriation cover recommended.

CURRENCY Bosnia and Herzegovina Konvertibilna Marka (KM) = 100 pfenings.

FINANCE Generally a cash-only economy, only deutschmarks and US dollars practical.

AIRPORTS Sarajevo (SJJ).

INTERNAL TRAVEL Rail links have generally been restored. The risk of andmines on major roads has been reduced, but caution should be used outside main cities. Some car hire available at the airport.

BUSINESS HOURS 0800-1600 Mon-Friday.

GMT +1/2.

VOLTAGE GUIDE 220 AC, 50 Hz.

RED TAPE

VISAS (AUS/CANADA/UK/US) Required by Australian travellers.

REPS IN UK/US/CANADA UK: 320 Regent Street, London W1R 5AB, tel 020 7255 3758, fax 020 7255 3760. US: 2109 E Street, NW, Washington, DC 20037, tel 202 337 1500, fax 202 337 1502, email: info@ bosnianembassy.org Also deals with enquiries from Canada .

CUSTOMS REGULATIONS Duty free allowance: 200 cigarettes or 20 cigars or 200 g of tobacco, 1 ltr of alcohol, 1 bottle of perfume, gifts to the value of DM150 .

DRIVING REQUIREMENTS International Driving Permit.

KEEPING IN TOUCH

BBC WORLD SERVICE MHz 15.40, 11.76, 6.190, 3.255.

ENGLISH-LANGUAGE NEWSPAPERS None.

EMERGENCIES

RED CROSS/CRESCENT SOCIETIES n/a.

UK/US/CANADIAN REPS UK: Tina Ujevica 8, 71000 Sarajevo, tel 71 444 429, fax 71 666 131, email britemb@bih.net.ba. US: Alipapina 43, Sarajevo, 71 445 700, fax 71 659 722. Canada: Logavina 7, 71000 Sarajevo, tel 71 447 900, fax 71 447 901.

Global weather guide p 818, Rainy seasons worldwide p 829, Vaccinations required p 832, Recommended reading p 848, Dependent territories p 812.

BOTSWANA

STATE OF THE NATION

SAFETY Safe.

LIFE EXPECTANCY M 46.2, F 48.4.

PEOPLE AND PLACE

CAPITAL Gaborone.

LANGUAGE English and Setswana.

PEOPLES Tswana (98%).

RELIGION Majority animistic beliefs, 30% Christian.

SIZE (KM) 581 730.

POPULATION 1,600,000.

POP DENSITY/KM 3.

FOOD Generally basic outside major hotels and restaurants.

TRAVEL PLANNING

WHEN TO GO Rainy season October-April, and is the hottest time of year. Drier and cooler weather from May-September, with an average temperature of 25°C.

MEDICAL CARE There is a nominal fee for hospital care and medicines supplied by government hospitals are free, but outside towns health facilities are basic and insurance is recommended.

CURRENCY Pula (P) = 100 thebe

FINANCE Limited acceptance of credit cards. Hotels accept travellers' cheques but the surcharge can be high.

AIRPORTS Gaborone Sir Seretse Khama International (GBE), 15 km from the city.

INTERNAL TRAVEL Major areas linked by air and rail. Some tarmac roads, four-wheel-drives necessary in many areas. Car hire can be arranged in Gaborone, Francistown or Maun.

BUSINESS HOURS 0800-1700 April-October, 0730-1630 October-April.

GMT +2.

VOLTAGE GUIDE 220-240 AC, 50 Hz.

RED TAPE

VISAS (AUS/CANADA/UK/US) None.

REPS IN UK/US UK: 6 Stratford Place, London W1N 9AE, 020 7499 0031, fax 020 7495 8595. US: 1531 New Hampshire Avenue, NW, Washington, DC 20036, tel 202 244 4990/1, fax 202 244 4164, email botwash@compuserve.com.

CUSTOMS REGULATIONS Duty free allowance: 400 cigarettes or 50 cigars or 250 g of tobacco, 2 ltrs of wine and 1 ltr of spirits, 50 ml of perfume and 250 *eau de toilette*, goods upto the value P500.

DRIVING REQUIREMENTS An International Driving Permit not legally required but recommended for longer stays.

KEEPING IN TOUCH

BBC WORLD SERVICE MHz 17.83, 15.40, 7.160, 6.005.

ENGLISH-LANGUAGE NEWSPAPERS *Botswana Daily News, The Botwana Gazette, The Botswana Guardian.*

EMERGENCIES

RED CROSS/CRESCENT SOCIETIES PO Box 485, Gaborone, tel 552 465, fax 312 352, email brcs@info.bw/admin@info.bw.

UK/US/CANADIAN REPS UK: Private Bag 0023, Gaborone, tel 353 841, fax 356 105, email british@bc.bw. US: PO Box 90 Gaborone, tel 353 982, fax 356 947, email usembgab@mega.co.za. Canada: The Canadian High Commission in Harare (Zimbabwe) deals with enquiries relating to Botswana.

Global weather guide p 818, Rainy seasons worldwide p 829, Vaccinations required p 832, Recommended reading p 848, Dependent territories p 812.

BRAZIL

STATE OF THE NATION

SAFETY Beware of petty crime (theft, pickpocketing).

LIFE EXPECTANCY M 63.1, F 71.

PEOPLE AND PLACE

CAPITAL Brasilia.

LANGUAGE Portugese.

PEOPLES Highly diverse population including Portuguese and African descendants, more recent Italian and Japanese immigrants and indigenous Indian groups.

RELIGION Mainly Roman Catholic.

SIZE (KM) 8,547,403.

POPULATION 165,200,000.

POP DENSITY/KM 20.

FOOD Each region has its own speciality. A Rio de Janeiro favourite is *feijoada* (a thick stew of black beans, beef, pork, sausage, chops, pigs ears and tails). A typical Bahain dish is *vatapá* (shrimps, fish oil, coconut milk, bread and rice). In the northeast dried salted meat and beans are the staple diet. The national drink is *caipirinha*, based on the phenomenally strong whisky liquer *cachaça,* mixed with sugar, ice and limes.

TRAVEL PLANNING

WHEN TO GO The Amazon basin has tropical temperatures and high humidity throughout the year. The coastlands also have a hot tropical climate. The south is more temperate. Rainy seasons occur from January-April in the north, April-July in the north-east, November-March in the Rio/Sao Paulo area.

MEDICAL CARE No health agreements with the UK. Medical costs are high, insurance strongly recommended.

CURRENCY Real (R$) = 100 centavos.

FINANCE Most international credit cards and travellers' cheques are accepted.

AIRPORTS Brasilia International (BSB), 11 km from the city, Rio de Janiero (GIG), Sao Paolo (GRU).

INTERNAL TRAVEL One of the largest internal air networks in the world. Limited rail services to most major cities and towns.

Extensive road network. Car hire available in major centres.

BUSINESS HOURS 0900-1800 Mon-Friday.

GMT from -3 to -5.

VOLTAGE GUIDE 220 AC , 60 Hz (Brasilia). 110AC, 60 Hz for the rest of the country.

RED TAPE

VISAS (AUS/CANADA/UK/US) Required by all apart from UK.

REPS IN UK/US/CANADA UK: 32 Green Street, London W1Y 4AT, 020 7499 0877, fax 020 7399 9100, email infolondres@infolondres.org.uk. US: 1185 Avenue of the Americas, 21st Floor, New York, NY 10036, 212 827 0976, fax 212 827 0225, email consulado@consuladobrasilny.org. Canada: Suite 1700, 2000 Mansfield Street, Montréal, H3A 3A5, tel 514 4993963, fax 514 499 3963, email: conbras@total.net.

CUSTOMS REGULATIONS Duty free allowance: 400 cigarettes and 250 g of tobacco and 25 cigars, 2ltrs of alcohol, up to US$500 worth of goods bought duty-free in Brazil. Prohibited: Meat and cheese products and other products of animal origin transported from Africa, Asia, Italy, Portugal and Spain.

DRIVING REQUIREMENTS International Driving Permit.

KEEPING IN TOUCH

BBC WORLD SERVICE MHz 17.84, 15.19, 9.915, 6.195.

ENGLISH-LANGUAGE NEWSPAPERS *The Brazil Herald.*

EMERGENCIES

RED CROSS/CRESCENT SOCIETIES Praça Cruz Vermelha No 10, 20230-130 Rio de Janeiro, tel 21 507 5543/4, fax 21507 1538.

UK/US/CANADIAN REPS UK: Praia do Flmengo, 284/2 andar, 22210-030 Rio de Janeiro, tel 21 553 3223, fax 21 553 6850, email britconrio@openlink.com.br. US: Avenida das Nações, Quadra 801, Lote 3, 70403-900 Brasilia, tel 61 321 7272, fax 61 225 9136, email administrator@americanembassy.org.br. Canada: SES, Avenida das Nações, Quadra 803, Lote 16, 70410-900, Brasilia, tel 61 321 2171, fax 61 321 4529.

Global weather guide p 818, Rainy seasons worldwide p 829, Vaccinations required p 832, Recommended reading p 848, Dependent territories p 812.

BRUNEI

STATE OF THE NATION

SAFETY Safe.

LIFE EXPECTANCY M 73.4, F 78.1.

PEOPLE AND PLACE

CAPITAL Bandar Seri Begawan.

LANGUAGE Malay and English.

PEOPLES Malay, Chinese, indigenous groups.

RELIGION Sunni Muslim, significant Buddhist, Confucian, Daoist, Christian communities.

SIZE (KM) 5765.

POPULATION 313,300.

POP DENSITY/KM 59.

FOOD Local food similar to Malay cuisine with fish and rice, often spicy. Malaysian, Chinese, Indian food widely served. European food served in hotel restaurants

TRAVEL PLANNING

WHEN TO GO Very hot, humid tropical climate most of the year. Monsoon season from November-December.

MEDICAL CARE Good, but repatriation may be necessary for certain treatments so insurance is recommended.

CURRENCY Brunei dollar (Br$).

FINANCE Major credit cards and travellers' cheques generally accepted.

AIRPORTS Bandar Seri Begawan (BWN)

INTERNAL TRAVEL No air travel. Water taxis. Self-drive or chauffeur-driven cars available for hire.

BUSINESS HOURS 0745-1215, 1330-1630 Mon-Thu, 0900-1200 Sat.

GMT +8.

VOLTAGE GUIDE 220/240 AC, 50 Hz.

RED TAPE

VISAS (AUS/CANADA/UK/US) Required by Australians and Canadians if staying more than 14 days.

REPS IN UK/US/CANADA UK: 19A Belgrave Mews West, London SW1X 8HT, tel 020 7581 0521, fax 020 7235 9717. US: 3520 International Court, NW, Washington DC 20037, tel 202 342 0159, fax 202 342 0158, email tutong@erols.com. Canada: 395 Laurier Avenue East, Ottawa, Ontario K1N 6R4, tel 613 234 5656, fax 613 234 4397, email bhco@mail.cyberus.com.

CUSTOMS REGULATIONS Duty free allowance: 200 cigarettes or 250 g of tobacco products, 2 bottles of liquor and 12 cans of beer (by non-Muslims for personal consumption only, must be declared on arrival), 60 ml of perfume and 250 ml *eau de toilette*. Prohibited: Firearms, drugs and pornography. The penalty for trafficking drugs is death. All medication must be declared.

DRIVING REQUIREMENTS International Driving Permit. A temporary licence is available on presentation of a valid driving licence from the visitor's country of origin.

KEEPING IN TOUCH

BBC WORLD SERVICE MHz 15.28, 9.740, 6.195, 3.195.

ENGLISH-LANGUAGE NEWSPAPERS *Borneo Bulletin*.

EMERGENCIES

RED CROSS/CRESCENT SOCIETIES PO Box 3065, Bandar Seri Begawan, BS8675, tel 2 339774, fax 2 382 797.

UK/US/CANADIAN REPS UK: Unit 2.01, 2nd Floor, Block D, Komplexs Bangunan Yayasan, Sultan Haji Hassanal, Bolkiah, Jalan Pretty, Bandar Seri Begawan BS8711, tel 2 226 001, fax 2 226 002, email brithc@brunet.bn. US: 3rd Floor, Teck Guan Plaza, Jalan Sultan, Bandar Seri Begawan BS8811, 2 229 670, fax 2 227 830, email amembbsb@brunet.bn. Canada: Suite 51/52, Britannia House, Jalan Cator, Bandar Seri Begawan BS8811, tel 2 220 043, fax 2 220 040.

Global weather guide p 818, Rainy seasons worldwide p 829, Vaccinations required p 832, Recommended reading p 848, Dependent territories p 812.

BULGARIA

STATE OF THE NATION

SAFETY Beware of hazardous drivers.
LIFE EXPECTANCY M 67.6, F 74.7.

PEOPLE AND PLACE

CAPITAL Sofia.
LANGUAGE Bulgarian.
PEOPLES Bulgarian, Turkish, Macedonian, Romany.
RELIGION Bulgarian Orthodox (85%), Muslim, Roman Catholic and Jewish.
SIZE (KM) 110, 994.
POPULATION 8, 427, 418.
POP DENSITY/KM 76.2.
FOOD Spicy, hearty dishes, including kebapcheta (strongly spiced minced meat rolls) and pastries stuffed with cheese or fruit. Standard west European food widely available. Heavily sweetened coffee is widely popular.

TRAVEL PLANNING

WHEN TO GO Climate varies according to altitude. Warm summers with some rainfall, cold winters with snow. Frequent rain during spring and autumn.
MEDICAL CARE Free health care for UK citizens, some specialised treatments may not be available.
CURRENCY Lev (Lv) = 100 stotinki.
FINANCE Credit cards and travellers' cheques accepted in major hotels and restaurants.
AIRPORTS Sofia (SOF) 10 km from city, Varna (VAR) 9 km from city, Bourgas (BOJ)13 kms from city.
INTERNAL TRAVEL Comparitively cheap air travel. Regular boat and hydrofoil services along the Danube link many centres. Roads generally of good quality, car hire can be arranged through hotels.
BUSINESS HOURS 0900-1730, Mon-Friday.
GMT +2/3.
VOLTAGE GUIDE 220 AC, 50 Hz.

RED TAPE

VISAS (AUS/CANADA/UK/US) None.
REPS IN UK/US/CANADA UK: 186-188 Queen's Gate, London SW7 5HL, tel 020 7584 9400, fax 020 7584 4948. US: 161 22nd Street, NW, Washington, DC 20008, tel 202 387 7969, fax 202 387 7969, email bulgaria@access.digex.net. Canada: 325 Steward Street, Ottawa, Ontario K1N 6K5, tel 613 789 3215, fax 613 789 3524.

CUSTOMS REGULATIONS Duty free allowance: 200 cigarettes or 50 cigars or 250 g of tobacco, 1ltr of spirits and 2ltrs of wine, 100 g of perfume, objects and foodstuffs intended for personal use (for travellers over 18). Prohibited: Arms, ammunition, narcotics and pornography.

DRIVING REQUIREMENTS Internatinal Driving Permit. Green Card is compulsory.

KEEPING IN TOUCH

BBC WORLD SERVICE MHz 15.65, 9.410, 6.195, 3.955.
ENGLISH-LANGUAGE NEWSPAPERS *Sofia News* (weekly).

EMERGENCIES

RED CROSS/CRESCENT SOCIETIES 76 James Boucher Boulevard, 1407 Sofia, tel 2 650 595, fax 2 656 937, email redcross@mail.bol.bg

UK/US/CANADIAN REPS UK: 38 Vassil Levski Boulevard, 1000 Sofia, Bulgaria, tel 2 980 1220, fax 2 980 1229, email brit.embsof@mbox.cit.bg. US: 1 Capitan Andrev, 1428 Sofia, tel 2 9362022, fax 2 963 2859. Canada: The Canadian Embassy in Bucharest (Romania) deals with enquiries relating to Bulgaria.

Global weather guide p 818,   Rainy seasons worldwide p 829,   Vaccinations required p 832, Recommended reading p 848,   Dependent territories p 812.

BURKINA FASO

STATE OF THE NATION

SAFETY Towns can be dangerous after dark. Take care in remote rural areas.

LIFE EXPECTANCY M 43.3, F 45.2.

PEOPLE AND PLACE

CAPITA Ouagadougou.

LANGUAGE French and several indigenous.

PEOPLES Mossi, Fulani, Tuareg, Songhai.

RELIGION Traditional beliefs, Muslim, Roman Catholic.

SIZE (KM) 274,200.

POPULATION 11,400,000.

POP DENSITY/KM 42.

FOOD Staple foods include sorghum, millet, rice, maize, nuts, potatoes and yams. Specialities include *brochettes* (meat cooked on a skewer) and chicken dishes.

TRAVEL PLANNING

WHEN TO GO During the dry season from November-February, when the *harmattan* winds from the east result in dry and cool weather. Rainy season from June-October.

MEDICAL CARE Limited, buy basic remedies before entering the country. Insurance strongly recommended including air evacuation cover.

CURRENCY Communauté Financiaire Africaine Franc (CFA) = 100 centimes.

FINANCE Limited acceptance of major credit cards.

AIRPORTS Ouagadougou (OUA), 8 km from the city.

INTERNAL TRAVEL Rail travel can become overcrowded. Roads generally impassable during the rainy season. Car hire is a relatively new development and cars may be in poor condition.

BUSINESS HOURS 0700-1230, 1500-1730 Monday-Friday.

GMT GMT.

VOLTAGE GUIDE 220 AC, 50 Hz.

RED TAPE

VISAS (AUS/CANADA/UK/US) Required.

REPS IN UK/US/CANADA
UK: 5 Cinnamon Row, Plantation Wharf, London SW11 3TW, tel 020 7738 1800, fax 020 7738 2820. US: 2340 Massachusetts Avenue, NW, Washington, DC 20008, tel 202 332 5577, fax 202 667 1882. Canada: 48 Range Road, Ottawa, Ontario K1N 8J4, tel 613 238 4796, fax 613 238 3812.

CUSTOMS REGULATIONS Duty free allowance: 200 cigarettes or 25 cigars or 250 g of tobacco, 1ltr of spirits and 1ltr of wine, 500 ml of *eau de toilette* and 250 ml of perfume (travellers over 18). Sporting guns may only be imported under licence.

DRIVING REQUIREMENTS International Driving Permit recommended although a temporary licence available on presentation of a valid national driving licence.

KEEPING IN TOUCH

BBC WORLD SERVICE MHz 17.83, 15.40, 11.83, 7.160.

ENGLISH-LANGUAGE NEWSPAPERS French papers only.

EMERGENCIES

RED CROSS/CRESCENT SOCIETIES 01 BP 4404, Ouagadougou 01, tel 361 340, fax 363 121.

UK/US/CANADIAN REPS UK: 01 BP 3769 Ouagadougou 01, tel 361 641, fax 361 640, email tmc@fasonet.bf. US: 01 BP 35, rue Raoul Folereau, Ouagadougou 01, tel 312 660, fax 312 368, email zoungranaj@ wo.state.gov. Canada: 01 BP 548, Canadian Development Centre, Ouagadougou 01, tel 311 894/5, fax 311 900, email ambrcanada@ fasonet.bf.

Global weather guide p 818, Rainy seasons worldwide p 829, Vaccinations required p 832, Recommended reading p 848, Dependent territories p 812.

BURUNDI

STATE OF THE NATION

SAFETY Extremely dangerous. Murder and violence widespread, and the rule of law cannot be guaranteed outside the capital.

LIFE EXPECTANCY M 41, F 45.2.

PEOPLE AND PLACE

CAPITAL Bujumbura.

LANGUAGE French and Kirundi.

PEOPLES Hutu (85%), Tutsi (14%).

RELIGION Mainly Roman Catholic.

SIZE (KM) 27, 834.

POPULATION 6, 600, 000.

POP DENSITY/KM 257.

FOOD Limited choice, hotel restaurants in Bujumbura serve meals of reasonable quality but at high prices.

TRAVEL PLANNING

WHEN TO GO Rainy season from October-May, dry season from June-September. Hot equatorial climate near Lake Tanganyika, the rest of the country is mild.

MEDICAL CARE Limited and payment will be demanded, insurance strongly recommended.

CURRENCY Burundi Franc (Bufr) = 100 centimes.

FINANCE Limited acceptance of travellers' cheques, MasterCard and Diners Club.

AIRPORTS Bujumbura International (BJM), 11 km from the city.

INTERNAL TRAVEL Many roads are sealed. Road travel difficult during the rainy season. Car hire may be possible in Bujumbura, through Avis or local garages.

BUSINESS HOURS 0730-1200, 14-1730 Mon-Fri.

GMT +2.

VOLTAGE GUIDE 220 AC, 50 Hz.

RED TAPE

VISAS (AUS/CANADA/UK/US) Required.

REPS IN UK/US/CANADA UK: 26 Armitage Road, London NW11 8RD, tel 020 8381 4092, fax 020 8458 8596, email ambabu.uk@btinternet.com. US: 2233 Wisconsin Avenue, Suite 212, NW, Washington, DC 20007, tel 202 342 2574, fax 202 342 2578, email burundiembassy@erols.com. Also deals with enquiries from Canada.

CUSTOMS REGULATIONS Duty free allowance: 1000 cigarettes or 1kg of tobacco, 1ltr of alcoholic beverages, a reasonable amount of perfume.

DRIVING REQUIREMENTS Driving licences issued by the UK are acceptable.

KEEPING IN TOUCH

BBC WORLD SERVICE MHz 17.83, 15.40, 11.76, 6.005.

ENGLISH-LANGUAGE NEWSPAPERS None.

EMERGENCIES

RED CROSS/CRESCENT SOCIETIES BP 324, Bujumbura, tel 216 246, fax 211 101.

UK/US/CANADIAN REPS UK: The British Embassy in Kigali (Rwanda) deals with enquiries relating to Burundi. US: BP 1720, avenue des Etats-Unis, Bujumbura, tel 223 454, fax 222 926. Canada: The Canadian High Commission in Nairobi deals with enquiries relating to Burundi.

Global weather guide p 818, Rainy seasons worldwide p 829, Vaccinations required p 832, Recommended reading p 848, Dependent territories p 812.

CAMBODIA

STATE OF THE NATION

SAFETY Politically calm at present. Highest incidence of landmines and unexploded ordnance in the world, so travel off the beaten track is very hazardous. Even local information on landmines is unreliable. Be wary in areas affected by covert activities such as drug-production or logging.

LIFE EXPECTANCY M 51.5, F 55.

PEOPLE AND PLACE

CAPITAL Phnom Penh.

LANGUAGE Khmer. Chinese and Vietnamese also spoken.

PEOPLES Khmer (94%), Small Chinese and Vietnamese communities.

RELIGION Mainly Buddhist.

SIZE (KM) 181,035.

POPULATION 10,800,000.

POP DENSITY/KM 61.

FOOD Influenced by Thai and Vietnamese cuisine. Restaurants and foot stalls abound in Phnom Penh.

TRAVEL PLANNING

WHEN TO GO Tropical monsoon climate, with the monsoon season from June-October. The best time to visit is from November-May, during the dry season.

MEDICAL CARE Limited. Immediate cash payments demanded, insurance strongly recommended.

CURRENCY Riel (CRI)= 100 sen.

FINANCE Very limited acceptance of major credit cards and travellers' cheques. US dollars widely accepted.

AIRPORTS Pochentong (PNH), 12 km from Phnom Penh.

INTERNAL TRAVEL Some rail services operate, but many need restoration. Boats and government run ferries frequently used. Driving can be hazardous, due to the poor conditions of the roads and accidents caused by reckless driving are relatively frequent. Reliable information about security should be obtained before considering extensive road journeys. Car hire is generally not recommended and visitors are advised to hire a car with driver for approximately the same cost.

BUSINESS HOURS 0700-1130 and 1400-1730 Monday-Friday .

GMT +7.

VOLTAGE GUIDE 220AC, 50 Hz.

RED TAPE

VISAS (AUS/CANADA/UK/US) Required.

REPS IN UK/US/CANADA UK: n/a, nearest in Paris: 4 rue Adolphe Yvon, 75116, Paris, 145 03 47 20, fax 1 45 03 47 40. US: 4500 16th Street, NW, Washington, DC 20011, tel 202 726 7742, fax 202 726 8381, email cambodia@embassy.org. Canada: n/a.

CUSTOMS REGULATIONS Duty free allowance: 200 cigarettes or an equivalent quantity of cigars or tobacco, 1 opened bottle of spirit, reasonable amount of perfume.

DRIVING REQUIREMENTS International Driving Permit not recognised.

KEEPING IN TOUCH

BBC WORLD SERVICE MHz 15.40, 11.94, 6.190, 3.255.

ENGLISH-LANGUAGE NEWSPAPERS *Phnom Penh Post, Cambodia Daily, Cambodia Times.*

EMERGENCIES

RED CROSS/CRESCENT SOCIETIES 17, Vithei deh Croix-Rouge, Cambodigienne, Phnom-Penh, tel 23 212 876, fax 23 212 875, email: crc@camnet.com.kh.

UK/US/CANADIAN REPS UK: 27-29 Street 75, Phnom Penh, tel 23 427 124, fax 23 427 125. US: 27 Street 240, Phnom Penh, 23 216 436/8, fax 23 216 437. Canada: Villa 9 Street 254, Sangkat Chaktomuk, Khan Daun Penh, tel 23 213 470, fax 23 211 389, email cdnemb1@camnet.com.kh.

Global weather guide p 818, Rainy seasons worldwide p 829, Vaccinations required p 832, Recommended reading p 848, Dependent territories p 812.

CAMEROON

STATE OF THE NATION

SAFETY Relatively safe, but Douala can be dangerous after dark.

LIFE EXPECTANCY M 53.4, F 65.5.

PEOPLE AND PLACE

CAPITAL Yaounde.

LANGUAGE French and English.

PEOPLES 230 ethnic groups, the Bamileke being the largest.

RELIGION Roman Catholic, Muslim, Protestant, traditional beliefs.

SIZE (KM) 475,442.

POPULATION 14,300,000.

POP DENSITY/KM 31.

FOOD Excellent street food, including spiced *brochettes* (meat on skewers) grilled over charcoal, meat dishes with spicy sauces served with rice or *fufu*, *pâte*, or *couscous* - mashes made from corn, manioc, plantains or bananas. French and Lebanese dishes widely available.

TRAVEL PLANNING

WHEN TO GO The south is hot and dry November-February, main rainy season is July-October. In the north the rainy season is May-October.

MEDICAL CARE Basic outside cities, insurance recommended.

CURRENCY Communauté Financiare Africaine Franc (CFAfr) = 100 centimes.

FINANCE Very limited acceptance of major credit cards, limited acceptance of travellers' cheques.

AIRPORTS Douala (DLA), 10 km from the city, Nsimalen (NSI), 25 km from the city.

INTERNAL TRAVEL Air travel most efficient, slow but cheap rail services. Paved roads between main towns but others poorly maintained and impassable in the rainy season. Limited car hire available.

BUSINESS HOURS 0730-1700 Mon-Friday.

GMT +1.

VOLTAGE GUIDE 220 AC, 50 Hz.

RED TAPE

VISAS (AUS/CANADA/UK/US) Required.

REPS IN UK/US/CANADA UK: 84 Holland Park, London W11 3SB, tel 020 7727 0771, fax 020 7792 9353. US: 2349 Massachusetts Avenue, NW, Washington, DC 20008, tel 202 265 8790, fax 202 387 3826. Canada: 170 Clemow Avenue, Ottawa, Ontario K1S 2B4, tel 613 236 1522, fax 613 236 3885, email cameroun@videotron.net.

CUSTOMS REGULATIONS Duty free allowance: 400 cigarettes or 50 cigars or 500 g tobacco, 1 bottle of alcoholic beverage, 2 botles of perfume.

DRIVING REQUIREMENTS International Driving Permit not legally required but recommended.

KEEPING IN TOUCH

BBC WORLD SERVICE MHz 15.40, 11.94, 6.190, 3.255.

ENGLISH-LANGUAGE NEWSPAPERS *The Herald, The Messenger, Cameroon Times, Cameroon Tribune.*

EMERGENCIES

RED CROSS/CRESCENT SOCIETIES BP 631, Yaoundé, tel/fax 224 177.

UK/US/CANADIAN REPS UK: BP 547, avenue Winston Churchill, Yaoundé, tel 220 545, fax 220 148, email bhccmy@ lom.camnet.cm. US: BP 817, rue Nachtigal, Yaoundé, tel 234 014, fax 230 512. Canada: BP 572, Immcuble Stamatiades, Yaoundé, tel 232 311, fax 221 090, email yunde@ dfait-maeci.gc.ca.

Global weather guide p 818, Rainy seasons worldwide p 829, Vaccinations required p 832, Recommended reading p 848, Dependent territories p 812.

CANADA

STATE OF THE NATION

SAFETY Safe.

LIFE EXPECTANCY M 76.1, F 81.8.

PEOPLE AND PLACE

CAPITAL Ottawa.

LANGUAGE French and English.

PEOPLES Of French, English and European origin (89%), Indigenous Indian and Innuit

RELIGION Roman Catholic, Protestant.

SIZE (KM) 9,958,319.

POPULATION 30,200,000.

POP DENSITY/KM 3.

FOOD As varied as the country. Excellent seafood along the coast, good beef from the central plains. Colonial influence still discernable in cuisine, European menus in all major cities and good French food in Québec.

TRAVEL PLANNING

WHEN TO GO March-April cool, May-September warm, October-Novemver cool, December-February cold with heavy snow.

MEDICAL CARE Good, but expensive; insurance recommended.

CURRENCY Canadian dollar (C$)

FINANCE Most major credit cards and travellers' cheques in Canadian dollars widely accepted.

AIRPORTS (With distances from the city) Calgary (YYC) 8 km, Edmonton (YEG) 28 km, Gander (YQX) 3 km, Halifax (YHZ) 42 km, Hamilton (YHM) 10 km, Montréal (Dorval) (YUL) 25 km, Montréal (Mirabel) (YMX) 53 km, Ottawa (YOW) 15 km, St John's (YYT) 8 km, Saskatoon (YXE) 7 km, Toronto (YYZ) 27 km, Vancouver (YVR) 15 km, Winnipeg (YWG) 10 km.

INTERNAL TRAVEL Numerous regional airlines, an extensive rail and road network. Car hire is easy to arrange for full licence holders aged over 21.

BUSINESS HOURS 0900-1700 Mon-Friday.

GMT From -3.5 to -8.

VOLTAGE GUIDE 110 AC, 60 Hz.

RED TAPE

VISAS (AUS/CANADA/UK/US) None.

REPS IN UK/US UK: 38 Grosvenor Street, London W1X 0AA, tel 09068 616 644 (recorded visa information), fax 020 7258 6506. US: 1251 Avenue of the Americas, New York, NY 10020-1175, tel 212 596 1628, fax 212 596 1790.

CUSTOMS REGULATIONS Duty free allowance: 200 cigarettes and 50 cigars and 200 g of loose tobacco and 400 sticks of tobacco, 1 bottle (1.1ltrs) spirits or wine or 24 bottles or cans of beer (355 ml), gifts to the value of C$60 per gift (not being advertising matter, tobacco or alcoholic beverages). NB Age requirements vary between provinces or territories. Prohibited: Fresh Fruit. Firearms, explosives, endangered species of animals and plants, animal products, meat, food and plant material are subject to certain restrictions and formalities.

DRIVING REQUIREMENTS International Driving Permit recommended, although not legally required. National driving licences will generally suffice for up to 3 months (shorter in some provinces).

KEEPING IN TOUCH

BBC WORLD SERVICE MHz 17.84, 15.22, 6.195, 5.975

ENGLISH-LANGUAGE NEWSPAPERS No national daily, Toronto's *The Globe and Mail* has national distribution. Numerous regional dailies in English.

EMERGENCIES

RED CROSS/CRESCENT SOCIETIES 1430 Blair Place, Gloucester, Ontario K1J 9N2, tel 613 740 1900, fax 613 740 1911, email cancross@redcross.ca.

UK/US REPS UK: 80 Elgin Street, Ottawa, Ontario, K1P 5K7, tel 613 237 1530, fax 613 237 7980. US: 100 Wellington Street, Ottawa, Ontario K1P 5T1, tel 613 238 4470, fax 613 238 8750.

Global weather guide p 818, Rainy seasons worldwide p 829, Vaccinations required p 832, Recommended reading p 848, Dependent territories p 812.

CAPE VERDE

STATE OF THE NATION

SAFETY Safe.

LIFE EXPECTANCY M 65.5, F 71.3.

PEOPLE AND PLACE

CAPITAL Ciudade de Praia.

LANGUAGE Portugese.

PEOPLES Mestico, African.

RELIGION Roman Catholic. Protestant minority

SIZE (KM) 4033.

POPULATION 417,000.

POP DENSITY/KM 103.

FOOD Main local speciality is *cachupa,* based on maize and beans. Increasing number of restaurants and cafes.

TRAVEL PLANNING

WHEN TO GO Generally temperate.

MEDICAL CARE Limited and expensive, insurance advised.

CURRENCY Cape Verde escudo (CVEsc) = 100 centavos.

FINANCE Credit cards rarely used, travellers' cheques accepted in main towns.

AIRPORTS Amilcar Cabral (SID) on Sal, 2 km from Espargos.

INTERNAL TRAVEL Cargo boats travelling between the islands take passengers. About one third of the roads are paved. Car hire is available on the main islands.

BUSINESS HOURS 0800-1230, 1430-1800 Monday-Friday.

GMT -1.

VOLTAGE GUIDE 220 AC, 50 Hz.

RED TAPE

VISAS (AUS/CANADA/UK/US) Required.

REPS IN UK/US/CANADA UK: n/a. US: 3415 Massachusetts Avenue, NW, Washington, DC 20007, tel 202 965 6820, fax 202 965 1207. Canada: 123 York View Drive, Etobivoke, Toronto, Ontario M8Z 2G5, tel 416 252 9881, fax 416 252 9924.

CUSTOMS REGULATIONS Duty free allowance: A reasonable amount of perfume, *eau de cologne* in opened bottles.

DRIVING REQUIREMENTS International Driving Permit recommended, although not legally required.

KEEPING IN TOUCH

BBC WORLD SERVICE MHz 17.64, 12.09, 9.410, 6.195.

ENGLISH-LANGUAGE NEWSPAPERS None.

EMERGENCIES

RED CROSS/CRESCENT SOCIETIES Caixa Postal 119, Praia, tel 611 701, fax 614 174.

UK/US/CANADIAN REPS UK: c/o Shell Cabo Verde, Sarl, Amilcar Cabral CP4, São Vincente, tel 314 470, fax 314 755. US: CP 201, Rua Abilio, Macedo 81, Praia, Santiago, 615 616, fax 611 355, email embusa@ mail.cvtelecom.cv Canada: The Canadian Embassy in Dakar deals with enquiries relating to Cape Verde.

Global weather guide p 818, Rainy seasons worldwide p 829, Vaccinations required p 832, Recommended reading p 848, Dependent territories p 812.

CENTRAL AFRICAN REPUBLIC

STATE OF THE NATION

SAFETY Potentially volatile and subject to occasional *coups d'état*. Banditry on remoter country roads.

LIFE EXPECTANCY M 42.9, F 46.9.

PEOPLE AND PLACE

CAPITAL Bangui.

LANGUAGE French and Sango.

PEOPLES Baya, Banda, Mandija, Sara.

RELIGION Mostly animist. Remainder Christian, and a small Islamic minority.

SIZE (KM) 622,984.

POPULATION 3,500,000.

POP DENSITY/KM 6.

FOOD Basic. Street food in towns is simple, burgers and *brochettes* (meat on a skewer). Restaurants serve French and other cuisines but otherwise travellers must call at local villages to barter for provisions.

TRAVEL PLANNING

WHEN TO GO Hot all year. The rainy season is from May-October.

MEDICAL CARE Limited, take own supply of basic medicines and full insurance cover.

CURRENCY Communauté Financiaire Africaine franc (CFA) = 100 centimes.

FINANCE Travellers' cheques and some credit cards accepted.

AIRPORTS Bangui M'Poko (BGF), 4 km from the city.

INTERNAL TRAVEL Domestic flying limited to charter planes. Ferries serve towns on the Ubangi River. Good roads connecting main towns, but often impassable during the rainy season. Car hire available.

BUSINESS HOURS 0730-15.30 Mon-Friday.

GMT +1.

VOLTAGE GUIDE 220/380 AC, 50 Hz.

RED TAPE

VISAS (AUS/CANADA/UK/US) Required.

REPS IN UK/US/CANADA UK: n/a. US: 1618 22nd Street, NW, Washington DC 20008, tel 202 483 7800. Canada: 500 Place d'Armes, Suite 1703, Montréal, H2Y 2W2, tel 514 849 8381, fax 514 849 8383, email constex@cam.org.

CUSTOMS REGULATIONS Duty free allowance: 400 cigarettes or cigarillos or 125 g of tobacco, 3 bottles of spirits (approximately 1 ltr, excluding prohibited types of spirits), personal jewellery not exceeding 500 g. Prohibited: Certain types of spirits.

DRIVING REQUIREMENTS International Driving Permit.

KEEPING IN TOUCH

BBC WORLD SERVICE MHz 17.88, 15.42, 11.86, 9.630.

ENGLISH-LANGUAGE NEWSPAPERS None.

EMERGENCIES

RED CROSS/CRESCENT SOCIETIES BP 1428, Bangui, tel 612 223, fax 613 561.

UK/US/CANADIAN REPS UK: The British Consulate is currently closed. The British High Commission in Yaoundé (Cameroon) deals with enquiries relating to the Central African Republic. US: BP 924, avenue David Dacko, Bangui, tel 610 200, fax 614 494, email emb-usa@intnet.cf. Canada: The Canadian Embassy in Yaoundé deals with enquiries relating to the Central African Republic.

Global weather guide p 818, Rainy seasons worldwide p 829, Vaccinations required p 832, Recommended reading p 848, Dependent territories p 812.

CHAD

STATE OF THE NATION

SAFETY Potentially dangerous. Seek latest information at time of visit.

LIFE EXPECTANCY M 45.7, F 48.7.

PEOPLE AND PLACE

CAPITAL Ndjaména.

LANGUAGE French, Arabic, 50 indigenous languages.

PEOPLES Sara, Toubou, Peul-Fulani, Tuareg.

RELIGION Muslim, traditional beliefs, Christian.

SIZE (KM) 1,284,000.

POPULATION 6,900,000.

POP DENSITY/KM 5.

FOOD French and African, grilled meat and fish at stalls, *tiéboudienne* (fish with mixed vegetables and rice). Shortages of some foodstuffs outside the capital.

TRAVEL PLANNING

WHEN TO GO Hot, tropical climate. Rainy season in the south from May-October, in the central region from June-September. Very little rain in the north.

MEDICAL CARE Very limited, take own supply of basic medicines and full insurance cover.

CURRENCY Communauté Financiaire Africaine franc (CFA) = 100 centimes.

FINANCE travellers' cheques, Diners Club and MasterCard accepted on a limited basis.

AIRPORTS N'Djaména (NDJ) 4 km from the city.

INTERNAL TRAVEL Some internal flights accepting cash payment only. Many roads need urgent repairs. Travelling outside N'Djaména only possible with 4-wheel-drives. Permits are usually needed. Due to security conditions and a lack of food, petrol and vehicle repair facilities, the government has prohibited travel in some parts of the country.

BUSINESS HOURS 0700-1530 Mon-Thurs, 0700-1200 Friday.

GMT +1.

VOLTAGE GUIDE 220/380 AC, 50 Hz.

RED TAPE

VISAS (AUS/CANADA/UK/US) Required.

REPS IN UK/US/CANADA UK: n/a. US: 2002 R Street, NW, Washington, DC 20009, tel 202 462 4009, fax 202 265 1937, email info@chadembassy.org. Also deals with enquiries from Canada.

CUSTOMS REGULATIONS Duty free allowance: 400 cigarettes or 125 cigars or 500g of tobacco (women are allowed to import cigarettes only), 3 bottles of wine, 1 bottle of spirits (for travellers over 18).

DRIVING REQUIREMENTS International Driving Permit.

KEEPING IN TOUCH

BBC WORLD SERVICE MHz 17.88, 15.42, 11.86, 9.630.

ENGLISH-LANGUAGE NEWSPAPERS None.

EMERGENCIES

RED CROSS/CRESCENT SOCIETIES BP 449, N'Djaména, tel 523 434, fax 525 218, email croix-rouge@intnet.td

UK/US/CANADIAN REPS UK: The British Embassy in Yaoundé (Cameroon) deals with enquiries relating to Chad. US: BP 413, avenue Félix Eboué , N'Djaména, tel 519 233, fax 515 654. Canada: The Canadian Embassy in Yaoundé (Cameroon) deals with enquiries relating to Chad.

Global weather guide p 818, Rainy seasons worldwide p 829, Vaccinations required p 832, Recommended reading p 848, Dependent territories p 812.

CHILE

STATE OF THE NATION

SAFETY Safe.

LIFE EXPECTANCY M 72.3, F 78.3.

PEOPLE AND PLACE

CAPITAL Santiago.

LANGUAGE Spanish.

PEOPLES Mixed Spanish-Indian descent, European, Indian.

RELIGION Roman Catholic.

SIZE (KM) 757, 626.

POPULATION 14, 800, 000.

POP DENSITY/KM 20.

FOOD Typical national dishes include *empanadas* (filled pastries), *humitas* (seasoned corn paste, wrapped in corn husks and boiled), *cazuela de ave* (soup with rice, vegetables, chicken and herbs) Meat and seafood of good quality. Chile is well known for its wine, and for *pisco*, a powerful grape liquer.

TRAVEL PLANNING

WHEN TO GO Hot and arid in the north. Very cold in the far south. Central areas have a mild Mediterranean climate with a wet season from May-Aug. Beyond Montt in the south is one of the stormiest, wettest areas in the world.

MEDICAL CARE Good, but insurance necessary.

CURRENCY Chilean peso (peso) = 100 centavos.

FINANCE Major credit cards accepted. May be some difficulty changing travellers' cheques outside major towns.

AIRPORTS Santiago (SCL), 21 km from the c ity.

INTERNAL TRAVEL Frequent air services between main towns. The state railway runs throughout Chile, from Santiago to Puerto Montt in the south. The Pan American Highway runs from the Peruvian border to Puerto Montt. Although most of the roads in Chile are in good condition, it is advisable in remoter areas to carry spare petrol and a spare tyre. Car hire available in major towns.

BUSINESS HOURS 0900-1830.

GMT -5.

VOLTAGE GUIDE 220AC, 50Hz.

RED TAPE

VISAS (AUS/CANADA/UK/US) None.

REPS IN UK/US/CANADA UK: 12 Devonshire Street, London W1N 2DS, tel 020 7580 6392, fax 020 7436 5204. US: Suite 302, 3rd Floor, 866 United Nations Plaza, New York, NY 10017, tel 212 355 0612, fax 212 888 5288 Canada: Suite 710, 1010 Sherbrooke Street West, Montréal, Quebec, H3A 2R7, tel 514 499 0405, fax 514 499 8914, email cgmontca@total.net

CUSTOMS REGULATIONS Duty free allowance: 400 cigarettes and 500 g of tobacco and 50 cigars, 2.5ltrs of alcohol (only for over visitors over 18), a reasonable quantity of perfume. Prohibited: Meat products, flowers, fruit and vegetables without prior permission from the Department of Agriculture in the country of origin before travelling.

DRIVING REQUIREMENTS International or Inter-American Driving Permit.

KEEPING IN TOUCH

BBC WORLD SERVICE MHz 17.84, 15.19, 9.915, 5.970.

ENGLISH-LANGUAGE NEWSPAPERS None but foreign papers available.

EMERGENCIES

RED CROSS/CRESCENT SOCIETIES Correo 21, Casilla 246V, Santiago, tel 2 777 1448, fax 2 737 0270, email cruzroja@rdc.cl.

UK/US/CANADIAN REPS UK: Casilla 72D, Avenida el Bosque Norte 0125, Las Condes, Santiago, tel 2 370 4100, fax 2 370 4180, email embsan@britemb.cl. US: Avenida Andrés Bello 2800, Las Condes, Santiago, tel 2 232 2600, fax 2 330 3710. Canada: Nueva Tajamar 481, North Tower, Piso 12, Santiago, 2 362 9660-3, fax 2 362 9393.

Global weather guide p 818, Rainy seasons worldwide p 829, Vaccinations required p 832, Recommended reading p 848, Dependent territories p 812.

CHINA

STATE OF THE NATION

Safety Safe.

Life expectancy M 67.9, F 72.

PEOPLE AND PLACE

Capital Beijing.

Language Mandarin Chinese.

Peoples Han, Hui, Zhaung.

Religion Buddhism, Confucianism, Daoism.

Size (km) 9,571,300.

Population 1,230,838,000.

Pop density/km 135.

Food Diverse regional styles. In the north, *Mongolian Hotpots* are popular, eaten in a communal style with meats and vegetables being cooked, fondue style, in a pot of simmering soup. Beijing is famous for *Peking Duck*. Southern cusine is probably the most exotic - markets in Guangzhou are full of the various (sometimes endangered) animals used. The east is noted for rich, sweet cooking, seafood, hot and sour soup, noodles and vegetables. In the west, spicy, peppery food is a speciality.

TRAVEL PLANNING

When to go Great diversity of climates. The north-east has hot, dry summers and bitterly cold winters. The north and central region has almost continuous rainfall, hot summers and cold winters. The south-east has substantial rainfall, semi-tropical summers and cool winters.

Medical care Good but some medicines unavailable, insurance recommended.

Currency Renminbi yuan (RMBY) = 10 chiao/jiao or 100 fen.

Finance Major credit cards and travellers' cheques accepted by designated establishments in major provincial cities .

Airports Beijing/Peking (BSJ/PEK), 26 km from the city, Guangzhou/Canton (Baiyun) 7 km from the city, Shanghai (SHA) 12 km from the city.

Internal travel Most long-distance internal travel is by air. Ferries serve major rivers. Railways are the principal means of transport for people and goods. 80% of settlements can be reached by road. These are not always of good quality, and vehicles should be reliable as mechanical services are few and far between. Car hire is available.

Business hours 0800-1130, 1300-1700, Monday-Friday.

GMT +8.

Voltage guide 220/240 AC, 50 Hz.

RED TAPE

Visas (Aus/Canada/UK/US) Required.

Reps in UK/US/Canada UK: 31 Portland Place, London W1N 3AG, tel 020 7631 1430, fax 020 7636 9756. US: 2300 Connecticut Avenue, NW, Washington, DC 20007, tel 202 328 2505-6, fax 202 328 2582. Canada: 515 St Patrick Street, Ottawa, Ontario K1N 5H3, tel 613 789 3434, fax 613 789 1911, email adoffice@buildlink.com.

Customs regulations Duty free allowance: 400 cigarettes (600 for stays over 6 months), 2ltrs of alcoholic beverages, a reasonable amount of perfume for personal use. Prohibited: Arms, ammunition, radio transmitters/receivers, exposed but undeveloped film, fruit and certain vegetables.

Driving requirements n/a.

KEEPING IN TOUCH

BBC World Service MHz 21.66, 15.28, 11.94, 5.99.

English-language newspapers *China Daily, China Travel*, weekly news magazine *Beijing Review*.

EMERGENCIES

Red Cross/Crescent societies 53 Ganmian Hutong, 100010 Beijing, tel 10 65 13 58 38, fax 10 65 12 41 69.

UK/US/Canadian reps UK: 11 Guang Hua Lu, Jian Guo Men Wai, Beijing 100600, tel 10 65 32 19 61-4, fax 10 65 32 19 30. US: 3 Xiu Shui Bei Jie, Beijing 100600, tel 10 65 32 38 31, fax 10 65 32 31 78. Canada: 19 Dong Zhi Men Wai Da Jie, Beijing 100600, tel 10 65 32 35 36, fax 10 65 34 43 11.

Global weather guide p 818, Rainy seasons worldwide p 829, Vaccinations required p 832, Recommended reading p 848, Dependent territories p 812.

COLOMBIA

STATE OF THE NATION

SAFETY VERY UNSAFE. Kidnapping and violence are commonplace. Do not accept sweets or drinks from strangers (even Westerners), they may be drugged. Many areasare subject to guerrilla warfare or covert activities (cocaine-growing, emerald-mining) and should be avoided.

LIFE EXPECTANCY M 67.3, F 74.3.

PEOPLE AND PLACE

CAPITAL Santa Fe de Bogotá.

LANGUAGE Spanish.

PEOPLES Mestizo, European, European-African, Black Amerindian, African.

RELIGION Roman Catholic.

SIZE (KM) 1, 141, 748.

POPULATION 37, 700, 000.

POP DENSITY/KM 36.

FOOD Varied, Spanish influenced local cuisine. Specialities include *ajiaco* (chicken stew served with cream, corn on the cob and capers) and *bandeja paisa* (meat dish with cassava, rice, fried plantain and red beans). Notable lobsters and seafood served on the Caribbean coast.

TRAVEL PLANNING

WHEN TO GO Very warm and tropical on the coast and in the north, with a rainy season from May-November. Cooler in the uplands and cold in the mountains. Bogotá has cool days and crisp nights.

MEDICAL CARE Limited outside cities.

CURRENCY Colombian peso (peso) = 100 centavos.

FINANCE Major credit cards accepted, travellers' cheques difficult to change in smaller towns.

AIRPORTS Bogotá (El Dorado) (BOG) 12 km from the city, Barranquilla (BAQ) 10 km from the city, Cali (CLO) 19 km from the city, Cartagena (CTG) 2 km from the city.

INTERNAL TRAVEL Excellent internal air network. Inter-city passenger rail services virtually non-existent. Good highways and other roads usually passable except during rainy seasons. Car hire available but driving in cities not recommended.

BUSINESS HOURS 0800-1200, 1400-1700 Monday-Friday.

GMT -5.

VOLTAGE GUIDE 110/120 AC, 60 Hz.

RED TAPE

VISAS (AUS/CANADA/UK/US) None.

REPS IN UK/US/CANADA UK: 15-19 Great Titchfield Street, London W1P 7FB, tel 020 7637 9893, fax 020 7637 5604. US: 2118 Leroy Place, NW, Washington, DC 20008, tel 202 387 8338, fax 202 232 8643, email enwas@colombiaemb.org. Canada: Suite 1002, 360 Albert Street, Ottawa, Ontario K1R 7X7, tel 613 230 3761, fax 613 230 4416, email embcolot@travel-net.com.

CUSTOMS REGULATIONS Duty free allowance: 200 cigarettes and 50 cigars and 500 g of tobacco, 2 bottles of wine or spirits, a reasonable quantity of perfume. Prohibited: Vegetables, plants or plant material, meat, food products of animal origin. Note: Emeralds, items made of gold or platinum need a purchase receipt which must be presented to customs on departure.

DRIVING REQUIREMENTS International Driving Permit.

KEEPING IN TOUCH

BBC WORLD SERVICE MHz 17.84, 15.22, 9.915, 9.590.

ENGLISH-LANGUAGE NEWSPAPERS *The Colombian Post.*

EMERGENCIES

RED CROSS/CRESCENT SOCIETIES Apartado Aéreo 11' 110 Bogotá DC, tel 1 437 6339, fax 1 428 1725, email: inter@andinet.com

UK/US/CANADIAN REPS UK: Carrera 9, No 76-49, Piso 9, Santa Fe de Bogotá, DC, tel 1 317 6690, fax 1 317 6265, email: britain@cable.net.co US: Calle 22D-bis, No 47-51, Santa Fe de Bogotá, DC, tel 1 315 0811, fax 1 315 2197. Canada: Carrera 7, No 115-33, Santa Fe de Bogotá, DC, tel 1 657 9800, fax 1 657 9914.

Global weather guide p 818, Rainy seasons worldwide p 829, Vaccinations required p 832, Recommended reading p 848, Dependent territories p 812.

COMOROS

STATE OF THE NATION

SAFETY Safe.

LIFE EXPECTANCY M 57.4, F 60.02.

PEOPLE AND PLACE

CAPITAL Moroni.

LANGUAGE French and Arabic.

PEOPLES Mainly mixed race, with Polynesians, Africans, Indonesians, Persians, Arabs, Europeans and Indians.

RELIGION Sunni Muslim (98%).

SIZE (KM) 1862.

POPULATION 672,000.

POP DENSITY/KM 301.

FOOD Spiced sauces, rice-based dishes, barbecued meat (mostly goat), plentiful seafood and tropical fruits, cassava, plantain, couscous. There may be restrictions on alcohol within Muslim circles.

TRAVEL PLANNING

WHEN TO GO Warm and tropical with a hot and rainy season from November-May and a cooler and dryer season from June-October.

MEDICAL CARE Full insurance recommended.

CURRENCY Comoros franc (Cfr) = 100 centimes.

FINANCE Limited acceptance of credit cards and travellers' cheques.

AIRPORTS Moroni International Prince Said Ibrahim (HAH), 25 km from the city.

INTERNAL TRAVEL Air and ferry connections between the islands. All the islands have tarred roads, 4-wheel-drive vehicles advisable for outlying islands and in the interior, particularly during the rainy season. Many roads are narrow and domestic animals roam freely, so drive slowly.

BUSINESS HOURS 0730-1430 Mon-Thurs, 0730-1100 Fri, 0730-1200 Saturday.

GMT +3.

VOLTAGE GUIDE 220 AC, 50 Hz.

RED TAPE

VISAS (AUS/CANADA/UK/US) Required.

REPS IN UK/US/CANADA UK: n/a. US: 2nd Floor, 336 East 45th Street, New York, NY 10017, tel 212 972 8010, fax 212 9384712. Also deals with enquiries from Canada.

CUSTOMS REGULATIONS Duty free allowance: 400 cigarettes or 100 cigars or 500 g of tobacco, 1ltr of alcoholic beverages, 75 cl of perfume (travellers over 18). Prohibited: Weapons, ammunition, radio transmission equipment, plants or soil.

DRIVING REQUIREMENTS International Driving Permit required.

KEEPING IN TOUCH

BBC WORLD SERVICE MHz 21.47, 17.88, 9.630, 6.005.

ENGLISH-LANGUAGE NEWSPAPERS None.

EMERGENCIES

RED CROSS/CRESCENT SOCIETIES n/a.

UK/US/CANADIAN REPS UK: The British Embassy in Antananarivo (Madagascar) deals with enquiries relating to Comoros. US: The American Embassy in Port Louis (Mauritius) deals with enquiries relating to Comoros. Canada: The Canadian High Commission in Dar es Salaam (Tanzania) deals with enquiries relating to the Comoros.

Global weather guide p 818, Rainy seasons worldwide p 829, Vaccinations required p 832, Recommended reading p 848, Dependent territories p 812.

CONGO (BRAZZAVILLE)

STATE OF THE NATION

SAFETY Politically volatile and subject to periodic rebellions. Seek latest information at time of visit.

LIFE EXPECTANCY M 48.3, F 50.8.

PEOPLE AND PLACE

CAPITAL Brazzaville.

LANGUAGE French.

PEOPLES Bakongo, Sangha, Teke, Mbochi.

RELIGION Animist, Roman Catholic.

SIZE (KM) 342,000.

POPULATION 2,800,000.

POP DENSITY/KM 8.

FOOD African dishes include *Mouamba* chicken in palm oil, palm cabbage salad and cassava leaves, *Saka Saka* (ground cassava leaves cooked with palm oil and peanut paste) and *Maboke* (fresh water fish cooked in large marantacee leaves). Excellent fish, giant oysters and shrimps on the coast. French cuisine in restaurants.

TRAVEL PLANNING

WHEN TO GO Equatorial climate. Short rains October-December and long rains between mid-January and mid-May. Main dry season from June-September.

MEDICAL CARE Limited, insurance strongly recommended.

CURRENCY Communauté Financiaire Africaine franc (CFA) = 100 centimes.

FINANCE travellers' cheques. Limited use of Master Card and Diners Club cards.

AIRPORTS Brazzaville (BZR) 4 km from the city, Pointe-Noire (PNR) 5.5 km from the city.

INTERNAL TRAVEL Regular air services between Brazzaville and Pointe-Noire. Rivers vital to inland transport and are served by steamers. Rail services can be erratic. Roads are sandy in the dry season and impassable in the wet, only suitable for 4-wheel-drive vehicles. Poorly marked army checkpoints throughout the country. Road travel at night can be dangerous. Several car-hire firms in Brazzaville.

BUSINESS HOURS 0700-1400 Mon-Friday, 0700-1200 Saturday.

GMT +1.

VOLTAGE GUIDE 220 AC, 50 Hz.

RED TAPE

VISAS (AUS/CANADA/UK/US) Required.

REPS IN UK/US/CANADA UK: 4 Wendle Court, 131-137 Wandsworth Road, London SW8 2LH, tel 020 7622 0419, fax 020 7622 0371. US: 4891 Colorado Avenue, NW, Washington, DC 20011, tel 202 726 0825, fax 202 726 1860. Canada: 2 Cedar Avenue, Pointe Claire, Montréal, Québec H9S 4Y1, tel 514 697 3781, fax 514 697 9860.

CUSTOMS REGULATIONS Duty free allowance: 200 cigarettes or 1 box of cigars or tobacco (women are permitted to import cigarettes only), 1 bottle of alcoholic beverages, a reasonable quantity of perfume in opened bottles (for travellers over 18).

DRIVING REQUIREMENTS International Driving Permit.

KEEPING IN TOUCH

BBC WORLD SERVICE MHz 17.83, 15.40, 11.83, 6.005.

ENGLISH-LANGUAGE NEWSPAPERS None.

EMERGENCIES

RED CROSS/CRESCENT SOCIETIES BP 4145, Brazzaville, tel 824 410, fax 828 825

UK/US/CANADIAN REPS UK: Côte de l'hôtel Méridien, rue Lyantey 26, Brazzaville, tel 838 527, fax 837 257. US: BP 1015 avenue Amilcar Cabral, Brazzaville, tel 832 070, fax 836 338. Canada: The Canadian Embassy in Kinshasha (Democratic Republic of Congo) deals with enquiries relating to Congo.

Global weather guide p 818, Rainy seasons worldwide p 829, Vaccinations required p 832, Recommended reading p 848, Dependent territories p 812.

CONGO (DEMOCRATIC REPUBLIC)

STATE OF THE NATION

SAFETY Highly unsafe. Continuing civil war in many areas. Lawlessness widespread.

LIFE EXPECTANCY M 49.2, F52.3 .

PEOPLE AND PLACE

CAPITAL Kinshasa.

LANGUAGE Officially French, many African languages used.

PEOPLES Bantu, Hamitic, Nilotic.

RELIGION Traditional beliefs, Roman Catholic, Protestant.

SIZE (KM) 2,344,885.

POPULATION 49,200,000.

POP DENSITY/KM 22.

FOOD National specialities include *moambe* chicken, cooked in palm oil with rice and spinach. Restaurants in Kinshasa and Lubumashi serving French, Belgian and local cuisine can be good but are expensive, catering essentially for business people.

TRAVEL PLANNING

WHEN TO GO The dry season in the north is from December-March, in the south from May October. Warm temperatures and high humidity throughout the year.

MEDICAL CARE Very limited and there is a shortage of supplies, insurance with repatriation cover recommended.

CURRENCY franc Congolais (FC) = 1000 centimes.

FINANCE Very limited use of MasterCard and Visa. Travellers' cheques are generally not recommended.

AIRPORTS Kinshasa (FIH) 25 km from the city.

INTERNAL TRAVEL Indefinite restrictions for tourist travel. Overland journeys by local public transport, hitch-hiking, or by foreign vehicle or motorcycle are forbidden. Over 40 internal airports, small planes may be available for charter. River and rail services available. Roads are among the worst in Africa. Hijackings/vehicle thefts at gunpoint do occur. Limited car hire available at the airport.

BUSINESS HOURS 0730-1500 Mon-Friday.

GMT From +1 to +2.

VOLTAGE GUIDE 220 AC, 50 Hz.

RED TAPE

VISAS (AUS/CANADA/UK/US) Required.

REPS IN UK/US/CANADA UK: 26 Chesham Place, London SW1X 8HG, 020 7235 6137, fax 020 7235 9048. US: 1800 New Hampshire Avenue, NW, Washington, DC 20009, tel 202 234 7690/1, fax 202 234 2609. Canada: 18 Range Road, Ottawa, Ontario, K1N 8J3, tel 613 230 6391, fax 613 230 1945.

CUSTOMS REGULATIONS Duty free allowance: 100 cigarettes or 50 cigars or 500 g of tobacco, 1 bottle of alcoholic beverages (opened), a reasonable amount of perfume for personal use. An import licence is required for arms and ammunition. Radios, tape recorders and gifts are subject to duty.

DRIVING REQUIREMENTS International Driving Permit.

KEEPING IN TOUCH

BBC WORLD SERVICE MHz 17.83, 15.40, 11.83, 6.005.

ENGLISH-LANGUAGE NEWSPAPERS None.

EMERGENCIES

RED CROSS/CRESCENT SOCIETIES BP 1712 Kinshasa 1, tel 12 34897, fax 88 04551, email secretariat@crrdc.aton.cd.

UK/US/CANADIAN REPS UK: BP 8049, 83 avenue de Lemera, Kinshasa-Gombe, tel 12 34775, fax 88 46102, email ambrit@ic.cd. US: BP 697, Unit 31550, 310 avenue des Aviateurs, Kinshasa, tel 12 21234, fax 88 03276, email usispin@compuserve.com. Canada: BP 8341, 17 avenue Pumbu, Commune de Gombe, Kinshasa 1, tel 12 34147, fax 88 03434.

Global weather guide p 818, Rainy seasons worldwide p 829, Vaccinations required p 832, Recommended reading p 848, Dependent territories p 812.

COSTA RICA

STATE OF THE NATION

SAFETY Safe (apart from strong tides when swimming).

LIFE EXPECTANCY M 74.3, F 78.9.

PEOPLE AND PLACE

CAPITAL San Jose.

LANGUAGE Spanish.

PEOPLES Mestizo, African descent.

RELIGION Mainly Roman Catholic.

SIZE (KM) 51,060.

POPULATION 3,700,000.

POP DENSITY/KM 72.

FOOD Common local dishes include *casado* (rice, beans, beef, plantain, salad and cabbage), *sopa negra* (black beans with a poached egg) and *picadillo* (vegetable and meat stew). Snacks, often sold at street stalls, are very popular, especially *gallos* (filled *tortillas*). Restaurants serve anything from French to Chinese cuisine.

TRAVEL PLANNING

WHEN TO GO Temperatures in the Central Valley average at 22C. Much hotter in the coastal areas. Rainy season May-November, dry season December-May.

MEDICAL CARE Good and free hospital treatment in emergencies, but insurance recommended.

CURRENCY Costa Rican colón (c) = 100 centimes.

FINANCE Major credit cards and travellers' cheques accepted.

AIRPORTS Juan Santamaria (SJO) 17 km from the city.

INTERNAL TRAVEL Some internal flights - reservations cannot be made outside Costa Rica. Standard of roads generally good. Car hire available in San José.

BUSINESS HOURS 0800-1200, 1400-1600, Monday-Friday.

GMT -6.

VOLTAGE GUIDE 110/220 AC, 60 Hz.

RED TAPE

VISAS (AUS/CANADA/UK/US) None.

REPS IN UK/US/CANADA UK: Flat 1, 14 Lancaster Gate, London W2 3LH, tel 020 7706 8844, fax 020 7706 8655, email info@embcrion.demon.co.uk. US: 2114 S Street, NW, Washington, DC 20008, tel 202 328 6628, fax 202 265 4795, email embassy@costarica.com Canada: 135 York Street, Suite 208, Ottawa, Ontario K1N 5T4, tel 613 562 2855, fax 613 562 2582, email embcrica@travel_net.com.

CUSTOMS REGULATIONS Duty free allowance: 500 cigarettes, 3ltrs of alcoholic beverages, a reasonable amount of perfume for personal use.

DRIVING REQUIREMENTS International Driving Permit or national driving licence.

KEEPING IN TOUCH

BBC WORLD SERVICE MHz 17.84, 15.22, 9.915, 9.590.

ENGLISH-LANGUAGE NEWSPAPERS *Costa Rica Today, The Tico Times* (both weekly).

EMERGENCIES

RED CROSS/CRESCENT SOCIETIES Apartado 1025, San José 1000, tel 233 7033, fax 223 7628, email bcrcsn@sol.racsa.co.cr.

UK/US/CANADIAN REPS UK: Apartado 815, 11th Floor, Edificio Centro Colón, 1007 San José, tel 221 5566, fax 233 9938. US: Calle 120 Avenida Central, San José, tel 220 3939, fax 220 2305. Canada: Apartado 351-1007, Centro Colón, San José, tel 296 4149, fax 296 4270, email canadacr@racsa.co.cr.

Global weather guide p 818, Rainy seasons worldwide p 829, Vaccinations required p 832, Recommended reading p 848, Dependent territories p 812.

COTE D'IVOIRE

STATE OF THE NATION

SAFETY Generally safe, apart from recent palace *coup*. Usual petty crime after dark.

LIFE EXPECTANCY M 46.1, F 47.3.

PEOPLE AND PLACE

CAPITAL Yamoussoukro.

LANGUAGE French.

PEOPLES Over 60 ethnic groups including Baoulé, Agri, Senufo, Dioula, Bété, and Dan-Yacouba.

RELIGION Mostly traditional beliefs, Islam, Christianity.

SIZE (KM) 322,462.

POPULATION 14,600,000.

POP DENSITY/KM 45.

FOOD Spicy African food. Traditional dishes include *kedjenou* (chicken and vegetables sealed in banana leaves), and *n'voufou* (mashed bananas or yam mixed with palm oil and served with aubergine sauce). Restaurants in main towns serve French, Italian, Lebanese and Vietnamese food.

TRAVEL PLANNING

WHEN TO GO Dry from December-April, long rains May-July, short dry season August-September, short rains from October-November. More extreme in the north with rains from May-October and dry from November-April.

MEDICAL CARE Fair, but insurance recommended.

CURRENCY Communauté Financiaire Africaine franc (CFA) = 100 centimes.

FINANCE American Express and Master-Card widely accepted, more limited acceptance of other cards and travellers' cheques.

AIRPORTS Abidjan (ABJ) 16 km from the city, Yamoussoukro (ASK).

INTERNAL TRAVEL Advanced rail service and good road system, with many surfaced roads. Car hire available in main towns.

BUSINESS HOURS 0730-1200, 1430-1800 Monday-Friday, 0800-1200 Saturday.

GMT GMT.

VOLTAGE GUIDE 220 AC, 50 Hz.

RED TAPE

VISAS (AUS/CANADA/UK/US) Required.

REPS IN UK/US/CANADA UK: 2 Upper Belgrave St, London SW1X 8BJ, tel 020 7235 6991, fax 020 7259 5320. US: 2424 Massachusetts Avenue, NW, Washington, DC 20008, tel 202 797 0300, fax 202 265 2454. Canada. 9 Marlborough Avenue, Ottawa, Ontario K1N 8E6, tel 613 236 9919, fax 613 563 8287, email ambaci@ican.net.

CUSTOMS REGULATIONS Duty free allowance: 200 cigarettes or 25 cigars or 250 g of tobacco or 100 cigarillos, 1 bottle of wine, 1 bottle of spirits, 0.5 ltrs of *eau de toilette* and 0.25 ltrs of perfume.

DRIVING REQUIREMENTS Insurance and International Driving Permit compulsory.

KEEPING IN TOUCH

BBC WORLD SERVICE MHz 17.88, 15.42, 11.86, 9.630.

ENGLISH-LANGUAGE NEWSPAPERS None.

EMERGENCIES

RED CROSS/CRESCENT SOCIETIES PO Box 1244, Abidjan 01, tel 321 335, fax 225 355.

UK/US/CANADIAN REPS UK: 01 BP 2581, Third Floor, Immeuble 'Les Harmonies', angle boulevard Carde et avenue Dr Jamot, Plateau, Abidjan, tel 226 850-2, fax 223 221, email britemb.a@africaonline.co.ci. US: 01 BP 1712, 5 rue Jesse Owens, Abidjan, tel 210 979, fax 223 259, email cca@globeaccess.net Canada: 01 BP 4104, Immeuble Trade Centre, 23 Nogues avenue, Le Plateau, Abidjan 01, tel 212 009, fax 217 728.

Global weather guide p 818, Rainy seasons worldwide p 829, Vaccinations required p 832, Recommended reading p 848, Dependent territories p 812.

CROATIA

STATE OF THE NATION

SAFETY Potentially affected by regional instability. Seek latest information at time of visit.

LIFE EXPECTANCY M 68.8, F 76.5.

PEOPLE AND PLACE

CAPITAL Zagreb.

LANGUAGE Croat-Serb and Serb-Croat.

PEOPLES Before the war Croats made up nearly 80% of the population, Serbs 12%.

RELIGION Roman Catholic (76%), Orthodox (11%), Muslim (1%), others.

SIZE (KM) 56,610.

POPULATION 4,500,000.

POP DENSITY/KM 80.

FOOD Interior specialities include *manistra od bobica* (bean and maize soup). The coast is renown for seafood dishes such as *brodet* (mixed fish stewed with rice) and good shellfish.

TRAVEL PLANNING

WHEN TO GO Varied climate, with continental conditions in the north, Mediterranean on the Adriatic coast.

MEDICAL CARE Free hospital care for UK citizens, some payment for medication may be demanded.

CURRENCY Kuna (K) = 100 Lipa.

FINANCE Most cards and travellers' cheques widely accepted.

AIRPORTS Zagreb (ZAG) 17 km from the city, Dubrovnik (DBV) 18 km from the city.

INTERNAL TRAVEL Some internal air services. Regular ferry services connect Rijeka and Split, services to Dubrovnik operate two or three times a week. Road and rail networks are adequate.

BUSINESS HOURS 0800-1600 Mon-Friday. **GMT** +1.

VOLTAGE GUIDE 220 AC, 50 Hz.

RED TAPE

VISAS (AUS/CANADA/UK/US) None.

REPS IN UK/US/CANADA UK: 21 Conway Street, London W1P 5HL, tel 020 7387 1144, fax 020 7387 0310, email croatianembassy_london@ compuserve.com. US: 2343 Massachusetts Ave, NW, Washington, DC 20008, tel 202 588 5899, fax 202 588 8936, email amboffice@croatiaemb.org. Canada: 229 Chapel Street, Ottawa, Ontario K1N 7Y6, tel 613 230 7351, fax 613 230 7388, email embcrott@sprint.ca.

CUSTOMS REGULATIONS Duty free allowance: 200 cigarettes or 50 cigars or 250 g of tobacco, 1ltr of wine and 1ltr of spirits, 250ml of eau de cologne and 1 bottle of perfume.

DRIVING REQUIREMENTS International Driving Permit or national licence. A Green Card should be carried by non-EU visitors taking their own car into Croatia. Passports should be carried at all times.

KEEPING IN TOUCH

BBC WORLD SERVICE MHz 17.64, 15.57, 9.410, 6.195.

ENGLISH-LANGUAGE NEWSPAPERS *Croatia Week*.

EMERGENCIES

RED CROSS/CRESCENT SOCIETIES Ulica Crvenogkriza 14, 10000 Zagreb, tel 1 465 5814, fax 1 455 0072, email redcross@hck.hr.

UK/US/CANADIAN REPS UK: Vlaska Street 121, 10000 Zagreb, tel 1 455 5310, fax 1 455 1685, email: britishembassy@ zg.tel.hr. US: Andrije Hebranga 2, 10000 Zagreb, tel 1 455 5500, fax 1 455 8585, email britishembassy@zg.tel.hr. Canada: Hotel Esplanade, Mihanoviceca 1, 10000 Zagreb, 1 484 8055, fax 1 457 7913, email zagreb@ dfait.x400.gc.ca.

Global weather guide p 818, Rainy seasons worldwide p 829, Vaccinations required p 832, Recommended reading p 848, Dependent territories p 812.

CUBA

STATE OF THE NATION

SAFETY Safe, apart from bag-snatchers.
LIFE EXPECTANCY M 74.2, F 78.

PEOPLE AND PLACE

CAPITAL Havana.

LANGUAGE Spanish.

PEOPLES Mainly of Spanish descent (70%), African descent, and European-African.

RELIGION Non-religious (49%), Roman Catholic (40%).

SIZE (KM) 110,860.

POPULATION 11,100,000.

POP DENSITY/KM 100.

FOOD Restaurants generally inexpensive although choice can be restricted by short-ages. Strong emphasis on seafood, other Cuban favourites include roast suckling pig, thick soups made from chicken and black beans, baked or fried plantains. Food in tourist hotels adequate, not exciting, but does feature a wide variety of exotic tropical fruit.

TRAVEL PLANNING

WHEN TO GO .Hot, sub-tropical climate all year. Most rain falls May-October. Hurricanes can occur from August-November.

MEDICAL CARE Limited, insurance recommended in case of need for repatriation.

CURRENCY Cuban peso = 100 centavos.

FINANCE American Express not accepted, limited acceptance of other cards. travellers' cheques accepted, but US dollar cheques issued by American banks are not acceptable.

AIRPORTS Havana (HAV) 18 km from the city.

INTERNAL TRAVEL Advance booking essential for iternal flights. Adequate rail system. Car hire relatively easy to arrange.

BUSINESS HOURS 0830-1230, 1330-1630 Monday-Friday.

GMT -5.

VOLTAGE GUIDE 110/120 AC, 60 Hz.

RED TAPE

VISAS (AUS/CANADA/UK/US) Required.

REPS IN UK/US/CANADA UK: 15 Grape Street, London WC2 8DR, tel 020 7240 6897, fax 020 7836 2602. US: (Cuba Interests Section) 2630 16th Street, NW, Washington DC 20009, tel 202 797 8515, fax 202 797 8521, email cubaseccion@prodigy.net. Canada: 388 Main Street, Ottawa, Ontario, K1S 1E3, tel 613 563 0068, email cuba@idirect.com.

CUSTOMS REGULATIONS Duty free allowance: 200 cigarettes or 50 cigars or 250 g of tobacco, 3 bottles of alcoholic beverages, gifts up to a value of US$50, 10 kg of medicines (for travellers over 18). Prohibited: Natural fruits, beans or vegetables, meat and dairy products, weapons and ammunition, video cassettes and household appliances, all pornographic material and drugs.

DRIVING REQUIREMENTS Valid national driving licence required. Drivers must be over 21.

KEEPING IN TOUCH

BBC WORLD SERVICE MHz 17.71, 15.22, 6.195, 5.975.

ENGLISH-LANGUAGE NEWSPAPERS Weekly *Granma*, fortnightly *Prisma de Cuba y las Américas*.

EMERGENCIES

RED CROSS/CRESCENT SOCIETIES CP 10400, tel 7 552 555, fax 7 662 057, email crsn@infomed.sld.cu.

UK/US/CANADIAN REPS UK: PO Box 1069, Calle 34 No 702, Entre 7 y 17, Miramar, 11300 Havana, tel 7 241 771, fax 7 248 104, email: embrit@ceniai.inf.cu. US: (US Interests Section) Swiss Embassy, Calzada entre Calle L y M, Vedado, 10400, Havana, tel 7 333 967, fax 7 334 728. Canada: Calle 30, No 518, Esquina a 7, Avenida Miramar, Havana, tel 7 242 516/7, fax 7 242 044.

Global weather guide p 818, Rainy seasons worldwide p 829, Vaccinations required p 832, Recommended reading p 848, Dependent territories p 812.

CYPRUS

STATE OF THE NATION

SAFETY Safe.

LIFE EXPECTANCY M 75.5, F 80.

PEOPLE AND PLACE

CAPITAL Nicosia.

LANGUAGE Greek.

PEOPLES Greek, Turkish minority.

RELIGION Greek Orthodox, small Muslim community.

SIZE (KM) 9251.

POPULATION 766,000.

POP DENSITY/KM 84.

FOOD Charcoal grilled meat and kebabs popular. Other Cypriot dishes include *dolmas* (vine leaves stuffed with meat and rice) and *tava* (a stew of meat, herbs and onions). Meals often preceded by a selection of snacks (*mezze*).

TRAVEL PLANNING

WHEN TO GO Warm Mediterranean climate. Hot, dry summers with mild winters during which rainfall is most likely.

MEDICAL CARE Good, but insurance recommended.

CURRENCY Cyprus pound (C£) = 100 cents

FINANCE Credit cards and travellers' cheques generally accepted.

AIRPORTS Larnaca (LCA) 5 km from the city, Paphos (PFO) 15 km from the city.

INTERNAL TRAVEL Efficient cheap bus service connects all towns and villages. Car hire widely available, but should be hired well in advance during the summer season.

BUSINESS HOURS 0800-1300, 1600-1930 in summer, in winter 0800-1300, 1430-1800 (shopping hours; business hours n/a)

GMT +2.

VOLTAGE GUIDE 240 AC, 50 Hz.

RED TAPE

VISAS (AUS/CANADA/UK/US) None.

REPS IN UK/US/CANADA UK: 93 Park Street, London, W1Y 4ET, tel 020 7499 8272, fax 020 7491 0691. US: 13 East 40th Street, New York, NY 10016, tel 212 686 6016-8, fax 212 683 5258. Canada: 356 Bloor Street, Suite 1010, Toronto, Ontario M4W 3L4, tel 416 944 0998, fax 416 944 9149.

CUSTOMS REGULATIONS Duty free allowance: 200 cigarettes or 50 cigars or 250 g of tobacco, 1 ltr of spirits or 750 ml of wine, 600 ml of perfume (to include no more than 150 ml of perfumed spirits), and 250 ml of *eau de toilette*, goods (excluding jewellery) up to C£50. Prohibited: Fruit and fresh flowers.

DRIVING REQUIREMENTS International Driving Permit or a national driving licence.

KEEPING IN TOUCH

BBC WORLD SERVICE MHz 17.64, 15.57, 9.410, 6.195.

ENGLISH-LANGUAGE NEWSPAPERS *Cyprus Mail* (daily), *Cyprus Weekly*.

EMERGENCIES

RED CROSS/CRESCENT SOCIETIES n/a.

UK/US/CANADIAN REPS UK: Alexander Pallis Street, Nicosia 1587, tel 2 861 100, fax 2 861 125. US: Metochiu and Ploutarchou Streets, Engomi, 2407 Nicosia, tel 2 776 400, fax 2 780 944, email amembass@ spidernet.com.cy. Canada: The Canadian Embassy in Damascus (Syria) deals with enquiries related to Cyprus.

Global weather guide p 818, Rainy seasons worldwide p 829, Vaccinations required p 832, Recommended reading p 848, Dependent territories p 812.

CZECH REPUBLIC

STATE OF THE NATION

SAFETY Safe.

LIFE EXPECTANCY M 70.3, F 77.4.

PEOPLE AND PLACE

CAPITAL Prague.

LANGUAGE Czech.

PEOPLES Czech (80%0, Morovians, Slovak and Romanian minorities.

RELIGION Atheist, Roman Catholic.

SIZE (KM) 78, 866.

POPULATION 10, 200, 000.

POP DENSITY/KM 129.

FOOD Often based on Austro-Hungarian dishes such as *Wiener Schnitzel*. Meat dishes are often served with *knedilky* (dumplings) and *zeli* (sauerkraut). Other specialities include *bramborak* (potato pancakes filled with garlic and herbs). Most popular drinks are beer and specialist brandies, including *Becherovka* (herb), *slivovice* (plum) and *merunkovice* (apricot).

TRAVEL PLANNING

WHEN TO GO Cold winters, mild summers.

MEDICAL CARE Free for UK citizens.

CURRENCY Koruna (Kc) or Crown = 100 hellers.

FINANCE Major cards and travellers' cheques widely accepted.

AIRPORTS Prague (PRG) 17 km from the city.

INTERNAL TRAVEL Extensive domestic air service. Several daily express trains between Prague and main cities and resorts, and the bus network covers areas not accessible by rail. Car hire easy to arrange.

BUSINESS HOURS 0800-1600 Mon-Friday.

GMT +1.

VOLTAGE GUIDE 220 AC, 50 Hz.

RED TAPE

VISAS (AUS/CANADA/UK/US) Required by Australians.

REPS IN UK/US/CANADA UK: 26-30 Kensington Palace Gardens, London W8 4QY, tel 020 7243 7943, fax 020 7727 9654, email london@embassy.mzv.cz. US: 3900 Spring of Freedom Street, NW, Washington, DC 20008, tel 202 274 9100, fax 202 966 8540, email washington@embassy.mzv.cz. Canada: n/a.

CUSTOMS REGULATIONS Duty free allowance: 200 cigarettes or 100 cigarillos or 50 cigars or 250 g tobacco, 1 ltr of spirits, 2 ltrs of wine (only half the above mentioned quantities for stays of 2 days or less), 500 ml of perfume or 250 ml *eau de toilette*, gifts up to a value of Kc3000 (for travellers over 18). Prohibited: The export of antiques.

DRIVING REQUIREMENTS Valid national driving licence.

KEEPING IN TOUCH

BBC WORLD SERVICE MHz 17.64, 15.57, 9.410, 6.195.

ENGLISH-LANGUAGE NEWSPAPERS *The Prague Post* (weekly).

EMERGENCIES

RED CROSS/CRESCENT SOCIETIES Thunovska 18, C2-118 04 Prague 1, tel 2 51 10 41 11, fax 2 57 53 21 13, email cck.zahranicni@iol.cz.

UK/US/CANADIAN REPS UK: Thunovská 14, 118 00 Prague 1, tel 2 57 32 03 55, fax 2 57 32 10 23, email info@britain.cz. US: Trziste 15, 118 01 Prague 1, tel 2 57 53 06 63, fax 2 57 32 09 20, email consular@ mbox.vol.cz. Canada: Mickiewiczová 6, 125 33 Prague 6, tel 2 72 10 18 00, fax 2 72 10 18 90, email embcanada2@chipnet.cz.

Global weather guide p 818, Rainy seasons worldwide p 829, Vaccinations required p 832, Recommended reading p 848, Dependent territories p 812.

DENMARK

STATE OF THE NATION

SAFETY Safe.

LIFE EXPECTANCY M 73, F 78.5.

PEOPLE AND PLACE

CAPITAL Copenhagen.

LANGUAGE Danish.

PEOPLES Danish. Very small Inuit and Faeroe population.

RELIGION Evangelical Lutheran (89%).

SIZE (KM) 43, 094.

POPULATION 5, 300, 000.

POP DENSITY/KM 125.

FOOD *Smørrebrød* - slices of bread topped, often smothered, with a variety of fish, cheese, meat and garnishes - is the most popular Danish dish. Seafood plays a large part in the diet and a variety of international dishes are widely available.

TRAVEL PLANNING

WHEN TO GO Summer from June-August, winter from December-March and very wet with long periods of frost. February is the coldest month, spring and autumn are generally mild.

MEDICAL CARE Very good. Free for UK citizens.

CURRENCY Danish krone (DKr) = 100 øre.

FINANCE Credit cards and travellers' cheques widely accepted.

AIRPORTS Copenhagen (CPH) 8 km from the city, Århus (AAR) 44 km from the city, Billund Airport (BLL) 2 km from Legoland.

INTERNAL TRAVEL Frequent ferry services between islands. The main cities on all islands are connected by rail. The road system makes frequent use of ferries.

BUSINESS HOURS 0800/0900-1600/1700 Monday-Friday.

GMT +1(+2 in the summer).

VOLTAGE GUIDE 220 AC, 50 Hz.

RED TAPE

VISAS (AUS/CANADA/UK/US) None.

REPS IN UK/US/CANADA UK: 55 Sloane Street, London SW1X 9SR, tel 020 7333 0200, fax 020 7333 0243, email dkembassy@compuserve.com. US: 3200 Whitehaven Street, NW, Washington, DC 20008-3683, tel 202 234 4300, fax 202 328 1470, email wasamb@wasamb.um.dk. Canada: Suite 450, 47 Clarence Street, Ottawa, Ontario K1N 9K1, tel 613 562 1811, fax 613 562 1812, email danemb@cyberus.ca.

CUSTOMS REGULATIONS Duty free allowance: For EU visitors with duty-paid goods purchased within: 1.5 ltrs of spirits or 20 ltrs of sparkling wine (under 22%), 90 ltrs of table wine, 300 cigarettes or 150 cigarillos or 75 cigars or 400 g of tobacco, other commodities, including beer, no limit. For non-EU visitors entering from outside the EU (excluding Greenland) with goods purchased in non-EU countries: 1 ltr of spirits or 2 ltrs of sparkling wine (under 22%), 2 ltrs of table wine, 200 cigarettes or 100 cigarillos or 50 cigars or 250 g of tobacco, 500 g of coffee or 200 g of coffee extracts, 100 g of tea or 40 g of tea extracts, 50 g of perfume, 250 ml of *eau de toilette*, other articles including beer up to DKr 1350 or DKr 750 if purchased on airline/ferry. Prohibited: Fresh foods unless vacuum-packed.

DRIVING REQUIREMENTS National driving licence. EU national taking their own cars are strongly advised to obtain a Green Card for insurance purposes.

KEEPING IN TOUCH

BBC WORLD SERVICE MHz 17.64, 15.57, 9.410, 6.195.

ENGLISH-LANGUAGE NEWSPAPERS None.

EMERGENCIES

RED CROSS/CRESCENT SOCIETIES PO Box 2600, DK-2100 Köbenhavn Ö, tel 35 259 200, fax 35 259 292, email drc@redcross.dk.

UK/US/CANADIAN REPS UK: Kastelsvej 36-40, DK2100 Copenhagen Ø, tel 35 44 52 00, fax 35 44 52 93, email brit-emb@post6.tele.dk. US: Dag Hammarskjølds Allé 24, DK-2100 Copenhagen Ø, tel 35 55 31 44, fax 35 43 02 23, email usis@usis.dk. Canada: Kr. Bernikowsgade 1, DK-1105 Copenhagen K, tel 33 48 32 00, fax 33 48 32 21.

Global weather guide p 818, Rainy seasons worldwide p 829, Vaccinations required p 832, Recommended reading p 848, Dependent territories p 812.

DJIBOUTI

STATE OF THE NATION

SAFETY Some areas closed to foreigners. Some risk of banditry after dark.

LIFE EXPECTANCY M 48.7, F 52.

PEOPLE AND PLACE

CAPITAL Djibouti.

LANGUAGE Arabic and French.

PEOPLES Issa, Afar.

RELIGION Muslim. Roman Catholic, Protestant and Greek Orthodox minorities.

SIZE (KM) 23.200.

POPULATION 652,000.

POP DENSITY/KM 28.

FOOD Local food is often spicy. Oven-baked or barbequed fish in the harbour area is popular. Restaurants serve French, Arabic, Vietnamese and Chinese food. Drink can be limited in Muslim areas.

TRAVEL PLANNING

WHEN TO GO Extremely hot and arid June-August when the dusty *khamsin* wind blows from the desert. Slightly cooler with occasional light rain October-April.

MEDICAL CARE Insurance highly recommended.

CURRENCY Djibouti franc (Dfr) – 100 centimes.

FINANCE Credit cards are only accepted by airlines and the larger hotels.

AIRPORTS Djibouti (JIB) 5 km from the city.

INTERNAL TRAVEL Ferry services to Tadjoura and Obock from Djibouti. The only rail service runs to the Ethiopian border, but travellers are prohibited from using this. 4-wheel-drive vehicles are recommended for the interior. Car hire available in Djibouti.

BUSINESS HOURS 0620-1300 Sat-Thurs.

GMT +3.

VOLTAGE GUIDE 220 AC, 50 Hz.

RED TAPE

VISAS (AUS/CANADA/UK/US) Required.

REPS IN UK/US/CANADA UK: n/a. US: Suite 515, 1156 15th Street, NW, Washington, DC 20005, tel 202 331 0270, fax 202 331 0302. Deals with enquiries from Canada.

CUSTOMS REGULATIONS Duty free allowance: For visitors over 17 from non-EU countries: 200 cigarettes or 50 cigars or 100 cigarillos or 250 g of tobacco, 1 ltr of spirits of more than 22° proof or 2 ltrs of up to 22° proof (eg fortified wine) and 2 ltrs of table wine, 60 ml of perfume, 250 ml of *eau de toilette*, other goods to the value of FRF 300. For visitors from EU countries: 800 cigarettes, 400 cigarillos, 200 cigars and 1 kg of tobacco, 10 ltrs of spirits, 20 ltrs of fortified wine, 90 ltrs wine (of this not more than 60 ltrs of sparkling wine), 110 ltrs of beer, no limit on perfume or *eau de toilette*. Firearms must be declared on entry and exit.

DRIVING REQUIREMENTS International Driving Permit recommended, although not legally required. A temporary licence is available from local authorities on presentaion of a valid British or Northern Ireland licence.

KEEPING IN TOUCH

BBC WORLD SERVICE MHz 21.47, 17.88, 17.64, 12.01.

ENGLISH-LANGUAGE NEWSPAPERS None.

EMERGENCIES

RED CROSS/CRESCENT SOCIETIES BP 8 Djibouti, tel 352 451, fax 355 049.

UK/US/CANADIAN REPS UK: c/o Inchcabe Shipping Service, BP 81, Djibouti, tel 353 844, fax 353 294, email iss@intnet.dj. US: Villa Plateau du Serpent, boulevard Maréchal Joffre, Djibouti, tel 353 995, fax 353 940, email amembadm@internet.dj. Canada: The Canadian Embassy in Addis Ababa (Ethiopia) deals with enquiries relating to Djibouti.

Global weather guide p 818, Rainy seasons worldwide p 829, Vaccinations required p 832, Recommended reading p 848, Dependent territories p 812.

DOMINICA

STATE OF THE NATION

SAFETY Safe.

LIFE EXPECTANCY 72.

PEOPLE AND PLACE

CAPITAL Roseau.

LANGUAGE English.

PEOPLES Of African descent.

RELIGION Mainly Roman Catholic. Protestant (15%)

SIZE (KM) 751.

POPULATION 74,000.

POP DENSITY/KM 99.

FOOD Island cooking includes Creole and American dishes. Creole specialities include *crabbacks* (backs of red and black crabs stuffed with seasoned crab meat), *lambi* (conch) and *tee-ree-ree* (tiny freshly spawned fish). Locally made *Bello Hot Pepper Sauce* served with almost everything. Island fruit juices combined with rum are excellent.

TRAVEL PLANNING

WHEN TO GO Hot, subtropical climate. Main rainy season between June-October.

MEDICAL CARE Cash payments demanded, insurance strongly recommended.

CURRENCY East Caribbean dollar (EC$) = 100 cents.

FINANCE Most major credit cards and travellers' cheques accepted.

AIRPORTS Melville Hall (DOM) 64 km from Roseau, Canefield (DCF) 5 km from Roseau.

INTERNAL TRAVEL Well mantained roads, car hire available.

BUSINESS HOURS 0800-1300, 1400-1700 Mon, 0800-1300, 1400-1600 Tues-Friday.

GMT -4.

VOLTAGE GUIDE 220/240 AC, 50 Hz.

RED TAPE

VISAS (AUS/CANADA/UK/US) None.

REPS IN UK/US/CANADA
UK: 1 Collingham Gardens, London SW5 0HW, tel 020 7370 5194/5, fax 020 7373 8743, email geninfo@dominica.co.uk.
US: 3216 New Mexico Avenue, NW, Washington, DC 20016, tel 202 364 6781, fax 202 364 6791, email embdomdc@aol.com.
Canada: 130 Albert Street, Suite 700, Ottawa, Ontario K1P 5G4, tel 613 236 8952, fax 613 236 3042, email echcc@travel-net.com.

CUSTOMS REGULATIONS Duty free allowance: 200 cigarettes or equivalent of tobacco products, 2 ltrs of alcoholic beverages (for travellers over 18). Prohibited: Various plants, including bananas, coconuts, coffee and avocados.

DRIVING REQUIREMENTS International Driving Permit recommended. A valid foreign licence can be used to get a Temporary Visitor's Permit.

KEEPING IN TOUCH

BBC WORLD SERVICE MHz 17.71, 15.22, 6.195, 5.975.

ENGLISH-LANGUAGE NEWSPAPERS All. Main papers are *The Chronicle* and *Tropical Star.*

EMERGENCIES

RED CROSS/CRESCENT SOCIETIES National Headquarters, Federation Drive, Goodwill, tel 448 8280, fax 448 7708, email redcross@cwdom.dm.

UK/US/CANADIAN REPS UK: c/o Courts (Dominica) Ltd, 29 Old Street, tel 448 7655, fax 448 7817. US: n/a. Canada: The Canadian High Commission in Bridgetown (Barbados) deals with enquiries relating to Dominica.

Global weather guide p 818, Rainy seasons worldwide p 829, Vaccinations required p 832, Recommended reading p 848, Dependent territories p 812.

DOMINICAN REPUBLIC

STATE OF THE NATION

SAFETY Safe.

LIFE EXPECTANCY M 68.9, F 73.1.

PEOPLE AND PLACE

CAPITAL Santo Domingo.

LANGUAGE Spanish.

PEOPLES Of Spanish and African descent.

RELIGION Roman Catholic.

SIZE (KM) 48,422.

POPULATION 8,200,000.

POP DENSITY/KM 169.

FOOD Spanish influences combined with local produce. Typical examples include *chicharonnes de pollo* (small pieces of seasoned, fried chicken), *sopa criolla dominicana* (soup of meat and vegetables), *la bandera* (rice, red beans, stewed meat with salad), *pastelon* (baked vegetable cake). Local rum drinks and beer are very good.

TRAVEL PLANNING

WHEN TO GO Hot with tropical temperatures all year. Rainy season and the occasional hurricane between June-October.

MEDICAL CARE Insurance recommended.

CURRENCY Dominican Republic peso (peso) = 100 centavos.

FINANCE Major credit cards accepted, travellers' cheques accepted by some banks.

AIRPORTS Santo Domingo (SDQ) 30 km from the city, Puerto Plata (POP), Punta Cana (PUJ) 10-30 minutes travel time to Punta Cana and Bávaro resorts.

INTERNAL TRAVEL Planes can be chartered. Reasonable network of roads, but not all roads are all-weather and 4-wheel-drive vehicles are recommended for wet weather.

BUSINESS HOURS 0830-1200, 1400-1800 Monday-Friday.

GMT -4.

VOLTAGE GUIDE 110 AC, 60 Hz.

RED TAPE

VISAS (AUS/CANADA/UK/US) Not required for stays up to 30 days. A tourist card will be issued.

REPS IN UK/US/CANADA UK: 139 Inverness Terrace, London W2 6JF, tel 020 7727 6214, fax 020 7727 3693. US: 1715 22nd Street, NW, Washington, DC 20008, tel 202 332 6280, fax 202 265 8057, email embdomrepusa@msn.com. Canada: 1470 Peel Street, Suite 263, Montréal, Québec H3H 1T1, email consudom@videotron.ca.

CUSTOMS REGULATIONS Duty free allowance: 200 cigarettes, 2 ltrs of alcoholic beverages, a reasonable amount of perfume (opened). Prohibited: All animal products, agricultural and horticultural products and drugs.

DRIVING REQUIREMENTS A national or International Driving Permit.

KEEPING IN TOUCH

BBC WORLD SERVICE MHz 17.71, 15.22, 6.192, 5.975.

ENGLISH-LANGUAGE NEWSPAPERS *Santo Domingo News* (weekly).

EMERGENCIES

RED CROSS/CRESCENT SOCIETIES Apartado Postal 1293, Santo Domingo, tel 682 3793, fax 682 2837, email cruz.roja@codetel.net.do.

UK/US/CANADIAN REPS UK: Edifico Corominas Pepin, 7th Floor, Avenida 27 dc Febrero 233, Santo Domingo, tel 472 7111, fax 472 7574, email brit.emb.sadom@codetel.net.do. US: Calle César Nicolás Pensón & Calle Leopoldo Navarro, Santo Domingo, tel 221 2171, fax 686 7437. Canada: Capt. Eugenio de Marchena 39, La Esperilla, Santo Domingo, tel 685 1136, fax 682 2691, email e.canada@codetel.net.do.

Global weather guide p 818, Rainy seasons worldwide p 829, Vaccinations required p 832, Recommended reading p 848, Dependent territories p 812.

ECUADOR

STATE OF THE NATION

SAFETY One of the safest countries in Latin America.

LIFE EXPECTANCY M 67.3, F 72.5.

PEOPLE AND PLACE

CAPITAL Quito.

LANGUAGE Spanish.

PEOPLES Mestizo (Indian-Spanish extraction), indigenous Indians.

RELIGION Roman Catholic.

SIZE (KM) 272,045.

POPULATION 12,200,000.

POP DENSITY/KM 44.

FOOD Specialities include *llapingachos* (pancakes mashed potato and cheese), shrimp or lobster *ceviche*, locro (stew of potatoes and cheese), *humitas* (flavoured sweetcorn tamale), and baked guinea pig.

TRAVEL PLANNING

WHEN TO GO Warm and subtropical all year. Andean regions are cooler. Rainfall is high in coastal and jungle areas.

MEDICAL CARE Good but expensive, insurance recommended.

CURRENCY Sucre (Su) = 100 centavos.

FINANCE Credit cards and travellers' cheques widely accepted.

AIRPORTS Quito (UIO) 5 km from the city, Guayaquil (GYE) 5 km from the city.

INTERNAL TRAVEL Flying is the usual mode of transport for intercity travel. Very limited passenger services between the mainland and the Galapagos Islands, but once there it is relatively easy to take boats between islands. Much of the railway network enjoys spectacular views. Road conditions remain variable as a result of frequent earthquakes and flooding over the last decade. Car hire available.

BUSINESS HOURS 0900-130, 1500-1900 Monday-Friday, 1000-2000 Saturday (shopping hours; business hours n/a).

GMT -5 (-6 Galapagos Islands).

VOLTAGE GUIDE 110/220 AC, 60 Hz.

RED TAPE

VISAS (AUS/CANADA/UK/US) Required for business only.

REPS IN UK/US/CANADA UK: Flat 3B, 3 Hans Crescent, London SW1X 0LS, tel 020 7584 1367, fax 020 7823 9701, email 101543.2243@compuserve.com. US: 2535 15th Street, NW, Washington, DC 20009, tel 202 234 7200, fax 202 265 6385, email mecuawaa@pop.erols.com. Canada: Suite 316, 50 O'Connor Street, Ottawa, Ontario K1P 6L2, tel 613 563 8206, fax 613 235 5776, email embcuca@sprint.ca.

CUSTOMS REGULATIONS Duty free allowance: 300 cigarettes or 50 cigars or 200 g of tobacco, 1 ltr of alcohol, a reasonable amount of perfume, gifts and personal effects. Prior permission is required for the import of firearms, ammunition, narcotics, fresh or dry meat and meat products, plants and vegetables.

DRIVING REQUIREMENTS International Driving Permit not required.

KEEPING IN TOUCH

BBC WORLD SERVICE MHz 17.84, 15.22, 9.915, 9.590.

ENGLISH-LANGUAGE NEWSPAPERS *Inside Ecuador, Q.*

EMERGENCIES

RED CROSS/CRESCENT SOCIETIES Casilla 1701 2119, Quito, tel 2 582 480, fax 2 570 424, email difusio@attglobal.net.

UK/US/CANADIAN REPS UK: Calle González Suárez 27-231, Quito, tel 2 970 800/1, fax 2 970 809, email britembq@ uio.telconet.net. US: Avenida 12 Octubre y Patria, Quito, tel 2 562 890, fax 2 502 052. Canada: Avenida 6 de Diciembre, 2816 y Paul Rivet, Quito, tel 2 506 162, fax 2 503 108, email quito~@dfait-maeci.gc.ca.

Global weather guide p 818, Rainy seasons worldwide p 829, Vaccinations required p 832, Recommended reading p 848, Dependent territories p 812.

EGYPT

STATE OF THE NATION

SAFETY Government claims that terrorist massacres of tourists are now over. Otherwise fairly safe, though women should beware sexual harrassment or worse. Observe Islamic customs.

LIFE EXPECTANCY M 64.7, F 67.9.

PEOPLE AND PLACE

CAPITAL Cairo.

LANGUAGE Arabic.

PEOPLES Eastern Hamitic (90%), Nubian, Armenian, Greek.

RELIGION Sunni Islam, small Coptic Christian minority.

SIZE (KM) 997,739.

POPULATION 65,700,000.

POP DENSITY/KM 66.

FOOD Middle Eastern in style and use of spices. *Foul* (bean) based dishes, kebabs and seasoned chickpeas are popular.

TRAVEL PLANNING

WHEN TO GO Warm all year. Hottest June-September. Negligible rainfall, except on the coast. In April the hot, dusty *Khamsin* wind blows from the Sahara.

MEDICAL CARE Insurance strongly recommended.

CURRENCY Egyptian pound (E£) = 100 piastres.

FINANCE Credit cards and travellers' cheques widely accepted.

AIRPORTS Cairo International (CAI) 22 km from the city, El Nouzha (ALY) 7 km from Maydan al-Tahir (Alexandria), Luxor (LXR) 5.5 km from the city.

INTERNAL TRAVEL Daily flights between main centres. A steamer service links Hurghada with Sharm el-Sheik in Sinai. Feluccas can be hired for sailing on the Nile and regular Nile cruises operate between Luxor and Aswan and sometimes between Cairo and Aswan. Comprehensive east-west rail network. The Nile Valley and Delta and the Mediterranean and Red Sea coasts are served by paved roads. Motoring in the desert without suitable vehicles and a guide is not recommended. Car hire available.

BUSINESS HOURS 0900-1900 every day except Monday and Thursday (0900-2000) in winter, 0900-1230, 1600-2000 Saturday-Thursday in summer (shopping hours; business hours n/a).

GMT +2.

VOLTAGE GUIDE 220 AC, 50 Hz most areas, 110-380 AC in some rural areas.

RED TAPE

VISAS (AUS/CANADA/UK/US) Required.

REPS IN UK/US/CANADA UK: 2 Lowndes Street, London SW1X 9ET, tel 020 7235 9719, fax 020 7235 5684. US: 3521 International Court, NW, Washington, DC 20008, tel 202 895 5400, fax 202 244 4319. Canada: 454 Laurier Avenue East, Ottawa, Ontario K1N 6R3, tel 613 234 4931, fax 613 234 9347.

CUSTOMS REGULATIONS Duty free allowance: 200 cigarettes or 25 cigars or 200 g of tobacco, 1 ltr of alcoholic beverages, a reasonable amount of perfume and 1 ltr of *eau de cologne*. Note: All cash, travellers' cheques, credit cards and gold over E£500 must be declared on arrival. Prohibited: Narcotics, firearms and cotton.

DRIVING REQUIREMENTS Own insurance and an International Driving Permit required.

KEEPING IN TOUCH

BBC WORLD SERVICE MHz 17.88, 15.42, 11.86, 9.630.

ENGLISH-LANGUAGE NEWSPAPERS *Egyptian Gazette* (daily), the *Middle East Observer* (weekly).

EMERGENCIES

RED CROSS/CRESCENT SOCIETIES 29 El Galaa Street, Cairo, tel 2 575 0558, fax 2 574 0450, email erc@brainyl.ie-eg.com.

UK/US/CANADIAN REPS UK: 7 Sharia Ahmad Ragheb, Garden City, Cairo, tel 2 354 0850/2, fax 2 354 0859, email commercial@cairo.mail.fco.gov.uk. US: 5 Latin America Street, Garden City, Cairo, tel 2 355 7371, fax 2 357 3200, email cacairo@ state.gov. Canada: Arab International Bank Building, 5 Midan El Saraya el Kobra, Garden City, Cairo, tel 2 354 3110, fax 2 356 3548.

Global weather guide p 818, Rainy seasons worldwide p 829, Vaccinations required p 832, Recommended reading p 848, Dependent territories p 812.

EL SALVADOR

STATE OF THE NATION

SAFETY Robbery and murder are not uncommon. Seek latest information at time of visit.

LIFE EXPECTANCY M 66.5, F 72.5.

PEOPLE AND PLACE

CAPITAL San Salvador.

LANGUAGE Spanish.

PEOPLES Mestizo.

RELIGION Roman Catholic, Evangelical.

SIZE (KM) 20,721.

POPULATION 6,100,000.

POP DENSITY/KM 294.

FOOD Th e popular stuffed tortillas (*pupusas*) come in several varieties including cheese (*queso*) and pork (*chicharrón*). Small dishes of yucca, avocado or chorizo, known as *boca*, are served with a drink before meals.

TRAVEL PLANNING

WHEN TO GO Hot subtropical climate. Coastal areas are particularly hot, with a rainy season between May-October. Upland areas have a more temperate climate.

MEDICAL CARE Cash payments demanded, insurance strongly recommended.

CURRENCY El Salvador colón ('peso') = 100 centavos

FINANCE Major credit cards and travellers' cheques accepted.

AIRPORTS San Salvador (SAL) 45 km from the city.

INTERNAL TRAVEL Flights between San Salvador and main centres, also linked by a rail network. About a third of the road system allows all-weather use. Car hijackings and burglaries are common. Car hire is available in San Salvador.

BUSINESS HOURS 0800-1230, 1430-1730 Monday-Friday.

GMT -6.

VOLTAGE GUIDE 110 AC, 60 Hz.

RED TAPE

VISAS (AUS/CANADA/UK/US) Not required by UK nationals. US nationals need a tourist card, Australian and Canadian visitors require a visa.

REPS IN UK/US/CANADA UK: Tennyson House, 159 Great Portland Street, London W1N 5FD, tel 020 7436 8282, fax 020 7436 8181. US: 2308 California Street, NW, Washington, DC 20008, tel 202 265 9671, fax 202 234 3834. Canada: 209 Kent Street, Ottawa, Ontario K2P 1Z8, tel 613 238 2939, fax 613 238 6940 email embagada@ elsalvador-ca.org.

CUSTOMS REGULATIONS Duty free allowance: 200 cigarettes or 50 cigars, 2 ltrs of alcoholic beverage, up to 6 units of perfume, gifts to the value of US$500. Prohibited: There are restrictions on the import and export of fruit, vegetables, plants and animals.

DRIVING REQUIREMENTS A national or International Driving Permit required.

KEEPING IN TOUCH

BBC WORLD SERVICE MHz 17.84, 15.22, 9.915, 9.590.

ENGLISH-LANGUAGE NEWSPAPERS None.

EMERGENCIES

RED CROSS/CRESCENT SOCIETIES Apartado Posta 2672, San Salvador, tel 222 7749, fax 222 7758, email crsalvador@ vianet.com.sv.

UK/US/CANADIAN REPS UK: Edificio Inter-Inversiones, Paseo General Escalōn 4828, San Salvador, tel 263 6527, fax 263 6516, email britemb@sal.gbm.net. US: Final Boulevard Santa Elena Sur, Antiguo Cuscatlán, San Salvador, tel 278 444, fax 278 6011. Canada: Calle Las Palmas, 111, Colonia San Benito, San Salvador, tel 279 4655, fax 279 0765.

Global weather guide p 818, Rainy seasons worldwide p 829, Vaccinations required p 832, Recommended reading p 848, Dependent territories p 812.

EQUATORIAL GUINEA

STATE OF THE NATION

SAFETY For the adventurer. Seek latest information at time of visit.

LIFE EXPECTANCY M 48.4, F 51.6.

PEOPLE AND PLACE

CAPITAL Malabo.

LANGUAGE Spanish.

PEOPLES Fang, Bubi and Creole minority.

RELIGION Roman Catholic.

SIZE (KM) 28,051.

POPULATION 430,000.

POP DENSITY/KM 15.

FOOD Most restaurants serve Spanish or continental cuisine.

TRAVEL PLANNING

WHEN TO GO Tropical all year, with heavy rainfall for most of the year, decreasing slightly between December-February.

MEDICAL CARE Limited, insurance cover for repatriation recommended.

CURRENCY Communauté Financiaire Africaine franc (CFAfr) = 100 centimes.

FINANCE Very limited acceptance of Diners Club. Travellers' cheques not recommended.

AIRPORTS Malabo (SSG), 7 km from the city, Bata 6 km from the city.

INTERNAL TRAVEL Regular flights between Malabo and Bata, and light aircraft can be chartered. However, it is reported that maintenance procedures on internal flights are not always properly observed. Roads of variable condition - not all are paved.

BUSINESS HOURS 0800-1300, 1600-1900 Monday-Saturday (shopping hours; business hours n/a).

GMT +1.

VOLTAGE GUIDE 220/240 AC.

RED TAPE

VISAS (AUS/CANADA/UK/US) Required.

REPS IN UK/US/CANADA UK: n/a. US: 2020 16th Street, NW, Washington, DC 20009, tel 202 518 5700, fax 202 518 5252 Canada: n/a.

CUSTOMS REGULATIONS Duty free allowance: 200 cigarettes or 50 cigars or 250 g of tobacco, 1 ltr of wine, 1 ltr of alcoholic beverage, a reasonable amount of perfume.

DRIVING REQUIREMENTS n/a.

KEEPING IN TOUCH

BBC WORLD SERVICE MHz 17.83, 15.40, 11.76, 6.005

ENGLISH-LANGUAGE NEWSPAPERS None.

EMERGENCIES

RED CROSS/CRESCENT SOCIETIES Apartado postal 460, Malabo, tel/fax 9 3701.

UK/US/CANADIAN REPS UK: The British Consulate in Yaoundé (Cameroon) deals with enquiries relating to Equatorial Guinea. US: The American Embassy in Yaoundé (Cameroon) deals with enquiries relating to Equatorial Guinea. Canada: The Canadian Embassy in Libreville (Gabon) deals with enquiries relating to Equatorial Guinea.

Global weather guide p 818, Rainy seasons worldwide p 829, Vaccinations required p 832, Recommended reading p 848, Dependent territories p 812.

ERITREA

STATE OF THE NATION

SAFETY Relatively safe, but avoid borders with Ethiopia and Sudan. Do not travel after dark, and register with embassy on arrival.

LIFE EXPECTANCY M 49.3, F 52.

PEOPLE AND PLACE

CAPITAL Asmara.

LANGUAGE Arabic and Tigrinya.

PEOPLES Tigrinya, Tigre, Afar and other indigenous groups.

RELIGION Islam and Christianity.

SIZE (KM) 124,330.

POPULATION 3,500,000.

POP DENSITY/KM 37.

FOOD Staple foods include *kitcha*, a thin bread made from wheat, and *injera*, a spongy pancake. Local specialities are often spicy. Massawa is renown for excellent seafood, particularly lobster and prawns. Italian cuisine dominates in restaurants in larger cities.

TRAVEL PLANNING

WHEN TO GO May-June, September-October. The short rainy season is March-April, long rains from end June to beginning of September. Temperatures can fall as low as freezing between December-February.

MEDICAL CARE Adequate, but insurance strongly recommended.

CURRENCY Nafka (Nfka) = 100 cents.

FINANCE Credit cards accepted on a limited basis, travellers' cheques are generally accepted.

AIRPORTS Asmara (ASM) 6 km from the city.

INTERNAL TRAVEL Internal flights between Asmara and Assab. Roads were badly damaged during the fighting, repairs are underway. Reasonable roads still connect business centres and holiday resorts. Car hire available through the Eritean Tour Servce in Asmara.

BUSINESS HOURS 0800-1200, 1400-1700 Monday-Friday, 0800-1200 Sat.

GMT +2 (+3 in summer).

VOLTAGE GUIDE 110/220 AC.

RED TAPE

VISAS (AUS/CANADA/UK/US) Required.

REPS IN UK/US/CANADA UK: 96 White Lion Street, London N1 9PF, tel 020 7713 0096, fax 020 7713 0161. US: 1708 New Hampshire Avenue, NW, Washington DC 20009, tel 202 319 1991, fax 202 319 1304. Canada: 75 Albert Street, Suite 610, Ottawa, Ontario K1P 5E7, tel 613 234 3989, fax 613 234 6213.

CUSTOMS REGULATIONS Duty free allowance: 200 cigarettes or 50 cigars or 250 g of tobacco, 1 ltr of alcoholic beverage.

DRIVING REQUIREMENTS International Driving Permit.

KEEPING IN TOUCH

BBC WORLD SERVICE MHz 17.88, 15.42, 11.86, 9.630.

ENGLISH-LANGUAGE NEWSPAPERS *Eritrea Profile* (weekly).

EMERGENCIES

RED CROSS/CRESCENT SOCIETIES n/a.

UK/US/CANADIAN REPS UK: PO Box 997, Asmara, tel 1 120 145, fax 1 120 104. US: PO Box 5584, Emperor Johannes Avenue 24, Asmara, tel 1 120 004, fax 1 127 584. Canada: 4 Dejat Chebremayam Street, Asmara, tel 1 181 940, fax 1 181 963. The Canadian Embassy in Addis Ababa (Ethiopia) also deals with enquiries relating to Eritrea.

Global weather guide p 818, Rainy seasons worldwide p 829, Vaccinations required p 832, Recommended reading p 848, Dependent territories p 812.

ESTONIA

STATE OF THE NATION

SAFETY Safe.

LIFE EXPECTANCY M 64.1, F 75.

PEOPLE AND PLACE

CAPITAL Tallinn.

LANGUAGE Estonian.

PEOPLES Russian, Estonian.

RELIGION Mainly Protestant (Lutheran).

SIZE (KM) 45, 227.

POPULATION 1, 476, 301.

POP DENSITY/KM 33.3.

FOOD Local specialities include *rosolje* (herring with vinagrette and beets), *sült* (jellied veal), *täidetud vasikarind* (roast stuffed shoulder of veal). Roast goose stuffed with apples and plums is another Baltic speciality.

TRAVEL PLANNING

WHEN TO GO Summer is warm with relatively mild weather in spring and autumn. Rainfall distributed throughout the year, heaviest in Aug. Winter, from November to mid-March, can be very cold and heavy snowfalls are common.

MEDICAL CARE Limited, cash payments demanded, insurance recommended.

CURRENCY Kroon (Ekr) = 100 sents.

FINANCE Credit cards and travellers' cheques widely accepted.

AIRPORTS Tallinn (TLL) 4 km from the city.

INTERNAL TRAVEL Domestic flights in summer from Tallinn to the islands of Saaremaa and Hiiumaa. Frequent ferry services between the mainland and islands. Underdeveloped rail system but major cities are connected. High density of roads. Car hire available at the airport or in Tallinn.

BUSINESS HOURS 0830-1830 Mon-Friday.

GMT +2 (+3 in summer).

VOLTAGE GUIDE 220 AC, 50 Hz.

RED TAPE

VISAS (AUS/CANADA/UK/US) Canadians need a visa for Latvia or Lithuania. Visas not required for UK/US/Australian visitors.

REPS IN UK/US/CANADA UK: 16 Hyde Park Gate, London SW7 5DG, tel 020 7589 3428, fax 020 7589 3430, email loa@estonia.gov.uk. US: 600 Third Avenue, 26th Floor, New York, NY 10016, tel 212 883 0636, fax 212 883 0648. Canada: 958 Broadview Avenue, Suite 202, Toronto, Ontario M4K 2R6, tel 416 461 0764, fax 416 461 0353, email estconsu@inforamp.net.

CUSTOMS REGULATIONS Duty free allowance: 200 cigarettes or 20 cigars or 250 g tobacco, 2 ltrs of alcohol up to 21% (passengers aged 18-20) or 1 ltr of alcohol over 21% and 1 ltr of alcohol up to 21% (passengers over 21) and 10 ltrs of beer, 10 kg of foodstuffs. Prohibited: Restrictions apply to certain items including plants and vegetable products, firearms and antiques.

DRIVING REQUIREMENTS EU nationals should have an EU pink format or national driving licence.

KEEPING IN TOUCH

BBC WORLD SERVICE MHz 17.64, 15.57, 9.410, 6.195.

ENGLISH-LANGUAGE NEWSPAPERS *The Baltic Times* (weekly).

EMERGENCIES

RED CROSS/CRESCENT SOCIETIES Lai Street 17, EE0001, Tallinn, tel 6 411 1643, fax 6 411 1641, email: didi@online.ee.

UK/US/CANADIAN REPS UK: Wismari 6, 10186 Tallinn, tel 6 674 700, fax 6 674 724, email uk.talli@netexpress.ee. US: Kentmanni 20, 15099 Tallinn, tel 6 312 021, fax 6 312 025/6. Canada: Toom Kooli 13, 2nd Floor, 10130 Tallinn, tel 6 273 311, fax 6 273 312, email canembt@zzz.ee.

Global weather guide p 818, Rainy seasons worldwide p 829, Vaccinations required p 832, Recommended reading p 848, Dependent territories p 812.

ETHIOPIA

STATE OF THE NATION

Safety Relatively safe, but avoid borders with Eritrea, Somalia and Sudan. Do not travel after dark, and register with embassy if travelling outside the capital by road.

Life expectancy M 42.4, F 44.3.

PEOPLE AND PLACE

Capital Addis Ababa.

Language Amharic.

Peoples Oromo, Amhara, Sidamo, Shankella, Somali.

Religion Ethiopian Orthodox, Coptic Church, Islam, traditional beliefs.

Size (km) 1, 133, 380.

Population 62, 100, 000.

Pop density/km 56.

Food Local food based on *we't* - meat, chicken or vegetables cooked in a hot pepper sauce, served with *injera* (a flat, spongy bread). Other dishes include *shivro* and *misir* (based on chickpeas and lentils) and *tibs* (crispy fried steak). Wide choice of fish available. *Tej* - an alcoholic drink based on fermented honey - is unique to Ethiopia.

TRAVEL PLANNING

When to go Most rainfall is from June-September. Hot and humid in the lowlands, warm in the hill country, cool in the uplands.

Medical care Limited, repatriation cover recommended.

Currency Ethiopian birr = 100 cents.

Finance Limited acceptance of travellers' cheques, very limited acceptance of Diners Club and MasterCard.

Airports Addis Ababa (ADD) 8 km from the city.

Internal travel Internal flights can be infrequent. The only operative rail line runs between Addis Ababa and Djibouti, via Dire Dawa. A good network of all-weather roads exists to most business and tourist centres, otherwise 4-wheel-drive vehicles are recommended. Frequent fuel shortages, and driving after dark outside Addis Ababa can be risky. Car hire available in Addis Ababa.

Business hours 0800-1200, 1300-1700 Monday-Friday.

GMT +3.

Voltage guide 220 AC, 50 Hz.

RED TAPE

Visas (Aus/Canada/UK/US) Required.

Reps in UK/USA/Canada UK: 17 Princes Gate, London SW7 1PZ, tel 020 7589 7212, fax 020 7584 7054. USA: 2134 Kalorama Road, NW, Washington, NW, Washington, DC 20008, tel 202 234 2281/2, fax 202 483 8407, email info@ ethiopi-anembassy.org. Canada: 151 Slater Street, Suite 210, Ottawa, Ontario K1P 5H3, tel 613 235 6637, fax 613 235 4638, email infoethi@magi.com.

Customs regulations Duty free allowance: 100 cigarettes or 50 cigars or 225 g of tobacco, 1 ltr of alcoholic beverages, 2 bottles or 500 ml of perfume, gifts up to the value of Birr 10.

Driving requirements British driving licence valid for 1 month, otherwise obtain a temporary Ethiopian driving licence.

KEEPING IN TOUCH

BBC World Service MHz 17.88, 15.42, 11.86, 9.630.

English-language newspapers *The Ethiopian Herald.*

EMERGENCIES

Red Cross/Crescent societies PO Box 195, Addis Ababa, tel 1 519 364, fax 1 512 643, email ercs@padis.gn. apc.org.

UK/USA/Canadian reps UK: PO Box 858, Fikre Mariam Abatechan Street, Addis Ababa, tel 1 612 354, fax 1 610 588, email britishembassy@telecom.net.et. US: PO Box 1014, Entoto Street, Addis Ababa, tel 1 550 666, fax 1 551 328, email usembassy@ telecom.net.et. Canada: PO Box 1130, Old Airport Area, Higher 23, Werede 12, House Number 122, Addis Ababa, tel 1 713 022, fax 1 713 033.

Global weather guide p 818, Rainy seasons worldwide p 829, Vaccinations required p 832, Recommended reading p 848, Dependent territories p 812.

FIJI

STATE OF THE NATION

SAFETY Generally safe, but from recent attempted *coup* has caused some civil unrest.

LIFE EXPECTANCY M 70.6, F 74.9.

PEOPLE AND PLACE

CAPITAL Suva.

LANGUAGE Fijian and Hindi.

PEOPLES Fijians, Indo-Fijians.

RELIGION Hindu, Methodist. Muslim and Roman Catholic minorities.

SIZE (KM) 18,333.

POPULATION 822,000.

POP DENSITY/KM 45.

FOOD Fijian/Indian cuisine such as *kakoda* (marinated local fish served in coconut cream and lime). Curries are popular, as are Fifian *lovo* feasts, where meat, fish and vegetables are cooked in covered pits.

TRAVEL PLANNING

WHEN TO GO Tropical climate, with southeast trade winds from May-October bringing dry weather. The rainy season is from December-April.

MEDICAL CARE Adequate, but insurance recommended.

CURRENCY Fijian dollar (F$) = 100 cents.

FINANCE Credit cards and travellers' cheques generally accepted.

AIRPORTS Nadi (NAN), 8 km from Nadi on Viti Levu island. Suba (SUV) is at Nausori, 21 km from Suva.

INTERNAL TRAVEL Air and sea services between islands. Roads in good condition and usable year round. Car hire is available.

BUSINESS HOURS 0830-1700 Mon-Friday.

GMT +12.

VOLTAGE GUIDE 240 AC, 50 Hz.

RED TAPE

VISAS (AUS/CANADA/UK/US) None.

REPS IN UK/US/CANADA UK: 34 Hyde Park Gate, London SW7 5DN, tel 020 7584 3661, fax 020 7584 2838, email fijirepuk@compuserve.com. US: Suite 240, 2233 Wisconsin Avenue, NW, Washington, DC 20007, tel 202 337 8320, fax 202 337 1996, email fijiemb@earthlink.net. Canada: 130 Slater Street, Suite 750, Ottawa, Ontario, K1P 6E2, tel 613 233 9252, fax 613 594 8705.

CUSTOMS REGULATIONS Duty free allowance: 500 cigarettes or 500 g of tobacco goods, 2 ltrs of spirits or 4 ltrs of wine or 4 litres of beer, 114 ml of perfume for personal use, goods to the value of F$400 (for travellers over 17). Prohibited: Firearms, ammunition, narcotics. The import of vegetables, seeds, meat and dairy products needs a special permit.

DRIVING REQUIREMENTS International Driving Permit.

KEEPING IN TOUCH

BBC WORLD SERVICE MHz 12.08, 11.77, 9.740, 7.145.

ENGLISH-LANGUAGE NEWSPAPERS *The Fiji Times, Daily Post.*

EMERGENCIES

RED CROSS/CRESCENT SOCIETIES GPO 569, Suva, tel 314 133, fax 303 818.

UK/US/CANADIAN REPS UK: PO Box 1355, Victoria House, 47 Gladstone Road, Suva, tel 311 033, fax 301 406, email ukinfo@bhc.org.fj. US: PO Box 218, 31 Loftus Street, Suva, tel 314 466, fax 300 081. Canada: PO Box 10690, Nadi Airport, tel 721 936, fax 750 666.

Global weather guide p 818,   Rainy seasons worldwide p 829,   Vaccinations required p 832,
Recommended reading p 848,   Dependent territories p 812.

FINLAND

STATE OF THE NATION

SAFETY Safe.

LIFE EXPECTANCY M 72.9, F 80.6.

PEOPLE AND PLACE

CAPITAL Helsinki.

LANGUAGE Finnish.

PEOPLES Finnish, small Sami population.

RELIGION Evangelical Lutheran.

SIZE (KM) 338, 144.

POPULATION 5, 200, 000.

POP DENSITY/KM 45.

FOOD Potatoes, meat, fish, butter and rye bread form the basis of Finnish diet, but the cuisine has been greatly influenced by French, Swedish and Russian cooking.

TRAVEL PLANNING

WHEN TO GO Relatively mild in spring and autumn, brief warm summers. Snow cover in the north lasts from October to mid-May.

MEDICAL CARE UK citizens eligible for a refund on some medical expenses.

CURRENCY Markka (Fmk) = 100 penni.

FINANCE Credit cards and travellers' cheques widely accepted.

AIRPORTS Helsinki (HEL) 20 km from the city, Turku (TKU) 7 km from the city, Tampere (TMP) 15 km from the city, Rovaniemi (RVN) 10 km from the city.

INTERNAL TRAVEL Excellent network of domestic flights. Rail travel is cheap and efficient. Lake steamers and motor vessels ply the inland waterways. Main roads are passable at all times. Car hire easily available.

BUSINESS HOURS 0800-1615 Mon-Friday.

GMT +2.

VOLTAGE GUIDE 220 AC, 50 Hz.

RED TAPE

VISAS (AUS/CANADA/UK/US) None.

REPS IN UK/US/CANADA UK: 38 Chesham Place, London SW1X 8HW, tel 020 7838 6212, fax 020 7838 9703. US: 3301 Massachusetts Avenue, NW, Washington, DC 20008, tel 202 298 5800, fax 202 298 6030, email: info@finland.org. Canada: Suite 850, 55 Metcalfe Street, Ottawa, Ontario, K1P 6LS, tel 613 236 2389, fax 613 238 1471, email finembott@synapse.net.

CUSTOMS REGULATIONS Duty free allowance: For travellers from EU countries: for travellers over 20, 1 ltr alcohol over 22%, for travellers over 18 3 ltrs of alcohol under 22% or sparkling wines and 2 ltrs other wines and 15 ltrs of beer. For travellers over 17, 300 cigarettes or 150 cigarillos or 75 cigars or 400 g of tobacco. For travellers from non-EU countries: for travellers over 20, 1 ltr alcohol over 22%; over 18, 2 ltrs of wine under 22% or sparkling wine, 2 ltrs other wines and 15 ltrs of beer. For travellers over 17, 200 cigarettes or 100 cigarillos or 50 cigars or 250 g of tobacco, 50 g perfume, 250 ml *eau de toilette*. Prohibited: Import of drinks containing more than 60% alcohol by volume.

DRIVING REQUIREMENTS National driving licence or International Driving Permit and insurance required.

KEEPING IN TOUCH

BBC WORLD SERVICE MHz 17.64, 15.56, 9.410, 6.195.

ENGLISH-LANGUAGE NEWSPAPERS None, but UK and American papers available.

EMERGENCIES

RED CROSS/CRESCENT SOCIETIES PO Box 168, FIN-00141 Helsinki, tel 9 12931, fax 9 129 3311.

UK/US/CANADIAN REPS UK: Itäinen Puistotie 17, 00140 Helsinki, tel 9 22 86 51 00, fax 9 22 86 52 62, email info@ ukembassy.fi. US: Itäinen Puistotie 14B, 00140 Helsinki, tel 9 171 931, fax 9 174 681, email arc@usembassy.fi. Canada: P Esplanadi 25B, 00101 Helsinki, tel 9 171 141, fax 9 601 060.

*Global weather guide p 818,   Rainy seasons worldwide p 829,   Vaccinations required p 832,
Recommended reading p 848,   Dependent territories p 812.*

FRANCE

STATE OF THE NATION

SAFETY Safe, apart from separatist activity in Corsica and the Basque area.

LIFE EXPECTANCY M 74.2, F 82.

PEOPLE AND PLACE

CAPITAL Paris.

LANGUAGE French.

PEOPLES French, North African, German, Breton.

RELIGION Roman Catholic. Protestant, Muslim, Jewish and Buddhist minorities.

SIZE (KM) 543,965.

POPULATION 58,700,000.

POP DENSITY/KM 107.

FOOD France boasts one of the most varied and developed cusines in the world. Haute-cuisine, bistro-fare and family cooking all rely on quality produce, and each region is proud of its own specialities. The country is famous for producing fine wine and over 365 different types of cheese.

TRAVEL PLANNING

WHEN TO GO Temperate and continental climate in the north, Mediterranean in the south, mountains are cooler with heavy snows in the winter.

MEDICAL CARE UK citizens eligible for a refund on some medical expenses.

CURRENCY French franc (FFr).

FINANCE Credit cards, travellers' cheques widely accepted.

AIRPORTS (And distances from the nearest city) Paris-Charles de Gaulle (CDG) 23 km, Paris-Orly (ORY) 14 km, Bordeaux (BOD) 12 km, Lille (LIL) 12 km, Lyon (LYS) 25 km, Marseille (MRS) 30 km, Nice (NCE) 6 km, Strasbourg (SXB) 12 km, Toulouse (TLS) 8 km.

INTERNAL TRAVEL All domestic networks (air, rail and road) are efficient.

BUSINESS HOURS 0900-1200, 1400-1800 Monday-Friday.

GMT +1 (+2 in summer).

VOLTAGE GUIDE 220 AC, 50 Hz.

RED TAPE

VISAS (AUS/CANADA/UK/US) None.

REPS IN UK/US/CANADA UK: 58 Knightsbridge, London, SW1X 7JT, tel 020 7201 1000, fax 020 7201 1053, email tourism@ambafrance.org.uk. US: 4101 Reservoir Road, NW, Washington, DC 20007, tel 202 944 6195, fax 202 944 6148, email infor@amb-wash.fr. Canada: 42 Sussex Drive, Ottawa, Ontario K1M 2C9, tel 613 789 1795, fax 613 562 3704, email consulat@amba-ottawa.fr.

CUSTOMS REGULATIONS Duty free allowance: For travellers over 17 from non-EU countries, 200 cigarettes or 50 cigars or 100 cigarillos or 250 g of tobacco, 1 ltr of spirits more than 22% or 2 ltrs of alcoholic beverage up to 22%, 2 ltrs of wine, 50 g of perfume and 250 ml of *eau de toilette*, goods up to the value of FFr 1200 (FFr 600 per person under 15). No limits on tobacco and alcohol for personal use only between EU countries. Prohibited: Restrictions on plants and plant products, pharmaceutical products (except those needed for personal use), works of art, collectors' items and antiques.

DRIVING REQUIREMENTS National driving licence acceptable. EU nationals taking their own car to france are strongly advised to obtain a green card.

KEEPING IN TOUCH

BBC WORLD SERVICE MHz 9.410, 6.195, 12.10, 0.648.

ENGLISH-LANGUAGE NEWSPAPERS International papers widely available. *International Herald Tribune* published from Paris.

EMERGENCIES

RED CROSS/CRESCENT SOCIETIES 1, Place Henry-Dunant, F-75384 Paris, Cedex 08, tel 1 44 43 110, fax 1 44 43 11 01, email cr@croix-rouge.fr.

UK/US/CANADIAN REPS UK: 35 rue de Faubourg St Honoré, 75383 Paris, Cedex 08, tel 1 44 51 31 00, fax 1 44 51 31 28. US: 2 rue St Florentin, 75382 Paris, Cedex 08, tel 836 701 488, fax 43 12 46 08. Canada: 35 avenue Montaigne, 75008 Paris, tel 1 44 43 29 00, fax 1 44 43 29 99.

Global weather guide p 818, Rainy seasons worldwide p 829, Vaccinations required p 832, Recommended reading p 848, Dependent territories p 812.

GABON

STATE OF THE NATION

SAFETY Generally stable.

LIFE EXPECTANCY M 51.1, F 53.8.

PEOPLE AND PLACE

CAPITAL Libreville.

LANGUAGE French.

PEOPLES Fang, Eshira and other Bantu.

RELIGION Christian (mainly Roman Catholic), Islam, Animist.

SIZE (KM) 267,667.

POPULATION 1,200,000.

POP DENSITY/KM 5.

FOOD Many restaurants serve Cameroonian, Congolese, French and Senegalese food. Bush meats such as wild boar and crocodile often form part of Gabonese cuisine.

TRAVEL PLANNING

WHEN TO GO Equatorial climate with high humidity. Dry season from June-August, main rainy season from October-May.

MEDICAL CARE Very limited, insurance strongly recommended.

CURRENCY Communauté Financiaire Africaine france (CFAfr) = 100 centimes.

FINANCE Relatively limited acceptance of credit cards, limited acceptance of travllers cheques.

AIRPORTS Libreville (LBV) 12 km from the city.

INTERNAL TRAVEL Some local flights. The Trans-Gabon railway connects Libreville with Ndjole, Booué and franceville. Most of the country consists of impenetrable rain-forest and the roads are generally of poor standard. Road travel during the rainy season is inadvisable. Car hire available at main hotels and airports.

BUSINESS HOURS 0730-1200, 1430-1800 Monday-Friday.

GMT +1.

VOLTAGE GUIDE 220 AC, 50 Hz.

RED TAPE

VISAS (AUS/CANADA/UK/US) Required.

REPS IN UK/US/CANADA UK: 27 Elvaston Place, London SW7 5NL, tel 020 7823 9986, fax 020 7584 0047. US: 2034 20th Street, NW, Washington, DC 20009, tel 202 797 1000, fax 202 332 0668. Canada: BP 368, 4 Range Road, Ottawa, Ontario K1N 8J5, tel 613 232 5301/2, fax 613 232 6916.

CUSTOMS REGULATIONS Duty free allowance: For travellers over 17, 200 cigarettes/cigarillos or 50 cigars or 250 g of tobacco (women - cigarettes only), 2 ltrs of alcoholic beverage, 50 g of perfume, gifts up to CFAfr 5000.

DRIVING REQUIREMENTS International Driving Permit and international insurance.

KEEPING IN TOUCH

BBC WORLD SERVICE MHz 15.40, 11.94, 6.190, 1.197.

ENGLISH-LANGUAGE NEWSPAPERS None.

EMERGENCIES

RED CROSS/CRESCENT SOCIETIES PO Box 2274, Libreville, tel/fax 766 160, email gab.cross@internetgabon.com.

UK/US/CANADIAN REPS UK: PO Box 486, Libreville, tel 762 200, fax 765 789. US: BP 4000, boulevard Bord de la Mer, Libreville, tel 762 003/4, fax 745 507. Canada: PO Box 4037, Libreville, tel 743 464/5, fax 743 466.

Global weather guide p 818, Rainy seasons worldwide p 829, Vaccinations required p 832, Recommended reading p 848, Dependent territories p 812.

GAMBIA

STATE OF THE NATION

SAFETY Calm since military *coup* of 1994.
LIFE EXPECTANCY M 45.4, F 48.6.

PEOPLE AND PLACE

CAPITAL Banjul.
LANGUAGE English.
PEOPLES Mandingo, Fulani, Wolof, Jola, Serahull.
RELIGION Islam 80%, Christian, Animist.
SIZE (KM) 11, 295.
POPULATION 1, 260, 000.
POP DENSITY/KM 119.
FOOD Typical dishes include 'Jollof Rice' or *benachin*, a mixture of spiced meat and rice with tomato puree and vegetables, *chere* (steamed millet flour balls), *base nyebe* (rich stew of chicken or beef with vegetables), *plasas* (meat and smoked fish cooked in palm oil with green vegetables).

TRAVEL PLANNING

WHEN TO GO Pleasantly tropical climate. Coastal areas dry November-May, rainy June-October. Inland very hot March-June.
MEDICAL CARE Adequate, but insurance recommended, take supplies of basic medicines.
CURRENCY Gambian dalasi (D) = 100 bututs.
FINANCE Limited acceptance of credit cards and travellers' cheques.
AIRPORTS Banjul (BJL).
INTERNAL TRAVEL Excellent river connections to all parts of the country. About a third of the roads are paved. Unsealed roads become impassable in the rainy season. Some car hire available, check with major companies before travelling.
BUSINESS HOURS 0800-1600 Mon-Thurs, 0800-1230 Friday.
GMT GMT.
VOLTAGE GUIDE 220 AC, 50 Hz.

RED TAPE

VISAS (AUS/CANADA/UK/US) Required by American and Canadian visitors.
REPS IN UK/US/CANADA UK: 57 Kensington Court, London W8 5DG, tel 020 7937 6316, fax 020 7937 9095. US: Suite 1000, 1155 15th Street, NW, Washington, DC 20005, tel 202 785 1399, fax 202 785 1430. Canada: n/a.
CUSTOMS REGULATIONS Duty free allowance: 200 cigarettes or 50 cigars or 250 g of tobacco, 1 ltr spirits, 1 ltr of beer or wine, 248 ml of perfume or *eau de toilette*, goods up to a value of D1000.
DRIVING REQUIREMENTS International Driving Permit. A temporary licence available from local authorities on presentation of a valid UK licence.

KEEPING IN TOUCH

BBC WORLD SERVICE MHz 17.83, 15.42, 11.86, 7.160.
ENGLISH-LANGUAGE NEWSPAPERS All papers published in English. Main papers are *The Gambia Weekly, The Nation, The Gambia Daily, The Gambian Times.*

EMERGENCIES

RED CROSS/CRESCENT SOCIETIES PO Box 472, Banjul, tel 392 405, fax 394 921.
UK/US/CANADIAN REPS UK: 48 Atlantic Road, Fajara, Banjul, tel 495 133/4, fax 496 134, email bhcbanjul@gamtel.gm. US: Kairaba Avenue, Fajara, Banjul, tel 392 856, fax 392 475. Canada: The Canadian High Commission in Dakar deals with enquiries relating to Gambia.

Global weather guide p 818, Rainy seasons worldwide p 829, Vaccinations required p 832, Recommended reading p 848, Dependent territories p 812.

GEORGIA

STATE OF THE NATION

Safety Avoid travelling at night outside the capital.

Life expectancy M 68.5, F 76.8.

PEOPLE AND PLACE

Capital Tbilisi.

Language Georgian, Russian.

Peoples Georgian (70%), Armenian, Russian, Azeri, Ossetian.

Religion Georgian Orthodox, Eastern Orthodox, Muslim, Jewish.

Size (km) 69,700.

Population 5,471,000.

Pop density/km 236.

Food Meals usually start with mixed hot and cold dishes, including grilled liver, *lobio* (bean and walnut salad), marinated aubergines, fresh and pickled vegetables. Walnuts used extensively - anything including the word *satsivi* will be served in a rich sauce flavoured with herbs, garlic, walnuts and egg. Roast suckling pig often served.

TRAVEL PLANNING

When to go Hot summers (May-September), mild winters.

Medical care Limited but free emergency care for UK citizens.

Currency Lari (GEL) = 100 tetri.

Finance Limited acceptance of credit cards and travellers' cheques.

Airports Tbilisi (TBS) 18 km from the city.

Internal travel Single-track, slow rail lines. Approximately 20,000 km of asphalted roads. Difficult to buy fuel outside cities without specialised local knowledge.

Business hours n/a.

GMT +4.

Voltage guide 220 AC, 50 Hz.

RED TAPE

Visas (Aus/Canada/UK/US) Required.

Reps in UK/US/Canada UK: 3 Hornton Place, London W8 4LZ, tel 020 7937 8233, fax 020 7938 4108, email goemb@dircon.com US: 1615 New Hampshire Avenue, Suite 300, NW, Washington DC 20009, tel 202 387 2390, fax 202 393 4537. Also deals with enquiries from Canada.

Customs regulations Duty free allowance: 200 cigarettes, 3 ltrs of wine or 10 ltrs of beer, personal goods up to 10 kg. Prohibited: Military weapons, ammunition, narcotics, drug paraphernalia, pornography, loose pearls, anything owned by a third party that is to be carried in for that third party. Prohibited exports: State loan certificates, lottery tickets, works of art and antiques without permits, saiga horns, Siberian stag, punctuate and red deer antlers, punctuate deer skins.

Driving requirements International Driving Permit.

KEEPING IN TOUCH

BBC World Service MHz 17.64, 15.58, 9.410, 6.195.

English-language newspapers *Georgian Times* (weekly).

EMERGENCIES

Red Cross/Crescent societies 15 Krilov St, 380002 Tbilisi, tel 32 954 282, fax 32 953 304.

UK/US/Canadian reps UK: Sheraton Palace Hotel, 380003 Tbilisi, tel 32 955 497, fax 32 001 065, email british.embassy@caucasus.net. US: 25 Ulitsa Atoneli, 380026 Tbilisi, tel 32 989 967, fax 32 933 759, email moodym@tbiliwpoa.us-state.gov. Canada: The Canadian Embassy in Ankara (Turkey) deals with enquiries relating to Georgia.

Global weather guide p 818, Rainy seasons worldwide p 829, Vaccinations required p 832, Recommended reading p 848, Dependent territories p 812.

GERMANY

STATE OF THE NATION

Safety Safe, apart from racist violence against non-white targets.

Life expectancy M 73.9, F 80.2.

PEOPLE AND PLACE

Capital Berlin.

Language German.

Peoples German (92%), other European and Turkish minorities.

Religion Protestant, Roman Catholic.

Size (km) 357,022.

Population 82,400,000.

Pop density/km 236.

Food Meals commonly based on meat, with typical dishes such as *Leberkäs* (pork and beef loaf) often served with dumplings. Sausages, from *Weisswurst* (white sausages), *Rostbratwurst*, to *Frankfurters* are popular. Beer is the national drink, although many German wines are notable.

TRAVEL PLANNING

When to go Temperate throughout the country with warm summers (May-September) and cold winters (November-March).

Medical care Free to UK citizens, with charge for prescribed medicines.

Currency Deutschmark = 100 pfennings. Single European Currency (Euro), currently only used as 'written money'. First Euro coins will be introduced in January 2002. The Deutschmark will be in circulation until Jul 2002. 1 Euro=DM 1.95583.

Finance Credit cards and travellers' cheques widely accepted.

Airports (And distances from nearest city): Berlin-Tergel (TXL) 8 km, Berlin-Schönefeld (SXF) 20 km, Berlin-Tempelhof (THF) 6 km, Cologne (CGN) 14 km, Düsseldorf (DUS) 8 km, Hamburg (HAM) 9 km, Munich (MUC) 28.5 km, Stuttgart (STR) 14 km, amongst others.

Internal travel Air, river, rail and road networks all well mantained and efficient in the western part, and is being improved in eastern Germany.

Business hours 0800-1600 Mon-Friday.

GMT +1 (+2 in summer).

Voltage guide 230 AC, 50 Hz.

RED TAPE

Visas (Aus/Canada/UK/US) None.

Reps in UK/US/Canada UK: 23 Belgrave Square, London SW1X 8PZ, tel 020 7824 1300, fax 020 7824 1435, email infoctr@german-embassy.org.uk. US: 4645 Reservoir Road, NW, Washington, DC 20007-1998, tel 202 298 8140, fax 202 298 4249. Canada: PO Box 379, Postal Station 'A', 1 Waverley Street, Ottawa, Ontario K2P 0T8, tel 613 232 1101, fax 613 594 9330, email 100566.2620@compuserve.com.

Customs regulations Duty free allowance: For visitors arriving from non-EU countries: 200 cigarettes or 100 cigarillos or 50 cigars or 250 g of tobacco, 1 ltr of spirits over 22% by volume or 2 ltrs of spirits or liquers under 22% by volume or 2 ltrs of sparkling or liquer wine, 2 ltrs of any other wine, 50 g of perfume or 250 ml of *eau de toilette*, 500 g of coffee or 200 g of coffee extracts, personal goods to the value of DM350. Alcohol and tobacco allowances are for travellers over 17. No limits on alcohol or tobacco imported for personal use within EU states.

Driving requirements International Driving Permit or national licence, car registration papers, insurance legally required.

KEEPING IN TOUCH

BBC World Service MHz 12.09, 9.410, 6.195, 0.648.

English-language newspapers None, but international press widely available.

EMERGENCIES

Red Cross/Crescent societies Postfach 1460, 53004 Bonn, tel 22 854 10, fax 22 854 112 90, email drk@drk.de.

UK/US/Canadian reps UK: Unter den Linden 32/34, 10117 Berlin, tel 30 201 840, fax 30 20 18 41 59. US: Neustädtische Kirchstraße 4, 10117 Berlin, tel 30 238 5174, fax 30 238 6290. Canada: Friedrichstraße 95, 23rd Floor, 10117 Berlin, tel 30 203 120, fax 30 20 31 25 90.

Global weather guide p 818, Rainy seasons worldwide p 829, Vaccinations required p 832, Recommended reading p 848, Dependent territories p 812.

GHANA

STATE OF THE NATION

SAFETY Usual petty crime, especially after dark. Otherwise relatively safe.

LIFE EXPECTANCY M 58.3, F 56.1.

PEOPLE AND PLACE

CAPITAL Accra.

LANGUAGE English.

PEOPLES Ashanti, Fanti, Mole-Dagbani, Ga-Adangbe, Ewe.

RELIGION Christianity, traditional beliefs, Islam.

SIZE (KM) 238,537.

POPULATION 18,900,000.

POP DENSITY/KM 82.

FOOD Dishes include traditional soups of palmnut and groundnut, *Kontomere* and *Okro* (stews) accompanied by *fufu* (pounded cassava).

TRAVEL PLANNING

WHEN TO GO Tropical, hot and humid. Rainy seasons from March-July, September-October.

MEDICAL CARE Adequate, but insurance recommended.

CURRENCY Cedi = 100 pesewas.

FINANCE Credit cards and travellers' cheques accepted in main towns.

AIRPORTS Accra (ACC) 10 km from the city.

INTERNAL TRAVEL Limited domestic air services and rail network - the rail service is a loop serving the coastal stri p and towns. Almost 40,000 km of roads. Car hire available but expensive.

BUSINESS HOURS 0800-1200, 1400-1700 Monday-Friday, 0830-1200 Saturday.

GMT GMT.

VOLTAGE GUIDE 220 AC, 50 Hz.

RED TAPE

VISAS (AUS/CANADA/UK/US) Required.

REPS IN UK/US/CANADA UK: 13 Belgrave Square, London SW1 8PN, tel 020 7201 5924/7, fax 020 7245 9552. US: 19 East 47th Street, New York, NY 10017, tel 212 832 1300, fax 212 751 6743, email ghanaembwash@cais.com. Canada: 1 Clemow Avenue, Ottawa, Ontario K1S 2A9, tel 613 236 0871, fax 613 236 0874.

CUSTOMS REGULATIONS Duty free allowance: 400 cigarettes or 100 cigars or 454 g of tobacco, 750 ml of spirits or 750 ml of wine, 227 ml of perfume, for travellers over 16. Duty must be paid on gifts. Prohibited: Animals, firearms, ammunition and explosives.

DRIVING REQUIREMENTS Intenational Driving Permit recommended. British driving licence valid for 90 days.

KEEPING IN TOUCH

BBC WORLD SERVICE MHz 17.89, 15.42, 11.60, 7.160.

ENGLISH-LANGUAGE NEWSPAPERS *The Ghanian Times, Daily Graphic, The Pioneer.*

EMERGENCIES

RED CROSS/CRESCENT SOCIETIES PO Box 835, Accra, tel 21 662 298, fax 21 667 226, email grcs@ghana.com.

UK/US/CANADIAN REPS UK: PO Box 296, Osu Link, off Gamel Abdul Nasser Road, Accra, tel 21 221 665, fax 21 701 0655, email high.commission@ accra.mail.fco.gov.uk. US: PO Box 194, Ring Road East, Accra, tel 21 775 347/8, fax 21 776 008. Canada: 46 Independence Avenue, Accra, tel 21 228 555, fax 21 773 792, email accra@accra01.x400.gc.ca.

Global weather guide p 818, Rainy seasons worldwide p 829, Vaccinations required p 832, Recommended reading p 848, Dependent territories p 812.

GREECE

STATE OF THE NATION

SAFETY Safe.

LIFE EXPECTANCY M 75.6, F 80.6.

PEOPLE AND PLACE

CAPITAL Athens.

LANGUAGE Greek.

PEOPLES Greek.

RELIGION Greek Orthodox.

SIZE (KM) 131,957.

POPULATION 10,600,000.

POP DENSITY/KM 81.

FOOD Charcoal grilled meat and kebabs, *dolmades* (stuffed vine leaves), *moussaka* and *avgolemono* (chicken broth with rice, eggs and lemon juice) found everywhere. Often preceded by a selection of *meze* (appetisers).

TRAVEL PLANNING

WHEN TO GO Warm Mediterranean climate with dry hot summers (April-September). Most rain falls between November-March.

MEDICAL CARE Refunds for hospital care for UK visitors can be obtained from IKA offices in Greece, but it will not be for more than 50% maximum, insurance strongly recommended.

CURRENCY Drachma (Dr)=100 lepta.

FINANCE Credit cards and travellers' cheques widely accepted.

AIRPORTS Athens (ATH) 14 km from the city. International airports on most major islands.

INTERNAL TRAVEL Cheap and easy to travel round the islands on frequent ferry and boat services. Good road network on the whole. Train services from Athens to northern Greece and Peloponnissos.

BUSINESS HOURS 0800-1430 Mon, Wed, Sat. 0800-1400, 1730-2030 Tue, Thu, Fri. (Shopping hours; business hours n/a)

GMT +2 (+3 in summer).

VOLTAGE GUIDE 220 AC, 50 Hz.

RED TAPE

VISAS (AUS/CANADA/UK/US) None.

REPS IN UK/US/CANADA UK: 1A Holland Park, London W11 3TP, tel 020 7229 3850, fax 020 7229 7221. US: 2221 Massachusetts Avenue, NW, Washington, DC 20008, tel 202 939 5818, fax 202 939 5824, email greece@greekembassy.org. Canada: 1170 place du Frére André, Suite 300, Montréal, Québec H3B 3C6, tel 514 875 2119, fax 514 875 8781, email con-grem@cite.net.

CUSTOMS REGULATIONS Duty free allowance for travellers over 18 as follows. For residents of European countries with goods bought duty-free outside the EU: 200 cigarettes or 50 cigars or 100 cigarillos or 250 g of tobacco, 1 ltr of alcoholic beverage over 22% or 2 ltrs of wine, 50 g of perfume and 250 ml of eau de cologne, gifts up to a total value of Dr 25,000. For residents of countries outside Europe with goods obtained duty-free outside the EU: 400 cigarettes or 200 cigarillos or 100 cigars or 500 g of tobacco, other items as above. Prohibited: Plants with soil. The export of antiquities is prohibited without permission of the Archaeological Service in Athens.

DRIVING REQUIREMENTS National driving licence acceptable for EU nationals, otherwise an International Driving Permit. EU nationals taking their own cars must obtain a Green Card.

KEEPING IN TOUCH

BBC WORLD SERVICE MHz 12.10, 9.410, 6.195, 3.955

ENGLISH-LANGUAGE NEWSPAPERS *Athens News, Athens Daily Post.*

EMERGENCIES

RED CROSS/CRESCENT SOCIETIES Rue Rycavittou 1, Athens 10672, tel 1 362 1681, fax 1 361 5666, email: hrc@ net-mode.ntua.gr.

UK/US/CANADIAN REPS UK: Odos Ploutarchou 1, 106 75 Athens, tel 1 723 6211, fax 1 727 2722, email britania@hol.gr. US: Leoforos Vassilissis Sophias 91, 101 60 Athens, tel 1 721 2951, fax 1 645 6282, email usembassy@usisathens.gr. Canada: Odos Ioannou Gennadiou 4, 115 21 Athens, tel 1 777 3400, fax 1 727 3460, email athns@ dfait-maeci.gc.ca.

Global weather guide p 818,   Rainy seasons worldwide p 829,   Vaccinations required p 832, Recommended reading p 848,   Dependent territories p 812.

GRENADA

STATE OF THE NATION

SAFETY Safe.

LIFE EXPECTANCY 71.

PEOPLE AND PLACE

CAPITAL St George's.

LANGUAGE English.

PEOPLES Of African descent. European and indigenous Indian minorities.

RELIGION Roman Catholic, Anglican.

SIZE (KM) 344.5.

POPULATION 98,600.

POP DENSITY/KM 290.

FOOD Specialities include seafood with vegetables, calaloo soup, crabs, conches (lambi), avocado ice-cream.

TRAVEL PLANNING

WHEN TO GO Tropical climate with a dry season from Jan-May.

MEDICAL CARE Adequate, but insurance advised because relocation to mainland may be necessary and payment is demanded for all treatment.

CURRENCY East Caribbean dollar (EC$).

FINANCE travellers' cheques widely accepted, limited acceptance of major credit cards.

AIRPORTS Point Salines International Airport (GND), 11 km from St George's.

INTERNAL TRAVEL Large fleet of charter yachts available for round-island trips. Most main roads in good condition. Car hire available in St George's and St Andrew's.

BUSINESS HOURS 0800-1330 Mon-Thurs, 0800-1600 Friday.

GMT -4.

VOLTAGE GUIDE 220/240 AC, 50 Hz.

RED TAPE

VISAS (AUS/CANADA/UK/US) None.

REPS IN UK/US/CANADA UK: 1 Collingham Gardens, London SW5 0HW, tel 020 7373 7809, fax 020 7370 7040, email grenada@high-commission.freeserve.co.uk. US: 1701 New Hampshire Avenue, NW, Washington, DC 20009, tel 202 265 2468, email gdaemb@worldnet.att.net. Canada: 439 University Avenue, Suite 930, Toronto, Ontario M5G 1Y8, tel 416 595 1343, fax 416 595 8278, email grenadator@sympatico.ca.

CUSTOMS REGULATIONS Duty free allowance: 200 cigarettes or 50 cigars or 225 g of tobacco, 1 ltr of wine or spirits . Prohibited: Narcotics, arms, ammunition, fruit and vegetables.

DRIVING REQUIREMENTS Temporary licences available on presentation of a valid driving licence.

KEEPING IN TOUCH

BBC WORLD SERVICE MHz 17.84, 15.22, 6.195, 5.975.

ENGLISH-LANGUAGE NEWSPAPERS *The Voice, Grenada Today, The Informer.*

EMERGENCIES

RED CROSS/CRESCENT SOCIETIES PO Box 551, St George's, tel 440 1483, fax 440 1829, email grercs@caribsurf.com.

UK/US/CANADIAN REPS UK: PO Box 56, 14 Church Street, St George's, tel 440 3222, fax 440 4939, email bhcgrenada@ caribsurf.com. US: PO Box 54, Lance aux Epines, St George's, tel 444 1173-6, fax 444 4820. Canada: The Canadian High Commission in Bridgetown (Barbados) deals with enquiries relating to Grenada.

Global weather guide p 818, Rainy seasons worldwide p 829, Vaccinations required p 832, Recommended reading p 848, Dependent territories p 812.

GUATEMALA

STATE OF THE NATION

SAFETY Possible low-level guerrilla conflict in some areas. Otherwise safe.

LIFE EXPECTANCY M 61.4, F 67.2.

PEOPLE AND PLACE

CAPITAL Guatemala City.

LANGUAGE Spanish.

PEOPLES Amerindian, Mestizo.

RELIGION Catholicism. Protestant minority.

SIZE (KM) 108,889.

POPULATION 11,600,000.

POP DENSITY/KM 107.

FOOD Traditional Central American food such as tortillas and tacos. Specialities include *Chiles rellenos* (stuffed chiles) and *pepián* (thick meat stew with vegetables).

TRAVEL PLANNING

WHEN TO GO Climate affected by altitude. Coastal regions and north-east hot all year. Rainy season May-September.

MEDICAL CARE Limited outside capital and all healthcare has to be paid for, insurance recommended.

CURRENCY Quetzal (Q) = 100 centavos.

FINANCE Visa, American Express accepted more widely than other cards. Limited acceptance of travellers' cheques.

AIRPORTS Guatemala City (GUA) 4 km from the city.

INTERNAL TRAVEL Air transport most eficient mode of internal travel. Extensive road network but less than a third of the roads are all-weather. Car hire available in Guatemala City.

BUSINESS HOURS 0800-1800 Mon-Friday, 0800-1200 Saturday.

GMT -6.

VOLTAGE GUIDE 110 AC, 60 Hz.

RED TAPE

VISAS (AUS/CANADA/UK/US) None.

REPS IN UK/US/CANADA UK: 13 Fawcett Street, London SW10 9HN, tel 020 7351 3042, fax 020 7376 5708, email 101740.3655@compuserve.com. US: 2220 R Street, NW, Washington, DC 20008, tel 202 745 4952-4, fax 202 745 1908, email info@guatemala-embassy.org. Canada: 130 Albert Street, Suite 1010, Ottawa, Ontario K1P 5G4, tel 613 233 7188, fax 613 233 0135, email embguate@webruler.com.

CUSTOMS REGULATIONS Duty free allowance: 80 cigarettes or 100 g of tobacco, 1.5 ltrs of alcoholic beverages, reasonable quantity of perfume (for travellers over 18). Prohibited: Fresh food.

DRIVING REQUIREMENTS Local licences issued on presentation of national licences.

KEEPING IN TOUCH

BBC WORLD SERVICE MHz 17.84, 15.22, 6.185, 5.975.

ENGLISH-LANGUAGE NEWSPAPERS *The Review, Guatemala Weekly.*

EMERGENCIES

RED CROSS/CRESCENT SOCIETIES 3a Calle 8-40, Zona 1, Guatemala City, tel 322 026/7, fax 324 649, email crg@guate.net.

UK/US/CANADIAN REPS UK: Avenida La Reforma 16-00 Calle Esquina Zona 10, Edificio Torre Internacional, Nivel 11, Guatemala City, tel 367 5425, fax 367 5430, email embassy@infovia.com.gt. US: Avenida La Reforma 7-01, zona 10, Guatemala City, tel 331 1541, fax 334 8477. Canada: 13 calle 8-44, zona 10, Paza Edyma, Guatemala City, tel 333 6102, fax 333 6153, email gtmla@dfait-maeci gc.ca.

Global weather guide p 818,   Rainy seasons worldwide p 829,   Vaccinations required p 832, Recommended reading p 848,   Dependent territories p 812.

GUINEA

STATE OF THE NATION

SAFETY High levels of street crime, do not carry valuables.

LIFE EXPECTANCY M 46, F 47.

PEOPLE AND PLACE

CAPITAL Conakry.

LANGUAGE French.

PEOPLES Fila (Fulani), Malinke, Soussou.

RELIGION Islam, Animist and Roman Catholic minorities.

SIZE (KM) 245, 857.

POPULATION 7, 700, 000.

POP DENSITY/KM 31.

FOOD Local dishes include *jollof rice* (rice with tomato puree, vegetables and spiced meat), stuffed chicken with groundnuts, spicy fish dishes served with rice.

TRAVEL PLANNING

WHEN TO GO Tropical and humid. Wet season from May-October, dry season from November-April.

MEDICAL CARE Limited, and all health treatments must be paid for, insurance recommended.

CURRENCY Guinea franc (F.G) = 100 centimes.

FINANCE Limited acceptance of credit cards and travellers' cheques.

AIRPORTS Conakry (CKY) 13 km from the city.

INTERNAL TRAVEL Rail travel is generally not recommended. Roads are generally in poor condition.

BUSINESS HOURS 0800-1630 Monday-Thursday, 0800-1300 Friday.

GMT GMT.

VOLTAGE GUIDE 220 AC, 50 Hz.

RED TAPE

VISAS (AUS/CANADA/UK/US) Required.

REPS IN UK/US/CANADA UK: n/a. US: 2112 Leroy Place, NW, Washington, DC 20008, tel 202 483 9420, fax 202 483 8688. Canada: 483 Wilbrod Street, Ottawa, Ontario K1N 6NI, tel 613 789 8444, fax 613 789 7560.

CUSTOMS REGULATIONS Duty free allowance: 1000 cigarettes or 250 cigars or 1 kg of tobacco, 1 bottle of alcoholic beverage (opened), a reasonable quantity of perfume.

DRIVING REQUIREMENTS International Driving Permit.

KEEPING IN TOUCH

BBC WORLD SERVICE MHz 17.83, 15.42, 11.86, 7.160.

ENGLISH-LANGUAGE NEWSPAPERS None.

EMERGENCIES

RED CROSS/CRESCENT SOCIETIES BP 376, Conakry, tel 443 825, fax 414 255.

UK/US/CANADIAN REPS UK: BP 834, Conakry, tel/fax 461 680. US: BP 603, 2nd Boulevard and 9th Avenue, Conakry, tel 411 520/1, fax 411 522. Canada: PO Box 99, Corniche Sud, Coleah, Conakry, tel 462 395, fax 464 235.

Global weather guide p 818, Rainy seasons worldwide p 829, Vaccinations required p 832, Recommended reading p 848, Dependent territories p 812.

GUINEA-BISSAU

STATE OF THE NATION

SAFETY Seek latest information at time of visit.

LIFE EXPECTANCY M 43.5, F 46.4.

PEOPLE AND PLACE

CAPITAL Bissau.

LANGUAGE Portugese.

PEOPLES Balante, Fulani, Malinke.

RELIGION Indigenous beliefs, Islam.

SIZE (KM) 36,125.

POPULATION 856,000.

POP DENSITY/KM 4.

FOOD Spicy chicken and fish dishes, *jollof rice* (rice with tomato puree, spiced meat and vegetables), cassava, yams and maize.

TRAVEL PLANNING

WHEN TO GO Tropical climate with a wet season June-October, dry December-April. High humidity July September.

MEDICAL CARE Limited, and immediate payment expected, insurance strongly recommended.

CURRENCY Communauté Financiare Africaine franc (CFA) = 100 centimes.

FINANCE Very limited use of credit cards, travellers' cheques rarely accepted.

AIRPORTS Bissau (OXB) 11 km from the city.

INTERNAL TRAVEL A few internal flights, some serving the outlying islands. Most towns are accessible by ship, riverboats or ferry. A small proportion of the roads all-weather.

BUSINESS HOURS 0730-1230, 1430-1830 Monday-Friday.

GMT GMT.

VOLTAGE GUIDE Limited supply on 220 AC, 50 Hz.

RED TAPE

VISAS (AUS/CANADA/UK/US) Required.

REPS IN UK/US/CANADA UK: 8 Palace Gate, London W8 5NF, tel 020 7589 5253, fax 020 7589 9590. US: Mezzanine Suite, 918 16th Street, NW, Washington, DC 20006, tel 202 347 3950, fax 202 872 4226. Canada: n/a.

CUSTOMS REGULATIONS Duty free allowance: A reasonable amount of tobacco products, 2.5 ltrs of alcoholic beverages (non-Muslims only), perfume in opened bottles.

DRIVING REQUIREMENTS International Driving Permit recommended. A temporary licence is available on presentation of a valid UK licence.

KEEPING IN TOUCH

BBC WORLD SERVICE MHz 17.83, 15.42, 11.86, 7.160.

ENGLISH-LANGUAGE NEWSPAPERS None.

EMERGENCIES

RED CROSS/CRESCENT SOCIETIES Caixa Postal 514-1036 BIX, Codex, Bissau, tel 202 408.

UK/US/CANADIAN REPS UK: CP 100, Bissau, tel 201 224, fax 201 265 (British Consulate, which can only provide limited assistance. The British Embassy in Dakar, Senegal, usually deals with enquiries relating to Guinea-Bissau) US: The US Embassy in Dakar (Senegal) deals with enquiries relating to Guinea-Bissau. Canada: The Canadian Embassy in Dakar (Senegal) deals with enquiries relating to Guinea-Bissau.

Global weather guide p 818, Rainy seasons worldwide p 829, Vaccinations required p 832, Recommended reading p 848, Dependent territories p 812.

GUYANA

STATE OF THE NATION

SAFETY Violent crime common in the capital.

LIFE EXPECTANCY M61.1, F 67.9.

PEOPLE AND PLACE

CAPITAL Georgetown.

LANGUAGE English.

PEOPLES Afro-Guyanese, Indo-Guyanese.

RELIGION Christian, Hindu. Muslim minority

SIZE (KM) 214, 969.

POPULATION 856, 000.

POP DENSITY/KM 4.

FOOD Mixed influences including Indian curries, African plaintain and coconut cooking, Portuguese stews and Amerindian dishes.

TRAVEL PLANNING

WHEN TO GO Warm and tropical all year, with generally high rainfall and humidity. Rainy seasons November-January and April-August.

MEDICAL CARE Limited supplies and hospital care, insurance recommended.

CURRENCY Guyanese dollar (G$) = 100 cents.

FINANCE Limited acceptance of credit cards. travellers' cheques not recommended for those wishing to change money quickly.

AIRPORTS Georgetown (GEO) 40 km from the city.

INTERNAL TRAVEL Air most reliable means of internal transport. Irregular river services. No scheduled passenger rail services. All-weather roads concentrated on eastern strip. Because of Guyana's many rivers, most journeys outside the capital will involve ferries and the attendant delays. Limited car hire in Georgetown.

BUSINESS HOURS 0800-1130, 1300-1630 Monday-Friday.

GMT -4.

VOLTAGE GUIDE 110 AC, 60 Hz.

RED TAPE

VISAS (AUS/CANADA/UK/US) None.

REPS IN UK/US/CANADA UK: 3 Palace Court, Bayswater Road, London W2 4LP, tel 020 7229 7684, fax 020 7727 9809. US: 3rd Floor, 866 UN Plaza, New York, NY 10017, tel 212 527 3215, fax 212 527 3229. Canada: Burnside Building, 151 Slater Street, Suite 309, Ottawa, Ontario, K1P 5H3, tel 613 235 7240, fax 613 235 1447, email guyanahcott@travel.net.com

CUSTOMS REGULATIONS Duty free allowance: 200 cigarettes or 50 cigars or 250 g of tobacco, spirits not exceeding 570 ml, wine not exceeding 570 ml, a reasonable amount of perfume (for travellers over 16).

DRIVING REQUIREMENTS International Driving Permit or foreign licence.

KEEPING IN TOUCH

BBC WORLD SERVICE MHz 17.84, 15.19, 6.195, 9.915.

ENGLISH-LANGUAGE NEWSPAPERS Local papers in English.

EMERGENCIES

RED CROSS/CRESCENT SOCIETIES PO Box 10524, Georgetown, tel 2 65174, email redcross@sdnp.org.gy.

UK/US/CANADIAN REPS UK: PO Box 10849, 44 Main Street, Georgetown, tel 2 65881, fax 2 53555. US: PO Box 10507, 100 Young and Duke Street, Kingston, Georgetown, tel 2 54900, fax 2 58497, email americanembassy@hotmail.com. Canada: PO Box 10880, High and Young Streets, Georgetown, tel 2 72081/2, fax 2 58380, email grgtn@dfait-maeci.gc.ca.

Global weather guide p 818, Rainy seasons worldwide p 829, Vaccinations required p 832, Recommended reading p 848, Dependent territories p 812.

HAITI

STATE OF THE NATION

SAFETY Highly unstable, subject to political violence and serious crime.

LIFE EXPECTANCY M 51.4, F 56.4.

PEOPLE AND PLACE

CAPITAL Port-au-Prince.

LANGUAGE French and Creole.

PEOPLES Mainly of African descent.

RELIGION Roman Catholic (80%), Protestant and other, including voodoo.

SIZE (KM) 27,750.

POPULATION 7,500,000.

POP DENSITY/KM 272.

FOOD Creole specialities combining French and African elements. Dishes include *langouste flambé* (local lobster), *grillot et banane pese* (pork chops and island bananas), *diri et djondjon* (rice and black mushrooms) and Guinea hen with sour orange sauce.

TRAVEL PLANNING

WHEN TO GO Tropical, with intermittent rain throughout the year.

MEDICAL CARE Unreliable, insurance strongly recommended.

CURRENCY Gourde = 100 centimes.

FINANCE American Express widely accepted, travellers' cheques generally accepted.

AIRPORTS Port-au-Prince (PAP) 8 km from the city.

INTERNAL TRAVEL Cancellations and delays common on scheduled internal flights. Planes may be chartered. All-weather roads from Port-au-Prince to Cap-Haiten and Jacmel. Car hire available in Port-au-Prince.

BUSINESS HOURS 0800-1600 Mon-Friday.

GMT -5.

VOLTAGE GUIDE 110 AC, 60 Hz.

RED TAPE

VISAS (AUS/CANADA/UK/US) Required by Australians.

REPS IN UK/USA/CANADA UK: The Embassy in Brussels is accredited to the UK (BP 25, 160A avenue Louise, B-1050 Brussels, Belgium, tel 2 649 7381, fax 2 640 6080). USA: 17th Floor, 271 Madison Avenue, New York, NY 10016, tel 212 697 9767, fax 212 681 6991, email haiti@dti.net. Canada: 112 Kent Street, Suite 205, Place de Ville, Tower B, Ottawa, Ontario, K1P 5P2, tel 613 238 1628/9, fax 613 238 2986.

CUSTOMS REGULATIONS Duty free allowance: 200 cigarettes or 50 cigars or 1 kg of tobacco, 1 ltr of spirits, small quantity of perfume or *eau de toilette* for personal use. Prohibited: Coffee, matches, methylated spirits, pork, all meat products from Brazil and the Dominican Republic, drugs and firearms (except sporting rifles with prior permission).

DRIVING REQUIREMENTS International Driving Permit.

KEEPING IN TOUCH

BBC WORLD SERVICE MHz 17.84, 15.22, 6.185, 5.975.

ENGLISH-LANGUAGE NEWSPAPERS None.

EMERGENCIES

RED CROSS/CRESCENT SOCIETIES CRH, BP 1337, Port-au-Prince, tel 231 035, fax 231 054, email croroha@haitiworld.com.

UK/USA/CANADIAN REPS UK: PO Box 1302, Hotel Montana, Bourdon, Port-au-Prince, tel 573 969, fax 574 048. USA: BP 1761, 5 boulevard Harry Truman, Port-au-Prince, tel 220 200, fax 231 641. Canada: BP Edifice Banque Nova Scotia, 18 route de Delmas, Port-au-Prince, tel 232 358, fax 238 720.

Global weather guide p 818, Rainy seasons worldwide p 829, Vaccinations required p 832, Recommended reading p 848, Dependent territories p 812.

HONDURAS

STATE OF THE NATION

SAFETY Usual petty crime.
LIFE EXPECTANCY M 67.5, F 72.3.

PEOPLE AND PLACE

CAPITAL Tegucigalpa.
LANGUAGE Spanish.
PEOPLES Mestizo. Small community of indigenous Indians.
RELIGION Roman Catholic.
SIZE (KM) 112,492.
POPULATION 6,100,000.
POP DENSITY/KM 55.
FOOD Typical dishes include *curiles* (seafood), tortillas, enchiladas, and *tamales de elote* (corn tamales).

TRAVEL PLANNING

WHEN TO GO Tropical climate with cooler weather in the mountains. Dry season from November-April, wet from May-October.
MEDICAL CARE Limited, insurance strongly recommended.
CURRENCY Lempira (La) = 100 centavos.
FINANCE Credit cards and travellers' cheques accepted.
AIRPORTS Tegucigalpa (TGU) 5 km from the city.
INTERNAL TRAVEL Frequent internal flights between Tegucigalpa and major towns. There are only three railways, mainly used for tansport between plantations. Some all-weather roads, and car hire is available at the airport.
BUSINESS HOURS 0800-1200, 1400-1700 Mon-Friday, 0800-1100 Saturday.
GMT -6.
VOLTAGE GUIDE 110/120/220 AC, 60 Hz.

RED TAPE

VISAS (AUS/CANADA/UK/US) None.
REPS IN UK/USA/CANADA UK: 115 Gloucester Place, London W1H 3PJ, tel 020 7486 4880, fax 020 7486 4550, email londres@ aol.com. USA: 3007 Tilden Street 4M, NW, Washington, DC 20008, tel 202 966 7702, fax 202 966 9751, email embhondu@ix.netcom.com. Canada: 151 Slater Street, Suite 805, Ottawa, Ontario K1P 5H3, tel 613 233 8900, fax 613 232 0193, email scastell@magmacom.com.
CUSTOMS REGULATIONS Duty free allowance: 200 cigarettes or 100 cigars or 454 g of tobacco, 2 bottles of alcoholic beverages, a reasonable amount of perfume for personal use, gifts up to a total value of US$ 1000.
DRIVING REQUIREMENTS Both foreign and international driving licences accepted.

KEEPING IN TOUCH

BBC WORLD SERVICE MHz 17.84, 15.22, 6.195, 5.975.
ENGLISH-LANGUAGE NEWSPAPERS *Honduras This Week.*

EMERGENCIES

RED CROSS/CRESCENT SOCIETIES 7a Calle, entre 1A, y 2A Avenidas, Comayagüela DC, tel 237 8876, fax 238 0185, email honducruz@datum.hn.

UK/USA/CANADIAN REPS UK: Apartado Postal 290, Edificio Palmira, 3er Piso, Colonia Palmira, Tegucigalpa, tel 232 0612, fax 232 5480, email rufus.legg@ tegucigalpa.mail.fco.gov.uk. USA: Avenida La Paz, Apdo 3453, Tegucigalpa, tel 238 5114, fax 236 9037. Canada: Apartado Postal 3552, Edificio Commercial Los Castonos, 60 Piso, Boulevard Morazan, Tegucigalpa, tel 232 6787.

Global weather guide p 818, Rainy seasons worldwide p 829, Vaccinations required p 832, Recommended reading p 848, Dependent territories p 812.

HUNGARY

STATE OF THE NATION

SAFETY Safe.

LIFE EXPECTANCY M 66.8, F 74.9.

PEOPLE AND PLACE

CAPITAL Budapest.

LANGUAGE Hungarian.

PEOPLES Magyar (90%), small groups of Slovaks, Germans, Romanies.

RELIGION Roman Catholic, Calvinist.

SIZE (KM) 93,030.

POPULATION 10,276,968.

POP DENSITY/KM 110.5.

FOOD Specialities include *halászlé* (fish soups) with pasta, *gulyás* or goulash soup and stuffed vegetables. Sweet pastries and *gundel palacsinta* (pancakes) are popular.

TRAVEL PLANNING

WHEN TO GO Spring and autumn are mild, summers are hot and winters are very cold with snowfall.

MEDICAL CARE Free health care for UK citizens.

CURRENCY Hungarian forint (Ft) = 100 fillér.

FINANCE Credit cards and travellers' cheques widely accepted.

AIRPORTS Budapest Ferihegy (BUD) 16 km from the city.

INTERNAL TRAVEL No scheduled internal air services. Efficient rail service and a good road network. Car hire is available at tourist offices and at the airport.

BUSINESS HOURS 0800 1630 Mon-Thurs, 0800-1400 Friday.

GMT +1 (+2 in summer).

VOLTAGE GUIDE 230 AC, 50 Hz.

RED TAPE

VISAS (AUS/CANADA/UK/US) Required by Australians.

REPS IN UK/USA/CANADA UK: 35 Eaton Place, London SW1X 8BY, tel 020 7235 2664, fax 020 7235 8630. USA: 3910 Shoemaker Street, NW, Washington, DC 2008, tel 202 362 6730, fax 202 966 8135, email huembwas@attmail.com. Canada: 299 Waverley Street, Ottawa, Ontario K2P 0V9, tel 613 230 2717, fax 613 230 7560, email h1embott@docuweb.ca.

CUSTOMS REGULATIONS Duty free allowance: 500 cigarettes or 100 cigars or 500 g of tobacco, 1 ltr of spirits, 1 ltr of wine and 5 litres of beer, gifts to the value of Ft270,0000.

DRIVING REQUIREMENTS Pink format EU licence accepted but International Driving Permit required if green licence held.

KEEPING IN TOUCH

BBC WORLD SERVICE MHz 15.58, 9.410, 6.195, 6.180.

ENGLISH-LANGUAGE NEWSPAPERS *Budapest Week, The Budapest Sun, The Hungarian Observer.*

EMERGENCIES

RED CROSS/CRESCENT SOCIETIES Magyar Vöröskereszt, 1367 Budapest 5, Pf 121, 1 331 3950, fax 1 533 988, email intdept@hrc.hu

UK/USA/CANADIAN REPS UK: Harmincad Utca 6, 1051 Budapest, tel 1 266 2888, fax 1 266 0907, email info@britemb.hu. USA: Szabadság tér 12, 1054 Budapest, tel 1 267 4400, fax 1 269 9337, email cons usembbudapest@pronet.hu. Canada: Budakeszi üt 32, 1121 Budapest, tel 1 275 1200, fax 1 275 1210.

Global weather guide p 818,   Rainy seasons worldwide p 829,   Vaccinations required p 832, Recommended reading p 848,   Dependent territories p 812.

ICELAND

STATE OF THE NATION

SAFETY Safe.

LIFE EXPECTANCY M 62.3, F 81.3.

PEOPLE AND PLACE

CAPITAL Reykjavik.

LANGUAGE Icelandic.

PEOPLES Icelandic.

RELIGION Evangelic Lutheran.

SIZE (KM) 103,000.

POPULATION 277,000.

POP DENSITY/KM 3.

FOOD Influenced by Scandinavian and European cuisines, and based heavily on fish and lamb. Salmon served in many forms, most popularly as *gravlax*. Specialities include *hangikjot* (smoked lamb) and *hardfiskur* (dried fish).

TRAVEL PLANNING

WHEN TO GO Mild summers (May-August) with nearly 24 hours of daylight. Very cold winters (November-March). The Aurora Borealis appears from the end of August. The weather can be very changeable throughout the year.

MEDICAL CARE Very good, insurance recommended.

CURRENCY Icelandic krona (Ikr) = 100 aurar.

FINANCE Credit cards and travellers' cheques widely accepted.

AIRPORTS Keflavik (REK) 51 km from Reykjavik.

INTERNAL TRAVEL Sea ferry services to all coastal ports. No rail system. Most roads are gravel. Use of headlights obligatory at all times. Car hire easily available.

BUSINESS HOURS 0800-1600 (summer) and 0900-1700 (winter), Mon-Friday.

GMT +1.

VOLTAGE GUIDE 220 AC, 50 Hz.

RED TAPE

VISAS (AUS/CANADA/UK/US) None.

REPS IN UK/USA/CANADA UK: 1 Eaton Terrace, London SW1W 8EY, tel 020 7590 1100, fax 020 7730 1683, email icemb.london@utn.stjr.is. USA: 1156 15th Street, Suite 1200, NW, Washington, DC 20005, tel 202 265 6653-5, fax 202 265 6656, email icembwash@utn.stjr.is. Canada: 250 Yonge Street, Suite 2400, Toronto, Ontario M5B 2M6, tel: 416 979 6740, fax 416 979 1234.

CUSTOMS REGULATIONS Duty free allowance: For passengers over 16 (tobacco products) or over 20 (alcoholic beverages) - 200 cigarettes or 250 g of tobacco products, 1 ltr of spirits or 1 ltr of wine (under 21%) or 12 bottles of beer (or a combination of two of these quantities). Prohibited: Drugs, firearms and uncooked meats.

DRIVING REQUIREMENTS International Driving Permit recommended. A temporary licence is available on presentation of a valid UK licence.

KEEPING IN TOUCH

BBC WORLD SERVICE MHz 12.01, 9.410, 6.195, 0.648.

ENGLISH-LANGUAGE NEWSPAPERS None, but international press available.

EMERGENCIES

RED CROSS/CRESCENT SOCIETIES Efstaleiti 9, 103 Reykjavik, tel 570 4000, fax 570 4010, email central@redcross.is.

UK/USA/CANADIAN REPS UK: Laufásvegur 31, 101 Reykjavik, tel 550 5100, fax 550 5105. USA: Laufásvegur 21, 101 Reykjavik, tel 562 9100, fax 562 9123, email usis@itn.is. Canada: Sudurlandsbraut 10, 108 Reykjavik, tel 568 0820, fax 568 0899, email cantrade@mmedia.is.

Global weather guide p 818, Rainy seasons worldwide p 829, Vaccinations required p 832, Recommended reading p 848, Dependent territories p 812.

INDIA

STATE OF THE NATION

SAFETY Safe, if sensible. Beware petty scams. Certain areas very unsafe (e.g. Kashmir and Bihar).

LIFE EXPECTANCY M 62.3, F 62.9.

PEOPLE AND PLACE

CAPITAL New Dehli.

LANGUAGE English, Hindi.

PEOPLES Indo-Aryan, Dravidian.

RELIGION Hindu (83%), Muslim, Sikh, Christian and Buddhist minorities.

SIZE (KM) 3,287,263.

POPULATION 976,000,000.

POP DENSITY/KM 328.

FOOD Scores of regional variations far removed from the *korma/madras/vindaloo* school of Indian restaurants the world over. Curries are based on individual *masalas*, each containing a unique blend of freshly ground spices. More meat dishes in the north, generally served with breads - *nan*, *chapatis* or *pooris*, mainly fish and vegetarian in the south, served with rice. *Chai* - tea ready brewed with milk and sugar - is the most popular drink.

TRAVEL PLANNING

WHEN TO GO Coolest from December-February, with fresh mornings and dry, sunny days. Very hot March-May. Monsoon rains June-September.

MEDICAL CARE Good in some places, limited in others, insurance recommended.

CURRENCY Rupee (Rs) = 100 paise.

FINANCE Credit cards and travellers' cheques accepted in most cities.

AIRPORTS (And distances from nearest city) Mumbai (BOM) 29 km, Calcutta (CCU) 13 km, Dehli (DEL), Chennai (MAA) 14 km .

INTERNAL TRAVEL Domestic air network connects over 70 cities. Second-largest rail system in the world, relatively inexpensive. Cars with drivers available for hire, self-drive cars not generally available.

BUSINESS HOURS 0930-1700 Mon-Friday, 0930-1300 Saturday.

GMT +5.30.

VOLTAGE GUIDE 220 AC, 50 Hz. Some areas have a DC supply.

RED TAPE

VISAS (AUS/CANADA/UK/US) Required.

REPS IN UK/USA/CANADA UK: India House, Aldwych, London WC2B 4NA, tel 020 7836 8484, fax 020 7836 4331. USA: 3 East, 64th Street, New York, NY 10021, tel 212 774 0600, fax 212 861 3788, email indiapvny@aol.com. Canada: 10 Springfield Road, Ottawa, Ontario K1M 1C9, tel 613 744 3751-3, fax 613 744 0913, email: hicomind@ottawa.net.

CUSTOMS REGULATIONS Duty free allowance: For passengers over 17, 200 cigarettes or 50 cigars or 250 g of tobacco, 1 ltr of alcoholic beverage, 250 ml of *eau de toilette*, goods for personal use or gifts to a value of Rs 750. Prohibited: Narcotics, plants, gold and silver bullion and coins not in current use.

DRIVING REQUIREMENTS International Driving Permit.

KEEPING IN TOUCH

BBC WORLD SERVICE MHz 17.64, 15.58, 12.10, 9.410.

ENGLISH-LANGUAGE NEWSPAPERS *The Times of India, Indian Express, The Hindu, Hindustan Times, The Telegraph.*

EMERGENCIES

RED CROSS/CRESCENT SOCIETIES Red Cross Building, Red Cross Road, New Dehli 110 001, tel 11 371 6441-3, fax 11 371 7454, email indcross@vsnl.com.

UK/USA/CANADIAN REPS UK: Shanti Path, Chanakyapuri, New Dehli 110 021, tel 11 687 2161, fax 11 687 0065. USA: Shanti Path, Chanakyapuri, New Dehli 110 021, tel 11 688 9033, fax 11 419 0017. Canada: 7/8 Shanti Path, Chanakyapuri, New Dehli 110 021, tel 11 687 6500, fax 11 687 0031, email: dehli@dehli01.x400.gc.ca.

Global weather guide p 818, Rainy seasons worldwide p 829, Vaccinations required p 832, Recommended reading p 848, Dependent territories p 812.

INDONESIA

STATE OF THE NATION

SAFETY Seriously volatile. Many islands have experienced rioting and murder due to ethnic/religious conflict and political tensions. Authorities unable to guarantee safety in some areas. Seek latest information at time of visit.

LIFE EXPECTANCY M 63.3, F 67.

PEOPLE AND PLACE

CAPITAL Jakarta.

LANGUAGE Bahasa Indonesian.

PEOPLES
Many island peoples, including Javanese, Sundanese, Malays, Madurese and Chinese.

RELIGION Muslim (87%), Christian, Hindu, Buddhist.

SIZE (KM) 1,919,317.

POPULATION 198,342,900.

POP DENSITY/KM 114.

FOOD Rice is the staple diet for most Indonesians, and is served in a variety of ways. One of the most popular is the Dutch influenced *rijstafel*, with a combination of meat, fish and vegetable curries. Satay and seafood are also common. Each island has regional specialities, from *gado-gado* in Java (a salad of raw and cooked vegetables and peanuts) to *babi guling* in Bali (roast suckling pig)

TRAVEL PLANNING

WHEN TO GO Tropical climate varies across the huge archipelago. Driest June-September, rainiest December-March.

MEDICAL CARE Limited outside cities, insurance with repatriation cover recommended.

CURRENCY Rupiah = 100 sen.

FINANCE Mastercard, Amex and visa accepted in cities; for remote areas take US dollars in small bills.

AIRPORTS Jakarta (CGK) 20 km from city. For Bali, Denpasar (DPS) 13 km is 13 km from city.

INTERNAL TRAVEL Extensive local flight network of Garuda Indonesia (national a ir-line) is good for island-hopping. Sea ferries operate slowly but efficiently. Larger islands have railways and good roads. Local buses goor for remoter places.

BUSINESS HOURS Private businesses 0900-1700 Mon-Friday. Government offices 0800-1430 Mon-Thurs, 0800-1200 Friday.

GMT +7.

VOLTAGE GUIDE 220 AC, 50 Hz (rural areas 110 AC, 50 Hz).

RED TAPE

VISAS (AUS/CANADA/UK/US) Not required for up to 60 days tourism for Australia, Canada, EU, USA. Required for all journalists and businesspeople.

REPS IN UK/USA/CANADA UK: 38 Grosvenor Square, London W1X 9AD, tel 020 7499 7661, fax 020 7491 4993. USA: 5 East 68th St, New York, NY 10021, tel 212 879 0600, fax 212 570 6206. Canada: 55 Parkville Ave, Ottawa, Ontario K1Y 1E5, tel 613 724 1100, fax 613 724 1105, email info@prica.org.

CUSTOMS REGULATIONS Duty free allowance: For over 18: 200 cigarettes or 50 cigars or 100 g tobacco, less than 2 litres alcohol opened, reasonable qty perfume, gifts worth US$100. Prohibited: Weapons and ammunition, non-prescription drugs, TV sets, some electronic equipment, cordless telephones, fresh fruit, Chinese publications/medicines, pornography.

DRIVING REQUIREMENTS International Driving Permit.

KEEPING IN TOUCH

BBC WORLD SERVICE MHz 15.28, 7.160, 6.195, 3.195.

ENGLISH-LANGUAGE NEWSPAPERS Many, notably *The Indonesian Times*, *Indonesian Observer*, *Jakarta Post*, *Bali Post*.

EMERGENCIES

RED CROSS/CRESCENT SOCIETIES PO Box 2009, Jakarta, tel 21 799 23 25, fax 21 799 5188.

UK/USA/CANADIAN REPS UK: Deutsche Bank Building, 19th floor, J1 Iman Bonjol 80, Jakarta 10310, tel 21 390 748 487, fax 21 316 0858. USA: Jalan Merdeka Selatan 4-5, Jakarta 10110, tel 21 344 2211, fax 21 386 2259. Canada: 5th floor, Wisma Metropolitan, Jalan Jendral Sudirman, Jakarta 12084, tel 21 525 0709, fax 21 571 2251.

Global weather guide p 818, Rainy seasons worldwide p 829, Vaccinations required p 832, Recommended reading p 848, Dependent territories p 812.

IRAN

STATE OF THE NATION

SAFETY Generally welcoming and safe. Observe Islamic customs strictly. Note that there is a total ban on video cameras.

LIFE EXPECTANCY M 60.9, F 63.9.

PEOPLE AND PLACE

CAPITAL Tehran

LANGUAGE Farsi.

PEOPLES Persian (50%), Azeri, Lur and Bakhtiari, Kurd, Arab.

RELIGION Shi'a Muslim (95%), Sunni Muslim.

SIZE (KM) 1,648,000.

POPULATION 73,100,000.

POP DENSITY/KM 36.4.

FOOD Rice based dishes, including chelo khoresh (rice topped with vegetables and meat in a nut sauce), polo sabzi (pilau rice with fresh herbs) and adas polo (rice, lentils and meat). Other popular dishes are kofte gusht (meatloaf) and badinjan (mutton and aubergine stew). The consumption of alcohol is strictly forbidden.

TRAVEL PLANNING

WHEN TO GO Dry and hot April-October, harsh winter December-February.

MEDICAL CARE Very limited outside the capital.

CURRENCY Iranian rial (IR) = 100 dinars.

FINANCE Travellers' cheques not usually accepted. Unlimited foreign currency can be imported.

AIRPORTS Tehran (THR) 5 km from city.

INTERNAL TRAVEL Good road network between main towns. Some railways.

BUSINESS HOURS 0800-1600 Sat-Wed, closed Thurs-Friday.

GMT +3.5

VOLTAGE GUIDE 220 AC, 50 Hz.

RED TAPE

VISAS (AUS/CANADA/UK/US) Required.

REPS IN UK/USA/CANADA UK: 50 Kensington Court, Kensington High St, London W8 5DB, tel 020 7937 5225, fax 020 7938 1615. USA: Pakistani embassy in Washington handles Iranian enquiries. Canada: 245 Metcalfe St, Ottawa, Ontario K2P 2K2, tel 613 235 4729, fax 613 232 5712.

CUSTOMS REGULATIONS Duty free allowance: 200 cigarettes, reasonable qty perfume, gifts on which import duty/tax does not exceed US$80. Prohibited: Alcohol, narcotics, guns and ammunition, aerial cameras, most CDs/films/videos/cassettes, any fashion magazines, pornography, transmitter-receiver equipment.

DRIVING REQUIREMENTS *Carnet de passage*, International Certificate of Vehicle Ownership, personal insurance. An International Driving Permit may prove useful but is not legally recognised.

KEEPING IN TOUCH

BBC WORLD SERVICE MHz 15.58, 12.10, 11.76, 9.410.

ENGLISH-LANGUAGE NEWSPAPERS *Teheran Times, Keyhan International, Iran News, Iran Daily*.

EMERGENCIES

RED CROSS/CRESCENT SOCIETIES Ostad Nejatollahi Avenue, Tehran, tel 21 884 9077, fax 21 884 9079, email helal@www.dci.co.ir.

UK/USA/CANADIAN REPS UK: 143 Ferdowsi Ave, tehran 11344, tel 21 670 0720, fax 21 670 5011. USA: n/a. Canada: 57 Shahid Sarafraz St, Ostad Motahari Ave, tehran, tel 21 873 2623, fax 21 873 3202.

Global weather guide p 818, Rainy seasons worldwide p 829, Vaccinations required p 832, Recommended reading p 848, Dependent territories p 812.

IRAQ

STATE OF THE NATION

SAFETY Highly dangerous. Possible hostility to Westerners. UK Foreign Office advise against travel. Seek latest information at time of visit.

LIFE EXPECTANCY M 60.9, F 63.9.

PEOPLE AND PLACE

CAPITAL Baghdad.

LANGUAGE Arabic.

PEOPLES Arab (79%), Kurdish, Persian, Turkoman.

RELIGION Shi'a Muslim (62%), Sunni Muslim (33%), Christian.

SIZE (KM) 438,317.

POPULATION 21,800,000.

POP DENSITY/KM 40.8.

FOOD Middle Eastern cuisine. Popular dishes include *quozi* (small lamb boiled whole and grilled, stuffed with rice, minced meat and spices), *tikka* (small cubes of charcoal-grilled mutton) and *dolma* (vine leaves, cabbage, lettuce, onions, aubergine, marrow or cucumbers stuffed with rice, meat and spices)

TRAVEL PLANNING

WHEN TO GO South has desert climate, hot and dry March-October, mild winters December-February. North has the same summers, but winter is harsh in the mountains.

MEDICAL CARE Limited. Insurance should include repatriation cover.

CURRENCY Iraqi dinar (ID) = 20 dirhams.

FINANCE Credit cards and travellers' cheques not widely used. Unlimited foreign currency can be imported.

AIRPORTS All air travel into Iraq is currently prohibited by the UN. Nearest permitted international airport is Amman in Jordan, 15 hours by road from Baghdad. If sanctions are lifted, use Baghdad (BGW) airport, 18 km from the city.

INTERNAL TRAVEL No land crossing into Kuwait. No internal flights at present. Good railway and road network.

BUSINESS HOURS 0800-1400 Sat-Wed,

0800-1300 Thursday, closed Friday.

GMT +3.

VOLTAGE GUIDE 220 AC, 50 Hz.

RED TAPE

VISAS (AUS/CANADA/UK/US) Required. Currently only being issued for business travel, not tourism. No Israeli passports or visa stamps.

REPS IN UK/USA/CANADA UK: 21 Queen's Gate, London SW7 5JG, tel 020 7584 7141, fax 020 7584 7716. USA: c/o Algerian Embassy, Washington. Canada: 215 McLeod St, Ottawa, Ontario K2P 0Z8, tel 613 236 9177, fax 613 567 1101.

CUSTOMS REGULATIONS Duty free allowance: 200 cigarettes or 50 cigars or 250 g tobacco, 1 ltr wine or spirits, 500 ml perfume. Prohibited: Electrical appliances other than personal effects, many fruits and plants.

DRIVING REQUIREMENTS International Driving Permit and third-party insurance.

KEEPING IN TOUCH

BBC WORLD SERVICE MHz 15.58, 11.76, 9.410, 6.195.

ENGLISH-LANGUAGE NEWSPAPERS *Baghdad Observer.*

EMERGENCIES

RED CROSS/CRESCENT SOCIETIES POBox 6143, Baghdad, tel 1 886 2191.

UK/USA/CANADIAN REPS UK: n/a. USA: c/o Polish Embassy, PO Box 2051, Hay Al-Wihda, Mahalla 904, Zuqaq 60, House 324, Baghdad, tel 1 719 0296, fax 1 719 0297. Canada: n/a.

Global weather guide p 818, Rainy seasons worldwide p 829, Vaccinations required p 832, Recommended reading p 848, Dependent territories p 812.

IRELAND

STATE OF THE NATION

SAFETY Safe, apart from areas affected by low-level civil conflict.

LIFE EXPECTANCY M 73.6, F 79.2.

PEOPLE AND PLACE

CAPITAL Dublin.

LANGUAGE English and Gaelic.

PEOPLES Irish (95%).

RELIGION Roman Catholic.

SIZE (KM) 70, 285.

POPULATION 3, 600, 000.

POP DENSITY/KM 52.

FOOD Ireland is noted for good meat, bacon and dairy produce. Irish Stew, *Colcannon* (mashed potatoes and cabbage cooked together), *crubeens* (pigs trotters) and soda bread are national favourites, and Irish oysters are notable, and often served with Guiness.

TRAVEL PLANNING

WHEN TO GO Warm summers between June and September, temperatures from October to March are much cooler. Rain falls all year.

MEDICAL CARE Free to UK citizens.

CURRENCY Irish punt (R£) = 100 pence.

FINANCE Credit cards and travellers' cheques widely accepted.

AIRPORTS Dublin Airport (DUB) 8 km from the city, Shannon (SNN) 26 km from Limerick, Cork (ORK) 8 km from the city.

INTERNAL TRAVEL EU-funded projects have improved roads, particularly around Dublin.

BUSINESS HOURS 0900-17.30 Monday-Friday.

GMT GMT.

VOLTAGE GUIDE 220 AC, 50 Hz.

RED TAPE

VISAS (AUS/CANADA/UK/US) None.

REPS IN UK/USA/CANADA UK: 17 Grosvenor Place, London SW1X 7HR, tel 020 7235 2171, fax 020 7245 6961. USA: 2234 Massachusetts Avenue, NW, Washington, DC 20008, tel 202 462 3939, fax 202 232 5993, email embirlus@aol.com Canada: 130 Albert Street, Suite 1105, Ottawa, Ontario K1P 5G4, tel 613 233 6381, fax 613 233 5835, email emb.ireland@sympatico.ca

CUSTOMS REGULATIONS Duty free allowance: For passengers over 17 with goods bought duty/tax free outside the EU: 200 cigarettes or 100 cigarillos or 50 cigars or 250 g of tobacco, 1 ltr of spirits over 22% or 2 ltrs of other alcoholic beverages, including sparkling or fortified wine, plus 2 ltrs of table wine, 50 g of perfume and 250 ml of *eau de toilette*, goods to the value IR£142 (IR£73 for passengers under 15 years old). There are no limits on tobacco and alcohol imported within the EU for personal use only. Prohibited: Meat, dairy products and raw vegetables.

DRIVING REQUIREMENTS International Driving Permit. For EU nationals: full EU driving licence and motor registration book. A Green Card strongly recommended. Vehicles must have nationality coding stickers.

KEEPING IN TOUCH

BBC WORLD SERVICE MHz 12.10, 9.410, 6.195, 0.648.

ENGLISH-LANGUAGE NEWSPAPERS Several, including *The Irish Times* and the *Irish Independent*.

EMERGENCIES

RED CROSS/CRESCENT SOCIETIES 16, Merrion Square, Dublin 2, tel 1 676 5135, fax 1 661 4461, email redcross@iol.ie.

UK/USA/CANADIAN REPS UK: 29 Merrion Road, Ballsbridge, Dublin 4, tel 1 205 3700, fax 1 205 3885, email bembassy@internet-ireland.ie. USA: 42 Elgin Road, Ballsbridge, Dublin 4, tel 1 668 9946, fax 1 668 9946. Canada: 65 St Stephen's Green, Dublin 2, tel 1 478 1988, fax 1 478 1285, email cdnembsy@iol.ie.

Global weather guide p 818, Rainy seasons worldwide p 829, Vaccinations required p 832, Recommended reading p 848, Dependent territories p 812.

ISRAEL

STATE OF THE NATION

Safety Mainly safe, but significant unrest in some areas due to ethnic conflict. Seek latest information at time of visit.

Life expectancy M 75.7, F 79.7.

PEOPLE AND PLACE

Capital Jerusalem.

Language Hebrew and Arabic.

Peoples Jewish (82%), Arab.

Religion Jewish. Sunni Muslim minority.

Size (km) 22,145.

Population 5,900,000.

Pop density/km 290.

Food A combination of Oriental and Western cuisines, as well as diverse dishes reflecting the previous nationalities of many Israelis - Russian *bortsch*, Viennese *schnitzel*, Hungarian *goulash* and Middle Eastern dishes such as *falafel* (chickpea fritters). Traditonal Jewish food includes *gefilte* fish, chopped liver and chicken soup.

TRAVEL PLANNING

When to go November-March is wet, but mild. Hot and dry from June-September.

Medical care Very good but insurance recommended.

Currency New shekel (IS) = 100 agorots.

Finance All major credit cards and travellers' cheques accepted.

Airports Tel Aviv (TLV) 14 km from the city, Eilat Central Airport (ETH) 8 km from the city.

Internal travel Excellent roads link all Israeli towns. Railroads are being extended. Ferries run across the Sea of Galilee. Car hire is available in major cities.

Business hours 0830-1200, 1600-1800 Sunday-Tuesday &Thursday, 0830-1230 Wednesday, 0830-1200 Friday .

GMT +2 (+3 from March to September).

Voltage guide 220 AC, 50 Hz.

RED TAPE

Visas (Aus/Canada/UK/US) None.

Reps in UK/USA/Canada UK: 15a Old Court Place, London W8 4QB, tel 020 7957 9500, fax 020 7957 9577, email consulate@israel-embassy.org.uk. USA: 3514 International Drive, NW, Washington, DC 20008, tel 202 364 5500, fax 202 364 5423, email ask@israelemb.org. Canada: Suite 1005, 50 O'Connor Street, Ottawa, Ontario K1P 6L2. tel 613 567 6450, fax 613 237 8865, email embisrott@cyberus.ca.

Customs regulations Duty free allowance: 250 cigarettes or 250 g of tobacco products, 1 ltr of spirits and 2 ltrs of wine, 250 ml of *eau de cologne* or perfume, gifts up to the value of US$125 (for travellers over 17). Prohibited: Firearms, animals, fresh meat, plants and seeds may not be imported without prior permission.

Driving requirements Full driving licence and insurance. An International Driving Permit is recommended.

KEEPING IN TOUCH

BBC World Service MHz 15.57, 11.76, 9.410, 6.195.

English-language newspapers *Jerusalem Post.*

EMERGENCIES

Red Cross/Crescent societies n/a.

UK/USA/Canadian reps UK: 6th Floor, Migdalor Building, 1 Ben Yehuda Street, Tel Aviv 63801, tel 3 510 0166, fax 3 510 1167, email bricontv@netvision.net.il. USA: 71 Rehov Hayarkon, Tel Aviv 63903, tel 3 519 7575, fax 3 517 3227, email usisisrl@usis-israel.org.il. Canada: 3 Nirim Street, Tel Aviv 67060, tel 3 636 3300, fax 3 636 3380.

Global weather guide p 818, Rainy seasons worldwide p 829, Vaccinations required p 832, Recommended reading p 848, Dependent territories p 812.

ITALY

STATE OF THE NATION

SAFETY Safe.

LIFE EXPECTANCY M 75, F 81.2.

PEOPLE AND PLACE

CAPITAL Rome.

LANGUAGE Italian.

PEOPLES Italian (94%).

RELIGION Roman Catholic.

SIZE (KM) 301,323.

POPULATION 57,268,578.

POP DENSITY/KM 188.4.

FOOD Although pasta, pizza, risotto, *minestre* (soups)and meat dishes can be found all over Italy, regions specialise in dishes based on local produce. Risottos are a northern dish, a classic example is *risotto alla milanese* (with saffron and white wine). Liguria is famous for pesto sauce made from local basil, Tuscany for bean soups and *bistecca alla fiorentina* (massive T-bone steaks grilled over charcoal), Umbria for truffles, Naples for pizzas.. More rice and dairy products are used in the north, the south uses tomato based sauces and seafood.

TRAVEL PLANNING

WHEN TO GO Hot from June-September, especially in the South. April-May, September October are generally mild. Mountain regions are cooler with heavy snow in winter.

MEDICAL CARE Good, but free treatment for emergencies only, insurance recommended.

CURRENCY Italian lira (L).

FINANCE Credit cards and travellers' cheques widely accepted.

AIRPORTS (And distances from nearest city) Rome, Fiumicino (FCO) 26 km, Bologna (BLQ) 6 km, Genoa (GOA) 6km, Milan, Malpensa (MXP) 45 km, Milan, Linate (LIN) 10 km, Naples (NAP) 7 km, Pisa (PSA) 2 km, Palermo (PMO) 30 km, Turin (TRN) 30 km, Venice (VCE) 10 km.

INTERNAL TRAVEL The Italian State Railways run a nationwide network at reasonable fares. Italian roads are often congested.

Car hire available in most cities and resorts.

BUSINESS HOURS 0900-1700 Mon-Friday.

GMT +1 (+2 in summer).

VOLTAGE GUIDE 220 AC, 50 Hz.

RED TAPE

VISAS (AUS/CANADA/UK/US) None.

REPS IN UK/USA/CANADA UK: 38 Eaton Place, London SW1X 8AN, tel 020 7235 9371, fax 020 7823 1609. USA: 690 Park Avenue, New York, NY 10021, tel 212 737 9100, fax 212 249 4945, email ItalConsNY@aol.com Canada: 21st Floor, 275 Slater Street, Ottawa, Ontario K1P 5H9, tel 613 232 2401, fax 613 233 1484.

CUSTOMS REGULATIONS Duty free allowance: For passengers over 17 from non-EU countries, 200 cigarettes or 50 cigars or 100 cigarillos or 250 g of tobacco, 750 ml of spirits over 22% or 2 ltrs of fortified or sparkling wine, 60 g of perfume and 250 ml of *eau de toilette*, 500 g of coffee or 200 g of coffee extract, 100 g of tea or 40 g of tea extract. No limits on importing tobacco and alcohol products for personal use within the EU.

DRIVING REQUIREMENTS International Green Card or other insurance. UK driving licence or EU pink formatlicences are valid but green-coloured licences must be accompanied by an International Driving Permit.

KEEPING IN TOUCH

BBC WORLD SERVICE MHz 12.10, 9.410, 6.195, 0.648.

ENGLISH-LANGUAGE NEWSPAPERS None, but international press easily available.

EMERGENCIES

RED CROSS/CRESCENT SOCIETIES Via Toscana 12, I-00187 Rome, tel 6 47591, fax 6 4424 4534.

UK/USA/CANADIAN REPS UK: Lungarno Corsini 2, 50123, Florence, tel 55 284 133, fax 55 219 112 USA: Via Vittorio Veneto 119A, 00187 Rome, tel 6 46741, fax6 4674 2356. Canada: Via Zara 30, 00198 Rome, tel 6 4459 8594, fax 6 4459 8905.

Global weather guide p 818, Rainy seasons worldwide p 829, Vaccinations required p 832, Recommended reading p 848, Dependent territories p 812.

JAMAICA

STATE OF THE NATION

SAFETY High murder rate, but generally safe for tourists.

LIFE EXPECTANCY M 72.9, F 76.8.

PEOPLE AND PLACE

CAPITAL Kingston.

LANGUAGE English.

PEOPLES African descent. Indian, Arab European and Chinese minorities.

RELIGION Mixed Christian (Church of God, Baptist, Anglican) and mixed beliefs, including Rastafarian.

SIZE (KM) 10,991.

POPULATION 2,500,000.

POP DENSITY/KM 231.

FOOD Firey, with pungent spices and peppers. Salt fish (dried cod) with *ackee* (the cooked fruit of the ackee tree), curried goat and rice, 'rice and peas' (rice with kidney beans, coconut milk and spring onions), pepperpot soup (salt pork, salt beef, okra and kale) and patties filled with spiced ground beef are all popular dishes.

TRAVEL PLANNING

WHEN TO GO Rainy between May and October, tropical for the rest of the year. Temperate in higher regions.

MEDICAL CARE Adequate, but insurance recommended.

CURRENCY Jamaican dollar (J$) = 100 cents.

FINANCE Credit cards and travellers' cheques accepted.

AIRPORTS Norman Manley International, Kingston (KIN) 17 km from the city, Montego Bay (MBJ) 3 km from the city.

INTERNAL TRAVEL Kingston harbour has been expanded. Main roads encircle the island and car hire is easily available.

BUSINESS HOURS 0830-1630 Mon-Friday.

GMT -5.

VOLTAGE GUIDE 110 AC, 50 Hz. Some hotel supply 220 AC, 50 Hz.

RED TAPE

VISAS (AUS/CANADA/UK/US) None.

REPS IN UK/USA/CANADA UK: 1-2 Prince Consort Road, London SW7 2BZ, tel 020 7823 9911, fax 020 7589 5154. USA: 767 Third Avenue, 2nd Floor, New York, NY 10017, tel 212 935 9000, fax 212 936 7507. Canada: Suite 800, 275 Slater Street, Ottawa, Ontario K1P 5H9, tel 613 233 9311, fax 613 233 0611, email jhcott@sympatico.ca.

CUSTOMS REGULATIONS Duty free allowance: 200 cigarettes or 50 cigars or 250 g of tobacco, 1 ltr of spirits (excluding rum), 1 ltr of wine, 340 ml *eau de toilette*, 150 g of perfume. Prohibited: Explosives, firearms, dangerous drugs (including marijuana), meat, flowers, fresh fruit, rum, vegetables (unless canned), honey, coffee in any form.

DRIVING REQUIREMENTS Full UK driving licence valid.

KEEPING IN TOUCH

BBC WORLD SERVICE MHz 17.84, 15.22, 6.195, 5.975.

ENGLISH-LANGUAGE NEWSPAPERS The *Jamaica Herald, The Daily Star.*

EMERGENCIES

RED CROSS/CRESCENT SOCIETIES 76 Arnold Road, Kingston 5, tel 984 78602, fax 984 8272, email jrcs@infochan.com.

UK/USA/CANADIAN REPS UK: PO Box 575, 28 Trafalgar Road, Kingston 10, tel 926 9050, fax 929 7869, email bhkingston@toj.com. USA: 3rd Floor, Jamaica Mutual Life Center, 2 Oxford Road, Kingston 5, tel 929 4850/9, fax 935 6019. Canada: PO Box 1500, National Commercial Bank Building, 30-36 Knutsford Boulevard, Kingston 5, tel 926 1500, fax 926 1702.

Global weather guide p 818, Rainy seasons worldwide p 829, Vaccinations required p 832, Recommended reading p 848, Dependent territories p 812.

JAPAN

STATE OF THE NATION

SAFETY Safe.

LIFE EXPECTANCY M 76.8, F 82.9.

PEOPLE AND PLACE

CAPITAL Tokyo.

LANGUAGE Japanese.

PEOPLES Japanese (99%).

RELIGION Shinto and Buddhist.

SIZE (KM) 377,829.

POPULATION 125,900,000.

POP DENSITY/KM 334.

FOOD Delicate flavours, crisp vegetables, bean curd and rice are the basis of Japanese food. Specialities include *tempura* (vegetables or seafood fried in a light batter), *teriyaki* (marinated chicken, beef or fish seared on a hot plate) and *sushi* - raw seafood served on lightly vinegared rice). Sake, hot rice wine, is popular.

TRAVEL PLANNING

WHEN TO GO Summer is between June and September and ranges from warm to very hot, while spring and autumn are generally mild across the country. Typhoons are likely to occur in September or October but rarely last more than a day.

MEDICAL CARE Very good, but expensive. Insurance strongly recommended.

CURRENCY Yen.

FINANCE Major credit cards widely used, travellers' cheques generally accepted.

AIRPORTS New Tokyo (TYO) 65 km from the city, Kansai (KIX) 50 km from Osaka, Fukuoka (FUK) 10 km from the city.

INTERNAL TRAVEL Extensive domestic air network covering Japan and its islands. The efficient rail network is widely used. Driving is complicated for visitors who cannot read the language, and therefore the roadsigns.

BUSINESS HOURS 0900-1700 Mon-Friday.

GMT +9.

VOLTAGE GUIDE 100 AC, 60 Hz in the west, 100 AC, 50 Hz in the east and Tokyo.

RED TAPE

VISAS (AUS/CANADA/UK/US) None.

REPS IN UK/USA/CANADA UK: 101-104 Piccadilly, London W1V 9FN, tel 020 7465 6500, fax 020 7491 9348, email jicc@jicc.demon.co.uk. USA: 2520 Massachusetts Avenue, NW, Washington, DC 20008, tel 202 238 6700, fax 202 328 2187. Canada: 255 Sussex Drive, Ottawa, Ontario K1N 9E6, tel 613 241 8541, fax 613 241 7415, email infocul@embjapan.can.org.

CUSTOMS REGULATIONS Duty free allowance: 200 cigarettes or 50 cigars or 250 g of tobacco, 3 bottles (approximately 0.760 ml each) of spirits, 57 ml of perfume, gifts up to the value of 200,000 yen. Tobacco and alcohol allowances are for travellers over 20. Prohibited: Articles which infringe upon rights in patents, utility-models, designs, trademarks, copyright or neighbouring right, counterfeit, altered or imitated coins, paper money, banknotes or securities, plants with soil, most meats, animals without health certificates, firearms, ammunition, narcotics, obscene articles and publications.

DRIVING REQUIREMENTS International Driving Permit.

KEEPING IN TOUCH

BBC WORLD SERVICE MHz 21.66, 15.28, 11.95, 5.965.

ENGLISH-LANGUAGE NEWSPAPERS The Asahi Evening News, The Daily Yomiuri, The Japan Times.

EMERGENCIES

RED CROSS/CRESCENT SOCIETIES 1-3 Shiba Daimon, 1-Chome, Minato-ku, Tokyo 105-8521, tel 3 34 38 13 11, fax 3 34 35 85 09, email rcjpn@ppp.bekkoame.ne.jp.

UK/USA/CANADIAN REPS UK: No 1 Ichiban-cho, Chiyoda-ku, Tokyo 102-8381, tel 3 52 11 11 00, fax 3 52 75 03 46, email-consular@tokyo.mail.fco.gov.uk
USA: 10-5, Akasaka 1-Chome, Minato-ku, Tokyo 107-8420, tel 3 32 24 50 00, fax 3 35 05 18 62. Canada: 7-3-38 Akasaka, Minato-ku, Tokyo 107-8503, tel 3 54 12 62 00, fax 3 54 12 63 03.

Global weather guide p 818,   Rainy seasons worldwide p 829,   Vaccinations required p 832,
Recommended reading p 848,   Dependent territories p 812.

JORDAN

STATE OF THE NATION

SAFETY Safe.

LIFE EXPECTANCY M 68.9, F 71.5.

PEOPLE AND PLACE

CAPITAL Amman.

LANGUAGE Arabic.

PEOPLES Arab (98%).

RELIGION Islam.

SIZE (KM) 97,740.

POPULATION 6,000,000.

POP DENSITY/KM 67.

FOOD Middle Eastern, with *meze* to start, followed by kebabs or specialities such as *mensaf* (stewed lamb in a yoghurt sauce) or *musakhan* (chicken in olive oil and onion sauce served on Arab bread). Sweets are popular, and include *baklava* (pastry filled with nuts or honey). Restrictions on alchohol during Ramadan.

TRAVEL PLANNING

WHEN TO GO May-September is hot and dry. Rain falls between November - March, and December and January can be cold.

MEDICAL CARE Good, but insurance recommended.

CURRENCY Dinar (JD) = 1000 fils.

FINANCE American Express and Visa widely accepted, other cards have more limited use. Travellers' cheques accepted.

AIRPORTS Queen Alia International (AMM) 32 km fromAmman.

INTERNAL TRAVEL Adequate roads link main cities. A railroad links Al Aqabah with the Syrian capital, Damascus. Car hire is available from hotels or travel agents.

BUSINESS HOURS .0900-1800 Saturday, Wednesday and Thursday.

GMT +2 (+3 in summer).

VOLTAGE GUIDE 220 AC, 50 Hz.

RED TAPE

VISAS (AUS/CANADA/UK/US) Required.

REPS IN UK/USA/CANADA UK: 6 Upper Phillimore Gardens, London W8 7HB, tel 020 7937 3685, fax 020 7937 8795. USA: 3504 International Drive, NW, Washington, DC 20008, tel 202 966 2861, fax 202 686 4491, email JordanInfo@aol.com. Canada: Suite 701, 100 Bronson Avenue, Ottawa, Ontario K1R 6G8, tel 613 238 8090, fax 613 232 3341.

CUSTOMS REGULATIONS Duty free allowance: 200 cigarettes or 25 cigars or 200 g of tobacco, 1 bottle of wine or 1 bottle of spirits, a reasonable amount of perfume for personal use, gifts up to the value of JD50 or the equivalent up to US$150. Prohibited: Narcotics.

DRIVING REQUIREMENTS National driving licences accepted if issued at least 1 year before travel. International Driving Permit recommended.

KEEPING IN TOUCH

BBC WORLD SERVICE MHz 15.57, 11.76, 9.410, 6.195.

ENGLISH-LANGUAGE NEWSPAPERS *The Jordan Times* (daily), *The Star* (weekly).

EMERGENCIES

RED CROSS/CRESCENT SOCIETIES PO Box 10001, Amman 11151, tel 6 773 142, fax 6 750 815.

UK/USA/CANADIAN REPS UK: PO Box 87, Abdoun, Amman, tel 6 823 100, fax 6 813 759, email british@nets.com.jo. USA: PO Box 354, Jabal, Amman 11118, tel 6 592 3293, fax 6 592 4102. Canada: PO Box 815403, Amman 11180, tel 6 666 124, fax 6 689 227.

Global weather guide p 818, Rainy seasons worldwide p 829, Vaccinations required p 832, Recommended reading p 848, Dependent territories p 812.

KAZAKHSTAN

STATE OF THE NATION

SAFETY Some reports of banditry on roads and railways. Seek latest information at time of visit.

LIFE EXPECTANCY M 62.8, F 72.4.

PEOPLE AND PLACE

CAPITAL Astana.

LANGUAGE Kazakh.

PEOPLES Kazakh, Russian. Ukrainian, German, Uzbek and Tatar minorities.

RELIGION Islam, Russian Orthodox.

SIZE (KM) 2,717,300.

POPULATION 16,900,000.

POP DENSITY/KM 6.2.

FOOD Kazakh dishes include *shashlyk* (skewered, grilled mutton), *lepeshka* (round, unleavened bread), *plov* (mutton, rice and yellow turnip) and *laghman* (noodles with a spicy meat sauce). Kazakh *chai* or tea is popular.

TRAVEL PLANNING

WHEN TO GO Hot from June to end-September, cold from October - March.

MEDICAL CARE Variable, supplies may be limited, insurance with repatriation cover recommended.

CURRENCY Tenge (T) = 100 tiyin.

FINANCE Larger establishments in cities accept credit cards and travellers' cheques.

AIRPORTS Almaty (ALA) 15 km from the city.

INTERNAL TRAVEL Some domestic flights. Rail links between main centres. Many roads are in need of repair but the network connects most towns and regional centres. Car hire available in Almaty and at the airport.

BUSINESS HOURS 0900-1700 Monday-Saturday (shopping hours, business hours n/a).

GMT +5 (+6 in summer).

VOLTAGE GUIDE 220 AC, 50 Hz.

RED TAPE

VISAS (AUS/CANADA/UK/US) Required.

REPS IN UK/USA/CANADA UK: 33 Thurloe Square, London SW7 2SD, tel 020 7581 4646, fax 020 7584 8481, email kazakhstan@zoo.co.uk USA: 1401 16th Street, NW, Washington, DC 20036, tel 202 232 5488, fax 202 232 5845, email kazak@ intr.net. Also deals with enquiries from Canada.

CUSTOMS REGULATIONS Duty free allowance: 1000 cigarettes or 1000 g of tobacco products, 1.5 ltrs of spirits and 2 ltrs of wine, a reasonable quantity of perfume for personal use, gifts up to the value of US$500 for personal use only. Prohibited imports: Military weapons, ammunition, narcotics, pornography, loose pearls and anything owned by a third party that is to be carried in for that third party. Prohibited exports: As imports, as wel as annulled securities, state loan certificates, lottery tickets, works of art and antiques without permits, saiga horns, Siberian stag, red deer and punctuate antlers, punctuate deer skins.

DRIVING REQUIREMENTS International Driving Permit.

KEEPING IN TOUCH

BBC WORLD SERVICE MHz 15.58, 11.76, 9.410, 6.195.

ENGLISH-LANGUAGE NEWSPAPERS None.

EMERGENCIES

RED CROSS/CRESCENT SOCIETIES n/a.

UK/USA/CANADIAN REPS UK: 173 Furmanova Street, Almaty 480091, tel 3272 506 192, fax 3272 506 260, email british embassy@kaznet.kz. USA: 99 Furmanova Street, Almaty 480091, tel 3272 633 639, fax 3272 633 883. Canada: 34 Karasai Batir, Almaty 480 100, tel 3272 501 151, fax 3272 581 1493.

Global weather guide p 818,   Rainy seasons worldwide p 829,   Vaccinations required p 832, Recommended reading p 848,   Dependent territories p 812.

KENYA

STATE OF THE NATION

SAFETY Not the safe haven it once was. Muggings and carjackings commonplace. Tourists frequently targetted in Nairobi (nicknamed 'Nairobbery'). Do not walk on the beach road, whatever you are told.

LIFE EXPECTANCY M 55.9, F 59.9.

PEOPLE AND PLACE

CAPITAL Nairobi.

LANGUAGE Swahili and English.

PEOPLES About 70 different ethnic groups, with the Kikuyu, Luhya, Luo, Kalenjin and Kamba most prominent. Europeans and Asians form 1% of the population.

RELIGION Christian 60%, traditional beliefs 25%, Islam and other15%.

SIZE (KM) 580, 367.

POPULATION 29, 292, 000.

POP DENSITY/KM 50.4.

FOOD Strong on meat, including game. *Nyama Choma* (charcoal grilled meat, usually goat) is found in many restaurants and street stalls. *Ugali* (maize meal porridge) is a staple for Kenyans, an acquired taste for most visitors. Curries can be found in most places, and reflect Indian home cooking, not Indian-restaurant-abroad cooking. *Chai* (tea) and beer (particularly the Tusker brand) are popular.

TRAVEL PLANNING

WHEN TO GO March to May sees the long rains, October to December the short rains. Coastal areas are hot and humid all year, the higher regions are more temperate.

MEDICAL CARE Adequate but insurance strongly recommended.

CURRENCY Kenya shilling (KSh) = 100 cents.

FINANCE Major credit cards and travellers' cheques widely accepted.

AIRPORTS Nairobi (NBO) 13 km from the city, Mombasa (MBA) 13 km from the city.

INTERNAL TRAVEL Extensive network of domestic flights, and charter aircraft available from Wilson airport. Major roads are paved, but vary in quality. Roads in the north are poor. Car hire easily available, can be expensive and most agents recommend 4-wheel-drive vehicles.

BUSINESS HOURS 0800-1300, 1400-1700 Monday-Friday.

GMT +3.

VOLTAGE GUIDE 220/240 AC, 50 Hz.

RED TAPE

VISAS (AUS/CANADA/UK/US) None for tourism, required by all for business.

REPS IN UK/USA/CANADA UK: 45 Portland Place, London W1N 4AS, tel 020 7636 2371, 020 7323 6717. USA: 424 Madison Avenue, Suite 1401, New York, NY 10017, tel 212 486 1300, fax 212 688 0911, email kenya2d@aol.com. Canada: 415 Laurier Avenue East, Ottawa, Ontario K1N 6R4, tel 613 563 1773-6, fax 613 233 6599 email kenrep@inpranet.ca

CUSTOMS REGULATIONS Duty free allowance: For passengers over 16, 200 cigarettes or 50 cigars or 225 g of tobacco, 1 bottle of spirits or wine, 568 ml of perfume.NB Firearms and ammunition require a police permit. Pets require a good health certificate, a rabies certificate and an import permit. Prohibited: Import of fruit, plants, seeds, imitation firearms. Export of gold, diamonds, game trophies or wildlife skin without government authorisation.

DRIVING REQUIREMENTS Full British driving licence valid, otherwise an International Driving Permit.

KEEPING IN TOUCH

BBC WORLD SERVICE MHz 15.40, 11.94, 6.190, 3.255.

ENGLISH-LANGUAGE NEWSPAPERS *Daily Nation, Kenya Times, The Standard.*

EMERGENCIES

RED CROSS/CRESCENT SOCIETIES PO Box 40712, Nairobi, tel 2 503 781, fax 2 503 845, email kenyarc@africaonline.co.ke.

UK/USA/CANADIAN REPS UK: Upper Hill Road, Nairobi, tel 2 714 699, fax 2 719 082, email bhcinfo@africaonline.co.ke. USA: Unit 64100, corner of Moi and Hailé Sélassie Avenues, Nairobi, tel 2 751 613, fax 2 749 590. Canada: Comcraft House, Hailé Sélassie Avenue, Nairobi, tel 2 214 804, fax 2 226 987, email nrobi@nrobi01.x400.gc.ca.

Global weather guide p 818, Rainy seasons worldwide p 829, Vaccinations required p 832, Recommended reading p 848, Dependent territories p 812.

KIRIBATI

STATE OF THE NATION

SAFETY Safe.

LIFE EXPECTANCY M n/a, F n/a.

PEOPLE AND PLACE

CAPITAL Bairiki.

LANGUAGE Kiribati and English.

PEOPLES Gilbertese. Banaban minority.

RELIGION Roman Catholic, Kiribati Protestant Church.

SIZE (KM) 810.5.

POPULATION 78,000.

POP DENSITY/KM 96.

FOOD A Kiribati favourite is *palu sami*, coconut cream with sliced onion and curry powder, wrapped in *taro* leaves and baked in an earth oven filled with seaweed. It is often served with roast pork or chicken. Local specialities in the southern islands include the boiled fruit of *pandanus* (screwpine), sliced and served with coconut cream.

TRAVEL PLANNING

WHEN TO GO March-October, when the trade winds temper the equatorial climate of the central islands. The highest rainfall (December to May) is concentrated on the northern islands. November to February is wet and humid.

MEDICAL CARE Insurance recommended.

CURRENCY Australian dollar (A$).

FINANCE Limited acceptance of travellers' cheques, very limited acceptance of cards.

AIRPORTS Tarawa (TRW), Christmas Island (CXI).

INTERNAL TRAVEL Internal flights to outlying islands. All-weather roads are limited to urban Tarawa and Christmas Island, the only places where car hire is available.

BUSINESS HOURS 0800-1230, 1330-1615 Monday-Friday.

GMT +12-14.

VOLTAGE GUIDE 240 AC, 50 Hz.

RED TAPE

VISAS (AUS/CANADA/UK/US) Required by Australian and American visitors.

REPS IN UK/USA/CANADA UK: The Great House, Llanddewi Rhyddderch, Monmouthshire NP7 9UY, tel/fax 01873 840 375. USA: 850 Richards Street, Suite 503, Honolulu, Hawaii 96813, tel 808 521 7703, fax 808 521 8304. Canada: n/a.

CUSTOMS REGULATIONS Duty free allowance: For travellers over 21, 200 cigarettes or 50 cigars or 225 g of tobacco, 1 ltr of spirits and one ltr of wine, a reasonable amount of perfume for personal use (subject to declaration), 1 pair of binoculars, 1 camera and 6 rolls, 1 cine camera and 200 m of film, 1 radio, 1 tape recorder, 1 typewriter, sports equipment for personal use.

DRIVING REQUIREMENTS International Driving Permit.

KEEPING IN TOUCH

BBC WORLD SERVICE MHz 15.36, 11.96, 9.740, 5.975.

ENGLISH-LANGUAGE NEWSPAPERS *Te Uekera* (weekly).

EMERGENCIES

RED CROSS/CRESCENT SOCIETIES .

UK/USA/CANADIAN REPS UK: The British High Commission in Suva (Fiji) deals with enquiries relating to Kiribati. USA: The US Embassy in Majuro (Marshall Islands) deals with enquiries relating to Kiribati. Canada: The Canadian High Commission in Wellington deals with enquiries deals with enquiries relating to Kiribati.

Global weather guide p 818, Rainy seasons worldwide p 829, Vaccinations required p 832, Recommended reading p 848, Dependent territories p 812.

KOREA (DEMOCRATIC PEOPLE'S REPUBLIC)

STATE OF THE NATION

SAFETY Unknown. Entire country closed to foreigners.

LIFE EXPECTANCY M 68.9, F 75.1.

PEOPLE AND PLACE

CAPITAL Pyongyang.

LANGUAGE Korean.

PEOPLES Korean (100%).

RELIGION Buddhism, Christianity, Chundo Kyo.

SIZE (KM) 122,762.

POPULATION 23,483,000.

POP DENSITY/KM 191.3.

TRAVEL PLANNING

Entire country closed to foreigners.

Global weather guide p 818, Rainy seasons worldwide p 829, Vaccinations required p 832, Recommended reading p 848, Dependent territories p 812.

KOREA (REPUBLIC)

STATE OF THE NATION

Safety Safe.

Life expectancy M 68, F 76.

PEOPLE AND PLACE

Capital Seoul.

Language Korean.

Peoples Korean (100%).

Religion Mahayana Buddhism, Protestant, Roman Catholic.

Size (km) 99,268.

Population 46,100,000.

Pop density/km 467.

Food Rice is a staple food, and a typical meal consists of rice, soup, rice water and at least eight side dishes of vegetables, poultry, eggs, bean-curd and sea plants. Red pepper is used in many dishes, and *kimchi*, a pungent, spicy pickle of cabbage or radish with turnips, onion, salt, fish, chesnuts and red pepper, is served as an accompaniment to most meals.

TRAVEL PLANNING

When to go The hottest part of the year is during the rainy season between July and August. December and January are very cold. The remainder of the year is mild and mainly dry.

Medical care Adequate but payment demanded, insurance advised.

Currency Won (W).

Finance Credit cards and travellers' cheques accepted in larger cities.

Airports Seoul (SEL) 17 km from the city, Pusan 27 km from the city, Cheju (CJU) on the island of Cheju-do.

Internal travel Steamers and ferries serve southern coastal ports and islands. Extensive, generally efficient rail service. The road network is also extensive, but while the motorways are in good condition, minor roads are often badly maintained. Car hire is available.

Business hours 0900-1800 Mon-Friday.

GMT +9.

Voltage guide 110/220 AC, 60 Hz

RED TAPE

Visas (Aus/Canada/UK/US) Required by American visitors.

Reps in UK/USA/Canada UK: 60 Buckingham Gate, London SW1E 6AJ, tel 020 7227 5505, fax 020 7227 5503. USA: 2450 Massachusetts Avenue, NW, Washington, DC 20008, tel 202 939 5663, fax 202 342 1597, email korinfo@koreaemb. org. Canada: 555 Avenue Road, Toronto, Ontario M4V 2J7, tel 416 920 3809, fax 416 924 7305.

Customs regulations Duty free allowance: For travellers over 20, 200 cigarettes or 50 cigars or 250 g of pipe tobacco (total quantity not exceeding 500 g), 1 ltr of alcoholic beverage, 2 oz of perfume, gifts up to the value of W300,000. Prohibited: Narcotics, drugs, fruit, seeds and printed material, films, records or cassettes considered by the authorities to be subversive or harmful to national security or public interest. Restricted items: Firearms, explosives and other weapons, textiles, radio equipment, articles considered to be for commercial use and any animals or plants prohibited by the relevant quarantine regulations. Korean antiques or valuable cultural items can only be exported with permission from the Seoul Metropolitan Government.

Driving requirements International Driving Permit.

KEEPING IN TOUCH

BBC World Service MHz 15.28, 9.740, 7.160, 6.195.

English-language newspapers *The Korea Herald, The Korea Times.*

EMERGENCIES

Red Cross/Crescent societies 32-3 ka, Namsan-dong, Choong-ku, Seoul 100-043, tel 2 37 05 37 05, fax 2 37 05 36 67, email knrc@redcross.or.kr.

UK/USA/Canadian reps UK: 4 Chung-dong, Chung-ku, Seoul 100-120, tel 2 735 7341, fax 2 725 1738, email beseoul@unitel.co.kr. USA: Unit 15550, 82 Sejong-ro, Chongno-ku, Seoul 110-050, tel 2 397 4114, fax 2 738 8845. Canada: 10th Floor, Kolon Building, 45 Mugyo-dong, Chung-ku, Seoul 100-170, tel 2 34 55 60 00, fax 2 755 0686.

Global weather guide p 818, Rainy seasons worldwide p 829, Vaccinations required p 832, Recommended reading p 848, Dependent territories p 812.

KUWAIT

STATE OF THE NATION

SAFETY Safe. But avoid the border with Iraq, and beware unexploded ordnance.

LIFE EXPECTANCY M 74.1, F 78.2.

PEOPLE AND PLACE

CAPITAL Kuwait City.

LANGUAGE Arabic and English.

PEOPLES Kuwaiti (45%), other Arab, South Asian, Iranian.

RELIGION Sunni Muslim.

SIZE (KM) 17,818.

POPULATION 1,800,000.

POP DENSITY/KM 101.

FOOD Arabic cuisine. Spicy meat and poultry dishes, often lamb, served with rice or flat bread. Alcohol is totally prohibited.

TRAVEL PLANNING

WHEN TO GO April to October is hot and humid with very little rain. November - March is cool with limited rain.

MEDICAL CARE Free emergency treatment at state medical centre but otherwise very expensive, insurance recommended.

CURRENCY Kuwait dinar (KD) = 1000 fils.

FINANCE Credit cards and travellers' cheques generally accepted.

AIRPORTS Kuwait (KWI) 16 km from Kuwait City.

INTERNAL TRAVEL Good road network between cities. Car hire available.

BUSINESS HOURS 0730-1230, 1600-1900 Saturday-Wednesday.

GMT +3.

VOLTAGE GUIDE 240 AC, 50 Hz.

RED TAPE

VISAS (AUS/CANADA/UK/US) Required.

REPS IN UK/USA/CANADA UK: 2 Albert Gate, London SW1X 7JU, tel 020 7590 3400, fax 020 7259 5042. USA: 2940 Tilden Street, NW, Washington, DC 20008, tel 202 966 0702, fax 202 966 0517. Canada: 80 Elgin Street, Ottawa, Ontario K1P 1C6, tel 613 780 9999, fax 613 780 9905, email info@ embassyofkuwait.com.

CUSTOMS REGULATIONS Duty free allowance: 500 cigarettes or 907 of tobacco. Prohibited: Alcohol, narcotics, unsealed milk products, salty fish, unsealed olives and pickles, food prepared abroad, fresh vegetables, shellfish and its products, fresh figs and mineral water. Penalties for attempting to smuggle restricted items are severe.

DRIVING REQUIREMENTS International Driving Licence.

KEEPING IN TOUCH

BBC WORLD SERVICE MHz 15.58, 11.76, 9.410, 6.195.

ENGLISH-LANGUAGE NEWSPAPERS *Arab Times, Kuwait Times.*

EMERGENCIES

RED CROSS/CRESCENT SOCIETIES PO Box 1359, 13014 Safat, tel 481 5478, fax 483 9114, email krcs@kuwait.net.

UK/USA/CANADIAN REPS UK: Arabian Gulf Street, Kuwait City, tel 240 3334, fax 242 5778, email britemb@ncc.moc.kw. USA: Area No 6, Al-Aksa Street, Bayan, tel 539 5307, fax 538 0282. Canada: Block 4, House No 24, Al-Mutawakel Street, Kuwait City, tel 256 3025, fax 256 4167.

Global weather guide p 818, Rainy seasons worldwide p 829, Vaccinations required p 832, Recommended reading p 848, Dependent territories p 812.

KYRGYZSTAN

STATE OF THE NATION

SAFETY Generally safe, beware theft.

LIFE EXPECTANCY M 64.3, F 72.4.

PEOPLE AND PLACE

CAPITAL Bishkek.

LANGUAGE Kyrgyz.

PEOPLES Kygryz, Russian, Uzbek.

RELIGION Predominantly Sunni Muslim with a Russian Orthodox minority.

SIZE (KM) 4,635,000.

POPULATION 4,500,000.

POP DENSITY/KM 23.

FOOD Cuisine shows some Chinese influences. Mutton is the staple meat, often cubed and grilled (*Shashlyk*). *Lipioshka*, an unleavened bread is often sold on street corners. *Laghman*, a noodle soup with mutton and vegetables is also popular.

TRAVEL PLANNING

WHEN TO GO Continental climate with relatively little rainfall and an average of 247 sunny days a year. Temperatures range between 20°-30° from June to August. Heavy snowfalls in winter.

MEDICAL CARE Limited, and cash payments demanded, insurance essential.

CURRENCY Som (KS) = 100 tyn.

FINANCE Limited acceptance of credit cards and travellers' cheques.

AIRPORTS Bishkek Manas (FRU) 30 km from Bishkek.

INTERNAL TRAVEL Rail travel can be dangerous - numerous robberies have been reported on some routes. Adequate road network although in bad condition in the mountains. Self-drive car hire not available. Cars with drivers may be hired for long distance journeys but petrol shortages make this an expensive option.

BUSINESS HOURS 0900-1800 Mon-Friday.

GMT +5.

VOLTAGE GUIDE 220 AC, 50 Hz.

RED TAPE

VISAS (AUS/CANADA/UK/US) Required.

REPS IN UK/USA/CANADA UK: Ascot House, 119 Crawford Street, London W1H 1AF, tel 020 7935 1462, fax 020 7935 7449, email email@kyrgyz-embassy.org.uk. USA: 1732 Wisconsin Avenue, NW, Washington, DC 20007, tel 202 338 5141, fax 202 338 5139, email embassy@kyrgyzstan.org. Also deals with enquiries from Canada.

CUSTOMS REGULATIONS Duty free allowance: 400 cigarettes or 100 cigars or 500 g of tobacco products, 2 ltrs of alcoholic beverages, a reasonable quantity of perfume for personal use, gifts up to an equivalent value of US$5000 for personal use only. Prohibited: Military weapons and ammunition, narcotics and pornography, loose pearls and anything owned by a third party that is to be carried in for that third party. Prohibited exports: as for imports. Also annulled securities, state loan certificates, lottery tickets, works of art and antiques without permits, saiga horns, Siberian stag, red deer and punctuate antlers and punctuate deer skins.

DRIVING REQUIREMENTS n/a.

KEEPING IN TOUCH

BBC WORLD SERVICE MHz 17.64, 15.56, 9.410, 3.955.

ENGLISH-LANGUAGE NEWSPAPERS The *Central Asian Post*, The *Kyrgyzstan Chronicle*.

EMERGENCIES

RED CROSS/CRESCENT SOCIETIES 720040 Bishkek, tel 312 222 414, fax 312 662 181email redcross@imfiko.bishkek.su.

UK/USA/CANADIAN REPS UK: The British Embassy in Almaty (Kazakhstan) deals with enquiries relating to Kyrgyzstan. USA: Prospekt Mira 171, 720016 Bishkek, tel 312 551 242-7. Canada: The Canadian Embassy in Almaty (Kazakhstan) deals with enquiries relating to Kyrgyzstan.

Global weather guide p 818, Rainy seasons worldwide p 829, Vaccinations required p 832, Recommended reading p 848, Dependent territories p 812.

LAOS

STATE OF THE NATION

SAFETY Safe, but be careful in drug-producing areas.

LIFE EXPECTANCY M 52, F 54.5.

PEOPLE AND PLACE

CAPITAL Vientiane.

LANGUAGE Laotian.

PEOPLES Lao Loum, Lao Theung, Lao Soung.

RELIGION Buddhist.

SIZE (KM) 236,800.

POPULATION 5,400,000.

POP DENSITY/KM 23.

FOOD Rice, especially sticky rice, is the staple food and dishes are Indo-Chinese in flavour. Good French restaurants in Vientiane. Rice whisky, known as *lao lao*, is popular.

TRAVEL PLANNING

WHEN TO GO Hot, tropical climate. Rainy season from May-October, dry from November to April.

MEDICAL CARE Limited and cash payments demanded, insurance strongly recommended.

CURRENCY Lao kip (Kip) = 100 cents.

FINANCE Limited acceptance of credit cards and travellers' cheques.

AIRPORTS Vientiane (VTE) 4 km from the city.

INTERNAL TRAVEL Rivers are a vital part of the country's transportation system. Many roads have been paved in recent years, but few are all-weather. Car hire can be made through hotels.

BUSINESS HOURS 0800-1200, 1330-1730, Monday to Friday.

GMT +7.

VOLTAGE GUIDE 220 AC, 50 Hz.

RED TAPE

VISAS (AUS/CANADA/UK/US) Required.

REPS IN UK/USA/CANADA UK: n/a. USA: 2222 S Street, NW, Washington, DC 20008, tel 202 332 6416, fax 202 332 4923, email laoemb@erols.com. Also deals with enquiries from Canada.

CUSTOMS REGULATIONS Duty free allowance: From countries not neighbouring Laos, 500 cigarettes or 100 cigars or 500 g of tobacco, 1 bottle of spirits, 2 bottles of wine, perfume for personal use, personal jewellery up to 500 g.

DRIVING REQUIREMENTS International Driving Permit recommended.

KEEPING IN TOUCH

BBC WORLD SERVICE MHz 15.28, 9.740, 7.160, 6.195.

ENGLISH-LANGUAGE NEWSPAPERS The *Vientiane Times*.

EMERGENCIES

RED CROSS/CRESCENT SOCIETIES PO Box 650, Vientiane, tel 21 222 398, fax 21 212 128.

UK/USA/CANADIAN REPS UK: The British Embassy in Bangkok (Thailand) deals with enquiries relating to Laos. USA: BP 114, rue Bartholonie, That Dam, Vientiane, tel 21 212 581/2, fax 21 212 584. Canada: The Canadian Embassy in Bangkok (Thailand) deals with enquiries relating to Laos.

Global weather guide p 818, Rainy seasons worldwide p 829, Vaccinations required p 832, Recommended reading p 848, Dependent territories p 812.

LATVIA

STATE OF THE NATION

SAFETY Safe.

LIFE EXPECTANCY M 62.4, F 74.4.

PEOPLE AND PLACE

CAPITAL Riga.

LANGUAGE Latvian.

PEOPLES Latvian (52%), Russian, Belorussian, Ukrainian.

RELIGION Mainly Lutheran. Roman Catholic and Russian Orthodox minorities.

SIZE (KM) 64,589.

POPULATION 2,529,500.

POP DENSITY/KM 39.7.

FOOD Local specialities include *kotletes* (meat patties), *skabu kapostu zupa* (cabbage soup), *piragi* (pastries filled with bacon and onions). Potatoes play a large part in the diet.

TRAVEL PLANNING

WHEN TO GO May to August is warm, although August sees the heaviest rainfall. Winter, from November-March can be very cold, with heavy snowfall.

MEDICAL CARE Limited and expensive. Insurance strongly recommended.

CURRENCY Latvian lat (Ls) = 100 santims.

FINANCE Credit cards and travellers' cheques generally accepted.

AIRPORTS Riga (RIX) 7 km from the city.

INTERNAL TRAVEL Reasonable rail network, good road connections from Riga to all parts of the country. Car hire available.

BUSINESS HOURS 0830-1730 Mon-Friday.

GMT +2.

VOLTAGE GUIDE 220 AC, 50 Hz.

RED TAPE

VISAS (AUS/CANADA/UK/US) Required by Australian and Canadian visitors.

REPS IN UK/USA/CANADA UK: 45 Nottingham Place, London W1M 3FE, tel 020 7312 0040, fax 020 7312 0042, email latemb@dircon.co.uk. USA: 4325 17th Street, NW, Washington, DC 20011, tel 202 726 8213, fax 202 726 6785, email latvia@ambergateway.com. Canada: 112 Kent Street, Tower B, Suite 208, Place de Ville Complex, Ottawa, Ontario, K1P 5P2, tel 613 238 6014, fax 613 238 7044, email latvia-embassy@magmacom.com.

CUSTOMS REGULATIONS Duty free allowance: For travellers over 18, 200 cigarettes or 20 cigars or 200 g of tobacco, 1 ltr of alcoholic beverages, up to Ls 15 of food, up to Ls 300 of new duty-free goods, up to Ls 225 of other new goods. Prohibited: Narcotics, guns and ammunition (without a police import permit).

DRIVING REQUIREMENTS EU pink format licence or an International Driving Permit.

KEEPING IN TOUCH

BBC WORLD SERVICE MHz 15.57, 9.410, 6.195, 6.180.

ENGLISH-LANGUAGE NEWSPAPERS *The Baltic Times* (weekly).

EMERGENCIES

RED CROSS/CRESCENT SOCIETIES 1, Skolas Street, LV-1010 Riga, tel/fax 731 0902.

UK/USA/CANADIAN REPS UK: Alunana iela 5, LV 1010 Riga, Latvia, tel 733 8126-31, fax 733 8132, email british.embassy@ apollo.lv. USA: Raina bulvaris 7, LV-1510 Riga, tel 721 0005, fax 782 0047, email us-emb@latnet.lv. Canada: Doma laukums 4, LV-1977 Riga, tel 783 0141, fax 783 0140, email canembr@bkc.lv.

Global weather guide p 818, Rainy seasons worldwide p 829, Vaccinations required p 832, Recommended reading p 848, Dependent territories p 812.

LEBANON

STATE OF THE NATION

SAFETY Currently safe, but be careful near the Israeli border.

LIFE EXPECTANCY M 68.1, F 71.7.

PEOPLE AND PLACE

CAPITAL Beirut.

LANGUAGE Arabic.

PEOPLES Of Arab descent (92%), large Palestinian refugee population.

RELIGION Islam (70%), Christianity.

SIZE (KM) 10,452.

POPULATION 3,855,000.

POP DENSITY/KM 271.1.

FOOD Lebanese cuisine has a good reputation, relying on fresh local produce and herbs. The traditional *mezza* may consistof up to 40 small dishes served as a starter, including *kebbeh* (lamb or fish paste with cracked wheat, served raw, baked or fried). Main courses are likely to include the staples of rice, vegetables and mutton, and include *lahm mishwi* (mutton with onions, peppers and tomato).

TRAVEL PLANNING

WHEN TO GO Summer (June to September) hot on the coast, cooler in the mountains. December to March is mostly rainy, with snow on the mountains. The rest of the year is warm and pleasant.

MEDICAL CARE Adequare, but insurance recommended.

CURRENCY Lebanese pound (L£) = 100 piastres.

FINANCE Limited acceptance of credit cards and travellers' cheques.

AIRPORTS Beirut (BEY) 16 km from the city.

INTERNAL TRAVEL Ports are served by coastal passenger ferries. Limited public transport. Car hire is available although chauffeur-driven vehicles are recommended.

BUSINESS HOURS 0800-1800 Monday-Saturday.

GMT +2 (+3 in the summer).

VOLTAGE GUIDE 220 AC, 50 Hz.

RED TAPE

VISAS (AUS/CANADA/UK/US) Required.

REPS IN UK/USA/CANADA UK: Palace Garden Mews, London W8 4RA, tel 020 7229 7265, fax 7243 1699, email emb.leb@btinternet.com. USA: 9 East 76th Street, New York, NY 10021, tel 212 744 7905, fax 212 794 1510. Canada: 40 Côte Ste-Catherine Road, Outremont, Québec H2V 2A2, tel 514 276 2638, fax 514 276 0090.

CUSTOMS REGULATIONS Duty free allowance: 200 cigarettes or 20 cigars or 200 g of tobacco, 2 bottles of alcohol. Prohibited: A valid import licence is required for any arms or ammunition. Antiques cannot be exported without relevant permits.

DRIVING REQUIREMENTS International Driving Permit and Green Card insurance.

KEEPING IN TOUCH

BBC WORLD SERVICE MHz 15.57, 11.76, 9.410, 6.195.

ENGLISH-LANGUAGE NEWSPAPERS *The Daily Star, Beirut Times.*

EMERGENCIES

RED CROSS/CRESCENT SOCIETIES Rue Spears, Beirut, tel 1 372 802, fax 1 378 207, email lrc-comme@dm.net.lb.

UK/USA/CANADIAN REPS UK: PO Box 60180, Autostrade Jal El-Dib, Coolrite Building, Jal El-Dib, Beirut, tel 1 406 330, fax 1 402 033. USA: Antelias, PO Box 70-840, Beirut, tel 1 402 200, fax 1 407 112. Canada: PO Box 613, 434 Autostrade Jal El-Dib, Coolrite Building, Jal El-Dib, Beirut, tel 1 521 163-5, fax 1 521 167.

Global weather guide p 818, Rainy seasons worldwide p 829, Vaccinations required p 832, Recommended reading p 848, Dependent territories p 812.

LESOTHO

STATE OF THE NATION

SAFETY Generally safe, but travel with caution.

LIFE EXPECTANCY M 55.5, F 60.5.

PEOPLE AND PLACE

CAPITAL Maseru.

LANGUAGE Sesotho and English.

PEOPLES Basotho (97%), European and Asian.

RELIGION Christian, mainly Anglican, Catholic and Lesotho Evangelical.

SIZE (KM) 30,355.

POPULATION 2,200,000.

POP DENSITY/KM 72.

FOOD Street stalls in towns sell good grilled meat. Much food has to be imported from South Africa, but freshwater fish is in abundant supply and is popular. Hotels and restaurants offer a wide variety of cuisines.

TRAVEL PLANNING

WHEN TO GO Most rainfall occurs from October-April. Snow occurs in the highlands from May-September. The hottest period is from January to February.

MEDICAL CARE Cash payments, insurance recommended.

CURRENCY Loti (M) = 100 lisente.

FINANCE Limited acceptance of credit cards, travellers' cheques widely accepted.

AIRPORTS Maseru (MSU) 18 km from the city.

INTERNAL TRAVEL Some main towns are connected by internal flights. The road system is underdeveloped.

BUSINESS HOURS 0800-1245, 1400-1630 Monday-Friday, 0800-1300 Saturday.

GMT +2.

VOLTAGE GUIDE 220 AC, 50 Hz.

RED TAPE

VISAS (AUS/CANADA/UK/US) Required by American visitors.

REPS IN UK/USA/CANADA UK: 7 Chesham Place, London SW1 8HN, tel 020 7235 5686, fax 020 7235 5023, email lesotholondonhighcom@compuserve.com. USA: 2511 Massachusetts Avenue, NW, Washington, DC 20008, tel 202 797 5533, fax 202 234 6815, email lesotho@afrika.com. Also deals with enquiries from Canada.

CUSTOMS REGULATIONS Duty free allowance: 400 cigarettes and 50 cigars and 250 g of tobacco, 1 ltr of spirits and 1 ltr of wine, 50 ml of perfume and 250 ml of *eau de toilette*. NB Nationals of South Africa may not import alcoholic beverages. Prohibited: Firearms, ammunition and pets require a permit.

DRIVING REQUIREMENTS International Driving Permit recommended. National driving licences are normally valid, if in English or accompanied by a certified translation.

KEEPING IN TOUCH

BBC WORLD SERVICE MHz 15.40, 11.97, 6.190, 3.255.

ENGLISH-LANGUAGE NEWSPAPERS *The Survivor, Lesohto Today, The Mirror.*

EMERGENCIES

RED CROSS/CRESCENT SOCIETIES PO Box 366, Maseru 100, tel 313 911, fax 310 166, email lesoff@lesred.co.za.

UK/USA/CANADIAN REPS UK: PO Box 521, Linare Road, Maseru 100, tel 313 961, fax 310 120, email hcmaseru@lesoff.co.za. USA: PO Box 333, Maseru 100, tel 312 666, fax 310 116 email amless@lesoff.co.za. Canada: The Canadian High Commission in Pretoria deals with enquiries relating to Lesotho.

Global weather guide p 818, Rainy seasons worldwide p 829, Vaccinations required p 832, Recommended reading p 848, Dependent territories p 812.

LIBERIA

STATE OF THE NATION

SAFETY Highly dangerous. Political violence and periodic *coups* are worsened by spillover from civil war in neighbouring Sierra Leone. Travel not recommended.

LIFE EXPECTANCY M 46, F 48.

PEOPLE AND PLACE

CAPITAL Monrovia.

LANGUAGE English.

PEOPLES Indigenous tribes (16 main groups), Americo-Liberians (5%).

RELIGION Officially a Christian state. Animist beliefs practised widely. Small Muslim community.

SIZE (KM) 97,754.

POPULATION 2,700,000.

POP DENSITY/KM 27.

FOOD West African cuisine can be found in 'chop bars' (streetside restaurants) or in 'cookhouses', where traditional Liberian dishes are served with rice. Only the most basic provisions are available in many towns outside the capital.

TRAVEL PLANNING

WHEN TO GO The rainy season is from May-October. Temperatures are consistently high.

MEDICAL CARE Very limited. Insurance with repatriation cover recommended.

CURRENCY Liberian dollar (L$).

FINANCE Very limited acceptance of credit cards, travellers' cheques generally not accepted.

AIRPORTS Monrovia (MLW) 60 km from the city.

INTERNAL TRAVEL Most roads unpaved. The railways are primarily used for mining goods and carry little other traffic.

BUSINESS HOURS 0800-1200, 1400-1700 Monday-Friday.

GMT GMT.

VOLTAGE GUIDE 110 AC, 60 Hz.

RED TAPE

VISAS (AUS/CANADA/UK/US) Required.

REPS IN UK/USA/CANADA UK: 2 Pembridge Place, London W2 4XB, tel 020 7221 1036. USA: 5201 16th Street, NW, Washington, DC 20011, tel 202 723 0437, fax 202 723 0436, email info@liberiaemb.org. Canada: 1080 Beaver Hall Hill, Suite 1720, Montréal, Québec H2Z 1S8, tel 514 871 4741, fax 514 397 0816, email lawyers@fieldbloom.com.

CUSTOMS REGULATIONS Duty free allowance: 200 cigarettes or 25 cigars or 250 g tobacco products, 1 ltr of alcoholic beverage, 100 g (4 fl oz) of perfume, goods to the value of US$125.

DRIVING REQUIREMENTS International Driving Permit. A temporary licence is available on presentation of a valid British or Northern Ireland driving licence.

KEEPING IN TOUCH

BBC WORLD SERVICE MHz 17.83, 15.40, 7.160, 6.005.

ENGLISH-LANGUAGE NEWSPAPERS *The Daily Observer, Inquirer, Sunday Express.*

EMERGENCIES

RED CROSS/CRESCENT SOCIETIES PO Box 20-5081, 1000 Monrovia 20, tel 225 172, fax 226 231.

UK/USA/CANADIAN REPS UK: The British Embassy in Abidjan(Côte d'Ivoire) deals with enquiries relating to Liberia. The British Consular Agent at UMARCO, Bush Rod Island, PO Box 1196, Monrovia, tel 226 056, fax 226 061 provides emergency assistance only. USA: 11 United Nations Drive, Mamba Point, Monrovia, tel 226 370, fax 226 148. Canada: The Canadian High Commission in Accra (Ghana) deals with enquiries relating to Liberia.

Global weather guide p 818, Rainy seasons worldwide p 829, Vaccinations required p 832, Recommended reading p 848, Dependent territories p 812.

LIBYA

STATE OF THE NATION

SAFETY Safe. Observe Islamic customs.
LIFE EXPECTANCY M 68.3, F 72.2.

PEOPLE AND PLACE

CAPITAL Tripoli.
LANGUAGE Arabic.
PEOPLES Arab and Berber.
RELIGION Islam (mainly Sunni Muslim).
SIZE (KM) 1,775,500.
POPULATION 6,000,000.
POP DENSITY/KM 3.

FOOD Based on *couscous*, served with vegetables, chicken, lamb or camel, and macaroni-based dishes influenced by the Italians. Libyan soup, a spicy minestrone with lamb and pasta, is served at most meals. The local fish along the coast is very good.

TRAVEL PLANNING

WHEN TO GO Summers (June to September) are very hot and dry, winters are mild with cooler evenings.
MEDICAL CARE Limited outside capital, insurance strongly recommended.
CURRENCY Libyan dinar (LD) = 1000 dirhams.
FINANCE Very limited acceptance of Diners Club and Visa, travellers' cheques generally not accepted.
AIRPORTS Tripoli (TIP) 35 km from the city, Benghazi (BEN) 19 km from Benghazi, Sebha (SEB) 11 km from the town.
INTERNAL TRAVEL Some internal flights between main centres. The National Coast Road runs from the Tunisian to the Egyptian border. All road signs are in Arabic only.
BUSINESS HOURS 0700-1400 Monday-Thursday, Saturday.
GMT +2.
VOLTAGE GUIDE 150/220 AC, 50 Hz.

RED TAPE

VISAS (AUS/CANADA/UK/US) Required.
REPS IN UK/USA/CANADA UK: Libyan Interests Section, c/o Royal Embassy of Saudi Arabia, 119 Harley Street, London W1, tel 020 7486 8387, fax 020 7224 6349. USA: (Permanent Mission to the UN) 309-315 East 48th Street, New York, NY 10017, tel 212 333 1192, fax 212 593 4787, email lbyun@undp.org. Also deals with enquiries from Canada.

CUSTOMS REGULATIONS Duty free allowance: 200 cigarettes or 250 g of tobacco or 250 cigars, 250 ml of perfume. Prohibited: All alcohol, obscene literature, pork, pork products, food. All goods made in Israel or manufactured by countries that do business with Israel are prohibited.

DRIVING REQUIREMENTS National driving licence valid for 3 months, after which a Libyan licence must be obtained.

KEEPING IN TOUCH

BBC WORLD SERVICE MHz 17.70, 15.40, 12.10, 6.005.
ENGLISH-LANGUAGE NEWSPAPERS n/a.

EMERGENCIES

RED CROSS/CRESCENT SOCIETIES PO Box 541 Benghazi, tel 61 909 5202, tel 61 909 5829.

UK/USA/CANADIAN REPS UK: British Interests Section, C/o Embassy of the Italian Republic, PO Box 4206, Sharia Uahran 1, Tripoli, tel 21 333 1192, tel 21 444 9121. USA: n/a. Canada: The Canadian Embassy in Tunis-Belvédère (Tunisia) deals with enquiries relating to Libya.

Global weather guide p 818, Rainy seasons worldwide p 829, Vaccinations required p 832, Recommended reading p 848, Dependent territories p 812.

LIECHTENSTEIN

STATE OF THE NATION

SAFETY Safe.

LIFE EXPECTANCY M 78, F 84.

PEOPLE AND PLACE

CAPITAL Vaduz.

LANGUAGE German.

PEOPLES Liechtensteiners, Swiss, German.

RELIGION Mainly Roman Catholic, Protestant and other minorities.

SIZE (KM) 160.

POPULATION 31,000.

POP DENSITY/KM 195.

FOOD Swiss with Austrian overtones. Specialities include *Kasknopfle*, small dumplings with cheese.

TRAVEL PLANNING

WHEN TO GO Temperate, Alpine climate, with warm wet summers from May-August, and mild winters.

MEDICAL CARE Very good. Free for UK citizens.

CURRENCY Swiss franc (sfr) = 100 centimes.

FINANCE Credit cards, travellers' cheques widely accepted.

AIRPORTS Nearest airport is Zurich, 130 km away.

INTERNAL TRAVEL Single track railroad with few stops, good roads.

BUSINESS HOURS 0800-1200, 1330-1700 Monday-Friday.

GMT +1.

VOLTAGE GUIDE 220 AC, 50 Hz.

RED TAPE

VISAS (AUS/CANADA/UK/US) As for Switzerland.

REPS IN UK/USA/CANADA Liechtenstein maintains very few overseas missions and is generally represented by Switzerland.

CUSTOMS REGULATIONS Duty free allowance: As for Switzerland.

DRIVING REQUIREMENTS National driving licences are valid.

KEEPING IN TOUCH

BBC WORLD SERVICE MHz 17.64, 12.09, 9.410, 6.195.

ENGLISH-LANGUAGE NEWSPAPERS None.

EMERGENCIES

RED CROSS/CRESCENT SOCIETIES Heiligkreuz 25, FL-9490, Vaduz, tel 75 232 2294, fax 75 232 2240.

UK/USA/CANADIAN REPS UK: 37-39 rue Vermont, 6th Floor, CH-1211 Geneva 20, tel 22 918 2400, fax 22 918 2322. USA: The American Embassy in Bern (Switzerland) deals with enquiries relating to Liechtenstein. Canada: The Canadian Embassy in Bern deals with enquiries relating to Liechtenstein.

Global weather guide p 818, Rainy seasons worldwide p 829, Vaccinations required p 832, Recommended reading p 848, Dependent territories p 812.

LITHUANIA

STATE OF THE NATION

SAFETY Safe.

LIFE EXPECTANCY M 64.3, F 75.6.

PEOPLE AND PLACE

CAPITAL Vilnius.

LANGUAGE Lithuanian.

PEOPLES Lithuanian (80%), Russian, Polish, Belorussian.

RELIGION Roman Catholic. Evangelical Lutheran, Evangelical Reformist, Russian Orthodox, Baptist, Muslim and Jewish minorities.

SIZE (KM) 65, 301.

POPULATION 3, 717, 700.

POP DENSITY/KM 57.

FOOD Specialities include smoked eel, *skilandis* (smoked meat), *cepelinai* (made from potatoes and filled with minced meat), *salti barsciai* (cold soup), *vedarai* (potato sausage), *bulviniai blynai* (dumplings).

TRAVEL PLANNING

WHEN TO GO Warm summers from May to August. August also sees heavy rainfall. Very cold winters from November to mid-March, heavy snowfalls are common.

MEDICAL CARE Free emergency treatment, but insurance recommended.

CURRENCY Litas (Lt) = 100 centas.

FINANCE Credit cards and travellers' cheques accepted in large towns.

AIRPORTS Vilnius (VNO) 6 km from the city centre.

INTERNAL TRAVEL Few domestic flights. Good rail connections and road network. Car hire available.

BUSINESS HOURS 0900-1300, 1400-1800 Monday to Friday.

GMT +1.

VOLTAGE GUIDE 220 AC, 50 Hz.

RED TAPE

VISAS (AUS/CANADA/UK/US) None.

REPS IN UK/USA/CANADA UK: 84 Gloucester Place, London W1H 3HN, tel 020 7486 6401/2, fax 020 7486 6403, email lralon@globalnet.co.uk. USA: 2622 16th Street, NW, Washington, DC 20009, tel 202 234 5860, fax 202 328 0466, email admin@ltembassy.org. Canada: 130 Albert Street, Suite 204, Ottawa, Ontario K1P 5G4, tel 613 567 5458, fax 613 567 5315, email litemb@storm.ca.

CUSTOMS REGULATIONS Duty free allowance: 200 cigarettes or 250 g of obacco, 1 ltr of spirits and 2 ltrs of wine and 1.5 ltrs of champagne and 5 ltrs of beer, a reasonable amount of perfume, 3 kg of chocolate, 2 kg of coffee, other foodstuffs not exceeding Lt200 in value.

DRIVING REQUIREMENTS EU pink format licences or national driving licences supported by photographic ID.

KEEPING IN TOUCH

BBC WORLD SERVICE MHz 15.58, 9.410, 6.195, 6.180.

ENGLISH-LANGUAGE NEWSPAPERS *Lithuanian Weekly, Lithuanian Worker.*

EMERGENCIES

RED CROSS/CRESCENT SOCIETIES Gedimino Avenue 3A, 2600 Vilnius, tel 2 628 037, fax 2 619 923, email redcross@tdd.lt.

UK/USA/CANADIAN REPS UK: Antakalnio 2, 2055 Vilnius, tel 2 227 071, fax 2 727 579, email bevilnius@post.omnitel.net. USA: Akmenu 6, 2600 Vilnius, tel 2 223 031, fax 2 312 819, email consec@state.gov. Canada: Gedimino 64, 2001 Vilnius, tel 2 220 853, fax 2 220 884, email canambv@aiva.lt.

Global weather guide p 818, Rainy seasons worldwide p 829, Vaccinations required p 832, Recommended reading p 848, Dependent territories p 812.

LUXEMBOURG

STATE OF THE NATION

SAFETY Safe.

LIFE EXPECTANCY M 73.3, F 79.9.

PEOPLE AND PLACE

CAPITAL Luxembourg-Ville.

LANGUAGE Lëtzeburgesch, German, French.

PEOPLES Luxembourgers, other western Europeans, mainly Italians and Portugese.

RELIGION Roman Catholic (97%).

SIZE (KM) 2586.

POPULATION 422,000.

POP DENSITY/KM 168.

FOOD German and Franco-Belgian influenced cuisine. Specialities include *carré de porc fumé* (smoked pork and broad beans or *sauerkraut*) and *cochon de lait en gelée* (jellied suckling pig). Good pastries and cakes, *kirsh* is liberally used in deserts.

TRAVEL PLANNING

WHEN TO GO Warm from May to September and snow likely during winter months.

MEDICAL CARE Good, and refunds can be obtained for all but basic medical costs.

CURRENCY Luxembourg franc (Luxfr) = 100 centimes.

FINANCE Credit cards and travellers' cheques widely accepted.

AIRPORTS Luxembourg (LUX) 8 km from city.

INTERNAL TRAVEL There is an excellent road network although congestion can be a problem. Rail and bus services are integrated.

BUSINESS HOURS 0830-1200, 1400-1800 Monday-Friday.

GMT +1.

VOLTAGE GUIDE 220 AC, 50 Hz.

RED TAPE

VISAS (AUS/CANADA/UK/US) None.

REPS IN UK/USA/CANADA UK: 27 Wilton Crescent, London SW1X 8SD, tel 020 7235 6961, fax 020 7235 9734. USA: 2200 Massachusetts Avenue, NW, Washington, DC 20008, tel 202 265 4171/2, fax 202 328 8270, email ambalux@earthlink.net. Also deals with enquiries from Canada.

CUSTOMS REGULATIONS Duty free allowance: For travellers arriving from countries outside the EU, 200 cigarettes or 100 cigarillos or 50 cigars or 250 g of tobacco, 1 ltr of spirits over 22% or 4 ltrs of wine, 50 g of perfume and 250 ml of *eau de toilette*, other goods to the value of Luxfr 2600 for passengers over 15 and Luxfr 1000 for passengers under 15. Alcohol and tobacco products only available to travellers over 17. No limits on tobacco on alcohol for personal use within the EU.

DRIVING REQUIREMENTS A valid national driving licence. A green card is strongly recommended.

KEEPING IN TOUCH

BBC WORLD SERVICE MHz 12.095, 9.410, 6.195, 3.955.

ENGLISH-LANGUAGE NEWSPAPERS *The Luxembourg News* (weekly).

EMERGENCIES

RED CROSS/CRESCENT SOCIETIES PO Box 404, L-2014 Luxembourg, tel 450 202, fax 457 269.

UK/USA/CANADIAN REPS UK: 14 Boulevard Roosevelt, L-2450 Luxembourg-Ville, tel 229 864-6, fax 229 867, email britemb@pt.lu. USA: 22 Boulevard Emmanuel-Servais, L-2535 Luxembourg-Ville, tel 460 123, fax 461 401. Canada: c/o Price Waterhouse and Co, PO Box 1443, 24-26 avenue de la Liberté, L-1930 Luxembourg-Ville, tel 402 420, fax 402 455.

Global weather guide p 818, Rainy seasons worldwide p 829, Vaccinations required p 832, Recommended reading p 848, Dependent territories p 812.

MACEDONIA

STATE OF THE NATION

SAFETY Generally safe, but unsettled by regional instability. Seek latest information at time of visit.

LIFE EXPECTANCY M 71, F 75.3.

PEOPLE AND PLACE

CAPITAL Skopje.

LANGUAGE Macedonian.

PEOPLES Macedonian (67%), Albanian (23%), Turkish, Serb, Romany.

RELIGION Christianity (Eastern Orthodox Macedonian), Islam.

SIZE (KM) 25,713.

POPULATION 2,200,000.

POP DENSITY/KM 86.

FOOD Similar to Turkish and Greek cuisine - kebabs and moussaka are popular. Local specialities are *gravce na tavce* (beans in a skillet) and Ohrid trout.

TRAVEL PLANNING

WHEN TO GO Continental climate with hot summers from June to September and very cold winters.

MEDICAL CARE Emergency treatment free but repatriation insurance cover recommended.

CURRENCY Macedonian denar (Den) = 100 deni.

FINANCE Limited acceptance of travellers' cheques, very limited acceptance of credit cards.

AIRPORTS Skopje (SKP) 25 km from the city.

INTERNAL TRAVEL No regular domestic flights. An east-west road and rail route is being built through Macedonia, linking Tirana and Sofia.

BUSINESS HOURS 0700-1500 Mon-Friday.

GMT +1 (+2 in summer).

VOLTAGE GUIDE 220 AC, 50 Hz.

RED TAPE

VISAS (AUS/CANADA/UK/US) Required, except for UK citizens.

REPS IN UK/USA/CANADA UK: 10 Harcourt House, 19A Cavendish Square, London W1M 9AD, email mkuk@btinternet.com. USA: (Permanent Mission to the UN) 866 UN Plaza, Suite 517, New York, NY 10017, tel 212 308 8504, fax 212 308 8724, email dzundev@spacelab.net. Also deals with enquiries from Canada.

CUSTOMS REGULATIONS Duty free allowance: 1 box of cigarettes, 1 bottle of alcohol, gifts to the value of 60 Deutschmarks.

DRIVING REQUIREMENTS n/a.

KEEPING IN TOUCH

BBC WORLD SERVICE MHz 15.57, 12.10, 9.410, 6.195.

ENGLISH-LANGUAGE NEWSPAPERS None, although the *Macedonian Times* is published monthly in English.

EMERGENCIES

RED CROSS/CRESCENT SOCIETIES No 13, Bul, Koko Racin 91000, Skopje, tel 91 114 355, fax 91 230 542.

UK/USA/CANADIAN REPS UK: ul. Dimitrija Chupovski 26, 91000 Skopje, tel 91 116 772, fax 91 117 005, email beskopje@nic.mpt.com.mk USA: Ilindenska bb, 91000 Skopje, tel 91 116 180, fax 91 117 103. Canada: 12 Udarna Brigada 2, tel 91 125 228, fax 91 122 681, email dfaitmk@unet.com.mk.

Global weather guide p 818, Rainy seasons worldwide p 829, Vaccinations required p 832, Recommended reading p 848, Dependent territories p 812.

MADAGASCAR

STATE OF THE NATION

SAFETY Safe, but some reports of muggings.

LIFE EXPECTANCY M 56, F 59.

PEOPLE AND PLACE

CAPITAL Antananarivo.

LANGUAGE Malagasy and French.

PEOPLES Of Malay-Indonesian, African and Arab descent.

RELIGION Traditional beliefs (52%), Christian (41%), Muslim.

SIZE (KM) 587,041.

POPULATION 16,300,000.

POP DENSITY/KM 28.

FOOD Rice dishes with sauces, meat, vegetables and seasoning, often served with red peppers. Some specialities include *vary amid'anana* (rice, leaves or herbs, meat and sometimes shrimps), and *ramazava* (leaves and pieces of beef and pork browned in oil).

TRAVEL PLANNING

WHEN TO GO Hot and subtropical. The rainy season is from November-March. Monsoons bring storms and cyclones to the east and north from December-March. The dry season is from April-October.

MEDICAL CARE Limited repatriation insurance cover recommended.

CURRENCY Malagasy franc (Mgfr) = 100 centimes.

FINANCE Limited acceptance of credit cards and travellers' cheques.

AIRPORTS Antananarivo (TNR) 17 km from the city.

INTERNAL TRAVEL Extensive domestic air network. Many roads are impassable during the rains. Car hire only available in main tourist towns. Limited rail network.

BUSINESS HOURS 0800-1200, 1400-1800 Monday-Saturday (shopping hours, business hours n/a).

GMT +3.

VOLTAGE GUIDE 220 AC, 50 Hz.

RED TAPE

VISAS (AUS/CANADA/UK/US) Required.

REPS IN UK/USA/CANADA UK: 16 Lanark Mansions, Pennard Road, London W12 8DT, tel 020 8746 0133, fax 020 8746 0134. USA: 2374 Massachusetts Avenue, NW, Washington, DC 20008, tel 202 265 5525/6, fax 202 483 7603, email malagasy@embassy.org. Canada: 649 Blair Road, Gloucester, Ottawa, Ontario K1J 7M4, tel 613 744 7995, fax 613 744 2530.

CUSTOMS REGULATIONS Duty free allowance: 500 cigarettes or 25 cigars or 500 g of tobacco, 1 bottle of alcoholic beverage.

DRIVING REQUIREMENTS A national driving licence is sufficient.

KEEPING IN TOUCH

BBC WORLD SERVICE MHz 15.40, 11.94, 6.190, 3.255.

ENGLISH-LANGUAGE NEWSPAPERS None.

EMERGENCIES

RED CROSS/CRESCENT SOCIETIES BP 1168, Antananarivo, tel 2022 22111, fax 2022 35457, email crm@dts.mg.

UK/USA/CANADIAN REPS UK: Première Etage, Immeuble 'Ny Havana', Cité de 67 Ha, 101 Antananarivo, tel 2022 27749, fax 2022 26690, email ukembant@simicro.mg. USA: BP 620, Antsahavola, 101 Antananarivo, tel 2022 21257, fax 2022 34539. Canada: c/o QIT - Madagascar Minerals, BP 4003, Villa Paula Androhibe, Lot II-M62C, Villa 3H, Ivandry, 101 Antananarivo, tel 2022 42559, fax 2022 42506.

Global weather guide p 818, Rainy seasons worldwide p 829, Vaccinations required p 832, Recommended reading p 848, Dependent territories p 812.

MALAWI

STATE OF THE NATION

SAFETY Generally safe, but avoid travelling after dark.

LIFE EXPECTANCY M 44.6, F 46.2.

PEOPLE AND PLACE

CAPITAL Lilongwe.

LANGUAGE English.

PEOPLES Mostly of Bantu origin, Asian minority.

RELIGION Protestant (55%), Roman Catholic (20%), Muslim (20%), traditional beliefs.

SIZE (KM) 118,484.

POPULATION 10,400,000.

POP DENSITY/KM 111.

FOOD Fresh fish from Lake Malawi is popular, *chambo* (Tilapia) being the main lake delicacy. River trout and local beef are also notable. Street stalls in Lilongwe Old Town serve cassava chips and roast meat. Hotel restaurants and many of those in the cities are of a high standard.

TRAVEL PLANNING

WHEN TO GO Winter, from May-July is dry, and nights can be chilly, particularly in the highlands. The rainy season runs from November to March.

MEDICAL CARE Very basic, take supplies with you, insurance with repatriation cover recommended.

CURRENCY Kwacha (K) = 100 tambala.

FINANCE Limited acceptance of credit cards and of travellers' cheques.

AIRPORTS Lilongwe (LLW) 22 km from the city, Blantyre (BLZ) 18 km from the city.

INTERNAL TRAVEL Reasonable air network. Planes are available for charter through local travel bureaus. Trains tend to be slow and crowded but major roads are tarmac and most secondary roads are all-weather. Car hire is available in major towns.

BUSINESS HOURS 0730-1700 Mon-Friday.

GMT +2.

VOLTAGE GUIDE 220/240 AC, 50 Hz.

RED TAPE

VISAS (AUS/CANADA/UK/US) None.

REPS IN UK/USA/CANADA UK: 33 Grosvenor Street, London W1X 0DE, tel 020 7491 4172, fax 020 7491 9916, email tourism@malawihighcomm.prestel.co.uk. USA: 2408 Massachusetts Avenue, NW, Washington, DC 20008, tel 202 797 1007, fax 202 265 0976. Canada: 7 Clemow Avenue, Ottawa, Ontario K1S 2A9, tel 613 236 8971, fax 613 236 1054, email malawi.highcommission@sympatico.ca.

CUSTOMS REGULATIONS Duty free allowance: For passengers over 16, 200 cigarettes or 250 g of tobacco in any form, 1 ltr of spirits and 1 ltr of beer and 1 ltr of wine. Prohibited: Firearms without a permit.

DRIVING REQUIREMENTS Nationals of certain countries, including the UK, do not require an International Driving Permit. A national driving licence is sufficient.

KEEPING IN TOUCH

BBC WORLD SERVICE MHz 21.66, 17.89, 11.94, 6.190.

ENGLISH-LANGUAGE NEWSPAPERS *The Daily Times, The Nation.*

EMERGENCIES

RED CROSS/CRESCENT SOCIETIES PO Box 30096, Capital City, Lilongwe 3, tel/fax 775 590.

UK/USA/CANADIAN REPS UK: PO Box 30042, Lilongwe 3, tel 782 400, fax 782 657, email britcomm@malawi.net. USA: PO Box 30016, Area 40, Flat 24, Kenyatta Road, Lilongwe 3, tel 783 166, fax 780 471, email dos-lilongwe@malawi.net. Canada: The Canadian High Commission in Lusaka (Zambia) deals with enquiries relating to Malawi.

Global weather guide p 818, Rainy seasons worldwide p 829, Vaccinations required p 832, Recommended reading p 848, Dependent territories p 812.

MALAYSIA

STATE OF THE NATION

SAFETY Generally safe. Easternmost islands possibly unsafe, following high-profile kidnapping of tourists by guerrillas from neighbouring Philippines.

LIFE EXPECTANCY M 69.9, F 74.3.

PEOPLE AND PLACE

CAPITAL Kuala Lumpur.

LANGUAGE Bahasa Malaysia.

PEOPLES Malay, Chinese, Indigenous tribes, Indian.

RELIGION Muslim, Buddhist, Chinese faiths, Christian, traditional beliefs.

SIZE (KM) 329,758.

POPULATION 21,500,000.

POP DENSITY/KM 65.

FOOD Every type of South-East Asian cooking. Many dishes are based on a blend of spices, ginger, coconut milk and peanuts. *Sambals* (ground chilli, onion and tamarind based pastes) are often used as side dishes. A national favourite is *satay*, a variety of meats barbecued on small skewers, with a spicy peanut dipping sauce and a salad of cucumber, onion and compressed rice cakes.

TRAVEL PLANNING

WHEN TO GO Tropical without extremely high temperatures. The main rainy season in the east is between November and February, August is the wettest period on the west coast.

MEDICAL CARE Good, but insurance recommended.

CURRENCY Ringgit (RM) = 100 sen.

FINANCE Credit cards and travellers' cheques generally accepted.

AIRPORTS Kuala Lumpur (KUL) 50 m from the city, Penang (PEN) 16 km from Georgetown, Kota Kinabalu (BKI) 6.5 km from the city, Kuching (KCH) 11 km from the city.

INTERNAL TRAVEL Reasonable internal air and rail networks. Most roads in the Peninsular states are paved. Car hire easily available.

BUSINESS HOURS 0830-1600/1730 Monday-Friday, 0800-1200 Saturday.

GMT +8.

VOLTAGE GUIDE 220 AC, 50 Hz.

RED TAPE

VISAS (AUS/CANADA/UK/US) None.

REPS IN UK/USA/CANADA UK: 45 Belgrave Square, London SW1X 8QT, tel 020 7235 8033, fax 020 7235 5161, email mhc.london-ny@btinternet.com. USA: 2401 Massachusetts Avenue, NW, Washington, DC 20008, tel 202 328 2700, fax 202 483 7661, email mwashdc@erols.com. Canada: 60 Boteler Street, Ottawa, Ontario, K1N 8Y7, tel 613 241 5182, fax 613 241 5214, email mwottawa@istar.ca.

CUSTOMS REGULATIONS Duty free allowance: 200 cigarettes or 50 cigars or 225 g of tobacco, 1 ltr of spirits or wine or malt liquor, 1 bottle of perfume up to the value of M$200, gifts and souvenirs not exceeding a total value of M$200, 100 matches. Prohibited: Goods from Israel, non-prescribed drugs, weapons, pornography and any cloth bearing the imprint or reproduction of any verses of The Koran. Drug-smuggling carries the death penalty.

DRIVING REQUIREMENTS An International Driving Permit. UK citizens may use a national licence which must be endorsed by the Registrar of Motor Vehicles in Malaysia.

KEEPING IN TOUCH

BBC WORLD SERVICE MHz 17.89, 15.40, 11.96, 6.190.

ENGLISH-LANGUAGE NEWSPAPERS *Malay Mail, New Straits Times, The Sun, The Star*.

EMERGENCIES

RED CROSS/CRESCENT SOCIETIES JKR 32, Jalan Ampang, 55000 Kuala Lumpur, tel 3 457 8122, fax 3 453 3191, email mrcs@po.jaring.my.

UK/USA/CANADIAN REPS UK: 185 Jalan Ampang, 50450 Kuala Lumpur, tel 3 248 2122, fax 3 244 9692. USA: 376 Jalan Tun Razak, 50400 Kuala Lumpur, tel 3 248 9011, fax 3 242 2207, email lrckl@usia.gov. Canada: PO Box 10990, 7th Floor, Plaza MBF, 172 Jalan Ampang, 50732 Kuala Lumpur, tel 3 261 2000, fax 3 261 3428, email klmpr@klmpr01.x400.gc.ca.

Global weather guide p 818, Rainy seasons worldwide p 829, Vaccinations required p 832, Recommended reading p 848, Dependent territories p 812.

MALDIVES

STATE OF THE NATION

SAFETY Safe.

LIFE EXPECTANCY M 66.2, F 63.2.

PEOPLE AND PLACE

CAPITAL Malé.

LANGUAGE Dhivehi.

PEOPLES Maldivian, of Arabic descent. Indian and Sri Lankan minorities.

RELIGION Sunni Muslim (100%).

SIZE (KM) 298.

POPULATION 282,000.

POP DENSITY/KM 940.

FOOD All foodstuffs, other than seafood, are imported and most resorts serve international cuisine. The local seafood is superb, and good curries can be had on most of the islands.

TRAVEL PLANNING

WHEN TO GO Hot and tropical. The best time to visit is between November and April. The south west sees monsoon weather from May to October.

MEDICAL CARE Adequate but repatriation insurance cover recommended.

CURRENCY Maldivian rufiya (Rf) = 100 laaris.

FINANCE Most island resorts accept credit cards and travellers' cheques.

AIRPORTS Hulule International (MLE) on Hulule Island, 2 km from Malé.

INTERNAL TRAVEL Internal air and ferry services between islands. Individual islands rarely take longer than half an hour to cross on foot.

BUSINESS HOURS 0730-1430 Sunday - Thursday.

GMT +5.

VOLTAGE GUIDE 220 AC, 50 Hz.

RED TAPE

VISAS (AUS/CANADA/UK/US) Issued on arrival.

REPS IN UK/USA/CANADA UK: 22 Nottingham Place, London W1M 3FB, tel 020 7224 2135, fax 020 7224 2157 email maldives.high.commission@virgin.net. USA: (Mission to the UN) Suite 800C, 820 Second Avenue, New York, NY 10017, tel 212 599 6195, fax 212 661 6405, email mdvun@undp.org. Canada: n/a.

CUSTOMS REGULATIONS Duty free allowance: A reasonable amount of cigarettes, cigars and tobacco, a reasonable amount of gifts. Prohibited: Pornographic literature, idols of worship, pork products and certain other animal products, explosives, weapons, drugs (the penalty for carrying drugs is life imprisonment), alcohol without an official licence. Prohibited exports: turtle shell and turtle shell products, black coral eel, pufferfish, parrotfish, skate and ray, big-eyed scad under 15cm, bait fish used in tuna fishery, dolphin, whale, lobster, all stony coral, triton shell, trochus shell and pearl oyster.

DRIVING REQUIREMENTS n/a.

KEEPING IN TOUCH

BBC WORLD SERVICE MHz 17.64, 15.57, 12.09, 9.410.

ENGLISH-LANGUAGE NEWSPAPERS The Maldives News Bulletin (weekly).

EMERGENCIES

RED CROSS/CRESCENT SOCIETIES n/a.

UK/USA/CANADIAN REPS UK, USA, Canada: All three countries have embassies or consuls in Colombo (Sri Lanka) dealing with enquiries related to the Maldives.

Global weather guide p 818, Rainy seasons worldwide p 829, Vaccinations required p 832, Recommended reading p 848, Dependent territories p 812.

MALI

STATE OF THE NATION

SAFETY Generally safe. Area north of Bamako potentially affected by ethnic tensions: seek latest information at time of visit.

LIFE EXPECTANCY M 52, F 54.6.

PEOPLE AND PLACE

CAPITAL Bamako.

LANGUAGE French.

PEOPLES Bambara, Malinke, Tuareg.

RELIGION Islam (mainly Sunni Muslim), traditional beliefs.

SIZE (KM) 1,240,192.

POPULATION 11,800,000.

POP DENSITY/KM 10.

FOOD Most towns have small restaurants serving north African and local dishes, including the Malian speciality of *La Capitaine Sangha*, a Nile perch served with hot chilli sauce, whole fried bananas, and rice. Beef *brochettes* and fried plantains are sold at street stalls.

TRAVEL PLANNING

WHEN TO GO The rainy season runs from June to October. October to February is cool, followed by extremely hot, dry weather until June.

MEDICAL CARE Very limited. Take medical supplies. Insurance with repatriation cover strongly recommended.

CURRENCY Communauté Financiaire Africaine franc (CFAfr) = 100 centimes.

FINANCE Limited acceptance of credit cards and travellers' cheques.

AIRPORTS Bamako (BKO) 15 km from the city.

INTERNAL TRAVEL Limited air travel. The rail link from Bamako to Kayes is used more than the roads, which range from moderate to very bad, with frequent stops at police checkpoints. Off the main roads, travel in convoy with a set of spare parts. Travel is difficult during the rainy season.

BUSINESS HOURS 0730-1230, 1430-1600 Monday-Thursday, 0730-1230, 1430-1730 Friday.

GMT GMT.

VOLTAGE GUIDE 220 AC, 50 Hz.

RED TAPE

VISAS (AUS/CANADA/UK/US) Required.

REPS IN UK/USA/CANADA UK: n/a. USA: 2130 R Street, NW, Washington, DC 20008, tel 202 332 2249, fax 202 332 6603. Canada: 50 Goulburn Avenue, Ottawa, Ontario K1N 8C8, tel 613 232 1501, fax 613 232 7429.

CUSTOMS REGULATIONS Duty free allowance: 1000 cigarettes or 250 cigars or 2 kg of tobacco, 2 bottles of alcoholic beverage, a reasonable amount of perfume for personal use. NB. Cameras and films must be declared. An import permit is needed for sporting guns. Plants, except fruit and vegetables need a certificate.

DRIVING REQUIREMENTS International Driving Permit required.

KEEPING IN TOUCH

BBC WORLD SERVICE MHz 17.71, 15.40, 12.10, 6.005.

ENGLISH-LANGUAGE NEWSPAPERS None.

EMERGENCIES

RED CROSS/CRESCENT SOCIETIES BP 280, Bamako, tel 244 569, fax 240 414.

UK/USA/CANADIAN REPS UK: rue 111, Badalabougou-Ouest, Porte 89, Bamako, tel 224 738, fax 220 853. USA: 3 rue de Rochester NY et rue Mohamed V, Bamako, tel 225 470, fax 223 712. Canada: BP 198, route de Koulikoro, Bamado, tel 212 236, fax 214 362.

Global weather guide p 818, Rainy seasons worldwide p 829, Vaccinations required p 832, Recommended reading p 848, Dependent territories p 812.

MALTA

STATE OF THE NATION

SAFETY Safe.

LIFE EXPECTANCY M 74.9, F 79.3.

PEOPLE AND PLACE

CAPITAL Valletta.

LANGUAGE Maltese, English.

PEOPLES Of mixed Sicilian, Norman, Spanish, English, Arabic and Italian descent.

RELIGION Roman Catholic (98%).

SIZE (KM) 316.

POPULATION 374,000.

POP DENSITY/KM 1,169.

FOOD Local dishes include *fenek* (rabbit cooked in wine), and pork and fish dishes are popular.

TRAVEL PLANNING

WHEN TO GO Warm for most of the year, and rain falls for very short periods. The hottest months are between July and September, but the heat is tempered by cooling sea breezes.

MEDICAL CARE Good and free for UK citizens.

CURRENCY Maltese lira (Lm) = 1000 mils.

FINANCE Credit cards and travellers' cheques generally accepted.

AIRPORTS Malta (MLA) 5 km from Valletta.

INTERNAL TRAVEL Helicopter and ferry services between Malta and Gozo. Roads are in good condition.

BUSINESS HOURS 0830-1245, 1430-1730 Monday-Friday, 0830-1200 Saturday.

GMT +1(+2 in summer).

VOLTAGE GUIDE 240 AC, 50 Hz.

RED TAPE

VISAS (AUS/CANADA/UK/US) None.

REPS IN UK/USA/CANADA UK: Malta House, 36-38 Piccadilly, London W1V 0PQ, tel 020 7292 4800, fax 020 7734 1831. USA: 2017 Connecticut Avenue, NW, Washington, DC 20008, tel 202 462 3611, fax 202 387 5470, email malta-embassy@compuserve.com. Canada: 3300 Bloor Street West, West Tower, Suite 730, Etobicoke, Ontario M8X 2X2, tel 416 207 0922, fax 416 207 0986.

CUSTOMS REGULATIONS Duty free allowance: 200 cigarettes or 250 g of tobacco, 1 ltr of spirits and 1 ltr of wine, perfume not exceeding Lm 2 in value. Prohibited: Firearms and ammunition, counterfeit goods and unlicenced drugs. Certain plants and meat products require an import licence.

DRIVING REQUIREMENTS Full national drivng licence.

KEEPING IN TOUCH

BBC WORLD SERVICE MHz 12.10, 9.410, 6.195, 0.195.

ENGLISH-LANGUAGE NEWSPAPERS *The Times, The Malta Independent.*

EMERGENCIES

RED CROSS/CRESCENT SOCIETIES 104 St Ursula Street, Valletta VLT 05, tel 222 645, fax 243 664, email redcross@waldonet.net.mt.

UK/USA/CANADIAN REPS UK: PO Box 506, 7 St Anne Street, Floriana, Valletta VLt 15, tel 233 134, fax 242 001, email bhc@vol.nct.mt. USA: PO Box 535, 3rd Floor, Development House, St Anne Street, Floriana, Valletta, tel 235 960, fax 243 229, email usismalt@vol.net.mt. Canada: Demajo House, 103 Archbishop Street, Valletta, tel/fax 243 147, email canhcon@malta.net.

Global weather guide p 818, Rainy seasons worldwide p 829, Vaccinations required p 832, Recommended reading p 848, Dependent territories p 812.

MARSHALL ISLANDS

STATE OF THE NATION

SAFETY Safe.

LIFE EXPECTANCY 64.

PEOPLE AND PLACE

CAPITAL Majuro.

LANGUAGE Marshellese, English.

PEOPLES Micronesian.

RELIGION Christian, mostly Roman Catholic.

SIZE (KM) 181.

POPULATION 59,000.

POP DENSITY/KM 325.

FOOD Coconut crabs, mangrove clams, langusta, octopus, sea cucumber and eels are all regional delicacies. Breadfruit, taro, rice and cassava are staples.

TRAVEL PLANNING

WHEN TO GO Tropical with frequent rain and cooling sea breezes. Little seasonal variation.

MEDICAL CARE Insurance recommended.

CURRENCY US dollar (US$).

FINANCE Credit cards and travellers' cheques accepted in tourist resorts.

AIRPORTS Majuro (MAJ).

INTERNAL TRAVEL Inter-island ships. All main roads are paved. Car hire available.

BUSINESS HOURS 0800-1700 Mon-Friday (shopping hours, business hours n/a).

GMT +12.

VOLTAGE GUIDE 110 AC, 50 Hz.

RED TAPE

VISAS (AUS/CANADA/UK/US) Required.

REPS IN UK/USA/CANADA UK: n/a. USA: 2433 Massachusetts Avenue, NW, Washington, DC 20008, tel 202 234 5414, fax 202 232 3236 email info@rmiembassyus.org. Canada: n/a.

CUSTOMS REGULATIONS Duty free allowance: 600 cigarettes or 454 g of cigars or tobacco, 2 ltrs of alcoholic beverage (alcohol allowance for passengers over 21 only). Prohibited: Firearms, ammunition, drugs and pornography. Coral, turtle shells and certain other natural resources, artefacts or objects of historical value cannot be exported.

DRIVING REQUIREMENTS National driving licence.

KEEPING IN TOUCH

BBC WORLD SERVICE MHz 15.36, 11.10, 9.740, 7.145.

ENGLISH-LANGUAGE NEWSPAPERS The *Marshall Islands Journal, The Pacific Daily News.*

EMERGENCIES

RED CROSS/CRESCENT SOCIETIES n/a.

UK/USA/CANADIAN REPS UK:n/a . USA: PO Box 1379, Majuro, MH 96960-1379, tel 247 4011, fax 247 4012. Canada: n/a.

Global weather guide p 818, Rainy seasons worldwide p 829, Vaccinations required p 832, Recommended reading p 848, Dependent territories p 812.

MAURITANIA

STATE OF THE NATION

SAFETY Fairly safe except in disputed border areas with Morocco.

LIFE EXPECTANCY M 51.9, F 55.1.

PEOPLE AND PLACE

CAPITAL Nouakchott.

LANGUAGE Arabic and French.

PEOPLES Maures, Havalin, Senegalese, Tukolor, Peulh and Wolof.

RELIGION Muslim (100%).

SIZE (KM) 1, 030, 700.

POPULATION 2, 500, 000.

POP DENSITY/KM 2.

FOOD Local cuisine is mostly based on lamb, goat and rice. Dishes include *mechoui* (whole roast lamb), dates, spiced fish and rice with vegetables, dried meat with *couscous*. Alcohol may be found in hotel bars.

TRAVEL PLANNING

WHEN TO GO Generally hot and dry. The south sees rainfall from July-September.

MEDICAL CARE Limited, insurance with repatriation cover strongly recommended.

CURRENCY Mauritanian ouguiya (UM) = 5 khoums.

FINANCE Credit cards generally not accepted, limited use of travellers' cheques.

AIRPORTS Nouakchott (NKC) 4 km from the city.

INTERNAL TRAVEL Limited internal flights but possible to charter light aircraft. Only one rail line serving the ore mines, services are free but the journeys are arduous. Main roads are paved and adequate, others are sand tracks requiring 4-wheel-drive vehicles. Car hire available.

BUSINESS HOURS 0800-1500 Saturday-Wednesday, 0800-1300 Thursday.

GMT GMT.

VOLTAGE GUIDE 127/220 AC, 50 Hz.

RED TAPE

VISAS (AUS/CANADA/UK/US) Required.

REPS IN UK/USA/CANADA UK: 140 Bow Common Lane, London E3 4BH, tel 020 8980 4382, fax 020 8980 2232. USA: 2129 Leroy Place, NW, Washington, DC 20008, tel 202 232 5700, fax 202 319 2623. Canada: 249 McLeod Street, Ottawa, Ontario K2P 1A1, tel 613 237 3283, fax 613 237 3287.

CUSTOMS REGULATIONS Duty free allowance: 200 cigarettes or 25 cigars or 450 g of tobacco (women - cigarettes only), 50 g of perfume, 250 ml *eau de toilette*. Prohibited: Alcohol.

DRIVING REQUIREMENTS International Driving Permit recommended.

KEEPING IN TOUCH

BBC WORLD SERVICE MHz 17.71, 15.40, 12.10, 6.005.

ENGLISH-LANGUAGE NEWSPAPERS None.

EMERGENCIES

RED CROSS/CRESCENT SOCIETIES BP 344, Nouakchott, tel 251 249, fax 254 784.

UK/USA/CANADIAN REPS UK: The British Embassy in Rabat (Morocco) deals with enquiries relating to Mauritania. USA: BP 222, Nouakchott, tel 252 660, fax 251 592 Canada: The Canadian Embassy in Dakar (Senegal) deals with enquiries relating to Mauritania.

Global weather guide p 818, Rainy seasons worldwide p 829, Vaccinations required p 832, Recommended reading p 848, Dependent territories p 812.

MAURITIUS

STATE OF THE NATION

SAFETY Safe.

LIFE EXPECTANCY M 67.9, F 75.1.

PEOPLE AND PLACE

CAPITAL Port Louis.

LANGUAGE English.

PEOPLES Of Indian descent and Creole. Minorities of Chinese and French descent.

RELIGION Hindu, Roman Catholic, Muslim.

SIZE (KM) 2040.

POPULATION 1,200,000.

POP DENSITY/KM 649.

FOOD French, Creole, Indian and Chinese cuisine, generally of a high standard although restaurants usually depend on imported foodstuff. Specialities include venison in season, *camarans* (freshwater prawns) in hot sauces, creole fish, fresh pineapple with chilli sauce, and rice with curry.

TRAVEL PLANNING

WHEN TO GO Warm coastal climate, particularly from January-April. The cyclone season is from December to March.

MEDICAL CARE Good, but insurance recommended.

CURRENCY Mauritian rupee (MRs) = 100 cents.

FINANCE Credit cards and travellers' cheques generally accepted.

AIRPORTS Mauritius (MRU) 48 km from Port Louis.

INTERNAL TRAVEL Good network of paved roads. Numerous car hire firms.

BUSINESS HOURS 0900-1600 Mon-Friday.

GMT +4.

VOLTAGE GUIDE 220 AC, 50 Hz.

RED TAPE

VISAS (AUS/CANADA/UK/US) None.

REPS IN UK/USA/CANADA UK: 32-33 Elvaston Place, London SW7 5NW, tel 020 7581 0294, fax 020 7823 8437, email londonmhc@btinternet.com. USA: 4301 Connecticut Avenue, Suite 441, NW, Washington, DC 20008, tel 202 244 1491, fax 202 966 0983, email mauritius.embassy@ CWIX.com. Canada: 606 Cathcart Street, Suite 200, Montréal, Québec H3B 1K9, tel 514 393 9500, fax 514 393 9324.

CUSTOMS REGULATIONS Duty free allowance: For travellers over 16, 250 g of tobacco products or 50 cigars, 1 ltr of spirits and 2 ltrs of wine or beer, 250 ml of *eau de toilette* and a small quantity of perfume for personal use. Prohibited: Sugar cane. Other fruit, vegetables, flowers, plants and seeds must be declared, as must firearms and ammuntition.

DRIVING REQUIREMENTS International Driving Permit recommended, although foreign licences are accepted.

KEEPING IN TOUCH

BBC WORLD SERVICE MHz 19.55, 15.31, 9.510, 5.975.

ENGLISH-LANGUAGE NEWSPAPERS *L'Express* and *Le Mauricien* are also published in English.

EMERGENCIES

RED CROSS/CRESCENT SOCIETIES Ste Thérèse Street, Curepipe, tel 230 676 3604, fax 230 674 8855.

UK/USA/CANADIAN REPS UK: PO Box 1063, Les Cascades Building, Edith Cavell Street, Port Louis, tel 211 1361, fax 211 1369, email bhc@bow.intnet.mu. USA: 4th Floor, Rogers House, John Kennedy Street, Port Louis, tel 208 2347, fax 208 9534, email usembass@bow.intnet.mu. Canada: The Canadian High Commission in Pretoria (South Africa) deals with enquiries relating to Mauritius.

Global weather guide p 818, Rainy seasons worldwide p 829, Vaccinations required p 832, Recommended reading p 848, Dependent territories p 812.

MEXICO

STATE OF THE NATION

SAFETY High levels of crime and violence, often linked to family honour, illegal border-crossing or drug-smuggling, but these may not affect foreigners. Central Chiapas region volatile: seek latest information at time of visit.

LIFE EXPECTANCY M 69.5, F 75.1.

PEOPLE AND PLACE

CAPITAL Mexico City.

LANGUAGE Spanish.

PEOPLES Mestizo, indigenous Indian, European.

RELIGION Roman Catholic (95%).

SIZE (KM) 1,953,162.

POPULATION 95,800,000.

POP DENSITY/KM 50.

FOOD Each region has its own specialities, but national dishes include *enchilidas* and *tacos* filled with pork, chicken, cheese, chilli or vegetables. *Guacamole*, an avocado salsa, is a popular accompaniment. A national favourite is *turkey mole*. *Moles* are sauces made from several ingredients including chillis, tomatoes, nuts and chocolate.

TRAVEL PLANNING

WHEN TO GO The plateau and high mountains are warm for much of the year. The Pacific coast has a tropical climate.

MEDICAL CARE Good but insurance recommended.

CURRENCY New peso (peso) = 100 centavos.

FINANCE Credit cards widely accepted, travellers' cheques generally accepted.

AIRPORTS (And distances from the nearest city): Mexico City (MEX) 13 km, Guadalajara (GDL) 20 km, Acapulco (ACA) 26 km, Monterrey (MTY) 24 km.

INTERNAL TRAVEL Good domestic air and rail networks. Extensive road network, but less than half is paved. Car hire available.

BUSINESS HOURS Vary considerably, usually 0900-1400, 1500-1800 Monday-Friday.

GMT -6 to -8.

VOLTAGE GUIDE 110 AC, 60 Hz.

RED TAPE

VISAS (AUS/CANADA/UK/US) Not required but tourist cards issued.

REPS IN UK/USA/CANADA UK: 8 Halkin Street, London SW1Y 7DW, tel 020 7235 6393, fax 0900 165 9927. USA: 2827 16th Street, NW, Washington DC 20009, tel 202 736 1000, fax 202 797 8458. Canada: Suite 1500, 45 O'Connor Street, Ottawa, Ontario K1P 1A4, tel 613 233 8988, fax 613 235 9123, email info@embamexcan.com.

CUSTOMS REGULATIONS Duty free allowance: For travellers over 18, 400 cigarettes or 50 cigars or 250 pipe tobacco, 3 ltrs of wine or spirits, a reasonable amount of perfume or *eau de toilette*, total of 2 photo, movie or video cameras for non-residents and up to 12 unexposed rolls of film or video cassettes for each camera, goods up to the value of US$300 or equivalent. Prohibited: Uncanned food, pork or pork products, plants, fruits, vegetables and their products.

DRIVING REQUIREMENTS International Driving Permit or full British driving licence.

KEEPING IN TOUCH

BBC WORLD SERVICE MHz 15.22, 9.590, 6.195, 5.975.

ENGLISH-LANGUAGE NEWSPAPERS *The News, Mexico City Times.*

EMERGENCIES

RED CROSS/CRESCENT SOCIETIES Calle Luis Bives 200, Colonia Palanco, Mexico DF 11510, tel 5 395 1111, fax 5 395 1598, email cruzroja@mexporta.com.

UK/USA/CANADIAN REPS UK: Rio Lerma 71, Colonia Cuauhtémoc, 06500 Mexico DF, tel 5 207 2089, fax 5 207 7672, email infogen@embajadabritanica.com.mx. USA: Paseo de la Reforma 305, 06500 Mexico DF, tel 5 209 9100, fax 5 208 3373, email embeuamx@usia.gov. Canada: Calle Schiller 529, Colonia Rincon del Bosque, 11560 Mexico DF, tel 5 724 7900, fax 5 724 7980, email www@canada.org.mx.

Global weather guide p 818, Rainy seasons worldwide p 829, Vaccinations required p 832, Recommended reading p 848, Dependent territories p 812.

MICRONESIA

STATE OF THE NATION

SAFETY Safe.

LIFE EXPECTANCY 67.

PEOPLE AND PLACE

CAPITAL Palikir (Pohnpei Island).

LANGUAGE English, Trukese, Pohnpeian, Losrean, Mortlockese.

PEOPLES Micronesian, Melanesian.

RELIGION Roman Catholic (50%), Protestant (48%).

SIZE (KM) 702.

POPULATION 109,000.

POP DENSITY/KM 156.

FOOD Local specialities include breadfruit, yams, and thin slices of raw fish dipped in peppery sauce. *Sakau* (known as *kava* in the rest of Polynesia) is made from the root of a shrub which yields a mildly narcotic substance when squeezed through hibiscus bark, and served at numerous bars.

TRAVEL PLANNING

WHEN TO GO Humid and hot all year round with abundant rainfall.

MEDICAL CARE Basic. Insurance recommended.

CURRENCY US dollar (US$).

FINANCE Credit cards and travellers' cheques are accepted on those islands with tourist facilities.

AIRPORTS Pohnpei (PNI) 5 km from Kolonia.

INTERNAL TRAVEL Ships visit outlying islands. Good roads in major island centres. Car hire available in larger towns.

BUSINESS HOURS 0800-1700 Mon-Friday.

GMT +10 to +11.

VOLTAGE GUIDE 110/120 AC, 60 Hz.

RED TAPE

VISAS (AUS/CANADA/UK/US) None.

REPS IN UK/USA/CANADA UK: n/a. USA: 1725 N Street, NW, Washington, DC 20036, tel 202 223 4383, fax 202 223 4391, email fsm@fsmembassy.org. Canada: n/a.

CUSTOMS REGULATIONS Duty free allowance: 600 cigarettes or 454 g of cigars or tobacco, 2 ltrs of alcoholic beverage (alcohol allowances for travellers over 21). Prohibited: Firearms and ammunition. Plants and animals must be declared and will be subject to restrictions.

DRIVING REQUIREMENTS International Driving Permit or national licence.

KEEPING IN TOUCH

BBC WORLD SERVICE MHz 15.36, 11.10, 9.740, 7.145.

ENGLISH-LANGUAGE NEWSPAPERS *Pacific Daily News.*

EMERGENCIES

RED CROSS/CRESCENT SOCIETIES n/a.

UK/USA/CANADIAN REPS UK: n/a. USA: PO Box 1286, Kolonia, Pohnpei FSM 96941, tel 320 2187, fax 320 2186, email USEmbassy@mail.fm. Canada: n/a.

Global weather guide p 818, Rainy seasons worldwide p 829, Vaccinations required p 832, Recommended reading p 848, Dependent territories p 812.

MOLDOVA

STATE OF THE NATION

SAFETY Seek latest information at time of visit.

LIFE EXPECTANCY M 63.5, F 71.3.

PEOPLE AND PLACE

CAPITAL Chisinau.

LANGUAGE Romanian.

PEOPLES Moldovan (65%). Ukranian, Russian, Gagauz.

RELIGION Eastern Orthodox Christian and other Christian denominations. Small Jewish community.

SIZE (KM) 33,700.

POPULATION 4,500,000.

POP DENSITY/KM 134.

FOOD Specialities include *tocana* (pork stew) served with watermelons and apples, *mititeyi* (grilled sausages with onion and pepper), *mamaliga* (sticky maize pie) served with *brinza* (feta cheese). Local wine can be excellent.

TRAVEL PLANNING

WHEN TO GO Warm summers from May - September. Cold, sometimes snowy winters.

MEDICAL CARE Free emergency treatment but supplies may be limited, insurance recommended.

CURRENCY Leu (MDL) = 100 bani.

FINANCE Very limited acceptance of both credit cards and travellers' cheques.

AIRPORTS Chisinau (KIV) 14.5 km from the city.

INTERNAL TRAVEL Reasonable rail and road network. Car hire available.

BUSINESS HOURS 0900-1700 Monday to Saturday (shopping hours, business hours n/a).

GMT +2 (+3 in summer).

VOLTAGE GUIDE 220 AC, 50 Hz.

RED TAPE

VISAS (AUS/CANADA/UK/US) Required.

REPS IN UK/USA/CANADA UK: n/a. USA: 2101 S Street, NW, Washington, DC 20008, tel 202 667 1130, fax 202 667 1204, email moldova@dgs.dgsys.com. Canada: n/a.

CUSTOMS REGULATIONS Duty free allowance: 200 cigarettes, 1 ltr of spirits and 1 ltr of wine, a reasonable quantity of perfume for personal use (for passengers over 18).

DRIVING REQUIREMENTS International Driving Permit.

KEEPING IN TOUCH

BBC WORLD SERVICE MHz 17.64, 12.10, 9.410, 6.195.

ENGLISH-LANGUAGE NEWSPAPERS None.

EMERGENCIES

RED CROSS/CRESCENT SOCIETIES n/a.

UK/USA/CANADIAN REPS UK: The British Embassy in Moscow (Russia) deals with enquiries relating to Moldova. USA: 103 Alexei Mateevici str., 2009 Chisinau, tel 2 233 772, fax 2 233 044. Canada: The Canadian Embassy in Bucharest (Romania) deals with enquiries relating to Moldova.

Global weather guide p 818, Rainy seasons worldwide p 829, Vaccinations required p 832, Recommended reading p 848, Dependent territories p 812.

MONACO

STATE OF THE NATION

SAFETY Safe.

LIFE EXPECTANCY M 73.1, F 81.3.

PEOPLE AND PLACE

CAPITAL Monaco.

LANGUAGE French.

PEOPLES French, Italian, American, British, Belgian, native Monégasque.

RELIGION Roman Catholic. Protestant minority.

SIZE (KM) 1.95.

POPULATION 32,000.

POP DENSITY/KM 16,410.

FOOD Similar to France. Local specialities include *barbagiuan* (pastry with rice and pumpkin), *socca* (chickpea flour pancakes) and *stocafi* (dried cod with tomatoes).

TRAVEL PLANNING

WHEN TO GO Mild, with most rain falling during the cool winter months. Hottest months are July and August.

MEDICAL CARE Good, but expensive, insurance strongly recommended.

CURRENCY French franc = 100 centimes.

FINANCE All major credit cards and travellers' cheques widely accepted.

AIRPORTS None, but plenty of helicopter pads.

INTERNAL TRAVEL Good rail and road connections.

BUSINESS HOURS 0900-1200, 1400-1700 Monday - Friday.

GMT +1 (+2 in summer).

VOLTAGE GUIDE 220 AC, 50 Hz.

RED TAPE

VISAS (AUS/CANADA/UK/US) None.

REPS IN UK/USA/CANADA UK: 4 Cromwell Place, London SW7 2JE, tel 020 7225 2679, fax 020 7581 8161. USA: 23rd Floor, 565 Fifth Avenue, New York, NY 10017, tel 212 286 3330, fax 212 286 9890, email mgto@monaco.mc/usa/. Canada: 1155 Sherbrooke West, Suite 1500, Montréal, Québec H3A 2W1, tel 514 849 0589, fax 514 631 2771.

CUSTOMS REGULATIONS Duty free allowance: As for France.

DRIVING REQUIREMENTS National driving licence.

KEEPING IN TOUCH

BBC WORLD SERVICE MHz 9.410, 6.195, 12.10, 0.648.

ENGLISH-LANGUAGE NEWSPAPERS None, but international press available.

EMERGENCIES

RED CROSS/CRESCENT SOCIETIES 27 boulevard de Suisse, Monte Carlo, tel 97 97 68 00, fax 93 15 90 47, email redcross@monaco.mc.

UK/USA/CANADIAN REPS UK: 33 boulevard Princesse Charlotte, 98005 Monaco, Cedex, tel 93 50 99 66, fax 97 70 72 00. USA: The American Consulate General in Marseille (France) deals with enquiries relating to Monaco. Canada: The Canadian Embassy in Paris deals with enquiries relating to Monaco.

Global weather guide p 818, Rainy seasons worldwide p 829, Vaccinations required p 832, Recommended reading p 848, Dependent territories p 812.

MONGOLIA

STATE OF THE NATION

SAFETY Safe.

LIFE EXPECTANCY M 62.4, F 67.3.

PEOPLE AND PLACE

CAPITAL Ulan Bator.

LANGUAGE Mongolian Khalkha.

PEOPLES Mongol (90%), Kazakh, Chinese and Russian minorities.

RELIGION Buddhist Lamaism.

SIZE (KM) 1,566,500.

POPULATION 2,600,000.

POP DENSITY/KM 2.

FOOD Meat based diet, with plenty of mutton and beef. A notable speciality is *boodog*, a whole carcass of a goat filled with burning stones and roasted from the inside. Mongolian vodka is excellent.

TRAVEL PLANNING

WHEN TO GO Winters (October to April) are severe. Summers (June to August) are short and mild.

MEDICAL CARE Limited, insurance with repatriation cover strongly recommended.

CURRENCY Tugrik (Tug) = 100 mungos.

FINANCE Limited acceptance of credit cards and travellers' cheques.

AIRPORTS Ulan Bator (ULN) 15 km from the city.

INTERNAL TRAVEL Internal flights are recommended for travel to remote regions. Limited rail network. Paved roads are only found in and around major cities. Car hire is available through tourism companies. Some fuel shortages. Camels and horses are often used.

BUSINESS HOURS 0900-1800 Mon-Friday, 0900-1500 Saturday.

GMT +9 (+8 in summer).

VOLTAGE GUIDE 220 AC, 50 Hz.

RED TAPE

VISAS (AUS/CANADA/UK/US) Required.

REPS IN UK/USA/CANADA UK: 7 Kensington Court, London W8 5DL, tel 020 7937 0150, fax 020 7937 1117. USA: 2833 M Street, NW, Washington, DC 20007, tel 202 333 7117, fax 202 298 9227, email monemb@aol.com. Canada: BCE Place, Suite 1800, 181 Bay Street, Toronto M5J 2TN, tel 416 865 7779, fax 416 863 1515, email consul@mongolia.org.

CUSTOMS REGULATIONS Duty free allowance: 200 cigarettes, 2 ltrs of alcoholic beverages, a reasonable amount of perfume. Prohibited: Guns, weapons, ammunition without special permission, explosive items, radioactive substances, narcotics, pornography, any publication, records, films or drawings critical of Mongolia, research materials, palaeontological and archaeological findings, collections of various plants and their seeds, birds and animals, wool, raw skins, hides and furs without permits.

DRIVING REQUIREMENTS n/a.

KEEPING IN TOUCH

BBC WORLD SERVICE MHz 17.76, 15.28, 11.96, 5.965.

ENGLISH-LANGUAGE NEWSPAPERS *The Mongol Messenger.*

EMERGENCIES

RED CROSS/CRESCENT SOCIETIES Central Post Office, PO Box 537, Ulan Bator 13, tel 1 312 578, fax 1 320 934, email redcross@magicnet.mn.

UK/USA/CANADIAN REPS UK: 30 Enkh Taivny Gudamzh, PO Box 703, Ulan Bator 13, tel 1 458 133, fax 1 458 036, email britemb@magicnet.mn. USA: The US Embassy in Beijing (China) deals with enquiries relating to Mongolia. Canada: PO Box 243, Peace and Friendship Palace, Peace Avenue, Ulan Bator 210644, tel 1 327 586, fax 1 325 530.

Global weather guide p 818,   Rainy seasons worldwide p 829,   Vaccinations required p 832,   Recommended reading p 848,   Dependent territories p 812.

MOROCCO

STATE OF THE NATION

SAFETY Safe, though women may experience harrassment. Beware offers of drugs, which may be a trap.

LIFE EXPECTANCY M 64.8, F 68.5.

PEOPLE AND PLACE

CAPITAL Rabat.

LANGUAGE Arabic.

PEOPLES Arab and Berber (99%).

RELIGION Muslim (98%).

SIZE (KM) 710,850.

POPULATION 28,000,000.

POP DENSITY/KM 63.

FOOD Typical specialities include rich, fragrant stews called *tajines*, made from marinated meat or poultry and often served with *couscous*. Also popular are *pastilla*, a pigeon-meat pastry, mchoui, pit-roasted mutton and *kab-el-ghzal*, almond pastries. Mint tea is drunk at every opportunity.

TRAVEL PLANNING

WHEN TO GO Warm Mediterranean climate on the coast, inland areas have a hotter, drier climate. Rain falls from November to March in coastal areas. April to August is the most popular time to visit.

MEDICAL CARE Good in cities and free for emergency treatment, otherwise insurance recommended.

CURRENCY Moroccan dirham (Dh) = 100 centimes.

FINANCE Limited acceptance of credit cards and travellers' cheques.

AIRPORTS Casablanca (CAS) 30 km from the city, Tangier (TNG) 12 km from the city.

INTERNAL TRAVEL Limited rail network but the services are cheap and regular. Major roads are all-weather, particularly in the north. Road travel in the interior is more difficult. Car hire can be expensive.

BUSINESS HOURS 0830-1200, 1430-1830 Monday-Friday.

GMT GMT.

VOLTAGE GUIDE 110/220 AC, 50 Hz.

RED TAPE

VISAS (AUS/CANADA/UK/US) None.

REPS IN UK/USA/CANADA UK: 49 Queen's Gate Gardens, London SW7 5NE, tel 020 7581 5001. USA: 1601 21st Street, NW, Washington, DC 20009, tel 202 462 7979, fax 202 265 0161, email sifamausa@trident.net. Canada: 38 Range Road, Ottawa, Ontario K1N 8.

CUSTOMS REGULATIONS Duty free allowance: 200 cigarettes or 50 cigars or 250 g of tobacco, 1 ltr of spirits and 1 ltr of wine, 50 g of perfume.

DRIVING REQUIREMENTS International Driving Permit or foreign driving licence.

KEEPING IN TOUCH

BBC WORLD SERVICE MHz 17.70, 15.40, 12.09, 6.005.

ENGLISH-LANGUAGE NEWSPAPERS None.

EMERGENCIES

RED CROSS/CRESCENT SOCIETIES BP 189, Rabat, tel 7 650 898, fax 7 759 395.

UK/USA/CANADIAN REPS UK: BP 45 RP, 17 boulevard de la Tour Hassan, Rabat, tel 7 729 696, fax 7 704 531, email sifamausa@ trident.net. USA: BP 120, 2 avenue de Marrakesh, Rabat, tel 7 762 265, fax 7 765 661, email iorabat@usia.gov. Canada: BP 709, 13 bis, rue Jaafar As-Sadik, Rabat-Agdal, tel 7 672 880, fax 7 627 187.

Global weather guide p 818, Rainy seasons worldwide p 829, Vaccinations required p 832, Recommended reading p 848, Dependent territories p 812.

MOZAMBIQUE

STATE OF THE NATION

SAFETY Generally safe, but many landmines remain.

LIFE EXPECTANCY M 43.9, F 46.6.

PEOPLE AND PLACE

CAPITAL Maputo.

LANGUAGE Portugese.

PEOPLES Makua Lomwe, Thonga, Malawi, Shona, Yao.

RELIGION Traditional beliefs (60%), Christianity (30%), Islam (10%).

SIZE (KM) 799,380.

POPULATION 18,700,000.

POP DENSITY/KM 24.

FOOD Many dishes are Portugese in origin. Specialities include *piri-piri* (spicy) chicken, Delagoa Bay prawns served with a hot sauce and *matapa* (sauce of ground peanuts and cassava leaves).

TRAVEL PLANNING

WHEN TO GO Hottest and wettest from October to March. The inland is cooler. The coast is warm and dry from April to September.

MEDICAL CARE Limited, insurance with repatriation cover recommended.

CURRENCY Mozambique metical (MT) = 100 centavos.

FINANCE Credit cards rarely used, very limited use of travellers' cheques.

AIRPORTS Maputo (MPM) 3 km from the city, Beira (BEW) 13 km from the city.

INTERNAL TRAVEL Air-taxi services are the safest means of transport outside the main cities. Train services are subject to disruption. Some major roads are tarred, but landmines may make travel by road outside the capital risky and up-to-the-minute advice should be sought. Hijackings are possible. Car hire is available - only hard currency is accepted.

BUSINESS HOURS 0730-1230, 1400-1730 Monday to Friday.

GMT +2.

VOLTAGE GUIDE 240 AC, 50 Hz.

RED TAPE

VISAS (AUS/CANADA/UK/US) Required.

REPS IN UK/USA/CANADA UK: 21 Fitzroy Square, London W1P 5HJ, tel 020 7383 3800, fax 020 7383 3801. USA: 1990 M Street, Suite 570, NW, Washington, DC 20036, email embamoc@aol.com. Also deals with enquiries from Canada.

CUSTOMS REGULATIONS Duty free allowance: 200 cigarettes or 250 g of tobacco, 1 bottle of spirits, a reasonable amount of perfume (opened). Prohibited: Narcotics. Firearms need a permit.

DRIVING REQUIREMENTS International Driving Licence.

KEEPING IN TOUCH

BBC WORLD SERVICE MHz 17.86, 11.94, 9.630, 6.005.

ENGLISH-LANGUAGE NEWSPAPERS None.

EMERGENCIES

RED CROSS/CRESCENT SOCIETIES CP 2986, Maputo, tel 1 490 943, fax 1 497 725.

UK/USA/CANADIAN REPS UK: CP 55, Avenida Vladimir 1 Lénine 310, Maputo, tel 1 420 111, fax 1 421 666, email bhc.maputo@teledata.mz. USA: CP 783, Avenida Kenneth Kaunda 193, Maputo, tel 1 492 797, fax 1 490 114, email usacomm@mail.tropical.co.mz. Canada: CP 1578, Avenida Julius Nyerere 1128, Maputo, tel 1 492 623, fax 1 492 667, email canembas@ecanada.uem.mz.

Global weather guide p 818, Rainy seasons worldwide p 829, Vaccinations required p 832, Recommended reading p 848, Dependent territories p 812.

MYANMAR (BURMA)

STATE OF THE NATION

SAFETY Foreigners may be required to keep to officially designated areas. Southern borders affected by low-level guerrilla war.

LIFE EXPECTANCY M 58.5 , F 61.8.

PEOPLE AND PLACE

CAPITAL Yangon (Rangoon).

LANGUAGE Burmese.

PEOPLES Burman (Bamah). Shan, Karen and Rakhine minorities.

RELIGION Buddhist (87%). Christian, Muslim, Hindu.

SIZE (KM) 676,552.

POPULATION 47,600,000.

POP DENSITY/KM 72.

FOOD Regional food is spicy. Dishes include *lethok son* (vegetarian rice salad), *oh-no khauk swe* (rice noodles, chicken and coconut milk), *mohinga* (fish soup with noodles). Fish, noodles, rice, vegetables, onions, ginger, garlic and chillies are the most common ingredients.

TRAVEL PLANNING

WHEN TO GO Monsoon climate. Hottest February-May. Rainy May-October, dry and cool October-February.

MEDICAL CARE Adequate but no free facilities, insurance recommended.

CURRENCY Kyat (Kt) = 100 pyas.

FINANCE Limited acceptance of credit cards. Travellers' cheques are accepted.

AIRPORTS Yangon (RGN) 19 km from the city.

INTERNAL TRAVEL Air travel is the most efficient and the only permissible means of transport for independent travellers. Rail services are subject to delays caused by climatic, technical and bureaucratic difficulties and tickets must be purchased as part of an organised tour group. Visitors can only use certain public bus services but privately operated buses have been introduced. Roads are being improved.

BUSINESS HOURS 0930-1630 Mon-Friday.

GMT +6.5.

VOLTAGE GUIDE 220/230 AC, 50 Hz.

RED TAPE

VISAS (AUS/CANADA/UK/US) Required.

REPS IN UK/USA/CANADA UK: 19a Charles Street, London W1X 8ER, tel 020 7499 8841, fax 020 7629 4169. USA: 2300 S Street, NW, Washington, DC 20008, tel 202 332 9044, fax 202 332 9046. Canada: Suite 902, The Sandringham, 85 Range Road, Ottawa, Ontario K1N 8J6, tel 613 232 6434, fax 613 232 6435.

CUSTOMS REGULATIONS Duty free allowance: For travellers over 17, 400 cigarettes or 100 cigars or 250 g of tobacco, 2 ltrs of alcohol, 0.5 ltrs of perfume or *eau de toilette*. Prohibited: Playing cards, gambling equipment, antiques, archaelogical items and pornography are prohibited. Jewellery, electrical goods and cameras must be declared or visitors may be refused to export the items on departure.

DRIVING REQUIREMENTS An International Driving Permit, which must be endorsed by local police.

KEEPING IN TOUCH

BBC WORLD SERVICE MHz 21.66, 15.36, 9.580, 6.035.

ENGLISH-LANGUAGE NEWSPAPERS *The New Light of Myanmar.*

EMERGENCIES

RED CROSS/CRESCENT SOCIETIES Red Cross Building, 42 Strand Road, Yangon, tel 1 296 552, fax 1 296 551.

UK/USA/CANADIAN REPS UK: 80 Strand Road, Yangon, tel 1 281 700, fax 1 289 566. USA: 581 Merchant Street, Yangon, tel 1 282 055, fax 1 280 409. Canada: The Canadian Embassy in Bangkok (Thailand) deals with enquiries relating to Myanmar.

Global weather guide p 818, Rainy seasons worldwide p 829, Vaccinations required p 832, Recommended reading p 848, Dependent territories p 812.

NAMIBIA

STATE OF THE NATION

SAFETY Safe, except possibly the Caprivi Strip and Angolan border, which have been affected by Angolan civil war.

LIFE EXPECTANCY M 51.8, F 53.

PEOPLE AND PLACE

CAPITAL Windhoek.

LANGUAGE English.

PEOPLES Ovambo (50%), Kavango, Damara, Herero.

RELIGION Christian majority.

SIZE (KM) 824,292.

POPULATION 1,700,000.

POP DENSITY/KM 2.

FOOD Game is a speciality. *Biltong* (air-dried meat) and *rauchfleisch* (smoked meat) are popular.

TRAVEL PLANNING

WHEN TO GO The coast is cool, damp and rain-free for most of the year, although coastal fog is common. Inland, the meagre rain falls from November to April (summer). Winter (June to September) is warm and pleasant, although nights can be cold.

MEDICAL CARE Adequate, but no free treatment. Insurance recommended.

CURRENCY Namibian dollar (NAD).

FINANCE Credit cards and travellers' cheques are generally accepted.

AIRPORTS Windhoek (WDH) 40 km from the city.

INTERNAL TRAVEL Flying is the quickest and sometimes most economical way to travel around the country. Planes can also be chartered. Efficient rail service, although limited in extent. Roads are generally well maintained. Car hire available.

BUSINESS HOURS 0800-1700 Mon-Friday.

GMT +2 (+1 from April-August).

VOLTAGE GUIDE 220/240 AC.

RED TAPE

VISAS (AUS/CANADA/UK/US) None.

REPS IN UK/USA/CANADA UK: 6 Chandos Street, London W1M 0LQ, tel 020 7636 6244, fax 020 7637 5694, email namibia-highcom@btconnect.com. USA: 1605 New Hampshire Avenue, NW, Washington, DC 20009, tel 202 986 0540, fax 202 986 0443, email embnamibia@ aol.com. Also deals with enquiries from Canada.

CUSTOMS REGULATIONS Duty free allowance: For travellers over 16, 400 cigarettes or 50 cigars or 250 g of tobacco, 2 ltrs of wine and 1 ltr of spirits, 50 ml of perfume and 250 ml of *eau de toilette*, gifts to the value of NAD 50,000 (including value of imported duty-free items). Prohibited: Handguns.

DRIVING REQUIREMENTS International Driving Permit.

KEEPING IN TOUCH

BBC WORLD SERVICE MHz 21.66, 15.40, 11.77, 6.190.

ENGLISH-LANGUAGE NEWSPAPERS *The Windhoek Advertiser, The Namibian.*

EMERGENCIES

RED CROSS/CRESCENT SOCIETIES PO Box 346, Windhoek, tel 61 235 216, fax 61 228 949, email namcross@iafrica.com.na.

UK/USA/CANADIAN REPS UK: PO Box 22202, 116 Robert Mugabe Avenue, Windhoek, tel 61 223 022, fax 61 228 895, email bhc@iwwn.com.na. USA: Private Bag 12029, 14 Lossen Street, Ausspannplatz, Windhoek, tel 61 221 601, fax 61 229 792. Canada: The Canadian High Commission in Pretoria (South Africa) deals with enquiries relating to Namibia.

Global weather guide p 818, Rainy seasons worldwide p 829, Vaccinations required p 832, Recommended reading p 848, Dependent territories p 812.

NAURU

STATE OF THE NATION

SAFETY Safe.

LIFE EXPECTANCY 67.

PEOPLE AND PLACE

CAPITAL Yaren District (no official capital).

LANGUAGE Nauruan and English.

PEOPLES Nauruan (62%), other Pacific islanders (25%), Chinese, Vietnamese, European.

RELIGION Christian, mainly Nauruan Protestant Church.

SIZE (KM) 21.3.

POPULATION 11,000.

POP DENSITY/KM 516.

FOOD Canned cuisine. Almost all foodstuff is imported. Very little fresh food -some fish and a little beef. No local fruit or vegetables.

TRAVEL PLANNING

WHEN TO GO March to October when the equatorial climate is tempered by northeast trade winds. November to February sees the western monsoon.

MEDICAL CARE Very basic, insurance recommended.

CURRENCY Australian dollar (A$).

FINANCE Credit cards accepted.

AIRPORTS Nauru Island (INU).

INTERNAL TRAVEL 19 km of sealed road circles the island, internal roads in good condition, car hire available.

BUSINESS HOURS n/a.

GMT +12.

VOLTAGE GUIDE 110/240 AC, 50 Hz.

RED TAPE

VISAS (AUS/CANADA/UK/US) Required.

REPS IN UK/USA/CANADA UK: Romshed Courtyard, Underriver, Nr Sevenoaks, Kent TN15 0SD, tel 01732 746 061, fax 01732 454 136, email info@weald.co.uk. USA: n/a. Canada: n/a.

CUSTOMS REGULATIONS Duty free allowance: 400 cigarettes or 50 cigars or 450 g of tobacco, 3 bottles of alcoholic beverage (for travellers over 21). Prohibited: Narcotics, firearms and pornography.

DRIVING REQUIREMENTS National driving licence.

KEEPING IN TOUCH

BBC WORLD SERVICE MHz 15.36, 11.77, 9.740, 5.975.

ENGLISH-LANGUAGE NEWSPAPERS *The Bulletin.*

EMERGENCIES

RED CROSS/CRESCENT SOCIETIES n/a.

UK/USA/CANADIAN REPS UK: The British Embassy is Suva (Fiji) deals with enquiries relating to Nauru. USA: The American Embassy in Suva (Fiji) deals with enquiries relating to Nauru. Canada: n/a.

Global weather guide p 818, Rainy seasons worldwide p 829, Vaccinations required p 832, Recommended reading p 848, Dependent territories p 812.

NEPAL

STATE OF THE NATION

SAFETY Safe, apart from a low-level Maoist insurgency in the far west, which has not so far affected foreigners.

LIFE EXPECTANCY M 57.6, F 57.1.

PEOPLE AND PLACE

CAPITAL Kathmandu.

LANGUAGE Nepali.

PEOPLES Nepalese, Sherpas, Newars.

RELIGION Hindu, Buddhist. Small Muslim minority.

SIZE (KM) 147, 181.

POPULATION 23, 200, 000.

POP DENSITY/KM 170.

FOOD *Dal Baht* - lentils and rice - is eaten most days. Newar cuisine includes spiced vegetables, chapatis and sweet snacks like *jelabis* (spirals of batter soaked in syrup and fried). Tibetan cooking inclues *thukba* (a hearty soup) and *momos* (ravioli). Meat is commonly goat, pork, chicken or buffalo as beef is forbidden.

TRAVEL PLANNING

WHEN TO GO Spring (March-May) and autumn (September-November) are the most pleasant seasons.

MEDICAL CARE Adequate in capital but no free treatment, insurance recommended.

CURRENCY Nepalese rupee (NRs) = 100 paisa.

FINANCE Major credit cards widely accepted, more limited acceptance of travellers' cheques.

AIRPORTS Kathmandu (KTM) 6.5 km from the city.

INTERNAL TRAVEL The road system is of unpredictable quality. Car hire available in Kathmandu.

BUSINESS HOURS 1000-1600/1700 Sun-Thursday.

GMT +5.45.

VOLTAGE GUIDE 220 AC, 50 Hz.

RED TAPE

VISAS (AUS/CANADA/UK/US) Required.

REPS IN UK/USA/CANADA UK: 12a Kensington Palace Gardens, London W8 4QU, tel 020 7229 1594, fax 020 7792 9861, email rnelondon@compuserve.com. USA: 820 Second Avenue, Suite 17B, 17th Floor, New York, NY 10017, tel 212 370 4189, fax 212 953 2038, email npln@undp.org. Canada: PO Box 33, 200 Bay Street, South Tower, 32nd Floor, Toronto M5J QJ9, tel 416 865 0210, fax 416 865 0904.

CUSTOMS REGULATIONS Duty free allowance: 200 cigarettes or 50 cigars, 1.15 ltrs of spirits or 12 cans of beer, a reasonable amount of perfume, 15 rolls of film. Prohibited: The export of goods over 100 years old. Permits required for the export of metal statues, sacred paintings and similar objects.

DRIVING REQUIREMENTS International Driving Permit valid for 15 days, thereafter a local licence is required.

KEEPING IN TOUCH

BBC WORLD SERVICE MHz 17.79, 15.31, 11.95, 5.975.

ENGLISH-LANGUAGE NEWSPAPERS *The Kathmandu Post* and *The Rising Nepal*.

EMERGENCIES

RED CROSS/CRESCENT SOCIETIES PO Box 217, Kathmandu, tel 1 270 650, fax 1 271 915, email nrcs@nhqs.wlink.com.np.

UK/USA/CANADIAN REPS UK: PO Box 106, Lainchaur, Kathmandu, tel 1 410 583, fax 1 411 789, email britemb@wlink.com.np. USA: PO Box 295, Pani Pokhari, Kathmandu, tel 1 411 179, fax 1 419 963. Canada: The Canadian High Commission in New Dehli deals with enquiries relating to Nepal.

Global weather guide p 818, Rainy seasons worldwide p 829, Vaccinations required p 832, Recommended reading p 848, Dependent territories p 812.

NETHERLANDS

STATE OF THE NATION

SAFETY Safe.

LIFE EXPECTANCY M 74.1, F 79.7.

PEOPLE AND PLACE

CAPITAL Amsterdam.

LANGUAGE Dutch.

PEOPLES Dutch (96%), Moroccan, Turkish.

RELIGION Roman Catholic, Protestant.

SIZE (KM) 33 920.

POPULATION 15,700,000.

POP DENSITY/KM 463.

FOOD Filled pancakes and 'green' herring are popular daytime snacks. More substantial dishes include *erwtensoep* (thick pea soup served with smoked sausage, bacon, pig's knuckle and bread), *hutspot* (potatoes, carrots and onions) served with *klapstuk* (stewed lean beef) and *rockworst* (kale and potatoes served with sausage).

TRAVEL PLANNING

WHEN TO GO Anytime, although winters can be fairly cold.

MEDICAL CARE Good and free for UK citizens.

CURRENCY Guilder (G) = 100 cents.

FINANCE Credit cards and travellers' cheques widely accepted.

AIRPORTS (And distances from nearest city): Amsterdam (AMS) 15 km, Rotterdam (RTM) 8 km, Eindhoven (EIN) 8km, Maastricht (MST) 8 km.

INTERNAL TRAVEL Efficient, cheap rail network, excellent road system.

BUSINESS HOURS 0830-1700 Mon-Friday.

GMT +1 (+2 in summer).

VOLTAGE GUIDE 220 AC, 50 Hz.

RED TAPE

VISAS (AUS/CANADA/UK/US) None.

REPS IN UK/USA/CANADA UK: 38 Hyde Park Gate, London SW7 5DP, tel 020 7590 3200, fax 020 7581 3458, email NLgovl@globalnet.co.uk. USA: 1 Rockefeller Plaza, 11th Floor, New York, NY 10020, tel 212 246 1429, fax 212 333 3603. Canada: 350 Albert Street, Ottawa, Ontario K1R 1A4, tel 613 237 5030, fax 613 237 6471, email nlgovott@netcom.ca.

CUSTOMS REGULATIONS Duty free allowance: For travellers from non-EU countries with goods purchased in non-EU countries: 200 cigarettes or 50 cigars or 100 cigarillos or 250 g of tobacco, 1 ltr of alcoholic beverages stronger than 22° proof or 2 ltrs less than 22% or 2 ltrs of fortified wine, 2 ltrs of wine, 8 ltrs of non-sparkling Luxembourg wine, 60 g of perfume and 250 ml of *eau de toilette*, other good worth G 125 if bought duty-free. For travellers from outside Europe: 400 cigarettes or 100 cigars or 500 g of tobacco, wine, spirits and perfume as for non-EU countries, other goods worth G 125. No limits on tobacco and alcohol imported within the EU for personal use.

DRIVING REQUIREMENTS National driving licence, EU pink format licence. Green Card advisable.

KEEPING IN TOUCH

BBC WORLD SERVICE MHz 12.10, 9.410, 6.195, 0.648.

ENGLISH-LANGUAGE NEWSPAPERS None. International press available.

EMERGENCIES

RED CROSS/CRESCENT SOCIETIES PO Box 28120, 2502 KC The Hague, tel 70 445 5666, fax 70 445 5777, email hq@redcross.nl.

UK/USA/CANADIAN REPS UK: Konigslaan 44, 1075 AE Amsterdam, tel 20 676 4343, fax 20 676 1069. USA: Museumplein 19, 1071 DJ Amsterdam, tel 20 575 5309, fax 20 575 5310. Canada: Sophialaan 7, 2514 GP The Hague, tel 70 311 1600, fax 70 311 1620 email info@canadatourism.nl.

Global weather guide p 818, Rainy seasons worldwide p 829, Vaccinations required p 832, Recommended reading p 848, Dependent territories p 812.

NEW ZEALAND

STATE OF THE NATION

SAFETY Safe.

LIFE EXPECTANCY M 74.1, F 79.7.

PEOPLE AND PLACE

CAPITAL Wellington.

LANGUAGE English.

PEOPLES European (82%), Maori (9%), Pacific Islanders.

RELIGION Christian denominations.

SIZE (KM) 266,171.

POPULATION 3,700,000.

POP DENSITY/KM 14.

FOOD New Zealand is a leading producer of meat and dairy products, and cuisine is largely based on these. Venison and game birds are also popular. A wide range of seafood is also available, including snapper, grouper, oysters and crayfish.

TRAVEL PLANNING

WHEN TO GO All year. Subtropical in the north and temperate in the south.

MEDICAL CARE Good and free state emergency treatment.

CURRENCY New Zealand dollar (NZ$).

FINANCE Credit cards widely accepted, travellers' cheques generally accepted.

AIRPORTS Auckland (AKL) 22.5 km from the city, Christchurch (CHC) 10 km from the city, Wellington (WLG) 8 km from the city.

INTERNAL TRAVEL Reliable rail service, good road networks.

BUSINESS HOURS 0900-1700 Mon-Friday.

GMT +12 (+11 in summer).

VOLTAGE GUIDE 230/240 AC, 50 Hz.

RED TAPE

VISAS (AUS/CANADA/UK/US) None.

REPS IN UK/USA/CANADA UK: New Zealand House, 80 Haymarket, London SW1Y 4TE, tel 020 7930 8422, fax 020 7839 4580. USA: 37 Observatory Circle, NW, Washington, DC 20008, tel 202 328 4800, fax 202 667 5227, email nz@nzemb.org. Canada: Suite 727, Metropolitan House, 99 Bank Street, Ottawa, Ontario, K1P 6G3, tel 613 238 5991, fax 613 238 5707, email nzh-cott@istar.ca.

CUSTOMS REGULATIONS Duty free allowance: For travellers over 17, 200 cigarettes or 50 cigars or 250 g of tobacco or a mixture of all three up to 250g, 4.5 ltrs of wine or beer, 1.125 ltrs or 40 oz of spirits or liqueurs, goods worth NZ$ 700. Prohibited: Firearms and weapons, ivory, toroise or turtle shell products, medicines using musk, tiger or rhino derivatives, products made from whalebone or bone from any other marine animals, cat skins, medicinal drugs unless covered by a doctor's prescription. Certain animal products, fruit, plant material or foodstuffs are prohibited, check with the nearest embassy.

DRIVING REQUIREMENTS National driving licences for most countries.

KEEPING IN TOUCH

BBC WORLD SERVICE MHz 15.36, 11.96, 9.740, 7.145.

ENGLISH-LANGUAGE NEWSPAPERS *New Zealand Herald, The Press, Evening Post.*

EMERGENCIES

RED CROSS/CRESCENT SOCIETIES PO Box 12140, Thorndon, Wellington 6038, tel 4 472 3750, fax 4 473 0315.

UK/USA/CANADIAN REPS UK: 44 Hill Street, Wellington, tel 4 472 6049, fax 4 473 4982. USA: PO Box 1190, 29 Fitzherbert Terrace, Thorndon, Wellington tel 4 472 2068, fax 4 471 2380. Canada: PO Box 12049, Wellington, tel 4 473 9577, fax 4 471 2082.

Global weather guide p 818, Rainy seasons worldwide p 829, Vaccinations required p 832, Recommended reading p 848, Dependent territories p 812.

NICARAGUA

STATE OF THE NATION

SAFETY Currently quiet, but stability cannot be entirely guaranteed.

LIFE EXPECTANCY M 65.8, F 70.6 .

PEOPLE AND PLACE

CAPITAL Managua.

LANGUAGE Spanish.

PEOPLES Mestizo, Indigenous Indian, of European descent, African descent, Zambos.

RELIGION Mainly Roman Catholic.

SIZE (KM) 130, 668.

POPULATION 4, 500, 000.

POP DENSITY/KM 37.4.

FOOD Spanish and Latin American in style. Dishes include *gallopinto* (rice and pinto beans), *mondongo* (tripe soup). Plantain and tortillas are staples.

TRAVEL PLANNING

WHEN TO GO From December to May, during the dry season.

MEDICAL CARE Limited, insurance recommended.

CURRENCY Nicaraguan gold córdoba (C$) = 100 centavos.

FINANCE Credit cards and travellers' cheques accepted on a limited basis.

AIRPORTS Managua (MGA) 12 km from the city.

INTERNAL TRAVEL No passenger rail service at present. Only a fraction of roads are paved. Car hire available.

BUSINESS HOURS 0800-1700 Mon-Friday.

GMT -6.

VOLTAGE GUIDE 110 AC, 60 Hz.

RED TAPE

VISAS (AUS/CANADA/UK/US) Required by Australian and Canadian nationals.

REPS IN UK/USA/CANADA UK: Vicarage House, Suite 31, 58-60 Kensington Church Street, London W8 4DB, tel 020 7938 2373, fax 020 7937 0952, email emb.ofnicaragua@virgin.net. USA: 1627 New Hampshire Avenue, NW, Washington, DC 20009, tel 202 939 6570, fax 202 939 6542. Also deals with enquiries relating to Canada.

CUSTOMS REGULATIONS Duty free allowance: 200 cigarettes or 500 g of tobacco, 3 ltrs alocholic beverage, 1 large bottle or 3 small bottles of perfume or *eau de cologne*. Prohibited imports: Canned or uncanned meats, leather and dairy products. Prohibited exports: Archaeological items, artefacts of historical or monetary value and gold.

DRIVING REQUIREMENTS National licence.

KEEPING IN TOUCH

BBC WORLD SERVICE MHz 15.22, 9.590, 6.195, 5.975.

ENGLISH-LANGUAGE NEWSPAPERS None.

EMERGENCIES

RED CROSS/CRESCENT SOCIETIES Apartado 3279, Managua, tel 651 307, fax 651 643, email nicacruz@ibw.com.ni.

UK/USA/CANADIAN REPS UK: Apartado A-169, Plaza Churchill, El Reparto 'Los Robles', 4ta Casa a Mano Derecha, Managua, tel 278 0014, fax 278 4085, email britemb@ibw.com.ni. USA: Apartado 327, Km 4.5, Carretera Sur, Managua, tel 266 6010, fax 266 6046. Canada: The Canadian Embassy in San José deals with enquiries relating to Nicaragua.

Global weather guide p 818,   Rainy seasons worldwide p 829,   Vaccinations required p 832, Recommended reading p 848,   Dependent territories p 812.

NIGER

STATE OF THE NATION

SAFETY Potentially unstable: seek latest information at time of visit.

LIFE EXPECTANCY M 46.9, F 50.1.

PEOPLE AND PLACE

CAPITAL Niamey.

LANGUAGE French.

PEOPLES Hausa, Djerma and Songhai, Fulani, Tuareg.

RELIGION Muslim (95%), Christian and Animist minorities.

SIZE (KM) 1,267,000.

POPULATION 10,100,000.

POP DENSITY/KM 8.

FOOD Local dishes usually based around millet, rice or *niebé*, a type of bean. Beef and mutton supplement these staples. Brochettes of meat are commonly sold on street stalls.

TRAVEL PLANNING

WHEN TO GO During the dry season from October to May. Heavy rains and very high temperatures common in July and August.

MEDICAL CARE Very limited, bring own supplies, insurance with repatriation cover recommended.

CURRENCY Communauté Financiaire Africaine franc (CFAfr) = 100 centimes.

FINANCE Credit cards and travellers' cheques accepted on a limited basis.

AIRPORTS Niamey (NIM) 12 km from the city.

INTERNAL TRAVEL Some domestic flights, and charter planes available. Only major roads are all-weather, and others are impassable during heavy rain. Petrol stations are infrequent. Car hire available but chauffeur-driven cars are compulsory outside the capital.

BUSINESS HOURS 0730-1230, 1500-1800 Monday to Friday, 0730-1230 Saturday.

GMT +3.

VOLTAGE GUIDE 220/380 AC, 50 Hz.

RED TAPE

VISAS (AUS/CANADA/UK/US) Required.

REPS IN UK/USA/CANADA UK: n/a.
USA: 2204 R Street, NW, Washington, DC 20008, tel 202 483 4224, fax 202 483 3168.
Canada: 38 Blackburn Avenue, Ottawa, Ontario K1N 8A2, tel 613 232 4291, fax 613 230 9808.

CUSTOMS REGULATIONS Duty free allowance: 200 cigarettes or 100 cigarillos or 25 cigars or 250 g of tobacco, 1 bottle of spirits and 1 bottle of wine, 500 ml of *eau de toilette* and 250 ml of perfume. Prohibited: Pornography.

DRIVING REQUIREMENTS International Driving Permit, *Carnet de Passage*.

KEEPING IN TOUCH

BBC WORLD SERVICE MHz 17.83, 15.40, 11.77, 7.160.

ENGLISH-LANGUAGE NEWSPAPERS None.

EMERGENCIES

RED CROSS/CRESCENT SOCIETIES BP 11386, Niamey, tel 733 037, fax 732 461.

UK/USA/CANADIAN REPS UK: The British Embassy in Abidjan (Côte d'Ivoire) deals with enquiries relating to Niger. USA: BP 11201, Niamey, tel 722 661, fax 733 167. Canada: PO Box 362, Niamey, tel 753 686, fax 753 107.

Global weather guide p 818, Rainy seasons worldwide p 829, Vaccinations required p 832, Recommended reading p 848, Dependent territories p 812.

NIGERIA

STATE OF THE NATION

SAFETY Very unsafe. High levels of street crime, business fraud and political violence. Avoid the Niger Delta entirely, scene of military operations and local rioting. Do not travel outside cities after dark.

LIFE EXPECTANCY M 48.7, F 51.5.

PEOPLE AND PLACE

CAPITAL Abuja.

LANGUAGE English.

PEOPLES Yoruba, Hausa, Ibo, Fulani.

RELIGION Muslim, Christian, traditional beliefs.

SIZE (KM) 923,768.

POPULATION 109,000,000.

POP DENSITY/KM 134.

FOOD. Typical West African fare, based on yams, sweet potatoes and plantains. Pepper soup, *kilishi* (spiced dried meat), *egussi soup* (meat, dried fish and melon seed stew) and goat and bush meat are popular.

TRAVEL PLANNING

WHEN TO GO November to April. The rainy season is from March to November.

MEDICAL CARE Very limited except for a few private hospitals in cities, insurance essential.

CURRENCY Naira (N) = 100 kobo.

FINANCE Credit card fraud is prevalent, and travellers' cheques are generally not recommended.

AIRPORTS Lagos (LOS) 22 km from the city.

INTERNAL TRAVEL Trains are generally slower than buses, but cheaper. National road system links main centres. Secondary roads become impassable in the rains. Advisable to hire cars through hotels, although chauffeur-driven cars are recommended.

BUSINESS HOURS 0830-1700 Mon-Friday.

GMT +1.

VOLTAGE GUIDE 220/250 AC, 50 Hz.

RED TAPE

VISAS (AUS/CANADA/UK/US) Required.

REPS IN UK/USA/CANADA UK: 56-57 Fleet Street, London EC4Y 1JU, tel 020 7353 3776, fax 020 7353 4352. USA: 828 2nd Avenue, 10th Floor, New York, NY 10017, tel 212 808 0301, fax 212 687 1476. Canada: 295 Metcalfe Street, Ottawa, Ontario K2P 1R9, tel 613 236 0521, fax 613 236 0529.

CUSTOMS REGULATIONS Duty free allowance: For travellers over 18, 200 cigarettes or 50 cigars or 200 g of tobacco, 1 ltr of spirits, and 1 ltr of wine, a small amount of perfume, gifts worth N300 (excluding jewellery, photographic equipment, electronics and luxury goods) Prohibited: Champagne, sparkling wine and beer, fruits, vegetables, cereals and fresh or preserved eggs, jewellery and precious metals.

DRIVING REQUIREMENTS International Driving Permit.

KEEPING IN TOUCH

BBC WORLD SERVICE MHz 17.83, 15.40, 7.160, 6.005.

ENGLISH-LANGUAGE NEWSPAPERS *Daily Times, Guardian, New Nigeria.*

EMERGENCIES

RED CROSS/CRESCENT SOCIETIES PO Box 764, Lagos, tel 1 269 5188, fax 1 269 1599.

UK/USA/CANADIAN REPS UK: 11 Louis Farrakhan Crescent, Victoria Island, Lagos, tel 1 261 9531, fax 1 261 4021. USA: PO Box 554, 2 Louis Farrakhan Crescent, Victoria Island, Lagos, tel 1 261 0097, fax 1 261 2218. Canada: 2 Louis Farrakhan Crescent, Victoria Island, Lagos, tel 1 262 8212, fax 1 262 8217.

Global weather guide p 818, Rainy seasons worldwide p 829, Vaccinations required p 832, Recommended reading p 848, Dependent territories p 812.

NORWAY

STATE OF THE NATION

SAFETY Safe.

LIFE EXPECTANCY M 75.2, F 81.1.

PEOPLE AND PLACE

CAPITAL Oslo.

LANGUAGE Norwegian.

PEOPLES Norwergian (95%), Lapp, other.

RELIGION Evangelical Lutheran.

SIZE (KM) 323, 758.

POPULATION 4, 400, 000.

POP DENSITY/KM 14.

FOOD *Koldtbord* (cold tables) consisting of smoked salmon, fresh lobster, shrimp and hot dishes are often found in hotels and restaurants. Open sandwiches topped with fish, cheese, meats and salads are also popular. Main dishes include roast venison, *lutefisk* (hot, highly flavoured cod) and herring prepared in a variety of ways.

TRAVEL PLANNING

WHEN TO GO Winters (November to March) are very cold. The rest of the year is mild and pleasant.

MEDICAL CARE Good, mostly free, total refunds for all medical treatment unlikely, insurance advisable.

CURRENCY Norwegian krone (NOK) = 100 øre.

FINANCE Credit cards and travellers' cheques widely accepted.

AIRPORTS (And distances from nearest city): Oslo (OSL) 47 km, Stavanger (SVG) 14.5 km, Bergen (BG)) 19 km.

INTERNAL TRAVEL Good domestic air network. Coastal towns and fjords served by ferries. Roads of variable quality, especially under freezing winter conditions in the north. Car hire easily available but costly.

BUSINESS HOURS 0800-1600 Mon-Friday.

GMT +1.

VOLTAGE GUIDE 220 AC, 50 Hz.

RED TAPE

VISAS (AUS/CANADA/UK/US) None.

REPS IN UK/USA/CANADA UK: 25 Belgrave Square, London SW1X 8QD, tel 020 7591 5500, fax 020 7245 6993, email embassy@embassy.norway.org.uk. USA: 2720 34th Street, NW, Washington, DC 20008, tel 202 333 6000, fax 202 337 0870. Canada: Suite 532, Royal Bank Centre, 90 Sparks Street, Ottawa, Ontario K1P 5B4, tel 613 238 6571, fax 613 238 2765, email nor-emb-ott@intronet.ca.

CUSTOMS REGULATIONS Duty free allowance: For residents of European countries: 200 cigarettes or 250 g of tobacco products and 200 leaves of cigarette paper (travellers over 18), 1 ltr spirits and 1 ltr of wine (travellers over 20) or 2 ltrs of wine and 2 ltrs of beer (travellers aged 18-20), goods worth NOK 1200. For residents of non-European countries: 400 cigarettes or 500 g of tobacco products and 200 leaves of cigarette paper (travellers over 18), alcohol as above, 50 g of perfume and 50 cl of *eau de cologne*, goods worth NOK 3500. Prohibited: Spirits over 60% volume (120° proof), wine over 22% volume, certain foodstuffs, including eggs, potatoes, meat, meat products, dairy products and poultry, narcotics, medicines, firearms and explosives.

DRIVING REQUIREMENTS International Driving Permit or national driving licence and log book. Green Card recommended.

KEEPING IN TOUCH

BBC WORLD SERVICE MHz 17.64, 15.57, 12.09, 9.410.

ENGLISH-LANGUAGE NEWSPAPERS None.

EMERGENCIES

RED CROSS/CRESCENT SOCIETIES Postbox 1, Gronland, 0133 Oslo, tel 22 05 40 00, fax 22 05 40 40.

UK/USA/CANADIAN REPS UK: Thomas Heftyesgate 8, 0244 Oslo, tel 23 13 27 00, fax 23 13 27 41 email britemb@online.no USA: Drammensveien 18, 0244 Oslo, tel 22 44 85 50, fax 22 43 07 77. Canada: Wergelandesveien 7, 0244 Oslo, tel 22 99 53 00, fax 22 99 53 01.

Global weather guide p 818, Rainy seasons worldwide p 829, Vaccinations required p 832, Recommended reading p 848, Dependent territories p 812.

OMAN

STATE OF THE NATION

SAFETY Safe. Observe Islamic customs.
LIFE EXPECTANCY M 68.9, F 73.3.

PEOPLE AND PLACE

CAPITAL Muscat.

LANGUAGE Arabic and English.

PEOPLES Omani, Baluchi, Jebali.

RELIGION Ibadhi Muslim.

SIZE (KM) 309, 500.

POPULATION 2, 500, 000.

POP DENSITY/KM 12.

FOOD Arabic, Lebanese and Indian food.
Biryanis, curries and felafel available everywhere. Visitors are only allowed to drink alcohol in licensed hotels and restaurants.

TRAVEL PLANNING

WHEN TO GO Pleasantly warm from October to March. June and July are particularly hot.

MEDICAL CARE Good, but expensive, insurance recommended.

CURRENCY Omani rial (OR) = 1000 baiza.

FINANCE Major cards widely accepted, travellers' cheques easily exchanged.

AIRPORTS Muscat (MCT) 40 km from the city.

INTERNAL TRAVEL Principal road routes run from north to south. Good roads to neighbouring states. Car hire available.

BUSINESS HOURS 0800-1300, 1600-1900 Saturday to Wednesday, 0800-1300 Thurs.

GMT +4.

VOLTAGE GUIDE 220/240 AC, 50 Hz.

RED TAPE

VISAS (AUS/CANADA/UK/US) Required.

REPS IN UK/USA/CANADA UK: 167 Queen's Gate, London SW7 5HE, tel 020 7225 0001, fax 020 7589 2505. USA: 2535 Belmont Road, NW, Washington, DC 20008, tel 202 387 1980, fax 202 745 4933. Also deals with enquiries from Canada.

CUSTOMS REGULATIONS Duty free allowance: A reasonable amount of tobacco products, 227 ml perfume. Non-Muslims are allowed to bring 1 ltr of alcohol into the country. Prohibited: Narcotics, fresh foods, firearms (including toys and replicas) and pornographic films/literature. Videos are subject to censorship.

DRIVING REQUIREMENTS A local licence must be obtained from the police by presenting a national driving licence or International Driving Permit.

KEEPING IN TOUCH

BBC WORLD SERVICE MHz 15.57, 11.76, 9.410.

ENGLISH-LANGUAGE NEWSPAPERS *The Times of Oman, The Oman Daily Observer.*

EMERGENCIES

RED CROSS/CRESCENT SOCIETIES n/a.

UK/USA/CANADIAN REPS UK: PO Box 300, Postal Code 113, Muscat, tel 693 077, fax 693 087. USA: PO Box 202, Medinat Al-Sultan Qaboos, Postal Code 115, Muscat, email aemctcns@gto.net.om. Canada: The Canadian Embassy in Riyadh (Saudi Arabia) deals with enquiries relating to Oman.

*Global weather guide p 818,   Rainy seasons worldwide p 829,   Vaccinations required p 832,
Recommended reading p 848,   Dependent territories p 812.*

PAKISTAN

STATE OF THE NATION

SAFETY Politically volatile, though his may not affect foreigners. Seek latest information at time of visit. Observe Islamic customs.

LIFE EXPECTANCY M 62.9, F 65.1.

PEOPLE AND PLACE

CAPITAL Islamabad.

LANGUAGE Urdu and English.

PEOPLES Punjabi, Sindhi, Pashtu, Mohajir, Baluch.

RELIGION Sunni Muslim (77%), Sh'ia Muslim (20%), Hindu and Christian minorities.

SIZE (KM) 803,950.

POPULATION 147,500,000.

POP DENSITY/KM 192.

FOOD Based on *masala* (spice) sauces with chicken, fish, lamb and vegetables. Typical dishes include *biryanis*, brain masala and *sag gosht* (spinach and lamb curry). Moghul cuisine is found in Lahore. Specialities include tandoori dishes and various kebabs. Alcohol may be bought at major hotels by visitors in possession of a Liquor Permit.

TRAVEL PLANNING

WHEN TO GO During winter (November to March) when it is warm and dry. April to July is extremely hot and the monsoon occurs from July to September.

MEDICAL CARE Limited, cash payments demanded, insurance strongly recommended.

CURRENCY .Pakistani rupee (PRe/PRs) = 100 paisa.

FINANCE American Express is widely accepted, other cards less so. Travellers' cheques are generally accepted.

AIRPORTS (And distances from nearest city) Karachi (KHI) 15 km, Lahore (LHE) 18 km, Islamabad (ISB) 15 km, Peshawar (PEW) 4km.

INTERNAL TRAVEL Several domestic flights between Lahore and main centres. Extensive rail system. Roads between cities generally well maintained. Car hire available.

BUSINESS HOURS 0800-1500 Monday to Thursday and Saturday, 0800-1230 Friday.

GMT +5.

VOLTAGE GUIDE 220 AC, 50 Hz.

RED TAPE

VISAS (AUS/CANADA/UK/US) Required.

REPS IN UK/USA/CANADA UK: 36 Lowndes Square, London SW1X 9JN, tel 020 7664 9200, fax 020 7664 9224. USA: 12 East 65th Street, New York, NY 10021, tel 212 879 5800, fax 212 517 6987, email pak-trade@mail.idt.net. Canada: Suite 608, Burnside Building, 151 Slater Street, Ottawa, Ontario K1P 5H3, tel 613 238 7881, fax 613 238 7269.

CUSTOMS REGULATIONS Duty free allowance: 200 cigarettes or 50 cigars or 500 g of tobacco, 250 ml of perfume and *eau de toilette* (opened), gifts worth PRs 2000. Prohibited: Alcohol, matches, plants, fruits and vegetables. The export of antiques is prohibited.

DRIVING REQUIREMENTS International Driving Permit.

KEEPING IN TOUCH

BBC WORLD SERVICE MHz 17.71, 15.31, 11.99, 5.965.

ENGLISH-LANGUAGE NEWSPAPERS *The Leader, The Pakistan Observer, The Pakistan Times, The Financial Post.*

EMERGENCIES

RED CROSS/CRESCENT SOCIETIES Sector H-8, Islamabad, tel 51 925 7404, fax 51 925 7408, email hilal@comsats.net.pk.

UK/USA/CANADIAN REPS UK: PO Box 1122, Diplomatic Enclave, Ramna 5, Islamabad, tel 51 822 131, fax 51 279 356, email bhcmedia@isb.comsats.net.pk. USA: PO Box 1048, Diplomatic Enclave, Sector G-5, Islamabad, tel 51 826 161, fax 51 276 427. Canada: PO Box 1042, Diplomatic Enclave, Sector G-5, Islamabad, tel 51 279 100, fax 51 279 110, email isbad@isbad01.x400.gc.ca.

Global weather guide p 818, Rainy seasons worldwide p 829, Vaccinations required p 832, Recommended reading p 848, Dependent territories p 812.

PALAU

STATE OF THE NATION

SAFETY Safe.

LIFE EXPECTANCY 71.

PEOPLE AND PLACE

CAPITAL Koror.

LANGUAGE English and Palauan.

PEOPLES Micronesian.

RELIGION Roman Catholic, Modekngei.

SIZE (KM) 508.

POPULATION 17,700.

POP DENSITY/KM 34.

FOOD Fresh local seafood is a highlight. International cuisine available, including Chinese and Japanese food.

TRAVEL PLANNING

WHEN TO GO Warm all year, with the heaviest rainfall between July and October.

MEDICAL CARE Basic. Insurance recommended.

CURRENCY US dollar (US$) = 100 cents.

FINANCE Some acceptance of credit cards and travellers' cheques on the main island.

AIRPORTS Koror Badeldaob (ROR), on Babeldaob Island.

INTERNAL TRAVEL Some inter-island boat services. Coral and dirt roads.

BUSINESS HOURS 0800-2100 Monday-Saturday (shopping hours, business hours n/a).

GMT +9.

VOLTAGE GUIDE 115/230 AC, 60 Hz.

RED TAPE

VISAS (AUS/CANADA/UK/US) Not required for visits of less than 30 days.

REPS IN UK/USA/CANADA UK: n/a. USA: 1150 18th Street, Suite 750, NW, Washington, DC 20036, tel 202 452 6814, fax 202 452 6281. Canada: n/a.

CUSTOMS REGULATIONS Duty free allowance: 200 cigarettes or 454 g of cigars or tobacco, 2 ltrs of alcoholic beverage. Prohibited: Narcotics and firearms.

DRIVING REQUIREMENTS n/a.

KEEPING IN TOUCH

BBC WORLD SERVICE n/a.

ENGLISH-LANGUAGE NEWSPAPERS *Pacific Daily News.*

EMERGENCIES

RED CROSS/CRESCENT SOCIETIES PO Box 6043, Koror, Palau 96940, tel 885 780, fax 884 540, email palredcross@ palaunet.com.

UK/USA/CANADIAN REPS UK: n/a. USA: PO Box 6028, Koror, Palau 96940, tel 488 2920, fax 488 291. Canada: n/a.

Global weather guide p 818, Rainy seasons worldwide p 829, Vaccinations required p 832, Recommended reading p 848, Dependent territories p 812.

PANAMA

STATE OF THE NATION

SAFETY Avoid the Colombian border. Beware muggings in tourist areas.

LIFE EXPECTANCY M 71.8, F 76.4.

PEOPLE AND PLACE

CAPITAL Panama City.

LANGUAGE Spanish.

PEOPLES Mestizo, of European and African descent, indigenous Indian, Asian.

RELIGION Roman Catholic.

SIZE (KM) 75,517.

POPULATION 2,800,000.

POP DENSITY/KM 37.

FOOD Native food is hot and spicy. Dishes include *ceviche* (raw fish marinated in lime juice and peppers), *sancocho* (chicken, meat and vegetable stew), *tamales* (pies wrapped in banana leaves) and *empanadas* (pastries filled with cheese, chicken or meat).

TRAVEL PLANNING

WHEN TO GO High temperatures throughout the year. Rainy season from May to November.

MEDICAL CARE Free emergency treatment, but insurance recommended.

CURRENCY Balboa (B) = 100 centésimos.

FINANCE Credit cards and travellers' cheques generally accepted.

AIRPORTS Panama City (PTY) 27 km from the city.

INTERNAL TRAVEL Some internal flights. Rail system currently only operating freight trains. The Trans-Isthman Highway links Panama City and Colón. Car hire available.

BUSINESS HOURS 0800-1200, 1400-1700 Monday-Friday.

GMT -5.

VOLTAGE GUIDE 120 AC, 60 Hz.

RED TAPE

VISAS (AUS/CANADA/UK/US) Not required by UK nationals, others issued with a tourist card.

REPS IN UK/USA/CANADA UK: 40 Hertford Street, London W1Y 7TG, tel 020 7409 2255, fax 020 7493 4499. USA: 870 Market Street, Suite 551, San Francisco, CA 94102, tel 415 391 4268, fax 415 391 4269. Canada: 130 Albert Street, Suite 300, Ottawa, Ontario K1P 5G4, tel 613 236 7177, fax 613 236 5775, email pancanem@travel-net.com.

CUSTOMS REGULATIONS Duty free allowance: 500 cigarettes or 50 cigars or 500g of tobacco, 3 bottles of alcoholic beverage, perfume and eau de cologne in opened bottles for personal use. Prohibited: Fruit, vegetable and animal products.

DRIVING REQUIREMENTS National driving licence.

KEEPING IN TOUCH

BBC WORLD SERVICE MHz 17.84, 15.19, 6.195, 9.915.

ENGLISH-LANGUAGE NEWSPAPERS None.

EMERGENCIES

RED CROSS/CRESCENT SOCIETIES Apartado 668, Zona 1, Panamá, tel 232 5639, fax 232 7450, email cruzroja@pan.gbm.net.

UK/USA/CANADIAN REPS UK: Apartado 889, 4th Floor, Torre Banco Suizo, Calle 53, Marbella, Panamá 1, tel 269 0866, fax 223 0730, email britemb@cwp.net.pa. USA: Apartado 5969, Avenida Balboa, Entre Calle 37 y 38, Panamá 5, tel 225 6988, fax 225 1595, email usispan@pty.com. Canada: Avenida Samuel Lewis, Edifico Banco Central Hispano, 4th Floor, Panama City, tel 264 9731, fax 263 8083, email panam@ dfait-maeci.gc.ca.

Global weather guide p 818, Rainy seasons worldwide p 829, Vaccinations required p 832, Recommended reading p 848, Dependent territories p 812.

PAPUA NEW GUINEA

STATE OF THE NATION

SAFETY Extremely dangerous: Westerners have been kidnapped by tribal protesters for propaganda purposes. High levels of violent crime (including rape) even in cities. Seek latest information at time of visit.

LIFE EXPECTANCY M 57.2, F 58.7.

PEOPLE AND PLACE

CAPITAL Port Moresby.

LANGUAGE English and Pidgin English.

PEOPLES Mixed race and tribal groups.

RELIGION Indigenous beliefs, Roman Catholic, Protestant, Lutheran, Anglican.

SIZE (KM) 462,840.

POPULATION 4,600,000.

POP DENSITY/KM 10.

FOOD Traditional dishes are based on root crops such as *taro, kaukau* and yams. A popular dish is *mumu*, a mixture of pork, sweet potatoes, rice and greens. Pigs are baked in earth for feasts.

TRAVEL PLANNING

WHEN TO GO May to November is the best time. Most rain falls between December and March, although Port Moresby is dry at this time.

MEDICAL CARE Very limited, cash payments demanded, it may be worthwhile getting a visa for Australia in case of medical emergencies, so that you can be evacuated to decent medical facilities. Insurance strongly recommended.

CURRENCY Kina = 100 toea.

FINANCE American Express is the most widely accepted card. Travellers' cheques are accepted by most shops and hotels.

AIRPORTS Port Moresby (POM) 11 km from the city.

INTERNAL TRAVEL Cargo/passenger services between some islands. Mountainous and rugged terrain limits roads in the interior. Car hire available in main towns.

BUSINESS HOURS 0800-1630 Mon-Friday.

GMT +10.

VOLTAGE GUIDE 240 AC, 50 Hz.

RED TAPE

VISAS (AUS/CANADA/UK/US) Required.

REPS IN UK/USA/CANADA UK: 14 Waterloo Place, London SW1Y 4AR, tel 020 7930 0922, fax 020 7930 0828. USA: 1779 Massachusetts Avenue, NW, Washington, DC 20036, tel 202 745 3680, fax 202 745 3679, email KunduWash@aol.com. Also deals with enquiries from Canada.

CUSTOMS REGULATIONS Duty free allowance: For travellers over 18, 200 cigarettes or 200 g of tobacco, 1 ltr of alcoholic beverages, goods worth Kina 250 (Kina 100 for persons under 18) excluding radios, tape recorders, television sets, video cameras, video tapes and record players. Prohibited: Plants and soil, uncanned foods of animal origin (unless from Australia or New Zealand) and all pig meat from New Zealand.

DRIVING REQUIREMENTS National driving licence.

KEEPING IN TOUCH

BBC WORLD SERVICE MHz 15.36, 11.96, 9.740, 6.195.

ENGLISH-LANGUAGE NEWSPAPERS *The National, The Papua New Guinea Post Courier.*

EMERGENCIES

RED CROSS/CRESCENT SOCIETIES PO Box 6545, Boroko, N.C.D tel 325 8577, fax 325 9714.

UK/USA/CANADIAN REPS UK: PO Box 212, NCD 131, Waigani, tel 325 1677, fax 325 3547, email bhcpng@datec.com.pg. USA: PO Box 1492, Douglas Street, Port Moresby, tel 321 1455, fax 321 3423. Canada: The Canadian High Commission in Canberra (Australia) deals with enquiries relating to Papua New Guinea.

Global weather guide p 818, Rainy seasons worldwide p 829, Vaccinations required p 832, Recommended reading p 848, Dependent territories p 812.

PARAGUAY

STATE OF THE NATION

Safety Volatile.

Life expectancy M 67.5, F 72.

PEOPLE AND PLACE

Capital Asunción.

Language Spanish and Guarani.

Peoples Of combined Spanish and native Guarani origin (Mestizo), small indigenous Indian minority.

Religion Roman Catholic.

Size (km) 406,752.

Population 5,200,000.

Pop density/km 13.

Food Local dishes include *chipas* (maize bread flavoured with egg and cheese), *soo-yosopy* (a soup of cornmeal and ground beef), *albondiga* (meatball soup), *boribori* (diced meat, vegetables and small dumplings mixed with cheese). Good local beef.

TRAVEL PLANNING

When to go December to March can be very hot and sees the most rainfall. June to September is mild, with few cold days.

Medical care Insurance strongly recommended.

Currency Guarani (G).

Finance Credit cards and travellers' cheques widely accepted.

Airports Asunción (ASU) 16 km from the city.

Internal travel Some internal flights but often disrupted by weather conditions. Unreliable rail service, with trains running weekly. Roads serving main centres are in good condition, other (unsurfaced) roads may be closed in bad weather. Car hire available.

Business hours 0800-1200, 1500-1730/1900, Monday to Friday.

GMT -4.

Voltage guide 220 AC, 50 Hz.

RED TAPE

Visas (Aus/Canada/UK/US) Required by Australian, Canadian and Irish nationals.

Reps in UK/USA/Canada UK: Braemar Lodge, Cornwall Gardens, London SW7 4AQ, tel 020 7937 1253, fax 020 7937 5687, email brembasu@mail.pla.net.py USA: 2400 Massachusetts Avenue, NW, Washington, DC 20008, tel 202 483 6960, fax 202 234 4508, email embapara@erols.com. Canada: 151Slater Street, Suite 501, Ottawa, Ontario, K1P 5H3, tel 613 567 1283, fax 613 567 1679, email embapar@magnacom.com.

Customs regulations Duty free allowance: A reasonable quantity of tobacco, alcoholic beverages and perfume for personal use, a reasonable quantity of personal and sporting equipment.

Driving requirements National driving licence or International Driving Permit.

KEEPING IN TOUCH

BBC World Service MHz 17.84, 15.22, 12.10, 5.970.

English-language newspapers None.

EMERGENCIES

Red Cross/Crescent societies Brasil 216 Esq. José Berges, Asunción, tel 21 222 797, fax 21 211 560/6, email cruzroja@pla.net.py

UK/USA/Canadian reps UK: Calle Presidente Franco 706, Asunción, tel 21 444 472, fax 21 446 385, email brembasu@ mail.pla.net.py. USA: Avenida Mariscal López 1776, Asunción, tel 21 213 715, fax 21 213 728, email cflasu@usia.gov. Canada: Casilla 883, El Paraguayo, Independiente 995, Colon 1, Entrepiso, Oficianas 1 y 2, Asunción, tel 21 449 505, fax 21 449 506.

Global weather guide p 818, Rainy seasons worldwide p 829, Vaccinations required p 832, Recommended reading p 848, Dependent territories p 812.

PERU

STATE OF THE NATION

SAFETY Relatively safe for travellers. Guerrilla conflict currently suppressed. Many reports of petty crime.

LIFE EXPECTANCY M 65.9, F 70.9.

PEOPLE AND PLACE

CAPITAL Lima.

LANGUAGE Spanish and Quechua.

PEOPLES Indigenous Indians, Mestizo, European.

RELIGION Roman Catholic.

SIZE (KM) 1, 285, 216.

POPULATION 24, 800, 000.

POP DENSITY/KM 19.

FOOD Hot pepper (*aji*) and garlic (*ajo*) flavour most Peruvian food. Typical dishes include *chupe de camarones*, a chowder-like soup made from shrimps, eggs, cream, potatoes and peppers, *sopa criolla* (spicy soup with beef and noodles), and *anticuchos* - beef or fish marinated in vinegar and spices, then barbecued.

TRAVEL PLANNING

WHEN TO GO Heavy rain in the mountains and jungle from December to April. It never rains in Lima nor most of the coast.

MEDICAL CARE Cash payments demanded, insurance strongly recommended.

CURRENCY New sol (S/.) = 100 céntimos.

FINANCE Most credit cards accepted. Changing travellers' cheques can be a slow process outside Lima.

AIRPORTS Lima (LIM) 16 km from the city, Cusco (CUZ).

INTERNAL TRAVEL Fairly extensive domestic air network. Peru is home to the highest railroad in the world. Roads are in reasonable condition but affected by landslides in the rainy season.

BUSINESS HOURS 0900-1700 Mon-Friday.

GMT -5.

VOLTAGE GUIDE 220 AC, 60 Hz.

RED TAPE

VISAS (AUS/CANADA/UK/US) Not required for stays upto 90 days.

REPS IN UK/USA/CANADA UK: 52 Sloane Street, London SW1X 9SP, tel 020 7838 9223, fax 020 7823 2789. USA: 1700 Massachusetts Avenue, NW, Washington, DC 20036, tel 202 833 9860, fax 202 659 8124. Canada: 130 Albert Street, Suite 1901, Ottawa, Ontario K1P 5G4, tel 613 233 2721, fax 613 232 3062, email emperu@magi.com.

CUSTOMS REGULATIONS Duty free allowance: 400 cigarettes or 50 cigars or 50 g of tobacco, 3 ltrs of alcoholic beverage, a reasonable amount of perfume for personal use, gifts or new articles for personal use worth US$300, 2 kg of processed food.

DRIVING REQUIREMENTS Foreign driving permit or an International Driving Permit.

KEEPING IN TOUCH

BBC WORLD SERVICE MHz 17.84, 15.22, 9.915, 9.590.

ENGLISH-LANGUAGE NEWSPAPERS None.

EMERGENCIES

RED CROSS/CRESCENT SOCIETIES Av. Arequipa N° 1285, Lima, tel 1 265 8784, fax 1 265 8788, email scrperu@mail.iaxis.com.pe.

UK/USA/CANADIAN REPS UK: Natalio Sanchez 125, 12th Floor, Plaza Washington, Lima 100, tel 1 433 4738, fax 1 433 4735. USA: Avenida La Encalada cuadra 17 s/n, Lima 33, tel 1 434 3000, fax 1 434 3037. Canada: Jiron Libertad 130, Lima 18, tel 1 444 4015, fax 1 444 4347.

Global weather guide p 818, Rainy seasons worldwide p 829, Vaccinations required p 832, Recommended reading p 848, Dependent territories p 812.

PHILIPPINES

STATE OF THE NATION

SAFETY Highly volatile, due to separatist guerrillas in the south and widespread Christian-Muslim violence. Recent mass-kidnapping of tourists from neighbouring Malaysia has inflamed the south, leading to military operations and rebel reprisals. Seek latest information at time of visit.

LIFE EXPECTANCY M 66.5, F 70.2.

PEOPLE AND PLACE

CAPITAL Manila.

LANGUAGE Filipino.

PEOPLES Malay, Indonesian and Polynesian, Chinese, Indian.

RELIGION Roman Catholic (83%), Protestant. Muslim and Buddhist minorities.

SIZE (KM) 300,000.

POPULATION 72,200,000.

POP DENSITY/KM 242.

FOOD More moderate use of spices than other Asian cooking. Seafood features on most menus, freshly caught and simply served with some lime. *Lechon* (whole roast pig) is served at feasts. *Adobo* (braised pork and chicken in soy sauce, vinegar and garlic) and *relleno* (boned, stuffed chicken or fish) are other specialities.

TRAVEL PLANNING

WHEN TO GO Rainy from June to September, cool and dry from October to February and hot and mainly dry from March to May.

MEDICAL CARE Adequate three-tier system, but insurance recommended.

CURRENCY Philippine peso (P) = 100 centavos.

FINANCE Credit cards and travellers' cheques accepted in big towns.

AIRPORTS Ninoy Aquino (MNL) 12 km from Manila, Mactan (NOP) on Cebu Island, 45 km from the city.

INTERNAL TRAVEL The local air network and ships connect the islands. Roads on the islands are in variable condition. Car hire available in Manila and major cities.

BUSINESS HOURS 0800-1200, 1300-1700 Monday-Friday.

GMT +8.

VOLTAGE GUIDE 220 AC, 60 Hz. 110 AC available in most hotels.

RED TAPE

VISAS (AUS/CANADA/UK/US) Not required for stays under 21 days.

REPS IN UK/USA/CANADA UK: 9a Palace Green, London W8 4QE, tel 020 7937 1600, fax 020 7937 2925, email embassy@philemb.demon.co.uk. USA: 1600 Massachusetts Avenue, NW, Washington, DC 20036, tel 202 467 9300, fax 202 328 7614. Canada: 130 Albert Street, Suite 606, Ottawa, Ontario K1P 5G4, tel 613 233 1121, fax 613 233 4165, email ottawape@istar.ca.

CUSTOMS REGULATIONS Duty free allowance: 400 cigarettes or 50 cigars or 250 g of tobacco, 2 ltrs of alcoholic beverage, clothing, jewellery and perfume for personal use worth US$100. Prohibited: Firearms, explosives, pornographic, seditious or subversive material, narcotics and other internationally prohibited drugs (unless accompanied by a medical prescription).

DRIVING REQUIREMENTS International Driving Permit and a national driving licence.

KEEPING IN TOUCH

BBC WORLD SERVICE MHz 21.66, 15.36, 7.110, 6.195.

ENGLISH-LANGUAGE NEWSPAPERS *Manila Times, Manila Bulletin, Philippine Daily Inquirer.*

EMERGENCIES

RED CROSS/CRESCENT SOCIETIES PO Box 280, Manila 2803, tel 2 527 0866, fax 2 527 0857, email secgen_pnrc@email.com.

UK/USA/CANADIAN REPS UK: LV Locsin Building, 6752, Ayala Avenue, 1226 Makati City, tel 2 816 7348, fax 2 815 4809, email bremb@skyinet.net. USA: 1201 Roxas Boulevard, Ermita 1000, Metro Manila, tel 2 521 7116, fax 2 522 4361. Canada: 9th-11th Floors, Allied Bank Center, 6754 Ayala Avenue, 1261 Makati, Metro Manila, tel 2 810 8861, fax 2 810 4299.

Global weather guide p 818, Rainy seasons worldwide p 829, Vaccinations required p 832, Recommended reading p 848, Dependent territories p 812.

POLAND

STATE OF THE NATION

SAFETY Safe.

LIFE EXPECTANCY M 68.2, F 76.9.

PEOPLE AND PLACE

CAPITAL Warsaw.

LANGUAGE Polish.

PEOPLES Polish (98%), German, other.

RELIGION Roman Catholic (93%), Eastern Orthodox.

SIZE (KM) 312,685.

POPULATION 38,700,000.

POP DENSITY/KM 127.

FOOD Dill, marjoram, caraway seeds, wild mushrooms and sour cream are added to many dishes. The national dish is *bigos*, made from *sauerkraut*, fresh cabbage, onions and leftover meat. Pike in aspic and marinated fish in sour cream and *barszcz* (beetroot soup) are popular starters. Vodka, drunk chilled, is the national drink, and *Wyborowa* is considered to be the best.

TRAVEL PLANNING

WHEN TO GO June to September are warm. Mid-December to April sees snow in the south.

MEDICAL CARE Free to UK citizens, except for a charge for 30% of prescribed medicines.

CURRENCY Zloty (Zl) = 100 groszy.

FINANCE Credit cards accepted in large establishments, travellers' cheques readily exchanged.

AIRPORTS Warsaw (WAW) 10 km from the city, Kraków (KRK) 14 km from the city, Wroclaw (WRO) 8 km from the city, Katowice (KTW) 34 km from the city.

INTERNAL TRAVEL Cheap, efficient rail network. Roads are in reasonable condition are car hire is available.

BUSINESS HOURS 0800-1600 Mon-Friday.

GMT +1 (+2 in summer).

VOLTAGE GUIDE 220 AC, 50 Hz.

RED TAPE

VISAS (AUS/CANADA/UK/US) Required by Australian and Canadian nationals. Not required by UK nationals for stays under 6 months and US nationals for stays under 90 days.

REPS IN UK/USA/CANADA UK: 73 New Cavendish Street, London W1M 8LS, tel 020 7580 0476, fax 020 7323 2320. USA: 2224 Wyoming Avenue, NW, Washington, DC 20008, tel 202 232 4517, fax 202 328 2152, email polconsul.dc@ioip.com. Canada: 433 Daly Avenue, Ottawa, Ontario K1N 6H3, tel 613 789 0468, fax 613 789 1218, email info@polonianet.com.

CUSTOMS REGULATIONS Duty free allowance: For travellers over 18, 250 cigarettes or 50 cigars or 250 g of tobacco, 3 ltrs of alcoholic beverages, goods worth US$ 100. Prohibited: Firearms, narcotics. The export of antiques and works of art is prohibited.

DRIVING REQUIREMENTS Visitors with their own cars require their national driving licence and Green Card. An International driving permit is also required.

KEEPING IN TOUCH

BBC WORLD SERVICE MHz 15.57, 12.10, 9.410, 6.195.

ENGLISH-LANGUAGE NEWSPAPERS *The Warsaw Voice* (weekly).

EMERGENCIES

RED CROSS/CRESCENT SOCIETIES PO Box 47, 00-950 Warsaw, tel 22 628 5201, fax 22 628 4168.

UK/USA/CANADIAN REPS UK: Aleje Róz 1, 00-556 Warsaw, tel 22 628 1001, fax 22 621 7161, email britemb@it.com.pl. USA: Aleje Ujazdowskie 29/31, 00-540 Warsaw, tel 22 628 3041, fax 22 628 8298. Canada: Ulica Matejki 1/5, 00-481 Warsaw, tel 22 629 8051, fax 22 629 6457.

Global weather guide p 818, Rainy seasons worldwide p 829, Vaccinations required p 832, Recommended reading p 848, Dependent territories p 812.

PORTUGAL

STATE OF THE NATION

SAFETY Safe.

LIFE EXPECTANCY M 71.8, F 78.5.

PEOPLE AND PLACE

CAPITAL Lisbon.

LANGUAGE Portuguese.

PEOPLES Portuguese (99%), African.

RELIGION Roman Catholic (97%).

SIZE (KM) 92, 345.

POPULATION 9, 902, 200.

POP DENSITY/KM 107.

FOOD Seafood features strongly. Many soups are main dishes, including *sopa de marisco* (shellfish soup cooked and served with wine), *caldo verde* (green soup with kale leaves). Other specialities are *caldeirada*, a stew with several types of fish, and *carne de porco á Alentejana*, pork covered with clam and tomato sauce.

TRAVEL PLANNING

WHEN TO GO March to October are warm with little rain in the south. The northwest has shorter summers.

MEDICAL CARE Good and free for UK citizens.

CURRENCY Escudo (Esc) = 100 centavos.

FINANCE Credit cards and travellers' cheques widely accepted.

AIRPORTS Lisbon (LIS) 7 km from the city, Faro (FAO) 4 km from the city, Oporto (OPO) 11 km from the city.

INTERNAL TRAVEL There is a rail service to every town and every town and village can be reached by an adequate system of roads. Car hire easily available.

BUSINESS HOURS 0900-1300, 1500-1900 Monday-Friday.

GMT +1 (+2 in summer).

VOLTAGE GUIDE 220 AC, 50 Hz.

RED TAPE

VISAS (AUS/CANADA/UK/US) Required by Australian nationals.

REPS IN UK/USA/CANADA UK: 11 Belgrave Square, London SW1X 8P, tel 020 7235 5331, fax 020 7245 1287. USA: 2125 Kalorama Road, NW, Washington, DC 20008, tel 202 328 8610, fax 202 462 3726. Canada: 645 Island Park Drive, Ottawa, Ontario K1Y 0B8, tel 613 729 0883, fax 613 729 4236, email embportugal@embportugal-ottawa.org.

CUSTOMS REGULATIONS Duty free allowance: For visitors over 18 arriving from countries outside the EU, 200 cigarettes or 100 cigarillos or 50 cigars or 250 g of tobacco, 1 ltr of spirits over 22% or 2 ltrs of spirit up to 22%, 2 ltrs of wine, 50 g of perfume and 250 ml of *eau de toilette*, 500 g of coffee or 200g of coffee extract, further goods worth Esc 7500. No limits within the EU on alcohol or tobacco for personal use.

DRIVING REQUIREMENTS International Driving Permit or foreign driving licence, a Green Card must be obtained.

KEEPING IN TOUCH

BBC WORLD SERVICE MHz 12.10, 9.410, 6.195, 3.955.

ENGLISH-LANGUAGE NEWSPAPERS *The News* (Algarve), *Anglo Portugese News* (Lisbon).

EMERGENCIES

RED CROSS/CRESCENT SOCIETIES Jardim 9 de Abril, 1a5, 1249-083 Lisbon tel 1 390 5571, fax 1 395 1045.

UK/USA/CANADIAN REPS UK: 33 Rue de São Bernardo, 1249-082, Lisbon, tel 1 392 4000, fax 1 392 4186, email britemb@mail.telepac.pt. USA: Avenida das Forças Armadas, 1600-081 Lisbon, tel 1 727 3300, fax 1 726 9109. Canada: 4th Floor, Avenida da Liberdade 144/56, 1269-121 Lisbon, tel 1 347 4892, fax 1 347 6466.

Global weather guide p 818, Rainy seasons worldwide p 829, Vaccinations required p 832, Recommended reading p 848, Dependent territories p 812.

QATAR

STATE OF THE NATION

SAFETY Safe. Observe Islamic customs.
LIFE EXPECTANCY M 66.9, F 71.8.

PEOPLE AND PLACE

CAPITAL Doha.
LANGUAGE Arabic.
PEOPLES Arab, Indian, Pakistani, Iranian.
RELIGION Sunni Islam.
SIZE (KM) 11,427.
POPULATION 600,000.
POP DENSITY/KM 136.

FOOD Curries, biryanis, kebabs, *shawarma* (Middle Eastern equivalent of the Turkish doner kebab) and felafel are widely available. Alcohol is prohibited and should not be consumed in public. Some international hotels do serve alcohol.

TRAVEL PLANNING

WHEN TO GO Summer (June to September) is very hot, spring and autumn are warm and pleasant.

MEDICAL CARE Good but expensive, insurance recommended.

CURRENCY Qatari riyal (QR) = 100 dirhams.

FINANCE Credit cards and travellers' cheques widely accepted.

AIRPORTS Doha (DOH) 8 km from the city.

INTERNAL TRAVEL Reasonable road system but conditions deteriorate during wet weather.

BUSINESS HOURS 0730-1230, 1430-1800 Saturday to Thursday.

GMT +3.

VOLTAGE GUIDE 240/415 AC, 50 Hz

RED TAPE

VISAS (AUS/CANADA/UK/US) Required.

REPS IN UK/USA/CANADA UK: 1 South Audley Street, London W1Y 5DQ, tel 020 7493 2200, fax 020 7493 2818. USA: 4200 Wisconsin Avenue, Suite 200, NW, Washington DC 20016, tel 202 274 1600, fax 202 237 0061. Also deals with enquiries from Canada.

CUSTOMS REGULATIONS Duty free allowance: A reasonable amount of tobacco and perfume for personal use. Prohibited: Alcohol.

DRIVING REQUIREMENTS International Driving Permit. A temporary licence can be obtained on presentation of a UK licence.

KEEPING IN TOUCH

BBC WORLD SERVICE MHz 15.57, 11.96, 9.140, 1.413.

ENGLISH-LANGUAGE NEWSPAPERS The *Gulf Times*.

EMERGENCIES

RED CROSS/CRESCENT SOCIETIES n/a.

UK/USA/CANADIAN REPS UK: PO Box 3, Doha, tel 364 189, fax 364 139, email british.embassy@doha.mail.fco.gov.uk. USA: 22nd February Street, Doha, tel 84 101, fax 884 298, email usisdoha@qatar.net.qa. Canada: The Canadian Embassy in Kuwait City (Kuwait) deals with enquiries relating to Qatar.

Global weather guide p 818, Rainy seasons worldwide p 829, Vaccinations required p 832, Recommended reading p 848, Dependent territories p 812.

ROMANIA

STATE OF THE NATION

SAFETY Bad reputation for petty crime, particularly bogus policemen.

LIFE EXPECTANCY M 66.6, F 73.1.

PEOPLE AND PLACE

CAPITAL Bucharest.

LANGUAGE Romanian.

PEOPLES Romanian (89%), Magyar, Romany.

RELIGION Romanian Orthodox (89%), other Christian denominations.

SIZE (KM) 230 340.

POPULATION 22, 730, 622.

POP DENSITY/KM 98.

FOOD Hearty and rich. Typical dishes include *ciorba de perisoare* (soup with meatballs), *ciorba tananeasca* (meat with vegetables) and *sarmale* (pork balls in cabbage leaves)

TRAVEL PLANNING

WHEN TO GO May to October. The rest of the year can be bitterly cold, with snow.

MEDICAL CARE Limited, free for UK citizens except for medicine from chemist.

CURRENCY Leu = 1000 bani.

FINANCE Limited acceptance of credit cards and travellers' cheques.

AIRPORTS Bucharest (BUH) 16 km from the city.

INTERNAL TRAVEL Efficient and cheap rail network. Road network needs some upgrading.

BUSINESS HOURS 0800-1600 Mon-Friday.

GMT +2 (+3 in summer).

VOLTAGE GUIDE 220 AC, 50 Hz.

RED TAPE

VISAS (AUS/CANADA/UK/US) Not required by US nationals for stays of up to 30 days, required by others.

REPS IN UK/USA/CANADA UK: Arundel House, 4 Palace Green, London W8 4QD, tel 020 7937 9666, fax 020 7937 8069. USA: 1607 23rd Street, NW, Washington, DC 20008, tel 202 232 4747, fax 202 232 4748, email romania@embassy.org. Canada: 655 Rideau Street, Ottawa, Ontario, K1N 6A3, tel 613 789 5345, fax 613 789 4365.

CUSTOMS REGULATIONS Duty free allowance: 200 cigarettes or 50 cigars or 200 g of tobacco, 2 ltrs of spirits, 4 ltrs of wine and 4 ltrs of beer, gifts worth US$ 1000. Prohibited: Ammunition, explosives, narcotics, pornography, uncanned meats, animal and dairy products. Articles of cultural, historical or artistic value may not be exported.

DRIVING REQUIREMENTS International Driving Permit or national driving licence an d Green Card insurance.

KEEPING IN TOUCH

BBC WORLD SERVICE MHz 17.64, 15.57, 12.10, 6.195.

ENGLISH-LANGUAGE NEWSPAPERS *Nine O'Clock, Romanian Business Journal.*

EMERGENCIES

RED CROSS/CRESCENT SOCIETIES Strada Biserica Amzei 29, Sector 1, Bucharest, tel 1 659 3385, fax 1 312 8452 .

UK/USA/CANADIAN REPS UK: 24 Strada Jules Michelet, 70154 Bucharest, tel 1 312 0303, fax 1 312 9652, email britemb@dnt.ro. USA: Strada Tudor Arghezi 7-9, Sector 2, Bucharest, tel 1 210 0149, fax 1 210 0395. Canada: PO Box 117, Post Office 22, Bucharest, tel 1 222 9845, fax 1 312 9680.

Global weather guide p 818, Rainy seasons worldwide p 829, Vaccinations required p 832, Recommended reading p 848, Dependent territories p 812.

RUSSIAN FEDERATION

STATE OF THE NATION

SAFETY Unsafe. Frequent murders for political or commercial reasons, though this may not affect tourists. High levels of theft and alcoholism. Strong presence of the so-called 'Russian mafia'. Avoid areas in the Caucasus (e.g. Grozny, Ingushetia) affected by separatist conflicts and kidnapping.

LIFE EXPECTANCY M 60.6, F 72.8.

PEOPLE AND PLACE

CAPITAL Moscow.

LANGUAGE Russian.

PEOPLES Russian (82%), Tatar, Ukrainian, Chuvash.

RELIGION Russian Orthodox (75%), other.

SIZE (KM) 17,075,400.

POPULATION 148,000,000.

POP DENSITY/KM 9.

FOOD Varies from region to region, but national favourites include well-known dishes like *borhsch* (beetroot soup with sour cream), blinis (small buckwheat pancakes) with sour cream and caviar or smoked salmon, and beef stroganoff. *Pirozhky* (filled rolls like ravioli) and *pelmeni*, (dumplings) are popular. Although vodka is the drink to drink, local champagne is cheap, and suprisingly good although a little sweet.

TRAVEL PLANNING

WHEN TO GO Warm summers (June to August), freezing winters.

MEDICAL CARE Free emergency treatment, but very expensive if further treatment is needed, insurance strongly recommended.

CURRENCY Rouble (Rbl) = 100 kopeks.

FINANCE Credit cards accepted in cities, cash is preferred to travellers' cheques.

AIRPORTS Moscow (SVO) 35 km from the city, St Petersburg (LED) 17 km from the city.

INTERNAL TRAVEL Some domestic flights. River transport is popular. The rail network is vital as the road system is poor. Self-drive and chauffeured car hire is available.

BUSINESS HOURS 0900-1800 Mon-Friday.

GMT from +3 to +12.

VOLTAGE GUIDE 220 AC, 50 Hz.

RED TAPE

VISAS (AUS/CANADA/UK/US) Required.

REPS IN UK/USA/CANADA UK: 5 Kensington Palace Gardens, London W8 4QS, tel 020 7229 8027, fax 020 7229 3215. USA: 2641 Tunlaw Road, NW, Washington, DC 20007, tel 202 939 8907, fax 202 438 7579. Canada: 52 Range Road, Ottawa, Ontario K1N 8J5, tel 613 236 7220, fax 613 238 6158.

CUSTOMS REGULATIONS Duty free allowance: 1000 cigars or cigarillos or 1 kg of tobacco, 1.5 ltrs of spirits and 2 ltrs of wine, a reasonable quantity of perfume for personal use, gifts worth US$ 1000 weighing no more than 50 kg. Prohibited: Photographs or printed matter directed against the Russian Federation, weapons, ammunition, narcotics, fruit and vegetables. Prohibited exports: Lottery tickets, electrical appliances, arms, some computer hardware, over 1.5 ltrs of vodka, works of art and antiques without permits, precious metals, furs. This list is subject to change at short notice, check with the relevant Embassy before travelling.

DRIVING REQUIREMENTS International or national driving licence with authorised translation.

KEEPING IN TOUCH

BBC WORLD SERVICE MHz 15.56, 12.09, 9.410, 6.195.

ENGLISH-LANGUAGE NEWSPAPERS The *Moscow Times*, the *St Petersburg Times*.

EMERGENCIES

RED CROSS/CRESCENT SOCIETIES Tcheryomushkinski Proezd 5, 117036 Moscow, tel 095 126 5731, fax 095 310 7048.

UK/USA/CANADIAN REPS UK: Sofiyskaya Naberezhnaya 14, Moscow 109072, tel 095 956 7200, fax 095 956 7420. USA: Novinskiy Bulvar 19/23, 121099 Moscow, tel 095 252 2451, fax 095 956 4261, email consulmo@moscowpoa.us-state.gov. Canada: Starokonyushenny Pereulok 23, 121002 Moscow, tel 095 956 6666, fax 095 232 9948.

Global weather guide p 818, Rainy seasons worldwide p 829, Vaccinations required p 832, Recommended reading p 848, Dependent territories p 812.

RWANDA

STATE OF THE NATION

SAFETY Apparently returning to normal. Some reports that travel is safe and easy. Potentially volatile, especially in all border areas.

LIFE EXPECTANCY M 39.4, F 41.7.

PEOPLE AND PLACE

CAPITAL Kigali.

LANGUAGE Kinyarwanda, French, Kiswahili.

PEOPLES Hutu (90%), Tutsi (8%), Twa.

RELIGION Animist (50%), Christian denominations and an Islamic minority.

SIZE (KM) 26,388.

POPULATION 6,500,000.

POP DENSITY/KM 261.

FOOD Maize meal eaten with a sauce of meat gravy or vegetables is a staple. Brochettes are available at street stalls and some restaurants serve Franco-Belgian cuisine.

TRAVEL PLANNING

WHEN TO GO Warm all year throughout the country, cooler in the mountains. The rainy seasons occur from mid-January to April and mid-October to mid-December.

MEDICAL CARE Extremely limited, insurance with repatriation cover strongly recommended.

CURRENCY Rwanda franc = 100 centimes.

FINANCE Credit cards and travellers' cheques rarely accepted.

AIRPORTS Kigali (KGL) 12 km from the city.

INTERNAL TRAVEL Sparse road network, many roads in bad condition. Driving is not recommended and visitors are advised to excercise caution.

BUSINESS HOURS 0800-1230, 1300-1700 Monday-Friday.

GMT +2.

VOLTAGE GUIDE 220 AC, 50 Hz.

RED TAPE

VISAS (AUS/CANADA/UK/US) Required.

REPS IN UK/USA/CANADA UK: 58-59 Trafalgar Square, London WC2N 5DX, tel 020 7930 2570, fax 020 7930 2572, email ambarwanda@compuserve.com. USA: 1714 New Hampshire Avenue, NW, Washington, DC 20009, tel 202 232 2882, fax 202 232 4544, email embrwawash@aol.com. Canada: 121 Sherwood Drive, Ottawa, Ontario K1Y 3VI, tel 613 722 5835, fax 613 722 4052, email embarwa@sympatico.ca.

CUSTOMS REGULATIONS Duty free allowance: 200 cigarettes or 50 cigars or 454 g tobacco, 2 bottles of spirits or wine (opened), a reasonable amount of perfume.

DRIVING REQUIREMENTS International Driving Permit.

KEEPING IN TOUCH

BBC WORLD SERVICE MHz 21.47, 17.90, 15.42, 9.630.

ENGLISH-LANGUAGE NEWSPAPERS None.

EMERGENCIES

RED CROSS/CRESCENT SOCIETIES BP 425, Kigali, tel 74402, fax 73233.

UK/USA/CANADIAN REPS UK: Parcelle No 1131, boulevard de l'Umuganda, Kacyiru-Sud, Kigali, tel 84098, fax 82044. USA: boulevard de la Révolution, Kigali, tel 75601/2, fax 72128. Canada: rue Akaera, Kigali, tel 73210, fax 72719.

Global weather guide p 818, Rainy seasons worldwide p 829, Vaccinations required p 832, Recommended reading p 848, Dependent territories p 812.

ST KITTS & NEVIS

STATE OF THE NATION

SAFETY Safe.

LIFE EXPECTANCY M 67.4, F 70.4.

PEOPLE AND PLACE

CAPITAL Basseterre.

LANGUAGE English.

PEOPLES African descent and of mixed-race origin.

RELIGION Christian denominations.

SIZE (KM) 168.4.

POPULATION 41,000.

POP DENSITY/KM 114.

FOOD Local dishes include roast suckling pig, spiny lobster, crab back and curries.

TRAVEL PLANNING

WHEN TO GO Driest from January to April, there is increased rainfall from May to October and towards the end of the year. Violent tropical hurricanes are most likely between August and October.

MEDICAL CARE Adequate, but insurance recommended with evacuation cover.

CURRENCY Eastern Caribbean dollar (EC$) = 100 cents.

FINANCE Major credit cards and travellers' cheques widely accepted.

AIRPORTS St Kitts (SKB) 3.2 km from Basseterre on St Kitts.

INTERNAL TRAVEL Ferries between St Kitts and Nevis, and a good road network on both islands. Cars and mopeds available for hire.

BUSINESS HOURS 0800-1200, 1300-1600 Monday to Friday.

GMT -4.

VOLTAGE GUIDE 230 Ac, 60 Hz (110 AC in some hotels).

RED TAPE

VISAS (AUS/CANADA/UK/US) None.

REPS IN UK/USA/CANADA UK: 10 Kensington Court, London W8 5DL, tel 020 7937 9522, fax 020 7937 5514, email sknhighcom@lineone.net. USA: 3216 New Mexico Avenue, NW, Washington, DC 20016, tel 202 686 2636, fax 202 686 5740. Canada: 365 Bay Street, Suite 806, Toronto, Ontario M5H 2V1, tel 416 368 6707, fax 416 368 3934, email skbnevcan@sympatico.ca.

CUSTOMS REGULATIONS Duty free allowance: For travellers over 18, 200 cigarettes or 50 cigars or 225 g of tobacco, 1.136 ltrs of wine or spirits.

DRIVING REQUIREMENTS Local Temporary Driver's Licence.

KEEPING IN TOUCH

BBC WORLD SERVICE MHz 17.72, 15.22, 6.195, 5.975.

ENGLISH-LANGUAGE NEWSPAPERS The *Democrat* (weekly).

EMERGENCIES

RED CROSS/CRESCENT SOCIETIES PO Box 62, Basseterre, tel 465 2584, fax 466 8129, email skbredcr@caribsurf.com.

UK/USA/CANADIAN REPS UK: The British High Commission in St John's (Antigua) deals with enquiries relating to St Kitts & Nevis. USA: n/a. Canada: The Canadian High Commission in Bridgetown (Barbados deals with enquiries relating to St Kitts & Nevis.

Global weather guide p 818, Rainy seasons worldwide p 829, Vaccinations required p 832, Recommended reading p 848, Dependent territories p 812.

ST LUCIA

STATE OF THE NATION

SAFETY Safe.

LIFE EXPECTANCY M 69.3, F 74.

PEOPLE AND PLACE

CAPITAL Castries.

LANGUAGE English.

PEOPLES Mixed race of African, Carib Indian and European descent.

RELIGION Roman Catholic.

SIZE (KM) 616.3.

POPULATION 142,000.

POP DENSITY/KM 233.

FOOD West Indian and Creole with French influences. Local dishes include *langouste* (native lobster) cooked in a variety of ways, *lambi* (conch) and other fresh seafood. Breadfruit and plantain are popular, and the local spicy *pepper pot* is worth trying.

TRAVEL PLANNING

WHEN TO GO Driest from January to April.

MEDICAL CARE Adequate but expensive, insurance recommended with evacuation cover.

CURRENCY Eastern Caribbean dollar (EC$) = 100 cents.

FINANCE Credit cards and travellers' cheques widely accepted.

AIRPORTS George F L Charles (SLU) 3 km from Castries, Hewanorra (UVF) 67 km from Castries.

INTERNAL TRAVEL All major centres served by a reasonably good road network.

BUSINESS HOURS 0800-1600 Mon-Friday.

GMT -4.

VOLTAGE GUIDE 220 AC, 50 Hz.

RED TAPE

VISAS (AUS/CANADA/UK/US) Not required for Australian nationals, not required by others for stays of up to 42 days.

REPS IN UK/USA/CANADA UK: 10 Kensington Court, London W8 5DL, tel 020 7937 9522, fax 020 7937 8704. USA: 3216 New Mexico Avenue, NW, Washington, DC 20016, tel 202 364 6792, fax 202 364 6723, email eofsaintlucia@aol.com. Canada: 130 Albert Street, Suite 700, Ottawa, Ontario K1P 5G4, tel 613 236 8952, fax 613 236 3042, email echcc@travel-net.com.

CUSTOMS REGULATIONS Duty free allowance: 200 cigarettes or 250 g of tobacco products or 50 cigars, 1 ltr of alcoholic beverage.

DRIVING REQUIREMENTS A local licence will be issued on presentation of a national driving licence or International Driving Permit.

KEEPING IN TOUCH

BBC WORLD SERVICE MHz 17.72, 15.22, 6.195, 5.975.

ENGLISH-LANGUAGE NEWSPAPERS *The Voice of St Lucia*, *The Star*, *The Crusader*.

EMERGENCIES

RED CROSS/CRESCENT SOCIETIES PO Box 271, Castries, tel 452 5582, fax 453 7811, email sluredcross@candw.lc.

UK/USA/CANADIAN REPS UK: PO Box 227, NIS Building, Waterfront, Castries, tel 452 2484, fax 453 1543, email postmaster@castries.mail.fco.gov.uk. USA: The American Embassy in Bridgetown (Barbados) deals with enquiries relating to St Lucia. Canada: The Canadian High Commission in Bridgetown (Barbados) deals with enquiries relating to St Lucia.

Global weather guide p 818, Rainy seasons worldwide p 829, Vaccinations required p 832, Recommended reading p 848, Dependent territories p 812.

ST VINCENT & THE GRENADINES

STATE OF THE NATION

SAFETY Safe.

LIFE EXPECTANCY M 69.3, F 74.

PEOPLE AND PLACE

CAPITAL Kingstown.

LANGUAGE English.

PEOPLES African, European and Carib-Indian descent.

RELIGION Christian denominations.

SIZE (KM) 344.

POPULATION 111,000.

POP DENSITY/KM 327.

FOOD Specialities include red snapper, kingfish, *lambi* (conch), *souse* (a sauce made from pigs' trotters) and sea-moss drink.

TRAVEL PLANNING

WHEN TO GO January to May before the rains, which are heaviest from June to November. Hurricanes are also likely during this period.

MEDICAL CARE Adequate, but insurance with evacuation cover recommended.

CURRENCY Eastern Caribbean Dollar (EC$) = 100 cents.

FINANCE Credit cards and travellers' cheques widely accepted.

AIRPORTS ET Joshua (SVD) 3 km from Kingstown.

INTERNAL TRAVEL Local and charter air services available. Regular boat and ferry services between islands.

BUSINESS HOURS 0800-1600 Mon-Friday.

GMT -4.

VOLTAGE GUIDE 220/240 AC, 50 Hz.

RED TAPE

VISAS (AUS/CANADA/UK/US) None.

REPS IN UK/USA/CANADA UK: 10 Kensington Court, London W8 5DL, tel 020 7565 2874, fax 020 7937 6040. USA: 801 Second Avenue, 21st Floor, New York, NY 10017, tel 212 687 4981, fax 212 949 5946, email svgtony@aol.com. Canada: 130 Albert Street, Suite 700, Ottawa, Ontario K1P 5G4.

CUSTOMS REGULATIONS Duty free allowance: 200 cigarettes or 50 cigars or 225 g of tobacco, 1.136 litres of alcoholic beverage.

DRIVING REQUIREMENTS A local licence, available on presentation of a national or international licence.

KEEPING IN TOUCH

BBC WORLD SERVICE MHz 17.72, 15.22, 6.195, 5.975.

ENGLISH-LANGUAGE NEWSPAPERS *The News, Crusader, The Vincentian.*

EMERGENCIES

RED CROSS/CRESCENT SOCIETIES PO Box 431, tel 456 1888, fax 485 6210, email svgredcross@caribsurf.

UK/USA/CANADIAN REPS UK: PO Box 132, Granby Street, Kingstown, tel 457 1701, fax 456 2750, email bhcsvg@caribsurf.com. USA: The American Embassy in Bridgetown (Barbados) deals with enquiries relating to St Vincent & the Grenadines. Canada: The Canadian High Commission in Bridgetown (Barbados) deals with enquiries relating to St Vincent & the Grenadines.

Global weather guide p 818, Rainy seasons worldwide p 829, Vaccinations required p 832, Recommended reading p 848, Dependent territories p 812.

SAMOA

STATE OF THE NATION

SAFETY Safe.

LIFE EXPECTANCY 71.

PEOPLE AND PLACE

CAPITAL Apia (Upolu Island).

LANGUAGE Samoan, English.

PEOPLES Samoan.

RELIGION Christian denominations.

SIZE (KM) 2831.

POPULATION 170,000.

POP DENSITY/KM 60.

FOOD Roast suckling pig cooked in the Samoan earthern oven, the *umu*, is a favourite at feasts. Other popular foods are breadfruit, chicken and seafood. Kava is the national drink.

TRAVEL PLANNING

WHEN TO GO Between May and September when the tropical climate is tempered by trade winds. Rainfall is heaviest between December and April.

MEDICAL CARE Insurance recommended.

CURRENCY Tala or Samoa dollar (Tala) = 100 sene.

FINANCE Master Card and travellers' cheques accepted on a limited basis.

AIRPORTS Apia (APW) 34 km from the city.

INTERNAL TRAVEL Inter-island ferries. Roads are in varying condition and drivers should be aware of roving lifestock.

BUSINESS HOURS 0800-1200, 1300-1630 Monday-Friday.

GMT -12.

VOLTAGE GUIDE 240 AC, 50 Hz.

RED TAPE

VISAS (AUS/CANADA/UK/US) Not required for visits up to 30 days for tourists.

REPS IN UK/USA/CANADA UK: n/a. USA: (Permanent Mission to the UN) 800 Second Avenue, Suite 400D, New York, NY 10017, tel 212 599 6196, fax 212 599 0797, email wsmun@undp.org. Also deals with enquiries from Canada.

CUSTOMS REGULATIONS Duty free allowance: 200 cigarettes or 50 cigars or 250 g of tobacco, 1 ltr of spirits. Prohibited: Firearms, ammunition, explosives, non-prescribed drugs and indecent publications. Restrictions on live animals and some plants.

DRIVING REQUIREMENTS International Driving Permit or national driving licence.

KEEPING IN TOUCH

BBC WORLD SERVICE MHz 15.36, 11.95, 9.740, 7.145.

ENGLISH-LANGUAGE NEWSPAPERS *The Samoa Observer, Savali.*

EMERGENCIES

RED CROSS/CRESCENT SOCIETIES PO Box 1616, Apia, tel 23686, fax 22676.

UK/USA/CANADIAN REPS UK: c/o Kruse, Enari and Barlow, PO Box 2029, Apia, tel 21758, fax 21407. USA: PO Box 3430, Apia, tel 21631, fax 22030. Canada: The Canadian High Commission in Wellington (New Zealand) deals with enquiries relating to Samoa.

Global weather guide p 818, Rainy seasons worldwide p 829, Vaccinations required p 832, Recommended reading p 848, Dependent territories p 812.

SAN MARINO

STATE OF THE NATION

SAFETY Safe.
LIFE EXPECTANCY 81.

PEOPLE AND PLACE

CAPITAL San Marino.
LANGUAGE Italian.
PEOPLES Sanmarinesi.
RELIGION Roman Catholic.
SIZE (KM) 60.5.
POPULATION 25,000.
POP DENSITY/KM 416.
FOOD Italian food widely available, with several pasta dishes eaten as starters. Main dishes include roast rabbit with fennel, devilled chicken, Bolognese veal cutlets, Roman veal escalopes.

TRAVEL PLANNING

WHEN TO GO Mediterranean climate moderated by sea breezes and height above sea level. Summer (June to September) is warm, moderate snow in winter.

MEDICAL CARE Good, free for locals, cost reduced for EU nationals. Insurance recommended.

CURRENCY Italian lira (L).

FINANCE Credit cards and travellers' cheques accepted.

AIRPORTS Nearest international airports are in Italy, Bologna (BLQ) 125 km away, and Rimini (RMI) 27 km away.

INTERNAL TRAVEL Good roads, no internal rail system.

BUSINESS HOURS 0830-1300, 1530-1930 Monday to Saturday (shopping hours, business hours n/a).

GMT +1 (+2 in summer).

VOLTAGE GUIDE 220 AC, 50 Hz.

RED TAPE

VISAS (AUS/CANADA/UK/US) None.
REPS IN UK/USA/CANADA UK: n/a. USA: n/a. Canada: 615 René Levesque Street West, Room 1010, Montréal, Québec H3B 1P9, tel 514 871 3838, fax 514 876 4217.

CUSTOMS REGULATIONS Duty free allowance: As for Italy.

DRIVING REQUIREMENTS As for Italy.

KEEPING IN TOUCH

BBC WORLD SERVICE MHz 12.10, 9.410, 6.195, 0.648.

ENGLISH-LANGUAGE NEWSPAPERS None.

EMERGENCIES

RED CROSS/CRESCENT SOCIETIES n/a.

UK/USA/CANADIAN REPS The relevant Embassies in Italy deal with enquiries relating to San Marino.

Global weather guide p 818, Rainy seasons worldwide p 829, Vaccinations required p 832, Recommended reading p 848, Dependent territories p 812.

SAO TOME & PRINCIPE

STATE OF THE NATION

SAFETY Safe.

LIFE EXPECTANCY 67.

PEOPLE AND PLACE

CAPITAL São Tomé.

LANGUAGE Portugese.

PEOPLES African descent (90%), Portugese and Creole (10%).

RELIGION Roman Catholic, other Christian denominations.

SIZE (KM) 1001.

POPULATION 131,000.

POP DENSITY/KM 137.

FOOD Most dishes are highly spiced, grilled meats and fish are popular.

TRAVEL PLANNING

WHEN TO GO The main dry season is from early June to late September, a shorter dry season runs from the end of December to the start of February. The rest of the year sees heavy rainfall. High temperatures throughout the year.

MEDICAL CARE Poor, insurance with evacuation cover strongly recommended.

CURRENCY Dobra (Db) = 100 cêntimos.

FINANCE Cards generally not accepted, limited acceptance of travellers' cheques.

AIRPORTS São Tomé (TMS) 5.5 km from the town.

INTERNAL TRAVEL Limited ferry service between São Tomé and Principe. Some roads are asphalt, much of the network is deteriorating. 4-wheel-drive vehicles are recommended for travelling beyond São Tomé.

BUSINESS HOURS n/a.

GMT GMT.

VOLTAGE GUIDE 220 AC.

RED TAPE

VISAS (AUS/CANADA/UK/US) Required.

REPS IN UK/USA/CANADA UK: n/a. USA: 400 Park Avenue, 7th Floor, New York, NY 10022, tel 212 317 0533, fax 212 317 0580. Canada: 250 Albert Street, Ottawa, Ontario K1P 6M1, tel 613 236 6163, fax 613 563 0815.

CUSTOMS REGULATIONS Duty free allowance: Reasonable quantities of tobacco products and perfume (opened).

DRIVING REQUIREMENTS International Driving Permit recommended.

KEEPING IN TOUCH

BBC WORLD SERVICE MHz 15.40, 11.94, 6.190, 1.197.

ENGLISH-LANGUAGE NEWSPAPERS None.

EMERGENCIES

RED CROSS/CRESCENT SOCIETIES BP 96, São Tomé, tel 12 22469, fax 12 22305, email cvstp@sol.stome.telepac.net.

UK/USA/CANADIAN REPS UK: c/o Hull Blythe Ltd, Avenida da Independencia, CP257, São Tomé, tel 12 21026, fax 12 21372. USA: The American Embassy in Libreville (Gabon) deals with enquiries relating to São Tomé e Principe. Canada: The Canadian Embassy in Libreville (Gabon) deals with enquiries relating to São Tomé e Principe.

Global weather guide p 818, Rainy seasons worldwide p 829, Vaccinations required p 832, Recommended reading p 848, Dependent territories p 812.

SAUDI ARABIA

STATE OF THE NATION

SAFETY Safe. Observe Islamic customs.
LIFE EXPECTANCY M 69.9, F 73.4.

PEOPLE AND PLACE

CAPITAL Riyadh.
LANGUAGE Arabic.
PEOPLES Arab (90%), Afroasian.
RELIGION Sunni Islam (85%), Shi'a Islam.
SIZE (KM) 2,240,000.
POPULATION 20,200,000.
POP DENSITY/KM 8.

FOOD Pitta bread accompanies every dish. Rice, lentils, chickpeas and cracked wheat (*burghul*) are common. Lamb and chicken are popular and usually served as kebabs, along with soup and vegetables. Most food is spicy. Alcohol is prohibited, even for visitors.

TRAVEL PLANNING

WHEN TO GO High temperatures for most of the year and very little rainfall. Winters can be cold, particularly in the northwest.

MEDICAL CARE Very high standard but expensive, insurance recommended.

CURRENCY Saudi Arabian riyal (SR) = 100 halalah.

FINANCE Credit cards and travellers' cheques widely accepted.

AIRPORTS Riyadh (RUH) 35 km from the city, Dhahran (DHA) 13 km from the city, Jeddah (JED) 18 km from the city.

INTERNAL TRAVEL Air travel is the most convenient way of travelling around the country. Adequate rail network, the road network is being improved and extended. Women are not allowed to drive vehicles or ride bicycles on public roads.

BUSINESS HOURS 0900-1300, 1630-2000 Saturday to Thursday.

GMT +3.

VOLTAGE GUIDE 125/215 AC, 50/60 Hz.

RED TAPE

VISAS (AUS/CANADA/UK/US) Required (Business only, no tourist visas issued).

REPS IN UK/USA/CANADA UK: 30 Charles Street, London W1X 8LP, tel 020 7917 3000, fax 020 77917 3255. USA: 601 New Hampshire Avenue, NW, Washington, DC 20037, tel 202 342 3800, fax 202 7337 4084. Canada: 99 Bank Street, Suite 901, Ottawa, Ontario K1P 6B9, tel 613 237 4104, fax 613 237 0567.

CUSTOMS REGULATIONS Duty free allowance: 600 cigarettes or 100 cigars or 500 g of tobacco, perfume for personal use, a reasonable amount of cultured pearls for personal use. Prohibited: Alcohol, narcotics, pornography, pork, contraceptives, firearms, natural pearls, most foods.

DRIVING REQUIREMENTS National driving licence with an officially sanctioned translation into Arabic. International Driving Permit (with translation) recommended.

KEEPING IN TOUCH

BBC WORLD SERVICE MHz 15.58, 11.96, 9.70, 9.410.

ENGLISH-LANGUAGE NEWSPAPERS *Arab News, Saudi Gazette, Riyadh Daily.*

EMERGENCIES

RED CROSS/CRESCENT SOCIETIES General Headquarters, Riyadh 11129, tel 1 4740027, fax 1 474 0430.

UK/USA/CANADIAN REPS UK: PO Box 94351, Riyadh 11693, tel 1 488 0077, fax 1 488 2373. USA: PO Box 94309, Riyadh, tel 1 488 3800, fax 1 488 7360. Canada: PO Box 94321, Diplomatic Quarter, Riyadh 11694, tel 1 488 2288, fax 1 488 1361.

Global weather guide p 818, Rainy seasons worldwide p 829, Vaccinations required p 832, Recommended reading p 848, Dependent territories p 812.

SENEGAL

STATE OF THE NATION

SAFETY Some unrest, seek latest information at time of visit.

LIFE EXPECTANCY M 50.5, F 54.2.

PEOPLE AND PLACE

CAPITAL Dakar.

LANGUAGE French and Wolof.

PEOPLES Wolof, Toucouleur, Malinke, Diola.

RELIGION Muslim (90%), Christian (5%), traditional beliefs.

SIZE (KM) 192,530.

POPULATION 9,000,000.

POP DENSITY/KM 47.

FOOD Dishes include *chicken au yassa* (chicken with lemon, pimento and onions), *tiebou dienne* (rice and fish) *dem á la St Louis* (stuffed mullet). Suckling pig is popular in the Casamance region.

TRAVEL PLANNING

WHEN TO GO During the dry season from December to May, when the trade winds cool the hot coastal area.

MEDICAL CARE Basic in rural areas, nsurance recommended.

CURRENCY Communauté Financiaire Africainc franc (CFAfr) = 100 centimes.

FINANCE American Express more widely accepted than other cards, which have limited use. Travellers' cheques generally accepted.

AIRPORTS Dakar (DKR) 17 km from the city.

INTERNAL TRAVEL Asphalt roads link major towns. Roads in the interior are rough and may become impassable in the rainy season.

BUSINESS HOURS 0800-1230, 1300-1600 Monday to Friday.

GMT GMT.

VOLTAGE GUIDE 220 AC, 50 Hz.

RED TAPE

VISAS (AUS/CANADA/UK/US) Required by Australian nationals. Not required for others for stays up to 90 days.

REPS IN UK/USA/CANADA UK: 39 Marloes Road, London W8 6LA, tel 020 7938 4048, fax 020 7938 2546. USA: 2112 Wyoming Avenue, NW, Washington, DC 20008, tel 202 234 0540, fax 202 332 6315. Canada: 57 Marlborough Avenue, Ottawa, Ontario K1N 8E8, tel 613 238 6392, fax 613 238 2695, email ambasseu@sympatico.ca.

CUSTOMS REGULATIONS Duty free allowance: For travellers over 18, 200 cigarettes or 50 cigars or 250 g tobacco, a reasonable amount of perfume for personal use, gifts worth CFAfr 5000. No free import of alcoholic beverages.

DRIVING REQUIREMENTS French or International Driving Permit and Green Card.

KEEPING IN TOUCH

BBC WORLD SERVICE MHz 17.83, 15.40, 11.76, 6.005.

ENGLISH-LANGUAGE NEWSPAPERS None.

EMERGENCIES

RED CROSS/CRESCENT SOCIETIES BP 299, Dakar, tel 823 3992, fax 822 5369.

UK/USA/CANADIAN REPS UK: 20 rue du Docteur Guillet, BP 6025, Dakar, tel 823 7392, fax 823 2766. USA: BP 49, avenue Jean XXIII, Dakar, tel 823 4296, fax 822 2991. Canada: 45 avenue de la République, Dakar, tel 823 9290, fax 823 8749, email dakar@dakar01.x400.gc.ca.

Global weather guide p 818, Rainy seasons worldwide p 829, Vaccinations required p 832, Recommended reading p 848, Dependent territories p 812.

SEYCHELLES

STATE OF THE NATION

SAFETY Safe.

LIFE EXPECTANCY M 65.3, F 74.1.

PEOPLE AND PLACE

CAPITAL Victoria.

LANGUAGE Creole, English, French.

PEOPLES Descendants from European, African, Indian and Chinese origins.

RELIGION Roman Catholic (90%).

SIZE (KM) 454.

POPULATION 78,500.

POP DENSITY/KM 173.

FOOD The Creole cuisine in the Seychelles is influenced by French, Indian and African traditions. Emphasis is placed on the careful blending of fresh spices, and coconut milk and breadfruit are commonly used. Specialities include coconut curries, *salade de palmiste* (palm heart salad) and seafood dishes. Lobster, octopus, pork and chicken feature more often than lamb or beef, which must be imported.

TRAVEL PLANNING

WHEN TO GO Hot all year. Humid during monsoon season (November-February).

MEDICAL CARE Adequate.

CURRENCY Seychelles rupee (Sre) = 100 cents.

FINANCE Amex, Visa and travellers' cheques are widely accepted.

AIRPORTS Mahé Island (SEZ) is 10 km from Victoria.

INTERNAL TRAVEL Good air and boat services. Roads are mostly sand-tracks.

BUSINESS HOURS 0800-1700 Mon-Friday.

GMT +4.

VOLTAGE GUIDE 240 AC, 50 Hz.

RED TAPE

VISAS (AUS/CANADA/UK/US) Not required.

REPS IN UK/USA/CANADA UK: Eros House, 111 baker Street, London W1M 1FE, tel 020 7224 1660, fax 020 7487 5756. USA: 800 2nd Avenue, 4th Floor, Suite 400c, New York, NY 10017, tel 212 972 1785, fax 212 972 1786. Canada: n/a.

CUSTOMS REGULATIONS Duty free allowance: 200 cigarettes or 50 cigars or 250 g tobacco. 1 ltr spirits and 1 ltr wine. 125 ml perfume or 250 ml *eau de toilette*. Gifts worth Srs2500. Prohibited: Drugs and firearms, including spear-fishing guns. Restrictions on importation of animals and agricultural produce.

DRIVING REQUIREMENTS National driving licence.

KEEPING IN TOUCH

BBC WORLD SERVICE MHz 15.40, 11.94, 6.190, 3.255.

ENGLISH-LANGUAGE NEWSPAPERS *The Seychelles Nation, The People* and others.

EMERGENCIES

RED CROSS/CRESCENT SOCIETIES BP 53, Victoria, tel 324 646, fax 321 663 .

UK/USA/CANADIAN REPS UK: PO Box 161, Oliaji Trade Centre, Victoria, tel 225 225, fax 225 127, email bhcsey@ seychelles.net. USA: Victoria House, Room 112, Victoria, tel 225 256, fax 225 189, email usoffice@seychelles.net. Canada: Handled by embassy in Tanzania.

Global weather guide p 818, Rainy seasons worldwide p 829, Vaccinations required p 832, Recommended reading p 848, Dependent territories p 812.

SIERRA LEONE

STATE OF THE NATION

SAFETY Highly dangerous. A war zone subject to kidnappings, mutilations and rape. UK Foreign Office warn against travel.

LIFE EXPECTANCY M 35.8, F 38.7.

PEOPLE AND PLACE

CAPITAL Freetown.

LANGUAGE English. Also Krio and tribal langauges.

PEOPLES Mende (35%), Temne (32%), Limba, other tribal origins.

RELIGION Animist (40%), Muslim (40%), Christian.

SIZE (KM) 71,740.

POPULATION 4,428,000.

POP DENSITY/KM 59.9.

FOOD Local dishes include excellent fish, lobster and prawns and a wide array of exotic fruit and vegetables. French, Armenian and Lebanese food is widely available.

TRAVEL PLANNING

WHEN TO GO Hot all year. Rainy May-November. Dry *Harmattan* blows December-January.

MEDICAL CARE Non-existent. Insurance with repatriation cover is vital.

CURRENCY Leone (Le) = 100 cents

FINANCE Amex and US dollars cash are the only widely accepted means of payment.

AIRPORTS Lungi (FNA) 13 km from the capital.

INTERNAL TRAVEL Roads are appalling and subject to ambush. Reasonable flight network.

BUSINESS HOURS 0800-1200 and 1400-1700 Monday-Friday.

GMT +0.

VOLTAGE GUIDE 220/240 AC, 50 Hz, when available.

RED TAPE

VISAS (AUS/CANADA/UK/US) Required.

REPS IN UK/USA/CANADA UK: Oxford Circus House, 245 Oxford Street, London W1R 1LF, tel 020 7287 9884, fax 020 7734 3822. USA: 1701 19th Street, NW, Washington, DC20009, tel 202 939 9261, fax 202 483 1793. Canada: n/a.

CUSTOMS REGULATIONS Duty free allowance: 200 cigarettes or 225 g tobacco. 1.136 ltrs wine or spirits. 1.136 ltrs perfume.

DRIVING REQUIREMENTS International Driving Permit.

KEEPING IN TOUCH

BBC WORLD SERVICE MHz 17.83, 15.42, 11.86, 7.160.

ENGLISH-LANGUAGE NEWSPAPERS *The Daily Mail.*

EMERGENCIES

RED CROSS/CRESCENT SOCIETIES PO Box 427, Freetown, tel 229 854, fax 229 083, email slrcs@sierratel.sl.

UK/USA/CANADIAN REPS UK: 5 Spur Road, Freetown, tel 22 232 563, fax 22 228 169. USA: corner of Walpole and Siaka Stevens Streets, Freetown, tel 22 226 481, fax 22 225 471, email usembsl@sierratel.sl. Canada: Handled by embassy in Ghana.

Global weather guide p 818, Rainy seasons worldwide p 829, Vaccinations required p 832, Recommended reading p 848, Dependent territories p 812.

SINGAPORE

STATE OF THE NATION

SAFETY Safe.

LIFE EXPECTANCY M 74.9, F 79.3.

PEOPLE AND PLACE

CAPITAL Singapore.

LANGUAGE Malay, English, Mandarin, Tamil.

PEOPLES Chinese (78%), Malay (14%), European, Tamil.

RELIGION Buddhist, Taoist, Muslim, Christian, Hindu.

SIZE (KM) 647.

POPULATION 3,163,500.

POP DENSITY/KM 4,793.

FOOD Over 30 different cooking styles, including local interpretations of Chinese, Indian, Malay, Indonesian, Korean, Japanese, French and Italian cuisine. *Satay*, cubes of skewered, grilled meat served with peanut sauce, is popular, as is *gado gado*, a fruit and vegetable salad in a peanut sauce. Curries such as beef *rendang* are another favourite, and are often based on coconut milk.

TRAVEL PLANNING

WHEN TO GO Hot and humid all year. Wettest November-January.

MEDICAL CARE Excellent but expensive. Be insured.

CURRENCY Singapore dollar (S$) = 100 cents.

FINANCE Credit cards and travellers' cheques widely accepted.

AIRPORTS Changi (SIN) is 20 km from the city.

INTERNAL TRAVEL Excellent roads. Also ferries around islands.

BUSINESS HOURS 0900-1300 and 1400-1700 Mon-Friday, 0900-1300 Saturday.

GMT +8.

VOLTAGE GUIDE 220/240 AC, 50 Hz.

RED TAPE

VISAS (AUS/CANADA/UK/US) Issued on arrival.

REPS IN UK/USA/CANADA UK: 5 Chesham Street, London SW1X 8SA, tel 020 7233 9189, fax 020 7630 6624, email shclondon@singcomm.demon.co.uk. USA: 3501 International Place, NW, Washington, DC 20008, tel 202 537 3100, fax 202 537 0876, email singemb@bellatlantic.net. Canada: Suite 1305, 999 West Hastings Street, Vancouver, BC V6C 2W2, tel 604 669 5115, fax 604 669 5153.

CUSTOMS REGULATIONS Duty free allowance: 1 ltr spirits and 1 ltr wine and 1 ltr beer. Gifts of varying value depending on status. Prohibited: Drugs, firearms, pornography.

DRIVING REQUIREMENTS National driving licence (for 1 month stays).

KEEPING IN TOUCH

BBC WORLD SERVICE FM 88.9.

ENGLISH-LANGUAGE NEWSPAPERS *The Straits Times* and others.

EMERGENCIES

RED CROSS/CRESCENT SOCIETIES Red Cross House, 15 Penang Lane, Singapore 238 486, tel 336 0269, fax 337 4360.

UK/USA/CANADIAN REPS UK: Tanglin Road, Singapore 247919, tel 473 9333, fax 474 0468, email info@britain.org.sg. USA: 27 Napier Road, Singapore 258508, tel 476 9100, fax 476 9232. Canada: 80 Anson Road, no 14-00, IBM Towers, Singapore 079907, tel 325 3200, fax 325 32967, email cdatanj@singnet.com.sg.

Global weather guide p 818, Rainy seasons worldwide p 829, Vaccinations required p 832, Recommended reading p 848, Dependent territories p 812.

SLOVAKIA

STATE OF THE NATION

SAFETY Relatively safe.

LIFE EXPECTANCY M 69.1, F 79.3.

PEOPLE AND PLACE

CAPITAL Bratislava.

LANGUAGE Slovak.

PEOPLES Slovak. Also Hungarian and Czech.

RELIGION Roman Catholic (60%), other Christian denominations, Jewish.

SIZE (KM) 49,034.

POPULATION 5,393,000.

POP DENSITY/KM 109.9.

FOOD Influenced over the ages by Hungarian, Austrian and German cooking. Soups, stews, hearty meat dishes with dumplings and a liberal use of dairy products typifies Slavic cuisine.

TRAVEL PLANNING

WHEN TO GO Very cold winters (November-March), warm summers June-August).

MEDICAL CARE Adequate. Free emergency treatment for UK citizens.

CURRENCY Slovenská koruna (Sk) = 100 halierov.

FINANCE Credit cards and travellers' cheques accepted, particularly in banks.

AIRPORTS Bratislava (BTS) is 10 km from city. (Vienna airport is only 50 km across the border from the capital.) Also Kosice (KSC) and Tatry-Poprad (TAT).

INTERNAL TRAVEL Good rod and rail links, also a network of navigable rivers and canals.

BUSINESS HOURS 0800-1600 Mon-Friday.

GMT +2.

VOLTAGE GUIDE 220 AC, 50 Hz.

RED TAPE

VISAS (AUS/CANADA/UK/US) Not required as follows: Canada 90 days, UK 180 days, USA 30 days. Required for Australia.

REPS IN UK/USA/CANADA UK: 25 Kensington Palace Gardens, London W8 4QY, tel 020 243 8935, fax 020 7727 5824, email skemb@netcomuk.co.uk. USA: 2201 Wisconsin Avenue, Suite 250, NW, Washington, DC 20007, tel 202 965 5160, fax 202 965 5166, email svkemb@concentric.net. Canada: 50 Rideau Terrace, Ottawa, Ontario K1M 2A1, tel 613 749 2496, fax 613 749 4989, email slovakemb@sprint.ca.

CUSTOMS REGULATIONS Duty free allowance: 200 cigarettes or 100 cigarillos or 50 cigars or 250 g of tobacco products. 1 ltr spirits and 2 ltrs wine. 50 g perfume or 250 ml *eau de toilette*. Gifts worth Sk3000.

DRIVING REQUIREMENTS International Driving Permit useful.

KEEPING IN TOUCH

BBC WORLD SERVICE MHz 15.57, 12.10, 6.195.

ENGLISH-LANGUAGE NEWSPAPERS *The Slovak Spectator, Slovak Foreign Trade.*

EMERGENCIES

RED CROSS/CRESCENT SOCIETIES Grösslingova 24, 81446 Bratislava, tel 7 52 92 53 05, fax 7 52 92 35 76.

UK/USA/CANADIAN REPS UK: Panská 16, 811 01 Bratislava, tel 7 54 41 96 32, fax 7 54 41 00 02, email bebra@internet.sk. USA: Hviezdoslavovo Námestie 4, 811 02 Bratislava, tel 7 54 43 33 38, fax 7 54 43 54 39. Canada: Handled by embassy in Czech republic.

Global weather guide p 818, Rainy seasons worldwide p 829, Vaccinations required p 832, Recommended reading p 848, Dependent territories p 812.

SLOVENIA

STATE OF THE NATION

SAFETY Safe.

LIFE EXPECTANCY M 70.6, F 78.2.

PEOPLE AND PLACE

CAPITAL Ljubljana.

LANGUAGE Slovene.

PEOPLES Slovene (88%), Serb, Croat.

RELIGION Roman catholic (90%).

SIZE (KM) 20,253.

POPULATION 1,984,923.

POP DENSITY/KM 98.

FOOD Slovenia's cuisine shows Austro-German influences, with *sauerkraut*, grilled sausage and strudels often appearing on menus. A national favourite is a wide range of breads made for special occasions. These are often stuffed with sweet or savoury fillings.

TRAVEL PLANNING

WHEN TO GO Warm summers (May-August), very cold winters (November-March).

MEDICAL CARE Good. Free emergency treatment for UK citizens.

CURRENCY Slovene tolar (SIT) = 100 stotins.

FINANCE Credit cards and travellers' cheques widely accepted.

AIRPORTS Ljubljana (LJU) is 26 km from city.

INTERNAL TRAVEL Good roads and railway. Some flights.

BUSINESS HOURS 0800-1600 Mon-Friday.

GMT +1.

VOLTAGE GUIDE 220 AC, 50 Hz.

RED TAPE

VISAS (AUS/CANADA/UK/US) Not required.

REPS IN UK/USA/CANADA UK: Cavendish Court, 11-15 Wigmore Street, London W1H 9LA, tel 020 7495 7775, fax 020 7495 7776, email slovene-embassy.london@virgin.net. USA: 1525 New Hampshire Avenue, NW, Washington, DC 20036, tel 202 667 5363, fax 202 667 4563, email slovenia@embassy.org. Canada: 150 Metcalfe Street, Suite 2101, Ottawa, Ontario K2P 1P1, tel 613 565 5781, fax 613 565 5783.

CUSTOMS REGULATIONS Duty free allowance: 200 cigarettes or 50 cigars or 250 g tobacco. 2 ltrs wine and 1 ltr spirits. 50 ml perfume and 250 ml *eau de toilette*. Gifts worth US$78 each.

DRIVING REQUIREMENTS National driving licence.

KEEPING IN TOUCH

BBC WORLD SERVICE MHz 15.58, 12.10, 9.419, 6.195.

ENGLISH-LANGUAGE NEWSPAPERS *Ars Vivendi, Slovenian Business Report, Slovenia Weekly.*

EMERGENCIES

RED CROSS/CRESCENT SOCIETIES PO Box 236, SI-1000 Ljubljana, tel 61 241 4300, fax 61 241 4344, email rdeci.kriz-slo@guest.arnes-si.

UK/USA/CANADIAN REPS UK: 4th Floor, Trg Republike 3, SI-1000 Ljubljana, tel 61 125 7191, fax 61 125 0174, email info@british-embassy.si. USA: Prazakova 4, SI-1000 Ljubljana, tel 61 301 427, fax 61 301 401, email email@usembassy.si. Canada: c/o Triglov Insurance Co Ltd, Miklosiceva 19, SI-6100, Ljubljana, tel 61 130 3570, fax 61 130, 3575, email cancons.lj@ciol.net.

Global weather guide p 818, Rainy seasons worldwide p 829, Vaccinations required p 832, Recommended reading p 848, Dependent territories p 812.

SOLOMON ISLANDS

STATE OF THE NATION

SAFETY Generally safe, but recent attempted *coup d'état* has stirred ethnic tensions.

LIFE EXPECTANCY M 69.9, F 73.9.

PEOPLE AND PLACE

CAPITAL Honiara.

LANGUAGE English, pidgin and 87 local dialects.

PEOPLES Melanesian.

RELIGION Various Protestant denominations (72%), Roman Catholic (19%).

SIZE (KM) 27,556.

POPULATION 404,000.

POP DENSITY/KM 14.2.

FOOD Traditional dishes include tapioca pudding and taro roots with taro leaves. Asian and European food is also popular.

TRAVEL PLANNING

WHEN TO GO Hot and humid all year. Rainy November-April.

MEDICAL CARE Adequate. Insurance should include evacuation cover.

CURRENCY Solomon Islands dollar (SI$) = 100 cents.

FINANCE Credit cards and travellers' cheques widely accepted.

AIRPORTS Honiara (HIR) on Guadalcanal island.

INTERNAL TRAVEL Poor roads. Ferries and small boats are best transport.

BUSINESS HOURS 0800-1200 and 1300-1630 Mon-Friday, 0730-1200 Saturday.

GMT +11.

VOLTAGE GUIDE 240 AC, 50 Hz.

RED TAPE

VISAS (AUS/CANADA/UK/US) Not required.

REPS IN UK/USA/CANADA UK: Tourism Council of the South Pacific, 203 East Sheen Lane, London SW14 8LE, tel 020 8876 1938, fax 020 8878 9876. USA: c/o Permanent Mission to the UN, Suite 400L, 800 Second Avenue, New York, NY 10017, tel 212 599 6192, fax 212 661 8925, email simny@s olomons.com. Canada: n/a.

CUSTOMS REGULATIONS Duty free allowance: 200 cigarettes or 250 cigars or 225 g tobacco. 2 ltrs wine or spirits. Other goods worth SI$400. Prohibited: Unlicensed weapons, offensive literature.

DRIVING REQUIREMENTS National driving licence.

KEEPING IN TOUCH

BBC WORLD SERVICE MHz 15.36, 11.76, 9.740, 7.145.

ENGLISH-LANGUAGE NEWSPAPERS *Solomon Star.*

EMERGENCIES

RED CROSS/CRESCENT SOCIETIES PO Box 187, Honiara, tel 22682, fax 25299, email sirc@solomon.com.sb.

UK/USA/CANADIAN REPS UK: Telekom House, Medana Avenue, Honiara, tel 21705, fax 21549, email bhc1@ welkam.solomon.com.sb. USA: Handled by embassy in Papua New Guinea. Canada: Handled by embassy in Australia.

Global weather guide p 818, Rainy seasons worldwide p 829, Vaccinations required p 832, Recommended reading p 848, Dependent territories p 812.

SOMALIA

STATE OF THE NATION

SAFETY Politically volatile. Seek latest information at time of visit.

LIFE EXPECTANCY M 45.4, F 48.6.

PEOPLE AND PLACE

CAPITAL Mogadishu.

LANGUAGE Somali and Arabic. Also Swahili, Italian, English.

PEOPLES Somali.

RELIGION Sunni Muslim (98%), Christian.

SIZE (KM) 637,657.

POPULATION 9,491,000.

POP DENSITY/KM 14.9.

FOOD The staple diet all over Somalia is rice, macaroni or spaghetti with a little sauce, or spiced mutton or kid, and for breakfast, fried liver of goat, sheep or camel with onions and bread.

TRAVEL PLANNING

WHEN TO GO Hot and dry January-February and August. Rainy March-June and September-December.

MEDICAL CARE Limted. Take own supplies and be insured, with evacuation cover.

CURRENCY Somali shilling (SoSh) = 100 cents.

FINANCE cash is only widely accepted means of payment. US dollars are best.

AIRPORTS Mogadishu (MGQ) is 6 km from city.

INTERNAL TRAVEL Poor roads. Reasonable flights.

BUSINESS HOURS 0800-1400 Saturday-Thursday.

GMT +3.

VOLTAGE GUIDE 220 AC, 50 Hz.

RED TAPE

VISAS (AUS/CANADA/UK/US) Required.

REPS IN UK/USA/CANADA UK: n/a. USA: n/a. Canada: n/a.

CUSTOMS REGULATIONS Duty free allowance: 400 cigarettes or 40 cigars or 400 g tobacco. 1 bottle wine or spirits.

DRIVING REQUIREMENTS International Driving Permit.

KEEPING IN TOUCH

BBC WORLD SERVICE MHz 21.47, 17.64, 12.09, 9.630.

ENGLISH-LANGUAGE NEWSPAPERS n/a.

EMERGENCIES

RED CROSS/CRESCENT SOCIETIES c/o ICRC, PO Box 73226, Nairobi, Kenya, tel 272 3963, fax 715598. The local telephone number is 131 2646, fax 131 2647

UK/USA/CANADIAN REPS UK: Handled by embassy in Ethiopia. USA: Handled by embassies in Kenya and Djibouti. Canada: Handled by embassy in Kenya.

Global weather guide p 818, Rainy seasons worldwide p 829, Vaccinations required p 832, Recommended reading p 848, Dependent territories p 812.

SOUTH AFRICA

STATE OF THE NATION

SAFETY Politically stable at last, but experiencing high levels of crime, especially in cities. Johannesburg infamous for car-jackings and muggings, Cape Town quieter. Rape a serious problem nationwide.

LIFE EXPECTANCY M 57.5, F 63.5.

PEOPLE AND PLACE

CAPITAL Pretoria.

LANGUAGE Afrikaans, English, Ndebele, Pedi, Sotho, Swati, Tsonga, Tswana, Venda, Xhosa, Zulu.

PEOPLES Zulu (23%), Xhosa, Ndebele, European descent (16%), Setswana, Sotho, Venda and other tribal origins.

RELIGION Various Christian denominations, Hindu, Muslim, Jewish.

SIZE (KM) 1,219,080.

POPULATION 42,130,500.

POP DENSITY/KM 33.8.

FOOD Excellent local produce, including meat, fruit and wine. The long coastline produces fresh, cheap seafood. Typical dishes include *sosaties* (a type of kebab), *bobotie* (a curried mince dish), *bredies* (meat, tomato and vegetable stews). *Poetoepap* or *Stywepap*, made with white maize meal, is often served with meat. *Biltong* (dried meat) is a speciality.

TRAVEL PLANNING

WHEN TO GO Warm all year.

MEDICAL CARE Good. Free for children and pregnant women.

CURRENCY Rand (R).

FINANCE Credit cards and travellers' cheques widely accepted.

AIRPORTS Cape Town (CPT) is 22 km from city. Johannesburg (JNB) is 24 km from city. Also Durban (DUR), Port Elizabeth (PLZ), Bloemfontein (BFN).

INTERNAL TRAVEL Ecellent roads and flights, slightly erratic trains.

BUSINESS HOURS 0830-1630 Mon-Friday.

GMT +2.

VOLTAGE GUIDE 220/230 AC (250 AC in Pretoria), 50 Hz.

RED TAPE

VISAS (AUS/CANADA/UK/US) Not required.

REPS IN UK/USA/CANADA UK: 15 Whitehall, London W1A 2DD, tel 020 7925 8900, fax 020 7930 1510. USA: 3051 Massachusetts Avenue, NW, Washington, DC 20008, tel 202 232 4400, fax 202 232 3402, email safrica@southafrica.net. Canada: 15 Sussex Drive, Ottawa, Ontario K1M 1M8, tel 613 744 0330, fax 613 741 1639, email rsafrica@sympatico.ca.

CUSTOMS REGULATIONS Duty free allowance: 400 cigarettes and 50 cigars and 250 g tobacco. 1 ltr spirits and 2 ltrs wine. 50 ml perfume and 250 ml *eau de toilette*. Gifts worth R1250.

DRIVING REQUIREMENTS International Driving Permit.

KEEPING IN TOUCH

BBC WORLD SERVICE MHz 21.66, 6.005, 3.255, 1.197.

ENGLISH-LANGUAGE NEWSPAPERS Many, notably

EMERGENCIES

RED CROSS/CRESCENT SOCIETIES Private Bag X26, Wynberg 7824, tel 21 797 5360, fax 21 797 4711, email sarcs@cyber-trade.co.za.

UK/USA/CANADIAN REPS UK: 15th Floor, Southern Life Centre, 8 Riebeek Street, Cape Town 8000, tel 21 425 3670, fax 21 425 1427. USA: 877 Pretorius Street, Pretoria, tel 12 342 1048, fax 12 342 2244. Canada: 1103 Arcadia Street, Hatfield 0083, pretoria, tel 12 422 3000, fax 12 422 3053.

Global weather guide p 818, Rainy seasons worldwide p 829, Vaccinations required p 832, Recommended reading p 848, Dependent territories p 812.

SPAIN

STATE OF THE NATION

SAFETY Safe, except for the Basque region, where separatist violence includes political assassinations and car-bombs.

LIFE EXPECTANCY M 74.5, F 81.5.

PEOPLE AND PLACE

CAPITAL Madrid.

LANGUAGE Spanish, Basque.

PEOPLES Castilian (72%), Catalan (17%), Galician, Basque, Gitano.

RELIGION Roman Catholic (96%).

SIZE (KM) 504,782.

POPULATION 39,371,147.

POP DENSITY/KM 72.47.

FOOD The excellent tradition of *tapas*, small portions of olives, cheese, meat and seafood, thrives in bars and restaurants. More substantial dishes include *zarzuelas* (fish stews), rice-based *paellas*, *butifarra* sausage stewed with beans, partridge with cabbage. *Gazpacho*, a refreshing tomato based soup, *chorizo* sausage and *Jamon Serrano* (air dried ham) are well known, as are the excellent Spanish sherries.

TRAVEL PLANNING

WHEN TO GO Hot all year, except the centre and north, which can be very cold in winter (November-April). Searing in summer (July-August).

MEDICAL CARE Good. limited free emergency treatment. Reciprocal arrangements for EU citizens.

CURRENCY Peseta (Pta), to be replaced by the Euro after July 2002.

FINANCE Credit cards and travellers' cheques widely accepted.

AIRPORTS Madrid (MAD) is 13 km from city. Also Alicante (ALC), Barcelona (BCN), Bilbao (BIO), Malaga (AGP), Santiago de Compostella (SCQ), Seville (SVQ), Valencia (VLC) and island airports.

INTERNAL TRAVEL Excellent road and flight network, railways good.

BUSINESS HOURS Variable. Generally start 0800 and finish 2000, with a *siesta* of 2-3 hours in the middle.

GMT +1.

VOLTAGE GUIDE 220 AC, 50 Hz.

RED TAPE

VISAS (AUS/CANADA/UK/US) Not required.

REPS IN UK/USA/CANADA UK: 20 Draycott Place, London SW3 2RZ, tel 020 7589 8989, fax 020 7581 7888. USA: 2375 Pennsylvania Avenue, NW, Washington, DC 20037, tel 202 452 0100, fax 202 833 5670. Canada: 74 Stanley Avenue, Ottawa, Ontario K1M 1P4, tel 613 747 2252, fax 613 744 1224, email spain@DocuWeb.ca.

CUSTOMS REGULATIONS Duty free allowance: from outside EU: 200 cigarettes or 50 cigars or 250 g tobacco. 1 ltr spirits over 22% or 2 ltrs alcohol under 22%. plus 2 ltrs wine. 250 ml *eau de toilette* and 50 g perfume. Gifts worth Pta 6200.

DRIVING REQUIREMENTS EU pink format licence. Third party insurance. Green Card recommended.

KEEPING IN TOUCH

BBC WORLD SERVICE MHz 17.71, 12.10, 9.410, 6.195.

ENGLISH-LANGUAGE NEWSPAPERS *Iberian Daily Sun, Majorca Daily Bulletin,* English edition of weekly *Sur.*

EMERGENCIES

RED CROSS/CRESCENT SOCIETIES Rafael Villa, s/n Vuelta Ginés Navarro, 28023, El Plantio, Madrid, tel 91 3354545, fax 91 335 4455, email informa@cruzroja.es/.

UK/USA/CANADIAN REPS UK: Marques de la Ensenada 16, 2nd Floor, Centro Colon, 28004 Madrid, tel 91 308 5201, fax 91 308 0882. USA: Serrano 75, 28006 Madrid, tel 91 587 2200, fax 91 587 2303. Canada: Edificio Goya, Calle Nunez de Balboa 35, 28001 Madrid, tel 91 423 3250, fax 91 423 3251.

Global weather guide p 818, Rainy seasons worldwide p 829, Vaccinations required p 832, Recommended reading p 848, Dependent territories p 812.

SRI LANKA

SAFETY Politically volatile. Separatist guerrilla war by the Tamil Tigers periodically sweeps across the north and east of the island, and sometimes causes bomb attacks in main cities. Seek latest information at time of visit.

LIFE EXPECTANCY M 70.9, F 75.4.

PEOPLE AND PLACE

CAPITAL Colombo.

LANGUAGE Sinhala, Tamil, English.

PEOPLES Sinhalese (74%), Tamil (18%), Arab or European descent.

RELIGION Buddhist. Most Tamils are Muslim.

SIZE (KM) 65,610.

POPULATION 18,552,000.

POP DENSITY/KM 278.9.

FOOD Spicy curries, of which basic curry, made with coconut milk, sliced onion, green chilli, cloves, nutmeg, cinnamon, saffron and aromatic leaves is a specialite. Local produce is excellent, particularly seafood and fruit.

TRAVEL PLANNING

WHEN TO GO Warm all year, except in highlands, which are cool and wet. Monsoons May-July and December-January.

MEDICAL CARE Free emergency treatment at government hospitals.

CURRENCY Sri Lanka rupee (SLRe) = 100 cents.

FINANCE Credit cards and travellers' cheques widely accepted.

AIRPORTS Colombo Bandaranayake (CMB) is 32 km from city.

INTERNAL TRAVEL Good roads and trains. Some flights.

BUSINESS HOURS 0800-1630 Mon-Friday.

GMT +6.

VOLTAGE GUIDE 230/240 AC, 50 Hz.

RED TAPE

VISAS (AUS/CANADA/UK/US) Issued on arrival as follows: for 30 days UK, Canada; for 90 days USA, Australia.

REPS IN UK/USA/CANADA UK: 13 Hyde Park Gardens, London W2 2LU, tel 020 7262 1841, fax 020 7262 7970, email lancom@easynet.co.uk. USA: 2148 Wyoming Avenue, NW, Washington, DC 20008, tel 202 483 4025, fax 202 232 7181, email slembasy@clark.net. Canada: 333 Laurier Avenue West, Suite 1204, Ottawa, Ontario K1P 1C1, tel 613 233 8449, fax 613 238 8448, email lankacom@magi.com.

CUSTOMS REGULATIONS Duty free allowance: 200 cigarettes or 50 cigars or 340 g tobacco. 2 bottles wine and 1.5 ltrs spirits. 250 ml *eau de toilette*. Precious metals including jewellery must be declared on arrival.

DRIVING REQUIREMENTS International Driving permit. (Temporary local driving licence can be obtained instead, but the red tape is formidable.)

KEEPING IN TOUCH

BBC WORLD SERVICE MHz 17.79, 15.31, 11.10, 5.975.

ENGLISH-LANGUAGE NEWSPAPERS *Daily News, The Observer, The Island.*

EMERGENCIES

RED CROSS/CRESCENT SOCIETIES PO Box 375, Colombo 10, tel 1 699 935, fax 1 695 434.

UK/USA/CANADIAN REPS UK: 190 Galle Road, Kollupitiya, Colombo 3, tel 1 437 336, fax 1 335 803, email blic@eureka.lk. USA: 210 Galle Road, Colombo 3, tel 1 448 007, fax 1 437 345, email amcenter@srilanka.net. Canada: 6 Gregory's Road, Colombo 7, tel 1 695 841, fax 1 687 049.

Global weather guide p 818, Rainy seasons worldwide p 829, Vaccinations required p 832, Recommended reading p 848, Dependent territories p 812.

SUDAN

STATE OF THE NATION

SAFETY Ongoing civil war in the south, which is very dangerous. Also avoid Ethiopian or Eritrean borders. Seek latest information at time of visit. Observe Islamic customs.

LIFE EXPECTANCY M 53.6, F 56.4.

PEOPLE AND PLACE

CAPITAL Khartoum.

LANGUAGE Arabic. Also English.

PEOPLES Arabic, Nubian, Nuer, Dinka, other tribal groups.

RELIGION Sunni Muslim (70%), Christian in south (9%), traditional beliefs (20%).

SIZE (KM) 2,505,813.

POPULATION 28,947,000.

POP DENSITY/KM 11.5.

FOOD Local staples are *ful mudamis* (stewed brown beans), *fasooliyya* (stewed white beans), *dura* (cooked maize or millet), often served with *kibda* (liver), *sheya* (charcoal barbecued meat) or *kalawi* (chopped kidney) or *chawarma* (lamb sliced fresh from a roasting spit).

TRAVEL PLANNING

WHEN TO GO Very hot all year. Sandstorms April-September.

MEDICAL CARE Limited outside capital. Insurance strongly recommended, to include evacuation cover.

CURRENCY Sudanese dinar (sD) = 100 piastres.

FINANCE Amex is widely accepted. Other cards and travellers' cheques not widely used.

AIRPORTS Khartoum (KRT) is 4 km from city.

INTERNAL TRAVEL Bad roads, erratic and slow railway, unsavoury ferries on Nile. Some good flights.

BUSINESS HOURS 0800-1430 Saturday-Thursday.

GMT +2.

VOLTAGE GUIDE 240 AC, 50 Hz.

RED TAPE

VISAS (AUS/CANADA/UK/US) Required.

REPS IN UK/USA/CANADA UK: 3 Cleveland Row, St James Street, London SW1A 1DD, tel 020 7839, 8080. fax 020 7839, 7560. USA: 2210 Massachusetts Avenue, NW, Washington, DC 20008, tel 202 338 8565, fax 202 667 2406, email tabaldi@aol.com. Canada: Suite 507, 85 Range Road, Ottawa, Ontario K1N 8J6, tel 613 235 4000, fax 613 235 6880.

CUSTOMS REGULATIONS Duty free allowance: 200 cigarettes or 50 cigars or 225 g tobacco. Prohibited: Goods from Israel, alcohol, fresh fruit and vegetables.

DRIVING REQUIREMENTS *Carnet de passage*, roadworthiness certificate (from embassy), adequate finance. Temporary driving licence obtainable on production of national driving licence.

KEEPING IN TOUCH

BBC WORLD SERVICE MHz 17.64, 15.42, 12.10, 9.770.

ENGLISH-LANGUAGE NEWSPAPERS *Sudan Now, New Horizons.*

EMERGENCIES

RED CROSS/CRESCENT SOCIETIES PO Box 235, Khartoum, tel 11 772011, fax 11 772 877, email srcs@sudanmail.net.

UK/USA/CANADIAN REPS UK: PO Box 801, Street 10, off Sharia Al Baladiya, Khartoum East, tel 11 770 767, fax 11 776 457, email dekhartoum@hotmail.com. USA: Handled by embassy in Kenya. Canada: Handled by embassy in Ethiopia.

Global weather guide p 818, Rainy seasons worldwide p 829, Vaccinations required p 832, Recommended reading p 848, Dependent territories p 812.

SURINAME

STATE OF THE NATION

SAFETY Safe.
LIFE EXPECTANCY M 67.5, F 72.7.

PEOPLE AND PLACE

CAPITAL Paramaribo.
LANGUAGE Dutch.
PEOPLES Creole (34%), Hinustani (34%), Javanese (18%), African or European descent.
RELIGION Christian (45%), Hindu, Muslim.
SIZE (KM) 163,265.
POPULATION 432,000.
POP DENSITY/KM 2.6.
FOOD Varied cuisine reflecting the diver sity of the population. Creole, Indian, Chinese and Indonesian dishes all feature. *Nasi goreng* (Indonesian fried rice) and *bami goreng* (Indonesian fried noodles), Creole dishes like *pom* (ground tayer roots and poultry) and *pastei* (chicken and vegetable pie), and Indian dishes like *roti* (flat bread) with curried chicken are popular.

TRAVEL PLANNING

WHEN TO GO Hot and humid all year. Short dry season February-April, long dry August-October.
MEDICAL CARE Good but expensive. Insurance recommended.
CURRENCY Surinam guilder (SG) = 100 cents.
FINANCE Amex more accepted than other cards. Travellers' cheques only accepted at banks.
AIRPORTS Johan Adolf Pengel (PBM) is 45 km from Paramaribo.
INTERNAL TRAVEL No railways. Patchy road network. Flights affected by rainy season.
BUSINESS HOURS 0700-1500 Mon-Friday, 0700-1430 Saturday,
GMT -3.
VOLTAGE GUIDE 110/220 AC, 60 Hz.

RED TAPE

VISAS (AUS/CANADA/UK/US) Required.
REPS IN UK/USA/CANADA UK: n/a. USA: Suite 460, Van Ness Centre, 4301 Connecticut Avenue, NW, Washington, DC 20008, tel 202 244 7488, fax 202 244 5878, email embsur@erols.com. Canada: Handled by embassy in USA.
CUSTOMS REGULATIONS Duty free allowance: 400 cigarettes or 200 cigarillos or 100 cigars or 500 g tobacco. 2 ltrs spirits and 4 ltrs wine. 50 g perfume. Other goods worth SG40. Prohibited: Many foodstuffs.
DRIVING REQUIREMENTS International Driving Permit.

KEEPING IN TOUCH

BBC WORLD SERVICE MHz 15.22, 12.10, 9.915, 6.195.
ENGLISH-LANGUAGE NEWSPAPERS n/a.

EMERGENCIES

RED CROSS/CRESCENT SOCIETIES Postbus 2919, Paramaribo, tel 498 410, fax 464 780, email surcross@sr.net.
UK/USA/CANADIAN REPS UK: Honorary Consulate, c/o VSH United Buildings, PO Box 1300, Van't Hogerhuysstraat 9-11, Paramaribo, tel 402 870, fax 403 824, email united@sr.net. USA: dr Sophie Redmonstraat 129, Paramaribo, tel 472 900, fax 420 800. Canada: Wagenweg Straat 50, First Floor, Paramaribo, tel 471 222, fax 475 718.

Global weather guide p 818, Rainy seasons worldwide p 829, Vaccinations required p 832, Recommended reading p 848, Dependent territories p 812.

SWAZILAND

STATE OF THE NATION

SAFETY Generally stable.

LIFE EXPECTANCY M 57.9, F 62.5.

PEOPLE AND PLACE

CAPITAL Mbabane.

LANGUAGE English and Siswati.

PEOPLES Siswati (95%), Zulu, European descent.

RELIGION Christian (60%), traditional beliefs (40%).

SIZE (KM) 17,363.

POPULATION 912,876.

POP DENSITY/KM 52.6.

FOOD The staple Swazi dish is meat stew with maize meal or stamped mealies. Roast corn on the cob. South African and Indian food is widely available.

TRAVEL PLANNING

WHEN TO GO moderate climate, though affected by altitude. Rainy October-March.

MEDICAL CARE Good private health care, insurance recommended.

CURRENCY Lilangeni (E) = 100 cents. Also South African rands (notes not coins).

FINANCE Amex, Mastercard and travellers' cheques widely accepted.

AIRPORTS Manzini (MTS) is 5 km from the city.

INTERNAL TRAVEL Extensive road network.

BUSINESS HOURS 0800-1300 and 1400-1645 Monday-Friday.

GMT +2.

VOLTAGE GUIDE 220 AC, 50 Hz.

RED TAPE

VISAS (AUS/CANADA/UK/US) Not required.

REPS IN UK/USA/CANADA UK: 20 Buckingham Gate, London SW1E 6LB, tel 020 7630 6611, fax 020 7630 6564. USA: 3400 International Drive, Suite M3, NW, Washington, DC 20008, tel 202 362 6683, fax 202 244 8059, email 73451.2752@ compuserve.com. Canada: 130 Albert Street, Suite 1204, ottawa, Ontario K1P 5G4, tel 613 567 1480, fax 613 567 1058, email shc@direct-internet.net.

CUSTOMS REGULATIONS Duty free allowance: 400 cigarettes and 50 cigars and 250 g tobacco. 750 ml alcohol. 50 ml perfume and 250 ml *eau de toilette*. Gifts worth E200. Married couples receive only one person's allowance.

DRIVING REQUIREMENTS International Driving Permit.

KEEPING IN TOUCH

BBC WORLD SERVICE MHz 21.66, 17.64, 15.40, 6.005.

ENGLISH-LANGUAGE NEWSPAPERS *The Times of Swaziland, Swazi Observer.*

EMERGENCIES

RED CROSS/CRESCENT SOCIETIES PO Box 377, Mbabane, tel 40 42532, fax 40 46108, email brcs@redcross.sz.

UK/USA/CANADIAN REPS UK: Allister Miller Street, Private Bag, Mbabane, tel 40 42581, fax 40 42585. USA: PO Box 199, 7th Floor, Central Bank Building, Warner Street, Mbabane, tel 40 46441, fax 40 45959, email usembswd@realnet.co.sz. Canada: Handled by High Commission in South Africa.

Global weather guide p 818, Rainy seasons worldwide p 829, Vaccinations required p 832, Recommended reading p 848, Dependent territories p 812.

SWEDEN

STATE OF THE NATION

SAFETY Safe.

LIFE EXPECTANCY M 76.3, F 80.8.

PEOPLE AND PLACE

CAPITAL Stockholm.

LANGUAGE Swedish.

PEOPLES Swedish (91%), Finns, Lapps.

RELIGION Lutheran (89%).

SIZE (KM) 449,964.

POPULATION 8,847,625.

POP DENSITY/KM 19.7.

FOOD The Scandinavian cold table, *smörgåsbord*, is traditional, and includes pickled herring with boiled potatoes, smoked salmon or anchovies, cold meat, sliced beef, stuffed veal or smoked reindeer, and hot dishes like small meatballs or omelettes.

TRAVEL PLANNING

WHEN TO GO Warm summers (June-August), very cold winters (October-April). Even colder further north. Midnight sun visible May-June.

MEDICAL CARE Good. Free to UK citizens.

CURRENCY Swedish krona (SKr) = 100 öre.

FINANCE Credit cards and travellers' cheques widely accepted.

AIRPORTS Stockholm (STO) is 42 km from city. Gothenburg (GOT) is 25 km from city. Malmö (MMA) is 31 km from city.

INTERNAL TRAVEL Excellent road, rail, air and ferry netowrk.

BUSINESS HOURS Flexible working hours.

GMT +1.

VOLTAGE GUIDE 220 3-phase AC, 50 Hz.

RED TAPE

VISAS (AUS/CANADA/UK/US) Not required.

REPS IN UK/USA/CANADA UK: 11 Montague Place, London W1H 2AL, tel 020 7917 6413, fax 020 7917 6475, email embassy@swednet.org.uk. USA: 1501 M Street, NW, Washington, DC 20005, tel 202 467 2600, fax 202 467 2699, email ambassaden.washington@ foreign.ministry.se. Canada: 377 Dalhousie Street, Ottawa, Ontario K1N 9N8, tel 613 241 8553, fax 613 241 2277, email info@ sweden-suede-can.org.

CUSTOMS REGULATIONS Duty free allowance: 200 cigarettes or 100 cigarillos or 50 cigars or 250 g tobacco. 1 ltr spirits and 2 ltrs wine. Goods worth SKr 1000. Prohibited: Firearms and ammunition, eggs, plants, endangered species, drugs, many meat and dairy products, alcohol over 60%.

DRIVING REQUIREMENTS National driving licence.

KEEPING IN TOUCH

BBC WORLD SERVICE MHz 17.64, 15.57, 9.410, 6.195.

ENGLISH-LANGUAGE NEWSPAPERS n/a.

EMERGENCIES

RED CROSS/CRESCENT SOCIETIES Box 27316, SE-10254, Stockholm, tel 8 665 5600, fax 8 661 2701, cmail int@redcross.se/.

UK/USA/CANADIAN REPS UK: Skarpögaten 6-8, 115 93 Stockholm, tel 8 671 9000, fax 8 661 9766. USA: Dag Hammarskjöldvag 31, 115 89 Stockholm, tel 8 783 5300, fax 8 660 5879. Canada: Tegelbacken 4, PO Box 16129, 103 23 Stockholm, tel 8 453 3000, fax 8 242 491.

Global weather guide p 818, Rainy seasons worldwide p 829, Vaccinations required p 832, Recommended reading p 848, Dependent territories p 812.

SWITZERLAND

STATE OF THE NATION

SAFETY Safe.

LIFE EXPECTANCY M 75.4, F 81.8.

PEOPLE AND PLACE

CAPITAL Berne.

LANGUAGE German, French, Italian.

PEOPLES German (65%), French (18%), Italian (10%).

RELIGION Roman Catholic (46%), Protestant (40%).

SIZE (KM) 41,285.

POPULATION 7,085,000.

POP DENSITY/KM 171.6.

FOOD The best known speciality is fondue, Gruyère and Vacherin cheese melted with white wine, *Kirsch* and a little garlic, eaten with cubes of bread. Regional dishes include *papet vaudois*, made from leeks and potatoes, *fondue bourguignonne* (cubed meat with various sauces), *rösti* (shredded, fried potatoes), specialist sausages and salamis, and Geneva's great speciality, *pieds de porc* (pigs feet).

TRAVEL PLANNING

WHEN TO GO Climate affected by altitude. Generally warm April-September, cold November-March.

MEDICAL CARE Good but expensive. Be insured.

CURRENCY Swiss franc (SFr) = 100 rappen or centimes.

FINANCE Credit cards, travellers' cheques and Eurocheques widely accepted.

AIRPORTS Zurich (ZRH) is 11 km from city. Geneva (GVA) is 5 km from city. Bern (BRN) is 9 km from city. Basel (BSL) is 12 km from city.

INTERNAL TRAVEL Excellent road, rail and air networks.

BUSINESS HOURS 0800-1200 and 1400-1700 Monday-Friday.

GMT +1.

VOLTAGE GUIDE 220 AC, 50 Hz.

RED TAPE

VISAS (AUS/CANADA/UK/US) Not required.

REPS IN UK/USA/CANADA UK: Portland Tower, 6th Floor, Portland Street, Manchester M1 3LD, tel 0161 236 2933, fax 0161 236 4689, email swis@cgmanchester.freeserve.co.uk . USA: 2900 cathedral Avenue, NW, Washington, DC 20008, tel 202 745 7900, fax 202 387 2564, email vertretung@was.rep.admin.ch. Canada: 5 Marlborough Avenue, Ottawa, Ontario K1N 8E6, tel 613 235 1837, fax 613 563 1394, email vertretung@ott.rep.admin.ch.

CUSTOMS REGULATIONS Duty free allowance: From EU: 200 cigarettes or 50 cigars or 250 g tobacco, 2 ltrs alcohol up to 15%, 1 ltr alcohol over 15%, gifts worth SFr100. Non-EU: 400 cigarettes or 100 cigars or 500 g tobacco, 2 ltrs alcohol up to 15%, 1 ltr alcohol over 15%, gifts worth SFr100. Prohibited: Meat products, drugs, absinthe. Restricted: importation of animals and firearms.

DRIVING REQUIREMENTS National driving licence.

KEEPING IN TOUCH

BBC WORLD SERVICE MHz 12.10, 9.410, 6.195, 0.648.

ENGLISH-LANGUAGE NEWSPAPERS International titles (e.g. *Internationa Herald Trubune*).

EMERGENCIES

RED CROSS/CRESCENT SOCIETIES Postfach 3001 Berne, tel 31 387 7111, fax 31 387 7122, email info@redcross.ch.

UK/USA/CANADIAN REPS UK: 37-39 Rue de Vermont, 6th Floor, 1211 Geneva 20, tel 22 918 2400, fax 22 918 2322. USA: Jubilaumsstrasse 93, 3001 Berne, tel 31 357 7011, fax 31 357 7344. Canada: Kirchenfeldstrasse 88, 3005 Berne, tel 31 357 3200, fax 31 357 3210, email bern-ag@dfait-maeci.gc.ca.

Global weather guide p 818, Rainy seasons worldwide p 829, Vaccinations required p 832, Recommended reading p 848, Dependent territories p 812.

SYRIA

STATE OF THE NATION

SAFETY Generally welcoming and safe. Take care to observe Islamic customs.

LIFE EXPECTANCY M 66.7, F 71.2.

PEOPLE AND PLACE

CAPITAL Damascus.

LANGUAGE Arabic.

PEOPLES Arab (98%), Kurdish (6%).

RELIGION Sunni Muslim (74%), Christian (10%).

SIZE (KM) 185,180.

POPULATION 17,459,550.

POP DENSITY/KM 94.2.

FOOD National dishes include *kubbeh* (minced meat and semolina suffed with minced meat, onions and nuts), *yabrak* (vine leaves stuffed with rice and minced meat, *ouzi* (pastry with minced meat stuffing), and meat dishes and vegetables cooked with tomatoes and served with rice.

TRAVEL PLANNING

WHEN TO GO Hot dry summers (May-October), cool winters (December-March).

MEDICAL CARE Emergency treatment is free for those who cannot afford to pay. Indurance recommended.

CURRENCY Syrian pound (S£) = 100 piastres.

FINANCE Amex widely accepted, others less so. Travellers' cheques not widely accepted.

AIRPORTS Damascus (DAM) is 29 km from city. Also Aleppo (ALP) and Latakia (LTK).

INTERNAL TRAVEL Good roads and cheap flights. Railways erratic.

BUSINESS HOURS 0830-1430 Saturday-Thursday.

GMT +2.

VOLTAGE GUIDE 220 AC, 50 Hz.

RED TAPE

VISAS (AUS/CANADA/UK/US) Required for all (Australia can obtain on arrival).

REPS IN UK/USA/CANADA UK: 8 Belgrave Square, London SW1X 8PH, tel 020 7245 9012, fax 020 7235 4621. USA: 2215 Wyoming Avenue, NW, Washington, DC 20008, tel 202 232 6313, fax 202 234 9548. Canada: n/a.

CUSTOMS REGULATIONS Duty free allowance: 200 cigarettes or 50 cigarillos or 25 cigars or 250 g tobacco. 570 ml spirits. 500 ml *eau de toilette*, gifts worth S£250. Prohibited: Firearms and ammunition.

DRIVING REQUIREMENTS International Driving Permit, insurance and importation certificates. Green Card not accepted.

KEEPING IN TOUCH

BBC WORLD SERVICE MHz 15.58, 11.76, 9.410, 6.195.

ENGLISH-LANGUAGE NEWSPAPERS *Syria Times.*

EMERGENCIES

RED CROSS/CRESCENT SOCIETIES Al Malek Aladel Street, Damascus, tel 11 442 9662, fax 11 442 5677, email SARC@net.sy.

UK/USA/CANADIAN REPS UK: Kotob building, 11 Rue Mohammad Kurd Ali, Malki, Damascus, tel 11 373 9242, fax 11 373 1600, email britemb.damascus@uk.damas.sprint.com. USA: Abou Roumaneh, Rue al-Mansur 2, Damascus, tel 11 333 0788, fax 11 331 9678. Canada: Lot 12, Mezzeh Autostrade, Damascus, tel 11 611 6851, fax 11 611 4000.

Global weather guide p 818, Rainy seasons worldwide p 829, Vaccinations required p 832, Recommended reading p 848, Dependent territories p 812.

TAIWAN

STATE OF THE NATION

SAFETY Safe.

LIFE EXPECTANCY M 72, F 77.4.

PEOPLE AND PLACE

CAPITAL Taipei.

LANGUAGE Mandarin. Also Taiwanese and some English.

PEOPLES Chinese (98%).

RELIGION Buddhist, Taoist, Confucian.

SIZE (KM) 36,000.

POPULATION 21,615,000.

POP DENSITY/KM 600.4.

FOOD Culinary styles come from all over China, including Canton, Peking, Szechuan and Shanghai. Fried shrimp with cashews, beef with oyster sauce, onion-marinated chicken, eels with pepper sauce, aubergine with garlic suace and seafood with thick sauces are all typical examples.

TRAVEL PLANNING

WHEN TO GO Typhoon season June-October. South is warm all year, north is cooler January-March.

MEDICAL CARE Good but expensive. Be insured.

CURRENCY New Taiwan dollar (NT$) = 100 cents.

FINANCE Credit cards and travellers' cheques widely accepted.

AIRPORTS Chiang-Kai-Shek Taipei (TPE) is 40 km from the city.

INTERNAL TRAVEL Good road and rail network.

BUSINESS HOURS n/a.

GMT +8.

VOLTAGE GUIDE 110 AC, 60 Hz.

RED TAPE

VISAS (AUS/CANADA/UK/US) Not required for 14 days (if no criminal record). For 30 days, available on arrival (need passport-sized photo).

REPS IN UK/USA/CANADA UK: 50 Grosvenor Gardens, London SW1W 0EB, tel 020 7396 9152, fax 020 7396 9151. USA: 4201 Wisconsin Avenue, NW, Washington, DC 20016, tel 202 895 1800, fax 202 895 0017. Canada: 151 Yonge Street, Suite 1202, Toronto, Ontario M5C 2W7, tel 416 369 9030, fax 416 369 1473, email tecotron@pathcom.com.

CUSTOMS REGULATIONS Duty free allowance: 200 cigarettes or 25 cigars or 454 g tobacco. 1 ltr alcohol. Goods up to NT$20,000 (over 20 yrs old). Prohibited: Toy pistols, real firearms, gambling articles, any items from mainland China, drugs, publications prmoting communism, non-canned meat products.

DRIVING REQUIREMENTS International Driving Permit.

KEEPING IN TOUCH

BBC WORLD SERVICE MHz 15.36, 11.955, 9.740, 6.195.

ENGLISH-LANGUAGE NEWSPAPERS *China News, China Post, Free China Journal.*

EMERGENCIES

RED CROSS/CRESCENT SOCIETIES n/a.

UK/USA/CANADIAN REPS UK: n/a. USA: section 7, Lane 134, Hsinyi Road, section 3, taipei, tel 2 27 09 20 00, fax 2 27 02 76 75, email aitarc@ait.org.tw. Canada: n/a.

Global weather guide p 818, Rainy seasons worldwide p 829, Vaccinations required p 832, Recommended reading p 848, Dependent territories p 812.

TAJIKISTAN

STATE OF THE NATION

SAFETY Politically unstable, but travel is possible. Seek local information.

LIFE EXPECTANCY M 64.2, F 70.2.

PEOPLE AND PLACE

CAPITAL Dushanbe.

LANGUAGE Tajik.

PEOPLES Tajik, Uzbeck, Russian,

RELIGION Sunni Muslim (80%).

SIZE (KM) 143,100.

POPULATION 5,945,903.

POP DENSITY/KM 41.6.

FOOD Traditional meals start with sweet dishes like *halva* and tea, followed by soups such as *shorpur* (made of meat and vegetables) and then a main dish of *plov*, a Central Asian staple of mutton, shredded yellow turnip and rice. *Shashlyk* (charcoal grilled mutton) served with *lipioshka* (unleavened bread) is also popular.

TRAVEL PLANNING

WHEN TO GO Extreme seasonal fluctuations: freezing December-January, searing July-August. Pamir Mts are near-polar.

MEDICAL CARE Very limited. Take own supplies and be covered for repatriation.

CURRENCY Tajik rouble (TR).

FINANCE Credit cards and travellers' cheques only accepted in some major hotels. US dollars in cash are best.

AIRPORTS Dushanbe (DYU) is 20 minutes from city.

INTERNAL TRAVEL Reasonable road network. Railways are limited and were subject to bomb attack in 1993. Flights are affected by fuel shortages.

BUSINESS HOURS 0900-1800 Mon-Friday.

GMT +5.

VOLTAGE GUIDE 220 AC, 50 Hz.

RED TAPE

VISAS (AUS/CANADA/UK/US) Required.

REPS IN UK/USA/CANADA UK: Handled by embassy of Russia. USA: Handled by embassy of Russia. Canada: n/a.

CUSTOMS REGULATIONS Duty free allowance: 200 cigarettes or 100 cigars or 500 g tobacco products. 2 ltrs alcohol. Other items worth US$500.

DRIVING REQUIREMENTS International Driving Permit and insurance documents.

KEEPING IN TOUCH

BBC WORLD SERVICE MHz 15.58, 12.10, 9.410, 6.195.

ENGLISH-LANGUAGE NEWSPAPERS n/a.

EMERGENCIES

RED CROSS/CRESCENT SOCIETIES 120, Omari Khayom Street, 734 017 Dushanbe, tel 240 374, fax 245 378, email rcstj@rcstj.td.silk.org.

UK/USA/CANADIAN REPS UK: Handled by embassy in Uzbekistan. USA: Handled by embassy in Kazakhstan. Canada: Handled by embassy in Kazakhstan.

Global weather guide p 818, Rainy seasons worldwide p 829, Vaccinations required p 832, Recommended reading p 848, Dependent territories p 812.

TANZANIA

STATE OF THE NATION

SAFETY Fairly safe, but be careful after dark. usual street crime.

LIFE EXPECTANCY M 46.8, F 49.1

PEOPLE AND PLACE

CAPITAL Dar es Salaam.

LANGUAGE Kiswahili and English.

PEOPLES 99% belong to 120 small tribal groups.

RELIGION Christian (33%), Muslim (33%), traditional beliefs (30%).

SIZE (KM) 945,087.

POPULATION 28,251,511

POP DENSITY/KM 29.9.

FOOD Both traditional African food, Afro-Indian and Indian meals are widely available, including roasted meat and maize, cassava, spicy curries and mutton *biryanis* and chicken and rice.

TRAVEL PLANNING

WHEN TO GO Rainy season March-June. Coast is hot and humid all year. Interior is hot and dry, northern highlands are cool and temperate.

MEDICAL CARE Adequate care is provided at private or religious hospitals, but can be expensive, so insurance is recommended.

CURRENCY Tanzanian shilling (TSh).

FINANCE Travellers' cheques widely accepted, credit cards less so.

AIRPORTS Dar es Salaam (DAR) is 15 km from city. Also international flights to Kilimanjaro International Airport (JRO) and Zanzibar (ZNZ).

INTERNAL TRAVEL Good road network, though of variable quality. Ferries on great lakes are erratic. Dar to Zanzibar is well served by ferries. Rail and air links are useful but limited.

BUSINESS HOURS 0800-1200 and 1400-1630 Monday-Friday, 0800-1300 Saturday.

GMT +3.

VOLTAGE GUIDE 240 AC, 50 Hz.

RED TAPE

VISAS (AUS/CANADA/UK/US) Required for all (except Australia).

REPS IN UK/USA/CANADA UK: 43 Hertford Street, London W1Y 8DB, tel 020 7499 8951, fax 020 7491 9321, email balozi@tanzania-online.gov.uk. USA: 2139 R Street, NW, Washington, DC 20008, tel 202 939 6125, fax 202 797 7408, email balozi@tanzaniaembassy-us.org. Canada: 50 Range Road, Ottawa, Ontario K1N 8J4, tel 613 232 1500, fax 613 232 5184, email tzottawa@synapse.net

CUSTOMS REGULATIONS Duty free allowance: 200 cigarettes or 50 cigars or 250 g tobacco. 500 ml spirits or wine. 250 ml perfume.

DRIVING REQUIREMENTS International Driving Permit ir equired for hiring cars, must be endorsed by police on arrival. For other situations, a temporary local driving licence should be obtained (available on presentation of national driving licence).

KEEPING IN TOUCH

BBC WORLD SERVICE MHz 17.85, 17.64, 15.42, 9.630.

ENGLISH-LANGUAGE NEWSPAPERS Many, notably *Daily News, Business Times, Guardian.*

EMERGENCIES

RED CROSS/CRESCENT SOCIETIES PO Box 1133, Dar es Salaam, tel 51 116 514, email redcross@unidar.gn.apc.org.

UK/USA/CANADIAN REPS UK: Social Security House, Samora Avenue, Dar es Salaam, tel 51 117 659 64, fax 51 112 951, email bhc.dar@dar.mail.fco.gov.uk. USA: 36 Laibon Road, Dar es Salaam, tel 51 666 010, fax 51 666 701, email usembassy-dar1@ cats-net.com. Canada: 38 Mirambo Street, Garden Avenue, Dar es Salaam, tel 51 112 831, fax 51 116 896.

Global weather guide p 818, Rainy seasons worldwide p 829, Vaccinations required p 832, Recommended reading p 848, Dependent territories p 812.

THAILAND

STATE OF THE NATION

SAFETY Safe, apart from border with Myanmar.

LIFE EXPECTANCY M 65.8, F 72.

PEOPLE AND PLACE

CAPITAL Bangkok.

LANGUAGE Thai.

PEOPLES Thai (80%), Chinese, Malay, Khmer.

RELIGION Buddhist (95%).

SIZE (KM) 513,115.

POPULATION 60,816,227.

POP DENSITY/KM 118.5.

FOOD Highly spiced and fragrant dishes, including *tom yam* (coconut-milk soup with ginger, lemon grass, prawns or chicken), *gang pet* (hot 'red' curry with shrimp paste, coconut-milk, garlic, chillies and coriander) and *kaeng dhiaw* ('green' curry with baby aubergines, beef or chicken). Curries are served with rice. The popular desert and breakfast dish of mangoes with sticky rice is worth trying.

TRAVEL PLANNING

WHEN TO GO Best November- February. Hot March-May. Monsoon June-October.

MEDICAL CARE Good.

CURRENCY Baht (Bt).

FINANCE Credit cards and travellers' cheques widely accepted.

AIRPORTS Bangkok (BKK) is 22 km from city. Chiang Mai (CNX) is 15 km from town. Phuket (HKT) is 35 km from town.

INTERNAL TRAVEL Excellent road, rail and air networks.

BUSINESS HOURS 0900-1700 Mon-Friday.

GMT +7.

VOLTAGE GUIDE 220 AC, 50 Hz.

RED TAPE

VISAS (AUS/CANADA/UK/US) Not required.

REPS IN UK/USA/CANADA UK: 29/30 Queen's Gate, London SW7 5JB, tel 020 7589 2944, fax 020 7823 9695, email thaiduto@btinternet.com. USA: 1024 Wisconsin Avenue, Suite 401, NW, Washington, DC 20007, tel 202 944 3600, fax 202 944 3611, email thai.wsn@thaiembdc.org. Canada: 180 island Park drive, Ottawa, Ontario K1Y 0A2, tel 613 722 4444, fax 613 722 6624, email thaiott@magma.ca.

CUSTOMS REGULATIONS Duty free allowance: 200 cigarettes or 250 g tobacco, 1 ltr wine or spirits. Prohibited: Export of Buddha images and other religious artefacts, also any archaeological or historical items.

DRIVING REQUIREMENTS International Driving Permit.

KEEPING IN TOUCH

BBC WORLD SERVICE MHz 17.76, 15.36, 9.740, 6.195.

ENGLISH-LANGUAGE NEWSPAPERS *Bangkok Post* and *The Nation.*

EMERGENCIES

RED CROSS/CRESCENT SOCIETIES Administration Office, Terd Prakiat Building, 1871 Henry Dunant Road, Bangkok 10330, tel 2 256 4037, fax 2 255 3064, email wmaster@redcross.or.th.

UK/USA/CANADIAN REPS UK: 1031 Wireless Road, Pathumwan, Bangkok 10330, tel 2 253 0191, fax 2 255 6051, email britemb@loxinfo.co.th. USA: 120-122 Wireless Road, Pathumwan District, Bangkok 10330, tel 2 205 4000, fax 2 205 4103. Canada: 15th Floor, Abdulrahim Place, 990 Rama IV, Bangkok 10500, tel 2 636 0540, fax 2 636 0555, email bngkk-td@dfait-maeci.gc.ca.

Global weather guide p 818, Rainy seasons worldwide p 829, Vaccinations required p 832, Recommended reading p 848, Dependent territories p 812.

TOGO

STATE OF THE NATION

SAFETY Safe for travellers, although politically troubled. Usual petty crime.

LIFE EXPECTANCY M 47.6, F 50.1.

PEOPLE AND PLACE

CAPITAL Lomé.

LANGUAGE French. Also Ewe, Watchi, Kabiyé.

PEOPLES Ewe, Kabye, Gurma.

RELIGION Traditional beliefs (50%), Christian, Muslim.

SIZE (KM) 56,785.

POPULATION 3,928,000.

POP DENSITY/KM 69.2.

FOOD Soups based on palm nut, ground-nut and maize are common, and meat, poultry and seafood is plentiful.

TRAVEL PLANNING

WHEN TO GO Dry and hot February-March. Long rains April-July, short rains October-November. *Harmattan* wind December-January.

MEDICAL CARE limited. Bring own supplies and be insured for repatriation.

CURRENCY Communauté Financiaire Africaine franc (CFA)= 100 centimes.

FINANCE Amex widely accepted, travellers' cheques and hard currency best in French francs.

AIRPORTS Lomé (LFW) is 4 km from city.

INTERNAL TRAVEL Poor roads, impassable during rains. Some train and ferry services.

BUSINESS HOURS 0700-1730 Mon-Friday.

GMT +0.

VOLTAGE GUIDE 220 AC, 50 Hz.

RED TAPE

VISAS (AUS/CANADA/UK/US) Required.

REPS IN UK/USA/CANADA UK: n/a. USA: 2208 Massachusetts Avenue, NW, Washington, DC 20008, tel 202 234 4212, fax 202 232 3190. Canada: 12 Range Road, Ottawa, Ontario K1N 8J3, tel 613 238 5916, fax 613 235 6425.

CUSTOMS REGULATIONS Duty free allowance: 100 cigarettes or 100 cigarillos or 50 cigars or 100 g tobacco. 1 bottle spirits and 1 bottle wine. 500 ml *eau de toilette* and 250 ml perfume.

DRIVING REQUIREMENTS International Driving Permit.

KEEPING IN TOUCH

BBC WORLD SERVICE MHz 17.89, 15.42, 7.160, 6.005.

ENGLISH-LANGUAGE NEWSPAPERS n/a.

EMERGENCIES

RED CROSS/CRESCENT SOCIETIES BP 655, Lomé, tel 212 110, fax 215 228, email crtogol@syfed.tg.refer.org.

UK/USA/CANADIAN REPS UK: Honorary Concul, c/o British School of Lomé, Lomé, tel 264 143, fax 214 989, email bsl@cafe.tg. USA: BP 852, angle RuePelletier Caventou et Rue Vauban, Lomé, tel 217 717, fax 217 952. Canada: c/o Société Nationale des Chemins de Fer du togo, Canac International Inc, Lomé, tel 212 211, fax 212 219 (also handled by embassy in Ghana).

Global weather guide p 818, Rainy seasons worldwide p 829, Vaccinations required p 832, Recommended reading p 848, Dependent territories p 812.

TONGA

STATE OF THE NATION

SAFETY Safe.

LIFE EXPECTANCY M 68.

PEOPLE AND PLACE

CAPITAL Nuku'alofa

LANGUAGE Tongan, English.

PEOPLES Tongan, European descent.

RELIGION Free Wesleyan (64%), Roma catholic (15%).

SIZE (KM) 748.

POPULATION 97,446.

POP DENSITY/KM 130.3.

FOOD Local staples are *'ufi* (white yam) and taro. Other dishes include *lu pullu* (meat and onions marinated in coconut-milk, baked in taro leaves in an underground oven), *feke* (grilled octopus or squid in coconut sauce) *'ota* (raw fish marinated in lemon juice), devilled clams. Feasts are an important part of the lifestyle and upto 30 different dishes may be served on a long tray of plaited coconut fronts, including suckling pig, chicken, crayfish, octopus, pork and vegetables steamed in an underground oven.

TRAVEL PLANNING

WHEN TO GO Best May-November. Heavy rains December-March.

MEDICAL CARE Adequate for minor problems. Insurance with evacuation cover recommended.

CURRENCY Pa'anga (T$) – 100 seniti.

FINANCE Travellers' cheques accepted in banks and tourist places, credit cards less so.

AIRPORTS Fua'Amotu (TBU) is 15 km from the capital.

INTERNAL TRAVEL Good roads, ferries and flights.

BUSINESS HOURS 0830-1630 Mon-Friday.

GMT +13.

VOLTAGE GUIDE 240 AC, 50 Hz.

RED TAPE

VISAS (AUS/CANADA/UK/US) Issued on arrival. Proof of onward ticket required.

REPS IN UK/USA/CANADA UK: 36 Molyneux Street, London W1H 6AB, tel 020 7724 5828, fax 020 7723 9074. USA: Suite 604, 360 Post Street, San Francisco, California ($108, tel 415 781 0365, fax 415 781 3964, email emeline@sfconsulate.gov.to. Canada: Handled by consulate in USA (San Francisco).

CUSTOMS REGULATIONS Duty free allowance: 500 cigarettes or 100 cigars. 2.25 ltrs spirits or 4.5 ltrs wine or one carton beer. Prohibited: Firearms and ammunition. Pornography.

DRIVING REQUIREMENTS Local driving licence (available from police headquarters on production of national driving licence).

KEEPING IN TOUCH

BBC WORLD SERVICE MHz 15.36, 11.96, 9.740, 7.145.

ENGLISH-LANGUAGE NEWSPAPERS *The Times of Tonga*, *Tonga Chronicle*.

EMERGENCIES

RED CROSS/CRESCENT SOCIETIES PO Box 456, Noku' Alofa, tel 676 21360, fax 676 24158.

UK/USA/CANADIAN REPS UK: PO Box 56, Nuku'alofa, tel 24285, fax 24109. USA: Handled by embassy in Fiji. Canada: Handled by High Comission in New Zealand.

Global weather guide p 818, Rainy seasons worldwide p 829, Vaccinations required p 832, Recommended reading p 848, Dependent territories p 812.

TRINIDAD & TOBAGO

STATE OF THE NATION

SAFETY Safe.

LIFE EXPECTANCY M 71.5, F 76.2.

PEOPLE AND PLACE

CAPITAL Port of Spain.

LANGUAGE English.

PEOPLES Asian descent (40%), African descent (40%), mixed race.

RELIGION Christian, Hindu and Muslim.

SIZE (KM) 5,128.

POPULATION 1,264,000.

POP DENSITY/KM 246.5.

FOOD Tobago offers notable seafood specialities, lobster and conch with dumplings amongst them. Both islands serve West Indian, Creole and Indian cuisine, including dishes such as peppery pigeon pea soup with pilau rice and *roti* (flat bread stuffed with curried chicken, fish, goat or vegetables. Bean sized oysters are a Trinidadian delicacy.

TRAVEL PLANNING

WHEN TO GO Dry season is November-May. Hottest June-October. Wettest May-July.

MEDICAL CARE Free and adequate in Trinidad, but Tobago more limited.

CURRENCY Trinidad & Tobago dollar (TT$) = 100 cents.

FINANCE credit cards accepted in many places but may be charged 50% extra. Travellers' cheques better.

AIRPORTS Port of Spain (POS) is 27 km from city. Crown point (TAB) is 13 km from Scarborough.

INTERNAL TRAVEL Good air, ferry and road links.

BUSINESS HOURS 0800-1600 Mon-Friday.

GMT -4.

VOLTAGE GUIDE 110/220 AC, 60 Hz.

RED TAPE

VISAS (AUS/CANADA/UK/US) Not required up to 3 months (except Australia).

REPS IN UK/USA/CANADA UK: 42 Belgrave Square, London SW1X 8NT, tel 020 7245 9351, fax 020 7823 1065. USA: 1708 Massachusetts Avenue, NW, Washington, DC 20036, tel 202 467 6490, fax 202 785 3130, email embttgo@erols.com. Canada: 75 Albert Street, Suite 508, Ottawa, Ontario K1P 5E7, tel 613 232 2418, fax 613 232 4349, email ottawa@ttmissions.com.

CUSTOMS REGULATIONS Duty free allowance: 200 cigarettes or 50 cigars or 250 g tobacco. 1.5 ltrs alcohol (opened).

DRIVING REQUIREMENTS National driving licence from Canada, UK, France, Germany, USA, Bahamas. Otherwise International Driving Permit.

KEEPING IN TOUCH

BBC WORLD SERVICE MHz 17.72, 15.22, 6.195, 5.975.

ENGLISH-LANGUAGE NEWSPAPERS All.

EMERGENCIES

RED CROSS/CRESCENT SOCIETIES PO Box 357, Por t of Spain, tel 627 8215, fax 627 8215, email ttrcs@carib-link.net.

UK/USA/CANADIAN REPS UK: PO Box 778, 19 St Clair Avenue, St Clair, Port of Spain, tel 622 2748, fax 622 4555, email ppabhc@opus.co.tt. USA: PO Box 752, 15 Queen's Park West, Port of Spain, tel 622 6372, fax 628 5462, email us_embtt@ trinidad.net. Canada: 3-3a Sweet Briar Road, St Clair, Port of Spain, tel 622 6232, fax 628 2581, email chcpspan@opus.co.tt.

Global weather guide p 818, Rainy seasons worldwide p 829, Vaccinations required p 832, Recommended reading p 848, Dependent territories p 812.

TUNISIA

STATE OF THE NATION

SAFETY Safe.

LIFE EXPECTANCY M 68.4, F 70.7.

PEOPLE AND PLACE

CAPITAL Tunis.

LANGUAGE Arabic.

PEOPLES Arab and Berber.

RELIGION Muslim.

SIZE (KM) 163,610.

POPULATION 9,214,900.

POP DENSITY/KM 59.6.

FOOD Tunisian dishes are often cooked with olive oil, spiced with aniseed, coriander, cumin, caraway, cinnamon or saffron. Lamb or *dorado* (bream) are often served with *couscous*, the *tajines* are generally excellent. *Brik*, a fried pastry envelope with a savoury filling, is a popular snack.

TRAVEL PLANNING

WHEN TO GO Warm all year. Very hot inland and June-September.

MEDICAL CARE Adequate. All supplies must be paid for and are expensive, so consider taking your own supplies. Insurance recommended.

CURRENCY Tunisian dinar (TD) = 1000 millimes.

FINANCE Credit cards and travellers' cheques widely accepted.

AIRPORTS Tunis (TUN) is 8 km from city. Monastir (MIR) is 8 km from city, Djerba (DJE) 8km, Sfax (SFA) 15 km, Tozeur (TOE) 10 km.

INTERNAL TRAVEL Excellent road and air network. Reasonable railway.

BUSINESS HOURS Winter: 0800-1230 and 1430-1800 Monday-Friday. Summer: 0800-1300 Monday-Saturday.

GMT +1.

VOLTAGE GUIDE 220 AC, 50 Hz.

RED TAPE

VISAS (AUS/CANADA/UK/US) Not required up to 3 months (except Australia, which can be obtained on arrival).

REPS IN UK/USA/CANADA UK: 29 prince's gate, London SW7 1QG, tel 020 7584 8117, fax 020 7225 2884. USA: 1515 Massachusetts Avenue, NW, Washington, DC 20005, tel 202 862 1850, fax 202 862 1858. Canada: 515 O'Connor Street, Ottawa, ontario K1S 3P8, tel 613 237 0330, fax 613 237 7939.

CUSTOMS REGULATIONS Duty free allowance: 400 cigarettes or 100 cigars or 500 g tobacco. 1 ltr alcohol over 25% or 2 ltrs alcohol less than 25%. 250 ml perfume and 1 ltr *eau de toilette*. Prohibited: Firearms, explosives, drugs, transmitter-receivers, pornography.

DRIVING REQUIREMENTS National driving licence, vehicle log book, insurance.

KEEPING IN TOUCH

BBC WORLD SERVICE MHz 17.64, 15.49, 12.10, 6.195.

ENGLISH-LANGUAGE NEWSPAPERS *Tunisia News.*

EMERGENCIES

RED CROSS/CRESCENT SOCIETIES 19 Rue d'Angleterre, Tunis 1000, tel 1 325 572, fax 1 320 151.

UK/USA/CANADIAN REPS UK: 5 Place de la Victoire, 1000 Tunis, tel 1 341 444, fax 1 354 877, email british.emb@planet.tn. USA: 144 Avenue de la Liberté, Belvédère, 1002 Tunis, tel 1 782 566, fax 1 789 719. Canada: 3 Rue du Sénégal, Place de l'Afrique, 1002 Tunis-Belvédère, tel 1 796 577, fax 1 792 371.

Global weather guide p 818, Rainy seasons worldwide p 829, Vaccinations required p 832, Recommended reading p 848, Dependent territories p 812.

TURKEY

STATE OF THE NATION

SAFETY Safe, except in Kurdish areas of the south-east, which can be affected by military-guerrilla operations.

LIFE EXPECTANCY M 66.5, F 71.7

PEOPLE AND PLACE

CAPITAL Ankara.

LANGUAGE Turkish.

PEOPLES Turkish (70%), Kurdish (20%), Arab and others.

RELIGION Muslim, mainly Sunni (99%).

SIZE (KM) 779,452.

POPULATION 62,510,000.

POP DENSITY/KM 80.7.

FOOD Lamb is featured on most menus, served as *shish* (cubed and grilled on a skewer) or *doner* (carved from roasting spit) kebabs. Red mullet and swordfish are also popular, as are *dolma* (vine leaves stuffed with nuts and currants) and *karniyarik* (aubergine stuffed with mince meat).

TRAVEL PLANNING

WHEN TO GO South and west coasts have a Mediterranean climate and are warm and sunny May-September. Inland has cooler winters and east can be very cold.

MEDICAL CARE Good but not free. Insurance recommended.

CURRENCY Turkish lira (TL).

FINANCE Credit cards and travellers' cheques widely accepted.

AIRPORTS Ankara (ESB) is 35 km from the city. Istanbul (IST) is 24 km from the city. Also Izmir, Dalaman, Antalya, Adana.

INTERNAL TRAVEL Excellent roads. Good railw and flight network.

BUSINESS HOURS 0830-1230 and 1330-1730 Monday-Friday.

GMT +2.

VOLTAGE GUIDE 220 AC, 50 Hz.

RED TAPE

VISAS (AUS/CANADA/UK/US) Not required up to 3 months.

REPS IN UK/USA/CANADA UK: Rutland Lodge, Rutland Gardens, London SW7 1BW, tel 020 7589 0360, fax 020 7584 6235. USA: 2525 Massachusetts Avenue, NW, Washington, DC 20008, tel 202 612 6742, fax 202 612 6744, email turkish@erols.com. Canada: 197 Wurtemburg Street, Ottawa, Ontario K1N 8L9, tel 613 789 4044, fax 613 789 3442, email turkish@magma.ca.

CUSTOMS REGULATIONS Duty free allowance: 200 cigarettes or 50 cigars or 200 g tobacco. Plus 50 g chewing tobacco or 200 g pipe tobacco or 200 g snuff. 5 ltrs alcohol, 120 ml perfume. Prohibited: Weapons and drugs.

DRIVING REQUIREMENTS Green Card International Insurance and Turkish third party insurance. International Driving Permit (if staying over 3 months).

KEEPING IN TOUCH

BBC WORLD SERVICE Mhz 15.57, 12.10, 9.410, 6.195.

ENGLISH-LANGUAGE NEWSPAPERS *Turkish Daily News.*

EMERGENCIES

RED CROSS/CRESCENT SOCIETIES Atac Sokak 1. No. 32, Yenisehir, Ankara, tel 312 430 2300, fax 312 430 0175.

UK/USA/CANADIAN REPS UK: Sehit Ersan Caddesi 46a, Cankaya, Ankara, tel 312 468 6230, fax 312 468 6643, email britembank@ankara.mail.fco.gov.uk. USA: Ataturk Bulvar 110, Kavaklidere 06100, Ankara, tel 312 468 6110, fax 312 468 6131. Canada: Nenehatun Caddesi 75, Gaziosmanpasa 06700, Ankara, tel 312 436 1275, fax 312 446 4437.

Global weather guide p 818, Rainy seasons worldwide p 829, Vaccinations required p 832, Recommended reading p 848, Dependent territories p 812.

TURKMENISTAN

STATE OF THE NATION

SAFETY Seek latest information at time of visit.

LIFE EXPECTANCY M 61.9, F 68.9.

PEOPLE AND PLACE

CAPITAL Ashgabat.

LANGUAGE Turkmen.

PEOPLES Turkmen, Uzbek, Russian.

RELIGION Sunni Muslim (87%), Eastern Orthodox Christian.

SIZE (KM) 488,100.

POPULATION 4,665,000.

POP DENSITY/KM 9.6.

FOOD Based on Central Asian staples such as *plov* (mutton, shredded yellow turnip and rice), *shashlyk* (chargrilled mutton kebabs) served with flat bread and raw onions, *shorpa* (meat and vegetable soup), *manty* (like ravioli, with a meat filling). A particular speciality is *ishkiykli*, dough balls filled with meat and cooked in hot sand.

TRAVEL PLANNING

WHEN TO GO Extreme continental climate, with freezing winters (November-April) and searing summers (May-September).

MEDICAL CARE Limted. Take own supplies. Insurance cover should include repatriations.

CURRENCY Manat (TMM) = 100 tenge.

FINANCE Credit cards only accepted at a few hotels. Travellers' cheques only accpeted from certain banks. US dollars cash is best.

AIRPORTS Ashgabat (ASB) is 4 km from city.

INTERNAL TRAVEL Reasonable road network, some internal flights, limited railway lines.

BUSINESS HOURS 0900-1800 Mon-Friday.

GMT +5.

VOLTAGE GUIDE 220 AC, 50 Hz.

RED TAPE

VISAS (AUS/CANADA/UK/US) Required.

REPS IN UK/USA/CANADA UK: St George's House, 14-17 Wells Street, London W1P 3FP, tel 020 7255 1071, fax 020 7323 9184. USA: 2207 Massachusetts Avenue, NW, Washington, DC 20008, tel 202 588 1500, fax 202 588 0697, email turkmen@earthlink.net. Canada: n/a.

CUSTOMS REGULATIONS Duty free allowance: 200 cigarettes or 200 g tobacco. 1.5 ltrs spirits and 2 ltrs wine (aged over 21). Prohibited: Weapons and ammunition, drugs, loose pearls, pornography, any third party's goods.

DRIVING REQUIREMENTS International Driving Permit with authorised translation.

KEEPING IN TOUCH

BBC WORLD SERVICE MHz 15.57, 12.10, 9.410, 6.195.

ENGLISH-LANGUAGE NEWSPAPERS n/a.

EMERGENCIES

RED CROSS/CRESCENT SOCIETIES 48a Navor Street, 744000 Ashgabat, tel 12 395 511, fax 12 351 750, email nrcst@cat.glasnet.ru.

UK/USA/CANADIAN REPS UK: 310 Office Building, Four Point Altin Hotel, 744014 Ashgabat, tel 12 510 616, fax 12 510 868, email postmaster@beasb.cat.glasnet.ru. USA: 9 Pushkin Street, 74400 Ashgabat, tel 12 350 037, fax 12 511 305. Canada: Handled by embassy in Turkey.

Global weather guide p 818, Rainy seasons worldwide p 829, Vaccinations required p 832, Recommended reading p 848, Dependent territories p 812.

TUVALU

STATE OF THE NATION

SAFETY Safe.

LIFE EXPECTANCY M 68.3, F 72.5.

PEOPLE AND PLACE

CAPITAL Funafuti.

LANGUAGE English.

PEOPLES Tuvaluan.

RELIGION Church of Tuvalu (97%).

SIZE (KM) 26.

POPULATION 9,800.

POP DENSITY/KM 376.9.

FOOD Fish and shellfish play a major part in the local diet, some restaurants serve international dishes.

TRAVEL PLANNING

WHEN TO GO Humid and hot all year. Rainy November-February.

MEDICAL CARE Good, but insurance with evacuation cover recommended.

CURRENCY Tuvaluan dollar (TV$) = 100 cents. Australian dollar (AS$) also used.

FINANCE No credit cards. Travellers' cheques in AS$.

AIRPORTS Funafuti (FUN) is 30 minutes outside town.

INTERNAL TRAVEL No air service. Few roads. A single passenger and cargo boat serves all the islands.

BUSINESS HOURS 0730-1615 Monday-Thursday, 0730-1245 Friday.

GMT +12.

VOLTAGE GUIDE 240 AC, 60 Hz.

RED TAPE

VISAS (AUS/CANADA/UK/US) Not required.

REPS IN UK/USA/CANADA UK: c/o Tourism Council of the South pacific, 203 East Sheen Lane, London SW14 8LE, tel 020 8876 1938, fax 020 8878 9876. USA: n/a. Canada: n/a.

CUSTOMS REGULATIONS Duty free allowance: 200 cigarettes or 225 g tobacco or ciagrs. 1 ltr spirits and 1 ltr wine. Prohibited: Pornography, drugs, pure alcohol, firearms and ammunition.

DRIVING REQUIREMENTS n/a.

KEEPING IN TOUCH

BBC WORLD SERVICE MHz 15.36, 11.96, 9.740, 5.975.

ENGLISH-LANGUAGE NEWSPAPERS *Tuvalu Echoes* (fortnightly).

EMERGENCIES

RED CROSS/CRESCENT SOCIETIES n/a.

UK/USA/CANADIAN REPS UK: Handled by High Commission in Fiji. USA: Handled by embassy in Fiji. Canada: Handled by High Commission in New Zealand.

Global weather guide p 818, Rainy seasons worldwide p 829, Vaccinations required p 832, Recommended reading p 848, Dependent territories p 812.

UGANDA

STATE OF THE NATION

SAFETY Potentially safe, despite murders of tourists on gorilla safari. Be wary in border areas, especially the north-west, haunt of bandits, rebels and religious militias.

LIFE EXPECTANCY M 38.9, F 40.4.

PEOPLE AND PLACE

CAPITAL Kampala.

LANGUAGE English.

PEOPLES 13 main ethnic groups (principally Luganda, Nkole, Chiga, Lango, Acholi, Teso, Lugbara).

RELIGION Roman Catholic (33%), Protestant (33%), traditional beliefs (13%), Muslim, Hindu.

SIZE (KM) 241,139.

POPULATION 18,592,000.

POP DENSITY/KM 77.1.

FOOD Popular dishes include *matoke* (made from bananas), millet bread, sweet potatoes, cassava, chicken and meat stews an d freshwater fish. Banana gin (*waragi*) makes a good cocktail base.

TRAVEL PLANNING

WHEN TO GO Heavy rains March-May and October-November. Otherwise warm all year, though cooler in hill country.

MEDICAL CARE Limited. Carry own supplies and insurance including repatriation cover.

CURRENCY Uganda shilling (USh).

FINANCE Visa and travellers' cheques widely accepted, other credit cards less so.

AIRPORTS Entebbe (EBB) is 35 km from city.

INTERNAL TRAVEL Rail network limited and timetables erratic. Fairly extensive roads, though in poor condition. Some internal flights. Ferries on great lakes efficient but not always safe.

BUSINESS HOURS 0800-1245 and 1400-1700 Monday-Friday.

GMT +3.

VOLTAGE GUIDE 240 AC, 50 Hz.

RED TAPE

VISAS (AUS/CANADA/UK/US) Required for all.

REPS IN UK/USA/CANADA UK: Uganda House, 58-59 Trafalgar Square,London WC2N 5DX, tel 020 7839 5783, fax 020 7839 8925. USA: 5911 16th Street, NW, Washington, DC 20011, tel 202 726 7100, fax 202 726 1727, email ugembassy@aol.com. Canada: 231 Cobourg Street, Ottawa, Ontario K1N 8J2, tel 613 789 7797, fax 613 789 8909, email ugacom@comnet.ca.

CUSTOMS REGULATIONS Duty free allowance: 200 cigarettes or 225 g tobacco. 1 bottle spirits or wine. 568 ml perfume.

DRIVING REQUIREMENTS International Driving Permit.

KEEPING IN TOUCH

BBC WORLD SERVICE MHz 17.64, 15.40, 11.73, 9.630.

ENGLISH-LANGUAGE NEWSPAPERS *East African*, *Financial Times*, *The Monitor* and many others.

EMERGENCIES

RED CROSS/CRESCENT SOCIETIES PO Box 494, Kampala, tel 41 258 701, fax 41 258 184.

UK/USA/CANADIAN REPS UK: PO Box 7070, 10-12 Parliament Avenue, Kampala, tel 41 257 054, fax 41 257 304. USA: PO Box 7007, 10-12 Parliament Avenue, Kampala, tel 41 259 792, fax 41 259 794, email usembassy@starcom.co.ug. Canada: IPS Building, Parliament Avenue, PO Box 20115, Kampala, tel 41 258 141, fax 41 234 518, email canada.consulate@ infocom.co.ug.

Global weather guide p 818, Rainy seasons worldwide p 829, Vaccinations required p 832, Recommended reading p 848, Dependent territories p 812.

UKRAINE

STATE OF THE NATION

SAFETY Be wary of carjackings and muggings.

LIFE EXPECTANCY M 63.8, F 73.7.

PEOPLE AND PLACE

CAPITAL Kyiv (Kiev).

LANGUAGE Ukrainian.

PEOPLES Ukrainian (73%), Russian (22%), Jewish and others.

RELIGION Ukrainian Orthodox.

SIZE (KM) 603,700.

POPULATION 50,500,000.

POP DENSITY/KM 83.6.

FOOD The cuisine is similar to Russian food, including *borshch* (beetroot soup), *varenniki* (parcels of dough containing cheese, meat or fruit), and *holubtsi* (stuffed cabbage rolls).

TRAVEL PLANNING

WHEN TO GO Warm summers (May-September), cold winters (November-March).

MEDICAL CARE Limited. Take own supplies and be insured.

CURRENCY Hryvnya = 100 kopiyok.

FINANCE Cash not credit cards.

AIRPORTS Kyiv (IEV)/Borispol (KBP) is 34 km from city.

INTERNAL TRAVEL Flights erratic due to fuel shortages. Railways slow but reliable, though difficult to book. Buses or self-drive not recommended.

BUSINESS HOURS 0900-1800 Mon-Friday.

GMT +2.

VOLTAGE GUIDE 220 AC, 50 Hz.

RED TAPE

VISAS (AUS/CANADA/UK/US) Required for all.

REPS IN UK/USA/CANADA UK: 78 Kensington Park Road, London W11 2PL, tel 020 7243 8923, fax 020 7727 3567. USA: 3350 M Street, NW, Washington, DC 20007, tel 202 333 0606, fax 202 333 0817, email infolook@aol.com. Canada: 310 Somerset Street West, Ottawa, Ontario K2P 0J9, tel 613 230 2961, fax 613 230 2400, email ukremb@cyberuf.ca.

CUSTOMS REGULATIONS Duty free allowance: 200 g tobacco products, 1 ltr spirits and 2 ltrs wine.

DRIVING REQUIREMENTS International Driving Permits.

KEEPING IN TOUCH

BBC WORLD SERVICE MHz 17.64, 15.57, 9.410, 6.195.

ENGLISH-LANGUAGE NEWSPAPERS *News From Ukraine.*

EMERGENCIES

RED CROSS/CRESCENT SOCIETIES 30 Pushkinskaya Street, 252004 Kiev, tel 44 235 0157, fax 44 235 1096, email redcross@ukrpack.net.

UK/USA/CANADIAN REPS UK: Sichnevoho Povstannyn 6, 252025 Kyiv, tel 44 290 2919, fax 44 290 7947, email ukembc@webber.net.ua. USA: vul. Yuria Kotsyubinskiho 10, 254053 Kyiv, tel 44 246 9750, fax 44 244 7350, email acs@usemb.kiev.ua. Canada: Yaroslaviv Val 31, Kyiv 01901, tel 44 464 1144, fax 44 464 1130.

Global weather guide p 818, Rainy seasons worldwide p 829, Vaccinations required p 832, Recommended reading p 848, Dependent territories p 812.

UNITED ARAB EMIRATES

STATE OF THE NATION

SAFETY Safe. Observe Islamic customs.
LIFE EXPECTANCY M 73.9, F 73.7.

PEOPLE AND PLACE

CAPITAL Abu Dhabi.
LANGUAGE Arabic.
PEOPLES Arab (42%), other Asian (50%).
RELIGION Sunni Muslim.
SIZE (KM) 77,700.
POPULATION 2,443,000.
POP DENSITY/KM 31.4.
FOOD Popular dishes include *tabbouleh* (bulghur wheat with mint and parsley), *hoummus* (chickpea and sesame paste), *warak enab* (stuffed vine leaves), *koussa mashi* (stuffed courgettes) and *makbous* (spicy lamb with rice).

TRAVEL PLANNING

WHEN TO GO Best October-May, very hot June-September.
MEDICAL CARE Good. Emergency treatment free, otherwise expensive, so insurance recommended.
CURRENCY UAE Dirham (Dh) – 100 fils.
FINANCE Credit cards and travellers' cheques widely accepted.
AIRPORTS Abu Dhani (AUH) is 35 km from city. Dubai (DXB) is 5 km from city. Ras al-Khaimah (RKT) is 15 km from sity. Sharjah (SHJ) is 10 km from city.
INTERNAL TRAVEL Good road and flight networks.
BUSINESS HOURS 0800-1300 and 1600-1930 Sat-Wednesday, 0800-1200 Thursday.
GMT +4.
VOLTAGE GUIDE 220/240 AC, 50 Hz.

RED TAPE

VISAS (AUS/CANADA/UK/US) Required for all (except UK up to 30 days).
REPS IN UK/USA/CANADA UK: 48 Prince's Gate, London SW7 1PT, tel 020 7589 3434, fax 020 581 9616. USA: 1255 22nd Street, Suite 700, NW, Washington, DC 20037, tel 202 955 7999, fax 202 337 7029. Canada: Handled by embassy in Washington.
CUSTOMS REGULATIONS Duty free allowance: 2000 cigarettes or 400 cigars or 2 kg tobacco. 2 ltrs spirits and 2 ltrs wine (non-Muslims only). Prohibited: Drugs, firearms and ammunition, unstrung pearls, fruit and vegetables from cholera-affected areas.
DRIVING REQUIREMENTS A local driving licence can be issued on presentation of a national driving licence and a letter from your sponsor. International Driving Permit useful but not mandatory.

KEEPING IN TOUCH

BBC WORLD SERVICE MHz 15.57, 12.00, 11.76, 9.410.
ENGLISH-LANGUAGE NEWSPAPERS *Gulf News, Emirates News.*

EMERGENCIES

RED CROSS/CRESCENT SOCIETIES PO Box 3324, Abu Dhabi, tel 2 621 9000, fax 2 621 2727.
UK/USA/CANADIAN REPS UK: PO Box 248, Abu Dhabi, tel 2 326 600, fax 2 345 968. USA: Al-Sudan Street, Abu Dhabi, tel 2 436 691, fax 2 435 441, email usisamem@ emirates.net.ae. Canada: Villa 440, 26th Street, Abu Dhabi, tel 2 456 969, fax 2 458 787, email canada@emirates.net.ae.

Global weather guide p 818, Rainy seasons worldwide p 829, Vaccinations required p 832, Recommended reading p 848, Dependent territories p 812.

UNITED KINGDOM

STATE OF THE NATION

SAFETY Safe, except for areas of Northern Ireland affected by separatist tensions.

LIFE EXPECTANCY M 74.5, F 79.8.

PEOPLE AND PLACE

CAPITAL London

LANGUAGE English.

PEOPLES European descent (96%), non-European descent (4%).

RELIGION Protestant and other Christian denominations. Jewish, Hindu and Muslim minorities.

SIZE (KM) 241,752.

POPULATION 58,801,500.

POP DENSITY/KM 243.2.

FOOD A diverse range of international cuisines can be found all over the country. There are regional specialities, based on the best local produce, such as black puddings in Lancashire and Yorkshire, sausages in Lincolnshire, and English cheese enjoys a growning reputation. Excellent meat, fish, game and the famous haggis (a sheep's stomach stuffed with oatmeal, spiced liver , onions and offal) can be found in Scotland. Welsh specialities include laver bread, a sea-weed and oatmeal cake and dishes based on high quality local lamb and the national vegetable, leeks.

TRAVEL PLANNING

WHEN TO GO Changeable climate, rainy all year. Cold wet winters (November-March).

MEDICAL CARE Free emergency treatment for travellers. Reciprocal arrangements for EU citizens.

CURRENCY Pounds sterling (£) = 100 pence.

FINANCE Credit cards widely accepted.

AIRPORTS Principally Heathrow (LHR) and Gatwick (LGW) which are 1 four from the capital. Also regional airports.

INTERNAL TRAVEL Good road and rail network. Flights limited but efficient.

BUSINESS HOURS 0930-1730 Mon-Friday

GMT Precisely.

VOLTAGE GUIDE 240 AC, 50 Hz.

RED TAPE

VISAS (AUS/CANADA/US) Not required.

REPS IN USA/CANADA USA: 3100 Massa-chusetts Avenue, NW, Washington, DC 20008, tel 202 588 6500, fax 202 588 7896. Canada: 80 Elgin Street, Ottawa, Ontario K1P 5K7, tel 613 237 1530, fax 613 237 7980.

CUSTOMS REGULATIONS Duty free allowance: (from outside EU) 200 cigarettes or 100 cigarillos or 50 cigars or 250 g tobacco, 1 ltr alcohol over 22% or 2 ltrs under 22%, 60 g perfume, 250 ml *eau de toilette*, other good worth £136. Prohibited: Animals/birds (except under licence), drugs, firearms, pornography.

DRIVING REQUIREMENTS National driving licence, Third Party insurance and vehicle registration documents.

KEEPING IN TOUCH

BBC WORLD SERVICE MHz 9.410, 6.195, 3.955, 0.648.

ENGLISH-LANGUAGE NEWSPAPERS All.

EMERGENCIES

RED CROSS/CRESCENT SOCIETIES 9 Grosvenor Crescent, London SW1X 7EJ, tel 020 7235 5454, fax 020 7245 6315, email information@redcross.org.uk/.

USA/CANADIAN REPS USA: 24-32 Grosvenor Square, London W1A 1AE, tel 020 7499 9000, fax 020 7629 8288, email weblond@usia.gov. Canada: 38 Grosvenor Street, London W1X 0AA, tel 09068 616 644, fax 020 7258 6506.

Global weather guide p 818, Rainy seasons worldwide p 829, Vaccinations required p 832, Recommended reading p 848, Dependent territories p 812.

UNITED STATES OF AMERICA

STATE OF THE NATION

SAFETY Safe, despite high levels of crime and murder.

LIFE EXPECTANCY M 73.4, F 80.1.

PEOPLE AND PLACE

CAPITAL Washington.

LANGUAGE English.

PEOPLES European descent incl Hispanic (84%), African descent (12%), Native American (1%), Chinese.

RELIGION Protestant (61%), Roman Catholic (25%), Jewish and other faiths.

SIZE (KM) 9,809,155.

POPULATION 270,298,524.

POP DENSITY/KM 27.6.

FOOD American breakfasts are legendary. Fast food from hamburgers to hotdogs is available everywhere and international cuisine is available in every city. There are numerous regional specialities, from Spanish flavours in the southwest to Creole or French in the deep south.

TRAVEL PLANNING

WHEN TO GO Climate varies hugely, check with individual states.

MEDICAL CARE Good but expensive. Some hospitals will not treat patients without proof of insurance cover.

CURRENCY Dollar ($) = 100 cents.

FINANCE Credit cards widely accepted, cheques less so.

AIRPORTS Numerous. Busiest 10 are: Atlanta (ATL), Chicago (ORD), Los Angeles (LAX), Dallas/Fort Worth(DFW), San Francisco (SFO), Denver (DEN), Miami (MIA), Newark (EWR), Phoenix (PHX), Detroit (DTW).

INTERNAL TRAVEL Excellent air, rail and road networks.

BUSINESS HOURS 0900-1730 Mon-Friday.

GMT Spans six time zones, from -5 (east coast) to -10 (Hawaii).

VOLTAGE GUIDE 110/120 AC, 60 Hz.

RED TAPE

VISAS (AUS/CANADA/UK) Not required up to 90 days.

REPS IN UK/CANADA UK: 24-32 Grosvenor Square, London W1A 1AE, tel 020 7499 9000, fax 020 7629 8288, email weblond@usia.gov. Canada: 100 Wellington Street, Ottawa, Ontario K1P 5T1, tel 613 238 5335, fax 613 238 8750.

CUSTOMS REGULATIONS Duty free allowance: 200 cigarettes or 100 cigars or 2 kg tobacco. 1 ltr alcohol. Articles up to $100 ($200 from US Virgin Islands, American Samoa, Guam; $300 from Hawaii). Prohibited: Drugs (except with doctor's prescription), firearms and ammunition, fireworks, meat products, pornography, switchblades, Cuban cigars, absinthe, biological materials, some seeds/fruits/plants.

DRIVING REQUIREMENTS National driving licence.

KEEPING IN TOUCH

BBC WORLD SERVICE East: MHz 17.84, 11,86, 6.185, 5.975. West: MHz21.66, 11.86, 9.590, 5.975.

ENGLISH-LANGUAGE NEWSPAPERS All.

EMERGENCIES

RED CROSS/CRESCENT SOCIETIES 431 18th Street NW, 2nd Floor, Washington DC 20006, tel 202 639 3400, fax 202 639 3595, email postmaster@usa.rcdcross.org.

UK/CANADIAN REPS UK: 3100 Massachusetts Avenue, NW, Washington, DC 20008, tel 202 588 6500, fax 202 588 7892. Canada: 501 Pennsylvania Avenue, NW, Washington, DC 20001, tel 202 682 1740, fax 202 682 7689

Global weather guide p 818, Rainy seasons worldwide p 829, Vaccinations required p 832, Recommended reading p 848, Dependent territories p 812.

URUGUAY

STATE OF THE NATION

SAFETY Generally safe, but seek local information.

LIFE EXPECTANCY M 70.4, F 78.

PEOPLE AND PLACE

CAPITAL Montevideo.

LANGUAGE Spanish.

PEOPLES European descent (90%), mestizo, African descent.

RELIGION Roman Catholic (66%), non-religious (30%), Jewish, Protestant.

SIZE (KM) 176,215.

POPULATION 3,203,000.

POP DENSITY/KM 18.2.

FOOD Most restaurants are *parrilladas* (grillrooms) serving the most famous traditional dish, the *asado* (barbecued beef). Other specialities include grilled chicken in wine, *morcilla salada* (salty sausage), *morcilla dulce* (sweet black sausage made from blood, orange peel and walnuts) and *puchero* (beef with vegetables, bacon, beans and sausages)

TRAVEL PLANNING

WHEN TO GO Mild all year. Best in summer (December-March).

MEDICAL CARE Good.

CURRENCY Peso Uruguayo (urug$) = 100 centécimos.

FINANCE Credit cards widely used. Travellers' cheques difficult to change unless in US dollars.

AIRPORTS Montevideo (MVD) is 19 km from city.

INTERNAL TRAVEL Internal flights are expensive. Road network is good.

BUSINESS HOURS 0830-1200 and 1430-1830 Monday-Friday.

GMT -3.

VOLTAGE GUIDE 220 AC, 50 Hz.

RED TAPE

VISAS (AUS/CANADA/UK/US) Required for Australia and Canada. Not required for UK and USA up to 3 months.

REPS IN UK/USA/CANADA UK: 140 brompton Road, London SW3 1HY, tel 020 7584 8192, fax 020 7581 9585. USA: 2715 M Street, 3rd floor, NW, washington, DC 20007, tel 202 331 4219, fax 202 331 8142, email uruguay@embassy.org. Canada: Suite 1905, 130 Albert street, Ottawa, Ontario K1P 5GA, tel 613 234 2937, fax 613 233 4670, email uruott@iosphere.net.

CUSTOMS REGULATIONS Duty free allowance: (foreigners) 400 cigarettes or 50 cigars or 500 g tobacco, 2 ltrs alcohol.

DRIVING REQUIREMENTS Temporary local licence must be obtained from a town hall; valid 90 days. National driving licence may prove useful.

KEEPING IN TOUCH

BBC WORLD SERVICE MHz 17.79, 15.52, 9.915, 5.970.

ENGLISH-LANGUAGE NEWSPAPERS None.

EMERGENCIES

RED CROSS/CRESCENT SOCIETIES Aveni-da 8 de Octobre 2990, 11600 Mondtevideo, tel 2 480 2112, fax 2 480 0714.

UK/USA/CANADIAN REPS UK: PO Box 16024, Calle Marco bruto 1073, 11300 Montevideo, tel 2 622 3630, fax 2 622 7815. USA: Lauro Muller 1776, 11100 Montevideo, tel 2 203 6061, fax 2 408 8611. Canada: Edificio Torre Libertad, Suite 1105, Plaza Cagancha 1335, 11100 Montevideo, tel 2 922 030, fax 2 902 2029.

Global weather guide p 818, Rainy seasons worldwide p 829, Vaccinations required p 832, Recommended reading p 848, Dependent territories p 812.

UZBEKISTAN

STATE OF THE NATION

SAFETY Avoid travelling at night.

LIFE EXPECTANCY M 64.3, F 70.7.

PEOPLE AND PLACE

CAPITAL Tashkent.

LANGUAGE Uzbek.

PEOPLES Uzbek (71%), Russian, Tajik, Kazakh.

RELIGION Sunni Muslim (88%), Eastern Orthodox Christian.

SIZE (KM) 447,400.

POPULATION 23,667,000.

POP DENSITY/KM 52.8.

FOOD Central Asian dishes such as *plov* (mutton, yellow turnip and rice) and *shashlyk* (charcoal grilled mutton kebabs) served with raw onions and flat bread are commonly eaten. *Samosas* are sold on street stalls, and a number of restaurants serve European and Korean food.

TRAVEL PLANNING

WHEN TO GO Extreme continental climate: but generally warmer in south, colder in north. Very cold winters (November-March), hot summers (May-September).

MEDICAL CARE Limited. Free for emergency treatment. Repatriation cover ecommended.

CURRENCY Uzbek sum = 100 tiyn.

FINANCE All bills normally settled in cash (US dollars best). Credit cards and travellers' cheques not widely accepted.

AIRPORTS Tashkent (TAS) is 6 km from the city.

INTERNAL TRAVEL Reasonably good air, road and rail networks, though trains can be vulnerable to theft.

BUSINESS HOURS 0900-1800 Mon-Friday.

GMT +5.

VOLTAGE GUIDE 220 AC, 50 Hz.

RED TAPE

VISAS (AUS/CANADA/UK/US) Required.

REPS IN UK/USA/CANADA UK: 41 Holland Park, London W11 2RP, tel 020 7229 7679, fax 020 7229 7029. USA: 1746 Massachusetts Avenue, NW, Washington, DC 20036, tel 202 887 5300, fax 202 293 6804. Canada: n/a.

CUSTOMS REGULATIONS Duty free allowance: 1000 cigarettes or 1 kg of tobacco products. 2 ltrs alcohol and 1.5 ltrs wine. Other goods worth US$10,000.

DRIVING REQUIREMENTS International Driving Permit.

KEEPING IN TOUCH

BBC WORLD SERVICE MHz 15.58, 13.23, 9.410, 6.195.

ENGLISH-LANGUAGE NEWSPAPERS n/a.

EMERGENCIES

RED CROSS/CRESCENT SOCIETIES 30 Yusuf Hos Hojib Street, 700031 Tashkent, tel 71 2563 741, fax 71 2561 801, email rcsuz@uzpak.uz.

UK/USA/CANADIAN REPS UK: 67 Gulymov Street, Tashkent 700000, tel 71 120 6288, fax 71 120 6549, email brit@emb.uz. USA: 82 chilanzarskaya Street, Tashkent 700115, tel 71 120 5450, fax 71 1205 444. Canada: Handled by Canadian embassy in Moscow.

Global weather guide p 818, Rainy seasons worldwide p 829, Vaccinations required p 832, Recommended reading p 848, Dependent territories p 812.

VANUATU

STATE OF THE NATION

SAFETY Safe.

LIFE EXPECTANCY M 65.5, F 69.5.

PEOPLE AND PLACE

CAPITAL Port Vila.

LANGUAGE Bislama (pidgin), English, French.

PEOPLES Melansesians (ni-Vanuatu) (94%).

RELIGION Various Christian denominations (92%), some traditional beliefs.

SIZE (KM) 12,190.

POPULATION 177,400.

POP DENSITY/KM 14.6.

FOOD Seafood features on most menus, and Chinese and French food is widely available.

TRAVEL PLANNING

WHEN TO GO Warm and wet November - April, windy May-October. Cyclones possible December and April.

MEDICAL CARE Adequate.

CURRENCY Vatu (Vt) = 100 centimes.

FINANCE Credit cards and travellers' cheques widely accepted.

AIRPORTS Port Vila (VLI) is 5 km from town.

INTERNAL TRAVEL Good flight and ferry network between islands.

BUSINESS HOURS 0730-1130 and 1330-1630 Monday-friday.

GMT +11.

VOLTAGE GUIDE 220/380 AC.

RED TAPE

VISAS (AUS/CANADA/UK/US) Not required.

REPS IN UK/USA/CANADA UK: 203 East Sheen Lane, London SW14 8LE, tel 020 8876 1938, fax 020 8878 9876. USA: 866 United Nations Plaza, Room 308, New York, NY 10017, tel 212 593 0144, fax 212 593 0219. Canada: n/a.

CUSTOMS REGULATIONS Duty free allowance: 200 cigarettes or 100 cigarillos or 50 cigars or 250 g tobacco. 1.5 ltrs spirits and 2 ltrs wine. 250 ml *eau de toilette* and 100 ml perfume. Other articles worth Vt 20,000.

DRIVING REQUIREMENTS National driving licence.

KEEPING IN TOUCH

BBC WORLD SERVICE MHz 12.08, 11.77, 9.740, 7.145.

ENGLISH-LANGUAGE NEWSPAPERS *Vanuatu Weekly.*

EMERGENCIES

RED CROSS/CRESCENT SOCIETIES PO Box 618, Port Vila, tel 27418, fax 22599.

UK/USA/CANADIAN REPS UK: PO Box 567, KPMG House, rue pasteur, Port Vila, tel 23100, fax 23651, email bhcvila@ vanuatu.com.vu. USA: handled by US embassy in New Guinea. Canada: handled by US embassy in Australia.

Global weather guide p 818, Rainy seasons worldwide p 829, Vaccinations required p 832, Recommended reading p 848, Dependent territories p 812.

VATICAN CITY

STATE OF THE NATION

SAFETY Safe.

LIFE EXPECTANCY n/a (possibly immortal).

PEOPLE AND PLACE

CAPITAL Vatican.

LANGUAGE Latin and Italian.

PEOPLES n/a.

RELIGION Roman Catholic.

SIZE (KM) 0.44.

POPULATION 1,500

POP DENSITY/KM 3,400

FOOD Italian.

TRAVEL PLANNING

WHEN TO GO As for Italy.

MEDICAL CARE Treatment would be in Italy.

CURRENCY Italian currency valid, but issues its own Vatican lire.

FINANCE Use Italian facilities.

AIRPORTS Use Rome airport.

INTERNAL TRAVEL Walking. There is a mini-railway from Rome into the Vatican City.

BUSINESS HOURS n/a.

GMT +1.

VOLTAGE GUIDE 220 AC, 50 Hz.

RED TAPE

VISAS (AUS/CANADA/UK/US) Not required, but entry is from Italy, so Italian requirements would apply beforehand.

REPS IN UK/USA/CANADA UK: Apostolic Nunciature, 54 Parkside, London SW19 5NE, tel 020 8946 1410, fax 020 8947 2494, email nuntius@globalnet.co.uk. USA: Apostolic Nunciature, 3339 Massachusetts Avenue, NW, Washington, DC 20008, tel 202 333 7121, fax 202 337 4036. Canada: Apostolic Nunciature, 724 Manor Avenue, Ottawa, Ontario K1M 0E3, tel 613 746 4914, fax 613 746 4786.

CUSTOMS REGULATIONS There are no customs or excise duties.

DRIVING REQUIREMENTS n/a.

KEEPING IN TOUCH

BBC WORLD SERVICE As for Italy.

ENGLISH-LANGUAGE NEWSPAPERS As for Italy, plus English edition of *L'Osservatore Romano*.

EMERGENCIES

RED CROSS/CRESCENT SOCIETIES n/a.

UK/USA/CANADIAN REPS UK: Via dei Condotti 91, 00187 Rome, tel 6 69 92 35 61, fax 6 69 94 06 84. USA: Via delle Terme Deciane 26, 00153 Rome, tel 6 46741, fax 6 57 30 06 82, email refrome@usis.it. Canada: Via della Conciliazione 4D, 00193 Rome, tel 6 68 30 73 16, fax 6 68 80 62 83, email vatcn@dfait-maeci.gc.ca.

Global weather guide p 818, Rainy seasons worldwide p 829, Vaccinations required p 832, Recommended reading p 848, Dependent territories p 812.

VENEZUELA

STATE OF THE NATION

Safety Beware violent crime in cities.
Life expectancy M 70, F 75.7.

PEOPLE AND PLACE

Capital Caracas.
Language Spanish, Amerindian languages.
Peoples Mestizo (69%), European or African descent, Amerindian (2%).
Religion Roman Catholic (89%), other Christian or traditional beliefs.
Size (km) 912,050.
Population 22,777,000.
Pop density/km 25.
Food Local specialities include *pabellón criollo*, a hash made with shredded meat and served with fried plantains and black beans on rice, *parrilla criolla*, marinated and grilled beef, *hervido*, soup made with beef, chicken or fish and vegetables, *chipi chipi* soup (made from tiny clams) and *empanadas* (meat pastries).

TRAVEL PLANNING

When to go January-April is best. Dry season December-April, rainy season May-December.
Medical care Good. Free emergency care for travellers.
Currency Bolivar (Bs) = 100 céntimos.
Finance Credit cards and travellers' cheques widely accepted.
Airports Caracas (CCS) (Simon Bolivar) is 22 km from the city.
Internal travel Good air network, excellent roads, limited railway links.
Business hours 0800-1800 Mon-Friday.
GMT -4.
Voltage guide 110 AC, 60 Hz.

RED TAPE

Visas (Aus/Canada/UK/US) Not required for up to 90 days.
Reps in UK/USA/Canada UK: 56 Grafton Way, London W1P 5LB, tel 020 7387 6727, fax 020 7383 3253. USA: 7 East 51st Street, New York, NY 10022, tel 212 826 1660, fax 212 644 7471. Canada: 32 Range Road, Sandy Hill, Ottawa, Ontario K1N 8J4, tel 613 235 5151, fax 613 235 3205, email embavene@travel-net.com.
Customs regulations Duty free allowance: 200 cigarettes and 25 cigars. 2 ltrs alcohol. 4 small bottles perfume. Prohibited: Flowers, plants, fruit, meat products.
Driving requirements National driving licence or International Driving Permit.

KEEPING IN TOUCH

BBC World Service MHz 17.84, 15.19, 9.195, 6.195.
English-language newspapers *The Daily Journal.*

EMERGENCIES

Red Cross/Crescent societies Apartado 3185, Caracas 1010, tel 2 571 4380, fax 2 576 1042, email diranacso@cantv.net.
UK/USA/Canadian reps UK: Apartado 1246, Edificio Torre Las Mercedes, 3°, Avenida la Estancia, Chuao, Caracas 1060, tel 2 993 4111, fax 2 993 9989, email embcarac@ven.net. USA: Calle F con Calle Suapure, Colinas de Valle Arriba, Caracas 1060, tel 2 975 6411, fax 2 975 6710, email embajada@usia.gov. Canada: Av los Chaguaramos, Centro gerencial Mohedano, PHC&D, La Castellana, Caracas, tel 2 263 3270, fax 2 263 8326.

Global weather guide p 818, Rainy seasons worldwide p 829, Vaccinations required p 832, Recommended reading p 848, Dependent territories p 812.

VIETNAM

STATE OF THE NATION

SAFETY Generally safe.

LIFE EXPECTANCY M 64.9, F 69.6

PEOPLE AND PLACE

CAPITAL Hanoi.

LANGUAGE Vietnamese.

PEOPLES Vietnamese (88%), Chinese, Thai, tribal groups.

RELIGION Buddhist (55%), Christian.

SIZE (KM) 331,114.

POPULATION 75,355,200.

POP DENSITY/KM 227.6.

FOOD Based on a mixture of Vietnamese, Chinese and French traditions. Breakfast is generally noodle soup, and noodles or rice provide the basis of most meals. Fish sauce (*nuac mam*) is an essential accompaniment. Specialities include *nem* (pork mixed with noodles, eggs and mushrooms, wrapped in rice paper and fried) and *banh chung* (glutinous rice, pork and onions).

TRAVEL PLANNING

WHEN TO GO Dry all year, except for the monsoon season (May-October).

MEDICAL CARE Limited. Insurance with repatriation cover recommended.

CURRENCY New Dong (D).

FINANCE Travellers' cheques in US dollars widely accepted. Visa and Mastercard becoming accepted.

AIRPORTS Noi Bai (HAN) is 45 km from Hanoi. Tan Son Nhat (SGN) is 7 km from Ho Chi Minh City (Saigon).

INTERNAL TRAVEL Good roads and good but limited railway.

BUSINESS HOURS 0730-1200 and 1300-1630 Monday-Saturday.

GMT +7.

VOLTAGE GUIDE 220 AC, 50 Hz.

RED TAPE

VISAS (AUS/CANADA/UK/US) Required.

REPS IN UK/USA/CANADA UK: 12-14 Victoria Road, London W8 5RD, tel 020 7937 1912, fax 020 7937 6108. USA: 1233 20th Street, Suite 400, NW, Washington, DC 20036, tel 202 861 0737, fax 202 861 0917, email vietnamembassy@msn.com. Canada: 226 MacLaren Street, Ottawa, Ontario K2P 0L6, tel 613 236 0772, fax 613 236 2704, email vietem@istar.ca.

CUSTOMS REGULATIONS Duty free allowance: changeable–check at time of trip. Prohibited: Firearms, drugs, pornography.

DRIVING REQUIREMENTS International Driving Permit and a test taken in-country.

KEEPING IN TOUCH

BBC WORLD SERVICE MHz 15.36, 9.740, 6.195, 5.965.

ENGLISH-LANGUAGE NEWSPAPERS *Saigon Times, Vietnam Economic Times, Vietnam News* and others.

EMERGENCIES

RED CROSS/CRESCENT SOCIETIES 82 Nguyen Du Street, Hanoi, tel 4 822 5157, fax 4 266 285, email vnrchq@netnam.org.vn.

UK/USA/CANADIAN REPS UK: 4th & 5th floor, Central building, 31 Hai Ba trung Street, Hanoi, tel 4 825 2510, fax 4 826 5762, email behanoi@fpt.vn. USA: Rose Garden, 6 Ngoc Khanh Street, Hanoi, tel 4 843 1500, fax 4 831 3017. Canada: 31 hung Vuong Street, Hanoi, tel 8 823 5500, fax 8 823 5333.

Global weather guide p 818, Rainy seasons worldwide p 829, Vaccinations required p 832, Recommended reading p 848, Dependent territories p 812.

YEMEN

STATE OF THE NATION

SAFETY Variable: Westerners have been kidnapped by tribal protesters, with fatal results. Seek latest information at time of visit.

LIFE EXPECTANCY M 57.4, F 58.4.

PEOPLE AND PLACE

CAPITAL Sana'a.

LANGUAGE Arabic.

PEOPLES Arab (95%).

RELIGION Shi'ite Muslim (55%), Sunni Muslim (42%).

SIZE (KM) 536, 869.

POPULATION 16,483,000.

POP DENSITY/KM 30.7.

FOOD Indian and Chinese cuisine served in restaurants. Elsewhere the food is typically Arabic. *Haradha*, a mincemeat and pepper dish is a speciality. Seafood is recommended.

TRAVEL PLANNING

WHEN TO GO Coastal areas hot and dusty all year. Highlands cooler October-March.

MEDICAL CARE Adequate, but insurance recommended.

CURRENCY Yemeny riyal (YR) = 100 fils.

FINANCE Amex widely accepted, check for other cards or travellers' cheques. Pounds sterling most useful currency.

AIRPORTS Sana'a (SAH) is 13 km from the city. Ta'izz (TAI) is 8 km from the city, Aden (ADE) 11km from the city, Hodeida (HOD) 8 km from the city.

INTERNAL TRAVEL Roads extensive but poor. Flights good.

BUSINESS HOURS 0800-1230 and 1600-1900 Mon-Wed, 0800-1100 Thursday.

GMT +3.

VOLTAGE GUIDE 220/230 AC, 50 Hz.

RED TAPE

VISAS (AUS/CANADA/UK/US) Required.

REPS IN UK/USA/CANADA UK: 57 Cromwell Road, London SW7 2ED, tel 020 7584 6607, fax 020 7589 3350. USA: 2600 Virginia Avenue, Suite 705, NW, Washington, DC 20037, tel 202 965 4760, fax 202 337 20217. Canada: 788 Island Park drive, Ottawa, Ontario K1Y 0C2, tel 613 729 6627, fax 613 729 8915.

CUSTOMS REGULATIONS Duty free allowance: 600 cigarettes or 60 cigars or 500 g tobacco. 2 bottles alcohol (non-Muslims only). 568 ml perfume or *eau de toilette*. Gifts up to YR 100,000. Prohibited: Firearms, narcotics, obscene literature, all products from Israel.

DRIVING REQUIREMENTS International Driving Permit is recommended but not mandatory.

KEEPING IN TOUCH

BBC WORLD SERVICE Mhz 15.58, 11.96, 9.750, 9.410.

ENGLISH-LANGUAGE NEWSPAPERS *The Yemen Times* and *Yemen Observer*.

EMERGENCIES

RED CROSS/CRESCENT SOCIETIES PO Box 1257, Sana'a, tel 1 283 132, fax 1 283 131.

UK/USA/CANADIAN REPS UK: 129 Haddah Road, Sana'a, tel 1 264 081, fax 1 263 059. USA: Sa'awan Street, Himyyar Zone, Sana'a, tel 1 238 843, fax 1 251 563, email usembassy01@y.net.ye. Canada: c/o Yemen Computer Co Ltd, Building 4, Mogadishu Street 11, Sana'a, tel 1 208 814, fax 1 209 523, email yccnet@y.net.ye.

Global weather guide p 818, Rainy seasons worldwide p 829, Vaccinations required p 832, Recommended reading p 848, Dependent territories p 812.

YUGOSLAVIA

STATE OF THE NATION

SAFETY Volatile after political upheavals in 2000. Potential hostility to Westerners following recent wars. Seek advice at time of travel.

LIFE EXPECTANCY M 70.2, F 75.5.

PEOPLE AND PLACE

CAPITAL Belgrade.

LANGUAGE Serbo-croat.

PEOPLES Serb (62%), Albanian, Montenegrin, Magyar and others.

RELIGION Christian (70%), Muslim.

SIZE (KM) 91,286 (Serbia & Montenegro).

POPULATION 8,473,830 (excl Kosovo).

POP DENSITY/KM 92.4.

FOOD Varies greatly between regions, but national specialities include *pihtije* (jellied pork or duck), *prsut* (smoked ham) and *sarma* or *japrak* (stuffed vine or cabbage leaves).

TRAVEL PLANNING

WHEN TO GO Cold winters (November-April), warm summers. Montenegro has a Mediterranean climate.

MEDICAL CARE Poor. Limited supplies, cash payments required. Insurance with repatriation cover essential.

CURRENCY New Yugoslav dinar (N Din) = 100 paras.

FINANCE Credit cards and travellers' cheques widely accepted, but US dollars and deutschmarks useful.

AIRPORTS All EU flights to Yugoslavia have been banned. Belgrade airport (Surcin) is 20 km from the city. Podgorica (TGD) serves Montenegro.

INTERNAL TRAVEL Railways poor. Road travel affected by fuel shortages, but bus network is efficient.

BUSINESS HOURS 0800-1500 Mon-Friday.

GMT +1.

VOLTAGE GUIDE 220 AC, 50 Hz.

RED TAPE

VISAS (AUS/CANADA/UK/US) Required.

REPS IN UK/USA/CANADA UK: Handled by Cyprus High Commission, 5 Lexham Gardens, London W8 5JJ, tel 020 7370 6105, fax 020 7370 3888. USA: 2410 California Street, NW, Washington, DC 20008, tel 202 462 6566, fax 202 797 9663, closed. Canada: 17 Blackburn Avenue, Ottawa, Ontario K1N 8A2, tel 613 233 6289, fax 613 233 7850, email ottambyu@capitalnet.com.

CUSTOMS REGULATIONS Duty free allowance: 200 cigarettes or 50 cigars or 250 g tobacco. 1 ltr wine or spirits. 250 ml *eau de toilette*, reasonable qty perfume.

DRIVING REQUIREMENTS National driving licence, car log books and Third Party Green Card insurance.

KEEPING IN TOUCH

BBC WORLD SERVICE Mhz 15.76, 15.57, 9.410, 6.195.

ENGLISH-LANGUAGE NEWSPAPERS n/a.

EMERGENCIES

RED CROSS/CRESCENT SOCIETIES Simina 19, 11000 Belgrade, tel 11 623 564, fax 11 622 965, email jckbg@jck.org.yu.

UK/USA/CANADIAN REPS UK: Generala Zdanova 46, 11000 Belgrade, tel 11 645 055, fax 11 659 651, closed. USA: Kneza Milosa 50, 11000 Belgrade, tel 11 645 655, fax 11 645 221, closed. Canada: Kneza Milosa 75, 11000 belgrade, tel 11 644 666, fax 11 641 480.

Global weather guide p 818, Rainy seasons worldwide p 829, Vaccinations required p 832, Recommended reading p 848, Dependent territories p 812.

ZAMBIA

STATE OF THE NATION

SAFETY Relatively safe.

LIFE EXPECTANCY M 39.5, F 40.6.

PEOPLE AND PLACE

CAPITAL Lusaka.

LANGUAGE English.

PEOPLES Bemba, Nyanja, Tonga, Kaonde, Lunda, Luvale, Lozi.

RELIGION Christian (63%), traditional beliefs, some Hindus and Muslims.

SIZE (KM) 752,614.

POPULATION 9,373,000.

POP DENSITY/KM 12.5.

FOOD Local specialities include bream, Nile perch, lake salmon and other freshwater fish.

TRAVEL PLANNING

WHEN TO GO Cool and dry May-September, hot and dry October-November, rainy and hot December-April.

MEDICAL CARE Limted, and cash payments required. Take own supplies and ensure you have repatriation cover.

CURRENCY Kwacha (K) = 100 ngwee.

FINANCE Travellers' cheques and Amex are widely accepted, other credit cards less widely.

AIRPORTS Lusaka (LUN) is 26 km from the city.

INTERNAL TRAVEL Reasonable road network, though delapidated in parts. Internal flights quite good.

BUSINESS HOURS 0800-1300 and 1400-1700 Monday-Friday.

GMT +2.

VOLTAGE GUIDE 220/240 AC, 50 Hz.

RED TAPE

VISAS (AUS/CANADA/UK/US) Required for USA. Not required for Australia, Canada. Not required for UK if in an organised tour group for up to 90 days.

REPS IN UK/USA/CANADA UK: 2 Palace Gate, London W8 5NG, tel 020 7589 6655, fax 020 7581 1353. USA: 2419 Massachusetts Avenue, NW, Washington, DC 20008, tel 202 265 9719, fax 202 332 0826, email zambia@tmn.com. Canada: Handled by embassy in USA.

CUSTOMS REGULATIONS Duty free allowance: 400 cigarettes or 500 g cigars or 500 g tobacco. 2.5 ltrs wine and 2.5 ltrs beer. 1 oz perfume. Other goods worth $150. Prohibited: Game trophies and animal products may be subject to export restrictions.

DRIVING REQUIREMENTS International Driving Permit.

KEEPING IN TOUCH

BBC WORLD SERVICE Mhz 17.88, 15.40, 11.94, 6.190.

ENGLISH-LANGUAGE NEWSPAPERS Mostly in English. Main dailes are *Times of Zambia* and *Zambia Daily Mail*.

EMERGENCIES

RED CROSS/CRESCENT SOCIETIES PO Box 50001, Lusaka, tel 1 250 667, fax 1 252 219, email zrcs@zamnet.zm.

UK/USA/CANADIAN REPS UK: Plot 5210, Independence Avenue, Ridgeway, Lusaka, tel 1 251 133, fax 1 253 798, email brithc@zam-net.zm. USA: Corner of Independence and UN Avenues, Lusaka, tel 1 250 955, fax 1 252 225, email usembass@zamnet.com. Canada: 5199 United Nations Avenue, Lusaka, tel 1 250 833, fax 1 254 176.

Global weather guide p 818, Rainy seasons worldwide p 829, Vaccinations required p 832, Recommended reading p 848, Dependent territories p 812.

ZIMBABWE

STATE OF THE NATION

SAFETY Usually safe, but recently subject to political violence. Possible hostility to white people. Seek latest information at time of visit.

LIFE EXPECTANCY M 43.6, F 44.7.

PEOPLE AND PLACE

CAPITAL Harare.

LANGUAGE English.

PEOPLES Shona (71%), Ndebele, other tribes and some whites.

RELIGION Christian (75%), traditional beliefs.

SIZE (KM) 390,310.

POPULATION 12,293,953.

POP DENSITY/KM 31.5.

FOOD International cuisine served in restaurants. A staple local dish is *sadza*, stiff maize meal, eaten with meat and/or gravy.

TRAVEL PLANNING

WHEN TO GO Best April-May, August-September. Hot and dry September-October, rainy November-March.

MEDICAL CARE Good, but insurance recommended.

CURRENCY Zimbabwe dollar (Z$) = 100 cents

FINANCE Credit cards and travellers' cheques widely accepted.

AIRPORTS Harare (HRE) is 12 km from the city. Bulawayo (BUQ) is 24 km from town. Victoria Falls (VFA) is 22 km from town.

INTERNAL TRAVEL Excellent network of roads and flights. Some rail lines, particularly to South Africa.

BUSINESS HOURS 0800-1630 Mon-Friday.

GMT +2.

VOLTAGE GUIDE 220/240 AC, 50 Hz.

RED TAPE

VISAS (AUS/CANADA/UK/US) Not required, though proof of onward travel may be required.

REPS IN UK/USA/CANADA UK: 429 Strand, London WC2R 0QE, tel 020 7836 7755, fax 020 7379 1167. USA: 1608 New Hampshire Avenue, NW, Washington, DC 20009, tel 202 332 7100, fax 202 483 9326, email zimemb@erols.com. Canada: 332 Somerset St West, Ottawa, Ontario K2P 0J9, tel 613 237 4388, fax 613 563 8269, email zim.highcomm@sympatico.ca.

CUSTOMS REGULATIONS Duty free allowance: Goods worth Z$1,000, including max 5 ltrs alcohol. Prohibited: Honey, drugs, toy firearms, pornography, knives.

DRIVING REQUIREMENTS National driving licence or International Driving Permit.

KEEPING IN TOUCH

BBC WORLD SERVICE Mhz 21.66, 15.40, 11.76, 6.190.

ENGLISH-LANGUAGE NEWSPAPERS Mostly in English. The *Herald* and *Chronicle* are the dailies.

EMERGENCIES

RED CROSS/CRESCENT SOCIETIES PO Box 1406, Harare, tel 4 775 416, fax 4 751 739, email zrcs@harare.iafrica.com.

UK/USA/CANADIAN REPS UK: Corner House, Samora Machel Avenue, Harare, tel 4 774 700, fax 4 774 617, email bhcinfo@id.co.zw. USA: 172 Herbert Chitepo Avenue, Harare, tel 4 794 521, fax 4 796 488, email aeharare@harare.iafrica.com. Canada: PO Box 1430, 45 Baines Avenue, Harare, tel 4 733 881, fax 4 732 917.

Global weather guide p 818, Rainy seasons worldwide p 829, Vaccinations required p 832, Recommended reading p 848, Dependent territories p 812.

Dependent territories of interest to travellers

American Samoa (USA)

Overview A group of seven tropical islands in the South Pacific offering some spectacular views and beaches.

Capital Pago Pago.

Language Samoan and English.

Size (km) 195.

Population 60,000.

When to go May-September is best. Heavy rains December-April.

Getting there Airport or harbour at Pago Pago. Airlines: Samoa Aviation, Hawaiian Airlines, Polynesian Airlines.

Visas Not required for tourist stays up to 30 days.

Anguilla (UK)

Overview Group of Caribbean islands largely dependent on tourism and offshore banking. Coral beaches and secluded hotels.

Capital The Valley.

Language English.

Size (km) 96.

Population 10,300.

When to go Hot all year round. July-October is hurricane season.

Getting there Wallblake Airport in The Valley is serviced by many airlines (BA, Delta, KLM, American Airlines, United Airlines, Air Canada etc). Also by sea.

Visas Not rquired for America, Australia, Canada, Commonwealth (most but not all), EU, and some others.

Aruba (Netherlands)

Overview Tiny Caribbean island whose beaches vary from white sand to rugged rocks. Mostly US tourists. US government involved in campaigns against drug trafficking and money laundering in late 1990s.

Capital Oranjestad.

Language Officially Dutch, also English and Spanish. Local pidgin is Papiamento.

Size (km) 193.

Population 88,000.

When to go Sunny all year round.

Getting there Flights from KLM, Continental, American Airlines. Also by sea.

Visas Not required by tourists up to 14 days. Not required for up to 3 months for America, Australia, Canada, EU, Japan.

Bermuda (UK)

Overview Tourist and tax haven in the Caribbean, with one of the world's highest concentrations of golf courses. Actually a chain of 150 islands, it has one of the largest flag-of-convenience shipping fleets.

Capital Hamilton.

Language English.

Size (km) 52.

Population 60,144.

When to go May-November is best. Night-time showers occur during November-December and March-April.

Getting there Regular flights from BA, American Airlines, Delta, Air Canada and Continental. Also by sea.

Visas Not required for up to 6 months for America, Australia, Canada, EU.

British Virgin Islands (UK)

Overview Caribbean archipelago of 40 islands, many uninhabited. Excellent diving and sailing. Thriving offshore finance sector.

Capital Road Town

Language English.

Size (km) 153.

Population 17,986.

When to go Sub-tropical climate with cooling winds all year round.

Getting there International flights via neighbouring islands (Antigua, Puerto Rico, ST Maaretn) and Miami. Airlines: BA, BWIA, Virgin, American Airlines, local airlines. Also by cruise ship or private yacht.

Visas Not required for up to 30 days for America, Australia, Canada, EU, Japan.

Global weather guide p 818,   Rainy seasons worldwide p 829,   Vaccinations required p 832, Recommended reading p 848.

Cayman Islands (UK)

OVERVIEW One of the world's largest off-shore finance centres. Big game fishing and diving very popular in its Caribbean waters.

CAPITAL George Town.

LANGUAGE English, also Spanish.

SIZE (KM) 259.

POPULATION 32,800.

WHEN TO GO Hot tropical climate all year round. Short rains May-October.

GETTING THERE Regular flights with main British and US airlines, plus Cubana or Cayman Airways. Very popular cruise ship stopover.

VISAS Not required for up to 30 days for America, Australia, Canada, Common-wealth (most), EU, Japan.

Channel Islands (UK)

OVERVIEW Small group of autonomous islands close to france. Haven for sailing and offshore finance.

CAPITAL St Helier (Jersey).

LANGUAGE English.

SIZE (KM) 192.

POPULATION 88,948.

WHEN TO GO As for Uk but milder.

GETTING THERE Well served by ferries and airlines from UK and france.

VISAS As for UK.

French Guiana (France)

OVERVIEW The last colony in South America, once home to the infamous Devil's Island penal colony. Luxuriant ranforest has yet to be exploited for eco-tourism

CAPITAL Cayenne.

LANGUAGE French and Creole.

SIZE (KM) 83,534.

POPULATION 152,300.

WHEN TO GO August-December is dry season. Hot all year.

GETTING THERE Air france from Paris to Cayenne airport. Also ships from france.

VISAS Fluctuating: check with French embassy (officially part of france).

French Polynesia (France)

OVERVIEW Huge shoal of Pacific islands centred around Tahiti. Idyllic for tourists, but subject to unrest due to dependence on france and unpopularity of nuclear tests.

CAPITAL Papeete.

LANGUAGE French, Tahitian and various Polynesian languages. Also English.

SIZE (KM) 4,167.

POPULATION 219,521.

WHEN TO GO April-October cool and dry, November- March humid.

GETTING THERE Papeete airport is well served by Air france, Qantas, Air New Zealand, Hawaiian Airlines and others.

VISAS Fluctuating: check with French embassy.

Gibraltar (UK)

OVERVIEW Drab offshore financial centre with few tourist attractions.

CAPITAL Gibraltar.

LANGUAGE English.

SIZE (KM) 6.5.

POPULATION 27,086.

WHEN TO GO Hot in summer (May-September), mild in winter.

GETTING THERE Drive from mainland Spain, or fly to Gibraltar airport.

VISAS Required for Australia, Canada, USA; not required from EU.

Greenland (Denmark)

OVERVIEW World's second largest island, almost entirely covered in ice. Possible arctic adventures include dog-sledging.

CAPITAL Nuuk.

LANGUAGE Inuit (Greenlandic), Danish.

SIZE (KM) 2,166,086.

POPULATION 56.076.

WHEN TO GO Arctic climate, especially in north and interior. Other areas milder in summer (July-September).

GETTING THERE Fly from Iceland or Denmark.

VISAS As for Denmark.

Global weather guide p 818, Rainy seasons worldwide p 829, Vaccinations required p 832, Recommended reading p 848.

Guadeloupe (France)

OVERVIEW Caribbean island group with attractive old colonial towns and some good beaches. Some islands quite undeveloped.

CAPITAL Basse-Terre

LANGUAGE French and Creole.

SIZE (KM) 1,780.

POPULATION 413,900.

WHEN TO GO Warm all year, rainy June-October.

GETTING THERE Air france, Air Canada, American Airlines, and Air Liberté to Pointe-à-Pitre airport.

VISAS Fluctuating: check with French embassy (officially part of france).

Guam (USA)

OVERVIEW Volcanic island in the Pacific, one-third occupied by US military base. Facilities for fishing, diving and golf.

CAPITAL Hagatna.

LANGUAGE Engliah and Chamorro.

SIZE (KM) 549.

POPULATION 1,139.

WHEN TO GO Rainy season is July-November, preceded by hot season.

GETTING THERE Virgin Atlantic, Japan Airlines, Northwest Airlines fly to Guam airport. Also by sea.

VISAS Not required for US citizens; nor for Australian/EU citizens up to 15 days.

Guernsey (UK)

OVERVIEW Pleasant group of islands in the English Channel, ideal for unstrenuous watersports and golfing holidays,

CAPITAL St Peter Port.

LANGUAGE English.

SIZE (KM) 65.

POPULATION 58,681.

WHEN TO GO May-October.

GETTING THERE Many ferries and flights from UK and france.

VISAS As for UK.

Isle of Man (UK)

OVERVIEW Pretty, unspoilt island between England and Ireland, famous for annual motorbike event (TTRaces).

CAPITAL Douglas.

LANGUAGE English and Manx.

SIZE (KM) 572.

POPULATION 71,714.

WHEN TO GO Warm July-September. Wet.

GETTING THERE Manx Air from UK to Ronaldsway airport. Or ferry from Dublin or Liverpool.

VISAS As for UK.

Martinique (France)

OVERVIEW Beautiful Caribbean island, rugged and volcanic

CAPITAL Fort-de-france.

LANGUAGE French

SIZE (KM) 1,100.

POPULATION 381,200.

WHEN TO GO Warm all year, rainy July-November.

GETTING THERE Air france, BWIA and Air Guadeloupe fly to Fort-de-france.

VISAS Fluctuating: check with French embassy (officially part of france).

New Caledonia (France)

OVERVIEW Island group off northern Australia, subject to serious interacial tensions. Origin of much fine tribal art. Beautiful beaches and mountains.

CAPITAL Nouméa.

LANGUAGE French

SIZE (KM) 19,103.

POPULATION 200,000.

WHEN TO GO Warm all year, hot October-May, cooler June-September.

GETTING THERE Air france, Qantas and Air New Zealand, among others, fly to Nouméa. Also by sea.

VISAS Fluctuating: check with French embassy (officially part of france).

Global weather guide p 818, Rainy seasons worldwide p 829, Vaccinations required p 832, Recommended reading p 848.

Niue (New Zealand)

OVERVIEW World's largest coral island and home to some of the least disturbed forests. Economy dependent on tourism and postage stamps. Excellent fishing, diving and snorkelling, and few tourists.

CAPITAL Alofi.

LANGUAGE Niuean and English.

SIZE (KM) 262.

POPULATION 2,080.

WHEN TO GO Warm days and cool nights. Rainy February-March.

GETTING THERE Royal Tongan Airlines connects with Niue International airport from Auckland and Sydney.

VISAS Not required for tourist stays up to 30 days.

Puerto Rico (USA)

OVERVIEW Densely populated and highly developed Caribbean island. Facilities for big-game fishing and other watersports.

CAPITAL San Juan.

LANGUAGE English and Spanish.

SIZE (KM) 8,959.

POPULATION 3,800,000.

WHEN TO GO Hot and tropical all year.

GETTING THERE BA, KLM, Northwest Airlines, Canadian Airlines, Iberia and American Airlines, among others, fly to Luis Muñoz Marin airport.

VISAS As for USA.

Reunion (France)

OVERVIEW Mountainous island in the India Ocean. Important military base.

CAPITAL Saint-Denis.

LANGUAGE French and Creole.

SIZE (KM) 2,512.

POPULATION 697,600.

WHEN TO GO Cyclone season is January-March. Otherwise hot and tropical.

GETTING THERE Air france to St Denis airport. Also by sea.

VISAS Fluctuating: check with French embassy (officially part of france).

Turks & Caicos Islands (UK)

OVERVIEW Coral archipelago in the Caribbean dominated by tourism and off-shore banking. Spectacular beaches, nature reserves and diving, often with few tourists.

CAPITAL Cockburn Town.

LANGUAGE English.

SIZE (KM) 430.

POPULATION 13,800.

WHEN TO GO Tropical all year. Some rain October-November.

GETTING THERE Grand Turk airport is served by American Airlines from Miami, Air Jamaica from Jamaica, Bahamasair from Bahamas. Few shipping lines.

VISAS For stays up to 90 days, not required for Australia, Canada, EU, USA.

Virgin Islands (USA)

OVERVIEW Major stopover for Caribbean cruises, these 50 islands offer good diving and sailing around fine beaches. But they also have the highest density of hotels in the entire Caribbean.

CAPITAL Charlotte Amalie.

LANGUAGE English.

SIZE (KM) 347.

POPULATION 101,809.

WHEN TO GO Hot all year. Wettest August-October.

GETTING THERE St Thomas and St Croix airports are well served by British and American airlines, particularly Britannia, Delta and American Airlines.

VISAS As for USA.

Global weather guide p 818, Rainy seasons worldwide p 829, Vaccinations required p 832, Recommended reading p 848.

Part 5: **The traveller's directory** ᘍ

Global information

Global weather guide

THIS CHART SHOWS THE AVERAGES for temperature, humidity and precipitation in various countries. Useful weather websites and helplines are listed on page 828.

TEMPERATURE These are shown as average daily maximum and minimum temperatures, taken in the shade. Maximum temperatures usually occur in the early afternoon, and minimum temperatures just before dawn.

HUMIDITY This is measured at one or more fixed hours daily. It is normally lowest in the early afternoon and highest just before dawn. High humidity combined with high temperatures increases human discomfort.

PRECIPITATION This includes all forms of moisture falling, mainly rain and snow.

		J	F	M	A	M	J	J	A	S	O	N	D
ARGENTINA (BUENOS AIRES)													
Temp °F	max	85	83	79	72	64	57	57	60	64	69	76	82
	min	63	63	60	53	47	41	42	43	46	50	56	61
Temp °C	max	29	28	26	22	18	14	14	16	18	21	24	28
	min	17	17	16	12	8	5	6	6	8	10	13	16
Hum %	am	81	83	87	88	90	91	92	90	86	83	79	79
	pm	61	63	69	71	74	78	79	74	68	65	60	62
Precip	mm	79	71	109	89	76	61	56	61	79	86	84	99
AUSTRALIA (MELBOURNE)													
Temp °F	max	78	78	75	68	62	57	56	59	63	67	71	75
	min	57	57	55	51	47	44	42	43	46	48	51	54
Temp °C	max	26	26	24	20	17	14	13	15	17	19	22	24
	min	14	14	13	11	8	7	6	6	8	9	11	12
Hum %	am	58	62	64	72	79	83	82	76	68	61	60	59
	pm	48	50	51	56	62	67	65	60	55	52	52	51
Precip	mm	48	46	56	58	53	53	48	48	58	66	58	58
AUSTRALIA (SYDNEY)													
Temp °F	max	78	78	76	71	66	61	60	63	67	71	74	77
	min	65	65	63	58	52	48	46	48	51	56	60	63
Temp °C	max	26	26	24	22	19	16	16	17	19	22	23	25
	min	18	18	17	14	11	9	8	9	11	13	16	17
Hum %	am	68	71	73	76	77	77	76	72	67	65	65	66
	pm	64	65	65	64	63	62	60	56	55	57	60	62
Precip	mm	89	102	127	135	127	117	117	76	74	71	74	74
AUSTRIA (VIENNA)													
Temp °F	max	34	38	47	58	67	73	76	75	68	56	45	37
	min	25	28	30	42	50	56	60	59	53	44	37	30
Temp °C	max	1	3	8	15	19	23	25	24	20	14	7	3
	min	-4	-3	-1	6	10	14	15	15	11	7	3	-1
Hum %	am	81	80	78	72	74	74	74	78	83	86	84	84
	pm	72	66	57	49	52	55	54	54	56	64	74	76
Precip	mm	39	44	44	45	70	67	84	72	42	56	52	45

		J	F	M	A	M	J	J	A	S	O	N	D
BAHAMAS (NASSAU)													
Temp °F	max	77	77	79	81	84	87	88	89	88	85	81	79
	min	65	64	66	69	71	74	75	76	75	73	70	67
Temp °C	max	25	25	26	27	29	31	31	32	31	29	27	26
	min	18	18	19	21	22	23	24	24	24	23	21	19
Hum %	am	84	82	81	79	79	81	80	82	84	83	83	84
	pm	64	62	64	65	65	68	69	70	73	71	68	66
Precip	mm	36	38	36	64	117	163	147	135	175	165	71	33
BAHRAIN													
Temp °F	max	68	70	75	84	92	96	99	100	96	90	82	71
	min	57	59	63	70	78	82	85	85	81	75	69	60
Temp °C	max	20	21	24	29	33	36	37	38	36	32	28	22
	min	14	15	17	21	26	28	29	29	27	24	21	16
Hum %	am	85	83	80	75	71	69	69	74	75	80	80	85
	pm	71	70	70	66	63	64	67	65	64	66	70	77
Precip	mm	8	18	13	8	0	0	0	0	0	0	18	18
BELGIUM (BRUSSELS)													
Temp °F	max	40	44	51	58	65	72	73	72	69	60	48	42
	min	30	32	36	41	46	52	54	54	51	45	38	32
Temp °C	max	4	7	10	14	18	22	23	22	21	15	9	6
	min	-1	0	2	5	8	11	12	12	11	7	3	0
Hum %	am	92	92	91	91	90	87	91	93	94	93	93	92
	pm	86	81	74	71	65	65	68	69	69	77	85	86
Precip	mm	66	61	53	60	55	76	95	80	63	83	75	88
BERMUDA (HAMILTON)													
Temp °F	max	68	68	68	71	76	81	85	86	84	79	74	70
	min	58	57	57	59	64	69	73	74	72	69	63	60
Temp °C	max	20	20	20	22	24	27	29	30	29	26	23	21
	min	14	14	14	15	18	21	23	23	22	21	17	16
Hum %	am	78	76	77	78	81	82	81	79	81	79	76	77
	pm	70	69	69	70	75	74	73	69	73	72	70	70
Precip	mm	112	119	122	104	117	112	114	137	132	147	127	119
BRAZIL (RIO DE JANEIRO)													
Temp °F	max	84	85	83	80	77	76	75	76	75	77	79	82
	min	73	73	72	69	66	64	63	64	65	66	68	71
Temp °C	max	29	29	28	27	25	24	24	24	24	25	26	28
	min	23	23	22	21	19	18	17	18	18	19	20	22
Hum %	am	82	84	87	87	87	87	86	84	84	83	82	82
	pm	70	71	74	73	70	69	68	66	72	72	72	72
Precip	mm	125	122	130	107	79	53	41	43	66	79	104	137
CANADA (OTTAWA)													
Temp °F	max	21	22	33	51	66	76	81	77	68	54	39	24
	min	3	3	16	31	44	54	58	55	48	37	26	9
Temp °C	max	-6	-6	1	11	19	24	27	25	20	12	4	-4
	min	-16	-16	-9	-1	7	12	14	13	9	3	-3	-13
Hum %	am	83	88	84	76	77	80	80	84	90	86	84	83
	pm	76	73	66	58	55	56	53	54	59	63	68	75
Precip	mm	74	56	71	69	64	89	86	66	81	74	76	66

		J	F	M	A	M	J	J	A	S	O	N	D
CANADA (VANCOUVER)													
Temp °F	max	41	44	50	58	64	69	74	73	65	57	48	43
	min	32	34	37	40	46	52	54	54	49	44	39	35
Temp °C	max	5	7	10	14	18	21	23	23	18	14	9	6
	min	0	1	3	4	8	11	12	12	9	7	4	2
Hum %	am	93	91	91	89	88	87	89	90	92	92	91	91
	pm	85	78	70	67	63	65	62	62	72	80	84	88
Precip	mm	218	147	127	84	71	64	31	43	91	147	211	224
CHINA (HONG KONG)													
Temp °F	max	64	63	67	75	82	85	87	87	85	81	74	68
	min	56	55	60	67	74	78	78	78	77	73	65	59
Temp °C	max	18	17	19	24	28	29	31	31	29	27	23	20
	min	13	13	16	19	23	26	26	26	25	23	18	15
Hum %	am	77	82	84	87	87	86	87	87	83	75	73	74
	pm	66	73	74	77	78	77	77	77	72	63	60	63
Precip	mm	33	46	74	137	292	394	381	367	257	114	43	31
CZECH REPUBLIC (PRAGUE)													
Temp °F	max	31	34	44	54	64	70	73	72	65	53	42	34
	min	23	24	30	38	46	52	55	55	49	41	33	27
Temp °C	max	0	1	7	12	18	21	23	22	18	12	5	1
	min	-5	-4	-1	3	8	11	13	13	9	5	1	-3
Hum %	am	84	83	82	77	75	74	77	81	84	87	87	87
	pm	73	67	55	47	45	46	49	48	51	60	73	78
Precip	mm	18	18	18	27	48	54	68	55	31	33	20	21
DENMARK (COPENHAGEN)													
Temp °F	max	36	36	41	51	61	67	71	70	64	54	45	40
	min	28	28	31	38	46	52	57	56	51	44	38	34
Temp °C	max	2	2	5	10	16	19	22	21	18	12	7	4
	min	-2	-3	-1	3	8	11	14	14	11	7	3	1
Hum	am	88	86	85	79	70	70	74	78	83	86	88	89
	pm	85	83	78	68	59	60	62	64	69	76	83	87
Precip	mm	49	39	32	38	43	47	71	66	62	59	48	49
EGYPT (CAIRO)													
Temp °F	max	65	69	75	83	91	95	96	95	90	86	78	68
	min	47	48	52	57	63	68	70	71	68	65	58	50
Temp °C	max	18	21	24	28	33	35	36	35	32	30	26	20
	min	8	9	11	14	17	20	21	22	20	18	14	10
Hum %	am	69	64	63	55	50	55	65	69	68	67	68	70
	pm	40	33	27	21	18	20	24	28	31	31	38	41
Precip	mm	5	5	5	3	3	0	0	0	0	0	3	5
FRANCE (PARIS)													
Temp °F	max	43	45	54	60	68	73	76	75	70	60	50	44
	min	34	34	39	43	49	55	58	58	53	46	40	36
Temp °C	max	6	7	12	16	20	23	25	24	21	16	10	7
	min	1	1	4	6	10	13	15	14	12	8	5	2
Hum %	am	88	87	85	82	83	83	83	87	90	91	91	90
	pm	80	73	63	54	55	58	57	61	65	71	79	82
Precip	mm	56	46	35	42	57	54	59	64	55	50	51	50

		J	F	M	A	M	J	J	A	S	O	N	D

FRENCH POLYNESIA (TAHITI)

		J	F	M	A	M	J	J	A	S	O	N	D
Temp °F	max	89	89	89	89	87	86	86	86	86	87	88	88
	min	72	72	72	72	70	69	68	68	69	70	71	72
Temp C	max	32	32	32	32	31	30	30	30	30	31	31	31
	min	22	22	22	22	21	21	20	20	21	21	22	22
Hum %	am	82	82	84	85	84	85	83	83	81	79	80	81
	pm	77	77	78	78	78	79	77	78	76	76	77	78
Precip	mm	252	244	429	142	102	76	53	43	53	89	150	249

GERMANY (BERLIN)

		J	F	M	A	M	J	J	A	S	O	N	D
Temp °F	max	35	37	46	56	66	72	75	74	68	56	45	38
	min	26	26	31	39	47	53	57	56	50	42	36	29
Temp °C	max	2	3	8	13	19	22	24	23	20	13	7	3
	min	-3	-3	0	4	8	12	14	13	10	6	2	-1
Hum %	am	89	89	88	84	80	80	84	88	92	93	92	91
	pm	82	78	67	60	57	58	61	61	65	73	83	86
Precip	mm	46	40	33	42	49	65	73	69	48	49	46	43

GERMANY (FRANKFURT)

		J	F	M	A	M	J	J	A	S	O	N	D
Temp °F	max	38	41	51	60	69	74	77	76	69	58	47	39
	min	29	30	35	42	49	55	58	57	52	44	38	32
Temp °C	max	3	5	11	16	20	23	25	24	21	14	8	4
	min	-2	-1	2	6	9	13	15	14	11	7	3	0
Hum %	am	86	86	84	79	78	78	81	85	89	91	89	88
	pm	77	70	57	51	50	52	53	54	60	68	77	81
Precip	mm	58	44	38	44	55	73	70	76	57	52	55	54

GHANA (ACCRA)

		J	F	M	A	M	J	J	A	S	O	N	D
Temp °F	max	87	88	88	88	87	84	81	80	81	85	87	88
	min	73	75	76	76	75	74	73	71	73	74	75	75
Temp °C	max	31	31	31	31	31	29	27	27	27	29	31	31
	min	23	24	24	24	24	23	23	22	23	23	24	24
Hum %	am	95	96	95	96	96	97	97	97	96	97	97	97
	pm	61	61	63	65	68	74	76	77	72	71	66	64
Precip	mm	15	33	56	81	142	178	46	15	36	64	36	23

GREECE (ATHENS)

		J	F	M	A	M	J	J	A	S	O	N	D
Temp °F	max	55	57	60	68	77	86	92	92	84	75	66	58
	min	44	44	46	52	61	68	73	73	67	60	53	47
Temp °C	max	13	14	16	20	25	30	33	33	29	24	19	15
	min	6	7	8	11	16	20	23	23	19	15	12	8
Hum %	am	77	74	71	65	60	50	47	48	58	70	78	78
	pm	62	57	54	48	47	39	34	34	42	52	61	63
Precip	mm	62	37	37	23	23	14	6	7	15	51	56	71

INDIA (BOMBAY)

		J	F	M	A	M	J	J	A	S	O	N	D
Temp °F	max	83	83	86	89	91	89	85	85	85	89	89	87
	min	67	67	72	76	80	79	77	76	76	76	73	69
Temp °C	max	28	28	30	32	33	32	29	29	29	32	32	31
	min	12	12	17	20	23	21	22	22	22	21	18	13
Hum %	am	70	71	73	75	74	79	83	83	85	81	73	70
	pm	61	62	65	67	68	77	83	81	78	71	64	62
Precip	mm	2.5	2.5	2.5	0	18	485	617	340	264	64	13	2.5

		J	F	M	A	M	J	J	A	S	O	N	D
INDIA (CALCUTTA)
Temp °F	max	80	84	93	97	96	92	89	89	90	89	84	79
	min	55	59	69	75	77	79	79	78	78	74	64	55
Temp °C	max	27	29	34	36	36	33	32	32	32	32	29	26
	min	13	15	21	24	25	26	26	26	24	24	18	13
Hum %	am	85	82	79	76	77	82	86	88	86	85	79	80
	pm	52	45	46	56	62	75	80	82	81	72	63	55
Precip	mm	10	31	36	43	140	297	325	328	252	114	20	5
INDIA (DELHI)
Temp °F	max	70	75	87	97	105	102	96	93	93	93	84	73
	min	44	49	58	68	79	83	81	79	75	65	52	46
Temp °C	max	21	24	31	36	41	39	36	34	34	34	29	23
	min	7	9	14	20	26	28	27	26	24	18	11	8
Hum %	am	72	67	49	35	35	53	75	80	72	56	51	69
	pm	41	35	23	19	20	36	59	64	51	32	31	42
Precip	mm	23	18	13	8	13	74	180	173	117	10	3	10
INDONESIA (JAKARTA)
Temp °F	max	84	84	86	87	87	87	87	87	88	87	86	85
	min	74	74	74	75	75	74	73	73	74	74	74	74
Temp °C	max	29	29	30	31	31	31	31	31	31	31	30	29
	min	23	23	23	24	24	23	23	23	23	23	23	23
Hum %	am	95	95	94	94	94	93	92	90	90	90	92	92
	pm	75	75	73	71	69	67	64	61	62	64	68	71
Precip	mm	300	300	211	147	114	97	64	43	66	112	142	203
IRAN (TEHRAN)
Temp °F	max	45	50	59	71	82	93	99	97	90	76	63	51
	min	27	32	39	49	58	66	72	71	64	53	43	33
Temp °C	max	7	10	15	22	28	34	37	36	32	24	17	11
	min	-3	0	4	9	14	19	22	22	18	12	6	1
Hum %	am	77	73	61	54	55	50	51	47	49	53	63	76
	pm	75	59	39	40	47	49	41	46	49	54	66	75
Precip	mm	46	38	46	36	13	3	3	3	3	8	20	31
ISRAEL (JERUSALEM)
Temp °F	max	55	56	65	73	81	85	87	87	85	81	70	59
	min	41	42	46	50	57	60	63	64	62	59	53	45
Temp °C	max	13	13	18	23	27	29	31	31	29	27	21	15
	min	5	6	8	10	14	16	17	18	17	15	12	7
Hum %	am	77	74	61	56	47	48	52	58	61	60	65	73
	pm	66	58	57	42	33	32	35	36	36	36	50	60
Precip	mm	132	132	64	28	3	0	0	0	0	13	71	86
ITALY (ROME)
Temp °F	max	52	55	59	66	74	82	87	86	79	71	61	55
	min	40	42	45	50	56	63	67	67	62	55	49	44
Temp °C	max	11	13	15	19	23	28	30	30	26	22	16	13
	min	5	5	7	10	13	17	20	20	17	13	9	6
Hum %	am	85	86	83	83	77	74	70	73	83	86	87	85
	pm	68	64	56	54	54	48	42	43	50	59	66	70
Precip	mm	71	62	57	51	46	37	15	21	63	99	129	93

		J	F	M	A	M	J	J	A	S	O	N	D
Japan (Tokyo)													
Temp °F	max	47	48	54	63	71	76	83	86	79	69	60	52
	min	29	31	36	46	54	63	70	72	66	55	43	33
Temp °C	max	8	9	12	17	22	24	28	30	26	21	16	11
	min	-2	-1	2	8	12	17	21	22	19	13	6	1
Hum %	am	73	71	75	81	85	89	91	92	91	88	83	77
	pm	48	48	53	59	62	68	69	66	68	64	58	51
Precip	mm	48	74	107	135	147	165	142	152	234	208	97	56
Kenya (Nairobi)													
Temp °F	max	77	79	77	75	72	70	69	70	75	76	74	74
	min	54	55	57	58	56	53	51	52	52	55	56	55
Temp °C	max	25	26	25	24	22	21	21	21	24	24	23	23
	min	12	13	14	14	13	12	11	11	11	13	13	13
Hum %	am	74	74	81	88	88	89	86	86	82	82	86	81
	pm	44	40	45	56	62	60	58	56	45	43	53	53
Precip	mm	38	64	125	211	158	46	15	23	31	53	109	86
Lebanon (Beirut)													
Temp °F	max	62	63	66	72	78	83	87	89	86	81	73	65
	min	51	51	54	58	64	69	73	74	73	69	61	55
Temp °C	max	17	17	19	22	26	28	31	32	30	27	23	18
	min	11	11	12	14	18	21	23	23	23	21	16	13
Hum %	am	72	72	72	72	69	67	66	65	64	65	67	70
	pm	70	70	69	67	64	61	58	57	57	62	61	69
Precip	mm	191	158	94	56	18	3	0	0	5	51	132	185
Malaysia (Kuala Lumpur)													
Temp °F	max	90	92	92	91	91	91	90	90	90	89	89	89
	min	72	72	73	74	73	72	73	73	73	73	73	72
Temp °C	max	32	33	33	33	33	33	32	32	32	32	32	32
	min	22	22	23	23	23	22	23	23	23	23	23	22
Hum %	am	97	97	97	97	97	96	95	96	96	96	97	97
	pm	60	60	58	63	66	63	63	62	64	65	66	61
Precip	mm	158	201	259	292	224	130	99	163	218	249	259	191
Mexico (Mexico City)													
Temp °F	max	66	69	75	77	78	76	73	73	74	70	68	66
	min	42	43	47	51	54	55	53	54	53	50	46	43
Temp °C	max	19	21	24	25	26	24	23	23	23	21	20	19
	min	6	6	8	11	12	13	12	12	12	10	8	6
Hum %	am	79	72	68	66	69	82	84	85	86	83	82	81
	pm	34	28	26	29	29	48	50	50	54	47	41	37
Precip	mm	13	5	10	20	53	119	170	152	130	51	18	8
Myanmar (Yangon)													
Temp °F	max	89	92	96	97	92	86	85	85	86	88	88	88
	min	65	67	71	76	77	76	76	76	76	76	73	67
Temp °C	max	32	33	36	36	33	30	29	29	30	31	31	31
	min	18	19	22	24	25	24	24	24	24	24	23	19
Hum %	am	71	72	74	71	80	87	89	89	87	83	79	75
	pm	52	52	54	64	76	85	88	88	86	77	72	61
Precip	mm	3	5	8	51	307	480	582	528	394	180	69	10

		J	F	M	A	M	J	J	A	S	O	N	D

NEPAL (KATHMANDU)

Temp °F	max	65	67	77	83	86	85	84	83	83	80	74	67
	min	35	39	45	53	61	67	68	68	66	56	45	37
Temp °C	max	18	19	25	28	30	29	29	28	28	27	23	19
	min	2	4	7	12	16	19	20	20	19	13	7	3
Hum %	am	89	90	73	68	72	79	86	87	86	88	90	89
	pm	70	68	53	54	61	72	82	84	83	81	78	73
Precip	mm	15	41	23	58	122	246	373	345	155	38	8	3

NETHERLANDS (AMSTERDAM)

Temp °F	max	40	42	49	56	64	70	72	71	67	57	48	42
	min	31	31	34	40	46	51	55	55	50	44	38	33
Temp °C	max	4	5	10	13	18	21	22	22	19	14	9	5
	min	-1	-1	1	4	8	11	13	13	10	7	3	1
Hum %	am	90	90	86	79	75	75	79	82	86	90	92	91
	pm	82	76	65	61	59	59	64	65	67	72	81	85
Precip	mm	68	53	44	49	52	58	77	87	72	72	70	64

NEW ZEALAND (AUCKLAND)

Temp °F	max	73	73	71	67	62	58	56	58	60	63	66	70
	min	60	60	59	56	51	48	46	46	49	52	54	57
Temp °C	max	23	23	22	19	17	14	13	14	16	17	19	21
	min	16	16	15	13	11	9	8	8	9	11	12	14
Hum %	am	71	72	74	78	80	83	84	80	76	74	71	70
	pm	62	61	65	69	70	73	74	70	68	66	64	64
Precip	mm	79	94	81	97	127	137	145	117	102	102	89	79

NEW ZEALAND (CHRISTCHURCH)

Temp °F	max	70	69	66	62	56	51	50	52	57	62	66	69
	min	53	53	50	45	40	36	35	36	40	44	47	51
Temp °C	max	21	21	19	17	13	11	10	11	14	17	19	21
	min	12	12	10	7	4	2	2	2	4	7	8	11
Hum %	am	65	71	75	82	85	87	87	81	72	63	64	67
	pm	59	60	69	71	69	72	76	66	69	60	64	60
Precip	mm	56	43	48	48	66	66	69	48	46	43	48	56

NIGERIA (LAGOS)

Temp °F	max	88	89	89	89	87	85	83	82	83	85	88	88
	min	74	77	78	77	76	74	74	73	74	74	75	75
Temp °C	max	31	32	32	32	31	29	28	28	28	29	31	31
	min	23	25	26	25	24	23	23	23	23	23	24	24
Hum %	am	84	83	82	81	83	87	87	85	86	86	85	86
	pm	65	69	72	72	76	80	80	76	77	76	72	68
Precip	mm	28	46	102	150	269	460	279	64	140	206	69	25

NORWAY (OSLO)

Temp °F	max	28	30	39	50	61	68	72	70	60	48	38	32
	min	19	19	25	34	43	50	55	53	46	38	31	25
Temp °C	max	-2	-1	4	10	16	20	22	21	16	9	3	0
	min	-7	-7	-4	1	6	10	13	12	8	3	-1	-4
Hum %	am	86	84	80	75	68	69	74	79	85	88	88	87
	pm	82	74	64	57	52	55	59	61	66	72	83	85
Precip	mm	49	35	26	43	44	70	82	95	81	74	68	63

		J	F	M	A	M	J	J	A	S	O	N	D
PERU (LIMA)													
Temp °F	max	82	83	83	80	74	68	67	66	68	71	74	78
	min	66	67	66	63	60	58	57	56	57	58	60	62
Temp °C	max	28	28	28	27	23	20	19	19	20	22	23	26
	min	19	19	19	17	16	14	14	13	14	14	16	17
Hum %	am	93	92	92	93	95	95	94	95	94	94	93	93
	pm	69	66	64	66	76	80	77	78	76	72	71	70
Precip	mm	3	0	0	0	5	5	8	8	8	3	3	0
PORTUGAL (LISBON)													
Temp °F	max	57	59	63	67	71	77	81	82	79	72	63	58
	min	46	47	50	53	55	60	63	63	62	58	52	47
Temp °C	max	14	15	17	20	21	25	27	28	26	22	17	15
	min	8	8	10	12	13	15	17	17	17	14	11	9
Hum %	am	85	80	78	69	68	65	62	64	70	75	81	84
	pm	71	64	64	56	57	54	48	49	54	59	68	72
Precip	mm	111	76	109	54	44	16	3	4	33	62	93	103
PHILIPPINES (MANILA)													
Temp °F	max	86	88	91	93	93	91	88	87	88	88	87	86
	min	69	69	71	73	75	75	75	75	75	74	73	70
Temp °C	max	30	31	33	34	34	33	31	31	31	31	31	30
	min	21	21	22	23	24	24	24	24	24	23	22	21
Hum %	am	89	88	85	85	88	91	92	93	92	91	90
	pm	63	59	55	55	61	68	74	73	73	71	69	67
Precip	mm	23	13	18	33	130	254	432	422	356	193	145	66
POLAND (WARSAW)													
Temp °F	max	32	32	42	53	67	73	75	73	66	55	42	35
	min	22	21	28	37	48	54	58	56	49	41	33	28
Temp °C	max	0	0	6	12	20	23	24	23	19	13	6	2
	min	-6	-6	-2	3	9	12	15	14	10	5	1	-3
Hum %	am	90	89	90	85	80	82	86	90	92	93	93	92
	pm	84	80	70	61	56	59	63	63	64	73	83	87
Precip	mm	27	32	27	37	46	69	96	65	43	38	31	44
RUSSIA (MOSCOW)													
Temp °F	max	15	22	32	50	66	70	73	72	61	48	35	24
	min	3	8	18	34	46	51	55	53	45	37	26	15
Temp °C	max	-9	-6	0	10	19	21	23	22	16	9	2	-5
	min	-16	-14	-8	1	8	11	13	12	7	3	-3	-10
Hum %	am	82	82	82	73	58	62	68	74	78	81	87	85
	pm	77	66	64	54	43	47	54	55	59	67	79	83
Precip	mm	39	38	36	37	53	58	88	71	58	45	47	54
SAUDI ARABIA (JEDDAH)													
Temp °F	max	84	84	85	91	95	97	99	99	96	95	91	86
	min	66	65	67	70	74	75	79	80	77	73	71	67
Temp °C	max	29	29	29	33	35	36	37	37	36	35	33	30
	min	19	18	19	21	23	24	26	27	25	23	22	19
Hum %	am	58	52	52	52	51	56	55	59	65	60	55	55
	pm	54	52	52	56	55	55	50	51	61	61	59	54
Precip	mm	5	0	0	0	0	0	0	0	0	0	25	31

		J	F	M	A	M	J	J	A	S	O	N	D
SINGAPORE													
Temp °F	max	86	88	88	88	89	88	88	87	87	87	87	87
	min	73	73	75	75	75	75	75	75	75	74	74	74
Temp °C	max	30	31	31	31	32	31	31	31	31	31	31	31
	min	23	23	24	24	24	24	24	24	24	23	23	23
Hum %	am	82	77	76	77	79	79	79	78	79	78	79	82
	pm	78	71	70	74	73	73	72	72	72	72	75	78
Precip	mm	252	173	193	188	173	173	170	196	178	208	254	257
SOUTH AFRICA (JOHANNESBURG)													
Temp °F	max	78	77	75	72	66	62	63	68	73	77	77	78
	min	58	58	55	50	43	39	39	43	48	53	55	57
Temp °C	max	26	25	24	22	19	17	17	20	23	25	25	26
	min	14	14	13	10	6	4	4	6	9	12	13	14
Hum %	am	75	78	79	74	70	70	69	64	59	64	67	70
	pm	50	53	50	44	36	33	32	29	30	37	45	47
Precip	mm	114	109	89	38	25	8	8	8	23	56	107	125
SPAIN (MADRID)													
Temp °F	max	47	52	59	65	70	80	87	85	77	65	55	48
	min	35	36	41	45	50	58	63	63	57	49	42	36
Temp °C	max	9	11	15	18	21	27	31	30	25	19	13	9
	min	2	2	5	7	10	15	17	17	14	10	5	2
Hum %	am	86	83	80	74	72	66	58	62	72	81	84	86
	pm	71	62	56	49	49	41	33	35	46	58	65	70
Precip	mm	39	34	43	48	47	27	11	15	32	53	47	48
SRI LANKA (COLOMBO)													
Temp °F	max	86	87	88	88	87	85	85	85	85	85	85	85
	min	72	72	74	76	78	77	77	77	77	75	73	72
Temp °C	max	30	31	31	31	31	29	29	29	29	29	29	29
	min	22	22	23	24	26	25	25	25	25	24	23	22
Hum %	am	73	71	71	74	78	80	79	78	76	77	77	74
	pm	67	66	66	70	76	78	77	76	75	76	75	69
Precip	mm	89	69	147	231	371	224	135	109	160	348	315	147
SWEDEN (STOCKHOLM)													
Temp °F	max	30	30	37	47	58	67	71	68	60	49	40	35
	min	23	22	26	34	43	51	57	56	49	41	34	29
Temp °C	max	-1	-1	3	8	14	19	22	20	15	9	5	2
	min	-5	-5	-4	1	6	11	14	13	9	5	1	-2
Hum %	am	85	83	82	76	66	68	74	81	87	88	89	88
	pm	83	77	68	60	53	55	59	64	69	76	85	86
Precip	mm	43	30	25	31	34	45	61	76	60	48	53	48
SWITZERLAND (ZURICH)													
Temp °F	max	36	41	51	59	67	73	76	75	69	57	45	37
	min	26	28	34	40	47	53	56	56	51	43	35	29
Temp °C	max	2	5	10	15	19	23	25	24	20	14	7	3
	min	-3	-2	1	4	8	12	14	13	11	6	2	-2
Hum %	am	88	88	86	81	80	80	81	85	90	92	90	89
	pm	74	65	55	51	52	52	52	53	57	64	73	76
Precip	mm	74	69	64	76	101	129	136	124	102	77	73	64

		J	F	M	A	M	J	J	A	S	O	N	D
THAILAND (BANGKOK)													
Temp °F	max	89	91	93	95	93	91	90	90	89	88	87	87
	min	68	72	75	77	77	76	76	76	76	75	72	68
Temp °C	max	32	33	34	35	34	33	32	32	32	31	31	31
	min	20	22	24	25	25	24	24	24	24	24	22	20
Hum %	am	91	92	92	90	91	90	91	92	94	93	92	91
	pm	53	55	56	58	64	67	66	66	70	70	65	56
Precip	mm	8	20	36	58	198	160	160	175	305	206	66	5
TRINIDAD (PORT OF SPAIN)													
Temp °F	max	87	88	89	90	90	89	88	88	89	89	89	88
	min	69	68	68	69	71	71	71	71	71	71	71	69
Temp °C	max	31	31	32	32	32	32	31	31	32	32	32	31
	min	21	20	20	21	22	22	22	22	22	22	22	21
Hum %	am	89	87	85	83	84	87	88	87	87	87	89	89
	pm	68	65	63	61	63	69	71	73	73	74	76	71
Precip	mm	69	41	46	53	94	193	218	246	193	170	183	125
TURKEY (ISTANBUL)													
Temp °F	max	46	47	51	60	69	77	82	82	76	68	59	51
	min	37	36	38	45	53	60	65	66	61	55	48	41
Temp °C	max	8	9	11	16	21	25	28	28	24	20	15	11
	min	3	?	3	7	12	16	18	19	16	13	9	5
Hum %	am	82	82	81	81	82	79	79	79	81	83	82	82
	pm	75	72	67	62	61	58	56	55	59	64	71	74
Precip	mm	109	92	72	46	38	34	34	30	58	81	103	119
UK (LONDON)													
Temp °F	max	43	44	50	56	62	69	71	71	65	58	50	45
	min	36	36	38	42	47	53	56	56	52	46	42	38
Temp °C	max	6	7	10	13	17	20	22	21	19	14	10	7
	min	2	2	3	6	8	12	14	13	11	8	5	4
Hum %	am	86	85	81	71	70	70	71	76	80	85	85	87
	pm	77	72	64	56	57	58	59	62	65	70	78	81
Precip	mm	54	40	37	37	46	45	57	59	49	57	64	48
USA (MIAMI)													
Temp °F	max	74	75	78	80	84	86	88	88	87	83	78	76
	min	61	61	64	67	71	74	76	76	75	72	66	62
Temp °C	max	23	24	26	27	29	30	31	31	31	28	26	24
	min	16	16	18	19	22	23	24	24	24	22	19	17
Hum %	am	81	82	77	73	75	75	75	76	79	80	77	82
	pm	66	63	62	64	67	69	68	68	70	69	64	65
Precip	mm	71	53	64	81	173	178	155	160	203	234	71	51
USA (NEW YORK)													
Temp °F	max	37	38	45	57	68	77	82	80	79	69	51	41
	min	24	24	30	42	53	60	66	66	60	49	37	29
Temp °C	max	3	3	7	14	20	25	28	27	26	21	11	5
	min	-4	-4	-1	6	12	16	19	19	16	9	3	-2
Hum %	am	72	70	70	68	70	74	77	79	79	76	75	73
	pm	60	58	55	53	54	58	58	60	61	57	60	61
Precip	mm	94	97	91	81	81	84	107	109	86	89	76	91

		J	F	M	A	M	J	J	A	S	O	N	D
USA (San Francisco)													
Temp °F	max	55	59	61	62	63	66	65	65	69	68	63	57
	min	45	47	48	49	51	52	53	53	55	54	51	47
Temp °C	max	13	15	16	17	17	19	18	18	21	20	17	14
	min	7	8	9	9	11	11	12	12	13	12	11	8
Hum %	am	85	84	83	83	85	88	91	92	88	85	83	83
	pm	69	66	61	61	62	64	69	70	63	58	60	68
Precip	mm	119	97	79	38	18	3	0	0	8	25	64	112
Zimbabwe (Harare)													
Temp °F	max	78	78	78	78	74	70	70	74	79	83	81	79
	min	60	60	58	55	49	44	44	47	53	58	60	60
Temp °C	max	26	26	26	26	23	21	21	23	26	28	27	26
	min	16	16	14	13	9	7	7	8	12	14	16	16
Hum %	am	74	77	75	68	60	58	56	50	43	43	56	67
	pm	57	53	52	44	37	36	33	28	26	26	43	57
Precip	mm	196	178	117	28	13	3	0	3	5	28	97	163

Useful weather phonelines

Metcall International
Tel UK + 09003 411 211
Provides weather forecasts worldwide.

Weather call
Tel UK + 0891 110 009
Provides weather forecasts worldwide.

UK Meteorological Office
Tel 0845 300 03000
Provides weather forecasts for the UK.

Useful weather websites

www.bbc.co.uk/weather
The BBC's weather website.

www.weather.com
Guide to weather conditions around the world.

www.meto.gov.uk
The UK's Meteorological Office site.

www.weather24.com
Short-term forecasts by email.

www.worldclimate.com
Global weather overview.

Rainy seasons worldwide

Tʜɪs ᴄʜᴀʀᴛ sʜᴏᴡs ᴛʜᴇ ᴀᴠᴇʀᴀɢᴇ ʀᴀɪɴꜰᴀʟʟ in various countries, per month and as an annual total.

Kᴇʏ ᴛᴏ sʏᴍʙᴏʟs
R the rainiest months   W wetter than average   D drier than average

	Annual total mm	J	F	M	A	M	J	J	A	S	O	N	D
Afghanistan (Kabul)	34.0	D	W	R	R	D	D	D	D	D	D	D	W
Algeria (Algiers)	76.5	W	W	W	D	D	D	D	D	D	W	R	R
Argentina (Buenos A.)	95.0	D	D	W	W	D	D	D	D	D	W	W	R
Argentina (Tucuman)	97.0	R	W	W	D	D	D	D	D	D	D	W	W
Australia (Cairns)	225.3	W	W	R	W	D	D	D	D	D	D	D	W
Australia (Darwin)	149.1	R	W	W	D	D	D	D	D	D	D	W	W
Australia (Melbourne)	65.3	D	D	W	W	D	D	D	D	W	R	W	W
Australia (Perth)	90.7	D	D	D	D	W	R	R	W	W	W	D	D
Australia (Sydney)	118.1	D	W	W	R	W	W	W	D	D	D	D	D
Benin (Cotonou)	132.6	D	D	W	W	R	R	D	D	D	W	D	D
Bolivia (Concepçion)	114.3	R	W	W	D	D	D	D	D	D	D	R	W
Bolivia (La Paz)	57.4	R	W	W	D	D	D	D	D	D	D	W	W
Brazil (Belem)	243.8	W	R	R	W	W	D	D	D	D	D	D	D
Brazil (Manaus)	181.1	W	W	R	D	D	D	D	D	D	D	W	W
Brazil (Recife)	161.0	D	D	W	W	W	R	W	W	D	D	D	D
Brazil (Rio de Janeiro)	108.2	W	W	W	W	D	D	D	D	D	D	W	R
Brazil (Salvador B.)	190.0	D	D	D	R	R	W	W	D	D	D	D	D
Chile (Santiago)	36.1	D	D	D	D	W	R	W	W	D	D	D	D
Chile (Valdivia)	260.1	D	D	D	W	W	R	W	W	D	D	D	D
China (Beijing)	134.1	D	D	D	D	D	D	W	R	R	W	D	D
China (Guangzhou)	164.3	D	D	D	W	W	R	W	W	D	D	D	D
China (Hong Kong)	216.1	D	D	D	D	W	R	R	R	W	D	D	D
China (Shanghai)	113.5	D	D	D	D	D	R	W	W	W	D	D	D
China (Wuhan)	125.7	D	D	D	W	W	R	W	D	D	D	D	D
Colombia (Bogota)	105.9	D	D	W	W	W	D	D	D	D	R	W	D
Congo (Kananga)	158.2	W	W	W	W	D	D	D	D	D	W	R	R
Congo (Kinshasa)	135.4	W	W	W	W	W	D	D	D	D	W	R	W
Cook Islands (Manih.)	248.2	R	W	D	D	D	D	D	D	D	W	W	W
Costa Rica (San Jose)	179.8	D	D	D	D	W	W	W	W	R	R	D	D
Cuba (Havana)	122.4	D	D	D	D	W	W	W	W	W	R	D	D
Dominican R. (S Dom.)	141.7	D	D	D	D	W	W	W	W	R	W	W	D
Ecuador (Guyaquil)	97.3	R	R	R	W	D	D	D	D	D	D	D	D
Ecuador (Quito)	112.3	W	W	W	R	W	D	D	D	D	D	D	D
Egypt (Cairo)	3.6	W	W	W	D	D	D	D	D	D	D	D	W
Ethiopia (Addis Ababa)	123.7	D	D	D	D	D	W	R	R	W	D	D	D
Ethiopia (Harar)	89.7	D	D	D	W	W	W	W	R	W	D	D	D
Fiji (Suva)	297.4	W	W	R	D	D	D	D	D	D	D	W	W
Fr. Polynesia (Tahiti)	162.8	R	R	W	W	D	D	D	D	D	D	W	R
Gabon (Libreville)	251.0	W	W	W	W	D	D	D	D	D	W	R	W
Ghana (Accra)	72.4	D	D	W	W	W	R	D	D	D	W	D	D
Guatemala (G. City)	131.6	D	D	D	D	W	R	W	W	W	W	D	D
Guyana (Georgetown)	225.3	W	D	D	D	W	R	W	D	D	D	D	W
Haiti (Port-au-Prince)	135.4	D	D	D	W	R	D	D	W	W	D	D	D

KEY TO SYMBOLS
R the rainiest months   W wetter than average   D drier than average

	Annual total mm	J	F	M	A	M	J	J	A	S	O	N	D
Hawaii (Honolulu)	64.3	R	W	W	D	D	D	D	D	D	D	W	R
Honduras (Tegucig.)	162.1	D	D	D	D	D	R	W	D	W	W	D	D
Iceland (Reykjavik)	77.2	W	D	D	D	D	D	D	D	W	R	W	W
India (Agra)	68.1	D	D	D	D	D	W	R	R	W	D	D	D
India (Bangalore)	329.2	D	D	D	D	D	R	R	W	D	D	D	D
India (Bombay)	181.4	D	D	D	D	D	R	R	W	W	D	D	D
India (Calcutta)	160.0	D	D	D	D	W	W	R	R	W	D	D	D
India (Delhi)	64.0	D	D	D	D	D	W	R	R	W	D	D	D
India (Hyderabad)	75.2	D	D	D	D	D	W	W	W	R	W	D	D
India (Madras)	127.0	D	D	D	D	D	D	D	W	W	R	R	W
Indonesia (Jakarta)	179.8	R	R	W	D	D	D	D	D	D	D	D	W
Iran (Tehran)	24.6	R	W	R	W	D	D	D	D	D	D	D	W
Iraq (Baghdad)	15.0	W	W	R	D	D	D	D	D	D	D	W	W
Israel (Jerusalem)	53.3	R	R	W	D	D	D	D	D	D	D	W	W
Jamaica (Kingston)	80.0	D	D	D	D	W	W	D	W	W	R	W	D
Japan (Nagasaki)	191.8	D	D	D	W	W	R	W	W	W	D	D	D
Japan (Osaka)	133.6	D	D	D	W	W	R	W	W	W	W	D	D
Japan (Tokyo)	156.5	D	D	D	W	W	W	W	W	R	W	D	D
Jordan (Amman)	27.9	R	R	W	D	D	D	D	D	D	D	W	W
Kenya (Nairobi)	95.8	D	D	W	R	W	D	D	D	D	W	W	W
Kenya (Mombasa)	120.1	D	D	D	W	R	W	D	D	D	D	D	D
Korea (Seoul)	125.0	D	D	D	D	D	W	R	R	W	D	D	D
Kuwait (Kuwait City)	12.7	W	W	R	D	D	D	D	D	D	D	W	R
Lebanon (Beirut)	89.7	R	W	W	D	D	D	D	D	D	D	W	R
Leeward Island (Dom.)	197.9	D	D	D	D	D	D	W	R	W	W	W	D
Liberia (Monrovia)	513.8	D	D	D	D	W	R	R	D	W	W	D	D
Libya (Tripoli)	38.9	W	W	W	W	D	D	D	D	D	W	W	R
Madagascar (Tamatav.)	325.6	W	W	R	W	D	W	W	D	D	D	D	D
Malaysia (K.L.)	244.1	D	D	W	R	W	D	D	D	D	W	W	D
Malaysia (Sandakan)	314.2	R	W	D	D	D	D	D	D	D	D	W	W
Malawi (Lilongwe)	78.7	R	R	W	D	D	D	D	D	D	D	D	W
Mali (Timbuctou)	24.4	D	D	D	D	D	W	R	R	W	D	D	D
Mexico (Acapulco)	154.2	D	D	D	D	D	R	W	W	W	W	D	D
Mexico (Mazatlan)	84.8	D	D	D	D	D	D	W	W	R	D	D	D
Mexico (Merida)	92.7	D	D	D	D	W	R	W	W	W	W	D	D
Mexico (Mexico City)	74.9	D	D	D	D	D	W	R	W	W	D	D	D
Morocco (Marrakesh)	23.9	W	W	R	W	D	D	D	D	D	W	W	W
Morocco (Tangier)	90.2	W	W	W	W	D	D	D	D	D	W	R	W
Mozambique (Maputo)	75.9	R	W	W	D	D	D	D	D	D	W	W	W
Myanmar (Mandalay)	82.8	D	D	D	D	R	R	W	W	W	W	D	D
Myanmar (Yangon)	261.6	D	D	D	D	W	R	R	W	W	D	D	D
Nepal (Kathmandu)	142.7	D	D	D	W	W	R	R	W	D	D	D	D
New Zealand (Auck.)	124.7	D	D	D	W	W	R	W	D	D	D	D	D
New Zealand (Christ.)	63.8	W	D	D	W	W	R	D	D	D	D	W	D
New Zealand (Welltn.)	120.4	D	D	D	W	W	R	W	D	W	D	D	D
Nigeria (Lagos)	183.6	D	D	D	W	R	W	D	D	W	D	D	D
Nigeria (Zungeru)	115.3	D	D	D	D	W	W	W	W	R	D	D	D
Pakistan (Karachi)	18.3	D	D	D	D	D	D	R	W	D	D	D	D
Panama (Balboa H.)	177.0	D	D	D	D	W	W	W	W	W	R	R	D
Papua NG (Port Msby.)	101.1	W	R	W	W	D	D	D	D	D	D	D	W

Key to symbols
R the rainiest months   W wetter than average   D drier than average

	Annual total mm	J	F	M	A	M	J	J	A	S	O	N	D
Paraguay (Asunçion)	131.6	W	W	D	W	W	D	D	D	D	W	W	R
Peru (Lima)	4.8	D	D	D	D	W	W	W	R	R	D	D	D
Philippines (Manila)	208.5	D	D	D	D	D	W	R	R	W	W	D	D
Samoa (Apia)	285.2	R	W	W	W	D	D	D	D	D	D	W	W
Saudi Arabia (Jeddah)	8.1	D	D	D	D	D	D	D	D	D	D	R	R
Saudi Arabia (Riyadh)	9.1	D	W	W	R	W	D	D	D	D	D	D	D
Senegal (Dakar)	155.4	D	D	D	D	D	D	W	R	W	D	D	D
Sierra Leone (Freetwn.)	343.4	D	D	D	D	D	W	R	R	W	W	D	D
Singapore	241.3	R	D	D	D	D	D	D	D	D	W	R	R
Sri Lanka (Colombo)	236.5	D	D	D	W	R	W	D	D	D	R	R	D
Solomon Islands (Tul.)	313.4	W	R	W	W	D	D	D	D	D	D	D	W
South Africa (Jo'burg)	70.9	W	W	W	D	D	D	D	D	D	D	W	R
South Africa (Cape T.)	50.8	D	D	D	W	W	W	R	W	W	D	D	D
Sudan (Khartoum)	17.0	D	D	D	D	D	D	W	R	W	D	D	D
Sudan (Mongalla)	94.5	D	D	D	W	W	W	R	W	W	W	D	D
Syria (Damascus)	22.4	R	RD	D	D	D	D	D	D	D	D	W	W
Taiwan (Taipei)	212.9	D	D	W	D	W	W	W	R	W	D	D	D
Thailand (Bangkok)	139.7	D	D	D	D	W	W	W	W	R	W	D	D
Turkey (Istanbul)	80.5	W	W	W	D	D	D	D	D	D	W	W	R
Uganda (Entebbe)	150.6	D	W	R	W	D	D	D	D	D	D	W	D
Uruguay (Montevideo)	95.0	D	D	R	R	W	W	D	D	D	D	D	D
Venezuela (Caracas)	83.3	D	D	D	D	W	R	R	R	R	R	W	D
Vietnam (Hanoi)	168.1	D	D	D	D	W	W	W	R	W	D	D	D
Yemen (Aden)	4.8	W	D	W	D	D	D	W	R	D	D	D	D
Zambia (Lusaka)	83.3	R	W	W	D	D	D	D	D	D	D	W	W
Zimbabwe (Harare)	82.8	R	W	W	D	D	D	D	D	D	D	W	W

Security information sources

E VERY JOURNEY INVOLVES A CERTAIN AMOUNT OF RISK, but this can be minimised by informing yourself properly about local conditions and events. The websites listed below carry the most up to date reports that you will find while still at home.

You might also check the chapter on *Countries in Conflict*, and the security summaries for countries, in Part 4.

But remember, the best information is local information. So if you're going somewhere risky, make sure you talk to local people. Their news will be fresher and more in touch. And, as with any travelling, be ready to set aside whatever preconceptions you brought with you.

UK GOVERNMENT WARNINGS www.fco.gov.uk/travel

US GOVERNMENT WARNINGS http://travel.state.gov/travel_warnings.html

GLOBAL HOTSPOTS www.traveller.org.uk (publisher, *The Traveller's Handbook)*

TROUBLESPOTS www.fieldingtravel.com/df/ (publisher, *The World's Most Dangerous Places*)

CIA WORLD FACTBOOK www.odci.gov/cia/publications/factbook

WORLD NEWS www.bbc.co.uk/worldservice (see Part 4 for BBC frequencies worldwide)

COUNTRY PROFILES www.pinkertons.com

Vaccinations required

THIS TABLE SHOWS IMMUNISATIONS that are recommended for each country. No immunisations are recommended for countries that are not listed here. Long-term travellers should also consider having the following vaccinations: BCG, diphtheria, hepatitis B, Japanese encephalitis (if travelling in Asia), rabies, tick-borne encephalitis (in European forests). See also the listing of *Travel health websites* on page 867.

YELLOW FEVER In some countries, yellow fever vaccination is an entry requirement. This is noted below with a superscript [1]. In other countries, it is an essential entry requirement only if the traveller has come from an infected area. This is noted with a superscript [2]. In either case, the immigration authorities will require documentary proof, such as a vaccination certificate, before allowing the traveller to enter their country. The superscript [3] indicates countries where we recommend yellow fever vaccination for all travellers, although officials require a certificate only for travellers from infected areas.

CHOLERA At some borders, officials may request a cholera certificate. This is an outdated requirement, since the international medical community no longer recognises cholera vaccines as significantly effective. Currently there is no cholera vaccine available in the UK. MENINGITIS This refers to meningococcal meningitis, for which vaccination is usually recommended only for long-stay travellers or during epidemics.

MALARIA In many of these countries, malaria may only be present in certain localities. Local disease conditions may vary and it is useful to ask your travel clinic for the latest advice.

Afghanistan	*Hep. A, Polio, Typhoid, Malaria, Y. Fever*[2]
Albania	*Hep. A, Polio, Typhoid, Y. Fever*[2]
Algeria	*Hep. A, Polio, Typhoid, Y. Fever*[2]
Angola	*Hep. A, Polio, Typhoid, Malaria, Y. Fever*[1]
Antigua & Barbuda	*Hep. A, Typhoid, Y. Fever*[2]
Argentina	*Hep. A, Typhoid, Malaria*
Armenia	*Hep. A, Polio, Typhoid, Malaria*
Australia	*Y. Fever*[2]
Azerbaijan	*Hep. A, Polio, Typhoid, Malaria, Diphtheria*
Bahamas	*Hep. A, Typhoid, Y. Fever*[2]
Bahrain	*Hep. A, Polio, Typhoid*
Bangladesh	*Hep. A, Polio, Typhoid, Malaria, Y. Fever*[2]
Barbados	*Hep. A, Typhoid, Y. Fever*[2]
Belarus	*Hep. A, Polio, Typhoid, Diphtheria*
Belize	*Hep. A, Typhoid, Malaria, Y. Fever*[2]
Benin	*Hep. A, Polio, Typhoid, Malaria, Y. Fever*[1]*, Meningitis*
Bermuda	*Hep. A, Typhoid*
Bhutan	*Hep. A, Polio, Typhoid, Malaria, Y. Fever*[2]*, Meningitis*
Bolivia	*Hep. A, Typhoid, Malaria, Y. Fever*[3]
Borneo (see Malaysia or Indonesia)	
Bosnia Herzegovina	*Hep. A, Polio, Typhoid*
Botswana	*Hep. A, Polio, Typhoid, Malaria*
Brazil	*Hep. A, Typhoid, Malaria, Y. Fever*[3]

British Virgin Islands	*Hep. A, Typhoid*
Brunei	*Hep. A, Polio, Typhoid, Y. Fever²*
Bulgaria	*Hep. A, Polio, Typhoid*
Burkina Faso	*Hep. A, Polio, Typhoid, Malaria, Y. Fever¹, Meningitis*
Burundi	*Hep. A, Polio, Typhoid, Malaria, Y. Fever³, Meningitis*
Cambodia	*Hep. A, Polio, Typhoid, Malaria, Y. Fever²*
Cameroon	*Hep. A, Polio, Typhoid, Malaria, Y. Fever¹, Meningitis*
Cape Verde	*Hep. A, Polio, Typhoid, Malaria, Y. Fever²*
Cayman Islands	*Hep. A, Typhoid*
Central African Rep.	*Hep. A, Polio, Typhoid, Malaria, Y. Fever¹, Meningitis*
Chad	*Hep. A, Polio, Typhoid, Malaria, Y. Fever, Meningitis*
Chile	*Hep. A, Typhoid*
China	*Hep. A, Polio, Typhoid, Malaria, Y. Fever²*
China (Hong Kong)	*Hep. A, Polio, Typhoid*
China (Macau)	*Hep. A, Polio, Typhoid*
Colombia	*Hep. A, Typhoid, Malaria, Y. Fever*
Comoros	*Hep. A, Polio, Typhoid, Malaria*
Congo (Brazzaville)	*Hep. A, Polio, Typhoid, Malaria, Meningitis, Y. Fever¹*
Congo (DRC)	*Hep. A, Polio, Typhoid, Malaria, Y. Fever¹*
Cook Islands	*Hep. A, Polio, Typhoid*
Costa Rica	*Hep. A, Typhoid, Malaria*
Côte d'Ivoire	*Hep. A, Polio, Typhoid, Malaria, Y. Fever¹, Meningitis*
Croatia	*Hep. A, Polio, Typhoid*
Cuba	*Hep. A, Typhoid*
Czech Republic	*Hep. A, Polio, Typhoid*
Djibouti	*Hep. A, Polio, Typhoid, Malaria, Y. Fever², Meningitis*
Dominica	*Hep. A, Typhoid, Y. Fever²*
Dominican Republic	*Hep. A, Typhoid, Malaria*
Ecuador	*Hep. A, Typhoid, Malaria, Y. Fever³*
Egypt	*Hep. A, Polio, Typhoid, Malaria , Y. Fever²*
El Salvador	*Hep. A, Typhoid, Malaria, Y. Fever²*
Equatorial Guinea	*Hep. A, Polio, Typhoid, Malaria, Y. Fever³, Meningitis*
Eritrea	*Hep. A, Polio, Typhoid, Malaria, Y. Fever², Meningitis*
Estonia	*Hep. A, Polio, Typhoid, Diphtheria*
Ethiopia	*Hep. A, Polio, Typhoid, Malaria, Y. Fever³, Meningitis*
Falkland Islands	*Hep. A, Polio, Typhoid*
Fiji	*Hep. A, Polio, Typhoid, Y. Fever²*
French Guiana	*Hep. A, Typhoid, Malaria, Y. Fever¹*
French Polynesia	*Hep. A, Polio, Typhoid, Y. Fever*
Gabon	*Hep. A, Polio, Typhoid, Malaria, Y. Fever¹*
The Gambia	*Hep. A, Polio, Typhoid, Malaria, Y. Fever³, Meningitis*
Georgia	*Hep. A, Polio, Typhoid, Diphtheria, Malaria*
Ghana	*Hep. A, Polio, Typhoid, Malaria, Y. Fever¹, Meningitis*
Greece	*Y. Fever²*

Grenada	*Hep. A, Typhoid, Y. Fever*[2]
Guadeloupe	*Hep. A, Typhoid, Y. Fever*[2]
Guam	*Hep. A, Typhoid*
Guatemala	*Hep. A, Polio, Typhoid, Malaria, Y. Fever*[2]
Guinea Republic	*Hep. A, Polio, Typhoid, Malaria, Y. Fever*[3]*, Meningitis*
Guinea-Bissau	*Hep. A, Polio, Typhoid, Malaria, Y. Fever*[3]*, Meningitis*
Guyana	*Hep. A, Typhoid, Malaria, Y. Fever*[1]
Haiti	*Hep. A, Typhoid, Malaria, Y. Fever*[2]
Honduras	*Hep. A, Typhoid, Malaria, Y. Fever*[2]
India	*Hep. A, Polio, Typhoid, Malaria, Y. Fever*[2]*, Meningitis*
Indonesia	*Hep. A, Polio, Typhoid, Malaria, Y. Fever*[2]
Iran	*Hep. A, Polio, Typhoid, Malaria*
Iraq	*Hep. A, Polio, Typhoid, Malaria, Y. Fever*[2]
Israel	*Hep. A, Polio, Typhoid*
Jamaica	*Hep. A, Typhoid, Y. Fever*[2]
Japan	*Polio, Typhoid*
Jordan	*Hep. A, Polio, Typhoid, Y. Fever*[2]
Kazakhstan	*Hep. A, Polio, Typhoid, Y. Fever*[2]*, Diphtheria*
Kenya	*Hep. A, Polio, Typhoid, Malaria, Y. Fever*[3]*, Meningitis*
Kiribati	*Hep. A, Polio, Typhoid, Y. Fever*[2]
Korea (North)	*Hep. A, Polio, Typhoid, Malaria*
Korea (South)	*Hep. A, Polio, Typhoid*
Kuwait	*Hep. A, Polio, Typhoid*
Kyrgyzstan	*Hep. A, Polio, Typhoid, Diphtheria*
Laos	*Hep. A, Polio, Typhoid, Malaria, Y. Fever*[2]
Latvia	*Hep. A, Polio, Typhoid, Diphtheria*
Lebanon	*Hep. A, Polio, Typhoid, Y. Fever*[2]
Lesotho	*Hep. A, Polio, Typhoid, Y. Fever*[2]
Liberia	*Hep. A, Polio, Typhoid, Malaria, Y. Fever*[1]*, Meningitis*
Libya	*Hep. A, Polio, Typhoid, Y. Fever*[2]*, Malaria*
Lithuania	*Hep. A, Polio, Typhoid, Diptheria*
Macedonia	*Hep. A, Polio, Typhoid*
Madagascar	*Hep. A, Polio, Typhoid, Malaria, Y. Fever*[2]
Madeira	*Y. Fever*[2]
Malawi	*Hep. A, Polio, Typhoid, Malaria, Y. Fever*[2]*, Meningitis*
Malaysia	*Hep. A, Polio, Typhoid, Malaria, Y. Fever*[2]
Maldives	*Hep. A, Polio, Typhoid, Y. Fever*[2]
Mali	*Hep. A, Polio, Typhoid, Malaria, Y. Fever*[1]*, Meningitis*
Malta	*Y. Fever*[2]
Martinique	*Hep. A, Typhoid*
Mauritania	*Hep. A, Polio, Typhoid, Malaria, Y. Fever*[1]
Mauritius	*Hep. A, Polio, Typhoid, Y. Fever*[2]*, Malaria*
Mexico	*Hep. A, Typhoid, Malaria, Y. Fever*[2]
Moldova	*Hep. A, Polio, Typhoid, Diphtheria*

Mongolia	*Hep. A, Polio, Typhoid*
Monserrat	*Hep. A, Polio, Typhoid*
Morocco	*Hep. A, Polio, Typhoid, Malaria*
Mozambique	*Hep. A, Polio, Typhoid, Malaria, Y. Fever[2], Meningitis*
Myanmar (Burma)	*Hep. A, Polio, Typhoid, Malaria, Y. Fever[2]*
Namibia	*Hep. A, Polio, Typhoid, Malaria, Y. Fever[2]*
Nauru	*Hep. A, Polio, Typhoid, Y. Fever[2]*
Nepal	*Hep. A, Polio, Typhoid, Malaria, Y. Fever[2], Meningitis*
Netherlands Antilles	*Hep. A, Typhoid, Y. Fever[2]*
New Caledonia	*Hep. A, Polio, Typhoid, Y. Fever[2]*
Nicaragua	*Hep. A, Typhoid, Malaria, Y. Fever[2]*
Niger	*Hep. A, Polio, Typhoid, Malaria, Y. Fever[1], Meningitis*
Nigeria	*Hep. A, Polio, Typhoid, Malaria, Y. Fever[1], Meningitis*
Niue	*Hep. A, Polio, Typhoid, Y. Fever[2]*
Oman	*Hep. A, Polio, Typhoid, Malaria, Y. Fever[2]*
Pakistan	*Hep. A, Polio, Typhoid, Malaria, Y. Fever[2]*
Panama	*Hep. A, Polio, Typhoid, Malaria, Y. Fever[3]*
Papua New Guinea	*Hep. A, Polio, Typhoid, Malaria, Y. Fever[2]*
Paraguay	*Hep. A, Typhoid, Malaria, Y. Fever[2]*
Peru	*Hep. A, Typhoid, Malaria, Y. Fever[1]*
Philippines	*Hep. A, Polio, Typhoid, Malaria, Y. Fever[2]*
Pitcairn Island	*Hep. A, Polio, Typhoid, Y. Fever[2]*
Portugal	*Y. Fever[2]*
Puerto Rico	*Hep. A, Typhoid*
Qatar	*Hep. A, Polio, Typhoid*
Réunion	*Hep. A, Polio, Typhoid, Y. Fever[2]*
Romania	*Hep. A, Polio, Typhoid*
Russian Federation	*Hep. A, Polio, Typhoid, Diphtheria*
Rwanda	*Hep. A, Polio, Typhoid, Malaria, Y. Fever[1], Meningitis*
St. Helena	*Hep. A, Polio, Typhoid, Y. Fever[2]*
St Kitts & Nevis	*Hep. A, Typhoid, Y. Fever[2]*
St. Lucia	*Hep. A, Typhoid, Y. Fever[2]*
St. Maarten	*Hep. A, Polio, Typhoid, Y. Fever[2]*
St.Vincent & Grenada	*Hep. A, Typhoid, Y. Fever[2]*
Samoa (American)	*Hep. A, Polio, Typhoid, Yellow Fever[2]*
Samoa (Western)	*Hep. A, Polio, Typhoid, Y. Fever[2]*
São Tomé & Príncipe	*Hep. A, Polio, Typhoid, Malaria, Y. Fever[1]*
Saudi Arabia	*Hep. A, Polio, Typhoid, Malaria, Meningitis, Y. Fever[2] ([1]for pilgrims)*
Senegal	*Hep. A, Polio, Typhoid, Malaria, Y. Fever[1], Meningitis*
Seychelles	*Hep. A, Polio, Typhoid, Y. Fever[2]*
Sierra Leone	*Hep. A, Polio, Typhoid, Malaria, Y. Fever[1], Meningitis*
Singapore	*Hep. A, Polio, Typhoid, Y. Fever[2]*
Slovak Republic	*Hep. A, Polio, Typhoid*
Slovenia	*Hep. A, Polio, Typhoid*

Solomon Islands	*Hep. A, Polio, Typhoid, Malaria, Y. Fever*[2]
Somalia	*Hep. A, Polio, Typhoid, Malaria, Y. Fever*[3]*, Meningitis*
South Africa	*Hep. A, Polio, Typhoid, Malaria, Y. Fever*[2]
Sri Lanka	*Hep. A, Polio, Typhoid, Malaria, Y. Fever*[2]
Sudan	*Hep. A, Polio, Typhoid, Malaria, Y. Fever*[3]*, Meningitis*
Surinam	*Hep. A, Polio, Typhoid, Malaria, Y. Fever*[3]
Swaziland	*Hep. A, Polio, Typhoid, Malaria, Y. Fever*[2]
Syria	*Hep. A, Polio, Typhoid, Malaria, Y. Fever*[2]
Taiwan	*Hep. A, Polio, Typhoid, Y. Fever*[2]
Tajikistan	*Hep. A, Polio, Typhoid, Malaria, Diphtheria*
Tanzania	*Hep. A, Polio, Typhoid, Malaria, Y. Fever*[3]*, Meningitis*
Thailand	*Hep. A, Polio, Typhoid, Malaria, Y. Fever*[2]
Togo	*Hep. A, Polio, Typhoid, Malaria, Y. Fever*[1]*, Meningitis*
Tonga	*Hep. A, Polio, Typhoid, Y. Fever*[2]
Trinidad & Tobago	*Hep. A, Typhoid, Y. Fever*[2]
Tunisia	*Hep. A, Polio, Typhoid, Y. Fever*[2]
Turkey	*Hep. A, Polio, Typhoid, Malaria*
Turkmenistan	*Hep. A, Polio, Typhoid, Malaria, Diphtheria*
Tuvalu	*Hep. A, Polio, Typhoid*
Uganda	*Hep. A, Polio, Typhoid, Malaria, Y. Fever*[3]*, Meningitis*
Ukraine	*Hep. A, Polio, Typhoid, Diphtheria*
United Arab Emirates	*Hep. A, Polio, Typhoid, Malaria*
Uruguay	*Hep. A, Typhoid*
Uzbekistan	*Hep. A, Polio, Typhoid, Diphtheria*
Vanuatu	*Hep. A, Polio, Typhoid, Malaria*
Venezuela	*Hep. A, Typhoid, Malaria, Y. Fever*
Vietnam	*Hep. A, Polio, Typhoid, Malaria, Y. Fever*[2]
Virgin Islands	*Hep. A, Typhoid*
Yemen	*Hep. A, Polio, Typhoid, Malaria, Y. Fever*[2]
Yugoslavia	*Hep. A, Polio, Typhoid*
Zambia	*Hep. A, Polio, Typhoid, Malaria, Y. Fever*
Zimbabwe	*Hep. A, Polio, Typhoid, Malaria, Y. Fever*[2]

City altitudes

Amsterdam (Netherlands)	5 *m*	Cape Town (South Africa)	8 *m*
Asuncion (Paraguay)	77	Caracas (Venezuela)	964
Athens (Greece)	0	Casablanca (Morocco)	49
Auckland (New Zealand)	0	Copenhagen (Denmark)	8
Bangkok (Thailand)	12	Damascus (Syria)	213
Beirut (Lebanon)	8	Frankfurt (Germany)	91
Bogota (Colombia)	2590	Geneva (Switzerland)	377
Buenos Aires (Argentina)	14	Glasgow (Scotland)	59

Guatemala City (Guatemala)	1478 *m*	Moscow (Russia)	191 *m*
Havana (Cuba)	9	Oslo (Norway)	12
Helsinki (Finland)	8	Panama City (Panama)	12
Istanbul (Turkey)	9	Quito (Ecuador)	2819
Jerusalem (Israel)	762	Rio de Janeiro (Brazil)	9
Kabul (Afghanistan)	2219	Rome (Italy)	14
Karachi (Pakistan)	15	Santiago (Chile)	550
La Paz (Bolivia)	3720	Stockholm (Sweden)	11
Lima (Peru)	153	Sydney (Australia)	8
Lisbon (Portugal)	87	Tegucigalpa (Honduras)	975
Madrid (Spain)	55	Tehran (Iran)	1220
Manila (Philippines)	8	Tokyo (Japan)	9
Mexico City (Mexico)	2240	Vienna (Austria)	168

Sea temperatures (°C)

	J	F	M	A	M	J	J	A	S	O	N	D
Algeria (Algiers)	15	14	15	15	17	20	23	24	23	21	18	16
Australia (Sydney)	23	24	23	20	18	18	16	17	18	19	19	21
Bahamas (Nassau)	23	23	23	24	25	27	28	28	28	27	26	24
Brazil (Rio de Janeiro)	25	25	26	25	24	23	22	22	22	22	23	24
Canada (Vancouver)	8	7	8	9	11	13	14	14	13	12	11	10
Canary Islands (Tenerife)	19	18	18	18	19	20	21	22	23	23	21	20
Croatia (Dubrovnik)	13	13	13	15	17	22	23	24	22	19	16	14
Denmark (Copenhagen)	3	2	3	5	9	14	16	16	14	12	8	5
Egypt (Cairo)	15	15	18	21	24	26	27	27	26	24	21	17
France (Nice)	13	12	13	14	16	20	22	23	21	19	16	14
French Polynesia (Tahiti)	27	27	27	28	28	27	26	26	26	26	27	27
Greece (Athens)	14	14	14	15	18	22	24	24	23	21	19	16
Greece (Corfu)	14	14	14	16	18	21	23	24	23	21	18	16
Hawaii (Honolulu)	24	24	24	25	26	26	27	27	27	27	26	25
Israel (Tel Aviv)	16	16	17	18	21	24	25	27	27	24	21	18
Italy (Naples)	14	13	14	15	18	21	24	25	23	21	18	16
Italy (Venice)	9	8	10	13	17	21	23	24	21	18	14	11
Jamaica (Kingston)	26	26	26	27	27	28	29	29	28	28	27	27
Kenya (Mombasa)	27	28	28	28	28	27	25	25	27	27	27	27
Majorca (Palma)	14	13	14	15	17	21	24	25	24	21	18	15
Malta (Valetta)	15	14	15	15	18	21	24	25	24	22	19	17
Mexico (Acapulco)	24	24	24	25	26	27	28	28	28	27	26	25
Morocco (Agadir)	17	17	18	18	19	19	22	22	22	22	21	18
New Zealand (Well'ton)	17	18	18	17	14	14	13	13	12	14	14	17
Portugal (Faro)	15	15	15	16	17	18	19	20	20	19	17	16
Spain (Barcelona)	13	12	13	14	16	19	22	24	22	21	16	1
Spain (Malaga)	15	14	14	15	17	18	21	22	21	19	17	16
Sweden (Stockholm)	3	1	1	2	5	10	15	15	13	10	7	4
Thailand (Bangkok)	26	27	27	28	28	28	28	28	28	27	27	27
Tunisia (Tunis)	15	14	14	15	17	20	21	22	23	23	21	20
Turkey (Istanbul)	8	8	8	11	15	20	22	23	21	19	15	11
USA (Los Angeles)	14	14	15	15	16	18	19	20	19	18	17	15
USA (Miami)	22	23	24	25	28	30	31	32	30	28	25	23
USA (New Orleans)	13	14	14	15	18	21	24	25	23	21	18	16
USA (San Francisco)	11	11	12	12	13	14	15	15	16	15	13	11

Preparing your trip

Useful websites

YOU WILL FIND USEFUL WEBSITES listed in every section of this Directory, relevant to the many specialist interests there.

By contrast, the websites listed below are for the more general traveller and could be useful for almost any kind of trip.

You might also like to check the special listings of global weather websites (page 828) and security information websites (page 831).

The Travellers' Handbook

www.travelleronline.com
Online version of *The Traveller's Handbook*. Also contains a library of Lonely Planet and Rough Guide guidebooks, *Traveller* magazine and trip-planning facilities.

Travellers' tips

www.tips4trips.com
Hundreds of travel tips by and for the international traveller.

www.vtourist.com
The Virtual Tourist - real travellers share their experiences.

www.geocities.com
Network of mostly local people living in various countries, who are willing to answer questions on their area.

Destination information

www.traveldex.co.uk
Efficient, quick site for checking destination details.

www.travel-guides.com
Travel virtually by clicking on the maps, get to your destination and get a comprehensive low-down.

www.traveldonkey.com
One-stop resource centre for travellers, and global database.

www.tourist-offices.org.uk
www.towd.com
The above two sites contain details of tourist offices world wide by destination, and where to find one country's offices in another country. Also links to country and destination sites.

www.officialtravelinfo.com
Destination overviews.

www.kropla.com
Help for world travellers, including a guide to electricity around the world.

www.national-holidays.com
Check here for details of public holidays worldwide.

www.isbister.com/worldtime
Find out the time anywhere in the world.

Foreign news

www.thepaperboy.com
www.onlinenewspapers.com
www.newsdirectory.com
The above three sites provide links to local newspapers around the world.

www.bbc.co.uk/worldservice
www.cnn.com/
World news coverage from the global networks - BBC and CNN, respectively.

Internet cafés

www.netcafeguide
Directory of cyber cafés around the world.

www.cybercaptive.com
Cyber cafés worldwide.

Finance

www.xe.net/ucc/
www.oanda.com
www.x-rates.com
The above three sites show currency rates and conversion guides.

www.travelex.co.uk
Buy foreign currency online and collect it at the airport

www.americanexpress.com
International information on travellers' cheques and flight insurance, plus links to currency converters.

www.trwl.com/visa.html
Part of the Thomas Cook travel money service, offering information on foreign currency, foreign cheque collection, travellers' cheques and currency guides.

www.globalrefund.com
Where and how to get hefty refunds on VAT when travelling.

www.Ftyourmoney.com
Information on currency rates, insurance deals, car-hire packages.

www.visa.com/pd/atm/main.html
www.mastercard.com/atm/
The above two sites locate ATM machines abroad.

Emergencies

http://travel.state.gov/judicial_assistance.html
How to get legal help when you're abroad, country-by-country.

See also: *Security information sources* (page 831) and individual country profiles in Part 4 for emergency contacts in each country.

Travel industry

www.airmiles.co.uk
Check your balance of airmiles - and find out about special offers.

http://flyaow.com
Links to almost every airline on the web.

www.travelsource.com
Free links to travel related businesses around the globe.

www.lastminute.com/
Late travel bargains.

www.airtickets.co.uk
Bookable discounted airfares.

Official representation

www.embpage.org
Contact details for embassies around the world

www.fco.gov.uk/links.asp
British Diplomatic Missions Finder

General interest

www.mumsnet.com
Good starting point for family travellers, with advice on flying with children and a bulletin board.

www.backpackessentials.com.au
Budget traveller's guide to the world.

www.artoftravel.com
Backpacker's guide to travel and travel guide books.

www.3.sympatico.ca/donna.mcsherry/airports.htm
Guide to sleeping in airports, for stranded or budget tavellers.

www.travel-library.com/rtw/html
The online guide to the ultimate trip - round the world.

www.charitychallenge.com
Travel and help charities at the same time.

www.dancexport.com
House and garage tracks, great graphics and info on deals in Europe's clubbing capitals.

www.ministryofsound.com
Click here to link up with their *Clubbers Guide to... Travel*

www.bikersadvice.co.uk
Good travelling tips for motor cyclists.

And finally

www.booktailor.com
Commercial service allowing you to create your own printed guidebook, based on information you choose from the internet.

Top travel periodicals

THERE ARE SURPRISINGLY FEW MAGAZINES devoted solely to travel journalism, but most ma stream magazines now include travel articles of one kind or another. This is partly because travel journalism is a hybrid genre, embracing aspects of consumer journalism ("What holiday shall I choose?"), literary writing ("I was there"), current affairs and foreign news. Many such outlets are included in the list below, alongside the specific travel titles.

Of the travel magazines, the best known in our listing are:

TRAVELLER Heavyweight and high-quality, closer to travel literature than consumer journalis Calls itself 'adventurous and authentic'. Grandaddy of the genre at 30 years old.

WANDERLUST In its first decade has established itself as the best practical magazine for adven turous travellers. Says it aims to help the 'free-spirited' traveller. Lively and useful.

CONDÉ NAST TRAVELLER Not to be confused with *Traveller*, this is the glamour-seeker's bibl Originally claimed to offer 'luxury on a budget'. Such stuff as dreams are made on.

NATIONAL GEOGRAPHIC Still the best in the world, though sometimes accused of blandness Explores the world in stunning photographs and highly accessible text.

For latest information on travel sections within national magazines and newspapers, check the *Writers' & Artists' Yearbook*, published annually by Black. This also has contact details for travel editors, as does the trade publication *Pimms United Kingdom Media Directory* (colo- quially known as 'PIMS'). If you are considering submitting your own work for publication, yo might find *The Writer's Handbook* (Macmillan/PEN) useful.

African Affairs
Prof. P. Woodward
Dept of Politics
University of Reading
PO Box 218
Reading, Berks
RG6 6AA, UK
Tel 0118 9875123
Quarterly journal,
featuring learned articles
on contemporary issues.

Australian Gourmet Traveller
Australian Consolidated
Press
PO Box 4088
54 Park Street
Sydney, NSW 2000
Australia
Tel 29 282 8000
Consumer publication for
travellers who enjoy food.

BBC Wildlife Magazine
Broadcasting House
Whiteladies Road
Bristol BS8 2LR, UK
Tel 0117 9732211
Monthly wildlife and
conservation issues.

BBC On Air Magazine
BBC World Service
227 NW Bush House
The Strand
London WC2B 4PH, UK
Tel 020 7557 2211
Monthly magazine with
world outlook and full
radio and television guide.

Bulletin Voyages
5115 Degaspe St 330
Montreal H2T 3B7
Canada
Tel 514 287 9773
Web www.acra.com

Business Traveller
Condor House
5-14 St Paul's Churchyard
London EC4V 5AA, UK
Tel 020 7580 9898
Web www.
businesstraveller.com
Monthly magazine aimed
at the business traveller
and featuring airfare cost-
cutting information.

Canadian Geographic
39 McArthur Avenue
Vanier
Ontario K1L 8L7
Canada
Tel 613 745 4629
Web www.
canadiangeographic.ca

Camping and Caravanning
Greenfields House
Westwood Way
Coventry CV4 8JH, UK
Tel 02476 694995
Web www.campingand
caravaningclub.co.uk
Monthly journal for
enthusiasts.

Condé Nast Traveller
Vogue House
1 Hanover Square
London W1S 1JU, UK
Tel 020 7499 9080
also at
4 Times Square
New York
NY 10036, USA
Tel 212 286 2860
Web www.
cntraveller.co.uk
See introduction to this
section.

Escape Routes
3rd Floor
Endeavour House
189 Shaftesbury Avenue
London WC2H 8JG, UK
www.escaperoutes.net
Tel 020 7437 9011
Fax 020 7208 3740
New magazine offering
practical information on
mainstream destinations,
aimed particularly at
women and families.

Essentially America
Phoenix Publishing and
Media Ltd
18-20 Scrutton Street
London EC2A 4TG, UK
Tel 020 7247 0537
Web www.
phoenix.wits.co.uk
Bi-monthly consumer
magazine on lifestyle and
travel in USA and Canada.

Explore
Suite 420
301-14 St N.W.
Calgary, Alberta
Canada T2N 2A1
Tel 403 270 8890
Web www.
explore-mag.com
Quarterly colour magazine
devoted to adventure travel
world-wide.

The Explorers Journal
The Explorers' Club
46 East 70th St
New York
NY 10021 , USA
Tel 212 799 6473
email
EXJOURNAL@aol.com
Official quarterly of The
Explorers Club. Established
1904. Interdisciplinary in
scope, highlights all areas of
exploration work.

Flight International
Reed Business Information
Oakfield House
Perrymount Road

Haywards Heath
West Sussex RH16 3DH,
UK
Tel 01444 445566
Web www.
reedbusiness.com
Highly respected weekly
journal covering everything
to do with the aviation
industry – both
commercial and military.

Food and Travel
51a George Street
Richmond
Surrey TW9 1HJ, UK
www.foodandtravel.com
Tel 020 8332 9090
Fax 020 8332 9991
Monthly glossy magazine
reporting on both topics
from around the world.

Geographical
47C Kensington Court
London W8 5DA
7 Chalcott Street
London NW1 8LX, UK
Tel 020 7938 4011
email magazine@
geographical.co.uk
Monthly magazine of the
Royal Geographical
Society. High quality
articles on geography,
exploration, travel.

Globe
The Globetrotters Club
BCM/Roving
London WC1N 3XX, UK
Newsletter of independent
travellers' club. Articles on
individual experiences,
news of members on the
move, tips, mutual-aid
column for members.

Great Expeditions
PO Box 64699
Station G
Vancouver
BC V6R 4GT, Canada
Tel 604 734 3938
For people who want to
travel and explore, offers

trips, a free classified ads
service, discounts on
books, an information
exchange, articles and
travel notes.

The Great Outdoors
SMG Magazines
200 Renfields Street
Glasgow G2 3PR, UK
Tel 0141 302 7700
Email tgo@calmags.co.uk
Monthly publication
featuring walking,
backpacking and
countryside matters.

Holiday Which?
2 Marylebone Road
London NW1 4DX
Tel 020 7830 6000
Web www.which.net
Excellent consumer issues
magazine, published by the
Consumers' Association.

Islands
3886 State Street
Santa Barbara
CA 93105
USA
Tel 805 682 7177
Glossy colour title devoted
to the world's islands, large
and small.

International Travel News
Martin Publications Inc
2120 28th Street
Sacramento
CA 95818, USA
Tel 916 457 3643
Web www.
intltravelnews.com
Email itn@ns.net
News source for the
business and/or pleasure
traveller who often goes
abroad. Contributions
mostly from readers. Free
sample copy on request.

The Lady
39-40 Bedford Street
The Strand
London WC2E 9ER, UK

Tel 020 7379 4717
Web www.lady.co.uk
Classified ads in this weekly
publication can be a useful
source for self-catering
accommodation and some
overseas jobs.

Lonely Planet Newsletter
Lonely Planet Publications
10A Spring Place
London NW5 3BH, UK
Tel 020 7428 4800
Web www.
lonelyplanet.com
Email go@
lonelyplanet.co.uk
Quarterly newsletter giving
updates on LP guidebooks
and lots of useful tips from
other travellers.

Mountain Biking UK
Beaufort Court
30 Monmouth St
Bath BA1 2BW, UK
Tel 01225 442244
Web www.futurenet.com
Monthly publication for
mountain bikers.

National Geographic
National Geographic
Society
1145 17th St, NW
Washington DC 20036-
4688, USA
Tel 202 857 7000
Web www.
nationalgeographic.com
See introduction to this
section.

*National Geographic
Traveller*
3000 University Center
Drive, Tampa
Florida 33612, USA
Tel 813 979 6625
Web
www.time.cust.serve.com
Quarterly consumer title
from the *National
Geographic* stable devoted
to travel and destination
reports.

New York Times website
website www.
nytimes.com/pages/travel
Register here to read some
classic travel writing.

Nomad
BCM-Nomad
London WC1V 6XX, UK
Newsletter aimed at people
on the move and written by
peripatetic publisher, with
many readers' reports.

Official Airlines Guide
Church Street
Dunstable
Bedfordshire LU5 4HB, UK
Tel 01582 600111
Web www.oag.com
Monthly airline timetable
in pocket format.

Outside Magazine
400 Market St
Santa Fe
Mexico 87501
Tel 505 9897100
Web www.outsidemag.com
Contemporary lifestyle
magazine featuring
adventure travel, sports,
fitness and photography.

The Railway Magazine
King's Reach Tower
Stamford Street
London SE1 9LS, UK
Tel 020 7261 5533
Email railway@
ipcmedia.com
Monthly established 1897.

Resident Abroad
Maple House
149 Tottenham Court Rd
London W1 P9LL, UK
Tel 020 7896 2525
Web www.ra.st.com
Monthly publication for
British expatriates.

Rough News
Rough Guides
62-70 Shorts Gdn
London WC2H 9AH

Tel 020 7556 5000
Web www.
roughguides.com
Newsletter of the Rough
Guides. Thrice-yearly.

Salon website
www.salon.com./travel
'Wanderlust' section of this
online magazine used to
contain some top travel
journalism – now it is
accessible through an
archive search.

*The South American
Explorer*
South American Explorers
Club , Casilla 3714
Lima 100, Peru
Web www.samexplo.org
Official journal of the
South American Explorers
Club. Accounts of scientific
studies, adventure, and
sports activities in South
America.

South East Asia Traveller
Compass Publishing
336 Smith Street
04-303 New Bridge Centre
Chinatown
Singapore 0105
Tel 221 1111
Glossy title geared at
frequent and business
travellers to the region.

Time Off
Time Off Publications
60 Berwick Street
Fortitude Valley
QLD 4006
Australia
Tel 7-252 9761

Travel and Leisure
1120 Avenue of the
Americas
New York
NY 10036, USA
Tel 212 382 5600
Web www.amexpub.com
Glossy title for American
Express members.

Travel Trade Gazette
United Business Media
City Reach
5 Greenwich View Place
Millharbour
London E14 9NN, UK
Tel 020 8861 6102
Email abergin@
unitedbusinessmedia.com
Weekly travel industry
newspaper.

Traveller
WEXAS International
45-49 Brompton Road
Knightsbridge
London SW3 1DE, UK
Tel 020 7581 4130
www.traveller.org.uk
See introduction to this
section.

Travel Smart
40 Beechdale Road
Dobbs Ferry
NY 10522, USA
Tel 914 693 8300
Web www.
travelsmartnews@aol.com
Newsletter for affluent
travellers.

Traveltips
PO Box 580188
Flushing
NY 11358, USA
Tel 718 939 2400
Web www.travltips.com
Email info@travltips.com
First-person accounts of
freighter and passenger
ship travel. Bi-monthly
publication includes
updated listing of
passenger-carrying
freighters, primarily
embarking in US ports.

Wanderlust
PO Box 1832
Windsro SL4 1YT, UK
Tel 01753 620426
website www.
wanderlust.co.uk
See the introduction to this
section.

Book and map sources

AA Publishing
Forum House
Priestly Road
Basingstoke
Hants RG21 2EA, UK
Tel 01256 491538
Web www.theaa.co.uk
Guide and map publishers
and distributors including
the Baedeker guides.

A & C Black
35 Bedford Row
London WC1R 4JH
Tel 020 7242 0946, UK
Web www.acblack.co.uk
Email postmaster@
acblack.co.uk
Publishes the Blue Guides.

John Bartholomew/Times
77-85 Fulham Palace Road
London W6 8JB, UK
Tel 020 8741 7070
Web www.
fireandwater.com
Tourist, road, topographic
andgeneral maps, atlases
and guides.

B.T.Batsford Ltd
9 Blenheim Court
Brewery Rd
London N7 9NT, UK
Tel 020 77007611
Email btbatsford@
crysalis books.co.uk
Guides and topographical
publications.

BBC Worldwide
80 Wood Lane
London W12 0TT, UK
Tel 020 8576 2000
Web www.
bbbcworldwide.com
Publishes books mainly
related to TV and radio
series. Also publishes
language learning books
and materials.

BFP Books
Focus House
497 Green Lanes
London N13 4BP, UK
Tel 020 8882 3315
Web www.thebfp.com
Email info@thebfp.com
Publishers of the industry
guide, *The Freelance
Photographer's Market
Handbook.*

Blackwell Map & Travel Bookshop
50 Broad Street
Oxford OX1 3BU, UK
Tel 01865 792792
Web www.
bookshop.blackwells.co.uk
Excellent selection of books
and knowledgeable staff.

The Booksellers' Association
Minster House
272-4 Vauxhall Bridge
Road
London SW1W 1BA, UK
Tel 020 7834 5477
Email 100437.2261@
compuserve.com
Web www.
booksellers.org.uk
Publishes an annual
directory of members
detailing information on
bookshops nationwide.

Books Etc.
26 James St
Covent Garden
London WC2E 8PA, UK
Tel 020 7379 6947
Central branch of a mainly
London-based chain, with
good travel sections.

Bradt Publications
Travel Guides
19 High Street
Chalfont St Peter
Bucks SL9 9QE, UK
Tel 01494 873478
Email info@
bradt_travelguides.com
Travel guides for the
adventurous traveller.

THE BRITISH CARTOGRAPHIC SOCIETY
Hon Membership Secretary
JK Atherton
12 Elworthy Drive
Wellington
Somerset TA21 9AT, UK
Tel 01823 663 965

CADOGAN GUIDES
West End House
11 Hills Place
London W1R 1AG, UK
Tel 020 7287 6555
Email cadoganguides@
morrispub.co.uk
Travel guide series.

CENTURY
Random House
20 Vauxhall Bridge Road
London SW1V 2SA, UK
Tel 020 7840 8400
Web www.
randomhouse.co.uk
Publishes travel narratives.

CHATTO & WINDUS LTD
Random House
20 Vauxhall Bridge Road
London SW1V 2SA, UK
Tel 020 7840 8400
Web www.
randomhouse.co.uk
Includes archaeology and
travel books.

CICERONE PRESS
2 Police Square
Milnthorpe
Cumbria LA7 7PY, UK
Tel 01539 562069
Web www.cicerone.co.uk
Email info@
cicerone.demon.co.uk
Outdoor books.

COLUMBUS TRAVEL GUIDES
Jordan House
47 Brunswick Place
London N1 6EB, UK
Tel 020 7608 6666
Fax 020 7608 6569
Website booksales@
columbus-group.co.uk
Publish *The World Travel
Guide*, the travel agents'
bible. Also atlases.

THE CROWOOD PRESS
The Stable Block
Crowood Lane
Ramsbury
Marlborough
Wilts SN8 2HR, UK
Tel 01672 520320
Web www.crowood.com
Email enquiries@
crowood.com
Mountaineering and
climbing books.

DAUNT BOOKS
83 Marylebone High Street
London W1M 3DE, UK
Tel 020 7224 2295
Email orders@
dauntbooks.com
Comprehensive travel
bookshop plus much else.
Mail order service.

**DEPARTMENT OF DEFENSE
AND MAPPING AGENCY**
Hydrographic Center
Washington, DC 20315
USA
Publishes charts of oceans
and coasts of all areas of the
world, and pilot charts.

FOOTPRINT HANDBOOKS
6 Riverside Court
Lower Bristol Road
Bath BA2 3DZ, UK
Tel 01225 469141
Web www.
footprintbooks.co.uk
Email handbooks@
footprint.cix.co.uk
High-quality guidebooks
for independent travellers,
including the famous *South
American Handbook*.

FOYLES
Travel Department
Ground Floor
119 Charing Cross Road
London WC2H 0EB, UK
Tel 020 7437 5660
Email sales@foyles.co.uk
Famous English bookshop.
Mail order available.

FODORS
20 Vauxhall Bridge Road

London SW1V 2SA
Tel 020 7840 8400
Fax 020 233 6058
website www.fodors.com
Guidebook publisher. The
website can be used to
generate itineraries based
on destination and budget.

FROMMERS
909 3rd Avenue
21st Floor
New York, NY 10022, USA
website
www.frommers.com
Leading publisher of
guidebooks. Website
features, specialist travel
sections and message
boards.

GLOBE PEQUOT PRESS
PO Box 480, Guilford
CT 06347-0480, USA
Tel 203 4584582
Email info@
globe-pequot.com
Web www.
globe-pequot.com
Good travel-only publisher,
especially on USA/Canada.

THE GOOD BOOK GUIDE
24 Seward Street
London EC1V 3PB, UK
Tel 020 7490 0900
Web www.
thegoodbookguide.com
Email enquiries@
gbgdirect.com
World-wide mail order
service based on *Good Book
Guide* catalogue.

HATCHARDS
187 Piccadilly
London W1V 0LE, UK
Tel 020 7439 9921
Web www.hatchards.co.uk
Email
books@hatchards.co.uk
Classic English bookshop.

HEFFERS
20 Trinity Street
Cambridge CB2 1TY, UK
Tel 01223 568400
Web www.heffers.co.uk

Email enquiries@
heffers.co.uk
Very good selection of
travel guides and books.

HIPPOCRENE BOOKS
171 Madison Avenue
New York, NY 10016, USA
Tel 718 454 2366
Web www.hippocrene.com
Email orders@
hippocrene.com
Publishers of travel guides,
international literature
and dictionaries.

HODDER HEADLINE
338 Euston Road
London NW1 3BH
Tel 020 7873 6000
Web www.hodder.co.uk
Publish mountaineering
and climbing narratives
plus Which? travel guides.

**HYDROGRAPHIC DEPT
UK MINISTRY OF DEFENCE
(NAVY)**
Admiralty Way
Taunton
Somerset TA1 2DN, UK
Tel 01823 337900
Publishes a global series of
Admiralty Charts and
hydrographic publications
used by the British Navy.
Available from appointed
Admiralty Chart Agencies.

ITCHY FEET
4 Bartlett St
Bath BA1 2Q2, UK
Tel 01225 337987
Web www.
itchyfeet online.com
Good range of guides,
maps and gear.

INSIGHT GUIDES
Geocenter international
The Viables Centre
Harrow Way
Basingstoke
Hants RG22 4BJ, UK
Tel 01256 817987

**INSTITUT GÉOGRAPHIQUE
NATIONAL**
107 Rue la Boétie

75008 Paris, France
Tel 1 43 98 80 00
Publish and sell maps of
France and many former
French possessions. Mail
order also available.

JAMES THIN LTD
53-59 South Bridge
Edinburgh EH1 1YS, UK
Tel 0131 5566743
Web www.jthin.co.uk
Email orders@jthin.co.uk
The largest of a UK
bookshop chain with good
travel sections.

KUMMERLY UND FREY LTD
Alpenstrasse 58
3052 Zollekofen
Switzerland
Tel 31 915 2211
Web www.swissmaps.ch
Publish charts and
political, topographic, road
and other maps.

LATITUDE
34 The Broadway
Darkes Lane, Potters Bar
Herts EN6 2HW, UK
Tel 01707 663090
Web www.latitude
mapsandglobes.co.uk
Email enquiries@
latitudemaps.demon.co.uk
Map and globe specialist
which also produces a mail
order catalogue.

**LONELY PLANET
PUBLICATIONS**
10A Spring Place
London NW5 3BH, UK
Tel 020 7428 4800
Web www.
lonelyplanet.com
Email go@
lonelyplanet.co.uk
Possibly the world's largest
guidebook publisher.
Extensive selection of off-
beat guidebooks, plus
health and food guides. The
website allows you to swap
tips at 'The Thorn Tree'.

MAPBLAST WEBSITE
www.mapblast.com
World wide maps and
driving directions.

MAP MARKETING
92-104 Carnwath Road
London SW6 3HW, UK
Tel 020 7526 2322
Web www.
mapmarketing.com
Email sales@
mapmarketing.com
Over 400 laminated maps,
framed or unframed,
including world maps,
country maps and over 300
section maps of the UK.

MAPQUEST WEBSITE
www.mapquest.com
Print out maps of most
major cities in the world.

THE MAP SHOP
15 High Street
Upton-upon- Severn
Worcs WR8 OHJ, UK
Tel 01684 593146
Web www.
themapshop.co.uk
Email themappshop@
btinternet.com
Agent for Ordnance Survey,
stocks large-scale maps and
guides worldwide. Send for
free catalogue by area.

MAPSWORLDWIDE WEBSITE
website www.
mapsworldwide.co.uk
Cut-price maps.

MICHELIN MAPS & GUIDES
Edward Hyde Building
38 Clarendon Road
Watford WD1 1SX, UK
Tel 01923 415000
Web www.michelin.co.uk
Email webinfo@
uk.michelin.com
Publish excellent maps and
the Red and Green Guides.

JOHN MURRAY
50 Albermarle Street
London W1S 4BD, UK
Tel 020 7493 4361
Email johnmurray.

genmark@dial.pipex.com
Publishes the Literary
Companion series and
excellent travel literature.

MOON PUBLICATIONS
PO Box 3040, Chico
CA95927-3040, USA
Tel 191 634 55473
website www.moon.com
Travel handbook
publishers, excerpted on
their webiste.

**NATIONAL GEOGRAPHIC
SOCIETY**
1145 17th St, NW
Washington
DC 20036-4688, USA
Tel 202 857 7000
Web www.
nationalgeographic.com
Publish maps to
accompany *National
Geographic* magazine.
Also sell atlases and globes,
magazines and books.

**THE NATIONAL MAP
CENTRE**
22-24 Caxton Street
London SW1H 0QU, UK
Tel 020 7222 2466
Web www.mapstore.co.uk
Email info@
mapsnmc.com
Main agent for Ordnance
Survey maps, and retailers
for all major publishers.

**THE NATIONAL OCEAN
SERVICE**
NOAA Distribution
Branch N/CG33
6501 Lafayette Ave
Riverdale
Maryland 20737, USA
Tel 301 436 6990
Email distribution@
noaa.gov
Publishes arial charts of the
USA and sells charts of
foreign areas published by
the Defense Mapping
Agency Aerospace Center.

NOMAD
781 Fulham Road

London SW6 5HA, UK
Tel 020 7736 4000
Email nomadbooks@
yahoo.co.uk
Travel book basement.

OAG
Church Street
Dunstable
Beds LU5 4HB, UK
Tel 01582-600111
Email central@oag.co.uk
Publishes a comprehensive
range of guides geared
towards the professional
travel planner.

ORDNANCE SURVEY
Romsey Road, Maybush
Southampton SO16 4GU
UK
Tel 02380 792416
Official mapping agency
for the UK. The Overseas
Surveys Directorate at the
same address publishes
maps of former and
current British possessions.

**PALLAS ATHENE
PUBLICATIONS**
59 Linden Gardens
London W2 4HJ, UK
Tel 020 7229 2798
Historical and cultural
guides to European cities.

DICK PHILLIPS
Whitehall House
Nenthead, Alston
Cumbria CA9 3PS, UK
Tel 01434 381440
Specialises in books and
maps of Iceland and Faroe.

GEORGE PHILIP & SON LTD
2-4 Heron Quay
London E14 4JP, UK
020 75318400
Web www.
philips-maps.co.uk
Email george philip@
philips-maps.co.uk
Publish a wide range of
topographical and thematic
maps, atlases and charts.

NIGEL PRESS ASSOCIATES
Crockham Park

Edenbridge
Kent TN8 6SR, UK
Tel 01732 865023
Web www.npagroup.com
Email info@
npagroup.com
Offers free satellite images
to *bona fide* expeditions.
Large archive covers most
of the world.

RAC PUBLISHING
RAC House
PO Box 100
Bartlett Street
South Croydon
Surrey CR2 6XW, UK
Tel 020 8686 0088
Publishers of guides,
handbooks and maps for
motorists and travellers in
the UK and the Continent.

**RALLYMAPS OF WEST
WELLOW**
PO Box 11. Romsey
Hampshire S051 8XX, UK
Tel 01794 515444
Web www.
rallymap.demon.co.uk
Email mike@
rallymap.demon.co.uk
Mail order specialists for
Ordnance Survey.

RAND MCNALLY & CO
8255 North Central Park
Ave, Skokie
Illinois 60076, USA
Tel 847 329 8100
Web www.
randmcnally.com
Large publisher of maps,
atlases, guides and globes.

ROGER LASCELLES
47 York Road
Brentford
Middlesex TW8 0QP, UK
Tel 020 8847 0935
Guide and map publisher
and distributor.

ROUGH GUIDES
1 Mercer Street
London WC2H 9QJ, UK
Tel 020 7379 3329
email mail@

roughguides.co.uk
Web www.
roughguides.com
Excellent travel guide series
for independent travellers,
also specialist in world
music guides and CDs.
Website includes 3,500
places and an e-zine of
articles and travel tips.

**ROYAL GEOGRAPHICAL
SOCIETY**
Publications Dept
1 Kensington Gore
London SW7 2AR, UK
Tel 020 7589 5466
Email maps@rgs.org
Sells maps from the
Geographical Journal, also
maps published separately
by the Society.

STANFORDS
12-14 Long Acre
London WC2 9LP, UK
Tel 020 7836 1321
Email sales@
stanfords.co.uk
The largest map seller in
the world, stocking a wide
range of maps, guides,
globes, charts and atlases.
Also in Bristol.

THAMES AND HUDSON
181a High Holborn
London WC1V 7QX, UK
Tel 020 7845 5000
Web www.
thameshudson.co.uik
Publisher of high-quality
illustrated books on world
cultures, usually of
academic standard, with
lavish photographs.

TIME OUT
Universal House
251 Tottenham Court Road
London W1P OAB
Tel 020 7813 3000
Fax 020 7813 6001
www.timeout.com
London-based listings
magazine with growing list
of international
guidebooks. Website is

updated monthly.

**TRAILFINDERS TRAVEL
CENTRE**
194 Kensington High St
London W8 7RG, UK
Tel 020 7938 3999
Stocks guides and maps as
well as travel equipment.

THE TRAVEL BOOKSHOP
13 Blenheim Crescent
London W11 2EE
Tel 020 7229 5260
Web www.
thetravelbookshop.co.uk
Email post@
thetravelbookshop.co.uk
Long-established and
dedicated travel bookshop.
Provides a 'complete
literary package' for the
traveller, including regional
guides, histories, cookery
books, relevant fiction and
so on. Also stocks old and
new maps and
topographical prints.

**ULYSSES TRAVEL
PUBLICATIONS**
4176 St. Denis
Montréal
Quebec H2W 2M5
Canada
Tel 514 843 9882
Email info@ulysses.ca
www.ulyssesguides.com
Guidebooks for
independent travellers.
Bookstores in Montréal
and Toronto.

**US DEPARTMENT OF
THE INTERIOR**
Geological Survey
Earth Science Information
Center (ESIC)
507 National Center
Reston, VA 20192, USA
Tel 703 648 5577
Web www.usgs.gov
Information about maps
and related data for US.

**VACATION WORK
PUBLICATIONS**
9 Park End Street

Oxford OX1 1HJ, UK
Tel 01865 241 978
Web www.
vacationwork.co.uk
Publishers of books for
budget travellers and for
anyone wanting to work or
study abroad.

WATERSTONES
82 Gower Street
London WC1E 6EQ, UK
Tel 020 7636 1577
Web www.
waterstones.co.uk
Email enquiries@
gowerst.waterstones.co.uk
Has a good travel section in
the basement. Branches
throughout the UK.

WILDERNESS PRESS
2440 Bancroft Way
Berkeley CA 94704, USA
Tel 415 843 8080
Natural history, adventure
travel guides and maps of
North America.

YHA BOOKSHOPS
14 Southampton Street
London WC2E 7HY, UK
Tel 020 7836 8541
Web www.
yhaadventure.co.uk
Books, maps, guides and
gear for backpackers,
hostellers, adventure
sportsmen and budget
travellers.

Web-only booksellers

AMAZON
www.amazon.co.uk
Pioneering website with
huge range of books on all
subjects.

THE INTERNET BOOKSHOP
www.bookshop.co.uk

ALPHABET STREET
www.alphabetstreet.infront
.co.uk

Recommended reading

O NE OF THE BEST WAYS to make any journey enjoyable and rewarding is to read up about the culture and history of your destination. Anyone can buy a guidebook, but the books listed below will add depth and quality to your travels. They are sorted by world regions.

You might also browse through *Anderson's Travel Companion*, a guide to the travel literature of the world. It was written by Sarah Anderson, founder of the Travel Bookshop in London, who has chosen the selection below.

Books are listed by region, as follows: Africa p 848, Americas p 850, Middle East p 852, Asia p 853, Australasia p 857, Europe p 857, Polar p 862.

NORTH AFRICA

Travels in Asia and Africa 1325-1354
Ibn Battuta
Ibn Battuta was born in Tangier and as a good Muslim made a pilgrimage to Mecca.

Letter from Egypt
Lucie Duff-Gordon
The author spent seven years in a ruined house in Luxor in the 1860s.

The Pyramids of Egypt
I.E.S.Edwards
One of the classic books on Egyptian archaeology.

Hideous Kinky
Esther Freud
Esther Freud was taken by her hippy mother to Morocco during the 1960s, aged five.

Morocco That Was
Walter Harris
Harris arrived in Tangier in 1886 and became the *Times* correspondent there until 1933.

Cairo Trilogy
Naguib Mahfouz
(*Palace Walk*, *Palace of Desire* and *Sugar Sweet*)
One of the most widely read authors and winner of the Nobel prize in 1988.

A Year in Marrakesh
Peter Mayne
Mayne lived in a small house in Marrakesh and wrote this book (originally published as *The Alleys of Marrakesh*) from his observations.

A Cure for Serpents
Duke of Pirajno
Pirajno arrived in North Africa as a doctor and stayed 18 years. His collection of reminiscences and stories makes wonderful reading.

In the Pharoah's Shadow
Anthony Sattin
A look at the ancient customs which survive in today's Egypt.

Old Serpent Nile
Stanley Stewart
A journey from the Nile Delta to the Mountains of the Moon.

WEST AFRICA

The Innocent Anthropologist
Nigel Barley
The hilarious account of Barley's first field trip to the Dowayo in the Cameroons.

A Good Man in Africa
William Boyd
A very funny novel set in Ghana and Nigeria.

The Viceroy of Ouidah
Bruce Chatwin
A poor Brazilian sailed to Dahomey (now Benin) in the early 1800s, determined to make his fortune and return triumphantly to Brazil.

Difficult and Dangerous Roads
Hugh Clapperton
Clapperton was one of the first British explorers to enter the central Sahara - this is the account of his travels in the Sahara and Fezzan in 1822-1825.

The Overloaded Ark
Gerald Durrell
Durrell's first book is about an expedition to the Cameroons to collect animals for his zoo.

Journey Without Maps
Graham Greene
This journey across Liberia with his cousin Barbara was Greene's first book.

Mali Blues
Lieve Joris
Four different tales of travelling through Senegal, Mauritania and Mali.

The Famished Road
Ben Okri
A lyrical and compelling book, full of flights of fancy, but also instructive about life in a village.

EAST AFRICA

Out of Africa
Karen Blixen
In 1914 Karen Blixen went to Kenya to run a coffee farm which failed. The friends and animals that she met are vividly portrayed, and we share her sense of loss both for the farm and, in a wider sense, for an era.

White Mischief
James Fox
The 'Happy Valley' clique in Kenya was thrown into confusion when Lord Erroll, founder of the set, was murdered in 1941.

I Dreamed of Africa
Kuki Gallmann
A haunting memoir capturing the magic, beauty and pain of Kenya.

The Weather in Africa
Martha Gellhorn
Three novellas set in East Africa: *On the Mountain*, *By the Sea* and *In the Highlands*.

Warriors
Gerald Hanley
Gerald Hanley spent several years in Somalia, where he got to know the local people very well.

The Flame Trees of Thika
Elspeth Huxley
Elspeth Huxley went with her parents to Thika to become pioneering settlers among the Kikuyu.

North of South
Shiva Naipaul
A brilliant travel narrative about journeying through Kenya, Tanzania and Zambia. Naipaul was extremely observant with a novelist's eye for detail.

Scoop
Evelyn Waugh
Journalist William Boot is sent mistakenly to Ishmaelia by press baron Lord Copper, to cover a war. As Boot blunders along, this becomes an hilarious satire on Fleet Street and war reporting.

CENTRAL AND SOUTHERN AFRICA

My Gorilla Journey
Helen Attwater
The author and her husband set up an orphanage for baby gorillas in the Congo.

The Rainbird
Jan Brokken
Travelling through the jungles of Gabon, Brokken is haunted by the hosts of his predecessors.

Heart of Darkness
Joseph Conrad
Conrad went to the Belgian Congo in 1890 to captain a river steamer, and it became the setting for this compelling novel.

My Traitor's Heart
Rian Malan
An extraordinarily powerful book about the reality of being brought up in South Africa.

Long Walk to Freedom
Nelson Mandela
Mandela's riveting memoirs recreate the experiences that helped shape his destiny.

The Ukimwi Road
Dervla Murphy
'Ukimwi' of the title is AIDS. Dervla Murphy made a 3,000-mile bicycle journey from Kenya through Uganda, Tanzania, Malawi and Zambia to Zimbabwe.

A Bend in the River
VS Naipaul
Salim travels to the town on a bend in the river and this is the story of his life as a trader in that town, a place which comes vividly alive in Naipaul's prose.

Congo Journey
Redmond O'Hanlon
A gut-wrenching adventure that is also filled with scholarly observations on natural history.

Cry the Beloved Country
Alan Paton
Even today this book remains one of the classics written about racial tension in South Africa.

AFRICAN ISLANDS

Paradise
Abdulrazek Gurnah
Set around Zanzibar in the early years of European involvement. Yusuf, a Muslim boy, is taken into the service of his merchant uncle and, through his eyes, we see the Europeans as colonisers.

Muddling Through in Madagascar
Dervla Murphy
Dervla Murphy travelled through Madagascar with her 14-year-old daughter Rachel.

Lemurs of the Lost World
Jane Wilson
An exploration of the forests and crocodile caves of Madagascar.

NORTH AMERICA

The New York Trilogy
Paul Auster
The trilogy consists of *City of Glass*, *Ghosts* and *The Locked Room* and has been described as 'A shatteringly clever piece of work'.

America Day by Day
Simone de Beauvoir
A fascinating record of de Beauvoir's first impressions of the US.

Midnight in the Garden of Good and Evil
John Berendt
Written as a novel, but based on the true eccentrics of Savannah, Georgia.

A Lady's Life in the Rockie Mountains
Isabella Bird
In 1873 Isabella Bird rode through the Wild West, meeting her 'dear (one-eyed) desperado', Rocky Mountain Jim, whom she described as 'a man any woman might love, but no sane woman would marry'.

The Penguin History of the United States of America
Hugh Brogan
A complete general history of the States, starting from British colonisation and ending at the fall of Nixon.

New York Days, New York Nights
Stephen Brook
Amusing and energetic observations of New York.

Bury My Heart at Wounded Knee
Dee Brown
The epic bestseller which tells the Indians' side of the Wild West story through the voices of such as Sitting Bull, Cochise, Crazy Horse and Geronimo.

The Lost Continent
Bill Bryson
Born in Des Moines, Bryson left as soon as he could, but after ten years in England he was lured back and drove around small-town America producing an hilarious acount of his travels.

Notes from a Big Country
Bill Bryson
Having lived in the UK for many years, Bryson at last returns to America with his family.

Almost Heaven
Martin Fletcher
An original look at the weird and wonderful things of small-town America.

Cold Mountain
Charles Frazer
A soldier wounded in the Civil War leaves for the long journey home to Ada, the the woman he had loved.

On the Road
Jack Kerouac
The classic book about Fifties underground America which has become the epitome of the Beat generation.

Into the Wild
Jon Krakauer
Chris McCandless disappeared in Alaska having reinvented himself andgiven all his possessions to charity. Why?

The Oatmeal Ark
Rory Maclean
The author traces his great-grandfather's voyage from Shetland to Nova Scotia and across Canada.

River Horse
William Least-Heat Moon
Moon's bid to cross America by its interior waterways rivals his previous book *Blue Highways*.

A Turn in the South
VS Naipaul
Naipaul aims to come to terms with themany complexities of the South, with all its paradoxes and contradictions.

Penguin Book of American Short Stories
Includes gems by Washington Irving, John Updike, Ambrose Bierce, Willa Cather, Herman Melville, Mark Twain and many others.

The Shipping News
E Annie Proulx
Pulitzer Prize-winning book about fishing and newspaper life in Newfoundland.

Old Glory
Jonathan Raban
Inspired by memories of reading *Huckleberry Finn* as a child, Jonathan Raban takes a boat up the Mississippi.

Life on the Mississippi
Mark Twain
Nostalgic and humourous mixture of journalism and autobiography, written in the heyday of steamboating on the Mississippi. Twain's love of the river shines through his prose.

CENTRAL AND SOUTH AMERICA AND CARIBBEAN

The House of the Spirits
Isabel Allende
A family saga spanning four generations in Chile. Full of unforgettable characters, spirits, history and forces of nature.

A Visit to Don Otavio
Sybille Bedford
Sybille Bedford describes the horrors of her train journey to Mexico in graphic detail.

Collected Fictions
Jorge Luis Borges
A collection of subtly ingenious stories.

In Patagonia
Bruce Chatwin
Chatwin never forgot the piece of skin with strands of hair from a Patagonian brontosaurus, which he found in his grandmother's cabinet; it was this that eventually inspired him to go to Patagonia.

Breaking the Maya Code
Michael D Coe
It is only in the last 20 years that the code to Mayan hieroglyphs has been discovered. This is a fascinating account of how it was done.

One River
Wade Davis
Science adventure and hallucinations in the Amazon basin.

The Spears of Twilight
Philippe Descola
Life and death in the Amazon jungle: modern anthropology at its best.

Havana Dreams
Wendy Gimbel
Four generations of Cuban women - one of whom is the illegitimate daughter of Fidel Castro.

The Lawless Roads
Graham Greene
Greene was commissioned to go to Mexico in 1938 to find out how people had reacted to the religious persecution and anti-clerical purges of the then President Calles. His trip formed the basis for *The Powr and the Glory*.

The Power and the Glory
Graham Greene
The 'whisky' priest of Greene's novel had done everything wrong in the eyes of the Church: taken a 'wife', fathered a daughter, had an addiction to brandy -and yet obstinately remained a priest.

Amazon Frontier
John Hemming
A definitive account, full of original research covering the period from the mid-eighteenth to the early twentieth century.

Personal Narrative of a Journey to the Equinoctial Regions of the New Continent
Alexander von Humboldt
From his youth, von Humboldt had been devoted to the study of nature and 'experienced in my travels, enjoyments which have amply compensated for the privations inseparable from a laborious and often agitated life.'

The Time of the Hero
Mario Vargas Llosa
Set in the Military Academy in Lima, this novel so outraged the Peruvian authorities that copies were publicly burned.

Under the Volcano
Malcolm Lowry
Set in Cuernavaca, where the alcoholic British consul has a breakdown and dies, this has now become a cult book (although when first published it sold only two copies in two years in Canada).

A House for Mr Biswas
VS Naipaul
Naipaul considers this book to be the one 'that is closest to me' and the one that contains some of his funniest writing.

The Fruit Palace
Charles Nicholl
Charles Nicholl first came into contact with the Colombian drug trade in the early Seventies. Twelve years later he went back to find out about this dangerous world.

The Labyrinth of Solitude
Octavio Paz
A collection of essays analysing Mexico's history and psyche and looking at relations with the USA.

Penguin History of Latin America
ed. Edwin Williamson
Starts with the pre-Columbian Indians and continues through savage colonisations.

Rites
Victor Perera
An autobiography of life in Guatemala City's Jewish community. Perera's father was a first-

generation immigrant who worked his way up from being an itinerant pedlar to a leading merchant.

The Final Passage
Caryl Phillips
The story of 19-year-old Leila's struggle to come to terms with life on a small Caribbean island in the 1950s.

Wide Sargasso Sea
Jean Rhys
This novel set in Dominica and Jamaica describes the lives of Edward Rochester and his mad wife before their introduction as characters into Charlotte Bronte's *Jane Eyre*.

The Vision of Elena Silves
Nicholas Shakespeare
Shakespeare's combination of magical realism with European traditions of fiction make an extremely effective mixture.

Touching the Void
Joe Simpson
A compulsivly readable book about a climbing accident in the Andes.

The Land of Miracles
Stephen Smith
Smith writes with ironic detachement about this country of paradox.

The Weather Prophet
Lucretia Stewart
A personal account of a single woman's foray into the wider reaches of the Antilles.

The Mosquito Coast
Paul Theroux
Allie Fox takes his family to live in the Honduran jungle and struggles to keep them alive with his inventions.

The Old Patagonian Express
Paul Theroux
Theroux's journey from Boston to Patagonia by train was full of contrast: some were ramshackle and old, others superb and new.

Ninety-Two Days
Evelyn Waugh
Often throughout this book, Waugh philosophises about travel: 'The delight of travel...is a delight just as incommunicable as the love of home.'

Travels in a Thin Country
Sara Wheeler
Sara Wheeler spent six months on her own travelling through Chile.

Time Among the Maya
Ronald Wright
An attempt to discover the ancient roots of the Maya civilization.

MIDDLE EAST

Wilder Shores of Love
Lesley Blanch
Biographies of four redoubtable nineteenth-century women travellers: Isabel Burton, Jane Digby, Aimee Dubucq de Rivery and Isabelle Eberhardt.

The Road to Oxiana
Robert Byron
One of the classic travel books about Persia and Afghanistan. Robert Byron made this journey in 1933-4 and vividly describes the people he met and scenes he saw.

From the Holy Mountain
William Dalrymple
Dalrymple followed in the footsteps of the sixth-century Byzantine monk

John Moschos on what has already become a classic journey.

The Hittites
OR Gurney
The Hittites created an advanced civilisation in Biblical times; they were politically well organised and their literature was inscribed on clay tablets in cuneiform writing.

The Gates of Damascus
Lieve Joris
An intimate portrait of contemporary Arab society.

Politics in the Middle East
Elie Kedourie
An historical analysis which attempts to explain why ideological politics, such as nationalism and fundamentalism, have triumphed in the Middle East and why democratic governments have not worked in Islamic countries.

Eothen
Alexander Kinglake
One of the classic travel books, written by the young Kinglake in 1844. The account of his travels to the East is interesting as much for the descriptions of what he saw as for the effect these places had upon him.

Seven Pillars of Wisdom
TE Lawrence
This book has been criticised for its historical inaccuracy, as it is a very personal account of the Arab Revolt, but Lawrence's lively prose ensures that it will remain a classic.

Yemen
Tim Mackintosh-Smith
Mackintosh-Smith lived in
the Yemen for 15 years and
wrote this quirky, learned
and poetic book.

The Arabs
Peter Mansfield
An introduction to the
modern Arab world from
political and
historical aspects; the
second half of the book
looks at each Arab state
separately.

*A Reed Shaken By the Wind
(A Journey through the
Unexplored Marshlands of
Iraq)*
Gavin Maxwell
In 1956 Gavin Maxwell
accompanied Wilfred
Thesiger to the marshlands
of Iraq. He describes the
people he met and his
experiences during these
travels.

Among the Believers
VS Naipaul
This first part of Naipaul's
Islamic journey visits Iran.

Arabia
Jonathan Raban
Raban was living in Earls
Court in the 1970s when it
began to fill up with Arabs;
he decided to go and see for
himself their countries
of origin - and produced
what has been called 'one of
the most delightful travel
books in 30 years'.

*The Oxford History of the
Crusades*
ed. Jonathan Riley-Smith
Written by a team of
scholars, the book covers
material from the First
Crusade in 1095 through to
ideas that we have about
the crusades today.

Arabian Sands
Wilfred Thesiger
Thesiger crossed the Empty
Quarter and says of the
book 'For me this
book remains a memorial
to a vanished past, a tribute
to a once magnificent
people.'

The Life of My Choice
Wilfred Thesiger
Thesiger's autobiography
explains how he got the
urge for travel and who
it was that influenced him.

The Marsh Arabs
Wilfred Thesiger
A book about the fast-
disappearing people who
live in the marshes in
Iraq, around the junction
of the Tigris and Euphrates.

Mirror to Damascus
Colin Thubron
The history of Damascus
from Biblical times until
the revolution of 1966.

SOUTH ASIA

*Memoirs of a Bengal
Civilian*
John Beames
Beames was in India from
1858-1893; this lively book
describes his time as a
district officer of the Raj.

An Indian Summer
James Cameron
Cameron captures the
sounds, smells and colours
of India. An invaluable
introduction.

*The Autobiography of an
Unknown Indian*
Nirad C Chaudhuri
Chaudhuri, a distinguished
scholar, was born in East
Bengal in 1897 and
did not finally settle in

England until 1970.

The Age of Kali
William Dalrymple
A series of essays which are
the distillation of ten years
travelling around the
sub-continent.

City of Djinns
William Dalrymple
After spending 12 months
in Delhi, Dalrymple
learned to peel away the
successive layers of history.

A Passage to India
E.M. Forster
An incident at the Marabar
caves between the
Englishwoman Adela
Quested and the Indian Dr
Aziz formsthe centre of this
classic novel: is one of
Forster's masterpieces.

Chasing the Monsoon
Alexander Frater
In 1987 Frater followed the
monsoon from Cape
Comorin in Southern India
to Bangladesh.

Liberty or Death
Patrick French
A controversial
reinterpretation of the last
years of British rule in
India.

Kim
Rudyard Kipling
A book to whet appetites
for travel in the
sub-continent.

The Snow Leopard
Peter Matthiessen
Although Matthiessen
primarily went in search of
the elusive snow leopard in
the remote Crystal
Mountains of northern
Nepal, this book is
essentially a spiritual
search. Inspiring

descriptions of the scenery and wildlife.

Calcutta
Geoffrey Moorhouse
An illuminating book about the city past and present, rich in anecdote and history.

Full Tilt
Dervla Murphy
Dervla Murphy fulfilled a childhood dream when she made a six-month journey riding her bicycle 3,000 miles across Europe, Persia, Afghanistan, Pakistan and into India.

Bachelor of Arts
RK Narayan
One of the Malgudi novels which gets to the heart of Indian life.

Slowly Down the Ganges
Eric Newby
The description of a 1,200-mile journey down the Ganges which Eric Newby made with his wife.

Travels in Nepal
Charlie Pye-Smith
Pye-Smith travelled throughout Nepal from Kathmandu to Namche Bazar, down the Kali Gandaki and south to the Terai along the Indian border.

Sorcerer's Apprentice
Tahir Shah
The gripping story of Shah's apprenticeship into the ways of Indian godmen.

Selected Poems
Rabindranath Tagore
A superb selection from a great poet.

No Full Stops in India
Mark Tully
Mark Tully was born in India and has worked there for the BBC for many years; his knowledge is almost unparalled among foreigners and his sympathy and understanding shine through all of these essays.

CENTRAL ASIA

The Search for Shangri-La
Charles Allen
An account of four recent journeys into far western Tibet.

First Russia Then Tibet
Robert Byron
Byron contrasts post-revolutionary Russia with pre-industrial Tibet, both of which he knew fairly well and both of which he describes lucidly.

In Xanadu
William Dalrymple
Dalrymple travelled from Jerusalem to Xanadu and Kubla Khan's palace, crossing Asia by a variety of transport.

Bayonets to Lhasa
Peter Fleming
An account of the Younghusband expedition to Lhasa in 1903/4 which paved the way for Anglo-Tibetan friendship.

News from Tartary
Peter Fleming
Fleming made this journey was to find out what was happening in Sinkiang (Chinese Turkestan).

Seven Years in Tibet
Heinrich Harrer
Probably one of the best known and most widely read books about Tibet.

Foreign Devils on the Silk Road
Peter Hopkirk
A highly readable account of the adventures of all the explorers who have made archaeological raids on the Silk Road.

The Great Game
Peter Hopkirk
The secret agents of both Britain and Russia were involved in a great struggle in Central Asia during the last century; this became known as the Great Game.

Setting the East Ablaze
Peter Hopkirk
The story of the Bolsheviks' attempt to 'set the east ablaze' with the doctrine of Marxism between the wars.

Trespassers on the Roof of the World
Peter Hopkirk
The account of how Tibet was forcibly opened to foreigners in the nineteenth and twentieth centuries.

Into Thin Air
Jon Krakauer
A personal account of the Everest disaster of May 1996.

Ancient Wisdom, Modern World
HH the Dalai Lama
The Dalai Lama's guide to living today using universal principles.

A Hero of Our Time
Mikhail Lermontov
Written between 1838-40,

this was the Russian poet
Lermontov's only
novel; it consists of five
stories set in Russian Asia.

*An English Lady in Chinese
Turkestan*
Lady Macartney
The author was a
diplomat's wife in Kashgar
from 1890 until 1918.

Eastern Approaches
Fitzroy Maclean
A tale of high adventure
and politics, superbly told,
set in the Caucasus, Central
Asia, Persia and Yugoslavia.

*A Short Walk in the Hindu
Kush*
Eric Newby
Eric Newby was working in
the rag trade in London
when he set off for
the Hindu Kush; his book
has now become a travel
classic.

From Heaven Lake
Vikram Seth
Seth hitch-hiked through
Chinese Central Asia
and Tibet to Nepal. A
delightful book.

Journey to Turkistan
Eric Teichman
In 1935 Teichman left the
British Embassy in China
and travelled through
Mongolia and Chinese
Turkistan to Urumchi by
motor truck and pony.

SOUTH-EAST ASIA

*Red Lights and Green
Lizards*
Liz Anderson
A doctor's account of her
new job in a brothel in
Phnom Penh in the
early 1990s.

*Freedom from Fear
and other writings*
Aung San Suu Kyi
A collection of pieces by the
Nobel Laureate, written
before her house arrest,
which reflect her beliefs,
hopes and fears for her
country and people.

Through the Jungle of Death
Stephen Brookes
Moving account of a boy's
escape from war-time
Burma.

Three Moons in Vietnam
Maria Coffey
An exploration of the coast
from the Mekong Delta in
the south to Halong
Bay in the north.

The Beach
Alex Garland
A fast-moving adventure
story in search of the
perfect beach.

The Quiet American
Graham Greene
Set in Saigon in the Fifties,
Graham Greene's novel
concerns an American on a
secret mission.

Playing with Water
James Hamilton-Paterson
An extraordinarily moving
and evocative book, which
combines fishing for
survival on the remote
Philippine island of
Tiwarik, with a journey of
inner exploration.

*A Dragon Apparent -
Cambodia, Laos and
Vietnam*
Norman Lewis
Poignant reading now, as
the last 40 years have seen
South-East Asia wracked by
war. Lewis was writing
about countries which no
longer exist as they did.

Golden Earth
Norman Lewis
Through sheer pesistence,
Lewis managed to travel all
over Burma, even though
much of the countryside
was under the control of
insurgent armies then.

Under the Dragon
Rory Maclean
A trip through today's sad
and beautiful Burma.

The Trouble with Tigers
Victor Mallet
An account of the turmoil
in South-East Asia after the
markets collapsed in 1997.

The Lost Tribe
Edward Marriott
When he hearrrd about the
'discovery' of the Liawep
tribe of Papua New
Guinea Marriott
determined to record their
stories, hopes and fears.

Into the Heart of Borneo
Redmond O'Hanlon
An extremely funny acount
of a journey which
O'Hanlon made with poet
James Fenton to the
mountains of Batu Tiban.

Burmese Days
George Orwell
Set when the British were
ruling in Burma. Flory, a
white timber merchant,
befriends Dr Veraswami, a
black enthusiast for Empire
who needs help.

A Bright Shining Lie
Neil Sheehan
Written through the eyes of
an American Colonel, John
Paul Vann, this book
encapsulates everything
that was most disturbing
about the Vietnam War.

A Fortune-Teller Told Me
Tiziano Terzani
Terzani was warned by a
Hong-Kong fortune-teller
not to fly for a year -
so he travelled by foot,
boat, bus, car and train.

The Great Railway Bazaar
Paul Theroux
Theroux takes the
Mandalay Express from
Rangoon and then the
local train to Maymyo and
Naung-Peng.

Islands in the Clouds
Isabella Tree
A journey to the remote
parts of Papua New Guinea
and Irian Jaya.

FAR EAST

*Tales from the South
China Seas*
Charles Allen
Relates the adventures of
the last generation of
British men and women
who went East in search of
their fortunes.

The Mummies of Urumchi
Elizabeth Wayland Barber
3,500 year-old mummies
were found in north-west
China. Where did they
come from?

Wild Swans
Jung Chang
An extremely moving
account of three
generations of Chinese
women, showing their
harrowing lives and
extraordinary resilience.

Memoirs of a Geisha
Arthur Golden
A novel that totally
transports you to another
time and place.

The Korean War
Max Hastings
The Korean War which
began in 1950 can today be
seen as the prelude to
Vietnam.

The Tyranny of History
W.J.F. Jenner
Jenner argues that China
has been both held together
and held back by
its deference to history.

*Twilight in the Forbidden
City*
Reginald F. Johnston
Johnston was a British
colonial official, scholar,
writer and poet, who
lived in Chinas as tutor to
the last Emperor between
1919 and 1924.

*The Japanese - Strange but
not Strangers*
Joe Joseph
The author was Tokyo
correspondent for *The
Times* and has a particular
insight into Japanese
institutions and customs.

Forbidden Colours
Yukio Mishima
CP Snow described
Mishima as 'A most
beautiful writer of prose -
clear, eloquent,
visual....Mishima's
characters are observed
with one of the sharpest of
eyes and with maximum
chill.'

The Silent Cry
Kenzaburo Oe
Awarding the Nobel Prize
for Literature, the
Committee said: 'his poetic
force creates an imagined
world, where life and myth
condense to form a
disconcerting picture of the
human predicament.'

East and West
Chris Patten
The experiences of the last
governor of Hong Kong.

The China Voyage
Tim Severin
Six men and one woman
sailed across the Pacific on
a bamboo raft to test
the theory that Asian
sailors reached America
2,000 years ago.

Frontiers of Heaven
Stanley Stewart
Stewart travelled from
Shanghai to the Indus.

Riding the Iron Rooster
Paul Theroux
Theroux spent a year
travelling by every kind of
train throughout China,
observing his companions
in razor-sharp detail.

Behind the Wall
Colin Thubron
Thubron is a perceptive
traveller who writes
beautiful prose; without
being in any way
pretentious, he manages to
teach us an enormous
amount about the country
and its people.

A History of Hong Kong
Frank Welsh
A comprehensive,
absorbing and up-to-date
book about the former
colony.

*Hand-Grenade Practice in
Peking*
Frances Wood
A remarkable account of
the year Wood spent as a
student in China in 1976 .

Slow Boats to China
Gavin Young
A journey to China by
every kind of boat.

AUSTRALASIA AND PACIFIC

Oscar and Lucinda
Peter Carey
A rich and complex novel which filled Angela Carter 'with a wild, savage envy'.

The Songlines
Bruce Chatwin
A compelling book: 'I have a vision of the Songlines stretching across the continents and ages.'

Tracks
Robyn Davidson
In 1977 Robyn Davidson set off from Alice Springs by camel to cross 1,700 miles of desert and bush.

The Kon-Tiki Expedition
Thor Heyerdahl
Six men sailed on a primitive raft from Peru to Polynesia to prove that 'the Pacific islands are located well inside the range of prehistoric craft from Peru.'

The Fatal Shore
Robert Hughes
An immensely readable yet scholarly history which traces the fate of those who were transported to Australia from 1787-1868.

The Bone People
Keri Hulme
Set on the South Island beaches of New Zealand, the book combines Maori myth and Christian symbols.

In the Land of Oz
Howard Jacobson
An entertaining and perceptive journey round Australia.

Kangaroo
DH Lawrence
A partly autobiographical novel in which Lawrence examines politics and power.

The Collected Stories of Katherine Mansfield
The 73 short stories and 15 unfinished fragments in this collection are representative of New Zealand-born Katherine Mansfield's writing.

Sydney
Geoffrey Moorhouse
A celebration - through history and culture - of this exciting city.

Promised Lands
Jane Rogers
An intertwining of the first years of the convict-colony with present-day lives.

In the South Seas
RL Stevenson
The record of Stevenson's first year in the Marquesas.

The Happy Isles of Oceania
Paul Theroux
Theroux travelled from the Solomons to Fiji, Tonga, Tahiti, the Marquesas and Easter Island.

The Singing Line
Alice Thomson
The story of the man who strung the telegraph line across Australia and of the woman who gave her name to Alice Springs.

The Tree of Man
Patrick White
The story of a man and woman who make their home in the outback; as their children grow up and the wilderness begins to disappear, changes occur.

NORTHERN EUROPE

Neither Here Nor There
Bill Bryson
Bryson's humourous sweep through Europe.

Notes from a Small Island
Bill Bryson
Before leaving Yorkshire for America, Bill Bryson made a last, hilarious trip round Britain.

On the Black Hill
Bruce Chatwin
Rural isolation and its effect on two brothers who lived and farmed a Welsh hill farm all their lives.

Walled Gardens
Annabel Davis-Goff
The author is called home from America to southern Ireland on the death of her father, and finds herself back in the world of her Anglo-Irish chilhood - with haunting memories of drafty houses, noisy rooks and faded chintzes.

Miss Smilla's Feeling for Snow
Peter Hoeg
A small boy falls to his death from a rooftop. Compulsive reading.

Journey to the Hebrides
Johnson & Boswell
Both Johnson's and Boswell's books are records of the same journey in the eighteenth century, to the Western isles and throughout Scotland.

Cider with Rosie
Laurie Lee
Classic account of rural childhood in the Cotswolds in the 1920s.

A Place Apart
Dervla Murphy
Northern Ireland from the inside out.

Round Ireland in Low Gear
Eric Newby
Eric and Wanda Newby went to Ireland by bicycle in the autumn of 1985 'to enjoy ourselves'.

Njal's Saga
This, the greatest of Icelandic sagas, was written by an unknown author in the late thirteenth century but based on the historical events of 300 years earlier.

The English
Jeremy Paxman
Good and amusing descriptions of the English today.

Coasting
Jonathan Raban
Jonathan Raban wanted to see his island home from the sea and, in 1982, set sail round the British Isles in a 30-foot ketch.

Berlin - the Biography of a City
Anthony Read & David Fisher
An essential guide to the past, present and future.

Stones of Aran: Pilgrimage and Labyrinth
Tim Robinson
An encyclopaedic survey of the Aran Islands.

The Embarrassment of Riches
Simon Schama
The social and cultural history of Holland in its golden age - and much more.

Kingdom by the Sea
Paul Theroux
An account of a three-month journey round Britain by foot, bus and train. An attempt not only to see Britain but to describe the British in all their aspects.

A Short Residence in Sweden, Norway & Denmark
Mary Wollstonecroft
The author travelled alone through Scandinavia in 1795, in search of happiness in the remote backwoods.

CENTRAL AND EASTERN EUROPE

Danube
Claudio Magris
A wide-ranging and excitingly original book about the Danube and the history, philosophy, people, war and politics that occur along its route.

Stalingrad
Antony Beevor
A brilliant and scholarly new look at the city and its wartime seige.

The Accursed Mountains
Robert Carver
A journey into wild and inaccesible Albania.

Utz
Bruce Chatwin
A novel about a compulsive porcelain collector in the Jewish quarter of Prague.

The Heart of Europe
Norman Davies
Although this history begins in 1945, Davies looks back to the past to illustrate his theories.

Prague in Black and Gold
Peter Demetz
A love-hate account of the author's obsession with Prague.

Stalin
Isaac Deutscher
The classic biography of one of Russia's more controversial figures.

One Hot Summer in St Petersburg
Duncan Fallowell
An honest, funny and passionate book.

The House by the Dvina
Eugenie Fraser
Russia before, during and after the revolution is delightfully evoked by Eugenia Fraser, who was half-Scottish and half-Russian.

The Fall of Yugoslavia
Misha Glenny
Causes, effects and dangers of the latest Balkan crisis.

On Foot to the Golden Horn
Jason Goodwin
A record of Goodwin's journey through Eastern Europe to Istanbul.

The Tin Drum
Günter Grass
A scathing dissection of the years 1925-1955 through the eyes of a dwarf.

The Good Soldier Svejk
J Hasek
A rambling but classic story about Svejk, an everyman figure who creates havoc in the Czech army during World War I.

The Castle
Franz Kafka
Modernist allegory about
K the unwanted Land
Surveyor, who is never
admitted to the Castle.

*The Unbearable Lightness of
Being*
M Kundera
A tragic and entertaining
novel which puts a new
perspective on living.

*Between the Woods and the
Water*
Patrick Leigh Fermor
The second part of the
trilogy describes Leigh
Fermor's journey from the
woods of Transylvania to
the waters of the Danube.

A Time of Gifts
Patrick Leigh Fermor
The first of a trilogy in
which Leigh Fermor
walked from London to
Istanbul in the 1930s.

The Drowned and the Saved
Primo Levi
Levi committed suicide
shortly after completing
this book which dispels the
myth that he forgave the
Germans for Auschwitz.

Kosovo - A Short History
Noel Malcolm
A brilliantly researched and
authoratative book.

The Bronski House
Philip Marsden
Marsden accompanies
exiled Polish poet Zofia
Ilinska back to her
childhood home.

The Crossing Place
Philip Marsden
A journey in search of the
Armenians through the
Middle East, Eastern
Europe and the Caucasus.

The Spirit-Wrestlers
Philip Marsden
A journey into the strange,
ambiguous world of the
Russia's ancient religions.

The Big Red Train Ride
Eric Newby
Eric Newby went from
Moscow to Nakhodka in
1977 with diverse
companions and some
vodka.

Queen of Romania
Hannah Pakula
Princess Marie of
Edinburgh was the grand-
daughter of both Queen
Victoria and Tsar
Alexander II.

Magic Prague
Angelo Maria Ripellino
All the mystery and
magnetism of Prague.

Echoes of a Native Land
Serge Schmemann
A lyrical look at two
centuries in a Russian
village.

And Quiet Flows the Don
M Sholokhov
Set in a Cossack village,
Sholokhov wrote this after
returning to his native Don
from Moscow.

The Pianist
Wladyslaw Szpilman
A young Jewish pianist
survived in Warsaw against
all odds.

Among the Russians
Colin Thubron
Thubron drove around
Russia by car when this was
still extremely difficult.

Pushkin's Button
Serena Vitale
The story of the duel which
killed the great poet.

MEDITERRANEAN EUROPE

France in the New Century
John Ardagh
Changes in French society
since 1945.

The Italians
Luigi Barzini
Barzini, being an Italian
himself, manages to get to
the real core of Italy and the
Italians by cutting through
the familiar clichés.

Captain Corelli's Mandolin
Louis de Bernieres
The young Italian officer
Corelli is posted to a Greek
island during World War II.

South from Granada
Gerald Brenan
Brenan lived in the village
of Yegen in the Sierra
Nevada for many years;
here he writes about his life
there and what Granada
was like in the 1920s.

The Golden Honeycomb
Vincent Cronin
Excellent descriptions of
Sicily's art, architecture and
folklore, written in the
form of a quest for the
golden honeycomb which
Daedalus is said to have
offered to Aphrodite in
return for his escape from
King Minos of Crete.

Bitter Lemons
Lawrence Durrell
Durrell was entranced by
Cyprus in 1953, buying a
house and becoming a local
teacher.

Prospero's Cell
Lawrence Durrell
A guide to the landscape
and manners on the island
of Corfu.

Reflections on a Marine Venus
Lawrence Durrell
'The marine Venus' is a statue which was found by sailors in their nets at the bottom of Rhodes harbour and which much appealed to Durrell.

The Journal of a Voyage to Lisbon
Henry Fielding
Fielding went to Portugal knowing he was dying.

Istanbul
John Freely
The imperial city of Romans, Byzantine and Ottoman Empires.

Lords of the Horizons
Jason Goodwin
A history of the Ottoman Empire.

For Whom the Bell Tolls
Ernest Hemingway
A novel which takes place during only four days of the Spanish civil war, but which feels as if it encompasses the whole of Spain.

Barcelona
Robert Hughes
Hughes places Barcelona firmly in its Catalan past, realising that there is little point in describing the new without the old.

Backwards out of the Big World
Paul Hyland
Hyland crosses Portugal and meets a cross-section of people.

Between Hopes and Memories
Michael Jacobs
Michael Jacobs travelled through every region of mainland Spain, meeting many prominent Spaniards as well as many lesser known poets, eccentrics and mystics.

Italian Journeys
Jonathan Keates
Over a period of twenty years, Keates wandered around northern Italy visiting off-beat places.

The Olive Grove
Katherine Kizilos
The author returns to her father's village in the heart of the Greek mountains.

The Leopard
Giuseppe di Lampedusa
In 1860 the old order still reigns in Sicily, but there are echoes of a new political movement, with Garibaldi on the mainland.

DH Lawrence and Italy
Lawrence's three books about Italy collected together: *Sea and Sardinia*, *Twilight in Italy* and *Etruscan Places*.

As I Walked Out One Midsummer Morning
Laurie Lee
Lee walked through pre-Civil War Spain from Vigo to Malaga in 1936, busking with his violin.

Mani and *Roumeli*
Patrick Leigh Fermor
Two of the best books on modern Greece, these are full of scholarship and anecdotes about the history and gradual demise of many rural communities in Greece, as well as offering superb descriptions of the countryside.

Christ Stopped at Eboli
Carlo Levi
Set in a remote region of Basilicata where Levi was exiled under the Fascists, a world cut off from history and the state: 'We're not Christians, Christ stopped short of here, at Eboli.'

Naples 44
Norman Lewis
Norman Lewis arrived in Naples as an Intelligence Officer attached to the American Fifth Army and after a year there decided that, given the chance to be born again, he would choose to be an Italian.

Voices of the Old Sea
Norman Lewis
Norman Lewis lived in a remote Catalan fishing village in the 1950s. This record of how life was then offers stark contrasts to the area today.

The Towers of Trebizond
Rose Macaulay
The book opens with a much quoted sentence: ' "Take my camel, dear," said my Aunt Dot, as she climbed down from this animal on her return from High Mass.'

The Stones of Venice and Florence Observed
Mary McCarthy
An interpretation of Florence in the 1950s.

Constantinople
Philip Mansel
Constantinople portrayed as the imperial capital of the Ottomans.

Under the Tuscan Sun
Frances Mayes
Captures the feeling of living in a foreign country.

The Turkish Embassy Letters
Lady Mary Wortley
Montagu
Lively letters from travels
through Europe to Turkey
in 1716.

Venice
Jan Morris
An essential companion to
Venice - entertaining,
ironical, witty and
high-spirited.

*Love and War in the
Apennines*
Eric Newby
The story of Newby's
capture in Sicily in 1942; he
escaped from the prison
camp with help from a
local girl, Wanda - who
later became his wife.

*On the Shores of the
Mediterranean*
Eric Newby
A Mediterranean journey
which took in Italy, the
Adriatic, Greece, Turkey,
the Levant, North Africa
and Spain.

Portrait of a Turkish Family
Irfan Orga
The author was born into a
prosperous family under
the Sultans, but in World
War I the family was ruined
and Turkey transformed.

Homage to Catalonia
George Orwell
The heady feelings of the
early days of the Spanish
Civil War, in Barcelona, are
followed by disillusion
as the Republicans are split
by factional in-fighting.

The Elusive Truffle
Mirabel Osler
A quest for the rapidly
disappearing traditional
cuisine and culture of
France.

Italian Education
Tim Parks
A look at the family in Italy,
through the eyes of the
author who lives near
Verona.

Italian Neigbours
Tim Parks
A very readable account of
how an Englishman copes
in the Veneto; he learns to
accept what the locals take
for granted, thereby getting
to grips with the real Italy.

History of the Italian People
Giuliano Procacci
Professor Procacci
pinpoints 1000 A.D. as the
time when European
supremacy began to take
root, and traces Italy's
progression within its
European context, through
the communes of the
eleventh century to the
birth of the European
Renaissance and the two
world wars.

Midnight in Sicily
Peter Robb
Robb uses history, painting,
literature and food in this
exploration of Sicily.

The Tuscan Year
Elizabeth Romer
An account of traditional
life and cooking in Italy.

Blindness
José Saramago
Blindness becomes
contagious and spreads
throughout the city.

Citizens
Simon Schama
A marvellous chronicle of
the French Revolution.

A Fez of the Heart
Jeremy Seal
Travels through Turkey.

The Volcano Lover
Susan Sontag
Based on the lives of Sir
William Hamilton, his wife
Emma and Lord Nelson
and set against the
backdrop of Vesuvius.

Within Tuscany
Matthew Spender
Spender went to live in
Tuscany and has written a
book about his experiences
which is 'by turns
informative, ruminative,
funny and touching'.

Travels with a Donkey
R.L. Stevenson
The account of Stevenson's
trip through the Cevennes
with his recalcitrant
donkey, Modestine.

Driving Over Lemons
Chris Stewart
A sympathetic account of
living in southern Spain, by
ex-Genesis drummer
Stewart.

The Spanish Civil War
Hugh Thomas
Huge and comprehensive
book about the Spanish
Civil War which traces in
scrupolous detail a
complicated story.

Journey into Cyprus
Colin Thubron
Thubron made a 600-mile
trek around Cyprus during
the last year of its peace.

The South
Colm Toibin
A painter on the run from a
broken marriage flits
between Spain and rural
Ireland.

Memoirs of Hadrian
Marguerite Yourcenar
As Hadrian was dying he
wrote a long valedictory

Medical kit checklist
by Dr Richard Dawood

THIS IS A CHECKLIST OF THE MAIN ESSENTIALS that you should consider. Some of the items listed require a doctor's prescription: they are intended for use in circumstances where skilled medical care is not available. Clearly, such medication needs to be prescribed for you by a doctor who has given you careful (and, ideally, written) instructions about its use, and about any side-effects and problems.

Make sure all medicines are easily identifiable: keep them in their original container. When possible, ask your pharmacist to dispense drugs in blister packs—these travel best and are easiest to identify. They also save space, and can be kept in small, resealable plastic bags or pouches.

ALLERGIES Antihistamine tablets are sometimes useful for treating allergic skin reactions; Piriton or Clarityn (less likely to cause drowsiness) are suitable choices. People suffering from severe or potentially life-threatening allergies should carry their own emergency supply of adrenaline.

ALTITUDE SICKNESS Some experts advise using the drug acetazolamide (Diamox) to prevent mountain sickness. For emergency use, it may also be worth carrying a supply of dexamethasone tablets to buy time in the treatment of acute mountain sickness.

ANTIBIOTICS For longer or high-risk trips, I also advise taking a broad-spectrum, prescription antibiotic for treatment of troublesome intestinal infections. The most suitable drug is ciprofloxacin, which can be taken either as a single dose, or as a more conventional course. In more remote places, medication for treatment of amoebic dysentery and giardia (such as Fasigyn) may also be worth carrying, in case skilled medical care can't be found.

ANTIBIOTICS AND ANTI-FUNGAL DRUGS For long-term travellers venturing far from the beaten track, a supply of broad-spectrum antibiotics may also be worthwhile. An antibiotic like co-amoxiclav can be used to treat a variety of infections, including common infections of the skin, sinuses, and chest. Fungal infections such as athlete's foot, groin infections and thrush, are common in tropical conditions—so it is also worth taking an anti-fungal preparation, such as Canesten.

ANTI-DIARRHOEAL DRUGS Diarrhoea is seldom a medically serious condition, but can turn a long journey into a sophisticated form of torture. For troublesome symptoms, it is strongly advisable to travel with a supply of loperamide (sold as Imodium or Arret), which is fast-acting and safe.

Anti-malarials The best choice of malaria medication for a particular trip is a matter for discussion at your travel clinic, prior to departure. Do allow plenty of time in advance of your trip—some anti-malarials need to be started between two and three weeks before you leave. If you need rabies vaccine, that course may need to be completed before you start taking the tablets. Besides taking preventive medication, we strongly recommend travelling with insect repellents, mosquito killers and mosquito nets.

Bite creams Take a tube of Eurax cream to relieve itching from insect bites (avoid anti-histamine creams—they may cause sensitisation). If you suffer from severe reactions to insect bites, your doctor may prescribe a more powerful, steroid cream if you need one.

Blood and intravenous fluids These are often talked about, but are quite impractical to travel with. Accidents are the commonest reason for travellers to need a transfusion, and taking precautions to avoid accidents is the most effective measure to avoid the necessity of a blood transfusion. Knowing your blood group can make it easier to find a donor in an emergency—embassies keep a record of screened donors willing to help. Alternatively, join the Blood Care Foundation, a charity that undertakes to supply blood for transfusion in an emergency.

Cold sores These are often triggered by strong sunlight, cold and wind. If you are prone to them, use high-factor sunblock on the lips, and consider taking acyclovir cream (Zovirax) for treatment.

Colds and sinusitis Travel with a decongestant spray (e.g. Sinex) to avoid discomfort caused by pressure changes during air travel.

Constipation Dehydration, jet lag, dietary changes (including low-fibre airline food) and an initial reluctance to use dirty toilets all add to this common problem. It may be worth travelling with a small supply of natural bran (or bran tablets).

Dental emergency kits These often seem appealing, but are in fact of very limited value. Any likely problems should be dealt with at a check-up prior to travel, and the best person to advise on the likelihood of DIY repairs becoming necessary is your own dentist.

Eye infections Minor infections are common in travellers to tropical countries and contact lens wearers. It is worth travelling with antibiotic drops in case of trouble (gentamicin drops do not need refrigeration, and can also be used as ear drops for infections caused by swimming).

First aid kit Minor injuries are common, and need much more care in hot climates than they normally would at home in order to avoid infection. It's worth buying a small pack of Band-aids and dressings, plus a small bottle of liquid antiseptic, such as betadine.

A supply of non-adherent dressings can also be helpful for dealing with slightly larger wounds. The other essential is something capable of holding together the edges of a clean, gaping wound if medical care cannot be obtained: Steristrips and similar adhesive tapes are useful.

'Flu Depending on the nature of your trip, consider travelling with a supply of Relenza, the new antiviral flu medication, which can be used to abort an attack of the disease. Research has shown that it may also be of value in preventing 'flu.

Insect repellents Insects spread not only malaria, but also dengue fever, many forms of encephalitis (such as the variety that caused such havoc in New York recently) and other diseases not easily preventable with vaccines or medication. Repellents dramatically reduce the risk. DEET is the chemical repellent most widely used, and comes as a liquid, spray, gel, on wipes and in sticks; high concentrations are more economical and long-lasting, but should be used carefully. DEET can be applied to exposed skin and also sprayed or impregnated onto clothing. In addition, the insecticide permethrin can be applied to clothing and mosquito nets; it lasts weeks or months (and survives washing) and it kills mosquitoes, rather than merely redirecting them towards somebody not using repellent. An alternative choice is a lemon eucalyptus preparation sold as Mosi-guard. Some people prefer the smell of this, though it is not as effective as DEET.

Mosquito killers

Use a mosquito killer at night—mosquito coils are suitable for use outdoors, or where there is no electricity. Otherwise, use the plug-in variety. Mosquito nets are increasingly important, with the continuing spread of drug-resistant malaria. Ideally, use a net that has been impregnated with permethrin—this means taking your own rather than buying a net of unknown origin on arrival at your destination.

Motion sickness

The best choice of medication is largely a matter of individual preference. There is very little objective difference in effectiveness between the many products available. Many products have side-effects such as drowsiness. Whatever your choice, take the medication well in advance of trouble—most tablets are useless once vomiting starts.

Oral rehydration solutions

Sachets containing oral rehydration powder (which is added to water to make the solution) are ideal for prompt treatment of dehydration caused by diarrhoea, which is the most important consequence especially in children and older travellers. You should also know how to make your own ORS if required.

Painkillers

The choice is between a milder type, such as paracetamol, and

something a little more powerful, such as ibuprofen.

Salt

Anyone travelling to extreme hot climates should increase salt intake to reduce the risk of heat illness. Take a small supply of ordinary table salt (rather than salt tablets, which may cause stomach irritation and do not always dissolve) to add to drinking water during acclimatisation: a quarter teaspoon per pint (just below the taste threshold) should be added to all drinking water.

Sterile needle kits

In many developing countries, there is a high potential for the spread of HIV and hepatitis B through non-sterile needles, syringes and other medical items. These simple, basic supplies may not be widely available; and even if they can be found in the capital city, don't expect them to be available in a poor, rural clinic at the moment you might need them. Most travellers to developing countries should take their own: the best way to do this is to buy a ready-made commercial kit rather than to attempt buying the items individually.

Sunburn

A supply of high-factor sunscreens (SPF 15 or higher) is essential for almost any outdoor activity, especially at altitude. Water-resistant sunscreens are also available, and last longer on the skin. Choose a brand that gives protection against UVA as well as UVB.

Water purification supplies

My own preference is either for

iodine tablets (such as Potable Aqua) or for solution (the dose is four drops of two per cent tincture of iodine per litre of water—wait 20 minutes before drinking). There is also a wide choice of water purification gadgets that are effective and simple to use, such as the PentaPure Travel Cup, if you have enough room in your luggage.

Medical kit suppliers

BCB
Moorland Road
Cardiff CF2 2YL, UK
Tel 02920 464464
Web www.bcb.ltd.uk
First aid and medical kits to any specification

Homeway Ltd
Fighting Cocks
West Amesbury
Salisbury, Wilts SP4 7BH
UK
Tel 01980 626361
Web www.
travelwithcare.co.uk
Email travelwithcare@
homeway.co.uk
Sterile medical packs.

John Bell and Croyden
50-54 Wigmore Street
London W1U 2AU, UK
Tel 020 7935 5555
Chemists specialising in travel and expedition supplies.

Medical Advisory Services for Travellers (MASTA)
London School of Hygiene and Tropical Medicine
Keppel Street
London WC1, UK

Tel 020 7636 8636.
Sells water-purifiers,
medical and dental kits.

**NOMAD TRAVELLERS
STORES**
40 Bernard Street
Russell Square
London WC1N 1LS, UK
Tel 020 7833 4114
also 3-4 Wellington
Terrace, Turnpike Lane
London N8 0PX, UK
Tel 020 8889 7014
also 4 Potters Road
New Barnet
Herts EN5 5HW, UK
Tel 020 8441 7208
also c/o STA Travel
43 Queens Road, Clifton,
Bristol BS8 1QH, UK
Tel 0117 922 6567
For catalogue/mail order,
tel 020 8889 7014
Email nomad.travstore@
virgin.net
Website www.
nomadtravel.co.uk.
Travel Health Information
Line: 09068 633414 (calls
cost 60p per minute).
Full medical centre,
vaccination service and
pharmacy, plus other gear.

OASIS
High Street
Stokeferry, King's Lynn
Norfolk PE33 9SP, UK
Tel 01366 500466
Website www.
lodgecottage1.freeserve.
co.uk
Sells mosquito nets and
provides a free malaria
advice sheet. Sells sterile
medical kits.

SAFETY AND FIRST AID
59 Hill Street
Liverpool L8 5SB, UK
Tel 0151 708 0397
Email catalogue@
safa.co.uk
General medical kits and
also prevention kits for
AIDS and Hepatitis B.

Vaccination centres

IN THE UK, MOST VACCINATIONS can be given by the
traveller's own doctor. Yellow fever vaccine can be given
by some general practitioners, or this and other unusual
vaccines can be obtained from the centres listed below. It
is best to consult your own doctor before ringing any of
the hospital-based clinics.

Vaccination requirements are listed in the *Vaccinations
Required* chart on page 832. Please note these are only
guidelines, as inoculations can change with new outbreaks
of diseases, so please check with your own doctor or with a
travel clinic as far in advance as possible

**BRITISH AIRWAYS TRAVEL
CLINICS**
Tel 01276 685 040 for your
nearest travel clinic: 25
clinics nationwide.

**BRITISH AIRWAYS
IMMUNIZATION CENTRE**
156 Regent Street
London W1, UK
Tel 020 7439 9584
Open Monday-Friday
9am-4.30pm and Saturday
10.00am -4.00pm. No
appointment necessary.

**BRITISH AIRWAYS'
VICTORIA CLINIC**
Victoria Plaza
Victoria Station
London SW1, UK
Tel 020 7233 6661
Open 8.15am-11.30am,
12.30pm-3.45pm
Also at North Terminal,
Gatwick Airport. Open all
day, evenings and weekends
for emergencies.

**CENTRAL PUBLIC HEALTH
LABORATORY**
61 Colindale Avenue
Colindale
London NW9 5HT, UK
Tel 020 8200 4400
Website www.phls.co.uk
Provides advice and
vaccines for doctors,
among other medical
professional services.

**CONVENIENCE CARE
CENTERS**
Suite 100
10301 East Darvey
Armani, CA 91733, USA
Undertakes all necessary
vaccinations.

**DEPARTMENT OF HEALTH
PUBLIC ENQUIRES OFFICE**
Richmond House
79 Whitehall
London SW1A 2NS, UK
Tel 020 7210 4850
Web www.doh.gov.uk
Email dhmail@
doh.gsi.gov.uk
Also publish a free booklet
Health Advice for
Travellers. Call tel 0800
555777 to order.

**DEPARTMENT OF
INFECTIOUS DISEASES AND
TROPICAL MEDICINE**
Birmingham Heartlands
Hospital
Bordesley Green East
Birmingham B9 5SS, UK
Tel 0121 4242000
Pre-travel telephone advice
and expertise in the
investigation and treatment
of tropical illness.

**DEPARTMENT OF
INFECTIOUS DISEASES &
TROPICAL MEDICINE**
North Manchester General
Hospital
Delaunays Road

Manchester M8 5AB, UK
Tel 0161-795 4567

DEPARTMENT OF INFECTIOUS DISEASES AND TROPICAL MEDICINE/TRAVEL INFORMATION

Ruchill Hospital
Glasgow G20 9NB
Tel 0141-946 7120
Together with
Communicable Disease
(Scotland) Unit, provides
telephone advice for
general practitioners and
other doctors and
maintains 'Travax', a
computerized database on
travel medicine that may be
accessed remotely by
modem. Pre- and post-
travel clinics and limited
travel health supplies.
Enquiries/referrals to
clinics are best initiated by
your doctor.

HEALTH CONTROL UNIT

Terminal 3 Arrivals
Heathrow Airport
Hounslow
Middlesex TW6 1NB, UK
Tel 020 8745 7209
Can give at any time
up-to-date information
on compulsory and
recommended
immunizations for
different countries.

HOSPITAL FOR TROPICAL DISEASES

4 St. Pancras Way
London NW1 0PE, UK
Tel 020 7637 6099
Centre for investigation
and treatment of tropical
illness. Comprehensive
range of pre-travel
immunisations and advice,
and post-travel check-ups
in travel clinic and large
travel shop. Pre-recorded
healthline gives country-
specific health hazards (you
will be asked to dial the

international dialling code
of the relevant country, so
have it ready).

INTERNATIONAL ASSOCIATION FOR MEDICAL ASSISTANCE TO TRAVELERS

417 Center Street
Lewiston, NY 14092, USA
Tel 716 754 4883
also at
40 Regal Road, Guelph
Ontario N1K 1B5, Canada
Tel 519 836 0102
Website www.
sentex.net/~iamat
Non-profit organisation
dedicated to the gathering
and dissemination of
health and sanitary
information worldwide.
Publishes a directory of
English-speaking medical
centres worldwide and
many leaflets on world
climates, immunisation,
malaria and other health
risks worldwide.

LIVERPOOL SCHOOL OF TROPICAL MEDICINE

Pembroke Place
Liverpool L3 5QA, UK
Tel 0151 708 9393
(pre-recorded pre-travel
advice and medical
queries)
or 0891 172111 (travel
clinic)
(calls charged at 50p per
minute)
Fax 0151-708 8733
Website www.
liv.ac.uk/lstm/travelmed.
html
International centre of
expertise and research on
venoms and snake bites,
and investigation and
management of tropical
diseases. Regular
immunisation and post-
travel clinics, limited range
of travellers' health
supplies.

MALARIA REFERENCE LABORATORY PHONELINE

Tel UK +020 7636 7921
Advice on malaria
prophylaxis.

MASTA

Moorfield Road
Yeadon
Leeds LS16 7BN, UK
Tel 0113 238 7575
Markets a wide range of
travel health products. For
detailed advice on all health
requirements for your
intended destinatio, ring
the Health Brief line.

ROSS INSTITUTE MALARIA ADVISORY SERVICE

London School of Hygiene
& Tropical Medicine
Keppel Street
London WC1E 7HT, UK
Tel 020 7636 7921
24-hour taped advice.

TRAVELLERS' HEALTHLINE

Tel 0891 224 100
This is a regularly updated
advice line (with inter-
active technology) for
travellers seeking
information about
vaccinations etc.

UDS DEPARTMENT OF HEALTH AND HUMAN SERVICES

Public Health Service
Centers for Disease
Control, Center for
Prevention Service
Division of Quarantine
101 Marietta Street
Room 1515, Atlanta
GA 30323, USA
Tel 404-331 2442
www.cdc.gov/travel
Internationally respected
centre for disease research
and information.

Travel health websites

www.cdc.gov/travel
Centers for Disease Control
(US Government).

www.
doh.gov.uk/hat/emerg.htm
www.
doh.gov.uk/hat/index.htm
Official UK government
site: find out what
vaccinations you require
for your trip and good local
information for out-of-the
way places.

www.
fitfortravel.scot.nhs.uk
Regularly updated
information and a
vaccination guide for each
country.

www.flyana.com
Healthy flying tips.

www.ifrc.org
Directory of Red Cross and
Red Crescent Societies
worldwide

www.
thirdworldtraveller.com/
Travel/TravelHealth.html
Information on diseases
and disease risks, health
alerts and precautions.

www.tmb.ie/
Tropical medical bureau.

www.
tmvc.com.au/info10.html
Country-by-country
vaccination guide

http://travelhealth.com
Repository of travel health
information

www.tripprep.com
Database of health and

safety issues, covering every
travel-related malady.

www.
tropicalscreening.com
Offers full check-ups for
unwell travellers returning
from exotic climes.

www.who.int
World Health Organisation

www.who.int/ctd
The World Health
Organisation's site for the
control of tropical diseases.

Specialist equipment suppliers

In the UK

AGFA UK
Customer Imaging
27 Great West Road
Brentford
Middlesex TW8 9AX
Tel 020 8231 4903
Photographic suppliers.

AVENTIS-PHARMA
Rainham Road South
Dagenham
Essex RM10 7XS
Tel 020 8919 3060
Web www.aventis.com
May & Baker are one of the
largest pharmaceutical
manufacturers in the UK.
They have several remedies
for the minor everyday
accidents that occur at
home or abroad.

BERGHAUS
Extern Centre
12 Olima Ave
Sunderland Enterprise Park
Sunderland SR5 3XV
www.berghaus.com
Tel 0191 5165600

Britain's leading suppliers
of specialist packs and
clothing for hiking and
climbing. Suppliers to
many expeditions.

**BLACKS CAMPING AND
LEISURE**
8-10 Old Hall Street
Hanley
Stoke on Trent ST1 1QT
Tel 01782 212870
Web www.blacks.co.uk
Have lightweight,
mountain and touring
tents; camp furniture,
kitchen kits, stoves and
lamps; clothing and
accessories and convertible
specialist and summer-
weight sleeping bags.

**THE BRASHER BOOT
COMPANY**
Storey House
Lancaster LA1 4XY
Tel 01524 841000
Web www.brasher.co.uk
Email brasher@
pentland.com

CALUMET
93-103 Drummond St
London NW1 2HJ
Tel 020 7380 1144
Web www.
calumetphoto.com
Major suppliers for all
photographic equipment
and accessories, including a
selection of second-hand
goods.

CAMERA CARE SYSTEMS
Vale Lane, Bedminster
Bristol BS3 5RU
Tel 0117 9635263
Web www.ccscentre.co.uk
Manufacture protective
casings for fine
photographic equipment.

CANON UK
Brent Trading Centre
North Circular Road
London NW10 0JF
Tel 01737 220001
Photographic suppliers.

CLOTHTEC
92 Par Green
Par, Cornwall PL24 2AG
Tel 01726 813602
Manufacturers of special
products that have been
supplied to expeditions all
over the world. Specialists
in jungle sleeping units,
mosquito nets, etc. Also
repairs equipment. Will
give advice over the
telephone to first time
expeditioners.

COLAB
Head Office
Herald Way
Coventry CV3 1BB
Tel 02476 455 007
UK's leading photographic
processing laboratory,
branches around country
and mail order.

COTSWOLD CAMPING
42-46 Uxbridge Road
London W12 8ND
Tel 020 8743 2976
Web www.
cotswold-outdoor.co.uk
Email sales@
cotswold-outdoor.co.uk
Supply a wide store of
outdoor equipment and
have a comprehensive
range of water filtering and
purification equipment.

FIELD AND TREK
105 Baker Street
London
Tel 020 7224 0049
also at
3 Palace Street
Canterbury Kent CT1 2DY
Tel 01227 470023
Web www.field-trek.co.uk
Mail order: Langdale
House, Sable Way
Laindon, Essex SS15 6SR
Tel 01277 233122
Illustrated catalogue with
products at discounted
prices on most leading
makes of expedition
equipment - tents,

rucksacks, boots,
waterproof clothing,
sleeping bags and
mountaineering gear.

FUJI UK
Fuji Film House
125 Finchley Road
London NW3 6HY
Tel 020 7586 5900
Photographic suppliers.

ILFORD IMAGING UK
54 Warren St
London W1P 5PA
Tel 020 7383 7050
Photographic suppliers.

JESSOP PHOTO CENTRE
63-69 New Oxford Street
London WC1A 1DG
Tel 020 7240 6077
Web www.jessop.com
Email sales@jessops.co.uk
Leading shop for low-price
film and cameras; other
branches around Britain.

KODAK
Kodak House
PO Box 66
Station Road
Hemel Hempstead
Herts HP1 1JU
Tel 01442 261122
Web www.kodak.co.uk
Photographic suppliers.

KARRIMORE INTERNATIONAL
Petre Road
Clayton-le-Moors
Accrington, Lancs, BB5 5JZ
Tel 01254 893000
Web www.
karrimore.com
Email webmaster@
karrimore.co.uk
Manufacturers of rucksacks
and other outdoor
equipment.

MINOLTA UK
Rooksley Park
Precedent Drive, Rooksley
Milton Keynes MK13 8HF
Tel 01908 200400
Web www.minolta.co.uk
Photographic suppliers.

MOUNTAIN EQUIPMENT
Peaco House
Dawson Street
Hyde, Cheshire, SK14 1RD
Tel 0161 366 5020
Web www.
mountainequipment.co.uk
Email info@
mountainequipment.co.uk
Equipment suppliers.

NIKON UK
Nikon House
380 Richmond Road
Kingston Upon Thames
Surrey KT2 5PR
Tel 020 8541 4440
www.Nikon.co.uk
Photographic suppliers.

OLYMPUS OPTICAL CO
2-8 Honduras St
London EC1Y 0TX
Tel 020 7253 2772
Web www.
olympus-europa.com
Email customer-service@
olympus.uk.com
Photographic suppliers.

PENRITH SURVIVAL EQUIPMENT
Morland, Penrith
Cumbria CA10 3AZ
Tel 01931 714444
Web www.
edirectory.co.uk/survial
Email hg@
survival.u-net.com
Mail order suppliers of
survival aids.

PENTAX UK
Pentax House
Heron Drive
Langley, Slough SL3 8PN
Tel 01753 792792
Web www.pentax.co.uk
Photographic suppliers.

ROHAN
30 Maryland Road
Tongwell
Milton Keynes MK15 8HN
Tel 0870 60122443
Web www.rohan.co.uk
Email post@rohan.co.uk
Makers of practical clothes

for the serious traveller and outdoor enthusiast.

TENT AND TARPAULIN MANUFACTURING COMPANY
101-103 Brixton Hill
London SW2 1AA
Tel 020 8674 0121
Web www.
tarpaulin-and-tent.co.uk
Email murban@cwcom.net

TRAVELLING LIGHT
The Old Mill
Morland, Penrith
Cumbria CA10 3AZ
Tel 01931 714488
Web www.
travelinglight.com
Email cats@
traveling light.com
Mail order available.

VIKING OPTICAL
Blythe Road
Halesworth
Suffolk IP19 8EN
Tel 01986 875315
Supplies Sunto compasses and binoculars, and other precision instruments.

YHA ADVENTURE SHOP
14 Southampton Street
London WC2E 7HY
Tel 020 7836 8541
Web www.
yhaadventure.co.uk

Related websites

www.adventuresports.com
/new/shopdir.htm
Wide range of supplies.

www.backpackgear.com
Mainly footwear but also tents and accessories.

www.footsloggers.com
All kinds of outdoor equipment.

www.gorp.com
Outdoor specialists.

In the USA

BASIC DESIGNS
1100 Stearns Drive
Sauk Rapids
Minnesota 56379
Tel 320 252 1642
Web www.stearnsinc.com
Email stearns@
stearnsnet.com
Makers of the H20 Sun Shower, a solar-heater portable shower.

LL BEAN
Freeport, ME 04033
Tel 207 865 4761
Web www.llbean.com
Operates a mail order service and has a salesroom which is open 24 hours a day, 365 days a year. Sells outdoor garments and accessories, boots and other footwear, canoes, compasses, axes, knives, binoculars, stoves, tents, sleeping bags, packs and frames, skis and snowshoes, campware, travel bags, lamps, blankets.

SIERRA WEST
121 Gray Avenue
3300 Santa Barbara
CA 93101
Tel 805 963 87 27
Web www.bigdogs.com
Manufacturer of high quality rainwear, outer-wear, tents and backpacking accessories. For further information, please write and request a free colour catalogue.

TAMRAC
9240 Jordan Avenue
Chatsworth
CA 91311
Tel 818 407 9500
www.tamrac.com
Makers of instant-access foam-padded weatherproof cases for 35mm systems.

TENDER CORP
After Bite, PO Box 290
Littleton, NH 03561
Tel 603 444 5464
Web www.tendercorp.com
America's leading treatment for the relief of pain and irritation due to insect bites or stings.

THINSULATE
3M Centre Building 275-6W-01
St Paul
MN 55114
Tel 800 328 1689
Insulation materials.

WYETH LABORATORIES
PO Box 8299
Philadelphia
PA 19101
Tel 215 878 9500
www.ahp.com
Manufacturer of anti-venoms against poisonous snakes of the United States. The serum is sold in a freeze-dried condition, making it ideally suited for expeditions (no need for refrigeration).

Passport offices and visa agencies

Passport offices in UK

UK PASSPORT WEBSITE
www.ukpa.gov.uk
The governments passport agency online

UK PASSPORT HOTLINE
Tel 0990 210 410
Call the above number for all passport enquiries. The addresses of all other passport offices are shown below, for those who need to obtain a passport at very short notice by applying in person rather than by post.

LONDON
Clive House
70 Petty France
London SW1H 9HD

ENGLAND (EAST)
Aragon Court
Northminster Road
Peterborough
Cambs PE1 1QG

ENGLAND (NORTH)
5th Floor
India Buildings
Water Street
Liverpool L2 0QZ

IRELAND
Hampton House
47-53 High Street
Belfast BT1 2QS

SCOTLAND
3 Northgate
96 Milton Street
Cowcaddans
Glasgow G4 0BT

WALES
Olympia House
Upper Dock Street
Newport
Gwent NP9 1XA

Visa agencies in UK

CORPORATE VISA SERVICES
1-2 Ramilles St, Room 307
Ramilles House
London W1F 7LN
Tel 020 7734 4537

FALCON MIDDLE EAST CONSULTANCY SERVICES
73 Kingsway
London WC2B 6TP
Tel 020 7243 4823

RAPID VISA SERVICE
Adventure Travel Centre
135 Earls Court Road
London SW5 9RH
Tel 020 7373 3026
Website www.
rapidvisaservice.com

ROSS CONSULAR SERVICES
Mill House, Mill Street
Slough, Berks SL2 5DD
Tel 01753 820881
Web www.rcsluk.com.uk

THAMES CONSULAR SERVICES
548 Chiswick High Road
London W4 5RG
Tel 020 8995 2492
Website www.
thamesconsular.com

THE VISA SERVICE
2 Northdown Street
London N1 9BG
Tel 020 7833 2709
Web www.visaservice.co.uk
Email mail@
visaservice.co.uk

Visa agencies in USA

INTERCONTINENTAL VISA SERVICE
Los Angeles World Trade Center
350 South Figueroa Street
Los Angeles, CA 90071
Tel 213 625 7175

VISAS INTERNATIONAL
3169 Barbara Ct Ste F
Los Angeles, CA 90068
Tel 213 850 1191

Travel insurance specialists

In the UK

A. SAUNDERS & CO
30 Aldenham Rd
Radlett, Herts. WD7 8AX
Tel 01923 858 339
Flexible all-risks insurance policies for photographers and equipment.

ASSOCIATION OF BRITISH INSURERS:
Tel 020 7600 3333
Website www.abi.org.uk
Professional association.

AUTOMOBILE ASSOCIATION
Fanum House
Leicester Square
London W1
Tel 0990 500 600
Policies for overland travel. Will also provide *carnets* and Green Cards.

HANOVER PARK INSURANCE BROKERS
Greystoke House
80-86 Westow St
London SE19 3AQ
Tel 020 8771 8844
Website www.
hanover-park.com
Can arrange insurance on motor vehicles throughout Europe including the CIS. Other countries in Near Middle and Far East as well as Africa are available by special arrangement. Also offers personal accident, sickness and baggage insurance.

CAMPBELL IRVINE
48 Earls Court Road
Kensington
London W8 6EJ
Tel 020 7937 6981
Website www.
campbellirvine.com

Email ci@netcomuk.co.uk
Specialises in unusual
insurance and can offer
insurance against medical
expenses, repatriation,
personal accident,
cancellation and
curtailment, and personal
liability. Vehicle insurance
can be arranged. *Carnet*
Indemnity insurance is
available so that travellers
can obtain *carnet de
passages* from the AA.

R.L. DAVISON & CO
Lloyd's Insurance Brokers
Bury House , 31Bury St
London EC3A5AH
Tel 020 7816 9876
Web www.rldavidson.co.uk
Offers *Carnet* indemnity
insurance.

WEXAS INTERNATIONAL
45-49 Brompton Road
London SW3 1DE
Tel 020 7589 3315
Website www.wexas.com
Email mship@wexas.com
Offers members a
comprehensive range of
travel insurance packages at
competitive prices,
including a year-round
policy allowing any
number of journeys lasting
up to three months.

In the USA

ASSIST-CARD
745 Fifth Avenue
New York, NY 10022
Tel 212 752 2788
(Outside New York
tel 1 800 221-4564)
An organisation to help
with travel crises such as
loss of passport, illness,
theft. legal trouble.
Cardholders may telephone
the office (collect) from 28
European countries and
both North and South
American countries.

KEMPER GROUP
1 Kemper Dr
Long Grove
IL 60049, USA
Tel 847 20 2000
Website www.
kemperinsurance.com
Inexpensive ravel accident
policies.

In France

**CENTRE DE
DOCUMENTATION
ET D'INFORMATION
DE L'ASSURANCE**
25 Boulevard Haessan
85009 Paris, France
Tel 1 42 47 90 00
Will give advice to travellers
on insurance problems.

PINON ASSUREUR
1719 Rue de Clichi
75009 Paris, France
Tel 1 48 78 02 98
Will insure cameras and
photographic equipment.

Language learning services

**ACCELERATED LEARNING
SYSTEMS**
50 Aylesbury Road
Aston Clinton, Aylesbury
Bucks HP22 5AH, UK
Tel 01296 631177
Website www.
acceleratedlearninguk.
co.uk
Range of open learning
packages with cassettes.

BBC WORLDWIDE
Woodlands, 80 Wood Lane
London W12 0TT, UK
Tel 020 8743 8000
Website www.bbc.co.uk
Good range of language
learning materials and

courses including videos,
audio cassettes and books.

**BERLITZ SCHOOLS OF
LANGUAGE**
9-13 Grosvenor Street
London W1A 3BZ, UK
Tel 020 7915 0909
Website www.berlitz.com
A range of language
learning materials and
courses including low-
budget and pocket books.

**CENTRE FOR INFORMATION
ON LANGUAGE TEACHING
AND RESEARCH (CILT)**
20 Bedfordbury
London WC2N 4LD, UK
Tel 020 7379 5101
Sponsored by the UK
Department of Education
and Science, offers
information and guidance
on language learning and
teaching.

LINGUAPHONE
124-126 Brompton Road
London SW3 1JD, UK
Tel 020 7589 2422
Website www.
linguaphone.com

FRENCH INSTITUTE
14 Cromwell Place
London SW7 2JR, UK
Tel 020 7581 2701
Website www.
institut.ambafrance.org.uk
French cultural centre with
extensive programme of
films, events, courses.

GOETHE INSTITUTE
50 Prince's Gate
Exhibition Road
London SW7 2PH, UK
Tel 020 7596 4004
Website www.
goethe.de/london
German cultural centre.

INSTITUTE OF LINGUISTS
Tel 020 7940 3100
Website www.iol.org.uk
Email info@iol.org.uk

KEY LANGUAGES
Douglas House
16-18 Douglas Street
London SW1P 4PB, UK
Tel 020 7630 6113
Fax 020 7630 6114
Email info@
keylanguages.com

THE LANGUAGE CENTRE
11 West Road
Cambridge , UK

RICHARD LEWIS COMMUNICATIONS
Riversdown House
Warnford
Nr. Southampton
Hants SO32 3LH, UK
Tel 01962-771111
Website www.
crossculture.com
Specialise in tailor-made
cours for the corporate
market, administered from
centres in UK and abroad.

TRAINING ACCESS POINTS (TAPS)
UK government interest in
promoting training and
vocational skills has
prompted the
establishment of TAPS
across the country. As the
name suggests, TAPS
identify where training -
including but not
exclusively language
training - is available from
providers in the public and
private sectors. Any local
Civic Library or Chamber
of Commerce should be
able to put you in contact
with the local office/
reference point.
Alternatively your local
TAPS office should be in
Yellow Pages.

Related websites

www.travlang.com

www.freetranslation.com

Consumer advice and complaints

ASSOCIATION OF BRITISH TRAVEL AGENTS (ABTA)
68-71 Newman Street
London W1T 3AH, UK
Tel 020 7637 2444
Web www.abtanet.com
Professional body of the
UK travel industry, with a
bond to protect travellers
against financial collapse.
Well-informed about new
legislation on provision for
disabled people.

AIR TRANSPORT USERS COMMITTEE
CAA House
45-59 Kingsway
London WC2B 6TE, UK
Tel 020 7240 6061
Web www.auc.org.uk
Helpline 2-5pm Mon-Fri
for complaints against
airlines. Small committee,
funded by CAA but acting
independently, to
investigate complaints.

CIVIL AVIATION AUTHORITY
CAA House
45-59 Kingsway
London WC2B 6TE, UK
Tel 020 7379 7311
Web www.caa.co.uk
Overall regulator of the UK
airline industry.

Related websites

www.passengerrights.com

www.holidaycomplaint.
com

Specialist organisations

Adventure and sports tourism

See also listings for
Expedition organisers and
Overland travel.

ADIRONDACK MOUNTAIN CLUB
174 Glen St, Glens Falls
NY 12801 , USA
Tel 518 793 7737
Membership organisation
aiming to conserve New
York's Adirondack and
Catskill parks.

ADRIFT
Wessex House
127 High Street
Hungerford
Berks RG17 0DL, UK
Tel 01488 684509
Website www.adrift.co.uk
Whitewater rafting
holidays worldwide.

ADVENTURE AND SPORTING
Access Tours
5th Floor, 58 Pitt St
Sydney, NSW 2070
Australia
Tel 2-241 1128
Activity holidays in the CIS
and South-East Asia.

THE ADVENTURE TRAVEL SOCIETY
6551 S. Revere Parkway
Suite 160, Englewood
CO 80111, USA
Tel 303-649 9016
Web www.
adventuretravel.com/ats
A professional corporation
devoted to natural resource
sustainability, economic
viability and cultural
integrity through the
development of tourism.

AIRTRACK SERVICES LTD
16-17 Windsor Street
Uxbridge
Middlesex UB8 1AB, UK
Tel 01895 810810
Web www.airtrack.co.uk
Email sales@airtrack.co.uk
Organises sporting
holidays around the world,
from bungy jumping in
Switzerland to tickets for
the IndyCar
championships in the US.

**ALTERNATIVE TRAVEL
GROUP OXFORD**
69-71 Banbury Road
Oxford OX2 6PE
Tel 01865 513333
Website
www.alternativetravel.
co.uk
Email info@
atg-oxford.co.uk
Walking and trekking
holidays for groups and
individuals in Europe.

**THE AMERICAN HIKING
SOCIETY**
1701 18th St NW
Washington, DC 20009
USA

**APPALACHIAN TRAIL
CONFERENCE**
Box 807, Harpers Ferry
WV 25425, USA
Tel 304 535 6331

ARCTURUS EXPEDITIONS
PO Box 850
Gartocharn Alexandria
Dunbartonshire G83 8RL
UK
Tel 01389 830204
Email arcturus@
btinternet.com
Specialise in the Arctic's
natural history,
archaeology and native
peoples. Also dog sledding,
kayaking and skiing.

BIG MOUNTAIN TOURS
25 Bury Hill, Woodbridge
Suffolk IP12 1JD, UK
Tel 01394 385416

Guided walking and
trekking in the Pyrenees.

BIKE EVENTS
PO Box 75
Bath BA1 1BX, UK
Tel 01225 480130

**BRITISH ACTIVITY
HOLIDAY ASSOCIATION
(BAHA)**
Orchard Cottage
22 Green Lane, Hersham
Walton-on-Thames KT12
5HD, UK
Tel 01932 252994
Website www.baha.org.uk.
Provides information on
activity holidays in the UK.

**BRITISH CANOE UNION
(BCU)**
Adbolton Lane
West Bridgford
Nottinghamshire NG2 5AS
UK
Tel 01159 821100
Website www.bcu.org.uk
Email info@bcu.org.uk
Advice and information on
courses, clubs, etc.

**BRITISH GLIDING
ASSOCIATION**
Kimberley House
Vaughan Way
Leicester LE1 4SE, UK
Tel 01162 531051
Website www.gliding.co.uk

**BRITISH MOUNTAINEERING
COUNCIL (BMC)**
177-179 Burton Road
Manchester M20 2BB, UK
Tel 0161 445 4747
Website www.thebmc.org
Reference books and
information on all aspects
of mountaineering.

**BRITISH ORIENTEERING
FEDERATION**
Riversdale
Dale Road North
Darley Dale, Matlock
Derbyshire DE4 2HX, UK
Tel 01629 734042
Website www.
cix.co.uk/~bof

**THE BRITISH PARACHUTE
ASSOCIATION**
5 Wharf Way, Glen Parva
Leicester LE2 9TF, UK
Tel 01162 785271
Website www.bpa.org.uk

BRITISH SUB-AQUA CLUB
Telford's Quay
Elsmere Port
Cheshire CH65 4FY, UK
Tel 0151 3506200
Website www.bsac.com
Diving instruction through
regional branches and a
diving holidays
information service.

**CANADIAN WILDERNESS
TRIPS**
187 College St, Toronto
Ontario M5T 1P7, Canada
Tel 416-977 3703
Whitewater rafting and
canoeing in Ontario.

**CONTINENTAL DIVIDE
TRAIL SOCIETY**
PO Box 30002, Bethesda
MD 20814, USA

**CORAL CAY CONSERVATION
EXPEDITIONS**
The Ivy Works
154 Clapham Park Road
UK
Tel 020 7498 6248
Website www.coralcay.org
Recruits qualified divers
over 18 to help establish a
marine park in Belize.

DESTINATION USA
14 Greville St
London EC1N 8SB, UK
Tel 020 7400 7000
Website www.
destination-group.co.uk
Golfing holidays.

ENCOUNTER OVERLAND
267 Old Brompton Road
London SW5 9JA, UK
Tel 020 7370 6845
Fax 020 7244 9737
Website www.
encounter-overland.com
Email adventure@
encounter.co.uk

Leading adventure/ overland travel organiser, with tours up to 29 weeks.

ERNA LOW CONSULTANTS
9 Reece Mews
London SW7 3HE, UK
Tel 020 7584 2841
Web www.ernalow.co.uk
Email info@ernalow.co.uk
Golfing and spa holidays.

EXODUS EXPEDITIONS
9 Weir Road
London SW12 0LT, UK
Tel 020 8675 5550
Fax 020 8673 0779
Website www.exodus.co.uk
Leading adventure/ overland travel organiser, with tours up to 29 weeks.

EXPLORE WORLDWIDE
1 Frederick Street
Aldershot
Hampshire GU11 1LQ, UK
Tel 01252 333031
Website www.info@explore.co.uk
Leading adventure/ overland travel organiser, with tours up to 29 weeks.

GO FISHING
6 Baron's Gate
33-35 Rothchilds Road
London W4 1RX, UK
Tel 020 8742 3700
Organises fishing trips to the Falkland Islands, Canada, and the USA.

THE GRAND TOURING CLUB
Model Farm, Rattlesden
Bury St Edmunds
Suffolk IP30 0SY, UK
Tel 01449 737774
Classic motoring rally/tours in France.
Website www.grandtouringclub.co.uk

GUERBA EXPEDITIONS
Wessex House
40 Station Road
Westbury
Wilts BA13 3JN, UK
Tel 01373 826611

Web www.guerba.co.uk
Email info@guerba.co.uk
Leading adventure/ overland travel organiser, with tours up to 29 weeks.

GUNG HO
6 Enys Road, Eastbourne
East Sussex BN21 2DH, UK
Tel 01323 431860
Website www.gungho.mistral.co.uk
Email gungho@mistral.co.uk
Adventure tours, particularly in Borneo.

HEADWATER HOLIDAYS
146 London Road
Northwich, Cheshire
CW9 5HH, UK
Tel 01606 813333
Website www.headwater-holidays.co.uk
Email info@headwater.com

THE INTERNATIONAL LONG RIVER CANOEIST CLUB
c/o Peter Salisbury
238 Birmingham Road
Redditch
Worcs B97 6EL, UK
Provides details of thousands of rivers around the world. Members in 26 countries ready to offer help and advice.

JOURNEY LATIN AMERICA
12-13 Heathfield Terrace
London W4 4JE, UK
Tel 020 8747 3108
Website www.journeylatinamerica.co.uk
Leading adventure/ overland travel organiser, with tours up to 29 weeks.

KE ADVENTURE TRAVEL
32 Lake Road, Keswick
Cumbria CA12 5DQ, UK
Tel 01768 773966
Website www.keadventure.com
Email keadventure@enterprise.net
Trekking, climbing and mountain biking holidays.

ORIGINS
Times Place, 45 Pall Mall
London SW1Y 5JG, UK
Website www.origin-it.com
Tel 020 7321 5700
Adventure holidays.

OUTWARD BOUND TRUST
Watermillock, Nr. Penrith
Cumbria CA11 0JL, UK
Tel 0990 134 227
Website www.outwardbound-uk.org
Email enquiries@outwardbound-uk.org
Adventure holidays in off-beat regions of UK.

PACIFIC CREST CLUB
PO Box 1907
Santa Ana
CA 92702

PAGE AND MOY
136-40 London Road
Leicester
Leics LE2 1EN, UK
Tel 0870 0106400
Web www.page-moy.co.uk
Email holidays@pageandmoy.co.uk
Specialist operator offering motor racing holidays to Grand Prix events worldwide, as well as golfing, music and archaeological tours.

THE RAMBLERS ASSOCIATION
2nd Floor Camelford Hse
8790 Albert Embankment
London SE1 7TW, UK
Web www.ramblers.org.uk
Email ramblers@london.ramblers.org.uk
Tel 020 7339 8500
Membership association for serious walkers in UK.

RAMBLERS HOLIDAYS
PO Box 43, 2 Church Road
Welwyn Garden City AL8 6PQ, UK
Tel 01707 331133
Website www.ramblersholidays.co.uk
Walking holidays

throughout Europe from an offshoot of the Ramblers' Association.

SAFARI DRIVE LTD
127 High Street
Hungerford
Berkshire RG17 0DL, UK
Tel 01488 681 611
Website www.
safaridrive.com
Email safari_drive@
compuserve.com
Organises self-drive safaris in Africa, also white water rafting and microlighting.

SCOTT DUNN
Fovant Mews
12 Noyna Road
London SW17 7PH, UK
Tel 020 8672 1234
Fax 020 8767 2026

SHEERWATER
PO Box 125
Victoria Falls, Zimbabwe
Experts in canoe and whitewater rafting trips along the Zambezi.

THE SIERRA CLUB
730 Polk St
San Francisco
CA 94109, USA
Tel 415-776 2211
Every sort of adventure holiday.

SKI CLUB OF GREAT BRITAIN
The White House
57/63 Church Road
London SW19 5SB, UK
Tel 020 8410 2000
Website www.skiclub.co.uk
Email info@skiclub.co.uk
Club benefits include unbiased advice on resorts, travel and equipment; snow reports; club flights and special discounts.

SOBECK EXPEDITIONS INC
Box 1089, Angels Camp
California 95222, USA
Leading adventure sports company, covers Africa as well as USA.

SPORTING INTERNATIONAL
13201 Northwest Freeway
Suite 800, Houston
TX 77040, USA
Owners of Ker Downey & Selby, who have vast concessions for safaris in the Okavango Delta.

TANA DELTA
PO Box 24988
Nairobi, Kenya
River journeys along the Tana Delta aboard *The African Queen*.

WORLD EXPEDITIONS
3 Northfields Prosect
Putney Bridge Road
London SW18 1PE
Tel 020 8870 2600
Website www.
worldexpeditions.co.uk
Email enquiries@
worldexpeditions.co.uk
Australian-based adventure tour operator.

Related websites

www.Adventure-Mag.com

www.adventurequest.com

www.adventuretravel.com
Adventure travel society

www.adventuroustraveler.
com/
Specialist bookshop: you can look for books by a combination of activity and location.

www.eDreams.com
Expert advice and extraordinary holidays - specialises in unusual and 'hard-to-find' holidays from leading operators.

www.gorp.com
'Great Outdoor Recreation Pages' site is an excellent starting point for research into adventure travel.

www.realworld-travel.com
Online adventure travel business: research, plan and book a trip.

www.serioussports.com
Pick your sport and pick your destination.

www.unmissable.com
One-stop shop for unusual and adventurous activities and destinations

www.wherewillwego.com

Websites for skiing and snowboarding

www.1ski.com
Resort guides, piste maps, web cameras, snow reports, a bulletin board for sharing advice or meeting skiers.

www.board-it.com

http://complete.skier.com
Resort profiles, fitness and technique tips, avalanche information, section for skiers with special needs

www.powderbyrne.com

www.skiin.com
Plenty of information on American resorts for both skiers and boarders. The 'Resort Finder' covers European resorts too.

www.skiclub.co.uk/cogs/
vauxhall
Snow and weather reports for major European, US and Canadian ski resorts, in conjunction with The Ski Club of Great Britain.

http://skiers-travel.co.uk
Comprehensive site with information on skiing and snowboarding holidays.

Diving sites

www.aquanaut.com
International diving
directory.

www.bsac.com
British Sub-Aqua Club
Sells travel insurance, trains
divers, awards certificates,
gives advice.

www.diving-uk.com
The National Diving
Directory, good links to
diving holiday companies.

Business travel

Many travel agencies offer
business travel services.
However, members of the
GBTA (Guild of Business
Travel Agents) specialise
in business travel
management. Leading
members are listed here.

GBTA
Artillery House
Artillery Row
London SW1P 1RT, UK
Tel 020 7222 2744
Web www.gbta-guild.com

AYSCOUGH TRAVEL
200 Great Dover Stt
London SE1 4WX, UK
Tel 020 7943 3711
Web www.ayscough.co.uk

BRITANNIC TRAVEL
230 Burlington Road
New Morden
Surrey KT3 4NW, UK
Tel 020 8336 4000
Web britannic-travel.com

**CARLSON WAGONLIT
TRAVEL**
8th Floor, Maple House
Potters Bar
Herts EN6 5RF, UK
Tel 01707 667788

Web carlsonwagonlit.com

GRAY DAWES TRAVEL
Dugard House
Peartree Road, Stanway
Colchester
Essex CO3 5UL, UK
Tel 08170 242 2422
Email ray.hopkins@
gray-doors.co.uk

**HOGG ROBINSON TRAVEL/
BUSINESS TRAVEL
INTERNATIONAL**
Abbey House
282 Farnborough Road
Farnborough
Hampshire GU 14 7NJ, UK
Surrey GU21 5XD
Tel 01252 372 2000

THE TRAVEL COMPANY
Marble Arch House
66/68 Seymour Street
London W1H 5AF, UK
Tel 020 7262 5040
Website www.
thetravelcompany.co.uk

PORTMAN TRAVEL
Hayley House
London Road, Bracknell
Berkshire RG12 2UX, UK
Tel 01344 867008
Website www.
portmantravel.co.uk

AMERICAN EXPRESS
Over 100 branches in UK.
Head office for business
travel enquiries is at Bank
House, 8 Cherry Sreet,
Birmingham B2 5AL, tel
0121 644 5560, fax 0121
644 5515.

WEXAS INTERNATIONAL
45-49 Brompton Road
London SW3 1DE
Tel 020 7589 3315
Web www.wexas.com
Email mship@wexas.com

Related websites

www.bradmans.com
Bradmans Business Guide
now on line, shows
restaurants and meeting

places around the world.

www.connectglobally.com
Make sure your PC works
in foreign countries.

www.crg.com
Travel safety tips aimed at
the business traveller, from
the Control Risks Group.

www.laptoptravel.com
Kit for your travelling
laptop.

www.thetrip.com
Aimed at frequent business
travellers, including airport
and city information with
maps. Will email you last-
minute deals.

www.iht.com
*The International Herald
Tribune* site, with a good
business travel column
called 'The Frequent
Traveler'.

www.businesstraveller.
co.uk
The website of *Business
Traveller Magazine*.

Recommended
reading

*The Survivor's Guide to
Business Travel* by Roger
Collis (Kogan Page).

Camping
associations
(by country)

AUSTRIAN CAMPING CLUB
Schubertring 1-3
Mandistrasse 28
D-80802 Munich, Germany
Tel 89 38 01 42

BELGIUM: CAMPING AND CARAVANNING CLUB
F.F.3C.B, Rue des Chats 104
B-1082 Brussels, Belgium
Tel 2-465 98 80

DANSK CAMPING UNION
Gammei Kongevej 74D
DK1850 Frederiksberg C
Denmark
Tel 33-21 06 00
Website www.dcu.dk

FINNISH TRAVEL ASSOCIATION
Atomit 5c
00370 Helsinki 10, Finland
Tel 00 3589 6226280

GERMANY: CAMPING AND CARAVANVERBAND DER DDR
Helmut Koch
Lichtenberger Str.27
DDR-1020
Berlin, Germany
Tel 3 02 18 060 71

GREECE: CAMPERS ASSOCIATION OF NORTHERN GREECE
16 Tsimiski Street
546 24 Thessaloniki, Greece
Tel 31-286897

HUNGARY: CAMPING AND CARAVANNING CLUB
Kalvin ter 6
1091 Budapest, Hungary
Tel 1 3171711

THE ISRAEL CAMPING CLUB
Mr. Baruch Preiss
PO Box 13029
61130 TelAviv, Israel
Tel 3-647 88 23

ITALIAN FED. OF CAMPING AND CARAVANNING
PO Box 23
50041 Calenzano, FI, Italy
Tel 055-88 23 91

JAPAN AUTOCAMPING FEDERATION
5F Yotsuya Takagi Building
2-9 Yotsuya ∂
Shinkjuku-Ku
Tokyo, Japan
Tel 33-357 2851

NETHERLANDS CAMPING RESERVATION SERVICE
Het Kolkije 4
NL-7606 CA Almelo
Netherlands
Tel 5490-18767

NEW ZEALAND CAMP AND CABIN ASSOCIATION
4A Kanawa Street
Waikanae, New Zealand

NORWEGIAN CARAVAN CLUB
Solheimveien 18
1473 Skaarer, Norway
Tel 6790 25 62

PARAGUAY: CASAGRANDE CAMPING CLUB
Calle 23 de Octubre #278
Recoleta, Asuncion,
Paraguay
Tel 21-663 730
www.camping-tour.com

POLISH FEDERATION OF CAMPING AND CARAVANNING
ul. Grochowska 331
03-838 Warsaw, Poland
Fax 22 81 06 050

PORTUGESE CAMPING AND CARAVANNING CLUB
Av. Colonel Eduardo
Galhardo #24 D
1170 Lisbon, Portugal
Tel 218 126 126 890
Web www.fpcampismo.pt

UK: CAMPING AND CARAVANNING CLUB
Green Fields House
Westwood Way
Coventry CV4 8JH, UK
Tel 02476 694995
Website www.
campingandcaravanning
.co.uk

UK: THE CARAVAN CLUB
East Grinstead House
Wood St, East Grinstead
W Sussex RH19 1UA, UK
Tel 01342 326 944
Website www.
caravanclub.co.uk

USA: CAMPGROUNDS OF AMERICA
PO Box 30558
Billings MT 59114
USA
Tel 406 248 7444
Web www.koa.com

Related websites

www.canvas.co.uk

www.campingandcaravann
ingclub.co.uk
Offers overseas travel
advice service for travel
tickets and pitch
reservations. Must be a
member.

www.eurocamp.co.uk
Searchable brochure, tour
of their family tent, map to
choose camp sites – so far
no online booking or late
deals

www.eurosites.co.uk

www.oginet.com/camping
Links to camping and
caravanning sites across
Europe.

www.reservcamerica.com
Register to book tents and
motorhomes onto sites in
the USA.

www.select-site.com
Reservations service for
independent campers

www.usacampsites.com

Cargo and freighter travel

BANK LINE
Dexter House
2 Royal Mint Court
London EC3N 4XX, UK
Tel 020 7265 0808
Website www.aws.co.uk
Email aws@aws.co.uk
Itineraries include round-the-world through the Pacific islands.

BLUE STAR LINE
20 Queen Elizabeth Street
London SE1 2LS, UK
Tel 020 7805 2500
Website www.ponl.com
Cargo/passenger services from Great Britain to Canada (West Coast) and the USA.

COMPAGNIE GÉNÉRAL MARITIME
22 rue de Gordot
009 Paris, France
Tel 1-49 24 24 73
The celebrated banana boats sailing between France and West Indies.

CURNOW SHIPPING
St. Helena Shipping Co. Ltd
48-50 Killigrew St
Falmouth TR11 3AP, UK
Tel 01326 211466
Website www.
rmf-st-helena.com
Email admin@
curnow-shipping.co.uk
From Great Britain to the Canary Islands, St. Helena, Ascension Island, South Africa.

EGON OLENDORFF
Villegrant allii 6
23554 Lubeck, Germany
Tel 451-15000
Company famous for its tramp ships, sailing on irregular routes worldwide.

FRACHTSCHIFF TOURISTICK
Exhöft 12
24404 Massholm, Germany
Tel 4642 6068
Created by an ex-sea captain, offers many routes.

FREIGHTER WORLD CRUISES
180 South Lake Avenue 335
Pasadena, CA 91101, USA
Tel 626 449 3106
Website www.
freighterworld.com
Publishes a fortnightly report with pictures.

GILL'S TRAVEL
23 Heol-Y-Deri, Rhiwbina
Cardiff CF4 6YF, UK
Tel 02920 693808
Web www.gillstravel.co.uk
Email gills-tvl@
business.ntl.com

GRIMALDI
Via Marchese Campodisola
13
80133 Naples, Italy
Tel 081 496111
www.grimaldi.napoli.it

MER ET VOYAGES
93 rue Notre Dame Victorie
75002 Paris, France
Tel 01-44 51 01 68
Fax: 01-40 07 12 72
website www.
mer.et.voyage.wanadoo.fr

N.S.B.
Violenstrasse 22
D-28195 Bremen, Germany
Tel 421-33 88 010
Big company with routes worldwide, including round-the-world.

POLISH OCEAN LINES
Gdynia America Lines
238 City Road
London EC1V 2QL
Tel 020 7251 3389
Very interesting routes at interesting prices.

STRAND CRUISE CENTRE
Charing Cross Shopping
Concourse, The Strand
London WC2N 4HZ, UK
Tel 020 7836 6363
Fax 020 7497 0078
Email voyages@
strandtravel.co.uk
Advice on passenger-carrying cargo ships.

TRAV'L TIPS
163-07 Depot Rd
PO Box 218, Flushing
NY 11358, USA
Tel 800-872 8584
Web www.travltips.com

Cruising

CARNIVAL CRUISE LINES
77/79 Great Eastern Street
London EC2A 3HU, UK
Tel 020 7729 1929
Fax 020 7739 7512
Email carnivaluk@
carnival.com
Website www.carnival.com
also at
Carnival Place
3655 NW, 87th Avenue
Miami, FLA 33178, USA
Tel 305 599 2600

CELEBRITY CRUISES
Royal Caribbean House
Addlestone Road
Weybridge
Surrey KT15 2UE, UK
Tel 01932 834325
Fax 01932 820286
Website www.
celebrity-cruises.com

CRYSTAL CRUISES
Quadrant House
80-82 Regent Street
London W1R 6JB, UK
Tel 020 7287 9040
Fax 020 7434 1410
Email cruise@
cruiseportfolio.co.uk
Web www.
crystalcruises.com

COSTA CRUISES
45/49 Mortimer Street
London W1N 8JL, UK

Tel 020 7323 3333
Fax 020 7323 0033
Email
costalonbookingmanager@
costa.it
Web www.costacruises.com

CUNARD SEABOURN
Mountbatten House
Grosvenor Square
Southampton SO15 2BF
UK
Tel 0800 052 3840
Fax 023 8063 4500
Website www.cunard.com

DISNEY CRUISE LINE
3 Queen Caroline Street
London W6 9PE, UK
Tel 020 8222 2846
Fax 020 8222 2491
Website www.disney.co.uk

FRED. OLSEN CRUISE LINES
Fred. Olsen House
White House Rd, Ipswich
Suffolk IP1 5LL, UK
Tel 01473 292222
Fax 01473 292345

HOLLAND AMERICA LINE
77/79 Great Eastern Street
London EC2A 3HU, UK
Tel 020 7613 3300
Fax 020 7739 7512
Email haluk@carnival.com
Website www.
hollandmerica.com

NORWEGIAN CRUISE LINE
1 Derry Street
London W8 5NN, UK
Tel 0800 181 560
Fax 020 7938 4515
Website www.ncl.com

**NORWEGIAN COASTAL
VOYAGES**
15 Bergham Mews
Blythe Road
London W14 0HN, UK
Tel 020 7559 6666
Fax 020 7559 4070
Web www.hurtigruten.com

ORIENT LINES
Michelin House
81 Fulham Road
London SW3 6RD, UK

Tel 020 7959 5900
Fax 020 7959 5910
Email cruise@
orientlines.com
Web www.orientlines.com

PETER DEILMANN
Suite 404, Albany House
324/326 Regent Street
London W1R 5AA, UK
Tel 020 7436 2931
Fax 020 7436 2607
Email gv13@
dial.pipex.com
Website www.
peter-deilmann-river-
cruises.co.uk

P&O CRUISES
77 New Oxford Street
London WC1A 1PP, UK
Tel 020 7800 2222
Fax 0207831 1410
Website www.
pocruises.com

PRINCESS CRUISES
77 New Oxford Street
London WC1A 1PP, UK
Tel 020 800 2468
Fax 020 800 1410
Website www.
princesscruises.com

PRINCESS CRUISES
10100 Santa Monica Blvd
Los Angeles
California 90067, USA
Tel 310 553 1770
Website www.princess.com

**ROYAL CARIBBEAN
INTERNATIONAL**
Royal Caribbean House
Addlestone Road
Weybridge
Surrey KT15 2UE, UK
Tel 0800 018 2020
Fax 01932 820286
Website www.
royalcaribbean.com

SILVERSEA CRUISES
77-79 Great Eastern Street
London EC2A 3HU, UK
Tel 0870 333 7030
Fax 0870 333 7040
Email information@
silverseacruises.com

Website www.
silverseacruises.com

STAR CLIPPERS
Fred. Olsen Travel
Fred. Olsen House
White House Rd, Ipswich
Suffolk IP1 5LL, UK
Tel 01473 292229
Fax 01473 292466
Email star.clippers@
fredolsen.co.uk
Website www.
starclippers.com

STAR CRUISES
1 Derry Street
London W8 5NN, UK
Tel 020 7591 8016
Fax 020 7938 1393
Website www.
starcruises.com

Cultural tours

ACE STUDY TOURS
Babraham
Cambridge CB2 4AP, UK
Tel 01223 835055
Web www.study-tours.org
Email ACE@
study-tours.org
Musical appreciation tours
combined with expert
interpretive sessions and
general sightseeing.

BLAIR TRAVEL
117 Regent's Park Road
London NW1 8UR, UK
Tel 020 7483 2297
Web www.blairtravel.co.uk
Email ablair@
blairtravel.co.uk
Music holidays with either
of two subsidiaries: Travel
for the Arts or Travel with
the Friends (Friends of
Covent Garden).

THE BRITISH INSTITUTE
Piazza Strozzi 2
Florence 50123, Italy
Tel 055 267781
Web www.britishinstitute.it

Email info@
british institute.it
Drawing and art history
holidays in Florence.

**THE BRITISH MUSEUM
TRAVELLER**
46 Bloomsbury Street
London WC1B 3QQ, UK
Tel 020 7323 8895
Website www.
britishmuseumtraveller.
co.uk
Email traveller@
bmcompany.co.uk

CRICKETER HOLIDAYS
4 The White House
Beacon Road
Crowborough
East Sussex TN6 1AB, UK
Tel 01892 664242
Email loraine@
cricketerholidays.co.uk
Painting and drawing.

**FESTIVAL TOURS
INTERNATIONAL**
73 Platts Lane
London NW3 7NL, UK
Tel 020 7431 3086
and at
15237 Sunset Boulevard
Suite 17, Pacific Palisades
CA 90272, USA
Tel 310 454 4080

**FRANCOPHILES DISCOVER
FRANCE**
66 Great Brockeridge
Bristol BS9 3UA, UK
Tel 0117 9621975
Light-hearted study tours.

**GALINA INTERNATIONAL
BATTLEFIELD TOURS**
711 Beverley High Road
Hull HU6 7JN, UK
Tel 01244 350888
European battlefields.

HOSKING TOURS
Pages Green House
Wetheringsett, Stowmarket
Suffolk IP14 5QA, UK
Tel 0172 8861113
Website www.
hosking-tours.co.uk
Email david@

hosking-tours.co.uk
Wildlife photographic.

JAMES KEOGH TOURS
138 Hanworth Road
Hounslow TW3 1UG, UK
Tel 020 8570 4228
Archaeology, art and
architecture tours.

JASMINE TOURS
55 Balham Hill
London SW12 9DR, UK
Website www.
mccabe-travel.co.uk
Tel 01628 531121
Long-haul archaeological.

**MAJOR AND MRS HOLT'S
BATTLEFIELD TOURS**
The Golden Key Building
15 Market Street, Sandwich
Kent CT13 9DA, UK
Tel 01304 612248
Web www.battletours.co.uk

MARTIN RANDALL
Andrew Brock Travel Ltd
10 Barley Mow Passage
London W4 4PH, UK
Tel 020 8742 3355
Web www.
martinrandall.com
Art history and
architectural tours.

**MIDDLEBROOK'S
BATTLEFIELD TOURS**
48 Linden Way, Boston
Lincs PE21 9DS, UK
Tel 01205 364555

PAGE AND MOY
136-40 London Road
Leicester
Leics LE2 1EN, UK
Tel 0870 0106400
Website www.
page-moy.co.uk
Email holidays@
pageandmoy.co.uk
Music and archaeology
(also golf and Grand Prix).

PHOTO TRAVELLERS
PO Box 58, Godalming
Surrey GU7 2SE, UK
Tel 01483 425448
Web www.

pentaxmagazine.co.uk
Escorted worldwide
photography tours.

PROSPECT ART TOURS LTD.
36 Manchester St
454-458 Chiswick High
Road
London W1U 7LH, UK
Tel 020 7486 5704
Web www.
prospecttours.com
Email enquiries@
prospecttours.com
Music and art history tours.

**SILK ROAD TRAVELLERS
CLUB**
39 Market Place
St Marys Court
Henley on Thames
Oxon RG9 2AA, UK
Website www.
silkroadtravel.co.uk
Tel 01491 410 510
Fax 01491 637 617
Email info@
silkroadtravel.co.uk
Along the ancient route.

SPECIAL TOURS LTD
2 Chester Row
London SW1W 9JH, UK
Tel 020 7730 2297
Email info@
specialtours.co.uk
Art history tours for the
National Art Collections
Fund (must be a member).

STEAMOND INTERNATIONAL
23 Eccleston Street
London SW1W 9LX, UK
Tel 020 7730 8646
Tailor-made birdwatching,
natural history and
archaeology tours.

SWAN HELLENIC
77 New Oxford St
London WC1A PP, UK
Tel 020 7800 2200
Web www.
swanhellenic.com
Email swanhellenic@
easynet.co.uk
Guided archaeological and
art history cruises.

Related websites

www.aredu.org.uk
Wide range of residential
courses covering most
subjects from archaeology to
wine appreciation.

www.councilexchanges.org

www.culturaltravels.com

www.eventsworldwide.com

www.festivalfinder.com

www.holidayfestival.com

www.museums.co.uk

www.webofculture.com/ed
u/gestures.html

www.whatsonwhen.co.uk

www.wherewillwego.com

Cycling associations and agencies

APEX CYCLES
40-42 Clapham High Street
London SW4 7UR, UK
Tel 020 7622 1334
Web www.apexcycles.com
Large retailer of bikes and
equipment with a number
of branches nationwide.

**BACK ROAD BICYCLE
TOURING**
801 Cedar St, Berkeley
California 94710, USA
Tel 510-527 1555
Web www.backroads.com

BENTS BICYCLE TOURS
The Priory, High Street
Redbourne

Herts AL3 7LZ, UK
Tel 01568 780800
Cycling tours overseas.

BICYCLE AFRICA
4887 Columbia Drive S
Seattle
Washington 981081919
USA
Tel 202 682 9314
Cycle tours through Africa
lasting 2 to 4 weeks.

BICYCLE AUSTRALIA
PO Box K499 , Haymarket
NSW 2000 , Australia
Tel 46-272 186

**BICYCLE ASSOCIATION OF
NEW ZEALAND**
PO Box 2454 , Wellington
New Zealand
Tel 4 472 3733/9 357 35 50

**BIKE EVENTS AND BIKE
TOURS**
PO Box 75
Bath Avon BA1 14X, UK
Tel 01225 310859
Email mail@
biketours.co.uk
Organises a range of
activities from day events to
touring holidays in Britain
and worldwide. Also
produces *BE Magazine*.

**BRITISH CYCLING
FEDERATION**
National Cycling Centre
Stuart St
Manchester M11 4DQ, UK
Tel 0161 230 2301
Web www.bcf.uk.com
Email info@bcf.uk.com
UK national association of
cycle-racing clubs.

**CANADIAN CYCLING
ASSOCIATION**
1600 James Naismith Drive
Gloucester
Ontario K1B 5N4, Canada
Tel 613 248 1353
Website www.
canadian-cycling.com
Email general@
canadian-cycling.com

CYCLE RIDES LTD
PO Box 2440
Bath BA1 5XG, UK
Web www.cycle-rides.co.uk
Tel 01225 428 452
Fax 01225 428 340

**CYCLISTS' TOURING CLUB
(CTC)**
69 Meadrow , Godalming
Surrey GU7 3HS, UK
Tel 01483 417217
Website www.ctc.org.uk
Email cycling@ctc.org.uk
UK national association for
all types of cyclists, with a
touring information
service. Also provides
insurance, magazine and
organised cycling holidays.

COVENT GARDEN CYCLES
2 Nottingham Court
Covent Garden
London WC2H 9BF, UK
Tel 020 7836 1752
Website www.
wheelie-serious.com

**LEAGUE OF AMERICAN
WHEELMEN**
190 West Ostend Street
Suite 120, Baltimore
MD 21230 , USA
Tel 301 944 3399

**LONDON TO PARIS BIKE
RIDE**
Sports Pro International
26A The Terrace
Riverside
London SW13, UK
Fax: 020 8392 1539
Fax the organisers, Sports
Pro, by mid-April for an
application form.

**SUSIE MADRON'S CYCLING
FOR SOFTIES**
2-4 Birch Polygon
Rusholme
Manchester M14 5HX, UK
Tel 0161 248 8282
Website www.
cycling-for-softies.co.uk
Email info@
cycling-for-softies.co.uk
Tours of rural France and

Italy, equipment provided, accommodation in 2 and 3 star hotels.

USA CYCLING FEDERATION
1 Olympic Plaza
Colorado Springs
CO 80909-577, USA
Tel 719 578 4581
Web www.usacycling.org

Related websites

www.GFOnline.org/
BikeAccess
Look here first if you're planning to cycle or take your bike anywhere in the world

www.rogergravel.com/wsl/
vh_for_a.html
List of cyclists willing to offer hospitality to other touring cyclists.

www.rough-tracks.co.uk
and
www.cycleactive.co.uk
cycle holidays in the UK and abroad

www.bolero.demon.co.uk/
bike.htm
European Bike Express – luxury bus travel for cyclists and their bikes, with pick up points throughout the UK for destinations in the Alps, Mediterranean and French Atlantic coasts.

Diabetic needs

BDA TRAVEL INSURANCE
Sussex House
Perrimount Rd
Haywards Heath
Sussex RH16 1DN, UK
Tel 0800 731 7431
Web www.diabetes.org.uk
Insurance.

BECTON-DICKINSON UK
21 Between Towns Road
Cowley
Oxford OX4 3LY, UK
Tel 01865 777722
Website www.bd.com
Diabetes supplies.

BEYER
Beyer House
Strawberry Hill, Newbury
Berkshire RG14 1JA, UK
Tel 01635 563000
Web www.beyer.co.uk
Diabetes supplies.

BRITISH AIRWAYS TRAVEL CLINICS
156 Regent St
London W1R 6DA, UK
Tel 020 7439 9584

ELI LILLY AND COMPANY
Dextra Court , Chapel Hill
Basingstoke
Hampshire RG21 5SY, UK
Tel 01256 315000
Web www.lilly.com
Diabetes supplies.

GOLDEN KEY COMPANY
1 Hare Street, Sheerness
Kent ME12 1AH, UK
Tel 01795 663403
Website www.
goldenkeyuk.com
Email golden_key@
hotmail.com
Identification.

HEALTH CARE ABROAD
DHSS Overseas Branch
Longbenton
Benton Park Road
Newcastle upon Tyne NE98 1YX, UK

INTERNATIONAL DIABETES FEDERATION
1 Rue Defacqz
1000 Brussels, Belgium
Tel 2 538 5511
Website www.idf.org
Email idf@idf.org

MEDIC ALERT FOUNDATION
1 Bridge Wharf
156 Caledonian Road
London N1 9UU

Tel 020 7833 3034
Web www.medicalert.co.uk
Email info@
medicalert.co.uk
Identification.

NOVO NORDISK PHARMACEUTICALS
Broadfield Park
Brighton Road
Pease Pottage , Crawley
West Sussex RH11 9RT, UK
Tel 01293 613555
Website www.
novonordisk.co.uk
Diabetes supplies.

ROCHE DIAGNOSTICS LTD
Bell Lane , Lewes
East Sussex BN7 1LG, UK
Tel 01273 480444
Web www.roche.com
Diabetes supplies.

SOS TALMAN CO LTD
21 Grays Corner
Ley Street, Ilford
Essex 1G2 7RQ, UK
Tel 020 8554 5579
Identification.

Disability services

THE ACROSS TRUST
70-72 Bridge Road
East Molesey
Surrey KT8 9HF, UK
Tel 020 8783 1355
Email across@across.org
Operates luxury fully-equipped ambulances taking disabled people on organised group pilgrimages and holidays.

ASSIST TRAVEL
P.O. Box 83, Lara
Victoria 3212, Australia
Tel 52 84 1284
Specialist tour operator.

ASSOCIATION OF BRITISH INSURERS
51 Gresham Street
London EC2V 7HQ
Tel 020 7600 3333
Web www.abi.org.uk
info@abi.org.uk
Information on travel
insurance for the disabled.

AUSTRALIAN COUNCIL FOR THE REHABILITATION OF THE DISABLED (ACROD)
PO Box 60, Curtin
ACT 2605, Canberra, Aus
Tel 62 82 4333
Australia's national
organisation for disability,
offers information for
disabled travellers.

BARRIER-FREE TRAVEL
36 Wheatley Street
North Bellingen
New South Wales 2454
Australia
Tel 66 552733
Offers a consultancy service
for disabled travel.

BREAK
20 Hooks Hill Road
Sheringham
Norfolk NR26 8NL
Tel 01263 823170
Holidays in Norfolk for the
physically and mentally
handicapped.

BRITISH RED CROSS
9 Grosvenor Crescent
London SW1 7EJ
Tel 020 7235 5454
Web www.redcross.org.uk
Can provide companions
for disabled travellers.

BRITISH SKI CLUB FOR THE DISABLED
Mr H.M. Sturgess
Spring Mount
Berwick St John
Shaftesbury
Dorset SP7 0HQ, UK
Tel 01747 828515

BRITISH SPORTS ASSOCIATION (FOR THE DISABLED)
Unit 4G 784-788 High Rd
London N17 0DA, UK
Tel 020 8801 4466
Web www.britsport.com

CAMPING FOR THE DISABLED
The Mobility Information
Service
Unit 2 , Atchim Estate
Shrewsbury
Shropshire SY 4 4UG, UK
Tel 01743 761889
Web www.mis.org.uk
Email mis@
nmcuk.freeserve.co.uk
Advice and information on
camping in the UK and
overseas.

CANADIAN REHABILITATION COUNCIL FOR THE DISABLED
45 Sheppard Avenue E
Toronto
Ontario M2N 5W9
Canada
Tel 52 84 1284
Gives advice and publishes
Handi-Travel, a book of
tips for the disabled
traveller.

CAREFREE HOLIDAYS
64 Florence Road
Northampton NN1 4NA
UK
Tel 01604 630382

CPA (CANADIAN PARAPLEGIC ASSOCIATION)
1550 Don Mills Road
Suite 201, Don Mills
Ontario M3B 3K4, Canada
Tel 416 391 0203

DEPARTMENT OF TRANSPORT DISABILITY UNIT
Great Minster House
76 Marsham St
London SW1P 4DR, UK
Tel 020 7944 4170
Web www.detr.gov.uk

DIAL UK
Park Lodge St Catherine's
Hospital
Tickhill Road, Balby
Doncaster DN4 8QN
Tel 01302 310123
Web www.
members.aol.com/dialuk
Email dialuk@aol.com

DISABLED DRIVERS ASSOCIATION
National Headquarters
Ashwellthorpe
Norwich NR16 1EX, UK
Tel 01508 489449
Web www.dda.org.uk
Email ddahq@aol.com

DISABLED DRIVERS' MOTOR CLUB
Cottingham Way
Thrapston
Northants NN14 4PL, UK
Tel 01832 734724
Web www.
ukonline.co.uk.ddmc
Email ddmc@
ukonline.co.uk

DISABLED KIWI TOURS (NZ) LTD
East Coast Highway
P.O. Box 550, Opotiki
New Zealand
Tel 7 315 7867 ∂
Personalised tours of New
Zealand for the disabled.

DISABLED LIVING FOUNDATION
380-384 Harrow Road
London W9 2H, UK
Tel 020 7289 6111
Web www.dlf.org.uk
Emaildlfinfo@dlf.org.uk

DISABLED PERSONS ASSEMBLY
P.O. Box 10-138
The Terrace, Wellington
New Zealand
Tel4 472 2626
National organisation for
the disabled.

DISAWAY TRUST
2 Charles Road
Merton Park

London SW19 3BD, UK
Tel 020 8543 3431
Holidays for groups
overseas and in the UK.

**HEALTH SERVICES
INFORMATION CENTRE**
Jewish Rehabilitation
Hospital
3205 Place Alton
Goldbloom, Chomedey
Laval, Quebec H7V 1R2
Canada
Tel 514 688 9550
Has over 800 access guides
and extensive information
on travel within Canada.

**HELP THE HANDICAPPED
HOLIDAY FUND**
147a Camden Road
Tunbridge Wells
Kent TN1 2RA, UK
Tel 01892-547474
Web www.
charitynet.org/~3hfund
Email 3hfund@
dial.pipex.com
Free holidays for the
physically disabled.

HOLIDAY CARE SERVICE
2nd Floor
Imperial Buildings
Victoria Road, Horley
Surrey RH6 7PZ, UK
Tel 01293 774535
Web www.
holidaycare.org.uk
Email holiday.care@
virgin.net
Travel advice and
information. Also has a
service called 'Holiday
Helpers' which matches
volunteer helpers with
elderly or disabled
travellers.

**HOLIDAYS FOR THE
DISABLED**
c/o Miss Linda Browning
9 Shapton Close, Holbury
Southampton SO45 1QY
UK
Tel 01703-892413
Organises holidays for
disabled people aged 30-60.

**JOHN GROOMS
ASSOCIATION FOR
DISABLED PEOPLE**
PO Box 36, Cowbridge
Vale of Glamorgan CF71
7GD, UK
Tel 01466 771311
This charity has launched
Grooms Holidays, which
specialises in holidays for
the disabled.

JUBILEE SAILING TRUST
Jubilee Yard, Merlin Quay
Hazel Road, Woolston
Southampton SO19 7GB
UK
Tel 01703-449138
Offers the opportunity of
working as a crew member
on a tall ship.

**LONDON REGIONAL
TRANSPORT UNIT FOR
DISABLED PASSENGERS**
172 Buckingham Palace Rd
London SW1W 9TN, UK
Tel 020 7918 3312

**MOBILITY ADVICE AND
VEHICLE INFORMATION
SERVICE (MAVIS)**
O Wing, MacAdam Avenue
Old Wokingham Road
Crowthorne
Berks RG45 6XD, UK
Tel 01344 661000
Web www.
mobilityunit.detr.go.uk/
mavis
Email mavis@detr.gov.uk

MOBILITY INTERNATIONAL
228 Borough High St
London SE1 1JX, UK
Tel 020 7403 5688
Exists to encourage the
integration of handicapped
people with the non-
handicapped. Publishes
*Mobility International
News*.

**MOBILITY INTERNATIONAL
USA**
P.O. Box 10767, Eugene
Oregon 97440, USA
Tel 541 343 1284

Web www.miusa.org
International club offering
travel and educational
exchanges for the disabled.

NEW ZEALAND CCS
P.O. Box 6349
Te Aro, Wellington
New Zealand
Tel 4 384 5677
Agency providing services
to help disabled travellers.

**PHYSICALLY HANDICAPPED
AND ABLE BODIED (PHAB)**
Summit House
Wandle Road
Croydon CRO 1DF, UK
Tel 020 8667 9443
Web www.
ukonline.co.uk/phab
Emailphab@
ukonline.co.uk
Holidays for all ages and
abilities.

**REHABILITATION INTER
USA**
25 East 21 Street, 4th Floor
New York , NY 10010 , USA
Tel 212 420 1500
Web www.
rehab-international.org
Email rehabintl@
rehabinternational.orgaol.
com
Disability society with
information on disabled
travel in North America.

**ROYAL ASSOCIATION FOR
DISABILITY AND
REHABILITATION (RADAR)**
Unit 12 City Forum
250 City Road
London EC1V 8AF, UK
Tel 020 7250 3222
Web www.radar.org.uk
Email radar@radar.org.uk
A registered charity
devoted to helping and
promoting the rights of the
disabled. RADAR finds
suitable accommodation
and facilities for holidays
for the disabled. Publishes a
wealth of useful reference
literature.

SOCIETY FOR THE ADVANCEMENT OF TRAVEL FOR THE HANDICAPPED (SATH)
347 Fifth Avenue, Suite 610
New York, NY 10016, USA
Tel 212 447 7284
Web www.sath.org
Email sathtravel@aol.com
Non-profit educational forum for the exchange of knowledge and the gaining of new skills to facilitate travel for the handicapped, the elderly and the retired. SATH publishes *The United States Welcomes Handicapped Visitors.*

TRIPSCOPE
Alexandra House
Albany Rd
Middlesex TW8 0NE, UK
Tel 020 8580 7021
Email tripscope@cableinet.co.uk
also at
Tripscope South West
Vassell Centre, Gill Ave
Bristol BS16 2QQ, UK
Tel 0117 941 4094
A registered charity, they provide reliable transport advice and information for local or international journeys.

UPHILL SKI CLUB OF GREAT BRITAIN
12 Park Crescent
London W1N 4EQ, UK
Tel 020 7636 1989
Organises wintersports for disabled people.

THE WHEEL RESORT
39-51 Broken Head Road
Byron Bay, NSW 2481
Australia
Tel 66 85 6139
Luxury cabins designed for disabled travellers and owned by wheelchair users.

WINGED FELLOWSHIP TRUST
Angel House
20-32 Pentonville Road
London N1 9XD, UK
Tel 020 7833 2594
Web www.wft.org.uk
Email admin@wft.org.uk
UK and overseas holidays for severely disabled adults.

Related websites

www.access-able.com
Practical information and searchable database on access, accommodation and adventure holidays.

www.canbedone.co.uk
Holidays and tours for people with disabilities.

www.disabilityworld.com
News, reports, travel ideas and good links page.

http://independentliving.org
Swedish organisation serves self-help organisations of disabled people. Includes section on home-exchange of accessible properties.

www.newmobility.com
Net magazine with travel articles, real-life stories and travel tips for adventurous wheelchair-bound people.

Environmental agencies

ACTION D'URGENCE INTERNATIONALE
2 Rue Belliard
75018 Paris , France
Tel 142 64 7588
Run training courses for people interested in helping rescue operations in times of natural disasters.

ARCTURUS EXPEDITIONS
PO Box 850
Gartocharn Alexandria
Dunbartonshire G83 8RL
UK
Tel 01389 830204
Email arcturus@btinternet.com
Specialise in the Arctic's natural history, archaeology and native peoples. Also dog sledding, kayaking and skiing.

BELLERIVE FOUNDATION
PO Box 3006, CH-1211
Geneva 3, Switzerland
Tel 22-7043500
New organisation devoted to protecting the Alps from pollution and thoughtless tourism.

CENTRE FOR THE ADVANCEMENT OF RESPONSIVE TRAVEL (CART)
Dr Roger Milman
70 Dry Hill Park Road
Tunbridge
Kent TN10 3BX, UK
Educational organisation specialising in "creative cultural interchange, economic sustainability and in environmental and cultural sensitivity".

CONVENTION ON INTERNATIONAL TRADE IN ENDANGERED SPECIES OF WILD FLORA AND FAUNA (CITES)
Conservation Monitoring Centre (CMC)
219 Huntingdon Road
Cambridge CB3 0DL, UK
Tel 01223 277314
Web www.unep-wcmc.org
The international agreement regulating trade in rare flora and fauna.

CORAL CAY CONSERVATION EXPEDITIONS
The Ivy Works
154 Clapham Park Road
London SW4 7DE, UK

Tel 020 7498 6248
Web www.coralcay.org
Recruits qualified divers
over 18 to help establish a
marine park in Belize.

DISCOVER THE WORLD LTD AND ARCTIC EXPERIENCE
29 Nork Way, Banstead
Surrey SN7 1PB, UK
Tel 01697 748356
Web www
.arctic-discover.co.uk
Email sales@
arctic.discover.co.uk
Organises tours on behalf
of the WWF and for the
Whale and Dolphin
Conservation Society.

EARTHWATCH
Belsyre Court
57 Woodstock Road
Oxford OX2 6HJ, UK
Tel 01865 318838
Web www.earthwatch.org
Email info@
uk.earthwatch.org
Charity which matches
paying volunteers to
research projects
worldwide.

ECUMENICAL COALITION ON THIRD WORLD TOURISM (ECTWT)
PO Box 24, Chorakhebua
Bangkok 10230
Thailand
Tel 662 510 7287
Church organisation
concerned with monitoring
tourism development and
preventing exploitation.

ELEFRIENDS
Born Free Foundation
3 Grove House
Foundry Lane, Horsham
W Sussex RH13 5PL, UK
Tel 01403 240170
Web www.bornfree.org.uk
Email wildlife@
bornfree.org.uk
Campaign for the
protection of the elephant.

ENGLISH NATURE
Northmister House
Northminster
Peterborough PE1 1UA
UK
Tel 01733 455 000
Web www.
englishnature.org.uk
Aims to raise public
awareness of conservation
issues and will act as a
consultancy on
environmental matters.

ENVIRONMENT INVESTIGATION AGENCY
2 Floor, 69-85 Old St
London EC1V 9HX, UK
Tel 020 7490 7040
Web www.
eia-international.org

EUROPA NOSTRA
Lange Voorhout 35
2514 EC, The Hague
Holland
Tel 70 356 0333
Email office@
europanostra.org
Devoted to preserving
Europe's national and
cultural heritage,
improving the
environment and
encouraging high
standards of town and
country planning.

EUROPE CONSERVATION
Col. Vilanna 6A
20143 Milano, Italy
Tel 02 8395475
Charity which runs
ecological and
archaeological holiday and
research programmes in
Europe's parks and nature
reserves.

FAUNA AND FLORA INTERNATIONAL
Great Eastern House
Tenison Road
Cambridge
CB1 2TT, UK
Web www.fauna-flora.org
Tel 01223 571 000

FIELD STUDIES COUNCIL
Head Office
Preston Montford
Montford Bridge
Shrewsbury SY4 1HW, UK
Tel 01743 850674
Web www.
field-studies-council.org
Email ffc.headoffice@
ukonline.co.uk
The council runs over 500
courses a year at its 11
centres in England and
Wales.

FIELD STUDIES COUNCIL OVERSEAS
Mrs Anne Stephens,
Overseas Expeditions
Co-ordinator
Montford Bridge
Shrewsbury SY4 1HW, UK
Tel 01743 852150
Runs environmental study
courses of one to four
weeks' duration worldwide.

FRIENDS OF CONSERVATION
Riverbank House
1 Putney Bridge Approach
London SW6 3JD, UK
Web www.foc-uk.com
Tel 020 7731 7803
Fax 020 7731 8213
Professional forum
bringing together travel
industry figures and
environmental
campaigners.

FRIENDS OF THE EARTH
26-28 Underwood Street
London N1 7JQ, UK
Tel 020 7490 1555
Web www.foe.co.uk
Email info@foe.co.uk
Campaigning organisation
promoting policies which
protect the natural
environment.

GREEN FLAG INTERNATIONAL
PO Box 396, Linton
Cambs CB1 6UL, UK
Tel 01223 893587
Environmental consultancy
for the tourism industry

and the general travelling public.

GREENPEACE
Canonbury Villas
London N1 2PN, UK
Tel 020 7865 8100
Website www.
greenpeace.org.uk
Email info@
uk.greenpeace.org.uk
International
environmental pressure
group.

INSTITUTE OF TRAVEL AND TOURISM
113 Victoria Street
St Albans, Herts AL1 3TJ
UK
Tel 01727 854395
Email admin@itt.co.uk

INTERFACE NORTH-SOUTH TRAVEL
Moulsham Mill
Parkway, Chelmsford
Essex CM2 7PX, UK
Tel 01245 252414
Website www.
northsouthtravel.co.uk
Email brenda@
nftravel.demon.co.uk
A travel agency which
devotes its profits to
development projects in
the Third World.

THE INTERNATIONAL ECOTOURISM SOCIETY
PO Box 668, Burlington
VT 05402, USA
www.ecotourism.org
Ph: 802 651 9818
Fax: 651 9819
ecomail@ecotourism.org

THE LAND IS OURS
Box E, 111 Magdalen Road
Oxford OX4 1RQ, UK
Tel 01865 722 016
A land rights charity.

MARINE CONSERVATION SOCIETY
9 Gloucester Road
Ross-on-Wye
Hereford HR9 5B, UUK
Tel 01989 566017

Web www.mcsuk.org
Email info@mcsuk.org

MEDITERRANEAN ACTION PLAN (MAP)
Lazriou Avenue 301
19002 Peania, Athens
Greece
Tel 1-665 7912
Conservation body which
carries out research into the
protection of the
Mediterranean coastal and
marine environment.

NATIONAL TRUST WORKING HOLIDAYS
PO Box84, Cirencester
Glocs GL7 1ZP, UK
Tel 01285-644 727
Web www.nationaltrust.
org.uk/volunteers
Runs over 400 volunteer
working projects/holidays a
year all over the UK.

NATIONAL TRUST FOR SCOTLAND
28 Charlotte Square
Edinburgh EH2 4ET, UK
Tel 0131 243 9470
Working holidays all over
Scotland as well as a variety
of cruises around the
world, the profits of which
go to the Islands Fund.

NATURETREK
Cheriton Mill, Cheriton
Nr. Alresford
Hants SO24 0NG, UK
Tel 01962 733051
Web www.naturetrek.co.uk
Email info@
naturetrek.co.uk
Birdwatching, natural
history and botanical tours
worldwide. Donates a
percentage of profits to
environmental charities.

REEF AND RAINFOREST TOURS
1 The Plains, Totnes
Devon TQ9 5DR, UK
Tel 01803 866965
Website www.
reefrainforest.co.uk

Email reefrain@
btinternet.com
Small outfit running
wildlife and diving tours to
Indonesia, Papua New
Guinea, Honduras,
Venezuela, Peru, Belize,
Ecuador and Costa Rica.

ROYAL SOCIETY FOR THE PROTECTION OF BIRDS (RSPB)
The Lodge, Sandy
Beds SG19 2DL, UK
Tel 01767 680551
Website www.rspb.org.uk
Email bird@
rspb.demon.co.uk

SAVE THE RHINO INTERNATIONAL
16 Winchester Walk21
Bentinck Street
London SE1 9AQ, UK
Tel 020 7357 7474
Website www.
savetherhino.com
Email save@
rhinos.demon.co.uk
Offer unique safaris to
Namibia to see desert
rhinos. Proceeds fund their
protection.

SURVIVAL INTERNATIONAL
11-15 Emerald Street
London WC1N 3QL, UK
Tel 020 7242 1441
Charity devoted to
protecting the human
rights of the world's tribal
peoples.

SUSTAINABILITY LIMITED
The People's Hall
91-97 Freston Road
London W11 4BD, UK
Tel 020 7243 1227

SYMBIOSIS EXPEDITION PLANNING
113 Bolingbroke Grove
London SW11 1DA, UK
Tel 020 7924 5906
Email 101456.2155@
compuserve.com
Ecologically and culturally
sensitive tailor-made

adventure holidays in
South-East Asia.

TOURISM CONCERN
Stapleton House
277-281 Holloway Road
London N7 8HN, UK
Website www.
tourismconcern.org.uk
Tel 020 7753 3330
Fax 020 7753 3331
email info@
tourismconcern.org.uk
Their *Community Tourism
Directory* lists details of
tour companies run by and
benefiting local
communities.

**UNIVERSITY RESEARCH
EXPEDITIONS PROGRAM**
University of California
Davis, CA 94720, USA
Tel 530 752 0692
Organises a range of
expeditions, from
environmental studies to
art and culture.

**WHALE AND DOLPHIN
CONSERVATION SOCIETY**
Alexander House
James Street West
Bath, Avon BA1 2BT, UK
Tel 01225-334511
Web www.wdcs.org
Email info@wcds.org

THE WILDLIFE TRUSTS
The Kiln, Waterside
Mather Road
Newark NG24 1WT, UK
Tel 01636 677711
Email info@
wildlife-trusts.cix.co.uk

**WORLD CONSERVATION
UNION (FORMERLY IUCN)**
28 Rue Mauverney
CH-1196 Gland
Switzerland
Tel 22-99 90001
Website www.iucn.org
Email mail@iucn.org
International organisation
co-ordinating the work of
various charities working
in the field of conservation.

**WORLD TOURISM
ORGANISATION**
Capitan Haya 42
28020 Madrid, Spain
Tel 91-571 0628
International forum for the
travel industry.

**WORLD WIDE FUND FOR
NATURE (WWF)**
Panda House, Weyside Park
Godalming
Surrey GU7 1XR, UK
Tel 01483 426444
Web www.wwf-uk.org
Major international
conservation charity,
including the problems
associated with tourism
development.

Related websites

www.btcv.org.uk
British Trust for
Conservation Volunteers

www.coralcay.org
Coral Cay protect and
restore tropical forests and
coral reefs – and help
sustain livelihoods and
alleviate poverty around
the world at the same time.

www.ecosourcenetwork.
com
Connects eco-minded
travellers and travel
organisers; section on jobs
in ecotourism.

www.ecotour.org
Travel that benefits the
environment and local
communities.

www.green-travel.com
Information about
environmentally
responsible travel an
tourism world wide.

www.gorp.com/rareearth
Eco-friendly safaris in
Africa and India.

Expatriate services

CORONA WORLDWIDE
Commonwealth Institute
Kensington High Street
London W8 6NQ, UK
Tel 020 7610 4407
Information for women
expatriates, especially their
Notes for Newcomers.

**EMPLOYMENT CONDITIONS
ABROAD**
Anchor House
15 Britten Street
London SW3 3TY, UK
Tel 020 7351 5000
Website www.
eca@eca-international.com

HOW TO BOOKS
Customer Services Dept
Plymbridge Distributors
Estover Road
Plymouth PL6 7PZ, UK
Website www.
howtobooks.co.uk
Tel 01752 202 301
Fax 01752 202 331
Country-specific
information on living and
working abroad.

WILFRED T FRY
Crescent House
Crescent Road, Worthing
W Sussex BN11 1RN, UK
Tel 01903 231545
Web www.wilfredtfry.com
Email Wilfred@
wilfredtfry.co.uk
Consultancy on the
financial aspects.

**WORLDWIDE EDUCATION
SERVICE**
Unit D2, Telford Road
Bicester, UK
Tel 01869 248682
Website www.
weshome.demon.co.uk
Email office@
weshome.demon.co.uk
Provides a service for those
teaching children at home.

Related websites

www.criterionworld.com

www.escapeartist.com

www.expatexchange.co.uk

www.expatexpert.com

www.expatspouse.com

www.expattax.co.uk

www.expatworld.com

www.expatnetwork.co.uk

www.livingabroad.com

www.telegraph.co.uk/globa
lliving

Expedition organisers

See also *Adventure and sports tourism*, and *Overland travel*, in this Directory.

ALPINE CLUB
55 Charlotte Road
London EC2A 3QF, UK
Tel 020 7613 0755
Website www.
alpine-club.org.uk
Email sec@
alpine-club.org.uk
Has an important reference collection of literature, guidebooks and maps. View by appointment only.

ARCHAEOLOGY ABROAD
31-34 Gordon Square
London WC1H 0PY, UK
Tel 020 7380 7495
Provides information about opportunities for archaeological field work and excavations abroad.

ARCTURUS EXPEDITIONS
PO Box 850
Gartocharn Alexandria
Dunbartonshire G83 8RL
UK
Tel 01389 830204
Email arcturus@
btinternet.com
Specialise in the Arctic's natural history, native peoples and archaeology. Also dog-sledding, kayaking and skiing.

BRATHAY EXPLORATION GROUP TRUST
Brathay Hall , Ambleside
Cumbria LA22 0HP, UK
Tel 01539 433942
Website www.
brathayexploration.org.uk
Emailadmin@
brathayexploration.org.uk
Provides expedition and training opportunities.

BRITISH SCHOOLS EXPLORING SOCIETY (BSES) EXPEDITIONS
Royal Geographical Society
1 Kensington Gore
London SW7 2AR, UK
Tel 020 7591 3141
Website www.rgs.org
Email bses@rgs.org.uk
Organises major adventurous and scientific expeditions annually for 17-to 20 -year-olds.

EARTHWATCH
Belsyre Court
57 Woodstock Road
Oxford OX2 6HJ, UK
Tel 01865 318838
Web www.earthwatch.org
Email info@
uk.earthwatch.org
Environmental charity, which matches paying volunteers to scientific research projects.

EXPEDITION ADVISORY CENTRE
Royal Geographical Society
1 Kensington Gore
London SW7 2AR, UK
Tel 020 7591 3030
Website www.rgs.org
The Expedition Advisory Centre provides an information and training service for those planning expeditions. Publishers of *The Expedition Planners' Handbook and Directory*.

EXPLORATION LOGISTICS
Floor 3 Bldg 8
Rank Xerox Business Park
Mitcheldean
Glocs GL17 0DD, UK
Tel 01594 545100
Web www.exlogs.com
Email michelle.neve@
exlogs.co.uk
Tailor-made support service for expeditions, with consultancy, design and purchase of equipment, survival courses and field support.

THE EXPLORERS CLUB
46 East 70th St, New York
NY 10021, USA
Tel 212 628 83 83
Web www.explorers.org
The Club has financed over 140 expeditions and awarded its flag to over 300 expeditions.

FOUNDATION FOR FIELD RESEARCH
PO Box 2010, Alpine
California 92001, USA
Sponsors research expeditions and finds volunteers to staff projects.

K & J SLAVIN QUEST
Cannon St House
Cannon St, Louth
Lincs LN11 9NF, UK
Tel 01507 313401
Expedition consultants offering complete support services to individual and commercial clients.

MOUNTAIN AND WILDLIFE ADVENTURES
Brow Foot , HighWray
Ambleside

Cumbria LA22 0JE, UK
Tel 01539 433285
Website www.
mountain-and-wildlife.
co.uk
Specialises in travel and
expedition advice for
Scandinavia.

**NATIONAL GEOGRAPHICAL
SOCIETY**
1145 17th and M Streets,
NW , Washington
DC 20036 , USA
Tel 202 857 7000
Website www.
nationalgeographic.com
The Society's aim is to
pursue and promulgate
geographical knowledge
and to promote research
and exploration. The
Society often sponsors
significant expeditions.

RALEIGH INTERNATIONAL
Raleigh House
27 Parsons Green Lane
London SW6 4HZ, UK
Tel 020 7371 8585
Fax 020 7371 5116
Web www.raleigh.org.uk
Email info@raleigh.org.uk
Leading project-based
organisation taking young
people overseas as
volunteers.

**ROYAL GEOGRAPHICAL
SOCIETY**
1 Kensington Gore
London SW7 2AR, UK
Tel 020 7591 3000
Web www.rgs.org
Email eac@rgs.org
UK's national centre for
geographers and explorers.
It directly organises and
finances its own scientific
expeditions and gives
financial support, approval
and advice to numerous
expeditions each year. The
RGS maintains the largest
private map collection in
Europe and has a large
library with books and

periodicals on geography,
travel and exploration. Also
hosts excellent lecture
programme.

**ROYAL SCOTTISH
GEOGRAPHICAL SOCIETY**
40 George Street
Glasgow G1 1QE
Tel 0141 552 3330
Website www.
geo.ed.ac.uk/~rsgs/
Email r.s.g.s.@Strath.ac.uk
Scottish affiliate of the
RGS.

**SCIENTIFIC EXPLORATION
SOCIETY**
Expedition Base
Motcombe, Shaftesbury
Dorset SP7 9PB, UK
Tel 01747853353
Web www.ses-explore.org
Email jbs@ses-explore.org
Organises its own
expeditions and 'approves
and supports' others, but
rarely provides funding.
Places on long- or short-
term expeditions available.

**SCOTT POLAR RESEARCH
INSTITUTE**
University of Cambridge
Lensfield Road
Cambridge CB2 1ER, UK
Tel 01223 336540
Web www.spri.cam.ac.uk
Has a specialist library
concerned with all aspects
of polar expeditions and
research.

**SOUTH AMERICAN
EXPLORERS CLUB**
Av. Portugal 146, Brena
Postal Casilla 3714
Lima 100 , Peru
Tel 1 425 0142
also at
Jorge Washington 311 y
L.Plaza
Postal Apartado 21-431
Quito, Ecuador
Tel/Fax: 2 225 228
also at
126 Indian Creek Road
Ithaca, NY14850, USA

Tel 607 277 0488
Web www.samexplo.org
Exists to promote travel
and sporting aspects of
exploration. Publications
include *The South
American Explorer*
magazine. The clubhouse,
with reading rooms, maps
and guidebooks, is at the
address in Lima listed
above, and people may visit
at any time.

SYMBIOSIS
205 St John's Hill
London SW11 1TH, UK
Website www.
symbiosis-travel.co.uk
Tel 020 7924 5906
Fax 020 7924 5907
Expedition planning.

TREKFORCE
34 Buckingham Palace Rd
London SW1W 0RE, UK
Tel 020 7828 2275
Web www.trekforce.org.uk
Email trekforce@
dial.pipex.com
Environmental trips.

**UNIVERSITY RESEARCH
EXPEDITIONS PROGRAM**
University of California
Berkeley
CA 94720
Tel 510 642 6586
Organises a range of
expeditions from
environmental studies to
art and culture.

**VANDER-MOLEN
FOUNDATION**
The Model Farm House
Church End
London NW4 4JS, UK
Tel 020 8203 2344
Helps to organise
expeditions, especially for
the handicapped.

**WORLD CHALLENGE
EXPEDITIONS**
Bklack Arrow House
2 Chandos Rd
London NW10 6NF, UK

Tel 020 8961 1122
Website www.
worldchallenge.co.uk
Month-long, fee-paying
projects with the emphasis
on personal development
for the 16-20 age group.

**YOUNG EXPLORERS TRUST
(THE ASSOCIATION OF
BRITISH YOUTH
EXPLORATION SOCIETIES)**
c/o The RGS
1 Kensington Gore
London SW7 2AR, UK
Tel 020 7591 3141
Website www.rgs.org
Provides a forum for
societies and individuals to
exchange information.

Related websites

www.adventureonline.com
Share an expedition
(virtually at least).

www.explorers.org
Interesting explorers' club

Freight
Forwarders

ALLIED PICKFORDS
345 Southbury Road
Enfield
Middlesex EN1 1UP, UK
Tel 0800 289 229
Website www.
allied-pickfords.co.uk

ATLASAIR
Unit 18
Heathrow Trading Estat
Green Lane, Hounslow
Middlesex TW4, UK
Tel 020 8707 7300

**BRITISH INTERNATIONAL
FREIGHT ASSOCIATION
(BIFA)**
Redfern House
Browells Lane

Feltham
Mids TW13 7EP, UK
Tel 020 8844 2266
Web www.bifa.org
Email bifa@btconnect.com
Trade association. Publish a
directory of members.

CLAYDON NCOY
Ensign House
42/44 Thomas Road
London E14 7BJ, UK
Tel 020 7987 8211

CONSTANTINE
134 Queen's Road
London SE15 2HR, UK
Tel 020 7635 0224

EXCESS BAGGAGE
Unit 1-9 Abbey Road
Industrial Park
Commercial Way
London NW10 6XF, UK
Tel 020 8965 3344
Fax 020 8961 2040

JEPPESEN HEATON
17 Church St , Epsom
Surrey KT17 4PF, UK
Tel 01372 745678
Email ian@
jeppesen.freeserve.co.uk

**SEALANDAIR TRANSPORT
COMPANY**
101 Stephenson Street
London E16 4SA, UK
Tel 020 7511 2288

Gay travel

THE DAMRON COMPANY
PO Box 422458
San Francisco, CA 94142
USA
Tel 415-255 0404

THE FERRARI GUIDES
PO Box 37887
Phoenix, AZ 85069, USA
Tel 602-863 2408
Website www.
ferrariguides.com
Email ferrari@q-net.com

MAN AROUND
89 Wembley Park Drive
Wembley Park
Middlesex HA9 8HS, UK
Tel 020 8902 7177
Web www.manaround.com
Gay holidays (Europe and
Australia).

OLIVIA TRAVEL
www.oliviatravel.com
Travel for women who like
women.

OUR WORLD MAGAZINE
Our World Publishing
1104 N Nova Road
#251 Daytona Beach
FLA 32117, USA
Tel 904-441 5367
Website www.
ourworldmag.com
Email ourworldmg@
aol.com

POSITIVE DISCOUNTS
PO Box 347, Twickenham
Mdsx TW1 2SN, UK
Tel 0870 345 3451
Web www.thecard.uk.com
Email hello@
thecard.uk.com
Travel insurance
whether or not you are
HIV-positive.

SENSATIONS
89 Wembley Park Drive
Wembley Park
Middlesex HA9 8HS, UK
Tel 020 7625 6969
Gay holidays (mainly in
Europe and USA).

**SPARTACUS CLUB
INTERNATIONAL GAY GUIDE**
Leuschnerdamm 31
Berlin 10999, Germany
Tel 30-2363 9377

URANIAN TRAVEL
Infocus House
111 Kew Road
Mdsx TW9 2PN, UK
Tel 020 8332 1022
Tour operator to mainly
European gay resorts.

Gourmet travel

ALTERNATIVE TRAVEL GROUP
69-71 Banbury Road
Oxford OX2 6PE, UK
Tel 01865 513333
Website www.
alternative-travel.co.uk
Email info@
atg-oxford.co.uk
Organises a number a
special interest holidays
including walking and wine
tours.

ARBLASTER AND CLARKE
Clarke House
Farnham Road, West Liss
Hants GU33 6AQ, UK
Tel 01730 895353
Website www.
arblasterandclarke.com
Email sales@
winetours.co.uk
Leading organisers of
worldwide wine tours.

SYMBIOSIS EXPEDITION PLANNING
205 St John's Hill
113 Bolingbroke Grove
London SW11 1TH, UK
Tel 020 7924 5906
Website www.
symbiosis-travel.co.uk
Email info@
symbiosis-travel.co.uk
Gastronomic and cultural
tours in South-East Asia.

TASTING PLACES
Unit 40 , Buspace Studios
Conlan Street
London W10 5AP, UK
www.tastingplaces.com
Tel 020 7460 0077
Fax 020 7460 0029
Email ss@
tastingplaces.com
Outstanding itineraries in
romantic destinations.
Expensive but exquisite.

Related websites

www.eatbug.com
Insect recipes, including
locust and mealy-worm.

www.eat-out.com
World wide guide to
restaurants and cafés.

www.globalgourmet.com/
destinations
Choose a country and
check out the cuisine.

www.orbweavers.com/
ultimate
Pick a cuisine, and a
destination and find a
matching restaurant.

www.restaurants.net

www.restaurantsrow.com

www.tudocs.com
Directory of culinary
websites worldwide.

www.zagat.com
The online version of the
reliable guide books, with
over 20,000 reviews world
wide.

Hitch-hiking associations

Allostop

Website www.allostop.com
Allostop is the collective
name for the associations
Allauto, Provoya and Stop-
Voyages. Allostop puts you
in contact with drivers with
a view to sharing petrol
costs. A small annual
subscription fee allows you
an unlimited number of
journeys in a year starting
from the date of enrolment
(If you wish to make only
one journey, the fee is less.)
Do remember to enrol
sufficiently in advance.
Allostop's main offices are:

Canada

ALLOSTOP
4317 Rue Saint Denis
Montreal H2J 2K9
Quebec
Tel 514-985 30 32
Web www.allostop.com

ALLOSTOP
665 Rue Saint-Jean,
61R Quebec
Tel 418 522 34 30

ALLOSTOP
185 Rue Alexandre
Sherbrooke JIH 4S8
Quebec
Tel 819 821 36 37

Czech Republic

AUTO TIP CESTOVNI CERNTALA
Lipova 12, Prague 2 120 00
Tel 2-20 43 83

GOMEZ TRAVEL AGENCY
Mrs Vera Rybova
Malatova 7, 150 00 Prague 5
Tel 2-53 52 48

Denmark

USE-IT-CENTRE
Raadhussteraede 13
DK 1466, Kopenhagen
Tel 1-15 65 18

France

ALLOSTOP
8 Rue Rochambeau, Paris
Tel 1-53 20 42 42 (out from
Paris), 4-53 20 42 43 (into
Paris)

AUTOPASS
21 Rue Patou , 59800 Lille
Tel 3-20 14 31 96

AUTOSTOP
190 Avenue du Pere Soulas
34094 Montpelier
Tel 4-67 04 36 66

C.R.I.J.
17 Rue de Metz
31000 Toulouse
Tel 5-61 21 20 20
Web www.crij.org

MAISON DES LANGUE ET DES VOYAGES
1 Place du Marichal Juin
3530 Rennes
Web www.mdl.fr
Tel 2-99 30 25 15

VOYAGE AU FIL
28 Rue du Calvaire
44000 Nantes
Tel 02 40 89 04 85

Germany

MITFAHRZENTRALE
Lammerstrasse 4,
8 Munich 2
Tel 89-19440
Autostop agency in
Germany; offices also in
Hamburg, Frankfurt,
Berlin.

Spain

IBERSTOP
Calle del Vira 85
18018 Granada
Tel 9 58 29 29 20

VIAJE FACIL
Apartado 336 Enrique
Granados 17
17310 Llorcta del Mar
Tel 972-308 301

IBERSTOP
Calle Maria 13/2
29013 Malaga
Tel 952 254

Switzerland

ALLOSTOP
Mitfahrzentrale
Ankerstr. 16
3006 Berne
Tel 31 444 707

Similar organisations

IN AUSTRIA

MITFAHRZENTRALE
Kapuzinerstrasse 14A4020
Linz
Tel 732-78 27 20

MITFAHRZENTRALE
Danngasse la. 1080 Vienna
Tel 22-408 2210

IN BELGIUM

TAXI-STOP
The Allostop card can be
used for Taxi-stop in
Belgium. Website
www.taxistop.be
Taxi-stop offices are:

INFOR-JEUNES
27 Rue Fosse aux Loups
1000 Brussels
Tel 2 223-2310

TAXI-STOP
51 Onderbergen, 9000 Gent
Tel 91-23 23 10

TAXI-STOP
21 Place de l'Universite
1348 Louvain la Neuve
Tel 10-45 14 14

Home exchange and timeshare associations

HOMELINK INTERNATIONAL
Linfield Hse, Gorse Hill Rd
Virginia Water
Surrey GU25 4AS, UK
Tel 01344 842642
Web www.homelink.org

HOMELINK INTERNATIONAL
1707 Platt Crescent
North Vancouver
BC V7J 1X9, Canada
Tel 604 987 3262

INTERNATIONAL HOME EXCHANGE
Level 2, 17 Sydney Road
Manly NSW 2095, Australia
Tel 8232 2022

INTERNATIONAL HOME EXCHANGE
PO Box 38615
11 Peach Parade, Ellerslie
New Zealand
Tel 9-522 2933

INTERVAC
3 Orchard Court
North Wraxall
Chippenham
Wilts SN14 7AD, UK
Tel 01225 892208
www.intervac.com

THE TIMESHARE COUNCIL
23 Buckingham Gate
London SW1E 6LB, UK
Tel 020 7291 0901
Free advice for members.

VACATION EXCHANGE CLUB
PO Box 820
Haleiwa, HI 96712, USA
Tel 800 638 3841
The longest-established
agency in the United States.

Related websites

www.heig.com

www.holi-swaps.com

www.homebase-hols.com

www.homeexchange.com

www.home-swap.com

www.seniorhomeexhange.com

www.timesharesdirect.com

www.timeshared.com
Timeshares for sale or rent.

www.tradinghomes.com

www.tug2.net
Unbiased opinions.

Honeymoon specialists

There are several British tour operators that specialise in honeymoon travel, some offering honeymoons worldwide, others concentrating on particular regions. Leading agencies are listed here.

ABERCROMBIE & KENT
Sloane Square House
Holbein Place
London SW1W 8NS, UK
Tel 020 7730 9600
Website www.
abercrombiekent.co.uk
Email info@
abercrombiekent.co.uk
Luxury travel agents.

ART OF TRAVEL
51 Castle St
Cirencester
Glos GL7 1QD, UK
Tel 020 7738 2038
Web www.artoftravel.co.uk
Emailsafari@
artoftravel.co.uk

ASIA WORLD
Forrester House
St Peter's St
St Albans
Herts AL1 3LW, UK
Tel 0870 0799788
Email reservations@
asiaworld.co.uk

BEACHCOMBER
Mauritius House
1 Portsmouth Road
Guildford
Surrey GU2 4BL
Tel 01483 533008
Fax 01483 532820
Web www.
beachcomber.co.za

BEST OF MOROCCO
Seend Park, High Street
Seend, Melksham
Wilts SN12 6NZ, UK
Tel 01380 828533

Website www.
morocco-travel.com
Email Vivienne@
dial.pipex.com

BRIDGE THE WORLD
47 Chalk Farm Road
London NW1 8AJ, UK
Website www.b-t-w.co.uk
Tel 020 7911 0900
Fax 020 7813 3350
Email sales@
bridge-the-world.co.uk
Offer 'honeymiles', so friends can buy a honeymoon as a present.

BRITISH AIRWAYS HOLIDAYS
Astral Towers, Betts Way
London Road
Crawley RH10 2XA, UK
Tel 0870 242 4245
Web www.baholidays.co.uk

CARIBBEAN CONNECTION
Concorde House
Canal St
Chester CH1 4EJ, UK
Tel 01244 355300
Email cc@itc-uk.com

COX & KINGS
Gordon House
10 Greencoat Pl
London SW1P 1PH, UK
Tel 020 7873 5000
Website www.
coxandkings.co.uk
Email Cox.Kings@
coxandkings.co.uk
Luxury travel agents.

CV TRAVEL
43 Cadogan St
London SW3 2PR, UK
Tel 020 7581 0851

ELEGANT RESORTS
The Old Palace
Chester CH1 1RB, UK
Tel 01244 897 888
Website www.
elegant resort.com
Email enquiries@
elegantresorts.co.uk

HAYES & JARVIS
Hayes House

152 Kings Street
London W6 0QU
Tel 0870 8989890
Fax 0208 741 0299
Luxury travel agents.

JOURNEY LATIN AMERICA
12-13 Heathfield Terrace
London W4 4JE, UK
Tel 020 8747 8315
Website www.
journeylatinamerica.co.uk
Email tours@
journey latinamerica.co.uk

KUONI
Kuoni House, Dorking
Surrey RH5 4AZ, UK
Tel 01306 742222
Web www.kuoni.co.uk
Email weddings.sales@
kuoni.co.uk

THE MAGIC OF SPAIN/ITALY/PORTUGAL/ ITALIAN ESCAPADES
2-7 Shepherds Bush Rd
London W6 7AS, UK
Tel 020 8741 4440
Web www.
magictravelgroup.co.uk

SANDALS RESORTS
32 Ives St
London SW3 2ND, UK
Tel 020 7581 9895
Web www.sandals.com
Email postmaster@
sandals.co.uk

SUNSET TRAVEL
4 Abbeville Mews
88 Clapham Park Road
London SW4 7BX
Tel 020 7498 9922
Email info@
sunsettravel.co.uk

THOMAS COOK HOLIDAYS
13-15Coningsby Road
Peterborough PE3 8AB, UK
Tel 01733 563200
Web www.
thomascook.com

WORLD ARCHIPELAGO
55 Fulham High St
London SW6 3JJ, UK
Tel 020 8780 5838

Website www.
tanzaniaodyssey.co.uk
Email worldarc@
compuserve.com

**WORLDWIDE JOURNEYS
AND EXPEDITIONS**
27 Vanston Place
London SW6 1AZ, UK
Tel 020 7381 8638
Email wwwj@
wjournex.demon.co.uk

Related websites

www.confetti.co.uk/travel/
weddings_abroad

www.wedaway.com

www.weddingsabroad.com

Horse-riding associations and agencies

**THE AMERICAN
HORSESHOWS ASSOCIATION**
4047 Iron Walks Parkway
Lexington
Kentucky 40511, USA
Tel 859 258 2472
Web www.ahsa.org

ARCTIC EXPERIENCE
29 Nork Way
Banstead SM7 1PB, UK
Tel 01737 362321
Riding in Iceland.

**CANADIAN EQUESTRIAN
FEDERATION**
1600 James Naismith Drive
Gloucester
Ontario K1B 5N4, Canada
Tel 613-748 5632

**THE NEW ZEALAND
EQUESTRIAN FEDERATION**
PO Box 47 , Hastings
Hawks Bay, New Zealand
Tel 6470 850 85

**EQUITOUR/ PEREGRINE
HOLIDAYS**
40/41 South Parade
Summertown
Oxford OX2 7JP, UK
Tel 01865 511642
Email mail@equitour.co.uk
Equestrian holidays
worldwide.

**THE EQUESTRIAN
FEDERATION OF AUSTRALIA**
52 Kensington Road
Rose Park
South Australia 5067
Australia
Tel 618 311 8411

EXPLORE WORLDWIDE LTD
1 Frederick St
Aldershot
Hants GU11 1LQ, UK
Tel 01252-344161
Web www.explore.co.uk
Emailinfo@explore.co.uk
Including pony-trekking.

INNTRAVEL
Hovingham
York YO6 4JZ
Tel 01653 628862
France and Spain.

**INTERNATIONAL HORSE
TRAVEL ASSOCIATION**
12 Rue du Rieensart 18
1331 Rosieres, Belgium
Tel 2 652 1010
Equestrian holidays
worldwide.

RIDE WORLDWIDE
Staddon Farm
North Tawton
Devon EX20 2BX, UK
Tel 01837 82544
Fax 01837 82179
Web www.
ridetheworld.co.uk
Adventurous riding trips.

SOBEK EXPEDITIONS INC
Box 1089 , Angels Camp
California 95222 , USA
Tel 800-777 7939
Riding in the Rockies.

STEAMOND INTERNATIONAL
23 Eccleston Street

London SW1W 9LX
Tel 020 7730 8646
Web www.easytravel.com
Riding tours in Argentina;
also polo-playing.

Related websites

www.apachestables.com
Riding trips in the Grand
Canyon.

www.equestrianvacations.
com

www.gorp.com/oldwest
Old West dude ranch

www.ranchweb.com
Holidays on dude and
cattle ranches.

www.ridingtours.com

Hostelling associations

Virtually every country has
a hostelling association of
some kind. For further
contact addresses, the
International Youth
HostelFederation publishes
an annual *Hostelling
International Book*. Their
website is www.iyhf.org/
iyhf/ehome.html.

In the UK

**YOUTH HOSTEL
ASSOCIATION**
Trevelyan House
8 St Stephens Hill
St Albans, Herts AL1 2DY
Tel 01727 855215
Web www.yha.org.uk
Emailcustomerservices@
yha.org.uk

**SCOTTISH YOUTH
HOSTELASSOCIATION**
7 Glebe Crescent

Stirling FK8 2JA
Tel 01786 891400
Web www.syha.org.uk
Email customerservices@
syha.org.uk

**YOUTH HOSTEL
ASSOCIATION OF
NORTHERN IRELAND**
22-32 Donegal Road
Belfast BT12 5JN
Tel 01232 324733
Web www.hina.org.uk
Email info@hin.org.uk

In the USA

American Youth Hostels
National Offices
PO Box 37613
Washington
DC 20013-7613
Tel 202-783 6161
Web www.hiayh.org

Related websites

www.hostels.com

www.backpackers.com.au

www.travel-ys.com
Central reservation system
for the YMCA and YWCA

Hotels and accommodation

There are so many hotels
and chains that this listing
can only cover the major
chains and brands. These
are continually subject to
takeover bids, so details
may change.

Addresses shown are for
UK or European offices,
not necessarily for global
headquarters.

**ACCOR HOTELS
AND RESORTS**
(Owns Sofitel, Mecure,
Ibis, Libertel, Novotel)
Hammersmith Int. Centre
1 Shortlands
London W8 8DR, UK
Tel (UK) 020 8283 4500
Web www.accor.com

BASS HOTELS & RESORTS
(Owns Inter Continental,
Southern Pacific, Holiday
Inn, Crowne Plaza)
The Thameside Centre
Kew Bridge Road
Brentford
Middlesex TW8 0EB, UK
Tel(UK) 0800 897121
Tel (USA) 0700 604 2000
Web www.basshotels.com

**BEST WESTERN
INTERNATIONAL**
7 Bridle Close
Kingston Upon Thames
Surrey KT1 2JW, UK
Tel (UK) 0800 393130
Tel (USA) 1 800 780 7234
Web www.bestwestern.com

CENDANT
(Owns Days Inn, Howard
Johnson, Travelodge,
Ramada USA)
26 Station Square
Petts Wood
Kent BR5 1NA, UK
Tel (UK) 01483 440470
Tel (USA) 407 370 2861
Web www.cendant.com

**CHOICE HOTELS
AND RESORTS**
(Own Sleep, Quality,
Clarion, Flag, Comfort)
Premier House
112-114 Station Rd
Edgware
Middlesex HA8 7BJ, UK
Tel (UK) 0800 444444
Tel (USA) 301 592 5000
Web www.
choicehotels.com

CONCORDE HOTELS
Grosvenor Gardnes House
35/37 Grosvenor Gardens

London SW1W 0BS, UK
Tel (UK) 0800 181 591
Tel (USA) 1 800 888 4747
Web www.
concorde-hotels.com

**DORINT HOTELS
& RESORTS**
Molasses House
Clove Hitch Quay
Plantation Wharf
London SW11 3TN, UK
Tel (UK) 00800 1367 4681
Tel (US A) 0 800 65 08 018
Web www.dorint.com

FAIRMONT HOTELS
(Owns Delta, Canadian
Pacific, Fairmont)
62-65 Trafalgar Square
London WC2N 5AF, UK
Tel (UK) 0800 515 070
Tel (USA) 1 800 866 5577
Web www.fairmont.com

FORTE
(Owns Le Meridien,
Posthouse, Heritage Hotels,
Travelodge)
166 High Holborn
London WC1V 6TT, UK
Tel (UK) 0800 404040
Tel (USA) 212 686 4081
Web www.forte-hotels.com

FOUR SEASONS
(Owns Four Seasons,
Regent Hotels)
7 Old Park Lane
London W1Y 3LJ, UK
Tel (UK) 0800 526 648
Tel (US A) 1 800 819-5053
Web www.fourseasons.com

HILTON
(Owns Hilton National,
International, Conrad,
Doubletree, Red Lion)
10th Floor
Hilton National Wembley
Empire Way
Middlesex HA9 8DS, UK
Tel (UK) 0990 445866
Tel (USA) 1 800 774 1500
Web www.hilton.com

**HYATT HOTELS
AND RESORTS**
Tolworth Tower

Ewell Road, Surbiton
Surrey KT6 7EL, UK
Tel (UK) 0345 581666
Tel (US A) 312 750 1234
Web www.hyatt.com

KEMPINKSI
Collingham House
Gladstone Road
London SW19 1QT, UK
Tel (UK) 00800 426 31355
Tel (US A)1 800 426 3135
Web www.kempinski,com

LEADING HOTELS OF THE WORLD
Avenfield House
118-127 Park Lane
London W1Y 4LH, UK
Tel (UK) 0800 181 123
Tel (USA) 1 800 223 6800
Web www.lhw.com

MANDARIN ORIENTAL
(Owns Mandarin Oriental,
Rafael Hotels)
Avenfield House
118-127 Park Lane
London W1Y 4LH, UK
Tel (UK) 00800 2823 3838
Web www.
mandarin-oriental.com

MARITIM HOTELS
1 Burgess Mews
38 Wycliffe Mews
London SW19 1UF, UK
Tel (UK) 0500 30 30 30
Tel (USA) 1800 8 43 33 11
Web www.maritim.de

MARRIOTT INTERNATIONAL
(Owns Marriott, Ramada
International, Renaissance,
Ritz Carlton, Marriott,
Courtyard by Marriot)
Bowater House East, 7th Flr
68 Knightsbridge
London SW1X 7XH, UK
UK) 0800 221222
USA) 1 888 236 2427
Web www.
marriothotels.com

MILLENNIUM COPTHORNE HOTELS
(Owns Millennium Hotels.
Copthorne Hotels, Regal
Hotels in USA)

Victoria House, Victoria Rd
Horely
Surrey RH6 7AF, UK
Tel (UK) 0800 414741
Web www.mill-cop.com

MOVENPICK
106 Zurichstrasse
Asliswil CH 8134
Switzerland
Tel (UK) 00800 1111 2222
Tel (US) 011 800 1111 2222
Web www.
movenpick-hotels.com

OBEROI
1 Thames Place
Lower Richmond Road
London SW15 1HF, UK
Tel (UK) 0800-96 20 96
Tel (USA) 800-562 37 64
Web www.
oberoihotels.com

PAN PACIFIC
4th Flr, 75-77 Margaret St
London W1N 7HB, UK
Tel (UK) 00800 777 96753
Tel (USA) 800 223 5652
Web www.panpac.com

PEGASUS
(Owns Utell, Golden Tulip,
Summit, Sterling)
14th Flr, Quadrant House
The Quadrant, Sutton
Surrey SM2 3AR, UK
Tel (UK) 08705 300 200
Tel (US A) 1 800 44 UTELL
Web www.pegsinc.com

THE PENINSULA GROUP
5 Lower Belgrave Street
London SW1W 0NR, UK
Tel (UK) 020 7730 0993
Tel (USA) 310 278 8777
Web www.peninsula.com

PREFERRED HOTELS AND RESORTS
34 Shepherds Hill
London N6 5AH, UK
Tel (UK) 00800 3237 5001
Tel (USA) 1 800 323 7500
Webwww.
preferredhotels.com

RADDISON HOTELS
4 Richview Office Park

Clonskeagh Road
Dublin 14, Ireland
Tel (UK) 0800 374411
Tel (USA) 1 800 333 3333
Web www.raddison.com

SHANGRI-LA HOTELS
5 The Courtyard
Swan Centre, Fishers Lane
London W4 1RX, UK
Tel (UK) 020 8747 8485
Tel (USA) 1 800 942 5050
Web www.shangri-la.com

SRS-WORLDHOTELS
4th Flr, 75-77 Margaret St
London W1N 7HB, UK
Tel (UK) 00 800 77 79 67 53
Tel (USA) 1 800 223 5652
Web www.
srsworldhotels.com

SMALL LUXURY HOTELS
James House, Bridge Street
Leatherhead
Surrey KT22 7EP, UK
Tel (UK) 00 800 525 48000
Tel (USA) 800 525 4800
Web www.slh.com

SOL MELIA
Melia White House
Regents Park
London NW1 3UP, UK
Tel (UK) 0800 962720
Tel (USA) 1 800 33 MELIA
Web www.solmelia.es

STARWOOD HOTELS
(Owns Westin, Sheraton,
Four Points, St Regis,
Luxury Collection, W
Hotels)
C c/o The Park Lane Hotel
Piccadilly
London W1Y 8BX, UK
Tel (UK) 00800 325 353535
Tel (USA) 800 325 3535
Web www.starwood.com

SUPRANATIONAL HOTELS
(Owns Achat Hotels, Acora,
Alfa Hotels, Andersen
Hotels, Austrotel, CCL,
Danubius, Fiesta, Caesar
Park, Jurys Doyle, Maritim,
Occidental, Protea, Rica
Hotels, Provobis, Sonesta,
Space)

The Butlers Wharf Building
Shad Thames
London SE1 2YE, UK
Tel (UK) 0500 30 30 30
Tel (USA) 1 800 843 3311
Web www.
supranational.co.uk

SWISSOTEL
Tel (UK) 00 800 637 94771
Tel (USA) 800 637 9477
Web www.swissotel.com

TAJ HOTELS
St James Court
Buckingham Gate
London SW1E 6AF, UK
Tel (UK) 0800 282699
Web www.tajhotels.com

Related websites

www.accomodata.co.uk
Accommodation by
country.

www.all-hotels.com
Linked to 55,000 online-
bookable hotels worldwide

http://asa.net
Find any kind of
accommodation anywhere.

http://cyberrentals.com
Private homes for hire.

www.holiday-rentals.co.uk
Private homes around the
world for rent.

www.hotelbook.com

www.hotelguide.com
Over 60,000 hotels to
choose from.

www.hotelstravel.com

www.hotelworld.com

www.innsite.com/index.ht
ml
International directory of
inns and bed-and-
breakfasts accommodation.

www.laterooms.co.uk
Late availability and
discounts.

www.placestostay.com

www.quikbook.com
Room availability and
reservations (often
discounted) for US hotels.

www.
1001-villa-holidaylets.com

Luxury tourism

ABERCROMBIE & KENT
Sloane Square House
Holbein Place
London SW1W 8NS, UK
Tel 020 7730 9600
Web www.
abercrombiekent.co.uk
Email info@
abercrombiekent.co.uk
also at
1420 Kensington Road
Suite 111, Oakbrook
IL 60521, USA
Tel 312 954 2944
Email info@
abercrombiekent.co

CARIBBEAN CONNECTIONS
Concorde House
Canal St
Chester CH1 4EJ, UK
Tel 01244 355300
Email cc@itc-uk.com

COX AND KINGS
Gordon House
10 Greencoat Place
London SW1P 1PH, UK
Tel 020 7873 5006
Fax 020 7630 6038
Web www.
coxandkings.co.uk

CUNARD SEABOURN
3rd Floor
Mountbatten House

Grosvenor Square
Southampton SO15 2BF
UK
Tel 02380 716634
Web www.cunard line.com

CV TRAVEL
43 Cadogan St
London SW3 2PR, UK
Tel 020 7581 0851

ELEGANT RESORTS
The Old Palace
Chester CH1 1RB, UK
Tel 01244 897 888
Fax 01244 897 990
Web www.
elegantresorts.co.uk
Email enquiries@
elegantresorts.co.uk

EXSUS TRAVEL LTD
23 Heddon Street
London W1R 7LG, UK
Web www.exsus.com
Tel 020 7292 5050
Fax 020 7292 5051
Email travel@exsus.com
Luxury tour operator for
South America, Mexico
and the Caribbean.

NOMADIC THOUGHTS
81 Brondesbury Road
London NW6 6BB, UK
Tel 020 7604 4408
Fax 020 7604 4407
Email uknomadic@
aol.com

RIVIERA RETREATS
52 Station Road
Petersfield
Hampshire GU32 3ES, UK
Tel 01243 575338

TUSCANY NOW
276 Seven Sisters Road
London N4 2HY, UK
Tel 020 7272 5469
Fax 020 7272 6184

VENICE SIMPLON ORIENT EXPRESS LTD
Sea Containers House
20 Upper Ground
London SE1 9PF
Tel 020 7928 6000
Fax 020 7805 5908

Web www.
orient-express.com
Email reservations@
orient-express.com

WESTERN & ORIENTAL TRAVEL LTD
King House
11 Westbourne Grove
London W2 4UA, UK
Tel 020 7313 6611
Fax 020 7313 6601
Email info@
westernoriental.com

WEXAS INTERNATIONAL
45-49 Brompton Road
London SW3 1DE
Tel 020 7589 3315
Web www.wexas.com
Email mship@wexas.com
Top UK travel club.

WORLD APART
PO Box 44209
Nairobi, Kenya
Tel 228961
and c/o
15 Clarence Pde
Cheltenham
Glos GL50 3PA, UK
Email info@
world-apart-travel.co.uk
Tel 01242 226578

Related websites

FIRST CLASS TRAVEL

www.bluetrain.co.za
South Africa's premier train

www.bookorbuy.com/
rovos
Luxury train travel through
Africa

www.flightfantasy.com

www.learjet.com

www.rajasthantourism.
com/rajtourism/pow/htm
India's Palace on Wheels

FIRST CLASS HOLIDAYS

www.islandhideaways.com

www.silk-steps.co.uk
Tailor-made tours of the
Far East and the Horn of
Africa.

www.spacevoyages.com
Book now for blast-off in
2002.

www.tailor-made.co.uk
Upmarket customised
itineraries.

www.tcs-expeditions.com
Private planes and private
trains, extravagant
itineraries.

www.turtlefiji.com
Turtle Island – 500 acres of
paradise.

www.unchartedoutposts.
com
Private ranches and
exclusive safaris

http://uncommonjourneys
.com

LUXURY ACCOMMODATION

www.quality-villas.co.uk

www.slh.com/slh
The Small Luxury Hotels of
the World group.

www.tuscanynow.com

www.villasofdistinction.
com

www.villa-rentals.com

www.unusualvillarentals.
com

www.worldexecutive.com
Directory to some of the
best hotels in the world.

Microlighting associations

BRITISH MICROLIGHT AIRCRAFT ASSOCIATION
Bullring, Deddington
Banbury
Oxon OX15 0TT, UK
Tel 01869 338888
Web www.bmaa.org
Email general@bmaa.org

EUROPEAN AIR SPORTS
Royal Belgium Aeroclub
1 rue Montoyre
Boite 12, 1040 Brussells
Tel 2 511 7947

UNITED STATES ULTRALIGHT ASSOCIATION
PO Box 667
Frederick MD21705, USA
Tel 301 695 9100

Mountaineering associations

ALPINE CLUB
55 Charlotte Road
London EC2A 3QF, UK
Tel 020 7613 0755
Web www.
alpine-club.org.uk
Email sec@
alpine-club.org.uk

BRITISH MOUNTAINEERING COUNCIL (BMC)
177179 Burton Road
Manchester M20 2BB, UK
Tel 0161 445 4747
Web www.thebmc.org
Everything of interest to
mountaineers, including
climbing walls in Britain.

MOUNT EVEREST FOUNDATION
Gowrie, Cardwell Close

Preston
Lancashire PR4 1SH, UK
Tel 01772 635346
Web www.mef.org.uk
Email bill.ruthven@
ukgateway.net

**MOUNTAIN MEDICINE
DATA CENTRE**
Department of
Neurological Sciences
St Bartholomew's Hospital
38 Little Britain
London EC1A 7BE, UK
Tel 020 737 77000

Related websites

www.americasroof.com
US high spots

www.highplaces.co.uk
Climbs and other high
altitude adventures around
the world.

www.megagrip.co.uk
Climbing and associated
activities.

Older travellers

ACE STUDY TOURS
Babraham
Cambridge CB2 4AP, UK
Tel 01223 835055
Web www.study-tours.org
Email ace@study-tours.org
Cultural study tours
throughout Europe.

AGE CONCERN ENGLAND
Astral House
1268 London Road
London SW16 4ER, UK
Tel 020 8679 8000
Web www.
ageconcern.org.uk
Provides holiday fact sheets
and books.

HELP THE AGED
16-18 St James's Walk
London EC1R 0BE, UK
Tel 020 7253 0253
Web www.
helptheaged.org.uk

SAGA HOLIDAYS
The Saga Building
Middelburg Square
Folkestone
Kent CT20 1AZ, UK
Tel 01303 771111
Web www.saga.co.uk
Extensive range of holidays
world-wide for the over
60's (companions can be
over 50). Also publish *Saga*,
a magazine for older
readers.

TIME OF YOUR LIFE
78 Capel Road
East Barnet
Herts EN4 8JF, UK
Tel 020 8449 4506
Organises retirement-
planning holidays.

TRIPSCOPE
Alexandra House
Albany Rd
Middlesex TW8 0NE, UK
Tel 020 8580 7021
Email tripscope@
cableinet.co.uk
also at
Tripscope South West
Vassell Centre, Gill Ave
Bristol BS16 2QQ, UK
Tel 0117 941 4094
Transport information
service for disabled or
elderly people.

WALLACE ARNOLD TOURS
62 George Street
Croydon
Surrey CR9 1DN, UK
Tel 020 8688 7255
Web www.
waworldchoice.com
Email info@
waworldchoice.com
Coach holidays on the
Continent.

WORLD EXPEDITIONS
3 Northfields Prospect
Putney Bridge Road
London SW18 1PE, UK
Tel 020 8870 2600
Web www.
worldexpeditions.co.uk
Email enquiries@
worldexpeditions.co.uk
Australian-based tour
operator who offer
adventure holidays for the
over-50s.

Further reading

*Life in the Sun: A guide to
Long-stay Holidays and
Living Abroad in Retirement*
(Age Concern)

*The Good Non-Retirement
Guide* (Kogan Page)

Related websites

www.eldertreks.com
Adventure travel company
for senior citizens.

www.poshnosh.com
Older women's travel.

www.senior.com/travel
Online travel magazine for
over-50s.

www.seniorhomeexchange.
com

Overland travel

See also *Adventure and
sports tourism*, and
Expedition organisers, in
this Directory.

AAT KINGS TOURS
15 Grosvenor Place
London SW1X 7HH, UK

Tel 020 8784 2801
Four-wheel-drive safaris in
the Australian Outback.

ACACIA EXPEDITIONS LTD
5 Walm Lane
London NW2 5SJ, UK
Tel 020 8451 3877
Camping safaris in Africa.

ADVENTURE CENTER
1311 63rd Street, Suite 200
Emmeryville
California 94608, USA
Tel 510-654 1879

**ADVENTURE TRAVEL
CENTRE**
131-135 Earls Court Road
London SW5 9RH, UK
Tel 020 7370 4555
Web www.
topdecktravel.co.uk
Email res@
topdecktravel.co.uk
Agency for overland
companies.

AFRICA TRAVEL CENTRE
21 Leigh St
London WC1H 9QX, UK
Tel 020 7387 1211
Web www.africatravel.com
Email info@
africatravel.co.uk
Offers a consultancy service
to overland travellers.

AMERICAN ADVENTURES
6762a Centinela Avenue
Colver City
California 90230, USA
Tel 800 864 0335 (Toll Free)

AMERICAN ADVENTURES
40 High Street
Tunbridge Wells
Kent TN1 1XF, UK
Tel 01892 511894
Email awwt@
btconnect.com
USA, Canada and Mexico.

AMERICAN PIONEERS
PO Box 229
Westlea, Swindon
Wiltshire SN5 7HJ, UK
Tel 01793 881882
Camping in Venezuela,

Mexico, Canada and USA.

BRIDGE THE WORLD
47 Chalk Farm Rd
London NW1 8AN, UK
Tel 020 7911 0900
Web www.b-t-w.com
Email sales@
bridgetheworld.com
Travel agency with most
overland brochures.

**DRAGOMAN ADVENTURE
TRAVEL**
Camp Green , Kenton Road
Debenham
Suffolk IP14 6LA, UK
Tel 01728 861133
Web www.dragoman.co.uk
Email info@
dragoman.co.uk
Overland trips in Asia,
South Africa and South
America.

ENCOUNTER OVERLAND
267 Old Brompton Road
London SW5 9JA, UK
Tel 020 7370 6845
Web www.
encounter-overland.com
Email adventure@
encounter.co.uk
Leading operator, founded
over 30 years ago: Asia,
Africa, Latin America.

EXODUS EXPEDITIONS
9 Weir Road
London SW12 OLT, UK
Tel 020 8675 5550
Web www.exodus.co.uk
Email sales@
exodustravels.co.uk
Leading operator:
expeditions worldwide.

EXPLORE WORLDWIDE LTD
1 Frederick St
Aldershot GU11 1LQ
Tel 01252 344161
Web www.explore.co.uk
Email info@explore.co.uk
Leading operator: 50
countries worldwide.

THE GLOBETROTTERS CLUB
BCM/Roving
London WC1N 3XX

An informal association of
travellers from all over the
world, sharing information
and experiences. Meet
monthly for talks.

GUERBA EXPEDITIONS
Wessex House
40 Station Road
Westbury BA13 3JN
Tel 01373-826611
Web www.guerba.co.uk
E:mail: info@guerba.co.uk
Leading operator: Africa
and Asia.

JOURNEY LATIN AMERICA
12-13 Heathfield Terr
London W4 4JE, UK
Tel 020 8747 8315
Web www.
journeylatinamerica.co.uk
Email tours@
journeylatinamerica.co.uk
Experts in South American
travel, guided tours using
local transport.

MOUNTAIN TRAVEL
6420 Fairmount Avenue
El Cerrito, CA 94530, USA
Tel 510 527 8100
Overland through
Patagonia.

**SUNDOWNERS TRAVEL
CENTRE**
151 Dorcas Street
South Melbourne
Victoria 3205
Australia
Tel 03-690 2499

SUN TRAVEL LTD
407 Great South Road
Penrose, Auckland
New Zealand
Tel 9-525 3074

TRAILFINDERS
194 Kensington High Street
London W8 7RG, UK
Tel 020 7938 3939
(longhaul)
Tel 020 7937 5400
(Transatlantic and
European)
Nowadays a mainstream
flights and travel agency,

but can organise some trips with overlanding companies.

TREK AMERICA
4 Waterperry Court
Middleton Road
Banbury
Oxon OX16 8QB, UK
Tel 01295256777
Web www.trekamerica.com
Email info@
trekamerica.com
North American adventure camping and trekking.

WEXAS INTERNATIONAL
45-49 Brompton Road
London SW3 1DE, UK
Tel 020 7589 3315
Web www.wexas.com
Email mship@wexas.com
Travel club for independent travellers, which can offer advice and book overlanding trips for its members.

Polar tourism

ABERCROMBIE & KENT
Suite 212
1520 Kensington Road
Oak Brook
IL 605232141, USA
Tel 630 954 2944
Web www.
abercrombiekent.com
Email info@
abercrombiekent.com
Various cruises to Antarctica from Argentina on *Explorer*, the vessel originally commissioned by Antarctic tourism pioneer Lars-Eric Linblad.

ARCTIC EXPERIENCE
29 Nork Way
Banstead
Surrey SM7 1PB, UK
Tel 01737 218800
Web www.
arctic-discover.co.uk

Email sales@
arctic-discover.co.uk
Arctic expeditions including Greenland.

ARCTURUS EXPEDITIONS
PO Box 850
Gartocharn Alexandria
Dunbartonshire G83 8RL
UK
Tel 01389 830204
Email arcturus@
btinternet.com
Specialise in the Arctic's natural history, native peoples and archaeology. Also dog -ledding, kayaking and skiing.

GMMS POLAR JOURNEYS
441 Kent Street, Sydney
NSW 2000, Australia
Tel 2 264 3366
Offers the chance to camp ashore in Antarctica overnight. Tours generally two weeks in length.

TRAVEL DYNAMICS
132 East 70th Street
New York, NY 10021, USA
Tel 212 517 7555
Web www.
classicalcruises.com
Operating for the past 25 years with small ships taking parties on educational voyages to Antarctica for non-profit organisations.

WILDWINGS
International House
Bank Road, Bristol
Avon BS15 8LX, UK
Tel 0117 984 8040
Web www.wildwings.co.uk
Email wildinfo@
wildwings.co.uk
Operates bird and wildlife tours to Antarctica.

Railway companies and tours

Foreign railway representatives in the UK

AUSTRALIAN RAILWAYS
c/o Longhaul Leisure Rail
PO Box 5
12 Coningsby Rd
Peterborough PE3 8XP
Tel 0870 7500222
Email andrea.page@
leisurerail.co.uk

AUSTRIAN FEDERAL RAILWAYS
13-14 Cork St
London W1S 3NS
Tel 020 7629 0461
Web www.
austria-tourism.at
Emailinfo@anto.co.uk

BELGIAN NATIONAL RAILWAYS
200a Blackfrairs Foundry
156 Blackfrairs Rd
London SE1 8EN
Tel 020 7593 2332
Email belrail@aol.com

CANADA: RAIL CANADA
c/o Longhaul Leisure Rail
PO Box 5
12 Coningsby Rd
Peterborough PE3 8XP
Tel 0870 7500222

DANISH STATE RAILWAYS
c/o Scandinavian Seaways
Scandinavia House
Parkeston Quay
Harwich
Essex CO12 4QG
Tel 01255 241234
Web www.
dsdsseaways.co.uk

EURO RAIL
c/o Norwegian State Railways

21-24 Cockspur St
London SW1Y 5DA
Tel 020 7387 0444

FINNISH STATE RAILWAYS
Finlandia Travel Agency
227 Regent Street
London W1R 8PD
Tel 020 7409 7334
Web www.norvista.co.uk
Email reservation@
norvista.com

GERMAN RAIL
Suite 6/8, The Sanctuary
23 Oakhill Grove
Surbiton
Surrey KT6 6DU
Tel 0870 2435363
Web www.bahn.de

INDIA RAIL
c/o S D Enterprises Ltd
103 Wembley Park Drive
Wembley HA9 8HG
Tel 020 8903 3411
Web www.indiarail.co.uk

**IRELAND: CORAS IOMPAIR
EIRANN**
185 London Road
Croydon
Surrey CR0 2RJ
Tel 020 86860994

JAPAN RAILWAYS GROUP
c/o East Japan Railway
Company
24-26 Rue de la Petiniere
75008 Paris
Tel 1 45 22 60 48
Web www.jreast.co.jp

**LUXEMBOURG NATIONAL
RAILWAYS**
122 Regent Street
London W1B 5SA
Tel 020 7434 2800
Web www.
luxembourg.co.uk
Email tourism@
luxembourg.co.uk

**NEW ZEALAND RAILWAYS
CORPORATION**
c/o Longhaul Leisure Rail
PO Box 5
12 Coningsby Rd
Peterborough PE3 8XP

Tel 0870 7500222

**NORWEGIAN STATE
RAILWAYS**
c/o European Rail
London SW1Y 5DA
Tel 020 7387 0444

POLISH STATE RAILWAYS
310-312 Regent Street
London SW1R 5HA
Tel 020 7580 8811

PORTUGUESE RAILWAYS
c/o Portuguese Trade &
Tourism Office
2nd floor
22-25a Sackville Street
London W1X 2LY
Tel 020 7494 1441

SOUTH AFRICA: SARTRAVEL
The Pipe Works
26-30 Prescott PL
London SW4 6BU
Tel 020 7627 3560287 1133
Email bee@satravel.co.uk

**SPANISH NATIONAL
RAILWAYS**
c/o Spanish National
Tourist Office
22-23 Manchester Square
London W1M 5AP
Tel 020 7486 8077

SWISS FEDERAL RAILWAYS
Swiss Centre
Swiss Court
London W1V 8EE
Tel 020 7734 4577

USA: AMTRACK
14 Greville St
London EC1N 8SB
Tel 020 7400 7099
Web www.amtrak.com

Specialist rail tour operators

ABERCROMBIE & KENT
Sloane Square House
Holbein Place
London SW1W 8NS, UK
Tel 020 7730 9600
Rail tours France,
Germany, Spain and
Switzerland.

COX & KINGS TRAVEL
Gordon House
10 Greencoat Place
London SW1P 1PH, UK
Tel 020 7873 5006
Palace on Wheels tour
through Rajasthan, and the
Andaluce Express in Spain.

EXPLORERS TOURS
223 Coppermill Road
Wraysbury TW19 5NW
UK
Tel 01753681999
Rail tours of the USA.

LONGHAUL LEISURE RAIL
PO Box 5
12 Coningsby Rd
Peterborough PE3 8XP, UK
Tel 0870 7500 222

RAIL EUROPE
10 Leak Street
London SE1 7NN, UK
Tel 0990848848

**RAILROAD ENTHUSIAST
TOURS**
PO Box 1997, Portoloa
California 96122, USA
Tel 916836 2105

**TEFS RAILWAY TOURS
LIMITED**
77 Frederick St
Loughborough LE11 3BH
UK
Tel 01509262745
Specialist rail holidays.

TRAINS UNLIMITED
PO Box 1997
Portola
California 96122, USA
Tel 916836 1745
also at
c/o GW Travel Limited
6 Old Market Place
Altrincham
Cheshire WA14 4NP, UK
Tel 0161928 9410

**VENICE SIMPLON
ORIENT-EXPRESS**
Sea Containers House
20 Upper Ground
London SE1 9PF
Tel 020 7620 0003

Further reading

ABC Rail Guide
(Reed Travel Group)
for UK and Europe

Eurail Guide
(Houghton Mifflin)

International Timetable
(Thomas Cook)

Overseas Timetable
(Thomas Cook)

Related websites

www.bluetrain.co.za
South Africa's premier train

www.bookorbuy.com/
rovos
Luxury train travel through
Africa.

www.amtrak.com
Timetables, online
bookings and route maps
for the US rail network.

www.eurorailways.com
Good site for finding out
about multi-country rail
passes.

www.eurostar.co.uk

www.indianrailway.com
Official and useful.

http://interrailer.net/
english
Information on inter-
railing across Europe.

www.orient-express.com

www.
rajasthan-tourism.com/
rajtourism/pow/htm
India's Palace on Wheels

www.railserve.com
Links to international

timetables

www.railtrack.co.uk

www.ribbonrail.com/
nmra/travelw2.html
Train timetables
worldwide.

www.
trainweb.com/indiarail
Indian railways: unofficial
but useful.

Sailing associations and agencies

**AUSTRALIAN YACHTING
FEDERATION**
Locked Bag 806
Post Office
Milsons Point
New South Wales 2060
Australia
Tel 2 9922 4333

**BRITISH MARINE
INDUSTRIES FEDERATION**
Marine House
Thorpe Lea Road
Egham
Surrey TW20 8BF
UK
Tel 01784473377
Body representing sailing
holiday companies, offers
Boatline, a holiday
information service.

**CANADIAN YACHTING
ASSOCIATION**
1600 James Naismith Drive
Gloucester
Ontario K1B 5N4
Canada
Tel 613748 5687

CENTRO VELICO CAPERA
Corso Italia 10
Milana 20122
Italy

Tel 289010826
Sailing courses and cruising
near Sardinia, min. age 17.

**CHICHESTER SAILING
CENTRE**
Chichester Marina
Sussex PO20 7EL
UK
Tel 01243 512557
Holidays for beginners and
experienced sailors, with
facilities for the physically,
visually and mentally
handicapped.

CRESTAR YACHTS LTD
Colette Court
125-126 Sloane Street
London SW1X 9AU
UK
Tel 020 7730 9962
Luxury charters in Europe,
the South Pacific and the
Caribbean, with crew.

**NATIONAL FEDERATION OF
SEA SCHOOLS**
Saddlestones
Fletchwood Lane
Totton
Southampton SO40 7DZ
UK
Tel 01703 869956
Full details of sail-training
nationwide, and affiliated
to the International Sailing
Schools Association.

**NEW ZEALAND YACHTING
FEDERATION**
PO Box 90900
Mail Centre
Auckland 1
New Zealand
Tel 649 303 2360

OCEAN YOUTH CLUB
South St
Gosport
Hampshire PO12 1EP
UK
Tel 0870 241 2252
Adventure sailing holidays
for young people.

**ROYAL YACHTING
ASSOCIATION (RYA)**
RYA House

Romsey Road
Eastleigh
Hampshire SO5 4YA
UK
Tel 01703 629962

UNITED STATES YACHTING RACING UNION
PO Box 209
Newport
Rhode Island 02840, USA
Tel 401 849 5200

YACHT CHARTER ASSOCIATION
c/o D. R. Howard
60 Silverdale
New Milton
Hampshire BH25 7DE
UK
Listing of approved members available.

Related websites

www.duhe.com
Worldwide sailing holidays.

www.saltyseas.com
Worldwide sailing guides, good links, travelogue and bookshop.

Self-catering holidays

AMERICAN DREAM HOLIDAYS
1/7 Station Chambers
High St North
London E6 1JE, UK
Tel 020 8470 1181
Villas and apartments in Hawaii and Florida.

AUSTRAVEL
44 Colcton Street
Bristol BS1 5AX, UK
Apartments in Australia and New Zealand.

INTERHOMES
383 Richmond Road

Twickenham
Middlesex TW1 2EF, UK
Tel 020 8891 1294
Apartments, chalets, villas all over Europe.

LAKES AND MOUNTAINS
The Red House
Garstons Close
Titchfield
Fareham
Hampshire PO14 4EW, UK
Tel 01329 844405
Alpine village homes.

LANDMARK TRUST
Shotterbroke
Maidenhead
Berkshire SL6 3SW, UK
Tel 01628825920

NATIONAL TRUST HOLIDAY COTTAGES
PO Box 536
Melksham
Wiltshire SN12 8SX, UK
Tel 01225 791199

SCANMERIDIAN
28b High Street
London NW3 1QA
UK
Tel 020 7431 5393
Traditional Scandinavian summer houses.

Student travel awards and agencies

Travel awards and grants

BP CONSERVATION PROGRAMME
C/o Expeditions Officer
BirdLife International
Wellbrook Court
Girton Road
Cambridge CB3 0NA, UK
Tel 01223 277318
Email eo@birdlife.org.uk

Is jointly administered by the International Council for Bird Preservation and the Fauna and Flora Preservation Society. Each year over £30,000 is given in grant funding.

MOUNT EVEREST FOUNDATION
Gowrie
Cardwell Close
Warton
Preston PR4 1SH, UK
Tel 01772 635346
Supports British and New Zealand expeditions only. Check dates for grant applications, they can be far in advance.

THE ROLEX AWARDS FOR ENTERPRISE
The Secretariat
PO Box 178
1211 Geneva 26
Switzerland
The Rolex Awards provide financial assistance in three broad fields: Applied Sciences and Invention, Exploration and Discovery, the Environment.

ROYAL GEOGRAPHICAL SOCIETY
1 Kensington Gore
London SW7 2AR, UK
Tel 020 7591 3030
Email awards@rgs.org
Administer not only their own awards and grants but those of many other sponsors. Details and applications from the Grants Secretary.

WEXAS INTERNATIONAL
Awards administered by The Royal Geographical Society on behalf of WEXAS. Write for details to the Grants Secretary at the RGS (see above).

WINSTON CHURCHILL MEMORIAL TRUST
15 Queens Gate Terrace

London SW7 5PR, UK
Tel 020 7581 0410
Awards about 100
travelling Fellowships
annually to enable British
citizens to carry out study
projects overseas in various
categories.

YOUNG EXPLORERS TRUST
c/o Royal Geographical
Society
1 Kensington Gore
London SW7 2AR, UK
Tel 020 7591 3030
Gives grants to school
expeditions.

Gap year projects

See also *Working your way
around the world* and *The
student traveller* in Part 2,
for the following key
organisations: Gap Activity
Projects, Gap Challenge,
Project Trust, Operation
Raleigh, Student
Partnership Worldwide.

CHANGING WORLDS
11 Doctors Lane
Chaldon
Surrey CR3 5AE, UK
Tel 01883 340960, website
Web www.
changingworlds.co.uk
Volunteers for teaching,
orphanage and rural work
in Tanzania, Zimbabwe,
Nepal, India, Australia,
New Zealand, Canada and
Argentina.

CORAL CAY CONSERVATION
154 Clapham Park Road
London SW4 7DE, UK
Tel 020 8498 6248
Web www.coralcay.org
Volunteers (especially
divers) needed for coastal
marine protection projects
in Honduras, Borneo, the
Philippines, etc.

FRONTIER CONSERVATION
77 Leonard St

London EC2A 4QS, UK
Tel 020 7613 2422
Website www.
frontierprojects.ac.uk
Environmental surveys and
other scientific research
projects in Tanzania,
Mozambique, Madagascar
and Vietnam.

**I TO I INTERNATIONAL
PROJECTS**
1 Cottage Road
Headingley
Leeds LS6 4DD, UK
Tel 0870 333 2332
Website www.i-to-i.com
Gap year students accepted
as volunteer teachers for Sri
Lanka, India, Bolivia, Costa
Rica, Russia, Uzbekistan,
and conservation
volunteers for Costa Rica,
Ghana and Australia. Also
paid English teachers
recruited for Taiwan and
Vietnam.

QUEST OVERSEAS
32 Clapham Mansions
Nightingale Lane
London SW4 9AQ, UK
Tel 020 8673 3313
Website www.
questoverseas.com
Three-phase gap year
programme in South
America.

RALEIGH INTERNATIONAL
Raleigh House
27 Parsons Green Lane
London SW6 4HZ, UK
Web www.
raleighinternational.org.uk
Tel 020 7371 8585
Fax 020 7371 5116
Leading organisation for
sending volunteers on
projects worldwide.

**TEACHING & PROJECTS
ABROAD**
Gerrard House
Rustington
W Sussex BN16 1AW, UK
Tel 01903 859911
Website www.

teaching-abroad.co.uk
Volunteers including gap
year students are sent for
short or long periods to
teach in schools and
companies in Ukraine,
Russia, India, Ghana,
Brazil, Mexico and China.
No experience required.

TRAVELLERS
7 Mulberry Close
Ferring
W. Sussex BN12 5HY, UK
Tel 01903 502595, website
Web www.
travellersworldwide.com
Gap year and other
volunteers to teach
overseas.

TREKFORCE
34 Buckingham Palace Rd
London SW1W 0RE, UK
Tel 020 7828 2275
Web www.trekforce.org.uk
Scientific and conservation
expeditions to Borneo,
Kenya and Belize.

VENTURE CO WORLDWIDE
Pleck House
Middletown
Moreton Morrell
Warwick CV35 9AU, UK
Tel 01926 651071
Web www.
venturecoworldwiude.com
Expeditions, voluntary
work and language courses
in South America and the
Himalayas.

Student travel
organisations

**COUNCIL ON
INTERNATIONAL
EDUCATION EXCHANGE
(CIEE)**
205 East 42nd Street
New York
NY10017, USA
Tel 212 661 1414

CULTURAL AND EDUCATIONAL SERVICES ABROAD
Western House
Malpas
Truro TR1 1SQ, UK
Tel 01872 225300
Web www.
csa.languages.com
Language learning courses in Europe, Russia and Japan.

EN FAMILLE OVERSEAS
The Old Stables
60b Maltravers Street
Arundel
W Sussex BN18 9BG, UK
Tel 01903 883266
Stay as a paying guest with a French family; language courses in Paris also available.

EUROPEAN COMMUNITY YOUNG WORKER EXCHANGE PROGRAMME
Central Bureau for Educational Visits and Exchanges
Vocational and Education Department
10 Spring Gardens
London SW1A 2BN, UK
Tel 020 7389 4004
web www.
centralbureau.org.uk
EC nationals aged 18 to 25 with vocational experience can apply for placements.

INSCAPE FINE ART TOURS
Austins Farm
High Street
Stonesfield
Witney
Oxon OX9 8PU, UK
Tel 01993 891726
Fine-art study tours to Europe.

INTERNATIONAL ASSOCIATION FOR THE EXCHANGE OF STUDENTS FOR TECHNICAL EXPERIENCE
10 Spring Gardens
London SW1A 2BN
Tel 020 7389 4004
Worldwide opportunities for undergraduates to gain industrial, technical or commercial experience.

INTERNATIONAL EDUCATIONAL OPPORTUNITIES
28 Canterbury Road
Lydden, Dover
Kent CT15 7ER, UK
Tel 01304 823631
An educational agency arranging language courses, homestays and term stays abroad.

INTERNATIONAL FARM EXPERIENCE PROGRAMME
YFC Centre
National Agricultural Centre, Kenilworth
Warwickshire CV8 2LG
UK
Offers opportunities for young agriculturist and horticulturists to further their knowledge through international exchanges.

LSG THEME HOLIDAYS
201 Main Street, Thornton
Leicestershire LE67 1AH
UK
Tel 01509 231713
Conversational French in all areas of France.

STA
Priory House
6 Wrights Lane
London W8 6TA, UK
Tel 020 7361 6100
Web www.statravel.co.uk
Student travel agent.

USIT CAMPUS
52 Grosvenor Gardens
London SW1W 0AG, UK
www.usitcampus.co.uk
Tel 0870 240 1010

YOUTH FOR UNDERSTANDING
International Exchange
3501 Newark St, NW
Washington DC 20016
USA
Tel 202 966 6800
Devoted to promoting world peace through high school student exchange programmes.

Student travel awards and agencies

www.bunac.org.uk/

www.istc.umn.edu/work
International study and travel centre - helps students combine work and travel.

www.netos.com.uct
Cheap holidays to interesting destinations, with the opportunity to work and cover some of the cost.

www.studentflights.co.uk
Student and youth discount fares on scheduled airlines.

Teaching English abroad

ANGLO-PACIFIC (ASIA) CONSULTANCY
Suite 32, Nevilles Court
Dollis Hill Lane
London NW2 6HG, UK
Tel 020 8452 7836
Educational consultancy specialising in recruitment of teachers for Thailand, Taiwan and the rest of Southeast Asia. Also offer careers guidance for TEFL teachers returning from overseas.

BÉNÉDICT SCHOOLS
PO Box 270
Rue des Terreaux 29
1000 Lausanne 9
Switzerland

Tel 21 323 66 55
Web www.
benedict-schools.com
Have over 80 business and
language schools in
Europe, Morocco and
Ecuador on a franchise
basis.

BERLITZ UK
9-13 Grosvenor Street
London W1A 3BZ, UK
Tel 020 7915 0909
Web www.berlitz.com
330 centres in 33 countries.

**CENTRAL BUREAU FOR
EDUCATIONAL VISITS &
EXCHANGES**
10 Spring Gardens
London SW1A 2BN, UK
Tel 020 7389 4004
Web www.
britishcouncil.org/cbeve
Administer various
exchange programmes for
certified teachers and
language assistant
placements to help local
teachers of English in many
countries of the world from
France to Venezuela.

**CFBT EDUCATION
SERVICES**
1 The Chambers
East Street
Reading RG1 4JD, UK
Tel 0118 952 3900
Web www.cfbt.com
TEFL qualified recruitment
in Africa, South East Asia,
Eastern Europe, the Gulf
and the Caribbean.

COUNCIL EXCHANGES UK
52 Poland St
London W1V 4JQ, UK
Tel 020 7478 2000
Fax 020 7734 7322
Web www.
councilexchanges.org
Administers the Japan
Exchange & Teaching (JET)
and Teach in China
Programmes.

**EF ENGLISH FIRST
TEACHER RECRUITMENT**
Kensington Cloisters
5 Kensington Church Street
London W8 4LD, UK
Tel 020 7878 3500
Web www.ef.com
Recruitment of up to 400
teachers for EF schools in
Ecuador, Colombia,
Mexico, Lithuania, Poland,
Russia, China, Indonesia
and Morocco.

**ELS LANGUAGE
CENTERS/BERLITZ**
International Division
400 Alexander Park,
Princeton, NJ 08540, USA
Tel 609 750 3512
Web www.els.com
TEFL-qualified teachers
recruited for 50 franchised
schools worldwide.

ELT BANBURY
49 Oxford Road, Banbury
Oxon OX16 9AH, UK
Tel 01295 263480
Maintains *Teacher
Directory* for worldwide
recruitment of teachers
with CELTA or Trinity
Certificate.

**INLINGUA TEACHER
TRAINING & RECRUITMENT**
Rodney Lodge
Rodney Road
Cheltenham
Glocs GL50 1JF, UK
Tel 01242 253171
Web www.
inlinguacheltenham.co.uk
Qualified teachers for 300
centres mostly in Spain,
Italy, Germany, Russia,
Poland, Turkey and
Singapore.

INTERNATIONAL HOUSE
Staffing Unit, 106 Piccadilly
London W1V 9FL, UK
Tel 020 7491 2598
Fax 020 7499 0174
Web www.
internationalhouselondon.
ac.uk

Largest independent
British-based organisation
for teaching English, with
110 schools in 30 countries.

**INTERNATIONAL
PLACEMENT GROUP**
Jezkova 9, 130 00 Prague 3
Czech Republic
Tel/fax 420 2 2272 0237
also at
72 New Bond St
London W1Y 9DD, UK
Tel 020 8682 1309
Web http://
business.fortunecity.com
EFL teacher recruitment
firm specialising in Eastern
Europe.

**I TO I INTERNATIONAL
PROJECTS**
1 Cottage Road
Headingley
Leeds LS6 4DD, UK
Tel 0113 217 9800
Fax 0113 217 9801
Web www.i-to-i.com
Independent TEFL training
organisation which recruits
teachers (many of them
graduates of the I-to-I
courses) for projects in Sri
Lanka, India, Bolivia,
Russia, Uzbekistan and
possibly Cuba.

LANGUAGE LINK
21 Harrington Road
London SW7 3EU, UK
Tel 020 7225 1065
Web www.
languagelink.co.uk
Training and recruitment
agency which places
qualified (including newly
qualified) teachers in its
network of affiliated
schools in Slovakia, Poland,
Russia, Czech Republic,
Germany, the Ukraine,
Vietnam, Colombia, etc.

LINGUARAMA
Group Personnel Dept
Oceanic House
89 High St, Alton
Hampshire GU34 1LG, UK

Tel 01420 80899
Web http://
www.linguarama.com/jobs
Specialist in language
training for business.
Recruits qualified teachers
for over 40 centres in
Finland, Germany, France,
Spain, Italy and Central
Europe.

**NORD-ANGLIA
INTERNATIONAL**
Overseas Recruitment Dept
10 Eden Place, Cheadle
Stockport
Cheshire SK8 1AT, UK
Tel 0161 491 8415
Specialises in EFL vacation
courses throughout the
UK, but recruits for
vacancies worldwide in
teaching English to adults,
teens and juniors on
business and general
courses.

**SAXONCOURT & ENGLISH
WORLDWIDE**
124 New Bond St
London W1Y 9AE, UK
Tel 020 7491 1911
Web www.saxoncourt.com
Specialist educational
recruitment agency places
qualified EFL teachers in
posts in Europe, the Middle
East, Latin America and the
Far East.

TEACHING ABROAD
Gerrard House, Rustington
W Sussex BN16 1AW, UK
Tel 01903 859911
Web www.
teaching-abroad.co.uk
Volunteer teaching
programmes in Ukraine,
Russia, India, Ghana,
Brazil, Mexico and China.
No TEFL background
required.

**UNIVERSITY OF
CAMBRIDGE LOCAL
EXAMINATIONS SYNDICATE**
Syndicate Buildings
1 Hills Road

Cambridge CB1 2EU, UK
Free job placement service
for graduates of the
Certificate in English
Language Teaching to
Adults (CELTA).

**WALL STREET INSTITUTE
INTERNATIONAL**
Rambla de Catalunya 2-4
Planta Baixa
08007 Barcelona, Spain
Tel 93 412 00 14
Chain of 250 commercial
language institutes for
adults, which employ
approximately 750
full-time EFL teachers in
Europe (Spain,
Switzerland, Portugal, Italy,
France and Germany) and
Latin America (Mexico,
Chile, Venezuela).

Further Reading

Teaching English Abroad,
published every other year
by Vacation Work
Publications, 9 Park End St,
Oxford OX1 1HJ, UK (tel
01865 241978, fax 01865
790885, website www.
vacationwork.co.uk)

Related websites

www.eslcafe.com.
Excellent resource for TEFL
job-seekers.

www.eslworldwide.com
Korean-based website with
international job listings

www.
jobsabroad.com/listings
Allows you to search for
ESL jobs by country.

http://tefl.com.
Job vacancy listings from
the TEFL Professional
Network

Tourist boards in the UK

If there is no Tourist Office
listed, the relevant embassy
or consulate may be able to
provide information.
  Some of the numbers
listed here are for tourist
departments within the
embassy. If you want to see
someone there, always ring
in advance to book an
appointment.

ANDORRA
63 Westover Road
London SW18 2RF
Tel 020 8874 4806
Email atbtour@
candw.com.ai
Website www.
andoraonline.ad

ANGUILLA
7 Westwood Road
London SW13 0LA
Tel 020 8876 9025
Web www.
anguilla-vacation.com

ANTIGUA & BARBUDA
Antigua House
15 Thayer Street
London W1U 3JT
Tel 020 7486 7073
Website www.
antigua-barbuda.com

ARGENTINA
27 Three Kings Yard
London W1Y 1FL
Tel 020 7318 1340

AUSTRALIA
Gemini House
10/18 Putney Hill
London SW15 6AA
Tel 020 8780 2227
Website www.aussie.net.au

AUSTRIA
13-14 Cork Street
London W1S 3NS
Tel 020 7629 0461
Website www.
austria-tourism.at

BAHAMAS
10 Chesterfield Street
London W1X 8AH
Tel 020 7629 5238
Website www.
interknowledge.com/
bahamas

BARBADOS
263 Tottenham Court Road
London W1P 0LA
Tel 020 7636 9448
Website www.barbados.org

BELGIUM
225 Marsh Wall
London E14 9FW
Tel 0906 3020245
Email info@ belgium-
tourism.org
Web www.
belgium-tourism.net

BERMUDA
1 Battersea Church Road
London SW11 3LY
Tel 020 7771 7001
Web www.
bermudatourism.com

BRAZIL
32 Green Street
London W1K 7AT
Tel 020 7 499 0877
Web www.brazil.org.uk

BRITISH VIRGIN ISLANDS
55 Newman Street
London W1T 3EB
Tel 020 7947 8200
Web www.bviwelcome.com

CANADA
Visit Canada
PO Box 5396
Northampton NN1 2FA
Tel 0906 871 5000
Email visitcanada@
dial.pipex.com

CARIBBEAN TOURISM
Vigilant House
120 Wilton Road
London SW1V 1JZ
Tel 020 7233 8382

CAYMAN ISLANDS
6 Arlington Street
London SW1A 1RE
Tel 020 7491 7771

Web www.
caymanislands.cy

CHINA
4 Glentworth Street
London NW1
Tel 020 0891 600188
(24-hr information line)

CZECH REPUBLIC
95 Great Portland Street
London W1N 5RA
Tel 020 7 291 9920

DENMARK
55 Sloane Street
London SW1X 9SY
Tel 020 7259 5959
Website www.
visitdenmark.com

DOMINICA
1 Collingham Gardens
London SW5 0HW
Tel 020 7835 1937

EGYPT
170 Piccadilly
London W1V 9DD
Tel 020 7493 5283
Website interoz.com/egypt

FALKLAND ISLANDS
14 Broadway
London SW1H 0BH
Tel 020 7222 2542

FINLAND
30-35 Pall Mall
London SW1Y 5LP
Tel 020 7839 4048
Web www.
finland-tourism.com

FRANCE
178 Piccadilly
London W1V 0AL
Tel 0891 244 123
Email info@mdlf.co.uk

GAMBIA
57 Kensington Court
London W8 5DG
Tel 020 7376 0093
Web www.
thegambia/touristoff.co.uk

GERMANY
PO Box 2695
London W1A 3TN
Tel 0891 600 100

Web www.
germany-tourism.de

GHANA
13 Belgrave Square
London SW1X 8PR
Tel 020 8342 8686

GIBRALTAR
Arundel Great Court
179 The Strand
London WC2R 1EL
Tel 020 7836 0777
Email giblondon@aol.com

GREECE
4 Conduit Street
London W1R 0DJ
Tel 020 7 734 5997
Website www.eexi.gr

GRENADA
1 Collingham Gardens
London SW5 0HW
Tel 020 7370 5164
Web www.grenada.org

HONG KONG
6 Grafton Street
London W1X 3LB
Tel 020 7533 7100
Website www.hkta.org

ICELAND
172 Tottenham Court Road
London W1P 9LG
Tel 020 8286 8008

INDIA
7 Cork Street
London W1X 2LN
Tel 020 7437 3677
Website www.
indiatouristoffice.org

IRELAND
Ireland House
150 New Bond Street
London W1Y 0AQ
Tel 020 7493 3201
Website www.
ireland.travel.ie

ISRAEL
UK House
180 Oxford Street
London W1N 9DJ
Tel 020 7299 1111
Website www.infotour.co.il

ITALY
1 Princes Street
London W1R 8AY
Tel 020 7408 1254

JAMAICA
1-2 Prince Consort Road
London SW7 2BZ
Tel 020 7224 0505
Website www.
jamaicatravel.com

JAPAN
Heathcote House
20 Saville Row
London W15 3PR
Tel 020 7734 9638
Website www.jnto.go.jp

JERSEY
7 Lower Ground
London Sw1W OEN
Tel 020 7630 8787
Email jtourism@itl.net
Website www.jersey.com

JORDAN
c/o Representation Plus
Representation House
11 Blades Court
121 Deodar Road
London SW15 2NU
Tel 020 8877 4524
Web www.
jordan-online.com
Email clare@
representationplus.co.uk

KENYA
25 Brook's Mews
London W1K 4DD
Tel 020 7355 3144
Website www.
africanvacation.com/kenya

KOREA (SOUTH)
3rd Floor
New Zealand House
Haymarket
London SW1Y 4TE
Tel 020 7321 2535
Website www.
visitkorea.co.uk

LUXEMBOURG
122 Regent Street
London W1B 5SA
Tel 020 7434 2800
Email tourism@

luxembourg.co.uk
Website www.
luxembourg.co.uk

MACAU
1 Battersea Church Road
London SW11 3LY
Tel 020 7771 7000

MALAWI
33 Grosvenor Street
London W1X 0DE
Tel 020 7491 4172

MALAYSIA
Malaysia House
57 Trafalgar Square
London WC2N 5DU
Tel 020 7930 7932
Website www.
tourism.gov.my

MALTA
36-38 Piccadilly
London W15 OLD
Tel 020 7 292 4900
Emailoffice.uk@
tourism.org.mt
Website www.
tourism.org.mt

MAURITIUS
32/33 Elvaston Place
London SW7 5NW
Tel 020 7581 0294

MEXICO
c/o Mexican Embassy
8 Halkin Street
London SW1X 7DW
Tel 020 7235 6393
Website www.
mexico-travel.com

MONACO
The Chambers
Chelsea Harbour
London SW10 0XF
Tel 020 7352 9962
 Website www.
monaco-tourism.com

MOROCCO
205 Regent Street
London W1R 7DE
Tel 020 7437 0073
Website www.
tourism-in.morocco.com

NAMIBIA
6 Chandos Street
London W1G 9LU
Tel 020 7636 2924
Email namibia@
globalnet.co.uk

NETHERLANDS
P.O. Box 523
London SW1E 6NT
Tel 0906 8717777
Website
www.goholland.co.uk

NEW ZEALAND
New Zealand House
Haymarket
London SW1Y 4TQ
Tel 020 7930 1662
Website www.nztb.org.nz

NORWAY
Charles House
5-11 Lower Regent Street
London SW1Y 4LR
Tel 020 7839 2650
Website www.
visitnorway.com

PERU
Embassy of Peru
Tourist Section
52 Sloane Street
London SW1X 9SP
Tel 020 7235 1917
Email postmaster@
foptur.gob.pe

PHILIPPINES
146 Cromwell Road
London SW7 4EF
Tel 020 7835 1100
Website www.
tourism.gov.ph
Email tourism@pdot.co.uk

POLAND
1st Floor
Remo House
310-312 Regent Street,
London W1R 5AJ
Tel 020 7580 8811
Email pnto@
dial.pipex.com
Website w3.poland.net/
travelpage

PORTUGAL
2nd Floor
22/25a Sackville Street
London W1X 2LY
Tel 020 7494 1441

ROMANIA
83a Marylebone High St
London W1M 3DE
Tel 020 7224 3692
Website www.
romtour.com/~tour/office

RUSSIA
Intourist
219 Marsh Wall
Isle of Dogs
London E14 9PD
Tel 020 7538 8600
Website www.
intourist.co.uk

SAUDI ARABIA
Cavendish House
18 Cavendish Square
London W1M 0AQ
Tel 020 7629 8803

SEYCHELLES
Eros House
111 Baker Street
London W1M 1FE
Tel 020 7224 1670
Web www.
seychelles.uk.com

SIERRA LEONE
33 Portland Place
London W1N 3AG
Tel 020 7636 6483

SINGAPORE
Carrington House
126/130 Regent Street
London W1R 5FE
Tel 020 7437 0033
Website www.
newasia-singapore.com

SLOVAK REPUBLIC
16 Frognal Parade
Finchley Road
London NW3 5HG
Tel 020 7794 3263
Website www. slovakia.net

SLOVENIA
49 Conduit Street
London W1R 9FB
Tel 020 7287 7133

SOUTH AFRICA
5/6 Alt Grove
London SW19 4DZ
Tel 020 8944 8080

SPAIN
22-23 Manchester Square
London W1M 5AP
Tel 020 7486 8077
Web www.tourspain.es

SRI LANKA
Claivalle House
26/27 Oxenden Street
London SW1Y 4EL
Tel 020 7930 2627
Web www.lanka.net/ctb

ST. KITTS & NEVIS
10 Kensington Court
London W8 5DL
Tel 020 7376 0881

ST. LUCIA
421a Finchley Road
London NW3 6HT
Tel 020 7431 3675

**ST. VINCENT & THE
GRENADINES**
10 Kensington Court
London W8 5DL
Tel 020 7937 6570

SWEDEN
11 Montague Place
London W1H 2AL
Tel 020 7724 5868
Email sttc-info@
swedish-tourism.org.uk

SWITZERLAND
Swiss Court
New Coventry Street
London W1V 8EE
Tel 020 7734 1921
Website www.
switzerlandtourism.ch

TANZANIA
80 Borough High Street
London SE1 1LL
Tel 020 7407 0566

THAILAND
49 Albermarle Street
London W1X 3FE
Tel 020 7499 7679
Website www.tat.or.th

TRINIDAD & TOBAGO
Mitre House
66 Abbey Road
Bush Hill Park
Enfield
Middlesex EN1 2RQ
Tel 020 8350 1015
Website www.visittnt.com

TUNISIA
77A Wigmore Street
London W1H 9LJ
Tel 020 7224 5561
Website www.
tourismtunisia.com

TURKEY
170-173 Piccadilly
London W15 9EJ
Tel 020 7629 7771
Website www.
tourist-offices.org.uk/
turkey

TURKS & CAICOS
Mitre House
66 Abbey Road
Bush Hill Park
Enfield
Middlesex EN1 2RQ
Tel 020 8350 1017
Web www.mki.ltd/uk

USA
Visit USA Association
24 Rosen Square
London W1A 1AE
Tel 0906 910 1020

US VIRGIN ISLANDS
Molasses House
Clove Hitch Quay
Plantation Wharf
London SW11 3PN
Tel 020 7978 5262

ZAMBIA
2 Palace Gate
London W8 5NG
Tel 020 7589 6343
Website www.
zamnet.zm/zamnet/
zntb.html

ZIMBABWE
429 The Strand
London WC2R 0QE
Tel 020 7240 6169

Travel agencies for tailor-made trips

ABERCROMBIE & KENT
Sloane Square House
Holbein Place
London SW1W 8NS, UK
Tel 020 7730 9600
Web www.
abercrombiekent. co.uk
Africa and more, in style.

BRIDGE THE WORLD
47 Chalk Farm Road
London NW1 8AN, UK
Tel 020 7911 0900
Australia and South Pacific.

COX AND KINGS
Gordon House
10 Greencoat Place
London SW1P 1PH, UK
Tel 020 7873 5006
Fax 020 7630 6038
Web www.
coxandkings.co.uk
India, Latin America,
Middle East and South
Africa. Luxurious.

CV TRAVEL
43 Cadogan St
London SW3 2PR, UK
Tel 020 7581 0851
Very upmarket,villas.

EXSUS TRAVEL
23 Heddon Street
London W1R 7LG, UK
Web www.exsus.com
Tel 020 7292 5050
Fax 020 7292 5051
Email travel@exsus.com
South America, Mexico,
Caribbean. Luxurious.

JOURNEY LATIN AMERICA
12-13 Heathfield Terrace
London W4 4JE, UK
Tel 020 8747 3108
Website www.
journeylatinamerica.co.uk
Latin America specialists.

NOMADIC THOUGHTS
81 Brondesbury Road
London NW6 6BB, UK
Tel 020 7604 4408
Fax 020 7604 4407
Email uknomadic@
aol.com
Anywhere, at any budget.

SILVERBIRD
4 Northfileds Prospect,
Putney Bridge Road,
London SW18 1PE
Tel 020 8875 9191
Fax 020 8875 1874
Web www.silverbird.co.uk
Far East specialists.

TAILOR MADE TRAVEL
18 Port Street, Evesham,
Worcs WR11 6AN, UK
Tel 01386 712000
Fax 01386 712071
Web www.
tailor-made.co.uk
Pacific, Australia, New
Zealand, Canada, Africa.

TRAILFINDERS
42/50 Earls Court Road
London W8 6EJ, UK
Tel 020 7937 5400
Worldwide itineraries.

TRAVELBAG
12 High Street. Alton
Hampshire GU34 1BN, UK
Tel 01420 541441
Worldwide itineraries.

WESTERN & ORIENTAL TRAVEL
King House
11 Westbourne Grove
London W2 4UA, UK
Tel 020 7313 6611
Fax 020 7313 6601
Email info@
westernoriental.com
India specialists.

WEXAS INTERNATIONAL
45-49 Brompton Road
London SW3 1DE
Tel 020 7589 3315
Web www.wexas.com
Email mship@wexas.com
Worldwide itineraries.

Travel writing & photography associations

THE ASSOCIATION OF AUTHORS' AGENTS
Drury House
37-43 Russell Street
London WC2B 5HA, UK
Tel 020 7344 1000

BOOK TRUST
Book House, 45 East Hill
London SW18 2QZ
Tel 020 8516 2977

BRITISH AMATEUR PRESS ASSOCIATION
Michaelmas
Cimarron Close
South Woodham Ferrers
Essex CM3 5PB, UK
Tel 01245 324059

BRITISH ASSOCIATION OF PICTURE LIBRARIES AND AGENCIES (BAPLA)
18 Vine Hill
London EC1R 5DX, UK
Tel 020 7713 1780

BRITISH GUILD OF TRAVEL WRITERS
178 Battersea Park Road
London SW11 4ND, UK
Web www.bgtw.org
Tel 020 7720 9009
Fax 020 7498 6153
Email bgtw@
garlandintl.co.uk

BRITISH INSTITUTE OF PROFESSIONAL PHOTOGRAPHY
Fox Talbot House
Amwell End
Ware, Herts SG12 9HN, UK
Tel 01920 464011
Web www.bipp.com

BUREAU OF FREELANCE PHOTOGRAPHERS (BFP)
Focus House
497 Green Lanes
London N13 4BP
Tel 020 8882 3315

**FOREIGN PRESS
ASSOCIATION IN LONDON**
11 Carlton House Terrace
London SW1Y 5AJ
Tel 020 7930 0445

**GENERAL PRACTITIONER
WRITERS ASSOCIATION**
Mr Wilfred Hopkins
633 Liverpool Road
Southport PR8 3NG
Tel& Fax: 01704 577 839
Email GPWA@
lepress.demon.co.uk

**THE INSTITUTE OF
JOURNALISTS**
Unit 2, Dock Offices
Surrey Quays Road
London SE16 2XU
Tel 020 7252 1187

**MASTER PHOTOGRAPHERS
ASSOCIATION**
Halmark House
1 Chancery Lane
Darlington
Co Durham DL1 5QP
Tel 01325 356555

**NATIONAL UNION OF
JOURNALISTS**
314-320 Gray's Inn Road
London WC1X 8DP
Tel 020 7278 7916

**PHOTOMARKETING
INTERNATIONAL**
Peel Place
50 Carver Street
Birmingham B1 3AS
Tel 0121 212 0299

PRESS COUNCIL
1 Salisbury Square
London EC4Y 85B
Tel 020 7353 1248

**THE ROYAL PHOTOGRAPHIC
SOCIETY**
The Octagon
Milsom St
Bath BA1 1DN
Tel 01225 462841

THE SOCIETY OF AUTHORS
84 Drayton Gardens
London SW10 9SB
Tel 020 7373 6642
Web www.

writers.org.uk/society

**SOCIETY OF WOMEN
WRITERS AND JOURNALISTS**
110 Whitehall Road
London E4 6DW

**THE WRITERS' GUILD OF
GREAT BRITAIN**
430 Edgware Road
London W2 1EH
Tel 020 7723 8074

Related websites

www.frenchfototours.com
Photographic workshops in
France, Italy, Greece and
Mexico.

www.ifwtwa.org
International food, wine,
travel writers association

www.michael-busselle.com
Travel photographs by one
of the UK's leading
photographers.

www.PhotoPro.co.uk
Advice and templates for
photographers who want to
design their own website

www.SATW.org
Society of American Travel
Writers

www.shutterchances.
com.au
Practice photography in
Africa, Australia, Japan and
New Zealand.

www.traveldonkey.com
Write your own travelogue
and win a prize.

www.travelwriters.com

www.voyagers.com/voyage
rs/photwork.htm
Workshops ranging from
nature photography to
digital imaging.

Volunteer organisations

**ACTION D'URGENCE
INTERNATIONALE**
10 Rue Felix-Aiem
75018 Paris
France
Tel 142 64 7588
Runs training courses for
people interested in helping
rescue operations in times
of natural disasters.
Branches in France, UK,
Morocco, India,
Dominican Republic and
Guadeloupe.

ACTION HEALTH
International Voluntary
Health Association
The Gate House
25 Gwydir St
Cambridge CB1 2LG
UK
Tel 01223 460853
Web www.skillshare.org
Charitable organisation
which places qualified
medics, nurses and
physiotherapists with at
least two years experience
in voluntary health
programmes in developing
countries.

**BRITISH EXECUTIVE
SERVICE OVERSEAS**
164 Vauxhall Bridge Road
London SW1V 2RB
UK
Tel 020 7630 0644
Web www.beso.org
Consider retired applicants
with lots of experience to
advise projects overseas
using technical and
managerial skills. Short-
term placements on an
expenses-only basis.

**BRITISH TRUST FOR
CONSERVATION
VOLUNTEERS**
36 St Mary Street

Oxford OX10 OEU
UK
Tel 01491 839766
www.btcv.org.uk
Practical conservation
work and training courses
for all age groups
throughout England,
Wales, Northern Ireland
and overseas (overseas
placements must be over
18). Also leadership courses

**CATHOLIC INSTITUTE FOR
INTERNATIONAL RELATIONS**
Unit 3
Canonbury Yard
190a New North Road
London N1 7BJ
UK
Tel 020 7354 0883
Web www.ciir.org
Recruits skilled, qualified
people for minimum of
two years work overseas.

CHRISTIAN OUTREACH
1 New Street
Leamington Spa
Warwickshire CV31 1HP
UK
Tel 01926 315301
Web www.cord-uk.co.uk
Welcomes well-qualified
applicants for one year
minimum for overseas
placements. Must have
Christian commitment.

CHRISTIAN VOCATIONS
St James House
Trinity Road
Dudley
W Mids DY1 1JB
Tel 01384 233511
Web www.
christianvocations.org
Short- and long-term
voluntary opportunities for
work overseas ranging
from missionary work to
engineering and farming.

**COMMUNITY SERVICE
VOLUNTEERS**
237 Pentonville Road
London N1 9NJ
UK

Tel 020 7278 6601
Web www.csv.org.uk
Provides volunteering
opportunities for people
aged 16-35, helping people
in need for period of 4-12
months, in the UK.
Volunteers work with
people with physical
disabilities and learning
difficulties.

**CONCORDIA (YOUTH
SERVICE VOLUNTEERS)**
Heversham House
20-22 Boundary Road
Hove
Sussex BN3 4ET
UK
Tel 01273 422293
International voluntary
work camps, should be over
17. Accommodation
provided but not expenses.

**COUNCIL OF CHURCHES
FOR BRITAIN AND IRELAND**
Inter Church House
35-41 Lower Marsh
London SE1 7RL
UK
Tel 020 7620 4444
Web www.ctbi.org.uk
Part of international
interdominational youth
service of the Ecumenical
Youth Council in Europe.
Groups of young people
carry out four-week
projects.

EARTHWATCH
57 Woodstock Road
Oxford OX2 6HJ
UK
Web www.earthwatch.org
Tel 01865 318 831
Fax 01865 311 383

**EAST EUROPEAN
PARTNERSHIP (EEP)**
Carlton House
27a Carlton Drive
London SW15 2BS, UK
Tel 020 8780 2841
Part of VSO. English
teachers needed in East
European countries.

Special education teachers
and others required for
Albania.

ECOVOLUNTEER WEBSITE
www.ecovolunteer.org

HEALTH UNLIMITED
Prince Consort House
27-29 Albert Embankment
London SE1 7TS
UK
Tel 020 7582 5999
Web www.
healthunlimited.org
Recruits medically
qualified volunteers for one
year or more to work on
projects worldwide.

**INTERNATIONAL
COOPERATION FOR
DEVELOPMENT (ICD)**
Unit 3, Canonbury Yard
190a New North Road
London N1 7BJ
UK
Tel 020 7354 0883
Qualified, experienced
argriculturalists, technical
and health people for two
years in Nicaragua, Peru,
Honduras, Ecuador, El
salvador, Dominican Rep,
Yemen, Zimbabwe and
Namibia.

**INTERNATIONAL HEALTH
EXCHANGE**
810 Dryden Street
London WC2E 9NA
UK
Tel 020 7836 5833
Provides details of job
vacancies and training for
health workers in
developing countries.

INVOLVEMENT VOLUNTEERS
PO Box 218
Port Melbourne
Victoria 3207
Australia
Opportunities for
voluntary conservation
projects.

KIBBUTZ REPRESENTATIVES
1a Accommodation Road
London NW11 8ED, UK
Tel 020 8458 9235
Working Holidays on
Kibbutz in Israel. Must be
18-32 years. Applicants pay
air fare and insurance. Free
board and small allowance.

**MERLIN (MEDICAL
EMERGENCY RELIEF
INTERNATIONAL)**
5-13 Trinity St
London SE1 1DB, UK
Tel020 7378 4888
Web www.merlin.org.uk
Charity placing suitably
qualified medical and
support staff in disaster
zones worldwide.

PEOPLE AND PLANET
51 Union Street
Oxford OX4 15P, UK
Tel 01865 245678
Organises student groups
in the UK.

PROJECT 67
10 Hatton Garden
London EC1N 8AH, UK
Tel 020 7831 7626
Kibbutz and *moshav*
voluntary work in Israel.

PROJECT TRUST
The Hebridean Centre
Bally Hough
Isle of Coll
Argyll PA78 6TE, UK
Tel 01879 230444
Web www.
projecttrust.org.uk
Opportunities for young
people aged 17-19 to serve
in developing countries on
12-month projects. Must
be in full-time education at
time of application.
Volunteer must raise part
of the costs.

RALEIGH INTERNATIONAL
Raleigh House
27 Parsons Green Lane
London SW6 4HZ, UK
Tel 020 7371 8585

Web www.
raleighinternational.org
Email info@raleigh.org.uk
Organises challenging
expeditions worldwide,
based around community
conservation, for young
people aged 17-25, also
skilled people over 25 years.

SKILLSHARE AFRICA
126 New Walk
Leicester LE1 7JA, UK
Tel 01162 541862
Web www.skillshare.org
Offers qualified and
experienced people
opportunities for working
in southern Africa for a
minimum of two years.

**TEAR FUND GAP
PROGRAMME**
100 Church Road
Teddington
Middlesex TW11 8QE, UK
Tel 020 8977 9144
Web tearfund.org
Email enquiry@
tearfund.dircon.co.uk
Christian organisation with
strong development
programmes, needing
qualified volunteers
prepared to serve 2-4 years.

UNIAS
57 Goodramgate
York YO1 7FX, UK
Tel 01904 647799
Agricultural, health and
engineering experts needed
for 2 years in Brazil, Bolivia,
Burkina Faso, Mali, West
Bank and Gaza.

**UNITED NATIONS
VOLUNTEERS (UNV)**
Palais des Nations
1211 Geneva 10
Switzerland
Tel 22 798 5850
Qualified volunteers from
all member nations of the
UN, with relevant
experience. Normally two
years but shorter
humanitarian relief work

also. British Passport
holders enquire through
VSO London.

**UNIVERSITIES'
EDUCATIONAL FUND FOR
PALESTINIAN REFUGEES
(UNIPAL)**
Volunteer Programme
Organiser
12 Helen Road
Oxford OX2 0DE, UK
Voluntary English teachers
for education and caring
programme in the West
Bank and the Gaza Strip.

**UNIVERSITY OF
CALIFORNIA RESEARCH
EXPEDITIONS PROGRAMME
(UREP)**
University of California
Berkeley
CA 94270, USA
Tel 415 642 6586
Will take inexperienced
volunteers on UREP
expeditions worldwide.
Wide variety of areas and
subjects.

US PEACE CORP
Washington, DC 20526
USA
Tel 202 606 3886
Places volunteers in 62
developing countries.
Volunteers with all kinds of
backgrounds are accepted.

**VACATION WORK
INTERNATIONAL**
9 Park End Street
Oxford OX1 1HJ, UK
Tel 01865 241978
Web www.
vacationwork.co.uk
Produces useful, regularly
updated, publications on
work, travel and study
abroad.

VOLUNTEERS FOR PEACE
43 Tiffany Road, Belmont
Vermont 05730, USA
Tel 802 259 2759
Publishes an *International
Work Camp Directory*.

VOLUNTARY SERVICE OVERSEAS
317 Putney Bridge Road
London SW15 2PN, UK
Tel 020 8780 2266
www.vso.org.uk
Volunteers for Third World development. Must have qualifications and useful experience.

VSO CANADA
35 Centennial Boulevard
Ottaw
Ontario KIY 2H8
Canada
Recruits experienced, qualified volunteers.

WORLD COUNCIL OF CHURCHES
Ecumenical Youth Action
150 Route de Ferney
PO Box 2100
1211 Geneva 2
Switzerland
Tel 22 791 6111
Opportunities for young volunteers aged 18-30 to work in international work camps contributing to local and national development in developing countries.

Further reading

International Directory of Voluntary Work

Directory of Work and Study in Developing Countries

Work Your Way Around the World

(All three titles above are published by Vacation Work, 9 Park End Street, Oxford OX1 1HJ, UK)

Volunteer Work
(Central Bureau for Educational Visits and Exchange, 10 Spring Gdns, London, SW1A 2BN, UK, tel 020 7389 4004).

Vegetarian societies

CANADIAN NATURAL HEALTH SOCIETY INC
6250 Mountain Sights
H3W 2Z3 Montreal
Canada

THE EUROPEAN VEGETARIAN UNION
Larensweg 26
NL 1221 CM Hilversum
Brussels, Belgium
Tel 31 35 834 796
Based at the offices of the Dutch Vegetarian Society, it aims to encourage better communications between the European vegetarian groups, and has a regular newsletter.

INTERNATIONAL JEWISH VEGETARIAN SOCIETY
853/5 Finchley Road
London NW11 8LX, UK
Tel 020 8455 0692
Email jvs@yahoo.com

THE INTERNATIONAL VEGETARIAN UNION (IVU)
c/o VSUK
Park Dale
Dunham Road
Altringham
Cheshire WA14 4QG, UK
Tel 0161 925 2000

IVU honorary regional secretaries

AFRICA
Mr Jan Beeldman
82 Darrenwood Village
First St, Darrenwood
2194 Randburg
South Africa

ASIA
Shah Jashu
114 Mittal Court
Nariman Point
Bombay 400 021
Tel 22 285 5755/56

AUSTRALASIA
Mark Berriman
AVS, PO Box 65
Paddington, NSW 2021
Australia
Email avs@moreinfo.com

EUROPE
John Mitchell
183 Folden Road
Great Barr
Birmingham B48 2EH, UK
Tel 0121 357 2772

MIDDLE EAST
Mr Mark Weintraub
8 Balfour Street
Jerusalem 92101
Israel

NEW ZEALAND VEGETARIAN SOCIETY INC
Box 77034, Auckland 3
New Zealand

NORTH AMERICAN VEGETARIAN SOCIETY (NAVS)
PO Box 72, Dolgeville
NY 13329, USA
Email darer@admin.njit.edu

USA
PO Box 9710, Washington
DC 20016, USA
Tel 301 577 5215
Email dalal@kcilink.com

VEGETARIAN AWARENESS NETWORK (VEGANET)
PO Box 76390, USA 20013
Tel 202 347 8343

THE VEGETARIAN SOCIETY OF THE UNITED KINGDOM
Parkdale
Dunham Road
Altrincham
Cheshire WA14 4QG, UK
Tel 0161 925 2000

THE VEGETARIAN SOCIETY OF RUSSIA
Moscow 109462
Volsky Bulwar
d39-k3-kv23
Moscow 109462, Russia
Tel 951728633

Further reading

The Vegetarian Travel Guide (The Vegetarian Society), a worldwide guide to vegetarian restaurants, societies and vegetarian meals in transit.

The Vegetarian Traveller (Grafton), Andrew Sanger's excellent guide to worldwide travel for vegetarians.

Related websites

www.vegdining.com

www.veg.org/veg/

Walking associations

LONG DISTANCE WALKERS ASSOCIATION
Janet Chapman
63 Yockley Clse, Camberley
Surrey GU15 1QQ, UK
Tel 01276 65169

RAMBLERS ASSOCIATION
Camelford House
87-90 Albert Embankment
London SE1 7TW
Tel 020 7339 8500
Web www.ramblers.org.uk
Publish the *Ramblers Yearbook* and
Accomodation Guide.

Related websites

www.countrywalks.org.co.uk
Conservation walks in areas of open access throughout England, by the Countryside Commission, including access for disabled users.

www.fs.fed.us
Comprehensive info on hiking (and mountain biking) routes in the US by the US forest service

www.gorp.com/ewt
European walking tours.

www.nps.gov/trails
Long distance footpaths in America provided by the American National Park Service.

www.ramblers.org.uk
The UK Ramblers' Association website.

www.
travelsource.com/trekking
Adventure trekking worldwide.

Wildlife and safari companies

ABERCROMBIE & KENT
Sloane Square House
Holbein Place
London SW1W 8NS, UK
Tel 020 7730 9600
Web www.
abercrombiekent.co.uk
Email info@
abercrombiekent.co.uk

ANDREWS SAFARIS
PO Box 31993
Lusaka, Zambia
Foot safaris in the Luangwa.

ANDREW BROCK TRAVEL
54 High Street East
Uppingham
Rutland LE15 9PZ, UK
Tel 01572 821330
Specialist in botanical, walking and garden Travel.

ART OF TRAVEL
51 Castle Street
Cirencester
Glocs GL7 1QD, UK
Tel 01285 650011
Web www.artoftravel.co.uk
Tailor-made safaris.

BIRDWATCHING BREAKS
26 School Lane
Herne Bay
Kent CT6 7AL, UK
Tel 01227740799
Bird-watching in Europe, Britain and North America.

CARRIER
London Road
Alderley Edge
Cheshire SK9 7JT, UK
Tel 01625 582006
Fax 01625 586818
Web www.carrier.co.uk

CAZENOVE AND LOYD SAFARIS
3 Alice Court
116 Putney Bridge Road
London SW15 2NQ, UK
Web www.caz-loyd.com
Tel 020 8875 9666
Fax 020 8875 9444

CHARIOTEER TRAVEL TOURS
10 Agias Sofias St
Thessaloniki
Greece GR 54322
Tel 31 229 230
Tailor-made bird-watching and natural history tours of Greece; 10 per cent of profits towards conservation.

DEFINITIVE AFRICA
Suite 5D
Parsonage Chambers
3 Parsonage
Manchester M3 2HF, UK
Web www.
designer-africa.com
Tel 0161 929 5151
Fax 0161 839 5160
email enquiry@
designer-africa.com

DISCOVER THE WORLD
29 Nork Way, Banstead
Surrey SM7 1PB
UK
Tel 01737218800
Web www.
arctic-discover.co.uk
Email sales@
arcticdiscover.co.uk
Whale-watching, wildlife
and wilderness holidays
worldwide.

EXPLORERS TOURS
223 Coppermill Road
Wraysbury TW19 5NW
UK
Tel 01753 681999
Web www.explorers.co.uk
Astronomical tours and
diving holidays.

FLAMINGO TOURS
PO Box 44899
Nairobi
Kenya
Camel safaris in the
Samburu.

**THE LEGENDARY
ADVENTURE COMPANY**
18 Albemarle Street
London W1X 3HA, UK
Tel 020 7629 2044
Tailor-made safaris in
Africa and trekking in
Nepal.

MOTOR SAFARI
Pinfold Lane
Buckley
Clwyd CH7 3NS, UK
Tel 01244 548849
Jeep mountain safaris,
quad-biking and
amphibious vehicles in
Wales and Cyprus.

NATURETREK
Cheriton Hall
Cheriton
Old Ford
Hants SO24 ONG, UK
Tel 01962 733051
Web www.naturetrek.co.uk
Bird-watching, natural
history and botanical tours
worldwide; donates a

percentage of profits to
environmental charities.

ORNITHOLIDAYS
29 Straight Mile
Romsey
Hants SO51 9BB
UK
Tel 01794 519445
Web www.
ornitholidays.co.uk
Established operator
offering a large variety of
bird-watching holidays
worldwide.

PAPYRUS TOURS
9 Rose Hill Court
Bessacarr
Doncaster DN4 5LY
UK
Tel 01302 530778
Wildlife tours in East
Africa.

PEREGRINE HOLIDAYS
41 South Parade
Oxford OX2 7JP, UK
Tel 01865 511642
Bird-watching, natural
history and horse safaris.

**REEF AND RAINFOREST
TOURS**
1 The Plains
Totnes
Devon TQ9 5DR, UK
Tel 01803 866965
Web www.
reefrainforest.co.uk
Small outfit running
wildlife and diving tours to
Indonesia, Papua New
Guinea, Honduras,
Venezuela, Peru, Belize,
Ecuador and Costa Rica.

SAFARI DRIVE
Wessex House
127 High Street
Hungerford
Berkshire RG17 0DL, UK
Tel 01488681 611
Web www.safaridrive.com
Organises self-drive safaris
in Africa, also whitewater
rafting and microlighting.

**SAVE THE RHINO
INTERNATIONAL**
21 Bentinck Street
London W1M 5RP, UK
Tel 020 7935 5880
Email save@
rhinos.demon.co.uk
Safaris to Namibia to see
desert rhinos; proceeds go
directly to protecting them.

WILD AFRICA SAFARIS
Mauritius House
1 Portsmouth Road
Guildford
Surrey GU2 5BL, UK
Tel 01483 579991
Fax 01483 532820
Web www.
wildafricasafari.com
Email was@
bctuk.demon.co.uk

**TIGER MOUNTAIN GROUPS
AND EXPEDITIONS**
PO Box 170
Lazimpat
Kathmandu
Nepal
Tel 1 411 225
Email tiger@
mtn.mos.com.np
Himalayan treks, jungle
lodges and wildlife camps.

WHALE WATCH AZORES
6B South Street
Banbury
Oxon OX16 7LF, UK
Tel 01295 267 652
Web www.whalewatch@
azores.freeserve.co.uk
Email whalewatch@
azores.freeserve.co.uk

WILDLIFE WORLDWIDE
170 Selsdon Road
South Croydon
Surrey CR2 6PJ
Tel 020 8667 9158
Email sales@
wildlifeworldwide.com

Related websites

www.africanet.com

www.bigfive.com

www.bushhomes.com
Stay in private homes and ranches in Kenya and Tanzania.

www.eagle-eye.com
Birdwatching tours around most of the world.

www.gorp.com
Good safari links, as well as links to national parks around the world and to tour operators in Africa.

www.offbeatsafaris.com
Horseback safaris in Kenya.

www.onsafari.com

www.onlinesafaris.com

www.outdoorns.com/whalewatching
Whale-watching.

www.safaris.com
African safari specialists.

www.unchartedoutposts.com
Private ranches and exclusive safaris.

www.widdl.com/wings
Small-group birdwatching tours around the world.

www.1alaskafishing.com
Whale watching tours and sports fishing.

Women's organisations

AMAZONIANS
c/o Kamin Mohammadi
Email kmohammadi@
msmail.condenast.co.uk
Association for professional travel writers.

OUTDOOR VACATIONS FOR WOMEN OVER 40
PO Box 200, Groton
MA 01450, USA
Tel 508 448 3331

RAINBOW TRAVEL
15033 Kelly Canyon Road
Bozeman, MT 59715, USA
Tel 406 587 3888
Adventure travel for women over 30.

SILVERMOON WOMEN'S BOOKSHOP
64-68 Charing Cross Road
London WC2H 0BB, UK
Tel 020 7836 7906

TRAVEL COMPANIONS
110 High Mount
Station Road
London NW4 3ST, UK
Tel 020 8202 8478
Non-profit service putting single travellers in touch with like-minded people.

WOMANSHIP
The Boathouse
410 Severn Avenue
Annapolis, MD 21403, USA
Tel 301 269 0784
Sailing cruises for women of all ages.

WOMEN'S CORONA SOCIETY/CORONA WORLDWIDE
c/o Commonwealth Institute
Kensington High Street
London W8 6NQ, UK
Tel 020 7610 4407
A support/advice group for expatriate women, offers advice to those moving abroad or returning home.

WOMEN'S TRAVEL ADVISORY BUREAU
Lansdowne, High Street
Blockley
Glocs GL56 9HF, UK
Tel 01865 310574
Supplies information packs tailored to individuals' travel plans.

WOMEN WELCOME WOMEN
88 Easton Street
High Wycombe
Bucks HP11 1DJ, UK
Tel 01494 465441
Organisation to promote international friendship by helping female travellers to stay with other members and their families.

WOODSWOMEN
25 W Diamond Lake Road
Minneapolis
MN55419, USA
Tel 612 822 3809
Adventure trips for women of all ages - some include facilities for children.

Related websites

www.adventurewomen.com
Exotic, high-adventure trips for women over 30.

www.goingplacestours.com
Walking tours for small groups of women.

www.womensquest.com
Action packed trips.

www.journeywoman.com
Quarterly e-zine with women-friendly travel tips and city sites.

www.dandelionadventures.com
Wilderness journeys, walks, nature retreats for women.

www.womentravelling.com

Transport issues

Rail passes

Tʜɪs ʟɪsᴛ sʜᴏᴡs ᴀ sᴇʟᴇᴄᴛɪᴏɴ of the many passes that are available worldwide. The passes shown are valid for the whole national rail network unless otherwise stated.

All prices are 2nd class. Validity is unlimited unless stated otherwise. We have not included summertime-only or limited availability tickets, or supplements.

ABBREVIATIONS USED

IR = Inter-Rail Card FP = Freedom Pass/Euro Domino
IR+ = Inter-Rail over 26 Card

Europe

As well as general passes, some passes to individual countries are also available.

INTER-RAIL CARD
You must be under 26 yrs when you start. You must have been resident in Europe for more than 6 months. Card includes 24-hour helpline; legal assistance; retail discounts. Card is divided into 7 zones. Prices as follows:
  Single zone ticket:
    £179/ 15 days
  Any 2 zones:
    £209 for 1 month
  Any 3 zones:
    £299 for 1 month
  All 7 zones:
    £249 for 1 month

INTER-RAIL 26+ CARD
You must be over 26 yrs when you start. Similar to Inter-Rail, but not valid in: Belgium, France, Italy, Macedonia, Morocco, Portugal, Spain, UK, Switzerland. Prices: 15 days or 1 month unlimited travel: £215 or £275.

FREEDOM PASS (EURO DOMINO)
3, 5 or 10 days unlimited travel within 1 month. Tickets: Adult 1st Class, Adult 2nd Class, Under 26, Child. Prices vary according to country. Includes some local supplements. A passport is required. Valid in all European countries except: Albania, Bosnia-Herzegovina, and ex-Soviet republics.

EURAIL PASS
Available to US citizens, these allow a variety of discount fares and types of pan-European rail travel.

Argentina

Argenpass: 30-90 day unlimited 1st class travel. Youth Pass: 25% discount for under-30s. Senior Pass: 25% discount for men 60+ and women 55+. Student Pass: 25% discount for students. Can only be obtained within Argentina.

Australia

Austrailpass: Validity 14, 21, 30 days. Austrail Flexi-Pass: Validity 8 days. Can only be obtained outside Australia, and is operated on a state-by-state basis.

Austria

Puzzle: Validity 10 days, max use 4 days. Puzzle Junior: similar to Puzzle, but for under 26s. IR, IR+, FP National Rail Pass: available for one month and valid on all Austrian railways. Environmental Ticket: purchase a half-fare pass and pay half fares for all train travel for one year. Environmental Tickets available for pensioners.

Belgium

B-Tourrail: Validity 1 month, max use 5 days. Reductie Kaart: Validity 1 month. 50% off all fares. Nettreinkaart: Validity 1 week. Benelux-Tourrail: Validity 1 month, max use 5 days. IR, FP

Canada

Canrailpass: Validity 12 days. Youth: same as Canrail. Senior: For travellers 60+. Alaska Pass: Validity 8-30 days. Alaska & BC only + buses. Must be obtained outside Canada.

Czech Republic

Kilometricka banka 2000: max 2000 kms travel. Kilometricka banka 5000: max 5000 kms travel. IR, IR+, FP

Denmark

Danmarkskort: Validity 1 month.
Scanrail, IR, IR+, FP

Finland

Finnrail Pass: Validity 1 month, max use 3-10 days.
Scanrail, IR, IR+, FP

Germany

DB Railcard: Allows you to buy unlimited 2nd class tickets at 50% discount.
IR, IR+, FP

Greece

Tourism Card: Validity 10, 20, 30 days. Unlimited 2nd class travel.
IR, IR+, FP

Hungary

Turistaberlet: Validity 7/10 days.
IR, IR+, FP

India

Indrail Pass : Permits travel on all trains.
Child Indrail: 50% discount.
Can be purchased inside or outside India. But in India can only be bought with £ or US$.

Ireland

Irish Explorer: Validity 15days, max use 5 days. 2nd class only.
Irish Explorer Rail & Bus: Validity 15 days, max use 8 days.
Irish Rover: Validity 15 days, max use 5 days.
Emerald Card: Validity 15/30 days, max use 8/15 days. 2nd class only + bus.
IR, IR+, FP

Italy

Italy Railcard: Validity 8-30 days.

Biglietto Chilometrico: Validity 2 months, max use 20 trips to max 2000 kms.
IR, FP

Japan

Japan Rail Pass: Must be obtained outside Japan.

Luxembourg

Ticket Reseau: Validity 1 day until 08:00 hrs next day.
Benelux-Tourrail
IR, IR+, FP

Malaysia

Malayan Railway Pass: Validity 10-30 days.

The Netherlands

Eurodomino Plus: Validity 3-10 days (buses, trams & metros).
Benelux-Tourrail: Cannot be obtained in Holland.
IR, IR+, FP (includes rail, bus, metro and tram).

New Zealand

New Zealand Travelpass: Unlimited travel on train, coach and ferry.

Norway

NIR Weelky Tourist Ticket: Validity 7-14 days or 1 month, max use 3 days. Prices increase 25% in summer.
Scanrail, IR, IR+, FP

Pakistan

Concessions for tourists on presentation of a certificate issued by the railway.
50% discount for students.

Poland

Polrail Pass: Validity 8 days-1 month.
IR, IR+, FP

Portugal

Bilhete Turisticos: Validity 7-21 days.
IR, FP

Singapore

The Malaysian-Singapore Rail Pass: Covers Singapore, Malaysia and Thailand, lasts for 10 days.

Slovakia

Kilometrica banka: Validity 6 months, max use 2000 kms of travel.
IR, IR+, FP

Slovenia

Slovenia Rail: Validity 10-30 days.
IR, FP

Sweden

Sweden Rail Pass: Validity 7-30 days, max use 3-14 days.
Scanrail, IR, IR+, FP

Switzerland

Swiss Pass: Validity 4 days-1 month (includes public transport in 35 towns).
Swiss Flexi Pass: Validity 15 days, max use 3 days (includes public transport in 35 towns).
Swiss Half-Fare: Validity 1 month. 50% discount on unlimited number of full tickets.
IR, FP

UK

Britexpress Card: 30% off on 30 consecutive days.
Tourist Trail Pass: unlimited travel for periods from 5-30 days.

USA

National Rail Pass: Validity 15-30 days.
Regional passes: Validity 15 or 30 days.

Air passes

AIRPASSES ARE ESSENTIALLY CONCESSIONARY AIRFARES offered by airlines for visitors to a particular country or region. When a journey requires a number of flights within a particular country or region, the airpass can be an attractive option, particularly if flights will be long-distance.

In most cases an airpass must be booked before departure from the country of origin, as it will not be available in the destination itself. A minimum number of flights (or 'coupons' as they are usually referred to) have to be pre-purchased. Typically, these are a minimum of two or three flights up to a maximum of ten. It is worth remembering that the airpasses are only valid for a specified number of days.

Airpasses can offer excellent value for money (when your itinerary includes the minimum number of flights) as they permit a greater degree of flexibility than most concessionary or discounted fares. Usually you can change the dates of travel (and in some cases the route) at little or no extra cost, whereas most other cheap or discounted airfares incur either penalties or do not allow changes. However, they are not always the cheapest way of simply getting from A to B.

Most IATA travel agents can sell airpasses as long as they are an accredited agent for the required airline. However, in the past few years, now that airlines are offering fares that include multiple stopovers as part of the main or international ticket, airpass sales have been dwindling, especially to North America. WEXAS International, or any good travel agent, will be able to advise which is the most suitable type of ticket for your particular journey.

While many of the airlines offer airpasses, no two are exactly the same. Below we have listed a selection of the most popular airpasses, but these are just a sample of what is available.

Africa

SOUTH AFRICAN AIRLINES (SA)
Africa Explorer Pass requires a minimum purchase of four coupons and a maximum of eight. Validity from three to 45 days. Prices vary according to the sectors flown and some destinations outside South Africa are included in the pass, which should be booked in conjunction with an international ticket either to or from South Africa.

Middle East

GULF AIR
The Visit the Gulf Pass is valid for flights within and between the United Arab Emirates, Bahrain, Qatar and Oman. A minimunm of three coupons must be purchased with prices from $40 to $80 per flight

depending on the route. The maximum validity is 3 months and unlimited coupons may be purchased. International travel to or from the Gulf must be on Gulf Air to qulaify for this airpass.

Latin America

AEROLINEAS ARGENTINAS
Visit Argentina Pass allows a minimum of four coupons for US$500 to a maximum of eight with additional coupons costing US$130 each. One stopover allowed per city. Valid for 30 days. International flights must can be with BA or AR.

MERCOSUR
Airpass links 36 Argentine cities with those of Brazil, Uruguay and Paraguay, valid on the services of AR and eight other carriers.

Fares are based on the number of kilometres travelled with a maximum of two stops per country. Valid for 30 days.

VARIG
Available in conjunction with international travel on BA or Varig, Brazilian Airpass costs from US$490 for up to five sectors to a maximum of nine from US$890. One stopover per city is allowed and the maximum validity is 21 days.

LAN CHILE
Various airpasses are available for routes within Chile from US$300 excluding Easter Island. Validity of 21 days.

MEXICO
MexiPass, from US$120, is used in conjunction with a return transatlantic ticket and valid for 90 days on Mexicana and Aeromexico

services. Coupons start at US$60, according to the route flown, and a minimum of two coupons must be purchased.

North America and the Carribean

AMERICAN AIRLINES
Visit USA Pass from £259 for a minimum of three couponsto a maximum of ten coupons from £679. Maximum of two stopovers at any one city and valid for 60 days. In conjunction with transatlantic travel on American Airlines, Virgin or British Airways to an American Airlines gateway city in the USA.

DELTA AIRLINE
Discover America from US$399, has a minimum of three coupons and a maximum of ten for CAD$1079 . It covers mainland USA and Delta services between USA and Canada with add-ons to Hawaii, Mexico and the Carribean available. Transatlantic flights need to be with Delta Airlines or Air France or higher levels apply from US$539 for three coupons. Valid for a maximum of 60 days.

UNITED AIRLINES
US Airpass from £259 has a minimum of three coupons to a maximum of eight in conjunction with international travel on United Airlines, British Airways or Virgin. For transatlantic travel on any other carriers higher fares are available. The airpass is valid for all routes in mainland US and some Canadian, Mexican and Alaskan destinations. To include Hawaii, an

additional supplement is payable.

Asia/Australia /Pacific

SOUTH PACIFIC PASS
Valid on Qantas, Air Pacific and several other Pacific Island carriers. A minimum of 2 sectors must be purchased, with prices ranging from $190 per sector to $340 per sector depending on the route. Maximum validity is 6 months and unlimited sectors can be purchased.

AIR NEW ZEALAND
Explore New Zealand Airpass from NZ$480,a minimum of three coupons, to a maximum of eight at NZ$1280. Valid up to one year and with any scheduled airline on international flights.

ANSETT AIRLINES AND AIR NEW ZEALAND
G'Day Pass from £190, available with any international airline to Australia and New Zealand. Fares from £95 (single zone) to £120 (multi-zone) per coupon with additional coupons up to a maximum of eight coupons per visit to Australia or New Zealand.

GARUDA INDONESIA
Visit Indonesia Airpass from US$300 covers domestic routes with one stopover permitted per city on Garuda or selected Merpati Nusantera services. Minimum purchase of three coupons for $300, with additional coupons at US$100 to a maximum of ten coupons. The maximum validity is 60 days. International flights must be booked with Garuda or British Airways

flight to Indonesia.

INDIAN AIRLINES
Discover India Pass US$500, unlimited travel valid on Indian Airlines network in India with one stopover at each point for 15 days. For 1 days travel the fare increases to $750.

QANTAS
Boomerang Pass from £220, for travellers to Australia, New Zealand or Fiji on any airline. The region is divided into four zones across Australia, New Zealand and selected islands of the South West Pacific. Sectors start at £110 (single zone) or £135 (multi-zone), with a minimum of two coupons to a maximum of ten.

THAI AIRWAYS
Amazing Thailand Pass from US$199 for four coupons with additional sectors at $49 each to a maximum of 8 coupons. The first sector must be prebooked and international travel can be with any airline. Valid for 3 months.

Airline head offices worldwide

ACES (AEROLINEAS CENTRALES DE COLOMBIA)
Calle 49, No 50-21
Edificio del Cafe , Piso 34
PO Box 6503, Colombia
Tel 456 053
Web www.
acescolombia.com

ADRIA AIRWAYS
Kuzmiceva 7, Ljubljana
Slovenia SI-1000
Tel 61 136 2500
Fax 61 136 9233
Web www.adria.si

AEGEAN AIRLINES
572 Vouliagmenis Avenue
Athens, Greece 16451
Tel 1 998 3850
Fax 1 995 7598

AER LINGUS
Dublin Airport , Dublin
Ireland
Tel 1 8862222
Fax 1 8863832
Web www.aerlingus.ie

AERO CALIFORNIA
Aquiles Serdan No.1995
La Paz, Baja California
Mexico 23000
Tel 112 208 33
Web www.
americanair.com/aahome/
servinfo/aerocal.htm

AEROCARIBE
Coba Ave, No 5 Local B1
Plaza America, Cancun
Quintana Roo
Mexico 77500
Tel 988 41231
Web www.
wotw.com/Aerocaribe

AEROCONTINENTE CHILE
Europa 1914, Santiago
Chile
Tel 56 2 2047784
Fax 56 2 3437638

AEROFLOT-RUSSIAN INTERNATIONAL AIRLINES
Leningradski Prospekt 37
Moscow 125167, Russia
Tel 155 54 94
Web www.aeroflot.org

AEROLINAS ARGENTINAS
Bouchard 547,
Buenos Aires, Argentina
Tel 4317 3000
Web www.
aerolineas.com.ar

AEROMEXICO
Paseo de la Reforma 445
Col. Cuauhtemoc
Mexico City 06500, Mexico
Tel 5 133 40 00
Web www.aeromexico.com

AERO ZAMBIA
Private Bag E717, Lusaka
Zambia
Tel 1 226194
Fax 1 226147
Web www. mbendi.co.za/
orgs/ccr5.htm

AFRICAN JOINT AIR SERVICE
13-15 Kimathi Avenue
Impala House
Kampala, Uganda
Tel 41 244011
Web www. imul.com/
uganda/alliance.html

AFRICAN STAR AIRWAYS
PO Box 783465, Sandton
Gauteng
South Africa 2146
Tel 11 390 2439/1204
Fax 11 390 1438

AIR 2000
Jetset House, Church Road
Lowfield Heath, Crawley
W Sussex RH11 0PQ, UK
Tel 01293 518966
Fax 01293 522927
Web www.air2000.co.uk

AIR AFRIQUE
01 BP 3927, Abidjan 01
Cote d'Ivoire
Tel 20 30 00
Fax 20 30 08
Web www.air-afrique.co.za

AIR ALASKA CARGO
6105 E.Rutter Avenue
Suite 201, Spokane
Washington 99212, USA
Tel 509 532 1000
Fax 509 532 8000

AIR ALGERIE
1 Place Maurice Audin
Algiers , Algeria
Tel 63 92 34/5/6
Web www.
cheapflights.co.uk/
Airlines/AirAlgerie.html

AIR ALLIANCE
611 6th Avenue
Jean Lesage Int'l Airport
Ste. Foy, Quebec
Canada G2E 5W1
Tel 418 872 7622
Fax 418 872 9716
Web www.
aircanada.ca/ac_world/serv
ices/connect/airalli.html

AIR AUSTRAL
B.P. 611, 4 rue de Nice
St Dennis Cedex
Reunion 97434
Tel 28 22 51
Web www.austral.com

AIR BALTIC CORPORATION
Riga Airport, Riga
Latvia LV-1053
Tel 7 207401
Web www.airbaltic.lv

AIR BERLIN LUFTVERKEHRS
Flughafen Tegel, Berlin
Germany 13405
Tel 30 41 013690
Fax 30 41 013695
Web www.airberlin.com

AIR BOTSWANA
Cycle Mart Building
Lobatse Road, PO Box 92
Gaborone , Botswana
Tel 52812
Fax 374802
Web www.
mbendi.co.za/orgs/cbjc

AIR BURKINA
Avenue Loudun
Siege Social 01 BP 1459

Ouagadougou
Burkina Faso
Tel 315324
Fax 301717
Web www.wtg.online.com/
country/bf/tra.html

AIR BURUNDI
PO Box 2460
40 Avenue du Commerce
Bujumbura, Burundi
Tel 257 224609
Fax 257 223452

AIR CALEDONIE
INTERNATIONAL
8 rue Frederic Surleau
BP 3736, Noumea
New Caledonia 98846
Tel 687 283333
Fax 687 272772
Web www.
pacificislands.com/airlines/
caledonie.html

AIR CANADA
PO Box 14000
Postal Station St-Laurent
Montreal, Quebec
Canada H4Y 1H4
Tel 514 422 5000
Fax 514 879 7990
Web www.aircanada.ca

AIR CHINA
Capital Int. Airport
Beijing 100621, China
Tel 10 456 3220
Fax 10 456 3348
Web www.airchina.com

AIR DJIBOUTI
PO Box 499, Djibouti
Tel 356723
Fax 356734
Web www.arab.
net/djibouti/transport/
di_air.html

AIR FRANCE
45 Rue de Paris
F-95747 Roissy CDG Cedex
France
Tel 43 23 81 81
Fax 43239711
Web www.airfrance.fr

AIR GABON
B.P 2206, Libreville, Gabon

Tel 73 21 97
Web www.
infoasis.com/people/
stevewt/airports_Airlines

AIR GEORGIA
49A Chavchavadze Avenue
Tbilisi, Georgia
380062
Tel 8832 23 51 56
Fax 8832 29 4053

AIR ICELAND
Reykjavik Airport
Reykjavik, Iceland 101
Tel 570 3000
Fax 570 3001
Web www.airiceland.is

AIR-INDIA
Air-India Building
218 Backbay Reclamation
Nariman Point
Mumbai 400 021 , India
Tel 22 202 4142
Fax 22 202 4897
Web www.airindia.com

AIR JAMAICA
72-76 Harbour St
Kingston, Jamaica
West Indies
Tel 876 922-3460
Fax 876 922-0107
Web www.airjamaica.com

AIR KAZAKSTAN
14 Ogareva, Almaty
Kazakstan 480079
Tel 3272 571693
Fax 3272 572503
Web www.airkaz.com

AIR LIBERTE
Immeuble le Delta
3 rue du Pont des Halles
F-94656 Rungis Cedex
France
Tel 247 54 21 45
Web www.air-liberte.fr

AIR LITTORAL
417 rue Samuel Morse
Le Millenaire , Montpellier
France 34961
Tel 467 20 67 20
Fax 467 64 10 61
Web www.air-littoral.com

AIR MACAU
693 Avenida da Praia
Grande
Edif. Tai Wah, 9-12 Andar
Macau
Tel 396 6888
Fax 396 6866
Web www.
airmacau.com.mo

AIR MADAGASCAR
31 Avenue de
l'Independance
Antananarivo
101 Madagascar
Tel 2 44222
Fax 2 44674
Web www.air-mad.com

AIR MALAWI
PO Box 84, Blantyre
Malawi
Tel 620 811
Fax 620 042
Web www.africaonline.
co.ke/airmalawi

AIR MALDIVES
26 Ameeru Ahmed Magu
Male, Maldives 20-05
Tel 322438
Fax 325056

AIR MALI
Immeuble SCIF Square
Lumumba, PO Box 2690
Bamako, Mali
Tel 22 93 94
Fax 22 94 03

AIR MALTA
Luqa Airport, Head Office
Luqa, Malta
Tel 824330
Fax 673241
Web www.airmalta.com

AIR MAURITANIE
B.P 41 , Nouakchott
Mauritania
Tel 52 22 11
Web www.
arab.net/mauritania/
transport/ma_air.html

AIR MAURITIUS
PO Box 441
Port Louis, Mauritius
Tel 208 7700

Fax 208 8331
Web www.
airmauritius.int.ch

AIR NAMIBIA
PO Box 731, Windhoek
Namibia 9000
Tel 61 223019
Fax 61 221916
Web www.
air-namibia.co.za

AIR NEW ZEALAND
Private Bag 92007
Level 21 Quay Tower
29 Customs Street West
Auckland, New Zealand
Tel 9 3662400
Fax 9 366 2667
Web www.airnz.com/
main_gateway.htm

AIR NIPPON
3-5-10 Haneda Airport
Otak-ku, Tokyo, Japan
100-6036
Tel 3 54 62 19 11
Fax 3 54 62 1950
Web www.ananet.or.jp

AIR PACIFIC
PO Box 9266, Nadi Airport
Fiji Islands
Tel 720777
Fax 720686
Web custom.supersites.net/
airpn2/docs/profile1.htm

AIR RAROTONGA
PO Box 79, Rarotonga
Cook Islands
Tel 22888
Fax 20979
Web www.ck/edairaro.htm

AIR SEYCHELLES
PO Box 386
Seychelles Int. Airport
Mahe, Seychelles
Tel 225300
Fax 225159
Web www.airseychelles.it

AIR SINAI
6 Adly Street, Cairo, Egypt
Tel 2 77 49 66
Fax 2 574 47 11
Web www.orca-air.com

AIR SLOVAKIA
PO Box 2
M.R. Stefanik Airport
Bratislava
Slovak Republic 82001
Tel 7 522 6805
Fax 7 522 2742

AIR TAHITI
PO Box 314
Boulevard Pomare
Papeete, Tahiti
French Polynesia
Tel 86400
Fax 864069
Web www.tcsp.com/
supps/sta519.htm

AIR TANZANIA
Tancot House, City Drive
PO Box 543, Dar-es-Salaam
Tanzania
Tel 51 38300
Fax 51 46545
Web www.
mwebmarketplace.co.za/
airtan

AIR TRANSAT
11600 Cargo Road A1
Montreal International
Airport, Mirabel
Quebec, Canada J7N 1G9
Tel 514 476 1011
Fax 514 476 7925
Web airlineinfo.com/
oiacarrier/airtransat.htm

AIR UKRAINE
14 Prospekt Pobedy
252135 Kiev, Ukraine
Tel 044 2262567
Fax 044 2168235
Web www.airukrainc.com

AIR VENEZUELA
Av. Francisco Solano
Caracas, Venezuela 1050
Tel 2 761 2149
Fax 2 761 8740

AIR ZIMBABWE
PO Box API
Harare Airport
Harare, Zimbabwe
Tel 4 575 111
Fax 4 575 068
Web www.home.earthlink.
net/-airzimbabwe

ALASKA AIRLINES
PO Box 68900
19300 Pacific Highway
South, Seattle
Washington 98188, USA
Tel 206 433 3200
Fax 206 433 3366
Web www.alaskaair.com/
contents.stm

ALBANIAN AIRLINES
R.R Durresi No. 202
Tirana, Albania
Tel 42 42857
Web www.higbee.db.erau.
edu/so.amer/nojava/
air1alba.html

ALITALIA
Viale Alessendro Marchetti
111
Alitalia Centro Direzionale
Roma1-00148, Italy
Tel 6 6562151
Fax 6 65624733
Web www.alitalia.it

ALL NIPPON AIRWAYS
3-5-10 Haneda Airport
Ota-Ku, Tokyo
Japan 144-0041
Tel 03 580 4711
Fax 03 592 3039
Web www.ana.co.jp/eng

ALM 1997 AIRLINE
Aeropuerto Hato
Willemstad, Curacao
Netherlands Antilles
Tel 9 338888
Fax 9 338300
Web www.empg.com/alm

ALOHA AIRLINES
371 Aokea St
PO Box 30028
Honolulu Int. Airport
Hawaii 96820 , USA
Tel 808 836 4210
Fax 808 833 3671
Web www.alohaair.com

AMERICAN AIRLINES
PO Box 619616
Dallas/Fort Worth Airport
Texas 75261-9616 , USA
Tel 817 967 1234
Fax 817 967 4318
Web www.aa.com

AMERICAN TRANS AIR
7337 West Washington St
PO Box 51609
Indianapolis
Indiana 46251, USA
Tel 317 247 4000
Fax 317 243 4165
Web www.ata.com

AMERICAN WEST AIRLINES
4000 East Sky Harbor Blvd
Phoenix Sky Harbor
International Airport
Phoenix
Arizona 85034, USA
Tel 602 693 0800
Fax 602 693 5546
Web www.
americawest.com

ANSETT AUSTRALIA
501 Swanston St
Melbourne
Victoria 3000, Australia
Tel 3 9668 1211
Fax 3 9668 1114
Web www.ansett.com

AOM - MINERVE
Strategic Orly 108
13-15 rue du Pont des
Halles, Paris, France 94526
Tel 149 79 10 00
Fax 149 79 10 12
Web www.aom.ch

ARIANA AFGHAN AIRLINES
Ansari Watt, PO Box 76
Kabul, Afghanistan
Tel 25541.45, 26541.45
Web www.
infoasis.com/people/
stevetwt/Airports_Airlines

ARKIA - ISRAELI AIRLINES
PO Box 39301, Dov Airport
Tel Aviv 61392, Israel
Tel 3 690 22 22
Fax 03 699 13 90
Web www.arkia.co.il

ARMENIAN AIRLINES
Airport Zvartnots
375042 Yerevan, Armenia
Tel 2 225 447
Fax 2 151 393
Web www.arminco.com/aa

AUSTRALIAN AIR EXPRESS
399 Elizabeth St
Melbourne
Victoria 3000, Australia
Tel 3 9297 3100
Fax 3 9297 3141
Web www.ausairx.com.au

AUSTRIAN AIRLINES
PO Box 50
Fontanastrasse 1
A-1107 Vienna, Austria
Tel 1 1766
Fax 1 68 55 05
Web www.aua.com

AVIANCA
Av Eldorado No 93-30
Bogota, Colombia
Tel 1 413 9511
Fax 1 269 9131
Web www.avianca.com.co

AVIATECA
Avenida Hincapie 12-22
Zona 13
Aeropuerto La Aurora
Guatemala City
Guatemala 01013
Tel 2 318261
Fax 2 317412
Web www.
flylatinamerica.com

AZERBAIJAN AIRLINES
Prospekt Azadlig 11
Baku 370000, Azerbaijan
Tel 12 243714
Fax 12 25 4466
Web www.
turkiye-online.com/air

BAHAMASAIR
Po Box N-4881
Nassau , Bahamas
Tel 809 327-8451
Fax 809 327 7408
Web www.bahamasair.com

BALKAN - BULGARIAN AIRLINES
Sofia Airport
1540 Sofia , Bulgaria
Tel 2 661690
Fax 2 723496
Web www.balkan.com

BANGKOK AIRWAYS
60 Queen Sirikit National

Convention Center
New Rajadapisek Road
Klongtoey, Bangkok
Thailand 10110
Tel 2 2293434
Fax 2 229 3450
Web www.bkair.co.th

BELAVIA - BELARUSSIAN AIRLINES
14 Nemiga Street
Minsk 220004, Belarus
Tel 172 250853
Fax 172 251566
Web www.higbee.db.erau.
edu/so.amer.nojava/
air1bela.html

BIMAN - BANGLADESH AIRLINES
Biman Bangladesh Bldng
100 Mitijheel
Dhaka 1000, Bangladesh
Tel 2 240151
Fax 2 863005
Web www.
bangladeshonline.com/
biman

BRAATHENS SAFE AIR TRANSPORT
Hd Office Oksenoyveien 3
PO Box 55-1330 Fornebu
Oslo Aiport, Norway
Tel 67597000
Fax 67591309
Web www.fly.braathens.no

BRIT AIR
B.P. 156
Aerodrome du Ploujean
Morlaix, Cedex
France F29204
Tel 98 62 10 22
Fax 98 62 12 58

BRITISH AIRWAYS
PO Box 365, Waterside
Harmondsworth
West Drayton UB7 0GB
UK
Tel 020 8738 5000
Fax 020 8562 9930
Web www.
britishairways.com

BRITISH MEDITERRANEAN AIRWAYS
Cirrus House, Bedfont Rd

Heathrow Airport
London TW19 7NL, UK
Tel 020 7493 3030
Fax 020 7493 9944
Web www.
britishairways.com

BRITISH MIDLAND
Donington Hall
Castle Donington
Derby DE7 2SB, UK
Tel 01332 854000
Fax 01332 854662
Web www.
britishmidland.com

BRITISH REGIONAL AIRLINES
Isle of Man (Ronaldsway)
Airport, Ballasalla
Isle of Man IM9 2JE
Tel 01624 826000
Fax 01624 826001
Web www.
manx-airlines.com

BWIA WEST INDIES AIRWAYS
Piarco Airport, PO Box 604
Admin. Building
Port of Spain
Trinidad and Tobago
Tel 664 4871
Web www.bwee.com

CAMEROON AIRLINES
BP 4092
3 Avenue General de Gaulle
Douala, Cameroon
Tel 42 25 25
Fax 42 24 87
Web www.undp.org/tcdc/
backup/ cmr/025.htm

CANADA 3000 AIRLINES
27 Fasken Drive, Toronto
Ontario, Canada M9W 1K6
Tel 416 674 0257
Fax 416 674 0256
Web www.canada3000.com

CANADIAN AIRLINES INTERNATIONAL
Suite 2800
700 2nd St SW, Calgary
Alberta T2P 2W2, Canada
Tel 403 294 2000
Fax 403 294 2066
Web www.cdair.ca

CATHAY PACIFIC AIRWAYS
Swire House, 5th Floor
9 Connaught Road Central
Hong Kong SAR, China
Tel 2745 5000
Fax 28 10 65 63
Web www.
cathaypacific.com

CAYMAN AIRWAYS
PO Box, 1101 George Town
Grand Cayman
Cayman Islands
Tel 949 8200
Fax 949 7607
Web www.
cayman.com.ky/com/cal

CHINA AIRLINES
131 Sec 3 Nanking East Rd
Taipei, Taiwan 10410
Tel 2 2514 5664
Fax 2 2717 4647
Web www.metro.co.uk/
travlog/ca.html

CHINA EASTERN AIRLINES
2550 Hong Qiao Road
Shanghai, China 200335
Tel 21 255 88 99
Fax 21 255 60 39
Web www.
chinaeasternair.com

CHINA NORTHERN AIRLINES
Dong Ta Airport
3-1 Xiaoheyan Road
Dadong District
Shenyang City
Liao Ning Province
China 110043
Tel 24 829 44 46
Fax 24 829 44 33

CHINA NORTHWEST AIRLINES
2 Feng Hao Lu, Xian City
Shaanxi Province
China 710082
Tel 29 729 8000
Fax 29 426 2022
Web www.
virtualairline.co.uk/
China-Northwest.html

CHINA SOUTHERN AIRLINES
Bai Yun Int. Airport
International Affairs Dept.

Guanzhou City
Guang Dong Province
China 510406
Tel 20 667 89 01
Fax 20 664 46 23
Web www.
chinasouthernair.com

CHINA SOUTHWEST AIRLINES
Shuangliu Airport
Chengdu
Sichuan Province, China
Tel 28 558 14 66
Fax 28 667 93 19
Web www.cswa.com

CITYFLYER EXPRESS
Beehive Ring Road
Gatwick Airport
Ian Stewart Centre
W Sussex RH6 0PB, UK
Tel 01293 567837
Fax 01293 567829
Web www.
britishairways.com

CITY JET
The Atrium, Level 5
Terminal Building
Dublin Airport
Co. Dublin, Ireland
Tel 1 844 5588
Fax 1 704 4753
Web www.
info.greenwich2000.com/
info/lcy/cityjet.htm

COMMERCIAL AIRWAYS
PO Box 7015
1622 Bonaero Park,
Gauteng, South Africa
Tel 11 921 01 11
Fax 11 973 39 13
Web www.
pix.za/business/travel/
tourism/96aprzb.html

CONGO AIRLINES
B.P. 12847
1920 Ave Kabambare
Kinshasa 1, Congo
Web www.
infoasis.com/people/
steven/Airports_Airlines

CONTINENTAL AIRLINES
PO Box 4607, Houston
Texas 77210-4607, USA

Tel 713 834 5000
Fax 713 639 3087
Web www.continental.com

CONTINENTAL MICRONESIA
Ab Won Pat Int.Airport
P.O. Box 8778 G
Tamuning, Guam 96931
Tel 671 646 0204
Fax 671 646 6821
Web www.magna.com.au/
-hideaway/mic.html

CROATIA AIRLINES
Savska Cesta 41
10000 Zagreb, Croatia
Tel 41 61 31 11
Fax 41 53 04 75
Web www.ctn.tel.hr/ctn

CROSSAIR
PO Box, Basel
Switzerland CH-4002
Tel 61 325 25 25
Fax 61 325 32 68
Web www.crossair.ch

CUBANA
Calle 23 No 64, Vedado
C.P. 10400, Havana, Cuba
Tel 7 36 775
Fax 7 36 190
Web www.
cubana.cu/contenido.htm

CYPRUS AIRWAYS
21 Alkeou Street
PO Box 1903-1514
Nicosia, Cyprus
Tel 2 443 054
Fax 2 443 167
Web www.cypnet.com/cta

CZECH AIRLINES
Kolejni 2, Praha 6
Czech Republic 160 00
Tel 2 2010 4400
Fax 2 2431 2696
Web www.csa.cz

DELTA AIRLINES
Hartsfield Atlanta
International Airport
P.O. Box 20706, Atlanta
Georgia 30320, USA
Tel 404 715 2600
Fax 404 767 8499
Web www.delta-air.com

DEUTSCHE BA
LUFTFAHRTGESELLSCHAFT
Wartungsallee 13
P.O. Box 231624
Munich, Germany 85356
Tel 89 97 1500
Fax 89 975 91503
Web www.deutsche-ba.de

DJIBOUTI AIRLINES
Place Lagarde, PO Box 2240
Djibouti
Tel 351006
Fax 352429

EASYJET
Easyland
London Luton Airport
Luton LU2 9LS, UK
Tel 01582 44 55 66
Fax 01582 44 33 55
Web www.easyjet.com

EGYPTAIR
Cairo International Airport
Cairo, Egypt
Tel 2 390 24 44
Fax 2 39 15 57

EL AL -ISRAEL AIRLINES
PO Box 41
Ben-Gurion Airport
Tel Aviv 70100 , Israel
Tel 3 971 6111
Fax 3 971 1442
Web www.elal.co.il

EMIRATES
PO Box 686 , Dubai
United Arab Emirates
Tel 4 82 2511
Fax 4 82 2357
Web www.emirates.com

ESTONIAN AIR
2 Lennujaama Street
Tallinn EE0011, Estonia
Tel 6 401 101
Fax 6 312 740
Web www.estonian-air.ee

ETHIOPIAN AIRLINES
PO Box 1755, Bole Airport
Addis Ababa, Ethiopia
Tel 1 61 22 22
Fax 1 61 14 74
Web www.
flyethiopian.com

EUROWINGS
LUFTVERKEHRS
Flughafenstrasse 21
D-44319 Dortmund
Germany
Tel 911 36 5560
Web www.eurowings.de

EVA AIRWAYS
EVA Air Building
376 Hsin-nan Road
Sec 1, Luchu
Tao-Yuan Hsien, Taiwan
Tel 3 351 2697
Fax 3 335 2246
Web www.
evaair.com.tw/english

FINNAIR
P.O. Box 15, Vantaa
Finland 01531
Tel 9 81881
Fax 0 818 8739
Web www.finnair.com

GARUDA INDONESIA
P.O. Box 1164
Jalan Merdeka Selatan 13
Jakarta 10110, Indonesia
Tel 3801901
Fax 21 363595
Web www.garuda.co.id

GHANA AIRWAYS
White Avenue
PO Box 1636
Ghana Airways House
Accra, Ghana
Tel 21 773321
Fax 21 777675
Web www.
ghana-airways.com

GILL AIRWAYS
Newcastle Airport
Newcastle upon Tyne
NE13 8BT, UK
Tel 0191 214 6600
Fax 0191 214 6699
Web www.eclipse.co.uk

GO
Enterprise House
Stanstead Airport
Essex CM24 1SB, UK
Tel 01279 666333
Fax 01279 681763
Web www.go-fly.com

GULF AIR
PO Box 138, Manama
Bahrain
Tel 322 200
Fax 330 466

HAWAIIAN AIRLINES
3375 Koapaka Street
Suite G-350, Honolulu
Hawaii 96819, USA
Tel 808 537 5100
Web www.hawaiianair.com

HELI AIR MONACO
Heliport De Monaco
Monaco 98000
Tel 93 30 80 88

HELI INTER RIVIERA
Aeroport International de
Cannes Mandelieu, NB 11
Cannes, France 06150
Web www.st-barths.com/
descriptivepgs/heli.html

**HONG KONG DRAGON
AIRLINES**
Taikoo Place, 979 Kings Rd
22nd Floor, Devon House
Quarry Bay
Hong Kong, China
Tel 25 90 13 28
Fax 25 90 13 33
Web www.dragonair.com

IBERIA
130 Calle Velazquez
Zona Industrial 2
La Munoza
E-28006 Madrid, Spain
Tel 1 587 8787
Fax 1 587 7193
Web www.iberia.com

ICELANDAIR
Reykjavik Airport
IS-101 Reykjavik, Iceland
Tel 354 5050 300
Fax 354 1 690 391
Web www.
arctic.is/Transport/
Icelandair/Icelandair.htm

INDIAN AIRLINES
Airlines House
113 Gurdwara Rakabganj
Road , Parliament St
New Delhi 110001, India
Tel 11 388951

Fax 11 381730
Web www.
nic.in/indian-airlines

IRAN AIR
Iran Air Building
Mehrabad Airport
PO Box13185-775
Tehran, Iran
Tel 21 882 9080
Fax 21 600 32 48
Web www.
aeolos.com/iranair.htm

ISLES OF SCILLY SKYBUS
Lands End Aerodrome
St Just, Penzance
Cornwall TR19 7RL, UK
Tel 07136 787017
Web www.
compulink.co.uk/~issco

ISTANBUL AIRLINES
Firuzkoy Yolu No. 26
Avcilar, Istanbul
Turkey 34850
Tel 212 509 2121
Fax 212 593 6035
Web www.turkish~airlines.
com/Istanbul-Airlines.htm

JAPAN AIRLINES
4-11 Higashi-Shinagawa
2-Chrome
Higashi-Shinagawa, Tokyo
Japan 140 8637
Tel 5460 3756
Fax 5460 5973
Web www.jal.co.jp

JERSEY EUROPEAN AIRWAYS
Exeter Airport, Exeter
Devon EX5 2BD, UK
Tel 01392 366 669
Fax 01392 366 151
Web www.
jersey-european.co.uk

JET AIRWAYS (INDIA)
41/42 Maker Chambers
Nariman Point, Mumbai
Maharashtra, India 400059
Tel 22 850 0423/8729
Fax 22 850 4270
Web www.jetairways.com/
visitind.htm

KAMPUCHEA AIRLINES
138/70 17th floor

Jewellery Center, Siphaya
Bangrak, Bangkok
Thailand 10500
Tel 23 427868
Web www.singnet.com/
~ajhunt/pix60.htm

KENYA AIRWAYS
PO Box 19002
Nairobi, Kenya
Tel 822171
Web www.
kenyaairways.co.uk

KLM CITYHOPPER
Schipol East Airport
P.O. Box 7700, Amsterdam
Netherlands 1117 ZL
Tel 20 6492227
Fax 20 6492379
Web www.klm.com

**KLM ROYAL DUTCH
AIRLINES**
PO Box 7700
NL-1117 ZL Schiphol
Airport, Amsterdam
The Netherlands
Tel 0120 6499123
Fax 0120 6488391
Web www.en.nederland.
klm.com/frame/default.asp

KLM UK
Endeavour House
Stanstead Airport
Stanstead
Essex CM24 1RS, UK
Tel 01279 680 146
Fax 01279 680 012
Web www.klm.com

KOREAN AIR LINES
1370 Gong Hang-Dong
Kang Seo-Gu, Seoul, Korea
Tel 2 7517 114
Fax 2 751 7522
Web www.koreaair.com

KUWAIT AIRWAYS
PO Box 528
Kuwait Int.Airport
Safat, Kuwait 13006
Tel 434 5555
Fax 431 9912
Web www.
kuwait-airways.com

KYRGHYZSTAN AIRLINES
Manas Airport, Bishkek
Kyrghyzstan 720062
Tel 331 313084
Fax 331 2 313084
Web www.frankfurtairport.
de/terminalexplorer/
airline/k2.html

LAN-CHILE
Estado 10
Piso 18~Casilla 147-D
Santiago, Chile
Tel 2 394 411
Fax 34 359 7714
Web www.lanchile.com

LAUDA AIR
PO Box 56
A-1300 Vienna Airport
Vienna, Austria
Tel 1 7 1110 2081/2/3/4
Fax 1 7 1110 3157
Web www.laudaair.com

LIAT
P.O Box 819
VC Bird Int. Airport
Antigua
Tel 462 0700
Fax 462 2682/4765
Web www.liat.com

LIBYAN ARAB AIRLINES
P.O Box 2555
Umer Mukhftar St.
Tripoli, Libya
Tel 21 602 083/5
Fax 21 30970

LITHUANIAN AIRLINES
A. Gutaicio 4
Vilnius 2023, Lithuania
Tel 2 63 01 16
Fax 2 22 68 28
Web www.lal.lt

LLOYD AEREO BOLIVIANO
Casilla No.132
Aeropuerto J Wilstermann
Cochabamba, Bolivia
Tel 5900
Web www.
labairlines.bo.net

LOT - POLISH AIRLINES
65/79 Jerozolmskie Av
00-697 Warsaw , Poland
Tel 22 630 50 07

Fax 22 630 55 03
Web www.lot.com

LUFTHANSA
Von-Gablenz-Strasse 2-6
D-5000 Koln 21
Germany
Tel 221 8260
Fax 221 826 3818
Web www.lufthansa.de

LUXAIR
Aeroport de Luxembourg
L-2987 Luxembourg
Tel 4798 2311
Fax 43 24 82
Web www.luxair.lu

MAERSK AIR
Copenhagen Airport South
DK-2791, Dragoer
Denmark
Tel 45 32 31 44 44
Fax 45 32 31 44 90
Web www.maersk-air.com

MALAYSIA AIRLINES
33rd Floor, Bangunan MAS
Jalan Sultan Ismail 50250
Kuala Lumpur , Malaysia
Tel 261 0555
Fax 6 37 746 2581
Web www.malaysiaair.com

MALEV - HUNGARIAN AIRLINES
Roosevelt Ter 2, Budapest
Hungary H-1051
Tel 1 266 9033
Fax 1 266 2685
Web www.malev.com

MANDARIN AIRLINES
13th Floor
134 Minsheng East Road
Sec 3, Taipei, Taiwan
Tel 886 2 717 1188
Fax 886 2 717 0716
Web www.
mandarinair.com

MANX AIRLINES
Isley of Man (Ranoldsway)
Airport, Ballasalla
Isle of Man, UK
Tel 01624 826000
Fax 01624 826031

MEA - MIDDLE EAST AIRLINES
PO Box 206
Beirut, Lebanon
Tel 01 316316
Fax 01 8711 754104
Web www.libanon.de/mea

MERPATI NUSTANTARA AIRLINES
P.O Box 1323
2&3 Jalan Angkasa
Block B-15, Jakarta
Indonesia 10720
Tel 21 413695
Fax 21 4207311/418
Web www.
garuda.co.id/merpati.htm

MEXICANA
Xola No 535
Piso 30, Col del Valle
PO Box 12-813
Mexico City 03100, Mexico
Tel 5 325 0909
Fax 5 543 4587
Web www.
mexicana.com/mx/
mx2/english/home.htm

MIAT - MONGOLIAN AIRWAYS
Buyant-Ukhaa Airport
Ulaanbaatar
Mongolia 210734
Tel 1-072 240
Web www.miat.com

MUSTIQUE AIRWAYS
P.O. Box 1232, St Vincent
Saint Vincent & Grenadines
Tel 458 4380
Fax 456 4586
Web www.caribisles.com/
mustique-air

MYANMAR AIRWAYS INTERNATIONAL
123 Sule Pagoda Road
Yangon, Myanmar
Tel 84566
Web www.myanmar.com

NICE AIRWAYS
Aeroport Nice 1, Cedex 3
Nice, France 06281
Tel 4 9321 3432
Fax 4 9321 3432

NIGERIA AIRWAYS
Airways House
M Muhammed Airport
PMB 21024, Lagos, Nigeria
Tel 900476
Web www.
escope/airlines/wt.html

NORTHWEST AIRLINES
5101 Northwest Drive
Minneapolis/St Paul
International Airport
St Paul, MIN 55111, USA
Tel 612 726 2111
Web www.nwa.com

OLYMPIC AIRWAYS
96 Syngrou Avenue
Athens 11741, Greece
Tel 929 2111
Fax 1 926 7156
Web agn.hol.gr/info/
olympic1.htm

OMAN AIR
P.O. Box 58, Code 111
Seeb International Airport
Muscat, Oman
Tel 519237
Fax 00968 510022
Web www.arabiantravel.
com/exhibs/al20.htm

**PIA - PAKISTAN
INTERNATIONAL AIRLINES**
PIA Building
Karachi Airport, Pakistan
Tel 412011
Fax 9221 727727
Web www.piac.com

PALESTINIAN AIRLINES
P.O.Box 4043
Althalathini Street
Gaza City, Israel
Tel 9727 822800
Fax 9727 821309

PHILIPPINE AIRLINES
10th Floor
Allied Bank Centre
6754 Ayala Avenue
Makati City
Philippines 0750
Tel 818 0111
Fax 818 3298
Web www.pal.com.ph

PIEDMONT AIRLINES
5443 Airport Terminal Rd
Salisbury, Maryland 21804
USA
Web www.
skipjack.net/le_shore/
members/piedmont.html

**PT. BOURAQ INDONESIA
AIRLINES**
1-3 Jalan Angkasa
Kemayoran, Jakarta
Indonesia 10720
Tel 21 65 52 89
Fax 21 629 8651
Web www.
promindo.com/tourism/
bouraq/friend.html

QANTAS AIRWAYS
Qantas Int. Centre
Building A
230 Coward Street-Mascot
Sydney, NSW 2020
Australia
Tel 2 691 3636
Fax 2 691 3277
Web www.quantas.com.au

QATAR AIRWAYS
Almana Tower
PO Box 22550, Airport Rd
Doha, Qatar
Tel 430707
Fax 352566
Web www.
qatarairways.com/qr

REGIONAL AIRLINES
Aeroport Nantes
Atlantique, Bouguenais
France 44340
Tel 02 40 84 81 38
Fax 02 40 84 83
Web www.
regionalairlines.com

ROYAL AIR MAROC
Aeroport De Casa-anfa
Casablanca , Morocco
Tel 36 16 20
Fax 36 05 20
Web www.maroc.net

ROYAL BRUNEI AIRLINES
PO Box 737, RBA Plaza
Bandar Seri Begawan
Brunei Darussalam 2085
Tel 02-240500

Web www.bdhclon.demon.
co.uk/rba.htm

**ROYAL JORDANIAN
AIRLINES**
Housing Bank Commercial
Centre
Queen Noor Street
PO Box 302, Amman
Jordan 11118
Tel 6 607300
Fax 6 672 527
Web www.rja.jo

ROYAL NEPAL AIRLINES
RNAC Building
Kanti Path, Kathmandu
Nepal
Tel 214511
Web www.catmando.com/
com/rnac/rnac.htm

ROYAL TONGAN AIRLINES
Private Bag 9, Nuku'Alofa
Tonga
Tel 22566
Web www.
tongatapu.net.to/tonga/
islands/royalt/contacts.htm

RWANDA AIRLINES
Avenue de la Justice
P.O. Box 3246
Kigali, Rwanda
Tel 77103
Fax 77669

RYANAIR
Dublin Airport
Co. Dublin, Ireland
Tel 01 844 4400
Fax 01 844 4402
Web www.ryanair.ie

**SAA - SOUTH AFRICAN
AIRWAYS**
Airways Towers
PO Box 7778
Johannesburg 2000
Transvaal, South Africa
Tel 011 28 1728
Fax 011 773 8988
Web www.saa.co.za

SABENA
Ave. E Mounierlaan 2
B-1200 Brussels, Belgium
Tel 02 723 23 23
Web www.sabena.com

SAS - Scandinavian Airlines
Fack
Stockholm S-195 87
Sweden
Tel 08 797 0000
Web www.sas.se

Saudi
PO Box 620
Jeddah 21231
Saudi Arabia
Tel 686 0000
Fax 686 4589
www.saudiairlines.com

ScotAirways
Cambridge Airport
Cambs CB5 8RT, UK
Tel 01223 292 525
Fax 01223 292 160
Web www.ds.dial.pipex.
com/suckling.airways

Shanghai Airlines
North Gate of Hongqiao
Int. Airport
Shanghai, China 200335
Tel 21 255 8558
Fax 21 255 9239
Web www.shanghi-air.com

Silk Air
5th Floor Core L
Cargo Airfreight Terminal
30 Airline Road (S)
Singapore 891830
Tel 225 4488
Fax 542 6286
Web www.silkair.com.sg

Singapore Airlines
P.O. Box 501
Airmile Transit Centre
Singapore 918101
Tel 542 3333
Fax 545 5749
Web www.
singaporeair.com

Slovak Airlines
Trnavska Cesta 56
Bratislava, Slovakia 82102
Tel 17 525 0096
Fax 17 525 4042

Solomon Airlines
PO Box 23, Honiara
Guadalcanal

Solomon Islands
Tel 20031
Web www.
pacificislands.com/airlines/
solomon.html

Southwest Airlines
2702 Love Field Drive
P.O. Box 36611, Dallas
Texas 75235, USA
Tel 214 904-4000
Web www.iflyswa.com

Sri Lankan Airlines
37 York Street, 3rd Floor
Grindlays Bank Building
Colombo, Sri Lanka 00100
Tel 1 73 5555
Fax 1 73 5122
Web www.airlanka.com

Sudan Airways
PO Box 253
SDC Building St. 15
New Extension
Khartoum, Sudan
Tel 41766

Swissair
Zurich Airport, Zurich
Switzerland CH-8058
Tel 812 1212
Fax 810 8046
Web www.swissair.com

Syrian Arab Airlines
PO Box 417, Damascus
Syria
Tel 22343 4/6
Web www.wtgonline.com/
country/sy/tra.html

TAAG - Angola Airlines
Rua Missao 123, PO Box 79
Luanda, Angola
Tel 336510
Web www.airtimes.com/
cgat/ao/taag.htm

Taca International Airlines
Edificio Caribe 2 Piso
San Salvador, El Salvador
Tel 298-5055
Web www.flylatinamerica.
com/acc_taca.html

TAM
R General Pantaleao, Teles
210 Jardim Aeroporto

Sao Paulo, 04355-040 Brazil
Tel 11 5777711
Fax 11 276 2691
Web www.tam.com.br

TAP (Air Portugal)
Aeroporto
(Apartado 50194)
P-1704-801 Lisbon Codex
Portugal
Tel 1 841 5000
Web www.tap.tp

TAROM (Romanian Air Transport)
Otopeni Airport
505 Bucuresti-Ploiesti Rd
Km 16.5, Bucharest,
Romania
Tel 333137
Web www.tarom.digiro.net

Thai Airways International
P.O. Box 1075
89 Vibhavadi Rangsit Road
Bangkok 10900, Thailand
Tel 513 0121
Fax 662 513-3341
Web www.thaiair.com

Tower Air
JFK International Airport
Hangar 17, Jamaica
New York 11430, USA
Tel 718 553-4300
Web www.towerair.com

Transavia Airlines
PO Box 7777
NL-1118 ZM
Schiphol-Centraal
The Netherlands
Tel 020 6046318
Fax 020 484637

TWA - Trans World Airlines
One City Centre
515 N 6th Street, St Louis
Missouri 63101, USA
Tel 314 589 7544
Fax 314 895 5428
Web www.twa.com

Tunis Air
Boulevard du 7 Novembre
Tunis Carthage 2035
Tunisia

Tel 700 100
Fax 700 008
Web www.tunisair.com

TURKISH AIRLINES
Genel Mudurlugu
Ataturk Havalimani
Yesilkoy, Istanbul
Turkey 34 830
Tel 0212 663 6300
Fax 0212 663 4744
Web www.
turkishairlines.com

UGANDA AIRLINES
M 92 Ssebugwawo Drive
Box 187, Entebbe
Uganda 5740
Tel 32990
Web www.
imul.com/uganda/qu.html

UKRAINE INTERNATIONAL AIRLINES
14 Avenue Peremogi
252135 Kiev, Ukraine
Tel 044 216 6758
Fax 044 216 7994
Web www.
iminet.com/SMS/Ukraine

UNITED AIRLINES
World Headquarters
PO Box 66100, Chicago
Illinois 60666, USA
Tel 847 700 4000
Web www.ual.com

URAL AIRLINES
6 Sputnikov Street
Ekaterinburg
Russia 620025
Tel 3432 268625
Fax 3432 266221

US AIRWAYS
2345 Crystal Drive
Arlington
Virginia 22227, USA
Tel 703 418 7000
Web www.usair.com

UZBEKISTAN AIRWAYS
41 Movarounnakhr
Tashkent
Uzbekistan 700060
Tel 3712 33 73 57
Fax 3712 33 18 85
Web www.

uzbekistan-airways.com

VARIG - BRAZILIAN AIRLINES
365 Avenida Almirante
Sylvio de Noronha
Edificio Varig
Rio de Janeiro
GB 20021-010 , Brasil
Tel 292 6600
Fax 55 21 240 6859
Web www.varig.com.br

VASP
Praca Comandante Lineu
Gomes Sno
Edifico Sede-VASP
Aeroporto de Congonhas
Sao Paulo, Brazil 04626 910
Tel 240 7011
Web www.vasp.com.br

VIETNAM AIRLINES
Phi Truong Road
Gia Lam District, Ha Noi
Viet Nam 10000
Tel 4 271 838
Fax 4 259 222

VIRGIN ATLANTIC AIRWAYS
Crawley Business Quarter
Manor Royal, Crawley
W Sussex RH10 2NU, UK
Tel 01293 562345
Fax 01293 561721
Web www.fly.virgin.com

VIRGIN EXPRESS
Building 116 Melsbroek
Airport
Regional Office, Melsbroek
Belgium B-1820
Tel 2 752 05 11
Fax 2 752 05 06
Web www.
virgin-express.com

VIRGIN EXPRESS (IRELAND)
Virgin House
Shannon Airport, Shannon
Co. Caire, Ireland
Tel 61 475233
Fax 61 704450

VLM
Internationale Luchthaven
Antwerpen
Luchthavengebouw Bus. 50
Antwerp, Belgium B-2100

Tel 10 437 9374
Fax 10 437 7932
Web www.vlm-air.com

YANGON AIRWAYS
22/24 Pansodan Street
Yangon, Myanmar
Tel 1 251932
Fax 1 251932
Web www.
myanmars.net/ygnair

YEMENIA - YEMEN AIRWAYS
PO Box 1183
Sana'a, Republic of Yemen
Tel 232389
Fax 252991
Web www.home.earthlink.
net/~yemenair

ZAMBIAN AIRWAYS
Lusaka Int. Airport
P.O. Box 310277
Lusaka, Zambia
Tel 1 271230
Fax 1 271278
Web www.africa-insites.
com/zambia/roanair.htm

ZIMBABWE EXPRESS AIRLINES
89 Nelson Mandela Avenue
Kurima House
P.O. Box 5130
Harare, Zimbabwe
Tel 4 739964
Web www.rapidttp.com/
travel/zzimcxpr.html

Airline offices in the UK

AER LINGUS
83 Staines Road
Hounslow
Middx PW3 3JB
Tel 020 8234 4333
Fax 020 8569 6264

AEROFLOT
70 Piccadilly
London W1V 9HH
Tel 020 7491 1764
Fax 020 7493 1852

AEROLINEAS ARGENTINAS
54 Conduit Street
London W1R 9FD
Tel 020 7494 1009
Fax 020 7494 1002

AIR ALGERIE
10 Baker Street
London W1M 1DA
Tel 020 7487 5709
Fax 020 7935 1715

**AIR CANADA &
CANADIAN AIRLINES**
Radius Park
Hatton Cross, Midsx
Tel 08705 247226
Fax 020 8750 8495

AIR CHINA
41 Grosvenor Gardens
London SW1W OBP
Tel 020 7630 7678
Fax 020 7630 7792

AIR FRANCE
Colet Court
100 Hamersmith Road
London W6 7JP
Tel 020 8759 2311
Fax 020 8782 8114

AIR GABON
19 Colonnade Walk
151 Buckingham Palace Rd
London SW1W 9SH
Tel 01293 596688
Fax 01293 596658

AIR INDIA
Great West House
Great West Road

Brentford, Mdsx TW8 9DF
Tel 020 8745 1000
Fax 020 8745 1059

AIR INTER
c/o Air France

AIR LANKA
c/o Sri Lankan

AIR MALTA
314/316 Upper Richmond
Rd, London SW15 6TV
Tel 020 8785 3199
Fax 020 8785 7468

AIR MAURITIUS
49 Conduit Street
London W1R 9FB
Tel 020 7434 7075
Fax 020 7439 4101

AIR NAMIBIA
Premiere House 3
Betts Way, Crawley
West Sussex
RH10 2GB
Tel 01293 596657
Fax 01293 596658

AIR NEW ZEALAND
Elsinore House
77 Fulham Palace Road
London W6 8JA
Tel 020 8600 7600
Fax 020 8741 4665

AIR SEYCHELLES
Oak House
County Oak Way
Crawley
W Sussex RH11 7ST
Tel 01293 596655
Fax 01293 596658

AIR ZIMBABWE
Colette House
52-55 Piccadilly
London W1V 9AA
Tel 020 7499 8947
Fax 020 7491 3164

ALITALIA
Plesman House
Cains Lane, Bedfont
Mdsx TW14 9RL
Tel 020 8745 8200
Fax 01603 778099

ALL NIPPON AIRWAYS
100 George Street

London W1H 5RH
Tel 020 7224 8866
Fax 020 7569 0860

AMERICAN AIRLINES
23/59 Staines Road
Mdsx TW3 3HE
Tel 0345 789789
Fax 020 8814 4230

ANSETT AUSTRALIA
c/o Air New Zealand

AUSTRIAN AIRLINES
5th Floor, 10 Wardour St
London W1V 4BQ
Tel 020 7434 7350
Fax 020 7434 7363

AVIANCA
15-17 Colonnade Walk
151 Buckingham Palace Rd
London SW1W 9SH
Tel 0870 6065040
Fax 0870 6065041

BALKAN BULGARIAN
322 Regent Street
London W1R 5AB
Tel 020 7631 1263
Fax 020 7637 2481

BIMAN BANGLADESH
17 Conduit Street
London W1R 9DD
Tel 020 7629 0161
Fax 020 7629 0736

BRITISH AIRWAYS
Waterside, PO Box 365
Harmondsworth UB7 0GB
Tel 0845 7799977
also at
156 Regent Street
London W1R 5TA

**BRITISH EUROPEAN
AIRWAYS**
Exeter Airport
Exeter EX5 2BD
Tel 01392 366669
Fax 01392 366151

BRITISH MIDLAND
Donington Hall
Castle Donington
Derby DE7 2SB
Tel 01332-854000
Fax 01332-854105

BWIA INTERNATIONAL
Central Hse, Lampton Rd
Mdsx TW3 1HY
Tel 020 8570 5552
Fax 020 8577 2112

CAMEROON AIRLINES
17 Clifford Street
London W1X 1RG
Tel 020 7494 7676
Fax 020 7494 7677

CANADIAN AIRLINES
c/o Air Canada

CATHAY PACIFIC
7 Apple Tree Yard
Duke of York Street
London SW1Y 6LD
Tel 020 7747 7000
Fax 020 7925 0445

CHINA AIRLINES
5th Floor, Nuffield House
41-46 Piccadilly
London W1V 9AJ
Tel 020 7494 4494
Fax 020 7439 4888

CONTINENTAL AIRLINES
Beulah Court
Albert Road, Horley
Surrey RH6 7HZ
Tel 01293-776464
Fax 01293-773726

CROATIAN AIRLINES
162-168 Regents Street
London W1R 5TB
Tel 020 8563 7080
Fax 020 8563 2615

CUBANA
49 Conduit Street
London W1R 9FB
Tel 020 7734 1165
Fax 020 7437 0681

CYPRUS AIRLINES
5 The Exchange
Brent Cross Gardens
London NW4 3RJ
Tel 020 8359 1350
Fax 020 8359 1340

CZECHOSLOVAK AIRLINES
72 Margaret Street
London W1W 8HA
Tel 020 7637 9152
Fax 020 7323 1633

DELTA AIRLINES
10 Warwick St
London W1B 5LZ
Tel 020 8601 6000
Fax 020 8601 6037

DRAGONAIR
c/o Cathay Pacific

EGYPTAIR
296 Regent Street
London W1R 6PH
Tel 020 7580 5477
Fax 020 7287 1728

EL AL ISRAEL AIRLINES
180 Oxford Street
London W1N OEL
Tel 020 7957 4200
Fax 020 7957 4299

EMIRATES
95 Cromwell Rd
Gloucester Park,
London SW7 4DL
Tel 020 7808 0033
Fax 020 7808 0061

ESTONIAN AIR
Terminal House
52 Grosvenor Gardens
London SW1W 0AU
Tel 020 7333 0197
Fax 020 7333 0068

ETHIOPIAN AIRLINES
Foxglove House
166 Piccadilly
London W1V 9DE
Tel 020 7491 2125
Fax 020 7491 1892

EVA AIR
Evergreen House
160 Euston Road
London NW1 2DT
Tel 020 7380 8334
Fax 020 7383 0809

FINNAIR
14 Clifford Street
London W1X 1RD
Tel 020 7629 4349
Fax 020 7629 7289

GARUDA INDONESIA
35 Duke Street
London W1M 5DF
Tel 020 7935 7055
Fax 020 7224 3971

GB AIRWAYS
Ian Stewart Centre
Beehive Ring Road
Gatwick Airport
Surrey RH6 0PB
Tel 01293-664239
Fax 01293-664218

GHANA AIRWAYS
100 Piccadilly
PO Box 2602
London W1A 3NY
Tel 020 7495 7969
Fax 020 7495 7966

GULF AIR
10 Albermarle Street
London W1X 3HE
Tel 020 7411 4440
Fax 020 7629 3989

IBERIA AIRLINES
Venture House
29 Glasshouse Street
London W1R 6JU
Tel 020 7413 1201
Fax 020 7830 1262

ICELANDAIR
172 Tottenham Court Rd
London W1P 9LG
Tel 020 7874 1000
Fax 020 7387 5711

IRAN AIR
73 Piccadilly
London W1V 0QX
Tel 020 7491 3656
Fax 020 7408 1360

JAPAN AIRLINES
5 Hanover Court
Hanover Square
London W1 R 0DR
Tel 0845 7747 7000
Fax 020 7499 1071

JERSEY EUROPEAN AIRWAYS
c/o British European

KENYA AIRWAYS
Bedfont Road
London Heathrow Airport
Staines, Mdsx TW19 7NL
Tel 01784 888233
Fax 01784 888299

KLM ROYAL DUTCH AIRLINES
Endeavour House
Stansted Airport
Essex CM24 1RS
Tel 01279 660400
Fax 01279 660330

KOREAN AIRLINES
66-68 Piccadilly
London SW1Y 4RF
Tel 020 7495 2299
Fax 020 7495 1616

KUWAIT AIRLINES
16-20 Baker Street
London W1M 2AD
Tel 020 7412 0006
Fax 020 7412 0008

LAN CHILE
150 Buckingham Palace Rd
London SW1W 9TR
Tel 01293 596607

LIAT
c/o Britih Airways

LUFTHANSA
World Business Centre
Newall Road
London Heathrow Airport
Mdsx TW6 2RD
Tel 020 8750 3500
Fax 020 8750 3545

LUXAIR
Aviareps house
County Oak Way
Crawley
West Sussex RH11 7ST
Tel 01293 596633
Fax 01293 596658

MAERSK AIR
Terminal House
52 Grosvenor Gardens
London SW1W 0AU
Tel 020 7333 0065
Fax 020 7333 0068

MALAYSIA AIRLINES
247-249 Cromwell Rd
London SW5 9GA
Tel 020 7341 2000
Fax 020 7341 2001

MALEV HUNGARIAN
1st Floor, 22-25 Sackville St
London W1X 1DE

Tel 020 7439 0577
Fax 020 7734 8116

MEXICANA
215 Chalk Farm Road
London NW1 8AF
Tel 020 7284 2550
Fax 020 7267 2004

MIDDLE EAST AIRLINES
45 Albermarle Street
London W1X 3FE
Tel 020 7493 6321
Fax 020 7629 4163

NIGERIA AIRWAYS
11-12 Conduit Street
London W1R 0NX
Tel 020 8745 0503
Fax 020 7491 9644

NORTHWEST AIRLINES
c/o KLM

OLYMPIC AIRWAYS
11 Conduit Street
London W1R 0LP
Tel 020 7399 1500
Fax 020 7629 9891

PAKISTAN INTERNATIONAL AIRLINES
1-5 King Street
London W6 9HR
Tel 020 8741 8066
Fax 020 8741 9376

QANTAS
395-403 King Street
London W6 9NJ
Tel 020 8846 0466
Fax 020 8471 8669

ROYAL AIR MAROC
205 Regent Street
London W1R 7DE
Tel 020 7439 8854
Fax 020 7734 6183

ROYAL BRUNEI AIRLINES
49 Cromwell Road
London W1R 7DD
Tel 020 7584 6360
Fax 020 7581 9279

ROYAL JORDANIAN
32 Brook Street
London W1 Y1AG
Tel 020 7878 6333
Fax 020 7629 4069

SABENA / SWISSAIR
Gemini House
10-18 Putney Hill
London SW15 6AA
Tel 020 8780 2270
Fax 020 8762 7199

SAS - SCANDANAVIAN AIRLINES
52 Conduit Street
London W1R 0AY
Tel 020 8990 7000
Fax 020 8990 7127

SAUDI ARABIA AIRLINES
508 Chiswick High Road
London W4 5RG
Tel 020 7798 9890
Fax 020 7798 9899

SINGAPORE AIRLINES
580-586 Chiswick High Rd
London W4 5RB
Tel 020 8563 6767
Fax 020 8742 1701

SOUTH AFRICAN AIRWAYS
61 Conduit Street
London W1R ONE
Tel 020 7312 5000
Fax 020 7312 5009

SRI LANKAN AIRLINES
Central House
3 Lampton Road
Mdsx TW3 1HY
Tel 020 8538 2000
Fax 020 8572 0808

SWISSAIR
c/o Sabena

TAP - AIR PORTUGAL
Gillingham House
38-44 Gillingham Street
London SW1V 1JW
Tel 020 7828 2092
Fax 020 8762 7199

TAROM - ROMANIAN AIRLINES
27 New Cavendish Street
London W1M 7RL
Tel 020 7935 3600
Fax 020 7487 2913

THAI AIRWAYS INTERNATIONAL
41 Albermarle Street
London W1X 3FE

Tel 020 7491 7953
Fax 020 7409 1463

TURKISH AIRLINES
11/12 Hanover Street
London W1R 9HF
Tel 020 7766 9333
Fax 020 7976 1738

TWA - TRANS WORLD AIRLINES
Central House
Lampton Road
Middlesex TW3 1TW
Tel 020 8754 2719
Fax 020 8754 2791

UNITED AIRLINES
United House
Southern Perimeter Road
London Heathrow Airport
Mdsx TW6 3LP
Tel 0845 8444777
Fax 020 8822 7755

VARIG BRAZILIAN
St. George House
61 Conduit Street
London W1R OHG
Tel 020 7287 1414
Fax 020 7478 2199

VIASA
c/o Iberia

VIRGIN ATLANTIC
Crawley Business Quarter
Manor Royal, Crawley
West Sussex RH10 2NU
Tel 01293-616161
Fax 01293-561721

YEMENIA - YEMEN AIRWAYS
11 Mayfair Place
London
W1J 8AN
Tel 020 7409 2171
Fax 020 7355 3062

Airline two-letter codes

The codes listed below are often used in timetables, brochures and tickets, to identify airlines.

AA	American Airlines
AC	Air Canada
AE	Mandarin Airlines
AF	Air France
AH	Air Algerie
AI	Air India
AJ	Air Belgium
AM	AERO MEXICO
AN	Ansett Australia
AO	AVIACO
AQ	Aloha Airlines
AR	Aerolineas Argentinas
AS	Alaska Airlines
AT	Royal Air Maroc
AV	AVIANCA
AY	Finnair
AZ	Alitalia
BA	British Airways
BD	British Midland
BG	Biman Bangladesh Airlines
BI	Royal Brunei Airlines
BL	Pacific Airlines
BO	Bouraq Indonesia Airlines
BP	Air Botswana
BR	EVA Airways
BU	Braathens SAFE
BV	Sun Air
BW	BWIA
CA	Air China
CF	Compania de Aviacion Faucett
CI	China Airlines
CM	COPA Compania Panamena
CO	Continental Airlines
CP	Canadian Airlines
CU	CUBANA
CW	Air Marshall Islands
CX	Cathay Pacific
CY	Cyprus Airways
CZ	China Southern Airlines
DL	Delta Airlines
DM	Maersk Air

DO	Dominicana
DS	Air Senegal
DT	TAAG Angolan Airlines
EF	Far Eastern Air Transport
EG	Japan Asia Airways
EH	SAETA
EI	Aer Lingus
EL	Air Nippon
EM	Empire Airlines
ET	Ethiopian Airlines
EU	Ecuatoriana
EW	Eurowings
FG	Ariana Afghan Airlines
FI	Icelandair
FJ	Air Pacific
FQ	Air Aruba
FR	Ryanair
GA	Garuda Indonesia
GE	Trans Asia Airways
GF	Gulf Air
GH	Ghana Airways
GN	Air Gabon
GU	Aviateca
GV	Riga Airlines
GY	Guyana Airways
HA	Hawaiian Airlines
HM	Air Seychelles
HP	America West Airlines
HV	Transavia Airlines
HY	Uzbekistan Airlines
IB	IBERIA
IC	Indian Airlines
IE	Solomon Airlines
IJ	TAT European Airlines
IL	Istanbul Airlines
IP	Airlines of Tasmania
IR	Iran Air
IV	Fujian Airlines
IY	Yemen Airways
IZ	Arkia Israeli Airlines
JE	Manx Airlines
JL	Japan Airlines
JM	Air Jamaica
JP	Adria Airways
JR	Aero California
JY	Jersey European Airways
KA	Dragonair
KB	Druk-Air
KE	Korean Air
KI	Air Atlantique

KL	KLM	QU	Uganda Airlines	VP	VASP
KM	Air Malta	QV	Lao Aviation	VR	Transportes Aereos
KQ	Kenya Airways	QW	Turks and Caicos		de Cabo Verde
KU	Kuwait Airways		National Airline	VS	Virgin Atlantic
KV	Eastern Air	RA	Royal Nepal Airline	VT	Air Tahiti
KX	Cayman Airways	RB	Syrian Arab Airlines	VU	Air Ivoire
LA	LAN Chile	RG	VARIG	WM	Windward Islands
LB	Lloyd Aereo	RJ	Royal Jordanian		Airways International
	Boliviano	RK	Air Afrique	WN	Southwest Airlines
LG	Luxair	RO	TAROM	WT	Nigeria Airways
LH	Lufthansa	RR	Royal Air Force	WY	Oman Air
LI	LIAT	RY	Air Rwanda	YT	Skywest Airlines
LO	LOT Polish Airlines	SA	South African	ZB	Monarch Airlines
LR	LACSA		Airways	ZQ	Ansett New Zealand
LX	Crossair	SD	Sudan Airways		
LY	El Al	SF	Shanghai Airlines		
LZ	Balkan	SH	Air Toulouse		
MA	MALEV	SK	SAS		
MD	Air Madagascar	SN	Sabena		
ME	Middle East Airlines	SO	Sunshine Airlines		
MK	Air Mauritius	SQ	Singapore Airlines		
MO	Calm Air	SR	Swissair		
	International	SU	Aeroflot		
MR	Air Mauritanie	SV	Saudia		
MS	Egyptair	SW	Air Namibia		
MW	Maya Airways	SZ	China Southwest		
MX	Mexicana	TA	Taca International		
NF	Air Vanuatu		Airlines		
NG	Lauda Air	TC	Air Tanzania		
NH	All Nippon Airways	TE	Lithuanian Airlines		
NN	Cardinal Airlines	TG	Thai Airways		
NW	Northwest Airlines		International		
NZ	Air New Zealand	TK	Turkish Airlines		
OA	Olympic Airways	TM	Linhas Aereas de		
OK	Czechoslovak		Mocambique		
	Airlines	TP	TAP Air Portugal		
ON	Air Nauru	TQ	Transwede		
OS	Austrian Airlines	TR	Transbrasil Linhas		
OU	Croatia Airlines		Aereas		
OV	Estonian Air	TS	Samoa Aviation		
PB	Air Burundi	TT	Airline Lithuania		
PC	Air Fiji	TU	Tunis Air		
PG	Bangkok Airways	TW	TWA (Trans World		
PH	Polynesian Airlines		Airlines)		
PK	Pakistan	UA	United Airlines		
	International Airlines	UB	Myanmar Airways		
PL	AeroPeru	UK	Air UK		
PR	Philippine Airlines	UL	Air Lanka		
PS	Ukraine	UM	Air Zimbabwe		
	International Airways	UP	Bahamasair		
PX	Air Niugini	UY	Cameroon Airlines		
PY	Surinam Airways	VA	VIASA		
PZ	LAPSA	VE	AVENSA		
QF	Qantas Airways	VJ	Royal Air Cambodge		
QL	Air Lesotho	VN	Vietnam Airlines		
QM	Air Malawi	VO	Tyrolean Airways		

Motorists' worldwide documentation

by Colin McElduff

THE FOLLOWING ADVICE is directed principally towards motorists from the UK and should be used as a general guide only, as each and every case produces its own requirements dependent on the countries concerned and the circumstances and regulations prevailing at the time.

As many travellers neglect documentation - some of which should be obtained well in advance of departure - it is advisable to list all that is known to be relevant to your trip and make enquiries as to the remainder.

I have included below only those documents which are specifically related to vehicles.

SUMMARY

For most overland trips you will need the following:

1. Driving Licence
2. Insurance - third party, and/or (3)
3. International Motor Insurance Certificate (Green Card)
4. International Registration Distinguishing Sign ('GB', etc.)
5. Vehicle Registration Certificate (depending on your country of departure and those through which you will be travelling)
6. Bail Bond
7. *Carnet* ATA
8. *Carnet Camping*
9. *Carnet de Passages en Douanes*
10. Letter of Authority to use borrowed, hired or leased vehicles
11. VE103 - Hired/Leased Vehicle Certificate
12. International Certificate for Motor Vehicles
13. International Driving Permit (IDP)
14. Motoring Organisation Membership Card
15. Petrol Coupons

DRIVING LICENCE

Most countries will allow you to drive for six months on your national driving licence. After this you must have an IDP or take a local test. In Italy a translation of the visitor's National Driving Licence is required if the National Licence is the older UK all green colour licence. The translation may be obtained from motoring organisations. Motorists in possession of an IDP do not require a translation. It is probably also useful to have a translation if travelling in Arab countries where males may only be allowed to drive. Also this may apply in some countries when hiring a vehicle, whatever, all or most of the above will need to be produced and Third Party Insurance is mandatory for it is essential to cover claims relating to death of or bodily injury to third parties as a result of the vehicle's use.

INTERNATIONAL MOTOR INSURANCE CERTIFICATE ('GREEN CARD')

When travelling in countries outside the scope of the 'Green Card' - which is generally outside Europe - Third Party insurance should be taken out at the first opportunity on entering the country. Whilst the 'Green Card' is technically no longer necessary in EC countries, it is extremely unwise to visit these countries without it as it remains readily acceptable as evidence of insurance to enable a driver to benefit from international claim-handling facilities. In any case, a 'Green Card' is required in all European countries outside the EC. It should be obtained from the insurance company that is currently insuring your vehicle.

THE INTERNATIONAL REGISTRATION DISTINGUISHING SIGN ('GB' ETC.)

This sign is mandatory and should be of the country in which your vehicle is registered, thus identifying your registration plates.

THE VEHICLE REGISTRATION CERTIFICATE

This is an essential document to take. However, further proof of ownership or authority to use the vehicle may sometimes be required.

Bail Bond

For visitors to Spain, it was always a wise precaution to obtain a Spanish Bail Bond from the vehicle insurers since the driver involved in an accident could have been required to lodge a deposit with the local Spanish Court and failure to meet that demand could result in imprisonment for the driver and detention of the vehicle until funds became available. Now that Spain is in the EU, this requirement is no longer technically applicable, but many insurers will still issue a Bail Bond at nil cost for anybody who wants to play doubly safe.

Carnet ATA

This is a customs document valid for 12 months, which facilitates the entry without payment of customs duties, etc., on professional equipment, goods for internal exhibition and commercial samples, temporarily imported into certain countries - a list of which may be obtained from the London Chamber of Commerce and Industry (33 Queen Street, London, EC4R 1AP, tel: 020 248 4444) or through one of their many offices throughout the UK. The LCCI is likely to move in the near future, so do check their address before writing to them.

Carnet Camping

An international document jointly produced by the three international organisations dealing with camping and caravanning - the Federation Internationale de l'Automobile, the Federation Internationale de Camping et Caravanign and the Alliance Internationale de Tourisme. It serves as an identity document and facilitates entry to sites under the wing of these organisations sometimes at - reduced rates. In addition, the document provides personal accident cover up to a specified sum for those names on it. You should approach a motoring organisation for this document.

Carnet de Passages en Douanes

This is an Internationally recognised customs document. If acceptable to a country, it will entitle the holder to import temporarily a vehicle, caravan, trailer, boat, etc., without the need to deposit the appropriate customs duties and taxes. The issuing authority of the *carnet* is directly responsible for the payment of customs duties and taxes if the *carnet* is not discharged correctly, i.e. if the owner violates another country's customs regulations by selling the vehicle illegally. Consequently, any substantial payment will be recovered from the *carnet* holder under the terms of the signed issuing agreement. Motoring organisations are issuing authorities and will provide issue documents upon receipt of a bank guarantee, cash deposit or an insurance indemnity from an agreed firm of brokers to cover any liability. The sum required is determined by the motoring organisation, taking into consideration the countries the vehicle will enter (destinations are declared when the application for the *carnet* is made).

Normally the amount of the bond required as security is related to the maximum import duty on motor vehicles required in the countries to be visited, which can be as high as 400 per cent of the UK value of the vehicle. In the case of a bank guarantee, you need to have collateral with the issuing bank or funds sufficient to cover the amount required to be guaranteed. These funds cannot be withdrawn until the bank's guarantee is surrendered by the motoring organisation. This is done when the *carnet* is returned correctly discharged.

The procedure is for the bank manager to provide a letter of indemnity to the motoring organisation, normally the motoring organisation's specially printed documents. If you have insufficient funds or security to cover the bond, you may pay an insurance premium (the AA and the RAC have their own nominated insurance companies with which they have *carnet* indemnity agreements) and the company will act as guarantor.

There are certain points to watch, however. The car must usually be registered in the country where the *carnet* is issued. In some cases (at the discretion of the issuing club or association), being a citizen of the country where the *carnet* is issued is an alternative - even though the car has been registered elsewhere. In all cases, membership of the issuing club is a requirement and a *carnet* is necessary for most long transcontinental journeys and should be obtained regardless of the fact that some of the countries on the itinerary do not require it. To be without one where it is required usually means being turned back if you have insufficient funds to cover the customs deposit for entry.

A *Carnet de Passages en Douanes* is valid for 12 months from the date of issue and may be extended beyond the expiry date by applying to the motoring organisation in the country you are visiting at the point of expiry. The name of the motoring organisation is shown in the front cover of the *carnet*. An extension should be noted on every page and not just inside the cover in order to avoid difficulties at border checks.

When a new *carnet* is required, the application must be made to the original issuing authority. *Carnets* are issued with five, 11 or 25 pages, depending on the number of countries to be visited, and a nominal fee is charged accordingly to cover administration. Each page contains an entry voucher (*volet d'entrée*), exit voucher (*volet de sortie*) and a counterfoil (*souche*). When the vehicle leaves the country, the customs officer endorses the exit part of the counterfoil and detaches the appropriate exit voucher, thus discharging the *carnet*. If you have not taken care to have this done, the validity of the *carnet* may be suspended until this is rectified.

CERTIFICATE OF AUTHORITY FOR A BORROWED OR HIRED VEHICLE

This is required when a vehicle is borrowed or hired and should bear the signature of the owner. This must be the same as on the Registration Certificate which must or should also be taken.

VE103: INTERNATIONAL CERTIFICATION FOR MOTOR VEHICLES ON HIRE/LOAN

In countries where the British Vehicle Registration Certificate is not accepted, this document is required and is issued by a motoring organisation.

INTERNATIONAL DRIVING PERMIT

An IDP is required by the driver of a vehicle in countries that do not accept the national driving licence of the visiting motorist. It is issued on request by motoring organisations for a small fee and is valid for twelve months from the date of issue. An IDP can only be issued in the country of the applicant's national driving licence.

MOTORING ORGANISATION MEMBERSHIP CARD

Most countries have a motoring organisation which is a member of the Alliance Internationale de Tourisme (AIT) or the Federation Internationale de l'Automobile (FIA) and provides certain reciprocal membership privileges to members of other motoring organisations.

PETROL COUPONS

These are issued to visiting motorists in some countries either to promote tourism or where there are restrictions on the residents' use of petrol. Motoring organisations can advise which countries issue petrol coupons.

ADDITIONAL DOCUMENTS

You may need your birth certificate, extra passport photographs and, as a precaution against theft, it is wise to have separate photostat's of these and other pertinent documents.

Off-road drivers' checklist

by Jack Jackson

IF YOU ARE AN EXPERIENCED OFF-ROAD MOTORIST and vehicle camper, you are, without doubt, the best person to decide exactly what you need to do and take for your trip. Even so, extensive experience doesn't guarantee perfect recall and everyone might find it useful to jog their memories by consulting other people's lists.

The lists that follow on the next page do assume some experience - without some mechanical expertise, for example, an immaculately stocked tool-box is of limited use. It is also assumed that the motorist in question will spend at least some time driving off-road, most probably in a four-wheel-drive vehicle.

Vehicle spares and tools

PETROL ENGINES

3 fan belts (plus power steering pump belts and air conditioning pump belts if fitted)
1 complete set of gaskets
4 oil filters (change every 5000 km)
2 tubes of Silicone RTV gasket compound
1 complete set of radiator hoses
2 metres of spare heater hose
2 metres of spare fuel pipe hose
0.5 metres of spare distributor vacuum pipe hose
2 exhaust valves
1 inlet valve
1 complete valve spring
Fine and coarse valve grinding paste and valve grinding tool
1 valve spring compressor
1 fuel pump repair kit (if electric type, take a complete spare pump)
1 water pump repair kit
1 carburettor overhaul kit
2 sets of sparking plugs
1 timing light or 12 volt bulb and holder with leads
3 sets of contact breaker points (preferably with hard fibre cam follower, because plastic types wear down quickly and close up the gap in the heat)
2 distributor rotor arms
1 distributor condenser
1 distributor cap
1 sparking plug spanner
1 set of high tension leads (older, wire type)
1 ignition coil
Slip ring and brushes for alternator or a complete spare alternator.
2 cans of spray type ignition sealant, for dusty and wet conditions
2 spare air intake filters, if you do not have the oil–bath type

EXTRAS FOR DIESEL ENGINES

Delete sparking plugs, contact breaker points, distributor, vacuum pipe hose, rotor arms, distributor cap and condenser, high tension leads, coil, and carburettor overhaul from the above list and substitute:
1 spare set of injectors, plus cleaning kit
1 complete set of high pressure injector pipes
1 set injector copper sealing washers plus steel sealing washers where these are used
1 set injector return pipe washers
1 metre of plastic fuel pipe, plus spare nuts and ferrules
A second in–line fuel filter
4 fuel filter elements
3 spare heater plugs, if fitted

BRAKES AND CLUTCH

2 wheel cylinder kits (one right and one left)
1 flexible brake hose
1 brake bleeding kit
1 brake, master cylinder seals kit
1 clutch, master cylinder seals kit
1 clutch, slave cylinder kit (or a complete unit for Land Rover series III or 110). (It is important to keep all these kits away from heat)
1 clutch centre plate
If you have an automatic gearbox, make sure you have plenty of the special fluid for this, a spare starter motor and a spare battery, kept charged.
If you have power steering, carry the correct fluid and spare hoses.
Some Land Rovers have automatic gearbox fluid in a manual gearbox.

GENERAL SPARES

2 warning triangles (compulsory in most countries)
1 good workshop manual (not the car handbook)
1 good torch and a fluorescent light with leads to work it from vehicle battery, plus spare bulbs and tubes
1 extra tyre in addition to that on the spare wheel. (Only the spare wheel and tyre will be necessary if two identical vehicles are travelling together.)
3 extra inner tubes (6 in areas of Acacia thorns)
1 large inner tube repair kit
1 set of tyre levers and 1 kg sledge hammer for tyres
5 spare inner tube valve cores and 2 valve core tools
4 inner tube valve dust caps (metal type)
1 Schrader tyre pump, which fits into sparking plug socket threads. Or a 12 volt electric compressor, which is the only system available if you have a diesel engine
Plenty of good quality engine oil
2 litres of distilled water or 1 bottle of water de–ionizing crystals
12-volt soldering iron and solder
Hand drill and drills
16 metres of nylon or terylene rope, strong enough to upright an overturned vehicle
1 good jack and wheel brace (if hydraulic, carry spare fluid)
1 (at least) metal fuel can, e.g. a jerry can

1 grease gun and a tin of multi–purpose grease
5 litres of correct differential and gearbox oil
1 large fire extinguisher suitable for petrol and electrical fires
1 reel of self–vulcanizing rubber tape, for leaking hoses
1 pair heavy-duty electric jump leads at least 3 metres long
10 push fit electrical connectors (of type to suit vehicle)
2 universal joints for prop shafts
0.5 litre can of brake and clutch fluid
1 small can of general light oil for hinges, etc
1 large can WD40
1 starting handle, if available
2 complete sets of keys, kept in different places
1 small Isopon or fibre glass kit for repairing fuel tank and body holes
2 kits of general adhesive eg. Bostik or Araldite Rapid
1 tin of hand cleaner (washing up liquid will do in an emergency)
Spare fuses and bulbs for all lights, including those on the dash panel, the red charging light bulb is often part of the charging circuit
1 radiator cap
Antifreeze —if route passes through cold areas
Spare windscreen wipers for use on return journey (keep away from heat)
Inner and outer-wheel bearings

A good tool kit

Wire brush to clean threads
Socket set
Torque wrench
Ring and open-ended spanners
Hacksaw and spare blades

Large and small flat and round files
Selection of spare nuts, bolts and washers, of type and thread/s to fit vehicle
30cm Stillson pipe wrench
1 box spanner for large wheel-bearing lock nuts
Hammer
Large and small cold chisels, for large and stubborn nuts
Self–grip wrench, e.g. Mole type
Broad and thin nosed pliers
Circlip pliers
Insulating tape
3 metres electrical wire (vehicle type, not mains)
1 set of feeler gauges
Small adjustable wrench
Tube of gasket cement, e.g. Red Hermetite
Tube Loctite thread sealant
Large and small slot head and Phillips head screwdrivers
Accurate tyre pressure gauge
Hardwood or steel plate, to support the jack on soft ground

Extras for off-road use

2 sand ladders per vehicle (4 if vehicle travels alone)
3 wheel bearing hub oil seals
1 rear gearbox oil seal
1 rear differential oil seal
1 rear spring main leaf, complete with bushes
1 front spring main leaf, complete with bushes
4 spare spring bushes
4 spring centre bolts
1 set (=4) of spring shackle plates
1 set (=4) of spring shackle pins
2 rear axle 'U' bolts
1 front axle 'U' bolt.
If instead of leaf springs you have coil springs, carry

one spare plus 2 mountings and 4 bushes
1 set of shock absorber mounting rubbers
2 spare engine mounting rubbers
1 spare gearbox mounting rubber
2 door hinge pins
1 screw jack (to use it on its side when changing springs and/or bushes)
2 metres of strong chain plus bolts to fix it, for splinting broken chassis axle or spring parts
Snow chains if you expect a lot of mud or snow
5cm paint brush, to dust off the engine, so that you can work on it
Large groundsheet for lying on when working under the vehicle or repairing tyres, so as to prevent sand from getting between the inner tube and the tyre
1 high lift jack
2 long-handled shovels for digging out
2 steering ball joints
2 spare padlocks
Radiator stop leak compound (dry porridge or raw egg will do in an emergency)

SPECIFIC TO SERIES IIA LAND ROVERS
1 set rear axle half shafts (heavy duty)

SPECIFIC TO SERIES III LAND ROVERS
1 complete gear change lever, if you have welded bush type (or replace with groove and rubber ring type)
4 nylon bonnet hinge inserts (or 2 home–made aluminium ones)
2 windscreen outer hinge bolts (No 346984)
2 windscreen inner tie bolts
2 rear differential drain plugs

1 set big end nuts
1 rear axle drive plate
(Salisbury)

**SPECIFIC TO LAND ROVER
TURBO DIESEL AND
TDI ENGINES**
2 spare glass fibre main
timing belts, stored flat and
in a cool place
3 pushrods
3 brass cam followers
2 air filter paper elements

Maintenance check before departure

1. Change oil and renew all oil and fuel filters
2. Clean air filter and change oil bath or air filter element
3. Lubricate drive shafts, winch, speedometer cable
4. Lubricate all locks with dry graphite
5. Adjust and lubricate all door hinges
6. Inspect undercarriage for fluid leaks, loose bolts, etc.
7. Rotate all tyres, inspecting for cuts and wear
8. Check and adjust brakes
9. Check adjustment of carburettor or injection pump
10. Check fan belts and accessory belts
11. Check sparking plugs. Clean and re–gap if necessary (replace as necessary). If diesel, clean or replace injectors.
12. Check ignition timing
13. Check and top up: front and rear differentials, swivel–pin housings, transmission, transfer case, overdrive, power steering pump, and air

conditioning pump (if applicable), steering box, battery, brake and clutch fluid, cooling system
14. Check that there are no rattles
15. Inspect radiator and heater hoses
16. Check breather vents on both axles, gearbox and fuel filler cap
17. Check all lights and direction indicators
18. Check wheel balance and steering alignment (always do this with new wheels and/or tyres)
19. Check battery clamps and all electrical wiring for faulty insulation

Specialist vehicle suppliers

BROWNCHURCH (LAND ROVERS)
1a Bickley Road
London E10 7AQ, UK
Tel 020 8556 0011
Web www. brownchurch.co.uk
Specialist safari preparation for Land Rovers, Range Rovers and Discovery: roof racks, light guards, bush bars, jerry can holders, suspension and over-drive modifications, winches, sand ladders, high-lift jacks, oil cooler kits etc. Covers all Land Rover needs for trips anywhere, including the fitting of jerry cans and holders, sand ladders, sump and light guards, crash bars, winches, water purifying plants, roof-racks

(custom-made if necessary), overdrive units. They also supply new vehicles and offer a maintenance and spares service for Land, Range Rovers and Discovery.

CROSS COUNTRY VEHICLES
Hailey, Witney
Oxon OX8 5UF, UK
Tel 01993 776622
Sell and convert vehicles, prepare them for safari use. Range Rover and Land Rover specialists - new and used vehicles and any other 4WD vehicle too. They offer service, special preparation, conversion parts (new and reconditioned). Parts and preparation quotes by return.

DUNSFOLD LAND ROVERS
Alfold Road, Dunsfold
Godalming
Surrey GU8 4NP, UK
Tel 01483 200567
Offers free travel advice to those contemplating overland travel: comprehensive stores, rebuilding to owner's specifications.

LAND ROVER
Direct Sales Department
Lode Lane , Solihull
West Midlands B92 8NW
UK
Tel 0121 722 2424
Manufacturers of Land Rovers and Range Rovers. Purchase must be through authorised dealers.

SANDERSON FORD
Ashton Old Road
Ardwick
Manchester M12 6JD, UK
Tel 0161 272 6000
Deal in Mevaride 4WD vehicles.

Vehicle shipping companies

Car ferry operators from the UK

BRITTANY FERRIES
Millbay
Plymouth PL1 3EW
Tel 0990 360360

CALEDONIA MACBRAYNE
The Ferry Terminal
Gourock PA19 1QP
Tel 01475 650100

CONDOR FERRIES
Condor House
Newharbour Road South
Poole
Dorset BH15 4AJ
Tel 01305 761551

DFDS SEAWAYS
Scandinavia House
Parkeston Quay
Harwich
Essex CO12 4QG
Tel 01255 240240

FRED OLSEN LINES
Whitehouse Road
Ipswich
Suffolk IP1 5LL
Tel 01473 292200

HOVERSPEED LTD
International Hoverport
Marine Parade
Dover
Kent CT17 9TG
Tel 0870 524 0241

IRISH FERRIES
2/4 Merrion Row
Dublin 2
Ireland
Tel 1 661 0511

ISLES OF SCILLY STEAMSHIP COMPANY
Quay Street, Penzance
Cornwall TR18 4BZ

Tel 0345 105555
Web www.
islesofscilly-travel.co.uk

NORFOLK LINE
Norfolk House
The Dock
Felixstowe
Suffolk IP11 3UY
Tel 01394 673676

ORKNEY FERRIES
Shore Street
Kirkwall
Orkney KW15 1LG
Tel 01856 872044

P&O EUROPEAN FERRIES
Channel House
Channel View Road
Dover
Kent CT17 9TJ
Tel 01304 203388

P&O FERRIES (ORKNEY & SHETLAND SERVICES)
PO Box 5
Jamiesons Quay
Aberdeen AB11 5NP
Tel 01224 572615

P&O NORTH SEA FERRIES
King George Dock
Hedon Road
Hull HU9 5QA
Tel 01482 377177

SHANNON FERRIES
Killimer
Kilrush
Co Clare, Ireland
Tel 65 53124

VIKING LINE
c/o Amagine UK
87-89 Church Street
Leigh
Manchester WN7 1AZ
Tel 01942 262662

WESTERN FERRIES
Hunters Quay
Dunoon
Argyll PA23 8HJ
Tel 01369 704452

Other helpful organisations

FEDERAL CHAMBER OF AUTOMOTIVE INDUSTRIES
10 Rudd St
Canberra City ACT
2601 Canberra
Australia
Tel 6 247 3811

MICHAEL GIBBONS FREIGHT
21 Berth
Tilbury Freeport
Tilbury Docks RM18 7JT
UK
Tel 01375 843461
One of the biggest shipment companies, with offices worldwide. Both the AA and the RAC refer their members to this company.

MOTOR VEHICLE MANUFACTURERS' ASSOCIATION (USA)
7430 Second Avenue
Suite 300
Detroit
Michigan 48202
USA
Tel 313 872 4311

VERBAND DER AUTOMOBILINDUSTRIE E
Westendstrasse 61
6000 Frankfurt am Main 1
Germany
Tel 69 75 70 0

Further reading

ABC Passenger Shipping Guide (Reed Travel Group)

International vehicle licence plates

A	Austria	GR	Greece	RSM	San Marino
AL	Albania	GUY	Guyana	RSR	Zimbabwe
AND	Andorra	H	Hungary	RU	Burundi
AUS	Australia	HK	Hong Kong	RUS	Russian Federation
B	Belgium	HKJ	Jordan	RWA	Rwanda
BDS	Barbados	HR	Croatia	S	Sweden
BG	Bulgaria	I	Italy	SD	waziland
BH	Belize	IL	Israel	SDV	Vatican City
BR	Brazil	IND	India	SF	Finland
BRN	Bahrain	IR	Iran	SGP	Singapore
BRU	Brunei	IRQ	Iraq	SME	Suriname
BS	Bahamas	IS	Iceland	SN	Senegal
C	Cuba	J	Japan	SY	Seychelles
CDN	Canada	JA	Jamaica	SYR	Syria
CH	Switzerland	K	Cambodia	T	Thailand
CI	Côte d'Ivoire	L	Luxembourg	TG	Togo
CL	Sri Lanka	LAO	Laos	TN	Tunisia
CO	Colombia	LAR	Libya	TR	Turkey
CR	Costa Rica	LB	Liberia	TT	Trinidad & Tobago
CZ	Czech Republic	LS	Lesotho	U	Uruguay
CY	Cyprus	M	Morocco	UA	Ukraine
D	ermany	MAL	Malaysia	USA	USA
DK	Denmark	MC	Monaco	VN	Vietnam
DOM	Dominican Republic	MEX	Mexico	WAG	Gambia
DY	Benin	MS	Mauritius	WAL	Sierra Leone
DZ	Algeria	MW	Malawi	WAN	Nigeria
E	pain	N	Norway	WD	Dominica
EAK	Kenya	NA	Netherlands Antilles	WG	Grenada
EAT	Tanzania			WL	St. Lucia
EAU	Uganda	NIC	Nicaragua	WS	Western Samoa
EAZ	Zanzibar	NIG	Niger	WV	St. Vincent
EC	Ecuador	NL	Netherlands	YU	Yugoslavia
EIR	Ireland	NZ	New Zealand	YV	Venezuela
ET	Egypt	P	Portugal	Z	Zambia
F	France	PA	Panama	ZA	South Africa
FJI	Fiji	PAK	Pakistan	ZR	Zaire
FK	Slovak Republic	PE	Peru	ZRE	Yemen
FL	Liechtenstein	PI	Philippines		
FLO	lovenia	PL	Poland		
G	abon	PY	Paraguay		
GB	United Kingdom	R	Romania		
GBA	Alderney	RA	Argentina		
GBG	Guernsey	RB	Botswana		
GBJ	Jersey	RC	Taiwan		
GBM	Isle of Man	RCA	Central African Republic		
GBZ	Gibraltar	RCB	Congo		
GH	Ghana	RCH	Chile		
GLA	Guatemala	RH	Haiti		
		RI	Indonesia		
		RIM	Mauritania		
		RL	Lebanon		
		RM	Madagascar		
		RMM	Mali		
		RNR	Zambia		
		ROK	Korea		

Metric conversions for drivers

Tyre pressures

lbs per sq inch	kg per sq cm	atmos -phere	kilo pascals (kPa)
14	0.98	0.95	96.6
16	1.12	1.08	110.4
18	1.26	1.22	124.2
20	1.40	1.36	138.0
22	1.54	1.49	151.8
24	1.68	1.63	165.6
26	1.83	1.76	179.4
28	1.96	1.90	193.2
30	2.10	2.04	207.0
32	2.24	2.16	220.8
36	2.52	2.44	248.4
40	2.80	2.72	276.0
50	3.50	3.40	345.0
55	3.85	3.74	379.5
60	4.20	4.08	414.0
65	4.55	4.42	448.5

Litre to gallon conversion

For converting	Multiply by
Gallons to litres	4.546
Litres to gallons	0.22

Units of quantity

2 pints = 1 quart = 1.136 litres
4 quarts = 1 gallon = 4.546 litres
5 gallons = 22.73 litres

Converting distances

1 yard = 0.91 metres
100 yards = 91 metres
1 mile = 1.6 kilometres

To convert miles to kilometres:
    divide by 5 then multiply by 8

To convert kilometres to miles:
    divide by 8 then multiply by 5

Acknowledgements

SPECIAL THANKS
Sarah Anderson, Simon Beeching, Richard Broadley, Chris Burnett, Andy Collings, Sam Dancey, James Dawson, Rajinder Ghatahorde, Charles Gordon, Rachel Hammond, Mick Kidd, Lara Marsh (and Tourism Concern), Duncan Mills, Carey Ogilvie, Katy O'Brien, Graham Pallett, Mark Richards, Douglas Schatz, Edwina Townsend, Sue Walsh, David Warne, Ian Wilson, Kim Winter.

SOURCES
World Travel Guide, published by Columbus Travel Guides, *World Desk Reference*, published by Dorling Kindersley, *Fielding's The World's Most Dangerous Places*, published by Fielding Worldwide.

ACKNOWLEDGEMENTS
Selected quotes from Earl MacRauch, Miriam Beard, Jon Carroll, Bettina Selby, Lin Yutang, Ken Welsh, Louis L'Amour, John Steinbeck, Douglas Adams, Paul Theroux, Orson Welles, Willie Nelson, Hunter S.Thomson, Tom Clancy and Larry McMurtry are reprinted with permission from *The Quotable Traveler*, A Running Press® Miniature Edition™, copyright © 1994 by Running Press Book Publishers, Philadelphia and London. We would also like to acknowledge the Trustees of the Joseph Conrad Estate, The Society of Authors, on behalf of the Bernard Shaw estate, The Society of Authors as the literary representative of the estate of Norman Douglas, Peters Fraser & Dunlop Group for permission to quote from Hilaire Belloc (*Complete Verse* published by Random House UK Ltd). Quotes from *My African Journey* by Sir Winston Churchill reproduced with permission of Curtis Brown Ltd, London, on behalf of the estate of Sir Winston Churchill. Copyright Winston S. Churchill 1908.

While every effort has been made to credit copyright holders and to acknowledge source material, the publishers would be happy to rectify any omissions in a future edition.

WEXAS membership offer

Free trial travel club membership

Wexas is the travel club for independent travellers. Our 35,000 members enjoy the unbeatable combination of low prices, travel ideas and information, and outstanding service.

As a reader of *The Traveller's Handbook* you can take out a month's free trial membership and then become a fully paid-up member for less than a pound a week.

Take a look at the benefits you'll receive and see how you'll save your subscription many times over.

- Discount rates on airfares, hotels and car hire worldwide

- Annual travel insurance from just £59 per year (2000 rates)

- FREE subscription to *Traveller*, the highly acclaimed travel magazine

- Expert service from experienced travel consultants, and access to our members-only phone numbers

- Privileged access to VIP airport lounges

- Currency and travellers' cheques available by post, commission-free

- Special rates for airport parking

- Discounts at British Airways travel clinics

- £50,000 free flight accident insurance with every flight booking

- BagTag lost-luggage retrieval service

- Free international assistance 24 hours a day

- Discounts on local tours and sightseeing worldwide

- Additional benefits for business travellers

- Access to WEXASonline (members-only website)

- Customised round-the-world itineraries

- Quarterly *Update* newsletter on special offers and discounts

---

COMPLETE THIS FORM AND POST IT TODAY FOR FULL DETAILS OF WEXAS MEMBERSHIP AND THE FREE TRIAL OFFER.

You can send post this form to us at WEXAS International, FREEPOST (no stamp required), London, SW3 1BR, UK.

Alternatively you can fax it to us on 020 7589 8418, or email mship@wexas.com for details.

Name (Mr/Mrs/Miss/Ms)

Address

Postcode

Telephone

Email

Index